American Literature Series

HARRY HAYDEN CLARK, General Editor

ALEXANDER COWIE

THE RISE OF THE
American Novel

AMERICAN BOOK COMPANY

New York   Cincinnati   Chicago   Boston

Atlanta   Dallas   San Francisco

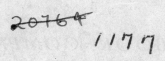

Acknowledgments

THE AUTHOR AND PUBLISHER OF *The Rise of the American Novel* AC-
KNOWLEDGE WITH THANKS PERMISSION GRANTED BY THE FOLLOWING PER-
SONS, JOURNALS, AND PUBLISHERS FOR THE USE OF THE SELECTIONS NAMED.

DUKE UNIVERSITY PRESS: Portions of Alexander Cowie's "The Vogue of the Domestic Novel, 1850-1870," from the *South Atlantic Quarterly*, Vol. XLI, No. 4
(October, 1942).

HARCOURT, BRACE & COMPANY: Five lines from T. S. Eliot's "Burnt Norton," from
his *Collected Poems*, 1909-1935, published by Harcourt, Brace & Company, 1936.

HARPER & BROTHERS: From Henry James's *The Awkward Age* (1899); Mark
Twain's *Personal Recollections of Joan of Arc* (1896), *The Mysterious Stranger*
(1916), *Pudd'nhead Wilson* (1894), *Tom Sawyer Abroad* (1894), *Letters*, edited by A. B. Paine (1917), *Autobiography* (1924), *Literary Essays*, "What Paul
Bourget Thinks of Us" (1895); also for passages from works of Mark Twain
out of copyright of which Harper & Brothers are the authorized publishers.

HOUGHTON MIFFLIN COMPANY: From Gamaliel Bradford's *American Portraits*;
W. D. Howells' *A Modern Instance* and *Indian Summer*; Henry James's *The
Tragic Muse* and *The Bostonians*; G. E. Woodberry's *Nathaniel Hawthorne*;
T. B. Aldrich's *Prudence Palfrey*, *The Stillwater Tragedy*, and *The Story of a
Bad Boy*; Holmes's *Elsie Venner*, *The Guardian Angel*, and *A Mortal Antipathy*;
various passages from Hawthorne; C. E. Stowe's *The Life of Harriet Beecher
Stowe*; H. B. Stowe's *The Minister's Wooing* and *My Wife and I*. All the fore-
going published by and reprinted by permission of and special arrangement with
Houghton Mifflin Company.

MISS MILDRED HOWELLS: From William Dean Howells: *The Landlord at Lion's
Head*, copyright 1900 by Harper & Brothers, copyright 1922 by Mildred How-
ells and John Mead Howells; *My Literary Passions*, copyright 1895 by Harper
& Brothers, copyright 1922 by Mildred Howells and John Mead Howells; *My
Mark Twain*, copyright 1910 by Harper & Brothers, copyright 1938 by Mildred
Howells and John Mead Howells; *The Son of Royal Langbrith*, copyright 1904
by Harper & Brothers, copyright 1931 by Mildred Howells and John Mead
Howells.

J. B. LIPPINCOTT COMPANY: From Forrest Wilson's *Crusader in Crinoline: The
Life of Harriet Beecher Stowe*, published by J. B. Lippincott Company, 1941.

THE MACMILLAN COMPANY: From Hamlin Garland's *A Son of the Middle Border*,
published by The Macmillan Company, 1927.

THE EDITORS OF THE NEW ENGLAND QUARTERLY: For Alexander Cowie's article
"Indian Summer Novelist," from *The New England Quarterly*, Vol. XV, No. 4,
(1942).

vi · *Acknowledgments*

PAUL R. REYNOLDS & SON, agents for Henry James: Henry James (editor), *The Letters of William James,* published by Little, Brown & Company, 1920.

CHARLES SCRIBNER'S SONS: From Lucy Leffingwell Biklé's *George W. Cable, His Life and Letters* (1928); G. W. Cable's *The Cavalier* (1901) and *The Grandissimes* (1880); Henry James's *The Sense of the Past* (1917) and *Letters,* edited by Percy Lubbock (1920); all published by Charles Scribner's Sons in the years indicated.

UNIVERSITY OF OKLAHOMA PRESS: From *Bayard Taylor: Laureate of the Gilded Age,* by Richard Croom Beatty. Copyright 1936 by University of Oklahoma Press. By permission.

. . . Art is long AND LIFE IS SHORT, AND SUCCESS IS VERY FAR OFF. AND THUS, DOUBTFUL OF STRENGTH TO TRAVEL SO FAR, WE TALK A LITTLE ABOUT THE AIM—THE AIM OF ART, WHICH, LIKE LIFE ITSELF, IS INSPIRING, DIFFICULT—OBSCURED BY MISTS. IT IS NOT IN THE CLEAR LOGIC OF A TRIUMPHANT CONCLUSION; IT IS NOT IN THE UNVEILING OF ONE OF THOSE HEARTLESS SECRETS WHICH ARE CALLED THE LAWS OF NATURE. IT IS NOT LESS GREAT, BUT ONLY MORE DIFFICULT.

JOSEPH CONRAD
PREFACE TO
THE NIGGER OF THE NARCISSUS

Preface

This volume presents materials for a critical history of the American novel from the beginning to the latter part of the nineteenth century, together with a concluding chapter intended as a rough indication of developments to the present time. It is not a complete and exhaustive study of all writers who have employed the novel form: such a work would require far more space. Rather, this book attempts to indicate the evolution of the American novel by means of comparatively full treatments of representative writers: all the major novelists, most of the secondary figures, and a considerable sprinkling of writers whose absolute value is very slight. Significant achievement has of course been the primary consideration. Yet the discussion of minor writers has seemed an essential part of the study: the peaks of accomplishment can be fully measured and appreciated only by one who has traversed the foot-hills on which they rest. Such minor writers as are included are accorded rather full treatment, for the mere citation of names and dates is of little use to the student of literary history. The number of pages devoted to any individual writer, therefore, is not to be regarded as a token of his intrinsic merit. Proportions are set not by space but by critical commentary.

Fundamentally the aim of this book is quite as much critical as historical. In evaluating the novelists, I have had occasion to offer revised estimates of many writers and of particular books. Although I have tried to avoid special pleading for minor novelists, it has seemed necessary to point out the merits of a few writers who have hitherto been condemned almost unread. Too often the reputations of major writers are sustained partly by unnecessary slurs upon writers little less distinguished: the runner-up in a race need not be far behind the winner. Moreover, although Americans have by now so far lost their sense of inferiority that they are prone to attach exaggerated values to new novels, a sort of retroactive provincialism causes them to disparage nineteenth-century authors. Accordingly, without becoming a missionary to obscure writers, I have aimed to re-set a number of critical judgments. Similarly I have often challenged the standard critical estimate of certain "major" books. The measuring rod in all cases has been the novelist's achievement *as* novelist; no social or political theory—whether Jeffersonian, Marxist, or New Humanist—is implicit in my criticism of the art of fiction.

The method here employed is in some respects new. Instead of presenting brief bibliographical, biographical, encyclopedia-like entries, this book offers extended and documented treatment of the authors selected or (in some cases) a few books of the author. Quotation has been liberally used, especially in cases of books difficult of access, to the end that the reader may observe the actual content and fibre of the novels discussed. The notes at the back of the volume contain entries of three principal types: detailed documentation; amplifying factual material yielded by the enormous activity of American scholars in the field of the novel; and miscellaneous items that seemed to me interesting. In most instances the various novelists have been discussed from the point of view of their development (or retrogression) as writers. Their economic, political, and religious views have been indicated as aids to the fuller understanding of their art. The older method of treating the history of literature as the history of "schools" has been largely discarded. The novelists here discussed are grouped only loosely—basted together rather than sewn. The attempt to force disparate and heterogeneous materials under confining captions—the romantic awakening, the realistic revolt, and the like—has often been responsible for curious, museum-like effects. Captions in this book, therefore, are intended to be flexible. For finally the history of the American novel is chiefly the history of American novelists.

A number of people have helped me in the preparation of this work. Professor Harry H. Clark, editor of the present series, has been ready at all times with very important assistance, both critical and scholarly. Professors Theodore H. Banks, Norman H. Pearson, and Harry R. Warfel have each read a chapter and made valuable suggestions. By far my greatest debt is to my wife, Elspeth Nicolson Cowie. She has not only borne the tremendous labor of typing but has added to this the far heavier and far more exacting task of acting as my research assistant throughout the project. In a very real sense her work is an integral part of this book.

Essential financial aid has been furnished by grants from the Wesleyan University Research Funds.

A. C.

Middletown, Connecticut

Contents

The Rise of the American Novel

At the Beginning

For the dearth of good American literature during the first 150 or 200 years of the white history of the country, apology is needed less than explanation. A new nation, like a new-born baby, requires time before its special characteristics become discernible. Doubtless a distinctive American literature could have been postulated at the moment when the first permanent colonist set foot on American soil: a heritage was established and an environment found. Yet generations had to pass before the emergence of those particular traits known as American. Change in physical characteristics of the people was so slow as to be almost imperceptible. At what time did Yorkshire speech give way to Yankee? When did the New Englander begin his nasal twang and the Southerner his drawl? No one can say with precision. And if physical changes are hard to record, cultural and literary evolution is still harder. Nor was the establishment of an American culture and literature a mere matter of throwing off the parental control of Great Britain—any more than a lad can achieve manhood by the simple process of cutting loose from home. Many other factors affected the development of a national literature. Most of these, to judge from our scanty artistic output before 1800, were unfavorable. As for the novel, it suffered from the general disabilities of all artistic enterprise in the early days as well as from special handicaps which will be referred to later. Our great achievements in fiction rose from humble beginnings.

If, as one writer has said, an American novel is simply "a novel treating of persons, places, and ideas from an American point of view," [1] it is no wonder that the form was so slow to appear. For there *was* no American point of view which could be agreed upon in the early days of the republic. Speech varied so sharply in different parts of the country that at the time of the First Continental Congress members from different localities had difficulty in understanding each other. The Revolution helped to bind the Colonies together and the Constitution gave them a common political dwelling, but even then the country was far from possessing the cohesion and solidarity and traditions which form the best matrix for the creation of art. Even in 1790 it was still true that "most citizens . . . if asked their country or nation, would not have answered American, but Carolinian, Virginian, Pennsylvanian, Jerseyman, New Yorker, or New Englander." [2] Only about three per cent of the population was urban and the rest was so scattered that easy communication was impossible. On account of the poor condition of the few roads that existed, farmers in the North often preferred to post-pone their heavy drayage until winter so as to take advantage of the snow. A journey by post-road from the northern colonies to the South took about a month under the best of conditions. Obviously it was dif-ficult to write a book which would be of interest to and could be dis-tributed to such a dispersed public. Favorable though some of these conditions might be to the later development of regional literature, they were a severe handicap in the beginning.

Other difficulties operated to prevent the development of literature of whatever sort. Elementary education thrived in New England—though even there most of a family's scholarly hopes were vested in one son—but in the South there were thousands of people (many of them slaves) who either couldn't read or preferred other amusements or con-fined their reading largely to newspapers, almanacs, and the Bible. The South had plenty of leisure and it was free from the religious preoccu-pation of New England. It was probably less prejudiced against the novel than New England. Yet its intellectual energies were largely absorbed in politics and economics; and its plantation system, essentially a quasi-aristocratic order, did not favor popular education. Free public education was established in New England fairly early, but in other parts of the country until well into the nineteenth century, schooling was obtained largely through "private initiative and benevolence." [3]

An additional difficulty in the early days was the lack of American publishers. By the end of the eighteenth century most of the big cities had printing presses, which poured forth elementary school books, re-ligious pamphlets, and political tracts in profusion. There were also a good many reprints of the classics and a fair number of reprints of modern foreign literature including novels. But native writers could seldom compete with established foreign writers, for books reprinted from foreign editions could be had without cost to the printer. [4] The lack of an international copyright law thus handicapped American writers, for if there had been a copyright fee, the local printers would have had to seek out local writers. As it was, the author had to seek out a printer, who, like as not, would refuse to print his book unless the author had secured enough subscriptions to guarantee the printer against loss. For in the late eighteenth century an author had in effect to bring out his own book: there were no publishers, only printers. [5]

Moreover, once printed, a novel was with difficulty made known to more than a local public, for before 1800 American book reviewing was practically non-existent, and after that it developed very slowly.

The newness of the country acted as a discouraging force also in less obvious ways. Those who speak of American literature as merely a continuation of English literature are forgetting the fact that a new beginning had to be made in a new country. Say that English culture was transplanted; yet in the process of transplantation, growth is certain to be suspended for a time. This was particularly true in America, where the first business on the Colonial agenda was establishing physical security. The comparatively large number of graduates of English universities who were among the early settlers of Massachusetts Bay indicates the presence of culture in the Colonies but not the impulse toward artistic expression. Art creeps in when necessity has ceased to tread, and the artist is loath to follow immediately in the footsteps of the pioneer. If, as Bliss Perry asserts, the sense of beauty was not "atrophied" [6] during our long minority in art, it was deeply dormant—and naturally so. Had Nathaniel Hawthorne been living in 1692 at the time when his great-great-grandfather Judge Hathorne was assenting to the conviction of Salem witches, his gifts as a writer would certainly have found no suitable literary outlet. Nor did Americans feel the need of producing literary work as long as America was a dependent of Britain. "We were contented," as William Cullen Bryant later said, "with considering ourselves as participating in the literary fame of that nation, of which we were a part, and of which many of us were natives, and aspired to no separate distinction." [7] These interlocking factors, then—the great size of the country, the scattering of its population, the slow progress of general education, the lack of publishers and of a copyright law, and the "psychology" of the pioneer—militated against the production of all belles lettres. As for the novel, it could not even be looked for until well into the eighteenth century. After all, the English novel was but a youngster itself. Its beginning may be dated from Defoe's *Robinson Crusoe* (1719), but the first novels of Richardson, Fielding, and Smollett did not appear until 1740, 1742, and 1749, respectively; and even Fielding, in the prefatory chapters of *Tom Jones* (1749), reminded his readers how difficult it was for a novelist to proceed without the benefit of any such body of tradition or critical principles as was available for the guidance of poets or dramatists. Moreover, although early American writers naturally imitated the English, the history of Anglo-American literary relationships up to approximately 1850 shows that there was a definite lag between English practice and American imitation. Thus, our writers continued to imitate

Addison and Pope long after those writers had passed their zenith in England; and the romantic poets of the early nineteenth century were almost unknown to the general public in America until well after 1825. In the novel it was almost inevitable that we should make a slow start, and it is not surprising that the first American novel—written long after the heyday of Richardson, Fielding, Smollett, and Sterne—did not appear until 1789.

In the meantime American readers had been enabled to sample the nature of the English product through reprints and importations. Such acquaintance as Americans made with the novel undoubtedly prepared our sterner moralists to resist home manufacture of such depraved compositions,[8] but at the same time these books created an appetite for fiction which sooner or later native novelists were bound to profit by. Probably in the early part of the eighteenth century there was more reading of fiction in the South, where a gentleman's library was likely to be less utilitarian than in the North. At all events there are signs that the English novel was well established in America long before 1789. *Robinson Crusoe* was advertised for sale by Benjamin Franklin as early as 1734, and Richardson's *Pamela* was actually brought out in a reprint by Franklin himself in 1744. A copy of Fielding's *Joseph Andrews* (1742) was read in Philadelphia as early as 1744.[9] The daughter of Jonathan Edwards was reading *Pamela* and *Joseph Andrews* in the mid-seventeen-fifties.[10] More general circulation of English novels was evidenced by their advertisement in newspapers from about 1770 onward.[11] Among the favorite works of fiction were Richardson's *Sir Charles Grandison* and Goldsmith's *Vicar of Wakefield*. Sterne's *Sentimental Journey* (1768) was for sale in America two years after it was published. Smollett, like Fielding, was probably regarded as in general too uncompromisingly realistic for household use,[12] but his *Humphrey Clinker* (1771) was circulated in a subscription library within a year, and it was advertised in the *Connecticut Journal* as early as February 12, 1776. From these and other examples that might be furnished it is clear that despite the preponderance of "improving" books in the intellectual diet available to the eighteenth-century American reader, the novel was reasonably well known. Yet when American authors began to write the novel, they produced, on the whole, only the most inferior stuff. No American Richardson or Fielding appeared in the eighteenth century to match our political independence with signs of literary parity. Before 1820, says Lyle Wright,[13] America had produced ninety novels. Yet excluding Charles Brockden Brown, H. H. Brackenridge, Cooper, and a few other writers, there were no novelists of real stature.

Reasons already given may account in part for the failure of our novelists to reach distinction. But to these influences must now be added an even more powerful deterrent, namely, the discouraging effects of that censure which greeted the first efforts of native novelists. For although novels were often indicted as evil influences long before America began to produce them, the wave of disapproval was vastly increased when American-made novels began to appear. No precise evaluation of the factors which account for our inferior production can well be made, but it is certain that the atmosphere of disapproval was unfavorable to good production. Almost every novelist who appeared in print betrayed a nervous apprehension lest his work be condemned as immoral or subversive. In short, novelists did not enjoy that freedom of intellectual and artistic climate without which few great or enduring books are born. They lived under a "perpetual childhood of prescription" [14] as to what they should and should not write. The same restraints hampered many writers of magazine fiction, which in general ran to the short tale rather than the novel. It is probable that the flood of censure aimed at fiction in general was evoked as much by magazine tales as by novels printed as books.[15] A virtual censorship was set up which must be considered before any attempt is made to understand pioneer fiction in America. For not only did such informal censorship appreciably discourage the production of fiction, but it helped to determine the character of such books as did appear. Its effect in many instances was that of devitalizing and paralyzing creative effort.

The first attempts to suppress the output or control the nature of the American novel were doubtless voiced from the pulpit. A typical attitude was that of Timothy Dwight, theologian and President of Yale College, who wrote, about 1796, that "Between the Bible, and novels, there is a gulph fixed, which few novel readers are willing to pass." [16] Magazines and newspapers, which sprouted in great numbers in the last decade of the eighteenth century, opened their columns to unrestrained attacks on fiction.[17] Sometimes the pages of fiction itself would carry pharisaical counsel against the folly and danger of indiscriminate novel-reading. Innumerable were the warnings issued to parents and children, but whatever the wording of the warning, the intention was almost always the same: novels were condemned because of their twofold threat—to morality (and religion) and to democracy.[18] Reading fiction tended to "inflame the passions" and "corrupt the heart." [19] It put ideas into girls' heads, gave them grossly inaccurate theories about life, made them discontented with their lot, opened the door to seduction, encouraged suicide, undermined religious beliefs, and vitiated democracy. No wonder it was asserted that novels are "one great engine in the hands of the fiends of darkness." [20] No wonder one editor uttered the warning that "It is as incumbent a duty to attend to the books a young lady reads, as to the company she keeps." [21] To judge from some of the diatribes against the novel, a girl was endangering her virtue almost as much by reading of a villain as by making an assignation with one.[22]

The result of such attacks as these could easily be predicted. Novelists vied with one another in making claims for the purity and usefulness of their products. In earnest prefaces they assured their readers that their stories were founded on fact. They attacked other novels as a way of establishing the innocence of their own. They made their morality unmistakably clear by the use of villains who were pitch black and heroes without a blemish. Heroines all but flew on wings. Heroes were well nigh impeccable. Hence the wide-spread acceptance of Richardson's *Sir Charles Grandison*. For finally what worried the Puritans most was the ambiguity of life and of human character. They wished to be sure of themselves. They wished to avoid admitting that there could be any good in a "bad person" or that a good person was far short of an angel. The attitude was grounded, of course, in the Puritans' anxiety to be "legally" secure, and to be able to draw a clear line between the elect and the damned. They constantly read Pope, but they would not have agreed with Pope's brilliant definition of man as "a being darkly wise and rudely great." Nor did they wish to encounter characters in fiction in whom the elements were so mixed as to make classification difficult. It is a fair guess that Fielding's *Tom Jones* was regarded as an evil book on account of the hero's mixture of traits: he was good at heart and generous in action, but intermittently prone to vice. A hero should be perfect. Thus by their insistence on categorical distinctions the moralists added to one of the very defects of the novel which they attacked, namely, unreal characterization. Joseph Dennie, the essayist, realized the probability that "the exhibition of real life has a more salutary influence on the taste of society, as well as a greater tendency to promote moral improvement and useful instruction than Richardson's 'faultless monsters, which the world ne'er saw.' " [23] But in general it was felt safer to label virtue and vice with unmistakable clarity. The novel was not to mirror life but to promote morality.

Yet although fictional characters were morally starched into mere caricatures of reality, it is doubtful if the cause of purity was served thereby, for novelists were not slow to learn that much undesirable excitement could be conveyed beneath the decorous drapery of didacticism. Even if a character is labelled as vicious, his actions may have a baneful effect. To see a character drink a glass of liquor with obvious gusto may arouse in the beholder a desire to do the same even if the author assures the reader that drinking is wrong. To read in detail of

the machinations whereby a profligate seeks to bring about the downfall of a pure maiden, wrote even such an emancipated critic as John
Trumbull, may instruct potential seducers as much as it warns female
readers.[24] Frequently the actions of the characters speak louder than
the words of the author. The factor which really determines the "morality" of a book, of course, is always the *intention* of the writer. Richardson, for example, often exhibited a morbid and prurient mind, dwelling with obvious relish on scenes which his pen pronounced evil; but
his books were in general regarded as acceptable on account of their
moral exteriors. Both he and Sterne were undoubtedly more harmful
to real virtue than the franker Fielding, for finally the only test of the
morality of a novel is the honesty and sincerity of the author's intentions: if he describes life truthfully, without seeking to exploit either
good or evil actions, he is performing the best service in his power. The
Puritans often erred in observing merely the appearances of things.
They insisted on the letter of morality.

But the attempts to curb and prescribe for the novel were in the
long run vain. Hysterical protest inevitably brings reaction. Sane people must have realized that books are only one means of education, and
that, as the author of *Areopagitica* had said, "evil manners are as perfectly learnt without books a thousand other ways which cannot be
stopped." Nor was the Puritan attitude toward life universal. In the
beginning the Puritans had something like a monopoly on publicity,
but they could not coerce the entire population even in Massachusetts,
where, even at the time of colonization, "not more than one in five adult
males . . . was sufficiently in sympathy with the religious ideas then
prevalent to become a church member." [25] At all events the reading of
novels went on. Young ladies could read them "while the governess
was gone out or mother not yet risen." [26] In some households, apparently, they could read openly without let or hindrance. In the diary
of Julia Cowles, for example, we find the intimate record of an apparently typical Connecticut girl of good family who did not scruple to
read novels, play cards, or engage in dancing. It is easy to see that the
young lady did not read merely to improve her mind, for she reported
finding Enos Hitchcock's *Memoirs of the Bloomsgrove Family* "very
entertaining as well as instructive." [27] Apparently she was at first disappointed in Richardson's *Sir Charles Grandison*—"a novel I don't in-
tend to read any more"—but the spell of Richardson must finally have
possessed her, for no less than five entries within the next few weeks
show that she returned to it, and she finally reported: "Been so much
engaged read[ing] 'Grandison' that other things have been neglected,
especially my journal." [28] Nor was Julia Cowles a merely frivolous

creature, for she was much preoccupied with religion. When she was fatally smitten with tuberculosis at the age of eighteen she committed to her diary the most exemplary sentiments and she faced her approaching death with abundant courage and the most amazing sangfroid. The satanic devices of cards, dancing, and fiction had not blasted her moral nature.

To what extent this example of novel-reading in an apparently conservative New England home is typical of its times cannot be proved. But signs of the spread of the novel are discernible in the increasing number of printers who ventured to offer fiction for sale. By 1800, despite all informal censorship, novels of American authorship had been printed not only in New York, Boston, and Philadelphia, but also in the smaller cities of Newburyport, Northampton, Leominster, Hallowell, Dedham, Walpole, and Portsmouth.[29] These books, added to the large number of foreign importations, made possible and profitable the development of circulating libraries. Of one of the most flourishing of these, Caritat's library in New York, it was reported in 1803:

> Novels are called for by the young and old; from the tender virgin of thirteen, whose little heart went pit-a-pat at the approach of a beau, to the experienced matron of three score, who could not read without spectacles.[30]

From this and other evidence it was clear by the turn of the century that whatever the objections urged against it, the novel had come to stay. The part of wisdom, then, was to encourage the production of better books and to guide readers in the wise selection of books. This much was obvious to Samuel Miller, who wrote in 1804:

> That by far the greater part of this species of fictitious history, now in circulation, is injurious to the manners, and subversive of the morals of youth, is a truth, which many lament, and which none will deny. But the pleasure with which they are read, and the eagerness with which they are sought after, will ever baffle the most sedulous attempts of parents and instructors, to keep them out of the hands of those, who are placed under their care. The best, and indeed the only remedy for this growing evil, is, the introduction of publications, of the novel class, which are unexceptionable in their moral tendency, and calculated to impress, on the young and tender mind, sentiments of honor, of virtue, and of religion; to represent things as they are, not as the wild imagination paints them.[31]

Under some such conditions as these, then, the American novel made its beginnings in the last decade of the eighteenth century. The nation was large, sparsely populated, and lacking in a strong sense of unity. Publishing enterprise was extremely slack, and printers were skeptical of native talent when successful foreign novels could be had for the pirating. Puritans were fearful of all art not directly dedicated to pious uses. Moralists thundered denunciation of the novel. Yet the public, though scattered, gradually made its demands known, and American novelists began to compete with foreign writers. Their first productions were timorously but craftily offered with every indication that the author hoped to produce a work which would satisfy the reader's craving for excitement without incurring the censure of the trustees of the nation's morals. An author's least concern, apparently, was whether his novel possessed artistic value: enough if he could reach his readers at all. It is not to be wondered at, therefore, that with few exceptions, early American novelists produced works whose principal importance is historical. For the most part they were tentative and experimental and imitative; their authors were groping to find a medium which would give play to their abilities and satisfaction to a vaguely felt public. For the first decade or so, no single species dominated the field; rather, the novels exhibited markings of various types. Yet in order to understand the nature of these early efforts, it is most convenient to view them as they approach or fall away from certain loose classifications: the sentimental or domestic, the Gothic, the historical, the "Indian," and the satirical.

HEART AND HOME: DOMESTIC, SENTIMENTAL, DIDACTIC FICTION

The Power of Sympathy (1789) is by general agreement regarded as the first American novel. There were a few American-born writers who had produced novels before 1789, but on account of the circumstances of their lives, they can hardly be reckoned as indigenous writers. Charlotte Lennox, author of *The Female Quixote* (1752), was born on American soil, but her adult life and literary career were wholly English.[32] *The History of Charles Wentworth Esq.* (London, 1770) was written by a native of Massachusetts, Edward Bancroft, who left America in early youth, never to return. Francis Hopkinson's *A Pretty Story* (1774) is indubitably American, but it can hardly be embraced in even a loose definition of the novel, for it is essentially a political satire taking the form of allegory.[33] With some reason *The Adventures of Alonso* (published anonymously at London in 1775) has been designated the first American novel, but although the author was apparently born in Maryland, the provenance of the book is only in limited degree American.[34] Though born in England, Susanna Rowson is generally regarded as an American writer by reason of her early emigration to this country and her profound impression upon American readers; yet though she had published three novels in England by 1788, it was not until she wrote *Charlotte Temple* (published in London in 1791 and in New York in 1794) that she laid the real basis for her enormous American popularity.[35] Therefore, although the point of priority is doubtless a minor one, it is at least plausible to date the beginning of the American novel from 1789 with the appearance of *The Power of Sympathy*, a comparatively long fictional work laid in Boston, published in Boston, written by an American, and grounded in purely local interests.[36] Published anonymously, the novel was for many years attributed to the pen of Mrs. Sarah Wentworth Morton, who had established herself as a poet more or less worthy of her sobriquet "the American Sappho." In the light of recent investigation, however, it appears that Mrs. Morton could not have been the author. Cogent, though not absolutely conclusive, evidence points rather to the authorship of a successful poet, dramatist, and essayist of the time, William Hill Brown (1765-1793).[37]

If American novelists hoped to gain a large constituency of readers, the best platform plank they could adopt was the promise of heavy moralizing. No rogue story like Fielding's or Smollett's with its emphasis on dupery and sex, no idle Gothic tale patterned after *The Castle of Otranto*, but a good domestic story calculated to impart unmistakable lessons to the young—that was the most likely to be acceptable. Richardson would be a good model. It was no accident that *The Power of Sympathy* carried its moral promises in its very dedication, which announced that the story was "Intended to represent the specious causes, and to expose the fatal consequences, of seduction; to inspire the female mind with a principle of self complacency, and to promote the economy of human life." Yet this didactic principle was hammered home by a story of such lurid violence that, despite the author's urbane language and his preservation of "decorum," the lesson it conveyed could hardly be considered suitable for young readers. The hero, one Harrington, falls captive to the charms of Harriott Fawcett, but because of her lowly station (as companion to Mrs. Francis) he has at first no intention of marrying her. Later, however, true love prompts him to defy the wishes of his patrician father by marrying Harriott secretly. This outcome is prevented when a friend conveys to Harrington the intelligence that Harriott is his half-sister by the unlawful union of his father and Maria Fawcett. These tidings arrive in time to prevent incest[38] but they precipitate the death of Harriott (by shock) and of Harrington (by suicide). This grim main plot is embellished with two insets, both instructive. The first of these tells of the triumph of one Mr. Martin over his wife's sister, Ophelia, who is subsequently so harshly treated by her father that she poisons herself. The other relates to the abduction of Fidelia by a ruffian a few days before her intended marriage with a true lover, who now hurls himself into a river.

Thus the American novel had its beginning in a story whose framework of action was sensational in the extreme. The text is as blameless as the action is sensational; and the impact of the tragedies is reduced somewhat by means of didactic padding and tearful sentimentalizing. Yet the final result must have been sufficiently horrible not only to act as a warning to the "female mind" but to induce nightmares. The episode of Ophelia was painfully real to contemporary readers because of its virtually undisguised analogy to a real tragedy which occurred almost precisely as related in the novel, to Fanny Apthorp, sister of the Mrs. Morton to whom the novel was for a long time ascribed. Indeed particular attention was called to the correspondence between the episode and the actual case by the use of a frontispiece which showed the dying agony of Ophelia.[39] So obviously did the author of the book attempt to trade upon a private scandal that steps were apparently taken, with only partial success, to suppress the book soon after publication.

The excitement created by the factual basis of *The Power of Sympathy* bears no ratio to the value of the novel. The story is readable only because it is reasonably brief: in a long novel the author's overwrought rhetoric and moral rant would have been intolerable. Its lack of detailed attention to setting is not remarkable in a novel written so early as 1789, but its poor characterization, loose motivation, graceless digressions, and generally careless structure are less excusable. Consequently the work is interesting chiefly for historical reasons. It provides the first American example of a novel embodying the Richardsonian theme of virtue in distress. Like many books in the seduction tradition it is uncomplimentary to men in that it represents them as frequently no better than wolves preying on the innocence of unprotected girls. It is written in the letter form,[40] and it is liberally dosed with strained moralizing. Like *Clarissa Harlowe*, this book emphasizes the sins "both of Parents and Children in relation to Marriage." [41] The evils of class distinction are of course exemplified in the fact that it is the senior Harrington's liaison with a woman "beneath him" in station which prepares for his son's tragedy.[42] It gives prominence to the subject of suicide, and Harrington's dying with a copy of Goethe's *Sorrows of Werther* lying open on his table establishes the use of that work as an indispensable manual for young men whose love falls fatefully in forbidden places. *The Power of Sympathy* is also representative of many novels in its author's attempt to disarm criticism by boldly referring to the dangers of novel-reading. Specific suggestions for more suitable reading for young ladies include the laborious epics of Dwight and Barlow, then newly published, and Noah Webster's (recent) *Grammatical Institute*.[43] Oddly enough, a good word is also put in for Laurence Sterne, who, despite the salacious elements in his writing, was evidently read a great deal in Puritan America—perhaps because his profession as a minister was felt to be a guarantee of his probity. On the other hand one of the young ladies is warned against Chesterfieldian principles as being not only inappropriate in a republic but also insidiously dangerous, for "affectation of fine breeding is destructive to morals." [44]

Thus viewed from whatever angle *The Power of Sympathy* was armed with admonitions calculated to cool any passions that its sensational action might have created. Yet the book was not destined for wide distribution, for the author, aware of the distress he was causing the members of the Apthorp family, apparently consented to its suppression. Sales were stopped, and unsold copies destroyed. The book fell from public sight; it seems to have been "mentioned in print only five times in 1789, only twice between 1790 and 1800, and not at all during the fifty years following." [45]

A second novel stemming from the Richardsonian tradition of the harassed female was Mrs. Rowson's *Charlotte Temple*, which had its first American edition at Philadelphia in 1794. Born in Portsmouth, England, in 1762, Susanna Haswell Rowson had a varied and exciting career exemplifying some of the same hardships which became stock experiences for sentimental fictional heroines in generations to come. The daughter of a Lieutenant in the British Navy, she came to Boston with him in 1767, and lived chiefly at Nantasket until 1778, when she and her father were deported for political reasons. She served as a governess in London; under pressure of friends she married a friend of her father; she endured poverty when her husband's business failed. An acting engagement at a Philadelphia theatre brought her to America in 1793. In 1796 she formed a new theatrical connection in Boston, but in the following year she gave up the stage in favor of teaching school. She died at Boston in 1824.[46]

Charlotte Temple is distinctly superior as a novel to *The Power of Sympathy*. The story is told rapidly and with signs of genuine power that cannot be laughed away in merriment over the inevitably ornate style in which the author wrote. The action begins in England. Under the influence of a dissolute French governess, Charlotte is induced to elope with a dashing young army officer, Montraville, who promises to marry her when they reach New York. Once arrived in America, Montraville prefers a wealthier match, leaving Charlotte to languish in a suburb of New York without friends or funds. The money which Montraville sends for her use is diverted by one Belcour, who wishes to win Charlotte to his own depraved purposes—not realizing that "a woman might fall a victim to impudence, and yet retain so strong a sense of honor, as to reject with horror and contempt every solicitation to a second fault." [47] Belcour assures Charlotte that Montraville has abandoned her and tells Montraville that Charlotte has been unfaithful to him. Charlotte walks several miles to ask assistance of Mrs. Crayton (her former governess), who repels her. She is finally given lodgings in the humble home of a kindly serving woman, but it is soon apparent that she will not survive the ordeal of childbirth. Her father arrives in time to witness her death and to cap the scene with a maximum of pathos and morality. Montraville, now filled with remorse and enraged at Belcour's duplicity, kills the latter in a duel at swords. Himself wounded in the fray, he suffers a serious illness. "He recovered," reports the author, "but to the end of his life was subject to severe fits of melancholy, and while he remained at New-York frequently retired to the church yard, where he would weep over the grave and regret the untimely fate of the lovely Charlotte Temple." [48]

The harsh attitude toward fallen women which is generally associated with Puritan morality is not fully illustrated in *Charlotte Temple*. The author's reproaches of Charlotte are at least equalled by her indignation at Montraville and Belcour, especially the latter. Observing Charlotte in her wretched betrayed condition, Mrs. Beauchampe asserts that Charlotte is worth saving, for "her heart may not be depraved," and even when the end is near Mrs. Beauchampe expresses a hope that Charlotte "might recover, and, spite of her former errors, become a useful and respectable member of society." [49] A far cry, this, from the common conviction that one step from rectitude should blast a girl's soul for eternity. Mrs. Rowson seems to have been aware that despite the indubitably moral bearing of her book, her humane attitude toward Charlotte might create disapproval among the unco guid:

My dear Madam, contract not your brow into a frown of disapprobation. I mean not to extenuate the faults of those unhappy women who fall victims to guilt and folly; but surely, when we reflect how many errors we are ourselves subject to, how many secret faults lie hid in the recesses of our hearts, which we should blush to have brought into open day (and yet those faults require the lenity and pity of a benevolent judge, or awful would be our prospect of futurity) I say my dear Madam, when we consider this, we surely may pity the fault of others.

Believe me, many an unfortunate female, who has once strayed into the thorny paths of vice, would gladly return to virtue, was any generous friend to endeavor to raise and reassure her: but alas! it cannot be, you say; the world would deride and scoff. Then let me tell you, Madam, 'tis a very unfeeling world, and does not deserve half the blessings which a bountiful Providence showers upon it.[50]

Obviously Mrs. Rowson was kinder to erring womanhood than most of her contemporaries and immediate successors among American novelists. Perhaps her experience of the world taught her a broader tolerance than was possible to the average female novelist, who too often gives the impression of having concocted her merciless morality on the basis of hatred and suspicion. Yet Mrs. Rowson is strong in her indictment of the one really corrupt character in her story, the French governess. The very last chapter of the book shows Mrs. Crayton, now reduced to the gutter, petitioning Mr. Temple for aid. He charitably and unsanctimoniously grants it, but she dies within a few weeks, "a striking example that vice, however prosperous in the beginning, in the end leads only to misery and shame." These are the last words in a book which has been one of the most popular ever published in America. It is easy, especially for the person without historical perspective, to laugh at the old-fashioned rhetoric of the author. It *is* amusing. When Mrs. Rowson meant that Mrs. Beauchampe wept for Charlotte, she referred to "the pellucid drop of humanity stealing down her cheek." [51] Yet to base a critical judgment of a whole book on trifles like this is illogical; over-embellished language was as much a part of the period as hoopskirts. The real question about *Charlotte*, as about any novel, is whether it has basic sincerity and power. Unquestionably it has; the wretchedness and loneliness of Charlotte and the quiet suffering of her parents are rendered with a simple vividness which can be felt even today. The book had something over two hundred editions.[52] The most striking thing about its sale, however, was not the size of the original editions but the long-continued demand for the book. It is a curious fact, that although the public is often misled for a short time into buying vast quantities of an inferior book, the public taste almost never errs over a long period of time; it never keeps alive a merely meretricious book. That *Charlotte* was in constant demand throughout the nineteenth century and has had a moderate sale even at the present time is a sign of real merit in the novel.[53]

Mrs. Rowson wrote a number of other novels which show a fair degree of skill and some originality but which for the most part deserve the oblivion which has overtaken them.[54] *Trials of the Human Heart* (Philadelphia, 1795) is a story which moves rapidly over land and sea on narrative errands which could hardly have edified conservative readers of the day. The heroine is a pure girl, but she finds her true love (a widower) only after glimpses of pretty seamy life, including an attempt at incest, a visit to a house of ill-fame, a loveless marriage. In *Reuben and Rachel: or Tales of Old Times* (1798) Mrs. Rowson uses American history and American scenes as ingredients in a romance so fantastic and so involved that even her comparatively sober study of the American Indian cannot redeem it. In 1803-04 *The Boston Weekly Magazine* (of which she was editor) serialized her *Sarah: or The Exemplary Wife*, a domestic story laid abroad and based in part on Mrs. Rowson's own experiences as a teacher and a governess.[55] In all these novels, as in a number of shorter tales, Mrs. Rowson repeatedly proved herself as an able delineator of dramatic episode with incidental realistic effects, but her plots showed that instability which was one of the principal weaknesses of the early novel. The stories are overloaded with poorly allocated episodes, and the scene shifts from place to place too rapidly to permit of orientation. Mrs. Rowson had a natural affinity with the adventure story. Her heroines are adventuresses of a superior sort, often displaying the author's own initiative and enterprise instead of the flabby passivity of many contemporary heroines. The underlying moral intention of the author is almost always felt, but Mrs. Rowson's fairly frequent use of the methods and atmosphere of what has come to be known as "chamber-maid fiction" raises the suspicion that she was occasionally thinking more of her own bread and butter than of a suitable intellectual diet for the young. The meek and lowly heroine of *Charlotte* was the only one of Mrs. Rowson's characters who really stirred the sympathies of the public.

A third extremely popular tale of seduction deriving in general from the Richardsonian pattern was Hannah Foster's *The Coquette* (1797).[56] It also was based upon an actual case whose details were familiar to a wide public. Elizabeth Whitman, the prototype of the heroine (called Eliza Wharton) was the beautiful, vain, and vivacious daughter of a well-known clergyman of Hartford. She rejected two substantial offers of marriage, fell victim to the wiles of a gay seducer, rode off to Danvers to conceal her pregnancy, and died in childbirth in July, 1788.[57]

The two rejected suitors were the Reverend Joseph Howe and the Reverend Joseph Buckminster, both of Yale College. The identity of the seducer has been the subject of much speculation—was he Jonathan Edwards' son Pierrepont, or Aaron Burr, or a foreign military officer? —but no record remains to prove the case.[58] In any case much of the blame for the tragedy was laid on the coquettish character of Miss Whitman herself. Nor did enemies of novel-reading fail to point out after her death that she had probably laid the foundation for her own ruin by becoming "*a great reader of romances.*" [59] The novel is in general faithful to the facts of the actual case so far as they are known. The principal change it makes is that Major Sanford (the villain in the story) is represented as having married another person and as being enabled to triumph over the heroine by assuring her that his heart had not gone with his hand. In any case Mrs. Foster had to alter real facts very little in order to make her novel "the most striking example in early American fiction of the pervasive influence of Samuel Richardson." [60] The letter form is employed with a great deal of skill—much more skillfully certainly than in *The Power of Sympathy*. The story moves with less speed than *Charlotte* and the author fills the interims of the action with the same sort of sentiment, didacticism, and stuffy analysis of the "heart" that clogs Richardson's *Clarissa*. *The Coquette* differs from *Charlotte* too in the pert attacks of its heroine on the conventions of the day. She regarded marriage as "the tomb of friendship" and she couldn't understand why people should try to "confine virtue to a cell." She found the conversation of her theological suitors extremely tedious and longed for a social sphere which would allow scope for her talents. No wonder that the gruesome result of such a rebellious and abandoned philosophy should have been felt to convey a salutary lesson which even the author's references to the mercy of God did not completely offset. Yet the book did not achieve instantaneous popularity. A second edition was not required for five years and a third not till 1811. The period of its greatest vogue was between 1824 and 1828, when it may have been regarded as a convenient resort for readers who did not fully relish the historical romance, at that time in the ascendancy.[61] In 1855, an enthusiastic reviewer greeted a new edition of *The Coquette* with the remark that the story had "attracted, perhaps, almost as much attention as that of the Waverley Novels." [62] From a literary point of view it has not weathered the years so well as *Charlotte Temple*. It is competently written in an agreeable prose style and it has that focus which early novels so often lack. Yet it is bookish in tone; it lacks *Charlotte Temple's* direct and simple appeal to the emotions. It depends for its effect too largely on a knowledge of the tragic facts to which it owed its origin.

These three novels, *The Power of Sympathy*, *Charlotte Temple*, and *The Coquette*, represented perhaps the most popular type of early American fiction, the sentimental novel. They were in many ways inferior—their settings were only bungled hints, their scanty dialogue was either puerile or incredibly formal, and their characters were little more than names. Of these three authors only Mrs. Rowson seems to have had that understanding of human nature which is essential to a novelist. Yet at least two of the novels were warmly received. Their authors at least had an eye for situation and they were crafty enough to select the ever-popular theme of seduction. They domesticated for American use the fascinating Richardsonian heroine. Their books were doubtless read for their thrills but they were accepted for their moral lessons. Didacticism was a *sine qua non* of the early novel.

Yet there were those who felt that the moral lessons might be learned at too great peril. Tender readers might be singed if they witnessed at too close range the blaze of passion which consumed the frail characters of a novel. The serpent of evil, if studied too intently, might claim a new victim in the observer. To be wholly innocuous a novel must recommend virtue without even describing vice. Accordingly some fiction-writers aimed directly at didacticism. Such a writer was the Reverend Enos Hitchcock, author of *Memoirs of the Bloomsgrove Family* (1790), the second American novel to be published in book form—if the term novel may be accurately applied to it. Anyone who feared that *The Power of Sympathy* was too strong a brew for tender systems could confidently recommend *Memoirs of the Bloomsgrove Family*, which is the very cambric tea of American fiction. Its action as such could almost be comprehended in the statement that after a due course of edifying lectures and object lessons Osander, the hero, marries Rozella, the heroine. The book distinctly recalls *Sandford and Merton* in its succession of lessons, projects, and anecdotes. The improving discourses on which the children dutifully sup are about as tasteless as barley water, and the anecdotes which Mr. Bloomsgrove distributes like cakes as a reward are frequently pretty musty. Moreover they were remote from American life, including such items as the "story of a grateful Turk," "anecdote of a noble Venetian," "anecdote of a French Lady," etc.

The author's direct observations on education have more pertinence, and they are of the sort which were to fill the intervals of action in domestic novels for decades to come. He aptly remarks that many educational systems fail because of their emphasis on "WHAT TO THINK rather than HOW TO THINK." [63] Some of the earlier manuals of education, the author believes, are useless as being "suited to a distant meridian." [64] He particularly stresses "the importance of the first seven years of education." Rousseau's *Émile* interests him greatly and to some extent pleases him. Yet he questions the advisability of allowing a child to forego books during the first twelve years of his life and to rely instead on the wisdom and learning of a preceptor, for

> every man to whom the care of children is committed is not a Rousseau, nor is every child an Emilius or a Sophia: neither are we aerial beings, that we should subsist on sentimental diet: application to labor, or some kind of employment, is NECESSARY for most people, and PROPER for all." [65]

The practical schoolmaster is seen also in his warnings against boarding schools, where girls are taught to "dissemble gracefully, rather than to think or act virtuously." Useless emphasis upon the arts and fancy needlework should be replaced by a grounding in "the science of economy" and "domestic business." A girl should learn to make a "pudding." As for general reading, she should acquire a certain amount of information, but she should avoid becoming a "learned lady" or bluestocking—a warning which is to be echoed in the American novel for the next sixty years. The usual warning against novel-reading in general is here: novels "excite romantic notions." Among those novelists who may be read without complete loss of integrity the safest is Richardson, whose books "unite sentiment with character, and present images of life." Yet the author shrewdly adds that there is some question whether "the moral view is not lost . . . in those love scenes [of *Clarissa*] which interest the passions more than the understanding." Therefore Richardson is to be read "with caution, and under direction of a guide." The same danger, he feels, is faced in Fielding's novels. Smollett is tolerantly allowed "merit" but, with a fine understatement, the author calls attention to his "unpolished humor." As for "books of infidelity" and other downright incitements to immorality, the author craftily avoids naming them but asserts that the "world abounds with them." The opinions of the author, naturally conservative in view of his clerical profession, are more mature than his art as a writer. A studious formality prevents his presenting effectively even such action as he deems suitable for young readers. The quality of his style may be judged from his elaborate muffling of a simple fact:

> On a day, when the declining sun had tinged the mountain tops
> with its milder rays, and reddening skies invited the tuneful choir
> to serenade the groves with the faint lays of their evening song;
> these happy parents were invited, by the serenity that followed the
> shower, to the gravel walk.[66]

It is difficult to believe that such a book could be widely read. It is true
that no second edition of it seems to have been called for, yet it was
not immediately lost from view, for we find a casual reference to it in
the diary of a young lady for the year 1799 as a book which she found
"very entertaining as well as instructive." [67]

In the early period there were many other novels which were so
flooded with didacticism that no spark of artistic merit could survive.
Helena Wells wrote two heavily didactic novels which, although published in London, seem to have been circulated successfully in America:
The Step-Mother (1799) and *Constantia Neville, or the West Indian*
(1800).[68] The former of these points out the "superior advantages of
religious education," and inveighs against the evil effects of fiction that
revels in "the marvelous and the terrible." The story itself is a fantastically "moral" narrative of an incredible female who renounces a
suitor because *she* possesses neither money nor social position—a finely
oblique suggestion of a truth seldom admitted by authors of romances
which are happily concluded, namely that a character's possession of
material resources is a great stimulus to the work of Cupid.

A didactic novel which apparently held the public longer than either
of these is Caroline Matilda Warren's *The Gamesters: or Ruins of Innocence*, first published in 1805 and reprinted as late as 1828. The plot
is compounded of exciting elements, including seduction and suicide,
but the language is maintained at a high level of formality. The narrow
path of the narrative is heavily hedged with morality. In this respect,
as well as in others, *The Gamesters* exhibits generic traits of the early
sentimental novel. The first business of the author is to deprive the
hero, Leander, of his parents. Accordingly Mrs. Anderson is

> suddenly dropped into eternity. It was a scene which angels might
> have contemplated with pleasure, to see the virtuous die.[69]

In the next chapter, following the burial of the mother, the father, feeling a twinge of something like apoplexy, announces to his son that the
latter "must shortly be an orphan." [70] In cases like this the author's
hints are never groundless; and soon Leander is thrown upon the wide,
wicked world, his devout parents lost, and his care committed to a

brother-in-law, who cannot save the lad from destruction. Bad company corrupts the young man; he goes so far in gambling that he even hazards the ornamental casket he has given his wife. There can be only one end to such a sordid tale, suicide; but it is true that in the death scene the author employs the "novelty of substituting Addison's *Cato* for the usual *Werther* opened at the appropriate passage." [71] Realism is almost wholly absent. There is no description, for example, of the tavern where Leander loses his moral course. The only relief from the stuffy atmosphere of sealed morality is the conventional nautical lingo of Tom Tarpaulin, who hopes "to tie the *grand reef* with Peggy, to sail one voyage in the ship, Matrimony" and whose most fearful imprecation expresses a wish that if he err he may be "soused with fresh water." [72] In her preface the author expresses the belief that the "light, unthinking mind, that would revolt at a moral lesson from the pulpit, will seize with avidity, the instruction offered under the similitude 'of a story.'" She further asserts that she will be satisfied if she can "lure one profligate from the arms of dissipation, or snatch from the precipice of ruin, one fair fabric of innocence." [73] It is a fair guess, however, that she also hoped her story would sell. And, though it is doubtful if any hardened gambler would read Mrs. Warren's remote admonitions "with avidity," the book does seem to have had a vogue among many comparable manuals of behavior.

Almost all early novels were to some extent didactic, but the ratio of instruction to entertainment varied greatly. In *The Hapless Orphans* (1793) "By an American Lady" the author pretty definitely set out to write first of all an interesting tale of adventure. Although it by no means flouts religion or morality, *The Hapless Orphans* lacks obvious marks of piety. It errs by the omission of underlined ethics. The heroine, Caroline Francis, is a bit worldly in her attitude. She does not flatten out under adversity and utter conventional phrases about the duty of submission. She acts for the most part out of a reasonable self-interest which she does not wholly obscure by moral posturing. She does not chant platitudes about meeting adversity and submitting to fate but avows her wish to "make as easy as possible the various incidents which occur in this journey of life." [74] Shocking! Here is a girl mainly interested in her own welfare—a girl with more than a hint of Becky Sharp in her. But she *has* her troubles. Forced out of her aunt's home by hard treatment, she vigorously takes charge of her own fortunes. She resists sundry predatory males, but when she falls in love with the betrothed of another girl, she does not renounce him heroically. As a result of the inevitable conflict that ensues, the young man commits suicide and Eliza, the first sweetheart, vows revenge. The details of Eliza's program of persecution, consisting among other things of slander, terror-devices, and attempted abduction, form the basis of most of the rest of the book. Meantime Caroline has become engaged to another man, but she must carry on without his protection while he is fighting the Indians in a distant place. In the end Eliza brings down her prey. What moral can be deduced from such a tale? True, the motivation of the story is often wobbly and the style needlessly pontifical, but the action in general is as objective and amoral as life itself must often have seemed to actual young ladies of the day. The author does not even mete out appropriate punishment to Eliza. Such a book as this could not fail to arouse protest, but it was likely to win readers. Other books of the same general type there were—books which were not flagrantly immoral but which failed to pay sufficient respect to the mores of Puritan America—but they enjoyed only a checkered prosperity until more emancipated times.[75] In the early days it was safer to use a conventional framework of reward and punishment, and make sure that the letters of morality were writ large.

THE GOTHIC ROMANCE

Nevertheless there was another type of novel which violated the implicit command that fiction must be first of all morally edifying— the Gothic romance. The complaint of the author of *The Step-Mother*[76] regarding fictional emphasis on "the marvelous and the terrible" was only one of many protests against a form of entertainment which consisted of nervous thrills and shudders at quasi-supernatural episodes involving pale heroines, haunted castles, bloody statues, trapdoors, ruthless bandits, etc. The Gothic romance, in point of fact, never really thrived upon American soil. It was practiced extensively by one of early America's most powerful novelists, Charles Brockden Brown,[77] but as a distinct species it languished. There were several reasons for this.

First, the Gothic novel had no ethical front. It might be provided with moral tags, but organically its function was not moral. In an era therefore when novels were often regarded as "a species of writing which can scarcely be spoken of without being condemned," [78] it behooved a writer to pick his vehicle carefully. There were three principal forms which the English novel took during the eighteenth century: the sentimental or domestic, the picaresque, and the Gothic. The picaresque, with its emphasis on dupery, sex, and satire, was naturally not welcomed, and in fact the picaresque novel did not prosper in America until the 1920's, when it flourished in a modified form. The sentimental novel was a better hope. Drenched in tears it might be, but it was provided with a solid rock of Christian ethics, and it often taught the supreme duty of self-sacrifice. Even in the form in which it first appeared in the American novel, namely, the tale of seduction, it was sometimes felt to serve a useful purpose. Reading novels like *Charlotte Temple* and *The Coquette* left a girl resolved never to trust any man— least of all a man in uniform. No such claim could be made for the Gothic novel. Reading *it* left the reader a mass of gooseflesh and fluttering nerves. How could such symptoms serve the cause of God and John Calvin? True, the Gothic novel was less objectionable than the picaresque, for it did not require an erotic content, but it had nothing positive to recommend it. It was sheer entertainment and as such to be condemned, whether written by Mrs. Radcliffe or by an American.

But there were technical difficulties as well as moral ones. The more romantic parts of the American landscape were shockingly devoid of castles in a suitable state of disrepair; we possessed few ancient portraits that leered or winked or dripped blood; our manuscripts were likely to be either spurious or imported or embarrassingly modern.[79] Our heroines could easily be pallid, and they could be trained to risk pneumonia, a nervous breakdown, or sudden death in the performance of nocturnal errands that brought them face to face with the apparently supernatural. A heroine could even be made to look proud and aristocratic, but, in a strictly republican country, she couldn't always be the daughter or ward of a depraved marquis. In short Cooper's later apology for the historical romance on the grounds that America lacked suitable antiquity and aristocracy was even more appropriate to the Gothic romance.

Perhaps another reason for our relative failure in the Gothic romance was our comparatively late beginning in the form. By the time our first Gothic romance appeared (in 1798), England had already built up a nice Gothic library—containing, among other items, *The Castle of Otranto*, *The Monk*, *Vathek*, *Caleb Williams*, and *The Mysteries of Udolpho*—which American publishers, profiting by the absence of copyright laws, were glad to make available to native readers at less than they would have to charge for doubtful American tales.[80] Later on, the Gothic temporarily wore out its popularity both in England and America. Scott's *Waverley* in 1814 created brand-new fictional interests. In 1818 Jane Austen's *Northanger Abbey* sprayed the Gothic form with noxious humor. In 1820 Cooper established the historical romance as the most popular American type of fiction. Thereafter straight Gothic was no longer a leader.[81]

Moral, technical, and chronological difficulties thus tended to hamper the growth of American Gothic, and even Charles Brockden Brown did not wholly surmount its difficulties. Yet the species was bound to appear. The first writer (excepting Brown) who made considerable use of the form was Sarah Sayward Barrell Keating Wood (usually referred to as Mrs. Sally Wood), a native of Maine. Although Mrs. Wood possessed only moderate ability, yet by virtue of her early position she repays attention in any study of the novel. Among the strains which she used to achieve interest was a mild infusion of the Gothic. This appears especially in her first novel, *Julia and the Illuminated Baron* (1800), a novel which, however, provides many other points of reference for a study of the literary taste of the times.

In the dedication and preface to *Julia*, Mrs. Wood is at great pains to introduce herself in a favorable light. Aware of the common prejudice against learned ladies who neglect the household arts, she assures the public that "not one social, or one domestic duty, have ever been sacrificed or postponed by her pen." [82] She also makes it clear that, although the story is laid in France during the period of the Revolution, her intentions are not political: indeed she avows her inability to understand politics. In choosing a foreign mise-en-scène she has aimed merely to avoid the unpleasantness of introducing living characters who might be recognized. That her story is a "Romance" she cannot deny, but she hopes to allay criticism by her service to morality: she proposes to show the horror of a general tendency toward "throwing off the shackles of religion, and becoming . . . infidels." She concludes humbly by asserting her "wish to do good." It is impossible to impugn Mrs. Wood's underlying morality but in view of the extravagant tale she has to unfold, one questions her complete ingenuousness. For, granted that she distributes moral judgments at appropriate points, it is hard to see how any Maine maiden or swain could be improved by being exposed to the mesh of intrigue and emotionalism that constitutes *Julia*.

As in many novels of the time and for years to come, the plot of *Julia* hinges finally on the identity of the principal character. Here is Julia, an affable, innocent, high-minded, and temptingly beautiful girl, living in a cottage in the south of France, mourning the death of a man referred to as (what he obviously is not) her "grandfather." Suddenly adopted as the protegée of one Countess de Launa and whisked away to the luxurious splendors of a château, she is thrown into the company of an equally high-minded (and, sh! apparently low-born) youth. These two must eventually marry each other: that is clear from the outset. Naturally, therefore, the author sets up a series of obstacles which must be surmounted before the union of the pair will be appreciated. The girl must be subjected to dishonorable proposals, arrested as a prisoner of state, stricken with smallpox, kidnapped by an unprincipled aristocrat, rescued in the nick of time from rape, reduced to roadside poverty by the burning of her temporary refuge, and in general forced through vicissitudes of fortune which shuttle her back and forth between states of "extreme agony" and "inexpressible joy." The hero in the meantime has had the comparatively easy assignment of going to America (a land he greatly admires as being possessed of "liberty without anarchy and confusion" [83]) on an errand of mercy—to rescue a cousin. Yet he too has his troubles (including shipwreck), and on his return he is falsely arrested for murder and imprisoned for a year. At the end it is revealed (to the surprise of the characters but not of the reader) that Julia is the niece of the Countess de Launa and that the young man is Ormond, the long-lost son of the Countess' first marriage. The young folks are therefore cousins, of noble blood and ample fortune. In grisly retrospect the reader realizes that the aristocratic cad who offered violence to Julia was none other than her half-brother— an oblique suggestion of incest which novelists of the day somehow found quite compatible with their vaunted wish to edify the young. Presumably the lesson of the story is chiefly found in its devout references to the "illustrious Washington" [84] and general implications of the advantages of a republican government. The hero, who is once rescued from shipwreck by the Negroes owned by Washington, declares himself free from the common "prejudice, that . . . a dark skin, cannot cover a fair heart." [85] Further instruction in democracy is implied by the decision of the happy pair to renounce the titles they have inherited, to dispense much of their fortunes to charity, and to live simply as Mr. and Mrs. Ormond. Yet no mere renunciation of titles at the end of a long story steeped in glamorous references to the lives of aristocrats can convert *Julia* into a primer of democracy. Mrs. Wood, like many other novelists, perfectly well knew that although American principles forbade titles, American readers loved to contemplate them. And it was to take almost as long to get foreign titles out of American fiction as to get the English skylark out of American poetry.

Indirectly, American ideals are emphasized by the author's treatment of the Baron (later Count) de Launa who figures in the title of the story. He it is who threatens the honor of Julia, and who has murdered his step-mother. In him Mrs. Wood presents a hideous embodiment of the vicious principles of the Illuminati, a secret society dedicated to the belief that humanity should enfranchize itself from petty principles of religion, marriage, property rights, and other negligible conventions. To them murder is only a practical means to an end, and incest is as acceptable as any other relationship.[86] The Baron scoffs at conventional mores, and he boasts to Julia: "I am to myself a God, and to myself accountable; I pursue my own pleasure . . ." [87] He refers to the membership of the Illuminati as being about 20,000, and he is confident that in time they will rule Europe. He invites Julia to join him in this organization of emancipated spirits, assuring her that its enrollment includes many of the "first characters" in literature and philosophy. Against such principles as these Mrs. Wood naturally pits all the energy she can spare from her chronicle of Julia's exciting adventures. Moreover the more Gothic elements of the story derive partly from the Baron's sinister pursuit of the heroine. Yet the scene most deeply dipped in horror was brought by the heroine upon herself when she insisted upon visiting a tomb at midnight. With two companions she sets out with only a candle and a lantern to combat a raging storm of hail and lightning. Once she is in the "mansion of death, a kind of chilling horror, seemed to pervade her whole frame, and congeal her blood." She even touches the countenance of one of the older residents of the place, whereupon the face "sunk into ashes, and mouldered into dust; not a feature remained; it was all an horrid chasm, for the affrighted imagination to fill up." Well might Julia's blood congeal at this Poe-like maneuver: it would have frozen utterly had she known that she was peering into the ex-countenance of her own mother. Meantime she has snipped a lock of the deceased's hair. Finally, she and her companions make their way from the place, not without glimpses of a "ghost," and, the candle having been extinguished at the exit of the tomb, they stumble home in the tempest. This godless scene must have been inserted by the author for the sake of sheer thrill, for it entirely lacks motivation beyond the fact that Julia has a curiosity to see the tomb and has the unfounded presentiment that she will be buried in it.

The story is the thing in *Julia*, but there are a few digressions and not the least of the horrors to which Julia is exposed is the necessity of listening to the irrelevant life stories of several characters—a distress which she shares with several characters in the novels of Charles Brockden Brown. Though the story is laid in France, Mrs. Wood is enabled to capitalize her own country by means of Colwort's letters, which comment on manners and government and miscellaneous matters including his visit to Mrs. Sarah Wentworth Morton, the eminent poet and essayist of Boston.[88] There is very little description, and that of the most amateur nature. The first description of the château of the Countess de Launa vouchsafes no single architectural detail which might enable the reader to visualize it.[89] Landscape receives the same general treatment, but it is slightly more effective, for, perhaps under the influence of Rousseau or St. Pierre, it is closely linked with the mood of the observer—as when at a point of vantage Julia under the "full orbed majesty" of the moon, "thought of various regions it overlooked, and asked her heart if one more wretched then [*sic*] herself now gazed upon it." [90] What makes the book difficult for the modern reader is its lack of relief from perpetual kaleidoscopic adventure alternating with breathless analysis of the emotions of characters who are not really alive anyway. Intellectually the book is almost a vacuum; stylistically it is no more than competent. Evidently it relied upon the novelty of the story for its appeal to the public. In many ways it typifies the second-rate fiction of the day.

Many of the same elements that appear in *Julia* are relied on to lend interest to Mrs. Wood's later novels. In *Dorval, or the Speculator* (1801) the villain gambles in Georgia lands, but there is the same problem of reclaiming lost relatives. *Amelia; or the Influence of Virtue: an Old Man's Story* (1802?) is slightly more original in tracing "the tremendous moral effect of an irritating paragon upon all who know her," [91] but is no better artistically. In *Ferdinand and Elmira: a Russian Story* (1804) Mrs. Wood returned to a foreign scene (Russia and Poland) where amid a wealth of titled folk she rings the changes on the themes of fradulent arrest and the long-lost father—leaving one finally with the conviction that what she needed most was a bureau of missing persons and a first-class corps of investigators. Maine, her homestead, she never wrote of except tangentially. [92] Her first story, the Gothic *Julia*, remains Mrs. Wood's most distinctive achievement.

REACTION

Mrs. Wood did not of course rely solely on the Gothic formula as a device to win readers. It is clear from her *Julia*, for example, that she, like many magazine writers of the day, knew how dearly young readers loved a story which, after carrying a heroine through a series of hazardous adventures, deposited her unscathed at the altar opposite a magnificent youth only lately discovered to be a wealthy aristocrat. The intrinsically low ideals and the false notions thus implanted in the minds of tender readers elicited plenty of serious condemnation, but seldom did critics of the novel resort to the corrective of humor. In 1801, however, there appeared a novel definitely designed to check the rank growth of the sentimental romance (with glances at the Gothic) by parodying it. This novel, *Female Quixotism: Exhibited in the Romantic Opinions and Extravagant Adventures of Dorcasina Sheldon*[93] by Mrs. Tabitha Tenney (1762-1837), stands in somewhat the same relationship to the sentimental romance as Charlotte Lennox's *The Female Quixote* (1752) to the English heroic romance and Jane Austen's *Northanger Abbey* (1817) to the Gothic romance. No parody, of course, could effectively stamp out a sturdy perennial like the sentimental romance, but if Mrs. Tenney couldn't laugh romance out of fashion, she doubtless helped to control its excesses; and in any case she wrote a book which is interesting in its own right. The story is set on "the beautiful banks of the Delaware" not far from Philadelphia. The heroine is a young woman neither remarkably pretty nor ill-favored but a "middling kind of person" whose head has been turned by the reading of too many novels and romances: "novels were her study, and history only her amusement." She is, moreover, heiress to £1000 a year. So saturated is her mind with romantic expectations that when at twenty she is the recipient of an offer of marriage from an estimable young man of the "middling kind" she rejects him disdainfully. But no story book hero appears to carry her off to a castle. For fourteen years she lives quietly with her father, her books, her little charitable activities, and her extremely realistic Sancho-Panza-ish maid, Betty. Being known for a bluestocking, she has very few admirers, for in her community there is a widespread prejudice against a woman who reads anything but "the bible, or perhaps the art of cookery." At the age of thirty-four Dorcasina (she has changed her name from plain Dorcas) has the first of a series of ludicrous adventures into which she is plunged chiefly because of her vanity and her bookish training. Her first suitor is an Irish rogue, O'Connor, who, having heard of the wealthy spinster, decides to marry her for her money. Though his true character is quickly known to others, including her maid, Dorcasina thinks of O'Connor as "a divine fellow, a perfect Sir Charles Grandison." She makes assignations to meet him in the woods. An amusing mock heroic scene, typical of Mrs. Tenney's robust manner, occurs when Dorcasina mistakes a Negro for her lover and sits embracing him while O'Connor, similarly in error, makes love to a Negro wench. Ultimately Dorcasina's name is clouded by her association with O'Connor, but despite overwhelming evidence she refuses to give him up until one day her father, finding O'Connor in his daughter's room with Dorcasina in his arms, firmly and finally dismisses him—leaving Dorcasina utterly disconsolate until the arrival of a new suitor.

A second lover, Philander, a wag recently graduated from Yale College, amuses himself by playing tricks on her by means of impersonations (with the help of a barber) and a pretended abduction. Dorcasina survives this second disillusionment to be solicited in marriage several years later by a respectable widower with three married children. She refuses, disgusted by his practical, unromantic manner. At the age of forty-eight the heroine again allows romance to dupe her. When under the influence of *Roderick Random* she fancies that one of the servants is a gentleman in disguise, she is prevented from marrying him only by being kidnapped by her friends and held prisoner for six months. The last misadventure of her aging heart brings her to the verge of matrimony with a married fortune-hunter who is finally exposed by his creditors. Now a disillusioned middle-aged woman still possessed of her virginity, Dorcasina is finally resigned to the life of an old maid trying to find happiness in her comfortable existence and in her charitable projects. Moreover, the experience of Harriot, her friend, who has refused to read novels because they "colour everything much too highly" [94] proves to her that even marriage is not the height of bliss, and she cautions Harriot not to allow her daughter to be ruined by novels.

Female Quixotism as a whole is not of course realistic, but many of the detailed scenes are handled with such freshness and such skill in phrasing that the book provides a pleasant contrast to much fiction of the times. The author, Mrs. Tenney, a native of New Hampshire, was clearly a woman of wide reading. She had a real sense of humor, and the reader laughs with her, not at her. Delightful humorous passages recall Fielding's Honour (in *Tom Jones*) and Sheridan's Mrs. Malaprop and Lydia Languish. The travesties on lovers' trysts recall the more inglorious episodes in the nocturnal parts of *The Merry Wives of Windsor* and *A Midsummer Night's Dream*. The rough tricks played on Dorcasina by Philander prove Mrs. Tenney's acquaintance with the picaresque tradition, which is but slightly represented elsewhere in early American fiction. Though apparently written in some haste, *Female Quixotism* is still a readable book. For Mrs. Tenney's principal aim seems to have been amusement, despite the lesson implied in her "true story" of a "country girl." That its lesson was not permanently learned by the American public is clear from the periodic recrudescence of vapid romance and domestic sentimentality and from its virtual domination of American fiction in the fifties and sixties.[95] *Female Quixotism*, however, was apparently not lost to view quickly, for it was reprinted at Newburyport in 1808 [96] and at Boston in 1829, and it remained so well known that as late as 1853 Mrs. Mowatt uses the adjective "Dorcasina-ish" as if confident that her allusion would be easily recognized.[97] A long life-span for an early American novel.

ANTIDOTE: THE EARLY HISTORICAL NOVEL

Though limited in quantity, an antidote to feverish sentimentalism was available in the form of the historical romance. Fiction dealing with themes from American history was rife long before Americans began to write it. Various causes coincided to delay *all* our fiction, and the historical novel was even slower than other forms to develop. Meantime in England there were dozens of novels dealing with the Revolutionary War and other phases of American history.[98] The emphasis of latter-day American text-book writers upon the contumely which a majority of British politicians (despite a few illustrious exceptions such as Burke and Fox) poured upon the Whig cause, hardly prepares the American reader to find most of the early British novelists taking a sympathetic view of the American struggle for independence. Yet the fact is that novel after novel attempts to generate sympathy for the rebels. Nor was the attitude of the novelists an unnatural one. Besides the general principle that the story-writer is constitutionally and professionally allied with persons in conflict with the law, there was for these writers the additional consideration that American soldiers were "warriors in the same cause for which many Englishmen at home were fighting—preservation of constitutional liberties." [99] Accordingly many British writers emphasized "colonial fortitude and pertinacity." The valor displayed by Americans in their fight for freedom was good grist for the British novelists' mill, and one "function of the American war was to provide a vent for a latent urge to hero-worship that . . . had found little outlet for many decades." [100] It is true that few of these British novelists were writers of great distinction, but as a group they were vigorous and often effective. American novelists, however, did not quickly follow the lead of the mother-country: the sentimental and the Gothic seemed easier avenues of popularity. Lack of research facilities, so important to the historical romance writer, was doubtless a handicap. Not until some fifty years after the Revolution did American writers—Cooper, Paulding, Child, Kennedy, Simms, etc.—really capitalize the greatest historical theme available to American novelists. References to "the illustrious Washington" and rhetorical allusions to Yorktown were sprinkled through many of our first novels, but in general our early novelists earned far less distinction in their treatment of the Revolution than other artists—essayists, orators, even poets.

The American historical romance as a type was adumbrated by Jeremy Belknap's allegorical narrative *The Foresters, an American Tale* (1792). *Amelia, or the Faithless Briton*, the first fairly extended piece of American prose fiction (hardly a novel) which dealt with the Revolution at all, was chiefly a tale of personal adventure with the Revolution used as a pretty dim background.[101] Eliza Bleecker's *History of Maria Kittle*[102] had made tangent use of the French and Indian War. Hilliard d'Auberteuil's *Miss MacRae* (1784), although composed and published in America, was written in French by a French writer.[103] The Revolutionary War again figures in the anonymous *History of*

Constantius and Pulchera, or Constancy Rewarded (1795), but the hero's seizure by a British press-gang and the heroine's experiences as a prisoner on various British vessels do not emphasize the national emergency so much as the amazing capacity of these characters to undergo hair-raising adventure on an itinerary which, starting at Philadelphia, touches at Halifax, London, Lisbon, and Bordeaux. If at the end the lovers were not united, the results might have been interesting, for it had been Pulchera's conviction that "the adamant would vegetate" before the hero's charms could be erased from her consciousness.[104] In both matter and manner, *Constantius and Pulchera* is one of the most extravagant American novels ever written. Its "history" is pale beside its plot. It may, in fact, have been intended as a burlesque.[105]

The heroine of *Constantius and Pulchera* had passed a good deal of time wearing men's clothing and occupied in masculine tasks—without being detected. In another anonymous tale, *The Female Review* (1797), the heroine likewise dons male attire as a prelude to adventures only slightly less incredible than Pulchera's. For two years she serves as a soldier in the patriot army, and though known as "the blooming boy," she escapes detection of her sex. Her adventures prove to be very taxing, what with her participation in the engagement at Bunker Hill and her adventures with the Indians ("the infernals"). After the War, she goes on an expedition to the Ohio territory, where, among other transactions, it becomes her duty to kill a bloodthirsty Indian guide. This intrepid girl, if one is to credit the copy of her discharge paper and other documents provided in the novel, was an actual person named Deborah Sampson. Doubtless part of Deborah's adventures were real; certainly in the aggregate they are incredible.[106] In any case the book is unimportant except for its early date as an historical novel.

Vapid stories like these did not augur well for the historical romance in America. They foretold no such powerfully original writer as Cooper. Such events of national significance as are woven into them are treated in a perfunctory fashion; military movements are scantily and inaccurately reported; and the Indians are mainly paper cut-outs rather than characters. Something of the same ineffectiveness characterizes most of the narratives in which the Indian plays a conspicuous part.

THE INDIAN IN THE NOVEL

Before Cooper no American novelist made conspicuously successful fictional use of the Indian. To the writer who really wished to make his book "native" in material, one would think, the Indian was a natural resort. Yet there were difficulties. By the time the American novel be-

gan to flourish, few cultivated Americans were meeting Indians on the
intimate terms created by missionary enterprise, warfare, or trade.
Christianizing the savages had proved to be an unsafe and unsavory
business, and in spite of eloquent reference to such aims in the charter
of Massachusetts Bay Colony, "missionary endeavors on the part of the
Puritans [were] conspicuous mainly by their absence." [107] Early settlers had known the Indian in battle, but the Pequot War and King
Philip's War had long since demonstrated the white man's supremacy with such finality that the redskins (depleted in numbers) had
withdrawn farther and farther from inter-racial contact. Trading, of
course, continued to go on at outposts, but in general the Indian, despite
his physical proximity, was not available for first-hand observation to
the late-eighteenth-century novelists. Legends there were; but mostly
the novelist had to rely upon the printed word, and the history of the
Indian had not yet been fully written. A better perspective would be
available to nineteenth-century writers like Cooper or Simms. Still it
was inevitable that American writers should soon seek to make some
use of a theme which even British novelists had employed as an interesting addition to their stock-in-trade for more than a century. Mrs.
Behn's *Oroonoko* (1688) had been the first of a considerable number
of tales and novels which traded upon the aborigine as a theme for fiction.[108] On the basis of hearsay, chronicle, and sheer imagination, plus
what might be gleaned from occasional appearances of actual Indians
in England, these writers alternately presented the Indian (whether in
the West Indies or North America) as a cruel and remorseless beast
and as a blossom of primitive virtue unsullied by the contagion of civilization. As a "noble savage" the Indian was used by English writers
who had political axes to grind: to such radical English thinkers as
Robert Bage and Thomas Holcroft he stood as a living embodiment of
those virtues which man might possess but for the debasing effects of
"civilization" and governmental malfeasance. Generally, however, the
Indian material, whether used for argument or embellishment, constituted but a subservient element in the British novel or tale, and among
such stories the only book by a major novelist was Smollett's *Humphrey Clinker*, in which the most painful details of the torture of Lieutenant Lismahago and Murphy, his companion, are ruthlessly recounted.

In America the commonest form of literary treatment devoted to the
Indian was the "captivity," a narrative reporting the actual experiences
of white people abducted by Indians. *The Narrative of the Captivity
and Restauration of Mrs. Mary Rowlandson* (1682) was a terrifyingly
vivid example of such "true relations." Following it "in never-ending

succession for the next hundred and fifty years" [109] came other narratives which are for the most part of scant interest to literary historians. Most of the early poetry touching on the Indian was undistinguished, excepting certain of the poems of Freneau, who displayed fine imaginative powers in "The Indian Burying Ground" and a few other pieces. Slowly the Indian assumed his place in fiction. The first considerable Indian story written by an American and issued in America was probably *The Female American; or, The Adventures of Unca Eliza Winkfield,* an adventure story purporting to be in basis autobiographical. First printed at London in 1767, it appeared in an American edition at Newburyport in 1790. About Mrs. Unca Eliza Winkfield (if the name be not a pseudonym) little is known beyond what may be accepted as factual in her "Adventures." [110] Her story is an extremely romantic one, beginning in Virginia, where her father was an early settler. There Winkfield experiences a John-Smith-like rescue and becomes married to an Indian Princess (mother of Unca). His wife is murdered by a jealous Indian, but Winkfield escapes with his daughter to England, where she is put to school and where she attracts great attention because of her strange dress and tawny skin. Later on, in this lumbering narrative, the father takes his daughter to Virginia. He soon dies, and Unca again sets out for England. But when she refuses to marry the son of the Captain of the ship, the latter takes his revenge by marooning her on a remote island. She carries on in a Crusoe-like way and finally becomes a missionary to Indians on nearby islands. Discovered by a cousin, she rejects his offer to return her to civilization and persuades him instead to collaborate with her in converting the Indians. [111] Clearly this was a story which lived mainly for its adventurous and exotic quality. The Indians are seen remotely through a romantic mist. They are capable of beheading prisoners, but they can also indulge in gentle reproof of the white men. Indeed the old chief who arraigns Winkfield in Virginia sheds tears as he quietly delivers one of the first of many protests in American fiction against the white man's conquest of the Indian lands:

> [W]e know you not and have never offended you; why then have you taken possession of our lands, ate our fruits, and made our countrymen prisoners? had you no lands of your own? Why did you not ask us? we would have given you some. Speak. [112]

After this winning speech the King orders heads off, but in general the author of this book treats the Indian as a remote, primitive, and picturesque person instead of as a relentless war-whooping harrier of white settlers. Unca's refusal to return to the settlements is likewise one of the first manifestations of a leit-motif which was characteristic of a romantic rather than a realistic approach to the theme of the "poor Indian."

Mrs. Winkfield's American residence was so transient and her literary point of view so patently European that she is not claimed as an indigenous American novelist at all by some literary historians. In any case her book was originally published in London. The first indubitably American story focussed upon American Indians was *The History of Maria Kittle* by Mrs. Ann Eliza Bleecker (1752-1783), a native of New York City. Written in 1781, the story was published serially in 1790-91 and in book form in 1793. It is rather a long tale than a novel, running to only about seventy small pages. Its action is devoted to the ghastly experiences of Mrs. Kittle of Tomhannock, New York. While her husband is away, Indians set upon her household and cruelly murder all its members but Mrs. Kittle herself, who is protected by an old Indian and carried off to Montreal. Later she is rejoined by her husband, now a member of Burgoyne's army. The story seems to have been partly founded on fact,[113] and it is "written in the manner of the Indian captivities," [114] but it carries the atmosphere of fiction. The Indians, excepting the one who aided Mrs. Kittle, are presented as a bloodthirsty crew whose onslaught is all the more harrowing for being set against the background of a pleasant friendship which has subsisted between them and the family. Nor does the author spare the reader the most revolting details of Indian cruelty.

The Indian tale, however, did not at once take its place as a definite genre for some years to come. The red man bobs in and out of various novels in the last decade of the eighteenth century as a minor and not very definitely characterized actor. In 1792 Brackenridge drafted the red man for brief periods of service as comic relief and as an instrument of political satire.[115] In 1793 an Indian abduction formed a slight thread of action in Imlay's *The Emigrants*.[116] In 1799 Charles Brockden Brown's *Edgar Huntly* employed Indians in a comparatively minor capacity.[117] Until 1802 no novel appeared which had capitalized Indian materials in a full-length story. In that year John Davis published his *The First Settlers of Virginia*.

John Davis was a native of Salisbury, England, but the fact may be waived in view of his insistence that "The United States is the country of my literary birth" [118] and in view of his ample demonstration of the possibilities of Indian life and legend. Davis was a vigorous traveler and a prolific, versatile writer. His first novel, *The Original Letters of Ferdinand and Elizabeth* (1798), was a "seduction-suicide-*Sorrows of Werther* concoction." [119] His other stories include *The Farmer of*

New Jersey (1800) and its sequel, *The Wanderings of William* (1801);
The Post Captain; and *Walter Kennedy, an American Tale* (1805).
He also published a volume of his *Travels* and a life of Chatterton. The
date of his death is not known.

Perhaps it was natural that the first idealistic fictional treatment of
the American Indian should have been set in "the sunny clime of Virginia" rather than in "bleak" New England.[120] Moreover the fascinating story (whether legend or gospel) of John Smith's rescue at the
instigation of lovely Pocahontas was a good foundation for the presentation of the Indian as a romantic character rather than a sordid menace.
Davis's story of *The First Settlers of Virginia* is the more romantic in
effect because of his knowledge of the mise-en-scène of the action. In
the subtitle of the book Davis denominates his work "An Historical
Novel, Exhibiting a View of the Rise and Progress of the Colony at
James Town, A Picture of Indian Manners, The Countenance of the
Country, and its Natural Productions." Needless to say, Davis's conception of a "novel" must have been a very loose one, for such action
as it reports is presented rather in the form of a chronicle than as a co-
ordinated series of interdependent episodes. No dialogue is vouchsafed
until page 47; and when it does occur, it consists of long formal
speeches. The author's meticulous citation of dates does nothing to add
to the pretence of fiction. The story as such recounts essentially the
events which were hinted at in the second edition of Smith's *New England Trials* (1622) and fully described in *The Generall Historie of Virginia, New England & the Summer Isles* (1624). Davis picks up John
Smith in the year 1606 when he arrived at Chesapeake Bay in command
of three vessels and carries him through his imprisonment, his rescue,
his captivity, his failure to respond to Pocahontas' passion, his return to
England, and his meeting with Pocahontas (now the bride of Rolfe) in
London. The narrative ends with the death of Pocahontas and the return of Rolfe to Virginia.

The distinguishing features of Davis's book are his fresh and intimate
description of the region inhabited by the Indians and his imaginative
reconstruction of the Indian attitude toward white men. Himself a
pioneer who had traversed sections of Virginia, he sketched the country with the eye of a keen observer, noting, for example, the varied
beauty of the scenery along the river Pamunkey bordered as it was by
marshes and savannas and "boundless forests." In 1802 his description
of the entourage was far from trite:

> Their road lay through a country well stocked with oaks, poplars,
> pines, cedars and cypress. The theatre of nature could be scarcely

more magnificent. For here rose tall forests, there rolled a large river, and herds of wild animals were seen browsing on its banks. The whole country displayed an exuberant verdure; the dog wood was shedding its blossoms in the wilderness, and the wild strawberry purpled the woods, the fields, the plains.[121]

Nor does he content himself with a few generalities. He dwells with obvious delight on the denizens of the region—"the timorous deer . . . courting the shade," the squirrel, the opossum, the raccoon, "millions of the changeable lizard," wolves, buffalo, turkey, and eagles. In many cases he expatiates on the habits as well as the habitat of the wild creatures, writing apparently from observation but frequently citing authorities for his statements. The mocking-bird's behavior particularly enlists his interest:

> But the mocking-bird mingles action with its song, and its measured movements accompany and express the succession of its emotions. Its prelude is to rise slowly with expanded wings, and soon sink back to the same spot, its head hanging downward. Its action now corresponds with the varied nature of its music. If the notes are brisk and lively, it describes in the air a number of circles crossing each other; or it ascends and descends continually in a spiral line. If they are loud and rapid, it with equal briskness flaps its wings. Is its song unequal? It flutters, it bounds. Do its tones soften by degrees, melt into tender strains, and die away in a pause more charming than the sweetest music? it gently diminishes its action, glides smoothly above its resting place, till the wavings of its wings begin to be imperceptible, at last cease, and the bird remains suspended and motionless in the air.[122]

Amid scenes so grateful to eye and ear it is no wonder that Davis writes romantically of the Indians as a race and as individuals. The beauty of Indian maidens is fully exploited not only in the person of the "admirably proportioned" Pocahontas but also by means of the "wild charms of the Indian nymphs" in general, whose woodland "allurements" proved so seductive to the Captain's followers that the men were with difficulty reassembled for duty. Nor is it surprising that Davis, aware of the final defeat destined for the Indian, should at times invest his story with a tone of melancholy. He was one of the first fiction-writers to be imbued with a poetic nostalgia for the vanishing American. At the end of the narrative when Rolfe returns to Virginia, he voices with considerable eloquence the natural feelings of the sensitive observer who envisions the dispossession of the Indian:

But alas! how changed is now the scene on the parent river of the Indian princess! No longer does the moon shed her silver light over the wigwams of the Indians sunk in profound repose. No more is the cry of arrival uttered by the young red warriors approaching the hamlet. No longer are the ebon tresses of the Indian nymph fanned by the evening gale, as she reclines her head upon the bosom, and listens to the vows of her roving lover. The race of Indians has been destroyed by the inroads of the whites! Surveyors with long chains have measured the wilderness, and lawyers contended for the right of possession. Beneath these forests once the favoured seat of freedom, the swarthy slave groans under the scourge of an imperious task-master; and the echoes multiply the strokes of the cleaving axe as he fells the proud tree of the melancholy waste. All alas! is changed. The cry of the hawk only is heard where the mock bird poured his melody; and no vestige is left behind of a powerful nation, who once unconscious of the existence of another people, dreamt not of invasions from foreign enemies, or inroads from colonists, but believed their strength invincible, and their race eternal![123]

It remained for later writers to make better novels of Indian activity, but Davis, inept as he was in the sheer mechanics of the novel, displayed an intimacy with Indian lore and a gift for regional description which comparatively few writers of the succeeding generation surpassed. *The First Settlers* seems, moreover, to have been well received. The second edition came forth in 1806 laurelled with extracts from letters of such commendation from Thomas Jefferson and Charles Brockden Brown and others that even *The Edinburgh Review's* condemnation of the book as "abominably stupid" could not spoil the general effect of panegyric. Englishman though he was by birth, Davis wrote a book the subject of which Charles Brockden Brown called "pure American," [124] and he knew his materials so well that *The Critical Review* dubbed him "the Teniers of Narrative" because "he paints from life." [125]

Only mediocre or less than mediocre art was displayed in most of the novels so far discussed—whether the sentimental, the didactic, the Gothic, the historical, the "Indian," or any mixture of these. Probably the most practical of these forms for American writers was the first— the sentimental. All the forms show defects attributable in part to generally unfavorable conditions—indifferent publishers or Anglophile readers. But the sentimental novel suffered least from that lack of American perspective which inevitably hampered early writers. It was hard to *feel* American in the new land. Such a condition was less serious to the writer who proposed to detail domestic or sentimental affairs: individual characters in America did not yet differ radically in their emotional make-up from individuals in England. But those forms which called for a merging of individual affairs with a tradition or outdoor intimacy with the American scene were harder. The Gothic couldn't flower until our buildings had mouldered a little and our legends had begun to get their growth. The historical romance had to wait until history itself could be written. The writer of Indian stories suffered similarly: the Indians had largely vanished, but their histories were not fully compiled. Many of the historical studies which were to prove such a boon to later writers of romance had not yet been written. Fully equipped libraries were rare in the land. Accordingly such novelists as were dependent on annals and archives were at a disadvantage. Such aids were obviously not so essential to the writer of sentimental romance. Satirists too could make a shift to subsist without complete geographical and historical orientation in the new country or complete psychological rapport with a given group of people, for by its nature satire tends to dwell on universal traits of men. Your true satirist is quickly at home anywhere in the international republic of letters. Greater maturity, therefore, characterized the work of the three early writers who, incidentally at least, trafficked in satire: Imlay, Brackenridge, and Tyler.

Early Satire and Realism

One reason for the ineffectiveness of many early American novels is their ceaseless dissection of the emotions of immature persons who seem to have no mental life whatever. Novelists wrote as if their whole vocation were endless agitation. Incredible situations were set up by crude and arbitrary methods in order that the "heart" of the heroine might be studied with cardiographical exactness. Understanding such "lessons" as they administered called for no greater cerebration than reading the *New England Primer*. Before the novel could grow up it badly needed some development of its intellectual content. This it received particularly at the hands of three writers during the first decade of its growth, Gilbert Imlay, Royall Tyler, and Hugh H. Brackenridge. These three men were not mere embodiments of intellect, but they had interests beyond discovering the outcome of a love affair or the sequel of a shipwreck. As is natural to the adult mind, they often resorted to satire and irony; and two of them, at least, possessed a sense of humor. They all discussed problems of interest to adult readers, but they were sufficiently skilled and interested in narrative per se to avoid being labelled as mere doctrinaire writers. The most able writer of the three was Brackenridge; the first to complete a novel was Gilbert Imlay.

GILBERT IMLAY (1754-1828 [?])

Imlay's *The Emigrants* was published in London in 1793.[1] Imlay's life was so "romantic" and so varied that even today certain data must rest upon hypothesis.[2] His birth-place seems to have been in Monmouth County, New Jersey. He fought in the Revolutionary War, attaining so far as records show only to the rank of First Lieutenant, though he later referred to himself as "Captain." He engaged in land speculations in Kentucky, and it is possible that he was associated with General James Wilkinson in the latter's conspiracy to separate Kentucky and part of the Southwest from the federal government in 1787.[3] At all events, his early experiences made him familiar with the region described in his first book, *A Typographical Description of the West-*

ern Territory of North America, published at London in 1792. About the same time he appears to have advised the French government on the subject of a plan to take Louisiana. In France he formed an attachment with Mary Wollstonecraft, author of *A Vindication of the Rights of Woman,* and became father of her illegitimate child, only to abandon mother and child later. Other affairs, mercantile and diplomatic, occupied him more or less mysteriously in various parts of Europe until his death on the isle of Jersey in 1828.[4] Imlay was evidently a man of energy and enterprise, but he seems to have been untroubled by conscientious scruples with respect to his business or personal affairs. As a writer, however, he gave no token of being animated by any but the most generous motives. Despite his cruel abandonment of Mary Wollstonecraft, he wrote his novel *The Emigrants* with the particular purpose of championing the cause of women rendered defenseless by being legally bound to faithless husbands. Imlay's proposed remedy for such women was easier divorce. The novel, however, was probably written before his association with Mary Wollstonecraft.[5]

As a story, *The Emigrants* is at least moderately interesting. It is presented in the form of letters. The action relates to the fortunes of the T——n family, which, having fallen into financial disaster (through debt) in England, seeks to rehabilitate itself in America, settling at Pittsburgh. The centre of the reader's attention is the seventeen-year-old Caroline, the youngest of three daughters, who is not only attractive personally but also a shrewd and amusing conversationalist and correspondent. Inevitably she captivates Captain Arl——ton, who has been acting as guide, philosopher, and friend to the T——n family during its journey to Pittsburgh. But a second daughter, Mary, who proves to be not only beautiful but also jealous, manages to create a misunderstanding between the lovers, as a result of which Arl——ton goes on to Louisville without declaring his love. The rest of the party subsequently follow Arl——ton to Louisville, but the confusion of Cupid is not clarified for a considerable time thereafter. Indeed a complete reconciliation is not effected until after Caroline has been abducted by Indians, to be rescued finally by Arl——ton. The young lovers are married, and Arl——ton sets up a Utopian colony on the Ohio river. In the meantime the affairs of other members of the family have been woven into the narrative. Eliza, the third daughter, has married a wastrel, gone to England, and returned finally to America, where she finds a more suitable spouse in the friend of Arl——ton. George, the only son, is a weakling who after a dissipated and quasi-criminal life in New York and London, is imprisoned for debt in London. At the end he is reclaimed, reformed, and destined by the author to be the husband of a lady whose first marriage had turned out badly. It is understood that he will prosper in the new Eden. Mary, who is contemptuous of American backwoods life, goes back to England with her parents. The debts of George and his parents have been paid by a long-lost uncle who turned up unexpectedly in America. Yet though the uncle has inherited an estate in England, he prefers to remain in America rather than to go back to the comparatively corrupt civilization of Europe.

The larger theme of *The Emigrants* is the contrast between the Old World and the New World, both of which Imlay's international experience fitted him to report. Though most of the presented action of the story occurs in America, it could not be fully seen in perspective without a reconstruction (in letters) of its European prologue. Imlay had plenty of models for the English scenes—of fashionable life and of conditions in a debtor's prison—but he had to fashion his American milieu without benefit of earlier fiction.[6] The bearing of the story as a whole is favorable toward America, but Imlay makes his book far more convincing than many partially doctrinaire novels by showing both sides of such controversial matters as come up. These matters are principally two: (1) the problem of marriage as an institution, and (2) the relative advantages of living in England and America. In general Imlay seems less inclined to study the welfare of society as a whole than to inquire into the condition of individuals; and he thinks that government must be judged not by the prosperity of the country but by the status of the individual.[7] As for the problem of marriage, he succinctly states in his preface that in his opinion "the many misfortunes which daily happen in domestic life, and which too often precipitate women of the most virtuous inclinations into the gulf of ruin, proceed from the great difficulty there is in England, of obtaining a divorce."[8] The problem arises because in too many cases marriages are unwisely entered into. It is for this reason that one of the characters in the story counsels parents against "urging a dutiful child to give her hand to a man when it is not an act of volition."[9] The unhappiness which often results is deplorable, for "of all the different prostitutions those of the feelings are the most ignominious." Yet it is "impossible for a woman of delicacy to be separated from her husband."[10] If the woman does break away, there is no course she can take which does not lead finally to her degradation and subsequently to the corruption of young men. Thus a vicious circle is drawn.

The problem is rendered concrete in the novel by the experiences of Eliza and of uncle P—— P——. Eliza is shamefully treated by her husband, but she is unable to get a divorce because she cannot *prove* either his impotence or his infidelity. (Finally her husband kills himself.) It was P—— P——'s experience to make the acquaintance of a lady restrained by her matrimonial vows from securing her freedom from a brute. When P—— P—— offered her his honorable sympathy, however, the husband cast his wife out and brought suit against the then penniless P—— P——, charging adultery. Despite the lack of evidence in this case, a judgment was entered against P—— P—— and he languished in prison nearly ten years. The wife was in the meantime divorced by her husband, who had planned the whole affair in order to marry another woman. Had Lady B—— been able to secure her freedom in the first place without surrendering her good name, all this misery, it is implied, would have been averted. Yet Imlay does not allow the implied opinions to prevail without opposition, and in fact it is the (somewhat precocious) heroine herself who seeks to confute P—— P——'s position by asserting that easy divorce would have "an effect equal to offering prizes to adultery." It is her opinion that since marital difficulties arise from "the manner and depravity of the age," the natural corrective for them should be education.[11] Yet the author appears finally to express his convictions through P—— P——, who insists that laws "oppress and restrain the acts of volition on the part of women." [12] In any case most of the distress visited on the characters in *The Emigrants* is directly or indirectly referred to defects in the institution of marriage. Views such as Imlay's were not unknown in the liberal and radical literature which preceded and accompanied the period of the French Revolution, but no novelist before Imlay had made such extensive use of the theme of divorce.[13]

Even more eloquent than his indictment of divorce laws is Imlay's praise of the New World: America is superior both in social organization and in natural advantages. He vividly draws a contrast between the sterility and drabness of sophisticated life in decaying Europe and the euphoria one experiences in America. Eliza, who goes back to England, writes to Caroline of her yearning for "those Arcadian regions" where manners are "simple and sincere." [14] Imlay also prefers "the unpolished wilds of America, with the honest affability and good humour of the people, to the refined address of the European world, who have substituted duplicity for candour, and cunning for wisdom." [15] As usual, Imlay lays open more than one view of a question, and we find the querulous Mary protesting against the "distressing ennui" she feels when exposed to "that honest [American] kind of manners." [16] Yet the whole tendency of the book is to glorify not only American institutions but also "the American scene." En route to Pittsburgh, Caroline praises the beauty of the country at great length, and she eagerly and realistically describes the various plants and animals that fall under her observation. The vicinity of Pittsburgh were Paradise enow, but Louisville evokes even warmer encomia from the pen of Arl—ton, and as for the regions farther west still, he found them so entrancing that he wrote: "It is impossible for any country to appear to advantage after you have seen the Illinois." [17] All this and more was written with the same fervor which had made Imlay's *Kentucky* so seductive—and so misleading—to certain English readers, including the poet Tom Moore.[18] Yet on the whole Imlay is not "romantic" in his approach to the subject: indeed he at one time points a contrast between ordinary sentimental rhapsodizing over "scenery" and Caroline's sounder method of learning to love a region by becoming acquainted with it at close range.[19] When Arl—ton writes to Il—ray that he must bring along fishing tackle on account of the good fishing near Pittsburgh, the reader knows he really is among anglers. The detailed agenda for the Utopian community on the Ohio not far from Louisville is set forth with a definiteness that suggests the hand of a practical organizer or entrepreneur (of the sort that Imlay actually was) rather than the dream of a visionary. Characteristically Imlay allows a margin for skepticism, which is expressed in the words of Sir T—— Mor—ly, who disbelieves in "perfectibility" and who thinks that "philosophers of the present day, by aiming at too much, will produce evils equivalent to those they have laboured to remove." [20] Yet the net result of such candor (or craft) on the part of Imlay is to present a conception of America extremely alluring to prospective colonists. The dangers of the frontier, the disadvantages of the wilderness, the comparative lack of culture in remote inland regions, remained for less patriotic and more disinterested writers to picture. Of these there were to be plenty among English travelers who, lured to America by idyllic accounts such as Crèvecoeur's and Imlay's, returned to England to write books severely critical of the New World.[21] Other writers, too, were to describe more fully and more realistically the behavior of the American Indian in his encounters with the invading white people.[22]

The Emigrants is both good story and good propaganda. Its style, with its somewhat formal eighteenth-century locutions, necessarily seems old-fashioned, but it has inherent strength and flexibility. The author was well read in eighteenth-century English and French writers, and he frequently embroiders a simple proposition with appropriate quotation, whether from Thomson, La Rochefoucauld, or Voltaire. Yet the work as a whole is not bookish. Imlay had a philosophical turn of mind which led him to speculate on the structure and validity of social institutions, but he was also a man of affairs who had promoted land schemes, acted as a government agent, and made his bow in diplomatic circles. He was at home in the saddle as well as in the study. Such a man was not likely to write a novel drenched in sentiment or dried up by argument.[23] *The Emigrants* is by no means a work of the first magnitude, but its mixture of action and reflection marks it as the product of a mature writer who aimed to match experience with art.

HUGH HENRY BRACKENRIDGE (1748-1816)

Hugh Henry Brackenridge, author of *Modern Chivalry*, belongs among the finest prose stylists, whether English or American, of the eighteenth century. The term novel must be stretched considerably to accommodate *Modern Chivalry*, a bulky, episodic, almost plotless book. Yet the history of fiction clearly shows that whereas a good plot may be the bait which first attracts readers to a novel, in the long run it is by no means the most important element of fiction. Such an inference is suggested by the solid reputations of such loose-jointed stories as *Vanity Fair, Pickwick Papers, The Way of All Flesh*, and many other novels. Of the things that weigh more heavily—characterization, setting, and a certain richness of texture betokening the author's understanding of life—Brackenridge had a goodly share. And he possessed abundantly the crowning glory of the novelist, namely, mastery of his medium, a perfect sense for the words which will obey the thought of the writer and gratify the ear of the reader. Not a really great novelist, Brackenridge is nevertheless a far more important writer than one would guess from the brief and cool entries accorded him by most historians of literature. He was the first distinguished American novelist to make substantial use of picaresque technique and of political satire.

LIFE AND CAREER. Brackenridge was born in Scotland, but his family moved to a frontier farm in Pennsylvania when he was only five years old. As a lad he was unusually well grounded in Latin and Greek —a fact which was later to account in part for his distinction as a writer. At fifteen he became a teacher in a public school in Maryland, but after five years at this post he resumed his own education at Princeton University (then the College of New Jersey). Here his horizon was immensely broadened in several ways. Among his classmates were the poet Philip Freneau, and James Madison, with whom he joined in devotion to belles lettres and Whig sentiment. Their literary society made satiric war on a rival society of Tory persuasion. Brackenridge and Freneau collaborated in a fragmentary prose satire called *Father Bombo's Pilgrimage to Mecca* and a poetical effusion, prophetic in content and epic in mood, called *The Rising Glory of America*. Both these pieces showed that Brackenridge was essentially a prose writer. At college, too, he indulged his life-long passion for reading in the classics —particularly his favorite authors, Lucian and Horace. A period of miscellaneous activity followed his graduation in 1771. He read divinity; taught school; served as a chaplain in the patriot army; and founded a periodical.[24] He also prepared himself for what was destined to be his vocation by reading law. Admitted to the bar at Philadelphia in 1780, he immediately set out for a region less rich in lawyers, settling finally in Pittsburgh, then a frontier village which afforded him intimate views of that backwoods life which in part forms the stuff of *Modern Chivalry*. Here he was to remain for the next twenty years, engaged in the law, journalism, politics, and the judiciary. From 1801 until the year of his death, 1816, he lived at Carlisle, Pennsylvania.

Brackenridge's career in public life was a checkered one. He was animated by the highest ideals and he never swerved from his support of the principles of enlightened democracy. Yet he was too independent, too objective in his judgments, to succeed for long in practical politics. Thus he was elected to the Pennsylvania legislature in 1786, but he angered his party by voting against bills which in his platform speeches he had promised to support. Actually he seems to have changed his views for good and sufficient reasons; but his defection was not forgotten and the following year he was defeated as candidate for delegate to the Constitutional Convention. He changed his opinions as conditions changed. He allied himself with the Federalists to support the Constitution, but he presently became critical of their administration. While Federalists were denouncing the French Revolution, he was asserting that the "cause of France is the cause of man, and neutrality is desertion." [25] Later, however, he became disgusted with the excesses of the revolutionists.[26] On the occasion of the Whiskey Insurrection of 1794, he managed to antagonize both sides: he affirmed the need of strong federal authority, but he expressed his sympathy with the farmers who resented the burdens of the excise tax. In 1801 he eulogized Jefferson as the ideal political philosopher, only to point out grievous defects in him later. In short Brackenridge, an independent observer, had the qualities of a statesman rather than of a politician: a reliable "party man" he could not be. In general he sought the golden mean, avoiding the extremes supported by whatever partisans.

MODERN CHIVALRY. Conscious of the integrity of his own motives, Brackenridge was embittered by his experience of public life; and his greatest work, *Modern Chivalry*, was begun as in some measure a retaliation against political enemies. Yet no partisan skulduggery could kill his love for democratic government, and no disillusionment could rob him of either his sense of humor or his artistry. Begun in rancor, *Modern Chivalry* developed into a brilliant but objective inquiry into the political principles and the actual conditions of the young republic. It is not, however, a treatise on government but an episodic narrative of the adventures of Captain Farrago and Teague O'Regan, whose peregrinations provide the basis of a panoramic view of American frontier life in Pennsylvania.

Brackenridge's first impulse had been to write a Hudibrastic poem on the theme of young democracy, and he actually composed a long narrative poem which he called *The Modern Chevalier*. Yet he was not really at home in verse forms and he presently adopted a prose vehicle. The composition of *Modern Chivalry* was begun in 1792, and the first section of the work appeared (in two volumes) in the same year. But Brackenridge was an extremely fertile writer and he kept adding large sections to his book from time to time. Additional volumes appeared in 1793, 1797,[27] 1804, 1805, and 1815. The whole work was published in four volumes in 1815.[28] In length it is equal to about four or five modern novels of average length. On account of its comparatively loose structure, no easy logical division of its parts is possible, but by custom it is now regarded as being comprised of two parts, Part One including the first two volumes of the 1815 edition; Part Two including volumes III and IV.

Part One itself does not make a perfect unity. It consists of the sections originally published as four separate volumes between 1792 and 1797. The first three of these consist mainly of satire directed at sundry American institutions which come under the observation of Captain Farrago on his wanderings from his home in the western part of Pennsylvania. Captain Farrago, a bachelor at fifty-three, is a sort of peripatetic philosopher who has decided to "ride about the world a little . . . to observe human nature,"[29] but his reflective nature is balanced by a practical strain which enables him to extricate himself from embarrassing situations into which he is plunged by the behavior of Teague O'Regan, his Irish foot-servant. Teague is an irrepressible ignoramus, amenable in general to his master's discipline but prone to get into scrapes on account of his credulity, his vanity, and his fondness for the less refined forms of amusement. A good-natured oaf, he has a certain plausibility in his bearing which leads people to credit him with intelligence, but he is utterly selfish, unscrupulous, and cowardly. His only accomplishment is that he can sing an Irish song.

Crude and illiterate as he is, Teague is everywhere invited to assume positions for which he is totally unqualified. Occasionally he is made the tool of vicious persons, but generally he is accepted out of sheer ignorance and stupidity on the part of the people. Thus happening upon a region where an election of a state representative is going forward, Teague volunteers to be a candidate against two others, an educated man and a weaver. The crowd presently prefers Teague to the others and is about to return him as legislator when Captain Farrago tells the multitude that Teague is only a "bog-trotter" who "can scarcely speak the dialect in which your laws ought to be written." Yet the people insist that it is "better to trust a plain man like him, than one of your high flyers, that will make laws to suit their own purposes." The situation is saved only when the Captain works on the fears of his servant by warning him of the ridicule his more skilled opponents will pour upon him. Teague finally withdraws and the crowd elects the weaver. Obviously Brackenridge is here pointing up one of the dangerous results of an unconsidered levelling tendency common to democratic procedure, the fallacy lying in the assumption that since in a free country everyone is equal before the law, everyone should have an equal right to participate in making the law. Such an attitude was perhaps an inevitable aftermath of the Revolutionary War: victory had produced a vague but powerful equalitarianism. "It is a very strange thing," said one of the speakers at the election, "that after having conquered Burgoyne and Cornwallis, and got a government of our own, we cannot put in it whom we please." [30]

Shortly after the fiasco of Teague's candidacy for office, he gets into a scrape of a different sort, for "as they would neither let him go to Congress, nor be a philosopher, he must be doing something." [31] While at an inn one night he creates a furore by attempting to get into bed with a chamber-maid, who resists his advances and screams for help. With what the Captain ironically calls "presence of mind," Teague manages to cast suspicion on a clergyman. When the case against the clergyman looks so serious that he is in danger of loss of reputation, the Captain pleads with Teague to confess the truth. Whereupon the graceless rogue finally agrees to tell the presbytery the real facts but insists that the clergyman "ought to pay a little smart money; for it was a thankless matter to do these things for nothing." [32] Utterly devoid of a sense of honor or a sense of decency but well versed in the lore of rogues, Teague is the closest approximation in the American novel to the picaresque characters of the eighteenth-century English novel.

Unsuccessful in his attempt to become a legislator, Teague is not discouraged from other attempts to rise in the world. Everywhere he is solicited to accept a post for which he is not fitted. The one adventure for which Teague is qualified by nature and training, namely, fighting a duel, he vigorously declines. On the other hand had it not been for the interference of Captain Farrago he would have become a preacher, a member of the Philosophical Society, and an Indian treaty maker. When on one occasion Teague disappears from view completely, Captain Farrago not unnaturally fears he will find him speaking in Congress or lecturing at a university. Both these hypotheses are wrong; but when the rascal is finally found, he is employed as a play actor. Material for satire of this sort is endless, for not only does Teague thrust himself ignorantly forward but, in many cases, authorities are quite eager to accept him. Hence there are prolonged passages of satire on legislation, the practice of law, the ministry, the press, higher education, duelling, scientific research, political chicanery, etc. The author's method is to show Teague in a ludicrously incongruous situation and then to pass on to general reflections of serious import regarding government or society.

One inevitable result of sending the wrong men to Congress is the spread of inefficiency and corruption in the central government. Thus it happens that the Captain is invited to hire out Teague to a treaty maker who wishes to use the bog-trotter as an Indian chief. The treaty maker answers the inquiries of the astonished Captain:

> My King of the Kickapoos, who was a Welch blacksmith, took sick by the way, and is dead. I have heard of this lad of yours, and could wish to have him a while to supply his place. The treaty will not last longer than a couple of weeks; and as the government will probably allow three or four thousand dollars for the treaty, it will be in our power to make it worth your while, to spare him for that time . . . You have heard of the Indian nations to the westward, that occasionally make war upon the frontier settlements. It has been a policy of government, to treat with these, and distribute goods . . . Now you are not to suppose that it is an easy matter to catch a real chief, and bring him from the woods . . . The commissioners will doubtless be glad to see us, and procure from government an allowance for the treaty. For the more treaties, the more use for commissioners. The business must be kept up, and treaties made if there are none of themselves . . . If your man is tractable, I can make him a Kickapoo in about nine days.

When the Captain is shocked to learn that government does not discover such corruption, the treaty man replies that the government

> is at a great distance. It knows no more of Indians than a cow does of Greek . . . Do you think the one half of those savages that

come to treat, are real representatives of the nation? Many of them are not savages at all; but weavers and pedlars, as I have told you, picked up to make kings and chiefs . . . These things are now reduced to a system . . .[33]

Appalled at the cool proposal of the treaty maker, the Captain somewhat disingenuously undertakes to save his servant from such ignoble service by telling him that the offer has been made for his red-haired scalp. Teague, as arrant a coward as Tom Jones' Partridge, is glad to forego the tempting opportunity to make a little money. No more is made of the episode as such, but Brackenridge indulges in ironical "observations" arising out of the case. The "policy of treating with the Indians is very good," he remarks, "because it takes off a great deal of loose merchandize . . . and cuts away superfluities from the finances of the government; at the same time, as every fresh treaty lays the foundation of a new war, it will serve to check the too rapid growth of the settlements." He goes further and suggests, in a passage of Swiftian satire, that treaties be made also with animals, only making the proviso that no liquor be given to them, for a "drunk wolf, or bear, would be a dangerous animal." [34]

Employing episode, conference, and reflection, then, Brackenridge delivers a series of ironical commentaries on the abuses of democratic government and on various social institutions. A certain sameness of approach and even of material marks the first three volumes of Part One. The fourth (and last) volume of Part One, however, grew out of one specific experience of the author, namely, the Whiskey Insurrection of 1794. Brackenridge's own plight during this disturbing uprising was a painful one, which he recorded directly in his *Incidents of the Insurrection* (1795).[35] In 1797 he incorporated some of the same facts in a fourth volume of *Modern Chivalry*. True to his satirical plan, however, he arranges that Teague shall play the leading role. The President of the United States, having heard of Teague, calls him into conference with a view to finding an office for him. The Captain as usual issues a warning about Teague and his qualifications. Accordingly the President forbears making Teague Secretary of War or Secretary of the Treasury and moderately assigns him to the role of an excise officer. Disaster falls upon the officer, and he is finally tarred and feathered—his own false excuses failing to save him and the Captain's reasoned suggestions for proceeding with due process of law also being of no avail. In his feathered state Teague makes such a picturesque appearance that he is sent to France as a scientific curiosity. His feathers having worn off by the time he reaches France, he is looked upon as a veritable *sans culotte* and as such warmly welcomed by the rabble. He has sundry adventures during his brief sojourn in France. A lady of royal blood falls in love with him on account of his resemblance to the Duke of Orleans, and he narrowly escapes being guillotined. In the meantime the Captain has had to avail himself of the services of a Scotsman named Duncan as servant, a person greatly superior to Teague. The Scotch dialect of the new servant, which is skillfully reported, enables Brackenridge to introduce variety into his narrative and Duncan's naive reactions to America (where he has but recently arrived) afford an opportunity for fundamental criticisms of the social order much after the fashion of the naive criticism of Oriental visitors employed for the same purpose by eighteenth-century European writers such as Montesquieu and Goldsmith. The Captain's own experience during the Whiskey Rebellion is not closely patterned after that of Brackenridge himself, but a parallel between the two is drawn when the Captain, who has tried to view the trouble philosophically from a vantage point outside the area of actual conflict is suspected of treason but finally exonerated. This episode concludes Part One of *Modern Chivalry*.

Teague does not remain long in France but manages (Brackenridge does not say under what circumstances) to return to America, where he resumes his position in the service of Captain Farrago and experiences the adventures which are included in *Modern Chivalry*, Part Two. In this part the action is even more deliberate than in Part One. Teague continues to aspire toward positions unsuitable to him, but new materials are also introduced. The impetus toward the first volume of Part Two (published in 1804) was Brackenridge's desire to express his scorn of the cheap journalists of the stripe of Peter Porcupine (the pen-name of William Cobbett) who had vilified Brackenridge's name on the occasion of his re-entrance into Pennsylvania politics in 1799-1800.[36] In the first volume of the second part of *Modern Chivalry* he satirizes the Peter Porcupine school of journalism by representing that a polecat had been brought in by villagers to whom Porcupine's paper had become obnoxious. When the polecat's stench became too much, it was proposed that a rival newspaper be established with, of course, the irrepressible Teague as editor. In this case, however, the Captain favors the selection of Teague for the journalistic post:

> The rogue has a low humour, and a sharp tongue; unbounded impudence . . . He has all the low phrases, cant expressions, illiberal reflections, that could be collected from the company he has kept since he has had the care of my horse . . . What is more,

he has been in France, and has a spice of the language, and a tang of Jacobinism in his principles, and conversation, that will match the contrary learning carried to an exorbitant excess in Peter Porcupine.[37]

Thus even while condemning Cobbett's jingoistic support of extreme conservative opinion, Brackenridge had inserted a warning against the opposite extreme, namely, rampant Jacobinism. To him, liberty of the press did not imply the license to indulge in unbridled scurrility. A similar tendency to hover near the golden mean characterized his attitude toward Jefferson. He admired Jefferson, and in 1801 he had written a warm panegyric, "Jefferson, in Imitation of Virgil's Pollio," which is "virtually a summary of the Jeffersonian political philosophy." [38] Yet now it pleased him to enter upon a sharp criticism of Jefferson's economy program as resulting in an unwise curtailment of public works.[39] In this part of the work he also showed his deepening despair of the populace on account of its attitude toward education. When public zeal for equalitarianism leads to the proposal that a college be burned down because "all learning is a nuisance," the Captain comments on the proposal with what for him is unusual bitterness, suggesting that the mob eject the professors but save the college building—for use as a hospital when the abolition of "learning and law" shall have reduced society to chaos and "trial by battle." [40] Similarly he is more caustic than usual in his protest against a man's being regarded as a poor candidate for office merely because he is educated. With fierce indignation at this perversion of the idea of democracy Brackenridge makes his point by means of irony, causing the candidate to protest:

I a scholar! I a learned man! it is a falsehood. See me reading! He never saw me read. I do not know a B, from a bulls foot. But this is the way to injure a man in his election. They report of me that I am a scholar! It is a malicious fabrication. I can prove it false. It is a groundless insinuation. What a wicked world is this in which we live. I a scholar! I am a son of a whore, if I ever opened a book in my life. O! The calumny; the malice of the report. All to destroy my election. Were you not seen carrying books, said a neighbour?

Aye, said the distressed man; two books that a student had borrowed from a clergyman. But did I look into them? Did any man see me open the books? I will be sworn upon the evangelists: I will take my Bible oath, I never looked into them. I am innocent of letters as the child unborn. I am an illiterate man, God be praised, and free from the sin of learning, or any wicked art, as I hope to be saved; but here a report is raised up, that I have dealings in books, that I can read. O! The wickedness of this world! Is there no protection from slander, and bad report? God help me! Here I am, *an honest republican; a good citizen,* and yet it is reported of me, that I read books.[41]

The principal innovation in Part Two, however, is concerned with the common law, the judiciary, and the Constitution. Here again the breach between the positions of Brackenridge and Jefferson became wider. At the turn of the century there was a growing popular tendency to distrust the common law, the federal judiciary, and the legal profession as a whole. Jefferson himself was convinced of the danger of investing too much power in the courts: "It is a misnomer to call a government republican, in which a branch of the supreme power is independent of the nation."[42] In general Brackenridge, himself a lawyer and a judge, defended the *status quo.* To the charge that our common law was unsuitable because it was derived in large part from English law, he replied that in reality the common law is ours for we "derive it from a common source with the inhabitants of Britain . . . Abolish the common law? why not abolish the art of medicine, because it has been cultivated in Great Britain? . . . Why not make war upon the apothecaries, because they sell English drugs?"[43] Undoubtedly a democrat and an "American," Brackenridge thus ventured to express opinions which could not be popular with proponents of a strong nationalism. Similarly he defended the judiciary at a time when radical thinkers were leading "an attack that was practically nationwide in its scope."[44] In Pennsylvania the war was particularly vehement; on one occasion, after an unpopular opinion had been handed down, all the members of the supreme court were impeached with the exception of Brackenridge, who was absent at the time of the trial.[45] Reform was in the air. Brackenridge was himself by no means a reactionary; yet with his usual desire to find the wise mean between extremes he was moved to write in a vein of caution against too great zeal for reform:

The idea of reform delights the imagination. Hence reformers are prone to reform too much. There is a blue and a better blue; but in making the better blue, a small error in the proportion of the drug, or alkali, will turn black. A great enemy to a judicious reform is a distrust of those skilled in the subject of the reform [*i.e.,* lawyers themselves] . . .

But the present idea of reform seems to be to pull down altogether, said the Captain. I do not know that you will see "down with the judges" just written upon fence-rails; or scored on tavern windows; but it is a very common language, among the more uninformed of the community. The danger is that it may be mistaken *for the voice of the people*, and under that idea, influence the constituted authorities.

That would be an error, said the blind lawyer. *For it does not follow, that, because a thing seems to have advocates, that it is the voice of the people. The noisy are heard; but the dissentients are silent.*[46]

Brackenridge thus deprecates both revolution and reform movements for their own sakes. Clearly his main concern is to counsel government by the intelligent and the trained. So much is implied, in connection with the controversy over the judiciary, by having the dauntless Teague made a judge.

In the last installment of Part Two Brackenridge analyzes yet another aspect of republican government, namely, the qualifications for voting—a subject which arises in connection with the move to revise the Constitution. It is his opinion that the property qualification for voting is utterly wrong. His Swift-like method of exposing the absurdity of such an institution is to develop a bizarre account of a community in which animals are represented as voting and otherwise carrying out the functions of ordinary citizens. Then he answers his objectors:

The preceding painting may be considered as extravagant; and exceeding all probability; the voting of beasts. But is it a new thing in the history of government that the right of suffrage should be made to depend upon property? No man shall be entitled to a vote unless he is worth so much, say some of the constitutions. In this case is it not his property that votes? If this property consists in cattle, can it be said that his cattle do not vote. Ergo, a cow or a horse, in some communities have the privilege of a vote in the enacting laws.[47]

In the last section, the fictional thread becomes even more tenuous than before. The author pronounces opinions on a great variety of subjects including war in general, the War of 1812 in particular, but always he sticks to his general position as observer of the commonwealth. A "visionary philosopher" is the mouthpiece of the author in much of this portion of the narrative. Teague, however, remains available for further mock-heroics, and in this section he becomes a popular military hero and almost reaches the rank of general. Thus to the last he serves as an embodiment of the author's conviction that private ambition is the "poison weed" of a republic. What a republic needs, the author finally avers, is "less eminence" and "more goodness." [48]

BRACKENRIDGE'S THEORY OF GOVERNMENT. *Modern Chivalry* is a book of such bulk and diversity that its outward appearance is one of disorder, almost anarchy. No principle of plot construction controls it, and the pretense of fiction becomes extremely shadowy toward the end. Brackenridge recognized as much, saying frankly on one occasion: "the fact is, that I mean this tale of a Captain travelling, but as a vehicle to my way of thinking on some subjects." [49] Chapters and episodes appear to exist of and for themselves as independent units. Opinions expressed in one chapter are found to be in apparent conflict with those expressed elsewhere. Thus at different times the author ridicules the farcical procedure of courts of justice and he defends the judiciary; he praises Jefferson's political principles and he pours obloquy on specific acts of Jefferson; he blows hot and blows cold on the subject of the French Revolution; he supports the Federalist creed of centralization and he resists Hamiltonian political maneuvers; he argues the need of reform (as of Indian treaties), but decries professional reformers; he at times seems to despair of popular sovereignty and at other times seems confident of the basic intelligence of the masses. *Modern Chivalry* is full of apparent inconsistencies. Yet examined as a whole the book is seen to contain a fairly coherent centre of thought which exercises sovereignty over its diverse parts. It is governed by the principle of balance or proportion. Brackenridge believed in the Greek maxim, nothing too much. The romantic democracy of Joel Barlow and of the youthful Charles Brockden Brown could never appeal to the level-headed Brackenridge. He feared excess of any sort. An enlightened democracy he believed to be the best form of government:

> A DEMOCRACY is beyond all question the freest government: because under this, every man is equally protected by the laws, and has equally a voice in making them. [50]

But a democracy is by its nature difficult to sustain. It is threatened on the one hand by the efforts of an aristocratic class to monopolize power and on the other hand by ignorance and wrongheadedness on the part of the rank and file. Frequently these two elements, the patrician and the popular, are engaged in a conflict which is in the main beneficial for it is by such opposition that "the spirit of democracy is kept alive." [51] Similarly, political parties may serve the purpose of curbing malfeasance. Yet only by eternal vigilance can either of these opposing interests be kept from violating that all-important principle of a wise "medium." The patrician or aristocratic class often "deserves to be checked by the populace," for "the evil [of misgovernment] most usually commences on this side." [52] Hence his frequent opposition to Hamiltonian Federalism. Yet the people also err. They may be misled by demagogues, who are just as malign as self-interested aristocrats:

> The demagogue is the first great destroyer of the constitution by deceiving the people . . . He is an aristocrat; and seeks after more power than is just. He will never rest short of despotic rule.[53]

They may also err by the "rage of *mere* democracy," that is, by blindly insisting on their rights. After the very earliest days of the French Revolution Brackenridge was not attracted by romantic radicalism in political thought; he did not echo the familiar eighteenth-century catchwords regarding the "natural rights of man." [54] A blind insistence on liberty without a concurrent willingness to use that liberty wisely, he thought, can only lead to disaster, for "democratic power unbalanced, is but the despotism of many instead of one." [55] The people may also err through the misuse of the right of suffrage, which ideally should be the "first spring of happiness in a republic." [56] Improper use of the right of suffrage in turn leads to the abuse of filling public office with incompetent persons. This is an abuse which may occur without malign intention, but it is an evil nevertheless, for the voters' concern should be "not only who is *honest*, but, who is *capable?*" [57] Such an equilibrium is not easy to achieve. Our Constitution was designed to create through its provision for representation, the separation of the powers, and the "*near equipoise of the legislative, judicial, and executive powers.*" But, adds Brackenridge, "the balance of the powers, is not easily preserved. *The natural tendency is to one scale.*" [58] Freedom, then, can be maintained only by persistent redress of errors as they appear. Yet finally Brackenridge was convinced that the American form of government was the best:

> But if justice cannot find *a certain residence in a democratic government; she must leave the earth.* I despair of finding it any where else.[59]

Modern Chivalry is often called a "satire on democracy." The term is partially appropriate, for the book gives more space to the condemnation and ridicule of popular errors than to the indictment of patrician arrogance. In fact the author himself said that the "great moral of this book is the evil of men seeking office for which they are not qualified." [60] Yet the term does not do justice to Brackenridge's political position. Had he lived in the days of the Puritan theocracy in Massachusetts, Brackenridge would undoubtedly have given proportionately more space to attacking the aristocratic political theories of Governor Winthrop and his associates. In Pennsylvania during the infancy of the nation a different emphasis seemed necessary. To be a self-appointed guardian of republican principles was a thankless task: Brackenridge alienated men and constituencies on both sides. Not that he was a fiercely aggressive man in an argument: like Franklin (whom he admired) he generally tried to "dominate his adversary by doubts." He employed the Socratic method instead of the doctrinaire. The Captain's (that is, Brackenridge's) "reflections" following the most outrageous conduct are always couched in the most temperate terms. His tolerance and breadth of observation prevented his joining heart and soul with any party. Life would have been easier for him if he could have accommodated himself permanently within the folds of one party. But he was constitutionally unable to commit himself to any platform which forbade freedom of inquiry. He had more wisdom for his country than for himself.

THEORY AND PRACTICE OF WRITING. Brackenridge as a writer has not yet received the full measure of praise to which he is entitled. Indeed, it is probable that comparatively few readers have explored fully the vast domain of *Modern Chivalry*, Brackenridge's only work of fiction. To the casual reader, moreover, its very real defects are at once apparent. The book is as unorganized as the weather. Clear and precise in smaller units—the sentence, the paragraph, and even the chapter—it becomes jumbled and unpredictable in the longer sequences. It is also repetitious—a fact to be accounted for partly by the intermittent nature of its composition. Brackenridge recognized this defect, saying in the last volume of the book that "if [he] were to go over the same ground again, [he] would make one word do where two were used." [61] The average novel-reader must be disappointed in its lack of a good plot. Characterization is excellent so far as typical human conduct is concerned, but individuals tend to be absorbed into generalizations. Readers seeking thrills of the sort that are crowded into the sentimental and Gothic novel must certainly have been disappointed.[62] Emotions tend to be understated or ironically expressed, or generalized out of all capacity to agitate the pulse of the popular reader.[63] Consequently although Brackenridge repeatedly said that he aimed to make his book agreeable to "Tom, Dick, and Harry, in the woods," rather than to "delegated authorities," [64] it is doubtful if he reached his "democratic" objective. For first and last *Modern Chivalry* is a book for the intelligentsia. It is the fruit of one of the ripest minds of the century. It is an aristocrat among books. Brackenridge's convictions embraced the welfare of the commoner, but his art could not stoop to the level of mass appeal, try as he would.

In a delightful introductory chapter Brackenridge playfully set himself up as a model of style. He avowed that he would "pay no regard to the idea," for it was useless to "expect good language and good sense, at the same time." First of all his book would help young minds to understand language; sense could come later. This point he presses home jocularly in a passage which well exemplifies an ironical method which appears time and again throughout the book:

> Being a book without thought, or the smallest degree of sense, it will be useful to young minds, not fatiguing their understandings, and easily introducing a love of reading and study. Acquiring language at first by this means, they will afterwards gain knowledge. It will be useful especially to young men of light minds intended for the bar or pulpit. By heaping too much upon them, stile and matter at once, you surfeit the stomach, and turn away the appetite from literary entertainment, to horse-racing and cock-fighting. I shall consider myself, therefore, as having performed an acceptable service, to all weak and visionary people, if I can give them something to read without the trouble of thinking. But these are collateral advantages of my work, the great object of which is, as I have said before, to give a model of perfect stile in writing.[65]

Actually Brackenridge believed that thought and language must never be regarded separately, for it is in the perfect fusion of the two that good writing consists. Embellishment as such is to be avoided.

> But can anything contribute more to form a taste for style than the study of these models of language, where there is every ornament of grace and expression: strength, at the same time, which will depend upon *conciseness and brevity:* perspicuity also, without which there is neither strength nor grace. For were I to lay down a rule of style, it would be to endeavour to obtain a *precise and clear idea* of what is to be said; and, to express it *with the utmost brevity*, and in the most *perspicuous phrase possible*. Where one is master of this . . . a diction may be indulged with the *embellishments of figure*, and the *flowers of imagination*. But until this *rib and bone* of clear thought is obtained, all garniture but wearies.[66]

The proof of good writing, he believed, is "that when you read the composition, you think of nothing but the sense." [67] Simplicity and lucidity he repeatedly held up as the prime objectives in style, and he quoted with approval Swift's famous mot regarding good style— " 'proper words in proper places.' " [68] Diction, in accordance with Aristotle's precept, should be common without being vulgar, and words should be placed in their natural order.[69] The final goal of the writer should be to complete effortlessness.

In one of his moods of humorous and amiable self-appreciation Brackenridge implied that he himself had achieved that effortless and flawless integration of matter and form which betokens "perfect mastery of all that relates to language." [70] The phrase is comprehensive but, as applied to Brackenridge, not grossly inappropriate; his style was close to perfection in its time. Some critics have called attention to petty rhetorical infelicities in his writing, but almost all of these characteristics (such as the floating participle) were inherent in the practice of the late eighteenth century. His now archaic punctuation also distorts his page. In all that pertains to good prose he was skilled: soundness and strength, as of good timber; precision of line that betokens clean craftsmanship; pattern that is stamped with individuality but escapes eccentricity; and surface finish that is at once luminous and natural—like the sheen of foliage—or the coat of an animal.

In many respects Brackenridge was representative of his own times— as thinker and writer. Yet it is a mistake to emphasize his obvious kinship with the neo-classical tradition in writing. The fashion of his phrasing sometimes recalls Augustan England, but his roots lay far deeper. His sinew and poise came from the classics which he read and loved from his earliest days. Greek and Roman writers supplied him with many of his "best thoughts" on government.[71] Other writers he read in great number but as the years rolled by he found that even Shakespeare and Milton occurred to his mind less and less, while the "best thoughts" of the classics continued to pour themselves onto his page. The other writers he read, however, were so numerous that even to cite those who receive mention in *Modern Chivalry* would suggest that Brackenridge was one of the most learned of American writers. Significantly enough his favorites, whether among the classical or more modern writers, were masters of humor or satire: Lucian, Horace, Rabelais, Montaigne, Cervantes, Butler, Scarron, Le Sage, Dryden, Pope, Swift, Smollett, Fielding, and Sterne. *Don Quixote* was a special model, and Brackenridge often invited attention to the obvious parallel between the Spanish knight with his follower and Captain Farrago with *his* Sancho.[72] There is a trace of tragedy, too, in the parallel, for Brackenridge in his own life had knightly ideals, and his tilting at windmills was as little profitable as Don Quixote's. But chiefly humor—that was what he quarried in greatest quantity from the past. Humor gleams from almost every page of *Modern Chivalry*. Sometimes a crude picaresque jest explodes upon the page, but Brackenridge's more characteristic humor is quiet, quizzical, reflective— perhaps quieter than that of his predecessors but no less pervasive. His wit is often incisive but it is not generally destructive, for finally it is subservient to his larger purpose of examining the bearings on which America's comparatively new machinery of government rested. Nevertheless Brackenridge's humor was often misunderstood. Like Fielding and Sterne he valued humor as a sanative or corrective agency, a device to cure one of the spleen, a rectifier of the mind. Yet he found to his sorrow that his ironical method was often beyond the intelligence of the persons it was intended to please. Accordingly he wrote half in seriousness and half in fun:

> [W]hen I came to have some acquaintance with the modern wits, such as Cervantes, Le Sage, and especially Swift, I found myself still more inclined to an ironical, ludicrous way of thinking and writing. But finding the bad effects of this, in many respects, leading me into broils with individuals, and rendering me obnoxious to public bodies, I saw the indiscretion, and bad policy of such indulgence; and have for several years past, carefully avoided every thing of this kind. It is indeed acting but a poor part in life, to make a business of laughing at the follies of others. It is injurious to one's self; for there is a great deal more to be gained by soothing and praising what men do, than by finding fault with them. It may be said of satire, what was said of anger by some philosopher, It never pays the service it requires. It is your scratching, rump-tickling people, that get into place and power. I never knew any good come of wit and humour yet. They are talents which keep the owner poor.[73]

Brackenridge was an American—and more than an American. He was in the main well pleased to make his home in the wilderness of the New World. Unlike many Americans of his time, he was content to be a citizen in a republic and he never yearned for the establishment of an American nobility.[74] He believed the American form of government to be potentially the best in the world. Yet as a man of letters he rose above nationality and above the comprehension of the average man. Born in Scotland, nourished on the classics of all ages and countries, keenly aware of his citizenship in the extra-national republic of letters, he could not trim and shape himself so as to fit in with what was after

all a very brief tradition of letters. Though he once said that English
was better written in America than England [75] his references to American writers are extremely rare.[76] His *Modern Chivalry* reports backwoods life in America in general terms—not with the intimacy implied
by many critics who iterate accurately but misleadingly, Parrington's
observation that *Modern Chivalry* was our "first backcountry book."[77]
Modern Chivalry is our first picaresque novel, but its roots are only
partly American. Captain Farrago is partly American—but, being a
literary creation, somewhat less American than Brackenridge himself.
American character was difficult to define in the early days of the
republic. Indeed Brackenridge went so far as to say that "the American has in fact, yet, no character; neither the clown, nor the gentleman." [78] As for Brackenridge the writer, he was a mixture. He addressed himself to contemporary problems and he knew the smell of
political warfare. But when he was in his study, it is fair to suppose,
he was a lonely and often dispirited soul. Like Miniver Cheevy, he
sighed for an earlier era. A vast and varied literary tradition lay behind
him, but he was consigned to an outpost of the youngest nation of all.
He craved more literary companionship than was available in the border village of Pittsburgh. His British heritage beckoned to him: "How
often have I sighed for the garrets of London . . ." [79] Such a writer
was not of the stuff of nationalism; he was at once an American and an
exile.

Brackenridge did not make much money from the various editions
of *Modern Chivalry*—though, if we may believe his statement, "Five
booksellers have made a fortune by it." [80] Yet he believed, or tried to
believe, that his work had had beneficial effects upon the body politic
in Pennsylvania. "And indeed," he wrote at the beginning of the last
chapter (in 1815), "I flatter myself, that it is not a little owing to this
book, published in portions, from time to time, that a very different
state of things now exists." [81] Yet such practical influence as *Modern
Chivalry* had is exceedingly hard to estimate, for other corrective
forces were in operation at the same time. The probability is that its
political influence was of brief duration in a limited area. Moreover
Brackenridge was no shirt-sleeves philosopher but a scholar, and his
book was packed with erudition that must have seemed obscure and
pedantic to the general reader. Its philosophy continued to be pertinent for years to come: Jacksonian America was to present a similar
set of problems for the nation to solve. Yet it is as a literary work, a
work of wisdom and wit rather than of propaganda, that *Modern
Chivalry* must chiefly endure. A Boston reviewer writing in 1808

seemed very much puzzled by the book. Treading warily amid the complexities of his subject, he finally came to the safe conclusion that it "will never, like its great model, the work of the immortal Cervantes, assume a commanding rank in the literature of the world." [82] The reviewer was right, but how far from Cervantes (or how close to him) Brackenridge might be, the reviewer never knew.

ROYALL TYLER (1757-1826)

The quality of Royall Tyler's writing is a sufficient reminder that even in the early days of the national literature it was not axiomatic that we should produce crude and naive fiction. Disadvantages there were, but after all much depended on the individual writer. With the rich legacy of English literature to draw upon—and beyond that, the wealth of the classics—no new writer needed to begin with the A B C's of his craft. No potentially good writer had to produce poor fiction because New York was in its infancy and Boston a small provincial city. With Tyler, as with most literary figures of his time, writing was an avocation, but he brought to it such talents that he earned a permanent, if modest, niche in American literary annals. A dramatist, he wrote our first American comedy, *The Contrast* (produced 1787), a play as enjoyable to witness even today as the average twentieth-century production. An essayist and poet, he collaborated with Joseph Dennie in a series of humorous papers, *Colon and Spondee*, which are now neglected not so much because of any lack of inherent merit as because of their topical nature. A novelist, he wrote one extended narrative, *The Algerine Captive* (1797), which, however deficient in the elements that make for popularity among readers in quest of "heart-thrills," was the work of one of the most interesting minds of his day. *The Algerine Captive* is picaresque in framework—being a narrative stitched together by road and maritime episode—and alternately satirical and humanitarian in tone.

Tyler was a New Englander through and through, and he seems to have been contented with his fate as such. Born in what his collaborator Dennie was later to refer to irritably as the "puddle called Boston," Tyler in due time passed on to Cambridge, where he was graduated from Harvard in 1776. During the Revolution he served in the patriot army, and he studied law. In 1779 he received the M.A. degree from Harvard and was admitted to the bar in Massachusetts. Though valedictorian of his class at Harvard and a successful student of the law, he seems to have been regarded as a somewhat volatile young man, for when he had wooed and won Abigail Adams, her father (John

Adams, in whose law office Tyler had studied for a time) foiled the marriage by shipping Abigail to France.[83] Tyler's military career was not ended by the Revolution, for he later assisted in the suppressing of Shays' Rebellion; but he presently settled down to law and letters in Guilford, Vermont. Letters were a sporadic, if a vital interest, but the law sustained him in comfort and renown throughout the rest of his life. He served for six years as Chief Justice of the Supreme Court of Vermont, and he was professor of jurisprudence at the University of Vermont from 1811 to 1814.

The Algerine Captive was published in 1797 at Walpole, New Hampshire, an active book-centre of the period. The narrative purports to record the experiences of an uncle of Tyler (called Updike Underhill in the novel), who was captured by pirates and never returned to his country despite the offer of ransom.[84] But the form of the book is autobiographical, and it is likely that in the account of the hero's early life, Tyler was drawing largely on the impressions (though not always the facts) of his own boyhood and youth. First of all he gives an account of the ancestors of his hero, who settled in Massachusetts in 1630. Tyler pauses to observe that the early Puritans were such zealots that they often saw sin where no sin existed. Thus in 1637 John Underhill was excommunicated for adultery on no better evidence than the fact that at a public lecture he looked too long at the hands of a certain lady who had appeared with "a pair of wanton open workt gloves, slit at the thumbs and fingers, for the purpose of taking snuff." It was assumed that these holes, called "Satan's port holes of firy temptatione," brought about the downfall of Underhill. The episode is handled by Tyler in a light, satiric tone which characterizes his treatment of the early life of his hero, a grandson of the erring lecture-goer.

The hero (Updike Underhill) was born in New Hampshire. As a lad and young man he is not a great success. He evinces bookish inclinations, and he spends four years under the tutelage of a minister. Unable, for financial reasons, to go to Harvard, he teaches school, but he is unequal to maintaining discipline. In local society he is a failure, being regarded as a pedant. He studies medicine, but fails to make a go of medical practice. He drifts about to Philadelphia, where he meets Franklin; to the South, where he again fails as a practicing physician, and where he scorns to enter into competition with inferior Southern schoolmasters. Instead, he accepts a position as ship's surgeon on a vessel bound first for London and later for Africa and the West Indies. In London he studies society, meets Tom Paine,[85] and reflects (anachronistically, for it is not yet 1789 in the story) on the French Revolution. In 1788 he sails for Africa on a ship engaged in the slave trade.

Up to this point—a little less than half-way through the story—the narrative has been conducted with a certain gaiety, even with facetiousness, and the incidental satire has been light. From this point forward, however, the tone is one of almost entire seriousness, and the satire is supported by deep indignation. At the same time the book gradually loses its character of an adventure story and takes on, toward the end, the quality of a travel book. The author follows Underhill on his voyage on a slave ship bound for Africa and thence via Barbados to South Carolina. Upon reaching Africa, Underhill is captured by a pirate ship and taken to Algiers as a slave. Here he sees and suffers the most atrocious treatment. He is solicited to adopt the Mahometan religion on the promise of freedom, but he finds that he cannot compromise with his honor. Various efforts to raise ransom money fail, and Underhill is not released until the United States makes a treaty with the Dey whereby all American captives are released and protection is guaranteed to American commerce. He returns to his country in 1797 —after being absent for a period of more than seven years, six years of which were spent in slavery.

Interest in *The Algerine Captive* must have centered partly in its topical content. For many years the piratical seizure of American vessels and enslavement of American citizens by the Barbary nations had been an outrage which had been only slightly lessened by the huge tribute paid to the African powers. The United States, a young nation without adequate army or navy, was particularly vulnerable. No aid could be expected from England. Indeed England's connivance at the practice of Algiers had drawn from Franklin the cynical remark that "if there were no Algiers, it would be worth England's while to build one." The problem as a whole was not solved until after America had proved her mettle in the War of 1812, and tribute continued to be paid to Algiers until 1815.[86] To Tyler, in the meantime, the situation was intolerably wrong and (through Underhill) he spoke his mind fully in *The Algerine Captive*. He believed that the pirates could have been curbed but for the private greed of European nations which prevented them from joining in "any common project, the result of which . . . may advantage its neighbour." [87]

The political causes of unhappy and unjust conditions, however, interest the novelist less than the actual conditions of slavery, which he presents with a vivid and excited pen. Arrived in Africa near the Congo River, Underhill has the opportunity of observing the whole sordid business of bargaining for slaves; yoking groups of them together; inspecting them medically (Underhill's job); consigning the "sound" ones, manacled, to the overcrowded and unsanitary hold of the ship; conniving at the sailors' assaults on female slaves; breaking a hunger strike by beating women and children. When Underhill makes suggestions regarding ordinary hygienic care, the captain scoffs at his "yankee nonsense about humanity." [88] Naturally the foul living conditions create illness among the slaves, who suffer a mortality of about twenty-five percent. A landing is necessary in order to try to cure some of the slaves, who are pathetically grateful to Underhill. Finally a return to the ship is ordered, but the vessel suddenly sails away, pursued by a pirate craft. Underhill (with one black slave) is presently captured by the crew of an Algerine rover bearing a black flag, and taken to Algiers.

Underhill is now sold into slavery by the Dey of Algiers. He is set to work digging a foundation for a wall. When an overseer strikes him with a whip, he responds by knocking the overseer down; but the overseer wins out, beats Underhill viciously, and assigns him to hard labor in a quarry. In general his fellow slaves are kind to him, but they make no attempt to aid him in the quarrel with the overseer. The realist in Tyler also forces him to observe that despite the romantic tales of Aphra Behn and George Colman, Underhill never saw "a man of rank, family, or fortune among the menial slaves." [89] Captives who were men of position or wealth were held for ransom instead of being made slaves. Manumission by the adoption of the Mahometan religion having been rejected by Underhill and actual escape being out of the question he is a thoroughly beaten man. All he can hope for is to raise money for a possible ransom, but in the effort to achieve this he is betrayed by a greedy Jew. Only his partial freedom as a physician mitigates the situation. All in all, he sees not only the wretchedness of slavery in Algiers but also a good deal of various aspects of Mahometan life. But he yearns to be released from a bondage which has made him think wistfully of his father's farm in America: "Let those of our fellow citizens, who set at nought the rich blessings of our federal union, go like me to a land of slavery, and they will learn to appreciate the value of our free government." [90]

Notwithstanding the power and the probable veracity of Tyler's presentation of Algerian oppression, the literary values of the book lie closer to home, and they are found largely in the earlier chapters. His true weapon as a satirist was not the howitzer but the rifle, and he excelled in puncturing follies and affectations which had come under his own observation or had long been familiar to him through reading. The targets of his satire were not new—education, medical quackery, duelling, social life—but it is a delight to observe his expert marksmanship. On the subject of education he spreads his fire so as to catch two types of abuse, the emphasis on idle erudition and the bigotry of the under-educated. Underhill did not attend Harvard, but on his travels he visited its museum which, he found, contained "the curiosities of all countries, but our own." [91] There is a jeering reference (probably the first in a long line of such references in fiction) to the credulity of Cotton Mather, one-time fellow of Harvard. At college, one finds, a great deal of time is wasted tussling with the classics in the original, whereas "all that is useful in them," says the minister, "is already translated into English." Young Underhill's father is accordingly against such studies, for he would wish that his son should learn "not *hard words*, but *useful things*." [92] On the other hand it is clear that Underhill (who seems interchangeable with Tyler in this part of the book) himself valued the classics, and was well repaid for his study of them. As a lad he devoted himself to Greek studies to such an extent that his farming technique was sadly impaired. Opposed to sterile philology as he was, Tyler could not have written this charmingly humorous passage unless he loved the true uses of the classics:

> It was resolved that I should labour on my father's farm; but alas! a taste for Greek had quite eradicated a love for labour. Poring so intensely on Homer and Virgil had so completely filled my brain with heathen mythology, that I imagined a Hamadryade in every sapling, a Naiad in every puddle; and expected to hear the sobbings of the infant Fauns, as I turned the furrow. I gave Greek names to all our farming tools; and cheered the cattle with hexameter verse. My father's hired men, after a tedious day's labour in the woods, inspecting our stores, for refreshment, instead of the customary bread and cheese and brandy, found Homer's Iliad, Virgil [*sic*] Delphini and Schrevelius's Lexicon, in the basket.
> After I had worked on the farm some months, having killed a fat heifer of my father's, upon which the family depended for their winter's beef, covered it with green boughs, and laid it in the shade to putrify, in order to raise a swarm of bees, after the manner of Virgil; which process, notwithstanding I followed closely the directions in the georgics, some how or other, failed, my father consented to my mother's request, that I should renew my career of learning.[93]

But Tyler also has his fun in peppering the under-educated. As a lad Updike once mortally offends a young lady by writing her a classically patterned letter in which he refers to her as "ox-eyed." Another young lady who pretends to love literature refers to Johnson's dictionary (which Updike had lent her) as "very pretty story books." [94] On another occasion he is taken for a Papist because he can speak French.[95] When he talks about Greek horses to some young bloods at a tavern, they respond with a challenge, saying that their horses could beat Achilles' Xanthus. He is called a pedant for presuming to read Homer to a company which would have listened in rapture if the language had been Indian, which the company understood no better than Greek.[96]

A general lack of education among local folk indirectly occasions Tyler's satire on duelling. The letter in which he classically described a young lady as "ox-eyed" has involved him in a challenge. At first he naively takes the badly spelled and generally incoherent but vaguely polite letter as an invitation to a partridge shoot. A gentleman from Carolina (where challenges are taken in one's stride) gladly explains the situation, and Underhill finally and in great trepidation accepts. The Carolinian assures him that he need have no fears, for the encounter will in any case be without bloodshed:

> You will . . . turn a copper for the first fire; but I should advise you to grant it to him. This will give him a vast idea of your firmness, and contempt of danger. Your antagonist, with banishment from his country, and the gallows staring him in the face, will be sure not to hit you, on his own account. The ball will pass, at least, ten rods over your head. You must then discharge your pistol, in the air, and offer him to fire again; as, in the language of the duellist, you will have given him his life, so it will be highly inconsistent, in him to again attempt yours. We seconds shall immediately interfere, and pronounce you both men of honour. The matter in controversy will be passed over. You will shake hands, commence warm friends, and the ladies will adore you.[97]

Actually the meeting does not occur at all, for, news of the matter having leaked out, Underhill and his challenger are arrested. Yet out of this farcical episode Underhill acquires the sobriquet "a man of honour," and he is no longer called a pedant.

Obviously Tyler's social purpose in this sort of satire is not exceedingly strong. So with his satire of the medical profession: it exists more as an amusing exposure of ignorance and stupidity than as a serious indictment of the profession as a whole. No profound criticism is implied when he reveals that as commencing medico he used the ancient trick (later to be used again by the inimitable Bob Sawyer in *Pickwick Papers*) of advertising his *busyness* by paying a lad to call him out of meeting. Indeed much of Tyler's satire has a slightly bookish tone, and it is pretty safe to assume that in several passages he had Fielding in mind. Yet light satire patently was his forte, and his crisp, classic prose was ideally suited to be its vehicle.

For all his exposure of the shortcomings of certain of his country-men, Tyler had a lively sense of the importance of being an American. The breath of freedom in the new republic was dear to the man who had studied the polity of European states. On Underhill's arrival at London, the author is at pains to sketch the city in terms none too complimentary to the late mother of the American colonies:

> Men of unbounded affluence, in plain attire, living within the rules of the most rigid economy; crowds of no substance, strutting in embroidery and lace; people, whose little smoky fire of coals was rendered cheerless by excise, and their daily draught of beer embittered by taxes; who administer to the luxury of pensioners and placemen, in every comfort, convenience, or even necessary of life they partake; who are entangled by innumerable penal laws, to the breach of which, banishment and the gallows are almost universally annexed; a motley race, in whose mongrel veins runs the blood of all nations, speaking with pointed contempt of the fat burgo master of Amsterdam, the cheerful French peasant, the hardy tiller of the Swiss cantons, and the independent farmer of America; rotting in dungeons, languishing wretched lives in foetid jails, and boasting of the GLORIOUS FREEDOM OF ENGLISHMEN: hered-itary senators, ignorant and inattentive to the welfare of their country, and unacquainted with the geography of its foreign pos-sessions; and politicians, in coffee houses, without one foot of soil, or one guinea in their pockets, vaunting, with national pride, of our victories, our colonies, our ministers, our magna charta, and our constitution! [98]

As for the French, the recent Revolution and the ruthless technique of Robespierre, "that Moloch of the French nation," [99] were reminders enough of the blessings of a nation firmly established on sane republi-can principles. America, New England in particular, was a place, more-over, in which literacy spread more easily than in the Old World, where the peasantry remained sodden and untutored.[100] Thus "Updike Underhill's" preface to *The Algerine Captive* called attention to the rapid increase in the public consumption of books of amusement, travel books and novels (even Mrs. "Ratcliffe's"), as opposed to books de-signed merely to instruct. This he cannot but regard as a token of our growth in culture. There are, however, "two things to be deplored. The first is that, while so many books are vended, they are not of our own manufacture . . . The second misfortune is that Novels, being the picture of the times, the New England reader is insensibly taught to admire the levity, and often the vices of the parent country. While the fancy is enchanted, the heart is corrupted. The farmer's daughter, while she pities the misfortune of some modern heroine, is exposed to the attacks of vice, from which her ignorance would have formed her surest shield. If the English Novel does not inculcate vice, it at least impresses on the young mind an erroneous idea of the world, in which she is to live. It paints the manners, customs, and habits of a strange country; excites a fondness for false splendour; and renders the homespun habits of her own country disgusting." [101]

It is perfectly plain that the malign influence of foreign importations can be counteracted if Americans see to it "that we write our own books of amusement, and that they exhibit our own manners." [102] This at least is what Updike Underhill gives out as the advice he received from a friend. Hence *The Algerine Captive*, which, besides telling a story of captivity abroad is intended to "display a portrait of New England manners, hitherto unattempted." [103]

Tyler's claim to priority as a delineator of New England manners can be pretty well substantiated, for those domestic books which preceded *The Algerine Captive* glanced no more than obliquely at many things that Tyler confronted intimately. It must be added—what is true of many early English and American "novels"—that his tale is really no novel in a modern sense. Like *Roderick Random*, it is picaresque in pattern, but it does not achieve even *Roderick Random's* flimsy semblance of a rounded plot.[104] Yet a novelist cannot live by plot alone; indeed his longevity depends more on other elements, especially the author's reflection of that general life of which the "action" purports to be a concrete example. Quite as important also is the author's ability to give memorable expression to those ideas, images, and emotions which form the raw material of fiction. In maturity of observation and in command of language, Tyler was far superior to the average popular novelist, whose book generally rendered up its final value as soon as certain arbitrarily withheld facts were divulged in the ultimate chapter.[105] It is Tyler's finished prose—swift, well-balanced, allusive but comparatively unembellished—which lends interest to his satire of what were inevitably temporary problems.

This is not to imply that *The Algerine Captive* is a great book. It has been unduly neglected by historians of literature (partly because it is almost inaccessible), but it can never claim a place of first importance. It possesses weight, but not *sufficient* weight. It is witty and apposite, but it lacks the general significance of, say, *Modern Chivalry*. Placed in his own period, Tyler appears to advantage, but forced into comparison with first-rank writers, he would inevitably diminish in stature. He was a good man of letters—not a towering genius.

With the appearance of Imlay, Brackenridge, and Tyler the American novel escapes from the swaddling clothes of didacticism, begins to evince signs of coming maturity. Sugary sentiment is exchanged for a more intellectual diet. Hysterical girls and handsome lifeless young men are replaced by persons capable of pondering problems relating to government, economics, "professional" life. Satire, a token of intellectual growth, is substituted for more elementary modes of instruction and criticism. Humor, a dividend on sound intellectual stocks, replaces whimsy. But satire is always regarded askance by readers less alert than its authors; and our early satirists, Brackenridge, Imlay, and Tyler, did not succeed so well with the multitude as did other writers. Moreover, all three of these men were a little cavalier with respect to the principles—loose though they were—of narrative writing: they allowed their stories to get cold while they followed intellectual trails. What the novel needed was capable writers who could merge problem and "human interest." It was to be a long time before such combinations became plentiful in American fiction.

Vaulting Ambition
Brockden Brown and Others

CHARLES BROCKDEN BROWN (1771-1810)

Charles Brockden Brown was possessed of more imaginative power than he ever successfully utilized as a novelist. His ambitions outran his preparation, his discipline, and his health. When he died at thirty-nine, he had written no book in which his extraordinary powers were concentrated, no novel which remained unblemished by glaring faults of structure or expression. Brown lacked ballast: when he soared into the higher reaches of the imagination, there was no assurance that he would reach a definite objective—if indeed he possessed one. His books seemed the brilliant but fumbling prelude of a journeyman prevented by death from achieving a full mastery of his technique. Yet readers who come to scoff at Brown as a Gothic bungler may remain to submit willingly to his undeniable spell and to acknowledge his high seriousness. His innate power was so great, his prose so interladen with passages of beauty, that he has survived defects which would have wrecked an average writer. Even his most imperfect stories carry the marks of extraordinary talent. The tone of his writing was that of a greater writer than he can ever be proved to have been. This was perceived by Shelley, who was strongly attracted by Brown:

> Brown's four novels, Schiller's *Robbers*, and Goethe's *Faust*, were, of all the works with which [Shelley] was familiar, those which took the deepest root in his mind, and had the strongest influence in the formation of his character . . . [He admired other writers] but admiration is one thing and assimilation is another; and nothing so blended itself with the structure of his interior mind as the creations of Brown.[1]

At all events he was the first American novelist who won recognition mainly on merit and he remains a distinguished if poorly proportioned figure on the threshold of our fictional art.

Brown spent a bookish and valetudinarian boyhood in Philadelphia, then a city of about 40,000 people. A Quaker, he attended the Friends School until November, 1786. He was exceedingly precocious. On one occasion when a visitor irritated him by calling him a "boy," this ten-year-old prodigy commented with asperity: "Why does he call me boy? Does he not know that it is neither size nor age, but understanding that makes the man? I could ask him an hundred questions, none of which he could answer." [2] Protracted formal education would hardly seem necessary for such a lad as this. In any case, a college was apparently not thought of; but, pressed by the neeed of preparing to earn a living, Brown submitted unwillingly to a plan whereby he should study law under a Philadelphia lawyer. Nominally he remained in this bondage until 1793, but his was a temperament "unfitted . . . for the duties of practical life," [3] and he learned nothing about the law so surely as that he did not wish to practice it. From the beginning of his legal training he had taken more interest in miscellaneous literary and philosophical studies than in Coke and Blackstone. Even as a lad he had been covetous of literary fame; and at sixteen years of age, fired by the poetic undertakings of the Hartford Wits, he contemplated a triad of epics involving North and South America, with such modest heroes as Columbus, Pizarro, and Cortez. Stimulation of his literary instincts was also provided by a Belles Lettres Club, of which he was the first president. His first printed pieces were moderate enough in scope, being a series of essays contributed to the *Columbian Magazine* for August, 1789. They foreshadowed his later writings, however, for they showed the young author "straining after unattainable perfection" and indulging in a "romancing vein." [4]

Science and philosophy, particularly political philosophy, interested him quite as much as literature during his early days. His was a nature easily rendered giddy by ideas of the universal, the ultimate, the absolute, and the Utopian. Idealism surged through his eager mind. Yet he made a pretense, at least, of being methodical. He was no more than sixteen when he made an attempt "toward classing and separating the several departments of knowledge," [5] It was characteristic of him that he surveyed more territory than he was ever able to possess himself of, much less to cultivate carefully. He was susceptible, also, to the advances of new philosophical conceptions. The radical doctrines of French writers—Voltaire, Rousseau, Diderot—took him by storm during his apprentice days. Later on Godwin was to fill his head with a welter of revolutionary doctrine. Such a youth was not likely to profit by following the well-worn paths of legal precedent. Brown never became a practicing attorney.

Having disappointed family and friends by rejecting the profession he was trained for, Brown felt at loose ends in his native city. It happened, moreover, that an epidemic of yellow fever attacked Philadelphia. Partly to escape its ravages and partly to seek new horizons, Brown journeyed to Litchfield in 1793, then the home of the Connecticut Wit Elihu Hubbard Smith, whom Brown had met at Philadelphia in the winter of 1790-91. Smith was a kindred soul, a physician whose professional duties did not prevent his taking a more than casual interest in literature. During the summer of this very year he published the first anthology of native verse, *American Poems* (1793). Dr. Smith helped to stabilize Brown at a difficult period, but he at the same time fed fuel to Brown's burning philosophical interests. Upon Smith's removal to New York, Brown accompanied him. Being largely without other connections in New York, the young man was invited to live for a time at the home of Dr. Smith and also at the home of his future biographer, the playwright William Dunlap. Smith introduced him to the "Friendly Club," a lively organization comprised chiefly of young professional men interested in the discussion of political, social, and literary subjects. Here, surrounded by patrons and practitioners of letters in an atmosphere charged with liberal doctrine, Brown determined to become a writer. Here too he became acquainted with that manual of radical and idealistic thinkers in England, France, and America—William Godwin's *Political Justice* (1793).[6] It was natural therefore that upon his return to Philadelphia later in the year he should commence work on a book dealing with Godwinian perfectionism.[7] By September, 1795, he was planning "a work equal in extent to *Caleb Williams*," and although this particular work did not materialize, Brown continued to regard *Caleb Williams* as a model for some time to come.[8]

Now followed a probationary period in which Brown's writing apparently consisted of a few Utopian sketches, bits of poetry, entries in his journal, and letters. He kept up his acquaintance with Dunlap, visiting him at Perth Amboy in 1796, and with Smith, whom he visited frequently at New York. It was the latter, apparently, who encouraged him in the writing of a series of papers on women's rights which were ultimately published in a small book, *Alcuin, A Dialogue*, in 1798.[9] By July, 1798, he had returned to New York to enjoy the intellectual ferment which had earlier been so stimulating. His valued friend E. H. Smith died in September of yellow fever, but there were many others who took an interest in the young author. He had brought with him the manuscript of an uncompleted novel, *Sky-Walk, or The Man Unknown to Himself*, as well as, probably, the manuscripts of some of the novels soon to be printed in rapid succession. It was not long, however, before he was set to work in the capacity of editor of a magazine sponsored by the Friendly Club, *The Monthly Magazine and American Review*. In conformity with the type of prospectus used at the time, the magazine announced its aims in grandiose terms—"to extract the quintessence of European wisdom; to review and estimate the labours of all writers, domestic and foreign." [10] Such a program could scarcely be expected to thrive even with the most industrious of staffs; with such meagre assistance as Brown actually received from his colleagues, it is surprising that the organ lasted as long as it did—from April 1, 1798 to December, 1800. Although Brown later said that magazines generally fail "by the fault or misfortune of the proprietors," [11] it is clear that the times were not propitious.

In the meantime Brown had made a serious beginning as a writer of fiction. *Wieland*, his first completed novel, was published in 1798. Little is known of what novelists Brown had read before this time. From such evidences of his reading as are available it would appear that "established writers of the eighteenth century were most in his eye." [12] Yet most of these were poets, and very few comments of his are available on novelists whose works appeared before *Wieland*. His reviews in *The Monthly Magazine* were mainly devoted to "obscure nobodies who have been totally forgotten." [13] His taste in fiction may be partially gauged by his subsequent remarks of approval on Richardson, Miss Edgeworth, Mrs. Opie, and Ann Radcliffe. [14] It is natural to assume that he was familiar with the various tales of terror which had appeared in England after Walpole's *The Castle of Otranto* had inaugurated the type in 1764. It is a matter of record that he had read and admired Godwin's *Caleb Williams* before he wrote *Wieland*. [15] It is clear also from the contents not only of *Wieland* but of his other novels as well that elements of Brown's fiction were often drawn from wide general reading, including science. The theme of *Wieland* was probably suggested to Brown by his reading of Cajetan Tschink's *Geisterseher*. [16] The basis of its plot, however, was taken directly from an actual case of murder committed under the influence of hallucination in Tomhannock, New York, seventeen years before *Wieland* was published. [17]

Wieland is a tale of mystery and violence originating in a religious psychosis and brought to its climax by unfortunate ventriloquistic experiments. The action occurs in the environs of Philadelphia, [18] where Wieland has lived a comparatively tranquil pastoral existence with Catharine his wife and Clara his sister until a mysterious voice begins to work havoc not only with the psychological well-being of the sensitive Wieland but also with the love affair of Clara and her fiancé Pleyel. Eight times the voice is heard, in situations ranging from the trivial to the tragic. Finally Wieland, now far gone in a religious psychosis, hears a voice which he takes as a heavenly command to slay his wife and children; and he is later prevented from killing Clara also, whom he believes to have "deserted him, and gone over to his enemies," only by the final command of the voice to "Hold!"

Wieland, Brown's first published novel, is as good and as bad as anything he wrote. It exhibits most of his equipment as a story-teller. There is the appealing persecuted heroine, an incredible mixture of eighteenth-century delicacy and Amazonian vigor. She promotes Brown's Gothic purposes by insisting on living in seclusion in a house architecturally ideal for nocturnal horror. Her fortitude in enduring trials and her facility in recounting them make her a worthy representative of Richardsonian tradition in America. The adventure she relates is so fraught with excitement that the breathless reader is willing to condone defects of which he would complain in a milder story. The structure of the whole narrative is poor. The Conway-Maxwell sub-plot bears no sensible relation to the rest of the story.[19] The author's plan to allow the reader to follow the action from the successive points of view of Clara, Pleyel, Wieland, and Carwin goes astray partly because Carwin's narrative gets out of hand.[20] Yet even the narrations of the other characters are exceedingly involved and disproportionate. Careless use of punctuation, tense, reference, and even of the names of the characters creates a condition that at times borders on chaos. Motivation is needlessly flimsy. Incoherence is so general that Brown's lavish use of coincidence seems almost a blessing: at least it brings a flash of clearness. It is obvious, however, that these errors, irritating as they are, testify to the haste, not the incapacity, of the author. He wrote at top speed under great pressure (at one time, it is said, composing five works concurrently) and he seldom revised. Other defects of the book—crudeness of dialogue and vagueness of setting—are such as might be expected in a novel written as early as 1798: even in England, where there was a novel-writing tradition of some decades, dialogue and setting were generally ineffective until a considerably later date.

How could a novel with so many sins upon its head ever come to be acknowledged as a significant piece of narrative writing? The answer lies in the intensity with which Brown pursued an important theme and his ability to invest single scenes with magnitude and significance. The book lacks order but it possesses weight. The religious mania of Wieland is its centre of gravity. To some extent Wieland's morbid interest in religion was a legacy from his father, a native of Germany, who settled near Philadelphia to act as missionary to the Indians. There the father purchased a farm and settled down to a life that was materially satisfactory: "The cheapness of the land, and the service of African slaves . . . gave him who was poor in Europe all the advantages of wealth." His missionary activities, however, were largely unsuccessful on account of the "license of savage passion, and the artifices of his depraved countrymen." More and more in later years he became a victim of religious melancholy. More and more, too, he frequented his "temple," a sort of summer house which he used for meditation. Here one day he met his death from a mysterious cause which is finally explained as spontaneous combustion.

The younger Wieland, however, always regarded the death of his father as the necessary outcome of "a direct and supernatural decree." Inclined toward religious introspection, he himself had become a morbid student of religious history. The simple faith of his sister Clara and the rational, unperturbed skepticism of her fiancé Pleyel had no effect on his thinking: he remained obedient to his belief in "moral necessity, and calvinistic inspiration." Finally his abnormality advances into a state of dementia, which it is one of Brown's distinctions to have treated fully and convincingly for the first time in American fiction. When the wandering ventriloquist Carwin first exercised his irresponsible powers on Wieland the effects were inevitably malign. Yet ventriloquism apparently did not cause but only hastened the growth of a pathological condition in Wieland.[21] At its greatest his religious frenzy reaches heights which (though the roots of the elder Wieland's mania were German) recall the testimony of Jonathan Edwards and other chroniclers of episodes proving the Puritans' capacity to contemplate cruelty complacently so long as it was apparently decreed by Heaven. Yet no earlier writer had woven the hideous strands of religious fanaticism into fiction with such power as Brown displayed in the scene in which Wieland exults in his dreadful deed. Here the author rises above the melodrama which elsewhere in the book is often unsuppressed:

> " 'I brought thee hither to fulfill a divine command. I am appointed thy destroyer, and destroy thee I must.' Saying this I seized her wrists. She shrieked aloud, and endeavoured to free herself from my grasp; but her efforts were vain . . .
>
> "Till her breath was stopped she shrieked for help—for mercy. When she could speak no longer, her gestures, her looks appealed to my compassion. My accursed hand was irresolute and tremulous. I meant thy death to be sudden, thy struggles to be brief. Alas! my heart was infirm; my resolves mutable. Thrice I slackened my grasp, and life kept its hold, though in the midst of pangs.

Her eye-balls started from their sockets. Grimness and distortion took place of all that used to bewitch me into transport, and subdue me into reverence . . .

"I was commissioned to kill thee, but not to torment thee with the foresight of thy death; not to multiply thy fears, and prolong thy agonies. Haggard, and pale, and lifeless, at length thou ceasedst to contend with thy destiny.

"This was a moment of triumph. Thus had I successfully subdued the stubbornness of human passions: the victim which had been demanded was given: the deed was done past recal [*sic*].

"I lifted the corpse in my arms and laid it on the bed. I gazed upon it with delight. Such was the elation of my thoughts, that I even broke into laughter. I clapped my hands and exclaimed, 'It is done! My sacred duty is fulfilled! To that I have sacrificed, O my God! thy last and best gift, my wife!'

"For a while I thus soared above frailty" . . .[22]

It was this scene which drew forth the high praise of Whittier. "In the entire range of English literature," he wrote, "there is no more thrilling passage than that which describes the execution of this baleful suggestion . . . The masters of the old Greek tragedy have scarcely exceeded the sublime horror of this scene from the American novelist." [23]

So intense a story as *Wieland* allows the reader little relief, but useful contrasts are not lacking. The raving and violence of Wieland himself are balanced by the cool deliberation of Carwin, whose scientific experiments finally help destroy the perilously-poised reason of the religious fanatic. Realism benefits by Brown's exonerating Carwin as the prime cause of Wieland's downfall, but Carwin's character remains at best ambiguous. He was born, one learns from the *Memoirs of a Biloquist*, with a sort of Faustian "thirst of knowledge" which was "augmented in proportion as it was supplied with gratification." This led him to various deeds which worked together toward the catastrophe. Only once did he use his voice with malicious intention—to persuade Pleyel that Clara was false to him. If he prowled unwarrantedly in Clara's rooms, he was interested primarily in her books and manuscripts. He pleads (on that occasion at least) that his "only crime was curiosity." [24] The fatal results of his Godwinian curiosity he professes to deplore deeply, but again he pleads that his originally innocent experiment had gone beyond his intentions: "had I not rashly set in motion a machine, over whose progress I had not control, and which experience had shewn me was infinite in power?" [25] Nor does the fact that it is Carwin's voice which saves Clara from Wieland's violence fully atone for all the destruction he has brought upon innocent people through his devotion to knowledge.[26] Yet as an embodiment of Brown's philosophical and scientific interests, Carwin is representative of a type of high-minded villains, experimenters on humanity, who manage to gain entry into almost all his novels. Retouched, Carwin would have made a good character for Hawthorne.

Yet the "supernatural" elements in *Wieland* account for only part of its compelling interest. If, as Thomas Love Peacock said, *Wieland* is "one of the few tales in which the final explanation of the apparently supernatural does not destroy or diminish the original effect,"[27] the reason is that Brown is interested in psychology quite as much as in horror. There can be no doubt that the effectiveness of *Wieland* as a story is dependent partly on the reality of the central situation: here was no mere bag of Gothic tricks[28] but a deadly serious account of terrible effects wrought by a man whose daily effort was to discern the will of God and who believed that "obedience was the test of perfect virtue." Here was a man who though proved to have slain his wife and children could still insist that his "supreme passion" had been to serve God with "a single and upright heart." Such a man had been and might be again. Some manufactured thrills there are in *Wieland* which bear the trademark of earlier writers, but these are largely confined to the episodes in which Carwin mystifies and persecutes Clara. The relationship between Clara and her brother is such as to inspire pity and terror in the reader. The device of ventriloquism, which might have been used merely theatrically, is employed in the service of so important a theme that, as Fitz-James O'Brien (himself a purveyor of horror) has said, the use of the voice becomes truly "awful."[29] Wieland's dignified address while a prisoner at the bar is charged with cold horror. Clara's situation when Carwin counterfeits a murderous dialogue in her closet can be accepted with equanimity by any seasoned reader of Gothic tales; but her desperate situation when she is confronted by a religious maniac, her own brother, who, having escaped from prison, wishes to complete his devotions by taking her life, is fraught with drama of the most intense sort, rising to peak after peak of horror.

After the horror, the pathos: in his last hour Wieland himself has lucid moments in which he realizes the result of his aberration. He is transformed, for the moment, into a man infinitely pathetic:

> "Sister," said he, in an accent sorrowful and mild, "I have acted poorly my part in this world. What thinkest thou? Shall I not do better in the next?"

Yet as these words are spoken Wieland has a knife in his hand. Presently there is a renewal of his malady, and Clara faces death at the hands of her crazed brother. Carwin's vocal intervention saves Clara, but in recalling Wieland from his hallucination converts him into "a monument of woe." There is left to Clara no hope but that the oblivion of death should finally minister to Wieland's mind:

> What can I wish for thee? Thou who has vied with the great preacher of thy faith in sanctity of motives, and in elevation above sensual and selfish! Thou whom thy fate has changed into paricide and savage! Can I wish for the continuance of thy being? No.

Her hope is fulfilled sooner than she expects, for seizing a knife, Wieland presently remedies his own condition:

> He plunged it to the hilt in his neck; and his life instantly escaped with the stream that gushed from the wound. He was stretched at my feet; and my hands were sprinkled with his blood as he fell.

In this moment Brown reaches true tragedy. In this moment no reader remembers the structural and stylistic faults elsewhere committed, for by some rare imaginative power Brown has carried his narrative to a level at which he inevitably recalls Shakespearian tragedy. Critics recoil from Brown's frequently blundering technique, but they must perceive in this erratic youth the signs of a genius which was destined never to find equilibrium.

After *Wieland*, Brown's first novel to be published was *Ormond; or The Secret Witness* (1799).[30] If Dunlap had found *Wieland* so "shocking" in its nature as to "lessen the attraction of the story," [31] he could hardly have taken comfort in *Ormond*. *Ormond* combines violent narrative with leisurely social theorizing in an unartistic but never wholly dull mélange. The story deals with the vicissitudes of Constantia Dudley and the sinister attentions of Ormond. Poverty, the blindness of her father, and the menace of yellow fever, are among the troubles which Constantia bravely meets before she is befriended by the brilliant Ormond, lately returned from participation in the French Revolution and contact with the revolutionary society of the Illuminati in Germany. Ormond is so charmed with Constantia that he rids himself of a mistress (who subsequently kills herself) in order to be free to court Constantia. He finally decides, however, that he will not offer her marriage, for he has a low opinion of women in general and he chooses not to submit himself to "the loathsome and impracticable obligations" of marriage." [32] When Constantia's father, Dudley, not unnaturally enters opposition to the informal suit of such a man as Ormond, the latter is provoked to violence which results in the death of Dudley and of the man Ormond had employed to kill him. Finally Ormond forces his way into the lonely mansion where Constantia is staying, and there, with two dead bodies lying about in grisly congruity, Ormond not only admits that he ordered the death of her father but avows that he is now ready to take by violence that which his irresponsible wooings had failed to win honorably. But Constantia defends her honor—which Ormond had ridiculed as a mere figment, an airy notion—with a very substantial little pen-knife. Subsequently Constantia finds peace and quiet happiness in England.

As a fictional character Ormond is unsatisfactory—in mind a mere patchwork of radical opinion, in action a robot assigned to a macabre role. His villainy is not at first apparent, being concealed by a glamorous exterior acquired in continental circles and by his air of benevolence.[33] Before his real villainy is made clear, he passes for a plausible if somewhat daring and headstrong individual, recklessly hostile to man-made institutions and unduly confident in his own powers and rectitude.[34] Yet his actual conduct is fearful in the extreme. His character may be in part inferred from an "exploit" of his eighteenth year when as a volunteer in the Russian army he had accomplished in one day the rape and stabbing of a helpless girl, the killing of a friend, and the slaughter of certain Turkish foragers whose "five heads, suspended, by their gory locks, to his horse's mane," he carried away as trophies. Such colossal rant as this does not create character in fiction, and Ormond remains a crude Gothic fabrication. Better drawn, he might have been a formidable villain and his death at the hands of Constantia might have been tragic.

Constantia is in part more realistically delineated. Her danger is an excess of merits. She is uncomplaining in adversity, resourceful in emergencies, modest and charming in demeanor. Her methodical habits and her constant reference to "reason" as a guide to conduct are results of the careful educational program of a father whose aim was to make her less "alluring and voluptuous" than "eloquent and wise." In all this she is seen in contrast to Helena Cleves, Ormond's coy, clinging mistress, who had been brought up amid luxurious surroundings according to the older principle that a woman should know little beyond music, French, and mild coquetry. Constantia was not perfect, however, for her education had failed to provide her with a good religious foundation: she was "unacquainted with religion," and had "formed her esti-

mate of good and evil on nothing but terrestrial and visible consequences." Yet even without this bulwark she is able to withstand the
worst the world could offer. She remains withal a charming and admirable, if somewhat shadowy character; and it is easy to understand
why she should have attracted Shelley.[35]

Ormond possesses elements of interest and power which the novel as
a whole does not sustain. Crass neglect of the principle of coherence
annoys the reader. More coincidence is used than can be rationalized
by Brown's observation that "Human life abounds with mysterious appearances." [36] Although there are occasional local references—to William Penn's house, to Amboy, to the Battery in New York—the story is
grounded nowhere. And the action, which is laid principally in Philadelphia, "might have taken place in any plague-ridden city." [37] The
philosophical elements are not assimilated by the story but remain as
fragmentary, essay-like intrusions. Most of all *Ormond* lacks the high-
seriousness and genuine tragedy of *Wieland*.

Brown's next book was the first part of *Arthur Mervyn*, published
in 1799; the second part appeared in 1800. When the first part reached
book form, it had already been "tried out" serially in the *Weekly Magazine* (Philadelphia), which published nine chapters in the year 1798.
If Brown was "the first American writer to envisage the possibilities
of . . . legitimate dual exploitation" [38] he did not employ the time between serial and book to improve the finish of his product. Evidently
the pressure of journalistic writing was responsible for the unfinished
nature of much of Brown's prose. *Arthur Mervyn* is as amorphous as
any book he wrote. Yet Brown managed to put something of real significance into each of his novels; in this case it is the vividness of his
account of the ravages of the yellow fever. He had seen and escaped
the disease at Philadelphia in 1793. In 1798 at New York he was attacked by it in the same epidemic that carried off his friend E. H.
Smith. In part *Arthur Mervyn* is more directly autobiographical than
anything he wrote. As a novel of purpose intended to show the
dreadful conditions in Philadelphia in 1793, it is written with all the
intensity of which Brown was master. Nor did his morbid mind recoil
from reporting in full the most repellent details of the course of the
disease.

The action of *Arthur Mervyn* is almost as chaotic as the condition of
the plague-ridden city. The exigencies of the situation account for
many of the abrupt exits and entrances of the characters, but the worst
foe of continuity in the story is Brown himself. He puts his hero
through enough unassimilated adventures to make the substance of
a half-dozen more efficient novels. He fails to name his characters

promptly, allows many of them autobiographical carte blanche, yanks them about like puppets, forgets their structural functions, and in general employs them as if they were labels instead of people. Some of the labels are marked for death, but no emotion is aroused for them as individuals: the reader does not really know them.

The hero, Arthur Mervyn, coming to Philadelphia and falling ill of the fever, tells his story to the man (the author) who befriends him. This involves the recital of how one Welbeck had taken Arthur as his secretary with the hope that the secretary might feel moved to marry Welbeck's cast-off mistress, now pregnant. Arthur escapes this snare, but he naively assists in disposing of the dead body of a man he has seen Welbeck in the act of murdering. On the way across the river Welbeck jumps overboard and is apparently drowned. In the meantime, of course, Welbeck has told Arthur his life-story in fatiguing detail. Upon Welbeck's disappearance Arthur is left with the ghastly secret of the murder he witnessed and also with some stolen Italian manuscripts which later embarrass him. Soon after, the narrative carries Arthur to the country, where he works as a day-laborer until he discovers how grievously the daughter of his employer is pining for an absent lover. Thereupon, with all that benevolence which is as typical of a Brunonian character as innocence and a turn for philosophy, Arthur rashly advances into the pestilence-stricken city (Philadelphia) to retrieve the object of her affections. He succeeds in his errand but falls ill of the fever, and, through his illness (as well as the author's facility in arranging coincidences), comes again under the baneful influence of Welbeck. Anyone but a Brown boy could recognize Welbeck for a villain to be shunned like the plague. Yet the author, who has a weakness for masterful criminals, manages to make some excuses for Welbeck as the victim of society. (Indeed there is no call to hiss the villain heartily in any of Brown's novels.) Arthur's association with Welbeck eventually lands him broken and penniless in jail, to be helped out later at the discretion of the narrator. In the meantime Arthur has gathered various morbid statistics including the deaths of his rustic employer, his lovelorn daughter, and her fiancé. Subsequently Welbeck also dies, rendering up at the last certain stolen money, which Arthur undertakes to return to its rightful owner at Baltimore. Here he meets and, despite having to listen to her long sad autobiography, forms an attachment for a wealthy widow. Innocent of love as of law, he dawdles about, unaware of the tumult he has stirred in her breast until a friend assures him of the truth, and he proposes—having completely forgotten a poor girl he was on the verge of marrying only a volume earlier. Now our hero returns to Philadelphia to study medicine under the patronage of the narrator. Thus is completed the main action of a story so involved with labyrinthine sub-plot and digression and dislocated episode that the reader is sure of practically nothing but that excitement will somehow be sustained.

There is little to praise in *Arthur Mervyn* except its authentic rendering of the mood of a great city under the shadow of plague.[39] Brown possessed a certain civic spirit which is revealed in his unflinching record of the awesome data of the epidemic and his hope that such an epidemic may not recur. He may have dabbled congenially in morbid symptoms, but behind his sensational case histories was a genuine humanitarian spirit which gives validity to his narrative. His tastes were morbid; but his motive was sound and his pen was effective when he detailed the horrors not only of victims left to die alone but even of those admitted to hospitals where their sufferings were unnecessarily increased by the dishonesty of paid attendants:

The atmosphere was loaded by mortal stenches. A vapour, suffocating and malignant, scarcely allowed me to breathe. No suitable receptacle was provided for the evacuations produced by medicine or disease. My nearest neighbour was struggling with death, and my bed, casually extended, was moist with the detestable matter which had flowed from his stomach.

You will scarcely believe that, in this scene of horrors, the sound of laughter should be overheard. While the upper rooms of this building are filled with the sick and the dying, the lower apartments are the scene of carousals and mirth. The wretches who are hired, at enormous wages, to tend the sick and convey away the dead, neglect their duty, and consume the cordials which are provided for the patients, in debauchery and riot.

A female visage, bloated with malignity and drunkenness, occasionally looked in. Dying eyes were cast upon her, invoking the boon, perhaps, of a drop of cold water, or her assistance to change a posture which compelled him to behold the ghastly writhings or deathful *smile* of his neighbour.

The visitant had left the banquet for a moment, only to see who was dead. If she entered the room, blinking eyes and reeling steps showed her to be totally unqualified for ministering the aid that was needed. Presently she disappeared, and others ascended the staircase, a coffin was deposited at the door, the wretch, whose heart still quivered, was seized by rude hands, and dragged along the floor into the passage.

Oh! how poor are the conceptions which are formed, by the fortunate few, of the sufferings to which millions of their fellow-beings are condemned. This misery was more frightful, because it was seen to flow from the depravity of the attendants. My own eyes only would make me credit the existence of wickedness so enormous. No wonder that to die in garrets, and cellars, and stables, unvisited and unknown, had, by so many, been preferred to being brought hither.[40]

If Poe read this scene with admiration for Brown's skill in merging the effects of carousal and mortal disease, his own studies of pestilence did not bear the marks of Brown's humanitarian interests.[41] Primarily, then, *Arthur Mervyn* is a novel of purpose. The plague was over, but there might be "periodic visitations of this calamity" unless the problem received intelligent attention, even in spite of such efforts.[42] In any case Brown deemed it essential to war on "the evils of poverty and disease . . . by calling forth benevolence in those who are able to afford relief."[43] To this end he wrote *Arthur Mervyn*. And if, as novelist, he had only a partial success in his attempt to "methodize his . . . reflections," as a humanitarian he more than proved his worth in an early day when, notwithstanding pioneer efforts like those of Benjamin Rush, the medical profession had taken but few effective steps toward the municipal control of disease.

Edgar Huntly, the next publication of Brown in the prolific year of 1799, is today accounted second of Brown's novels in point of popularity and intrinsic value.[44] Apology and applause must go hand in hand in any discussion of it. It is a fine detective story—until Brown allows what should have been a minor episode to develop into a structural unit demanding parity with the original plot. It is brilliantly written—except where the author fails to correct the incoherencies and extravagances of first-draft writing. On the whole it has less imaginative power than *Wieland*, but it suffers less from crude error, and in passages it exhibits an extremely fine prose style.

The first problem implicit in the action of the story is to discover the identity of the murderer of one Waldegrave, found mysteriously slain without apparent motive or clue to the assassin. Since calling in the aid of the sheriff is out of the question in Brown's novels, Edgar Huntly, friend of the deceased, seeks his own solution—as much to gratify his insatiable curiosity as to further the ends of justice. Believing that the murderer might return to the scene of the crime, Huntly loiters at midnight near the elm beneath which Waldegrave had met his end. Here in fact he espies a suspicious-looking character—a fellow bearing a spade with which he digs a pit, only to sit down in it and emit sobs of a "mighty anguish." He is obviously no ghost but he is as hard to interview as the ghost of Hamlet's father—for he is asleep! A new element in the fiction of thrillers—somnambulism—and Brown makes the most of it. The mysterious visitant walks the night a second and third time. On the third occasion Huntly succeeds in following the sleepwalker to his lodging and lays preparation for an interview in clear daylight. The man proves to be one Clithero Edny, the only "foreigner" in the little settlement where the story begins. Finally Huntly accosts the man and, discreetly, charges him with being aware of the circumstances of Waldegrave's death. Clithero replies with a sixty-page account of his life. Clithero, it appears from his own account, has had a shocking experience in Ireland. In the process of trying to protect the woman (Mrs. Lorimer) who employed him, from her violent brother, he was obliged to kill the brother in self-defense. He then feared for the well-being of Mrs. Lorimer, for he knew of her obsession with the idea that her own death would be bound up with the death of her brother.[45] With a curiously distorted conception of benevolence, therefore, he plans to kill her also—to save her the horror of dying consciously. This part of the tragedy of errors reaches its climax in a gruesome night-scene when his dagger is arrested by Mrs. Lorimer just as it was about to descend by mistake on Clarice, Mrs. Lorimer's niece, whom he loves. Overcome by a sense of his crimes, Clithero vows never to seek Clarice again, and goes to the States.

This recital ended, Clithero neglects to answer Huntly's charge regarding Waldegrave's death, but scoots off into a suburban wilderness, leaving Edgar to meditate on whether there can be guilt where there has been no evil design. Edgar now transfers his detective energies to finding Clithero, whom he wishes to study and to aid. But the story receives still another turn when Edgar is plunged into a hideously enthralling experience as a result of a little somnambulism on his own part: for there are two sleepwalkers in this book! He wakes up from one of his unconscious peregrinations in the bottom of a pit, whence he emerges only after the most incredible but fascinating maneuvers. Thrill follows upon thrill, for at the exit from his cave the spent Edgar encounters Indians. It appears that he can escape only by dispatching one of them with a hatchet—a bloody deed from which he recoils momentarily (despite remembering that Indians had rendered him an orphan) but which he finally perpetrates with considerable vigor. Exhausted, he still has a long trek to safety at his uncle's house. Here he subsequently learns the facts in the case of Waldegrave's death—facts which, after so much excitement from other sources, the reader receives in apathy. Nor is the reader much interested to learn, after endless ramifications, that Clithero finally drowned himself in order to escape being committed to a hospital for the insane.

Edgar Huntly is a story that recalls Godwin in its emphasis upon the morbid curiosity that impelled Huntly to sleuth Clithero, the unhappy effects of Clithero's bungling benevolence, and the ever-present theme of the relationship of good and evil to motive. Yet Brown's "psychology," though keen in detail, is shaky in assembly, and the novel as a whole is unconvincing on this level. The novel lives rather for "new springs of action and new motives to curiosity" on which Brown prided himself:

> Puerile superstition and exploded manners, Gothic castles and chimeras, are the materials usually employed for this end. The incidents of Indian hostility, and the perils of the Western wilderness, are far more suitable; and for a native of America to overlook these would admit of no apology. These, therefore, are, in part, the ingredients of this tale, and these he has been ambitious of depicting in vivid and faithful colours.[46]

The action takes place near "Norwalk" in "one of the western counties of Pennsylvania." [47] Brown believed that he had provided the setting with enough specific indications so that "those who have ranged along the foot of the Blue-Ridge from the Wind-Gap to the Water-Gap will see the exactness of the local descriptions." [48] But *Edgar Huntly* is most famous for two scenes which point the way toward Poe and Cooper—the pit scene and the Indian encounter which immediately follows it. The ratiocinative processes and physical dexterity which enable Edgar to find his way out of a situation so desperate that he was fain to eat tiger's flesh and drink his own perspiration are suggestive of Poe both in *Gordon Pym* and in "The Pit and the Pendulum." [49] Nor need Brown's work in these scenes be accounted any less successful than Poe's. In another way, not yet noted, Brown may have provided Poe with a handy precedent, namely, in building up the horror of a scene by preliminary statement of the author's reluctance and probable inability to recount such enormities at all. Poe's manner is distinctly adumbrated when Brown writes:

> Here, my friend, thou must permit me to pause. The following incidents are of a kind to which the most ardent invention has never conceived a parallel. Fortune, in her most wayward mood, could scarcely be suspected of an influence like this. The scene was pregnant with astonishment and horror. I cannot, even now, recall it without reviving the dismay and confusion which I then experienced.
>   Possibly, the period will arrive when I shall look back without

agony on the perils I have undergone. That period is still distant. Solitude and sleep are now no more than the signals to summon up a tribe of ugly phantoms. Famine, and blindness, and death, and savage enemies, never fail to be conjured up by the silence and darkness of the night. I cannot dissipate them by any efforts of reason. My cowardice requires the perpetual consolation of light. My heart droops when I mark the decline of the sun, and I never sleep but with a candle burning at my pillow. If, by any chance, I should awake and find myself immersed in darkness, I know not what act of desperation I might be suddenly impelled to commit.

I have delayed this narrative longer than my duty to my friend enjoined. Now that I am able to hold a pen, I will hasten to terminate that uncertainty with regard to my fate in which my silence has involved thee. I will recall that series of unheard-of and disastrous vicissitudes which has constituted the latest portion of my life.[50]

The Indian episode, a briefer one, is less successful than the subterranean adventure, but it is sufficiently exciting and it is no more implausible than many in Cooper, who later scoffed at Brown,[51] and still later imitated him.[52] In any case the entire cave scene, of which the Indian encounter is really only the appendix, is one of the most brilliant and fascinating in early American fiction.

To come upon *Clara Howard* after reading the three lurid narratives which preceded it, is to be shocked by its comparative mildness. Reasons for the new tone discernible in Brown are partly economic. After his prodigal production during the years 1798 and 1799 it must have been discouraging to him to observe that though his books had brought him personal prestige,[53] they had done little to advance his financial interests. By April, 1800, he was pretty much disillusioned about the profits of literature:

> Book-making . . . is the dullest of all trades, and the utmost that any American can look for, in his native country, is to be re-imbursed his unavoidable expenses.[54]

He did not, however, like his fellow-townsman, Joseph Dennie, rest in his gloomy generalizations about the state of letters in America, but bestirred himself to alter his own fictional technique to make it more conformable with public taste.[55] To certain objections his brother had raised regarding the extravagance and improbability of his first three published novels he replied:

Your remarks upon the gloominess and out-of-nature incidents of Huntley, if they be not just in their full extent, are, doubtless, such as most readers will make, which alone, is a sufficient reason for dropping the doleful tone and assuming a cheerful one, or, at least substituting moral causes and daily incidents in place of the prodigious or the singular. I shall not fall hereafter into that strain.[56]

In his next two novels he did not rid himself entirely of his "doleful tone"; indeed humor and mirth seem to have been entirely strangers to his temperament. But he did make some attempt to descend to the level of everyday affairs, and he succeeded in substituting "moral causes" for the "prodigious or the singular."

Clara Howard is not a new departure in every respect, for it again shows that Brown was obsessed by the "inextricability of human events." [57] Yet its quiet tone is new. The novel, a short one, is related in a series of letters. It purports to be an account of the troubled romance of Clara Howard and Philip Stanley, a country boy whom Clara's step-father (fathers are rare in Brown) has befriended. A prior claim on Philip is held by Mary Wilmot, nine years his senior, with whom his engagement had failed, for lack of financial cultivation, to blossom into marriage. Mary disappears, but, in spite of all temptation, Clara's sense of honor forbids her taking advantage of her rival's absence. This delicate complication is protracted for some time before by an elaborate and none-too-plausible arrangement the author brings about a happy ending—an innovation for Brown—with the "purest delight" for Philip and "unruffled felicity" for Clara.[58]

The lack of murders, ghosts, suicides, and general violence in *Clara Howard* does not obscure Brown's authorship entirely, for a number of his favorite elements recur. The hero goes through many mental crises and one nearly mortal illness before he is honorably able to take Clara for his bride. The character of the well-to-do patron is by now a familiar one. Impostors are so familiar that when Morton's claim to $5000 turns out to be fraudulent, no seasoned reader of Brown is surprised. The cloud on the good name of a presumably virtuous girl (Mary) one confidently expects to see dispelled. Poor proportion obtains even in this short novel when an unnecessarily full account of Mary's mother is given and when Brown uses the clumsy device of having the past years of a character recounted in a letter to a friend who does not otherwise figure at all in the story. Time relationships are dubious throughout. There is the usual discovery of an unsuspected kinship—apparently a thrilling discovery to all readers, here and abroad, at the time: Mary turns out to be a second cousin of Mrs. Howard.

Again, as in earlier books, the stronger of the two principal characters is the woman. .

Social distinctions continue to interest Brown. The characterization of Philip is apparently partly a by-product of Brown's interest in leveling principles. Philip, a country boy, is made to regard himself as fortunate in being allowed by Mrs. Howard to court Clara, daughter of a well-to-do man. Yet Philip reminds himself that it is only because of tradition that the country-bred person ever regards himself as inferior:

> The ideas annexed to the term *peasant* are wholly inapplicable to the tillers of the ground in America . . . Our books are almost wholly the productions of Europe, and the prejudices which infect us are derived chiefly from this source.[59]

Thus Brown adds his bit to the democratic American credo voiced a little earlier by Crèvecoeur and, almost at the same time as Brown, by Brackenridge. Brackenridge, however, observed more fully and wrote more discriminatingly of the actual problems of insuring democracy without losing quality. Brown as usual was influenced mainly by general principles—drawn from the radical writing, not from the actual conditions, of Europe.

Clara Howard, though more simple than some of Brown's stories, is not notably realistic. The "daily incidents" he promised are not many or well drawn. There are few signs that the author felt any obligation to provide a recognizable setting: perhaps he instinctively felt that American readers, many of whom were nostalgic for the mother country, did not wish to be reminded of their own back yards or of their proximity to the wild frontier. Only seldom in *Clara Howard* does the reader realize that he is in the vicinity of Philadelphia. Mention is made, when Philip is setting out for Baltimore, of the fact that a bridge over the Schuylkill has been carried away by floods. New York is referred to as the "second city of our country." Philip expresses surprise at the "proportions" of the Battery, which he finds a mere "mound" serving the "double purpose of pleasure and defence." Moreover Brown had the impulse to sketch in, if not the ability or the patience to work out thoroughly, suggestions of extent and distance: perhaps this was a lingering sign of the epic interests of his early youth. One interesting passage is that in which the hero, now at an apparent cul de sac in his fortune, contemplates (not very seriously) a journey westward over the breadth of the continent. He envisions the trip in some detail, even describing the difficulties of battling the current of the Mississippi river and going portage over the Rockies before finding still another river which wanders "through as many realms as the Wolga [*sic*] or the Oronoco [*sic*]." At last, in imagination he reaches "the shores of the great Pacific" only to project his fancy from there across the ocean "to China, or along the coast to the dominions of the Spaniards." Here obviously is the romantic visionary indulging in grandiose speculation about remote lands while what should be the interesting domain of the story proper remains vaguely limned. The poverty of local imagery and domestic detail drives the reader back upon the central problem of the novel: how Clara can secure Philip to herself without violating her own ethical sense. The situation was not new in Anglo-Saxon fiction, yet in America, where the love interest of novels was likely to centre either in seduction or Sunday-school, *Clara Howard* was a pioneer novel which, in however rudimentary fashion, adumbrates the love casuistry of the domestic novelists of the sixties and seventies[60] and even of Henry James.

"I am very far from being a wise girl," the opening sentence of Brown's last published novel, *Jane Talbot,* slightly exaggerates the heroine's weaknesses but effectively introduces the theme which dominates the book. Jane needs wisdom in order to extricate herself from a marital problem. Encouraged by her adopted mother, Mrs. Fielder, Jane has made a loveless marriage with Talbot despite having met Henry Colden, apparently her real affinity, before the wedding took place. Colden does not relax his attentions to Jane even after her marriage—with the result that Jane's reputation became spotted with slander, a malady of heroines that was almost epidemic in the period. The death of Talbot would seem to prepare the way for more honorable advances by Colden, but Colden's suit is highly distasteful to Jane's guardian, for she has learned that he is a reader of Godwin's *Political Justice*. She threatens to disinherit Jane if she marries Colden, and Colden receives a comparable warning from his parents. Ultimately love triumphs, for Mrs. Fielder relents.

For Brown this is a terribly thin novel—no carnage, few hysterics, no science but the alchemy of love. Perhaps Brown had learned by this time the truth of his own epigram: "Experience . . . is the antidote of wonder." [61] In any case, the reader is obviously not intended to be awed by "striking" effects but absorbed by close analysis of a psychological and social problem. Some narrative excitement is provided by the slandering of the heroine, but interest in the explanation—a letter forged by a disappointed lover—is sustained merely by the withholding of information. One striking example of dialogue shows what Brown could have done toward the development of realistic speech, but he does not sustain the effort.[62] Bungling use of the letter form again calls attention to Brown's careless narrative technique. Yet these flaws do not seriously interfere with his social purpose, which actually injures the story through overemphasis. The characters are not so much individuals as devices for clarifying the issues of the problem. Mrs. Fielder represents the conservative point of view; Colden, the radical. Jane, equidistant between them, vacillates for the duration of the argument. Mrs. Fielder's conservative position is sufficiently indicated by her unqualified statement to Jane: "The preservation of your virtue was unspeakably of more importance in my eyes than of your life." Her objections to Colden are based on the latter's subversive attitude toward the family and marriage, an attitude referable to his adoption of "that pernicious philosophy which is now so much in vogue." To her he is an atheist and a libertine. Nor is it surprising that she should have objected, considering what she had learned through letters purporting to have been written by him: "[T]hese letters showed Colden as the advocate of suicide; a scoffer at promises; the despiser of revelation, of Providence and a future state; an opponent of marriage, and as one who denied (shocking!) that any thing but mere habit and positive law stood in the way of marriage, nay, of intercourse without marriage, between brother and sister, parent and child." Her final decision to permit the marriage of course hinges on the fact that Colden is finally shorn of his most extreme opinions. As a Godwinian disciple, however irresolute, Colden is obviously destined by Brown to be a hero, but, reversing Ormond's evolution,[63] Colden is at first allowed to look considerably like a villain. Jane is fully equipped with conventional defensive armor, having been brought up to "regard religion not only as the safeguard of every virtue, but even as the test of a good understanding." Yet she avows that she admires Colden for his free inquiry into controversial subjects, and for a time she deplores her own previous condition as one of "superstitious ignorance" because it allowed for no free play of inquiry. She even writes to him in terms of gratitude as the person responsible for her "piety,—all of it that is permanent and rational." Under his influence her "piety ha[d] become more rational and fervent." Likewise she regarded it as a blessing that he had given a "new spring" to her "curiosity." To her, Colden is admirable in his "simplicity and frankness." On the other side the twin menaces of parental displeasure and poverty restrain her. At one time she is on the point of eloping with Colden, but she renounces the plan and dismisses him. When she does accept him he has abdicated his most radical positions: he has admitted his "past misconduct and . . . former degeneracy." Most important of all he possesses a new faith, having "awakened from [his] dreams of doubt and misery, not to the cold and vague belief, but to the living and delightful consciousness, of every tie that can bind man to his Divine Parent and Judge." The conclusion is not a real solution of the general problems involved, but it is a satisfactory equation of the particular forces in this story.

This story with its free discussion of sex (even to the point of mentioning incest without condemning it) and marriage in general can have done little to improve Brown's popular status as a novelist. William Hill Brown, Susanna Rowson, and Hannah Foster had proved that Americans would read novels of seduction so long as they contained no argument against virtue, but there was obviously no large public for the "advanced" thought introduced by Brown's characters. Even news of Colden's reform could not purify the text that preceded it. *Clara Howard* and *Jane Talbot* were not exactly thesis novels, but their intellectual content must have seemed a little formidable to the general reader. A higher ratio of sentiment to theory would probably have improved Brown's product from the point of view of sales. In any case his attempt to increase his sales by turning from the Gothic to the social did not profit him financially. He was therefore more and more dependent on other resources for a livelihood.

One of the resources had been adopted in the summer of 1801, when Brown went into the commission-merchant business with two of his brothers. The Napoleonic wars and maritime disasters, however, almost foundered the firm in 1804, and its last two years, with one of the brothers withdrawn from the partnership, were only a gloomy descent into actual failure. Thereafter Brown was brought so low that in order to eke out a living he even "sold pots and pans across the counter." [64] His needs were the greater, for he had been married (in 1804), and his energies were the less, for tuberculosis was gaining its hold on him. Yet he never wholly relinquished the trade of writing. If the novel would not pay, he could still return to periodical work.[65] And during the years that remained to him (he died in 1810), he devoted himself to the functions of critic and editor. He found criticism, too, precarious as a source of livelihood, but he persisted amid difficulties and he became one of the pioneers of American criticism.[66] In 1803 he became editor of a magazine wholly devoted to literature, *The Literary Magazine and American Register*, which ran until 1807. From 1806 to his death he edited *The American Register*, an historical magazine. One other project on which he was engaged when he died, "A System of General Geography," might well have brought him the financial returns he never actually received from writing, but it was uncompleted and it has remained unpublished. The editorial and critical work of his last six or seven years revealed no completely new aspects of Brown as a writer. Yet they emphasized what is clear to any close student of the novels, that Brown's critical and scholarly interests were quite as natural and deep-seated as his imaginative tendencies and creative instincts. He was an enormous reader and he was keenly interested in facts and affairs. Indeed by 1803 he even spoke disparagingly of his earliest efforts in writing which had been largely fictional:

> I am far from wishing, however, that my readers should judge of my exertions by my former ones. I have written much, but take much blame to myself for something [*sic*] which I have written, and take no praise for any thing. I should enjoy a larger share of my own respect, at the present moment, if nothing had ever flowed from my pen, the production of which could be traced to me.[67]

By this time he was immersed in periodical and pamphlet writing. His social and political ideas, however, had by now changed substantially from what they were in his youth.

SOCIAL VIEWS

To regard Brown merely as a Gothic writer, an escapist from real life, is manifestly absurd. Yet his political and social and religious views were so fluid that it is difficult to reduce them to a unity. In general, however, he moved from a radical or at least liberal position to a comparatively conservative one. During his youth, his enthusiasm for social amelioration led him to grasp at many hopeful hypotheses which time could not verify. In his fiction he handled radical doctrine which he did not necessarily endorse. Originality was not his strong point. As a young man he eagerly circulated the bright coins of other political writers, but he minted few of his own. Nor was he practical enough to translate opinion into program or even system. He remained for a time a bubbling optimist, a visionary who dreamed of making over society, of founding an ideal commonwealth. He penetrated the causes of our social ailments, but his remedies were too simple. In short he was, even more than Godwin, a theorizer or a closet philosopher. Only he was less cynical than Godwin, and he wrote more in hope and love than in hatred.

The revolutionary tastes of young Brown were stimulated principally by the influx of ideas from England and France. His specific indebtedness to the English radicals cannot always be discerned, but it is clear that he fingered many of the concepts implicit in their teaching. Mary Wollstonecraft and William Godwin he definitely studied. In addition there was the influence of the French philosophers and encyclopedists

—Voltaire, Diderot, Rousseau, d'Alembert—who, as a group at least, so attracted the youthful Brown that, the better to read them, he set about learning French. Moreover, he may have acquired some of his philosophy orally, for French political refugees were plentiful in both New York and Philadelphia. And he was doubtless the more aware of French thought because of his early association with Franklin, whose home Brown as a lad frequented.[68] From these sources, supplemented by occasional rills of radical thought from Germany,[69] Brown seems to have drawn inspiration for his own philosophizing, which, like the continental, was "distinguished by the ideas of progress, human perfectibility, humanitarianism, conscious benevolence, and by a strong belief in reason." [70] In addition he may have picked up ideas from the revolutionary novelists, Robert Bage, Thomas Holcroft, and others.[71] Brown's liberal political thought had plenty of precedent in America, but the advanced social ideas intermingled with them (especially with respect to sex) were not so frequently circulated here as abroad. In adopting these Brown was turning his back on one of America's principal bulwarks of moral suasion, the doctrine of original depravity, which, with its various corollaries, was a powerful deterrent to sinful living but no great spur to seeking the more abundant life on this earth. Brown thought men better than the systems devised to control them.[72] Thus he was convinced that humanity need not rest in the cheerless tenets of Calvinism, the effects of which he showed in *Wieland*. People could be improved by improved environment, errors could be rooted out by reason, and misery could be relieved by general benevolence.[73] Especially was this true of a democratic society where wealth and rank do not "pervert the understanding." [74] The frequency with which he invests his fictional characters with these and kindred ideas[75] shows how congenial the philosophy of enlightenment was to Brown's mind.

Brown was obviously infected with revolutionary thought. Yet he did not betray all of its most violent symptoms. In politics his reaction was less marked than that, say, of Tom Paine. There is no direct evidence that Brown was particularly interested in the purely political aspects of revolutionary doctrine. He favors a democratic state but he does not often fulminate against monarchy. A proletarian revolution he does not seem to have desired. In a vague way he deplores all government as inimical to liberty and the highest perfection of the individual, but he has no single point of attack. Nor does he appear ever to have contemplated atheism as favorably as did many French political radicals; at his most unorthodox stage he probably allowed his preference for "reason" to triumph over earlier ideas of special revelation:

he was perhaps a deist. No more definite statement than this can be made on the basis of the opinions uttered by his fictional characters.[76]

Brown was most radical on the social side. Along with his preference for the rule of reason went a natural distrust of institutions maintained by tradition and habit. His first published book, *Alcuin*, is a radical study of the rights of women and an appraisal of the institution of marriage. True, the author in a degree screens himself behind the device of dialogue, but it is clear from the protests of his friends that in this case at least he personally stood behind some of the doctrine he allowed his characters to express.[77] Precedent there was for such a tract—in Condorcet's *Sur l'Admission des Femmes au Droit de Cité* (1790), parts of Godwin's *Political Justice* (1793),[78] and Mary Wollstonecraft's *A Vindication of the Rights of Women* (1792)—but Brown wrote in *Alcuin* with enough force to make source-hunting only a subordinate interest here. The dialogue is conducted by Alcuin, a somewhat stuffy but not wholly illiberal schoolmaster, and Mrs. Carter, one of the most vigorous champions "the sex" had in the literature of the eighteenth century. In the first part Mrs. Carter offers the now-familiar arguments for the emancipation of women. The education vouchsafed women, she says, is so trivial and unbalanced that they must become the virtual slaves of men. They lack industrial and professional opportunity and, politics being too crude an arena for the delicate female, they have no means of remedying their disabilities. Marriage only confirms their bondage and calls for deference to their oppressors. In her anger she even castigates the Constitution as an iniquitous instrument. In the second part, however, Alcuin reports an experience which is too rich for the blood even of Mrs. Carter. He has just come back from a "paradise" of women in France, where there is absolute equality, political and economic, for women. When Mrs. Carter learns that equality has been achieved partly by the complete abolition of marriage, she draws the line firmly. She is "prejudiced" in favor of marriage, and the only palliative she will tolerate in this respect is unrestricted divorce to be initiated either by the man or by the woman.

Brown seems at his most modern in *Alcuin* when he discusses the relationship between what is legal and what is moral. Mrs. Carter upholds divorce not only as a means whereby a woman may escape from tyranny but also as an expedient to put an end to a legal union between people who have become hateful or indifferent to each other. Such a union seems to her loathsome, almost immoral: "That a man continues to associate with me contrary to his judgment and inclination is no subject of congratulation . . . If the heart of my husband be estranged from me, I may possibly regard it as an evil."[79] That Brown himself was strongly inclined toward this view is suggested by his subsequent use of similar sentiments in *Ormond*.[80]

In all this as in other arguments it can be seen that Brown is testing society by the application of reason. If he was inclined to be romantic politically, he was too rational for his own good as a novelist in the treatment of love. The original expression of that reasoning habit, that penchant for analysis, which characterizes many of Brown's fictional lovers, is found in *Alcuin* in the speech of Mrs. Carter. Love, she says, is often

> "an empty and capricious passion . . . In the majority of cases it is nothing but a miserable project of affectation. The languishing and sighing lover is an object to which the errors of mankind have annexed a certain degree of reverence. Misery is our title to compassion, and to men of limited capacities the most delicious potion that can be administered is pity. For the sake of this, hundreds are annually metamorphosed into lovers. It is graceful to languish with an hopeless passion; to court the music of sighs and the secrecy of groves. But it is to be hoped that these chimeras will, at length, take their leave of us." [81]

Granted the common sense of much of what Mrs. Carter says, her opinions constituted no good school for novelists—deflating love by ruthless analysis. If Brown was dismayed at the relatively poor pecuniary returns he received from his novels, he might well have considered whether he ought not to have given his readers more sugared sentiment and less cold analysis. His theories confounded his fiction.

By temperament, then, Brown was somewhat radical. But the heady doctrine which intoxicated the youth seemed less and less acceptable to the more mature man. The most radical words from his pen had all been published by 1801. At some time thereafter his liberalism began to recede. With the passage of years conservative thoughts naturally found readier acceptance. Increasing ill health robbed him of the feverish energy he had displayed in the first flush of Godwinism. His buoyancy waned, and his opinions contracted. Moreover, it was hard to nurse Utopian ideals in a breast embittered by private misfortune— for he had failed to prosper financially in either books or business. In any case the political horizon was hard on radical eyes: the dazzling career of Napoleon only reminded men of the futility of revolution as an escape from tyranny.[82] Even Jeffersonian democracy, which would have won the heart of a younger Brown, now seemed a thing to scrutinize pretty carefully. With his increasing attention to periodical work Brown began to exhibit symptoms of the occupational disease of editors, namely, timidity or over-caution. When in 1804 a zealous Kentuckian Jeffersonian, relying no doubt on Brown's earlier reputation for liberalism, wrote to enlist Brown's aid as editor, the latter temporized:

> I have received a letter [he wrote to his father-in-law] full of respect and compliment, from Kentucky. The writer is a man who has acquired no small credit with the leaders of his party, by two publications, an invective against Adams, and a eulogy of Jefferson. He desires their republication in the Magazine, but I mean to write him a private letter excusing myself as I can on the score of our political neutrality.[83]

In short, by this time the volatile opinions of Brown's youth had vanished, leaving him to all intents and purposes a Federalist. Along with his recession from extreme political positions went an abdication of any religious unorthodoxy he may have temporarily entertained. Probably never very radical in this respect, he made his position unmistakably clear in the prospectus to the *Literary Magazine* in October, 1803:

> In an age like this, when the foundations of religion and morality have been so boldly attacked, it seems necessary in announcing a work of this nature, to be particularly explicit as to the path which the editor means to pursue. He, therefore, avows himself to be, without equivocation or reserve, the ardent friend and the willing champion of the Christian religion.[84]

Brown, like Godwin, was the very tinder of inflammable doctrine in youth, but, like Godwin, he found his opinions dampened by experience and he became finally a pretty safe conservative citizen of the republic. He even evinced a definite patriotic sentiment, and the three political pamphlets which he published in the last years of his life were distinctly nationalistic in tone.[85] When the Louisiana territory was ceded to the French, he was one of the first to regard the probable effects as unfortunate, and he looked forward with approval to all necessary steps, even if they led to war, "for the expulsion of foreigners from this land; for securing to our own posterity the possession of this continent." [86] A far cry, this partisan pamphlet, from the sort of opinion Brown had voiced a few years before when, beaming with benevolence, he had looked forward to a time when the rule of reason would bring about the brotherhood of man.

LITERARY THEORY

Brown's book reviews, as has been noted,[87] were devoted largely to foreign authors, many of whom were obscure even in their day. In ten reviews of poetry in the *Monthly Magazine*, the only writer of even secondary rank he discussed was Southey. Burns and Wordsworth are barely mentioned in his critical writing. In contemporary British fiction he discusses larger figures—Edgeworth and Radcliffe—but his reviews in general are comparatively unimportant except by virtue of their priority in the history of American criticism.[88] More interesting are his miscellaneous remarks on the theory of fiction. American fiction being still in its infancy, Brown's critical observations consist largely of generalizations regarding the form and function of fiction. These are occasionally illustrated by reference to the development of his own art as a writer.

Brown did not share the general feeling of many respectable people in his time that novels were necessarily bad for one's mind and morals. Granting that cheap novels existed, he did not fear them excessively, and he welcomed the better ones as productive of fruitful reflection in the reader. It is obvious that his critical position was dictated partly by the nature of his own fictions:

> They who prate about the influence of novels to unfit us for solid and useful reading are guilty of a double error: for in the first place, a just and powerful picture of human life in which the connection between vice and misery, and between felicity and virtue, is vividly portrayed, is the most solid and useful reading that a mortal and social being (exclusive of particular cases and professional engagements) can read; and in the second place, the most trivial and trite of these performances are, to readers of certain ages and intellects, the only books which they will read. If they were not thus employed, they would be employed in a way far more trivial or pernicious . . . My fancy has received more delight, my heart more humanity, and my understanding more instruction from a few novels I could name, than from any other works.[89]

From the very beginning of his writing career Brown had definitely in mind the major objectives of his art as a novelist. In the prospectus to his unpublished story *Sky-Walk* he made these clear. Fiction should be national, plausible, moral, and exciting:

> He who shall examine objects with his own eyes, who shall employ the European models merely for the improvement of his

taste, and adapt his fiction to all that is genuine and peculiar in the scene before him, will be entitled at least to the praise of originality . . . He, therefore, who paints, not from books, but from nature, who introduces those lines and hues in which we differ, rather than those in which we resemble our kindred nations beyond the ocean, may lay some claim to the patronage of his countrymen. The value of such works lies without doubt in their moral tendency. The popular tales have their merit, but there is one thing in which they are deficient. They are generally adapted to one class of readers only . . . The world is governed, not by the simpleton, but by the men of soaring passions and intellectual energy. By the display of such only can we hope to enchain the attention and ravish the souls of those who study and reflect . . . To gain their homage it is not needful to forego the approbation of those whose circumstances hindered them from making the same progress. A contexture of facts capable of suspending the faculties of every soul in curiosity may be joined with depths of views into human nature and all the subtleties of reasoning . . .[90]

Obviously fiction, to have the values here suggested, must centre around important matters. Significance of theme and seriousness of purpose are of the highest importance:

The selection of a theme truly important, adorning it with the lustre of eloquence, supplying, with judicious hand, the deficiencies of history, in the statements of motives and the enumeration of circumstances; fashioning falsehood by the most rigid standard of probability, and suggesting to the reader beneficial truths, is the sublimest province that can be assigned to man.[91]

To the natural question of whether prose or verse could best achieve the high ends Brown cherished for fiction, he answered in favor of the former:

All that constitutes the genuine and lasting excellence of narratives; all the subtilties of ratiocination, the energies and ornaments of rhetoric, and the colours of description, are compatible with prose. Numbers are equivocal, or, at least, not an essential attribute of a moral and useful tale.[92]

These were general aims. To be effective, fiction should be not only in a good sense didactic but also persuasive and entertaining per se. This Brown believed could best be brought about by the skilful union of the natural and the exciting:

Give the human agents you employ qualities to command good will and esteem; let their manners be natural, and their sentiments the genuine effusions of the human heart, in such circumstances as those they are placed in; and then, perhaps, the more singular their adventures, the wilder the scenes in which they are exposed, the more capricious the beings to whose power they are subjected, and the more seemingly inadequate the means by which all the changes in their fate are accomplished; so much the more irresistibly will they engage, and transport, and chain down the attention, and sway the passions of the spectator or reader.[93]

Except to a slight extent in *Jane Talbot* and *Clara Howard*, Brown did not of course attempt to make his characters realistic by the use of the small detail and incident of everyday life. The period was too early for that. What he had in mind undoubtedly was what would now be regarded as realistic characterization. That he deplored the artificial portraiture of women that marked most fiction is clear from a somewhat caustic passage in his incompleted fiction, *Stephen Calvert*:

We are taught to expect that a woman will assiduously counterfeit indifference till the man has avowed his affection; that the secret of her heart, instead of spontaneously flowing to her lips, can only be extorted; that tremours, flutterings, and misgivings; a proneness to recede and delay, are to accompany every act of condescension, and every acquiescence in necessity; that these are feminine attributes, and are not only dictated by reason and duty, but are interwoven with the female constitution.[94]

Similarly he responded to a criticism of his having finally shorn Arthur Mervyn of wealth by saying that such a procedure was necessary in the interests of "consistency and congruity." [95] Perhaps he could have won more popularity by a freer use of bonuses and blessings to his characters, but in this respect at least he was true to his theory that "nature" should be the novelist's guide.

That in general Brown's theory of natural writing fitted his practice is too fantastic to be argued. Yet as a writer of novels in a genre already being denounced and burlesqued as ludicrously artificial, namely, the Gothic romance,[96] Brown attempted to defend such "Gothic" practices as he did employ. He showed, in his preface to *Edgar Huntly*, that his methods were new and that his materials were native.[97] When it is added that Brown believed also in giving rational explanations to apparently supernatural phenomena, the most has been made of his theories of natural and national fiction. Obviously his practice conforms to his theories with the looseness customary in the cases of most American authors except Henry James. Yet by virtue of his substantial inquiries into the rationale of fiction Brown must be regarded as a significant American critic.

REPUTATION

In the absence of many contemporary critical reviews of Brown's novels, their immediate reception can only be inferred from incidental remarks of the author[98] and from the fact that only one of his novels (*Edgar Huntly*) was reprinted in this country as a separate volume during his lifetime. It is probable that each of his first four novels, *Wieland, Arthur Mervyn, Ormond,* and *Edgar Huntly* won a succès d'estime but brought little financial emolument. English reprints soon appeared, however, and there were translations in France and Germany.[99] In England his first reception was not flattering. Several periodicals reviewed the early novels, but these early notices were "almost all unfavorable"; the stories were regarded as "improbable and horrid" and one reviewer referred to the author as a "pragmatic enthusiast! a mad-headed metaphysician." [100] The statement that "English readers and reviewers showed more interest in Brown, for a century and a half after his death, than Americans have ever proclaimed," [101] begins to find justification only a little later when Brown was gradually discovered by various of the English literati. Shelley had read much of Brown by 1815,[102] and Mary Shelley almost certainly knew *Wieland* well.[103] William Godwin, who was both a creditor and a debtor of Brown, acknowledged the inspiration of *Wieland* in the preface to his *Mandeville* (1817), and referred to Brown as "a person certainly of distinguished genius." [104] In 1819 Keats, egged on by Hazlitt to read Brown,[105] enthusiastically recommended *Wieland* as a "very powerful" book "something like Godwin . . . Between Schiller and Godwin," but "More clever in plot and incident than Godwin." [106] The publication of a collection of Brown's stories in London in 1822 elicited much more favorable periodical criticism, with some iterated grumbling over his faults, than Brown had formerly received; apparently Irving's success had opened the door to more impartial appraisals of American productions.[107] Thomas Hood was familiar with Brown's works by 1823 and made merry over Edgar Huntly's sleepwalking in a trifling rhyme in his poem "The Fall." [108] In 1824 (after Cooper had written *The Spy* and *The Pioneers*), Lockhart's remark to Scott that "Brockden Brown was the most remarkable writer of fiction that America had produced," drew forth Scott's judgment that although Brown possessed "wonderful powers" he had so wasted and misused them in an outworn and un-"wholesome" species of writing (*i.e.*, the Gothic) that his fame would be "ephemeral." [109]

By 1824, then, Brown's reputation had taken on so much weight as to be considered very satisfactory. It remained for an American, however, to claim credit for this growth. Writing in October, 1824, John Neal asserted in *Blackwood's Magazine* that it was he who first recognized Brown's ability. In recounting this service to his fellow-writer he complained that subsequent criticism had gone too far in the direction of encomia:

> Some years ago, WE took up CHARLES BROCKDEN BROWN; disinterred him; embalmed him; did him up, decently; and put him back again—(that is—one of us did so.)—Since then, poor Brown has had no peace, for his countrymen. We opened upon the North American creature—making him break cover; and riding after him, as if he were worth our while. *Then*—but never till then—(we were the first)—did they give tongue, on the other side of the Atlantic.—We puffed him a little. They have blown him up—'sky-high.' We went up to him, reverently—they, head-over-heels. We flattered him somewhat—for he deserved it; and was atrociously neglected. But they have laid it on with a trowel. —He would never have been heard of, but for us.—They are determined, now, that we shall never hear of any thing else.—We licked him into shape; they have slobbered him . . .[110]

Following this, Neal reviews his own opinions of Brown's novels— entirely from his memory, which was none too accurate—and finally decides that although Brown at times bungled his plots atrociously, yet he was "undeniably the most original writer, that American has produced."[111]

Neal claims to have discovered Brown before the appearance of E. T. Channing's well-known article in *The North American Review* for June, 1819. Shortly after this a proposal for a collected edition of Brown's novels came out, but made little headway: "They talked about his books; but nobody thought of subscribing."[112] The first American collected edition came out in Philadelphia and Boston in 1827.[113] Jared Sparks' *American Biography* included a rather long study of Brown by William H. Prescott in 1834. Thereafter Brown took hold among good critics everywhere. His radical opinions continued to raise eyebrows here and there.[114] Yet political and moral considerations finally died away,[115] and Brown was read and remembered for his fiction itself.

In 1845 Poe, who had been fascinated by Brown ever since his boyhood,[116] complimented W. G. Simms by asserting that "Grayling, or 'Murder Will Out'" was "forcibly conceived, and detailed throughout with a degree of artistic skill which has had no parallel among American story-tellers since the epoch of Brockden Brown." [117] In the following year, so far had Brown's fame gained in breadth, Hawthorne observed that "no American writer enjoys a more classic reputation on this side of the water." [118] That Hawthorne's statement was not merely the expression of a privately nursed fondness for Brown is evident from the fact that in the next year Griswold's popular anthology, *Prose Writers of America* (1847), used extracts from four of his novels.[119]

Thus by the middle of the century, despite Whittier's statement (in 1848) that "his merits have not yet been sufficiently acknowledged," [120] Brown's novels had reached a very respectable height of fame—far higher, certainly, than their author could have hoped for them during the impecunious years that preceded his death in 1810. After the middle of the century, more and more writers were competing for public attention. Despite the 1857 (Philadelphia) edition, there is reason to suspect that he fell off in popular esteem. Critically also he received less attention for a time, but during the twentieth century his stock has again risen, partly as a result of a number of scholarly studies that have appeared, beginning in 1904.[121]

"I have sometimes been mortified," Brown once wrote, "in looking over the catalogue of heroes, sages and saints, to find not a single Brown among them. This indeed may be said of many other names, but most others are of rare occurrence, while the most common appellation in almost all languages is *Brown*. It must then be a strange fatality which has hitherto excluded it from the illustrious and venerable list." [122] In these whimsical but humble remarks to an acquaintance who had named a child after him, Brown called attention to his comparatively obscure position three years before his death. The subsequent expansion of his reputation he could hardly have foreseen. Hero, sage, or saint he has never become, but he is now recognized as a better novelist than he was known for in his lifetime.

His faults were as conspicuous as his virtues. As a thinker he was eager and courageous but too excitable to work out problems thoroughly. In his youth he was warmly receptive to liberal ideas, but, as *Alcuin* shows, he was unable to marshal them into an orderly progression. His actual performance always fell short of his aspirations. He harbored grand conceptions: he would master a classification of all knowledge—become (like Franklin) a sort of universal scholar; he would write great epic poems; he would point the way to an ideal planned society; he would become a successful novelist; he would establish important magazines. In each of these fields he had only a partial success. The rudimentary state of the national culture and the pressure under which Brown wrote account for a good deal of his trouble, but he was also a victim of his own peculiar mental makeup. He could not transform his enthusiasm into effective work. If he had courage, he lacked concentration and continuity. He had great energy but could not secure and sustain the right leverage for his efforts. He was so dazzled by Utopian visions that he had no eye for detail or design. His broad conceptions of social progress—through democracy, "reason," and general benevolence—were lacking in decisiveness. He could illuminate a subject but not penetrate it. In a sense he was too simple in his ideas, and there is a note of naiveté in his writings that makes one wonder if, despite all his "psychologizing," he understood the complexity of human nature. He was a youthful romantic in thought.

As a writer he betrayed the same lack of conclusiveness and clearness. What he himself said of an early unfinished work may be applied to a considerable portion of his production, namely, that it was "written in an hasty and inaccurate way." [123] He had great stores of power but his transmission was faulty. For various reasons, the reader of the novels experiences constantly a feeling of partial frustration. In the first place, the stories are deficient in concrete detail, in imagery. To a considerable extent Brown the novelist answers to his own description of Arthur Mervyn, who is made to say:

> My existence is a series of thoughts rather than of motions. Ratiocination and deduction leave my senses unemployed . . . Sensations do not precede and suggest, but follow and are secondary to, the acts of my mind.[124]

Other defects contribute to the blurred effect of Brown's narrative: chaotic chronology, ill-proportioned in-set stories, unallocated incidents. Brown explained the "supernatural" in his Gothic stories, but he left many mundane matters in doubt. The reader is not reassured by his air of starting a new story every few chapters and forgetting what he has written, of going on detours so protracted that the main road is forgotten. He breaks camp so often that the reader cannot become oriented. The autobiographical privileges accorded many of his characters become a source of irritation to the reader. At times Brown seems to have shared the sentiment ascribed to Stephen Calvert: "There is but one mode of appeasing your wonder . . . and that is, the relation of the events of my life." [125] Certain it is that he should have hearkened closely while he caused Edgar Huntly to utter the understatement: "I am not sure that I shall relate in an intelligible manner." [126] Other limitations Brown shared with many writers of the period—the repetition of stock devices (mistaken identity, fraudulent property claims, overheard conversations, etc.) and excess of coincidence, comparatively poor characterization and dialogue—but his most radical fault was want of clearness and decisiveness. His thoughts, like those of Edgar Huntly, were too often "wildering and mazy."

To offset such a list of debits as this with a like number of credits is manifestly impossible. Brown prevailed not by the number of his merits but by the strength of a few. He succeeded by intensity, eloquence, and imagination. His high seriousness is felt beneath even his most improbable stories. He has the rare faculty, as John Neal observed, of giving the impression that he was "altogether in earnest, and believe[d] every word of his own story." [128] Even the most thrilling midnight horrors of his stories, one feels, were no mere fabrications of a littérateur but were in part, at least, the natural expression of a mind that was morbidly, almost abnormally, sensitive. The spectres of his books were no more real than those of his mind. His persistent linking of fiction with scientific and psychological themes—dementia, claustrophobia, euthanasia,[129] epidemic disease—marks a novelist who knew higher motives than the merely pecuniary. The cloudy exposition of his social opinions does not detract from their genuineness, and it is clear that he strove to make his fiction more than ephemeral amusement. Despite his penchant for analysis, he was intensely emotional, and, as with Poe, it is difficult to say whether the rational or the emotional dominated. At all events he succeeded best as a writer by virtue of his emotional pitch and power. If he did not understand the subtlety of individual characters, he was painfully aware of the quality of strong human emotions—fear, sorrow, religious ecstasy. Feeling often surges through his pages with torrential force. *Wieland*, at times, has the quality of a great natural phenomenon. In language too, Brown rose to heights seldom reached in early American fiction. An electric quality runs through his prose which compels attention. Its circuit may be broken from time to time by Brown's careless mechanics, but its flow is renewed ere long, and in certain passages it causes his art to glow with a radiance which more than one critic has dared to call genius. In his later years Brown affected to dislike being thought of as a literary man, preferring to be regarded as a gentleman who used literature as an avocation. The time was not yet arrived in America, he felt, when much prestige could attach to the profession of writing, and he was more or less reconciled to our literary dependence on England. Literature was a "commodity" and like other commodities it would not be produced in profusion until the public demanded it and was willing to pay well for it.[130] Yet literary reputation is finally independent of commercial conditions; and Brown had done enough, before he took to selling pots and pans, to insure the permanence of his name on the rolls of minor novelists.

INTERIM: BETWEEN BROWN AND COOPER

Between Brown and Cooper no novelist of importance came into view. The number of novels produced, in any case, was small and the quality at best second-rate. It is true that by about 1810 the reading public had grown enormously, but unknown native authors continued to operate at a disadvantage.[131] In 1817 a reviewer of John Neal's *Keep Cool* wrote in the (Baltimore) *Portico* that this was "the only American Novel that has come under our notice for many years." [132] The remark testifies to the limited area of the reviewer's observation, but it is doubtful if the quality of the books he missed, some of which are now extremely rare or inaccessible, was such as to merit much analysis. In books of the period which had a commercial success, however, one may read certain signs of the times. Among these are two novels which appeared shortly after the turn of the century, Isaac Mitchell's *Alonzo and Melissa* and George Watterston's *Glencarn*.

BELATED GOTHIC: *Alonzo and Melissa*

Competition for public attention was so keen after, say, 1800, that no student of the times can afford to ignore *Alonzo and Melissa*, probably one of the most popular works of fiction written in nineteenth-century America. Fustian it may now seem, but it gave the public what it craved during something like sixty years, continuing to be read even through decades that burgeoned with new best-sellers. What was the secret of its success? One may answer accurately enough that it was a variation of the ancient formula: young love, minus money, plus romantic scenery, divided by parental displeasure and fate. Yet only a perusal of the book will reveal exactly what were the right proportions in a tale of this variety.

The authorship and first publication of *Alonzo and Melissa* have long been matters of debate. It seems finally certain that the original be-getter of the story was Isaac Mitchell, over whose signature it first appeared serially between June 5 and October 30, 1804, in *The Political Barometer* of Poughkeepsie. The book achieved its astonishing record of popularity, however, in a shortened form, generally entitled *Alonzo and Melissa, or the Unfeeling Father*, and ascribed to Daniel Jackson.[133]

The story itself concerns the romantic love affair of Alonzo, recently graduated from Yale College, and Melissa, daughter of a well-to-do

Connecticut farmer.[134] Under the influence of pastoral Connecticut scenery and voluptuous ball-room music, the couple become affianced lovers, a secondary candidate for Melissa's heart having been shuffled off; but it is not long before the loss of the fortune of Alonzo's father, a New London merchant, convinces Melissa's father that the match is not an ideal one. To protect Melissa from a wealthless marriage her father immures her in a Gothic castle, complete with moat, drawbridge, and drafty corridors—all this on Long Island Sound. Here the heroine experiences terrors long familiar to readers of Mrs. Radcliffe's romances, such as icy hands, bloody daggers, and ghostly apparitions, which were presumably none the less effective for being finally explained as the work of smugglers who hoped to scare Melissa away. The smugglers' methods may be judged from Melissa's experience on the second night of her imprisonment when she is awakened out of her sleep in time to see "a horrible form" by her bed:

> Its appearance was tall and robust, wrapped in a tattered white robe, spotted with blood. The hair of its head was matted with clotted gore. A deep wound appeared to have pierced its breast, from which fresh blood flowed down its garment. Its pale face was gashed and gory! its eyes fixed, glazed, and glaring;—its lips open, its teeth set, and in its hand was a bloody dagger.[135]

Under these circumstances—with her limbs suffering an "ague" and her face bathed in "chilling sweat"—our heroine may be pardoned if "a thought darted into her mind to leave the house immediately." In the meantime Alonzo, temporarily foiled in his quest for the missing girl, is plunged into the deepest despair by reading an account of the death of Melissa. To forget his grief he enlists in the patriot army (the Revolution is in progress), is thrown into a British prison, escapes by a homemade rope, crosses the channel to Paris. Here he has an interview with Benjamin Franklin—a procedure that becomes almost routine for lonely American heroes of fiction stranded in Paris. The apostle of common sense lectures the hero on the folly of moping, for, says Franklin, "the fancied value of an object ceases with the attainment." He recommends that Alonzo return home to the service of his country. After his return to America, Alonzo makes a pilgrimage to Charleston to shed a few tears on the grave of his lost one. He finds a grave marked Melissa, but he also finds Melissa, for the death he had heard reported was the death of a cousin Melissa: his sweetheart had given currency to the report to escape from her father's persecution. The lovers are now united and only await the conclusion of the War before they shall settle down to love in a cottage.

In a story so exciting as this, it is not surprising to find a prefatorial avowal of the author's hope that it is "not unfriendly to religion and to virtue" and his assurance that it "contains no indecorous stimulants." Yet although no crude offenses against decency blemish its pages, the story is clearly of the type calculated to alarm those persons who thought that novels "put notions into girls' heads." Nor can it be relieved from this charge by the author's boast that the book contained no "unmeaning and inexplicated incidents, sounding upon the sense but imperceptible to the understanding." [136] To make a claim of realism for this story is, in fact, to make the book the more harmful to young minds. For even if doubtful events are "elucidated by the consequence," the story is basically fantastic. Judged by criteria of a later day, the technique of the author seems naive and artificial. The outdoor scenes, derived apparently by the crossing of neo-classical poetic diction and Radcliffean pastoral strains, suggest that the author was bent on proving that he wrote nature descriptions without looking at nature:

> A soft and silent shower had descended; a thousand transitory gems trembled upon the foliage glittering the western ray.—A bright rainbow sat upon a southern cloud; the light gales whispered among the branches, agitated the young harvest to billowy motion, or waved the tops of the distant deep green forest with majestic grandeur. Flocks, herds, and cottages were scattered over the variegated landscape.
>
> Hills piled on hills, receding, faded from the pursuing eye, mingling with the blue mist which hovered around the extreme verge of the horizon.[137]

Moreover, although the author made a creditable attempt to draw his birds and flowers from their own habitats instead of importing skylarks and nightingales from abroad, his use of whippoorwills is not only so repetitious that "they are treated practically like hired musicians," [138] but it is ornithologically inaccurate. Similarly the dialogue, although it is reported in short speeches instead of the incredibly large blocks favored by most of the author's contemporaries, seems laughably stilted:

> "This is a most delightful scene," said Melissa.
> "It is indeed," replied Alonzo; "can New-London boast so charming a prospect?"
> Melissa. No—yes; indeed I can hardly say. You know, Alonzo, how I am charmed with the rock at the point of the beach.

Alonzo. You told me of the happy hours you had passed at that place. Perhaps the company which attended you there, gave the scenery its highest embellishment.

Melissa. I know not how it happened; but you are the only person who ever attended me there.

Alonzo. That is a little surprising.

Mel. Why surprising?

Al. Where was Beauman?

Mel. Perhaps he was not fond of solitude. Besides he was not always my Beauman.

Al. Sometimes.

Mel. Yes, sometimes.

Al. And now always.

Mel. Not this evening.

Al. He formerly [*sic*] addresses you.

Mel. Well.

Al. And will soon claim the exclusive privilege so to do.

Mel. That does not follow of course.

Al. Of course, if his intentions are sincere, and the wishes of another should accord therewith.

Mel. Who am I to understand by another?

Al. Melissa. [A pause ensued.]

Mel. See that ship, Alonzo, coming up the sound; how she ploughs through the white foam, while the breezes flutter among the sails, varying with the beams of the sun.

Al. Yes, it is almost down.

Mel. What is almost down?

Al. The sun. Was you not speaking of the sun, madam?

Mel. Your mind is absent, Alonzo; I was speaking of yonder ship.

Al. I beg pardon, madam. O yes—the ship—it—it bounds with rapid motion over the waves.[139]

As for the moral effect of the book, the author does avoid scenes likely to corrupt the young. His references to the emotion of love are decorously phrased. Yet it is hard to believe that any young girl could be *improved* by reading such claptrap as the author writes when Alonzo and Melissa are discovered in a (proper) embrace:

> Sneer not, ye callous hearted insensibles, ye fastidious prudes, if we inform you that their tears fell in one intermingling shower, that their sighs wafted in one blended breeze.[140]

With all its faults, *Alonzo and Melissa* was accepted by countless readers as an ideal story. Its papier-maché scenery, its stumbling dialogue, its bogus Gothic effects, its elementary stratagem seem feeble enough to a later generation, but to our rude forefathers they sufficed as the principal ingredients of a breathless and touching story. Moreover, despite his period elegance the author wrote with ease and pace, and withal as if the fate of his characters mattered deeply to himself: a kind of sincerity pervades the book. Young love and hair-raising adventure were seldom more successfully merged in the early American novel. At least twenty editions of the book appeared by 1850,[141] and an unknown (but lesser) number thereafter. The book became a part of American tradition. Doubtless, as Edmund Pearson suggests,[142] it was regarded as so worldly that young ladies sometimes had to smuggle it to their bedrooms to read it, but it was also found sometimes as part of the family library.[143] In any case its history is proof that Isaac Mitchell had found a popular formula which, though apparently simple enough, has eluded many an ambitious novelist. There is no record of its foreign experience, but when Sydney Smith a few years later sneeringly asked, who reads an American book?, the rejoinder might well have been that *Alonzo and Melissa* would certainly have found plenty of British readers if British publishers had seen fit to pirate it.

EDUCATION OF A GOTHIC HERO: *George Watterston's Glencarn.*

Charles Brockden Brown founded no school, for the Gothic market that flourished in the 1790's was pretty much played out by the turn of the century. Yet part of the public is always lagging, and considerable currency was apparently vouchsafed to the fictional production of one George Watterston, who was in some respects a follower of Brown. Watterston appears to have had very little originality, for there are also Godwinian strains in his work. Moreover, his first story, *The Lawyer, or Man as he ought not to be* (1808), a tale of chicanery and cruelty, was obviously a literary reaction to Robert Bage's novels, *Hermsprong or Man as He Is* and *Man as He Is Not*. Watterston's more ambitious work of fiction, *Glencarn; or, The Disappointments of Youth* (1810), is hardly more original. It uses new but dimly outlined parts of America as a background for extremely desiccated romantic plot materials. One can only guess that the book prevailed by the sheer bulk (three volumes full) of its bizarre adventure and by the tone of heavy romantic melancholy that reverberates through the whole tale. Yet really to understand a literature—or a nation—one must know something of its weakness as well as its strength. *Glencarn* may serve as an example of the American novel at a very low ebb.

Ostensibly the story of *Glencarn* stems from the rather vague thesis that "happiness is the result of a certain physical organization of the

nerves, modified by habits of virtue." [144] But the tale which is unfolded proves no such thing: indeed the happiness which finally comes
to the hero is derived from the far less subtle elements of a bride and a
bank account. A better key to the appalling cycle of grief assigned to
the protagonist is the author's further remark that he has sent his hero
out "in pursuit of what the stoics termed the *summum bonum* of existence" but that the hero was "like the Rasselas of Dr. Johnson, frequently without success" on account of "the malevolence of envy and
the stratagem of malice." The calendar of Glencarn's woes is so great
that only a myth-man could have sustained them. "Malevolence" first
strikes at him through Mrs. Richardson, second wife of the man who
took him in when as a foundling Glencarn was laid at his doorstep.
Not very subtle but certainly false and treacherous, Mrs. Richardson
lives in a perpetual winter of discontent, for she hates Glencarn as the
rival of her own son Rodolpho and she hates her husband for fostering
the lad. Throughout the book she persecutes Glencarn, and at the end
she nearly succeeds in securing his conviction for the murder of her
son, whom Glencarn has unwittingly killed in self-defense when Rodolpho, at his mother's instigation, attempted to assault him feloniously.
Ultimately Mrs. Richardson is proved guilty of conspiracy—as well as
of poisoning her husband. In the meantime Glencarn has fallen in love
with Amelia, daughter of Mr. Richardson's first wife. But slanderous
remarks by a friend break off temporarily the ideal engagement. A
duel follows, and Glencarn has to hide out to avoid the law. He lives
much in exile amid the most wildly romantic scenery in the Appa-
lachian mountains and points west. Between crises he studies medicine,
writes essays, and discusses literature; but generally he is involved in
a scrape of some sort—being attacked by enemies (fomented by Mrs.
Richardson), being captured by bandits, trying to shake himself free
from a young lady who has foolishly fallen in love with him. When
he has nothing else to occupy him, he can always manage to get lost
in the woods. In his last crisis, the murder charge, he is aided by a
mysterious stranger who has been popping in and out of the story on
benevolent errands for some time: it is none other than his father!
Mother is finally unearthed too, and Amelia, of course, is reclaimed.
And so, outfitted at last with parents, sweetheart, and a goodly financial
prospect, Glencarn, now graduated from the school of adversity, commences a life so free from "disappointments" that the author has nothing further to say. He has said plenty, as it happens, for this story has
wheels within wheels and the reader is distinctly relieved when its
machinery runs down.

Glencarn recalls the stories of Brown not only by direct reference to their author but also by narrative modes and materials that suggest imitation. The hero's solitary wandering "in the darkest recesses of the woods" and "the deepest caverns of the Alleghany" [145] had its prototype in the peregrinations of Edgar Huntly in western Pennsylvania. Glencarn spends hours in seclusion and meditation in a vaguely located bower built by his own hands in a region of "wild simplicity and beautiful disorder" which recalls the scenery of *Wieland*. *Wieland* is also apparently in Watterston's mind when he has his hero use ventriloquism in order to escape from a bandit's cave and, later, to baffle a posse pursuing him as an alleged murderer.[146] Other Brownlike details may have been used coincidentally, such as a brief reference to a yellow fever epidemic—a theme which Brown exploited in *Arthur Mervyn*. Like Brown, too, Watterston has his say on "philosophical" topics—including education and politics.[147] How much Brown was in Watterston's mind may be judged also from a long literary conversation engaged in by several men. One of the speakers affirms that Brown's *Wieland* is "highly unnatural and extravagant" in action as well as "low, mean and unmusical" in style. This opinion, however, is opposed by Glencarn, who evidently speaks with the approval of Watterston:

> I think, sir, it displays great vigour of fancy, and originality of genius, like all romances it is extravagant, but it is an extravagance which is consistent with the laws of versimilitude [*sic*]. In a production of that sort, the reader is always prepared for something unnatural, and therefore receives it, without disgust, as to Mr. Brown's stile it is chaste, and vigorous, its only defect is I think the want of ornament, and is consequently deficient in what Blair terms elegance, yet on the whole, as to correctness of composition, Mr. Brown is without doubt much the best writer this country has produced.[148]

Watterston further echoes his master when he attributes the lack of good American fiction to the public taste for "descriptions of balls and masquerades, or inflated delinieations [*sic*] of Alpine scenery, rustic innocence and stupidity." [149] Yet that fresh reality which he believes American fiction could have through reliance on native character and native scenery, he finally forfeits by his too bookish manner of developing his fiction. How unreal his characters are may be inferred from his description of one person, Amelia, who is on the same page referred to as a girl "as simple and unaffected, as the meanest child of rural innocence" and as a young lady of "heated imagination" who dreams all day of love.[150] It is this falsity of characterization more than any technical narrative blunders or stylistic blemishes which must mark such a book as *Glencarn* as essentially an inferior work. The hero is likewise incredible in toto, being mainly an ill-wrought synthesis of moods of the author. Yet Glencarn is endowed with physical powers which are exhibited in one of the finest examples of unintentionally humorous writing in the early American novel. His assignment is to rescue Amelia from a bear:

> I beheld the bear grasp her in his paws, it almost deprived me of the power of action; I had no time, however, to hesitate, and rushing with the rapidity of lighting [*sic*] to her assistance, caught the animal by the neck, and plunged a knife which I had brought with me for the purpose of digging up roots, into his breast, instantly he drooped [*sic*] his victim, and seized me round the body—I repeated the blow, still he grasped me more firmly—we stood near a precipice of considerable depth, the water of the Susquehanna rolled below, I attempted to cast him over it. Amelia seized me by the back, and endeavored to rescue me from his grasp, but to no purpose. I struck him again in the throat, he became more enraged, and making a leap, carried me with him headlong into the river. I was not so much stunned by the fall, as not to know where I was and what I did—we struggled in the water for several minutes, I found my strength decreasing, and determined to make one desperate effort to conquer my opponent. With great difficulty, I liberated my other arm from his grasp, and thrusting it down his throat as far as I could reach, kept his head under water until he expired, then swam towards shore, which I had no sooner reached then [*sic*] I sunk into a swoon.[151]

It may seem incredible that such balderdash as this should have been reckoned worthy of print, but the fact has its significance for the student of early American fiction. For the slow evolution of the novel between 1800 and 1820 cannot be fully understood without some consideration of what books, however defective, were paid for by the public. Watterston seems to have written two other works of fiction, *The L—— Family at Washington, or A Winter in the Metropolis* (1822) and *Wanderer in Washington* (1827).[152] No wonder that American booksellers posted their agents at the slips of trans-Atlantic packet-boats which might bring piratable copies of the latest works of Miss Edgeworth and Walter Scott. No wonder that American readers rubbed their eyes in astonishment when they read the first successful novel of the American Scott, the author of *The Spy*.

THE HISTORICAL ROMANCE FLICKERS FITFULLY: Samuel Woodworth's The Champions of Freedom.

Samuel Woodworth (1784-1842), who is still a tiny point of reference in the history of American poetry as the author of "The Old Oaken Bucket," was the author also of a now pretty-much-forgotten historical romance written four years before Cooper's *The Spy.* It is unlikely that Woodworth's romance, *The Champions of Freedom, or the Mysterious Chief* (1816), provided the fecund Cooper with idea or inspiration. Yet it contains many of the same elements as Cooper's productions and is by that token of some significance to those interested in the progress of the historical romance.

Even if he had been a writer of more force and weight, Woodworth would probably have had difficulty in finding a course in the dark chaos that was American literature in the second decade of the nineteenth century. His early efforts were discouraging. He tried time and again to establish himself as a successful publisher and editor of periodicals. Between 1805 and 1823 he had his hand in at least seven periodical ventures—with titles employing such beguiling words (typical of the period) as "Repository," "Chronicle," "Cabinet," "Casket," "Mirror" —but most of these promptly had to shut down.[153] He wrote one successful play, *The Forest Rose* (1825), a comedy which capitalized the American rustic character as "Jonathan Ploughman." *The Forest Rose* was "one of the longest-lived American plays before the Civil War,"[154] but none of Woodworth's other plays had a comparable success. Woodworth never struck it rich again. He had charm and taste, but what was needed in order to attract attention in the callow days of our national boyhood was more novelty or more sheer power. Even Bryant had found it expedient to move to the security of a daily newspaper in 1827: mere literature promised but a lean living.

In the preface to *The Champions of Freedom* Woodworth makes some show of courting originality, but his effort seems forced and inconsistent. When a friend who has seen the manuscript is reported as having characterized the book as a "monster" in which "'the grand fundamental rule of composition is violated in every chapter,'" the author's rejoinder is jaunty after the fashion of Laurence Sterne: "'The very thing I aimed at.'"[155] But the mantle of Sterne could not well be worn by a writer temperamentally as conventional as Woodworth. The preface contains, however, a promise which must have heartened readers lately surfeited with news and stories of the War of 1812. The author plans to use a minimum of martial detail:

> To furnish this relief without alluring [*sic*] from the subject—
> to soften the rough notes of the bugle by the gentler tones of the
> lyre—to mingle the flowers of fancy with the laurels of victory—
> and to shift the scene occasionally from the hostile camp to the
> mansion of love, has been the author's aim . . .[156]

Fine writing, this, and little else—for with the very next flourish of his
pen, Woodworth attempts to appeal to readers interested in the War
(of 1812):

> Although termed a ROMANCE, and embellished with a few fic-
> titious scenes, incidents, and characters, it will, nevertheless, be
> the most correct and complete History of the recent War, that
> has yet appeared. Every event of importance will here be found
> detailed in order . . .[157]

In politics such straddling technique as this might have been useful; in
the preface to a novel it is merely confusing. The story which ensues
is also confusing. It does contain both military and civil elements; the
trouble is that they do not unite to form a coherent whole. As it happens, the military part (no inconsiderable portion of the story) is the
least effective, having been got up from "sources." Detailing the pre-
service career of the hero was obviously more to the taste of the contemplative author of "The Old Oaken Bucket."

The birth of the hero, George Washington Willoughby, was attended by a singular (romantic) circumstance: his father, who had
received a sword as the personal gift of General Washington, had taken
an oath never to part with it as long as life remained in him. It happened, however, that during an engagement with Indian fighters, his
sword hand had been severed—whereupon the father cried out: "O
that I had a son to redeem my vow." [158] Heaven, it seems, not only
heard his vow but had anticipated his need, for at that very moment,
eight hundred miles away, his son was born. This much the astonished
father learns from a voice that seems to emanate from a Miami chief,
who is dead nearby. Clearly this son of Willoughby is to be no ordinary lad. To make sure that all his noble potentialities are realized, the
father later decides to bid "an eternal adieu to the busy haunts of
civilization" and hie him to a forest on the southern shore of Lake
Erie—there to live, not as a hermit, but as a "Grecian philosopher"
with children for pupils. Young George becomes a "child of nature"
and "an infant Hercules." He makes a companion of the son of the big
Indian chief Logan, and under his tutelage he becomes, at the age of
ten, "quite an accomplished savage." [159] The Indians of this part of

Pennsylvania are friendly to the white people because of William Penn's having treated them with a "noble spirit of equity and sound policy." [160]

George's delightful sylvan boyhood, however, must come to an end, for his father decrees that Harvard College—"the first literary institution in the United States"—can best minister to his son's needs. The primitive life is over for George. It now becomes the father's ambition to coach the lad in the ways of conservatism and security. Federalism and centralization become the watch words. The young man is admonished to cherish Washington's Farewell Address: "read [it] next to your Bible." Mindful of the danger of sectionalism, he must "[f]rown indignantly on the first dawning of an attempt to alienate any portion of this country from the rest, or enfeeble the sacred ties which now link its various parts." [161]

But there isn't much time for George to meditate on political principles. He is busy as a young man is busy at college. Evil companions try to lead him astray; on one occasion he discovers only in time that he has been introduced to a brothel. But all this life—of books, sociability, and temptation—is presently to be banished, for the War of 1812 begins and the hero must join the colors. Phases of the War occupy most of the rest of the book—in the form of letters. The personal adventures of George receive attention and there is relief from military matters when the author writes of such things as Mrs. Madison's levées. Yet the book lists heavily with the dull minutiae of campaign and maneuver. The miraculous coincidence that occurred at the time of the hero's birth is not forgotten, for the apparition of the mysterious Miami chief who had announced George's birth turns up from time to time with helpful hints for George. At the end the "vow" motif is resolved, and of course there are matrimonial vows as well. But by that time the story has nearly died. For Woodworth was not equal to the task he had staked out for himself. The early life of his hero he could make shift to report—not with complete originality but with general effectiveness and some charm. Woodland scenery and philosophical speculation were congenial to Woodworth. He handled detail well and coined sententious comments freely. But when he deployed his characters on a national frontier, although his "sources" were adequate[162] his own resources failed him. He had sprightliness but not much vigor. As for the "mysterious chief," he was a spirit too difficult for Woodworth to wrestle with. Let such figures await the more competent attention of Cooper and Simms.

James Fenimore Cooper
and the Historical Romance

With the appearance of Washington Irving and James Fenimore Cooper, America for the first time entered international literary competition on something like even terms. Of the two writers Cooper was the more surprising phenomenon, for whereas Irving easily accommodated his talents to a well-established English tradition in letters, Cooper, who was contemptuous of Irving as "denationalized and sycophantic," [1] was straight American through and through. If he was called "the American Scott," the sobriquet implied his parity with, more than his imitation of, the author of *Waverley*. Cooper quickly became, and still remains, one of the great novelists in English: whatever may be made of defects in his method or style, this fact is undeniable. Indeed the furious critical attacks to which he has been subjected from the time of his first publication to the present tend to prove his case: a lesser writer would have been blasted to oblivion. Cooper still lives as the first strongly original delineator of the American scene and as the creator of one of the immortal characters of fiction, Natty Bumppo.

It was but natural that Cooper should make his success in the historical romance. For decades American writers had been trying vainly to produce an indigenous literature appropriate to an independent nation of enormous geographical area. The burning desire to celebrate the nation in epic poem had lured Barlow and Dwight to their ultimate ruin in morasses of heroic couplets. Many creditable poems had been written in imitation of Augustan writers of England, but no clear American note had been struck by an important poet until Bryant shuffled off most of his British models and began to stamp his page with American images. The essay too had suffered from general acceptance of the premise that all progress must start from Addison and Steele; to this rule Irving was a partial exception. As for drama, our theatres were leagues away from London, but our playwrights were still within the gravitational field of Sheridan, Shakespeare, and Beaumont and Fletcher. The novel, despite a few laudable gestures toward autonomy, had failed to declare its independence of foreign domination in theme and method. Even Cooper's first attempt at fiction was in effect merely another English novel written by an American, and not a very good one at that.

But the historical romance opened up vast possibilities. True, all danger of foreign influence was not absent in this field, what with the enormous flow of romantic narrative emanating from the pen of Sir Walter Scott. Yet the American writer had certain unique assets. He had territorial extent which dwarfed the British Isles even if trans-Allegheny regions should remain untouched. He had different climate, topography, and wild life. He had uncharted inland lakes, trackless forests, frontiers so vast that no single writer could master them. He had the Indian—a new race to lend strength to a new literature. And he had a nation lately sprung into independence. Lately—yes, there was the rub for Cooper and many of his followers: *too* lately for the historical romancer, who likes his traditions encrusted with age, his legends extending back in time to a vanishing point, his historical events remote enough to be redolent of romance rather than smudged by politics. America, alas, had no Middle Ages! Yet much could be done —and was to be done—with the Revolutionary War, now to be viewed through a perspective of almost fifty years! Couldn't the victories of Washington and the daring exploits of John Paul Jones or Francis Marion be as thrilling to Americans as the campaigns of Marlborough or of Bonnie Prince Charlie to Britishers? Even the War of 1812 could yield good material for a writer bent on celebrating the struggles of a young nation against unjust aggression by a tyrannous foe. For, whatever the terrain, patriotism was the atmosphere of the historical romance: the life-breath of the nation was the memory of her heroes. More fictional wealth was at hand than Cooper realized, but once he learned that to him an encampment on Lake Erie was as useful as a Northumberland fortress to Scott, he began to write amain (albeit not without occasionally grumbling at the newness of things American), and he became the first and greatest of a long line of American writers of the historical romance, extending from 1821 to the present. The genre has altered in some important respects—witness the new methods employed by Kenneth Roberts and others—but its essentials remain much the same: a tale of high adventure set in the past, centering in a situation crucial in the life of a nation or a people, involving persons, places, and actions partly invented and partly historical.[2]

The time was ripe for Cooper, but he was slow to perceive his opportunity. No consuming literary passion impelled him into authorship. Not a prodigy of the library like Charles Brockden Brown, he spent a rugged outdoor boyhood and youth. He seems not to have thought of authorship until he was thirty. Even if he had, it is doubtful if he would have had much hope of succeeding, given the situation in the world of letters. His buoyant temperament and rugged vitality did not prepare him to write fashionable sentimental romances, whether reeking with piety or smouldering with erotic intrigue. Gothic corridors and subterranean horrors were not to his taste. Within four walls Cooper was all but helpless; in a forest or in the saddle or on the quarterdeck he was master. Yet who would be interested in an American forest when Mrs. Radcliffe's scenic studies of France and Italy were available? How, unless you were a Defoe or a Smollett, could you sell a sea novel to landlubbers? Moreover why write at all when American publishers shared the "general impression . . . that we had not, and could not have, a literature"? What hope for native production when it was believed to be "positively injurious to the commercial credit of a bookseller to undertake American works, unless they might be Morse's geographies, classical books, school-books, devotional books, or other utilitarian works"? [3] Yet upon retrospect, Cooper's early life proved to have been in many respects ideal for the purposes he finally adopted. If he was articled to life instead of to letters, he was later able to capitalize much of his experience in ways undreamt of by American novelists before his time.

LIFE AND PUBLICATIONS

He was born in 1789 at Burlington, New Jersey. His father, William Cooper, was an energetic man possessed of many talents, including a gift for vigorous narrative.[4] A Federalist in politics, the elder Cooper held office (as a judge and a Congressman) on several occasions, but his principal occupation was that of a land agent. He firmly believed in the domination of a landed gentry. He bought and sold immense tracts of land, and it was his boast that he had "settled more acres than any other man in America." [5] Among his purchases had been a 50,000-acre tract of upper New York land put on the market by William Franklin, son of Benjamin Franklin. Shortly after young Cooper's birth, the family moved to New York state, where Judge Cooper established himself on Otsego Lake in an imposing three-story house, later to be described by his son in *The Pioneers*. Here the future novelist lived in an environment which was friendly to culture and adjacent to the wilds. Distinguished society naturally circulated in the home of his father, the "Sir Roger de Coverley of Otsego Hall," [6] and it was undoubtedly through observation of the squire's life led by his father that Cooper got his first love of aristocratic ease which was to rise as a ghost at his Republican banquets. But that came later. Meantime young Cooper had his own life to begin. He was apparently an avid reader of romances, but was always ready to drop his books in favor of hunting, sailing, or riding. After his elementary training in a village academy, his preparation for college was entrusted to Thomas Ellison, a bigoted Episcopalian clergyman of Albany, who was well versed in Virgil and Cicero and who "detested a democrat as he did the devil." [7] Sufficiently trained to meet the rather light entrance requirements of Yale College at the time, Cooper entered with the class of 1806, but he was prevented from graduating by reason of his excessive love of fun, which led him on one occasion to explode gunpowder in the keyhole of a hallmaster's door. Expelled from college in his junior year for this prank, Cooper never again submitted himself to that academic discipline which, in the opinion of his biographer, might have given him greater interest in "perfection of form" than was shown in his novels.[8]

For the wooded environs of New Haven, Cooper now substituted a freer life aboard ship, where as a common sailor before the mast and, after a year's apprenticeship, as midshipman, he acquired much of that experience which he was later to draw upon heavily in the composition of *The Pilot, The Pathfinder,* and other stories. His naval service took him abroad as far as London and Gibraltar, inland to Lake Ontario. He at first enjoyed the experience, but in 1810 his budding critical sense found so much cause for dissatisfaction in "the blasted prospect of the service" that he contemplated resigning.[9] He was persuaded by a superior officer to defer his resignation for one year (till 1811). Despite his critical attitude, Cooper's experience of the Navy left no "burden on his spirit" comparable to that which later tormented Melville.[10] He continued to love the sea, and the Navy remained "one of his chief interests to the last." [11]

Cooper's next adventure was matrimony. Susan De Lancey, his bride, was a descendant of a family which had been strongly Loyalist during the Revolution. One of her kinsmen, James De Lancey, had been the originator of the freebooting "Cow-Boys" whose habit of harrying neutrals Cooper later described (with a degree of sympathy doubtless ascribable to his marriage to Susan) in *The Spy*.[12] When Cooper took Susan to wife, the De Lancey family was a cultivated and prosperous one. In a letter to his brother, Cooper jocosely confessed that Susan would inherit an ample estate upon the death of her aunt, who—then seventy-two—could not "weather it long." He added that he was himself "indifferent to anything of this nature." [13] Cooper was married on January 1, 1811, and in May of the same year, at the instigation of his wife, he formally ended his service in the Navy. For three years he lived principally at the estate of his father-in-law near Mamaroneck, but about 1814 he moved back to one of the Cooper farms, which he called Fenimore, not far from Otsego Hall in Cooperstown. Here he began to build a stone house, and he settled down to the life of a gentleman farmer, studying crop development, keeping his estate in repair, lending a hand in community affairs. He became secretary of the local Bible association, producer of a provincial play, part owner of a whaling ship, and amateur architect. As secretary of the Otsego Agricultural Society he introduced Merino sheep to the region. Named an aide-de-camp with the rank of colonel by Governor Clinton, he participated in full dress military reviews. Amid a growing family Cooper led a full and varied life at Fenimore. Yet it appears that his wife yearned to be closer to her family home, and when the aunt (who in 1810 couldn't "weather it long") finally died in 1817, Cooper abandoned Fenimore (with its house still incompletely built) and began to build a new home, on French château lines, on the farm near Scarsdale which his wife had inherited. Angevine—so the farm was named, after early Huguenot settlers—was close enough to the Mamaroneck De Lanceys to please his wife but far enough away to permit Cooper to resume the life of independent country squire. Here he was to live until his move to New York City in 1822.

The observable influences that had played upon Cooper up to this time were largely conservative—his father, his boyhood tutor, Yale College, and his wife's family tradition. His commission in the Navy and his honorary colonelcy in the Army can have done nothing to lessen his patrician outlook or to shake his acquiescence in a moderately aristocratic way of life. It is to be presumed that his contacts with the lowlier manifestations of democracy had been slight, and not wholly congenial; indeed he never became a champion of humble folk as such: at most he would try to see that they received adequate protection and sound leadership. The sources of his liberal beliefs are hard to search out: perhaps their essence was mainly an anti-monarchical feeling natural to a free-born out-door-loving American. Somewhere within himself he harbored republican convictions which were not wholly smothered by the life of comparative personal ease which he led. Later these embers of political liberalism were to be fanned into a blaze of Jacksonian feeling: for when the aristocratic order he grew up in was threatened with extinction, he resisted the imminent displacement of the landed gentry by the aggressive methods of a scheming capitalistic class. But that was in the future, and in the early days of his manhood it would have been hard to predict that the complacent squire of Angevine would ever become embroiled in national issues.

It also would have been hard to prophesy the spectacular career as a popular author he was shortly to commence. That a man who was even "averse to writing" letters[14] should at the age of thirty not only begin to write novels but also prove to be one of the most prolific writers in the history of our literature was indeed astonishing. The circumstances under which he began were more or less accidental. The story of his start occurs in at least three slightly different versions from the pen of his daughter Susan, but the essential fact is that one night when he was reading an English novel aloud to his wife he was so impressed by its feeble quality that he tossed aside the volume, remarking at the same time: "I could write you a better book than that myself." Despite polite scoffing he forthwith began to write such a book, and the result was his first novel, *Precaution: or, Prevention is Better than Cure*, published in two volumes in November, 1820.[15] As the composition of the book proceeded, the author read chapters to his family. His wife thought it excellent—what other Westchester squire could equal it?—and little Susan was once found shedding (serious) tears over its pathos. But to offer an intra-family exercise to the general public was a procedure to be avoided without more impartial testing. Accordingly the story was read in part to various friends and almost entire to the family of John Jay before Cooper determined upon publication. And so his first novel appeared in two volumes over the imprint of A. T. Goodrich & Co. on November 10, 1820.

The story of *Precaution* was based on the theme of the judicious selection of a spouse. The blessings of Providence, says Cooper, are "too often hazarded by a neglect of duty that springs from too great security, or an indolence which renders us averse to the precaution necessary to insure their continuance." [16] Emily Moseley, the heroine of the story, is well provided with advice from the lips of the ever watchful Mrs. Wilson, sister of her widowed father. The theory of husband-choosing is simple enough: the girl must be religious, scrupulously delicate in taste, prudent in conduct, and responsive to parental guidance. She must learn to look for those qualities in a husband which mark him as a man of principle rather than of mere taste and fashion. Armed with such rules and guarded by the vigilance of Mrs. Wilson, Emily succeeds in eluding undesirable suitors and, after surviving a number of difficulties caused in part by her aunt's excessive zeal, she wins a wholly admirable young man—who turns out to be a lord! In the meantime the wages of careless or abandoned conduct are illustrated (discreetly) in the experiences of some of the other dramatis personae, particularly that of Julia, who reposed too much trust in an army officer. At the end, the reader is assured that "the consequences of [Julia's] imprudence are likely to continue" while only happiness is in store for Emily. Thus it is clear that—in the last words of the book—"prevention is at all times better than cure."

It is interesting and illuminating, though perhaps unfair, to compare *Precaution* with Cooper's later works. The book was, as Boynton says, a deliberate "fraud"—an anonymous story, sure to be taken as the work of an English gentlewoman—a story set in a country which the author knew chiefly through the glimpses of shore afforded from the deck of a ship. Cooper merely wished to see how well he could imitate a school of novel-writing. Here was no chance to exhibit his full equipment as a writer. The result was inevitable: the book was not a very good one. One critic has offered the extreme judgment that in many ways it is "the best novel written in America before 1821," and that if it were "republished today as a newly-discovered early work by Jane Austen it would deceive most readers." [17] Well, hardly: anyone familiar with the sharp economy and tidy technique of Jane Austen would scarcely suspect her of having produced this overstuffed afternoon-tea novel. Other critics (among them many who have not read the novel at all) have been equally sure that *Precaution* is nothing but piffle. The unexciting truth is near the middle—if anything, closer to the latter judgment than to the former. *Precaution* is most suggestive of Cooper in its ethical tone: the lessons implied in it were congenial to him. Whereas Jane Austen shows how people act in given situations, Cooper tells how they ought to act. Yet the moral tone of *Precaution* gives it a certain weight that is partly an asset. In characterization *Precaution* is not distinguished. People are adequate types: that is all, in most cases. Perhaps the best-drawn person is the crotchety old bachelor, Mr. Benfield—a minor person in the plot. Occasionally the language has epigrammatic point—as when the author observes that "it was the great error of Mrs. Wilson to attempt to convince, where she might have influenced." [18] But Cooper's faults are here in even greater array than elsewhere. The language drags, and the grammar creaks. The story is needlessly long—almost twice as long as *Persuasion* and far more complicated. A whole chapter is devoted to telling how the various characters appeared as they entered church one day. Conversation is not only bookish but clumsily so. The minutiae of daily existence of indoor people are set forth with exasperating detail by a writer who never excelled in such matters anyway. Such exciting actions as are resolutely introduced to break the monotony of social palaver—a

buggy accident, an accidental shooting, etc.—seem pretty petty tactics
for a writer destined to electrify thousands of readers by thrilling exploits of immense magnitude and national significance on land and sea.
Such minor episodes do occur in the later novels incidentally, but in
Precaution they are central. Really major events, such as Napoleon's
defeat at Waterloo, receive only tangential reference: Cooper is writing a novel, not an historical romance. In short *Precaution* represents
only part of Cooper—the lesser part. Most of all one misses in *Precaution* a strong sense of place. It is astonishing that Cooper could have
kept his characters so long in one place (Northampton) without appearing to realize that he has not *rendered* that place. When his characters go to Bath for several chapters, the reader is aware of the fact
only because the author says so. All of this is an indirect reminder of
how important a part the setting generally plays in Cooper's tales.

The story of *Precaution* thus called for strength where Cooper was
weak—in the study of domestic relationships—and made little demand
on his real powers—the presentation of vivid action set against large
open-air backgrounds. Even so it seems to have had a fair initial success, to judge from pleasant reviews and the appearance of an English
edition. The book was quickly forgotten, however, by everyone but
its author.[19]

In *The Spy* Cooper wisely forsook the dimly imagined English countryside which had formed the background of his first novel and set his
narrative in a region whose soil was fresh on his boots. For plot he took
material from a portion of our history so close to him that some of the
facts could be learned in conversation with persons still living. Notwithstanding his partial success in *Precaution,* however, he undertook
the new work with diffidence, well knowing that for most Americans
imported fiction seemed as much of a necessity as imported tea. After
he had finished the first volume, he secured a publisher. Yet doubts
refused to be dissolved, and Cooper laid the book aside for several
months.[20] When the publishers succeeded in reviving his confidence,
he resumed writing with such copiousness (finally more characteristic
of him than diffidence) that they feared the tale might reach imprac-
tically large proportions. To still this anxiety Cooper wrote the last
chapter and gave it to the printer even before the intervening action
had been conceived—a circumstance which he referred to later as an
explanation of the many slips in language in the novel as well as its
somewhat bungled plot structure. *The Spy* was published on December 22, 1821. Like many American books of the period, and all Cooper's novels, it was published anonymously, but Cooper obstinately
ascribed it on the title page to "the author of 'Precaution.'" The re-

ception of the first small edition was so favorable that two large editions, totalling 8000 copies, were called for within four months,[21] and the book held its ground so well that by 1829 it had reached a seventh edition.[22] In England, where Murray had refused the book even on the recommendation of Irving, *The Spy* had several editions from 1822 on. Numerous French and German editions (the first being in 1822 and 1824 respectively) further testified to Cooper's strong popular appeal. An ample recognition, this, of the genius of an American writer at a time when Irving was believed to be the only American capable of competing in popularity with Scott. Critical opinion at home was mixed but generally favorable. Many critics complained of crudities in style, unnecessarily revolting detail, and the "lame and impotent conclusion" of the story,[23] but praise preponderated, and one early critic averred that *The Spy* was "the best American novel that has been written." [24] The (Philadelphia) *Port Folio* was extremely laudatory, and even *The North American Review*, representing a constituency hardly ideal from the point of view of a New York novelist, paid the book so many compliments that its reservations were comparatively inconspicuous. The reviewer (W. H. Gardiner) concluded that Cooper had "laid the foundations of American romance" and had become "the first who has deserved the appellation of a distinguished American novel writer." [25] Critical judgments by British reviewers,[26] almost uniformly condescending in tone, were often contradictory but generally friendly and sometimes enthusiastic. What was undoubtedly one of the most valued encomia Cooper received came from the extremely popular Maria Edgeworth, who, though she condemned Harvey Birch as vulgar, referred to the no less vulgar Betty Flanagan as "incomparable" and vouchsafed that "an Irish peer could not have drawn her better." [27] *The Literary Chronicle and Weekly Review* thought Cooper a worthy successor of Brown and his book "one of the best novels that we have met with." [28]

Time has pretty well sustained the mixed judgments of a hundred years ago; *The Spy* is still loved by Americans and continental readers and still criticized for crass defects. The story of Harvey Birch, the peddler-spy whose prototype in actuality Cooper learned of from John Jay, was a moving one embodying one of the most useful themes in any romance writer's kit, namely, unflinching loyalty under hazardous conditions. The scenery was startlingly vivid and almost wholly new. The action of the book as a whole is ill-proportioned but in separate scenes, such as the hanging of the "Skinner," superbly effective. Harvey Birch is, as Gardiner pointed out, a "finely conceived character," [29] and his rapidly varying fortunes are as touching as they are thrilling. Genuine comedy abounds in the passages involving several of the characters.[30] Best of all, the whole book is invested with a note of high seriousness suitable to the national issues at stake. Defects there are which cry out to the most rapid reader: the use of Washington (Mr. Harper) in plain clothes;[31] certain badly done scenes such as the death of Miss Singleton; the general ineffectiveness of the treatment of love; the frequently poor style; the curious over-emphasis upon unimportant minutiae, creating an air of naive literalness not unlike that which later characterized Mark Twain in his less inspired moments; and an over-reliance on "stage-tricks and claptraps." [32]

Precaution had represented "the real Cooper" very inadequately; *The Spy* was a much fuller (though not complete) indication of what might be expected of him in the future. Certain favorite characters and devices are brought into initial prominence: the flight and pursuit motif (with sympathy focussed on the pursued); the solitary horseman (founder of a prolific line in American romance) mysteriously approaching a solitary farmhouse at nightfall; the split in family affections created by the difficult conditions of war;[33] the unnamed historical character; the pair of extremely sensitive girls—a sort of female counterpart to Rosencrantz and Guildenstern; the supposedly amusing bore (Col. Sitgreaves); the admirably drawn hearty campaigner (Lawton); the "female" with impaired mental faculties; the low-life comics; the amateur rescue which defies logic but thrills the imagination (Captain Wharton changes clothes with Caesar and masks himself to simulate the Negro servant); and in general the alternation between boyish prank and stark tragedy. In Caesar the novelist presented his first full-drawn portrait of a Negro.[34] Furthermore he had been original enough, as *The North American Review* was quick to point out, to discover that "the American Revolution is an admirable basis, on which to found fiction of the highest order of romantic interest." [35] He had given New York state its full franchise in fiction, for whereas Scott "loved strange adventure and sought it in the Middle Age," [36] Cooper had found romance in his own back yard without benefit of antiquity. He was himself later to join the chorus of woe at America's poverty in tradition, yet when he substituted a Westchester farmhouse for a medieval castle as a mise-en-scène, he had put American fiction on the road to great indigenous achievement. He had also turned the first page of his own success as a writer.

On the other hand, Cooper achieved a major success in *The Spy* without heavy reliance on at least three of the principal elements which were to be "featured" in later books. First, notwithstanding some description of native scenery, including one of the best passages Cooper ever wrote (the description of the Hudson in Chapter XXXII) nature is used far less than in many later books. Secondly, the Indian is used only incidentally. Thirdly, of course, Natty Bumppo has yet to be born. All three of these omissions were largely to be repaired in Cooper's next novel, *The Pioneers*. That *The Spy* succeeded so astonishingly without their reinforcement is further evidence of the sheer power of Cooper as a writer.

In 1822 Cooper moved to New York City. A strange thing, one might think, for the devotée of nature to desert a rural estate for the very heart of a metropolis, even the comparatively tiny metropolis of New York. But Cooper was now an author, and as such he owed his first allegiance to his work. Angevine farm was only twenty-five miles out of the city, but even so you couldn't drop in on your publisher at will, couldn't consult with the printer about proof, couldn't meet literati in professional or convivial camaraderie. So the Coopers—there were five children now, and the girls needed good schooling—moved to New York, which would be their home until the move to Europe in 1827. There followed a comparatively happy and prosperous period for Cooper. Although he had already shown himself to be allergic to adverse criticism, so far he had suffered only minor rashes. Dismay at the conduct of his countrymen in general would come later. Libel suits and wars with the press were largely in the future. In the meantime the author of *The Spy* wore his laurels complacently (even ostentatiously, some thought[37]) and enjoyed domination among the literati. With Irving in Europe and Bryant not yet migrated southward from the Berkshires, the Knickerbockers weren't an overpoweringly brilliant coterie: Halleck and Drake and Percival seemed big men then. Cooper showed his instinct for eminence by founding and presiding over a pleasant organization, The Bread and Cheese Club, devoted to superior cuisine, literary chit-chat, and miscellaneous discourse—for its membership included a variety of prominent professional and mercantile men of the day.[38] Best of all, perhaps, Cooper had pleasant and fruitful hours of shop talk in the back room at the establishment of Charles Wiley, who had published *The Spy* and was soon to publish *The Pioneers*.

Cooper expressed himself as exceedingly fond of *The Pioneers*, for he wrote it happily, sometimes haphazardly, out of impressions that rose easily to the surface of his mind. Incongruously, he united these warm boyhood memories to a superannuated plot involving the temporary dispossession of an estate, the whole being set in an upper-New York settlement in 1793. The action stems from the fact that Major Effingham has given his estate to his son on the occasion of the latter's marriage. The son, being of an indolent disposition, in turn has consigned his affairs into the hands of Marmaduke Temple, judge of the settlement—taking care to keep the arrangement secret because of Temple's (unpopular) Quaker allegiance. Upon the outbreak of the Revolution, Effingham the younger joins the Royalists and subsequently settles in England. After his death, *his* son, introduced in the story as Oliver Edwards, comes out to the States to search for his grandfather. Edwards conceives a suspicion that Temple has embezzled his father's estate (which Temple now occupies) but it turns out that the Judge has duly sent proper remittances to Effingham up to the time of the latter's death and that he had been holding the estate in trust. There is no bar, therefore, to Edwards' marriage to Elizabeth, the Judge's daughter, a move which permanently unites the assets of Temple and Effingham.

To this ancient piece of plot machinery is geared a looser but more original action relating to Natty Bumppo, here hight Leatherstocking. Arrested and incarcerated for shooting a buck out of season, Natty breaks jail partly by means of a canister of powder brought to him by Elizabeth Temple: it was the least she could do for a man who had saved her and another female nonentity from a real panther. Natty continues to be the object of legal molestation, but he holds out for a time in an improvised fort—if the flight-and-pursuit theme is absent from this book, at least the hero is on the defensive. Finally after grandfather Effingham is produced and has testified that Leatherstocking has been the faithful servant of his long retirement, Natty is pardoned and invited to settle down in village security and comfort. But Natty, intuitively aware of what is expected of an epic hero, declines the offer and turns westward to the woods.

There is in *The Pioneers* a more definite disjunction of the action from the illustrative material than in any of Cooper's tales of the frontier; consequently, once the plot has begun slowly to turn over, the setting and characterization may be enjoyed for their own sake.[39] The author indulges himself in unhurried descriptions of pioneer life: going to meeting, inn-visiting, turkey-shooting, fishing, and sap-collecting—as well as in more nature description than he had ever before attempted. Fine characterizations are given to persons who are minor in the action of the story but integral parts of the complete representation of the settlement contemplated by Cooper: the clergyman, the physician, the sheriff, the store-keeper, the servants, etc. French and Dutch elements are embodied in M. le Quoi and Major Hartmann, whose foreign accents are clumsily reproduced but whose general characteristics are convincingly set forth. The whole book is leisurely in tone, as if Cooper were disposed to enjoy himself as much as to entertain the reader. A good deal of humor arises from small causes, as when Remarkable and Benjamin shrewdly discuss their "betters." We learn of a white pine wood so soft that "it is commonly chosen by the hunters for pillows" and (from Dr. Todd) of a patient who had pains in his amputated leg because the removed part was buried in too small a box. Then there is the sheer frivolousness of an allusion to a pedestal bust as being that of Julius Caesar or Dr. Faustus: " 'there were good reasons for believing either.' " Trivia, these, but Cooper was equal to bigger game also. Thomas Hardy furnishes few instances of more delightful comedy than the court-room scene in which, when the auditors are struck dumb by an unexpected revelation, the sheriff strikes his sword on the table and shouts "Silence!" On the side of serious social criticism there is less in *The Pioneers* than was to appear in later books, but Cooper can be seen sharpening his weapons on the subject of wrongs inflicted on the Indian and on the subject of justice in general. Some of the social comment emanates from Leatherstocking himself.

Natty makes his first appearance in the Leatherstocking series in a book which, reckoning by his age (sixty), should be fourth in the series. He is vivid and picturesque, having been modelled partly on a certain leatherstockinged hunter named Shipman, whom Cooper knew in boyhood, and partly on an idealized conception of Daniel Boone. He is attractive in his fine gift for friendship, and his loyalty to Chingachgook (who, despite scenes which reveal his weakness for fire-water, finally dies a very moving death in this volume) establishes a tone which will be sustained throughout the series. So too with his humane attitude toward wild creatures: Natty it is who voices an objection to the pioneers' lust for killing more pigeons than one needs. His single yellow tooth, however, and his peculiar silent laugh, as well as a certain querulousness in his manner, prevent his being the ideal romantic character which in subsequent additions to the series he became. Here too one gets the first impressions of his boastfulness and his loquacity. His woodcraft and general resourcefulness stand him in good stead in his first tests, too, but it would have been pleasant to find him under legal restraint for some nobler reason than shooting a buck out of season! And his prevarication about the matter does not go down well with the reader who happens to have heard Natty stress the importance of truth in some of his other serial appearances. Likewise, readers who come to *The Pioneers* after having sampled some of Natty's high eloquence in *The Pathfinder* and *The Deerslayer* may be disconcerted at Natty's untutored vernacular, appropriate though such language is to the simple hunter. The union of these diverse traits in Natty clearly marks him as the child of a realistic phase in his creator. It was a phase which would reappear often in parts of books to come and would be dominant in some entire stories (such as *Satanstoe*), but it was not his most popular phase.[40]

Even so *The Pioneers* was immensely successful from the first. The public was so eager to learn the latest inventions of the author of *The Spy* (though Cooper clung on the title page to the sobriquet "author of Precaution") that on the morning of publication (February 1, 1823) *The Pioneers* sold 3500 copies.[41] The work continued to be popular for some years, reaching a sixth edition by 1832. Objections to it were based upon its monotony and upon its exploitation of "low-life." *The North American Review* had held that Cooper's skill in delineating low-life was one of his chief assets[42] but there were many readers and critics so devoted to the satin and plush of current English and American sentimental novels that they were revolted by Cooper's honest denim fabric and the coarse (though naturally never indecent) idiom of his frontier folk. James Gates Percival referred to *The Pioneers* as one of a class of "long, dirty, straggling tales." [43] Criticism of this type soon received substantial rebuttal from the vigorous pen of James Kirke Paulding:

> With certain people, perhaps a large portion of those who read novels, every thing which is not fashionable is vulgar. A worthy farmer or mechanic, in a clean white frock, and thick-soled shoes is vulgar, and therefore ought not to be introduced into a novel. In short, with this class of readers and critics, every trait of nature, and every exhibition of manners, or dress, which does not come up to the standard of fashionable elegance, is of necessity low and vulgar.
>
> If we trace this vulgar error to its source, we shall find it, in general, flowing from a false opinion with regard to what constitutes real refinement. In the general estimation, refinement or gentility, as opposed to vulgarity, consists not in intellectual, or moral superiority, but in outward manners and outward splendors, in station, title, or wealth. This opinion is the offspring of ignorance and vulgarity combined.[44]

Indeed it is clear that Cooper was one of the first American novelists to make frequent and realistic use of actual shirt-sleeve characters (as opposed to romantic "ploughmen" and "foresters") who were to receive widespread attention in fiction only after the Civil War. Notwithstanding Paulding's able defense, however, and the vigorous success of *The Pioneers* in its first decade (as well as Cooper's own fondness for it), the first of the Leatherstocking Tales has gradually become the least prized of the series. And doubtless this is an indication of the reading public's judgment that Cooper's forte was the mastery of illusion and suspense, not, mainly at least, his faithfulness to actual data of the life he knew.[45]

Confirmed as a popular author, though not committed to one fictional type, Cooper opened still another avenue of interest in *The Pilot* (1823).[46] It was at a dinner party in New York that he conceived the idea of writing a sea story. When someone argued that *The Pirate*, which had just appeared anonymously, could not have been written by Scott on account of the seamanship it showed, Cooper asserted that the nautical data were the best reason for believing that Scott *had* written the book: a real seaman would do these things better. And so Cooper wrote *The Pilot*, a packed tale of military exploit, naval maneuver, and heart adventure off and on the coast of Northumberland. The characters include the customary charming girls, for whom, after the usual amount of blushing and misunderstanding, suitable mates are found among the male dramatis personae. Cooper's reasonably sympathetic attitude toward Loyalists is again seen in his delineation of the expatriated Col. Howard, who finally relaxes his opposition to the marriage of his ward with a Yankee. The mysterious pilot, Mr. Gray (John Paul Jones), though sufficiently dull as a character, pitches the story on a national scale and enables Cooper to show his nautical stuff: Mr. Gray saves the frigate in a storm and later engages the British fleet in a vivid and exciting action. Men of lesser rank have more individuality: the spunky Manual (of the Marines), the alcoholic Borroughcliffe (a British officer), and the fluent and energetic American Captain Barnstable. Most effective of all the portraits is the Nantucketer Long Tom Coffin, who, in spite of the comparative brevity of his life span, is one of Cooper's memorable portraits—the saltwater counterpart of Natty Bumppo. His capable hands, his racy, practical discourse, his grand indignation at injustice, and his capacity for self-sacrifice are integrated in one of those fine masculine creations belying critics who have asserted that Cooper could not draw character.[47] In a grimly effective scene, as Long Tom watches the villain swim helplessly from the wrecked "Ariel" toward shore, he cannot refrain from giving the poor man (vain) advice as to how the undertow may be avoided—while at the same time Long Tom himself is waiting to go down with the doomed schooner: for "when the death watch is called, none can skulk from the muster." While Cooper was preparing to write *The Pilot*, his friend R. H. Dana, remembering Cooper's satirical portraits of New Englanders in his earlier books (such as Hiram Doolittle and Dr. Todd in *The Pioneers*) im-

plored him to "have some mercy on the Yankees this time." [48]   In the
characterization of Long Tom Coffin of Nantucket Cooper made handsome amends.[49] Indeed with Long Tom for "human interest" and John
Paul Jones for patriotic appeal, the story could hardly fail. One critic
expressed a fairly widespread conviction when he asserted that "Scott's
Pirate was a mere daub to the *Pilot*." [50] *The Pilot* in fact was so much
appreciated by the general public, whether acquainted with ships or
not, that scores of imitations of it soon appeared. Few of these were of
great account—before 1850 only Dana and Melville and (the English)
Marryat seriously challenged Cooper's supremacy in the sea-tale—and
even to the present day *The Pilot* holds a respectable position.

Cooper had now established mastery of three genres: the historical
romance, the narrative of the frontier, and the sea romance. His next
story, *Lionel Lincoln* (1825), was a variation of the first type. It was
intended to be the first of a series of historical novels dealing, as the
half-title of *Lionel Lincoln* indicates, with "Legends of the Thirteen
Republics." The series remained uncompleted, however, for the first
unit was a partial failure.[51] Two things militated against the success of
Lionel Lincoln. First, Cooper's fundamental and ineradicable antipathy
toward "Yankees" prevented his entering con amore upon a narrative of
New England of the period of Lexington, Concord, and Bunker Hill.
The confused psychology of Lionel Lincoln himself (who, though
American-born, had lived all his life in England until the outbreak of
the Revolution), is perhaps partly an indirect expression of Cooper's
mixed feelings. The facts and setting he worked up industriously
through the study of scores of sources, but documents could not im-
pregnate him with the atmosphere of time and place: illusion is not to
be wooed in research. Secondly, the melodramatic co-plot (involving
the parentage of Lionel and his illegitimate half-brother) is poorly handled. Cooper liked a bit of mystery as a complement to more open plot
elements, but he lacked subtlety. The analysis of the effects of crime
and sin upon personality which Poe and Hawthorne were to handle so
well and which even Simms was to treat with moderate success, Cooper
found beyond his powers. Mrs. Lechmere, with her grisly burden of
recollection and her melodramatic gestures, carries no conviction and
little interest. Cooper's ability to report objective action did not, of
course, desert him utterly in *Lionel Lincoln*, but exciting episodes are
finally interesting only when they centre around an interesting character. Certain minor characters are again well-drawn, chiefly Captain
Polwarth, but Lionel Lincoln was no worthy occupant of the boots
of Birch or Bumppo or Long Tom Coffin. Cooper's readers wanted
Bumppo back. And in his next novel Cooper restored him, much al-

tered, but from the point of view of romance greatly improved. In *The Last of the Mohicans* Cooper perfectly integrated his powers with ideal materials: Natty, New York, and the Indians.

The Spy had dealt with events of 1780; *Lionel Lincoln*, of 1775. For *The Last of the Mohicans* Cooper went back to the year 1757. The book was written partly under the handicap of Cooper's serious illness, but it shows the author's amazing invention at its peak. From the moment when Magua undertakes to act as a guide for Duncan Heyward and his party, there is no slackening of suspense until the *katharsis* following the unusually heavy mortality which brings the story to a conclusion. The pale-face youth are again pretty pale as characters—Cora, Alice, and Duncan—but there is no lack of variety and color. Magua is a superb Indian villain; Chingachgook and his son Uncas perfectly embody all the aborigine's most fascinating attributes—physical strength and grace, nobility of character, and a certain poetic strain bred of their forest life. The mysterious Uncas, last of his race, is a fragment of America's epic. Certainly if Cooper was slow to capitalize the Indian in his fiction, here in *The Last of the Mohicans* he utilized their resources to the fullest extent. Hawkeye is perfectly harmonized with the rest of the characters. Cooper's intuition stood him in good stead when he decided to reissue Natty in the prime of his young manhood, less garrulous and critical than in *The Pioneers*, more lithe of step and keen of eye, equally devoted to high ideals, assigned to more harrowing and heroic exploits in a rapidly shifting scene. David Gamut the psalm-singer, with his debatable humor, is regarded as a bore by juvenile readers, but he provides a useful contrast to the romantic characters. Adult readers, in turn, are a little wearied by the itemized adventure of the book. Yet *The Last of the Mohicans* is filled with those elements for which Cooper was and is still most prized: the running fight, the pendulum-like swing between temporary triumph and cruel reversal, the capture, the rescue (or partial rescue: one is often lost), torture, massacre, generosity toward a foe, breath-taking surprise, ineffable courage and silent suffering, the ultimate triumph (though not without the toll of a life or two) of the right side, and poetic justice. The adventure story here attains perfection. The success of *The Last of the Mohicans* was instant and phenomenal,[52] nor has its popularity abated greatly with the passing years. Not so rich a book as *The Deerslayer*, it remains Cooper's most famous novel and perhaps the best known American novel in the world.

Cooper had now reached a peak of fame which he maintained for a time but could not surpass. His name was familiarly known wherever English was spoken and in many foreign lands as well, for as William

Cullen Bryant noted,[53] Cooper was an ideal writer for translation: he dealt little in subtlety or nuance and his simple elemental powers lost hardly at all in a good translation. His works from this time forward were often published simultaneously in England, France, and America, and since Cooper gave some attention to managing his publishing ventures, he reaped profits with which only Irving's could be compared. Yet there were certain leaks in an author's returns on account of the lack of international copyright laws, and it was partly to safeguard his interests that Cooper left America for Europe in 1826. Additional motives were his hope of improved health, his desire to give his children a continental education, and a strong curiosity to observe European political and social institutions at first hand. He stopped briefly in England—transacting publishing business in London and noting by the way that the Thames was "a stream of trifling expanse" [54]—but he was headed for France. He stayed abroad seven years.

Socially the experience was not always a success. Cooper's brusque manner, his pronounced individualistic tendencies, his habit of wearing his democracy on his sleeve, at first made him a somewhat difficult visitor. He refused to use most of his letters of introduction; resentful of the superiority implied by aristocratic titles but fearful of showing his provincialism, he exhibited a defense-mechanism. After a time, however, things became easier, and once Cooper had made his bow at a swank diplomatic dinner given by the American minister, he was over the threshold of Parisian society. In the meantime he had met (again) Lafayette, who was Cooper's beau idéal: "a patrician and fine gentleman by birth and habit, but also a confirmed democrat in political theory and practice." [55] Upon Lafayette's warm invitation Cooper visited him several times at his château at Rozoy-en-Brie. He also met Scott, who was, like Cooper, suffering from royalty-deficiency, and they commiserated with one another. They also inspected each other warily as representative provincial types. The results of their observation were amusingly similar: Scott noted in his diary that Cooper had "a good deal of the manner, or want of manner, peculiar to his countrymen"; Cooper was impressed by the fact that Scott "wanted the ease and *aplomb* of one accustomed to live with his equals." [56] But the important thing is that they appeared to respect and like each other, with no sense that they were more than friendly competitors or rivals.[57]

Political orientation was in some respects as painful as social adjustment. Before he left, he had surveyed Europe from England to Italy, but with unpleasant results. No number of aristocratic dinners, no hobnobbing with the élite, no display of priceless objets d'art, no pilgrim view of cathedral or forum, could break down his disapproval of the feudalism he found surviving in European social and political institutions. By contrast, his own country (which he would berate as soon as he got home) began to seem a paradise. He wrote about the contrast. One of the most egregious examples of Cooper's bumptious Americanism and want of tact was his publication in 1828 of *Notions of the Americans, Picked Up by a Traveling Bachelor*. If Cooper had been snubbed by Europeans from the Rialto to the Strand, his rank celebration of America at the expense of Europe, and particularly England, would not have been justified. The book purports to contain the observations of an Englishman traveling in the United States. The fiction adopted by Cooper forces the traveler to find excellence everywhere he goes. The data contained in the book would have been useful and entertaining if the whole work had not been drenched in a nauseating solution of super-patriotism. Freedom, prosperity, progress—these were the notes he harped upon. The vices of America (soon to be entered in Cooper's books just as unstintedly) were almost overlooked. Only one letter was devoted to the cancerous growth of slavery.[58] Even New Englanders, generally the butt of Cooper's satire, are here given a grand puff.[59] Worst of all, considering Cooper's later emphasis upon the need for spiritual progress, was his open glorification of material advancement in America. The book was bad manners and a diplomatic blunder; Cooper never lived down its effect in England. But this attack on an effete European political and social order—if attack it was—was delivered indirectly. Soon Cooper was to follow up by writing three novels which directly and concretely revealed the sores on the European body politic. But before that, he added to the canon of his American tales.

Although many imitators of Cooper sprang up, no rival author could offer to the public a character who was the peer of Natty Bumppo, of whom a contemporary reviewer (in discussing *The Last of the Mohicans*) remarked that "there never was a hero that could be so often brought before the public." [60] The reviewer also expressed hope that readers might be allowed to "know something of his early life, and what should be still more gratifying, shed a few tears over his grave that were so feelingly shed by him over the grave of Uncas." [61] Cooper deferred gratifying the former of these wishes for many years but soon gratified the latter—in *The Prairie* (1827). In *The Prairie* Natty, withdrawn in disgust from the corruption of settlement life, is a stalwart though somewhat enfeebled figure of the age of eighty years, whose failing eyesight has reduced him to the employment of trapping on the plains of Missouri. With his dog Hector—whose keen scent is no more essential to the trapper than his companionship—Natty ranges the plains, seldom stopping more than a month in one place. After he falls in with Ishmael Bush (Cooper's character names are often good), he finally becomes involved in many adventures between the Pawnees (noble Indians) and the Sioux (bad Indians) over the possession of land and the custody of a number of persons. Cooper had no first-hand experience of the mise-en-scène of his new story,[62] but he added the prairie to his fictional domain with almost the same ease and brilliance that he had shown in mastering the forest and the sea. Indeed he frequently conceived of the prairie as a vast ocean.[63] He skilfully absorbed into his narrative new and picturesque elements: Indians on horseback (harder to catch and thrilling to behold); cattle-rustling; prairie fires and prairie sunsets; the degenerate white man who has gone over the Alleghenies to escape law and plunder land—a sort of inland pirate; and various types of white men, including the French and the Spanish, who were more legitimately engaged in the westward expansion of the country. For several of the minor characters Cooper had merely to find new names and new costumes: their essential attributes he had often enough described elsewhere. The valiant Hardheart, too, has traits in common with Chingachgook. Doctor Obed Bat, a pedant and a coward, is expected to supply diversion much in the manner of David Gamut in *The Last of the Mohicans*—with about the same results. Ishmael Bush is new, however, and so is his wife—"nearly the most memorable figure among Cooper's women." [64] Her lonely, sordid life as the wife of a renegade squatter reaches a point of heavy tragedy when Ishmael, dispensing a rude frontier justice, condemns her brother to self-execution for the murder of his own nephew. But above all the characters towers Natty—who has " 'lived too long to disturb the close of life with quarrels,' " [65] but who gallantly sets about doing his share for friends beset by "miscreants." He is ready in counsel, cunning in action, and philosophic in spirit. He personifies courage and rectitude; he interprets the prairie; he dies "without kith or kin in the world," the last of his race. Yet a certain family pride sustains him, and he tells the awed circle gathered around in his last moments: "We have never been chiefs; but honest, and useful in our way, I hope it cannot be denied we have always proved ourselves." When offer is made to move his remains to the side of his father "near the sea," he demurs, saying that his "bones will whiten on the prairies . . . beyond the din of the settlements." And so the old hunter, his work done and his mind at rest, prepares to answer the final roll-call:

> Suddenly . . . Middleton felt the hand which he held grasp his own with incredible power, and the old man, supported on either

side by his friends, rose upright to his feet. For a moment he looked about him, as if to invite all in presence to listen (the lingering remnant of human frailty), and then, with a fine military elevation of the head, and with a voice that might be heard in every part of that numerous assembly, he pronounced the word— "Here!" [66]

The Prairie, coming in the wake of *The Last of the Mohicans*, did not enjoy a relatively warm popular reception, nor has it ever caught up popularly with certain other books in the Leatherstocking series. An eighty-year-old protagonist, however skilled and admirable *per se*, does not easily stir youthful pulses; to many young people Natty is an old duffer. Nor is the book without its blemishes, mostly stylistic. Eloquence often swells into grandiloquence, and clumsy syntax sometimes marches with both. Yet fundamentally Cooper's evocation of the beauty and magnitude and peril of the prairie is richly poetic, and his loving last rites for Natty Bumppo confer upon *The Prairie* a spiritual elevation found in few novels. Among American novels *The Prairie* deserves a high place.

Repeated editions of *The Pilot* having proved the public appetite for romances of the sea, Cooper responded handsomely in his next novel, *The Red Rover* (1828). The story begins off the coast of Rhode Island in 1759 according to orthodox Cooper formula: a journey (in this case a voyage) is undertaken against apparently good but guarded advice. The principal party (from Newport) falls into the hands of a pirate ship, which in turn is attacked by the British in a fine sea fight interrupted by a fine storm. There are a few deaths, including the very affecting one of the black Scipio, who is found to be wearing a dog-collar (for a bracelet) with an inscription that solves one of the mysterious family relationships which, here as often, Cooper used to lend romance to his relatively obvious surface action. The circumstances of the death of the pirate twenty years later (Cooper was fond of the epilogue) adds another nugget of surprise. It is fair to recall Cooper's own avowal that the work was "hastily-composed" and as such is vulnerable to attack. The book refused to sink under criticism, however, and it still has a faithful following.[67]

Among the other products of Cooper's very active pen during his residence abroad was *The Wept of Wish-ton-Wish*, begun in Switzerland, completed in Italy, and printed in Florence, "at Dante's Head," in 1829. The story proved to be another disastrous journey into "Yankeeland"; Cooper was unable to bring this Connecticut tale completely to life, chiefly, in Lounsbury's opinion, because he could not draw Puritan characters.[68] Nor was his treatment of the theme of the "Angel of

Hadley" as authentic in ring and atmosphere as Hawthorne's briefer treatment of it in "The Gray Champion." [69] As for the dreadful fighting and suffering incidental to King Philip's War, Cooper had already done that sort of thing better in earlier books. The modern reader is inclined to set more store by Cooper's description of early customs in New England. Yet somehow, in spite of the promise held out by Gardiner for the American novelist who should attempt romance set in early Colonial times,[70] *The Wept of Wish-ton-Wish* does not come off very well.[71]

The Water-Witch, another souvenir of his Italian residence, was published (at Dresden)[72] in 1830. Although it was this novel, set largely in the harbor at Rome, which drew from Cooper's friendly critic Shubrick the observation that he liked Cooper "better afloat than ashore," [73] the general judgment of novel readers has not sustained Shubrick's judgment with respect to this book—despite one chase in Cooper's best manner. This novel completed the stories Cooper wrote on American subjects during his European residence. It was also "his last sea story for eight years, and his last pure romance for a full ten." [74]

The prodigality of Cooper's narrative invention was almost equalled by the enormous activity of his critical eye. This is apparent in the next ten years, which showed him as prolific as ever, but much more given to critical comment. Observing the political scene wherever he went became a passion with him. Everywhere what he observed in Europe he contrasted, for the moment at least, with superior conditions in America. Attention has already been called to his chauvinistic compendium, *Notions of the Americans*.[75] During the last three years of his European residence he reasserted his Americanism by writing three novels holding up to view the rottenness of feudal Europe. He seems to have aimed incidentally at dispelling the "glamor" with which Scott had invested remnants of medieval institutions in Europe: his theme was "the decline of the old order before the growing liberalism of the new." [76] Nor was his interest in liberty purely a theoretical one, for during a crisis in the Polish struggle for freedom in 1831 Cooper presided at a meeting of Americans in Paris who were working for Polish relief.[77]

The three tales which indirectly expressed Cooper's liberal republicanism—*The Bravo* (1831), *The Heidenmauer* (1832), and *The Headsman* (1833)—mark the beginning of a protracted but not permanent retrogression in Cooper's art as a novelist. They are rarely read now. By common agreement *The Bravo* is the best of the three.[78] The weakest is *The Heidenmauer*, dubbed by Lounsbury "one of the most

tedious novels that Cooper ever wrote"— no mean distinction.[79] All
have European settings: *The Bravo* in Venice; *The Heidenmauer* in the
Palatinate; *The Headsman* in Switzerland. The cause of liberalism is
supported by various fictional methods. In *The Bravo* the oligarchical
control of Venice (in the days of her decline) is brought into prominence by the fate of the admirable Jacopo Frontini, who is executed
for instigating a much-needed revolt. In *The Heidenmauer* the issue is
drawn between the age-old domination of the Benedictine order and the
growing power of Lutheranism. In *The Headsman* an ancient tradition,
namely, that the son of a headsman must adopt his father's profession,
gives birth to actions illustrating the need of emancipating humanity
from the bondage to the past. Of the three stories, only the first has a
tragic ending.[80] In writing these stories against continental backgrounds
Cooper did not completely alter his fictional technique. Certain of the
new materials were congenial to him. Thus in *The Bravo* the theme of
espionage was a "natural" for him; and Jacopo, who is the *unwilling* spy of a decadent government, reveals admirable traits of character which led William Gilmore Simms to compare him with Natty
Bumppo.[81] Similarly, no reader of Cooper is surprised when Sigismund,
supposedly the son of a headsman, turns out to be the son of the Prince
of Genoa (in *The Headsman*). Other elements are as easily handled as
their American counterparts: a bit of natural scenery, a snow-storm, a
fire, a riot, the sacking of an abbey, etc. Occasionally Cooper seems
hampered by the narrow confines and unfamiliar materials of his European milieu—perhaps no more so than in the race of the *gondolas:* a
tolerably tame diversion for an author who had pitted ships of the line
against each other and deployed Indians against pioneers on the Great
Prairie! Nevertheless, Cooper was largely unsuccessful in these novels
because of his inability to get inside the psychology of individual
characters: his imagination was unequal to the effort. Moreover his
mind was on other things, chiefly, of course, using his story as a mirror
of liberal propaganda. He wished to write stories which should tell the
truth about medieval institutions instead of investing them with a false
romantic glamor such as characterized them in Scott's novels.[82] The
general tendency of the trilogy was expressed at the conclusion of *The
Heidenmauer:*

> Our object has been to show, by a rapidly-traced picture of life,
> the reluctant manner in which the mind of man abandons old to
> receive new impressions—the inconsistencies between profession
> and practice—the error in confounding the good with the bad,

in any sect or persuasion—the common and governing principles that control the selfish, under every shade and degree of existence—and the high and immutable qualities of the good, the virtuous, and of the really noble.[83]

In general the evil that men do is described fully in its nature and its consequences, but Cooper who, though a harsh critic, was no pessimist, generally contrived to show humanity triumphing over superstition and corruption. Even in *The Bravo*, which ends in the death of Jacopo, one senses the author's belief in the ultimate triumph of the *principle* of good. And that *principle*, he believed, could survive only when the cruelty and inertia of monarchical or oligarchical government was opposed by republican thought and action. America's free institutions, of course, could be seen in pleasant contrast to Europe's bondage, yet Cooper's purpose seems to have been not so much "to instruct Europe" as to provide America (for which he always really wrote) with "awful examples" of what might happen to the nation "if she permitted the selfish aims of a minority to get control of the machinery of democratic government." [84]

For America herself was soon to come in for her share of criticism from the candid critic of Europe's short-comings. There were signs of his impatience with his countrymen as early as 1832, when he wrote: "I know of no country that has retrograded in opinion, so much as our own within the last five years." [85] Doubtless his judgment was partly personal: he was somewhat irked, as his letters during the last few years of his European residence show, by adverse criticism of his writings.[86] But there were other causes as well. He returned to America in 1833 in no very good mood. When Irving had come home the year before, there had been a grand public dinner of welcome. But a similar dinner offered by admirers and public-spirited citizens of New York was cold-shouldered by the irascible Cooper, who immediately upon his arrival posted off to Washington on private business. He was back in America for good, and he soon returned to Cooperstown, where he acquired his father's old mansion, Otsego Hall, now dilapidated, and began to re-build his life as an American gentleman. But he could not pick up his old life where he had left off. He had gone through the vicissitudes of authorship; he knew the honey and gall of popular attention—and he was now (as he thought) in an unfortunate phase of his reputation: he seriously considered quitting authorship. His health was not good—would never, in fact, be perfectly sound again. Upon his arrival he had gloomily conceded that "the heart of the nation . . . is sound," [87] but he didn't at all like its outward appearances, and he feared for its future.

Under such conditions Cooper was not the man to be silent. Though he wrote less fiction, he by no means gave up authorship. Indeed for the rest of the thirties he wrote as actively as ever, but the more he wrote the more unhappiness he created for himself as well as for others. Not until 1840, when he wrote *The Pathfinder*, would he regain anything like the pleasant relationship with a large public which he had enjoyed in the early twenties.

Cooper's apparent reversal of opinion about his native land was shocking to his contemporaries. While abroad he had carried himself with an air which had plainly said that a republican out of the west was as good as a no-matter-how-ancient aristocratic family in decayed Europe. He had written books extolling his country's form of government and degree of progress. But when he came home, he seemed to think that the country had deteriorated while he was away! Doubtless it had in some respects: seven years is a long time. Possibly there had actually been a cultural retrogression during the era of expanding industry. In any case Cooper was depressed by what he saw. In the progress of growing "from gristle to bone" the country was exhibiting signs of crudeness and corruption. Cooper knew one reason for it: the shift in economic leadership from the landed classes to Wall Street: for "banking and the manipulation of credit seemed to him mean and sordid, and the spirit of speculation that was overrunning the land he believed was destructive of common morality." [88]

But there were other and more specific aspects of the national life that made Cooper unhappy. These he expounded in one of the most unfortunate publications he ever signed, *A Letter to His Countrymen* (1834). It is a document not entirely coherent but extremely forceful. It attacks the press, the Congress, the President. The press, which is subservient to foreign opinion, is largely responsible for the deterioration of democratic American ideals. The President has exceeded his powers in making certain diplomatic appointments. The Congress— the most dangerous branch of the government, for it cannot be impeached—has wrongfully censured Jackson for his action in removing deposits from the Bank of the United States. He fears that the Congress is emulating the English Parliament—a dangerous move toward the assumption of undue power that threatens to enslave the people. The American people, in turn, are to blame for their spineless acceptance of malfeasance. Thus Cooper manages to irritate both his country and her neighbors. He has a shaft for everyone. Worst of all, perhaps, is the aggressive and ill-tempered tone of the whole attack. Even William Gilmore Simms, who thought that Cooper was often maligned unjustly, referred to this publication as an "imprudent pamphlet" [89]—an understatement of a sort seldom employed by Cooper. For actually the centre of Cooper's thought—if one can reach to it amid so much confused polemic—is not either extremely unreasonable or uncomplimentary to his fellow-countrymen. He stands in this paper for strict construction of the Constitution and for a careful balance of executive, legislative, and judicial powers. For finally, he thought, the distinguishing feature of our government is popular sovereignty. Moreover in this scorching document Cooper utters final words of confidence:

> But the democracy of this country is in every sense strong enough to protect itself. Here the democrat is conservative and, thank God, he has something to conserve.[90]

In short it was Cooper's manner more than his matter that antagonized readers. There is no question that his original impulse in writing the *Letter to His Countrymen* was largely a personal and emotional one. He attacked the press because he believed the press, here and abroad, was conspiring against him. His book sales had fallen off for a number of years; as a writer he was discouraged and disgusted. Accordingly at the end of the *Letter* he announces his retirement from authorship. Actually, of course, he was far from through as a writer.

Only a year after the *Letter*, Cooper returned to the novel, publishing his most difficult story, *The Monikins*, in 1835. In this book, Cooper's "only attempt at sustained satire," [91] the literary tradition of Defoe and Swift is seen in an allegorical narrative in which the actions of monikins (manikin-monkeys) are intended to interpret the author's social views of England, France, and America. Cynical and supposedly humorous axioms on the nature of man are sprinkled through the book amid more or less serious discussion of such principles as the "social-stake" theory of society: "Cooper is attempting to examine the theory of a property qualification for suffrage, in its broadest and most humanitarian form, and to prove it unsatisfactory as a foundation principle for social government." [92]

Miscellaneous writing occupied Cooper between 1835 and 1838. He wrote two pieces on the Navy, several volumes of recollections of his travel years in Europe, an article on the relationship between himself and Sir Walter Scott, an historical sketch of Cooperstown, and *The American Democrat*.[93] The last-named carries additional views on the nature of a democracy. Believing that the power must rest with a people capable of exercising it intelligently, and that "power ought always to be chidden rather than commended," [94] Cooper gives plenty of fairly acid advice. Characteristically he attacks the press as a chief foe of democracy: for "The press tyrannizes over publick men, letters, the arts, the stage, and even over private life." [95]

Next came *Homeward Bound; or the Chase* and *Home As Found*, both published in 1838. *Homeward Bound*, as its preface indicates, was intended to be a sort of novel of manners describing "the present state of society in the United States" as it might be seen through the eyes of persons lately resident in Europe.[96] But the spell of the sea took hold of Cooper during composition with the result that the book describes very few "manners" and much sea adventure including a chase of "The Montauk" by a British frigate, fighting off the coast of Africa, and a great deal of hocus-pocus devoted to straightening out concealed and misunderstood identities among the personnel of the narrative. Not much new Cooper here—and not much of the best Cooper.

Home As Found hewed to its course better, but it isn't a successful novel. Social criticism is here aplenty: criticism of manners, dress, social intercourse, commerce, literature, the law, and the national temper in general. Fictional characters do the talking, but Cooper is obviously prompting them. New York is a disappointing "commercial town" instead of a "capital." The older generation of people depend too much on English opinion, while young America is raucously selfish. The inevitable levelling of pioneer society produces at first neighborliness and good will but later a jealous struggle for money and position. Despite advantages in a democracy, there is an "irresistible tendency to mediocrity, in a nation where the common mind so imperiously rules." [97] Many incidental opinions favorable to America are also aired, but the general effect is one of a fairly severe indictment of "Home As Found." Through the maze of description and polemic runs a thread of romantic love which finally unites Eve Effingham and Paul Powis—the only semblance of "plot" in the book. But a great deal of "plot" arose *out* of the book, for it was closely associated with the "Three Mile Point Controversy" and the "Effingham" libel suits. The facts in brief are that Cooper wished to put an end to the townspeople's use of certain property belonging to the Cooper estate and posted a notice to that effect. The townspeople resented the notice and presently a controversy began which embittered Cooper's life from 1837 to 1845. Newspapers which commented unfavorably on his conduct of the dispute were sued for libel on several occasions. The issue was at first privately discussed, but the publication of *Home As Found* gave it a much larger arena.

For *Home As Found* not only contained Cooper's opinions, but it was also to a considerable extent autobiographical. The Edward Effingham who is shown returning from a ten-year sojourn abroad (with his daughter Eve) is represented as a descendant of the Effingham family of *The Pioneers,* but he was naturally identified with Cooper when he was described as returning to a village hall, "The Wigwam" at "Templeton," patently modelled upon Otsego Hall at Cooperstown, recently bought by Cooper. And in fact Cooper devotes three entire chapters of his story to an episode closely paralleling the conditions of the "Three Mile Point Controversy." In the actual quarrel Cooper was well within his rights, and he won most of his libel suits (though the damages awarded were generally small),[98] but the affair caused needless unhappiness. Cooper was right, but in this instance as in many others, he showed a singular ability to make the better appear the worse reason. At the very outset of the controversy the folk of Cooperstown had voted to remove all Cooper's books from the local library—a sufficient suggestion that Cooper, though legally justified, had not handled the initial stages of the matter with tact and discretion. The loss to his popularity in the nation as a whole must have been considerable. In any case the merits of *Home As Found*—except for its wealth of social data of the period—were extremely slight. Even the general social criticism contained in the book was delivered with a blundering rudeness.[99]

After having wasted too much of his substance in critical writing for nearly a decade, Cooper fortunately returned in 1840 to the coadjutor of his best work—Natty Bumppo.[100] His disappointment in his country had been deep, but his diatribes, motivated in many instances by personal rancor, must have seemed fruitless after a time, for instead of meekly accepting the wisdom of the prophet Cooper, the public and the press had countered every criticism with equally energetic rebuttal: let this novelist stick to his last instead of meddling in politics. When Cooper did divest himself of his critical toga, he proved that his defection from the practice of straight fiction had not permanently impaired his art, for *The Pathfinder* and *The Deerslayer* are at least the equal of any two other books in the Leatherstocking series.

The Pathfinder: or, The Inland Sea carried the readers back to 1760 to follow an adventure set in a region that Cooper learned to know and love during his career in the Navy, namely, the Lake Ontario country. When Mabel Dunham and her uncle Charles Cap, presently to be joined by Natty (now in the prime of manhood) and Chingachgook, set out on a long trip under the guidance of Arrowhead, a train of romantic adventure is set in motion which only increases after the party reaches its destination. The campaign against the French provides plenty of excitement, of which the gale and the defense of the blockhouse are the principal focuses. Type characters are guilelessly repeated, but compensating variations are numerous. Charles Cap, who thinks fresh-water sailing immoral, is a splended creation of Cooper's humor. The garrison yields not only new action (the shooting match is exciting) but new types of men, some of them dissolute. Most of the men agree, however, in admiration for Mabel's charms. Handsome young Jasper Western, suspected of duplicity (chiefly, it appears, because he can speak French), is a stock specimen of ideal young manhood, but he is brought into a new situation when he finds that Natty (here called Pathfinder) is his unwitting rival for the hand of Mabel: Mabel's dying father had signified his hope that Pathfinder should marry Mabel. Natty's conduct when, after incredible blindness, he discovers what should have been immediately apparent—namely, that Mabel loves Jasper—is noble in extreme. Indeed the renunciation scene would have been a very fine one were it not for Cooper's commenting on the action (with a vestigial respect for European aristocracy that he never quite sloughed off) by saying that Pathfinder "had withdrawn, with a tact and a delicacy that might have done credit to the sensibility and breeding of a courtier." [101] Yet notwithstanding Cooper's tinkering as well as the hero's growing garrulousness, Natty is as interesting a character as ever—a mixture of the preacher and the woodsman—"a saint with a gun." [102] The action, as usual, exhibits lapses from realism at critical junctures, but the veil of illusion covers most of these for all readers but the prying critic. Certainly such logical lapses as occur in the book are less inimical to illusion than the critical digressions in his novels of manners. *The Pathfinder* is probably the best balanced book of the series: character, region, and action support each other perfectly.[103]

In *The Deerslayer*, a fictitious tale "of the First War-path," Cooper finally reached Natty's youth.[104] The action takes place around 1740 near lake "Glimmerglass," in a region easily identified as Cooper's own section of New York. Deerslayer (so called because he never took human life wantonly) is engaged in assisting Chingachgook to recover the maid, Hist, who has been abducted. This project, the outcome of which is deferred for some chapters, is sufficient to set in motion a vivid cycle of adventures involving an unusually interesting set of characters. Hurry Harry March, a frontiersman possessed of an exceedingly rude code of ethics, provides a good contrast for Deerslayer's honorable (though slightly priggish) character. Hurry's love for Judith Hutter, the glamorous toast of the British garrison, also sets him off from Natty, who successfully, if somewhat ludicrously, resists Judith's wooing. Judith's father, Tom Hutter, dissolute lord of Muskrat Castle (a house built on the lake), is a brute who unites with Hurry Harry March in believing that no deception or cruelty is too great to be practiced on an Indian. He ultimately suffers scalping and death. Hutter's other daughter, Hetty, is a half-wit useful because of the Indian partiality for white people who are known to be subnormal mentally. Deerslayer sometimes uses language of a lofty order that comports but badly with the uncouth idiom that Cooper granted him in previous books and to some extent in *Deerslayer*. Occasionally, also, he is too holy for rugged readers. Yet he is a hero of adventure par excellence—capable in action, noble in victory or defeat, and at once attractive to "the sex" and endowed with good defenses against it. The Indians are mixed beings capable of scalping a foe but also of allowing the captured Natty to go on a furlough—from which he honorably returns, presumably to be tortured. Ultimately the British provide a rescue. The love affair of Chingachgook, which precipitated all these adventures, evokes some of Cooper's most beautiful prose passages. Chingachgook, too, has been greatly altered from the Indian John who had been depicted during his last days—shiftless and drunken he was then—in *The Pioneers*. Here he embodies the romantic traits of the "noble savage." [105] Hist is a lovely Indian maid with no talent for understanding the discrepancy between the counsels of the Bible and the actions of the white people who read it. The landscape, which was a part of Cooper's boyhood memories, is painted without subtle technique but with a breadth and a grandeur suitable to the tale. The action, it is true, is full of those inaccuracies which Mark Twain listed in his enormously funny essay, "The Literary Offenses of James Fenimore Cooper." But it is idle to apply scientific tests to a romance, or even to insist too vigorously on the rule of common sense. After all discounts are made, *The Deerslayer* remains a fine story. With *The Pathfinder* it represents the height of Cooper's art as a writer of Indian romance, for it has most of the elements which made a success of *The Last of the Mohicans*, with added finish of language and higher flights of the imagination. It was a matter of course that these two books should be fiercely attacked by the hostile press, but there were enough commendations to minister to the *amour propre* of the author. One anonymous friend in England prayed that Cooper would henceforth produce "no more [books] like *The Heidenmauer*, or *The Monikins*" but would assign new adventures to Leatherstocking, for, said the admirer, "You have succeeded in making the Leather-Stocking as great a Hero as Homer has Achilles, or Virgil, Aeneas." [106] Undoubtedly extreme praise, perhaps good counsel, but it came too late: Cooper had permanently closed the book of Natty Bumppo's life.

But Leatherstocking's fame went marching on. Despite all difficulties —a partially hostile press, increasing competition from new American writers, and the dissemination of cheap pirated editions of English books—the time seemed ripe in 1849 for a collected edition of Cooper's works. This edition, published by Putnam and illustrated by F. O. C. Darley, was corrected in many minor details, revised in a few organic matters, and provided with a number of new prefaces. The famous preface to the Leatherstocking series appears in the new edition of *The Deerslayer*. In it Cooper comments on the "very desultory and in-artificial manner" in which the parts of the series were written. To this fact he ascribes certain defects and inequalities in the whole work; yet he expresses his confidence that

> If anything from the pen of the writer of these romances is at all to outlive himself, it is, unquestionably, the series of "The Leather-Stocking Tales." To say this, is not to predict a very lasting reputation for the series itself, but simply to express the belief it will outlast any, or all, of the works from the same hand.[107]

To those readers who have wished to know whether Natty Bumppo was based on an original in the flesh, Cooper remarked that physically his hero had "models" but that "in a moral sense this man of the forest is purely a creation." [108] The Natty he has tried finally to evolve has lived with white men and with Indians, and, though mainly "white" in his gifts, has been steeped in "the better qualities of both conditions." Thus Natty is a man who

> sees God in the forest; hears him in the winds; bows to him in the firmament that o'ercanopies all; submits to his sway in a humble belief of his justice and mercy; in a word, a being who finds the impress of the Deity in all the works of nature, without any of the blots produced by the expedients, and passion, and mistakes of man.[109]

In the same preface Cooper answers, in what for him are surprisingly moderate terms, those detractors who have insisted that his Indians didn't check with actuality. The point has been brought up time and again, and considerable nonsense has been written on both sides. Cooper, like most of his critics, knew little of the aborigines at first hand.[110] He had visited Indian reservations and had seen Indian deputa-tions; probably he had met some of the half-breeds that were roving about in New York even as late as the second quarter of the century.[111] But chiefly he had read about Indians in histories, journals, and treatises. Principal among his sources was John Heckewelder's *Indian Nations*

(1819), which reported, from direct observation, a Moravian missionary's opinion that the Delaware Indians were in general an admirable tribe and that the Iroquois were a pack of rascals. Cooper obviously took over not only Heckewelder's favorable opinion of the Delawares but many factual details as well. He also took the name Chingachgook. Such other sources as he used were subordinated to Heckewelder's book.

Attacks on Cooper's Indians had been prompt and sharp. One of the chief critics was General Lewis Cass, who had actually known some Indians. In 1826 Cass criticized Cooper for having relied upon Heckewelder, whose account he said was "mere unmixed panegyric." He asserted, moreover, that " 'The Last of the Mohegans' [was] an Indian of the school of Mr. Heckewelder, and not of the school of nature." [112] Later General Cass regretfully (for he liked Cooper's tales) admitted that "his Uncas and his Pawnee Hardheart, for they are both of the same family, have no living prototype in our forests." [113] Still later (in 1851) the historian Parkman remarked that Cooper's Indian characters were "for the most part either superficially or falsely drawn; while the long conversations which he puts into their mouths are as truthless as they are tiresome." [114] In short Cooper was repeatedly subjected to the same sort of critical fire as he had himself employed in his famous attack on the cave scene in Charles Brockden Brown's *Edgar Huntly*, an attack delivered from the platform of realism.[115]

Modern scholarly critics (not including the remorseless Mark Twain) have tended to defend Cooper. Some of them have gone too far. It is certain, however, that the early critics failed to take account of the different types of Indians drawn by Cooper: his Indians were by no means all of the genus Heckewelder. In general he drew two types of Indians: the treacherous and murderous Indian of the wild (generally Iroquois or Huron or Narrangansett or Sioux) and Indians (of whatever tribe) in the process of absorbing a measure of civilization from contact with white people.[116] He shows the virtues of both groups, but he also shows their vices, including drunkenness and abject cowardice. It is certainly wrong to imply as R. M. Bird did in 1837,[117] that Cooper failed to record the sins of the Indians. On the other hand he made a number of errors with respect to Indian lore, mixing his tribes, and mistaking certain of their military exploits.[118] Professor Gregory L. Paine, author of an admirable study of Cooper's Indians, insists that "Cooper's portraiture of Indians . . . is generally realistic." [119] So, too, Albert Keiser, who has examined most of the evidence: on the whole Cooper "has given the world a remarkably complete and faithful picture of the character and life of the aborigines of primitive America." [120] Here we find zeal for defense carried too far. Undoubtedly some of Cooper's Indians (especially perhaps Saucy Nick in *Wyandotté*, who figures little in these controversies) are realistic. Yet realism is not the fundamental aim of the Leatherstocking series, and it does not serve Cooper to try to make his red men realistic any more than it does to try to give Natty Bumppo a clean bill of logical health. The Indians would not have played their true part in Cooper's epic if their conduct had been checked by a board of experts in Indian lore. It is best to let literal critics have their say: it is idle to deny realistic errors. The best defense is Cooper's own defense in the preface to the Leatherstocking series in 1849. Admitting the depravity and degradation of many Indians, he begs to be excused from confining his descriptions to such characteristics. He craves the privilege of the imaginative writer:

> It is the privilege of all writers of fiction, more particularly when their works aspire to the elevation of romances, to present the *beau-idéal* of their characters to the reader. This it is which constitutes poetry, and to suppose that the red man is to be represented only in the squalid misery or in the degraded moral state that certainly more or less belongs to his condition, is, we apprehend, taking a very narrow view of an author's privileges. Such criticism would have deprived the world of even Homer.[121]

Natty's dossier was complete and filed away, but Cooper was far from having reached the end of the road as novelist. The books that remained to be written have, with a few definite exceptions, added little to his permanent fame. In general their quality suggests that their author's creative force was waning. No longer did he essay the higher ranges of imagination. It must be remembered, however, that the second wave of popularity of the historical romance (that of the thirties) had passed away.[122] *The Pathfinder* and *The Deerslayer* were in a sense autumn roses; soon would come a winter of discontent for writers of the historical romance, including Simms and others as well as Cooper. Aware that his métier was beginning to be outmoded, Cooper to some extent tried to write the sort of books he believed were in demand—especially "the novel of facts and ideas," [123] but his success, from a popular point of view, was variable and seldom great. Devotées of Cooper value some of these later books highly, however, and historians can find useful data in the amazingly copious and detailed descriptions which Cooper wrote to the last. From the point of view of the art of Cooper, the best of these later books are those which are richest in mellowing autobiographical matter—revealing the reminiscent, not the critical, Cooper.

First among the novels of this period come two sea stories. In *The Two Admirals* (1842), Cooper went back to the period of the Young Pretender's Rebellion. The rupture of friendship between two old English admirals over the respective merits of the House of Hanover and the Stuarts almost assures victory to the French in a vigorous naval battle, one of Cooper's best episodes, in the Bay of Biscay. But finally Admiral Bluewater's old loyalty to Admiral Oakes revives, and he dashes off to the rescue in standard story time. *The Two Admirals* is an inherently exciting but hastily told story showing relatively little of Cooper's abilities and weakly (although elaborately) supported by a hackneyed sub-plot involving the ambiguous parentage of a beautiful, dutiful young girl: as much as anything in Cooper, these naive but entangling sub-plots alienate the modern reader's interest. In *Wing-and-Wing* (1842) the marine maneuvers centre around a French privateer in the Mediterranean. The collateral theme is more interesting than that of *The Two Admirals*, being grounded in the dilemma of a young girl of the Catholic faith who finds herself in love with and loved by an infidel. When she fails to convert him, tragedy is the result. Cooper preaches a great deal in this novel, which, he professed, was one of his favorites.

Wyandotté; or the Hutted Knoll (1843) brings Cooper back to New York state in the period of the Revolution. As often in Cooper, there is distress over divided family allegiance: one member of the family is Royalist and one, Colonist. In between these, Captain Willoughby (retired British) favors neutrality. Of course the hutted knoll is besieged: this time the United States Marines are assigned rescue duty—though they do not arrive in time to save the fair Beulah from one of Cooper's stray bullets. There is also the fortunate discovery that Maud is only an adopted daughter of Captain Willoughby and therefore eligible to live happily ever after the war with young Major Willoughby. But the more original and valuable part of *Wyandotté* is Cooper's long account (taking almost half the book) of how Captain Willoughby obtains and develops his "patent"—a large grant of land south of Otsego Lake. Gradually he transforms the wild forested land into an organized settlement presided over by himself and provided with a stockade for defense. Here he lives with his family and his dependents as a kind of benevolent patron. Among his dependents is one of Cooper's most realistically drawn Indians, a Tuscarora who is alternately given to proud reminiscences of his chiefdom as "Wyandotté" and to periods of sloth, prevarication, and sullenness, when he is known as Saucy Nick. He never forgets kindness or injury, and his belated revenge for a flogging given him by Captain Willoughby is one of the grisliest scenes Cooper ever drew.

Edgar Allan Poe was one of the first readers of *Wyandotté*. He found in it a good many things to object to, particularly glaring faults of style and several structural weaknesses: he doubted if Cooper was "capable" of plot. Yet Poe admired Cooper's skill in "Robinson-Crusoe-like detail" in several of the portraits, particularly that of Wyandotté (alias Saucy Nick), the half-civilized Indian. He added that the "negroes are, without exception, admirably drawn"—high praise from an authoritative source.[124] Time, if not the general public, has endorsed Poe's opinion: for *Wyandotté*, stemming in large part from the author's early memories and observation of a cherished region, is not far inferior to Cooper's best works.[125]

A curious manifestation of Cooper's realistic mood, seen in *Wyandotté*, was his tendency to disparage American scenery. A large part of his reputation had been based on his exploitation of phases of American landscape that called for repeated use of such epithets as "grand," "awesome," "gigantic," "proud," "majestic," "sublime," etc. Now, in the very first chapter of *Wyandotté*, he was at pains to point out limitations of the scenes he had for these many years capitalized in the grand manner:

> There is a widespread error on the subject of American scenery. From the size of the lakes, the length and breadth of the rivers, the vast solitudes of the forests, and the seemingly boundless expanse of the prairies, the world has come to attach to it an idea of grandeur; a word that is in nearly every case misapplied. The scenery of that portion of the American continent which has fallen to the share of the Anglo-Saxon race very seldom rises to a scale that merits this term; when it does it is more owing to the accessories, as in the case of the interminable woods, than to the natural face of the country. To him who is accustomed to the terrific sublimity of the Alps, the softened and yet wild grandeur of the Italian lakes, or to the noble witchery of the shores of the Mediterranean, this country is apt to seem tame and uninteresting as a whole; though it certainly has exceptions that carry charms of this nature to the verge of loveliness.[126]

If the conception Cooper here seeks to dispel was a "widespread error," certainly he had done his part to foster it in almost every book he wrote before going abroad and in some later ones as well. Only three years before, in fact, he had found the very "principle of grandeur" in "the vastness of the view, the nearly unbroken surface of verdure" of a setting in *The Pathfinder*.[127] The explanation for this and other unenthusiastic references to his native land is doubtless partly artistic: in *Wyandotté* Cooper was writing under the aegis of realism more than in *The Pathfinder*. But doubtless, too, there is also, in the passage quoted, an indirect emotional expression of Cooper's dismay in the mid-eighteen-forties when his reputation seemed to be on the wane and his finances were undoubtedly so. In 1838 the British had passed a copyright law which heavily cut his profits both there and at home, for the law resulted in a flurry of cheap American pirated editions of English writers. Books by American writers had to be sold cheaply or not at all. From 1842 to 1849, therefore, "most of Cooper's novels were brought out at twenty-five cents a volume." [128] In 1846 Cooper complained of his situation:

> The cheap literature has destroyed the value of nearly all literary property, and after five and twenty years of hard work, I find myself comparatively a poor man . . . I do not think the last three books will nett me much more than $500 a book . . . I am unpopular with the country generally . . .[129]

In the same year when he was asked to write a story set in the South, he replied gloomily:

> My time is nearly done. At 57 the world is not apt to believe that a man can write fiction, and I have long known that the country is already tired of me. Novelties are puissant in this country, and new names take the names of old ones so rapidly that one scarcely learns to distinguish who are in favor before a successor is pointed out. My clients, such as they are, are in Europe, and long have been, and there is no great use in going out of my way to endeavor to awaken a feeling in this country that has long gone out.[130]

Thus various factors—age, literary fashion, and his slightly declining artistic powers—combined to make Cooper thoroughly disheartened. No wonder he began to speak more admiringly of foreign scenes and to disparage his own land. But authorship must go on.

Two shorter pieces next occupied Cooper: *Ned Meyers* (1843), a true biographical account of a sailor whom Cooper had known on his first voyage and who turned up many years later full of "copy," and

The Autobiography of a Pocket Handkerchief (1843), a brief and unsuccessful sketch of New York social life. Then came the two parts of a series called *Afloat and Ashore*, which appeared in June and December, 1844.[131] These two volumes followed the hero through a mélange of adventures interrupted by sessions of social and sociological discourse (frequently of a caustic order, for Cooper had begun to pull out the *laudator-temporis-acti* stop) on the follies of the present day. It seems clear that Miles Wallingford was charged with some of the same adventurous errands that Cooper had run in his youth (though the geography does not tally) and that Lucy Hardinge was the fictional portrait of his wife during the time when Cooper was courting her.[132]

There seemed no limit to the fertility of Cooper's brain or the vigor of his production. The so-called Littlepage Manuscript series, which occupied him soon after the *Afloat and Ashore* series, consisted of three large volumes: *Satanstoe* (1845), *The Chainbearer* (1845), and *The Redskins* (1846).[133] All three of the stories deal, directly or indirectly, with the Anti-Rent War that originated in the Rensselaer holdings (first granted in 1630 by the Dutch) in upper New York state in 1839. The issue in its simplest form was whether the patroon system of leasing land to small farmers should continue to operate or should be broken down by the outright sale of lands to individuals. Anti-Rent associations were formed in order to consolidate the strength of dissatisfied tenants, and many concessions were won. In 1846 the tide was turned in favor of the Anti-Renters when at the constitutional convention a clause was inserted "abolishing all feudal tenures and prohibiting the leasing of agricultural lands for more than twelve years."[134] In the whole affair Cooper was found, as he often was, on the side of those whom the common people regard as their enemies: he favored the patroon system. Yet he firmly believed that a primary error of the new democracy in America "lay in confusing the present will of the majority with the rule of the people."[135] He did *not* believe that democracy is predicated on the "notion that every husbandman is to be a freeholder."[136] In the case of the New York lands, he was convinced that the landed proprietors, who served as stabilizers and cultural influences in a prosperous community, were extremely valuable and that they "would do the most good at the least social risk of any social caste known."[137] Certainly they were infinitely superior, he thought, to the capitalistic (Wall-Street-dominated) aristocracy that seemed the ultimate alternative. Much as he admired Jackson, Cooper was revolted by a levelling equalitarianism. Not all he had ever said in his palmiest republican days about the superiority of American government to European could be construed to mean that Cooper believed all men equally capable of sharing administrative responsibilities. That everyone should be "on the same level in fortune, condition, education, and habits" was a "utopian" theory which, said Cooper (using an argument often invoked by theocratic founders of the Massachusetts Bay Colony as a justification of rule by a minority), "was probably never designed by divine wisdom." [138] He had respect for the honest artisan or peasant *as* artisan or peasant, but he felt that leaders were as important as workers:

> The column of society [he characteristically wrote] must have its capital as well as its base. It is only perfect while each part is entire, and discharges its proper duty. In New York the great landholders long have, and do still, in a social sense, occupy the place of the capital.[139]

Besides using these general grounds of argument, Cooper, who, as has been seen, was strongly property-minded, insisted that it would be wrong to invalidate existing land contracts.

Cooper's trilogy bearing on the Anti-Rent War is not severely polemical throughout. In fact the first volume, *Satanstoe*, is what Cooper called it—mainly a "chronicle of manners." [140] It forms a background for the climax of the Anti-Rent War (dealt with most fully in *The Redskins*), but it is occupied with the life and adventures of Cornelius Littlepage long before that climax—the main events of the story occurring in 1757-58 when the hero was twenty years old. The story is autobiographical in form, and like the other two in the series it purports to be part of the fictitious "Littlepage Manuscripts." Cornelius Littlepage is a Dutch-American lad, heir of a well-to-do and aristocratic family living at "Satanstoe," a neck (or "toe") of land in Westchester County. Without the least sign that he is in a hurry to get on toward critical events, the author details many phases of his young manhood. At Nassau Hall (Princeton) he gets a classical education and has fun baiting the New Englander Jason Newcome. Here and at New York (in Chapters III-V) Cooper's satire may be seen at its best. On his first visit to New York "Corny" is enthralled at miscellaneous metropolitan sights and by the amateur theatricals. He makes his bow in New York society—awkwardly, for he feels very much out-of-place as a provincial from Westchester County. In New York, too, Corny performs one of the least heroic rescues that Cooper ever devised: he saves a girl from a *caged* lion! The incident serves a romantic purpose, however, and when the young man rescues the girl again at Albany (this time from a Hudson River flood—with danger), the reader realizes that the two must marry. But before that can happen, the story must be carried on to Lake George, where the hero fights the Frenchmen and the Indians. In the northern part of the state, he also gets his first view of the Littlepage patent at "Mooseridge"—where the next unit of the trilogy will take up its action. *Satanstoe* is obviously put together in a mood of reminiscence, rather than built by the professional story-teller. It lives as a re-creation of olden days in New York, city and state. A score of pages are devoted to the Negro Pinkster festival—which has only the vaguest connection with the "action." There is time to visit Wall Street, Trinity Church Yard, and the Battery; time to note matters of pronunciation, dress, food, convivial drinking, and general deportment. British regiments are at hand, and our hero is thus introduced to several social strata in the city—all very different from the landed gentry he has left at Satanstoe. Interesting and authentic data for the historian, however, do not constitute the whole of *Satanstoe*, for all these items are registered upon the consciousness of one of Cooper's most attractive characters. Somehow the simplest actions of youthful Cornelius—in whom clearly runs some of the blood of Cooper—are endowed with an agreeably nostalgic air, an aura of gentle romance. Cooper could be very charming when his satiric sock was off, and there are passages in this book that are among the most delightful he ever wrote.[141]

In *The Chainbearer*, set after the Revolution, Cornelius' son, Mordaunt Littlepage, is seen on the family patent, improving the land and coming into conflict with squatters. In *The Redskins*, Hugh Roger Littlepage, grandson of Cornelius, is an actor in events brought about by the organization of the Anti-Rent groups to fight the descendants of the original patroons. Blood is spilled amid scenes which are given a touch of the picturesque by the fact that the Anti-Renters appear in the disguise of Indians. *The Redskins*, which is contemporary in its material, brings the series to an end. It is the most controversial of the three novels. By common consent the weakest of the three is *The Chainbearer*, which bogs down in detail, and the best is *Satanstoe*, which while merely providing an historical introduction to the Anti-Rent problem, proved to be the key which unlocked some of Cooper's most valuable memories. Cooper was at his best when he relied on old memories or on imagination. In contemplating the immediate scene critically, he wrote vigorously but without sufficient insight.

Cooper wrote on copiously to the end of his life. He had the habit of writing, and he had need of the added income, however shrunken, that it might bring. The stories he wrote after the Littlepage trilogy do not include any that are now considered among his best. On the

other hand, nothing that Cooper wrote is wholly negligible: if he wrote
pot-boilers, they contain more substance than most books so labelled
—for, however wrongheaded he may have been at times, however
tediously detailed at others, he seemed incapable of writing vacuously.
He had a keen and ranging mind, though not a flexible one. In *The
Crater* (1847) he uses a fabulous and short-lived island in the Pacific as
the setting for a story of a Utopia which exists happily enough until,
with the arrival of several clergymen, a lawyer, and an editor, seeds of
dissension are sown which presage the failure of the colony. It is a
book akin to *The Monikins* as an expression of the deep disillusionment
of Cooper. On account of its mood of disillusionment with democratic
procedure, *The Crater* also ranges Cooper alongside Melville and Mark
Twain. Although believed by Cooper to be a creditable book, *The
Crater* apparently did not take on. His bitter remarks to his wife
proved to be prophetic: "I like my new book [*The Crater*] exceedingly, and the part which I was afraid was ill done, is the best done. I
mean the close. Altogether, it is a remarkable book, and ought to make
a noise. If any one else had written it, it would be the next six months'
talk. As it is, it will probably not be much read in this country. Well,
there is not much love lost between us. It is a contemptible public
opinion at best." [142]

Cooper went to sea again in *Jack Tier* (1848),[143] but he used a good
deal of the same equipment, now badly worn, that he had used in *The
Red Rover* years before. Its comedy is jejune, its tragedy unconvincing. It had, however, a topical interest in its protest against the
Mexican War. Another novel of scant value appeared in 1848—
Oak Openings; or the Bee-Hunter. Though in one sense the book had
a fresh inspiration, Cooper having recently made a trip into the Mid-
Western milieu used in the story, in another it was vieux jeu, for in
it the author took to the pulpit to show how a war-like Indian turned
Christian upon observing the way in which a Methodist minister could
die. Doubtless a fine lesson is here, but the story is lost in absurdity.
The Sea Lions (1849), erring on the side of dullness more than of absurdity, is also an inferior narrative, but it is harnessed to some interesting disquisitions on the theme of Unitarianism as opposed to Trinitar-
ianism. As in *Wing-and-Wing*, the religious problem is also a romantic
problem, for hero and heroine are divided on the issue. In this case
the hero gives in and avows that henceforth he will no more "set up
his own feeble understanding . . . in opposition to the plainest language of revelation as well as the prevalent belief of the Church." The
victory is arbitrarily wrested from the young man by the author rather
than decided by the strategy of the story.[144] The *mise-en-scène* in the

extreme South Seas is in part well described, but in one writer's opinion it serves chiefly to help establish the moral: "that dwellers in the chilly spiritual clime of Unitarianism can be cured of their fault in that icy creed by being subjected to the horrors of a polar winter." [145]

Only one novel remained to be written by Cooper, *The Ways of the Hour* (1850). The germ of this book (like that of the preceding) was undoubtedly intellectual: Cooper wished to descant on the current issue of trial by jury. Naturally he gave an unfavorable verdict, for by now Cooper definitely refused to believe that one man was as good as another.[146] Here was subject matter for an essay or a treatise, but Cooper was too confirmed a story-teller to forbear providing the usual pictorial framework. As usual he managed to spur his energies to the creation of a few good scenes (such as the climax of the trial),[147] and, as often, he failed to weld story and disquisition without crude patchwork.

Cooper's hour was at hand, too, but he laid one more offering before the American public before he died—a satirical comedy called *Upside Down; or, Philosophy in Petticoats*, which was played for three June nights in 1850.[148] In September the author was dead. His astonishing force and tenacity as a productive writer had over-matched his physical capacity at last.

CRITICISM OF GOVERNMENT AND SOCIETY

Cooper's written comments on government and the structure of society in general are in the aggregate enormous. They are also full of real and apparent contradictions. The complexity and rapidly shifting nature of national politics during the thirty-year period of his authorship doubtless explain some of his changes of front. Sheer inconsistency and emotional bias may explain others. At heart, however, Cooper was not quite so vacillating as has sometimes been held.

What, then, if anything, was constant in Cooper? Probably only one thing essentially—his deeply rooted love of country: about that there is no doubt. Far more than Irving he was dependent on America for his happiness. Even during his bitterest wars with the press, even when he was obsessed by the idea that he was being persecuted by people and press in a vast conspiracy, even when he expressed a wish that he could leave the United States for good and all,[149] Cooper's deepest suffering lay in the thought that he was being attacked in the land he loved.

But the land changed. Cooper was conservative by nature, and he always disapproved of the people who "court change for its own sake." [150] He dreaded innovation, and such pressure as he exerted by his pen was predicated on a belief that America had retrogressed. He merely wished to remold things nearer to his original conception of an ideal society. That ideal society, in the simplest terms, was a society founded on patriarchal principles, with a benevolent and respected chief at the centre surrounded by contented retainers and tenants who gladly tilled his land for the sake of his protection and guidance. These retainers were, as he conceived them, a quiet corps of peasantry perfectly willing to live out their days as peasants—not a potential band of revolutionists clamoring for more and yet more "rights." The vigorously independent "coonskin democracy" that existed farther west would have been hard to fit into this scheme. The true son of his aristocratic father, Cooper coveted an old order in a new land—a sort of innocent *ancien régime américain*. The "squire" would cherish his retainers in true Roger de Coverley fashion, and the retainers would nurse no unruly ambition to "rise" in the world. Even slavery Cooper looked upon with little horror, and although he professed himself as in favor of a slow emancipation program, he furiously condemned Northern violators of the Fugitive Slave Law: [151] such acts of property-violation alienated landlords of the South. Slaves, too, could lead a contented plantation life. It was an implied condition of Cooper's plan that people should live mainly in the country. He liked a woodsman who would stay a woodsman (didn't Natty Bumppo?)—not a restless fellow who was planning to go off to the city and become a real estate operator. Cooper himself liked occasionally to sample the society of the city, but first and last he spilled a great deal of ink denouncing various urban capitals, including New York City. Commerce was a hideous necessity perhaps, but no logic could force him to approve of it: he hated the smell of mercantilism. There were overlords in the city, too, and of the worst class: they were money barons of Wall Street. The landed proprietor in the country exercised rights, yes, but he did so benevolently. He cared for his people equally. His leadership was not inconsistent with democracy, for all the interests of the community were basically unified. His "aristocracy" was in reality a blessing to the people. [152]

There were two things which could threaten such an idyllic state as Cooper imagined: malfeasance by a corrupted (financial) aristocracy and aggression from below. Cooper feared both. Abuse of the squire-archical system in America Cooper seems not to have regarded as a serious danger, but in his younger days he vigorously denounced European countries for tolerating governments in which a traditional "nobility" tramples on simple human rights. During the Revolution of 1830 he even feared that the Whig party in America "represented a threat to restore monarchy itself" in this country.[153] During his own European residence, healthy republican convictions stabilized him. He might wish his daughters to have the advantages of Old World culture, and he might himself enjoy the amenities of dining with French aristocrats; but he could not approve their form of government or their essential contempt for the lower classes. Much of Cooper's invective for years to come would be based on his disapproval of foreign modes of life and foreign opinion.

The other threat to Cooper's ideal society was bumptious class assertion from below, with its inevitable corollary, namely, domination by that metropolitan moneyed class which ultimately takes advantage of an unprotected proletariat. In some ways, aggression of the lower classes bothered Cooper more than corruption of feudal lords: it was just as wrong and even more odious. In his discussion of the ideal "democratic gentleman," Cooper asserted that the "same principles and manliness that would induce him [*i.e.*, the "democratic gentleman"] to depose a royal despot, would induce him to resist a vulgar tyrant." [154] Indeed after his return to America in 1833 Cooper spent more energy in attacking vulgar pretensions to power than aristocratic.[155] Much of that vulgarity he found in the Whig party, which, he thought, was responsible for the spread of low ideals among the common people. Doubtless it was the Whig party, too, which fostered the spread of that irresponsibility which is one of the greatest dangers to a democracy.[156] The country, it seemed to Cooper at times, was going to the dogs. Manners were being corrupted; the simple life was almost gone. And when the Anti-Rent War began to threaten one of the last strongholds of enlightened aristocracy, Cooper was completely disheartened and embittered. He could only mourn the past. For Cooper was not really a progressive person: he did not wish to reform but to restore. He yearned nostalgically for something like the life he had known in his father's mansion at Otsego many years before.

All this is of course a little too simple an explanation to fit Cooper's varied and unpredictable conduct during the last twenty-five years of his life. Lover of the past, he had to live in the present. Cooper was at first an "unconscious aristocrat," but he had later to decide rationally upon a socio-political creed; he had to *join,* whereas at first he merely *belonged.* It was a necessity which exasperated him. Which of the various political evils available to him would he regard as the least objectionable? Superficially one might have expected him to become a member of the Whig party, traditionally regarded as the lineal descendant of the Federalist party. But the Whig party was by no means the reincorporation of the Federalist party,[157] and, in fact, "Cooper identified Americanism with Jacksonian Democracy as positively as his father's generation before him had identified it with Federalism." [158] Moreover, even American politics were perhaps not utterly hopeless. He did not "quit" politics any more than he did letters. He grumbled but he worked. It was Cooper's misfortune to voice his dissent and his pessimism so eloquently that such courageous or optimistic observations as he delivered have been relatively neglected. Even in his extremely unlucky *Letter to His Countrymen* he had spoken of the essential soundness of the nation. There, too, as frequently, he exhorted his compatriots to cherish and be proud of their democracy, which, he assured them, was strong enough to survive. Cooper was cantankerous; he scolded and fretted and fumed about this and that defect of America, but underneath all his querulousness lay a deep affection. He was like the parent who nags but loves his erring child. If he had become the self-appointed guardian and critic of his country, he had partly earned the right to do so by his devotion to its welfare.

LITERARY THEORY

No strongly original or completely articulated theory of literature emerges from Cooper's many references to the art of writing. Yet his literary creed, in its broadest aspect, was closely related to his political thought. He was keenly aware of the need of being national. By being national he meant giving expression to those aspects of American life and thought which were most distinctive, namely, our political and religious institutions; all else we share with England:

> It is quite obvious that, so far as taste and forms alone are concerned, the literature of England and that of America must be fashioned after the same models . . . The only peculiarity that can, or ought to be expected in their [*i.e.*, American] literature, is that which is connected with their distinctive political opinions.[159]

He did not of course wish writers to confine their efforts to discussing large issues of religion or politics but counseled them to describe such "customs" as are "connected with principles, in their origin, development, or end." [160]

Truth he held up as the great ideal of the writer, but he interpreted the term with the same breadth that characterized much of his thinking and writing. He was greatly interested in detail and he knew that imaginative literature thrives upon it, but factual accuracy he did not propose always to observe. As early as 1823 he began to create critical justification for his own methods by drawing the distinction between the obligations of the historian and the historical-romance writer:

> The privileges of the Historian and of the writer of Romances are very different, and it behooves them equally to respect each other's rights. The latter is permitted to garnish a probable fiction, while he is sternly prohibited from dwelling on improbable truths . . .[161]

He repeatedly asserted—what later became routine prefatorial matter for historical romance writers—that the writer need not manacle his imagination by writing as if under oath, for it is "possible to render that which is purely fictitious even more useful than that which is strictly true, by avoiding extravagance, by portraying with fidelity, and . . . by 'generalizing' with discretion." [162] In *Wyandotté* he is more concerned to tell the broad truth, even if it be unpalatable, than to be scrupulously accurate in "historical" detail. If the story has an anachronism, he is not worried, for "the incidents of this tale are believed to be sufficiently historical for all legitimate purposes of fiction." [163] He appeared to think that unpleasant truths needed more substantiation than pleasant ones. In any case he had an answer for critics who accused him of excessive idealization: "A leading character in a work of fiction," he wrote in his preface to the Leatherstocking series (in 1849), "has a fair right to the aid which can be obtained from a poetical view of the subject." [164] The same sort of defense he offered in reply to those who criticized his Indians as too sweet.[165] In short Cooper believed that the imaginative writer should present truth, pleasant or unpleasant, with fidelity to its broad outlines but not necessarily with complete observation of literal accuracy.

Holding such views as these Cooper naturally set a high value on a novelist's skill in invention—an aspect of fiction in which he excelled—and, next in importance, upon *vraisemblance*.[166] With precise motivation, by the same token, he was comparatively little concerned. Closely knit and carefully ordered sequences of events carried forward with an air of inevitability one does not look for in an author so much given as Cooper was to the apt aid of coincidence and "fate." Indeed he was inclined to make a virtue of the use of fortuitous elements in stories, for:

> Chance has usually as much to do with the fortunes of states, as with those of individuals; or, if there be calculation connected with them, at all, they are the calculations of a power superior to any that exists in man.[167]

Philosophy and psychology as aids to fiction Cooper appeared to scorn. He was himself an active critic but nothing of a philosopher, and he frequently took digs at writers who conceived of themselves as "metaphysicians." Similarly he laid no claim to what would now be called psychological insight. Nor did he deem it part of his responsibility to probe into the deepest recesses of the human mind: enough if one could touch the mainsprings of behavior. This point he brought out with some asperity in response, apparently, to criticism of the simplicity of his characters, their conduct, and their emotional patterns:

> Our business is solely to treat of man, and this fair scene on which he acts, and that not in his subtleties, and metaphysical contradictions, but in his palpable nature, that all may understand our meaning as well as ourselves—whereby we manifestly reject the prodigious advantage of being thought a genius, by perhaps foolishly refusing the mighty aid of incomprehensibility to establish such a character.[168]

Nearly everything in Cooper's observations on the theory of writing points to his reliance upon the elementary virtues of clarity and naturalness. He had only contempt for the methods of the sophisticated New York literati whom he encountered after he returned to New York in 1833, and whom he satirized in *Home As Found*. Too many ephemeral writers were likely to substitute sound for sense:

> To them it is a profound mystery that the "strongest writing" is that in which the just ideas are expressed in the simplest language, and the "weakest writing" is that in which, when the froth has gone, it is found that the substance has disappeared along with it.[169]

In short Cooper's literary theory at its basis is predicated on the belief that the writer must possess substantial thoughts which he will set down honestly and plainly. What he wrote in a letter to his son Paul in 1843 briefly expresses his cardinal convictions: "Nature and simplicity are the great secrets, as to style, as well as to declamation. All fine writing must have its root in the ideas." [170]

"Nature and simplicity"—how well the words apply to Cooper's own production as a writer. His literary output, like his capacity for dissent, was so enormous that generalizations about it are likely to break down—even if, for the moment, one leaves out of consideration the stories of "fact and ideas." Yet it is clear that Cooper lived chiefly by a few rules for writing. Coming late to a craft for which he had no technical training, he remained an amateur to the last in many respects, but his millions of readers are sufficient testimony to his having possessed important keys to reader-interest. His main plots (leaving out the mislaid relative motif) are generally simple in design, and although they are slow in getting under way, they gather tremendous momentum.[171] The flight-and-pursuit pattern on which many of the stories are based is perhaps the simplest of all story devices, but Cooper uses it with uncommon skill, employing pursuit, capture, renewal of peril, and final reckonings with a fine sense for the maintenance of suspense. Good fortune generally attends good people, but Cooper keeps his readers guessing, for occasionally there is considerable carnage and not *all* the good people can be saved. As for the miscellaneous miraculous exploits his characters perform on land and sea, their story value is partly proved by the parodies they evoked.[172]

Cooper's landscape, like his action, is of a simple sort: it generally consists of a magnificent back-drop to which the author calls attention at intervals. Descriptive strokes are of the broadest sort, for Cooper did not wish to itemize nature. No violet by a mossy stone could detain the author of adventures which would embrace leagues of virgin wilderness. While Bryant was stooping over a fringed gentian, Cooper was covering acres. His magnificent description of the Hudson in *The Spy* embraces almost the whole river in a paragraph. Nor did Cooper command the language necessary for discriminating study of the nuances of nature. He was content to produce minor variations of a few formulas in which either "sublimity" or "picturesqueness" was the preponderant element. Hardly any writer has rivalled him in the power to suggest the solitude and vastness of the American continent—forest, mountain, inland lake, and plain—centuries before man's original occupation of the land. Nor is the average reader likely to demand more than the general descriptive outlines afforded by Cooper. If Cooper could not describe natural scenes subtly, he felt them strongly.

People were harder to devise than action or setting. When Balzac, one of the strongest champions Cooper ever had, said that "If Cooper had succeeded in the painting of character as well as he did in the painting of the phenomena of nature he would have uttered the last word of our art," [173] he was at once too complimentary to Cooper's nature description (a natural error in one who read in translation) and unduly severe in his criticism of Cooper's characters. It is true that Cooper paints characters with primary colors, but the colors are often vividly applied. No doubt, too, there are dozens of undifferentiated characters (especially gentlewomen) who seem absurd to the sophisticated generation of a hundred years later. But these simple folk were necessities in stories. Scott is full of them. They are not really characters at all but people in costume. They are described adequately from top to toe in such a way as to make one feel that one might recognize them again "if they happened to be wearing the same clothes." [174] But to compensate for these wooden people there are scores of characters (from high life as well as low) who are well drawn. They are not studied with psychological finesse, but they are humanly credible and humanly interesting. They are now laughed at for irrelevant details of literary fashion by a generation which has produced few novelists capable of characterizations as real. Betty Flanagan, Charles Cap, Aristabulus Bragg, Mike O'Hearn, Hiram Doolittle, Saucy Nick, Ishmael Bush, Admiral Bluewater, Cornelius Littlepage—these and dozens of other intermediate characters in Cooper are of such quality that no apology is needed for their existence. They will live longer than many a "complex" character got 'twixt the Freudian sheets of the novel of the 1920's. Other creations of Cooper reach an even higher level of achievement: Harvey Birch, Chingachgook, and Tom Coffin. And Natty Bumppo: the folly of denying Cooper the ability to depict human character is climaxed by those who fail to see the distinction of Leatherstocking. One may not *like* Natty; one may find faults in the loose synthesis of traits with which Cooper endowed his hero between 1823 and 1841. One may protest at the inconsistent language Natty is made to speak. One may yawn at his ethical essays. Yet, all cavilling admitted, Natty Bumppo claims rank with the greatest fictional creations. More than one disinterested critic has linked Cooper's hero with the great imaginative embodiments of earlier days. In the course of a not exclusively favorable estimate of Cooper, Lowell affirmed (in his *Fable for Critics*) that

> . . . Natty won't go to oblivion quicker
> Than Adams the parson or Primrose the vicar.

Sainte-Beuve assigned him to the company of Panurge, Gil Blas, and Clarissa Harlowe. Thackeray had no hesitation in granting Cooper highest honors:

> I have to own . . . that I think the heroes of another writer, viz.,
> Leatherstocking, Uncas, Hardheart, Tom Coffin, are quite the
> equals of Scott's men; perhaps Leatherstocking is better than any
> one in 'Scott's lot.' *La Longue Carabine* is one of the great prize
> men of fiction. He ranks with your Uncle Toby, Sir Roger de

Coverley, Falstaff—heroic figures all, American or British—and the artist has deserved well of his country who devised them.[175]

Surely a character who can command such panegyric as this is not to be lightly dismissed; the enemies of Cooper err when they centre their attack on his characterization.

No, it is not Cooper's action or setting or characterization which imperils his fame but another aspect of his work, namely, his style. This it is which places in jeopardy all his distinguished resources as a novelist. Undoubtedly one of the most widely read writers in the history of Anglo-Saxon fiction, Cooper is probably the most inferior of this group in point of style. His blundering ineptitude of phrase casts its malign effect on scene, setting, and character. It is rhetorical infelicities which tend to convert his characters into caricatures, his descriptions into copy book platitudes, his actions into farce or melodrama. The explanation of Cooper's stylistic faults is probably two-fold: (1) skill in sheer language was not his gift, and (2) he wrote too rapidly: by forcing the growth of his books he forfeited flavor. He was ready in conception but impatient of the processes of nurture. His art was largely based upon inspiration. Nor did it avail him to write at slower speeds; when he labored in research, he lost energy and he made no compensating gains. In the naively literal and elaborate detail of certain "realistic" passages he can be unutterably tedious—a kind of rural Theodore Dreiser. High-flown embellishments in the worst possible taste vitiate crucial episodes in the life of Leatherstocking. There is no denying the fact that in the sheer manipulation of language Cooper was often a supreme bungler.

This is Cooper's principal defect—his style. But there are in him also certain limitations which reduce his interest for large sections of the reading public. He is by nature a surface writer. He has more energy than insight. Certain areas of interest he never explored or even understood. He strode blindly over many human problems with very little sign that he comprehended sociological phenomena. Sailors as a class he tended to be aloof from. The social and political disabilities of women interested him little: he was old-fashioned on this score. Nor did his stories interest women readers greatly; his minutiae were not of the sort, as he noted in *The Pilot*,[176] to make him "a favorite with females." He had a sharp sense of legal justice, but he was not notably humanitarian. Complexities of many sorts eluded him. He wrote often of love but seldom of "passion." Philosophical abstractions and ambiguities did not detain him long. He combatted "wrong," but hardly came to grips with the essential nature of evil: enough if he could round up "miscreants" and "varmints" in the flesh! Even in his stronger areas, he disclosed limitations. He expressed the force and attraction of the sea, but not the subtlety. Melville's oracular utterances and brooding cosmic speculations must have been lost on Cooper. For Conrad's Marlow, there is reason to believe, he would have had mostly scorn. Cooper was a plain man with simple ideas to which he gave forthright expression.

More than many writers Cooper has need of that fundamental and primary charity of criticism: that a writer should be judged on the basis of what he attempted to accomplish. Cooper must be taken at his best, whether it be in the comparatively realistic re-creation of early American life of such books as *Satanstoe* and *The Pioneers* or in the grossly improbable but spiritually truthful tales of Leatherstocking. The great error in estimating Cooper is to apply the wrong set of principles to his epic of America. To test an epic hero by laboratory devices is as palpably unfair as it is naive. One does not measure the *Beowulf* by its conformity to physical laws governing cause and effect. One does not scrutinize the *Iliad* for lapses from logic. Longfellow's *Hiawatha* is not the less valuable for being poetic rather than realistic. So with the Leatherstocking series. No harm in Mark Twain's superbly clowning analysis of *The Deerslayer*—if one does not use it as a critical text. Much better to follow the advice of D. H. Lawrence, a writer whose gifts were in most ways the antithesis of Cooper's, but whose intuitions taught him how to read Cooper. Do not read *The Deerslayer*, Lawrence advised, as a study in realism: "Read it as a lovely myth . . ." [177] A lovely myth—that is the essence of epic. Time and distance are its aids; suspension of disbelief is its commandment. Read in this fashion Cooper's tales, too, take on epic proportions. Their faults are for the moment lost in that larger view which lends national significance to individual deeds. If, as one critic has recently said, "intelligent people find they can no longer read Cooper," [178] something is obviously wrong. It should be easier to change "intelligent people" than to change Cooper.

— V —

Contemporaries and Immediate
Followers of Cooper, I

JOHN NEAL (1793-1875)

Among the contemporaries of Cooper none was more original than John Neal (1793-1875), a Maine Yankee of Scotch or English or Irish descent.[1] He was possessed of a limitless exuberance which explained both his success and his failure as a writer. His enormous ambition, his warm imagination, his generous sympathies, his passionate convictions, his genially quarrelsome nature, and his boundless egotism tempered by keen humor marked him as a man who must write vividly if at all. Unable or unwilling to discipline himself, however, he substituted a sort of wild improvisation for hard work. The violence and velocity of his early novels commanded instant attention but soon wearied the public. Story and style alike were splintered by the hurricane of his inspiration; and the reader, stunned by his experience, scarcely knew what had happened. With more art Neal might have rivalled Cooper as a writer of romance or Poe as an exponent of the tale of terror. In his rarer moods of quiet reflection he might have produced charming regional stories of New England. As it was, he never fully developed any one of his brilliant abilities. Accordingly Neal is now remembered chiefly as the eccentric and slightly choleric author of a few freakish novels and as a friend of Poe. Most of his books are out of print and they are largely inaccessible. Nevertheless no writer can be wholly ignored whose romances could intoxicate Hawthorne's "boyish brain." [2] In any case Neal deserves attention as an early experimenter with native materials in fiction and as a colorful critic of literature during the difficult days when American writers were just beginning to *be* American.

Neal was born in Portland, Maine. Destined to be a fighter all his life, he was brought up a Quaker. Capable of the most prodigious literary productivity, he spent twelve years in mercantile life. He was the commercial partner for a time of the poet John Pierpont, but they were forced into bankruptcy not long after the War of 1812. Neal profited, however, by his association with Pierpont, whose *Airs of Palestine,* published in 1816, presently made him one of the best-known poets in America. In Baltimore, Pierpont was one of the founders of a literary club, the "Delphians," and out of that club grew a magazine, the *Portico,* which was destined to be the theatre of Neal's first literary appearance. One day when Pierpont declined to write a review of Byron's works, Neal, who happened to be present at the time, intrepidly offered himself as a substitute. The offer was regarded as a joke by everyone but Neal. Then followed four frenzied days, during which "Jehu O'Cataract" (such was Neal's nickname and pen-name) read all of Byron's published works and produced a fifty-five page review, which was greeted enthusiastically upon its serial appearance in the *Portico.*[3] Thus Neal's career as a writer was characteristically launched. At the same time he was studying law, but although he was admitted to the Maryland bar in 1819, he practiced only intermittently: letters would be his prime vocation for the next decade or so at least.

Contributing to the *Portico* brought fame but not funds. Accordingly Neal dashed off a novel, peddled it unsuccessfully, rewrote it, changed its title, and finally "entrapped" a publisher, who paid him two hundred dollars for it. This, Neal's first novel, was published in 1817 under the title *Keep Cool: A Novel.* It is a story of a man who suffers remorse after killing his opponent in a duel. On the title page Neal facetiously referred to the book as "Written in Hot Weather, by Somebody." Apparently cold weather soon overtook the novel, and its author remained a nobody except to a small circle of friends who kept insisting that Neal was a genius. Neal himself later admitted that *Keep Cool* contained much of which "even a young writer might well be ashamed; much indeed that was boyish, if not absolutely childish."[4] During the interval between *Keep Cool* and his next novel, Neal was busy with a number of projects including writing poetry[5] and considerable literary hackwork, besides his law studies. In 1822 he reappeared as a novelist with *Logan,* which, though crude in many respects, was successful enough to encourage the author to write stories furiously for a number of years to come.

Logan, A Family History (1822) arose out of Neal's desire to see justice done to the Indian. The humanitarian interest in it—which, besides the plight of the Indian, touches on slavery,[6] imprisonment for debt, and capital punishment—is in fact considerable, but it is overshadowed by the amazing narrative of Logan and his family. Neal's Logan, an Englishman, is a partly real and partly legendary character—

a sort of superman—married to an Indian queen. His gigantic stature and his implacably cruel temperament make him an ideal warrior-leader among the Indians. When part of his wife's family is murdered by white people he vows vengeance, but is prevented from consummating it when the Indians discover that *he* is a white man and attempt to kill him. On what he supposes to be his death bed he entreats Harold, his son, who has been brought up as an Indian, to take up the red man's burden. This ultimately involves Harold's going to England and addressing Parliament on behalf of the Indians. Returned to America, he is shot down by his father on the spot where his father was believed to have died. Actually Logan had lived on, a raving maniac, killing everyone who crossed his path. Harold's brother now completes the catastrophe by shooting Logan before he recognizes him as his own father. He himself soon after dies a madman. In the meantime many complications have been brought about by Harold's synchronous love for the wife of a governor who has befriended him and for Loena, an Indian princess, the last direct descendant of the historic old Indian chief Logan. Harold had taken Elvira (the governor's wife) by violence, but later suffered remorse, which was rendered the more acute by his discovery that his brother had once loved her too. His final devotion, however, had been to Loena—who upon Harold's death herself fell dead upon his body. It should be added in a story in which four out of the five principal characters apparently die and are reanimated, that these last-cited deaths are permanent.

Logan is not a nice story. Superstition, supernatural suggestions, brutality, sensuality, colossal hatred, delirium, rape, insanity, murder are the stuff out of which Neal weaves a Gothic tapestry never quite paralleled by Charles Brockden Brown or Poe. Characters live constantly on the peak of extreme emotions generally of the more horrible sort. On one occasion the heroine is fain to restore her failing strength by drinking the blood of a pigeon shot by Harold:

> He fired, and a pigeon came fluttering, from mid-heaven, almost to his feet. Loena started at the sound of the shot, and in the first terrour of the moment, shrieked to find herself alone. The next, her head was supported upon his knee, the bosom of the bird was laid open, and applied, bleeding, to her lips. She shut her eyes, in her loathing, but still, with an unconquerable eagerness, that showed how nearly famished she was, she pressed her mouth to it, and, if her newly opened eyes told true, she drew new life with the red moisture from its heart. Harold leant over her with looks of unutterable fondness.[7]

A fight is not complete without the most harrowing and sometimes incredible details:

> Their blades met. Harold was the more wary, the more lightning-like, but the stranger was bolder, and stronger. Both were resolute as death. Several wounds were given, and received. Harold's sword broke to the hilt. He threw himself upon the stranger and bore him to the earth, wrenched his sword from him, and twice, in his blindness and wrath attempted, in vain, to pass it through and through his heart, as they grappled together. But twice the Englishman caught the sharp blade in his hands, and twice Harold drew it, by main force, through his clenched fingers, slowly severing sinew, and tendon, and flesh, and grating on the bones, as it passed. Harold gasped—the Englishman held him by the throat—the blood gushed from his ears and nostrils—once more!—he has succeeded! The blood has started through the pores of the brave fellow below him! His arteries are burst—He is dead—dead!—nailed to the earth, and Harold is sitting by him, blinded, and sick.
>
> A half hour has passed. The horse stamps, impatiently, by the corse. Why stands Harold thus, gazing upon the red ruin before him, with such a deadly hatred? [8]

The reader is at first shocked by the ghastly detail of the book, but he soon becomes calloused to further attack on his sensibilities, the more so because of the fact that in his hot pursuit of blood and bombast Neal allows the larger action of the story to become almost hopelessly confused.

Sometimes, however, Neal's penchant for horror carried him into psychological realms where his methods are a trifle less objectionable. His analysis of Harold's mental distress is distinctly suggestive of Poe in this respect:

> Alas, for Harold! A continual and confused ringing was about him, all night long. Worn, and trembling, and sick at heart, time appeared to stand still, as he turned, again and again, and adjusted his limbs to the rugged cordage, upon which he lay, until he was utterly exhausted.
>
> .   .   .   .   .
>
> And then his conscience would awake, and put on her bloody robes, and sit over him with a terrible countenance—and he would feel himself pinioned, naked, hand and foot—helpless, alone—with just enough of light to see the far off and dim movement of innumerable feet, incessantly approaching in the darkness, as of

some cumbrous, and interminable monster—and to feel ten thousand detestable and obscene creatures crawling slowly over his very lips and eyes, which he had no power to shut—slimy, loathsome reptiles, slipping lazily over his naked fingers; while his very flesh crawled and quivered, and rotted, in the poison that they left in their trail. Anon, this would be changed. The light would break out upon him—he would be sleeping in a delicious green solitude —the earth flowering all about him, with fountains flowing 'in odour and gold'—and violets—'but the trail of the serpent was over them all.' He would lie, *so* happy, so purely, so perfectly happy—he would feel an approaching face—his hair would be stirred by a gentle breathing—he would awake, and behold two miniature pictures of himself—a pair of the loveliest blue eyes over him, dissolving in lustre—with an image of himself in each— damp, luminous—transparent—like the swimming azure of heaven —or violets exhaling colour, and substance, and perfume, all in the red sunshine!

Then, a strange obscurity would arise, like the vapour of charnel houses, offensive and sickening—and some other violent transition would succeed, alternately—from heaven to hell, from hell to heaven, would he vibrate, like a pendulum.

> 'It was, as if the dead could feel
> The icy worm around them steal;
> And shudder, as the reptiles creep,
> And revel in their rotting sleep;
> Without the power to scare away
> The cold consumers of their clay;'

And then, as if the very dead were suddenly thrilling with life, and borne away—to the tranquillest climes:

> Where—'light breezes *but* ruffle the flowers sometimes.' [9]

A gruesome scene certainly, and yet a scene betokening uncommon literary powers. Poe was guilty of similar extravagant indulgences in *The Narrative of A. Gordon Pym* and elsewhere, but on other occasions Poe exercised that artistic restraint which was almost completely foreign to Neal. *Logan* maintains its dizzying pace throughout. The public read it with astonishment. Some persons took it seriously as an almost epic work; others "took it as they took opium, or exhilarating gas." [10]

Having once well begun to write novels Neal continued with the feverish intensity which characterized his activity throughout life. No less than three novels appeared bearing the date 1823. *Seventy-Six* was avowedly suggested by, though not imitative of, Cooper's *Spy*.[11] Its psychological content is greater than that of Cooper's Revolutionary stories, and it gives space to discussions of love and passion that Cooper, if he read the book, must have regarded as unwholesome. Mainly, however, *Seventy-Six* was a patriotic tale of adventure. Not Neal's most original work, it was possibly, as Neal thought, his best story.[12]

Randolph (1823) is a story (in letter form) so full of inflammable comment on current events and on celebrities of all sorts—writers, painters, orators, statesmen—that it was "received like a lighted-thunderbolt, dropped into a powder magazine." [13] Neal was not a malicious man by nature, but he was sometimes dreadfully plain-spoken in his adverse comments. At all times he was supremely confident in his judgments. The story of *Randolph* as such is slight and chaotic: its burden is to dispel the clouds around a mysterious, fascinating young "villain" and finally show him forth as a hero. A contemporary reviewer remarked that "the various incidents have about as much coherence as the thoughts of a maniac." [14] At the same time the reviewer discerned signs of real power in Neal—power which, in the reviewer's opinion, was destined never to be controlled:

> We think Mr. Neal a man of unquestionable and inexhaustible resources. We know him personally, and have wondered at his energy and power of achievement. We always believed him possessed of a moral and intellectual nature, which, with due culture and discipline, might have borne most rare and valuable fruits. But it is too late . . . and . . . we cannot resist the conviction, that either from some inherent defect in his disposition or faculties, or from the irresistible dominion of confirmed habit, he never will be other than what he is—a man whose talents are various and powerful, but perverted and worse than useless.[15]

But Neal was soon to be visited with more material protest against his arbitrary judgments of men. The book had appeared anonymously, and indeed the author gravely included his own literary portrait (with his name deliberately misspelled "Neale") among the celebrities. But the authorship was soon guessed. One of the sparks from *Randolph* inflamed Edward C. Pinkney, the poet, to the point of challenging Neal to a duel on account of his disparaging comments on Pinkney's father, who died just after the book was written. Here was an irony indeed: that a man who had written a book (*Keep Cool*) in denunciation of duelling should himself be called to the "field of honor." Neal conceived that he could best show his originality by ignoring the challenge (even though he was stigmatized as "craven" for his restraint and, it was whispered, "soundly thrashed" as well), and he utilized the whole affair in his next novel, *Errata, or the Works of Will Adams* (1823), "purporting to be the confessions of a coward." [16]

Despite the mixed reception of his books, Neal had received enough commendation, including favorable foreign comment,[17] to lead him to believe that he could swing a literary career abroad. Accordingly, having made arrangements for the accommodation of his legal clients, he sailed for England, arriving there January 8, 1824. The *Quarterly's* impudent inquiry as to "who reads an American book" had aroused his ire as it did Paulding's, and he proposed to

> see what might be done, with a fair field, and no favor, by an American writer. Irving had succeeded; and, though I was wholly unlike Irving, why shouldn't I? Cooper was well received; and I had a notion, that, without crossing his path, or poaching upon his manor, I might do something, so American, as to secure the attention of an Englishman.[18]

He was confident of his own high powers, and he knew that he could "write faster than any man that ever yet lived." [19] Personally he was well received, and he lived for a time with Jeremy Bentham in the capacity of secretary. His literary work consisted chiefly of articles written for *Blackwood's Magazine*.[20] In his first article he pretended to be an English traveler writing his impression of America—even referring again to "Neal" as if to another writer—for he "had good reason to believe, that communications from an American, if he did not abuse America, would go into the Balaam-basket." [21] After an initial success he became a regular contributor to *Blackwood's* and received very satisfactory sums for his work, though nothing comparable to what Irving could ask. His aim in his periodical writing was to present a series of brief, vivid sketches of American writers from an impartial point of view. The sketches, done entirely from memory, were often faulty in factual detail, occasionally unfair in judgments, but generally rich in acute critical perceptions.

Neal came to London with high hopes of becoming a permanent addition to the literary coterie there. He expected to pour forth novels which would make his name forever illustrious. But despite the fact that *Logan* and *Seventy-Six* had been promptly pirated in England, he found London publishers strangely indifferent to his actual presence and his proffer of new manuscripts. Indeed it was only after he had completely rewritten it a second time that he finally secured a publisher (Blackwood of Edinburgh) for his next novel *Brother Jonathan: or, The New Englanders* (1824).

Brother Jonathan, the longest of Neal's novels, is about as much of a hodge-podge as anything he wrote: reviewers complained that they couldn't even follow the story. It differs from the other novels in containing (besides rant and rubbish) a considerable amount of local realism pertaining to New England.[22] The action of the story is set in Ginger Town, Connecticut, beginning about a year before the Battle of Lexington. Here a stranger arrives—one Jonathan Peters, a mysterious, sorrowful person about whose past nothing can be learned. He can talk down the preacher, the lawyer, and the military, and he is a vaguely awe-inspiring man—not unlike a character out of Hawthorne. Perhaps he is the spirit of the times: "It was [says Neal] a time of rebellion. A whole people had become rebels. It was a time of warfare and sedition.—The face of Jonathan Peters corresponded finely with it . . ." [23] Presently Peters is swept up in the welter of the Revolutionary War: he is suspected as a spy, his house is burned. But he has a personal problem as well as a political one, for he enters into a controversy with one Abraham Harwood, a minister, over the latter's too harsh treatment of his son. A reader oriented in the American novel of this period naturally suspects that Harwood's "son" is in reality the son of Peters—and this proves to be the case. But many, far too many, other matters arise to complicate the story of *Brother Jonathan;* and in the end, the reader, wearied by an anarchy of incident, takes what comfort he may in the incidental New England lore distributed throughout the book. The book is drenched with superstition, prophecy, and legend. It contains pages of Yankee dialect, carefully marked by Neal to indicate proper stresses in pronunciation. It tells of a New England husking, a "raising," a quilting "frolick." [24] Quaker dialect, dress, and customs receive authoritative and none too complimentary treatment by Neal.[25] To see unity in the vast conglomeration of *Brother Jonathan* is impossible. Perhaps Neal thought he was expressing all of New England in its various aspects—political, personal, domestic, household—at the time of a crisis. A few reviewers were favorable toward the book, but almost all of them were puzzled by it. One critic compared Neal with Charles Brockden Brown, to the disparagement of the former:

> The characters described in Brown are downright men and women, whom, with all their weaknesses and eccentricities, we are almost sure we know or have known. Neal's dramatis personae are for the most part stalking moody spectres with glaring eyeballs and inflated nostrils, towering above the common height, and exhibiting the play of their muscles and veins through their clothes in the most trivial action; atrocious two-legged nightmares such

as might have been engendered in the brains of Edgar Huntley, if he had washed down his raw panther collop with new Yankee rum, and slept in the reeking skin.[26]

The same critic suggested that Jonathan Peters was plagiarized from Brown's Carwin, and added his regret that Neal should have

> devote[d] three huge closely-printed volumes to the adventures of profligates, misanthropes, maniacs, liars, and louts, for such are the serious personages of "Brother Jonathan." We are really at a loss to divine any thing like a moral or a leading idea in the book . . .[27]

In 1827, after about three and a half years spent abroad, Neal returned to America. He was received none too warmly by his compatriots at Portland, Maine. Occasionally he was assailed in language as unrestrained as his own.[28] His works were not being reissued in this country. New writers were competing for public favor, and Neal's flare as a novelist would seem to have burned out. Yet he was as cocky as ever, and he was far from finished with literature. Many more stories were yet to come from his pen, and he was to be connected with a number of journalistic ventures. The first of these latter after his return from Europe was the establishment of *The Yankee*, a weekly newspaper, as editor of which Neal gave Poe "the very first words of encouragement" he remembered having received in print.[29] As for fiction, he wrote *Rachel Dyer* (1828), *Authorship* (1830), *The Down-easters* (1833), *True Womanhood* (1859), besides a number of dime novels produced in the 1860's. Of the novels, perhaps the most fruitful for modern readers is *Rachel Dyer* (1828), not only because it constitutes an early treatment of an important American theme but because it reveals a new aspect of Neal as a writer.

Rachel Dyer is in several respects Neal's best novel. He seems to have turned to the subject of witchcraft not as a professional writer in quest of "copy" but as a genuine student of early American history. Nor was he interested merely in the external history of the Salem tragedies, with their gruesome data of torture and death; rather, he sought to incorporate these data in a story which should lead finally to a philosophical understanding of the whole phenomenon. He does not indicate his sympathy with the victims of witchcraft by the simple expedient of railing at the judges. He tries, as his preface shows, to be objective:

> I would call the attention of our novel-writers and our novel-readers to what is undoubtedly native and peculiar, in the early

history of our Fathers; I would urge them to believe that though
there is much to lament in that history, there is nothing to conceal;
that if they went astray, as they most assuredly did in the judgments, they went astray conscientiously, with what they understood to be the law of God in their right hands.[30]

An introductory first chapter bespeaks the reader's imaginative sympathy even with those of our ancestors who were deluded. After all,
they had their warrant in Scripture, their precedent in the statutes of
the mother-country. Most of all, the belief in witchcraft was a natural
one in man:

> We may smile now to hear witchcraft spoken seriously of; but
> we forget perhaps that a belief in it is like a belief in the after ap-
> pearance of the dead among the blue waters, the green graves, the
> still starry atmosphere and the great shadowy woods of our earth;
> or like the beautiful deep instinct of our nature for worship,—
> older than the skies, it may be, universal as thought, and sure as the
> steadfast hope of immortality.[31]

The tale itself, of course, does not attempt to exculpate the leaders of
the Salem persecutions.[32] Rather it is focussed upon the victims of the
delusion and on their heroic, pitiful efforts to oppose it. Action begins
with the partly mischievous, partly nervous behavior of the children
whose complaints led to the rapid spread of hysteria, and it ends with
brief allusion to the recantation of Sewall. Dynamic courtroom scenes
bring out the full horror of the situation. Persons actually involved in
the Salem tragedies appear in active roles: Samuel Parris (called Matthew Paris in the novel), Samuel Sewall, Increase and Cotton Mather,
the Indian Tituba, Sarah Good, George Burroughs, and others.[33] The
hero of the story is George Burroughs, the minister, who carries on
courageously against impossible odds, including distorted evidence.
The heroine is Rachel Dyer, a Quaker woman "without youth or
beauty," [34] who is drawn into the vortex of suspicion and hatred by
reason of her association with the minister Burroughs. Toward the
end of the book a moving scene occurs in a dungeon cell when Burroughs beseeches Rachel to save herself by confessing: her confession,
he believes, will delay her execution until the accusers are themselves
accused. But Rachel disdains to "save herself by a lie." When she in
turn asks him if he means to confess, he pleads that as "a preacher of
the word of truth" he would be unable to force his conscience. Elizabeth, a sister of Rachel, who also refuses to confess, is saved by an illness which delays legal action. But Burroughs is executed, and Rachel's

execution is appointed for the following day. As it turns out, Rachel is spared the gallows, for when the executioners come for her, she is found in her last "sleep," her arm thrown over the Bible she has been reading. The novel ends as quietly as it had begun. No unnecessary exploitation of physical or mental distress has been resorted to, for Neal was so deeply moved by the cruel errors he was recording, that he was fain to let the most agonizing events speak for themselves. A kind of sombre repose characterizes the style of *Rachel Dyer*. Constrained, perhaps, by his great theme, Neal for once abandoned his literary monkeyshines and wrote in simple sincerity of real people whose tragedy was the heavier for having resulted from the religious convictions of their oppressors.

Even *Rachel Dyer*, arresting as it is, has now passed into oblivion for all but historians and special students.[35] Neal left no single work of fiction which deserves to be revived for its sheer merit. In most of his stories he was the victim of his own lust for words. In his torrential flow of uninhibited language he surprisingly foreshadows Thomas Wolfe, but he is even less controlled than Wolfe. Whatever idea or image came to the surface of his subconscious mind was hastily tumbled on to his page, wholly unedited by his judgment. Inevitably he reaped the harvest of haste: poor proportion, loose ends, slip-shod diction, and general incoherence. As if to make up for these defects, he tried to hold the reader by the passionate intensity of his expression. But the reader finally fled from such disorder and violence.

What, then, can be the excuse for regarding Neal as of any consequence in the history of American literature? The answer can only be that, however badly he used them, he possessed extraordinary literary powers. Flashes of something very like genius gleamed from his most gaudy pages. Critics who were aghast at Neal's excesses could not forbear to praise his brilliance. Poe regarded him highly.[36] Hawthorne fed—selectively, one may be sure—at the mountainous repast Neal offered. Moreover in a day when the average literary ambition of Americans yearned toward an Irving-like success in the Anglo-American essay, Neal sturdily mined his native land for materials. Crude ore he undoubtedly turned up for the most part, but along with it came more valuable materials which the curious amateur of Americana may yet discover in John Neal of Portland, Maine.

For it never could be forgotten that Neal was staunchly loyal, first to his section[37] and then to his nation. From a practical point of view perhaps this has been his greatest service: that he energized American literature at a time when such a service was badly needed. Sometimes he wrote scornfully of his fellow-American writers as sycophantic;

sometimes he singled out individual writers for attack. But always his aim was to stimulate more and better narrative production. His gibes were tonic in effect. Thus in the second preface to *Rachel Dyer* he wrote:

> The British are a nation of writers. Their novel-writers are as a cloud. True—true—but they still want something which they have not. They want a real American writer—one with courage enough to write in his native tongue. *That* they have not, even at this day. *That* they never had. Our best writers are English writers, not American writers. They are English in every thing they do, and in every thing they say, as authors—in the structure and moral of their stories, in their dialogue, speech and pronunciation, yea in the very characters they draw. Not so much as one true Yankee is to be found in any of our native books: hardly so much as one true Yankee phrase. Not so much as one true Indian, though you hardly take up a story on either side of the water now, without finding a red-man stowed away in it; and what sort of a red-man? Why one that uniformly talks the best English the author is capable of—more than half the time perhaps out-Ossianing Ossian.
>
> I have the modesty to believe that in some things I am unlike all the other writers of my country—both living and dead; although there are not a few, I dare say who would be glad to hear of my bearing a great resemblance to the latter. For my own part I do not pretend to write English—that is, I do not pretend to write what the English themselves call English—I do not, and I hope to God—I say this reverently, although one of their Reviewers may be again puzzled to determine "whether I am swearing or praying" when I say so—that I never shall write what is now worshipped under the name of *classical* English. It is no natural language—it never was—it never will be spoken alive on this earth: and therefore, ought never to be written. We have dead languages enough now; but the deadest language I ever met with or heard of, was that in use among the writers of Queen Anne's day.[38]

It was not easy to produce a good indigenous literature; Neal recognized as much in 1822 when (in *Randolph*) he cited the usual obstacles to such an end. Yet it is to be observed that Neal answered his own objections and that at bottom he is optimistic:

> But in our country, there is every thing to discourage a novelist —nothing to incite him. The very name . . . of a novel writer would be a perpetual reproach to a man of genius . . . We have no old castles—no banditti—no shadow of a thousand years to

penetrate—but what of that. We have men and women—creatures that God himself hath fashioned and filled with character. And what more do we want? . . . You laugh at my enthusiasm. I am sure of it. But why need we go back to the past for our heroes?—There is no such necessity; and he who shall first dare to grapple with the *present*, will triumph, in this country. Remember, my prediction.

Another very serious reason why, whatever were the merit of our writers, we could not enter into competition with the men of Europe is, that we cannot afford to write for nothing; and yet, if we would write for nothing; and *give* the copy right of a novel, for instance, to a publisher, it would still be a perilous adventure to him. Shall I tell you the reason? Our booksellers here can publish your costliest poems, and novels, and dramas, without any expense for the copy-right. You give Byron or Moore five thousand guineas for a poem; and, in forty days, there will be an American edition published here, for the copy right of which, our publishers have not given a cent. Names will sell anything. We all know that . . .

But will this last forever? No. The time is rapidly approaching, when, it will be enough to sell a work, if it be called American. We are getting to feel a national pride; and men are already beginning to put in their title pages, *"by an American"*—and *"an American Tale"*—words, that, a few years ago, would have been as politick, as "by a Choctaw" or *"or a Narragansett tale."* [39]

It was in this spirit that John Neal wrote. He could be pugnacious, whimsical, blood curdling, or idealistic in his own writing. He could attack his contemporaries smartly. But finally he was an eager apostle of American literature. He lived so long that he was lost to view the nation over. In 1846 Hawthorne wrote that Neal must be dead: "else he never could keep himself so quiet." [40] No, Neal was not dead, he had merely contracted his circle of activity. Within that circle (finally no larger than Portland, Maine) he lived on until 1875.

LYDIA MARIA (FRANCIS) CHILD (1802-1880)

The historical romance, in which she first achieved fame, was finally only a secondary interest of Lydia Maria (Francis) Child. Primarily she was a reformer, and she is now best known for her extremely active work as an abolitionist and agitator. She turned her hand to many activities. She taught school in Massachusetts, her native state, for three years, and in 1826 she established the first American monthly magazine for children, the *Juvenile Miscellany*. After her marriage to David Lee

Child in 1828, she became deeply devoted to abolitionism, a cause which her husband also supported. Her first anti-slavery book, *Appeal in Favor of That Class of Americans Called Africans* (1833), was widely acclaimed. She edited the *National Anti-Slavery Standard* from 1840 to 1844. Her writings and her strongly partisan actions aroused tremendous admiration and much violent protest. The Child farm at Wayland, Massachusetts, was known to be a station in the Underground Railroad for fugitive slaves. When John Brown was wounded at Harper's Ferry, Mrs. Child offered to nurse him. Other reform movements of the day drew her interest and support, including woman's suffrage and sex-education.[41] Mrs. Child also wrote four novels and a good many short tales. Sales of her later stories were undoubtedly increased by her national prominence, but her first two novels had to stand strictly on their merits, for they were written when the author was in her early twenties: *Hobomok* was published in 1824, and *The Rebels* in 1825. Both were published anonymously.

Hobomok: A Tale of Early Times is interesting by reason of its early position among historical romances treating of the American Indian in relationship to seventeenth-century life in Massachusetts. At twenty-two years of age, it is safe to say, Mrs. Child (then Lydia Maria Francis) knew little about the Indians or about life or about novel writing. But she was stimulated to attempt authorship by reading Dr. J. G. Palfrey's review of *Yamoyden, A Tale of the Wars of King Philip* (1820), a narrative poem which had a tremendous popular success. In the course of his review, which appeared in the *North American Review* for April, 1821, Dr. Palfrey had said apropos of *Yamoyden's* theme:

> We are glad that somebody has at last found out the unequalled fitness of our early history for the purposes of a work of fiction. For ourselves, we know not the country or age which has such capacities in this view as N. England in its early day; nor do we suppose it easy to imagine any element of the sublime, the wonderful, the picturesque and the pathetic, which is not to be found here by him who shall hold the witch-hazel wand that can trace it. . . . Whoever in this country first attains the rank of a first rate writer of fiction, we venture to predict will lay his scene here. The wide field is ripe for the harvest, and scarce a sickle has yet touched it.[42]

Doubtless many a pen went into action in response to such a glowing promise. Our author didn't see Dr. Palfrey's prophecy until one Sunday in 1824, but when she did, she pounced upon it as her warrant and she wrote the first chapter of *Hobomok* instanter. The rest of the story, less than two hundred pages long, was soon completed. "Hobomok" is the name of a young Indian chief of the stamp vaguely alluded to in the term "noble savage." He is friendly to the white people in and about Salem and Plymouth, and he finally falls in love with one Mary Conant, a granddaughter of an English earl and a more or less unwilling pioneer in "this wilderness life" of America. She is engaged to marry Charles Brown, but the latter is reported lost in a shipwreck. Not having read many pale-face novels, Hobomok takes this news at face value, and Mary herself finally gives up Charles for lost. The two are married. Mary is not entirely happy as the bride of an Indian, but in time she gives birth to a son, whom she loves deeply (and finally sends to Cambridge, England, for his education). Of course Charles must be re-introduced after three years—he was only *stranded* on the African coast—and it is up to the two men to be noble indeed. Hobomok proves to be the winner in the contest of magnanimity; and, securing an Indian divorce, he trots off into the wilderness without any formality of farewell beyond leaving Mary a newly killed deer.

It is obvious that *Hobomok* contains strong elements of reader-interest—the theme of Enoch Arden in the main plot, a love affair among secondary characters which anticipates Longfellow's "Speak for yourself" scene in "The Courtship of Miles Standish," [43] and the problem of miscegenation. The marriage of a white girl to an Indian, however "civilized," was a move to be taken only with the greatest caution by a novelist. Catharine Sedgwick was shortly to make use of the theme in *Hope Leslie*[44] and Cooper was to use it in *The Wept of Wish-ton-Wish*, but there was a great risk of alienating readers, particularly in the North. A similar attitude was soon to be shown toward miscegenation involving the white and black races in the South. Accordingly Mrs. Child did well, from the point of view of romance, to send her noble Indian back to the forest. In any case, he will not really suffer much, for he is but a lay figure, artificial in language and action. The whole action of the book is pretty much askew anyway. The love affair of Sally Oldham (who tells her suitor to speak for himself) is treated at first as if it were to form an important part of the story, but Sally is practically ignored by the author thereafter. Sally is a pretty good character, though, with plenty of sparkle in her eye and pepper on her tongue. She can talk like a person instead of a copybook—as when she says with monosyllabic fervor: "Folks who have the least to do with love are the best off." [45] But Sally is an exception, and Mary is accorded those rhetorical flourishes that are the unhappy rule in most early novels. Mary's appearance must remind the reader of "a Parian statue, or one of those fair visions which fancy gives to slumber," [46] and when it

is her lot to see Charles go away on his shipwreck assignment, she is described as "a lily weighed down by the pitiless pelting of the storm; a
violet shedding its soft, rich perfume on bleakness and desolation . . ." [47]
She becomes a vessel of sentimentality and in many ways she anticipates
the pallid, neurotic heroines of the school of Edna Earl in Mrs. Wilson's
St. Elmo. The imaginative reconstruction of early Salem and Plymouth
days, though on a slight scale, is rather better than the characterization.
The details of domestic life among well-to-do people are well suggested
and due attention is given to religion in the lives of the early settlers.
The author roguishly exposes the local minister as quite willing to give
"a sly look and word" to Sally if "his good-woman was out of the
way." [48] Yet in general the Puritan community is viewed favorably
and Governor Endicott makes a genial entrance into the narrative. Indeed the novel opens with praise of New England and the Puritans:

> In this enlightened and liberal age, it is perhaps too fashionable to
> look back upon those early sufferers in the cause of the Reforma-
> tion as a band of dark, discontented bigots. [49]

The humanitarian crusader that the author was later to become is not
clearly implicit in *Hobomok*, however, and it is obvious that Mrs. Child
was beginning her career as a writer of historical romance in accordance
with the encouraging words of Dr. Palfrey in the *North American Review*. She was to write one more "historical" novel before discovering
her real mission in society.

The *Rebels, or Boston Before the Revolution* (1825) was inferior to
Hobomok. Although the author in part lived up to her promise that
she would write "the domestic annals" of the period (*i.e.*, 1765) [50] the
major narrative events of the book are unnecessarily complex, and the
style is over-wrought and over-allusive. The turgid political discussion
arising out of the national emergency (emphasis is on the Stamp Tax
crisis) reveals the author's youthful limitations. Again the most effective elements are the details of everyday life and the sprightly treatment of female characters. There is variety (if not subtlety) in the
author's portrait of Miss Sandford—a spinster who looks like "an ante-
diluvian image," speaks in "the squeaking tones of antiquated coquetry," and conducts herself in such fashion as to elicit Dr. Mather
Byles's query: "Has Aunt Sandford been backbiting her neighbours till
her double teeth ache?" [51] But lively, brash phrasing could not save
The Rebels from rather harsh treatment at the hands of the *North
American Review*, the very magazine which had encouraged her youthful attempts to coin fiction out of history. The reviewer regretfully

refers to the book as a partial failure. The grounds of his criticism are interesting as calling attention to one difficult task of all writers of historical romance: they must compete with the vivid pages of history itself. As for *The Rebels*, it consists largely of

> mere copy from real history, a narrative of events possessing an interest which fiction can do little to heighten . . . a repetition of political sentiments which we find expressed with far more force and eloquence in the writings of Adams and of Quincy.[52]

The reviewer voices objections, too, to that part of the action which takes place in the tomb of the Osbornes: it is too revolting. Better, he implies, if the author will capitalize further the gift which she had shown in *Hobomok* and which she shows to some extent elsewhere in *The Rebels*, namely, a gift for "passages . . . of a pathetic kind."

Sad tidings, these critical pronouncements, to an ambitious youngster. It was clear enough by now that Mrs. Child would not challenge the supremacy of Cooper! It did not seem likely that she would ever master *any* form of writing: she clearly lacked discipline. She did not return to the novel until 1836. In the meantime she began to live more in the present, taking a husband and writing on avowedly domestic subjects: *The Frugal Housewife* (1829), *The Mother's Book* (1831), both of which were tremendously popular. At this stage of her career Mrs. Child for a time ran a course parallel to that of Catharine M. Sedgwick, who began by writing fiction and, when romance temporarily lost prestige, turned successfully to non-fictional works designed to interest feminine readers. But she was to go farther afield than Miss Sedgwick and to delve deeply into problems of social reform which Miss Sedgwick was never able to observe more than tangentially.[53] In 1833 Mrs. Child found her métier as a writer by publishing *An Appeal in Favor of That Class of Americans Called Africans*, a book which had an electrical power of drawing attention. From now on, Mrs. Child was a figure of national importance and it is not too much to say that she began to *make* history—as an abolitionist. She wrote two more novels and a considerable number of short tales and poems—as well as one of the best-selling books of the 1840's, *Letters From New York*.[54]

Philothea (1836), her third novel, shows greater ability in novel-construction than Mrs. Child's earlier stories, but its merits are not sufficient to lift it above the level of mediocre fiction which was prolifically produced in the thirties.[55] It constitutes, however, one of the early signs of a vogue for novels laid in early eras—whether Greek or Roman or early Christian. *Philothea* is a tale of Greek life—mainly a love story—

in the days of Pericles.[56] Its subject-matter enabled Mrs. Child to capitalize her respectable knowledge of antiquity, but the author erred in her artistry by grafting New England morality upon Greek life.[57] It is superior to the earlier novels in its style, which Poe referred to with needless extravagance as "a model for purity, chastity, and ease." [58] Mrs. Child's last novel, *A Romance of the Republic,* published in 1867, should logically have been her best fiction, for its theme was that which had dominated the active middle years of her life, namely, abolition. But a new disadvantage rose to prevent her from reaching high distinction as novelist, and this time it was the hampering grip of propaganda. Interested in political and civil freedom for humanity, she could not emancipate her fictional characters from ideological bondage. Her quadroons are hardly more than one-quarter real. The book finally fails to achieve authenticity. Mrs. Child knew slavery as an institution, but she did not know the South intimately and she had to resort to artificial coloring of the local scene. Moreover her narrative suffers from having "too large a framework, too many *vertebræ* to the plot." [59] Appearing in the same year as De Forest's *Miss Ravenel's Conversion,*[60] Mrs. Child's novel cannot challenge comparison with De Forest's on any major point.

Mrs. Child died in 1880, recognized as one of the most able women of her generation. But fiction was not her forte. Her brave little attempts at the historical romance it now seems a folly to compare with Cooper's brilliant enterprises. Yet she had a great deal of force as a writer of nonfiction and at one or two points her ideas on social problems converged with those of Cooper. She saw and deplored some of the same conditions that Cooper energetically denounced upon his return from Europe, particularly the unfortunate conditions under which young folk grew up in commercial New York. These ideas she expressed in various places, notably in *Letters From New York* (1843, 1845), a work which, from the point of view of the general student of literary history, is probably Mrs. Child's most valuable legacy. Like Cooper, she was disheartened by America's tendency to ape European ways and to establish unwholesome class cleavages on the basis of money. Her pen was quite equal to the description of devastating contrasts:

> Rapid approximation to the European style of living is more and more observable in this city. The number of servants in livery visibly increases every season. Foreign artistic upholsterers assert that there will soon be more houses in New-York furnished according to the fortune and taste of noblemen, than there are either in Paris or London; and this prophecy may well be believed, when the fact is considered that it is already not very un-

common to order furniture for a single room, at the cost of ten thousand dollars. There would be no reason to regret this lavishness, if the convenience and beauty of social environment were really increased in proportion to the expenditure, and if there were a progressive tendency to equality in this distribution. But, alas, a few moments' walk from saloons superbly furnished in the style of Louis 14th, brings us to Loafers' Hall, a dreary desolate apartment, where shivering little urchins pay a cent apiece, for the privilege of keeping out of watchmen's hands, by sleeping on boards arranged in tiers.[61]

The enervating effects of soft living among the gentle-born she also notes with due concern:

But the effects of a luxurious and artificial life are sad enough on those who indulge in it, without seeking for painful contrast among the wretchedly poor. Sallow complexions, feeble steps, and crooked spines, already show an obvious deterioration in beauty, grace, and vigour. Spiritual bloom and elasticity are still more injured by modes of life untrue to nature . . . It is one of the saddest sights to see a young girl, born of wealthy and worldly parents, full of heart and soul, her kindly impulses continually checked by etiquette, her noble energies repressed by genteel limitations. She must not presume to love anybody till father and mother find a suitable match; she must not laugh loud, because it is vulgar; she must not walk fast, because it is ungenteel; she must not work in the garden, for fear the sun and wind may injure her complexion; she must sew nothing but gossamer, lest it mar the delicacy of her hands; she must not study, because gentlemen do not admire literary ladies. Thus left without ennobling objects of interest, the feelings and energies are usually concentrated on frivolous and unsatisfactory pursuits, and woman becomes a by-word and a jest, for her giddy vanity, her love of dress and beaux.[62]

Young men in the city, deprived of the normal ranges of activity in simple environments, are the victims of mal-formed society. Mrs. Child deplores the mania for speculation which so distressed Cooper:

The natural, spontaneous influences of society should be such as to supply men with healthy motives, and give full, free play to the affections, and the faculties. It is horrible to see our young men goaded on by the fierce, speculating spirit of the age, from the contagion of which it is almost impossible to escape, and then see them tortured into madness, or driven to crime, by fluctuating changes of the money-market. The young soul is, as it were, entangled in the great merciless machine of a falsely-constructed society . . .[63]

Mrs. Child saw many of the same symptoms of an ailing society that Cooper saw, but her diagnosis was different. Whereas Cooper was inclined to ascribe many socio-economic evils to a corrupt press and to political causes (the waning prestige of landed proprietors, etc.), Mrs. Child, who was a social worker, came to grips with evil as she saw it on the Bowery and on Blackwell's Island. She did not look at the problem of general social amelioration from a political angle or from, what was just as frequent in her day, a religious angle. She took a sociological stand. She felt that poverty was the greatest menace to society: "If we can abolish *poverty*, we shall have taken the greatest step toward the abolition of crime." [64] Nor can poverty be cured by perfunctory (even if organized) charitable or correctional treatment:

Benevolent institutions and reformatory societies perform but a limited and temporary use. They do not reach the ground-work of evil; and it is reproduced too rapidly for them to keep even the surface healed.[65]

The problem, she grants, is a difficult one, but she sees most hope in an educational program with respect to correctional media: society must not merely punish criminals but must educate them and provide economic opportunity for them. Here was a line of thought which Cooper never followed, for he almost never met the lower classes, excepting his own servants, at close range. Sooner or later, novelists would have to reckon with underprivileged folk. The domestic sentimentalists of the fifties and sixties would finger some of the issues delicately for a Victorian public,[66] but the real battle for social security would not be waged by novelists until after the Civil War. As for Mrs. Child, perhaps at first she instinctively recoiled from trying to express deeply felt social lessons in the artificial medium of the novel. At any rate she never quite worked out a plan whereby her social studies could be used to nourish her art as a novelist. Her short stories occasionally traversed ground that their author had known in actuality, but the stories she left untold or told only in the form of treatise or tract were the more numerous. She had, as Lowell said, a "great heart," [67] but not a great gift as a fiction-writer.

JAMES KIRKE PAULDING (1778-1860)

The ruthless winnowing process of time removes from general view not only scores of worthless writers but also a considerable number of writers whose productions are but a little short of first-rate. Among the latter group is James Kirke Paulding. In his day he was so popular that some of his works were translated into as many as five languages. Critically he was so well received that there seemed little reason to question Poe's assertion (about 1835) that there was "no better literary *manner* than the manner of Mr. Paulding." [68] He appealed to many tastes and offended few. For a number of years he was accorded honors virtually on a par with those received by Cooper. This was the more remarkable in that Paulding was a competitor in Cooper's own field of operations, the historical romance. In retrospect it is clear that Paulding was a writer of less weight and power than Cooper. It is clear, too, that some of his many literary gifts tended to cancel each other. Nevertheless a tidy balance of credit remains, and Paulding is still respected and admired for his colorful stories of Colonial life in the Middle states, especially New York. [69]

New York was Paulding's native state and New York City became his principal place of residence from the time he was about nineteen years old. He received little formal schooling, but read enormously under the tutelary eye of his mother, who largely supported the family after the father's mercantile business had failed. He lived for eight years (1815-1822) at Washington, and he returned there when he became Secretary of the Navy under Van Buren in 1838. He also from time to time traveled in the South and the West. But he was essentially a loyal New Yorker, and about 1846 he moved to an estate near Hyde Park, where he lived in amicable retirement until his death in 1860.

Although he lived to enjoy a mellow old age, Paulding was by nature an aggressive and even contentious person. Well might he refer to writers as members of the "genus irritabile," [70] for his own career as a writer was marked by many a battle of book and pamphlet. His strong opinions were matched by his somewhat testy disposition. At one time his friend Henry Brevoort referred to him as having "a mind at war with everything." [71] Nor were these traits completely effaced when he ·came to write the historical romance, for which he is now best remembered. [72] Indeed he imperiled his success as a writer of romance by his persistent habit of satire.

Paulding's earliest writing, it seems odd to recall, was the result of a collaboration with Irving, gentle Washington Irving. In 1807-08 he participated in those ebullient, bantering studies of social life in adolescent New York which were published as *Salmagundi*. Although the wit he there displayed never deserted him, Paulding later lost the amateur charm of youth and acquired in its place the purposeful and occasionally acerb manner of a vigilant observer of the political scene and of human motive and behavior in general. Political issues, foreign and domestic, interested him passionately. He became one of the most conspicuous champions of America during that literary warfare with England which became an inglorious substitute for powder and ball as a means of expressing hostility between the nations. Irving deplored such warfare and sought to allay it. But if Irving was oil, Paulding was acid, and he etched many a satiric portrait of John Bull in the years between 1812 and 1822. Other literary interests had not entirely lapsed during this period, witness *The Backwoodsman* (1818), a long poem celebrating the life and exploits of a New Yorker who emigrated to the Ohio Valley. But Paulding's poem was dull, and it was not until 1823 that he made a fair popular success with non-controversial material. In that year he published *Koningsmarke, the Long Finne: A Story of the New World*.

Brought out in the same year and by the same publisher as Cooper's *The Pioneers*, Paulding's story was clearly in the same genre as Cooper's.[73] It was set, however, in an earlier period than Cooper generally used, being a tale of the Swedes in Delaware during the mid-seventeenth century. The town of Elsingburgh, on the west bank of the Delaware River, is the main scene of the action. Owning allegiance to Gustavus Adolphus, the little community has incidental boundary troubles with the Quakers under William Penn and treaty troubles with the Indians. The "romantic" action begins with the introduction of Koningsmarke, a Finnish fellow of such noble stature and demeanor that the lovely, lonely Christina Piper, daughter of the local governor, is inevitably attracted to him. Arrested for carrying illegal (English) coin, Koningsmarke is imprisoned but escapes when the prison burns. Thereafter he becomes a guest in the house of the Governor, and the indicated romance between him and Christina would seem to be free to develop except for one or two obstacles. First, there are the prophecies of a "frizzle-" headed hag named Bombie, an African slave, who keeps muttering warnings about Koningsmarke's essential villainy. Christina, too, has her doubts about her hero when she chances to observe a certain scar on his neck. This makes a mystery, the solution to which the author obviously intends to defer until near the end of the book. Meantime Koningsmarke can establish his status as a hero. In an exciting scene he rescues Christina from being raped by a maniacal hermit, and from time to time throughout the story he furnishes additional illustrations of his prowess: rescuing a man from drowning, surviving the horrible experience of being lost in the woods during a snowstorm, etc. But the heaviest drafts on his fortitude occur when the Indians strike. Dissatisfied with a bargain which had bereft them of lands in exchange for lethal whiskey and worthless gewgaws, they seek redress in a council with the white people. When satisfaction is denied them, they burn the village and capture the principals of the story. Four settlers are brutally murdered: Paulding does not spare the reader the ghastly details. Christina is adopted as a sister by an Indian maid; and Koningsmarke, now the object of both their affections, becomes the slave of an Indian widow. When the widow wants to change his status from slave to husband, a general escape is attempted but ends in recapture. Death for the romantic couple (plus a comic constable called Lob Dotterel) now seems imminent, but in the nick of time William Penn arrives and buys their freedom: Paulding on several occasions pays his respects to Penn and the Quakers.[74] Restored to Elsingburgh, now rebuilt, Koningsmarke and Christina are still harried by the exigencies of romance, for the English have arrived to demand (and secure) the surrender of the Swedes. They also arrest Koningsmarke, and sentence him to be transported as a slave to Barbados. It is now so near the end of the story that a pardon or an escape must obviously be arranged, the former expedient being finally chosen by Paulding. Only the black clouds of Bombie's disapproval and Christina's doubt remain to be dispelled. In a long explanation (which, coming sooner, might have ruined the romance but improved the story), it is made clear that Koningsmarke had *not* been involved willingly in the outrage that led to the death of Christina's mother in Sweden many years before.

This synopsis may serve to show how well Paulding had conned the rules for making an historical romance. But *Koningsmarke* is more— and also less—than an historical romance. It is more in that it has greater variety than generally characterized the form. The personnel is more real and more diversified than was usual. Christina's father, Governor Piper, is made vivid by close attention to his speech and person. At times Paulding's treatment of the doughty Swedish governor recalls Irving's treatment of the Dutch governors of New Amsterdam, but Paulding is on the whole less burlesque in his treatment and also less kindly. Lob Dotterel, the constable, is an excellent comic character, and Dominie Kanttwell, the hypocritical minister, realistically reveals the sorry results of fanatical sectarianism. The Indians in council speak an incredible philosophical jargon, but in action they are formidably real. Even the hero and the heroine, though mainly types, share in Paulding's effort to make his characters psychologically plausible. They

are attracted by love at first sight but become partially estranged by the
unspoken doubts of Christina and Koningsmarke's obstinate silence.
However arbitrarily arranged, the impasse is handled with skilful detail. On one occasion, oppressed by the situation, they returned home
from a walk "without uttering a word, and were received with a very
bad grace by the Heer, who did not much like their walking so late by
moon-light." [75] On another occasion, the "lovers returned home, little
satisfied with themselves, or each other." [76] This type of comment was
something new under the romantic sun. Paulding was good in describing adventure, but he was finally more interested in character and motive than in mere excitement. He was also interested in natural scenery,
and his skill in describing outdoor scenes was distinctly superior to that
of most of his confrères in the historical romance. To some modern
readers, *Koningsmarke* may seem more valuable as a regional story than
as an historical romance. For others the chief value of the story may
lie in the author's mastery of a terse, epigrammatic style. Paulding's
humor, obviously inspired in part by Shakespeare (Falstaff was an especial favorite), imbues *Koningsmarke* with vitality throughout. Few
writers of the historical romance offered so much variety to their
readers. A partial statement of what Paulding offered occurs in *Koningsmarke* itself:

> It is in order to accommodate, as far as possible, every class of
> readers, that we have endeavoured, in the course of this work, to
> do what we are fully convinced can easily be done, namely, please
> all sorts of people . . .
> Our introductory chapters are intended for the deepest philos-
> ophers, who will find therein matters of weighty import; our his-
> torical details are for the inveterate lovers of truth; our love scenes
> for all whom it may concern; our gravity for the aged; our jests
> for the young; our wisdom is at any body's service that can find
> it out; and the sublime declamation of the Frizzled Head is par-
> ticularly intended for the refreshment of ladies and gentlemen of
> colour, who, it is presumed, will become ere long sufficiently en-
> lightened to scold their masters, and bully their mistresses, into a
> proper sense of equality. [77]

Koningsmarke is also less than a good historical romance. The reason for this is implicit in the paragraph quoted above: the critic and the
satirist in Paulding obtruded too often. He had the defects of his qualities. That same vitality which raises *Koningsmarke* to distinction is associated with the partial defeat of his romance as such. Too often he
adopted a tone of mockery which either irritates or puzzles the reader

of romance. The bantering tone he adopts with respect to his own story proves disconcerting, for example, when upon Koningsmarke's failing to clear up the mystery of the scar on his neck, Paulding interpolates a facetious remark:

> Now, though it is in our power, by a single flourish of the pen, to account for this singularity, we are too well acquainted with the nature of the human mind, to deprive our history at the very outset of that indescribable interest which arises from the author's keeping to himself certain secrets, which, like leading strings, as it were, conduct the reader to the end, in the hope of at length being fully rewarded by a disclosure, a hope in which, it must be confessed, he is often sadly disappointed, seeing it is much easier to knit, than to unravel a mystery.

Paulding's comment makes sense, but it impairs the pleasure of your thoroughgoing reader of romance, who can endure endless absurdities if delivered with sufficient solemnity but grows restive under jocose treatment. It is particularly disconcerting to the open-mouthed reader of romantic fiction if the author playfully mocks his own story, as Paulding sometimes did—a procedure which produces much the same effect as that of a magician who explains his magic, namely, the loss of glamor and illusion. Paulding's inveterate habit of dissecting motives was often embarrassing. Not only Dominie Kanttwell but other characters as well feel the effects of Paulding's personal disapproval. Wolfgang Langfange, with his passion for an internal improvements program, is too patently an oblique characterization of Henry Clay to serve well in a romance laid in the seventeenth century. Too often the critic superseded the creator in Paulding. Romance that was cultivated by his right hand was slashed by his left. He provided *Koningsmarke* with introductory chapters containing brilliantly written comments, but these comments, which were apparently inspired by Fielding's prefatory comments in the picaresque and comic story of *Tom Jones* do the author no good in an ostensibly imaginative tale. A friend and erstwhile collaborator of Irving, Paulding lacked Irving's genial nature. Irving wanted to make the reader laugh; Paulding wanted to make him laugh and think. A writer of historical romance par excellence is not troubled by afterthoughts, and it is as well if his humor is used sparingly—and never at the expense of his principal characters. Doubtless the satirical characterization of Langfange is furthered by Paulding's definition of political economy as being (according to Langfange's practice at least) "the science of starving on philosophical principles," [79] but such a mot does not enhance the aura of romance. A typical example of

Paulding's violation of tone occurs when he is describing the night of the Indian raid:

> The vigilant sentinels, whose turn it was to watch at the gates of the palisades, which surrounded the place, were fast asleep at their posts, like their legitimate successors, the trusty watchmen of New-York and Philadelphia; and nothing disturbed the repose of midnight but the barkings of some sleepless curs, baying each other from afar.[80]

Clearly it is an acceptable fact that the sentinels are not alert, but the allusion to contemporary policemen in New York and Philadelphia is gratuitous as well as destructive. Less objectionable but still of doubtful wisdom is Paulding's habit of insisting upon a commonsense interpretation of character or action. After the hero has recovered from an illness, the author refers to him as seeking out

> the charming Christina, who had ministered to his sick bed, like a guardian sylph—Pshaw! like a gentle, compassionate, sweet-souled woman! who is worth all the sylphs that ever sung or flitted in the vacuum of a poet's brain.[81]

Doubtless all this is sound and sensible, but there are readers who prefer their sentiment straight: they want no peppery particles in a sugar stick.

Thus Paulding varied the genre of the historical romance—for better or worse as the reader may decide. When he wrote straight adventure he was thoroughly competent. When his witty or satiric vein is quiescent the story goes through phases that are as thrilling or chilling as one may care to read. Such are the attack on the village, the attempts at escape, and the death of Bombie with her deformed grandson, Cupid. Paulding's serious manner is well exemplified in his account of the last moments of the slave woman and Cupid. Cupid, having been found guilty of treason by the Indians, is hanged in full sight of his grandmother. Bombie, like a terrifying sybil, utters dire imprecations upon the "accursed race of the white man" as she watches his last struggles. Then she dies:

> The tough old heart-strings that had so often been tested, in the hard gales of life, now cracked, and gave way; the strong frame that had endured so many hardships, all at once refused to endure any more, and in less than a minute after Bombie uttered these words, she sunk to the ground, overwhelmed by the agony of her feelings.

Numbers flocked around, as is usual in these cases, and one of the crowd exclaimed to the others, "raise her up." "Raise her!" repeated the Frizzled Head, the last energies of life trembling on her tongue—"Raise her! none but Him who broke down the eternal barriers between the quick and the dead; who called at the mouth of the sepulchre, and awoke the sleeping dust; who triumphed over death and the grave, can raise this withered old trunk. The hour is come—it is past. Wait, boy—I come." Her eyes closed, and she departed to a better world.

The crowd dispersed, overwhelmed with terror.[82]

Derivative as this scene patently is in some respects, it is one of the types of scene which helped to sustain the historical romance as the leading form of fiction for many years. Paulding, when he chose, could write in the popular vein.

After publishing *Koningsmarke*, which seems to have been a moderate success,[83] Paulding turned to other literary ventures, especially the short story, in which he was amazingly prolific. In 1830 he stumbled on a popular success with his drama *The Lion of the West*, which introduced a rugged, untutored, and unmistakably American frontiersman to the stage. The play won a three-hundred dollar prize, and it formed one of the main foundations of Paulding's great popularity in the years just ahead. In the following year he rounded out his development as a really successful author by publishing *The Dutchman's Fireside* (1831).

The Dutchman's Fireside is probably the best of Paulding's novels. Most of the characteristics observable in *Koningsmarke* reappear in *The Dutchman's Fireside*, but the author's mocking and satiric tone is heard less frequently. *The Dutchman's Fireside* is mainly a story, a very good story, of the Dutch in New York before the Revolutionary War. For the principal setting of the narrative near Albany, Paulding drew upon personal memories and family traditions which gave the book an authentic charm. The hero, Sybrant Westbrook, a shy youth, seems to have been in part autobiographically conceived. A mild thesis holds the action together, namely, that a life of action is the cure for one who suffers from the mental or psychological ills of civilization. Sybrant Westbrook's introverted nature is what stands in the way of his successful wooing of his distant cousin, Catalina Vancour, recently returned from a fashionable boarding school in New York. To her, Sybrant's sincere but uncouth advances seem simply boorish. Even after rescuing Catalina from drowning, Sybrant makes no apparent progress as a suitor: the girl seems to prefer one Sydenham, an English Colonel. Sybrant takes to the woods, hoping for dangerous adventure—which he finds to such good purpose that he himself has to be rescued. His rescuer, the great woodsman Sir William Johnson, undertakes to cure the lad by converting him into a man of action. From this remedial course Sybrant returns with his social kinks pretty well straightened out. He rescues Catalina a couple more times, on one occasion from a sinister old Indian, Hans Pipe, who had a grudge against the girl's family. You would think the hero now entitled to claim the heroine's hand, for she begins to see that he is the real McCoy. But no, there is a scheming aunt and there are (in smartest New York) other candidates for Catalina's hand: the silent, substantial Sir Thicknesse Throgmorton and the witty Irish Captain Gilfillan. Sybrant performs the action of challenging Gilfillan, but the French and Indian War forestalls the event. Gilfillan dies, and Sybrant is reported killed in action; but the report is false, and it is now merely a matter of time until the hero returns to Catalina and his inherited estate.

The story manifestly is based in good American sentiment: an inarticulate rural lad finally carries off the prize of a fashionable but virtuous girl in the face of heavy competition by moneyed, titled suitors with glamorous European backgrounds. The hero is not a hero at the beginning but must prove himself one by pluck and resourcefulness. This is one advantage *The Dutchman's Fireside* has over Cooper's yet-to-be-written *Satanstoe*, which it resembles in much of its narrative agenda and portions of its setting. It is also a livelier and more varied book than *Satanstoe*, and its re-creation of old Dutch life seems more authentic than that of Cooper's story. Likewise, as one reviewer points out, its "machinery" was "not involved or complex," and it was free from "supernumerary characters." [84] Chiefly in its masterful treatment of sheer adventure Cooper's story excels Paulding's. Whatever its absolute or comparative merits, *The Dutchman's Fireside* became a successful book, reaching its fourth New York edition within a year and appearing in scores of editions, reprints, and translations at home and abroad. Its press was mixed but prevailingly good. Even the British reviewers (who were aware of Paulding's inveterate animus against John Bull) wrote in terms of commendation. [85]

Paulding's popularity now made him such a good publisher's risk that the Harpers soon began (1833) a collected edition of his works. In the meantime they felt confident enough of the success of his next novel, *Westward Ho!* (1832) to print a first edition of 5000 copies. This book and the two novels which succeeded it added more to Paulding's royalties than to his permanent reputation, for in none of them did he marshal his abilities with sustained success. Yet each has substantial elements which refuse to be dismissed lightly.

Westward Ho! proved to be a none-too-happy blending of adventure and psychology. The westward trek of Cuthbert Dangerfield from Virginia (which Paulding knew) to Kentucky (which he had read about—especially in Timothy Flint's *Recollections of the Last Ten Years*) entailed dangerous adventures which had been common matters of record in the period just after the Revolution. This aspect of the story is well handled. Dudley Rainsford, however, a religious fanatic in love with Dangerfield's daughter Virginia, is the subject of more psychological analysis than the action can well sustain. Rainsford, who fears that he will inherit his family's strain of madness, does in the end become a madman, obsessed by religion. Here was a theme, religious fanaticism, that Paulding had treated before (in *Koningsmarke*) and would treat again (in *The Puritan and His Daughter*). Here was a character, Dudley Rainsford, a shade too clinical for the good of the fiction in which he appeared. A mild impatience with the story moved one reviewer to say: "In fact, he [Rainsford] is so good a madman that it is almost a pity he should have recovered his wits through the persevering affection of Virginia." [86] *Westward Ho!* is superlatively good neither as a novel nor as romance.

More short tales, a life of Washington, miscellaneous political writing, and official duties (as Secretary of the Navy) occupied Paulding in the interval between *Westward Ho!* and his next novel, *The Old Continental: or, The Price of Liberty* (1846). The latter is a lively narrative of the Revolutionary War, in which Paulding made his closest approach to the materials and methods of Cooper. The setting in the Neutral Ground of Weschester County and the theme of espionage constitute the fundamental points of similarity. Paulding's hero is a young patriot who falls under suspicion as a spy. After having been imprisoned both ashore and afloat, the hero escapes to take part in the expedition which resulted in the capture of André. The action is taken very largely from historical accounts, in which Paulding took a peculiar interest by reason of the fact that his hero, John Paulding, was a distant relative of the author. The tale as a whole is vigorous and racy, but it falls off in power toward the end. Whereas Cooper gloried in "big scenes" and capitalized them to the full, Paulding again proved in *The Old Continental* that he found climaxes uncongenial or too taxing. He excelled in detail rather than in mass. In *The Old Continental* the capture of André, which should have called forth all the author's powers as a writer of adventure, proved to be very inadequate as a climax. Paulding's novels as a whole, in fact, suggest that he might have been more at home in a sort of satirico-picaresque narrative with frequent philosophical stop-overs somewhat after the fashion of Brackenridge's

Modern Chivalry. But satirical fiction (as Robert Montgomery Bird was learning at about the same time)[87] was not the wanted type in America of the forties and fifties. Paulding was doing his best to splice his talents to a form, the historical romance, to which they were not perfectly suited.

The last of Paulding's novels, *The Puritan and His Daughter* (1849), was at once the author's favorite and his poorest long story. Beginning in the England of Oliver Cromwell and moving successively to Virginia and to an unspecified region probably on the Connecticut River,[88] the novel exhibits a geographical dispersion that is not compensated for by focus of character or action. Nor is the story completely redeemed by Paulding's use of the interesting thesis that the noxious gases of New England sectarianism can best be dissipated in the beneficent air of the freer West. Paulding's political preferences and critical propensities long survived his creative vigor.

In retrospect it appears that at the very centre of his talents Paulding was a commentator first and a story-teller second. He was always brimful of opinion, which he often managed to suppress for moderate intervals but which he took his keenest pleasure in expounding. The stories should in effect be illustrations or examples of the author's views. He himself admitted almost as much when he described the introductory chapters of the eight books of *Koningsmarke* as the "very cream" of the book.[89] One of the reviewers of *The Dutchman's Fireside* expressed a comparable opinion: "The best parts of our author's work are the digressions, wherein he drops the novelist and speaks for the author." [90] The point is perhaps debatable, but it is certain that Paulding never ceased airing strong opinion from his first book to his last. Broadly speaking, his opinions may be classified as political, ethical or religious, and literary.

The permanent feature of his political thought was his sturdy Americanism. This implied a love of his country, especially New York and points south-west, but it also implied a corresponding vindictiveness toward England. Paulding came to maturity at a time of extremely difficult relations between Britain and America. His first book, *The Diverting History of John Bull and Brother Jonathan* (1812), was an allegory that only perfunctorily clothed the bare facts that the author regarded John Bull as an overbearing, quarrelsome, jealous, and iniquitous old tyrant. Thereafter Paulding took every possible occasion to ridicule England and to impress his fellow-countrymen with the need of throwing off her influence, political, mercantile, and cultural. No English traveler's vituperation of American manners and institutions ever convinced Paulding that democracy was not superior to "Toryism," and although his contentious nature frequently involved him in local embroilments over ways and means in his own country, he never swerved essentially from liberal ideals implanted in him by Jefferson and rooted more deeply by Jackson. As far as America was concerned, he had no extreme love of New England (the land of fanatics), but his affections were not limited to his native state of New York. His intimacy with Virginia led him to voice approval of her social and political ideals even to the point of allowing that slavery was not so bad as it had been painted.[91] Doubtless he was somewhat beguiled by the plantation-owners' adaptation of the patriarchal system with its warrant in Scripture. In Virginia, at least, which was the Southern state Paulding knew best, slavery showed perhaps its most benign aspects.[92] Furthermore, slavery was part of an agrarian framework with which Paulding was in warm sympathy. For the one feature of American life which Paulding felt stood most in need of correction was the trend toward urban life with all its attendant evils of speculation and capitalistic exploitation of the working classes: wage slaves could be worse off than plantation slaves. Like Cooper, but with even more fervor, he hated Wall Street. Bankers as a class were anathema to him. Hence in his *Letters from the South* he deplored the fact that "we have too many people living in cities, in proportion to our farmers, who, after all, are the backbone of every country, whence originates its riches and its solid strength." [93]

As for ethics and religion Paulding stood for right living and joyous living. He stood in reverent awe of Creation, but to him it was no part of the Creator's plan to make his people permanently unhappy. Yet such was the effect of certain systems devised in His name. New England was rife with fanatical zeal to stamp out innocent pleasures. Blue laws were hateful in Paulding's eyes, and religious oppression irked him everywhere he met with it, whether in Connecticut or in the fictional region of Elsingburgh, Delaware. In *Koningsmarke* hardly any character comes off so badly at the author's hands as Dominie Kanttwell, the two-faced minister. For Kanttwell is the fictional representative of Paulding's idea

> that *excess* is in itself the root of all evil, and that whenever the blessed institution of religion interferes with our social and moral obligations, it ceases to be the conservator of human happiness, as well as of human virtue. As the excesses of sensual indulgence destroy the capacity for more refined gratifications, so do those of a fanatical religion blight and wither the most amiable feelings of the heart, rendering us insensible to many of the purest, the most exalted delights of which our nature is susceptible.[94]

Paulding's literary theories and criticisms are scattered through a score of volumes dating from his young manhood to his old age. The itch to comment on writing, whether his own or others', was one of his most persistent traits. Consistency he did not always maintain, but most of his detailed criticism stems from his creed of "rational fictions." Inasmuch as he himself often traveled the popular route of the historical romance, it is easy to understand that on occasion he was not a little pinched by his own insistence on common sense as the basic literary virtue. Indeed he never did achieve a comfortable coalition of opposing forces in his own theory and practice. While ostensibly writing romance he was in the position of sabotaging his own efforts by ridiculing the form or at least needlessly exposing its machinery.

It is certain that Paulding was no dyed-in-the-wool romanticist. So much might be guessed of a writer who referred to Dryden as "the best critic of modern times." [95] His roving imagination was firmly tethered to a stake of realism in his most exciting tales. He believed that the facts of history can be as exciting as extravagant concoctions of "Gothic or Grecian" wonders, and real characters as interesting as synthetic ideals or mechanized villains. His robust Americanism explains his preference for national themes and his independent spirit forbade slavish imitation—especially imitation of supercilious British writers. An admirer of Charles Brockden Brown's studies of American Indians, he was in agreement with Brown in protesting against derivative Gothic tales. He deprecated the constant resort to "the aid of superstition, the agency of ghosts, fairies, goblins, and all the antiquated machinery which till lately was confined to the nursery." Good material for romantic fiction need not be strikingly novel, but it should be plausible:

> The best and most perfect works of imagination appear to me to be those which are founded upon a combination of such characters as every generation of men exhibits, and such events as have often taken place in the world, and will again. Such works are only fictions, because the tissue of events which they record never perhaps happened in precisely the same train, and to the same number of persons, as are exhibited and associated in the relation. Real life is fraught with adventures, to which the wildest fictions scarcely afford a parallel; and it has this special advantage over its rival, that these events, however extraordinary, can always be traced to motives, actions, and passions, arising out of circumstances no way unnatural, and partaking of no impossible or supernatural agency. [96]

He adds that whereas it is easy to write stories involving irresponsible supernatural agents, it calls for a rare ability to manage materials out of life itself. Citing *Tom Jones* as the type of good romance, he pretty well sums up the qualities of a good writer of fiction as being the "rare and happy combination of invention, judgment, and experience." And he adds that the founders of the American nation possessed in their characters those things which should be the best guides to imaginative writing: "The only second-sight they possessed was founded on the solid basis of a keen recollection of the past, a rational anticipation of the future." This in effect was Paulding's theory of "rational fiction" as set forth in an essay called "National Literature," which appeared in the second series of *Salmagundi*, August, 1820. Appearing as it did on the threshold of an era of romantic fiction that in many cases knew no bounds of probability, Paulding's remarks called attention to his essential difficulty as a follower of the tradition of Scott and Cooper. Cooper he admired for his more realistic studies, especially *The Pioneers*. Scott, as part of the British tradition which Paulding fought so fiercely during more than a decade, he ridiculed vigorously. To him he devoted a burlesque poem of five cantos entitled *The Lay of the Scottish Fiddle* (1813). Whether in prose or poetry Sir Walter irritated the proponent of "rational" fiction.

The essay called "National Literature" is a remarkable document for the period. It is also unlike much, perhaps most, of Paulding's other reflections on the art of authorship in that it is coolly and objectively written. Its direct style is in strong contrast to the ironical vein in which he wrote in many of his prefatory chapters in *Koningsmarke* and in other words such as *Letters from the South* which incidentally touch the same subject. Time and again he lashes out against the feeble British writers who overinfluence their American colleagues for the worse. Imitation he thought was responsible for hundreds of soft, ephemeral books written by American authors. Virginian writers he liked particularly because their "independence of character, in a great degree preserves them from the degrading habit of perpetual imitation. They will not suffer the Edinburgh or the Quarterly to think and decide for them . . ."[97] Moreover imitating the English entailed a great deal of fawning upon noble and royal characters. This positively sickened Paulding:

> Hence the vast advantages accruing to an author from a discreet choice of his characters, whose actions, provided they are persons of a proper rank, may be both vulgar and insignificant, without either tiring or disgusting the reader. The hero, provided he is right royal, or even noble, may turn his palace into a brothel, or commit the most paltry meannesses, without losing his character;

and the heroine, if of sufficient rank, may, by virtue of her prerogative, swear like a fishwoman, without being thought in the least vulgar. The most delicate and virtuous female, properly imbued with a taste for the extempore historical novel, does not mind being introduced, by a popular author, into the company of strumpets, pimps, and their dignified employers, whose titles and patents of nobility give them the privilege of doing things that would disgrace the vulgar, who, poor souls, have no way of becoming tolerably respectable, but by conforming to the common decencies of life. So also, a Buckingham, a Rochester, or a Sir Charles Sedley, or any other distinguished person, historically witty, may be made by an author as coarse, flat, and vulgar in his conversations, as the said author himself, who puts the words into his mouth, and, ten to one, the reader will think he is banqueting on the quintessence of refined wit and humour. Not to multiply particular instances, we may lay it down as a general rule, that the dignity of actions, the refinement of morals, and the sharpness of wit, is exactly in proportion to the rank and quality of the characters to whom they appertain. . . .

We have endeavoured to make all the amends possible for the absence of what constitutes the quintessence of the interest arising from works of imagination, by the introduction of persons coming as near to kings and nobility, as any that are the natural product of our country. But, after all, we are obliged to confess, that Indian monarchs, provincial governors, nay, our good friend William Penn himself, though the illustrious founder of what may almost be called an empire, are but poor substitutes for dukes and earls, whose very titles tickle the fancy so delightfully, that the reader seems all the while swimming in an ocean of peacock's feathers . . .

To confess the honest truth, we are, as has been most likely discovered ere this, rather new in the trade of novel writing, having been partly induced to enter upon it, as people engage in the tobacco or grocery line, from seeing others prosper mightily in the business. But we shall do better hereafter, having felt the want of a hero and heroine of proper rank most sorely in the course of this work. We take this opportunity of advertising our friends, and the public in general, that we have at present six new historical novels on the anvil, one of which, we have contracted with our bookseller to hammer out every twelvemonth, and each of which shall contain one legitimate, tyrannical king, at least, provided there should be a sufficient number remaining unhanged at that time. We have also stipulated with our publisher, that not one of the characters shall be below a right-honourable, or an *Irish peer*, at least.[98]

Paulding was also exasperated by the vogue of certain popular authors (unspecified) who wrote in a facile, flimsy vein without bothering to perfect the motivation of their stories. He inveighed against what he called "extempore writing":

> But whatever may be the profit of the reader, certain it is, that of the author is amazingly enhanced by the increased velocity attained by this new mode of writing. Certain plodding writers, such as Fielding, Smollet, and others, whom it is unnecessary to name, wrote not above three or four works of this sort in the whole course of their lives; and what was the consequence? They lived from hand to mouth, as it were, for want of a knowledge of the art of writing extempore; and were obliged to put up with an immortality of fame, which they could never enjoy. Instead of making their fortune in a few years by the power of multiplying their progeny, they foolishly preferred to pass whole years in the unprofitable business of copying nature, and running a wild-goose chase after probability.[99]

These examples of Paulding's criticism, caustic in content, ironical in form, help to explain the malaise which always affected him more or less. The historical romance was vogue when he came into his maturity, but he could not hope to marry his art to a form he was only half in love with. His perpetual harping on what a novel or romance should and should not be must have wearied his readers as much as the fashionable writers irritated him. Often the only party to be hurt by glancing blows during the critical battles which Paulding introduced into his stories was romance, an innocent bystander. It would have been well if Paulding could have established himself as a satirical writer: his gifts were not very different from those of Brackenridge and Tyler. But for such fiction there might have been no market. Perhaps it was true in Paulding's time that, as Lowell said, "before we have an American literature, we must have an American criticism." [100] Certainly there were few critical canons to guide American novelists in the 1820's and 1830's except for the rather loose criteria for the historical romance. In this confused period, Paulding made a substantial success based partly on his conformity to apparent popular demand and partly on his inherent ability. His heyday was during the early 1820's. When, however, N. P. Willis savagely condemned Paulding as "flat, pointless, and essentially vulgar" on the occasion of the publication of Paulding's collected works, he severely damaged their author in critical quarters.[101] This was followed by a lag in public interest, though new editions of individual works continued to come out from time to time. As late as

1868, Scribner listed *The Dutchman's Fireside* as among its "popular books." [102] At present, more than a century after the period of his greatest success, Paulding is little known. He has a small faithful following of readers who value him for his vivid portrayals of "olden times in the new world," his occasionally spirited scenes of adventure, his loving evocation of a loved region. Most of all, perhaps, connoisseurs of fine prose recognize in Paulding a master of a keen, incisive idiom ready to serve alike the purposes of humor and critical reflection. But the broad public insists on story and sentiment, and from the point of view of maintaining popularity it would appear that a certain idyllic charm in his descriptions of rural and village life might well have been more fully capitalized by Paulding. His greatest defect—and the measure of his inferiority to Cooper—was his lack of illusion in scenes devoted to high adventure. In his studies of character and light episode on a less grandiose scale, he needed no "illusion," for he was drawing from the life.

CATHARINE MARIA SEDGWICK (1789-1867)

One of the first of a large number of women writers to win a considerable popularity in the second quarter of the nineteenth century was Catharine Maria Sedgwick. She began to publish in a period when few American novels but Cooper's were deemed worth reading, [103] but before many years she proved that a very good market was available to other native novelists. Finally eschewing the religious themes toward which her nature and training inclined her, as well as the sentimental matter which had been the basis of the most successful books of Hannah Foster and Mrs. Rowson, she cast in her lot with the writers of historical romance who followed in the wake of Cooper. She wisely forbore direct competition with Cooper, however, and mined particularly those veins in which he did not excel. She laid the scene of her most distinguished novel, *Hope Leslie* (1827), in Massachusetts, where, by common consent, Cooper was regarded as relatively unsuccessful. Moreover she merged elements from the novel of manners with the historical romance more successfully than Cooper. She was more adept than most of her contemporaries at recounting domestic detail and the small social transactions of village life. Consequently she elicited the interest of a large public of feminine readers for whom the too steady contemplation of bloody adventure on sea and in forest proved wearisome. She was withal a well-poised, tidy writer, and she focussed her work more rigidly than the blustering romancers. Whereas Cooper's proclivity was for expansiveness and spaciousness, Miss Sedgwick, operating on a smaller radius, proved what may be achieved by greater centripetal force. Yet she was sufficiently identified with the romantic genre to find her reputation sharply reduced when the type passed its peak of popularity. Her other resources, though respectable and even, in the case of her juvenile books, profitable, were not substantial enough from the point of view of belles lettres to create a lasting reputation. Today she is remembered chiefly for *Hope Leslie*, which still receives a measure of critical approval not to be wholly explained on the basis of local pride or patriotism.

Miss Sedgwick belonged to a distinguished family in which she took an inoffensive pride. Her grandmother was a sister of the founder of Williams College, and her father, a prominent lawyer and statesman, and for a number of years a member of Congress, stood high in the regard of the Federalist party during its declining days. From her father she naturally derived conservative political preferences, and she dissented only moderately from his distrust of any movement aimed to grant much political power to "the people." Yet, though in later years she adopted a social manner that "vacillated . . . between cordiality and a reserve amounting to hauteur," [104] she regarded herself as a true devotée of republican ideals; and she congratulated herself upon the fact that the earliest known representative of her family, "a Puritan and an Independent," received his political advancement from Cromwell "who achieved his own greatness, and not from the King Charleses who were born to it, and lost it by their own unworthiness." [105] At all events, the wholesome lessons written into her stories prove her faith in a relatively simple and pious life such as she herself lived as a girl and young woman in Stockbridge. Frequent trips to New York, however, balanced her rural life and gave her what she regarded as a primary educational advantage, namely, "country life with outlets to the great world." [106] Upon reaching womanhood she spent more and more time among the literati of New York but she retained her New England residence also.

Miss Sedgwick's strong religious bent was shown in her first book, *A New England Tale* (1822), which she undertook because she felt "spiritless and sad" and "wanted some pursuit." [107] Originally intended as a religious tract celebrating "some of the humbler and unnoticed virtues," it outgrew its author's intentions and reached the status of a somewhat amorphous story, which her friends persuaded her to publish. Miss Sedgwick set little store by the book, but notwithstanding some persons who were "miffed" because New England characters did not receive entirely complimentary attention, the reception of the book was so enthusiastic that her family confidently looked forward to her "future eminence." [108] The tale was read, as Bryant said, by "thousands who were by no means habitual readers of novels, and who found themselves none the worse for having read it." [109]

Miss Sedgwick's next work of fiction, *Redwood* (1824), was dedicated to Bryant, who had become acquainted with the brilliant Sedgwick family while he was living in Great Barrington. Beginning briskly on the assumption that "It is not a conclusive objection to a new book, that there are better ones already in existence that remain unread," she sets out to write a novel of manners which she hopes will be acceptable, for each new generation needs its own amusement and instruction: she is sure, at least, that her "efforts . . . will do no harm." [110] She has no idea of rivalling Cooper in his own domain: "There is but one individual (whom it would be affectation to call *unknown*) who has had eminent success in the delineations of former periods, or what is called historical romance." [111]

Notwithstanding some materials drawn from observation, the plot of *Redwood* is compounded of elements fairly familiar to readers of earlier American novels and minor novels of the later eighteenth century in England. Henry Redwood is the son of a rich planter of Virginia, "that State of the Union where the patrician rank has escaped in the greatest degree, the levelling principle of republicanism." As a youth he is obsessed by a desire for intellectual power much after the fashion of Godwinian young men in the eighteenth-century English novel and in C. B. Brown's novels. He contracts a secret marriage with a loveable creature, Mary Erwine, an orphan, whose blood is insufficiently blue to suit his father. When under the influence of the "poisonous society" of one Alsop he neglects her and goes to Europe, he receives in Rome a letter from a clergyman telling him (what no reader experienced in this period of the American novel will believe) that his wife has pined away and died. Subsequently he marries his cousin, "a spoilt child and flattered beauty," but his second wife soon indubitably dies, leaving a daughter, Caroline. At fourteen (it is characteristic of such a novel in this period that much time is consumed in the progress of the story) Caroline, who has been educated in South Carolina by a French governess under the careful eye of Grandmother Olney, is "brought out." At eighteen she is the darling of fashionable society and as accomplished as "a veteran belle of five and twenty." Upon becoming reacquainted with his daughter, Redwood, in whom aristocratic tastes are held in check by republican ideals, is mortified to discover that she has been spoiled by her education. He soon takes her on a tour of the Great Lakes and Canada. Upon the return journey a carriage accident (a device used with shameless frequency by novelists of the time) brings his party to an abrupt halt at the home of Farmer Lenox in Eton, Vermont. Here commences what threatens to be a very dull interval for a belle of so many ball rooms as Caroline. But while the party is waiting for Mr. Redwood's arm to mend, a pretty little enmity grows up between Caroline and Ellen Bruce, a wholesome type of local girl, who threatens to enlist too much of the attention not only of Caroline's father but also of a young man, Westall, whom Caroline hoped, with the approval of her father, to marry. Ultimately, as the reader has by now guessed, Ellen Bruce is revealed as the daughter of Redwood. Poetic justice assigns Westall to Ellen and grants to the spoiled Caroline for a husband a military officer.

Redwood sold well over a thousand copies in less than six months.[112] It was promptly reprinted in England, where it elicited a favorable comment from Mrs. Barbauld, and it was translated into French.[113] Booksellers spoke of it as better than *Redgauntlet*. Miss Sedgwick was freely compared with Scott, and there was a dispute in Parisian newspapers as to whether *Redwood* was written by Cooper.[114] It is obvious that the popularity of the book was due in part to the unexploited (American) field in which Miss Sedgwick was working. In some respects, to be sure—its rambling structure, its hackneyed plot, certain stock characters, and the frequent resort to letters—it looks backward rather than forward as far as the technique of the novel is concerned. Yet there is in it enough that is new—in the delineation of New England landscape, in the picture of the Shaker community (which despite the author's avowed intention of avoiding sectarian embroilments, is described with some emphasis on its "wild fanaticism"),[115] and in the undeniably fresh and real characterization of Debby Lenox, the farmer's unmarried daughter—to account for the enthusiasm with which the book was received.

In *Hope Leslie* (1827), Miss Sedgwick's best known novel,[116] she remedied some of the defects she had exhibited in her earlier writing. Although the action, like that of most novels of the time, covers a great many years, the story is coherently and plausibly related. Most of the dramatis personae are possessed of real individuality, especially Hope Leslie, who is one of the most natural heroines in the early American novel. The action takes place in the seventeenth century. William Fletcher, a young Englishman prevented by parental interference from marrying the girl of his choice, finally marries an orphan girl who willingly accompanies him on Winthrop's expedition to the New World. Soon after settling at Springfield, Massachusetts, however, he learns that his former fiancée, who subsequently married one Leslie, has died en route to America and has left her daughters under his guardianship.

He proceeds promptly to Boston to meet his new charges, who are now rechristened Hope and Faith. Detained in Boston by business and illness, Mr. Fletcher keeps Hope with him, but he sends Faith, with her aunt and her tutor, to Springfield, where the Fletcher ménage has recently been augmented by two Indian servants, Magawisca and Oneco. These are the children of a discontented Pequod chief whose "humane virtues" [117] had been replaced by a fierce hatred of the oppression of the white people. Before Fletcher's return to Springfield, discord between the Indians and the white settlers reaches a fearful climax in a brutal attack resulting in the death of his wife and younger children, as well as the capture of his boy, Everell, and Faith. Everell's death has been prevented by the intervention of Magawisca, daughter of the wrathful Pequod chief, Monomotto. Further difficulties with the Indians menace the white people. Hope is captured once, but the heroine experiences her greatest peril through the machinations of a polished villain of Popish persuasion, Sir Philip Gardiner, whose ardent and reckless pursuit of Hope culminates in a thrilling attempt at abduction. To these sufficiently exciting materials Miss Sedgwick adds the theme of Hope's renunciation of the man she really loves, but in the end an appropriate disposition is made of all the persons still remaining alive after many mortuary episodes. Faith, however, has become so accustomed to Indian ways that she chooses at the end to return to the wigwam with Oneco. As in *The Last of the Mohicans*, the fate of the "vanishing American" is sympathetically presented, for Miss Sedgwick was deeply impressed by the injustice which the Indians suffered at the hands of the white people.[118]

Though exciting as a story, *Hope Leslie* is "no romantic fiction," but a compound of controlled invention plus history. A great many authentic sources are behind (sometimes not far enough behind) the march of her narrative. Events, persons, and customs from the pages of history are freely drawn upon—the settlement of Springfield, the Pequod wars, Governor Winthrop's leadership, Thomas Morton's heterodoxy, the Blue Laws, the Puritan sabbath, witchcraft, the quarrel over Popish encroachments on Puritan America. Yet the historical material, if not always perfectly assimilated, is not emphasized to the serious detriment of the narrative, which is everywhere plausible and coherent. The treatment of the Indians is able, especially with respect to the brooding Magawisca, who is torn between loyalty to her race and affection for the Fletcher family, but Miss Sedgwick modestly waives the right to be considered in this respect a competitor of the author of "a recent popular work" (doubtless Cooper's *Last of the Mohicans*).[119] The reader to whom Indian wars are tedious finds plenty of collateral interests, for here, as in (the later) *The Linwoods*, the author centres attention less on the action, however exciting, than on the people: her books are not adventure stories. The characterizations are not always successful—Everell is just a type of an impetuous and attractive young man and Sir Philip is only slightly altered from conventional villains—but the whole story is given vraisemblance by the colloquial speech and natural action of Hope Leslie. Hope's reactions to various situations in which her emotions are deeply involved are indicated with far more plausible psychology than had been evident in the heroines of Charles Brockden Brown or Cooper or any of the lesser novelists who preceded her. Hope shares, moreover, the comic abilities with which some of the minor characters, notably Aunt Grafton, are more fully endowed. Sentiment there is in the story, but Miss Sedgwick's fine common sense keeps it from reaching that saturation point which was one of the abuses of the domestic novel both before and after her time.

Hope Leslie was very favorably received. It went through several editions, and it strengthened Miss Sedgwick's position as one of the few American novelists whose works were consistently read even amid a vast influx of English books. Even Mrs. Trollope, whose peregrinations through America did not often move her to eulogy, spoke of its "great merit." [119a] Indeed *Hope Leslie* brought Miss Sedgwick's reputation to such dizzy heights that the author counselled herself against undue pride in her accomplishments:

> I hear from all quarters what honestly seems to me very extravagant praise of "Hope Leslie." I trust I shall not be elated by it. At present I certainly am not, for I feel too heavily oppressed, too firmly grappled to the earth to mount in the balloon of vanity. [120]

Sismondi, however, to whom she sent a copy, complained of her severe treatment of the Pilgrim fathers. His point was not very well taken, for Miss Sedgwick regarded the early Puritans with reasonable pride. [121] Her reply to the criticism shows that although she was anxious to treat the early settlers with impartiality, she had a strongly realistic vein:

> The notice you have bestowed on "Hope Leslie" has made me anxious to redeem a fault I have unintentionally committed in so delineating the Pilgrims as to degrade them in your estimation. I meant to touch their characters with filial reverence. Their bigotry, their superstition, and, above all, their intolerance, were too apparent on the pages of history to be forgotten. But these were the vices of their age, and they were only partially disengaged from the chains that bound their contemporaries . . . They had

a most generous and self-devoting zeal to the cause of liberty, so far as they understood it, but they were still in the thraldom of Judaic superstitition, and adhered steadfastly, as unhappily a majority of their descendants do, to Calvin's interpretation of Scripture, even now the popular dogmas of our enlightened country.[122]

Sismondi's comment was not typical of the popular reaction, however, and the book seems to have been read chiefly for its entertainment value. Although some critics, Poe among them,[123] regarded *The Linwoods* as her best work, *Hope Leslie* apparently retained its popularity longer.[124]

Miss Sedgwick's rather obvious use of documentation for the background of *Hope Leslie* (which curiously enough emphasizes the invented characters of the plot as such even while it gives authenticity to the atmosphere) showed her limitations as a writer of historical romance. She herself seems to have felt that she lacked Cooper's power of creating illusion. In *Hope Leslie* she speaks of her difficulty in this respect:

> The mighty master of fiction has but to wave his wand to preserve the past to his readers with all the vividness and distinction of the present; but we, who follow him at an immeasurable distance—we, who have no magician's enchantments, wherewith we can imitate the miracles wrought by the rod of the prophet—we must betake ourselves to the compass and the rule, and set forth our description as minutely and exactly as if we were making out an inventory for a salesman.[125]

Consequently it was perhaps a natural instinct which led her to try her talents in a novel of contemporary life. To this decision she was also urged by the "cheap reprints of popular English novels [which] have reduced the value of coypright productions . . ." [126] In the novel of contemporary manners, moreover, she had the opportunity of exploiting her ability in reporting those details of domestic life which had thus far received relatively little attention at the hands of American novelists. Unfortunately, in her next novel, *Clarence* (1830), she merged her undeniably real episodes from daily life of contemporary New York, where from her youth onward Miss Sedgwick spent a great deal of the year, with a superannuated plot involving mistaken identity, parental tyranny, the perils of an heiress, concealed crime, mysterious manuscripts, overheard conversations, synthetic villains, and other badly worn devices. Her legacy from Miss Edgeworth, whom she refers to both in this novel and elsewhere,[127] included not only a gift for small

realism but also antiquated devices for producing action. Miss Edgeworth's wholesome domestic ideals also animate her, as, for example,
when Frank Carrol rebukes his wife for setting up for a social star
merely because her sister is *haut ton:* "I thank God [says Frank] there
is a barrier between us and the fashionable world . . ." [128] Similarly
satire is implied in a woman of fashion's comment on the latest novels:
" 'No,' said another lady, 'I never read *American* novels, there's no high
life in them.' " [129] Miss Sedgwick, who herself moved in good society of
the enlightened sort, resolutely supported sound middle-class ideals, and
she praised Miss Edgeworth as "the beneficent genius who has made the
actual social world better and happier." [130] Miss Sedgwick's own works
are provided with a vein of intelligent and inoffensive moralizing, but
she had insufficient depth to offer any significant interpretation of
urban life.

Clarence was brought out in 1830 by a publisher who was optimistic
enough to pay $1200 for the copyright of an edition of 2000 copies;[131]
but despite the author's belief that it was better than any book she
had written and was "better adapted to the general taste of novel-
readers," [132] *Clarence* appears to have been less read than any of Miss
Sedgwick's long stories.[133] Her vivacious transcript of manners was
unsuccessfully grafted to an old and devitalized plot structure. In her
next novel Miss Sedgwick wisely returned to the species in which she
had made her greatest success—the historical romance crossed by the
novel of manners.

In this new novel, *The Linwoods* (1835), Miss Sedgwick showed no
more inventive genius than before, but she displayed with even greater
success her special ability to handle a social milieu. The story is on the
surface a tale of Revolutionary days, but the rataplan of military life is
heard only from a distance, and the author's main concern is for the
personal lives of individual characters whose fortunes are only partially
determined by the national crisis.[134] The scene of action changes frequently but is laid most of the time in New York and a country town
near Boston. Linwood, a patrician paterfamilias, is such a strong Tory
during the Revolution that when his son Herbert joins Washington's
army, the boy is promptly disowned—to be reclaimed only at the
happy ending. A complete foil to Herbert is his friend Jasper Meredith,
who is definitely Tory in sympathies but, for the sake of personal
safety, an avowed neutral. He is seen to be a cad in his trifling with the
affections of Bessie Lee, the charming and ingenuous daughter of an
affluent farmer. Unable to consider marrying her, he finally responds to
his mother's plan to have him marry Lady Anne Seton, his cousin, who
is an English heiress under Mrs. Meredith's guardianship. But Lady

Anne, having had opportunities to observe the fine character of Herbert Linwood, spurns the proposal of the weaker Jasper. Thereupon Jasper turns his attention to the radiantly beautiful Isabella, sister of Herbert—only to find that Isabella, aware of the perfidy of Jasper toward Bessie, is by now hearkening to the wooing of Eliot Lee, poor Bessie's brother, described disdainfully by her father as "the portionless son of a New-England farmer." [135] Having lost both the heiress and the beauty, Jasper in a fit of pique plunges into an unhappy marriage with a giddy creature who "cannot be bound by those petty axioms and frigid rules that shackle [her] sex." [136] In the meantime, Bessie, the victim of Jasper's trifling, has gone mad, is now recovered, and plans to devote herself to a saintly life helping the poor. Obviously Miss Sedgwick's interest is focussed on this love tangle rather than on the events of the Revolution. She manages to bring in (often with imperfect success) many allusions to the campaigns of the middle years of the war and to celebrate a number of heroes of the American army as well as sympathizers from abroad—Washington, Putnam, Lafayette, Kosciusko, etc. Though allusions to Washington were routine in American historical romances, Miss Sedgwick wrote of him with special authority, for her father had been well acquainted with the President.[137] Her action, moreover, if sometimes too dispersed, is frequently made exciting through siege, capture, and the minor exigencies of warfare. Yet action *per se* is not her forte, and her most advantageous use of the Revolution as a theme lay in her analysis of the critical social relations partially induced by the issue between Tory and Whig.

The characterization is again competent without being profound. The men are on the whole less well drawn than the women. Isabella, the nominal heroine, is sketched in a manner so often employed by later novelists in America that she seems conventional, and yet earlier American novels had provided no complete model for her portrait. Bessie Lee, called by Poe "one of the most effective personalities to be found in our fictitious literature," [138] undoubtedly has her counterpart among the distressed females of Scott's stories, but her mental decline is recorded with a psychological insight that was probably rare before Miss Sedgwick's time.[139] Even the minor characters, perhaps, less original in type, are sketched with enough individuality (sometimes expressed in humor) to afford entertainment and a sense of reality, especially Herbert's bodyguard, Kisel. Miss Sedgwick was in fact very skilful in the light delineation of character. Her dialogue, too, is exceedingly well-phrased and, despite occasional interludes of language a bit more elaborate than fits the character, very real.[140] Her style here, as in almost all her work, is marked by both fluency and precision. She was, if not a bluestocking,[141] at least a very well-read person and a carefully disciplined writer.

The Linwoods had appeared at about the height of Miss Sedgwick's popularity as a writer of novels. Several editions were called for. It seemed likely that another book in a similar vein would be welcomed, but whether because of a realization that she probably could never surpass *The Linwoods* and *Hope Leslie*, or because she wished to devote herself more definitely to humanitarian projects, Miss Sedgwick never resumed the historical romance. Her prolific writing after this time fell into two classes of books, juveniles and tales with a moral or sociological purpose. The latter concerned themselves largely with the education of girls and with social justice. She devoted herself to doing good to society with much the same zeal that animated the "sweet singer of Hartford," Lydia Huntley Sigourney. *Live and Let Live*, for example, is a story treating of "the manifold trials and discouragements of the mistress of a family in relation to her domestics." [142] The book is more humanitarian than democratic, and the point of view is always that of the enlightened lady speaking of her "inferiors in position." The author urges American women to instruct their daughters in managing and ministering to a household—for "emergencies constantly occur where a *lady* must perform the primitive offices of women, or her family will be comfortless." [143] Like Enos Hitchcock, author of *Memoirs of the Bloomsgrove Family*, Miss Sedgwick deplores the tendency of the times to confine a young lady's training to "French, Italian, drawing, music, &c." [144] Miss Sedgwick is not radical in her attitude, and most of her discussion of the emancipation of woman is qualified by the implied premise that woman's place is in the home. Yet she dimly discerns a day of something like social equality and of a greater range of intellectual activity for women. In the meantime she argues the need of a housewife's being practical and the justice (as well as wisdom) of treating servants so that there will be a minimum of suffering and discord. If her humanitarian thought does not now seem advanced, it was relatively so in her time, for an anecdote is told of a person who professed to having been improved by reading *Live and Let Live* for previously he "had supposed the Irish were to be treated as you would treat slaves!" [145] As a novel, *Live and Let Live* is ineffective; Miss Sedgwick wrote too early to appreciate fully the possibilities of a story based on the condition of slaves. Nor could she foresee the deluge of tears soon to be wrung from thousands of readers by the plight of governesses who, once the vogue was established by Charlotte Brontë in *Jane Eyre*, became the heroines of many sentimental romances.[146] Hence although she was keenly interested in the improvement of conditions in almshouses and prisons (which she personally visited)[147] and was occasionally in contact with such advanced thinkers as Harriet Martineau, Lucy Stone, Fredrika Bremer,[148] and Margaret Fuller, she confined her analysis of social problems to tracts and her lesser tales. A close liaison between social justice and the novel remained for American writers of a slightly later generation. Moreover Miss Sedgwick always wrote of social improvement with a great awareness of the gulf between classes. The implication is that the lower classes should be aided *as* lower classes rather than encouraged to ascend to a higher class. She was not a crusader for "democracy"; charity interested her more than any radical revision of the social system. She was strongly American, however, and particularly disapproved of imitating the ways of the French, even by the interspersion of too many French phrases in conversation.[149]

As Miss Sedgwick grew older (she lived until 1867), it became clear that writing had become essentially an avocation for her. Indeed as early as 1835 she had expressed the opinion that the art of writing was secondary:

> My author existence has always seemed something accidental, extraneous, and independent of my inner self. My books have been a pleasant occupation and excitement in my life. The notice, and friends, or acquaintance, they have procured me, have relieved me from the danger of ennui and blue devils, that are most apt to infest a single person. But they constitute no portion of my happiness—that is, of such as I derive from the dearest relations of life. When I feel that my writings have made any one happier or better, I feel an emotion of gratitude to Him who has made me the medium of any blessing to my fellow-creatures. And I do feel that I am but the instrument.[150]

The emphasis upon utility (perhaps an afterglow of Puritanism in her) explains much in Miss Sedgwick's writing. The passion for writing as such she did not have. She judged not only her own books but the writings of others by the same criteria. Thus she regarded Thackeray as a "libeler of humanity." She read Byron but believed that he "ought to be ashamed of wasting his noble genius upon Giaours and Corsairs." [151] Her criticism of Hawthorne's *The House of the Seven Gables* is a clear indication that in her old age at least she was unable to think of art as entirely separate from practical uses:

> There is marvelous beauty in the diction; a richness and originality of thought that give the stamp of unquestionable genius; a microscopic observation of the external world, and the keenest

analysis of character; an elegance and finish that is like the work of a master sculptor—perfect in its artistic details. And yet, to my mind, it is a failure. It fails in the essentials of a work of art; there is not essential dignity in the characters to make them worth the labor spent on them. A low-minded vulgar hypocrite, a weak-minded nervous old maid, and her half-cracked brother, with nothing but beauty, and a blind instinctive love of the beautiful, are the chief characters of the drama. 'Little Phoebe' is the redemption, as far as she goes, of the book—a sweet and perfect flower amidst corruption, barrenness, and decay. The book is an affliction. It affects me like a passage through the wards of an insane asylum, or a visit to specimens of morbid anatomy. It has the unity and simple construction of a Greek tragedy, but without the relief of divine qualities or great events; and the man takes such savage delight in repeating and repeating the raw head and bloody bones of his imagination. There is nothing genial, excepting always little Phoebe, the ideal of a New England, sweet-tempered, 'accomplishing' village girl. I might have liked it better when I was younger, but as we go through the tragedy of life we need elixirs, cordials, and all the kindliest resources of the art of fiction. There is too much force for the subject. It is as if a railroad should be built and a locomotive started to transport skeletons, specimens, and one bird of Paradise! [152]

On the other hand she warmly approved George Eliot's *Mill on the Floss* for its "heart-probings and knowledge of human life"; and despite her dubiousness in regard to the French she read *Les Misérables* with great interest as a book dealing with "the greatest topics of humanity." [153] The writer whose art *per se* appears to have evoked her greatest admiration was Charlotte Brontë.[154]

Miss Sedgwick's increasing preoccupation with juvenile and social studies toward the latter part of her career did not detract greatly from the position of eminence she enjoyed in American letters during her lifetime, but it perhaps serves to explain her later loss of fame. She was not a strongly original writer. She was facile, intelligent, and versatile, but she lacked intensity and great power of imagination. A contemporary judgment of *Redwood* might well be applied to her writing as a whole: "it is work of much talent and of excellent taste, but not of high and commanding genius." [155]

As a follower of Cooper she was exceedingly able and shrewd. She coped valiantly with Indian raids and military campaigns, and she recreated an earlier social atmosphere with more fidelity and finesse than most writers of her period. She was praised by a contemporary critic for "portraits drawn with singular fidelity from life, and incidents so natural that the New Englander can scarcely doubt that they are his village's history." [156] Nevertheless she has suffered somewhat from occupying a position between two eras. Her sobriquet, "the Maria Edgeworth of America," is a reminder not only of her warm humanity, her wit, and her command of phrase, but also of her tendency to fall back on somewhat threadbare narrative devices. Had she come to maturity as a writer a little bit later, she might have capitalized her talents as a social historian more fully, for in her best work she distinctly looks forward to the novel of manners at its best. Moreover in her sharply defined studies of New England manners, she even forecasts dimly the well-balanced social studies of Howells. Like him she possessed a goodly portion of common sense and a style distinguished for naturalness and clarity. She avoided the extremes of both sentiment and melodrama. In her own time she won a vast public—including a larger share of women readers than Cooper or Charles Brockden Brown had been able to win—for her honest, well-proportioned tales compounded of history, light invention, humanitarian sentiment, "cheerful philosophy" [157] and the easy delineation of domestic manners. Good ideals dominated her life and her art.

TIMOTHY FLINT (1780-1840) AND EARLY WESTERN FICTION

Cooper had a considerable trans-Allegheny public, but it was generally agreed by those who lived in the West that his *The Prairie* had failed to interpret the spirit of the region. The failure of the book to succeed in this respect was not attributed principally to the author's defects as a writer, for, as one critic wrote, "in delineating the West, no power of genius, can supply the want of opportunities for personal observation on our natural and social aspects." [158] Such opportunities to observe the West were available, however, to an increasing number of settlers, some of whom were or became writers. In the twenties and thirties a considerable literature of the West grew up. A great deal of the publication that emanated from such flourishing centres as Cincinnati and Lexington (Kentucky) was of course purely utilitarian and much was controversial. Yet the major fields of belles lettres—poetry, fiction, the drama—were also tilled by Westerners, who hoped to prove that pioneer life was not incompatible with the production of art. Magazines earnestly tutored their readers in "sectional loyalty," and leaders among the literati insisted that "native materials" were best for Western writers.[159] In general the results of their efforts before the middle of the century were not distinguished. In general, also, their interpretation of Western territory, though undertaken with a view to displacing spurious accounts, proved to be blurred by a certain "romantic haze." It seemed hard to write about the West without trying to express its vastness and future promise more than the actual conditions in a given locality.[160] It was hard not to make a rough backwoodsman into a "romantic" figure. A certain provincial pride prevented the West from assessing its own civilization at its actual value. When in his *Legends of the West* James Hall *did* dwell realistically upon pioneer people—with all their faults and crudity as well as their virtues—he was attacked as disloyal: he was "no true son of the border." [161] Moreover Western writers sensed that there was more potential profit in romanticizing the West than in itemizing its reality, just as later on, in the far West, Bret Harte was to succeed best by throwing a romantic color over the glare of actuality. For whatever reason, the Ohio Valley writers seemed to prefer to handle the promissory notes of romance rather than the petty cash of realism. There were exceptions to this rule, but in general the more gifted Western writers of belles lettres attempted to celebrate rather than to record the growth of the West. Not unnaturally they felt the need of "advertizing" a region either ignored or misrepresented by Eastern writers. As a group they are now largely unknown today except to special students.[162] The most important writer of fiction in the group, James Hall, devoted himself chiefly to short narratives. The most realistic fiction writer was Caroline M. Kirkland. The earliest and most prolific novelist among them was Timothy Flint.

Just as most of the earliest "American" writers were born in England, many of the founders of Western fiction were emigrants from the Atlantic states. Timothy Flint was born at North Reading, Massachusetts. He never completely severed the emotional bond between himself and his native region, and he frequently made visits to New England, but he spent many of his most active years in Western travel or residence, and his literary service—as novelist, travel-writer, and editor—was almost entirely devoted to the West. He was one of the persons chiefly responsible for the rapid literary growth of Cincinnati in the early twenties and thirties. By apprenticeship a schoolmaster, by profession a minister, by temperament a mixture of the dreamer and the adventurer, he led a life of much color and variety. Dissatisfaction with his professional status and the impairment of his health seem to have motivated his first journeyings.[163] He did not wholly give up religious work, and indeed he acted as a missionary at St. Charles, Missouri, for three years. He was an indefatigable traveler, however, and at one time or another he had visited most of the country east of the Rocky Mountains as well as the West Indies, Canada, (probably) South America, and (possibly) Europe.[164] During most of the last six years of his life his home was in Louisiana, but he spent summers in New England.

Cincinnati was a town of nearly twenty thousand people when Flint lived there from 1827 to 1832.[165] His son at the same time operated a publishing business (which issued some of his father's books) and a retail book store. Already the author of two books, *Francis Berrian* (1826) and *Recollections of the Last Ten Years,* Flint began at once the publishing of the *Western Monthly Review,* a magazine dedicated to belles lettres. The West, he said in his first editorial pronouncement, was possessed of its "thousand orators and poets" but thus far had "not a solitary journal expressly constituted to be the echo of public literary opinion." [166] He was irked, too, because he knew "with what a curl of the lip . . . an Atlantic reviewer contemplates the idea of a work written west of the Allegheny mountains." [167] But like several similar ventures, Flint's magazine soon failed, for the West "was not ready for a literary review." Its reading public was small and such material as it required could easily be supplied by Eastern publications or reprints of British periodicals.[168] But Flint had other irons in the Cincinnati fire. One of them was establishing a church "like those of the fathers in New England." Though he was by now tending toward Unitarianism, the church was to be nameless and non-sectarian: so much did Flint dislike doctrinal wrangling. Another interest was writing fiction; by 1830 he had published three additional novels.

Flint's endowment as a writer may be judged from his first novel, *Francis Berrian, or The Mexican Patriot* (1826). The story is represented as having been told to the narrator by Francis Berrian during a voyage down the Ohio and Mississippi rivers toward "the Spanish frontier." Francis Berrian was born in a New England village near Boston. He admired the devotion to high principle and strong discipline which characterized the "substantial yeomanry" among whom he grew up, and he thought of their schoolhouses as "those thousand nurseries of New England's greatness." [169] Yet after being graduated from Harvard College he is seized by a wanderlust which makes him break away from the home land he praised: like the Emerson of "The Problem," he could admire without wishing to emulate. He packs for the West without any very clear view of his probable course of action. He boats it down the Ohio and the Mississippi and begins to explore the romantic Southwest in the company of a band of young men engaged in "traffic with the Spanish and Indians for mules." He aims not to make money but to release his spirit. His romantic hunger is fed by the vast plains and by the "sublime chain" of the Rocky Mountains. He enjoys living as a neighbor of the primitive Commanche [*sic*] Indians. He quotes Virgil and thinks of Byron. Here, far away from the competitive life of "civilization," the soul can fulfill itself. But another sort of romantic excitement presently fills his breast when he is besought by a beautiful girl to save her from Indian abductors. It is the radiant Doña Martha Miguela d'Alvaro who needs his assistance.

Thus far the book has had the leisurely air of travel-book and idyll, but now it is suddenly converted into an exciting tale of adventure roughly analogous to the historical romance of Cooper and his confrères. In brief, Berrian delivers the damsel from her immediate danger and restores her to the grateful arms of her aristocratic father, the Conde d'Alvaro, at Santa Fe. Berrian is received graciously by all the household of the Conde, but he is at once hated by the dashing Don Pedro Guttierez, who, it is understood, is to become the husband of Doña Martha. Gratitude dictates that the Conde shall do something for the young rescuer of his daughter. A staunch royalist, he offers to give Berrian an officer's commission under Don Pedro, but Berrian is sure that he cannot bring himself to "draw a sword in defence of the claims of Ferdinand VII. [*sic*] upon any part of Spanish America." [170] The Conde then engages Berrian to teach English to Doña Martha and certain other girls, but he puts him on his honor not to attempt to unsettle the marital arrangements already contemplated. Berrian is on his honor for the rest of the book—throughout all the complicated phases of a Mexican revolution in Durango. Berrian, of course, serves the rebels. Against his own interest he twice saves the rascally life of his rival for the hand of Doña Martha, but fate (or Timothy Flint) finally steps in to tip the scales of romance in his favor: the treacherous Don Pedro is finally captured and "literally torn to pieces" by the angry citizenry. Thus Doña Martha reverts permanently to the arms that had first saved her life and honor. Berrian takes his trophy on a visit back to New England, where he is forced to tell and retell his adventures to the astonished yeomanry. All are agog at the beauty of Doña Martha, but Berrian's spinster aunt sniffs at the Popish bride because she has never heard of the "five points" of Calvinism. Berrian plans to build a "firstrate house of pure Chelmsford granite" in New England for a part-time residence, but he intends to make his home in New Spain. His father is astonished at such a decision, for he "would not swap that orchard, and the broad meadow, and the barn hill field for all the lands in Mexico," and, as for him, you would never catch him "beyond the great river Connecticut." [171]

Returning his dramatis personae to New England at the end of *Francis Berrian* was an effective stroke on the part of the author: it gives a semblance of form to a novel which is on the whole poorly constructed.

Flint wrote hastily and haphazardly. His language was seldom more than adequate and often less. The finer points of the technique of narrative he did not bother to acquire. When Doña Martha's tale of distress on one occasion is interrupted by her "burst of irrepressible grief," she at once resumes her statement with a precision that seems to indicate a complete divorce between her emotions and her speech centres:

> "Stranger! you are of our race. You are instructed and must be a man of humanity. Surely my confidence in you cannot be misplaced. Should it appear, after the arrival of the deputation, that I am not to be set at liberty, or in any event, if I am to be persecuted by that being, I put every thing dear into your hands, and appeal to you to aid me to escape to my parents. Whatever motives detain one of your pursuits in this place, they could not but operate to induce you to such an act of honor and humanity; and there is nothing of reward, or gratitude, that such an act would not claim from my parents." [172]

Even in 1826 such balderdash could not have been condoned; Cooper by comparison seems realistic. That Flint, who was natural and plausible, though not adroit, in reporting simple experience as such, should stuff his book with such twaddle must be attributed to the conventions of his day: nobody wanted a realistic heroine. Not until the time of Eggleston would the West produce novelists who dared to take the whalebone and starch out of their leading characters.

Flint's romance is turgid, but interesting realistic details crop out. When Berrian is received into the d'Alvaro household, he is accepted warmly as the rescuer of Doña Martha, but as a New Englander he is only tolerated. Only gradually does it appear to the Spanish aristocrats that he is an exception in a "nation of pedlars and sharpers, immoderately addicted to gain." Berrian replies briskly, though diplomatically, to this disparagement of his kinfolk: "For a man to know the force of his patriotism, it is necessary that he should be in a foreign country, and hear his own vilified." [173] Occasionally, too, Flint lets a little breath of humor creep into his closely packed adventure. When, for example, a particularly sleazy-looking band of men gather to form a defense for Doña Martha, Flint reports that the group was "in appearance not unlike the regiment of Falstaff. I did not doubt that they would all have scampered away in view of twenty Commanches." [174] Here Flint writes somewhat in the simple manner he adopted in his autobiographical writing.

Francis Berrian is, of course, partly autobiographical in its representation of a maladjusted New Englander seeking surcease of sorrow in the broad bosom of the West. Although the story reaches more distant regions (in New Spain) than Flint ever traversed, yet Francis Berrian who describes himself (after Rousseau) as "a dreamer with my eyes open" is patently a stand-in for Timothy Flint taking vicarious satisfaction in contrasting the rigors of a winter on the Atlantic coast—enduring the sleety power of a "Northeaster"—with a life of dreamy ease in the land of the catalpa and the mocking bird. "I suspected [Berrian (speaking for Flint) tells the Condesa] there was a sufficient leaven of romance in my composition to unfit me for the hard struggle and the dry competition of actual experience." [175] Obviously here was a man ripe to appreciate the sentiments of Chateaubriand, whose books had lately been published in America. Add mouldy ruined monuments and agreeably melancholy thoughts of the tomb to Cooper's experience of forest solitudes, and you get something like the tone of Chateaubriand.[176] And so we find Francis Berrian announcing this new note in American fiction—a sympathetic response to Chateaubriand's variety of tender mysticism in forest fastnesses. Berrian tells the Condesa of his passion for the author of *Atala* (which he quotes from memory), and he vouchsafes that Chateaubriand's travels afford passages of poetic fervor which provide "abundant aliment for day-dreams." When asked why such passages brought him to her country, he replies with a long speech which may be regarded as the emotional nucleus of *Francis Berrian*:

> "Such passages, particularly that, 'une belle nuit,' &c. gave me back more beautifully the image of my own thoughts. I was determined to converse with nature alone in those prairies, and those boundless deserts, that he so delightfully painted to my imagination. I could not hope to find these places, except in the western regions of my own country, and that part of yours contiguous to them. My journey from the Mississippi to this place has, thus far, more than realized my images. I worshipped in all the forms of nature, from the lowly and inaccessible swamp of the Mississippi, the abode of gloom and fever, and vocal only with the notes of the owl, and the howling of wolves, to the extended plantation, with its mansion, surrounded by the little village of hovels, and from the region of the plantations, to the grassy sea of the prairies, and the sublime scenery of yonder chain of mountains, to the beautiful valley, in which dwelt the ruthless, but primitive Commanches; a place so exquisitely beautiful in its scenery, that even your daughter, under all the gloom and apprehension of her residence there, felt that beauty; to this place, where all the contrasts of social and primitive life, of wealth and poverty, refinement and simplicity, are brought side by side . . ." [177]

Dissatisfaction and disillusionment with civilization is also a conspicuous theme in Flint's second novel, *The Life and Adventures of Arthur Clenning* (1828), but the setting for most of the action is far removed from that of *Francis Berrian*. Flint seems to have been obsessed by the Robinson-Crusoe motif, and here he gives it full rein. The hero goes to sea to make his fortune on a ship bound from Liverpool to New Holland (Australia). The ship is wrecked and Arthur is cast ashore on an uninhabited volcanic island. Virtually destitute of man-made equipment, he finds a beautiful grotto, where he can make a shift to live, sustenance being provided by a bread-fruit tree, an oyster bed, and a spring of fresh water. Presently he discovers and revives the unconscious body of one of the women passengers of the ship, Augusta Wellman. An English heiress and prone to be snobbish, Augusta is grateful for Arthur's aid, but she means to maintain propriety and each night assigns him to the hall bedroom of the grotto. The story passes through routine phases of desert-island experience—making the raft, salvaging the precious items from the hulk, resisting the savages arrived from island suburbs, and domesticating the savage (female, this time) rescued from cannibalism. Of course Arthur finally wins Augusta, and he himself marries the happy pair by reading the Episcopal service. A daughter is born to them in whose interest they finally leave their idyllic island—after a period of three mainly happy years. Father Defoe of course has stood sponsor for much of the detail in this part of the book, but Flint has also added imaginative touches learned, apparently, from Bernardin de Saint-Pierre. But the story is far from ended when the island is abandoned. Further adventures (too detailed even for brief synopsis) carry Arthur and family to New Holland, where the convict-ridden society is exceedingly disagreeable; to England, where patrician papa Wellman snubs them; and to America, where they establish themselves at the Morris Birbeck settlement on the Mid-Western prairies. There young Arthur Clenning (the family has increased) will grow up as a genuine "Buckeye." He will also, by a barefaced convention, have plenty of money, for at the very end Flint goes back to England and retrieves old Wellman's fortune for Arthur and Augusta.

Behind all this hodge-podge of adventure one is constantly aware of the critical and didactic author. Flint points out several lessons. First, society is often so mean and unfair that a retreat to nature seems the only solution of the problem of personal unhappiness. Even as she contemplates their return to civilization (so that the daughter may be educated!) Augusta declares that "man is neither so good, or true as those kind animals that I leave, nor can any thing equal this grand and lovely nature." [178] Flint also looks askance at American politics. He speaks sarcastically of a local congressman—

> a man who had obtained his place by crouching and purring to the people in the first instance, who was alternately a toad eater to the great and a tyrant to the small—a union much more common, than is generally imagined. [179]

With a tincture of the same sort of bitterness that characterized Cooper he makes it clear that Arthur failed to secure a certain position because he possesses "honesty, and conscience, and [is] scrupulous." [180] Village life, even in the blessed West, is often petty and cruel. Yet there is another side to all this, and Flint, who has had his own conflicts, is not the man to deny it. One of man's duties is to get on with his fellow-men in as much amity as possible. Charity and tolerance must be tested amid the strains and stresses of daily intercourse with common people. This is lesson number one for the snobbishly bred Augusta. And she learns it well enough. She learns it when she has to take in sewing in order to help support the family in London. She can then look back on her

> foolish and degrading prejudices towards people in humble life. How often have I smiled at the miserable wit of novel writers and play makers, when attempting to ridicule the million, the great mass of society. [181]

The ordeal of Augusta, however, is not the centre of the book, nor does the action end in London. Society or solitude—the point is not formally debated, but Flint's final preference is suggested by the happiness allotted to the Clennings on a farm in Illinois. *Arthur Clenning* is a book full of faults, [182] but it lays bare many of the problems and possibilities of American novelists during their lehr- and wanderjahre.

Flint wrote three other novels. *George Mason, the Young Backwoodsman; or, 'Don't Give Up the Ship'* (1829) could have been his most valuable contribution to American fiction, for it is laid in the Mississippi Valley and it is rooted in Flint's own experiences. [183] Yet the honest roots of the book served mainly to rear a structure of soft sentiment and copybook morality. It is his most poorly written novel. Its most interesting aspect today is its revelation of how the "complication of minute difficulties and vexations . . . during a ministry of sixteen years" had so broken the "health and spirits" of George Mason that he determined to try his luck in those western regions which accidentally he had found described in "the romances of Imlay and Chateaubriand." [183a]

The Lost Child, published about 1830, has proved to be a lost book.[184] In 1830 there appeared what was probably the last and certainly the most extravagant of Flint's novels, *The Shoshonee Valley; a Romance*. Set in the Far West, the book did not arise out of Flint's experiences but, probably, out of first hand accounts of travelers to that region. The period of the action antedates those of Irving's Western tales in *Astoria* and *The Adventures of Captain Bonneville, U. S. A.*, still to be written. The action is again precipitated by the desire of a major character to shuffle off the deadening coils of civilization. This time it is William Weldon, a New Englander, who makes the break-away—with Yensi, his Chinese wife. They head for Oregon, to live among the Indians. The melodramatic action centres in a struggle for the hand of their daughter Jessy. Before he is through, the author has assembled a cast of characters racially and morally varied enough to form a good nucleus for a study of ethnology and anthropology. But he puts them through such bloody vicissitudes that few are left at the end, the heroine climaxing the action by committing suicide to forget the horrors she has experienced.[185] But the Indians are not wholly stamped out, and it is among them that Flint finds the substance of his most interesting observations. As could be expected of a writer in love with primitivism and largely unacquainted with Indians in their own habitats, Flint paints the Shoshonees as the noble savages of tradition: "It is the white intruders who spoil the paradise of the Indians." [186] But the reader of Flint's earlier novels needs no further proof of the author's yearning for a life of sylvan ease and natural benevolence. Least of all does the reader care to be deluged with melodrama in a milieu the author never saw.

Though now almost forgotten, except as the author of *Recollections*, Flint received widespread comment in his day. His travel and historical books quickly persuaded critics that here was no idle tourist, no mere journalist covering a region for "copy," but a serious, if somewhat romantic student of the West. The critical press at home and abroad gave ample space and considerable eulogy to the *Recollections*.[187] The novels seem to have been less often cited but favorably received. In 1829 N. P. Willis praised Flint's work as editor and historian but also liked the novels, particularly *Francis Berrian*.[188] In 1833 the editor of the *Knickerbocker Magazine* referred to Flint as "one of the very best of our native writers." [189] Flint was read widely also in England. Miss Mitford put in a good word for *George Mason* and asserted that it was "almost equal to Defoe." [190] Praise from a particularly interesting quarter appeared in Mrs. Trollope's *Domestic Manners of the Americans* (1832). Mrs. Trollope's book was based upon experiences in much of the same territory as Flint's *Recollections*. In general she found her American experiences extremely trying, and she was very sparing of her compliments to American writers. Flint, however, delighted her— both as man and as writer:

> The most agreeable acquaintance I made in Cincinnati, and indeed one of the most talented men I ever met, was Mr. Flint, the author of several extremely clever volumes, and the editor of the *Western Monthly Review*. His conversational powers are of the highest order; he is the only person I remember to have known with first-rate powers of satire, and even of sarcasm, whose kindness of nature and of manner remained perfectly uninjured. In some of his critical notices there is a strength and keenness second to nothing of the kind I have ever read. He . . . is the only American I ever listened to, whose unqualified praise of his country did not appear to me somewhat overstrained and ridiculous . . . Mr. Flint's *Francis Berrian* is excellent; a little wild and romantic, but containing scenes of first-rate interest and pathos . . . They [the Americans] are great novel readers, but the market is chiefly furnished by England. They have, however, a few very good native novels. Mr. Flint's *Francis Berrian* is delightful. There is a vigour and freshness in his writing that is exactly in accordance with what one looks for in the literature of a new country; and yet, strange to say, it is exactly what is most wanting in that of America.[191]

Such praise as Mrs. Trollope's would be misleading if taken as a sign that Flint's popularity would last. His novels, at least, seem not to have had a very long life. *Francis Berrian* was reprinted at least twice in the thirties, but Flint's novels in general soon languished, and they were referred to in 1839 as "now almost forgotten." [192]

Timothy Flint never really capitalized the fictional wealth available to him. Beneath his feet in the Middle West was all the material he needed, but he perversely sought the gold of farther and always farther hills. America did not need his imitations of Cooper or Scott or Defoe.[193] Bird would presently do stories of the Spanish Southwest far better than Flint's *Francis Berrian*. But Flint knew chapter and verse of the New England exodus to Ohio and other promised western lands: this is clear from his *Recollections*. Had he been able to do a realistic study of Ohio or Illinois in his best manner (the *George Mason* being negligible), American fiction might have been the richer, especially if he had written it with that air of "familiar talk" which had pleased readers of the *Recollections*.[194] The villages then growing up would have afforded ample material. Indeed Flint was vaguely aware that such a story might be written—a story (or a study) emphasizing the restricted and often mean life of the mid-western small town. Long before Howe wrote his *Story of a Country Town* (1883), and Lewis his *Main Street* —neither book really a novel—Flint suggested the idea of such a study —together with reasons for not writing it:

> A fair history of the society of a country village [would be a thousand times more interesting than a novel; and besides the interest of the picture, it would be one of the most useful views of society that can be presented. But taste has not yet matured sufficiently to relish such a picture, and, perhaps, the historian does not yet exist who has the requisite discrimination and felicity to draw it!][195]

What, then, was the "taste" which had not "matured sufficiently" to appreciate fidelity to common facts? In Flint's day in Ohio, there was apparently a preference for highly embellished writing. Highly rhetorical writing, in fact, had its apologists in the West. What was noted as the chief difference between Eastern and Western pulpit eloquence could be observed in written discourse as well:

> The eloquence of the East . . . is sober, passionless, condensed, metaphysical; that of the West is free, lofty, agitating, grand, impassioned . . . The West defies and transcends criticism.[196]

It is natural, said Daniel Drake, that young writers should feel their rhetorical oats:

> The literature of a young and free people, will of course be declamatory, and such, so far as it is yet developed, is the character of our own. Deeper learning will, no doubt, abate its virtuosity and intumescence; but our natural scenery, and our liberal political and social institutions, must long continue to maintain its character of floridness. And what is there in this that should excite regret in ourselves, or raise derision in others? Ought not the literature of a free people to be declamatory? . . . Whenever the literature of a new country loses its metaphorical and declamatory character, the institutions which depend on public sentiment will languish and decline.[197]

It is pretty clear that Timothy Flint felt strongly the urge to be "declamatory"; it was the way to impress people. It is true that he once confessed that his "attachment to ornamental speech" was "pernicious,"[198] but one questions a little the sincerity of his confession. Flint was doubtless proud of having made his heroine talk like a manual of rhetoric.[199] The quieter tones that breed conviction he confided to his journal. Yet his confidence in declamation was not wholly misconceived. At the time it was useful. The West needed open-throated songs of praise as well as minute records of daily transactions. The man who was to celebrate a Chateaubriand-like faith in primitivism should cultivate expansiveness as much as finesse. The trumpet is in its own way quite as useful as the flute. The trouble was that Flint did not really master his instrument. Declamation is well enough, but only if one excels in it. Still Flint served his purpose as a pioneer Western writer. If he could not wholly write the constitution of the West, he could at least help to declare its independence.

Among the other spokesmen of Western independence was James Hall (1793-1868). A native of Philadelphia, Hall lived almost fifty years in the West, chiefly in Illinois and Ohio. For thirty-five years he was a banker at Cincinnati. Most of his literary work—as travel-writer, essayist, editor, historian, and fiction-writer—was done in the twenties and thirties.[200] His *Letters From the West* (1828) was a compound of adventure, sentiment, and picturesqueness in proportions that the gift-books and annuals of a slightly later date were to find favorable to popularity. He wrote innumerable short tales, many of which originally appeared in anthologies and magazines. The first separate publication of his collected tales and sketches, *Legends of the West*, appeared in 1832. He also wrote one story, *The Harpe's Head; A Legend of Kentucky* (1833), long enough to be called a novel but not radically different in technique from his short tales. He had a good sense for materials rich in "human interest," and he wrote with fluency and charm. The public quickly responded to so pleasant a synthesis of gifts; and as early as 1832 Miss Mitford, a close observer of things American, selected one of his tales for her anthology, *Lights and Shadows of American Life*.

Hall's long residence in the West and his fairly steady adherence to Western themes, however, did not fashion him into a strongly original delineator of the trans-Allegheny territory. As a reader he had grown up largely on the romantic diet of Scott, Byron, and Cooper. It would not be rash to infer from his style that he also had a fondness for the polished periods of N. P. Willis, whose essays and sketches were enormously popular in the 1820's and 1830's: America was full of young writers who hoped to emulate Willis. He also seems to have known Brackenridge's *Modern Chivalry*, a book which must have confirmed him in such realistic tendencies as he possessed.

How "Western" was Hall? He himself took a stand on the "accurate descriptions" in his *Legends of the West* and asserted that their "only merit" was "fidelity." [201] His interest in data relating to the West is attested further by his detailed factual studies such as *Statistics of the West* (1836), which goes so far as to list all the (several hundred) steamboats of the period with full data on time and place of construction, tonnage, date and cause of loss. Yet as a popular writer he seems to have felt the need of drawing a veil over the uncouth aspects of Western life and at the same time stepping up its fresh charm and picturesqueness. And small wonder that he did, for when he descended to homely realism, there were squawks at his lack of sectional loyalty.[202] Verily his public was hard to please, and Hall not unnaturally tried to please its larger part. Thus the Western camp-meeting—an institution frequently characterized by a mixture of offensive emotionalism and religious sincerity—he euphemistically described on one occasion as an experience which left "the mind elevated by the noble pursuit of a high object." [203] What Hall said was of course the truth—but not the whole truth. He tended to romanticize frontier characters—who needed no such treatment. Like Cooper, he was interested in the "scale of greatness [which] pervaded all the works of nature." [204] His Daniel Boone was right enough in most of his actions, but he was made to speak "the purest English of a rather stilted kind." [205] In his novel *The Harpe's Head*, Hall writes a story of authentic Kentucky adventure involving actual outlaws of the region, but he draws back from uttering the last word of realism, for certain of the "real incidents" in the lives of these desperadoes were "too atrocious for recital . . ." [206] The pioneer writer should be made of sterner stuff. Accordingly, Hall was criticized even by his fellow-Westerners as an "on-looker" rather than an "actor," and his writings were called "less western" than those of Timothy Flint.[207] *The North American Review* probably held no brief for Western writers in general, but it did object strenuously to Hall's unestablished Westernism:

> He professes to be a western man; the scene of his stories is generally in the west; his incidents are taken from western life; but of the western character he knows little, and of the western spirit he possesses nothing. He wants the intellectual *openness*, which would enable him to catch the spirit of society. His mind is shut up in its own ways of thinking and feeling, and his writings, in consequence, give no true reflection of western character.[208]

Clearly the objection was not to Hall's matter but to his manner. He devoted hundreds of pages to genuine Western people—the boatman, the woodsman, the Indian, the Methodist circuit-rider—in authentic

Western scenes. His fault (if any) was more in his procedure than in his agenda. It was not that he did not know his West; he merely gave a romantic gloss to basically realistic materials. As for the novel, he was not at home in the form, and after *The Harpe's Head* he "wisely limited himself to shorter fiction." [209]

James Hall is now admittedly a writer of small importance to belles lettres. Yet the history of the West's attempt to be itself in literature is implicit in his irresolute regionalism. Another aspect of the same effort is to be seen in the work of a Western writer of more definite convictions, Caroline M. Kirkland. Mrs. Kirkland dealt in a minimum of those candied accounts of the West that Hall had found profitable, and her kit contained certain bitter pills of realism, which she advertised just as freely. Her wares, moreover, seem to have been well received, for *A New Home—Who'll Follow? or, Glimpses of Western Life* (1839), her principal work, had reached a fourth edition by 1850.[210]

Like many another writer, Mrs. Kirkland had gained much of her conception of the West from the facile pen of Chateaubriand. When she moved to Michigan, she had a chance to check up. Her dreamy ideas were presently corrected by experience. It is one thing to range philosophically over romantic scenes and quite another to buckle down to the mundane task of preparing a dinner under difficulties. *A New Home*, Mrs. Kirkland said, was almost "a veritable history; an unimpeachable transcript of reality . . ." [211] Certainly such "glosses, and colorings, and lights" as she added to reality did not constitute a very heavy draft on the privileges of romance. Indeed *A New Home* is interesting as an early (though no doubt partly unconscious) attempt to see how successful a narrative could be without the lavish use of "adventure." It chronicles the arrival and the settling and the daily life: housekeeping, borrowing from neighbors, trading with Indians, building a dam, confronting the lesser foes of the frontier from snakes to the ague, the recital of personal histories, the development of "culture" through schooling and reading.[212] Little threads of action remain undeveloped into plot, and the whole book has a fragmentary, anecdotal air—as if it lived, as undoubtedly it did, chiefly as an outlet for the author's interest in commentary. The most interesting commentary, from the point of view of emerging realism, touched on the physical discomfort of the westward journey and the narrowness of life in the little village of Montacute. The carriage the author rides in is frequently in trouble because of innumerable mudholes, which, together with other inescapable irritations, convinced her that "Hoffman's Tour, or Captain Hall's 'graphic' delineations" gave one "but incorrect notions of a real journey through Michigan." [213] Once arrived, Mrs. Kirkland finds the petty irritations of life just as objectionable as they would be in a less "romantic" region than remote Michigan—perhaps more so. Clothes have to be ironed; boisterous children exasperate their elders. Hearts are not necessarily ennobled by the proximity of magnificent forest solitudes and the vast splendor of the Great Lakes. Universal emotions find their way to the frontier, among them jealousy. Hence the Montacute Female Beneficent Society, though dedicated to a whole list of laudable objectives, proved to be also "the fountain of village scandal, the hot-bed from which springs every root of bitterness among the petticoated denizens of Montacute." [214] Of course not all Mrs. Kirkland's entries in this journal-like story are debits. On the credit side, one finds occasional appreciative references to natural scenery (when she was not jolted by carriage or weighed down by housework), as well as downright enthusiasm for the flowers of Michigan.[215] Social organization viewed in the large also has its better side, for here men live in a democracy so deeply felt that even kindness toward a needy neighbor has to be extended with extreme caution lest a soupçon of condescension be suspected: "In cities we bestow charity—in the country we can only exchange kind offices, nominally at least." [216] Here one enjoys a "simplification of life," a "bringing down the transactions of daily intercourse to the original principles of society." [217] All this, Mrs. Kirkland implies, is ultimately to the good—though to cultivated emigrants from the East there may be at first a certain amount of shock. *A New Home,* therefore, is not continuously satirical or pessimistic in its rationale. Moreover the sprightliness of Mrs. Kirkland's style and the evident relish with which she inlays her discourse with quotations (far too many) from a wide range of authors indicate that the author keenly enjoyed composing the work for its own sake. Yet amid its impartial display of life on the frontier, the book affords glimpses of realism which suggest that the author's eager reading of Chateaubriand had been a prelude to disillusionment. Later on Mrs. Kirkland's son, Joseph Kirkland (1830-1894), the author of *Zury*, would dig only a little deeper in the soil of realism in the neighboring state of Illinois.

A number of other writers may be loosely denominated as "Western," but few of these made important contributions to frontier literature. John A. McClung showed his interest in the West by compiling *Sketches of Western Adventure* (1832), but his one novel *Camden* (1830) was an historical romance of the Revolution, laid in Carolina and patterned after Scott.[218] Frederick William Thomas commenced author after his establishment at Cincinnati in 1831, but his novels as a whole show that he "had no such serious interest in the rise of Western literature as inspired Hall and Flint." [219] Caroline Lee Hentz, who wrote an intersectional novel (*Lovell's Folly*, 1833) during her residence in Ohio, may more appropriately be designated a "domestic" rather than a "frontier" writer.[220] Flint and Hall and Kirkland, then, may be regarded as, in spirit at least, the most Western of the early Westerners.[221] Their books promise more than they perform. Their faults and virtues—poor coördination, awkward phrasing, uncertainty of final aims, sudden bursts of enthusiasm, equally sudden (and often poorly motivated) outbreaks of despair, and withal a certain freshness and frankness—are the qualities of adolescence. Yet the adolescence of art, like that of persons, must be taken seriously by one who would understand the adult. The maturity of the novel in the Middle West would not be reached for many years. Howells was to turn his back on his native Ohio in 1861. Eggleston would delineate Indiana scenes with more intimacy than power in the seventies. E. W. Howe in his *Story of a Country Town* (1883) and Joseph Kirkland's *Zury* (1887) would add sinew and strength to the novel without mastering its movement. Not until the twentieth century would the novel really come into its own in the Ohio and Mississippi valleys.

Contemporaries and Immediate Followers of Cooper, II

WILLIAM GILMORE SIMMS (1806-1870)

In the year of Cooper's return from Europe there appeared the first full-length novel of a writer destined to be remembered as Cooper's most distinguished competitor in romance. Simms entered the field after the first great wave of romance had passed its crest, and he was largely responsible for the revivification of the genre in the 1830's. He adopted some of the technique of Cooper, whom he greatly admired, but he had a strong original bent as well, and he opened veins of romance in regions untouched by Cooper. Like Cooper, he was also an alert political observer and a strong partisan. His prolific and trenchant commentaries on political and economic issues as well as on literary themes, are invaluable to the student of history. Yet he seldom opened the pages of his stories to his personal convictions, and he is now known to the general public chiefly as a vigorous writer of straight narrative.

Simms was born on April 17, 1806, in Charleston, South Carolina, of a family considerably less affluent and less distinguished socially than Cooper's. During his earliest years the bankruptcy of his father and the death of his mother presaged the misfortunes of his none-too-happy childhood. From a "worthless and scoundrelly" public school [1] he was removed after a few desultory years by his grandmother, who cared for the lad after his father had gone west to recoup his fortunes. Later she apprenticed him to a druggist as the first step toward preparing him for a career (which did not eventuate) in medicine. In the meantime she encouraged the boy's natural interest in letters, which he had shown by writing verses at eight years of age; and she began to fill his capacious mind with those Southern legends, superstitions, and historical episodes which were later to become such an important part of his equipment as a writer of historical romance.

Ultimately Grandmother Gates had to tell young Simms the saga of his father. The elder Simms, a witty, improvident Irishman, wholly de-

voted to Jacksonian politics, had left South Carolina upon his bankruptcy to lead a wandering, soldiering life for a number of years in
Tennessee, Florida, Alabama, and Mississippi. He settled in the territory
of Mississippi. Young Simms (now a law student) at first resisted his
father's attempt to lure him to Mississippi's rude frontier; but after his
father had come back and supplemented Grandmother Gates's stories
with further tall tales told in his best raconteur's fashion, the adventurous spirit in Simms was awakened. Accordingly when another opportunity came (in 1824 or 1825), he finally went out to see the country
where his father "killed his own horse for food, and lived on it for seven
days." [2] Arrived in New Orleans, he presently undertook an arduous
journey to his father's plantation near Georgeville, Mississippi. He
visited the Cherokee and Creek Indians, and he traveled about in the
backwoods from settlement to settlement, where if he occasionally encountered buoyant optimism on the part of the more enterprising pioneers, he also observed border conditions far cruder than those experienced by Cooper on the New York frontier. The Mississippi territory
that Simms saw was a gloomy ague-stricken region peopled by a heterogeneous collection of border characters—rugged backwoodsmen,
Indians, half-breeds, Negro slaves, poor whites, farmers, and social out-
casts, as well as itinerant gamblers, gunmen, Yankee peddlers, and Methodist preachers—living on the whole a pretty seamy sort of existence,
reflections of which later appeared as a lurid streak of realism in Simms's
romances of the border. Growing up with this sort of country, glorified by legend and history[3] but peopled by inferior breeds of men, did
not appeal to Simms; and he accordingly returned against his father's
advice to Charleston, a city which, though then containing only 28,000
inhabitants, stood in much the same relationship to South Carolina and
the South as Boston to New England.

At this time Simms's primary interest was literature, but since (being
now married) he was faced with the necessity of making a living, he
renewed his study of the law. His alternate reading in Blackstone and
Byron bore fruit in the same year, 1827, when he gained admittance to
the bar and published two books of verse.[4] Besides practicing law, he
also dabbled in politics and journalism, but without financial success.
Moreover personal misfortune dogged him: within a few years he suffered the loss of his wife, his father, and his grandmother. His house
was destroyed by fire. Encumbered by debt but now relatively free
from domestic ties (his daughter being cared for by a relative), Simms
determined to stake his fortune on literature. To this end he naturally
betook himself northward, for though Charleston was the cultural
centre of South Carolina, its culture was a somewhat static one: the

spirit of the eighteenth century lasted a long time in the South. Nor could Simms, born outside the pale of Charleston society, hope to rival or share Legaré's claim to supremacy as the city's literary dictator. Bent on new projects he therefore went to New York, where he made literary contacts which were to be valuable to him in the years ahead. In 1833, after a few minor literary successes in New York, he settled temporarily at New Haven, where he completed his first novel, *Martin Faber*, a tale which was well received. The next year he scored an even greater success with his border romance, *Guy Rivers*.

Now definitely established as a writer, Simms continued to pour forth stories, articles, poems, plays, history, and biography, with unabated energy until his death. He was also widely known as an orator of extraordinary energy and eloquence. His home remained in South Carolina, where he lived at Charleston and, after his second marriage, on his father-in-law's plantation near Barnwell; but publishing arrangements necessitated frequent and sometimes protracted stays in New York amid a friendly circle of Knickerbocker literati. His increasing rancor against the North, however, finally lost him many friends there, especially after certain ill-advised remarks he made in a lecture in November, 1856.[5] About this time, also, the popularity of his stories began to wane. On the other hand, it was a satisfaction to him to be the acknowledged leader of a coterie of Charleston writers—among them the brilliant younger poets Paul Hayne and Henry Timrod—whose enthusiastic gatherings at "the wigwam" (Simms's house) and at Russell's Bookshop were the prelude to the establishment of Charleston's best literary organ, *Russell's Magazine*, in April, 1856. Himself beginning to be outmoded, Simms thus aided the growth of a new generation of Southern writers. His later years were to be saddened and embittered by personal bereavements and by the ravaging of the South during the Civil War as well as by Northern interference after the War.[6] He died at Charleston on June 11, 1870.

FICTION

During his early years, Simms experimented a good deal, but his fiction as a whole falls naturally into a few large classifications. His first successful work of fiction was the relatively brief story of crime, *Martin Faber*, a tale not wholly original in type[7] but effectively enough written to enable the publisher to sell out the entire edition. Yet, though an interest in the psychology of crime is obvious in later books of Simms's, *Martin Faber* was not fully indicative of Simms's forte as a writer; for he made his greatest reputation with his so-called border romances and historical novels.

The first of Simms's "regular novels" [8] was *Guy Rivers* (1834). This is a thrilling tale arising out of the nefarious operations of a gang of desperadoes, comprising the "Pony Club," who waylay lonely travelers in the gold fields of Georgia. Their overlord, Guy Rivers, is an intelligent outlaw capable of arguing the case against society with considerable acumen. He is a sort of Robin Hood without Robin Hood's mercurial temperament and good will.[9] When Ralph Colleton, a stereotyped young hero, not only triumphs over the robber upon the latter's attempt to relieve him of his small change but also proves to have been his unwitting rival in love, a plot to murder Colleton is launched by Rivers and his henchman, Wat Munro, a dissolute innkeeper who for a bit of money is "always ready to blow out a man's liver with a brace of bullets." In the end Rivers is foiled, but not before a fearfully exciting and bloody narrative has been unfolded. Yet rich as the story is in action, it is quite as notable for its description of border conditions in a barren section of upper Georgia after the cry of gold [10] brought an influx of miscellaneous characters, many of them of a shady sort, into a community poorly organized to control them by law or religion.[11]

Although *Guy Rivers* was promptly recognized as a brilliant and fascinating story,[12] Simms did not immediately try to duplicate his triumph, but turned for his next book, *The Yemassee,* to the annals of Indian warfare in his own state. *The Yemassee,* Simms's "most widely read" romance, was in progress by August 2, 1834, and it was published in the spring of 1835.[13] Its theme, the Yemassee war of 1715 in South Carolina, was obviously capable of a type of treatment not far different from that of Cooper's Indian stories. Sanutee, aged chief of the Yemassees, is determined to fight the English, notwithstanding the tendency of certain members of the tribe (including his son, Occonestoga) to absorb British propaganda with British rum. The hope of a successful revolt is greatly augmented by the activities of one Chorley, a dissolute lad who has become a renegade with pirating and kidnapping propensities and who is in league with certain scheming Spaniards. The issue of the rebellion is presumably made the more interesting by the doubt it creates regarding the fortunes of the Matthews family including the lovely Bess, who resists all suitors but the resourceful and mysterious Captain Harrison. Harrison it is who is mainly responsible for the final safety of the principal dramatis personae and for the suppression of the rebellion. But, the reader is thrilled to learn, the man who has won Bess's hand is not really "Harrison" but Governor Craven in disguise! The culmination of the action so far as adventure is concerned is the exciting attack on the blockhouse. The latter part of the narrative relates how the Yemassee attack on Charleston was repelled and how, by Governor Craven's orders, most of the Yemassees were finally extirpated. Sanutee dies heroically at the end of a vivid story which reveals how helpless the Indians are to resist the encroachments of the white people.

The Yemassee inevitably recalls Cooper's tales, which it resembles in many details of style and structure. The seasoned reader of Cooper finds himself very much at home when Simms introduces a scene:

> The gray soft tints of an April dawn had scarcely yet begun to lighten in the dim horizon, when the low door of an Indian lodge that lay almost entirely embowered in a forest thicket, less than a mile from Pocota-ligo, might be seen to open, and a tall warrior to emerge slowly and in silence from its shelter.[14]

Occasionally, too, a flight of metaphorical language suggesting Cooper is put into the mouths of the Indians, as in Sanutee's lament:

> Why comes the English to the lodge of our people? Why comes he with a red coat to the Chief—why brings he beads and paints for the eye of a little boy? Why brings he the strong water for the young man? Why makes he long speeches, full of smooth words —why does he call us brother? He wants our lands. But we have no lands to sell. The lands came from our fathers—they must go to our children. They do not belong to us to sell—they belong to our children to keep. We have sold too much land, and the old turkey, before the sun sinks behind the trees, can fly over all the land that is ours.[15]

In addition there is the Cooper-like background of historical fact, much of it undigested; the broadly effective painting of scene; the poetical chapter mottoes; the exasperating failure of the author to mention a character's name promptly; the attack on a young girl by a wild animal; the humorous Negro; the blustering soldier-adventurer; the notable in disguise; the attack on the blockhouse, with appropriate miracles; the inclusion of horrible detail—such as the broken bone protruding through a savage's arm. Moreover, the best scene in the story, that in which Matiwan kills her son Occonestoga to prevent his being dishonored by a tribal ceremony, recalls the superb scene of the death of Abiram White at the orders of his sister's husband in *The Prairie*.

As in Cooper, the Indians are treated with moderate sympathy bred of the author's conviction that their worst traits have been brought out by association with white people. Yet a writer of romance cannot regard the aborigines mainly as sociological problems; consequently although Simms often evokes admiration for their better qualities, he does not shrink from describing most gruesome results of their cunning and cruelty. Their ultimate defeat he accepts philosophically as dictated by destiny. Simms's portrayal of Indian character is probably closer to reality than Cooper's, for he had better sources of information.[16] He exposes for example the popular fallacy that Indians are uniformly stoical by showing that they frequently shed tears. In general it was his aim to show both their virtues and their defects in due proportion.[17] In addition to Cooper's influence one may discern that of Scott especially in the relationship of the Cavalier Craven (the "unknown") to the Puritan Matthews and his daughter. What is most original in *The Yemassee* is Simms's fine use of his mise-en-scène, his dynamic narrative manner, and his realistic treatment of the Indians.

The reception of *The Yemassee* showed that the public was quite as much interested in his Indians as in his border romances. Yet although Simms wrote one other long story involving the Indians, *The Cassique of Kiawah* (1859), and two volumes of sketches containing Indian legend and lore, *The Wigwam and The Cabin* (1845-46), he never utilized Indian warfare as fully as his early success would seem to have warranted. At all events, not long after the publication of *The Yemassee*, his versatile mind led him to open still another vein of fiction, the historical novel dealing with the events of the American Revolution.

Beginning, like Cooper's first Revolutionary novel, in the year 1780, *The Partisan* (1835) relates actions emphasizing the wisdom of Marion and the folly of Gates, with the defeat of Cornwallis at Camden as the climax of the military maneuvers. Beyond this, the principal interest derives from the familiar conflict between the Tories and the Partisans (patriots). The wavering of Colonel Walton prepares the way for exciting events, and the love of Major Singleton for Walton's daughter provides the story with a tepid sentiment. Although a marriage is in sight at the conclusion of the story, it is not achieved in this volume; for at the behest of Simms, who has a trilogy in mind, Miss Walton tells the Major to wait. The story is somewhat carelessly constructed, but it contains an excellent re-creation of Old Dorchester (which Simms had personally visited), a basically true account of military affairs during a critical period, and sufficient invented material to provide variety of interest. The principal characters are a trifle too conventionally drawn to be interesting, but the secondary characters, including the revenge-mad Frampton, the half-breed spy Blonay, and the Falstaffian Porgy, are invested with the esprit and vitality common to many of

Simms's supporting characters. Porgy, indeed, who is subordinate in the action of this story, proved to be so interesting that Simms used him in subsequent novels.

Thus within two years Simms had written one book in each of three genres for which he is best known, the border romance, the romance of Indian warfare, and the Revolutionary romance. The last of these proved to be his most fruitful field. In the next year he resumed the trilogy begun in *The Partisan*. The lovers of the first story must needs be patient, however, for in the second unit, *Mellichampe* (1836), Simms introduces new (and more interesting) love matter in the rivalry of Ernest Mellichampe, a patriot, and Barsfield, an English officer (who has killed Mellichampe's father), for the hand of Janet Berkeley, a faithful Partisan. The military action, however, carries on immediately from Camden, and is centered in the opposition between Marion and Tarleton. The third unit of the series, *Katharine Walton* (1851), resumes the narrative of Colonel Walton (rescued from hanging at the end of *The Partisan*) and of the lovers, Katharine Walton and Major Singleton, who after an interlude with an ugly brute, Balfour (whom the heroine consents to marry in order to save her father from hanging) are eventually united. Colonel Walton, however, is hanged. In the meantime Simms has relieved the monotony of military adventure (following Camden) by inserting some lively, if not very subtly drawn, pictures of Charleston society. Besides this trilogy, Simms wrote four Revolutionary tales.[18]

The Scout (1841), originally called *The Kinsmen*, pits two half-brothers against each other in love and war in a discursive narrative of the year 1781. *Woodcraft*, which appeared in 1854 (under the better title *The Sword and the Distaff*), is a medley of post-war social intrigue, practical jokes, and plantation problems (including slave abduction) in and near Charleston at the time of the British evacuation in December, 1782. It gives greater prominence to Simms's best comic character, Lieutenant Porgy, whose misadventures in courtship delightfully recall the Falstaff of *The Merry Wives of Windsor*.[19] In *The Forayers* (1855) and a sequel, *Eutaw* (1856), Simms went back to his exciting military operations of the year 1781 culminating in the battle of Eutaw,[20] but these tales fell on a public beginning to tire of the historical romance. Like almost all of Simms's stories, these last two were competently written. Simms handled the Revolutionary romance well, but not supremely well. In expository and background material he frequently overshot the mark of thoroughness, and he trespassed on the reader's patience by introducing quantities of technical military detail relating to military matters.[21] Moreover, seen as a whole, the

Revolutionary romances lack a good focus of the reader's hopes and affections. Generals Marion and Greene are admirable men, and there are fictitious juvenile heroes aplenty, as well as a host of splendid minor characters, but there is no single character comparable in power and interest to Natty Bumppo in the Leatherstocking series. Nor could the exciting plots of his stories wholly conceal the slipshod style into which Simms was often betrayed by the speed of his production. Yet most of the Revolutionary tales are avowedly stories "of events, rather than of persons," [22] and regarded as stories of adventure they are still among the most readable in the history of the American novel.

Long before completing his Revolutionary romances Simms had added to the series of border romances of which *Guy Rivers* was the first. In *Richard Hurdis* (1838) he tells a sensational tale of love and adventure in which the son of an Alabama planter seeks to avenge the murder of a friend by disguising himself as a gambler and joining a gang of marauders. Ultimately the gang is routed, but their leader, Foster, escapes into Mississippi and into the pages of Simms's next border romance, *The Border Beagles* (1840). In the latter book the bandit carries on his machinations until his capture is achieved amid scenes which, having visited the territory as a young man, Simms was able to re-create vividly.[23] Both these books are loosely compounded of picaresque and Gothic elements, and although there are humorous interpolations and occasional parleys on the quality of justice, they are frankly sensational tales designed to appeal to a public that found *Guy Rivers* enthralling. They were published anonymously.

Simms's next border story, *Beauchampe* (1842), a "tale of passion," is unrelated in its action to the preceding ones, but although it showed Simms tending toward the psychological novel it is equally sensational. His plot Simms found ready-made in the (then recent) story of Colonel Beauchampe, of Frankfort, Kentucky, who killed the man guilty of having seduced his wife before her marriage.[24] Approximately the first half of the story is devoted to the story of Colonel Sharpe's conquest of Margaret Cooper[25] after, as an ambitious village girl, she has rejected the honorable attentions of a local swain. Sharpe promises her marriage but deserts her. Upon the death of her child, she leaves Charlemont, swearing vengeance. The second phase of the action begins with her introduction (now as Anna Cooke) to Orville Beauchampe, to whom she is finally married. Upon learning of his wife's history Beauchampe is resolved to avenge the crime—the more so since Sharpe reappears to harass his former victim. A challenge follows, which Sharpe refuses to accept. Beauchampe subsequently stabs Sharpe fatally. Beauchampe is found guilty, but the ends of justice are thwarted by his suicide pact with his wife.[26] In his narrative Simms is apparently concerned to keep close to the facts in the case,[27] but the result is a story exhibiting the most sustained emotional tension of any that Simms ever wrote. *Beauchampe* (with *Charlemont*) has been disparaged as "salacious" and "barbarously ornate," [28] but although lacking in restraint and crude in artistry, it has a good deal of power, and it is more than mere melodrama (if by melodrama we mean thrills for the sake of thrills), for Simms was sincerely interested in the social problem involved. Less can be said for *Confession; or the Blind Heart* (1841), which is a pretentious and over-written "domestic story" based upon the motif of jealousy and avowedly developed partly under the influence of Godwin's *Caleb Williams*. Simms had a good general understanding of human passions, but when, deliberately rejecting incident, he made it his business to "analyze the heart . . . in its obliquities and perversities," [29] he was less successful than in handling the more tangible problems that fill his border and Revolutionary romances. Psychology was not Simms's forte.

Although Simms was a thoroughly indigenous writer, he followed Cooper's precedent in writing a few stories set in foreign countries. And, like Cooper, he largely failed in them. The first of these, *Pelayo* (1838), a Spanish tale, was coldly received, but Simms obstinately undertook a sequel, *Count Julian* (1845), which was no better. *The Damsel of Darien* (1839), a perfunctory story of Balboa, was so little appreciated that when Simms next essayed a foreign romance, *Vasconselos* (1854), he used a pseudonym, "Frank Cooper," in order to gain a fresh critical appraisal of his ability. *Vasconselos* is a rather colorful chronicle of the conflict between De Soto and the adventurer Vasconselos, who responds to unfair treatment at the hands of his chief by turning traitor and "going native" as the mate of a savage princess. Despite the brilliance of Simms's narrative, the sordid evolution of his hero impaired the popularity of the book with readers accustomed to more idealistic protagonists.[30] Thus although Simms came honestly and early by his interest in Spanish history and legend,[31] he (like Robert Montgomery Bird) was less successful with his Spanish stories than with those that sprang from soil nearer home and from events less remote in time. For his last novel published in book form, *The Cassique of Kiawah* (1859), Simms returned to Colonial history and told a story interwoven of Indian warfare and contraband traffic at sea just before the end of the seventeenth century. Four other novels were serialized in magazines now difficult of access: *Paddy McGann, or The Demon of the Swamp* (1863), *Joscelyn: a Tale of the Revolution* (1867), *The Cub of the Panther: a Mountain Legend* (1869), and *Voltmeier, or The*

Mountain Men (1869). Besides his novels Simms wrote a great many short stories, of which the most famous is "Grayling," called by Poe "the best ghost story he ever read," [32] but they are on the whole inferior to his novels. A writer of more force than finesse, Simms preferred the ampler opportunities of the novel to the rigid requirements of the short story.

POLITICAL, RELIGIOUS, AND SOCIAL IDEAS.

Simms's interests were by no means confined to belles lettres but included every aspect of the social order in which he lived. In general, however, he did not allow his opinions to intrude on his fiction,[33] but committed them to paper in the form of articles and reviews.[34] His thought was seldom very profound or very subtle, and not infrequently his views were prejudiced. Yet his non-fictional writing is not only useful as an aid to the interpretation of his stories, but it is interesting and significant in itself.

Simms had a Southerner's characteristic fondness for discussing political economy, but unfortunate experiences as an office-seeker gave him something of a distaste for politics as such.[35] He remained an interested student of political theory and an alert observer of current affairs. Although the Civil War greatly embittered his later years, he fundamentally believed in the Union and in an enlightened democracy. The secret of good government, he believed, lay in safeguarding the home, whence "spring all the virtues and securities of a nation," and to him the state was "durable rather as a social than a political edifice." [36] He was therefore convinced of the wisdom of depending less on "policy" than on a knowledge of "the real nature of the race to be governed." [37] It was for these reasons that he condemned history as being "usually the history of princes rather than of the people." [38] On the other hand he had no naive faith in the will of the populace and he sounds a warning against the aberrations of "popular justice." [39] He naturally espoused those measures which were favorable to an agrarian section. He believed in free trade and (limited) states' rights.[40] Especially he feared undue centralization. One of the greatest dangers to good government, he felt, was that through overweening ambition for power a leader might be transformed into a tyrant or a despot. On this account he looked askance at such men (useful though they might be in romance) as De Soto, Cortez, and Cromwell.[41] Yet until the Civil War he never completely lost his faith in the ability of a sound society to survive the machinations of petty politicians and political opportunists; indeed he once remarked that "politicians rarely destroy anything—but themselves and one another!" [42] It was only when he fully realized what might be the result of the consolidation of political power in the North that he had bitter reason to revise this optimistic view.

NATIONALISM. Although Simms ultimately became a fierce antagonist of the North, he was in the beginning an ardent nationalist. His first foe was Great Britian. Born between the period of the Revolution and the War of 1812, he nursed his anti-British wrath on memories of both wars. But even more than he hated England's arms, he feared that cultural domination of Europe which deferred the hope of an autochthonous American civilization. As late as 1844, in an address on "Americanism," he wrote bitterly:

> The writers think after European models, draw their stimuli and provocation from European books, fashion themselves to European tastes, and look chiefly to the awards of European criticism. This is to denationalize the American mind. [43]

He never completely relinquished hope, however, and in the same address he says, in a passage finely reminiscent of Emerson's Phi Beta Kappa address at Harvard in 1837 (*The American Scholar*): "Let the nation but yield a day's faith to its own genius, and that day will suffice for triumph." [44] As time went on, the theme of nationalism was overshadowed in his mind by a new issue, and he became absorbed in the strife between the North and South. He lost much of his Anglophobia, and finally all the rancor he had once entertained for England was now renewed and redoubled and redirected against the North. He even came (in 1850) to contemplate with satisfaction the possibility that the British might aid the South in the event of secession of the Southern states. [45]

NORTH VERSUS SOUTH. Although Simms was originally a firm believer in the Union[46] and even as late as 1850 he referred to the Constitution as the "source and living Spirit" of the Union,[47] his strong national feeling began to contract into a fierce Southern partisanship when he realized that the North contemplated the abolition of a basic essential of the Southern economy, namely, slavery. It now mattered little that he had won his literary spurs in the North, that among his best friends were the New York literati, including Bryant, and that on occasion he had even used the North as a refuge from the menace of cholera. He began to vilify all things Northern, especially New England things. He urged Southerners to discontinue the practice of spending their vacations in Saratoga and other Northern resorts where they were in danger of "subservience to northern opinion," [48] and he began to sing the praises of Virginia and the Carolinas as summer resorts. He complained that "Yankee historians" were falsifying the South,[49] and that the New England states seemed to think they alone had won the Revolutionary War.[50] He sneered at Northern writers, especially at that "school too much on stilts," the transcendentalists.[51] He thundered indictments at the "wild philosophies" bred in the North and depraved political practices that threatened the social order, such as Fourierism.[52] But most of all he raged at abolitionists.

Simms had always believed in slavery. Although it was his practice largely to avoid controversial subjects in his fiction, it is clear from Craven's attempt to give Hector his freedom in *The Yemassee*[53] that even in 1835 he was convinced of the beneficence of slavery as an institution quite apart from its economic importance to the South. In 1837 his extended review of Harriet Martineau's *Society in America*[54] written before the issue had become critical, clearly revealed his position as that of a person willing to see slavery modified but under no circumstances abolished. Goaded by what he conceived to be Northern arrogance, however, Simms gradually changed from a strong champion of slavery to an infuriated opponent of the "abolition mania." He conceded that the "fanatics of abolition" in the North might be numerically a minority, but he asked: "Why do they shape the laws, dictate the policy, control the whole action of society?"[55] *Uncle Tom's Cabin* (published serially in 1851) seemed to him a gross libel, based partly on fact but proceeding to inferences that were "wholly false."[56] With bitter irony he writes of the typical freed slave who "walks off with two loving white brothers, who soon show him how much more moral it is to become a burglar than to remain a slave." Presently, after a brief experience of "freedom" ex-slaves write home from Northern jails to complain of the wrongs they have suffered at the hands of their "sympathizing brethren, whose object has been, not the good of the wretched slave, but the injury and annoyance of the 'soft-head' owner." Then when the former owner responds to the pitiful appeal by paying necessary fines, the abolitionists prevent the slaves' departure—"the poor darkies all the while struggling against the cruel fate of freedom, for which they are so totally unfit."[57] In 1852 he unequivocally states what he believes to be the Southern conviction as to the benefits of slavery:

> We beg, once for all, to say to our Northern readers, writers, and publishers, that, in the South, we hold slavery to be an especially and wisely devised institution of heaven; devised for the benefit, the improvement, and safety, morally, socially, and physically, of a barbarous and inferior race, who would otherwise perish by famine or by filth, by the sword, by disease, by waste,

. and destinies forever gnawing, consuming, and finally destroying.[58]

And the North proposed to abolish this blessing! This was a proposal
so iniquitous to Simms that he became wholly sectional in his interests.
Although formerly an opponent of nullification, he now subscribed to
secession as the only means of fighting a movement that threatened to
become fatal to Southern existence. The national sentiments he had
once entertained were now replaced by a hope expressed unequivocally
to a compatriot in 1859: "Let all your game lie in the constant recognition and assertion of a *Southern nationality*." [59]

MISCELLANEOUS SOCIAL IDEAS. The narrowly sectional view
of politics finally held by Simms is suggestive of a rather conservative
nature which characterized him in some other fields as well. He wrote
very little about what was perhaps the major need of the South in his
time, namely, some improvement in the system of public education
which he had himself once suffered under. He was far from progressive
with respect to the social status of women.[60] And although he was less
squeamish about sex than Cooper was, he was pretty careful to keep
his allusions to sex on a plane that comported with the bourgeois morality that on the whole he favored. On the other hand he exhibited
more liberal views in connection with religion and social responsibility.
He appears to have lived in accordance with Christian precept, but he
was not orthodox in the light of the teaching of any one of its branches.[61]
His general fear of fanaticism and tyranny extended to the churches,
for he believed that the "rigid exactions of the clergy" were sometimes
provocative of evil and that "ultraism, in matters of religion, is the most
malignant and bitter despotism that ever afflicted or degraded man, and
misrepresented and defamed his Creator." [62] Historically, he viewed
the Puritans with disfavor as a physically feeble class of men possessed
by a fanatical zeal for discipline.[63] In general he held the view that religion should be confined to its "offices of unpretending charity, and
quiet persuasive tuition." [64]

Sex may have been tabooed in the fiction of Simms's time, but murder
was not, and Simms made the most of it. The theme of crime is prominent in a number of his books. There was nothing he preferred to a
good gory crime replete with all its ghastly details. Some of his stories
so reeked with blood that even Poe was revolted.[65] It is true, however,
that Poe's horrors were slightly more refined. Moreover, except in
Martin Faber, Simms showed much less interest in the *detection* of
crime than Poe. In fact in *Beauchampe* he amusingly satirizes the
writers who waste time on the "dreary details" connected with the solu-

tion of a murder case.[66] On the other hand, Simms, more than Poe, was interested in the social implications of crime. He gave voice to theories of crime which, although they did not wholly excuse the offender, at least showed to what extent social conditions may favor the growth of crime. In *Guy Rivers* he made much of this theme. Rivers is no common illiterate thug but an intelligent robber (once a lawyer) with a turn for philosophy; and he is quite capable of showing that his antisocial acts were in part provoked by society through "favoritism and prejudice." [67] In *Beauchampe*, a story of the "unwritten law," Simms does not wholly condone the murderer's act, but he believes that the wrong he suffered should be regarded as an "offset" to his crime, for

> There are a thousand respects . . . where to await for law, or to hope for law is to leave the feeble and the innocent to perish . . . Law is a very good thing in its way, but it is not every thing; and there are some honest impulses, in every manly bosom, which are the best of all moral laws.[68]

Much as he was interested in sociological problems, however, Simms did not often burden his stories with his own views. His literary opinions also received separate treatment.

LITERARY THEORY.

As a successful writer of popular romances, Simms realized the importance of entertaining his readers, but he believed nevertheless that the ultimate function of an artist was to arrive at "moral truth." Fiction, he believed, can be useful, "only . . . when it ministers to morals, to mankind and to society." [69] Yet he was no didactic prig, and he objected to writers whose lessons were conveyed too baldly. Nor did he believe that the ends of morality could be served only through the representation of pious people engaged in exemplary actions. In fact, he was often criticized for his use of "low" characters and sordid materials. His defense against this charge was that his stories were always drawn truthfully from life and that the best way to define good and evil was to show them in contrast to each other. In his opinion, any true representation of life, properly interpreted, was in the best sense moral.[70]

Besides serving the ends of "humanity and virtue," Simms thought, literature should be an organic part of the national life, for a nation's

> institutions must grow out of her own conditions and necessities, and not be arbitrarily framed upon those of other countries. Her poets and artists, to feel her wants, her hopes, her triumphs, must be born of the soil, and ardently devoted to its claims.[71]

Simms deplored the fact that, long after coming of age politically, America remained a cultural dependent of England. Nor did it seem easy to stem the tide of British opinion so long as, in the absence of an international copyright law, it was cheaper for American publishers to pirate English works than to offer adequate compensation to native writers.[72] It was impossible to deny, of course, that our culture was born of English culture, but Simms felt that unless we were weaned from British influence, we could never develop that indigenous literature which he regarded as essential to national unity: "Our language is English, but such need not be the case with our literature." Consequently he praised those American writers who, like Paulding, had "never made any concessions to . . . foreign sway," [73] and he had the utmost scorn for the American author who took the easiest way to literary recognition, namely, by flattering British prejudices:

> You have but to frame your books so as to flatter British nobility—conciliate their prejudices—show the most habitual deference for their preposterous claims to controlling dignity—studiously forbear all freedom of opinion—all independence of thought—and let them see that you value a breakfast with Mr. Rogers, as a matter of too serious importance to be foregone for the pitiful object of proving that you are at once a man and an American.[74]

Simms did not insist, of course, that every writer should directly celebrate his own country, but he believed that "national themes seemed to be among the most enduring." [75] There is, consequently, an intimate relation between the historian and the artist. The historian who marshals and chronicles the facts, however, is less important than the artist who interprets them, for "the chief value of history consists in its proper employment for the purposes of art." History is useless for "moral and human ends" unless it is freed from hampering detail:

> To lay bare the tombs of . . . buried kings, to find their names, to retrace their experience, to declare their histories, would really add no desirable measure to the amount of human knowledge.[76]

But the artist (who, of course, may be an historian as well) can so reclothe the "dry bones" of history that useful lessons will arise out of the past. He integrates isolated facts:

> Hence, it is the artist only who is the true historian. It is he who gives shape to the unhewn fact,—who yields relation to the scat-

tered fragments,—who unites the parts in coherent dependency, and endows with life and action the otherwise motionless automata of history. It is by such artists, indeed, that nations live.[77]

There is, however, a still further use of history, namely, its use for the purpose of a writer of romance, whose "privileges . . . begin where those of the historian cease." [78]

The writer of romance differs from the historian in his freer use of invention and imagination. What, then, are the proper proportions of fact and fiction in romance? Perhaps more than most romance writers Simms valued factual accuracy. He was a zealous student of history.[79] For the basis of his own stories he went, whenever possible, to original sources—manuscripts, court records, state papers, military memoranda, and contemporary newspapers. In his prefaces he repeatedly assures his readers of the authenticity of the historical portions of his narrative. On the other hand, he claimed the privilege of a romance writer to throw a coloring of the imagination over his factual framework:

> A certain degree of obscurity . . . must hang over the realm of the romancer. The events of history and of time, which he employs, must be such as will admit of the full exercise of the great characteristic of genius—imagination. He must be free to conceive and to invent—to create and to endow;—without any dread of crossing the confines of ordinary truth, and of such history as may be found in undisputed records.[80]

Speaking of stories in general, Simms once said that fiction is "probable truth under intenser conditions than ordinary." [81] In romance, which he carefully distinguished from the novel,[82] he believed that an author might allow himself even greater latitude, for a good romance "does not confine itself to what is known, or even what is probable. It grasps at the possible." [83] He objected, however, to "unnatural" bases for fiction such as that used by Mrs. Shelley in *Frankenstein*, a work which he praised for its "fearlessness and ingenuity" but condemned for its "extreme violation of natural laws." [84] It must not be inferred, therefore, that Simms approved of crudely exaggerated effects. Rather, once having selected "wild and wonderful" materials,[85] he sought to invest every exciting situation with as much verisimilitude as he could. He well knew the value of the careful treatment of detail.[86] His practice in fiction, indeed, was very largely in conformity with Aristotle's dictum: "A likely impossibility is always preferable to an unconvincing possibility." [87]

It is natural, then, that of all the qualifications necessary to the writer of romance, Simms appears to have regarded invention as the most important. Despite his own constant reference to "tradition and authority," [88] he felt that the best novelist was he who possessed in a high degree "the constructive faculty." [89] It is this faculty, of course, which enables a writer to provide his story with sufficient action; and Simms regarded action, in the Revolutionary romances at least, as more important than characterization.[90] Next to invention he prized "design," or harmony between all parts of a work. This is a quality difficult to command:

> It is a tolerably easy thing to write a spirited sketch—a startling event—a hurried and passionate delineation of an action . . . But the perfecting of the wondrous whole—the admirable adaptation of means to ends—the fitness of parts,—the propriety of the action—the employment of the right materials,—and the fine architectural proportions of the fabric,—these are the essentials which determine the claim of the writer to be the BUILDER . . .[91]

Finally, the gift which is most necessary of all is intuition, for the artist "works by intuition, quite as much as by calculation and common reasoning." [92] Himself an incredibly rapid and fecund writer, Simms believed that a person who aspires to authorship must have a "nature for it," for "no sort of drudgery" will achieve the end desired. Discipline meant little to him. He was averse to too much revision lest it rob the text of "freshness and freedom." [93] He distrusted publishers' readers, professional critics, and in general all people too literary. Like Scott, he thought that unlettered persons often make the best judges of a work of art, and he suggested reading one's manuscript to one's cook in preference to the so-called intelligentsia.[94] Simms was a natural writer with a talent for copious but unstudied expression carrying the ring of eloquence, and he wanted no critical refinements to impair his gift for that "energetic and passionate utterance" which he regarded as the prime essential of the art of writing.[95]

Deeply as Simms was interested in political and social issues as well as literary theory, he is now remembered chiefly as a story-teller. As such he relied upon a relatively simple equipment, which he handled well. Like Cooper, he painted his characters in primary colors, leaving the subtle shades to the romance-writers of the last decade of the century. He relied on range and variety rather than depth of characterization. His heroes are generally little more than animated ideals and his heroines are likely to be "high-souled creatures that awe while they attract." [96] His good Indians too are very very good; they are labelled "noble." A bad Indian is known by the epithet "sullen." But in addition to these, Simms peoples his stories with many picturesque types truthfully but simply characterized with frequent resort to humor and rude dialect: [97] half-breeds, witch women, Negro servants, stevedores, flunkies, renegades, gangsters, innkeepers, gold-diggers. The great lack of course is a single figure who bears comparison with Natty Bumppo. Lieutenant Porgy is fine, but he is subordinate throughout most of the Revolutionary novels. The actions which Simms devised for his motley dramatis personae are sufficiently spectacular and horrible. The depredations of bandits, Indian warfare, and "that saturnalia of crime, the Tory warfare in Carolina," proved to be rich in the violence that Simms loved. The regions described were in their way just as terrifying and sordid as the Georgia, North Carolina, and Mississippi described with latter-day realism by Caldwell, Wolfe, Faulkner, and others. When readers shuddered at the recurrence of brutality and violent death in Simms's novels, especially the border romances, Simms replied by pointing out the factual basis of his stories. [98] Yet the fact remains that his weakness was a love for melodrama. Even Poe complained of Simms's "fondness for the purely disgusting or repulsive, where the intention was or should have been merely the horrible." [99] Indeed Simms, like Neal, seems to have revelled in blood and the exploitation of jealousy and revenge. Moreover although the conventions of the day forbade his treating the theme of sex in as robust a manner as his observation of border life would have warranted, he was a great deal freer than Cooper —and not so "wholesome." He generally confined illicit love to his humbler characters, and he was far from achieving the erotic realism that some of his successors in the Southern novel have gloried in. Yet it is clear that his border stories were of sterner stuff than could be recommended for young ladies trained to believe that "novel reading produces a morbid appetite for excitement." [100]

Probably the reason why Simms encountered the charge of being too "gloomy and savage" is that although he was on the side of right living, he was not rich in the vein of ready moralizing that characterized the domestic novel of his time. Moreover though capable of strong indignation at political chicanery and literary skulduggery, he was not keenly sensitive to those economic problems which have formed the basis of so many modern novels of the South. He was militantly and fiercely sectional. He was unable to take the enlightened view which characterized Joel Chandler Harris a generation later, who had love for the South but deplored sectionalism. He was extremely sensitive politically, but his social purposes were slight—for all his eloquence on the uses of the historical novel. Generally there is at the end of his novels a sort of elementary justice: Tories are defeated, the bandit is hunted down, the Indian is subjugated, and the lovers are united. Simms seems to have had an interest in the psychology of behavior, and he shows some skill in handling characterizations of abnormal characters. But all of these interests are submerged in Simms's desire to write a good story. As a story-teller he succeeded because of his fertile invention and the air of vitality with which all his writing is invested. He was a writer of tremendous exuberance. At the same time, curiously enough, he seems to have assumed the reader's capacity for assimilating huge chunks of documentation—he was an expert in military tactics and a student of court procedure—but the reader is likely to avoid these in order to get on with the story. His style was at times good; and his frequent citation of Elizabethan dramatists, especially Shakespeare, shows how he revered great language,[101] but he wrote too fast to maintain a high standard of excellence.[102] Historically Simms is important as complementary to Cooper. Between them they surveyed most of the Atlantic seaboard from Maine to Florida and many points inland. They were both writers of immense vigor and range, with corresponding defects in the treatment of detail. In the historical romance they found a medium which called out their best powers and was kind to their weaknesses.

ROBERT MONTGOMERY BIRD (1806-1854)

Authorship was no merely fortuitous or fleeting phase of the career of Robert Montgomery Bird. A versatile person, he dabbled in many activities, but from his earliest days the one essential element was printer's ink. His first literary interest (if one ignores certain inevitable juvenile verses, some of which found their way into print) was in the drama. When certain unfortunate business experiences temporarily destroyed his interest in the theatre, he turned to the novel with such success that he is now remembered as one of the principal representatives of the historical romance in the second phase of its popularity, namely, in the thirties. One of his stories, indeed—*Nick of the Woods* (1837) —created so powerful an impression that its title is familiar today even to persons to whom the author's name is unknown.

Bird was born in New Castle, Delaware, in 1806. Conservative influences surrounded him as a youngster. Upon the death of his father, the boy was committed to the guardianship of his uncle Van Dyke, a man of "stern integrity, with views on education and religion that bordered on the severe." [103] A harsh schoolmaster, later satirized as McGoggin ("an Irishman just caught") in *The Adventures of Robin Day*, gave Bird a distaste for institutional education but did not kill his love of books. Later he prepared at Germantown for the medical school of the University of Pennsylvania. In 1827 he was graduated from the medical school but, like Oliver Wendell Holmes (three years his junior), he practiced medicine only a short time before discovering that he was temperamentally unsuited to the work. Subsequently he capitalized his medical knowledge by drawing on it in his fiction and (again like Holmes) by teaching.

In the meantime even as a medical student he had exhibited an uncommon interest in the anatomy of books other than those pertaining to materia medica. His specialty was Elizabethan plays, whose influence is observable not only in the chapter mottoes of his novels but also, it is fair to guess, in his proneness toward complicated plots revolving around the thrilling device of mistaken identity. His notebooks also disclose an ambitious array of literary plans including especially poetry and drama (tragedy). A good lyric poet Bird never became, but as a dramatist he was famous by the age of twenty-five.

Bird's success as a dramatist was all the more remarkable in view of special handicaps to American playwriting. Besides that lack of international copyright which hampered almost all contemporary authors, there was for the dramatist the added irritation that a play could be pirated (stenographically) even before it was printed. Moreover, the theatrical world had not worked out adequate types of contracts between authors and producers. Bird triumphed for a time over all these obstacles by dint of a combination of hard work and good fortune. He studied the art of playwriting with the most faithful attention to both the artistic and the practical needs of the theatre. Moreover, he was fortunate enough to mature his playwriting ambitions at the very time when Edwin Forrest, the popular tragedian, was offering cash prizes for manuscripts of plays suitable to his repertoire. Bird won four of Forrest's prizes, and his name, coupled with that of the celebrated actor, soared to heights reached by few nineteenth-century American dramatists. The best known of his plays were *The Gladiator* (1831) and *The Broker of Bogota* (1834). But mutually profitable as the association of Bird and Forrest was for a time, it was finally ruptured (in 1837) by financial disagreement, with the result that Bird forswore the theatre completely. In the meantime he had already become distrustful enough of playwriting as a means of livelihood to try his hand at novels as being likely to "immortalize one's pocket much sooner."[104] His first novel, *Calavar*, appeared in 1834.

If only to avoid direct competition with Cooper, it was natural for

Bird to have sought his setting in regions remote from New York and New England. Yet his choice of Mexico as a setting was also dictated in part by his knowledge of the Spanish language and his wide reading in Spanish-American history. He even projected a trip into Mexico with Edwin Forrest in 1833, but an epidemic of cholera interrupted the trip at New Orleans. He had recourse to books, therefore, not only for the plot but also for the settings of *Calavar*. The plot is formidably complicated. History provides the central situation: Governor Velasquez, after dispatching Cortez to conquer Montezuma, experiences a revulsion of feeling against Cortez and sends Narváez to replace him. Cortez, however, ignores orders, triumphs over Narváez at Zempoala, and proceeds with the difficult task of subjugating Mexico. In disastrous retreat from the capital city the Spaniards lose some five thousand men—the famous *noche triste*—but when battle is joined shortly thereafter on the field of Otumba the Spanish forces and allies inflict a decisive defeat upon the Mexicans. To this framework of fact (with its multifarious ramifications, including the revolt in which Montezuma is killed by his own men) Bird adds the story of Calavar, Don Amador (the juvenile lead), and Jacinto, page and cup-bearer assigned to Amador. Calavar, an aged knight of "wan and even ghastly" appearance but touched by distinction which makes him resemble a "ruin majestic in its decay," is obviously burdened by remorse for acts he has committed years before in Spain. Don Amador, a gallant youngster newly dedicated to the service of Cortez, also has his secret woe, the loss of his dear one, Leila. Amid all the turmoil of battle, the recital of glamorous legend, and the march over romantic scenery, the mystery is finally solved: during the Moorish wars in his youth Calavar had allowed jealousy to impel him to the murder of his sweetheart, the wounding of his benefactor and blood-brother, a noble Arab, and the firing of a whole village. The young lady whose loss Don Amador has bewailed proves to be Jacinto, with whom he is presently united. Jacinto, it also appears, is the daughter of the slain sweetheart of Calavar. Calavar's grief is further assuaged by the discovery that the friend he had wounded did not die but has been the guardian of Jacinto. Now purged of earthly passion and convinced of the folly of bloodshed, Calavar urges Amador to forswear warfare and to try to convert pagans by the cross instead of by the sword. Soon thereafter he dies. Much later, after Amador has returned to Spain, it is reported to him that Cortez has completed the conquest of Mexico. The final stages of the conquest, however, are reserved by Bird for use in *The Infidel*, which was published in May, 1835.

In *The Infidel* Cortez, possessed of a new commission and furnished with reinforcements, renews his assault upon Tenochtitlan (Mexico City). Upon the authority of Charles V, a Mexican leader has been named king by Cortez, but rebel forces under the Emperor Guatimozin continue to resist the Spanish. Only after a ninety-day siege does Cortez succeed in completing the conquest. In the meantime an exceedingly involved tale has been told concerning Cortez, his followers, and certain invented characters. Lerma, the youthful hero, is named in Spanish history,[106] but Bird assigns him a romantic role of which no historian gives the details. He is a handsome but singularly passive youth of noble bearing who first appears as the protégé of Cortez. Subsequently, slander turns his leader against him, and Lerma is sent on exceedingly perilous expeditions and is unjustly allowed to languish in prison. Throughout his persecution Lerma exhibits the most incredible magnanimity, forgiving his enemies and refusing to believe the worst of Cortez. Ultimately the slanderer, now at the point of death, confesses his sins, Lerma is returned to favor, and events prove that he is the nephew of Cortez! He finally marries Lellahualla, daughter of Montezuma, and returns with his bride to Spain to settle down upon his rightful estate, long withheld from him by the machinations of a wicked kinsman.

Both *Calavar* and *The Infidel* are crowded with the most complicated (though not always fast-moving) action from beginning to end. The spectacular subject-matter of Cortez' conquest provides Bird with manifold opportunities to display his gifts for reporting exciting action (both in individual exploits and in mass movements) and for colorful description, whether of exotic natural scenery in Central America, the barbarous splendor of an ancient civilization, or the brilliant appearance of the invaders. Scott is often recalled by Bird's use of pageantry and by his treatment of the mysterious Calavar, but there is in both books also an epic tone attributable, doubtless, to the theme of the dispossession of an ancient race and the founding of a new empire. It follows that characterization is largely confined to general outlines. In this respect, however, *Calavar* is superior to its sequel, for there is no single character in *The Infidel* who commands so much interest as the monumentally sorrowful knight Calavar.

Bird's preparation for *Calavar* and *The Infidel* had been to read enormously in the period. Probably he overestimated the public's capacity to absorb the results of research. At all events he later recognized that his success in his Mexican stories had been "nothing to compare with Simms's, which I esteem quite extraordinary: I feel very envious about him, but not in a malicious way." [107] It was difficult for the average reader of romance to centre his interests in stories set so far away in time and place. The patriotic heart that had thrilled to historical romances featuring John Paul Jones or Washington or Francis Marion could respond only feebly to stories of the brilliant but remote Cortez. Nor were Bird's non-historical characters endowed with sufficient originality to emerge clearly from the welter of historical incident. Yet critics were on the whole favorable. English editions appeared,[108] and Prescott the historian (later) added his word of praise,[109] but the public's enthusiasm was not long-lived over Bird's long-drawn-out stories. Perhaps a general reaction may be inferred from the frank expression of relief of one of Bird's own friends, James Lawson, when Bird had decided to try new pastures:

> 'Twixt you and me . . . I am not sorry you are done with Mexico. I fear the novel-reading world do not feel the same interest in the semi-civilized portion of our hemispheres, which you entertain. We want something, though not exactly at our door, yet near us.[110]

For the setting of his next novel, *The Hawks of Hawk Hollow* (1835) Bird had only to consult the memory of his frequent visits to the picturesque region of the Delaware Water Gap. The action is set in the year 1782, when, although the Revolutionary War was virtually over, there was still some sporadic back-woods fighting. The hero is a gentle soul (recently returned from Jamaica) who settles down to do some amateur painting. Promptly upon his arrival near the estate of Colonel Falconer, a patriot, he is accused of a recent attempt upon Falconer's life, and he is soon thereafter identified as "Hyland Gilbert," associated with a desperate gang of Tory marauders, The Hawks of Hawk Hollow. The Gilberts, originally patriots, had turned Tory during the war; but the reader's sympathy is not wholly withdrawn from them, for it is their family grievance that Falconer, now possessed of their former estate, had in bygone days seduced their Jessie. "Hyland Gilbert's" arrival at the Water Gap precipitates a long story whose involutions no brief outline can more than suggest. He falls in love with the object of young Harry Falconer's attentions. Later he is falsely imprisoned for the killing of Harry, but actually he was innocent both of Harry's death and the (earlier) attempt on Colonel Falconer's life. In the end it proves that the hero is not the original Hyland Gilbert, but his half-brother, the original bearer of the same name having died years before. It also appears that he is the legitimate son of Colonel Falconer, who had actually married Jessie but who, when opportunity for a richer match occurred, had told her that the marriage was false. It remains for Harriet Falconer, who thought she was the legitimate daughter of Falconer, to die of shame, and for Hyland, now known for the true "American" he is, to marry a local patriot nymph.

The critical reception of *The Hawks of Hawk Hollow* was not enthusiastic. After many quixotic comments, Poe concluded that it was "inferior, as a whole, to *The Infidel* and vastly inferior to *Calavar*." [111] The book did not have a quick sale but its "steady appreciation" over a period of seven months[112] proves that it was fairly congenial to contemporary readers. Today it appears as almost unreadable by reason of the author's remorseless piling up of confusing incident, his neglect of proportion, his ludicrously poor motivation, and his clumsy use of old narrative devices such as the changeling child and the unrevealed marriage. Disguise, mis-identification, and false leads are used to the point of exasperation. Only Neal's *Logan* can compare with this book in point of incoherence. The characterization is mostly perfunctory. The setting, which as a part of Bird's own observation might have been a saving thing, is disappointingly meagre in detail and confused in presentation—far inferior to that of the author's contemporary, J. P. Kennedy, whose *Horse-Shoe Robinson* appeared in the same year. But most serious of all the defects of the story is its excess of poorly linked incident. It was to this that N. P. Willis referred, with fine understatement, upon receiving a set of Bird's books: "I wonder . . . how you could afford to put so much *material* into a book. You see I look at it with an author's eye." [113] Yet the author appeared to pride himself on this very feature of his book. In the midst of the second volume he pauses to allude to Cooper's comparison of the course of a story to that of a stone rolled down a mountain side: its momentum is "communicated" to other stones, "which, increasing in number as they grow in velocity, are at last seen rattling down to the vale below, in a perfect avalanche, as confounding to the senses as it is hurrying to the spirits." [114] *The Hawks of Hawk Hollow* is indeed "confounding to the senses" of a modern reader, who would be contented with something less than a "perfect avalanche"—a few well-selected boulders tumbled one at a time would do.

As will be seen, Bird was to reach his one great popular success, *Nick of the Woods*, by a devious route. His next book was even more different from *The Hawks of Hawk Hollow* than the latter had been from his Mexican romances. So complete a departure, in fact, was the anonymous *Sheppard Lee* (1836) that a close friend, upon hearing it ascribed to Bird, dubbed the hypothesis "an absurd notion." [115] A brief analysis of the content of the book will readily account for the friend's skepticism. *Sheppard Lee* is a blending of eighteenth-century picaresque narrative, social satire, and psychological analysis of abnormality recalling in about equal proportions the methods of C. B. Brown and Poe. Bird equalled neither Brown nor Poe in originality and emotional power, but his *Sheppard Lee* is an ingenious tale. For the first time in his fiction Bird achieved clarity and proportion. The structural problem, to be sure, was relatively simple. Sheppard Lee, an amiable but shiftless gentleman farmer, loses his estate through a dishonest overseer and his money through speculation. Political plans also miscarry, and Sheppard Lee, now accused of being defective in the "upper story," takes to digging for Captain Kidd's treasure.[116] In the process he falls into a trance from which he emerges as a disembodied spirit. Envious of the prosperity of one Colonel Higginson, who conveniently suffers a broken neck nearby, Sheppard Lee by an effort of the will projects his spirit into the body of the dead man—"vanishing, as it were, into the dead man's nostrils . . ."[117] Now commences a series of episodes in which Lee successively inhabits the bodies of persons recently dead. As Colonel Higginson, Lee is so harassed by a shrewish wife and a bad case of the gout that he is glad to abandon the Colonel's carcass and assume the identity of I. Dulwer Dawkins, a fop whose complicated affairs have just led him to suicide. As Dawkins, however, Sheppard Lee finds that the fashionable career of his host had exhausted his patrimony and that he (Lee) must live a picaresque existence by his wits. A plan to marry for money goes astray, and Sheppard Lee jumps into a new existence—as Abraham Skinner, a usurer, father of one of the girls he had hoped to marry. This move proves to him that avarice is the root of most of the evil in the world. It also subjects him to abuse at the hands of his children. The daughter wheedles him for money; one son, imprisoned for forgery, dies a suicide; the other son attempts to murder his father and later becomes insane. Relief from these woes is briefly delayed by a dearth of dead men, but Sheppard Lee finally manages to take spiritual possession of a philanthropical Quaker just murdered. Disillusionment promptly follows, for all his good deeds only prove that "man is an unthankful animal . . ." In time Sheppard Lee (*qua* Quaker) is kidnapped by Yankee peddlers to be sold down the river as an abolitionist suitable for lynching. At a critical moment Sheppard Lee leaps into the body of a Negro lad, and leads for a time the contented life of a well-cared-for slave. But an anti-slavery pamphlet causes an insurrection in the course of which Tom (Sheppard Lee) is hanged and buried. He revives two days later and optimistically enters the body of a youth who has no care in the world. Even this move brings its train of trouble, for having no real ills, Sheppard Lee invents some and become first a hypochondriac and then a maniac. The treatment for his condition gradually brings back his consciousness—as

Sheppard Lee. His mental disorder has been cured. As himself, Sheppard Lee is disturbed because no one will believe in his adventures, but he is happy to learn that his farm has been recovered.

As a story, *Sheppard Lee* is sprightly and entertaining throughout. The theme of metempsychosis naturally attracted Poe's attention to the book and it elicited critical remarks in Poe's best manner.[118] Though he praised the work for its "directness," Poe was of the opinion that a better artistic effect might have been gained by omitting rational explanation of the situation and "by leaving the result as a wonder not to be accounted for." [119] Poe was, of course, less interested in the social satire which was a large part of the raison d'être of the book.

In *Nick of the Woods* (1837) Bird so successfully synthesized his best qualities and suppressed his weaknesses that he produced a story of quick and lasting popularity. The use of Kentucky as a setting was fortunate not only because Bird's own travels had furnished him with regional data but also because public interest was already firmly rooted in a section made glamorous by the exploits of Daniel Boone and (in the neighboring state of Tennessee) of Davy Crockett,[120] not to mention the prominence of Henry Clay. Speculation in public lands was at its height.[121] Bird's romance, though set back in time (the date assigned for the action is 1782) was of topical interest, therefore, in that it recounted the adventures of folk emigrating from Virginia to settle bounty land in Kentucky territory. Yet *Nick of the Woods* can stand on its own merits as story. The action is not without trite complications relating to an inheritance, but it has stronger unity and greater clarity than that of Bird's Spanish-American stories. At the same time, there is a mystery (the identity of the Jibbenainosay), which is shrewdly managed and adequately resolved. The central theme, a white man's cleverly contrived mode of revenge for Indian atrocities, was far from new in 1837, but Bird's relentless attack on Indian character gave it a new piquancy. The gradual revelation of the Jibbenainosay's implacable purpose is managed with a maximum of skill. Telie Doe, daughter of a renegade white man, has at least the pin-feathers of realism, and the blustering border character, Roaring Ralph Stackpole (largely drawn from the life), is genuinely comic.[122] With such interesting dramatis personae the reader does not murmur if the young lovers, Roland and Edith, are mostly costume and the villain Braxley is mainly mustache. Characterization, however, is less important than the action, which is brilliantly described. Bird the dramatist is recalled in the magnificent scene in which Nathan is tempted to slay Wenonga.[123] Like any writer of the period who essayed an Indian tale after Cooper, Bird almost of necessity seemed unoriginal in certain situations and de-

vices, among them the false Indian guide, the preference of the hero
for the more dangerous of two alternatives, the dispossession of a rightful heir, the refusal of the woodsman (Nathan) to leave the frontier and
return to the settlements. But his Indians differed sharply from the
stereotype. He was not unaware that "there is something deeply melancholy . . . in the fate of the Indian," but he was not disposed to shed
tears over the situation, for "the earth is the dwelling of man, not the
brute . . ." [124] As far as Bird was concerned, the vanishing American
should vanish. The "noble savage" to him was largely a noxious myth.
Here was a new attitude toward Indian stock characters, and Bird noted
as much in his preface:

> We owe, perhaps, some apology for the hues we have thrown
> around the Indian portraits in our picture,—hues darker than are
> usually employed by the painters of such figures. But, we confess,
> the North American savage has never appeared to us the gallant
> and heroic personage he seems to others. The single fact that he
> wages war—systematic war—upon beings incapable of resistance
> or defence,—upon women and children, whom all other races in
> the world, no matter how barbarous, consent to spare,—has hith-
> erto been, and we suppose, to the end of our days will remain, a
> stumbling-block to our imagination: we look into the woods for
> the mighty warrior, 'the feather-cinctured chief,' rushing to meet
> his foe, and behold him retiring, laden with the scalps of miser-
> able squaws and their babes. Heroical? *Hoc verbum quid valeat,
> non vident.*[125]

Thus after four attempts Bird finally wrote a best seller. Despite the
depression in the book trade following the panic of 1837, *Nick of the
Woods* seems to have held a steady public and it has received in all
some twenty editions.[126] Dr. Bird's scholarship and his social interests
are only slightly reflected in the story, but its wealth of exciting and
well-proportioned action compounded of invented material and historical fact[127] proved to be a formula capable of pleasing a vast public.

That Bird did not capitalize the new-found formula is to be explained
partly by his ill health (which became serious in 1837) and partly by
the timidity of publishers during the economic depression following
1837. No great success attended his collection of tales and sketches,
Peter Pilgrim (1838) or his novel *The Adventures of Robin Day* (1839).
Robin Day provides an interesting study in fictional modes during
the interval between the heyday of the historical romance and the
rise of the domestic novel.[128] Bird's last long fiction, it also reveals in
part the reasons for his decline in popularity. The hero is first seen as a

nameless infant cast up from a wreck off the New Jersey coast near Barnegat in 1796. For seven years he lives with a worthless thieving hag who uses him as a drudge until he is bought (for the price of a keg of rum) by the villainous Captain Day, owner of a fishing boat. Five years of hardship, cruelty, and undernourishment in Day's service are brought to an end when Robin is rewarded for saving a boy from drowning by being taken into the home of the boy's father. Robin responds favorably to his improved home environment, but the school to which his new patron sends him is so badly managed that the rebellious boys assault (and apparently kill) the brutal McGoggin.[129] Robin flees to Philadelphia with a letter of introduction to a merchant; but, misled by a thief who represents himself as the merchant, Robin is subsequently apprehended and detained as an accomplice in an attempted robbery. Once escaped, he is submerged in a welter of adventures recounted at tedious length by Bird: fighting and being taken prisoner in the War of 1812; selling quack medicines in company with the aforesaid thief; skirmishing against Indians in the South; being taken prisoner and barely escaping death at the stake; adventuring in Florida until captured by the Spanish at Pensacola and imprisoned by the order of one Colonel Aubrey; escaping and going pirate (this changes the scene to Cuba and waters adjacent thereto); and, finally, rescuing a lovely maiden, Isabel. At the end there is the usual startling check-up of the personnel: Colonel Aubrey is revealed as Robin's uncle and Isabel as his sister. The love which has sprung up between the latter two, however, is easily modified, and Robin's more romantic affection reverts to a shadowy creature met earlier in the story.

The book as a whole is disappointing. Robin's early adventures as apprentice to disreputable characters seem for a time to promise interests comparable to those of *Oliver Twist*, which had recently appeared, but his subsequent career is largely a throwback to older picaresque narratives. In this story identification problems are still solved by lockets, rosaries, portraits, and long-armed coincidences. Nor are the characters fully enough individualized to lend significance to the action. The author's language is as usual vigorous and racy, but it seems largely wasted in this mediocre tale.

After 1839 Bird wrote no long fictions, and the rest of his life was a somewhat harassing miscellany. His precarious physical condition had already necessitated trips to the West and frequent intervals of retirement in the country (in Maryland and Pennsylvania). He had become much interested not only in the joys of farm life but also in the science of agriculture. Increasing financial pressure, however, forced him to do periodical writing which he did not enjoy,[130] to enter upon a disastrous career as newspaper editor and part-owner, to revise his plays and novels for re-publication,[131] and to project two histories, one of the United States and one of the Mexican War. For a short time he taught medicine. An active Whig, he stumped for Henry Clay. On one occasion he also announced his candidacy for Congress, but he shortly withdrew. These and other projects revealed versatile abilities but did little to relieve his financial stringency. He died in 1854, the days of his greatest celebrity far behind him, his debts haunting him to the end.

In temperament Bird was conservative but not reactionary. A certain skepticism tinctured his "philosophy of life." If *Sheppard Lee* be taken as even a partial indication of his view of man and society, it is apparent that Bird was aware of many sad defects in human nature. Nor did he have much faith in social nostrums or even specific acts of benevolence: in *Sheppard Lee* there is a catalogue of nineteen attempts to benefit mankind, each one of them ineffective in the end. Bird seemed to think that progress was up to the individual, but he did not look for miracles. His medical training had taught him (as it did Holmes) how often an individual's physical state conditions his moral outlook.[132] In his broad tolerance Bird seemed modern. On the other hand he had no taste for frivolous new-fangled notions, and he disapproved, for example, of the agitation over women's rights.[133] Moreover although he was aware of defects in the social order in general, he thought that conformity had its uses, for it was related to intellectual progress:

> The whole system of social federation is a state of enthrallment and captivity, although undoubtedly a wholesome one; and he who publicly rejects its fetters, though he may personally enjoy his independence, violates that compact which separates the refined from the primitive and uncivilized states of existence, and encourages others to rush back upon the savage freedom of the latter. The preservation of a certain share of dignity is incumbent upon men, not merely as a means of holding caste, but of preventing a downslide in manners and mind.[134]

Politically also Bird was conservative. As a Whig, he favored the protective tariff and he deplored upstart parties such as the Locofocos.[135] Slavery he was opposed to on principle and he seems to have been irritated by the insolence of Negroes in Northern cities,[136] but he was no fanatical abolitionist, for he realized how much affection subsisted between a good owner and his contented charges.[137] He was a patriot but no chauvinist, a republican but no lover of the masses.[138] He could love his home and celebrate his own region[139] without ceasing to venerate the entire Anglo-Saxon tradition of which America was only the latest manifestation. The shrill demand of his contemporaries for an unequivocally national literature awakened no response in his placid bosom. This is clear from his generous use of English literary sources, his selection of themes, and his literary theory.

Bird's literary theory gave no central place to national pride. In the introduction to *The Hawks of Hawk Hollow* he describes his story as "rather a domestic tale, treating of incidents and characters common to the whole world, than one of which these components can be considered *peculiarly* American." [140] He recognized of course that this treatment might be "unfortunate"—

> the tendency of the public taste seeming to require of American authors that they should confine themselves to what is, in subject, event, and character, indigenous to their own hemisphere; although such a requisition would end in reducing their materials to such a stock as might be carried about in a nut-shell. America is a part of the great world, and, like other parts, has little (that is, suited to the purposes of fiction) which it can call exclusively its own: and how far that little has been already *used up*, any one may tell, who is conversant with our domestic literature. Some little, however, of that little yet remains; and, by and by, we will perhaps ourselves join in the general scramble after it.[141]

As for the technique of novel-writing as such, Bird was prone to be a little slothful. He cherished the most rigorous ideas of what constituted good dramatic writing,[142] but he was inclined to regard the novel as a vehicle for relaxation:

> A tragedy takes, or should take, as much labor as two romances; and one comedy as much as six tragedies. How blessedly and lazily, in making a novel, a man may go spinning and snoring over his quires.[143]

He thought of the novel less as a structure requiring the most careful design than as a catch-all of vivid fact and impression:

> A novel is, at best, a piece of Mosaic-work, of which the materials have been scraped up here and there, sometimes in an unchronicled corner of the world itself, . . . sometimes from the little mine of precious stones that is found in the human brain—at least as often as the pearl in the toad's head, of which John Bunyan discourses so poetically, in the Apology for his *Pilgrim's Progress*.[144]

"Snoring over his quires"—perhaps that is exactly what caused the comparative failure of most of Bird's novels. Perhaps too he was more of an antiquarian than comports with being a popular novelist. He wrote with more vigor than Kennedy (another antiquarian) but with less clarity—and less obvious charm. The personal attractiveness of Bird is little reflected in his novels except the autobiographical story of *Robin Day*. He did not excel in small talk. The fashion recently set by Bulwer, who used "the hero of observation and reflection, who did not do great things, but who said good things," [145] Bird did not choose to imitate. He underestimated the current demand for sentiment; a certain classical quality in his prose which recommends it to the connoisseur made his books seem a little austere to readers accustomed to a more popular style and a freer flow of emotion. Those fine intellectual gifts which Bird exhibited in his many avocations were never fully capitalized in his novels.

If there had been a public demand for satirical novels, the author of *Sheppard Lee* might have responded. Certainly there were satirical impulses in the pen that could write epigrammatic lines such as: "I never . . . knew a lawyer to believe any thing unless he was paid for it." [146] Like Paulding, Bird had a penchant for caustic commentary that did not always fit with the type of tale he was telling, and his finely articulated irony may well have perplexed readers in quest of simple entertainment. His characterization is good but it is not distinguished by full realization of individuals: Bird knew man in general better than he knew individuals. Some of his gifts, therefore, remained unused in his career as a novelist. *Nick of the Woods* was no more mellow than Bird's other novels, but it had the qualities that make for popular success. Kentucky instead of Mexico, history instead of antiquarianism, Shawnees instead of Aztecs, a living national frontier instead of a remote gladiatorial arena, well-shaped, forward-driving narrative instead of labyrinthine fictional tapestry—these shifts of aim and tactic between Bird's first stories and his most popular romance explain his final success. For the rest, it is unlikely that the early novels will ever be widely read again—heavily veined as they are with the rich ore of Bird's capacious mind. Bird will continue to live as a distinguished ornament to his time, as a dramatist, and as the author of *Nick of the Woods*.

JOHN PENDLETON KENNEDY (1795-1870)

Generally regarded as a Southern writer, J. P. Kennedy answers to that description but poorly in several respects. It is possibly an overstatement to say that he was "not Southern in birth or in political sympathy";[147] yet he was not a Southerner in the sense that, for example, Simms was. Born in 1795 in Baltimore, a city which even in his youth was "growing less and less Southern," [148] he lived all his life, except for summer visits to Virginia, above the Potomac River. He had a number of family connections in Philadelphia, New York, and Cincinnati. The manufacturing interests of Baltimore and the protectionist convictions of his father-in-law, a wealthy Baltimore manufacturer, naturally made him an atypical Southerner. His real views on slavery (which are not to be hastily inferred from his novels) marked him as a "mild abolitionist." [149] He was an avid student of politics; yet although he occasionally supported a cause with vehemence, he was not a strong partisan after the fashion of Simms. Well versed in classical authors, he developed a mental horizon that transcended sectional interests. Temperamentally he was a spectator, an amateur of life and letters. He had a connoisseur's love of good company and fine cuisine; the art of living called for a knowledge of viands, whether on the occasion of a "neat repast . . . light and choice" or a Lucullan feast. In writing, too, he exhibited his fine breeding and unerring taste. His literary gifts were comprised mainly in the ability to distill the flavor of life, to sketch character, and to indulge a pleasant philosophizing vein which was often vigorously ironic but seldom cynical. A story-writer par excellence Kennedy was not, but the times drew him into fiction, and his three long novels added genuine distinction to the novel of the thirties.[150]

American literary biography is so strewn with names of those who reached literature after an apprenticeship in law that it is almost a routine matter to relate how as a young man Kennedy stole time from his law practice to write "essays, treatises, notes, journals, farces, poems, travels," and even to toy with pencil-sketching and painting.[151] Like many another young American writer he was early smitten with the idea that he might reach fame as a metropolitan wit. Accordingly in 1818 he joined his talents with those of Peter Hoffman Cruse in a small magazine, *The Red Book*, which aimed to do much the same thing for Baltimore as had been done by Irving and Paulding for New York in the *Salmagundi* papers and as was shortly to be resumed by Halleck and Drake in *The Croakers*. His models included the common sire of many such literary progeny, Addison, but he had an especial fondness for Horace, and he gave to local verse satires included in *The Red Book* the title of "Horace in Baltimore." [152]

Kennedy's early use of Horace as a model perhaps helps to account for the quality of his first extended work of fiction, *Swallow Barn* (1832), which is rather less a novel than a series of descriptive essays, character sketches, digressory episodes, and miscellaneous wisdom set forth in language which is at once leisurely in tone and brilliantly epigrammatic in style. Kennedy himself asserted that *Swallow Barn* is "not a novel," [153] but the public has persisted in making the most of its fictional quality.[154] Such slender right as it has to be called a novel is vested in its account of a dispute over a boundary-line between two estates in Virginia. The feud is an old and silly one, and its prosecution is marked by many ludicrous episodes before the time comes to prove whether or not Manning Diana, the sybil, is correct in her prophecy that it will remain unsettled "until Swallow Barn shall wed the Brakes."

Setting and characterization are superbly handled in *Swallow Barn*, and they have been a source of inspiration to countless later novelists who have used a Virginian entourage. Although Kennedy's political and economic views were affected by Northern opinion, his mellowest story is set in the middle South. Swallow Barn is an estate on the southern bank of the James River twenty miles below Richmond. Around its principal building, a brick-walled mansion more than a century old, numerous frame structures have grown up to form a "domain" which is "inefficient" but largely self-sustaining, and full of drowsy picturesqueness. Kennedy describes the life of the whole ménage, man and beast, and he lingers over his characters—as one might linger over a favorite dish at dinner. Few American novels are richer in characterization that is searching without being profound. Addison and Irving and the "character" writers were Kennedy's models, but he added much from his own observation. Whether a plot is forthcoming or not, the reader is content to know the people. Frank Meriwether—forty-five, handsome, good-tempered, indolent, disillusioned with politics but a vigilant observer of affairs, inclined toward literature as a hobby—controls the estate of Swallow Barn. He is hospitable but "apt to be impatient of contradiction" and "always very touchy on the point of honor." Naturally he finds it hard to reach agreement with the master of The Brakes, Isaac Tracy, a testy old patrician addicted to fashions in dress of days gone by, and so completely absorbed in the litigation over the boundary line that when the long-standing controversy is decided in his favor, he loses his zest for life. Other residents of the two estates are brought to life in leisurely portraits: Meriwether's wife, famous for her breakfasts and passionately concerned for the protection of home manufactures; Prudence Meriwether, Frank's unmarried sister, who showed "a little too much girlishness, which betrays a suspicion of its opposite"; Parson Chubb, victim of many jokes but "a philosopher after the order of Socrates"; Barbara Winkle, an old retainer who takes care of the "little infantry." These and many others go to make a group of people who inevitably recall Irving's *Bracebridge Hall* and sometimes people out of Sheridan but who were undoubtedly observed by the author in a section of Virginia as it was in the first quarter of the nineteenth century. Gradually the life is sketched through accounts of the quiet occupations and amusements of the characters: attending sessions of the court; hunting the opossum; conversations on poetry, politics, and history; equestrianism; minstrelsy; domestic theatricals; a Fourth of July celebration; a visit to the Negro quarters.

The condition of the Negroes is represented as moderately good. Frank Meriwether does not approve of slavery, but he believes that its evils have been greatly magnified and that a sudden emancipation would be disastrous, for the Negroes are virtually children, unable to take care of themselves industrially. Such a move would be the "most cruel of all projects." Rather he looks forward to a scheme of gradual emancipation whereby those Negroes who have shown themselves capable should be allowed to "hold small tracts of land under their masters, rendering for it a certain rent . . ."[155] In Frank Meriwether's views one may read roughly Kennedy's own opinions, but his attitude toward slavery was fundamentally more critical than Frank Meriwether's.[156]

Swallow Barn, the "first important fictional treatment of Virginian life," [157] is by and large an accurate study of the social order in Virginia during the first part of the nineteenth century, but the social organization was even then changing on account of Jeffersonian policies which were splitting up the large plantations[158] and inducing the westward migration from Virginia to Kentucky and other Western states.[159] The result of these changes was not immediately taken into account by novelists. When Kennedy revised *Swallow Barn* for a new edition twenty years later, his book had lost some of its social application, for by that time a new aristocracy had been built up, to be described later by Thomas Nelson Page. Kennedy erred slightly in one respect in which many subsequent historical writers were grievous offenders, namely, in neglecting the small planter and the poor white. The great planters were never numerous, and the

> chief charm of old Virginia life lay not in its luxury or grandeur but in its homespun simplicity. The Virginian planter was a gentleman farmer, not an English lord; and his estate was not an English manor, but a tobacco farm.[160]

Most of the novels in the Virginia tradition with which the general reading public is acquainted were written after *Swallow Barn* and most of them are basically less true to the social fabric of the South. With Caruthers' *The Cavaliers of Virginia* (1834-35) there began a long line of books more attractive than accurate in their accounts of Virginian life. They have been widely read, of course, both in the South and the North, for the fiction reader has always regarded Virginia as a romantic fairyland where debonair young men may ride to the wars but always return to marry a supernally beautiful (if fragile) heroine under the slightly suspicious eye of a patrician father given to drinking mint juleps and quarrelling over points of honor but mainly devoted to managing a glamorous estate on a placid river where the wood-pigeons coo and contented darky dependents sing joyously at their intermittent tasks. Accuracy is not the demand of the readers of historical romance. Kennedy proved in *Swallow Barn* that many of these elements may be found in a story that is close to reality and written with far more beauty of style than has been displayed by later writers in the Virginia tradition. Cooper had used Virginian characters in *The Spy*, but Kennedy was the first to reveal them in their homes much as they really were.[161]

When in his next book Kennedy forswore the indolent habit of an essayist to join "the industrious tribe of chroniclers" of the American Revolution[162] he found a larger public, but he disclosed no important new aspects of his art as a writer. *Horse-Shoe Robinson* (1835) is an historical romance patterned broadly after Cooper. The locale was new (for Simms had barely begun to produce his vast studies of the Southern terrain) and the plot utilized new episodes in the history of the nation; but the situations and for the most part the characters were already somewhat stereotyped when Kennedy began to write. The action takes place in South Carolina during the year 1780. The plot is largely invented insofar as it pertains to the central characters, but Kennedy, who was more of an antiquarian than Cooper, was at pains to make the details of the setting, costume, and even the major military movements as authentic as research could accomplish.[163] The military movements reach a climax in a full description of the battle of King's Mountain. Yet in reporting history accurately Kennedy did not seriously impair the "romantic" plot, which is a perfectly adequate one if the test of originality is not too rigorously applied. The situation revolves about the familiar poles of love in conflict with parental displeasure and lovers endangered by exigencies of warfare. To this may be added the special interest that derives from the political ambiguity of the times, which was such that "it wasn't safe to meet a man on the road: you couldn't tell whether he was friend or enemy." [164] As in Cooper's *Spy* good men were in doubt whether to cast their fortunes with the Loyalists or the Whigs—for in many respects the Revolutionary War was "in reality a civil war." [165] An excellent portrait is that of

Tory-tempered Philip Lindsay, the harassed father of the heroine. The hero and heroine are, however, indubitably "patriotic," and the story is a conventional romance in most respects. Kennedy's attempt to give it a new turn by concealing the true relationship between Major Butler and the heroine is at best a clumsy variation on older formulas for romance. Invention was not Kennedy's forte. This much is proved by the number of elements which he seems to have borrowed from Cooper: the hazardous journey, the incognito celebrity, the frail heroine finally goaded by fate into undertaking a desperate mission, the treacherous guide, the overheard conversation, the exhibition of wanton cruelty toward animals, the eccentric, big-hearted woodsman, and the darky comic. The fortunes of the hero have a rhythmic rise and fall that could be graphed much as in a Cooper story. Even the titular hero has his counterpart in Natty Bumppo.

For Galbraith (called Horse-Shoe) Robinson and not Major Butler, the juvenile lead, is the centre of interest in the book for the modern reader. It is perhaps a wearisome business to be obliged to handle the small change of every transaction involving the corporal safety of a handsome young hero destined to be rescued at last anyway; but it is a delight to move in the company of a hearty old campaigner whose salty vernacular and unstudied reactions provide an adult antidote to that code of elegant propriety which dictated every thought, word, and action of hero and heroine.[166] Undignified actions, however natural, were strictly forbidden the juvenile leads in an historical romance. No hero, for example, could snore. But the illiterate Horse-Shoe Robinson was not expected to have "manners" and he could snore with astonishing range and volume:

> The speed of Horse Shoe's journey through this pleasant valley of sleep might be measured somewhat in the same manner that the route of a mail stage may sometimes be traced through a mountain defile, by the notes of the coachman's horn; it was defined by the succession of varying intonations through which he ascended the gamut, beginning with a low but audible breathing, and rising through the several stages of an incipient snore, a short quick bark, and up to a snort that constituted the greatest altitude of the ascent. Occasionally a half articulated interjection escaped him, and words that showed in what current his dreams were sailing: "No pistols! Look in the water, James! Ha ha!" These utterings were accompanied with contortions of body that more than once awaked the sleeper; but, at last, the huge bulk of Horse Shoe grew motionless in a deep and strong sleep.[167]

Compensation for the prim speeches of the juveniles may be found in Horse-Shoe's preamble to a rough and tumble fight with a (damnable) Tory named Curry:

> "When I observed, just now," replied Robinson, somewhat sternly, "that I couldn't be instigated, I meant to be compre-hended as laying down a kind of general doctrine that I was a man not given to quarrels; but still, if I suspicioned a bamboozlement, which I am not far from at this present speaking, if it but come up to the conflagrating of only the tenth part of the wink of an eye, in a project to play me off, fore God, I confess myself to be as weak in the flesh as e'er a rumbunctious fellow you mought meet on the road." [168]

These words are unmistakably reminiscent of Natty Bumppo, but though the two are kin spirits, Kennedy's man is also largely original and he was in fact modelled upon a backwoodsman whom the author met on one of his rambles through a remote section of the western part of South Carolina.[169] Transmuted into literature he is one of the best-drawn characters in the American historical romance, and he has kept *Horse-Shoe Robinson* from the utter neglect into which it otherwise might have fallen. Each new age demands new apparatus and para-phernalia and turns of action for young lovers, but genuine characters survive changing fashions. Despite its prolixity (Kennedy's action is slower than Cooper's) *Horse-Shoe Robinson* is read even today. It has other virtues—an almost flawless (if seldom elevated) style and mo-ments of good description as well as unity of time and of tone (the en-tire action taking place in three months), but these would not have kept the book alive without Galbraith Robinson.

Horse-Shoe Robinson won an immediate success—a much greater popular success than *Swallow Barn*, which is in most respects a superior book. Irving, to whom the book was dedicated, promptly wrote to Kennedy of the "great gusto" with which he read the story.[170] Poe oracularly announced that it would "place Mr. Kennedy at once in the very first rank of American novelists," and he praised Kennedy for a virtue hitherto but little practiced among American romance-writers:

> The writer has also made another innovation. He has begun at the beginning. We all know this to be an unusual method of pro-cedure. It has been too, for some time past, the custom, to delay as long as possible the main interest of a novel—no doubt with the very laudable intention of making it the more intense when it does at length arrive. Now for our own parts we can see little

difference in being amused with the beginning or with the end of a book, but have a decided preference for those rare volumes which are so lucky as to amuse us throughout. And such a book is the one before us.[171]

He likewise praised Kennedy for his delineation of "female characters"; and for a style that is "simple and forcible, and . . . at the same time, richly figurative and poetical." [172] Poe's pronouncement about the probable success of the book proved prophetic, for *Horse-Shoe Robinson* took hold quickly and remained popular for decades.[173]

No such welcome awaited Kennedy's next novel, *Rob of the Bowl: A Legend of St. Inigoe's* (1838), despite the fact that critically it is now accounted his best long narrative. Its mixed legend and history of seventeenth-century Maryland did not afford such ample opportunity for the exploitation of patriotism as Revolutionary themes. Moreover, the quarrel between Catholic and Protestant in days long before our nation was even established was somehow harder for the general reader to grasp. In *Rob of the Bowl* Kennedy tells a good story, but he tells it to please himself as much as the reader. He writes in a ruminative, meditative, almost muted manner that is full of charm. To be sure, no gourmet of the historical romance could be disappointed at the spicy ingredients of the story: resplendent nobility, blustering soldiers, picturesque tavern scenes, a beautiful heroine, a debonair hero with a cloud over his name, a band of freebooters plying their trade from a haunted house on a fearsome shore, a villainous pirate chief, an abduction, a rescue, an adequate solution of the genealogical problem of the hero, and withal enough gaiety and blood to fashion out any romantic narrative. Yet one suspects that the author was not mainly interested in the action as such. Certainly the plot was not highly original. Nor were the characters wholly unknown before *Rob of the Bowl* was published. Rather they are brilliant transitional figures borrowed, relimned, and passed over to later writers. Captain Dauntrees stands between Bobadil and other Elizabethan hearties and Miles Standish. Dame Dorothy is a bit of Elizabethan tavern life transplanted, bag and baggage, in Maryland. Her husband, as fine a coward as American fiction can boast, is driven to rationalizing expedients that unfailingly recall Falstaff. The crippled freebooter, Rob of the Bowl, with his awesome machinations, looks backward to Irving's *Money Diggers* and forward to Stevenson's *Treasure Island*. The gallery of characters in *Rob of the Bowl*, indeed, is so brilliant that complaint has been made of Kennedy's failure to create one central figure.[174] The point is unimportant in view of the rich texture of the whole book. The American historical romance is not often pitched so brilliantly as in this passage describing the Weasel Garret's attempt to avoid a hazardous adventure:

"You must know, Garret," said Dauntrees when the serving-maid had retired, "that we go to-night to visit the Wizard's Chapel by his Lordship's order; and as I would have stout fellows with me, I have come down here on purpose to take you along."

"Heaven bless us, Master Jasper Dauntrees!" exclaimed Garret, somewhat confounded with this sudden appeal to his valour, which was not of that prompt complexion to stand so instant a demand, and yet which the publican was never willing to have doubted—"truly there be three of you, and it might mar the matter to have too many on so secret an outgoing"—

"Tush, man,—that has been considered. His Lordship especially looks to your going: you cannot choose but go."

"But my wife, Captain Dauntrees"—

"Leave that to me," said the Captain; "I will manage it as handsomely as the taking of Troy. Worthy Garret, say naught against it—you must go, and take with you a few bottles of Canary and a good luncheon of provender in the basket. You shall be our commissary. I came on set purpose to procure the assistance of your experience, and store of comfortable sustenance. Get the bottles, Garret,—his Lordship pays the scot to-night."

"I should have my nag," said Garret, "and the dame keeps the key of the stable, and will in no wise consent to let me have it. She would suspect us for a rouse if I but asked the key."

"I will engage for that, good Weasel," said Dauntrees: "I will cozen the dame with some special invention which shall put her to giving the key of her own motion: she shall be coaxed with a device that shall make all sure—only say you will obey his Lordship's earnest desire."

"It is a notable piece of service," said the innkeeper, meditating over the subject, and tickled with the importance which was ascribed to his co-operation—"and will win thanks from the whole province. His Lordship did wisely to give it in charge to valiant men."

"In faith did he," replied the Captain; "and it will be the finishing stroke of thy fortunes. You will be a man of mark for ever after."

"I am a man to be looked to in a strait, Captain," said Weasel, growing valorous with the thought. "I saw by his Lordship's eye yesternight that he was much moved by what I told him. I have had a wrestle with devils before now." [175]

Kennedy dared to tune his phrases by remembered notes of Shakespeare and Ben Jonson, a procedure far from inappropriate considering that the Elizabethans were not long in their graves at the time of. the imagined action of *Rob of the Bowl*. Antiquarian that he had to be in order to dig up the forgotten facts of Lord Baltimore's quarrel over the threatened dispossession of Catholic office-holders, Kennedy turned poet when he began to transcribe his findings. Nor did he fall into the hollow imitative manner of the *forsooth*-and-*quotha* school of romance-writers. *Rob of the Bowl* is one of the minor classics in a semi-popular genre. For though a purveyor of historical romance, Kennedy, like Leonard Merrick, was a novelist's novelist. Reaching the general public was no more important to him than obeying his highest instincts as a craftsman.

Notwithstanding the hope expressed by a writer in the *North Atlantic Review* that the author of *Swallow Barn* would "withdraw his attention from other objects, and devote himself entirely to the elegant pursuits of polite literature," [176] Kennedy had allowed politics to absorb his energies more and more. Antiquarian though he was, Kennedy took a keen interest in governmental affairs, and he held several public offices, including that of Secretary of the Navy. His activity in public life largely explains why, although he never ceased writing, he produced no other avowedly literary work. Indeed despite his success as a writer he appeared to regard literature as a pastime.[177] Politically he expressed himself frequently. His best known political work is *The Annals of Quodlibet* (1840), which has been called "the most vivacious criticism of Jacksonianism in our political library." [178] His *Life of William Wirt* (1849) in two large volumes was an exceedingly able expression of admiration for his distinguished friend. These works like a number of short political tracts show the same care for literary expression that Kennedy always evinced. He never returned to belles lettres, but the voluminous journal in which he recorded his impressions of Europe during a period of more than two years, promises, when it is published, to afford rich plunder to the literary connoisseur. He died in 1870.

Kennedy's literary reputation (he was of course well known as an orator and a statesman also) was at its height at about the middle of the century, but he had been widely known and respected ever since the publication of *Swallow Barn* in 1832. T. W. White, publisher of the *Southern Literary Messenger*, referred to him in 1834 as among the five men to whom he looked to bring credit upon his magazine.[179] *Horse-Shoe Robinson* and, to a less extent, *Rob of the Bowl*, placed him among the few writers of historical romance who compared with Cooper and Simms in popularity. Gradually the public tended to value Kennedy chiefly for one book, *Horse-Shoe Robinson*, but the literati respected his entire output. In 1858 Thackeray (whom he met more than once) showed his confidence in Kennedy's judgment by drawing upon him for notes to be used in a chapter of *The Virginians*.[180] The publication of a five-volume edition of his works in 1860 elicited a favorable review from the editor of the *North American Review*.[181] At the time of his death a great deal of panegyric comment was passed on the man and his works. The president of the Massachusetts Historical Society asserted that Kennedy had made "no common mark . . . in a line of literature in which . . . Charles Brockden Brown and Washington Irving and James Fenimore Cooper had . . . been so conspicuous." [182] J. R. Lowell and Holmes, however, were more temperate in their praise, Holmes confining himself almost entirely to personal eulogy. Lowell remarked, with perhaps a shade of patronage, on the pleasure of spending time in the company of writers who though not geniuses contribute to the enjoyment of life: "it is wholesome to unbend our faculties now and then from the strain of that Alpine society in the company of authors who simply know how to be agreeable." [183] Nevertheless it is apparent that by 1873 Kennedy's vogue was largely past as a popular writer. He went out of fashion, to be remembered mainly for one book, *Horse-Shoe Robinson*.

Hervey Allen's remark that Kennedy's "'only genuine claim to literary remembrance" is the kindness he showed to Poe obviously fails to do justice to Kennedy.[184] It calls attention, however, to an interesting chapter in Kennedy's literary career. Kennedy was one of a committee of three who decided to award the prize of the *Baltimore Visitor* to Poe for his "MS Found in a Bottle" in 1833. Shortly thereafter he made the acquaintance of Poe, then in a state of extreme destitution. He assisted Poe by gifts of clothes and money and he entertained him in his home. Poe was touched by the interest shown him, and he traded upon it with his customary frankness—even to the extent of responding to an invitation to dinner by saying that he would come if Kennedy advanced him twenty dollars to enable him to revise his "personal appearance." Kennedy further assisted Poe by helping to bring about the publication of some of his stories at a time when many people including Carey the publisher questioned Poe's sanity. Moreover he recommended Poe to the attention of T. W. White, publisher of the *Southern Literary Messenger*, as a candidate for the post of assistant editor. The poet thereafter looked upon Kennedy as his patron, though after leaving Baltimore he did not see him again. Kennedy recognized Poe's gifts and his defects equally, and in 1836 he gave him this piece of excellent advice:

Your fault is your love of the extravagant. Pray beware of it.
You find a hundred *intense* writers for one *natural* one.[185]

To such kindness and interest as Kennedy had shown Poe in his early
days, Poe could only respond by reviewing *Horse-Shoe Robinson* in
favorable terms[186]—more favorable perhaps than he would have used
had he not been under an obligation to Kennedy.[187]

When Kennedy advised Poe to prefer naturalness to intensity he
was speaking from a predilection for that quality in his own writing
which has given it rank among critics without serving to sustain his
popular reputation. He gave to literature only what came easily to
him, and he frequently deserted the cloister for the forum. Such intensity as lay in his nature was evoked more by politics than by literary
inspiration. His espousal of the Northern economic program and his
insistence that the Union must be preserved marked him as a man
capable of warmth of emotion and of personal courage. It was no
easy matter for a Marylander to oppose the South as he did, for
although he generally avoided public utterance on the subject of slavery, his views were known, and he lost friends because of them. Although only a "mild abolitionist," he was a strong Unionist. In the
privacy of his notebook he wrote after the Civil War had begun:
"Undoubtedly the States have rights, the question is have they sovereignty?" and he referred to the Southern military movements as a "rebellion." [188] Though a man of convictions, Kennedy was not a writer
of great power. Some of his critics also felt a lack of profundity in his
writing: he was a humanitarian but no philosopher. Lowell remarked
that Kennedy's works "attempt no solution of the Infinite." [189] Kennedy's horizon was not broad and his ethical content was slight. The
field of letters he cultivated was largely restricted to urbane studies
of manners and relatively light characterization. Yet in his domain he
was one of the most finished writers in the history of American fiction.
In *Swallow Barn* and *Rob of the Bowl* he wrote prose of even more
subtlety and sustained beauty than Washington Irving generally exhibited. He was more finely formed than Cooper but of less stature.
He had little explosive strength or dynamic power. He was more interested in orientation than progress, satisfied to feel the texture of a
fabric without measuring its length. But his fine technique could not
save him. The tincture of the classics that gives character and poise
to his prose marked him as a writer of rarer quality than readers of
romance are likely to appreciate. He was a "literary man" rather than
a professional author, and his fate has been that of many a charming

writer who exercised his own best inclinations more than he consulted the public taste.

DANIEL PIERCE THOMPSON (1795-1868)

The critical attention accorded the novels of Daniel Pierce Thompson during his lifetime was very meagre despite the fact that his *Green Mountain Boys* was "the most popular romance of the immediate school of Cooper." [190] A first-rate novelist Thompson never became. His originality was not great, and his style bordered on the commonplace. Yet his talents were sufficient to enable him to earn widespread popular favor as a chronicler of historical events and fictional episode centred about the activities of one of the most fascinating figures in American history, Ethan Allen. His other novels, now little heard of, are intrinsically little inferior to *The Green Mountain Boys*.

Thompson was born at Charlestown, Massachusetts, but soon moved to Vermont, where he lived most of his life. As a farm lad in a district remote from cultural centres he supplemented his ineffective schooling by a substantial course of reading that included, besides Scott and Cooper, a great many English poets of the eighteenth century and earlier. In preparation for college he quickly read all of Virgil. After considerable financial strain he was able to attend Middlebury College, where he was graduated in 1820. A few years spent as a private tutor in Virginia preceded his return to Montpelier, where he was admitted to the bar. He soon received a minor political office, and for the next thirty years or more he supported himself largely by holding a variety of political offices. He also practiced law intermittently and he edited newspapers, occupations not wholly irrelevant to the type of historical fiction he wrote. His avocations, principally trapping and fishing, were equally important to his career as a novelist, for he is still valued for his authentic descriptions of outdoor life in Vermont.[191]

Like Cooper, whom he obviously imitated, Daniel Pierce Thompson came late to the craft of writing. His love of literature blossomed earlier than Cooper's, but a literary career naturally seemed out of the question for a man without independent means. Until he was thirty-nine years old Thompson wrote nothing that has been preserved. In 1835, however, he published three works. The first of these was a compilation of Vermont Statutes. The second, *The Adventures of Timothy Peacock*, possessed literary overtones, but it was essentially a political work—in denunciation of Free-Masonry. Not long after this, however, Thompson produced his first piece of belles lettres, *May Martin, or the Money Diggers*, a long short story about buried treasure and counterfeiting. Submitted as an entry in a competition conducted by *The New England Galaxy*, Thompson's story not only won the prize but it became so popular that it received fifty editions, mostly pirated, before the Civil War. *May Martin* received little critical attention but its popular approval encouraged Thompson to continue writing, and in 1839 he published what proved to be one of the best-selling books of the entire school of the historical romance, *The Green Mountain Boys*.

The Green Mountain Boys exhibited only a few facets of the now slowly rolling ball of historical romance but it traversed a new territory. Cooper would have loved the litigation (between the New Yorkers and residents of the New Hampshire Grant) that formed the factual background for the narrative, but he would not have been at home in the Vermont terrain—its hills, forests, creeks, and caves. If Thompson lacked Cooper's gift for illusion, he proved what could be achieved by earnest realism and a genuine love for Vermont countryside. There was also Ethan Allen, one of the richest legacies ever bequeathed to a novelist by history. A burly fellow, warmhearted in his natural affections, cool-blooded in the hour of danger, tempestuous in his assault upon injustice and inhumanity, and a bit of an egoist withal, Allen was almost the beau ideal of historical romance. His contempt for legal procedure was a great advantage: a good outlaw is a cousin only once removed from a hero. Ethan Allen's exploits may raise the eyebrows of the historian or the jurist, but the lay readers of Thompson's romance are completely satisfied with the elementary justice dispensed by this neo-Robin Hood of Vermont. Especially is this so because the author is partial enough to his hero to omit details found in the archives of history where they do not fit the ideal of Ethan Allen cherished by the novelist.[192] Moreover, for the sake of capitalizing two major interests, namely, the land litigation that brought the Green Mountain Boys into action and the Revolution (especially the brilliant episode at Ticonderoga), Thompson conveniently telescoped time. Other shifts from fact there are, but they are the result not of imperfect knowledge on the novelist's part (for Thompson was exceedingly well versed in document and legend of the period) but of deliberate fictional aims. Other historical characters are introduced in actions not grossly at variance with history's record, and one of these characters, Colonel Seth Warner (called Warrington) provides part of the principal "love interest" in the book. The devised action is so far from original that in summary the plot could hardly be distinguished from one of Cooper's. The theme of dispossession had been vieux jeu in the historical romance ever since *The Pioneers*. Even Jones, the comic rustic, who is perhaps the most individual character in the book, belongs in the goodly company of many comic characters who have spiced the dull details of many an historical campaign or conventional love scene. Yet the style would betray Thompson, for even more than Cooper he sinned against idiom and syntax. One looks in vain for satisfaction of a purely literary sort. Nevertheless the romantic facts and the vividly drawn background were sufficiently good to hold the attention of the readers whom Thompson wrote for, namely, the younger generation. *The Green Mountain Boys* took hold immediately and even with the advent of newer matters for romance it has retained a tolerably conspicuous place as a "standard book for boys." [193]

If *The Green Mountain Boys* offered little for the mind to feed on but adventure, Thompson's next book was more reflective. *Locke Amsden* (1847) was provided with a hackneyed plot, but it was essentially a doctrinaire study based on the author's own struggle for an education and on his later observation of a common school system much in need of improvement. Within a rough fictional framework the author delivers a number of shrewd comments regarding the location and construction of the school building, ventilation, seating arrangements, and above all the character of the institution. Thompson's educational creed was simple: the principal thing needed, beyond adequate physical condition, is instruction that correlates "book learning" with an independent habit of thought. Simple as Thompson's recommendations were, they were far from irrelevant among people still not wholly emancipated from belief in witchcraft.[194] The story which serves as the bait for Thompson's theories is a dilute concoction of elements much over-used even in Thompson's day—especially the foul slandering of the hero, the rescue of the heroine from a burning building,[195] the return of the given-up-for-dead father, the marriage of the poor lad to the girl thought poor until the last chapter. The characters, though drawn in many instances from life, are hammered into conventional designs in the novel. Rather better, however, is the author's recreation of farming scenes familiar to him in boyhood, for though his style is rhetorical, he is faithfully reporting native scenes which few American novelists were then qualified to treat:

> Our story, contrary perhaps to fashionable precedent, opens at a common farm-house . . . The old white mantle of the frost-king was also becoming sadly dingy and tattered. Each stump and stone was enclosed by a widening circle of bare ground; while the tops of the furrows, peering through the dissolving snows, were beginning to streak, with long, faint, dotted lines, the self-

disclosing plough-fields. The cattle were lazily ruminating in the barn-yard, occasionally lowing and casting a wistful glance at the bare hills around, but without offering to move towards them, as if they thought that the prospects there were hardly sufficient to induce them yet to leave their winter quarters. The earth-loving sheep, however, had broken from their fold, and, having reached the borders of the hills by some partially trod path, were busily nibbling at the roots of the shriveled herbage, unheedful of the bleating cries of their feebler companions, that they had left stuck in the treacherous snow-drifts, encountered in their migrations from one bare patch to another.[196]

Locke Amsden, like most of Thompson's novels is practically forgotten today, but it was a fairly popular book in its time. It was the first of Thompson's stories to receive extended analysis in an important magazine[197] and it received nine editions between 1847 and 1892. Moreover it was a forerunner of Eggleston's *Hoosier Schoolmaster* (1871), to which it is remarkably similar in plot.[198] Nevertheless for his next novel Thompson chose to ignore Jared Sparks' advice to continue to mine his personal memories, and he returned to the Revolution for the substance of *The Rangers or the Tory's Daughter* (1851).

The decision was a poor one, for *The Rangers* exhibited no new powers on the part of the author, and it appeared too late to be carried on the miscellaneous flood of the historical romance; the domestic novel had definitely displaced the historical romance, which had been losing popularity for some years past. The massacre at Westminster and the battle of Bennington were sufficiently good focuses for interest, but the welter of routine incidents involving poorly delineated characters of outmoded types soon carried the book to oblivion for all but the staunchest devotées of local antiquities.

A similar fate has overtaken *Gaut Gurley* (1857), but the latter is a much more readable story. Its action is so sensational that the book could easily be classified as a specimen of the melodramatic school that had a vogue about the middle of the century, but it is clear from the author's notes that he modelled his action on a real murder that occurred in Maine nearly forty years before. The story deals with a prosperous Boston merchant, Mark Elwood, who is forced into bankruptcy partly because of the evil machinations of Gaut Gurley, who holds a mysterious power over him. Vividly drawn gambling and drinking scenes (with timely moralizing on the evils of intemperance)[199] precede the decision of Elwood to recoup his moral and economic fortunes by living the life of a trapper in the Maine woods. But his evil angel Gurley reappears just as Elwood has reëstablished himself in more healthful surroundings. Subsequently Gurley is accused of robbery and arson in connection with a trapping expedition in the north woods. When Elwood testifies against him, Gurley plots a revenge by murder. In a remote wilderness Gurley consummates his revenge, but he is brought to justice partly through the testimony of an Indian girl who has witnessed the crime. At the end the secret of Gurley's power over Elwood is explained: many years before while engaged in smuggling silk with Gurley, Elwood had killed a Customs officer in order to retain his smuggled goods. This knowledge had been kept secret by Gurley and he had himself not troubled Elwood until financial difficulties pointed toward blackmail as the easiest solution of his own troubles. Finally the desire for revenge on Elwood became the ruling passion of Gurley. The narrative of Gurley's revenge and the retribution he suffered form one of the most thrilling murder stories in the early history of the novel. The malignity of Gurley recalls the more ruthless characters in the border romances of W. G. Simms. The attractive north-woods background in which the trappers operate tends to accentuate the sordidness of the action of the villain. Much as he loved the country, Thompson makes it clear in *Gaut Gurley* that the primeval forest does not necessarily promote human virtues. The text of Cowper's famous line appeals to him:

> "God made the country and man made the town." Yet the poet's moral application of this statement he cannot accept, for although there may be more "mere *vices*" in the city, yet of "those flagrant crimes which stand first in the graduation of human offences . . . the country ever furnishes the greatest proportions." [200]

In *Gaut Gurley* Thompson provided one formidable example of his thesis.

Thompson continued to write until his death (in 1868), but his remaining works had comparatively poor success. *The Doomed Chief; or Two Hundred Years Ago* (1860) is a mediocre romantic story of King Philip's War; Thompson seemed unable to project himself imaginatively as far back as the seventeenth century. *Centiola; or the Maid of the Mounds* (1864), a story set in Wisconsin, proved to be another illustration of his inability to produce purely imaginative fiction. Rather more effective among his later writings were a number of short stories (published in the same volume with *Centiola*) that were set amid New England scenes. Obviously Thompson was severely handicapped unless he was dealing at first hand with the Vermont mise-en-scène or the well-conned events of the Revolution.[201]

During his lifetime Thompson received scant attention from the critical press. Even *The Green Mountain Boys* despite its tremendous sales elicited little comment. When it was published in 1839 Thompson sent a copy to Longfellow with the request that the latter review it. Longfellow, himself at the threshold of his greatest popularity, expressed his confidence that the book was a tale calculated to interest those who "love to contemplate the stern face of history reflected in the mirror of romance," but he politely declined to review it, pleading a general disinclination to all reviewing. He suggested, however, that Thompson send a copy to *The North American Review*.[202] The reason for the failure of the "great guns of the press" to appraise the book was perhaps, as was suggested by *The Literary World* in 1851, partly that it was printed in such a cheap format.[203] Yet there is reason to believe that even in the beginning Thompson's limitations were clearly realized. In 1846 Griswold's comprehensive anthology *Prose Writers of America* gave him no space. The publication of *Locke Amsden* in the following year brought him to the attention of the New York literati, and he was accorded a generous notice in Duyckinck's *Cyclopaedia of American Literature*. On the whole, however, Thompson has received little formal approbation. His talents in fact were not distinguished. His hackneyed plots, his mechanical characterizations, and his faltering style prevent all but the most unsophisticated readers from thoroughly enjoying his books. A certain literalness in his make-up prompts him to give the dull details of unimportant matters. He did not possess Cooper's faculty for creating an illusion and suspending disbelief. Instead, he hoped to achieve his ends by honest verisimilitude. Perhaps he set too much store by "faithful descriptions . . . , instructive thought and wholesome moral sentiment," forgetting that factual accuracy and right thinking are not at a premium in romance.[204] Much as he owed to Cooper, he complained of the latter's impossible woodcraft. He also objected to Cooper's apparent subserviency to aristocratic foreign influences.[205] Indeed he made disparaging comments on the entire school of the American historical romance on the grounds that our authors were too prone to "borrow English wings for American muses." [206] Yet some wings it is essential to have, and Thompson's occasional superiority to Cooper in the meticulous transcription of the lives of trappers and hunters does not entirely compensate for his lack of imaginative range. In *The Green Mountain Boys*—"the classic of Vermont"—Thompson triumphed over his own limitations by giving adequate treatment to historical events that are inherently thrilling.

The Mixed Thirties

WILLIAM ALEXANDER CARUTHERS
(1800 [?]-1846)

In Old Virginia

Distinguished politically by her primacy among the American colonies and uniquely honored by being accorded the royal distinction of dominion status, Virginia was from the beginning rich in literary potentialities of many sorts. Yet she has been comparatively slow to take her place in belles lettres. Only gradually did American writers (Virginian or not) learn to take advantage of the state's physical beauty, its wealth of tradition, its distinctive social order. Reasons within the state are obvious: the lack of general popular education; inadequate facilities for printing, publishing, and distributing books for people scattered over a wide area not yet knitted together by railroad; the indolence of affluent classes;[1] and the preoccupation of the intelligentsia with politics. Observers from without were needed, and despite Virginia's traditionally bad roads, they finally came. As for the novel, its tardy beginnings owed little to local enterprise, and indeed "[u]ntil after the Civil War, the best which the South gave to literature was written by outsiders."[2] In the 1820's and 1830's, however, there was a brisk efflorescence of fiction by Virginian writers.

Among the most familiar titles of American fiction belonging to the thirties is W. A. Caruthers' *The Cavaliers of Virginia* (1834). A follower of Scott more than of Cooper, Caruthers added little distinction to the American historical romance, but *The Cavaliers of Virginia* attracted a great deal of attention as an early example of fiction with a Virginian background.[3] Caruthers also gave interesting expression to ideas on political and social topics, particularly slavery and sectionalism at a time when it was just becoming fully apparent that differences in economic interests between the North and the South were almost certain to lead to a major struggle of some sort. Caruthers' works, therefore, are of some historical importance. He didn't write a great deal—indeed he didn't live a very long life. About the details of his life, little is known; and even the spelling of his surname is not finally established.[4] It appears, however, that he came of a cultivated family. He attended Washington (now Washington and Lee) College, and he at some time studied medicine, for by 1840 he was a practicing physician at Savannah, Georgia. When his own health became irretrievably bad, he moved to the hills of northern Georgia, where he died in 1846.[5]

Caruthers' first book, *The Kentuckian in New York: or, The Adventures of Three Southerns* (1834) is a pleasant story that clearly demonstrates Caruthers' happy ability to see good in both the North and the South. The story is intersectional with a vengeance, for two of the "Southerns" fall in love on a visit to New York, while a third, a Virginian, finds his soul's mate in a New York girl living at Charleston. The Kentuckian himself, Montgomery Damon, is a hearty borderman who bears himself in a manner that calls to mind the dauntless Davy Crockett.[6] Throughout the book there is a good deal of talk and letter-writing indicative of a tolerant and friendly attitude toward the North. It was an attitude rarely to be encountered in early Virginian fiction. George Tucker, whose *The Valley of Shenandoah* (1824) was probably the first Virginian novel,[7] had confined himself pretty much to a faithfully realistic portrayal of rural Virginian manners. Nathaniel Beverley Tucker, his son, whose novels *George Balcombe* and *The Partisan Leader* were to appear in 1836, was steeped in a Southern allegiance which he showed by insisting on sectional rights and by warning his fellow-Southerners against the sinister intentions of the federal government.[8] W. G. Simms, now (in 1834) in the first stages of his prolific authorship, was to prove a staunch and at times arrogant sectionalist. Only J. P. Kennedy, among the "Southern" novelists of the time approached Caruthers in the breadth of his outlook. Not that Caruthers abdicated his Southern loyalties; rather he expanded his sympathies to include his Northern neighbors. For Northerners are also human beings!

> Every southern should visit New-York. It would allay provincial prejudices, and calm his excitement against his northern countrymen. The people here are warm-hearted, generous, and enthusiastic, in a degree scarcely inferior to our own southerns. ... Many of these Yorkers are above local prejudices, and truly consider this as the commercial metropolis of the Union, and all the people of the land as their customers, friends, patrons, and countrymen. Nor is trade the only thing that flourishes. The arts of polished and refined life, refined literature, and the pro-

founder studies of the schoolmen, all have here their distinguished votaries,—I say distinguished, with reference to the standard of science in our country.[9]

But friendliness toward the North must be based upon more than the mere interchange of civilities and pleasantries. It undergoes its greatest strain from the problem of slavery. Caruthers did not bait the Northerners on the subject of abolition, nor could he wholly acquiesce in the simple belief that slavery was a necessity to the agrarian South. He had no single solution in mind, but his attitude may be guessed from passages (sometimes offered as the opinions of characters) in his books. He realized that the conditions of slavery were very different in different parts of the South: in Virginia slavery may be "tolerable," for "the slaves are more in the condition of tenants to their landlords—they are viewed as rational creatures, and with more kindly feelings"; in the deep South slaves are likely to live under conditions that are "intolerable." It is likely that in general Caruthers believed the slaves to be "an incubus upon our prosperity." On the other hand, emancipation by one legislative stroke would not only "dissolve the social compact" but would probably precipitate catastrophe, for liberated, unprotected Negroes would form themselves into mobs capable of threatening the very foundations of the nation. A dilemma there was, for which no peaceable solution seemed at hand, what with increasing pressure from abolitionists and the most bitter remonstrances from the South. Caruthers feared the horror of a war which he was not destined to live long enough to see:

> Revolutions, whether sudden or gradual [says one of Caruthers' characters], are fearful things; we learn to feel attachments to those things which they tear up, as a poor cripple feels attached to the mortified limb, that must be amputated to save his life. A line of demarkation in such a case is distinctly drawn between the diseased and the healthy flesh. Such a line is now drawing between the slave and free states, I fear. God send that the disease may be cured without amputation, and before mortification takes place.[10]

Caruthers did not live to see the "mortification" take place, but he did sense the decline of Piedmont Virginia, a decline attributable in part no doubt to that same institution of slavery, for slavery was part of the system which had lulled Virginia to sleep: "Poor, exhausted eastern Virginia! she is in her dotage . . ." A new order must succeed the old. The big plantations would be disintegrated, and a more active agricultural class would restore vigor to old Virginia. But the process would be slow, and in the meantime many of her sons would migrate to the teeming western state of Kentucky, itself partly a way-station in the vast movement to the far West. There, in imagination, Caruthers had found Montgomery Damon, "The Kentuckian."

But Caruthers' imagination also projected itself far back into the annals of his own state. In *The Cavaliers of Virginia* (1835) he is a romance-writer pure and simple. The historical basis of the narrative is Bacon's Rebellion, but, despite his frequent citation of authorities, the author's zest as a story-teller is keener than his conscience as an historian. The subject chosen by Caruthers was in itself a promising one, for Bacon's Rebellion involved two major interests—the questions of Crown versus Colonials and Indians versus settlers—both of which are handled with considerable veracity in their broad outlines. To these Caruthers adds the mysterious movements of Regicide Whalley, whose appearance, the author asserts, conforms to historical record, but whose presence in a Gothic cave in Virginia in 1676 is harmless romantic license. Caruthers tampers with history in other ways also, chiefly by setting up competition between Bacon and Frank Beverly, adopted son of Governor Berkeley, for the hand of Virginia Fairfax. The spark which ignites the action occurs in a conversation at the Governor's ball when Bacon, having overheard Beverly slandering his unknown father, challenges Beverly to a duel. At the same function the "historical" part of the tale also begins, for the growing resentment of Roundheads is signalized by an explosion: the rebels have blown up the powder magazine. The dance is broken up by a fight during which the mysterious "Recluse" (so the Regicide is called until the end of the story) appears as an ally of the Cavaliers. In the meantime there has already been "Indian trouble." These three elements—the personal, the political, and the Indian—are carried through the book, coalescing to form a fairly homogeneous story. The resolution is reached only after many ramifications. Bacon's suit for Virginia is favored by her mother but forbidden by the Governor, who has two reasons for opposing it: (1) he wants Virginia for the bride of his adopted son, and (2) he hates Bacon as the instigator of the popular uprising against a Royal Governor. The Governor, in turn, is harassed by the people for his failure to take measures to quell the Indian uprising—a thing he is loath to do because of his profitable trade with the Indians. Berkeley's defection as a defender of his people causes Bacon to form an independent army, which moves successfully against the Indians. Upon his return to Jamestown, he is acclaimed by the people but taken prisoner by the Governor and condemned to death. But the rebel forces, greatly augmented by now, free

Bacon, burn Jamestown, and depose the Governor. In the register of history Bacon dies (of fever or poison) at the very height of his triumph, but romance saves him for the arms of the lovely Virginia. They had *almost* been wedded during a lull in the revolution, but the Recluse had stalked in to prevent the crime: they were, he said, brother and sister! This routine threat to lovers' bliss is finally quashed by a comic opera dénouement (worthy to be compared with standard devices later used by Gilbert and Sullivan) in which a locket miniature and an aged nurse's testimony unfold a story of misfiled children. The phases of the story are extremely intricate, but notwithstanding a few loose ends, the whole is well coördinated. The action is sometimes extravagant but almost always clear: the reader knows where the characters are, why they are there, and how much time elapses during and between episodes. Such care for construction is rare in novels of the period, and in fact of the plot of *The Cavaliers of Virginia* is its most distinguished feature.

Other elements, however, are interesting and significant. The basis of the conflict between Colonists and His Majesty's governor is well set forth. The Roundheads are not glorified without stint: their "desperate, reckless and restless" membership is described, in its nucleus of Cromwellian exiles, at least, as being made up of "veteran soldiers and furious bigots." [11] On the other hand a reasoned explanation of the rebel position is given, along with an actual speech of Bacon justifying his course of action. And fundamentally the author's sympathies go with the Roundhead cause. Caruthers insists, however, that the origins of independent movements among Americans—even at the time of the Revolution—were grounded in practical necessities rather than in any abstract love of freedom:

> Here [in Berkeley's refusal to fight the Indians] was sown the first germ of the American revolution. Men have read the able arguments—the thrilling declamations, the logical defence of natural and primitive rights, which the men of '76 put forth to the world, with wonder at the seeming intuitive wisdom that burst so suddenly upon the world at the very exigency which called it into action. But in our humble opinion, the inception of these noble sentiments was of much earlier date—their development not so miraculous as we would like to flatter ourselves. Exactly one hundred years before the American revolution, there was a Virginian revolution based upon precisely similar principles. The struggle commenced between the representatives of the people and the representatives of the king. The Cavaliers and citizens of the colony now arrived at the infant capital, resolved to take upon

themselves as much power as was necessary for the defence of life, freedom, and property.[12]

The Indians also are allowed free expression of their plaint. They are brutal, but they have been dispossessed. It falls to the lot of Wyanokee, Virginia's Indian servant girl, to utter most of the protest against the white man's aggression. She is a charming and graceful creature, whose face wears an expression of "that calm sadness which has been remarked as characteristic of the domesticated aborigines from that day to the present." [13] No satisfaction she might herself take in living in comfort and amity with white persons can make her forget that she is under the protection of the destined conquerors of her race. There are, she realizes, only two hundred warriors of the Chickahominies left. She foresees that in time the aboriginal Americans will all have vanished:

> Her soul seemed fully capable of realizing the melancholy destiny which awaited all the nations of the aborigines then inhabiting the country, from the sea board to the blue mountains, and whose fiat was· fast bearing her race from the loved places which had known them so long. It was doubtless in her mind a poor compensation for the destruction of her native tribe and their contemporaries, that she herself had been reclaimed from the happy ignorance of savage, to the more painful knowledge of civilized life.[14]

Exciting, well-coördinated action and interesting collateral materials *The Cavaliers of Virginia* possesses, but it falls down in two essentials of the novelist's art, characterization and style. Occasionally, particularly when politics was his theme, Caruthers turned a good phrase, but his style in this book is on the whole ineffective—generally verbose and often banal. His fault was not so much awkwardness as a certain flat and dull quality. He had a fairly good ear for cadence but a poor eye for original image. Certainly he cannot compare as a stylist with his fellow-novelist, J. P. Kennedy. That he was writing as early as 1834 cannot extenuate Caruthers' offenses against good taste. Even in 1834 the reader must have shuddered to hear that

> the feathered tribes, luxuriant in beauty, warbled forth their richest strains of nature's melody as they hopped from twig to twig, flashing their brilliant colours in dazzling contrast to the pendant dew-drops glittering in the sunbeams.[15]

The author's passion for trite phraseology is perhaps responsible for the unreality of his characters. Certainly no heroine could live as a character after being inundated by the flood of clichés which submerge Virginia Fairfax:

> Her dress was simple, tasteful, and exquisitely appropriate to her style of beauty. She had apparently scarce passed her sixteenth birthday; and of course her figure was not yet rounded out to its full perfection of female loveliness. So much of her neck as was visible above a rather high and close cut dress, was of that pure, chaste and lovely white which gives such an air of heavenly innocence to the budding girl of that delightful age. The face although exceeding the neck in the height, variety and richness of its colouring, was not disfigured by a single freckle, scar or blemish. The features were generally well proportioned and suited to each other, the lips full and gently pouting, with a margin of as luxurious tinting as that with which nature ever adorned the first budding rose of spring, and when parted, as they often were, by the most gentle and *naïve* laughter, displayed a set of teeth as beautifully white and regular. Yet one could scarcely fasten the eye upon them for the admiration excited by the exquisite expression of the dimpled mouth, ever varying, and as it seemed, more lovely with each succeeding change. The motion of her eyes was so rapid that it was difficult to ascertain their colour; but certain it is they were soft and brilliant, the latter effect produced in no small degree by long fair dewy lashes which rose and fell over the picture, as lights and shadows fall from the pencil of an inspired painter.
>
> The fair flaxen ringlets fell beneath the small gipsey hat in short thick curls, and were clustered around her brow, so as to form the most natural and appropriate shade imaginable to a forehead of polished ivory. She was about the medium height, symmetrically proportioned, with an exquisitely turned ankle and little foot . . .[16]

The sheer length of this description is a mark of an artistic myopia which is still further manifested when Caruthers calls upon Virginia to converse with her lover:

> Bacon: "But see, the long shadows of the trees are already extending across the river and the birds are seeking their resting places for the night."
> Virginia: "Oh, happy little songsters! would to Heaven that my rest could be as sweet and tranquil as theirs this night? [*sic*]"[17]

If *The Cavaliers of Virginia* contained a good story, it was clearly vulnerable to critical attack. Its reception, however, seems to have been prevailingly favorable. One reviewer, in fact, was so irritated by the encomia with which it was "literally plastered . . . from Maine to Georgia" that he gave vent to his reaction in language more picturesque than judicial:

> We read the first chapter, and yawned—we read the second, and yawned again; at the third, we threw the volume down. However, we took it up again, and, with desperate exertion, got through the whole. We tried as hard to like the work as we could; but, neither patriotism, good nature, nor gratitude to the Harpers, could make it endurable. Nevertheless, as we had seen it strangely puffed in the public prints, we were willing to believe, that the fault might be in our own bad taste; so we gave the book to a friend, in whose judgment we have confidence, and requested his opinion. He returned it, saying, that if the second volume were like the first, nothing but a literary boa-constrictor could swallow it.[18]

The reviewer also gave his reasons for damning the book—chiefly that its non-historical "materials are . . . common, ill-chosen, unnatural, and impossible" and that they are "awkwardly put together." It is clear that the reviewer didn't like this book, but he failed to attack it for its real defect, namely, stylistic ineptitude. Perhaps he didn't like the historical romance in general and, in any case, he seems to have misunderstood its function. A romance is not to be "swallowed" as a bolus of logic but enjoyed (or disliked) regardless of its credibility. That hosts of readers could enjoy *The Cavaliers of Virginia* is clear from the reviewer's own testimony.

The reputation of the book, however, has been badly corroded during the century since its appearance. Virginian fiction has since then passed through so many phases that Caruthers' book seems completely outmoded. Miss Ellen Glasgow, who has done as much as anyone to distinguish her state in fiction, speaks impatiently (and without a full perspective, it must be added) of *The Cavaliers:*

> Why old Virginia, with a mode of living as gay, as gallant, as picturesque, and as uncomfortable as the life of England in the eighteenth century, created, not a minor *Tom Jones*, the crown of English fiction, but merely *Cavaliers of Virginia* and *Knights of the Horseshoe?*—this is a question which no Southern gentleman, however Georgian his morals or Victorian his manners, would have dignified with an answer.[19]

Caruthers was aware of the character traditionally ascribed to Virginian life in its more picturesque aspects. Indeed at the opening of *The*

Cavaliers he remarks that his story takes place not long after Virginia became the home of "the immediate ancestors of that generous, fox-hunting, wine-drinking, duelling and reckless race of men, which gives so distinct a character to Virginians wherever they may be found." [20] He does give some conception of that sort of life—with its "julip"-drinking young men and its gay assemblies and its fox-hunting—but *The Cavaliers* was after all a story of 1676 and much of the famed picturesqueness of Virginian life doubtless developed during the eighteenth century. It was later to be described in Cooke's *The Virginia Comedians*. It was also to be falsified into a sort of cheap romantic tradition from which Miss Glasgow herself was later to rescue the Virginian novel.

The end-pages of *The Cavaliers* in its 1834 edition carried an advertisement of the author's next book *The Tramontane Order, or the Knights of the Golden Horseshoe*. Though probably completed at about the same time as *The Cavaliers* it was not published until 1845, when it appeared under the title *The Knights of the Horse-shoe: A Traditionary Tale of the Cocked Hat Gentry in the Old Dominion*. A tale woven about the career of Governor Spotswood with emphasis upon the juvenile hero's loyalty to the Stuarts, the book disclosed no radically new gifts of Caruthers, but it possesses antiquarian and historical interest because of its account of Governor Spotswood's discovery of West Virginia lands.[21] Caruthers' first two books had placed him as a writer: *The Kentuckian in New York* as a social critic, and *The Cavaliers of Virginia* as a practitioner of the historical romance. Neither book sufficed to carry his fame permanently to great heights. Of late there has been a tendency to "rediscover" Caruthers. Finding that his social and political doctrines of *The Kentuckian* marked him as a liberal, Parrington has extended his approval to cover *The Cavaliers of Virginia* as well. Actually *The Kentuckian*, though probably never so popular as *The Cavaliers*, more fully exhibits Caruthers' real talents as a writer. If he could not create character, he could report conditions. By nature, he was more an observer than an originator. His concern for his country's present plight touched deeper chords in him (and therefore evoked better writing) than the vicissitudes of real or imaginary characters of the year 1676. It will not do to "rediscover" Caruthers too zealously: he cannot be made over into an important writer. Yet that which he is, he is—a sincere student of the Old Dominion and a creditable craftsman.

THEODORE FAY (1807-1898)

Fashion and Foul Play in the New York Manner

If asked in December 1835 what had been the most widely read novel of the year, the average New Yorker would undoubtedly have replied *Norman Leslie*. Today few people have heard of *Norman Leslie*. Yet anyone who wishes to know what was regarded as good fictional entertainment in the middle of the fourth decade of the nineteenth century would do well to read Theodore Fay's best seller.[22] Nor need the modern reader gird his loins too strenuously in preparation for the ordeal; in fact he will find his task a pleasant one. And if he cannot praise the book as an example of high art, he will perhaps be surprised at its sheer readability.

Fay was not primarily a literary man, but made the law his profession. Yet his literary interests were strong, and he was early associated with G. P. Morris and N. P. Willis in editing the New York *Mirror*. Between 1833 and 1836 he traveled abroad, supplying the *Mirror* meanwhile with travel sketches of the same sort that his co-editor Willis had written a few years before under the title of *Pencillings By the Way*. *Norman Leslie* was Fay's first novel. Not long after its publication he went abroad as Secretary of Legation at Berlin, and he spent the rest of his life abroad filling various diplomatic posts and writing miscellaneously. Besides *Norman Leslie*, he wrote three novels. *Sydney Clifton* (1839) is a species of Gothic romance set in New York and London. *The Countess Ida* (1840), a story laid in Prussia, is a didactic novel which inveighs against duelling—a subject which seems to have preoccupied Fay, for it is discussed in three of his novels.[23] *Hoboken; a Romance* (1843) is a sensational tale which works out the complications resulting from a duel between an American youth and a Captain in the British army.[24] Fay also wrote a novelette (of sixty-nine pages), *Robert Rueful*, published in 1844.

The central motivating factor in the plot of *Norman Leslie*, a murder charge brought against a fashionable young man of good family, the author avowedly took from an actual case that occurred in New York "many years since." [25] His hero, Norman Leslie, is the handsome and accomplished son of United States Senator Mordaunt Leslie, a gentleman who "would have been instantly received with delight at the most fastidious and polished court of Europe." [26] After discovering that his first love, Rosalie Romain, is no more than a flirt, Norman falls in love with Flora Temple. But serious complications arise, for Flora is sought in marriage by one Clairmont, a recently arrived "French" Count, whom

Flora's mother instantly recognizes as a more eligible suitor. The Count, of course, is a cad—and a very mean one. Unable to avoid quarrelling with him, Leslie not only incurs the Count's fierce enmity but is regarded askance by many of the beau monde who have been fascinated by the foreigner's distinguished air. When Rosalie Romain suddenly disappears it is easy to fix suspicion on Leslie, and, although the only corpse provided by the prosecution obviously cannot be proved to be Rosalie's body, Leslie is indicted and tried for murder. He is acquitted, but many persons believe him guilty—saved only by wealth and influence. Actually Rosalie is not dead but, having possessed herself of plenty of diamonds, has been sent abroad by the Count, who will join her later: for Flora has refused the rogue! Norman also goes abroad presently and searches for Rosalie through most of the second volume. Many unoriginal plot devices are rehandled by Fay during Leslie's residence abroad (chiefly in Italy) and many coincidences enable the author to create a brilliant dénouement. Eventually with the help of Clairmont's deserted wife (in the mid-century American novel and drama it was axiomatic that glamorous, amorous "French" Counts should have deserted their wives) Leslie finds Rosalie—long incarcerated by Clairmont and now insane. It also appears that Clairmont was not only not a count at all but not even a Frenchman: he was a Neapolitan and his real name was Rinaldo! The action is virtually concluded at Rome in the Coliseum when Clairmont, in attempting to kill Leslie and Rosalie, is himself killed by a fall. It remains for Rosalie to die and for Leslie to be united with Flora, who has been faithful to him back in New York these many years.

But *Norman Leslie* had more than an exciting plot to interest its readers. The hero's social station necessitated a full description of life among the wealthy in New York—their promenades, their carriage-driving, their assemblies, their dinner-parties, their sartorial habits, their manipulation of the marriage market, their peregrinations to fashionable watering places. All this is reported by the hand of one who has observed the details from within the élite circle itself. Norman's father being a Senator, the author naturally brings in a description of Washington. Politics were in Fay's line, and he discusses them with an intimate understanding found in few novels of the period excepting G. W. Curtis's *Trumps*.[27] But he also has social detail to offer the reader. He describes a President's *levée*, which he refers to as "the American court"—though, to be sure, the "flower of American talent" is "necessarily blended with dashes of more homely material."[28] The years spent abroad are pleasantly sketched by a writer who could set down the details of European sights from his own recollections instead of (as too often was patently the case in American novels written before about 1875) digging them out of travel books and Baedekers. But the great boon to romance-hungry New Yorkers was the introduction of the Count. The Count, though a liar, is no farcical mustached stage villain, but a plausible and impressive rascal with gifted tongue, easy address, and ruthless intention. Though destined finally to be stripped to his black-guardly essentials, he furnishes forth the novel with a full complement of glittering data relating to the life and adventures of a member of the foreign nobility—a subject very dear to republican readers. For Fay was perfectly aware that "nowhere are the badges of nobility more reverently and indiscriminately hailed than by the gay votaries of fashion in a republic, where all men are 'born equal' and where titles are excluded by the constitution." [29] Yet, though it trafficked in a mild form of snob-appeal, the book is prevailingly American in viewpoint. The theory of republican government is fully endorsed, and American political institutions are set off in sharp contrast to those of Italy, which are represented as frightfully degraded.[30] Moreover, though a globe-trotter, Fay is at pains to praise American scenery and show-places.[31]

Obviously here, in *Norman Leslie,* is a tale planned according to a very popular recipe. Garnished with wit and sprinkled with French phrases (not too difficult) it was calculated to win the approval of most devotées of the light novel of manners. Fay wrote with an easy, well-bred, rather gay and cosmopolitan air—as one long acquainted with good literature, important people, famous places. He was a facile writer, at home in sentiment or epigram, skilled in both persiflage and melodrama, always ready with the polished phrase. Yet he wished to be more than a glib entertainer, and he was evidently thinking partly of himself when he wrote of his belief that "the art of novel-writing, however long associated with heartbroken boarding school girls and sentimental chambermaids, is now as dignified as that of Canova, Mozart, or Raphael." [32] In *Norman Leslie* he reveals his acquaintance with much important literature, particularly the plays of Shakespeare, several of which he refers to directly or indirectly. A quotation from *Hamlet* graces the title page. An inept suitor of Flora is dubbed a "Malvolio." There are echoes of *Othello.* But chiefly *Romeo and Juliet* is used as a "background" for the star-crossed lovers of metropolitan New York. The play is quoted directly, and analogies are offered—even forced on the reader—from time to time. Thus Norman Leslie has lately recovered from his infatuation with Rosalie (even the name is a hint), meets his true love at a ball, is troubled by dire premonitions of catastrophe, is chastised for quarrelling in public, and is in effect banished. The Nurse's slow articulation of her news to Juliet is clearly the model for a long scene in which the banished Norman tries to elicit information about Flora from an American friend. These and other literary allusions reveal Fay as an accomplished student of literature. Yet ably as this Shakespearean plunder is used, it proves too heavy for the comparatively frail craft Fay is sailing, and the reader is embarrassed rather than elevated by the transactions: to evoke Shakespeare's memory amid episodes devoted to such vapid and pallid people seems a sacrilege. Fay remains a facile, graceful writer, able to report ripples on the surface of society but unqualified to plumb the depths of human character and motive. But for a simple-minded public *Norman Leslie* was deep enough: 'twould serve the purposes of entertainment for the patrons of the rapidly growing circulating libraries of the period. Read critically, *Norman Leslie* quickly reveals its vulnerability at many points, most of which were seized upon by Poe in his crushing review of the book as "an inestimable piece of balderdash." [33] Poe's review was unfair in that it failed to credit Fay with such merits as he possessed, and his sardonic humor was little short of insulting; but most of the points he made were pertinent. Yet his review evoked bitter blasts of retaliation by New York critics and friends of the author.[34] Most of the public doubtless was sublimely unaware of this critical tilting, but in any case it went on reading *Norman Leslie*.[35] Doubtless, as in any era, the public did not care whether the novel was "art": enough if it proved an absorbing narrative.

JOSEPH HOLT INGRAHAM (1809-1860)

Historical Romance à la Louisiane

The thirties were rife with historical romances produced by Cooper, Simms, Paulding, Kennedy, and others, but in 1836 there appeared a romance which imparted an unmistakably new flavor to the genre. The book was *Lafitte, The Pirate of the Gulf*, and its author was Joseph Holt Ingraham (1809-1860), one of the most prolific and popular writers during the three middle decades of the nineteenth century.[36]

Jean Lafitte the man has been so inextricably bound up with Jean Lafitte the legend that even after the resources of modern scholarship have been brought to bear on the subject, many details of the "life" remain ambiguous or unallocated.[37] It is known, however, that he was born in France in 1780; that he became a smuggler and freebooter (possibly a pirate) operating chiefly out of Barataria and St. Domingo with the coöperation of his brother Pierre; that he was granted an amnesty by the American government in consideration of his aid to General Jackson at the Battle of New Orleans, January 8, 1815;[38] and that both during his outlawry and after it he was regarded by the people of Louisiana as something of a hero.[39] The date of his death is uncertain.[40]

By the time Ingraham came to the subject, Lafitte's exploits had already been used abundantly in song and story. Oddly enough, Lord Byron was "responsible for the beginning of the Lafitte legend" [41] when he appended certain notes to his poem *The Corsair* (1815) suggesting an analogy between his own hero and the Baratarian outlaw. In 1826 appeared a long tale entitled *Lafitte, or the Baratarian Chief*, which had a considerable vogue—though it did not elaborate the pirate's exploits at New Orleans.[42] In 1831 *The Casket* published serially a sentimentalized narrative of the "pirate's" life—endowing him with a sweetheart responsible for his regeneration—under the title, *The Baratarian Chief*. Yet J. H. Ingraham stole the pirate from these and other writers in 1836 when he published his substantial romance *Lafitte, The Pirate of the Gulf*, now by far the best known fiction dealing with Lafitte. The explanation of Ingraham's success lay probably in his peculiar ability to appeal to a mass public. He used many of the verifiable facts of Lafitte's life; he grafted a love story to the chronicle of fact; and he fused the factual with the imaginary in a glamorous climax occurring at the time of the Battle of New Orleans. In addition he infused the entire narrative with a sort of spurious romanticism compounded of elements borrowed from Scott and Byron—two high favorites of the period.[43] In his *Red Rover* Cooper had proved equal to handling some of Scott's favorite romantic devices, but no novelist before Ingraham had given a Byronic turn to the American historical romance.

Ingraham's hero is a proud, moody, and defiant lad, originally named Achille, who brutally stabs his brother Henri when the latter proves to be the preference of the fair Gertrude. Conscience-stricken at his murderous act, Achille leaves home (in the Kennebec country)[44] forever, and ultimately becomes Lafitte, the pirate. A brief interlude in the book tells of his experiences of fifteen years as an adventurer in the Mediterranean: he is captured by Algerine pirates, whom he later joins and commands; he is captured by Turks and later leads *them;* turned pirate, he is taken by Spaniards, but he escapes and recommences pirate; he has in the meantime added to his experience by raping a Moorish girl (who had rescued him from prison) and by adopting the Mohammedan religion. This, then, is the ruthless but romantic character who is to be the hero of notorious exploits carried on between Barataria and the West Indies and New Orleans. Too full of action for complete recital in brief compass, the main plot revolves (or spins) round the opposition between Lafitte and one Count D'Oyley, fiancé of the lovely Constanza. The daughter of a wealthy Mexican exile living in Jamaica, Constanza first falls into the pirate's hands during the latter's raid on the home of her father. From such a perfidious monster as the reader has discovered Lafitte to be, one expects no less than violation of Constanza's innocence. But, no, the freebooter guarantees her safety from all attack: for he has been stricken by her beauty, and although, despite his handsome appearance, he cannot hope to win her love, he can at least look upon her as the regenerator of his own wicked heart. He is as good as his word, but Count D'Oyley, who doesn't know of the pirate's conversion, manages to give him a nasty wound at the Battle of New Orleans, where Lafitte, having spurned British offers of negotiation, is fighting on the American side. Lafitte is nursed at New Orleans —so long is the arm of coincidence—by Gertrude, now in religious orders! Now thoroughly penitent, Lafitte sets out to restore all the money and plunder he has relieved his victims of—buying a ship for the purpose. But trouble lies ahead, for Constanza has been once more abducted and the furious Count D'Oyley, assuming that Lafitte has been at it again, strikes him down without waiting for the pirate's "story." Before he dies, however, Lafitte becomes the beneficiary of another romantic policy: the author hasn't allowed brother Henri to die after all, and he is now restored to the sight of his dying brother as none other than the Count D'Oyley! The father of the two "boys" is there also: he had been cunningly disguised. Amid these distracting disclosures Lafitte dies. There is a final reunion of the lovers—Henri and Constanza, of course: Gertrude has presumably ceased to experience worldly longings.

Such is the précis of one of the most eagerly read books of the 1830's and after. It is not hard to see why it captivated a certain type of guileless reader. The author is facile in the use of language and fertile in invention. Large-scale operations he engineers with comparative ease. He is adept at an elementary sort of "psychologizing": he shows the fierce churning and chafing of young Achille's turbulent spirit with considerable skill. He is capable of broad romantic effects in description; he excels in vivid tableaux and in the Byronic posturing of his hero.[45] His action is brilliant and varied, and he produces a striking dramatic effect by synchronizing the climaxes of the love-theme and the pirate-theme at New Orleans. Moreover, the story as a whole is provided with what looks like a moral tendency: the bad man is redeemed by the purity of a woman. This point is pressed home in language that has a kind of unctuous religiosity. There are many invocations of the Virgin Mary and many Scriptural references which to the laity must have passed for signs not only of genuine piety but of high literary skill as well. Similarly, Ingraham's frequent comparisons of Lafitte with Cain and Lucifer give his hero a kind of literary glamor popular with the masses.

Yet examined coolly *Lafitte* may be seen for what it essentially is, a tour de force, an expert job of literary fabrication. A good narrative of romantic adventure it remains: nothing more. The descriptions, though glittering with brilliant phrase, suffer from a kind of baroque over-ornamentation which finally seems false. And as Poe noted, there is too much unimportant detail: "Not a dog yelps, unsung." [46] Most serious of all is a fundamental lack of sincerity in the character of Lafitte as presented by Ingraham. Outrageous use of coincidence and other unrealistic devices may be condoned in romance, but not shoddy characterization: so much we learn from Cooper, whose wood lore may be defective but whose Natty Bumppo prevails by the artistic integrity of Cooper: we believe in the *character* of Natty Bumppo. But Lafitte is finally incredible.[47] A fratricide, a rapist, a bandit, an overweening brute he has been, but the sight of a beautiful woman presently turns him, we are expected to believe, into an epic hero. The imagination refuses to make the effort. The outlaw's snivelling cant and forced self-accusations are revolting despite Ingraham's easy borrowing of Scriptural cadences for their expression:

> "What matters it," he suddenly exclaimed, "that I have gained the wealth of princes—that I have waded through crime and blood to the acquisition of the guilty fame that makes my name terrible!—that my hand has been against every man! I am at last but a miserable being—penitent, without the power to repent— remorseful, without hope—a lover of virtue, without daring to seek it—banned of God—outlawed of my race—fratricide and murderer!—the mark of Cain branded upon my brow, and burnt deep—deep into my soul. Oh, God!—if there be a"—he cried, clasping his hands and lifting his eyes to heaven—"be merciful unto my iniquities, for they are very great!" [48]

As for style, Ingraham is fluent, at times even graceful, but his full-bodied prose finally impresses one unpleasantly as being composed of fatty tissue: it makes a show of ruggedness that is not really present. By comparison with the muscular idiom of Simms and the sturdy power of Cooper, Ingraham's writing seems flaccid. Yet these aspects of *Lafitte*, though apparent certainly to Poe and probably to other critics of the day, passed unnoticed, one may be sure, by the rank and file of readers, who looked upon *Lafitte* as a glamorous story set in regions hitherto seldom available to American novel-readers. And thus it was that better artists of the day—Poe and Hawthorne—had much ado to eke out a living while a facile romancer mechanically plied a trade which finally brought him a handsome annual income.[49]

RICHARD HILDRETH (1807-1865)

Are Slaves People?

If anything were needed to provide a contrast to the gaudy romance of Ingraham's *Lafitte* (1836) and the perfumed furbelows of Fay's *Norman Leslie* (1835), it could have been found in Richard Hildreth's powerful novel of purpose, *The Slave: or Memoirs of Archy Moore*, published in 1836.[50] A good deal of youthful rhetoric chops and churns the surface of Hildreth's book, but underneath is a full tide of effective sincerity. It is a bitter book, written with a clenched fist; no tearful eye blurred the author's view of injustice. Though not the first novel to touch on the theme of Negro slavery, *The Slave* is the first full-blown anti-slavery novel. It is a tremendously powerful piece of writing; until the appearance of Richard Wright's *Native Son*, written a hundred years later, few novels treating of any aspect of the Negro's disabilities have been written with such burning intensity as Hildreth's *The Slave*. Its outmoded style of course unfits it for general reading today, but some acquaintance with it is essential to anyone seeking a full knowledge of how anti-slavery sentiment affected, and was affected by, the novel. Long before Mrs. Stowe thought of writing *Uncle Tom's Cabin*, Hildreth's book itemized the charges which were to form the standard indictment of slavery in fiction for a generation to come.

The Slave has little more organization than a picaresque novel, merely following the fortunes of the protagonist from his earliest days to a convenient stopping-point. The first person is used throughout. Archy Moore is born to slavery on the Virginian plantation of Colonel Charles Moore, who is "a democrat in politics, . . . an aristocrat and an exclusive in his feelings." [51] As was common enough in those days—the story starts in the late eighteenth century—Col. Moore had children not only by his wife but also by various "favorites" among the female slaves. Among these favorites was Archy's mother, a beautiful creature with only a modicum of African blood in her veins: in fact her father was a Randolph—a name to conjure by in Virginia. Archy the slave, therefore, was actually of distinguished and aristocratic descent, but the tincture of Negro blood in him was the master determinant in his heredity: it made him a "prisoner for life." In his bitter reference to this basic injustice Hildreth sounds a note which will be reiterated innumerable times in stories of octoroons and persons of even less Negro blood:

> Alas! she [my mother] did not seem to recollect that though I might count all the nobles of Virginia among my ancestors, one drop of blood imported from Africa—though that too, might be the blood of kings and chieftains,—would be enough to taint the whole pedigree, and to condemn me to perpetual slavery, even in the house of my own father![52]

Archy's life as a young slave is in some ways tolerable, for instead of being told off to heavy manual labor in the fields he is assigned as a personal servant to James, one of Col. Moore's all-white children—Archy's own half-brother. Although generally the custom of presenting young white boys with slaves only initiates the boy in an "apprenticeship of tyranny,"[53] James proves a kindly young master. But James dies early, and when Col. Moore gives Archy the alternative of becoming the servant of William, another son, or going into the fields, he chooses the fields, well knowing that William is a sadistic young aristocrat. In the fields he learns to know the ways of overseers. The character of Stubbs, his first overseer, is suggested by his language: " 'You damned black rascal' was pretty sure to begin every sentence, and 'by God' to end it."[54] He learns the miseries of field slaves: long hours, contaminated food, shamefully inadequate quarters, bullying, and flogging. He learns that a "hypocritical humility" is the only thing which will enable one to escape the most hideous physical punishment. But Archy's mental suffering is just as great, for when he falls in love with Cassie, the daughter of Col. Moore by another slave, Col. Moore thwarts the marriage because he wishes to make Cassie, too, one of his "favorites." Archy circumvents the Colonel by uniting himself in an exceedingly informal secret marriage with Cassie. But when the Colonel persists in his incestuous intentions, Archy makes the desperate (and generally futile) move of the slave who is hounded beyond endurance: he runs away with Cassie. A short period of more or less happy existence in the wilderness hideout is ended when Archy decides to make a break for the North. The clothes needed as a disguise in such a project he is finally promised by a poor-white storekeeper, whose life Archy had once saved. But the poor-white cruelly betrays him—for the five hundred dollars reward. When he is brought back, the most exquisite torture Col. Moore can devise is to require Cassie to flog him herself. Upon her refusal, the enraged Colonel fells her with his fists and stamps on her prostrate body. Archy is sold to North Carolina, the first remove of many which carry him farther and farther South and which gradually disclose to him every horrible phase of slavery. Not the least of his miseries for a time is the thought of his wife's probable fate at the hands of Col. Moore, but Cassie runs away (with the assistance of another servant who herself covets the favors of the master) and passes as free for a time. But she is kidnapped by white men and sold as a slave:

> The business of kidnapping is one of the natural fruits of the American system of slavery; and is as common, and as well organized in several parts of the United States, as the business of horsestealing is, in many other countries.[55]

By a coincidence Cassie is taken to a plantation not far from Archy's new home, and the two are re-united (with the permission of their masters) as man and wife. A son is born to them, and Archy later looks back upon the year spent with Cassie as "the happiest" of his life. Even so, the thought that their child is born to slavery so depresses Archy that he is tempted to kill the infant in order to save it from certain misery.

Financial difficulties of Cassie's employer finally separate husband and wife once more. Archy is never to see her again. His own remove to South Carolina opens his eyes to new abuses of the slave system on a plantation owned by one of the "absentee aristocracy" of Charleston. Here he is not even allowed to call himself "Archy Moore"—one name suffices for a slave. In every way conditions are worse in South Carolina than in Virginia. Among Archy's new experiences is that of being required to act in the degrading capacities of spy and slave driver. It is at this time that he meets with one Thomas, a slave noted for his religious zeal acquired under Methodist auspices. So strong is the Christian spirit of vicarious service in him that he confesses to crimes he has not committed. It has been suggested that Thomas's "emotional piety . . . may possibly have had its effect upon Mrs. Stowe," [56] but the actions of Hildreth's Thomas finally make the reader forget his "piety." For he vows revenge on an overseer who had stripped and flogged his recently confined wife into insensibility for the crime of walking instead of running from one field to another. The wife becomes ill and is denied proper medical care: Thomas "returned one night, and found her dead." [57] Having lost his drivership, Archy joins with Thomas (now taken to drink) and other slaves in a gang bent upon reprisal against their oppressors. They live a precarious existence as fugitive outlaws, lodging in the natural defenses of the wilderness of "pine barrens" and preying on neighboring plantations for sustenance. Thomas's hour of triumph comes when Overseer Martin (who had flogged his wife) falls into his power. No religious thought now restrains Thomas: he gives the overseer thirty minutes to repent and then shoots him. Commences a flight toward the North. Thomas, wounded and in any case handicapped by his color, insists that Archy leave him and take his chances in the North: he can easily pass for white. Though feeling guilty of a "base desertion, which not even the love of liberty could excuse," Archy breaks with the altruistic Thomas and makes his way (in a few pages) to the North: Philadelphia, New York, Connecticut, and Boston. In New York he is recognized by one of his former overseers and seized, but he breaks away from an officer—with the passive aid of nearby citizens.

Hildreth could have made a whole book of Archy's remaining adventures, but he compresses them into a few chapters. At Boston Archy signs as a sailor on a ship for Bordeaux, leaving his native land with "a mingled feeling of safety and disdain." [58] He is seized and impressed by the British—the War of 1812 being in progress—and "no patriotic scruples" prevent his signing articles to command a British privateer. Chance later brings him face to face with one Captain Osborne, formerly commander of a slave-ship in which Archy had endured a minor hell. Archy, like Thomas, is too full of anger against society to parley: he stabs Osborne to his death. Subsequent adventures take him far abroad—to Turkey, Persia, South America—but he still plans to come back to America to find his son, whom he had brought into the world a slave.[59]

The adventures of Archy could speak for themselves—they are sufficiently harrowing—but the author does not let them. Throughout the book he uses the situations of his hero as texts for fierce invective against the system of slavery and against the nation that tolerates such a system. He relentlessly exposes every type of tyranny that contributes to the bondage of slaves. He goes behind every euphemism used to condone the system. Nor does he regard Archy's wretched case as exceptional: for after saying that Archy was "hard worked, ill fed, and well whipped," he adds that these words would "suffice to describe the whole lives of many thousand Americans." [60] Every abuse elicits the author's angry remonstrance. The slave must not learn to read: it will make him a less contented slave. He must not complain of overwork or injustice. He is denied every vestige of domestic and social or civil right. He cannot testify in court against a white man. The security of his marriage depends upon the caprice of a licensed tyrant. His very child becomes property at the moment of birth. To offset these and scores of other abuses, the slave enjoys none but negligible benefits. There are a few masters who treat their slaves kindly, but, no matter how kind, they cannot make Archy forget his real status. The affectionate relationships between master and slave so often cited by "sophists" intent upon making a "eulogium of slavery" occur but seldom.[61] Grudgingly Hildreth admits the existence of kind employers:

> No doubt, through the broad extent of slave-holding America, there are many amiable women and kind-hearted mistresses. Yet how little does their kindness avail! [62]

He also admits that slaves are often heard to sing at their tasks, or even at an auction—a fact which he says has been viciously used as a defense of slavery.[63] In any case the death of a good master is likely to expose the slave to a new cycle of suffering. Moreover, no matter how charitable the master's impulses may be, the slave generally sees less of the master than of the overseer, who, if only for economic reasons, is given supreme authority: the estate must show a profit. For overseers, whether of the Northern or Southern variety, Hildreth has nothing but contempt:

> Take the American overseers together, and they are the most ignorant, intractable, stupid, obstinate, and self-willed race that ever existed.[64]

Under all these woes it is not to be wondered at if the slave's life seems unendurable.

But Hildreth does not merely ask the reader's tears for the plight of the slave: *The Slave* is no *Uncle Tom's Cabin*. Hildreth is less evangelical than critical; he seeks to create indignation more than pity. He writes with a certain truculence which must have irritated many readers. He makes sardonic comments designed to sting the sponsors of slavery unpleasantly into a recognition of the evil they are perpetuating. He wishes to shame and goad them into correcting the conditions. He scoffs at the widespread talk of liberty in "slave-holding America,— for anti-republican as it may seem, in no part of the world is the distinction between *gentlemen* and the *common people*, more distinctly marked . . ." [65] He pauses, while Archy is being conducted through the city of Washington, to expatiate sarcastically on "that head quarters of a great nation, the spot in which its concentrated wisdom is collected, to devise laws for the benefit of the whole community,—the just and equal laws of a free people and a great democracy!" There in Washington, "within a stone's throw of the Temple of Liberty," he finds in active operation that "most brutal, odious and detestable tyranny"—a slave-market.[66] He tries to bring home to the slave owner his final responsibility:

> The young lady who dines heartily on lamb, has a sentimental horror of the butcher who killed it; and the slave-owner who lives luxuriously on the forced labor of his slaves, has a like sentimental abhorrence of the man who holds the whip and compels the labor. He is like a receiver of stolen goods, who cannot bear the thoughts of stealing himself, but who has no objection to live upon the proceeds of stolen property . . . The slave owner prides himself upon the honorable appellation of a planter; and the receiver of stolen goods assumes the character of a respectable shop-keeper. By such contemptible juggle do men deceive not themselves only, but oft-times the world also.[67]

Individuals are invited to explore their own bosoms for feelings of guilt, and the nation is taunted for smudges on her scutcheon. In a final thrust Archy, now a world traveler, reminds his countrymen that the reduction of slavery is occurring far more rapidly in the supposedly less advanced regions of Spanish and Portuguese America. Even in Brazil, bondsmen are "lisping in the language of freedom." [68] Only in the United States does statute-provision make emancipation impossible; it is only in the United States that "oppression riots unchecked by fear of God." Thus the book ends on a sombre, not to say pessimistic, note. It is a characteristic note, for notwithstanding one full-throated passage on the tenacity of the principle of freedom[69] and occasional quavers of hope, Hildreth's method is not so much to appeal to better instincts as to try to scourge out the evil in man.

It is clear that a good deal of Hildreth's writing is rhetorical. It is not rant, for he deeply feels the cogency of the problem implicit in *The Slave*. Yet his constant resort to superlatives in the long run weakens his story. His denunciatory passages are generally not so long as to interrupt the narrative unduly, but they occur at too frequent intervals. Thus the reader is confident that if Archy is snatching a little pleasure or satisfaction from life, the author will soon come along with his acid spray: present happiness will only seem bitter upon recollection during the trouble to come. Moreover the oases in Archy's grief are too briefly described: the whole year of his "happiest" experience (as Cassie's husband) is disposed of in a page or two. Probably Hildreth was not completely successful in reporting slave psychology. In any case Archy is not a typical slave, being almost entirely white and possessed not only of a very keen sensitiveness but also of some surreptitiously acquired education. Archy does not seem able to understand the genuine black man's ability temporarily to forget the trouble he's seen: he assumes that all slaves brood as constantly as he does himself. And even Archy himself seems at times to speak like a mechanical dummy, ventriloquistically, with Hildreth's voice. In short *The Slave* cannot be taken at face value as an appraisal of the institution of slavery.

Yet *The Slave* contains a good deal of realistic data hitherto unavailable to readers of American fiction. William Dean Howells testified to the fact that the book created in him "an indelible impression of [Hildreth's] imaginative verity." *The Slave* was, he said, "a powerful piece of realism." [70] Himself unacquainted with the slave problem, Howells no doubt valued the book for its compelling sincerity: Hildreth has the air of uttering gospel. Howells may also have been impressed by one important aspect of Hildreth's Negro-portraiture, namely, that Hildreth's Negroes are not sentimentalized or idealized. Archy may be too articulate to be typical, but he is not too good to be true. Hildreth tries not to violate character traits. If Archy and Thomas have been fiercely vindictive toward tyrants, Hildreth does not try to make them over into conventional heroes at the last by having them forgive their enemies. Their weaknesses are freely described. Nor are the Negroes as a group too tenderly treated. Hildreth frequently refers to their mean, cruel, depraved conduct. They plunder one another's cabins, turn state's evidence, indulge in disgusting drinking bouts, snub slaves of less social station (*i.e.*, generally with less white blood), and exercise extreme cruelty when elevated to the position of spy or slave driver.[71] To be sure, Hildreth attributes these faults to the system of slavery, for "such is the baneful effect of slavery, that it almost destroys the very germ of virtue." [72] He shows too the depths of degradation of slaves who take pleasure in commanding a higher price at auction than their mates—"the lowest form" of "that love of superiority, which exercises so principal an influence over the feelings and actions of men." [73] Most conspicuous, perhaps, of the "realistic" material used by Hildreth is the weeping at the funeral of a certain kind master. Traditionally this would later become a symbol of the affectionate relationship between slave and owner, but Hildreth interprets it differently—as an expression of self-pity. The slaves feared future owners more than they loved their dead master: "Doubt not [says Archy] the sincerity of our sorrow! It was for ourselves we were lamenting." [74]

Less spectacular, and perhaps more convincing, efforts to report facts faithfully are found in Hildreth's reference to the economic status of Virginia during the disintegration of the large plantation system.

Archy was easily able to find a hideout in a wilderness comparatively near Col. Moore's estate:

> Lower Virginia had already begun to feel the effects of that blight, which has since lighted so heavily upon her, and which in truth, she has so well deserved. Already her fields were beginning to be deserted; already impenetrable thickets had commenced to cover plantations, which, had the soil been cultivated by freemen, might still have produced a rich and abundant harvest.[75]

The large number of poor-whites in Virginia is explained partly by the fact that "there are more persons who desire to be overseers than there are plantations to oversee." [76] Instead of plantations there are farms.[77] Moreover the economic distress of Virginia is increased by two other factors, namely, the habit of selling slaves to the far South and the tendency of the white population toward western emigration:

> But the slave-trade in America, as well as in Africa, carries with it the curse of depopulation; and, together with the emigration which is constantly going on, has already unpeopled great tracts of country in the lower part of Virginia, and is fast restoring the first seats of Anglo-American population to all their original wildness and solitude. Whole counties, almost, are grown up in useless and impenetrable thickets, already retenanted by deer and other wild game, their original inhabitants.[78]

Later Virginian fiction would revert to the earlier plantation system as being better fitted to "romance," but Hildreth tried at least to hew to the facts as he saw them. If his temperament was that of a Jeremiah, his mind was that of a realist.[79]

Actually Hildreth's observation of the scenes he describes was somewhat limited. He was a Northerner, born at Deerfield, Massachusetts, and educated at Harvard. He practiced law and journalism in Boston. Failing health, however, necessitated his removing to Florida, where he stayed for two years and where, apparently, he wrote *The Slave*.[80] He read and wrote widely on abolition, even editing two anti-slavery papers in British Guiana, whither he went on a second quest to regain his health in 1840.[81] Among other reforms, he advocated prohibition of liquor. He was a dauntless opponent in debate, whether written or spoken. In recent years emphasis has centred upon his historical works. Yet *The Slave*, with its flaming condemnation of an iniquitous system and its vivid story of imagined slaves in imagined situations, may yet be reckoned his most important contribution to "history." The author had trouble launching a book so packed with social and political dynamite. No New York company "dared to publish it" and the Boston house which finally printed it took care to remain anonymous.[82] The first edition was quickly sold, but magazines and newspapers shied away from mentioning the book. Moreover the panic (of 1837), said the author, made a new edition unfeasible until 1840.[83] The book then took hold and became a best seller, reaching a seventh edition by 1848.[84] It was translated into French and Italian.[85] After the Civil War the book became more or less obsolete. Now it is rarely mentioned. It has recently been characterized as possessing a "tone . . . of romantic propaganda" [86]—a sorry term for a book so sincerely written. Recently it has also been dubbed "unreadable." [87] Perhaps so—its florid phraseology is likely to irritate persons unoriented in the period. Almost any book written more than a hundred years ago presents a similar problem to readers: its accurate appraisal calls for historical perspective. *The Slave* is not suited to be re-established as a popular novel. It is an uncomfortable book to read, for it is a tale not of "silken sorrows" but of horrid wrongs.[88] Nevertheless Hildreth's power, courage, and originality deserve credit at the hands of literary historians. His book died after a score or more of years: how many twentieth-century books have survived for a decade?

EDGAR ALLAN POE (1809-1849)

Readers Prefer Novels

"Readers in this country have a decided and strong preference for works (especially fiction) in which a single and connected story occupies the whole volume, or number of volumes, as the case may be . . ." [89] Perhaps these words, written to Poe in 1836 by Harper and Brothers, were mainly responsible for Poe's turning his attention to the composition of *The Narrative of Arthur Gordon Pym, of Nantucket,* his first long fiction. Two installments of the story were published in the *Southern Literary Messenger* for January and February, 1837; and Harper brought out the book in 1838. Poe was now a "novelist." Two years later he would produce another extended fiction (inferior in quality to his first), *The Journal of Julius Rodman.*

Yet Poe is now associated with the history of the novel principally as a reviewer and a critic. A master of the tale, he could not readily adapt his great gifts to the pace and pattern of long narrative. He was comparatively ineffective in dialogue, deficient in characterization, and, though given to the theatrical, not essentially dramatic. From the point of view of popularity with the masses he was also handicapped by being unable to treat the themes of love and sex except in a somewhat shadowy fashion with disquieting intimations of the abnormal. Here was no man, surely, to dabble in the clear swift stream of the historical romance.[90] Nor was it likely that the author of "Ligeia" could write a cozy domestic novel which would find favor on the average citizen's hearth. Poe was, however, intensely interested in the novel, and he was one of the most acute American critics who ever exercised the reviewer's art. Emotional biases often led him into extremes of abuse and praise, but they seldom caused him to fumble his judgments completely: he seldom puffed a bad book or, despite exasperating qualifications, wholly damned a good book. His pontifical manner was superimposed upon, instead of offered as a substitute for, generally sound criticism. His judgments, moreover, were likely to be related strictly to the craftsmanship of a novelist, and this in a day when ethical or political considerations heavily influenced the judgments of most reviewers.

In his reviews of novels Poe did not use a set of principles wholly alien to the forms of writing he himself mainly practiced. Thus his preference for brevity and unity of tone in poetry comported with his insistence that

> A long story does not appear to us necessarily twice as good as one only half so long. The ordinary talk about "continuous and sustained effort" is pure twaddle and nothing more. Perseverance is one thing and genius is another . . .[91]

Not even his friendly obligation to J. P. Kennedy could prevent his murmuring at the excessive length of *Horse-Shoe Robinson*.[92] Many of the defects of novels that came under his eye he attributed to the "absurd fashion of periodical novel-writing,"[93] but he believed that plot was difficult to sustain in any long fiction. On the other hand, despite the excellence of his own short-story plots, he apparently regarded plot as less important than other narrative elements.[94] That Cooper seemed almost incapable of good plot structure did not constitute a grave defect in the eyes of Poe.[95] The general public, he believed, was interested in incident and action but not in plot as a whole. In any case, a more important objective was "naturalness." Hence Poe's frequent patronizing references to the dramatic method (whether in stage plays or in fiction), for the concentration which is essential to dramatic writing is likely, he thought, to lead the writer into orgies of coincidence and artificiality.[96] The later history of the American theatre has proved that the drama need not labor under the artificial restrictions Poe objected to and that it may in fact achieve that "unity or totality of effect" which he coveted for novelists. Yet in his day Poe was consistent enough in drawing a distinction between his own ideals and those of more widely popular writers, whether of plays or novels. For, whatever his blunders in performance, Poe attempted to follow his own canons. True, in his fiction he constantly sought to exploit the unique experience; yet it is a mistake to endorse the trite corollary that the essence of Poe's *method* was exaggeration. Almost the reverse is true: having selected an extraordinary theme or situation, Poe expended his efforts in a desperate but quiet attempt to induce belief in the reader. He tried to make the unique imaginatively credible; he documented the abnormal and the anomalous. The most outré of his materials do not escape his literary discipline.[97] Proud as he obviously was of capitalizing unparalleled experiences, he would have defeated his own ends if he had deliberately pushed the unparalleled into the impossible. In his reviews he repeatedly rebuked the writer who trafficked in shoddy "supernatural" materials. His frequent failure to win the reader's acceptance of his own stories does not argue the falsity of his principles.

Among Poe's failures many critics would list his only long invented prose fiction of consequence, *The Narrative of Arthur Gordon Pym, of Nantucket*. Such a decision may be justified if one applies to the story Poe's own principle of unity of effect. Yet, taking the story as a succession of episodes (just as, Poe said, one must take *Paradise Lost* as made up, in part, of brief poems), one may allow *The Narrative of Arthur Gordon Pym* a great deal of merit. It contains passages as gripping as Poe ever wrote, details as carefully capitalized as any in his best short stories, imaginative effects seldom equalled by Poe elsewhere in prose or verse. Its chief fault is that which J. P. Kennedy had long before warned Poe against, namely, too great intensity. Intermittently in the story, Poe either forgets or deliberately foregoes that "severity" of technique which was often his goal even amid materials the most fantastic.[98] In this plotless, nightmare-ridden book Poe almost turns inside-out the bag of melodramatic tricks he used from time to time in his other stories.

Arthur Gordon Pym is a Nantucket lad with a passion for the sea of which his family disapproves but which his friend Augustus Barnard manages to gratify by stowing him in the hold of a New Bedford whaler, the "Grampus." Pym's stay in the hold is protracted so far beyond the agreed-upon time that he almost perishes of hunger and thirst and an attack by a dog. He nearly loses his sanity before Augus-

tus finally retrieves him—at the same time revealing to him that a mutiny has occurred in which all the loyalists but Augustus have been
either killed or set adrift in open boats. Partly by means of hoaxing a
superstitious sailor (through the impersonation of a dead man), Augustus and Pym and one Peters (who has deserted the mutineers) manage
to retake the brig, killing all the rebels but one, whom they keep to
work at the pumps.

A gale now reduces the brig to a mere hulk, filled with water but
unsinkable because of her cargo of oil. The four men are faced with
the dangers of being washed overboard, starving to death, and dying
of thirst. The attempts at reaching the store room are fruitless. A
Coleridgean vessel which comes directly toward them is found to be
manned only by dead men, upon whose bodies the sea-gulls are feeding.
When a bird flying over the "Grampus" drops a piece of liver-like substance, however, the starved wretches are tempted to eat it. Pym
throws it overboard just in time. A bottle of port wine, accidentally
retrieved, makes them all drunk except Pym. When a vessel on the
horizon fails to approach them, they draw lots to see who shall die
in order to preserve the rest. Parker, who has proposed the plot, is
stabbed and eaten (except for hands, feet, and entrails) during the
succeeding four days. Pym finally thinks of cutting a hole in the deck
in order to get at the store room. Result: a bottle of olives (as interesting as anything in *Robinson Crusoe*), ham, Madeira, and a live tortoise.
Augustus, poisoned by a sore arm which evinces symptoms of mortification, dies in a state of putrefaction, weighing only 45 pounds: when
Peters tries to lift him, a leg comes off in his grasp. All this time the
men are hard put to it for water, which they can get in small quantities
by holding their shirts in the rain. The hulk now overturns, but they
manage to regain her, and are provided with food in the barnacles.
Sharks prevent their bathing to relieve their thirst. From their now
impossible position they are shortly rescued by the "Jane Guy," a
whaling schooner out of Liverpool for the South Seas. In the "Jane
Guy," Pym and Peters reach an island somewhere near the South Pole.
The savages there express themselves as delighted to see the white men,
most of whom they later kill by arranging an avalanche of soapstone,
which is there curiously stratified. Then they go after the remainder
on the ship, and tear them to pieces—only to be themselves killed by
the hundreds in an explosion that occurs when the ship is fired. Peters
and Pym have been saved from death by being hurled into a chamber
in the rocks which bids fair to be their tomb. Finally emerging alive,
they escape from the island in a canoe of the savages, but the native
whom they have taken with them to aid their navigation presently dies,

and with him their hope of final escape. The story ends as the boat rushes into a chasm presumably very near the South Pole. There they see "a shrouded human figure, very far larger in its proportions than any dweller among men. And the hue of the skin of the figure was of the perfect whiteness of the snow."

This is the story which Poe began to publish in the *Southern Literary Messenger* for January and February, 1837. It was common in books of the sort to make a claim of authenticity for the adventures, but with his characteristic flair for originality, Poe decided to have wheels within wheels. Accordingly he provided the book with a Preface (purporting to have been written by Pym) explaining that Pym had allowed Poe to write down some of his adventures *"under the guise of fiction."* Pym added that the public refused to accept the narrative as fictitious despite the "air of fable" with which Poe had so "ingeniously" invested it. Consequently, he said, he had himself compiled the remainder of the adventures (following those parts which had appeared in the *Messenger*), and this new part he incorporated with "Poe's" part—adding with a fine show of naiveté that "the difference in point of style will be readily perceived." Surely one of the cleverest prefaces ever written for a book of strange adventure.[99]

Of course part of the *Narrative* was in a sense true. Scenes in New Bedford were drawn from observation—as well as certain descriptive bits re-allocated from Richmond. The schoolmaster "Ricketts" of the story bears the same name as a schoolmaster Poe knew in Richmond. Pym's grandfather seems to have been drawn from John Allan. The yachting adventure in which, during a preamble to the main story, Pym and Augustus almost lose their lives, suggests that Poe was looking back upon early boating adventures he had had with Ebenezer Burling on the James River.[100] Much of the knowledge of seafaring shown in the book was a reflection of Poe's own experiences; as a matter of fact few American novelists except Cooper were doing authentic "sea stories" as early as 1838. These realistic details most of Poe's readers could not verify, but many of his readers were aware of a current interest in Antarctic adventure which was stimulated by government plans to fit out an expedition to South Pole waters—an expedition promoted largely by Jeremiah N. Reynolds, whom Poe probably knew.[101] Poe evidently drew upon contemporary publications which could aid him, such as Morrell's *Narrative of Four Voyages to the South Sea and the Pacific,* a current version of *Mutiny on the Bounty,* and possibly Irving's *Astoria.* For the rest, there were also standard literary sources—Coleridge, Defoe, Smollett, Brown, etc. Poe could be as circumstantial as Defoe, as emotional as Brown, as haunting as Coleridge. The story which he pieced together does not bear the marks of homogeneity, but it possesses features of real interest. Only a genuine artistic impulse could have prompted Poe to narrate the gripping but wholly credible story of the rammed sloop-rigged sailboat as a prelude to the more heightened experiences on the "Grampus" and the "Jane Guy." Concrete detail is skilfully used in many parts of the more melodramatic action, for Poe constantly aimed to create sober credence even when the odds were most against him:

> I have been thus particular in speaking of Dirk Peters, because . . . I shall have frequent occasion to mention him hereafter in the course of my narrative—a narrative, let me here say, which, in its latter portions, will be found to include incidents of a nature so entirely out of the range of human experience, and for this reason so far beyond the limits of human credulity, that I proceed in utter hopelessness of obtaining credence for all that I shall tell, yet confidently trusting in time and progressing science to verify some of the most important and most improbable of my statements.[102]

His detailed, almost didactic, observations on the proper mode of stowing a cargo are designed not merely to show off knowledge but to nurse the reader's acceptance of the story. His passion for exact detail also crops out in his comments on the elucidation of hieroglyphs at the end of the story—the first known example of Poe's expression of interest in ciphers.[103] It has frequently been remarked that the story is best at the beginning and at the end. The beginning excels in Defoe-like circumstantiality; the end brings to view Poe's individual interest in phantasmagoria. He tells "wildly well" the Antarctic adventures of Pym. His admirably drawn description of the white curtain-like mist observed by Pym made a deep impression even on Henry James.[104] Melville may well have read *Pym;* in any case there is a similarity between him and Poe in their common use of a white object as an instrument calculated to inspire terror.[105] Hervey Allen declares that the *Narrative* had "a very small success." There were several British editions, but in America the book never became really popular. As part of Poe's canon it has been an embarrassment to critics, many of whom have trampled on it unnecessarily. Granted its defects, it exhibits flashes of genuis that have interested many special students of the craft of fiction.[106] As to the masses, they might cull out bits of the action for exciting reading, but the book as a whole must have been too horrible for some tastes and too elusive for some minds. As for the ending of the story, it was not only "unhappy" but disturbingly vague. Well, Poe could return to the short story, in which his most popular period lay only a few years ahead. His comparatively unsuccessful venture into longer narrative he could perhaps write off in the consideration that many books by lesser writers succeeded only because they were of "that secondary character which never fails of the fullest public appreciation." [107] Some rationalization or consolation he must have needed, for his *Narrative*, despite the jaunty journalistic manner of its launching, was no mere occupation of an idle hour. Parts of it may have been written from his cuff, but other parts were fetched up out of deep personal experience, for when Poe came to die, the literary fragments that rose to the surface of his breaking mind were scenes from his only novel, *The Narrative of Arthur Gordon Pym, of Nantucket*.[108]

WALT WHITMAN (1819-1892)

Temperance Tractarian

By 1842 the novel seemed a tempting form for writers without other definite projects. Amid many failures there had been a number of novels which had succeeded startlingly. What more natural than that Walt Whitman should have his fling? He was "at liberty" at the moment, his various literary and editorial projects having proved somewhat unfruitful. Moreover a subject and a manner of approach suggested themselves easily enough: he could capitalize a current public interest by writing a "temperance" novel, and he could mold his wares to a popular pattern by imitating Dickens, recently a visitor in America. True, the labor of constructing the framework for a novel was foreign to his vagrant temperament. Nor would the production of detailed character studies be easy for a man so prone to lyrical celebration of his own ego as Whitman. Still if a needy man is offered seventy-five dollars for a literary piece, he is not likely to spurn the opportunity of testing himself in a possibly lucrative field. And so *Franklin Evans* was presented to the American public in 1842. It was only a moderate success: Whitman would have to try still other angles of approach before he attained that publicity which his egocentric nature apparently required. When he finally found his métier in the poetry of the *Leaves of Grass*, less and less attention was paid to *Franklin Evans*. Whitman himself made no effort to save it for posterity, and copies became rare.[109] Today hardly anyone refers to it except to damn it vaguely. Apparently few people have read it.

The story is that of a lad who, upon arrival in the city, falls under the influence of a dissolute acquaintance. In due time, drinking is responsible for his failure to deliver an important packet: he loses his job. Presently his wife pines away and dies. His happiness wrecked, he attempts to kill the man who had first led him astray. Selling his household effects, he departs from the city which has been the scene and in part the cause of his degradation. His subsequent career, though brightened by intervals of prosperity and partial reform, is mainly a record of relapse and misery. His wandering carries him ultimately to Virginia, where heavy drinking bouts are the prelude to many scenes of violence and suffering for which he is partly responsible: murder, suicide, attempted rape. An epidemic of pestilence is thrown in for good measure: so far had Whitman's literary intemperance carried him. From these sordid scenes Evans finally rescues himself, and he comes back to New York, convinced that nothing but total abstinence will save him from completely ruining his life. Incredibly enough, in New York he receives a timely bequest from the very man who had discharged him years before: the motive of the employer is to make amends for not having taken better care of the country boy years ago. Evans now identifies himself smugly with a temperance movement, and, happy in the knowledge that somehow his physique has escaped being shattered by dissipation, he settles down to an honorable and contented life.

On the title page *Franklin Evans* was designated a "Tale of the Times." The times in fact were propitious, for the foundation of a "Washingtonian Temperance Society," two years before, had given impetus to the temperance movement. Only two months before the publication of *Franklin Evans*, another society had been formed, "The Sons of Temperance," which was destined within seven years to attain a membership roll of 300,000 people. The move to control spirituous liquors would not reach a conspicuous political phase until 1846 (when Maine adopted an amendment prohibiting the sale of spirituous liquors), but reform was definitely in the air when *Franklin Evans* appeared. Whitman, with a gesture which later became characteristic, announced that he wrote the book "for the mass." He was aware, he said, that the story was not equipped with "profound reflections, or sentimental remarks." It was, he implied, a "romance" designed to be useful. As such, he believed, it would succeed: it was "not written for the critics, but for the PEOPLE." [110] Reliable figures are not available, but its sale was said to have been about 2000 copies—a good sale, one must think, for a book of the quality of *Franklin Evans*.[111] For, granted a certain effectiveness in the account of the hero's first slips from the path of virtue, *Franklin Evans* possesses little to recommend it. Despite Whitman's prefatorial claim for his work as a pioneer book in the field, it was not the first book of the kind.[112] As an avowed imitator of Dickens (whose studies of low life he praised) Whitman was far from successful: the thinness of *Franklin Evans* suggests the unwisdom of Whitman's ever attempting to emulate the author of *Oliver Twist.* Whitman's references to Charles Lamb's "Confessions of a Drunkard" serve mainly to remind the reader of the enormous gulf between Lamb's prose and Whitman's.[113] The great powers that lay in the future author of *Leaves of Grass* were little evidenced by his perfunctory protests against liquor:

> A wretched scene! Half-a-dozen men, just entering the busy scenes of life, not one of us over twenty-five years, and there we were, benumbing our faculties, and confirming ourselves in practices which ever too surely bring the scorn of the world, and deserved disgrace to their miserable victims! It is a terrible sight, I have often thought since, to see *young men* beginning their walk upon this fatal journey! To reflect that those faculties which have been given us by God, for our own enjoyment, and the benefit of our fellows, are, at the very outset rendered useless, and of not so much avail as the instinct of the very beasts. To know that the blood is poisoned, and that the strength is to be broken down, and the bloom banished from the cheek, and the lustre of the eye dimmed, and all for a few hours' sensual gratification, now and then—is it not terrible! If there were no other drawback, the mere physical prostration which follows a fit of drunkenness were enough. But to the young, it saps the foundations, not only of the body's health, but places a stigma for the future on their worldly course, which can never be wiped out, or concealed from the knowledge of those about them.[114]

The structure of the book is wobbly at best, and it is rendered the more defective in this respect by several interpolated stories.[115] There are near the beginning of the story several good descriptive bits reflective of Whitman's knowledge of Long Island and New York, but such local color as exists is pretty well washed away when the story reaches a Virginian plantation, of which Whitman knew nothing from firsthand observation. He missed a chance to speak eloquently on slavery,[116] a topic which the Mexican War would soon bring sharply into focus. Verisimilitude almost completely vanishes in the face of crude melodramatic action until the story returns to New York, where it comes to a perfunctory conclusion. *Franklin Evans*, in short, forms no important part of Whitman's permanent reputation. Readable it is, but its apparent flimsiness suggests that its brief contemporary vogue was owing largely to its comparative novelty.

Years after its publication Whitman called *Franklin Evans* "damned rot," [117] and he implied that he wrote it (partly with the inspiration of liquor) merely for the sake of the money it might bring in. He added, what was probably not true, that he wrote it in three days. Yet he thought well enough of his story four years after its first appearance to reprint it serially (with a few alterations intended to integrate its action) in the *Brooklyn Eagle*.[118] The explanation of the contemptuous attitude he later took toward the story is that he finally wished to dissociate himself from any specific reform movement: the author of *Leaves of Grass* had by that time shown himself to be above fanatical organized attempts to curb human vices.[119] By that time he had long since decided to leave to others the problem of reckoning with evil while he chanted hymns of faith and liberation. Walt Whitman's gift was not for admonishing transgressors or condemning petty culprits. He was a liberator, not a judge. His poetry preached spiritual emancipation to thousands. His disparagement of *Franklin Evans*, therefore, was natural. He had been a clerk for the times: his hand wrote the book, but his soul did not consent to the deed. *Franklin Evans* proved that the novel was an uncongenial medium for Whitman, but it did not prove that its subject was unsuited to fictional treatment. Indeed it was only twelve years later that T. S. Arthur's *Ten Nights in a Bar-Room* took hold of the public so firmly that it became one of the most popular books of the century.

HENRY W. LONGFELLOW (1807-1882)

"Romance, Who Loves to Nod and Sing"

Longfellow began to write at an early age, but he matured his art slowly. Leading personally a somewhat protected (though not opulent) life, he was not, like Poe, obliged to publish in order to live. The impulse to write was persistent in him, but it was seldom urgent or ungovernable. He blossomed lazily when conditions were propitious. Steady growth, not spurts, revealed the law of his nature. The ambition to succeed was no stronger in him than the instinct to perfect his work. His productions were quiet-toned; his colors were pastels. He uttered few piercing notes of sudden grief or shouts of exultant joy. All was measured, settled, and slow. The poet of the fireside was at his best when the fire had reached the stage of embers. The prose writer too was unhurried, pensive, dreamy. He waited for his thoughts to mature; he was content if growth continued. He may be said to have ripened his stories rather than constructed them. Accordingly they are stories to be enjoyed for their flavor and texture, rather than for the stimulation they afford. Longfellow was a good prose writer but not a very good narrative writer.

Most of his prose exhibits the same properties. *Outre-Mer* was a skilful blending of the same sort of sentiment and picturesqueness as Irving had purveyed in the *Sketch Book*. His two long stories, *Hyperion* (1839) and *Kavanagh* (1849), were almost wholly lacking in the dynamic qualities that are popularly associated with novel and romance. They are both drowsy books—bred out of dream and mist, heavy with reminiscence, reluctant to deliver their burden of plot. Generations since their time have largely passed these books by with a vague phrase of recognition. Yet they deserve better than the fate that has befallen them. Their defects of plot are obvious to him who runs; their pallid characterizations are as easy to overlook as many of Hawthorne's. Nevertheless in most respects they are quite the equal of most of the poetical pieces of Longfellow that appear perennially in the "litercher books" of our school children. They are not so well proportioned as many of the poems, but they contain much extremely skilful writing, and they contain more that is of interest to the adult mind than do most of the poems. Their practical defect is that they are books of miscellany. Likewise, although they are "earnest" books, they lack profundity. Their general aspect is one of tameness and simplicity. Yet it is a mistake to reserve the laurel for those writers who undertake an enterprise of obvious magnitude, weight, and scope. A writer should not be condemned because it is not his gift to plumb the depths of the ocean in its farthest reaches; he may be reflecting life with as much truth and brilliance in cove or estuary. Not timidity but a true discernment of his real powers kept Longfellow from the truly sublime and terrible. He could translate, but not emulate, the author of *The Divine Comedy*.

When he wrote *Hyperion*, Longfellow had no idea of furthering the cause of a "national literature." The genesis of the book was strictly personal, and in so far as there was an "outside" influence on its form, that influence was German. By the time he came to write *Hyperion*, Longfellow had succumbed to the fascination of German romanticism as embodied in the gleaming phrases of Jean Paul Richter and the autobiographical reflections of Goethe. No doubt he felt inwardly that he could not really rival Goethe, and yet what more natural than that he should follow in the footsteps of the master: *Hyperion* should be Longfellow's *Wilhelm Meister!* Perhaps a glance or two at Goethe's *The Sorrows of the Young Werther* would be useful in helping to shape the progress of his own sorrowful hero's love story.

The story of *Hyperion* is fundamentally the story of Longfellow, just as Goethe's life was shadowed forth in *Wilhelm Meister*. Facts are of course occasionally altered for expediency's sake, but the basic pattern was so close to reality that Longfellow was made to smart for his temerity when the lady of his choice found out that she had been made public property in a "romance." The book covers that part of Longfellow's life after the death of his first wife in Rotterdam and during the unsuccessful first stages of his courtship of Frances Appleton. In *Hyperion* the integrated action is slight. Paul Flemming goes about Europe in a sober attempt to shake off the heavy incubus of a "sick and morbid soul" [120] and to search out the blue flower, the symbol of German romanticism. Among the people whom he meets is the pure and beautiful Mary Ashburton, to whom he makes love desperately but decorously. She does not respond. Shocked, but not angered or embittered, he continues his Childe Harold-like trek over Europe until one day, in a hotel, he hears her praying in the next room. The old love prompts him to seek her again, but a proud and high resolve restrains him and he flees from the inn—to see her no more. He was now resolved "no longer to waste his years in vain regrets, nor wait the fulfilment of boundless hopes and indiscreet desires; but to live in the Present wisely, alike forgetful of the Past, and careless of what the mysterious Future might bring." [121]

The action is not the main thing in *Hyperion*. It is Flemming's discovery of Germany that fires the ardor of the writer and kindles the pages of the book. Flemming visits the shrines of Richter and Goethe. He moons about in Heidelberg castle (next to the Alhambra "the most magnificent ruin of the Middle Ages") and other castles less famous but little less picturesque. He climbs mountains, stares at lakes and gorges, reads the tales of Hoffmann, hears the legends of monks, observes the pathetic lives of humble peasants, sees the university students at their revels and their duels, discusses transcendentalism with a professor. Part of the time he travels with a witty older man, Berkley, who tries to cure Paul of his vain love. But mostly he woos the spirit of the Middle Ages—which comes back to him in a shimmering pattern whose recurring elements in a sense compensate for the lack of a plot: lakes, mountains, flowers, bells, ballads, legends, love stories; churches, castles, and inns. Much of the story takes place in the mists of the morning or amid the calm or loneliness of night.

It is true that Longfellow conceived *Hyperion* as a narrative: he refers to it in fact as a "romance." He does have a leading character whom he calls a "hero," and he puts his hero into circulation with a narrative assignment. He does provide motive and counter motive: Flemming is in search of a dream that will heal his spirit, and he is opposed by circumstance as well as by the counsel of Berkley. There is, moreover, a definite, if too abrupt, outcome of this tenuous transaction. But the hero makes little appreciable progress; he floats through his assignment like a figure in a dream. For pages at a time he does nothing but absorb atmosphere and collect legends. On his first day he achieves no more, as far as "action" is concerned, than to receive a warning from the ruins of Stolzenfels castle: "Beware of dreams!" [122] Progress in the usual narrative sense is slowed down because the plot must carry so many bagfuls of tradition, legend, emblems, and analogies. The hero can hardly venture out of the house for five minutes without encountering a spate of popular superstitions and legends. He becomes the willing victim of the first widow, hausfrau, or "old inhabitant" he meets. He develops a gluttonous appetite for antiquities of all sorts. Enormously distended by his consumption of legends, he is no bad counterpart for "the watchman's wife, in the Tower of Waiblingen, who grew to such a size, that she could not get down the narrow staircase" and had to be married to her new husband in the Tower. [123]

Some of these legends, however, are interesting, and the reader learns to accept them in lieu of action. Many of them are grim or morbid, some merely picturesque. Most of them are extremely well told—for Longfellow was like Irving (his earliest American model) in that although he fumbled the construction of a long narrative, he was expert in fashioning his smaller units. The *Tales of a Wayside Inn* were later to emphasize this fact. In *Hyperion* the story of the old man who lived with his two sons in the castle of Liebenstein, for example, attains absolute perfection. [124] Descriptions tend to be over-elaborate but are often successful of their kind. The book abounds, too, in folk wisdom and literary plunder. Longfellow's mind was like an old chest of drawers into which one tosses knick-knacks, items hard to assemble into a coherent whole but interesting each in its own way. He was pleased by ribbons of sentiment, and detached crystals of thought. Flemming quotes Jean Paul's sentiment: "Life in every shape should be precious to us, for the same reason that the Turks carefully collect every scrap of paper that comes in their way, because the name of God may be written upon it." [125] He hears the Baron define ballads as "the gypsy-children of song, born under green hedgerows, in the leafy lanes and by-paths of literature,—in the genial Summer-time." [126] He engages in many provocative discussions of fame, faith, art, and literary life. He is beguiled by older customs and medieval thought, but his visit to the home of Goethe leads him into discussions of transcendentalism—a theme which, after all, appears in *Wilhelm Meister*. Longfellow is not deeply interested in philosophical systems, but in earnest contemplation of simple and practical modes of right living. Although his hero is often morbid, the book is bathed in gentle piety. This piety he discerned even in an earlier day when amid superstition, people at least clung to faith. He liked to recall an olden time when faith struggled with ignorance:

> It was a warm, vapory morning, and a struggle was going on between the mist and the rising sun. The sun had taken the hilltops, but the mist still kept possession of the valley and the town. The steeple of the great church rose through a dense mass of snow-white clouds; and eastward, on the hills, the dim vapors were rolling across the windows of the ruined castle, like the fiery smoke of a fierce conflagration. It seemed to him an image of the rising of the sun of Truth on a benighted world; its light streamed through the ruins of centuries; and, down in the valley of Time, the cross on the Christian church caught its rays, though the priests were singing in mist and darkness below.[127]

At times he seems guileless and naive, at times possessed of a fine intuition. Has any better analogy been drawn than his emblem of the nature of art?

> Art is the revelation of man; and not merely that, but likewise the revelation of Nature, speaking through man. Art preëxists in Nature, and Nature is reproduced in Art. As vapors from the ocean, floating landward and dissolved in rain, are carried back in rivers to the ocean, so thoughts and the semblances of things that fall upon the soul of man in showers, flow out again in living streams of Art, and lose themselves in the great ocean, which is Nature. Art and Nature are not, then, discordant, but ever harmoniously working in each other.[128]

In *Hyperion,* then, the novel is unrecognizable. Even the "romance" gets lost if by romance one means a knot of adventure cunningly tied and untied by a conscious craftsman. But the romantic quest of Paul Flemming exists in the warm emotion created by contemplation of an ancient atmosphere and old pageantry. This dreamy re-creation of old Germany and some of its modern exemplars serves as a matrix wherein is born a pattern of faith, a mode of life for a hero in the strife of life. The book is as unordered as a field of flowers; its atmosphere uncertainly alternates between mist and sunshine. The hero stumbles from time to time on his uneasy pilgrimage but finally reaches a resolution of his doubts. *Hyperion* is a sort of spiritual journal of Paul Flemming.

Kavanagh, Longfellow's only other extended piece of prose fiction, appeared in 1849. By this time Longfellow had had the narrative experience of writing *Evangeline*, but he had not tasked himself in the stricter demands of the story-writer's art. He succeeded in narrative in spite of rather than because of his narrative habits. Only about half as long as *Hyperion*, *Kavanagh* is somewhat more unified than its predecessor, but it is just about as guileless in narrative technique. Compared with a narrative of Poe, it would seem to be the work of an amateur story-teller. Once this defect has been granted, the book can be enjoyed for its idyllic tone—its utterly simple and natural quality. Passing through summer into the first frosts of autumn, it is not without sadness for some of its characters, but it preserves an air of tranquillity. *Kavanagh*, for all its technical defects is a charming book, and a valuable contribution to the literary history of New England—a kind of extended elegy of a village people.

The story is just such a story as was later to appeal to men like Holmes and Aldrich, bunglers both in plot structure but adept in the art of atmosphere creation. The locale is a quiet and remote village, its chief male character a gentle and ineffectual schoolmaster who, through lack of strong enough will and purpose, was unable to write, or even begin, the romance he constantly thought he was going to write. The first sentences of the book at once describe the schoolmaster and set the tone for the book:

> Great men stand like solitary towers in the city of God, and secret passages running deep beneath external nature give their thoughts intercourse with higher intelligences, which strengthens and consoles them, and of which the laborers on the surface do not even dream!
>
> Some such thought as this was floating vaguely through the brain of Mr. Churchill, as he closed his school-house door behind him; and if in any degree he applied it to himself, it may perhaps be pardoned in a dreamy, poetic man like him, for we judge ourselves by what we feel capable of doing, while others judge us by what we have already done. And moreover his wife considered him equal to great things. To the people in the village, he was the school-master, and nothing more. They beheld in his form and countenance no outward sign of the divinity within. They saw him daily moiling and delving in the common path, like a beetle, and little thought that underneath that hard and cold exterior, lay folded delicate golden wings, wherewith, when the heat of day was over, he soared and revelled in the pleasant evening air.[129]

Mr. Churchill felt "capable," but proved to be non-productive. Had he really been able to get down to work, he would not have dawdled over

vague imaginings but would have found the substance of a good romance lying under his very eyes in Fairmeadow. This romance in actual life concerned the turmoil created in Fairmeadow by the arrival of
Kavanagh, the handsome young preacher who replaced old Mr. Pen-
dexter. Two girls (among many) fall in love with Kavanagh, and these
two are friends of each other. One, Cecilia Vaughan, is a beautiful girl
and a rich one; the other, Alice Archer, is a poor girl devoted to her
poor partially blind mother. The romance will call upon one of these
girls to show great fortitude. She must finally bear up bravely under
the news—brought directly by the happy girl herself—that the minister's engagement to Cecilia has taken place. Alice must act out her
part to the end, never telling her love. But not for long will she suffer:
within a few months this "Patience" will have a "monument" of her
own in the village graveyard. Kavanagh will take his bride abroad, stay
three years, return to Fairmeadow, sadly observe signs of progress—
the railroad had transformed the "simple village" into "a very precocious town"—revisit Mr. Churchill, and deliver a few final admonitions.
Only a few things will seem the same, among them the "workhouse,
standing alone in the pasture by the river" and "that other workhouse,"
the school. Mr. Churchill will be the same—correcting school exercises
and trying vainly to get on with his "romance," wholly oblivious of the
romance that has occurred but a few steps away. He will never complete his book.

Kavanagh is a pleasant tale. Its major romantic characters, Kavanagh,
Cecilia, and Alice, aren't very real, but Mr. Churchill is and some of the
villagers are. There is Hiram A. Hawkins, who changes his name to
H. Adolphus Hawkins when he falls in love with Cecilia Vaughan. He
has no chance of winning Cecilia, but is himself the object of tenacious
affection, for when he died, "two elderly maidens went into mourning
simultaneously, each thinking herself engaged to him." There is Miss
Sally Manchester, chambermaid and cook of the Archer family, who
dabbles in veterinary practices in spare moments—"administering lamp-
oil to the cock, when she thought he crowed hoarsely." [130] A traveling
dentist fills not only her teeth but also a place in her heart. When it becomes apparent that his repeated postponement of their marriage was
prophetic, she vows permanent spinsterhood. She is from time to time
sought in marriage by Mr. Vaughan's hired man Silas, but she refuses
to respond to his somewhat sanguinary courtship: "In vain did he send
her letters written with his own blood,—going barefooted into the
brook to be bitten by leeches, and then using his feet as inkstands." [131]
A community problem is Lucy, the Churchill's servant girl, who finally
runs away with a shoe peddler. Fairmeadow's comparative isolation is

emphasized also by the bad boy of the community, Wilmerdings' boy, who runs away to serve on a whaling ship. For mostly the village is self-contained and tradition-locked. Its population has little mobility. Although Wilmerdings' boy runs away, signs of the village conformity to routine may be seen in

> Mr. Wilmerdings, the butcher, standing beside his cart, and surrounded by five cats, that had risen simultaneously on their hind legs, to receive their quotidian morning's meal. Mr. Wilmerdings not only supplied the village with fresh provisions daily, but he likewise weighed all the babies. There was hardly a child in town that had not hung beneath his steelyards, tied in a silk handkerchief, the movable weight above sliding along the notched beam from eight pounds to twelve. He was a young man with a very fresh and rosy complexion, and every Monday morning he appeared dressed in an exceedingly white frock. He had lately married a milliner, who sold "Dunstable and eleven-braid, open-work and colored straws," and their bridal tour had been to a neighbouring town to see a man hanged for murdering his wife. A pair of huge ox-horns branched from the gable of his slaughterhouse; and near it stood the great pits of the tannery, which all the school-boys thought were filled with blood![132]

Indeed the static quality of Fairmeadow is its greatest charm. And yet the charm is not without its realism. Longfellow was not one to itemize vice and misery, but he included them in his totals. At significant junctures he exhibits a surprising attention to unromantic detail. At the very moment when the two girls are locked in exciting discourse over Kavanagh's choice, the rest of the village carried on as usual: "And below sat the two old women, talking of moths, and cheap furniture, and what was the best remedy for rheumatism . . ."[133] All this is seen from the point of view of an outsider, it is true, but a very observant outsider. Howells was to do the same sort of thing with greater success: *he* was able to get on with his story.

Lack of grip and impact—that is perhaps the explanation of the gradual loss of public interest in *Kavanagh*. Longfellow wrote it quickly (he said) but not (one may be sure) energetically. Even so it had sold ten thousand copies at the end of less than a decade.[134] It was prized in discerning quarters. Emerson told Longfellow he thought it the "best sketch we have seen in the direction of the American Novel."[135] Hawthorne seems to have been genuinely delighted, but had his doubts about the public's probable appreciation of it. He referred to *Kavanagh* as a most precious and rare book . . . Nobody but yourself would dare to write so quiet a book; nor could any other succeed in it. It is entirely original, a book by itself; a true work of genius if ever there were one. And yet I should not wonder if many people (confound them!) were to see no such matter in it. In fact, I doubt whether anybody else has enjoyed it so much as I . . .[136]

Howells wrote of his "peculiar devotion" to the book, which he valued as a "touching and lightly humorous tale" about a village not far different from his own: he could appreciate the "delicate realism" of the story.[137]

Probably everyone, friendly or not toward *Kavanagh*, would agree that it was a natural book for Longfellow to have written. In it there is no sign of strain after effect. It was one of Longfellow's most useful traits that he took himself as he was. *Kavanagh*, for example, is largely American in its texture but its author does not feel it necessary to be clamorously national: better to be natural than noisily national, he thought. One of the most interesting passages in *Kavanagh* takes up this very issue when Mr. Churchill quietly outpoints Mr. Hathaway, an editor who has strong convictions about native literature:

> "I think, Mr. Churchill," said [Mr. Hathaway], "that we want a national literature commensurate with out mountains and rivers —commensurate with Niagara, and the Alleghanies, and the Great Lakes!"
> "Oh!"
> "We want a national epic that shall correspond to the size of the country. . . We want a national drama in which scope enough shall be given to our gigantic ideas . . . In a word, we want a national literature altogether shaggy and unshorn, that shall shake the earth, like a herd of buffaloes thundering over the prairies!"
> "Precisely," interrupted Mr. Churchill; "but excuse me!—are you not confounding things that have no analogy? Great has a very different meaning when applied to a river, and when applied to a literature. Large and shallow may perhaps be applied to both. Literature is rather an image of the spiritual world, than of the physical, is it not?—of the internal, rather than the external. Mountains, lakes, and rivers are, after all, only its scenery and decorations, not its substance and essence. A man will not necessarily be a great poet because he lives near a great mountain. Nor, being a poet, will he necessarily write better poems than another, because he lives nearer Niagara. . . ."
> "But, at all events," urged Mr. Hathaway, "let us have our literature national. If it is not national, it is nothing."

"On the contrary, it may be a great deal. Nationality is a good thing to a certain extent, but universality is better. All that is best in the great poets of all countries is not what is national in them, but what is universal. Their roots are in their native soil; but their branches wave in the unpatriotic air . . ."

"But you admit nationality to be a good thing?"

"Yes, if not carried too far; still, I confess, it rather limits one's views of truth. I prefer what is natural. Mere nationality is often ridiculous. Every one smiles when he hears the Icelandic proverb, 'Iceland is the best land the sun shines upon.' Let us be natural, and we shall be national enough. Besides, our literature can be strictly national only so far as our character and modes of thought differ from those of other nations. Now, as we are very like the English,—are, in fact, English under a different sky,—I do not see how our literature can be very different from theirs. Westward from hand to hand we pass the lighted torch, but it was lighted at the old domestic fireside of England."

"Then you think our literature is never to be any thing but an imitation of the English?"

"Not at all, it is not an imitation, but, as some one has said, a continuation." [138]

Here indeed lay Longfellow's strength: he quietly cultivated his natural resources wherever they were and wherever they came from. It was his genius to woo the reader, not to storm his defenses. And many a reader yields to the sunny page who would resist the blasts of more dynamic writers. True, Longfellow is always the butt of the sophisticated critic. The reader who has been overstimulated by violent fictional methods will pass by a man who makes so few demands upon him. Such readers and such critics Longfellow was not writing for. To them he would have addressed the sage words that Mr. Churchill wrote one day for his own edification:

Many readers judge of the power of a book by the shock it gives their feelings,—as some savage tribes determine the power of muskets by their recoil; that being considered best which fairly prostrates the purchaser. [139]

The reader of Longfellow experiences no recoil. He may even doze off as he listens to the soft accent of the narrator. And when he wakes —whether in a picturesque inn on the Rhine with Paul Flemming or in the sleepy village of Fairmeadow—he will not bother to know what action he has missed. For the dream and the charm will be as before.

GEORGE LIPPARD (1822-1854)

Horror and Humanitarianism

George Lippard had a career that was in some ways as colorful as the books he wrote. In temperament he seems to have been a curious mixture of the moral crusader and the sensation-monger. The tone of his writing often surprisingly adumbrates that of the modern tabloid writer. He entered training for the ministry, but gave up "in disgust at the contradiction between theory and practice" of Christianity. For a similar reason he gave up the law (after four years of preparation): he felt that the law did not sufficiently serve the ends of real justice. Journalism, which he tried next, seems not to have inspired in him any comparable aversion, for he filled several posts with a good deal of success and satisfaction, the first of these being a position as police-court reporter for the (Philadelphia) *Spirit of the Times* in 1841. Ill health from overwork sent him from journalism to independent authorship. It was not long before his popular story appeared, first serially and soon in book form, *The Monks of Monk Hall* (1844).[140] Lippard dramatized the story of *The Monks of Monk Hall,* but its performance was prevented by municipal authorities. At about the same time Lippard began a brilliant career as a lecturer, his subjects generally being drawn from people and episodes of the Revolutionary War. A facile writer, Lippard continued to produce stories and romances until his death in 1854. His other activities included various humanitarian but unorthodox moves for the improvement of mankind. In general he opposed institutions. His early dislike of formal religion and law was matched by his later attacks upon capitalism. Lippard had a passionate interest in the amelioration of the social order, and he earnestly tried to promote the brotherhood of man. His program in this respect was finally made concrete in the Brotherhood of Union (now called the Brotherhood of America), which he organized in 1850.[141]

Little is generally known about the works of Lippard for the simple reason that historians of literature have chosen to ignore them.[142] Yet to omit consideration of Lippard is to distort the history of the novel of the forties. For there was apparently a large percentage of truth in the author's claim that *The Quaker City* had been "more attacked and more read than any work of American fiction published for the last ten years." [143]

Lippard's characteristics as a writer are best observed in *The Quaker City*, probably the most extravagant compound of Gothic terror, intense melodrama, and social invective ever written on this continent. It is a Gargantuan work in its narrative scope. Nothing less than a small volume could adequately summarize its content. Monk Hall itself, called by the author "one of the vilest rookeries in the world," is a sort of combination of house of ill fame, fashionable club, and gambling hell. Its chief denizens are not the dregs of society but "respectable" ministers, lawyers, doctors, and other professional people who repair to its gorgeous club accommodations to indulge in the most extreme revelry and the most sordid orgies—a kind of metropolitan counterpart of "Young Goodman Brown." Beneath the hall, which is itself three stories under the surface of the ground, is a pit tended by a porter called Devil-Bug—an ugly, deformed, one-eyed, moronic, and generally depraved creature. It is a place of dark horror, permeated by foul humors, filled with the débris of years, and tenanted by the most loathsome vermin and reptiles. A subterranean stream flows momently through the pit and then buries itself in the earth again. Here on one occasion it is Devil-Bug's congenial assignment to bury an unconscious victim alive . . . Thus a section of the setting.

The story, though extremely complex, is well organized, and the whole action occurs within three days. One of its three main strands deals with Dora Livingstone, a beautiful, vain, and heartless creature, who has formed a liaison with one Col. Fitz-Cowles, a millionaire, whom she plans to marry in order that she may become the titled mistress of his English estate. But her husband one day discovers her sleeping in the arms of her paramour. Resisting an impulse to slay them at once with a dagger, he cuts off a ringlet of the hair of each as a proof of their guilt and plans a later revenge—by poison. The idea of poison is not his exclusively, however, for Mrs. Livingstone presently begins to acquire the technique of Dr. McTorniquet. But in this race for armament the man wins out. On Christmas Eve he takes his wife to a country house on what she thinks a pleasure junket. Here he plays upon her cupidity by telling her that *he* has inherited an English estate. Then, with a touch of the same genius for refined revenge which Montrésor shows in Poe's "The Cask of Amontillado" (yet to be written), he presents her with her Christmas gift—a coffin fully equipped with name-plate—Dora's name-plate—and two locks of hair! Meantime he has gaily poisoned her coffee. He now refuses her the antidote she pleads for, and watches her die. Her paramour, Fitz-Cowles, is presently invited by one of Livingstone's retainers to fight a duel in a nearby chapel, but he manages to escape alive. A little later the retainer enters the room in which Dora died, in time to see the raving Livingstone bending over her naked body, engaged in an act too monstrous for the author to mention in print. Livingstone presumably dies also in a spectacular fire which now consumes the entire mansion—in a scene which viewed from a nearby hill, proves to be "an awful sight, awful and sublime as tho' the Book of Revelations had started into action." [144]

Another strand of action concerns the daughter of Devil-Bug, the porter. Depraved though he is, Devil-Bug has a human and humane side which shows itself in his fierce struggle to save his daughter Mabel Pyne (unaware of her parentage) from a ghastly series of dangers, including being drugged and almost violated by a minister. Without revealing his relationship to her, he manages to bring her safely out of all her troubles and into the arms of Luke Harvey, a young man who is far from perfect but who seems little less than a saint in this unclean chronicle. Devil-Bug himself dies a terrible death on the scene of one of the murders he has committed.

A third strand of action, interwoven with these, tells the story of Mary Byrnewood's ruin at the hands of a wealthy libertine named Lorrimer. The daughter of a respectable merchant, Mary is lured to the scene of her doom on the promise of marriage and is there (in Monk Hall) violated after a faked ceremony. Her brother, who by a well-contrived coincidence has been present just before Mary is dishonored, vows revenge, but he is immediately made the object of a series of murderous attempts captained by Devil-Bug. Falling through trap-doors becomes almost a routine for Byrnewood; but he somehow survives all the outrages planned for him, and he finally dispatches Lorrimer in the last chapter. Thus is verified the prophecy of an astrologer who in the first chapter had predicted that one of the young men would kill the other within three days.

These three lurid strands appear and reappear throughout the story of *The Quaker City*, but they do not suggest the abundance of excitement that characterizes the book as a whole. Lippard does not fail to exploit every standard device for creating sensation: torture, murder, seduction, rape, incest, arson, insanity, hallucination, hypnotism, disease (including small-pox), drug-taking, alcoholism, forgery, blackmail, living inhumation, and the reanimation of a "corpse." Most of the tested Gothic properties are here too: subterranean vaults, trap-doors, skeletons, rodents, poisoned potions, mysterious lights. Dedicated to Brockden Brown, this book is ghastly enough to have given even that experienced terrorist a bad nervous turn. *The Quaker City*, however, is clearer than most of the stories of Brown. Lippard had a quite extraordinary gift for organization, and his narrative, although extremely involved, is held firmly in hand by its ingenious author.

An exciting story, *The Quaker City*, but a frightful arraignment of the social order in Philadelphia as well. [145] The charges against the social order in Philadelphia are many and detailed, but their burden is that hypocrisy and gross connivance are everywhere employed to conceal the most hideous subversions of justice and the foulest crimes. The handicaps under which common people live are known to the wealthier classes, but are utterly ignored. Even the depraved Devil-Bug, the author implies, is nothing but the logical development of a kind of vicious environment tolerated with the full knowledge of the city fathers. Indeed in this whited sepulchre which is Philadelphia, the persons who commit the direst crimes against society are those in the upper ranks of society:

> And the Monks of Monk-hall—who are they?
> Grim-faced personages in long black robes and drooping cowls? Stern old men with beads around their necks and crucifix in hand? Blood-thirsty characters, perhaps, or black-browed ruffians, or wan-faced outcasts of society?
> Ah no, ah no! From the eloquent, the learned, and—don't you laugh—from the pious of the Quaker City, the old Skeleton-Monk had selected the members of his band. Here were lawyers from the court, doctors from the school, and judges from the bench. Here too, ruddy and round faced, sate a demure parson, whose white hands and soft words, had made him the idol of his wealthy congregation. Here was a puffy-faced Editor side by side with a Magazine Proprietor; here were sleek-visaged tradesmen, with round faces and gouty hands, whose voices, now shouting the drinking song had re-echoed the prayer and the psalm in the aristocratic church, not longer than a Sunday ago; here were solemn-faced merchants, whose names were wont to figure largely in the records of 'Bible Societies,' 'Tract Societies' and 'Send Flannel-to-the-South-Sea-Islanders Societies;' here were reputable married men, with grown up children at college, and trustful wives sleeping quietly in their dreamless beds at home; here were hopeful sons, clerks in wholesale stores, who raised the wine-glass on high with hands which, not three hours since, had been busy with the cash-book of the employer. here [*sic*] in fine were men of all classes,—poets, authors, lawyers, judges, doctors, merchants, gamblers, and—this is no libel I hope—*one* parson, a fine red-faced parson, whose glowing face would have warmed a poor man on a cold day.[146]

Lippard does not pause to prove his charges but he reiterates them from time to time with explosive force. To Luke Harvey he assigns a speech on justice:

"*Justice,* and in the Quaker City!" said Luke, with a quiet sneer, as folding his arms across his breast, he gazed from face to face—"Justice and in the Quaker City! A Strange Monster I trow! One moment it unbolts the doors of the prison, and bids the Bank-Director, who boasts his ten thousand victims, whose ears ring forever with the curses of the Widow and the Orphan, it bids the *honest* Bank-Director, go forth! The next moment it bolts and seals those very prison doors, upon the poor devil, who has stolen a loaf of bread to save himself from starvation! One day it stands grimly smiling while a mob fires a Church or sacks a Hall, the next, ha, ha, ha, it hurries from its impartial throne, and pastes its placards over the walls of a Theatre, stating in pompous words, and big capitals, that THE TRUTH *must not be told in Philadelphia!*" [147]

The law and the church receive the fiercest vituperation at the hands of Lippard. Foreign missions were an especial abomination to the author, for, he says, missionaries are sent "to the Isles of the Sea, to the Hindoo, the Turk, and the Hottentot" while the need of correction at home is enormous:

> And in this great city, there are thousands upon thousands hidden in the nooks and dens of vice, who, like Devil-Bug of Monk-Hall, have never heard that there is a Bible, a Savior, or a God! True, when dragged before the bar of Justice (as by a lively stretch of fancy the mockery is called) for the commission of crimes, to which the very evils of this most Christian community had driven them, hungry and starving as they were, these wretches have seen that Bible lifted up in Court, heard that Savior's name lipped over by some official, anxious for his dinner, or heard the name of that God profaned by some witness, greedy to sell his soul for the price of a hat! [148]

But it was not only spectacular suffering that elicited his interest. He was also concerned at the plight of thousands of underpaid workers. His relentless analysis of their poverty and of the effects of poverty presages the later fictional studies of Theodore Dreiser. In *New York: Its Upper Ten* he speaks bitterly and sincerely (albeit in tawdry prose) of the connection between poverty and crime:

> Poverty! Did you ever think of the full meaning of that word? The curse of poverty is the cowardice which it breeds, cowardice of body and soul . . . Poverty in the city, is not mere want of bread, but it is the lack of the means to supply innumerable wants,

created by civilization,—and that lack is slow moral and physical death . . . Proud lady, sitting on your sofa, in your luxurious parlor, you regard with a quiet sneer, that paragraph in the paper (you hold it in your hand), which tells how a virtuous girl, sold her person into the grasp of wealthy lust for—bread! You sneer, —virtue, refined education, beauty, innocence, chastity, all gone to the devil for a—bit of bread! Sneer on! but were you to try the experiment of living two days without—not your carriage and opera-box,—but without bread or fire in the dead of winter, working meanwhile at your needle, with half-frozen fingers for just sixteen pennies per day, you would, I am afraid, think differently of the matter. . . . And you, friend, now from the quiet of some country village, railing bravely against southern slavery, and finding no word bitter enough to express your hatred of the slave market, in which black men and black women are sold—just look a moment from the window of your quiet home, and behold yonder huge building, blazing out upon the night from its hundred windows. That is a factory. Yes. Have you no pity for the white men . . . who are chained in hopeless slavery, to the iron wheels of yonder factory's machinery? Have you no thought of the white wom[e]n . . . who very often are driven by want, from yonder factory to the grave, or to the—brothels of New York? You mourn over black children, sold at the slave block,— have you no tear for white children, who in yonder factory, are deprived of education, converted into mere working machines (without one tithe of the food and comfort of the black slave), and transformed into precocious old men and women, before they have ever felt one free pulse of childhood?[149]

There can be no question that Lippard was a sincere champion of the oppressed and distressed. He was possessed of a strong evangelical fervor.[150] Unfortunately a good deal of his invective reads like rant. Moreover he has no time to give the data which might substantiate his charges. Certainly the melodramatic story he tells cannot be accepted as evidence of the conditions he harps on. No wonder his book created resentment. The way of the crusader is hard unless he uses more diplomacy and discretion than Lippard could summon up. Moreover his books seemed immoral on the grounds of sex. Here Lippard was plainly vulnerable. It is no part of the obligation of the reformer to give a voluptuous description of a woman about to be seduced. Time and again Lippard exploits the female form (with *1844* freedom) far beyond the needs of a moral crusader. The explanation of all this must be left to psychologists: Lippard was a vivid writer who seems to have aimed both at sensationalism and at humanitarianism.

Lippard's humanitarian purpose lends weight to *The Quaker City*, but it is of course not constantly in the foreground. For the most part the story itself claims attention. Occasionally moral ideas are blended easily with the narrative, as in the following characteristic passage:

> There may be some of our readers who have never been within the confines of one of those oyster-caverns which abound in the Quaker City. For their especial benefit, we will endeavor to pencil forth a few of the most prominent characteristics of the "Oyster Saloon by Mr. Samuel Chiffin."
>
> Lighted by flaring gas-pipes, it was divided into two sections by a blazing hot coal stove. The section beyond the stove, wrapt in comparative obscurity, was occupied by two opposing rows of 'boxes,' looking very much like conventual stalls, ranged side by side, for the accommodation of the brothers of some old-time monastery. The other section, all light, and glitter, and show, was ornamented at its extreme end, by a tremendous mirror, in which a toper might look, time after time, in order to note the various degrees of drunkenness through which he passed . . .
>
> These Oyster Cellers are queer things. Like the caverns of old story, in which the Giants, those ante-diluvian rowdies, used to sit all day long, and use the most disreputable arts to inveigle lonely travellers into their clutches, so these modern dens, are occupied by a jolly old Giant of a decanter, who too often lures the unsuspecting into his embrace. A strange tale might be told, could the stairway leading down into the Oyster Celler be gifted with the power of speech. Here Youth has gone down laughing merrily, and here Youth has come up, his ruddy cheek wrinkled and his voice quavering with premature age. Here Wealth has gone down, and kept going down until at last he came up with his empty pocket, turned inside out, and the gripe of grim starvation on his shoulder. Here Hope, so young, so gay, so light-hearted has gone down, and came up transformed into a very devil with sunken cheeks, bleared eyes, and a cankered heart. Oh merry cavern of the Oyster Celler, nestling under the ground so close to Independence Hall, how great the wonders, how mighty the doings, how surprising the changes accomplished in your pleasant den, by your jolly old Giant of a Decanter!
>
> It is here in this Oyster Celler, that we open the fearful tragedy which it is the painful object of our narrative, to tell. Here amid paint, and glitter and gilding, amid the clink of glasses and the roar of drinking songs, occurred a scene, which trifling and insipid as it may appear to the casual observer, was but the initial letter to a long and dreary alphabet of crime, mystery and bloodshed.[151]

It is clear that, whatever his faults, Lippard was at least a vivid writer.

He was unable to create memorable characters. Instead of character he produced ingenious mechanisms or marionettes who were operated arbitrarily at his whim. He somehow managed, moreover, to create a slight effect of mountebankery in even his most vivid scenes. Yet he possessed a very considerable literary *skill*. He was extremely apt in phrasing and he was abundant in the invention of striking scenes. A wide reader, he inevitably calls to mind a number of English writers who were contemporary, especially Dickens, Bulwer, and Ainsworth.[152] His dedication of *The Quaker City* to Brockden Brown was a serious gesture. His bow to Fenimore Cooper—"the greatest Novelist that ever gave a literary name to our country abroad, or enchained his million-readers at home" [153]—is flamboyant but sincere. He probably learned tricks of the trade also from Poe, who with greater finish and concentration treated themes similar to Lippard's.[154] He was no mere penny-dreadful writer coming to his trade all untutored but a skilled and trained writer with a strong moral sense, a somewhat deficient artistic sense, and a keen discernment of what constitutes popular fictional material. At all events the public liked his books. Perhaps they read them surreptitiously, but read them they did, for *The Quaker City* reached its twenty-seventh edition within a few years, and F. O. C. Darley thought it worth his while to illustrate the story. Enough reason, surely, for considering Lippard as an American novelist. In the forties the more enduring work in American literature was being produced by the Cambridge and Concord groups and a few other writers like Poe and Melville, but at the same time a large public was gazing with rapt attention at the gigantic canvases of George Lippard. He foreshadowed the modern mystery thriller and the modern sociological novel. He proved that even in the forties there was a market for literature of a sort not ordinarily associated with the gift-book era.[155]

Nathaniel Hawthorne
(1804-1864)

When Hawthorne diffidently published *The Scarlet Letter* in 1850, he won tardy recognition of distinguished gifts which he had exercised with discouraging results for a score of years in the field of the short tale. Perhaps it was the failure of his ambitious juvenile novel *Fanshawe* (1828) which kept him for a long time from trying to share honors in fictional types which proved so profitable to Cooper, Simms, Paulding, Sedgwick. Uninterested in Indian. legend,[1] inexperienced on the sea, meagre in powers of invention, not gifted in characterization, possessed of no ready fund of tearful sentiment, seldom moved by the comic, inclined toward careful finish rather than intensity, interested in line more than color or mass, he produced faint, ethereal etchings which were tossed aside by the multitude who stood agape before the larger, more lurid canvases of Cooper and Simms and the charming Dutch realism of Irving. He steadily practiced a genre in which mingled realism and fantasy contended for empire with a heavier strain of philosophizing than most readers of fiction welcomed. He cultivated a highly specialized type of tale. To be sure, the delicate modulations of his shy voice were heard by the discriminating, but he had small chance of competing successfully for public favor that was granted to the robust, ringing narrative tones of Cooper and Simms. Like Poe, he was for a long time a misfit in an America intent upon industrial expansion rather than the cultivation of fine arts. But he was unable or indisposed to imitate Poe by capitalizing fully a strain of the macabre which was native to him. He did not possess a vein of that genial humor which enabled Irving to compensate for guileless plots and thinness in thought. Aware of his deficiencies, he sometimes scorned a public that was indifferent to his talents but no thought of journalistic success ever caused him to swerve from his ideals. Consequently even after the publication of *Twice-Told Tales* (1837) he remained for many years "the obscurest man of letters in America."[2] With the passing of time the friendship of men who had access to publishing ventures helped Hawthorne to achieve a minor celebrity proved by the second (enlarged) edition of *Twice-Told Tales* in 1842, but his popularity was slight and inconstant until 1850. A master of his craft, he received the recognition and emolument of an apprentice, but he did not seek to escape the terms of an indenture drawn by fate.

From his earliest articulate years, he evinced that love of reading and writing which marked him for the service of art. His boyish reading in Smollett, Neal, Radcliffe, Scott, Godwin, and *The Arabian Nights* aroused his interest in narrative fields never more than adjacent to his true province in fiction.[3] Nor did his early practice in versification, inspired in part by Burns, do much more than prove that prose was his medium. But they both showed, as did his prolific letters, that some sort of literary expression was native to this lad whose shyness made him more at home brooding over a book or courting solitude in the Maine woods than in easy intercourse with people. With his retiring disposition went a proneness to melancholy. Even in his youth he was subject to gloomy depression, which, as he cautiously confided to his sister, he sought on occasion to alleviate in a somewhat surprising manner: "I . . . have taken to chewing tobacco with all my might, which, I think, raises my spirits. Say nothing of it in your letters . . ."[4]

By the time he was ready for college, he had "almost given up" poetry but not the thought of authorship:

> I have not yet concluded [he wrote his mother] what profession I shall have. The being a minister is of course out of the question. I should not think that even you could desire me to choose so dull a way of life. Oh, no, mother, I was not born to vegetate forever in one place, and to live and die as calm and tranquil as—a puddle of water. As to lawyers, there are so many of them already that one half of them (upon a moderate calculation) are in a state of actual starvation. A physician, then, seems to be "Hobson's choice;" but yet I should not like to live by the diseases and infirmities of my fellow-creatures. And it would weigh very heavily on my conscience, in the course of my practice, if I should chance to send any unlucky patient "ad inferum," which being interpreted is, "to the realms below." Oh that I was rich enough to live without a profession! What do you think of my becoming an author, and relying for support upon my pen? Indeed, I think the illegibility of my handwriting is very author-like. How proud you would feel to see my works praised by the reviewers, as equal to the proudest productions of the scribbling sons of John Bull!

Then he adds with a prophetic insight which he had occasion to recall bitterly: "But authors are always poor devils, and therefore Satan may take them." [5] He appears not to have believed that the way to authorship lay through academic distinction despite the stimulating example of his ambitious classmate, Longfellow, for upon graduation at Bowdoin he was to stand no higher than eighteenth in his class.[6] Moreover, now escaped from the largely feminine environment which home and illnesses had naturally subjected him to, he expanded his slight talent for conviviality by taking part in forbidden card-playing and wine-drinking. These dissipations, however, fell far short of excess, and his relative innocence may be gauged by his indignant protest when the President implied that he had been led astray by bad company: "I was full as willing to play as the person he suspects of having enticed me . . ." [7] Easy intimacy, however, was not one of his gifts, and though a member of a college society referred to as "democratic," he formed few friendships. With Longfellow he may have been formally acquainted, but the temperamental differences between them militated against a close association. He associated freely with Franklin Pierce and Jonathan Cilley but appears to have regarded them as companions rather than as friends.[8] Horatio Bridge alone of the men Hawthorne met at Bowdoin was able slowly to penetrate the shy reserve of Hawthorne. That "cursed habit of solitude" which Hawthorne deplored but was unable to remedy in himself was relaxed under the influence of Bridge to such an extent that Hawthorne even confided to Bridge his literary ambitions, and it was Bridge who later bolstered Hawthorne's frequently wavering self-esteem and helped him variously in connection with the publication of his earlier works.

Meanwhile part of the energy Hawthorne withheld from his studies he devoted to a volume of tales and the first draft of a novel. The tales, which were to be called "Seven Tales of My Native Land," were finally burned by Hawthorne in exasperation at a publisher's delay.[9] *Fanshawe*, the novel, Hawthorne sent to a number of publishers, but none was willing to underwrite it. As he bitterly complained later, American authors without renown had small chance of being published. Accordingly he had the book printed at his own expense in 1828.[10] It received a moderate number of reviews, but the public seemed little interested. Hawthorne gave vent to his anger and despair by arranging for the destruction of all the copies he could find—despite the fact that the work had appeared anonymously like those of his god of inspiration, Scott.[11]

Fanshawe came into the world at the very height of the reputation of Cooper, but Hawthorne was not the man to compete with the author of *The Last of the Mohicans*. Nor could he hope to match the vigorous actions of Scott. Yet he had read Scott voraciously in his early youth, and to some extent he imitated him in *Fanshawe*. To Longfellow, *Fanshawe* carried "a suggestion of Bowdoin days," but it derived pretty directly from Scott in its "low-life tragedy, its romantic scenery, and its bookish humor." [12] Yet Scott was but a poor model for Hawthorne.[13] The plot of *Fanshawe* is potentially an exciting one. Fanshawe and his friend Edward fall in love with the same young woman. The situation becomes critical when the less preferred young man, Fanshawe, rescues the heroine from a villain. But Fanshawe (with a sense of chivalry comparable to that of Natty Bumppo) refuses to allow Ellen to sacrifice love to gratitude. He dies slowly of consumption, leaving Edward to marry Ellen after an interval of four years. Unfortunately, although Hawthorne could imitate Scott with a degree of success in details, he was quite unable to match Scott's power in handling dramatic scenes.[14] His characters in *Fanshawe* are not strongly felt and the dialogue, never a strong point with Hawthorne, is very crude. Nor does Hawthorne compensate for his somewhat amorphous narrative by investing it with that wealth of fancy and moral speculation which enriched his later novels. Consequently although the book contains some faint prophecies of the mature Hawthorne—the delicate youth (Fanshawe) deficient in human qualities, and the deliberate villain with a dark past full of unspecified crime—there are reasons to believe that Hawthorne's judgment was good when he sought to suppress *Fanshawe*. Only his graceful prose partially redeemed the failure of his first novel.

Graduated from Bowdoin in 1825, Hawthorne had returned to Salem, where he remained, except for brief annual trips in New England and New York, until 1837.[15] The interval of companionship at college had not destroyed his appetite for solitude, however, and he soon settled down to a quiet routine of reading and writing in a household so considerate of individual privacy that the members of the family (Hawthorne, his mother, and two sisters) seldom met each other except by appointment.[16] He ignored the more aristocratic society of Salem in favor of limited companionship with the less literate but perhaps wiser citizens, especially one William Pike, a carpenter. He seldom left the house except for short walks at night. Occasionally there was an evening at cards with some of the simpler folk. Most of his time was spent in the room under the eaves which gave upon the wharves and admitted the afternoon sun he so loved. His deliberately contrived isolation perhaps closed the door to happiness that he might have enjoyed more abundantly in a freer social life; yet although he later complained that he knew little at first hand of the "deep and warm realities" of life,[17] it is idle to suppose that his art would have been greater if he had led the more robust life which Julian Hawthorne later said he was more naturally fitted for.[18] At all events he soon began, with the painful deliberation always characteristic of him, to write those short stories which ultimately brought him fame.

The public indifference to *Fanshawe* blasted Hawthorne's confidence to such an extent that he did not essay another extended narrative for more than twenty years. Yet the publication of the book was fortunate, for S. G. Goodrich, editor of *The Token*, discovered in it signs of a talent which he thought worth while encouraging. He sought out Hawthorne, and listened sympathetically to the young writer's plan of publishing a volume of tales, to be called "Provincial Tales." When even Goodrich's friendly aid failed to secure a publisher, Hawthorne invited Goodrich to use such stories from the collection as he saw fit for his annual, *The Token*. Finding that Hawthorne's tales were at least as good as the average of what he was able to secure for *The Token*, Goodrich took four tales,[19] which were published anonymously in 1832. Other Hawthorne items appeared in subsequent issues as well as a few pieces in other magazines.[20] Later in 1834 he also began to contribute to *The New England Magazine*, then under the editorship of Park Benjamin, who had commented favorably on Hawthorne's anonymous contributions to *The Token*.[21] A further step toward that recognition in the world of letters which Hawthorne so coveted was taken when through the influence of Goodrich, Hawthorne secured the editorship of *The American Magazine of Useful and Entertaining Knowledge*, a monthly magazine published in Boston. Yet misfortune still dogged him, for the magazine shortly became insolvent and Hawthorne went back to Salem, profoundly discouraged at the small returns, financial or artistic, which his devotion to letters had yielded: "May my hand wither when it would write another [tale]" says Oberon (speaking for young Hawthorne) in "The Devil in Manuscript." [22] Well might he have repined, for some of his best pieces in *The Token* "extorted hardly a word of either praise or blame, while columns were given to pieces since totally forgotten." [23]

The explanation for Hawthorne's continued obscurity lay partly, doubtless, in his perverse desire to remain anonymous. In 1837, he was induced by friends, especially Horatio Bridge (who without Hawthorne's knowledge made a financial guarantee), to gather up a number of his best tales and to print them in a volume bearing his own name. *Twice-Told Tales*, the volume which resulted, contained eighteen pieces, and was brought out over the well-known imprint of the American Stationer's Company, Boston. Its immediate reception was not overwhelmingly favorable despite Longfellow's sympathetic if not very understanding review,[24] but it at least did not drop completely from view, and a year later "a breeze seemed to rise and fill its sails." [25]

Now first after years of vexation and despair Hawthorne had won a modest complement of prestige. Though many years were to pass before he gained widespread fame comparable to Longfellow's sudden accession of fame (in 1839), he now received enough acclaim to keep his self-esteem alive if not to stop his grumbling.[26] Intervals of depression constantly recurred during which he alternately castigated the American public for neglecting him and regretted his inability to get at "the real secret" of his powers.[27]

Hawthorne's self-imposed exile came to an end in 1837. It was about this time that the Peabody family of Salem reestablished an old acquaintance with the Hawthornes, especially Nathaniel. Elizabeth Peabody thought that Hawthorne was "handsomer than Lord Byron," [28] and it appeared to Sophia that although he was shy, he was "by nature profoundly social." [29] Apparently Hawthorne merely needed opportunity and encouragement to emerge from his shell of isolation. Indeed he co-operated with those who tried to get him to circulate among people, for he felt the danger of "walking in a shadowy world." [30] The Peabodys drew him out socially and the confluence of literary men in the Peabody shop in Boston where the *Dial*, short-lived organ of transcendentalism, was published later, gave Hawthorne new opportunities for establishing rapport with the sages of Concord thought.

In time Sophia Peabody, long an invalid, partially recovered her health and, responding to Hawthorne's "magnetic personality," accepted his offer of marriage. In the meantime Hawthorne had begun to seek a more gainful occupation than authorship, which seemed hopeless. At the instigation of Franklin Pierce and other friends, he had seriously considered the possibility of joining an Arctic expedition, as historiographer, a venture that might have been salutary for a man who for many years had "not lived, but only dreamed of living," but the plans for the expedition collapsed. In January, 1839, he became weigher and gauger at the Boston Custom House. At first he enjoyed the common work in companionship with men, but he came in time to regard it as a "grievous thralldom." Similarly the manual labor he engaged in at Brook Farm, whither he went after leaving his customs appointment in 1841, he found to be a "bondage" detrimental to literary production.[31] A decade later he was to realize profits from his investment of time and money ($1000) when he wrote *The Blithedale Romance*. In 1842 he married Sophia Peabody and moved to Concord where he established himself in the Manse hallowed by the recent occupancy of Emerson, in a happy frame of mind shadowed only by the menace of poverty. The "indicated" friendship with Emerson failed to ripen, but Hawthorne had all the companionship necessary to his cautious nature. He remained at Concord until in 1846 Bridge secured him an appointment to the Customs position at Salem, an appointment at which Whitman, one of the early appreciators of Hawthorne, rejoiced.[32] Three years later he was removed for political reasons,[33] and he again experienced a period of despair which was to be terminated only by the surprising success of *The Scarlet Letter* in 1850.

During these years of doubt and insecurity tempered by his domestic felicity his pen had not been exceedingly prolific. His connection with S. G. Goodrich had yielded editorial and hack-work jobs; he had published *Grandfather's Chair* in 1840, and he had brought out a new and enlarged edition of the *Twice-Told Tales* in 1842. Life at Concord amid "customary associates" of an "anti-literary" sort[34] had for Hawthorne an idyllic quality which did not favor great activity on the part of a man for whom literary composition was at best painfully slow. For two years he composed practically nothing. Yet by 1846, he had assembled enough tales and sketches, old and new, to form two small volumes. These were published at New York in 1846 as *Mosses From an Old Manse*. Their reception was favorable but not enthusiastic. Melville indeed exhibited rare insight in his review of the work, which he valued so highly that he felt safe in asserting that no matter what Hawthorne might write thereafter, the *Mosses* would be "ultimately accounted his masterpiece." [35] The journalistic pen of Poe probably came nearer expressing the general reaction. Although he had professed himself delighted with Hawthorne upon the publication of the first volume of the *Twice-Told Tales*, which he regarded as "original at all points," Poe with his customary fickleness was now disposed to cavil at Hawthorne for his peculiarities and for his growing tendency to load his stories with allegory, the bane of public interest. Hawthorne himself was not sanguine about their success, and he wearily looked about for another source of income. Thus when he returned to Salem to enter the Custom House he was in no cheerful mood—despite the fact that he had written the two collections of short tales which, artistically at least, gave him a parity with Irving and Poe, his major competitors.

The quality of Hawthorne's stories and essays, like that of the novels to come, was too rare to enlist a great deal of public interest. Action was almost always more subordinate than in Poe and the tone was seldom so merry as Irving's. The subject matter reflected an interest in native material (for Scott's influence lingered and historical fiction from other hands was prospering), but it partook more of sombre local antiquities than of the picturesque legends that Irving dug up. Moreover although Hawthorne occasionally tried to report the outward world with a degree of objectiveness, as in the "Seven Vagabonds," he was less successful in them than in imaginative studies centred in some problem of conduct. His passion for ethics prompted him to stop his characters in the midst of action in order to probe their inner lives. What he found there he frequently reported by means of symbol and allegory. Consequently the action lost its sharp edge of general interest and became vague. He dodged back and forth between fantasy and reality with an elfin sportiveness that irritated readers in quest of plain tales with plain conclusions and obvious justice, such as characterized the historical romance. Whereas the general reader wanted to know, for example, exactly what Goodman Brown did when he left home, Hawthorne gradually retreated from the specific lines he had commenced on and before the reader is through he is not sure whether he has had a story or an essay. The stories as such are generally incompletely articulated. "Popular" elements are reduced or diluted. "Instead of passion there is sentiment" and in place of tragedy there is a mild pathos.[36] By a kind of involution the characters dry up into abstractions of moral qualities, and the drama tapers off into tableau. The action is almost imperceptibly transformed into a species of fantasy which is as unstable as the reality, for if the reader reconciles himself to a bit of the supernatural, Hawthorne is likely to drop his wizardry and restore the clear air of reality most disturbingly—leaving the reader a bit ashamed of the fantastic ideas he has been harboring. Hawthorne generally lays his facts and fancies so close together that in the half light the reader is prepared to find them merging. Thus in "Dr. Heidegger's Experiment" the rose and the butterfly *were* in part rejuvenated, and it is easy for the reader to carry on the enchantment begun by Hawthorne. "The Maypole of Merry Mount" is founded on fact and the characters at first have a strong reality, but the philosopher soon wrests the pen from the story-teller, and before the end the reader finds himself sitting in sorrow for mankind instead of attending to the fortunes of a hero and heroine. Hawthorne daringly subsisted on the thinnest fringe of narrative. "Roger Malvin's Burial" begins with a potentially dramatic situation suited to the talents of Scott or Cooper, but after a few pages the author commences his subtle process of evolving a generalized truth in the moral sphere with the result that the narrative interest lags in ratio to the rise in moral content. Generalization is the thief of character, and by it Hawthorne robbed countless readers of an interest in the climax. It is significant that the reader is not concerned over the ultimate fortunes, for example, of Giovanni in "Rappaccini's Daughter." The fast narrative of "Mr. Higginbotham's Catastrophe" is not typical of Hawthorne. Hawthorne experimented on his characters and nourished his philosophy on their life's blood. But the transfusion was sometimes fatal to the story, as Hawthorne sadly inferred from his failure to become popular. It is not surprising that the most popular piece in either of these collections, "The Gentle Boy," retains character and story in a primary sense until the end. The *Twice-Told Tales* and the *Mosses* include some of the finest pieces in our literature, but their purely popular appeal has always been qualified by the inconclusiveness of their objective action.[37] Of course the real glory of Hawthorne lay not in verisimilitude of character or action but in his power to provide illuminating, if tentative, comment on the mysteries of existence which appear in different guise to different persons. It was so in his longer stories also: those characters who are so real that they seem to have been drawn from the life are less valuable than those portraits whose shifting light and shadow never yield a full complement either of reality or fantasy.

The three years at Concord had "hastened away with a noiseless flight," [38] and Hawthorne had gone to Salem, there in 1847 to begin work on his greatest novel. When Hawthorne commenced *The Scarlet Letter*, he had small hope of becoming a well-known man of letters. The prejudice against the novel was slowly breaking down, and there was a demand for fiction to fill the shelves of circulating libraries.[39] But the demand was filled by stories with a "liberal admixture of the horrible and the sentimental." [40] As for the better writers, Cooper and Simms held on pretty well, and there were flurries of popularity for a number of other writers: Paulding, Kennedy, Bird, Ingraham, and others. If Scott was falling off a trifle in popularity here, he was being replaced by Dickens and Thackeray. Bulwer's polished tales were still in demand. But no American novelist had created a taste for the sort of fiction Hawthorne was capable of writing. Our national ideals were to that extent still in need of improvement.

Hawthorne wrote *The Scarlet Letter* under difficult circumstances, for the family was not far from poverty, and there was scant happiness for him in a house where his mother lay dying and his children innocently doubled his sorrows by re-enacting her struggle with death. When the book was near completion he set so little store by it that James T. Fields the publisher very nearly missed seeing it on a visit to Salem to secure "copy" from Hawthorne. He wrote the story under the stress of great emotional excitement, a fact which probably accounts for its having an artistic unity so strong that it would have drawn praise even from finical Poe. There is not an ounce of excrescence in it. Indeed Hawthorne perhaps imperilled his story as such by omitting all but brief and indirect comment on the unfortunate events which led up to the tragedy.

The first plank in the tragic platform of the story had been laid two years before when Hester Prynne was married to a man, an English scholar, unsuited to her in age and temperament. Sent on to America in advance of him, she had formed a liaison with the minister, Arthur Dimmesdale. The novelist picks up the narrative at the door of the prison where Hester, now the mother of Pearl, awaits her sentence. Her husband is there, arrived in time to witness her ignominy. It will be his sole aim to find and punish her lover. Dimmesdale is there; it will be for him to wrestle in agony with his conscience. For Hester there begins the long slow reconstruction of her life. She suffers but grows stronger through her suffering because her sin has been confessed and because her lowly life is at least a life of action. Dimmesdale suffers but grows weaker as long as his guilt remains clamped in his bosom. Chillingworth's implacable purpose hardens him into a hideous image of hatred. For seven years the burden is borne. It is Hester who proposes a way out—flight across the ocean. It is Dimmesdale who finds the solution—public confession on the scaffold. He has found strength at last—and in his strength he dies. It remains for Hester, always robust in her grip on life, to re-establish herself and Pearl. Pearl, who with the fortune left her by Chillingworth has become "the richest heiress of her day, in the New World," is taken abroad by Hester and there finds happiness. Later Hester returns to her old cottage, voluntarily resumes her scarlet letter, and lives out the days of her years in sober toil. Herself the survivor of "a mighty trouble," she has learned the art of aiding others in their time of need.

Hawthorne's allusion to Pearl as "the richest heiress of her day" strikes a popular fictional note which is elsewhere unheard in this chronicle of woe. For *The Scarlet Letter* exists as an artistic demonstration of "the stern and sad truth . . . that the breach which guile has once made into the human soul is never, in this mortal state, repaired." [41] The theme of the book is sin, but the action can have no attraction for readers in quest of shocking delineations of sinful behavior. For Hawthorne's interest was not in wrong-doing per se but in the psychological implications of sin.[42] The theme of concealed sin was not a new one with the author of the *Twice-Told Tales* and *Mosses From an Old Manse,* but nowhere had he explored the theme with such a steady focus. The charming air of leisure that would soon pervade *The House of the Seven Gables* and *The Blithedale Romance* is largely excluded from *The Scarlet Letter*. Although imaginatively authentic, the setting is spare rather than full in detail—a conspicuous example, as Willa Cather was noted, of "the novel démeublé." [43] Humor is absent: Pearl's naive irrelevancies increase rather than relieve tension. The characters are few and their reality is never stressed more than their significance in the moral allegory that Hawthorne was producing by means of a series of tableaux of incomparable though subdued beauty. The book is a gloomy one, so much so that Hawthorne doubted its success. The ideal novel he had projected at Concord in 1846 had been one "that should evolve some deep lesson and should possess physical substance enough to stand alone." [44] The formidable lesson of *The Scarlet Letter* was inescapable.

The lesson was inescapable but not simple. It was easy to understand that the impingement upon the moral laws of society would bring severe punishment, and that even more dreadful than the displeasure of the community was the corrosion of the spirit which occurred when the sin was concealed. Yet almost equally disastrous, the author implies, is an indirect result of the sin of the lovers, namely, the "injured" husband's perverse effort to trespass on the Lord's prerogative of vengeance. If Hester and Dimmesdale were the sinners, Chillingworth became the "villain of the piece." Hawthorne even allows the lovers to discriminate between sinning through weakness or passion and the deliberate cultivation of a profane pursuit:

> "We are not, Hester, the worst sinners in the world. There is one worse than even the polluted priest! That old man's revenge has been blacker than my sin. He has violated, in cold blood, the sanctity of a human heart. Thou and I, Hester, never did so!"
>
> "Never, never!" whispered she. "What we did had a consecration of its own. We felt it so!" [45]

Nevertheless the reader feels a certain remorselessness on Hawthorne's part as he records the outward tragedy of Hester and Dimmesdale and Chillingworth and Pearl. For although he appears to have regarded Chillingworth's violation of the "sanctity of the human heart" as a greater sin than the illicit love of Hester and Dimmesdale, he is not disposed to minimize the effects of the lovers' uncontrolled passion. The reader who is horrified at the grim revenge of Chillingworth can find small comfort in any comments of the author, for Hawthorne preserves an almost scientific detachment as he observes and records the outcome of this experiment in transgressions of law. Notwithstanding the intimation of pardon at the end, the book has on its literal level an air of hopelessness that comports well with its seventeenth-century setting. Nor has the principal psychological lesson of the book been wholly outmoded by later conceptions of morality; Hawthorne's interpretation stands the test of time.[46] The tragic nature of the book is somewhat relieved, however, by the fact that the characters are not strongly realistic. Indeed Hawthorne referred to the dramatis personae as the "shadowy beings" of his story.[47] The unlucky Pearl who appears to have been drawn, by an inverse process, from Hawthorne's daughter Una[48] hovers near the edge of the supernatural. Hester at times seems a real individual, a deeply suffering woman, especially in that moment when she exclaims to Dimmesdale (in language not far from Shakespearean in tone): "Surely, surely, we have ransomed one another, with all this woe!" Yet she mainly helps to sustain Hawthorne's magnificent allegory of the interaction of good and evil. The characters seem often to move in that quasi-somnambulistic state which characterized Dimmesdale when he sought "a moment's peace" by visiting the scaffold at night. Thus the story is relieved of that acute sense of pain which the reader experiences in books like George Eliot's *Adam Bede*. Moreover in a larger sense there is a wisdom in the book that tempers the sadness of the human story. It is not to be forgotten that the physician's passion for revenge is what finally brings Dimmesdale's confession—good out of evil. Hawthorne's speculation on things unseen convinced him that the moral organization of the world is capable of no easy analysis. Though pessimistic in attitude, he does not presume to be the final judge. In his dying speech Dimmesdale dares to feel a faint hope that divine mercy will rescue the lovers from the eternal wrath to come. Even Chillingworth may be only an illustration of slight spiritual maladjustment which will be finally set right:

> It is a curious subject of observation and inquiry, whether hatred and love be not the same thing at bottom. Each, in its utmost development, supposes a high degree of intimacy and heart-knowledge; each renders one individual dependent for the food of his affections and spiritual life upon another; each leaves the passionate lover, or the no less passionate hater, forlorn and desolate by the withdrawal of his subject. Philosophically considered, therefore, the two passions seem essentially the same, except that one happens to be seen in a celestial radiance, and the other in a dusky and lurid glow. In the spiritual world, the old physician and the minister—mutual victims as they have been—may, unawares, have found their earthly stock of hatred and antipathy transmuted into golden love.[49]

Many of the characteristics that Hawthorne had revealed in his shorter pieces reappear in *The Scarlet Letter*, which indeed is more akin to the short story in structure than to the novel. It was for this reason that Hawthorne opposed the serial publication of his novel.[50] Very little external action is employed and what there is is geared to the slow tempo that Hawthorne always preferred. There is nothing new in the use of symbolism, the disposition to linger over scenes until the last significance has been drained from them, the light veil of fantasy which obscures the outlines of the action, or that frequent evasion of literal statement at critical junctures in the narrative which results in the reader's being forced to "choose among these theories." [51] By using a minimum of physical movement, Hawthorne invites attention to spiritual changes. Certainly never before had Hawthorne sustained the focus of his art so long on a moral problem, nor did he ever again achieve a comparable feat. Nor did he ever sustain his prose with such tranquil beauty and classic poise for so many pages. *The Scarlet Letter* marked the apogee of Hawthorne's power to unite narrative with metaphysic —without serious loss to either. It remains one of the great examples of fictional art in the English language.

Hawthorne's long and vexatious probation had now fully justified the faith of friends who had assisted him with encouragement, tips on marketing, appointments, and even the proffer of outright financial gift.[52] After *The Scarlet Letter* his critical reputation was never again the cause for the slightest concern. Though moralists complained of the treatment accorded sexual ethics in the book[53]—perhaps partly *because* of their complaint—the book took hold rapidly and the original edition of five thousand copies was quickly exhausted.[54] Critical encomia from the most distinguished sources flooded the author's mail. After a brief reaction Hawthorne resumed writing, and the next few years were the most prolific and happy he ever spent. *The House of the Seven Gables*, written at Lenox, Massachusetts, was in Hawthorne's opinion a "more natural book" for him to write, and his relaxation of mind and spirit is evident in the new volume. A discreet discursiveness replaces the rigid focus of *The Scarlet Letter*, and more of Hawthorne's rather rustic humor creeps in. The author seemed after the "cloudy and gusty morning" of his life[55] to expand and bloom with the belated sunshine of success, and he wrote with apparent friendliness to his prospective readers. A favorite moral there is, namely, that the ugly past imposes its wickedness on succeeding generations, and indeed Hawthorne was in a sense writing "family history." [56] As a young man Hawthorne seems to have brooded over the guilty part played by his great-great-grandfather at the time of the Salem witch trials, and he certainly had heard the legend that John Hathorne had been cursed.[57] Yet he obviously did not feel constrained to attend to his problem so strictly as in *The Scarlet Letter*. Judge Pyncheon's persecution of Hepzibah and Clifford is so exaggerated that harsh reality fades gently into romance. Even the gruesome scene of the "drinking of blood" is felt to be mostly "story." And so Hawthorne intended, for, as he says in his Preface, "the personages of the tale . . . are . . . of the author's own making, or, at all events, of his own mixing." It was his hope that the book would be read "strictly as a romance." *The House of the Seven Gables* seems to have been written *con amore*. Hawthorne's pen dwelt with obvious satisfaction on the description of the house, the leisurely portraiture, the tiny traffic of the shop, the garden on a Sunday afternoon, the purchase of the hens (Hawthorne was now living in the country), the development of picturesque Gothic plot-elements, the Quixotic railway journey of Hepzibah and Clifford, and the mildly picaresque strain represented by the daguerreotypist Holgrave.[58] If the action is sluggish and digressive, there is a great deal more variety of mood in the book than in *The Scarlet Letter*. The book is less austere and more entertaining. To be sure the marriage of a Maule and a Pyncheon does not remedy the wrong done to Hepzibah and Clifford, but Hawthorne was more disposed to see chinks of light in the moral gloom overshadowing the world. "Life is made up of marble and mud," he says; but he adds that "poetic insight is the gift of discerning . . . the beauty and the majesty which are compelled to assume a garb so sordid." [59] *The House of the Seven Gables* is Hawthorne's most mellow book, and it established a bond of affection between Hawthorne and the public of the sort that existed between Dickens and his readers. People had written to Hawthorne to inquire whether the scarlet "A" of *The Scarlet Letter* existed, but they were certain that the House of the Seven Gables was drawn from life, despite Hawthorne's assurance to the contrary in the preface to the book.[60] In any case *The House of the Seven Gables* possessed that body and that sense of physical intimacy (the result in part of Hawthorne's own observation) which *The Scarlet Letter* by its very nature as a "period" book necessarily lacked. Melville, who eagerly watched for Hawthorne's productions, was delighted. "This book," he wrote to Hawthorne, "is like a fine old chamber, abundantly, but still judiciously, furnished . . . ," and in a postscript he testified to the reality the story had for him, by issuing the gay order: "If you pass Hepzibah's cent-shop, buy me a Jim Crow (fresh) and send it to me by Ned Higgins." [61]

Notwithstanding pleasant experiences and pleasant neighbors (including Melville) at Lenox, Hawthorne soon moved to Roxbury, where his next book, *The Blithedale Romance* (1852) was written. Its thesis is that a good ideal brings a man to a worthy end only if it does not alienate him from the natural order of life. More specifically, the book reflects Hawthorne's profound distrust of reform movements as such. He was convinced of "the folly of attempting to benefit the world." [62] With the monomaniacal Hollingsworth as its centre, the book virtually becomes a *"reductio ad horrendum* of the philanthropist who loves man in the abstract to the final exclusion of the least affection for real men, and who ends by loving only his theory." [63] The story tells how Miles Coverdale (one of Hawthorne's many aliases) came to Blithedale farm; experienced the disillusionment resulting from the attempt to harmonize the (to him) unreconcilable elements of hard physical labor and high thinking; witnessed the dire effects of Hollingsworth's vague but fanatical program of reforming criminals; observed with dismay how mesmerism was used as a means of subjugating Priscilla; wept over the tragic end of Zenobia's love for a reformer who made love to her for her money; and sorrowed for the loss of Priscilla, half-sister of Zenobia, who after suffering keen anguish at the hands of Zenobia, lives to be the disconsclate bride of Hollingsworth. Sombre though many of the incidents and implications of the book are,[64] there is much sunshine on its pages and Hawthorne's elfin humor plays confidently at frequent intervals. Despite his usual flight from contemporary materials, Hawthorne boldly based the charming narrative of *The Blithedale Romance* on memories hardly more than a decade old—though taking consolation, doubtless, in the fact that Brook Farm, the real setting for the story, was in itself a retreat from reality. The degree to which Zenobia represents Hawthorne's conception of the character of Margaret Fuller is debatable.[65] Miles Coverdale is assuredly the Hawthorne who under the influence of Sophia Peabody tried to exorcise the demons of his solitude by joining the ranks of those zealots who consecrated themselves to plain living and high thinking at Brook Farm in 1842. Allusions to Transcendentalism, for the most part casual or facetious, indirectly remind the reader of the reality of the experiment Hawthorne had made. But although Hawthorne had started out on firm earth (in a very real snow storm), and although Zenobia's gruel is gruel without a metaphor, and no veil of allegory flutters over Silas Foster's pigs, and the discovery of Zenobia's body in the brook is terribly real,[66] Hawthorne was not the man to confine himself to verifiable matters of fact very long; he was never able to coin fact into truth without a considerable alloy of fancy or fantasy. The history of old Moodie and his daughters (finely reminiscent of *Père Goriot,* published in 1834) doubtless had come from some niche or nook of fact just as the Veil episode shows Hawthorne's interest in mesmerism of the day, but even in this, the most nearly contemporary of Hawthorne's long stories, the embroidery of fancy completely obscures much of the woof of fact.[67] If Brisbane sat for the portrait of Hollingsworth, Hawthorne occasionally flecked the portrait with fancy, looking beyond his sitter into the realm of the slightly grotesque. Again Hawthorne uses the theme of the wickedness of attempting to subjugate a personality, and, using the example of Hollingsworth, he again preaches the folly of reform through the intellect; but the essence of this romance, "the lightest, the brightest, the liveliest" that Hawthorne ever wrote,[68] came from the same obscure inspiration as the finer parts of all of Hawthorne's books.[69]

The years after the publication of *The Scarlet Letter* brought Hawthorne compensation for his immured, almost monastic, state during youth and early manhood. He had fame and, if not wealth, at least a competency.[70] In 1852 he served his former college-mate, Franklin Pierce, by writing a campaign biography of him. As President, Pierce promptly discharged the debt by appointing Hawthorne to the consulate at Liverpool. In 1853 he betook himself and family to England and thence, in 1857, to Italy. For six years his writing was largely confined to official business and voluminous notebooks. He stayed abroad long enough to banish "all feeling of homesickness," [71] and to orient himself more fully than might have been expected in a man of his temperament and history. After a bitter-sweet experience of England (recorded in *Our Old Home,* published in 1863, and in many letters) he found in Rome the genesis of his last great work of fiction, *The Marble Faun* (1860). The change was good for man and writer. After a brief period of disgust at the cold weather and dirty streets of Rome, he began to feel at home. He enjoyed a leisurely country where "Spring is not compelled to burst into Summer with such headlong haste." [72] He revelled in the romantic atmosphere of Rome. He now fully realized how barren America was as a field for romance. Perhaps it was ungracious of the author of *The Scarlet Letter* to write as he did in the preface to *The Marble Faun:*

> Italy, as the site of his Romance, was chiefly valuable to him as affording a sort of poetic or fairy precinct, where actualities would not be so terribly insisted upon as they are, and must needs be, in America. No author, without a trial, can conceive of the difficulty of writing a romance about a country where there is no shadow, no antiquity, no mystery, no picturesque and gloomy

wrong, nor anything but a commonplace prosperity, in broad and simple daylight, as is happily the case with my dear native land. It will be very long, I trust, before romance-writers may find congenial and easily handled themes, either in the annals of our stalwart republic, or in any characteristic and probable events of our individual lives. Romance and poetry, ivy, lichens, and wall-flowers, need ruin to make them grow.[73]

Posterity can only be grateful, however, for the imaginative power which enabled Hawthorne to give new root to his art in the rich soil of old-world civilization: *The Marble Faun* is one of Hawthorne's most lovable books.

The faun of Praxiteles had set his imagination spinning on the pos-sibility of a romance arising out of a love between the faun and a human being. Here was a magificent opportunity to study the birth of sin and the evolution of conscience. For this purpose Hawthorne united the faun theme with the story of a richly endowed and darkly passionate creature (Miriam) of mixed English and Jewish blood who was suffering from the consequences of a vaguely outlined act of re-bellion that threatened her destruction. Followed by a spectre who is none the less terrifying for being unaggressive, Miriam lives in a half-free state[74] that becomes unbearable. Finally, with her ocular consent, the faun pushes the fleshly spectre off the battlement to his death. This act brings Miriam and Donatello closer together than they have ever been, but the humanizing of the faun has the effect of awaken-ing in him a conscience that torments him with his crime. When the law steps in, he is finally consigned to a dungeon. In the meantime Hawthorne has inlaid the whole narrative with allegory, philosophy, and fantasy. In this fantasy the faun symbolized a glorious golden age which Hawthorne was fond of postulating as a background for the study of sin's effect on the human soul. The story of Miriam embodied the artificial problems of civilized life. The setting in Rome enabled Hawthorne to gratify his passion for great sculpture as well as for resplendent ruins connoting the pageant of man's brief progress. He loved it every inch—it's gorgeous palaces, its sylvan retreats, its gush-ing fountains, and its "sunless alleys." [75] The dust of ages lies on the monuments, and the alternating sunshine and shadow symbolize Haw-thorne's ebb and flow of belief in the beneficence of the Creator. Moonlight and marble are leitmotifs that announce the mysterious beauty of the Roman story. Reality and fantasy again coalesce and disintegrate in even more than usually baffling manner. Moral truth rides through the entire story and, equally with Hawthorne's descrip-tion of Rome, sins against the narrative interest. The theme is again the true nature of good and evil, symbolized on the first page as the dove and the serpent. As in *The Scarlet Letter* it becomes difficult, before Hawthorne finishes, to decide where the two part company, for the thesis which Hawthorne apparently endorses is that the commission of sin may humanize the soul.[76] The book is unusually poor in proportion but lovers of Rome value every paragraph of its description and students of Hawthorne's thought find its summation in this, the last long novel Hawthorne completed.

As story, *The Marble Faun* is often defective, but its power to interest the general reader was proved by the clamor for more definite statements about the outcome which was quieted only when Hawthorne wrote an additional chapter. The book contains much unorganized wealth. Emerson called it "mere mush" [77]—an opinion which must be regarded as a minority report in the light of later criticism. In a sense *The Marble Faun* epitomizes Hawthorne's art, for excepting the New England scene, it treats at least briefly almost every major element that he had employed in his earlier fiction. The people are sometimes as cold as the marble in the moonlight, but Hawthorne's luminous intuitions glow throughout the book. With this book Hawthorne took his place beside Ruskin and Browning as an interpreter of the grandeur and enchantment of Rome. Both Howells and James were later to use Rome (and Florence) as the mise-en-scène for realistic narrative, but neither James nor Howells ever wrote a single book which was so indissolubly linked with the Eternal City as *The Marble Faun*. Nor did many nineteenth-century writers attain the level of Hawthorne's simple, lucid, finely cadenced prose. The mark of his greatness as a prose-writer is his subtle, almost magical, creation of beauty out of word and phrase brought together in apparently very simple sequences—as in his description of Miriam:

> She was very youthful, and had what was usually thought to be a Jewish aspect; a complexion in which there was no roseate bloom, yet neither was it pale; dark eyes, into which you might look as deeply as your glance would go, and still be conscious of a depth that you had not sounded, though it lay open to the day. She had black, abundant hair, with none of the vulgar glossiness of other women's sable locks; if she were really of Jewish blood, then this was Jewish hair, and a dark glory such as crowns no Christian maiden's head. Gazing at this portrait, you saw what Rachel might have been, when Jacob deemed her worth the wooing seven years, and seven more; or perchance she might ripen to be what Judith was, when she vanquished Holofernes with her beauty, and slew him for too much adoring it.[78]

Upon his return to America in 1860 with some fear that he had "lost [his] country by staying away too long," [79] Hawthorne's vital force, never very great, commenced to ebb, and his delicate artistic gifts showed a synchronous tendency to fade. His charm and subtlety never abandoned him and his conversational powers, as Holmes testified,[80] remained brilliant to the end, but his power to sustain an organic problem was gone. Perhaps he might have succeeded again in the shorter pieces which had first brought him into minor prominence, but his mind had "lost the plan and measure of those little narratives, in which it was once so unprofitably fertile," [81] and he had "lost the habit of writing magazine articles." [82] Instead, he now made three rather ambitious attempts to finish full-length romances, all of which, despite intermittent flashes of the author's old powers, must be regarded as comparative failures. A favorite theme of Hawthorne's, the elixir of life, was to be merged with a study of the return of an American to England for the purpose of coming into an hereditary estate. The first of these drafts, *Septimius Felton,* was conceived and begun before *The Marble Faun,* but it was never finished artistically. It was published posthumously in 1871. Its setting in place and time are much the same as in Cooper's *Lionel Lincoln,* and there are also minor analogies to the plot of *Lionel Lincoln,* but the theme of the elixir of life dominated Hawthorne's work. The story ends in anticlimax, and the book is mainly a miscellany of observations on life and incompletely drawn characters. An appendix, "The Ancestral Footstep," is a nebulous study for a story recounting the attempt of a younger brother, long thought lost in America, to piece together evidence which should prove his right to an English estate. *Dr. Grimshawe's Secret* is complete in plot but not in detail. Despite its title, the book makes little of the elixir motif and a great deal of the theme of reclaiming an estate. When a certain New England lad, who had been brought up as a foundling by Dr. Grimshawe, goes to England to look up his claim, he makes a number of surprising discoveries, one of which is that not he but his tutor is the rightful heir of an estate long held by an Italian lord. The jumbled action is surprisingly rich in Gothic elements, generally used in moderation in Hawthorne's earlier stories: the lost key, the "curiously-shaped Italian dagger," [82a] the rusty coffer (supposed to contain gold but actually full of golden hair), the old manuscript, the secret chamber, the mysterious prisoner, the poisoned potion. Hawthorne did not complete the story, but his son Julian prepared it for publication, in 1882.

The Dolliver Romance reverts to the elixir of life for its emphasis, but in this story the ancestral inheritance proves to be the elixir of life itself—a characteristically Hawthornesque refinement. Dr. Dolliver, who has experimented with herbs in the hope of deferring old age and death, finally devises a concoction which, taken in small quantities, actually appears to renew his vigor. But one day an eccentric old Colonel turns up and at the point of a pistol demands the elixir as his proper inheritance. He secures it, drains it at one gulp, and with a cry of exultation leaps into the air, to fall down dead in a moment—leaving Dr. Dolliver with the vague impression that just before death occurred, the old Colonel exhibited "a young man's face . . . with all the passionate energy of early manhood." Dr. Dolliver was quickly acquitted of responsibility for the Colonel's death. So much of *The Dolliver Romance* appeared in *The Atlantic Monthly* in 1864; but Hawthorne, who had promised no more than that he would proceed with the story "at such a pace as suits the feeble gait of an old man," [83] became so ill that he was obliged to abandon its composition and concern himself with his own approaching dissolution. He died in May, 1864. His declining years had filled his mind with echoes and shadows of countless stories he had written in earlier days, but no elixir enabled him to achieve their synthesis into what he hoped would be the crowning achievement of his career.[84] His crowning achievement had long since been written and entered to his credit in the register of fame in 1850 —*The Scarlet Letter*.

Hawthorne's limited but fine art rose to high levels of universality. Yet he was one of the most strictly indigenous of our eminent men of letters. His New England heritage and residence confirmed in him a strong individuality which was modified by very few exterior influences. His Italian period was an Indian summer. European experiences, which exerted so strong an influence on Longfellow and Irving and even Emerson and Cooper in their early manhood, Hawthorne did not know until his native proclivities were so set that they could not be substantially altered. Indeed Hawthorne moved in the opposite direction, for not only did he remain a New Englander but he severely limited his contacts in his native land. He was as deeply rooted in New England as Bryant.[85] His isolation and his restricted horizon explain much of the good and the bad in his art. Henry James believed that New England's lack of certain types of tradition was a real handicap—an opinion with which Hawthorne was at times in perfect accord.[86] On the other hand, Joel Chandler Harris attributed much that was finest in Hawthorne to his New England milieu.[87]

Hawthorne's intensely private life obviously did not fit him to write novels of manners or romances of external adventure. He was capable of great authenticity in background material: there is much faithful Salem detail in *The House of the Seven Gables; The Blithedale Romance* carries a few real descriptions of Roxbury which may be searched out; *The Marble Faun* has a secondary value as a "guide-book to Rome"; and although the setting in *The Scarlet Letter* never reveals crudely Hawthorne's patient investigation of seventeenth-century conditions it is much more authentic than most novels which wear history on the sleeve.[88] Yet Hawthorne is not superficially a specialist in setting. Objective detail employed as sheer verisimilitude is relatively rare, and though his note-books show how often he began a story with a basis in actuality, they do not show by what path he went from reality to that borderland between reality and fantasy which was always his preferred milieu.

For most of his stories he wisely chose scenes remote from the crowded haunts of men. He worked on native soil but only in selected areas. He generally avoided the Revolution and Indian warfare because, though once a disciple of Scott, he could seldom handle large scenes effectively. He was uneasy in crowds, and wary of the contemporary scene. He feared the harm which critics might do "by bringing his fancy-pictures almost into positive contact with the realities of the moment." [89] The varied clash of social life on a large scale would have been fatal to his high purposes. Brook Farm (the real setting for *The Blithedale Romance*) was preëminently a communal centre, but in the story Hawthorne "escape[s] as promptly as possible . . . to Coverdale's sick chamber, and then to the shadowy recesses of the woods lying about the farm." [90] The march of men is seldom heard in the Rome of *The Marble Faun*. Even the market place scenes of *The Scarlet Letter* imposed a strain on Hawthorne's pen, and he muffled the public utterance incidental to them. Though not averse to a bit of theatre or pageantry, he was seldom robustly dramatic. For his shorter tales especially, he needed a small theatre with subdued lights, impalpable gauze-like backdrops, exotic costumes, and muted music —with which to contrive his airy metaphysical interludes ("Young Goodman Brown"), his dainty fantasies ("David Swan"), his masque-like episodes ("The Maypole of Merry Mount"), as well as his more macabre studies like "Rappaccini's Daughter." Even the setting for "The Ambitious Guest," defined though it is by the surrounding mountains at Crawford Notch, is finally made to seem unreal. Hawthorne's swains and witches perform little that is dynamic; they are the vessels of sorcery or the agents of transactions that to the outward eye seem petty. Hawthorne dealt more in a species of necromancy than in drama, and the traffic of his stage depended much on subdued tones and half-lights. Quiet and isolation were essentials. When the moonlit streets of Rome were all but empty, when Dimmesdale was confronting his conscience on the scaffold at night, when the shop of Hepzibah was still, and the garden of Rappaccini was invested with an unreal twilight, and when Eliot's pulpit was shrouded in loneliness, the shadowy muse of Hawthorne crept out to engage in antic play and impish caper. The best milieu for Hawthorne's wizardy was a remote and dimly seen one. Yet it was integral with the action; for whereas in Cooper the setting is so mechanically wrought that it seems detachable, in Hawthorne it is no more capable of easy separation from the action than old ivy from old walls. Remove the web of his setting and the action is destroyed.

Yet the delicate web of setting throughout all Hawthorne's stories must bear the weight of serious themes. Cooper's preoccupation with the bodily safety of his characters is the measure of his difference from Hawthorne. The injured soul interested Hawthorne more than the maimed body. Most of his themes centre in some act baneful to the soul. It may be an overt act of sin like that of Hester and Dimmesdale or of Donatello or of Reuben Bourne which gives the story outward substance, but the essence of the narrative is generally the irreparable harm done to the soul of the violator of a spiritual law. Hawthorne used principally three or four types of such violation. Unconfessed sin he found to be the chief enemy of the spirit not only of Arthur Dimmesdale but of Reuben Bourne, Roderick Elliston, Mr. Hooper, and many another haunted character who proved that "what was hidden must be therefore evil" [91] Equally harmful was the attempt to violate or subjugate the spirit of another person whether by persecution (as in Chillingworth) or by insistence upon reform (as in Hollingsworth) or by experimentation (as in Rappaccini, Holgrave, Westervelt, and others). The unpardonable sin of Ethan Brand was a variation of this type of misused power, for it consisted in a "want of love and reverence for the Human Soul." [92] Sometimes an individual innocently gains a species of control over others, as in "The Prophetic Pictures," but the possessor of such a power is saddened by it, and his actions may imperil both himself and others.[93] Allowing the past to dominate the present constituted little less than a sin in *The House of the Seven Gables*. The wickedness and folly of experimenting on mankind through science or psychology was a theme which interested Hawthorne almost to the point of obsession.[94] Mesmerism was a special interest in *The Blithedale Romance* and *The House of the Seven Gables*.[95] His morbid interest in the idea of prying into the secrets of nature and of possibly defeating her laws led him frequently to speculate on an elixir of life,[96] and though he commented freely upon possible benefits of such a means of prolonging earthly existence (especially in *The Dolliver Romance*, which was to have had a happy conclusion) the general end of attempts at rejuvenation was ludicrous physical frustration and philosophical rejection of the idea. Most of these themes are suggestive of the morbid, especially in conjunction with Hawthorne's obsession for isolation.[97] Their adequate treatment seems to call for the offices of a philosopher or a scientist, for demonstration or experiment. Hawthorne's essential difference from Poe (whom he resembles in some points) is here made clear, for stories for the general reader are more easily made from the attempt to escape the tangible consequences of crime in a verifiable physical setting than from observing the disintegration of a soul in a metaphysical laboratory.[98]

The major characters in Hawthorne's novels are generally endowed with an initial realism which falls into shadow in the progress of the story. Their dress is reported in some detail and they are often seen, especially near the beginning of a story, engaged in petty actions which tend to create versimilitude. Thus his presentation of the workers at Blithedale, though fanciful in its comparisons, shows that Hawthorne was capable of objective description:

Arcadians though we were, our costume bore no resemblance to the beribboned doublets, silk breeches and stockings, and slippers fastened with artificial roses that distinguish the pastoral people of poetry and the stage. In outward show, I humbly conceive, we looked rather like a gang of beggars or banditti than either a company of honest laboring men or a conclave of philosophers. Whatever might be our points of difference, we all of us seemed to have come to Blithedale with the one thrifty and laudable idea of wearing out our old clothes. Such garments as had an airing whenever we strode abroad! Coats with high collars and with no collars, broad-skirted or swallow-tailed, and with the waist at every point between the hip and arm-pit; pantaloons of a dozen successive epochs, and greatly defaced at the knees by the humiliations of the wearer before his lady-love; in short, we were a living epitome of defunct fashions, and the very raggedest presentment of men who had seen better days. It was gentility in tatters. Often retaining a scholarlike or clerical air, you might have taken us for the denizens of Grub street intent on getting a comfortable livelihood by agricultural labor, or Coleridge's projected Pantisocracy in full experiment, or Candide, and his motley associates at work in their cabbage-garden, or anything else that was miserably out at elbows and most clumsily patched in the rear. We might have been sworn comrades to Falstaff's ragged regiment. Little skill as we boasted in other points of husbandry, every mother's son of us would have served admirably to stick up for a scarecrow. And the worst of the matter was, that the first energetic movement essential to one downright stroke of real labor was sure to put a finish to these poor habiliments. So we gradually flung them all aside, and took to honest homespun and linsey-woolsey . . .[99]

But Hawthorne quickly abandons that domain of everyday psychology which is employed by most popular novelists. Once he begins to spin the fabric of fantasy, his characters lose their identity as real people—so much so that, in some cases, the reader is startled to learn that they possess names other than their Christian names.[100] They are transfixed by a symbol (like Hester, Roderick, Elliston, Priscilla), or they become philosophical clearing-houses for Hawthorne's ideas on sin and redemption (like Miriam). "Roger Malvin's Burial" begins with an episode arising out of an historical event, Lovell's Fight, but by the time Hawthorne is through probing the conscience of his hero (Reuben Bourne), the reader has lost all grasp of objective reality. Young Goodman Brown leaves his house at night a common working man and comes back in the morning reeking with metaphysics. Priscilla enters Blithedale a charming girl in need of protection, but the reader's original affection for her gradually changes into a speculative curiosity regarding a "subject." She vanishes into an experiment. Chillingworth becomes dimmer and dimmer as a character the longer he is forced to sustain Hawthorne's illustration of the malign influence of a ruling passion for revenge. The general reader ceases to fear Hawthorne's villains and to love his heroes. This is true even when, as in the case of Zenobia, Hawthorne found the inspiration for his portrait in real persons and even based his action on real incidents.[101] The most real characters are likely to be the least important in the action—Silas Foster in *The Blithedale Romance*, Uncle Venner in *The House of the Seven Gables*. The major characters often act as if under an enchantment.

Moreover, although individual markings distinguish the various characters somewhat, Hawthorne had a tendency to rely rather heavily on a few types most useful in the working out of his themes. Thus one meets the aggressive, somewhat predatory female, richly endowed physically and bearing a hint of "exotic" paganism in her nature (Zenobia, Miriam); the attractive, home-loving girl with a shade more independence than her charming exterior prepares the reader to expect (Hilda, Phoebe); and the pale victims of stronger personalities (Priscilla, Alice Pyncheon). So with Hawthorne's various villains, idealists, broken down old men, young students, village derelicts, and emblematic children—they have more kinship with each other than with reality. Indeed Hawthorne saved himself the trouble of creating completely new dramatis personae by ransacking his tales for types which could be altered. By a species of inbreeding "each character became a source of traits for characters to follow." [102] This is not to say that Hawthorne failed in characterization utterly, for each of his characters retained a zone of reality which for the purposes Hawthorne had in mind was quite sufficient.[103] Why the zone of reality did not become enlarged is explained by Hawthorne's narrative method.

Stevenson assuredly reckoned without Hawthorne when he said: "There are . . . three ways, and three ways only, of writing a story. You may take a plot and fit characters to it, or you may take a character and choose incidents and situations to develop it, or . . . get action and persons to realize and express it." [104] Hawthorne appears to have employed a fourth method: to begin with a theme and then to find character types and a situation which may illustrate it without dominating it.[105] The explanation of this type of procedure is that Hawthorne's recluse life did not supply him with direct observation of life or exercise his human sympathies sufficiently. The initial impulse for a story was often intellectual rather than emotional. This was perhaps coming close to the "unpardonable sin," but Hawthorne was reprobate enough to continue in his iniquity. He was aware of the danger of losing his readers' interest by digressions on the history of Rome,[106] but he appears willing to have risked such dullness. The greater hazard of excess philosophical content bothered him equally little. Few writers who have adopted fiction as a form have adopted a method so inimical to entertainment as Hawthorne.[107] Preoccupied with an idea, he summoned up characters who would work his will.

The method he employed in general involves a flight from reality. "Drowne's Wooden Image," to take one example from a short tale, begins concretely enough (in all reality) on a "sunshiny morning" with a wood carver "contemplating a large oaken log, which it was his purpose to convert into the figure-head of a vessel." [108] He has been commissioned to do the job for the "jolly captain" Hunnewell. All this is tangible enough—a craftsman, a client, and an oak log. But presently it appears that Captain Hunnewell has a secret wish which must be communicated to the artist "in so low a tone that it would be unmannerly to repeat what was evidently intended for the carver's private ear." Thus begins the witchery, the necromancy. Genius in Drowne enables him to produce a work not only beautiful in itself but, to the amazement of the villagers, an exact reproduction of a Portuguese lady who is one day seen emerging from Captain Hunnewell's residence, a figure "so airy and yet so real . . . that people knew not whether to suppose the magic wood etherealized into a spirit or warmed and softened into an actual woman." [109] Captain Hunnewell and his ambiguous consort make for Drowne's shop, but at the moment of their entry, they are both whisked away and the carver is left with his original image, now bereft of all animation, a mechanical thing. All of this, says Hawthorne, may be held to show that "the very highest state to which a human spirit can attain, in its loftiest aspirations, is its truest and most natural state . . ." In the meantime what has happened to the story as such? It has been lost in a beautiful borderland between reality and fantasy. The use of local color and the presence of the painter Copley are a guarantee of the partial reality of the tale, but the theme of Pygmalion is used so equivocally that the reader is sure of only one thing, namely, that Hawthorne has employed the materials to present moral truth. Thus Hawthorne devises actions which shall illustrate his theme, but the tempo is generally slow and the action seldom reaches a dramatic climax with subsequent relief of tension. The same conditions obtain also in the longer stories: at most he wishes to secure a "foothold between fiction and reality." [110] Plot is sometimes reduced to little more than diagram or design. Conventional means of advancing action are discarded. Chillingworth, for example, is finally convinced of the guilt of his victim not by devices common in stories of infidelity—a glove, a letter, a handkerchief, a chance meeting—but by a *fantastic* "discovery" of an "A" on Dimmesdale's breast. Nor does Hawthorne's occasional use of the threadbare fictional device of clearing up a mistaken identity in the last chapter restore his narrative to popular standards: his real quarry remains the philosophy yielded by the facts. If the reader engages his affections on the characters or focuses his interest on external action, therefore, he is generally destined to disappointment. *The Scarlet Letter* is the least culpable of the long stories from this point of view and *The Marble Faun* the most flagrant.

The constant iteration of a theme exemplified in action reduced to a slow tempo and interrupted by pauses becomes even more subtly disturbing to readers of romance because such progress as *is* made comes about indirectly.[111] Hawthorne observed life intermittently in a mirror. His avoidance of direct approach to truth (which was his aim more than fiction) was deliberate. In the preface to *Our Old Home* he tells of his hope that by means of implication he can "convey more of various modes of truth than [he] could have grasped by a direct effort." [112] Hence his stories are heavily allegorical [113] and his scenes are often parables. He resorts much to the use of half-finished pictures and delayed or unconsummated actions.[114] In detail, he sought indirection by means of symbol. Thus Hooper's black veil, Zenobia's exotic flower, Westervelt's false teeth, Roderick Elliston's snake, Donatello's furry ears, Felton's spider, Chillingworth's hunched shoulder, etc., are indirect comment on character and are merged with the action in such a way as to deepen meaning if not to further the story. The line of Hawthorne's art is often circular; his force is centripetal. Instead of constantly traversing new territory, he tends to swing around a point. The Maypole of Merry Mount is a good symbol of his art.

Symbols are commonly believed to impair realism, but Hawthorne valued them as being, at least, completely natural. In a scene between Miriam and Donatello, Hawthorne indicated why he relied so much on symbols:

> With every step she took, he expressed his joy at her nearer and nearer presence by what might be thought an extravagance of gesticulation, but which doubtless was the language of the natural man, though laid aside and forgotten by other men, now that words have been feebly substituted in the place of signs and symbols.[115]

Yet though the symbol has an immediacy which is artistically useful in bringing narrative art to the borders of the plastic arts, it is wanting in explicitness. Many readers find Hawthorne's sermons in stones unpleasantly cold, his snow-images merely irritating. The habit of allegory was deepened in Hawthorne as he grew older, and it accounted in part for Poe's loss of enthusiasm for Hawthorne's narrative.[116] But Hawthorne persisted in his search for final truths. Although he once referred to clay as "more interesting than even the final marble," he seems ultimately to have preferred marble. Miriam's indictment of Kenyon, the sculptor, might well be turned against Hawthorne: "You turn feverish men into cool, quiet marble." [117]

Marble statuary, however, suggests more definiteness, more firmness of line, than Hawthorne generally achieved. His shadowy characters are sent on ambiguous errands in eerie realms where little can be settled by the tests of reality. He deliberately wooed fantasy because it yielded poetic truth and beauty. "We artists purposely exclude sunshine," says Miriam in *The Marble Faun*.[118] Hawthorne himself sought dim scenes "where there are glimpses, sketches, and half-developed prints of beings and objects grander and more beautiful than we can find anywhere in reality." [119] When Miriam hearkens to the two separate voices of her dual nature, she slips into an unreality comparable to that of masked characters in plays of Eugene O'Neill, but she serves her purpose of bringing out truth. The dark forces that mold the inner lives of Miriam and Young Goodman Brown are no more capable of easy analysis than the problem of evil in Melville's *Pierre*.[120] Hence the characters lack definition, the forces they grapple with are intangible, and the outward action, like as not, ends in rumor. Readers and reviewers rebelled against this apparent betrayal of their interest. They were exasperated by Hawthorne's habit of setting up a fleet of hypotheses among which the reader must choose—without ultimate corroboration or correction by the author.[121] The incompleteness of *The Marble Faun* caused the English reviewers to remark petulantly: "a mystery is set before us, and at the end the author turns round and asks us what is the good of solving it."[122] In response to many requests Hawthorne added a chapter of elucidation, most of which, as he virtually admitted, proved to be "clear as a London fog."[123] Some things Hawthorne cleared up, but he staunchly refused to capitulate to those literal-minded readers who wished to know definitely whether Donatello had furry ears or not, for said Hawthorne, to "all who ask such questions, the book is, to that extent, a failure."[124] Hawthorne was not interested in factual resolution, but in disclosing glimpses of beauty and facets of truth. *The Scarlet Letter* does not "settle" anything. The beauty in Hawthorne is apprehensible everywhere, but the meaning is often elusive, for Hawthorne knew that the scheme of the universe requires that "truth" itself be constantly oriented. He was interested in dangerous corners in the spiritual life of his characters, but the wisest course to take he seldom trusted himself to indicate. The quest for ultimate truth, he knew, must go on forever.

Explicit conclusions are rarely to be found in Hawthorne's work, but the bearing of his thought is understandable. He is dealing with intangibles, seeking the metaphysical link which should bind the spiritual world to the universe we live in. He seeks principally to understand the nature of good and evil and the extent to which these are subject to human control. Matters long settled for conservative thinkers by the *Institutes* of John Calvin reappear on the agenda of Nathaniel Hawthorne: what is the true nature and source of sin; are a person's acts foreordained or can he really control his conduct by free will; is a certain amount of "depravity" inborn; can a sinner hope for grace through repentance? Hawthorne's conclusions with reference to these and kindred questions have a certain homogeneity, but they are neither comprehensive nor constant. Readers accustomed to finding a "moral" at the end of each story may be disappointed.[125] Nor does the sum of his conclusions equal a system, for Hawthorne reaches results "by intuition, not by logic."[126]

One thing is certain, that although sunshine and shadow intermingle in Hawthorne's stories, the shadows are more powerful. Occasionally Hawthorne postulates a Providence controlling human events, as in "David Swan." It was by "God's providence" that his daughter Una recovered from a serious illness in Italy.[127] Once he seems to advocate prayer.[128] Pardon seems possible even for the chief sinner of *The Scarlet Letter* for "to own a sin is to disown it." [129] The resolution of a moral knot by confession and expiation sometimes brings a sober satisfaction which may be set down on the side of optimism.[130] Donatello's fearful experience of human sin appears to have been salutary in that by it he was brought within the pale of natural experience. Says Miriam:

> He has travelled in a circle, as all things heavenly and earthly do, and now comes back to his original self, with an inestimable treasure of improvement won from an experience of pain . . . Was the crime a blessing in disguise? [131]

Establishing a bond with humanity—that seems to be the great good. At the end of those stories in which such a bond is established there is consequently an effect of *katharsis*. Yet it seldom removes the last vestiges of Hawthorne's dark speculations. Says Melville: "For spite of all the Indian-summer sunlight on the hither side of Hawthorne's soul, the other side—like the dark half of the physical sphere—is shrouded in a blackness, ten times black." [132] A modified pessimism is the normal mood of Hawthorne. The influences that he received during the "frozen purgatory" of his childhood were never removed from his heart. Even as a lad he had picked out his grave,[133] and throughout his life as a writer he never ceased to be preoccupied with scenes in which children are seen weeping or playing over graves. Hawthorne's imperfectly articulated philosophy only supplements impressions created by mood and image.

Generalizations about Hawthorne's religion are somewhat hazardous because his comments on it are often indirect and sometimes contradictory. They are found in story and essay. He apparently had something like Emerson's distrust of the "official goodness" of ministers. Theological treatises held very little of value for him. When in the garret of the Manse he found a number of old religious books, he sharply evaluated their contents:

> Then there was a vast folio body of divinity—too corpulent a body, it might be feared, to comprehend the spiritual element of religion. Volumes of this form dated back two hundred years or

more, and were generally bound in black leather, exhibiting precisely such an appearance as we should attribute to books of enchantment . . .

The rain pattered upon the roof and the sky gloomed through the dusty garret windows, while I burrowed among these venerable books in search of any living thought which should burn like a coal of fire, or glow like an inextinguishable gem, beneath the dead trumpery that had long hidden it. But I found no such treasure; all was dead alike; and I could not but muse deeply and wonderingly upon the humiliating fact that the works of man's intellect decay like those of his hands. Thought grows mouldy. What was good and nourishing food for the spirits of one generation affords no sustenance for the next. Books of religion, however, cannot be considered a fair test of the enduring and vivacious properties of human thought, because such books so seldom really touch upon their ostensible subject, and have, therefore, so little business to be written at all. So long as an unlettered soul can attain to saving grace, there would seem to be no deadly error in holding theological libraries to be accumulations of, for the most part, stupendous impertinence.[134]

Ritual may have interested him more than doctrine, but his austere temperament and background prevented his taking much consolation in it. In mature years he seldom, if ever, attended church services.[135] Although Rome captured his imagination so completely that he seemed to have a certain fondness for Catholicism[136] it is inconceivable that he felt deeply attracted to the Romish church. On a rare visit to York Cathedral he felt uncomfortable in the presence of Anglican forms: "The spirit of my Puritan ancestors was mighty in me."[137] The austerity of his early life bound him to simple if vague articles of belief. In his seclusion he might almost as well have been in the eighteenth century as far as new thought was concerned. Lloyd Morris has called Hawthorne a "rebellious Puritan." Some distrust of orthodox religious pronouncements must indeed be inferred from his tentative plan of using his energies at the Manse in setting down "a layman's unprofessional and therefore unprejudiced views of religion."[138] Certainly he harbored Calvinistic thoughts from time to time, but to what extent he endorsed them intellectually it is hard to estimate because, like Milton, he had artistic uses for outmoded systems of thought. Even the doctrine of universal depravity appears to have had fascination for him, and although he probably did not accept it literally he may have found it "empirically true."[139] This view is borne out by his frequent references to the Fall of Man and to a hypothetical "Golden Age, before mankind was burdened with sin and sorrow."[140] A modified predestination he also found a convenient basis for explaining man's apparent inability to cope successfully with regeneration in this world. A cloud of determinism darkened his outlook. In *The Marble Faun* he allows Miriam to meditate on fatalism:

> "As these busts in the block of marble," thought Miriam, "so does our individual fate exist in the limestone of time. We fancy that we carve it out; but its ultimate shape is prior to all our action." [141]

In this case the determination is antecedent philosophically. But in other instances Hawthorne implies that an unfortunate impulsion toward sin may be made active only in "favorable" circumstances, that is, only if environment brings out evil:

> There is evil in every human heart, which may remain latent, perhaps, through the whole of life; but circumstances may rouse it to activity. [142]

In one of his tales he speaks of his desire to "exemplify how an influence beyond our control lays its strong hand on every deed which we do, and weaves its consequences into an iron tissue of necessity." [143] Like Hardy, he seems at times to have believed that "tragedy is true guise; comedy lies." [144] Like Hardy, too, he exhibits a certain tenderness toward sinners, for in reality chance often determines their "character." Yet such tenderness is more conspicuous in Hardy than in Hawthorne, for Hawthorne is less interested in exonerating men than in dwelling on their unhappy condition. It is clear that Calvinism constituted a real challenge to Hawthorne's mind and that emotionally, at least, he often surrendered to its spirit. Indeed he seems to have taken a melancholy comfort in exploring its gloomy negations.

Hawthorne's Calvinism remains indefinite but his gloom is undeniable. His stories are pervaded by a constant sense of the loss of Eden. He employs references to sunlight more repeatedly than almost any writer of fiction, but for him sunlight always connotes shadow. He seems to have believed with Miriam that man's "moments of gloom and despondency [are] his moments of deepest insight." [145] He is puzzled by the approximation of innocence and evil, symbolized by the dove and the serpent,[146] but his stories are governed more by the serpent than by the dove. Wrong-doing weaves itself sinuously through his works, and he is not sure that its power does not exceed that of innocence: "Sin, alas! is careful of her bond slaves" and the powers of darkness may even "snatch a guilty soul from the gate of heaven." [147] Formal attempts to eradicate evil he regarded as futile, for such attempts do not reach the real fortress of evil, which is that " 'foul cavern' " the human heart.[148] Redemption in another life is a possibility but the "moral gloom of the world overpowers all systematic gayety." [149] It is significant that Hawthorne uses the words "gayety" and "mirth" a great deal and seldom "happiness." There is in his pages much gayety, but it is generally a carnival clown's strained gayety, not far removed from hysteria and despair. Unalloyed happiness and enjoyment come to man "seldom or never," [150] and when it does come it comes after pain. Says Miriam to Donatello: "You cannot suffer deeply; therefore you can but half enjoy." [151] Such shadows as these trouble most of Hawthorne's characters. The very blackest despair Hawthorne generally avoids, but he functions in a heavy philosophical twilight. At the bottom of his well of mysticism lurked a terrible spectre of doubt.

Hawthorne's complete absorption in the moral domain led him into a pessimism that corresponds to his captiousness as a critic. He was not a keen observer of the outward life of his generation; but when he did relax from his moral studies, he beheld no very edifying conditions in the fields of social, political, and literary life of his contemporaries.

A friend of Pierce at Bowdoin, he later wrote a partisan book that showed his leaning toward conservatism.[152] He was a strong Democrat. The slavery issue irked him perhaps because he had no solution in mind for "the present generation of negroes, the childhood of whose race is now gone forever, and who must henceforth fight a hard battle with the world." [153] He sympathized with "poor fugitives" [154] but his hatred of reformers included abolitionists.[155] He himself summed up his views on the subject by saying that he was "rather more of an abolitionist in feeling than in principle." [156] He thought John Brown "justly hanged." [157] He was so strongly sectional that he even thought favorably of the hypothesis that New England might some day become a "separate nation." [158] National problems held relatively small interest for him, and though he loved his native land he despised petty patriotism. He looked for no quick amelioration of national (or human) affairs, for although he felt that each generation must fight to escape evils of the past it was a mistake to suppose "that this age, more than any past or future one, is destined to see the tattered garments of Antiquity exchanged for a new suit, instead of gradually renewing themselves by patchwork." [159] He was by nature conservative. He wisely forswore politics after the unhappy experience of being dislodged from the Custom House at Salem—and he wanted nothing to do with politicians thereafter, for "their hearts wither away, and die out of their bodies." [160] In general, Hawthorne was much less a critic of his generation than Cooper, for he was more of an artist and could not give himself for long as a partisan to any cause however honorable.

Nor was Hawthorne prone to comment extensively on the state of society generally. He believed in formal education but did not worship it, for he shared with Emerson a distrust of organization. The education of women, he believed, needed improvement in the direction of solidity. The social behavior of advanced women was apparently not to his liking. Both Zenobia (in *The Blithedale Romance*) and Hester Prynne reflect traces of his animosity toward presumptuous feminism.[161] Yet he did not endorse the widely accepted Victorian view that the only criteria of success for a woman were domestic and emotional.[162] Hawthorne seems to have had a certain scorn for America because of her lack of tradition.[163] Yet with a lingering resentment on account of undue British contempt for America, he frequently lashed British social behavior.[164] He always looked with a certain suspicion on professional men, as a group. Lawyers were largely parasites, physicians were often the subject of indirect censure in his stories: their danger was needless experiment on human lives.[165] Ministers did not escape his reproof, for notwithstanding his temperamental sympathy with Puritanism, he feared the assumption of too great authority on their part.[166] As an artist, he was nourished by the past, but he chafed against the bondage it imposed on the living present. Into the mouth of Holgrave he puts one of his most eloquent social tirades:

> "Shall we never, never get rid of this Past?" cried he, keeping up the earnest tone of his preceding conversation. "It lies upon the Present like a giant's dead body! In fact, the case is just as if a young giant were compelled to waste all his strength in carrying about the corpse of the old giant, his grandfather, who died a long while ago, and only needs to be decently buried. Just think a moment, and it will startle you to see what slaves we are to bygone times,—to Death, if we give the matter the right word!" . . .
>
> "For example, then," continued Holgrave: "a dead man, if he happen to have made a will, disposes of wealth no longer his own; or, if he die intestate, it is distributed in accordance with the notions of men much longer dead than he. A dead man sits on all our judgment-seats; and living judges do but search out and repeat his decisions. We read in dead men's books! We laugh at dead men's jokes, and cry at dead men's pathos! We are sick of dead men's diseases, physical and moral, and die of the same

remedies with which dead doctors killed their patients! We worship the living Deity according to dead men's forms and creeds. Whatever we seek to do, of our own free motion, a dead man's icy hand obstructs us! Turn our eyes to what point we may, a dead man's white, immitigable face encounters them, and freezes our very heart! And we must be dead ourselves before we can begin to have our proper influence on our own world, which will then be no longer our world, but the world of another generation, with which we shall have no shadow of a right to interfere. I ought to have said, too, that we live in dead men's houses; as, for instance, in this of the Seven Gables!" [167]

Yet Hawthorne was a trifle difficult to please on the issue of past-versus-present and in the *Mosses*, after a long meditation on the subject of books, old and new, he concludes that there

appeared no hope of either mounting to the better world on a Gothic staircase of ancient folios or of flying thither on the wings of a modern tract. [168]

A certain modicum of new thought he welcomed, but his hatred of cranks and reformers led him to condemn new-fangled religion and the "vaguely liberal clergymen" of his day. [169] Especially did he condemn a "terrible giant . . . German by birth . . . called Giant Transcendentalist" which looked "like a heap of fog and duskiness." [170] He admired Emerson's poetry but "sought nothing from him as a philosopher." [171] A certain vagueness in Hawthorne's own philosophical speculations as well as his residence in Concord led Poe to ascribe to Hawthorne more sympathy with transcendentalism than he actually had and to suggest that he "cut Mr. Alcott" in order to escape the habit of allegory. [172] But there was little need to fear that Hawthorne would be intoxicated by the bubbling optimism of Concord: he much preferred his own slightly bitter brew drawn from the musty vats of Calvinism.

A man who was obliged to wait as long as Hawthorne for recognition could hardly be expected to have much respect for the literary criticism of his day. Yet Hawthorne showed comparatively little rancor. The literary production of America before his day he appraised with a fairly dispassionate eye. He made merry over the epic productions of Barlow and Dwight; he had a word of praise for Brown; Bryant he thought had "gone to his last sleep, with the Thanatopsis gleaming over him like a sculptured marble sepulchre by moonlight." [173] In general he thought that our literature was growing up slowly. [174] For other contemporary poets he had more praise, especially Emerson and Lowell. [175]

To Whittier, the militant Quaker, however, the Muse had "perversely assigned a battle trumpet." [176] In fiction he deplored poor characters drawn by writers of romance for being "lukewarm and abortive characters, composed of heterogeneous materials, used for the thousandth time." [177] His most fervid criticisms were leveled at "the d———d mob of scribbling women," [178] whose prolific productions, he felt, were partly responsible for his own failure to get recognition.

Hawthorne's contemporary reputation has already been indicated in part. From the first he was appreciated by the more discriminating, including S. G. Goodrich, Horatio Bridge, Park Benjamin, Poe, Melville, James T. Fields, Whitman, Ellery Channing, and others. Emerson's disapproval, which Hawthorne must have sensed, was no doubt a real discouragement to a man of Hawthorne's extreme diffidence.[179] Melville's public avowal of admiration was a great compensation: "I found that but to glean after this man, is better than to be in at the harvest of others." [180] Even the burly William Gilmore Simms, whose rugged writing was so different from Hawthorne's, saw signs of great power in the author of *The Scarlet Letter* and *The House of the Seven Gables*.[181] After 1852 praise flowed in from all quarters, and in 1879 Henry James expressed what was undoubtedly a widely held opinion when he wrote that "in the field of letters, Hawthorne is the most valuable example of the American genius." [182]

Hawthorne now has an understanding public, never large but renewed constantly, which embraces readers who have learned to take him for what he is. These readers know his reticences and his perversities. They know he mixes reality and history with allegory and metaphysics in such a way as to produce a beautiful and baffling fantasy. They know he is a conscienceless repeater of somewhat cheerless conclusions. They understand he is obsessed by the danger of that "perverted wisdom" of science which results in alienating man from his fellows. They realize that his art is so special that he largely ignores the simple melodies of daily life, but they are not rendered uncomfortable by his strange, subtle orchestration or by his eerie harmonics. They have heard it said that he lacked "ardour," [183] but they know that an icy exterior does not preclude the possibility of a tidy fire glowing on the hearth inside. They are not dismayed by his prophetic pictures—gloomy in tone but rich in beauty and truth. On a small margin of "insulated emotion" his readers (like his characters) learn to subsist soberly but much alive to the magic of his stories and the witchery of his prose. They look for no tides of violence in his stories but for gentle osmotic pressure. They know that the tiny rill of his allegory will carry more meaning and delight than the torrential stream of many a tale of bluster and passion or the oceans of tears in which the domestic novel foundered. They know that he is shy of definite conclusions in fable or philosophy, but they believe he seldom leaves more than a reasonable doubt in a world of relativity.[184] They know that although he tells no more exciting tale than Wordsworth told in "Simon Lee," yet after the story is over much wisdom will be found lingering in the mind. They know that there is a sense in which he who loses his story shall find it. The tales that Hawthorne left half-told will call him up in men's minds for generations to come.

This long term public is a specialized public. Men of his own generation, accustomed to the throbbing romances of Cooper and Paulding and Simms, fumbled long before finding his light pulse; but once they found the real Hawthorne, they valued him for his quiet vitality and they were delighted by his quaint humor, his sombre wisdom, and his enchanting voice. The better readers among them discovered in him one of the first great literary artists of America.

Herman Melville
(1819-1891)

When Melville dedicated *Moby-Dick* to Nathaniel Hawthorne, he happily linked the names of two major novelists who had reached the meridian of their powers almost at the same moment in the middle of the century. Both were artists who had much ado to fit their genius to the times. Though "novelists," both were finally less interested in tidy narratives designed to provide entertainment than in using a fictional theme for searching out the secrets of the universe and of the nature of man. Melville realized as much as Hawthorne the danger of the quest for final meanings, for "all the eyes we get beyond our own but minister to infelicity," [1] but no more than Hawthorne could he forbear to exercise his intuitions. Yet Melville also had a taste for more robust narrative, and his stories are not only great works of artistry, but, with some exceptions, extremely readable. His narrative abilities were recognized immediately upon the publication of his first book in 1846 (*Typee*). Certain idiosyncrasies appeared in a few years, however, which accounted for the neglect into which his books later fell, to be rescued only within relatively recent years. Now, with Hawthorne, he stands as one of our indubitably great writers.

LIFE AND EARLY WORKS. The great renascence of interest in the works of Herman Melville which may be said to have begun in 1921 with the publication of Weaver's biography[2] has scotched two principal errors. The first is that except for a little attention bestowed upon *Moby-Dick* Melville was almost entirely unappreciated until the twentieth century. Actually Melville was so widely read on account of his first two books *Typee* (1846) and *Omoo* (1847) that he seemed destined for a substantial career as a writer of popular fiction. The other erroneous idea is that after *Moby-Dick* Melville wrote only "incomprehensible" books that could in no way bear comparison with his earlier works. For the past twenty years, however, Melville has received an amount of attention which can best be compared with the enormous attention accorded Walt Whitman slightly earlier. Editions not only of *Moby-Dick* but of earlier and later works have flooded the popular market, and Melville's life has been studied to the last detail. Even in academic circles, where for many years he was coldly received, he has been accorded the full meed of recognition. At this moment there is probably more scholarly interest in Melville than in any other major American writer, Poe not excepted.

All this is cold comfort for Melville, who lived in comparative seclusion for nearly three decades and who died in personal obscurity in 1891. For whatever the present reputation of Melville it is certain that between 1852 and approximately 1920 his reputation with the arbiters of American letters was but low.[3] Reasons for Melville's loss of prestige after his brief period of popularity are fairly clear. He was in many ways a misfit in his generation. His *Typee* and *Omoo* (properly expurgated) were regarded as good "travel books." For the rest, *Moby-Dick* was spoiled by digression and documentation: *Mardi* was obscure; and *Pierre* was profane. The last charge was the most serious: Melville "sinned blackly against the orthodoxy of his time."[4] He was perhaps basically no more unorthodox than Emerson, but whereas Emerson's individualism ultimately carried him to uplands of optimism which he shared with people who reached the same goal by more conventional paths, Melville's dissent pitched him into moods of bleak despair and bitter cynicism which barred his later books from the firesides of Victorian America. Like Hawthorne he was too much preoccupied with evil to be continuously entertaining as a novelist. But whereas Hawthorne managed his pessimism without arousing doubts about his essential godliness, Melville's sharp invective of missionary practices and free satire of orthodox religions smelled like blasphemy, and his frank exposure of what he conceived to be the hypocritical basis of ordinary moral codes made him an uncomfortable prophet. Nor could conservative folk fully trust a man who in his youth had led a vagrant sort of life in the pagan islands of the South Seas. The books of such a man could hardly be "safe."

To recover Melville the artist from these *argumenta ad hominem* has been the work of years. Nowadays one hears of distaste for Melville's prolixity, but those who do not find him attractive are more prone to avoid him than to condemn him. More and more readers are found who agree with the panegyric comments of Barrie and Masefield[5] as well as the enthusiastic endorsement of a British critic who ranked the author of *Moby-Dick* "with Rabelais, Swift, Shakespeare, and other minor and disreputable worthies."[6] Personal predilections have been supported by critical judgments. In a thoroughly considered study, John Freeman called Melville "the most powerful of all the great American writers." [7] Nor is Melville's reputation, any more than Conrad's, to be ultimately based on his ability to write mere "sea romances"; rather he is valued for his fundamentally real approaches to universal problems. Probably few discerning critics now differ radically from Lewis Mumford's pronouncement that "in depth of experience and religious insight there is scarcely any one in the nineteenth century, with the exception of Dostoyevsky, who can be placed beside him." [8] Whether Melville's fame will remain on the high level it has now reached can only be conjectured, but in view of his belated recognition it is unlikely that he will ever suffer a serious loss of prestige. He will doubtless always remain one of the great writers in English.

Although Melville tasted popularity while Hawthorne was still nursing his wrath as a neglected writer, he was fifteen years younger than Hawthorne. He was born on August 1, 1819, at 6 Pearl Street, New York City. Upon principle Melville objected to undue pride in one's lineage, but he frequently recalled in later years that he was a descendant, on his mother's side, of a family of Dutch origin distinguished for service during the Revolutionary War and, on his father's, of a strain of worthy Scotch blood that could be traced to the time of Edward the First.[9] His paternal grandfather, Thomas Melville, genially described by Holmes in "The Last Leaf," was a well-to-do and slightly eccentric Boston merchant whose patrician instincts had not prevented him from being a patriot during the Revolution. His father, Allan Melville, was apparently a man with access to more avenues to culture than he ever fully explored. An importer of French goods, he traveled a great deal, but the secrets of the sea like those of his fairly good library remained for his son Herman Melville to unlock. Both Melville's grandfather and his father died in 1832, when Melville was thirteen, and although his mother lived on for nearly forty years, Melville soon had to turn his hand to earning a living, for his father's business had fallen away considerably before his death and Melville naturally did not look to his rather distinguished circle of affluent relatives for support.

The early years of Melville's minority by no means prophesied his career except insofar as they brought him a fair share of hardship and unhappiness. His education at Albany Academy was of necessity interrupted. Doing a clerk's work in a bank and selling hats neither fattened his purse nor nourished his spirit. Next came a brief interval at farmwork near Pittsfield, helping Uncle Thomas. Then a period at teaching school before he returned to his mother's board. All this time the lad was becoming reconciled to the family's loss of position and prestige, the likelihood that he would never go to college, and his dreary bondage to work-a-day commercial life. Yet he longed for greater personal independence and spiritual latitude. And so, observing how hard it was for his mother to feed eight children, he bethought himself that his absence might be a blessing to his family and the means of satisfying his "naturally roving disposition."[10] He shipped for Liverpool on the merchantman *Highlander* in June, 1837.[11] A mere lad of seventeen, unacquainted with the hard discipline of marine life, Melville was sharply initiated into the discipline of the ship, the filth of the forecastle, the culinary atrocities of a cook whom Melville never saw wash but once,[12] and the general brutality of life aboard a trader. Nor did the weeks he spent in Liverpool and a possible trip to London prove to be merely a tourist's Paradise. Historic England he saw, but he also saw at a tender age the shockingly degraded excesses of drunken and diseased sailors in waterfront dens designed to despoil them of their wages.

After this initiation into crass reality, Melville returned to an environment (upper New York State) less abrasive to his sensitive nature but little more congenial to his spirit. The years between 1837 and 1841 are meagre in biographical remains, but it is clear that he led a decorous existence as a (probably itinerant) schoolmaster in Greenbush (now East Albany) and Pittsfield and as an amateur of letters. Those examples of his juvenile attempts that have been identified show that he was seeking to find a focus for his art. He contributed letters to *The Democratic Press and Lansingburgh Advertiser*[13] that revealed typical adolescent faults of a potentially good writer: a harmless indulgence in over-polished phrasing and excessive literary allusion. They were, he was later to say satirically, "characterised throughout by Perfect Taste."[14] Certainly more action and less verbal dalliance would seem to have been the best prescription for the author of this account of a girl's eyes:

> And then her eyes! They open their dark, rich orbs upon you like the full noon of heaven, and blaze into your very soul the fires of day! Like the offerings laid upon the sacrificial altars of the Hebrews, when in an instant the divine spark falling from the propitiated God kindled them in flames; so, a single glance from that Oriental eye as quickly fires your soul, and leaves your bosom in a perfect conflagration! Odds Cupids and Darts! with one broad sweep of vision in a crowded ballroom, that splendid creature would lay around her like the two-handed sword of Minotti, hearts on hearts, piled round in semicircles! But it is well for the more rugged sex that this glorious being can vary her proud dominion, and give to the expression of her eye a melting tenderness which dissolves the most frigid heart, and heals the wounds she gave before.[15]

Melville later realized that his originality had scarcely budded in these early leaves, but it is likely that he took his first "creative agonies" quite seriously.[16]

If action was what Melville needed to cure him of his painted-porcelain habits of composition, the remedy was at hand in plentiful measure. Full twenty-one years of age Melville sailed from Fairhaven for the South Seas on January 3, 1841. He returned to Boston in 1844 with most of the outward experience in hand which, when supplemented by his metaphysical speculations, was to provide the material for his novels. The motives leading to this prolonged adventure were mixed. Melville had been no great success in the various capacities in which he had tested himself—as clerk, salesman, farmer, school-teacher. It is clear from the books later to be written, that he regarded himself as unfitted to cope with a competitive industrial order. Furthermore he was apparently oppressed by the iron mores of the respectable society in which he moved. There were no signs of a proneness to dissolute living in him, but he vaguely yearned to be free. Possibly there were personal disappointments and frustrations natural to a lad of his years. On the positive side, Melville seems to have been endowed with a strange wanderlust. From his earliest years he was (like the Ishmael of *Moby-Dick*) possessed of an "itch for things remote . . . forbidden seas . . . barbarous coasts." [17] One may even read "Melville" for "Ishmael" when the latter avows that one of his "[c]hief . . . motives was the overwhelming idea of the great whale himself." [18] These desires were fed by Melville's reading, of that one may be sure. The oft-repeated statement that he was inspired by Dana's *Two Years Before the Mast* is of somewhat doubtful validity, for Dana's book was not published until October and Melville arrived at the port of New Bedford in December.[19] But other books and journals there were, and some of these dealt with whaling. One of them recounted adventures of a ship which had carried one of Melville's uncles as far as Nukahiva (also spelled Nukuheva) in the Marquesas Islands, the future scene of Melville's *Typee*.[20] These were the influences—economic, personal, and literary—which sent Melville to the South Seas. Their exact proportions one cannot know, but their aggregate weight must have been considerable, for Melville not only went to extremely remote coasts but he stayed far longer than there was necessity for.

The facts of Melville's life during his Odyssey in the South Seas may be found in broad outline in those books which he subsequently spun from his experiences—*Typee*, *Omoo*, *White Jacket*, and (to a less extent) *Mardi*, but recent research has shown that Melville freely mixed fact and fiction at many points.[21] The major facts are clear. Aboard the whaler *Acushnet*, which was his "Yale College and [his] Harvard," Melville went as a common seaman as far as Nukahiva, in the Marquesas Islands.[22] By this time (the summer of 1842) he had found the educational program of the *Acushnet* so little to his liking that, in the company of a shipmate, Richard Tobias Greene, he played truant and remained hidden on the island of Nukahiva until the *Acushnet* had departed. In the valley of Typee he spent several weeks in "indulgent captivity" among cannibals who although not viciously inclined could not be relied upon to forbear exercising their talents indefinitely.[23] Melville escaped and signed on an Australian whaler which carried him to Tahiti, where he had adventures later to be recorded in *Omoo*. A mutiny broke out which neither the Captain nor port authorities could cope with, and after a few weeks of confinement on a French man-of-war and in a British jail ashore Melville was free to explore the tropical wonders and observe the discouraging conditions of people living in the Society Islands. Wearying of this idyllic vagabondage and disheartening survey, made in the company of a physician, he appears to have sailed early in 1843 on another whaler for a protracted voyage of which he left no detailed account. The route seems finally to have been northward and westward through the Pacific, though the coast of Japan (referred to vaguely in *Omoo* as the ship's destination) was probably never reached. At all events it was on this whaler that Melville arrived at the Sandwich Islands, reaching Honolulu in April, 1843. Here he worked for a short time as a clerk before shipping (August 17, 1843) on the man-of-war *United States* for Boston. Melville's memories of his earlier months in the Polynesian Islands were briefly renewed when the *United States* stopped at Nukahiva and Tahiti. After a fourteen-month voyage, the vessel reached Boston October 4, 1844. Melville was sharply restored to a civilized environment in which as the years went by he would find much to criticize. "The identical trees in the Boston common blotted out the same patterns against New England stars; none of the streets had swerved from off their prim and angular respectability." [24] Melville had shipped at Honolulu as an ordinary seaman, but he had come back with his head full of rich and strange memories which he would soon transmute into some of the greatest prose of our literature. Meantime he repaired to his mother's home at Lansingburgh, and thence, after his marriage to Elizabeth Shaw in 1847, to New York.

Tired of wandering, unfitted for a profession, disinclined toward commercial life or pioneering in the West, yet faced with the necessity of making a living, Melville naturally thought of authorship as a means of livelihood. His first book, *Typee* (1846), was based mainly on his experiences after he recklessly abandoned the *Acushnet* in the Marquesas Islands. It has less homogeneity than some of Melville's other books, being a mélange of adventure, idyll, and satire. The flight from the ship is recounted with bare dispatch reminiscent of Defoe, and with shrewd narrative emphasis on the danger of the undertaking; and the thrilling escape at the end is described in a straightforward manner. Yet soon after reaching the island Melville swerves from the conciseness of the Defoe-like style adopted at the beginning and shows more of that power to invest relatively unimportant detail with more than passing interest, a gift more characteristic of him than terse reporting. Humor plays near the surface throughout much of the central part of the book. Picturesque and humorous episodes gradually dissolve most of the reader's fears for the safety of Melville. The simple but relatively effective economic system and the highly informal marital arrangements are amusingly described. Leisurely descriptions of local conditions please his pen. Thus he pauses to describe a certain species of fly that infests the island:

> The tameness of the birds and lizards is as nothing when compared to the fearless confidence of this insect. He will perch upon one of your eyelashes, and go to roost there, if you do not disturb him, or force his way through your hair, or along the cavity of the nostril, till you almost fancy he is resolved to explore the very brain itself. On one occasion I was so inconsiderate as to yawn while a number of them were hovering around me. I never repeated the act. Some half-dozen darted into the open apartment, and began walking about its ceiling; the sensation was dreadful. I involuntarily closed my mouth, and the poor creatures, being enveloped in inner darkness, must in their consternation have stumbled over my palate, and been precipitated into the gulf beneath. At any rate, though I afterward charitably held my mouth open for at least five minutes, with a view of affording egress to the stragglers, none of them ever availed themselves of the opportunity.[25]

Good-natured elaboration of trivial detail, however, sometimes gives way to rather sharp satire of those white persons who, under the banner of civilization and religion, are introducing elements that ultimately must prove baneful to the simple islanders. As a primitive people—as "noble savages"—the natives of Typee have enjoyed that ideal existence which is the natural condition of people uncontaminated by contact with civilization. Melville knew of Rousseau's theories and he had observed a concrete situation in Typee. Certainly he did not understate the advantages of the simple native life:

There were none of those thousand sources of irritation that the ingenuity of civilised man has created to mar his own felicity. There were no foreclosures of mortgages, no protested notes, no bills payable, no debts of honour in Typee; no unreasonable tailors and shoemakers, perversely bent on being paid; no duns of any description; no assault and battery attorneys, to foment discord, backing their clients up to a quarrel, and then knocking their heads together; no poor relations everlastingly occupying the spare bed-chamber, and diminishing the elbow-room at the family table; no destitute widows with their children starving on the cold charities of the world; no beggars; no debtors' prisons; no proud and hard-hearted nabobs in Typee; or, to sum up all in one word—no Money! That 'root of all evil' was not to be found in the valley.

In this secluded abode of happiness there were no cross old women, no cruel step-dames, no withered spinsters, no love-sick maidens, no sour old bachelors, no inattentive husbands, no melancholy young men, no blubbering youngsters, and no squalling brats. All was mirth, fun, and high good-humour. Blue devils, hypochondria, and doleful dumps went and hid themselves among the nooks and crannies of the rocks.[26]

Yet this ideal condition must be blighted if the happy valley is subjected to the same "civilizing" and "Christianizing" processes which have occurred elsewhere in the Pacific, notably in the Sandwich Islands:

Ill-fated people! I shudder when I think of the change a few years will produce in their paradisiacal abode; and probably when the most destructive vices, and the worst attendances on civilisation, shall have driven all peace and happiness from the valley, the magnanimous French will proclaim to the world that the Marquesas Islands have been converted to Christianity! . . .

How little do some of these poor islanders comprehend when they look around them, that no inconsiderable part of their disasters originate in certain tea-party excitements, under the influence of which benevolent-looking gentlemen in white cravats solicit alms, and old ladies in spectacles, and young ladies in sober russet low gowns, contribute sixpences toward the creation of a fund, the object of which is to ameliorate the spiritual condition of the Polynesians, but whose end has almost invariably been to accomplish their temporal destruction!

Let the savages be civilised, but civilise them with benefits, and not with evils; and let heathenism be destroyed, but not by destroying the heathen . . .

Among the islands of Polynesia, no sooner are the images overturned, the temples demolished, and the idolaters converted into *nominal* Christians, than disease, vice, and premature death make their appearance . . .

There is something decidedly wrong in the practical operations of the Sandwich Island Missions . . . The demoralising influence of a dissolute foreign population, and the frequent visits of all descriptions of vessels, have tended not a little to increase the evils alluded to. In a word, here, as in every case where civilisation has in any way been introduced among those whom we call savages, she has scattered her vices, and withheld her blessings.[27]

The satirical elements, however, constitute in bulk the smallest part of *Typee*. Adventure and idyll are the principal ingredients in this, the gayest book that Melville ever wrote. In his next book (*Omoo*) he would return to the theme of social ills.

Typee was hailed from the first by a majority of reviewers as a delightful book to be enjoyed as "travels, romance, poetry or humor." [28] Not always regarded as truthful, Melville's account of the "paradise" of the valley of Typee was accepted as a charming idyll. The author's command of prose was compared favorably with that of Irving, Dr. Johnson (the comparison was with *Rasselas*), and Defoe.[29] Most common was the analogy drawn between Melville and Defoe, and the generally conservative *John Bull* wrote enthusiastically: "Since the joyous moment when we first read Robinson Crusoe, and believed it all . . . we have not met with so bewitching a work as this narrative of Herman Melville's." [30] There was also from the first much protest of persons who were offended by Melville's reflections on missionaries and his occasionally roguish (though never indecent) description of native habits of courtship and marriage. Despite the fact that *Typee* was accepted for publication in London only on Melville's assurance to Murray that it was a true relation,[31] there was a great deal of skepticism about its veracity which was dissipated only when Richard Tobias Greene, the "Toby" of *Typee*, who had escaped from the island before Melville and whom Melville thought to be dead, turned out to be living in Buffalo, New York.

Subsequent editions of *Typee* carried a sequel narrative of the exciting adventures of Toby. American editions also differed materially from the original by reason of a "revision" which amounted to a wholesale expurgation of passages regarded as likely to offend the public, principally those that satirized the missionaries or dwelt too freely on the charms of the Polynesian girls.[32] Melville appears to have consented to censorship and he even referred to the book as "measurably unscathed" by the process.[33] Yet actually the deletions were considerable, and it is likely that this instance of public displeasure bothered him later on as one of the first signs of that cloud of disapproval which gradually gathered over him. In the meantime he expanded in the warmth of measurable approval from critics and prevailing goodwill on the part of the public. Socially, too, he seems to have been happily adjusted, for upon his arrival at New York in 1847 he was admitted to parity in the influential literary coterie dominated by the Duyckinck brothers and initiated into the punch bowl parties of that somewhat patrician group. As time went on, he was to feel stifled by the literary and social climate he lived in at New York, but for many months he lent himself with apparent enjoyment to social living. Outwardly, at least, these first years in New York were "the happiest of his life." [34]

The initial success of *Typee* was great enough to spur Melville on to the composition of the second unit of what proved finally to be a trilogy based on his experiences in the South Seas and homeward bound.[35] *Omoo*, which appeared in 1847, was advertised as "the true sequel and counterpart of the author's popular production—*Typee*." [36] The "most strictly autobiographical of all Melville's works," [37] it begins with Melville's reception on board the ship (called the "Julia") to which he escaped from Typee. After the solution of the difficulties between the crew and their superiors at Tahiti, Melville set out on a desultory but delightful tour of the islands in company with Doctor Long Ghost, one of the first notable examples of Melville's ability in character-drawing, which was to be so pronounced in *Moby-Dick*. The book is even more amorphous than *Typee*, but it is equally rich in piquant reporting of a region that had not yet been exploited in American fiction. Most of the characters are "focussed with a slight distortion, through Melville's sense of the comic," [38] and the whole book is characterized by his somewhat quixotic and irresponsible tone. D. H. Lawrence, however, thought that *Omoo* shows Melville "at his best, his happiest." [39] Even here, it is true, the canker of evil troubles Melville. The satire of "civilization" is more direct than in *Typee*, and Melville's hostile comments on the Protestant mission at Tahiti evoked the charge that he was "guilty of deliberate and elaborate misrepresentations." [40] Yet the book was so well received that five printings appeared in America in its first year, and in London it was printed in 1848, 1849, and 1850. Melville's subsequent loss of popular prestige was so marked that his first accession of popularity, created by *Typee* and *Omoo*, has been lost sight of. In reality after a relatively brief apprenticeship, he became popular almost overnight,[41] and he was much more widely known in 1850 than Nathaniel Hawthorne, who had first fixed his nets for fame while Melville was but a lad.

Now a sufficiently good risk to be the object of publishers' importunities,[42] Melville next wrote a book, *Mardi* (1849), which evoked the first of those critical broadsides that seriously damaged his reputation. In this book Melville responded to the iterated assertion that his first two books were romantic fabrications by writing a tale that was avowedly romantic—"to see whether the fiction might not, possibly, be received for a verity: in some degree the reverse of my previous experience." [43] The book is so packed with extravagant fancy that it was by no means received as a "verity." Rather, despite a few laudatory notices, it was generally damned heartily as "a rubbishing rhapsody" (*Blackwood's Magazine*) and as "one of the saddest, most melancholy, most deplorable and humiliating perversions of genius in the language" (*The Dublin University Magazine*).[44] This story it was which first evoked the complaint of "incomprehensibility," later to be so often held up as a reproach to Melville.

Mardi is indeed a difficult book, very little read even now during the renascence of Melville's fame. In it Melville emerges, after introductory material not radically unlike that of *Typee* and *Omoo*, from his reliance on external fact and begins to draw on his subconscious mind. For the first time, his ideas begin to take the forms of symbol and allegory. It was a change of method fraught with peril, for readers accustomed to reckoning their narrative by ordinary instruments were unable to get their bearings in the vast reaches of Melville's imagination. In fact navigating in *Mardi* is at times little short of bewildering. Yet this erratic book represents Melville's first move in the direction of his greatest imaginative flight, in *Moby-Dick*.

The story begins in the clear light of fact with the hero's desertion, in company with the sturdy Jarl, from a whaling vessel in the Pacific. Subsequently they join forces with a strange pair, man and woman, subsisting on an otherwise deserted brigantine. The brigantine is lost in a gale, and further adventures bring the hero to an island (presumably in the Polynesian group) where he rescues an enchanting, elusive creature named Yillah. After a serene and vaguely romantic period on the island, the hero is dismayed by the disappearance of Yillah. Taji (so the hero has been dubbed) commences a long quest, accompanied by a king, an historian, a philosopher, and a poet. Naturally the gentlemen engage in unchecked discourses on assorted topics—from the meaning of eternity to a session of Congress. They visit various countries—including England, Africa, and the United States—whose identities are not completely concealed by the fanciful names applied to them. Nowhere do the wanderers discover a satisfactory haven until they reach Serenia, where the final control of action is Love. The philosopher would fain abide here, but Taji is not to be permanently deterred from his search, and he moves on. Finally they reach a region ruled by Queen Hautia, a beautiful Circe-like creature who appears to have transformed Yillah into one of her "black-eyed maidens." But Taji cannot find the "warm ray" he seeks, and despite the openly seductive wiles of Hautia he turns seaward again, leaving his companions at last to swim desperately for their lives.

The straight adventure which opens *Mardi* is understandable and even credible, but the rest of the book makes difficult reading because of the obliqueness of its presentation. It consists, however, of two elements, the satirical and the idealistic. The satirical reveals the inadequacy of most of the institutions man has established. Some of the shafts of Melville's satire are delivered with a Swiftian savagery against man in general. Others are more specific in their application and more Socratic in tone. Reflecting, perhaps, some of the ideas that were conservatively discussed at the Duyckinck soirées, Melville introduces into his satire of the United States (Vivenza) several matters of contemporary national interest: "the gold rush, the jury system, the exploitation of the Indian, the blatant spirit of nationalism, the controversy over slavery, the Mexican War, and national figures like Clay, Webster, and General Zachary Taylor." [45] The satire of *Mardi* can with patience be allocated, but the idealistic quest of Taji is less susceptible of confident analysis. For certainly the temporal objects of Melville's satire— government, law, industry—are not central in Taji's mind. In pursuing Yillah, the hero seems to be seeking a "fixed beatitude" which forever eludes him. Taji's companions counsel him wisely, using age-old maxims such as the philosopher's simple statement: "Within our hearts is all we seek." [46] It may be, that as related in Babbalanja's vision, man is destined never to know "the last mystery which underlieth all the rest." [47] But Taji, "fixed as fate," is impelled to go on "beyond the reef," forever seeking that which he can scarcely define for himself. In general terms it is clear that his search is for absolute or ultimate truth, and the probability is that for Melville the possession of ultimate truth meant the revelation of the nature of good and evil. The quest is an old one, stated and restated in various ages. In Melville's time—so recent and so complete had been the triumph of Calvinistic dogma—the sluices of speculation naturally needed to be reopened in order to cope with the new findings of science. Yet this simple statement of Melville's purpose very imperfectly suggests the nature of *Mardi*, which is a vehicle not of logic but of intuition and art. One never forgets the germ of desperate aspiration in which the book began, but one is beguiled by the tree of fractional knowledge to which it finally gives life. Its growth is irregular, its form less than symmetrical. Yet as one turns its leaves of image, fable, vision, and satire, one is overwhelmed by the sincere fervor of Melville's thought, the prodigality of his invention, the artfulness of his literary borrowings, and his dazzling display of language. For the stylistic tone of the book is as mixed as its ideology. The bare idiom of an adventure story gives way to the most elaborate involutions of archaic syntax and diction. Corrosive satire is sometimes put away in favor of "a snow of softest syllables." [48] Passages of lyric beauty are jostled by commonplace phraseology. The frequent citation of remote places— a device which in *Moby-Dick* helps to create the effect of magnitude— here seems forced and rhetorical. Perhaps beauty preponderates in *Mardi*, but the total effect of the book, both in substance and style, is at first baffling.

At all events Melville's general public was disappointed by *Mardi*. Clearly what it valued in Melville's earlier books was his faculty of reporting Robinson-Crusoe-like adventures and distilling exotic perfumes in a South Sea paradise. All this had been comprehensible enough, and whether it was fact or fiction mattered little so long as the effect was that of a slightly superior travelogue. But when in *Mardi* Melville began to explore the turbulent recesses of his subconscious mind, his public and many critics felt betrayed. They were revolted by the buckets of dark philosophy that were offered for their examination. They recoiled when Melville challenged the very bases of hallowed traditions, moral, religious, and political, of the day. They were puzzled by his Thoreau-like comments on faith: "And it is only of our easy faith, that we are not infidels throughout; and only of our lack of faith, that we believe what we do." [49] *Mardi* could hardly be a welcome book to a public which had recently been buying thousands of copies of *Evangeline* and would soon be devouring Susan Warner's *The Wide, Wide World*. *Mardi*'s world was too remote, and its fantasy-born characters were too illusory. The forty-niners could understand a gold-rush but hardly a metaphysical El Dorado. Readers suspected the existence of veiled cynicism in whimsically obscure passages. Worst of all, perhaps, the book didn't get anywhere; it reached no conclusion. The general public craves happy certainties and snug finalities; Melville could offer it only endless quest:

> Thus deeper and deeper into Time's endless tunnel, does the winged soul, like a night-hawk, wend her wild way; and finds eternities before and behind; and her last limit is her everlasting beginning. [50]

Yet when all is said, all faults counted in, *Mardi* is even yet not appreciated properly. The lover of Melville finds in it so much wealth, so much honest effort to face eternal problems, so many pools of poetry on the shimmering isles of fantasy, so much Puckish humor, that he no more resents its occasional gaucherie and extravagance than he is offended by the awkward age of a boy becoming a man. *Mardi* is Melville's spiritual adolescence. True critical charity will be kind to it.

The brutal invective hurled at *Mardi* created wounds from which Melville never recovered, for though he lived a long life, his spirit was as sensitive as that of a Keats. His jocose manner had covered intimate elements in his creed, and his Quixotic linguistic front was not entirely burlesque. He cherished his own art even if he did not wear his pride upon his sleeve. A young man (he was but thirty), he had essayed a higher flight than before; but, he exclaimed, when a writer in need of money "attempts anything higher, God help him and save him!" [51] So much did he take criticism of his writing to heart that instead of hitting back he resolved never to speak harshly of another's book:

> In a little notice of the "Oregon Trail" I once said something "critical" about another man's book—I shall never do it again. Hereafter I shall no more stab at a book (in print, I mean) than I would stab at a man.[52]

Mardi was a book that, as Weaver points out, belongs in the category of many great books: "*Penguin Island, Figures of Earth, Gulliver's Travels, Erehwon, Candide, The New Republic*, and *Alice in Wonderland*," [53] but it evoked the first wave of those hostile criticisms that ultimately bruised Melville irremediably. Even the friendship of the Duyckinck brothers could not save him. Melville had turned a corner.

Though *Mardi* was "driven forth like a wild mystic Mormon into shelterless exile," [54] a better commercial fate, at least, befell another book published in the same year, 1849, for *Redburn* was written "for the million," [55] in the vein that the public had first valued in Melville. Though there are passages of whimsicality and Dickensian interludes, the main narrative is simple and clear. It is a chronicle touched up in detail doubtless but essentially reporting Melville's external experience in his first extended voyage—on the trader *Highlander* to Liverpool and back. Redburn starts out with a romantic conception of sailing and sailors that would have been expected in Longfellow or Irving, but the fresh breezes of realism soon begin to blow about his head. Realism was as true a facet of Melville's art as philosophizing, and the book is full of ruddy description and narrative based on his maiden voyage. The portrait of Jackson—"the foul lees and dregs of a man" who nevertheless "understood human nature to a kink"—is a masterpiece. Redburn's experiences as a novice are graphically reported on the outward voyage, though a little side-tracked on the return. Despite the fact that the narrative is confined to a single comparatively brief voyage Melville manages to sandwich in many interesting themes. *Redburn* is in fact like most of Melville's books, a miscellany, and after the reader has galloped through the surface "story" he may go back afoot to enjoy at leisure passages on the beauty of the sea, the habits of whales, the English countryside, echoes from Elizabethan days, contemporary London and its great land-marks, as well as a number of literary knick-knacks and a delightful chapter on old guide books. From the point of view of Melville's concern with the theme of evil, there is not so much material in *Redburn* as in some of the other books. The author reports rather than describes the depravity of sections of Liverpool: the "lanes and alleys" that are "putrid with vice and crime," houses that have a "reeking, Sodom-like, and murderous look," and characters to whom "kidnappers, burkers, and resurrectionists are almost saints and angels." [56] He speaks briefly of sailors as a tough lot who will need a good deal of help to arise from the "mire" in which they exist.[57] The dependence of Liverpool upon the slave-trade calls to mind the "struggle between sordid interest and humanity" to which slavery had given rise.[58] He dwells on the large number of beggars and frequent instances of extreme poverty he observes. Yet all these subjects, though serious, are treated with far more detachment than is observable in most of Melville's comments on evil and suffering. *Redburn* is mainly story and episode. The London interlude is perhaps overlong for general readers, but for the most part the book can be enjoyed (despite much unsavory detail) on the plane of objective fact. It may be added that inasmuch as Melville was of all "sea-writers" the least interested in the actual technique of sailing, the reader is spared those nautical details that often confound the landsman reader. *Redburn* has had a fair share of enthusiastic readers, and Masefield preferred it to all of Melville's other books. He loved it, however, as a "boy's book about running away to sea." [59] *Redburn* pricks the balloon of popular notions of sailing[60] without losing that essential romance which Masefield, Conrad, and Melville himself so fully enjoyed. But the outward eye of Melville, keen as it was, ultimately conferred less distinction upon him than his rare imagination. And although *Redburn* put "money into an empty purse" Melville himself expressed an at least partially sincere hope that he would "never write such a book again." [61]

The author of four books, Melville "had made reputation, but fortune was still to make." [62] Indeed despite the fair success of three of his books, overdrafts on the Harpers had left him by February 22, 1850, in debt to the company more than seven hundred dollars.[63] As pater-familias Melville felt his responsibilities fairly heavily, and accordingly he planned henceforth to market his books with what acumen he could muster. In 1850 he took the manuscript of *White Jacket* abroad to sell the English rights as advantageously as possible. In London he found that people were far from indifferent to the author of *Typee* and *Omoo*. He also found a publisher, Bentley, who was willing to pay him £ 200 for the English rights to *White Jacket*, and the book was published both at New York (Harper) and London in 1850. Before leaving for home, Melville took a brief trip to Paris, an experience that was to be of use to him in retrospect when he came to write *Israel Potter*.

In *White Jacket* Melville returned to his old base of experience—the cycle of South Sea adventure (begun on the *Acushnet*), of which it reports the last three months—from Callao to Boston. The book differs from Melville's earlier "travel" stories in that its action has nothing to do with island paradises but is limited to what takes place, in reality and imaginatively, on board the *United States*, here called the "Neversink." The life of a seaman on a man-of-war is described with a great deal of detail—from the crow's nest to the fearsome quarters of the master gunner. The nautical duties and simple recreations of the tar are treated in a leisurely fashion, and the life of the officers is reported a little less freely. This account of what goes on in a "floating box of live-oak" is in itself interesting enough, but special peaks of popular interest are provided by a few episodes calculated to win readers who insist upon "action." These include flogging, a near drowning, the amputation of a leg, the smuggling of liquor from Rio, the "massacre" of the sailors' beards, and the man-of-war race with the English and French. Yet these incidents, though partly invented, do not unite to form a "plot," and Melville again stakes his reputation partly on his ability to invest minor material with significance: the Queequeg-like Polynesian servant's attempt to collect and preserve hailstones for glass beads to give his sweetheart, the grotesque colloquy between the two sail makers (surely akin to Shakespeare's grave diggers in *Hamlet*) touching the nice question of whether the customary last stitch should be taken through the nose of a dead sailor being enshrouded in canvas for sea-burial. Characterization is even richer here than in the earlier books, and Melville's genial wit, philosopher, and friend, Jack Chase, is a memorable portrait drawn from life. Jack Chase's name on naval records testifies to his actual existence. Recent research, however, has shown that, despite Melville's assertion that in writing the book he was "inventing nothing," [64] *White Jacket* must not be taken as a literal account of the last three months of the *United States*' homeward voyage. The absence of official record is almost certain proof of the fictitious origin of the amputation scene,[65] Melville's fall overboard, and the "massacre" of the beards. Many other incidents were heightened or shifted so as to lend dramatic climaxes to his medley of exposition. Roughly one-half the book must be regarded as fictitious.[66]

Despite the embroidery of fancy that constitutes a large part of *White Jacket*, no one denies that Melville's attack upon naval abuses was motivated by a real desire to bring about reform. Though he himself did not come so close to flogging as he implies,[67] flogging had by no means been abolished, and Melville's humanitarian propaganda had a real target. The results of his propaganda have, however, been exaggerated despite an angry remonstrance written by Rear-Admiral Selfridge four months after the publication of *White Jacket*.[68] Melville's position was not so radical as has been hinted, and what he recommended was legislation which would improve the common sailor's position "without relaxing the subordination, in which he should by all means be retained," and without divesting officers of their "legitimate dignity and authority." [69] Moreover this recommended reform is not so basic as to warrant agreeing with the judgment that *White Jacket* is to any considerable extent a "novel of purpose." [70] The essential Melville again is the Melville who is adept at "concocting information into wisdom," [71] and who finds his pleasure in the crow's nest reading lessons in the stars or communing in literary rhapsody with Jack Chase. Even his best satire is more literary than practical as in his revelation of the ceremony by which the cook was apprised of the wish to have pickles served to the crew,[72] and other details designed to show that "there still lingers in American men-of-war all the stilted etiquette and childish parade of the old-fashioned Spanish Court of Madrid." [73] It is not what Melville's reportorial eye observes that makes him great but what flows through the channels of his subconscious mind. This explains why *White Jacket*, though less "documented" than Dana's *Two Years Before the Mast*, is a more valuable record among the early novels telling of what may be seen elsewhere than from the bridge. The physical point of view (the forecastle) from which Melville generally wrote was lower than that employed by the more aristocratic Cooper, but in imagination he sprang from the forecastle to regions Cooper never knew. The meditations on Surgeon Cuticle and his victim[74] and the chapter on the Gunner's hold [75] are the measure of Melville's imaginative superiority to both Cooper and Smollett.

The frigate *United States* moved in its course, but on it was scant possibility for roving of the sort that lent charm to *Typee* and *Omoo*. Indeed as Melville said in *Billy Budd*, "the people of a great warship [are] in one respect like villagers . . ." [76] Hence many readers who were interested in exotic retreats and gay savage girls were not attracted by *White Jacket*. Nor did it have much currency as a document. It was not, as has been incessantly implied, placed on every Congressman's desk, and it had apparently very little weight in a movement (started in 1821) to correct naval abuses. It did not have a second edition for five years or a third until 1892. Yet in recent years the book has come into its own, and it is now rightfully regarded as one of Melville's richest books.

MOBY-DICK. In 1850 Melville left the "Babylonish brick-kiln of New York" for the more congenial surroundings of Pittsfield, where he lived for the next thirteen years, and where he wrote *Moby-Dick*. He was now entered upon the most enjoyable "literary" friendship of his life, for Hawthorne settled at about the same time in Lenox, six miles away. Melville had by now pretty well "out-grown the New York 'literati,' " [77] and in Hawthorne he found his "spiritual equal," a man who had arrived at something like "his own tragic vision of human life." [78] Much younger than Hawthorne, Melville had long been an admirer of Hawthorne's writing, and he was at the very time of their first meeting engaged in writing a review (shortly to appear in *The Literary World*) of *Mosses From an Old Manse*. In *White Jacket* he had referred to Hawthorne in playfully affectionate terms: "And would that my fine countryman, Hawthorne of Salem, had but served on board a man-of-war in his time, that he might give us the reading of a '*rill*' from the scuttle-butt." [79] And he was soon to testify further to his respect and affection for Hawthorne by dedicating *Moby-Dick* to him. The younger man poured out to Hawthorne all the cries of his lonely spirit and he confided to him his hopes and despair as a writer. Hawthorne's response to this devotion was probably not so enthusiastic as Melville could have wished, for Hawthorne's art was inspired by that seclusion which brought desolation to Melville's spirit. To establish a new friendship was not so easy for a man of Hawthorne's age. Perhaps Melville with his "infirmity of jocularity" forced himself upon Hawthorne.[80] The two never came to an open break, but in later years their friendship reached a disastrous pocket. In the meantime the association was a comforting one. A considerable measure of comradeship must be inferred from Melville's high-spirited command when he wrote Hawthorne of a plan to visit him: "Have ready a bottle of brandy, because I always feel like drinking that heroic drink when we talk ontological heroics together." [81] Certainly Hawthorne must have thawed a trifle, and if he didn't drink heroically he doubtless was valiant in conversation. Hawthorne had reviewed *Typee*[82] and in a letter to E. A. Duyckinck he had expressed warm approval of what Melville had written:

> I have read Melville's works with a progressive appreciation of the author. No writer ever put the reality before his reader more unflinchingly than he does in "Redburn" and "White Jacket." "Mardi" is a rich book, with depths here and there that compel a man to swim for his life. It is so good that one scarcely pardons the writer for not having brooded long over it so as to make it a great deal better.[83]

This was not extreme adulation, but it was highly satisfactory to one who admired Hawthorne as Melville did. Even the comments on *Mardi* must have pleased Melville, for they were more favorable than the average of contemporary critical opinion and they suggested Hawthorne's capacity for being interested in those audacious adventures of the spirit which were to reach their zenith in *Moby-Dick.*

Fundamentally Melville needed neither Hawthorne's approval nor anyone else's, for he felt the presence of great powers within him. In 1849, in a letter in which he referred to his *Redburn* as a "beggarly" book, he avowed he would yet "write such things as the Great Publisher of mankind ordained ages before he published The World." [84] In a letter to Hawthorne he later spoke whimsically of Hawthorne and himself as possessed of "divine magnet[s]" and he candidly queried, "which is the bigger." [85] Yet the period of the composition of *Moby-Dick* was a harassing one, for he "knew . . . the painful pauses and hesitations of creation, the despairing lapses and slow renewals." [86] The book was finally published on October 18, 1851.

Moby-Dick; or, The Whale is a book of such great original power, that readers are generally surprised to discover that a considerable literature of whaling existed before Melville's book appeared. How much of what had been previously written was known to Melville cannot be definitely stated, but it is clear that he was a wide reader and an antiquarian with a passion for documentation. The extracts on cetology prefixed to *Moby-Dick* indicate with what care he had culled allusions from a wide variety of books in most cases not wholly devoted to whaling. Most of the "source" books available in his time are mentioned in Weaver's *Life of Melville.*[87] Of these the principal sources acknowledged by Melville were William Scoresby's *An Account of the Arctic Regions* (1820), Obed Macy's *History of Nantucket* (1836), Owen Chase's *Narrative of the . . . Wreck of the Whale Ship Essex* (1821), and F. D. Bennett's *Narrative of a Voyage Round the World* (1833-36).

The first two of these were historical in nature and the last two, personal narratives. From the *Narrative of the Essex* by Owen Chase (whom Melville knew) Melville drew the inspiration and many of the details for the final catastrophe of the "Pequod" in *Moby-Dick*.[88] It is likely also that Joseph Hart's *Miriam Coffin* (1834), mentioned in the "Extracts," was of definite assistance to him.[89] One other account of whaling not mentioned by Melville may conceivably have fallen into his hands, for it bears a rough analogy to elements in *Moby-Dick*. This brief narrative, called *Mocha Dick or the White Whale*, by "J. N. Reynolds, Esq.," appeared first in the *Knickerbocker Magazine* in 1839.[90] In it a whaleman and a sealer engage in a lively debate during the course of which the former finally gives an account (probably highly embellished by fancy) of Mocha Dick, who was first seen and attacked some time before 1810 and finally captured after many mischances and much loss of life.[91] Particularly impressive are the fierce determination of the mate and the emphasis upon the temporary neglect of men in danger. Yet all these sources, useful as they may have been, would have been as nothing without Melville's own sea-going experiences, his wide reading of a more general character, his high imagination, and his growing concern with the problem of evil.

Outwardly *Moby-Dick* is a tale of revenge. From the very first, critics have condemned it as an amorphous story in which "all the regular rules of narrative or story are spurned and set at defiance." [92] So much has been made of its defects as a story that it is worth while to observe that, although its leisurely tempo and so-called digressions preclude compactness, it contains most of the elements of popular narrative. Ishmael (the narrator) is a poor lad who encounters some difficulty in getting signed for his first whaling voyage. Bad omens attend the ship from the first. The monomania of Captain Ahab dominates the entire story even when it is not the surface theme. Conflicting forces are at work from the beginning. The white whale, who has already maimed the protagonist, is a foe worthy of the relentless Ahab, and Ahab manages to imbue the crew with some of his madness. He also provides a golden doubloon for the man who shall first sight the "huge island bulk" of Moby-Dick. The history and horror of typical whaling scenes and detailed characterizations of officers and crew gradually give place to more and more action and more and more exciting reports of other whalers that have seen or sought Moby-Dick. This amplifying matter is fatal to the interest of the languid reader, but read with patience it immensely heightens the reader's suspense regarding the outcome of the final encounter with Moby-Dick. Nor are traditional story elements wanting near the end. The dire prophecy of Fedallah is a dark thread running through the book, and his grotesque figure is a perpetual memento mori.[93] His malign countenance is "subdued to an earthly passionlessness" in a momentous scene as he watches Ahab take his last observation on the quadrant before, cursing the "vain toy" of science, he dashes it to the deck and determines to guide his course toward Moby-Dick by dead reckoning. It is a sinister portent, and the titanic contest is henceforth to be conducted upon a basis of individual enmity, man against leviathan. Nor are all the crew at one in their support of Ahab in his extremely hazardous project. Thoughts of wife and child almost induce Starbuck, who was "no crusader after perils," to murder Ahab in his sleep. On the verge of the great chase Ahab himself pauses to hear the plea of Starbuck to give over his mad quest and return to a serene old age in Nantucket, where "they have some such mild blue days, even as this . . ." But he blackly denies the human impulses of his own heart and turns to the colossal struggle soon to be concluded in a catastrophe that verifies the Parsee's prophecy. The cycle is now complete. The most avid reader of adventure yarns must agree that interwoven in the vast fabric of *Moby-Dick* is a tale as thrilling as Cooper could scarce compass. Yet *Moby-Dick* is more than a story of outward events.

The structure of *Moby-Dick* is such that it has baffled many readers and irritated not a few. Hence a great deal of fruitless comment on Melville's "digressions." One might almost as well say that the occupations of daily life are "digressions" from eating meals because the day begins with breakfast and ends with dinner. *Moby-Dick* begins with an action, to be sure, and there is a culmination of an exciting nature in the last three chapters, but it is merely naive to assume that the intervening material is padding or digression. The chapter on cetology and the details of whaling and whaling ships reinforce the book and give weight and reality to its meaning. It makes little difference whether *Moby-Dick* is called a "symphonic poem" or a "poetic allegory." No true reader of Melville resents one paragraph of the amplifying material in the book. Significance often arises from the most trivial details. Small, innocent-looking nimbus clouds coalesce and darken to form the thunder-cloud of doom. Melville was not the man to approve heartily of Emerson's writings; yet he exemplified a theory dear to Emerson's heart and central in his philosophy, namely, that any object, rightly viewed, faithfully renders up the secret of the universe. In *Moby-Dick* the tiniest filings are ultimately polarized with the power that invades the whole book. Commonplace details of the ship's equipment are used to illustrate important motifs. Thus the superstitious Stubb (who thinks Fedallah is the devil incarnate) undertakes to tell the Parsee's age:

"How old do you suppose Fedallah is, Stubb?"

"Do you see that mainmast there?" pointing to the ship; "well, that's the figure one; now take all the hoops in the *Pequod's* hold, and string 'em along in a row with that mast, for oughts, do you see; well, that wouldn't begin to be Fedallah's age. Nor all the coopers in creation couldn't show hoops enough to make oughts enough." [94]

Even the prosaic chapter on "The Line" proves to have its fearful import for Ahab when, at the ghastly catastrophe, its "flying turn caught him round the neck, and voicelessly as Turkish mutes bowstring their victim, he was shot out of the boat . . ." Each of the "Pequod's" encounters with other ships steps up the current of horrible anticipation. The key to the structure of *Moby-Dick* is the gradual accretion of detail; the law of its narrative is deliberate speed. The vast globe finally created by Melville is moved with difficulty, but once under way it gathers heavy momentum, and its cosmic career is terrific before the end is reached.

The labor and emotional stress involved in the composition of *Moby-Dick* followed by the exceedingly wearying process of seeing it through the press led Melville to say that the book had been "broiled in hell-fire." When this "hardest possible day's work" [95] was over, Melville's first reaction was one of peace, almost of apathy. The book was written, that was all that counted. He did not look for praise: "not one man in five cycles, who is wise, will expect appreciative recognition from his fellows, or any one of them." [96] Yet the reception of *Moby-Dick* was finally a blow to his great heart. It was received "with a little respect and a great deal of derision." [97] To Melville, exhausted by the birth of his great work, any derision must have been crushing. In England where the "uninspired revision" of Bentley's editor was responsible for the cancellation of sixty passages[98] it was damned as belonging to the "worst school of Bedlam literature" and generally condemned both for its poor narrative and its extravagant style.[99] Fortunately from the first there were friendly critics both in England and America, Hawthorne among them. Although there is reason to believe that Hawthorne failed to perceive its greatness fully, he at least wrote warmly enough of it to elicit Melville's grateful reference to "A sense of unspeakable security" on account of Hawthorne's "having understood the book." [100]

Understanding the book was indeed the great difficulty. If, prepared by *Typee*, one embarked upon *Moby-Dick* as a narrative of adventure, there were huge blocks of material which seemed to delay the action. If, on the other hand, beguiled by the "philosophical" aspects of the book, one attempted to stitch them together into a coherent pattern, the result was failure. *Moby-Dick* is neither a yarn nor a system of philosophy. It is obvious, however, that it copes with a colossal problem: in it Melville seems to be trying to understand the meaning of the universe. In a sense the book comes to a "conclusion," but it certainly contains no final "solution" of the problem. Many truths are turned up, but not that one truth which should coordinate and integrate the rest. And this was inevitable. The artist, like the philosopher or the scientist, must finally fail if he seeks the ultimate. And, like the scientist and the philosopher he is to be valued for such incomplete findings as he is able to deliver. In *Moby-Dick* these fractional results are in the aggregate so great as to suggest that totality of comprehension which is never achieved. The very bulk and diversity of Melville's data tempt the reader to try to find finality where Melville offered only hypothesis. *Moby-Dick* is indeed a "difficult" book. It is not, however, an obscure book. It is full of hints, half-truths, and hypotheses, but it contains no "hidden meanings." Melville told all he knew. Much ink has been expended in elaborate attempts to find a subtle allegory in *Moby-Dick*, but, though provocative (for *any* fact may be construed as a symbol), these attempts are finally misleading. Melville foresaw and deprecated the possibility that his book might be regarded as "a hideous and intolerable allegory." [101] He knew of course that significant writing often yields meanings on two planes at once,[102] but he did not deliberately implant a coherent and complete allegory in *Moby-Dick*. Like Shakespeare, he cultivated openness and directness (not simplicity) of expression. He was rich in symbol and allusiveness, but he did not write riddles. *Moby-Dick* is difficult only because of the difficulty of the problem incorporated in it.

The problem is essentially the problem of evil in the universe. *Moby-Dick* is in a sense complementary to *Mardi*, for the protagonist in each case is seeking something beyond the bounds of human understanding. In *Mardi*, Taji seeks ultimate good; in *Moby-Dick* Ahab tries to confront absolute evil. Ahab's search for Moby-Dick has a double motive. His pursuit of the whale is an enterprise of revenge—for Moby-Dick's having "reaped" his leg. Its general or universal significance is felt to be man's effort to understand and struggle against universal evil. The whale is inevitably taken to be the brute embodiment of the principle of evil. This basic bit of "allegory" is inescapable.[103] Ahab is well suited to his great role, for he is no common "hero." He not only has an iron will to succeed but, unlike the simpler sort of hero, he "add[s] intensity of thought and feeling to mere intentness of will.[104] He wishes to understand the nature of that malignity which menaces life.

And this in a sense he achieves. For although as the tragic hero he is destined for the external defeat implied by his death, yet he has a momentary insight into the nature of things which enables him at the very end to refer to Moby-Dick as "all-destroying but unconquering." [105] His "topmost greatness lies in [his] topmost grief" [106] because he has learned that "good and evil derive their meaning from one another." [107] As finite man he could not extirpate an infinite thing—evil—but he could see its destined place in the scheme of things. Melville clearly gives concrete expression to this view through the symbol of the skyhawk which, coming accidentally under Tashtego's hammer, goes down with the "Pequod"—

> which, like Satan, would not sink to hell till she had dragged a living part of heaven along with her, and helmeted herself with it.[108]

There is much miscellaneous wisdom in *Moby-Dick*, but one of the centres of Melville's thought is surely here. Man's victory lies not in the exercise of power but in understanding. This view has been stated by a recent critic:

> The end of Ahab is not unrelieved defeat, but victory in defeat; and the main point of *Moby Dick* is that any great human action will show that the heavens and the deeps, eternal symbols of man's triumphs and disasters, are merely the limits of his experience, related to each other through that experience and dependent upon each other and upon him for their meaning.[109]

Of course this simple statement does not elucidate all the problems that are tangent to the central one. Granted that Ahab was imprudent to attempt to break through the limits of human capacities, there is still the problem of how he conceived his Promethean enterprise. It merely begs the question to say (as Ishmael does) that his "thoughts have created a creature" in Ahab.[110] Who first put those thoughts there? This problem, too, receives intermittent attention throughout the book. Ahab has an indomitable will which he pits against an adamant system of nature: he determines to be captain of his fate. Yet at times he feels as if he were "the Fates' lieutenant," acting "under orders." [111] This conviction is perhaps a phase of Ahab's monomania, but it raises the question of whether or not the universe is operated by a vast determinism. Free will was a subject on which Melville constantly debated with himself. In *Moby-Dick* he raises but does not decide the issue. The reader knows that Ahab has won the ambiguous victory of learning that good and evil fulfill each other, but the reader does not know to what extent man's actions are self-determined, to what extent character molds circumstance. In later years Melville tended bitterly to deny freedom of the will, but in *Moby-Dick* he is not prepared to be dogmatic. Indeed if Ishmael may be taken as his spokesman, Melville seems to straddle the issue, for in the chapter in which he most elaborately considers it ("The Mat-Maker") he reaches the conclusion that "chance, free will, and necessity—no wise incompatible—[are] all interweavingly working together." [112] Logically this was an impasse as formidable as could be found in the conflicts of Calvinistic theology which Melville knew as a boy. But Melville was concerned with logic no more than with comprehensive allegory, and the "meaning" of *Moby-Dick* exists in a multitude of fragments of which each reader must gather as many as he can. For the reader, as for Ishmael, there must remain mysteries too deep for man's solution: "all this to explain, would be to dive deeper than Ishmael can go." [113] This is not to imply that Melville in any sense "failed" in *Moby-Dick*. The scope of the book is so great that incompleteness in rationale was one of the inevitable conditions of its composition. But the book is "not a philosophical essay, not a dance of symbolic phantoms," but "a tragic interpretation of an action." [114] As such it challenges comparison with other great works of fiction and drama.

The greatness of *Moby-Dick* was not fully perceived by his contemporaries. True, there were at least three friendly reviews in major periodicals,[115] and one of these (in *Harper's*) was really intelligent. But even well-disposed critics seemed on the whole not to understand the book. A review in the *Literary World* (probably by Evert Duyckinck) preposterously referred to *Moby-Dick* as "an intellectual chowder." Such a pygmy phrase for the gigantic undertaking that was *Moby-Dick* must indeed have been a sore trial to Melville. In any case the gaps between editions of *Moby-Dick*—it was reprinted in 1863, 1892, 1896, and 1899—are the best proof of the obscurity into which the book soon fell. In 1856, the Duyckinck brothers, his friends though they were, granted the author of *Moby-Dick* but three and a half pages in an encyclopaedia that allowed more than twice as much space to Longfellow. In academic circles Melville was very curtly treated for more than a generation. In 1892 W. P. Trent endorsed Poe's opinion that Simms was superior to Melville in "quantity as well as quality." [116] As late as 1900 Barrett Wendell dismissed Melville in less than a page by referring to his "career of literary promise, which never came to fruition." [117] In the following year W. D. Howells silently passed by Melville when he expressed the opinion that "if we put aside the romances of Hawthorne and the romantic novels of Cooper, we can hardly find much fiction of American scope and import before the Civil War. . . ." [118] W. C. Brownell's *American Prose Masters* (1909) had no word for Melville! Although there were various attempts to secure for Melville and *Moby-Dick* their true places in American literature,[119] and there have been individual commentators who have said a good word for *Moby-Dick* (among them, Stevenson, Masefield, and Barrie), no full and general approbation has been accorded Melville until the last ten or fifteen years, when Frank Jewett Mather, Archibald MacMechan, Raymond Weaver, Lewis Mumford, John Freeman, and D. H. Lawrence have spoken for him. More than one critic has invoked *Paradise Lost* for comparison with *Moby-Dick*.[120] There is now no lack of eulogy. Indeed, so many have been the eulogies of *Moby-Dick* that, incredible as it may seem, there are again signs that a brief periodic reaction against Melville may yet set in:

> Although Herman Melville has a throne in our literary Valhalla, it may perhaps be seen, after the rosy clouds have rolled away from the pedestal, that he is balanced precariously on a chair with a single leg, and that made of whale-bone, like the leg of Captain Ahab.[121]

LATER WORKS. Melville's letters about the time when *Moby-Dick* was being completed are jauntier in tone than his spirits vouch for. His eyes had already begun to trouble him, and even before the book was printed he plaintively expressed to Hawthorne a hope that they might "hit upon some little bit of vagabondage before autumn comes" in order to "bury all Blue Devils." [122] All the causes of these "blue devils" are not readily discoverable, but one biographer has hazarded the hypothesis that Melville's marriage had not developed into a happy union.[123] Certainly the reception of *Moby-Dick* was a sufficient cause for the appearance of new "devils." No direct statement reveals his disappointment at the relative failure of *Moby-Dick*, but a chasm between it and his subsequent works indicates his despair. In that chasm he wrote *Pierre*.

During the composition of *Moby-Dick*, Melville had told Duyckinck of his having "fifty" works in his head. Most of these perished in his brain (where they were at least "safer from criticism,")[124] but *Pierre* appeared only a year after *Moby-Dick*. So prompt a re-entry into literary waters now so frigid can be explained partly by Melville's need of expressing the gloom engendered in his spirit by his literary career. *Pierre* is "an anatomy of despair." [125] Most of the plot is obviously invented, but biographers of Melville generally agree that the book is basically autobiographical in that it reports the reaction he suffered from his treatment at the hands of critics. Certainly many of the factual details of the book are autobiographical,[126] and it may be guessed that psychologically and philosophically *Pierre* pretty much represents Melville's own point of view.

It is easy to understand from a brief analysis of the action why the book was not acceptable to Victorian America. Pierre Glendinning, about to marry Lucy Tartan, is dissuaded from doing so by his discovery of the existence of an illegitimate daughter of his father. Abandoning his patrician mother (who could not have accepted Isabel) and his fiancée, he sets about righting the wrong done to Isabel by taking her away and, the better to protect her, letting it be known that they are man and wife. They live perilously in an "ambiguous" but innocent relationship, until Lucy insists upon coming to live with them in one of the strangest ménages known in fiction. When Lucy's brother and his cousin impugn his honor and the cousin strikes him, Pierre shoots the cousin and is handed over to the police. In the jail to which he has been committed Lucy dies upon hearing of Isabel's relationship to Pierre. Isabel and Pierre complete the catastrophe by taking poison.

The thesis upon which the book rests is that a virtuous action may lead to the most terrible injustice and tragedy. What makes the book peculiarly distressing to many readers is that whereas in *Moby-Dick* Melville had treated evil against a background of ships and whalingmen, in *Pierre* he found poison in personal and family relationships. The hints of abnormality in the relationship between Pierre and his mother as well as between Pierre and his half-sister must have been disturbing to the average reader.[127] Nor could the monitors of American morals have been pleased with Melville's frank comments on incest in the latter part of the book.[128] The satire of the clergy in the fifth chapter fell harshly on orthodox ears, and the generally gloomy, not to say cynical, tone of the book banished it from the domestic circle. In short Melville brashly opened doors which a majority of novel-readers preferred to keep closed or at most to peek through. His book plainly showed how an altruistic action, *i.e.*, Pierre's protecting Isabel, may form the prologue to untold misery. Pierre ultimately becomes "the fool of Truth, the fool of Virtue, the fool of Fate." [129] All this was disturbing and disagreeable to the American public in general. People did not want to be lectured on "the relativity of what we have called virtue, the ambiguous and even awful possibilities in what we call love, the cheat in sacrifice, the evanescence of parental affection, the granite nature of pride and vanity, and the pit which may yawn suddenly in this world at the touch of an idealist." [130] Philosophically, *Pierre* is a book "bottom-less" and "out of soundings." [131] Artistically it is blemished by sensationalism. The Duyckincks referred to it as being "in the worst school of the mixed French and German melodramatic." [132] This criticism is of course wide of the mark, for although there are melodramatic morasses (suggestive of Byron rather than German or French writers) [133] in *Pierre*, there are also peaks of magnificent prose which, when they echo any writer, show how closely Melville read Shakespeare and Dante. *Hamlet, Timon,* and *Romeo and Juliet* are repeatedly called to mind, and the *Inferno* is clearly a background for much of Melville's more sombre thought. The plot of course naturally suggests the unhappy story of the Cenci, and Guido's Cenci is in fact mentioned by Melville.[134] There are also touches of Hawthorne, deepened and more embittered, in Melville's use of the theme of corroding secret sin, and in the play of light and shadow in a portrait. Despite areas of prose bordering on the great, most of Melville's generally sympathetic critics, even among modern writers, have deemed *Pierre* a failure.[135] Yet it seems likely that more and more critics in the future will agree with H. M. Tomlinson in finding the book full enough of brilliance and depth to compensate for its melodramatic action and passages of overwrought prose.[136]

The meagrely appreciative reception of *Moby-Dick* and the wave of scorn accorded *Pierre* confirmed Melville in his belief that he could look for no satisfactory livelihood from the profession of letters. His South Seas experience had long since been exhausted as literary material and the best that he had to offer in other kinds was not suited to the gift-book era. A beaten man at thirty-two, he was now convinced that "All fame is patronage," [137] and he was fast losing his few profitable connections with his generation. In 1854 a story of his was refused by an editor who feared "offending the religious sensibilities of the public and the Congregation of Grace Church." [138] His health became a cause for anxiety. Yet he had somehow to support a large family, and when even with the support of Richard H. Dana he failed to get a consular appointment he was forced to resume writing for what slight emolument it might yield.

His next novel, *Israel Potter*, was more of a success than could have been expected in the circumstances. It was first published serially, in *Putnam's Monthly Magazine*, from July 1854 to March 1855; in book form it had three printings at New York in its first year (1855).[139] Based upon an undistinguished narrative purporting to be true, *The Life and Remarkable Adventures of Israel R. Potter* (1824), it showed Melville's capacity (to be demonstrated also in *Benito Cereno*) to take over large sections of "source material" and still produce a book in his own image. The book follows the adventures of a Vermont youth through Bunker Hill, a voyage abroad in an American cruiser, capture by the British, escape to France with despatches entrusted to him by English radicals, diplomatic duties under the eye of Benjamin Franklin, impressment into the British navy, service under John Paul Jones in the famous battle between the *Bonhomme Richard* and the *Serapis,* and miscellaneous adventures in England, where he finally marries and lives in obscurity and poverty until the age of eighty. When he returns to Boston and later to his home, there is little left for him but to die. All this is good reading for anyone. Perhaps taught by his experience with *Pierre,* Melville for the most part avoided subjects likely to disturb bourgeois morality and religion. A mild cynicism crops out occasionally, and there is some bitterness about war and this thing called civilization; but the story is mainly an adventure story, and its celebration of national heroes—Ethan Allen and John Paul Jones—made for popularity with patriotic readers. The description of the battle between the *Bonhomme Richard* and the *Serapis* has been called by Frank J. Mather "the best account of a sea fight in American fiction." [140] Mumford asserts that Melville's portrait of Jones is much better than Cooper's.[141] The episode of Israel's meeting the King in Kew Gardens is an example of Melville's delightful humor. The interlude with Franklin in Paris is a masterpiece of humorous characterization—a slightly acid one, for Melville's ranging imagination could have small sympathy with that "professor of housewifery . . . maxim-monger, herb-doctor, wit" who was "everything but a poet." [142] Among Melville's lesser known books this should be better known in the future: in it Melville returns frequently to the sea, he offers the diversions of travel, and he carries enough philosophical baggage to fill in the moments of travel-weariness.

After 1855 Melville produced no long fiction of great value, but he was far from finished with the craft of writing. Short story, sketch, poetry, journal, and longer narrative—he wrote more or less continuously, though not prolifically, throughout the remaining thirty-five years of his life. No longer "popular," he could write to please himself. The confident mood of his earlier years seemed gone forever, but his distinguished powers survived. Two of his best tales remained to be written. Indeed, the first of these, "Benito Cereno," which appeared among a collection of miscellaneous pieces entitled *Piazza Tales* in 1856,[143] is one of the finest long short-stories in American literature. The adventure is based upon an experience reported in the *Voyages and Travels* (1817) of one Captain Amasa Delano of Duxbury, Massachusetts. Melville freely borrowed large sections from this journal but the story he told is essentially as different from its source as *Romeo and Juliet* is from Brooke's *Romeus and Juliet*.[144] Whether regarded as mere narrative or as an example of impressionistic art, it possesses true distinction.

As a story "Benito Cereno" creates as strong a suspense as any that Melville ever wrote. In his attempt to give aid to Don Benito Cereno, Captain of the "San Dominick" which is in apparent distress off the coast of Chile, Captain Delano of the "Batchelor's Delight" is puzzled by the alternating friendliness and curtness of Cereno. Particularly ominous is the perpetual attendance of a black servant, Babo, who cringes to his master but seems somehow in authority at the same time. When the "Batchelor's Delight" has completed its friendly office and Captain Delano's boat is about to leave the "San Dominick," Captain Benito suddenly jumps into the boat, to be followed immediately by Babo, brandishing a dagger which he attempts to plunge into the body of Cereno. The explanation of Cereno's equivocal conduct is now made clear: the vessel had been taken in a mutiny by the blacks and Benito was only the nominal captain: his scabbard contained no sword but was artificially stiffened. The superior man has been in silent subjugation to rogues— a theme now greatly to Melville's taste.

Most of the facts used in the story come from the *Voyages* of Delano, but the story has outdistanced its sources. Mr. H. H. Scudder, who discovered the source, is somewhat misleading in his remarks. He observes that Melville "found his story ready-made" and that he "merely rewrote" a chapter of Captain Delano's book, "including a portion of one of the legal documents there appended, suppressing a few items, and making some small additions." [145] Yet Mr. Scudder later adds that Melville made certain changes and supplied certain additional materials including the description of the "San Dominick," the shaving of Cereno by Babo, and Babo's leap into the boat after Cereno. These are in fact among the principal elements which make "Benito Cereno" a "short masterpiece." [146] For "Benito Cereno" is not, as Mr. Scudder implies,[147] a "typical tale of terror," but a tale which, although compounded partly of terror, is by no means comparable to a thriller by Poe. If any American writer influenced its conception, it was Hawthorne, himself a specialist in the theme of "subjection." In execution it exhibits a subtle psychology and an austere artistry to be matched by very few writers of sea-stories except Conrad. "Benito Cereno" is too long to be called a short story, hardly long enough to be called a novel. But whatever its classification as to genre, it must be reckoned one of the greatest fictions in American literature.

There is possibly an autobiographical content in "Benito Cereno" as well as in "Bartleby," a brief study of an "exile in city life" [148] that also appeared in the *Piazza Tales*. There are also strains of autobiography in *The Confidence-Man*, Melville's last novel, which, though never completed, was published in 1857. Unhappily the book does not reflect the whole Melville, but only a jaundiced likeness. Satire which had trickled moderately through earlier books—*Typee, Omoo, Mardi*—almost submerges *The Confidence-Man*. The lover of Melville must be saddened by the transformation it betokened in the author. The playfulness, the boyish enthusiasm, the bold flights of imagination that characterized Melville when he was in health, are now largely gone. Ahab's titanic struggle with the principle of evil in *Moby-Dick* at least manifested the author's capacity for resistance. Even the stormy pessimism of *Pierre* was an indirect expression of a nature still capable of a strong idealism. The bitterly sardonic tone of *The Confidence-Man*, however, is that of a man who has given up hope. Hence the reader moves sorrowfully among Melville's portraits of beggars, sharpers, cripples, herb-doctors, conycatchers, fortune-hunters, philosophers, and "metaphysical scamps" that represent humanity gathered on board the steamer "Fidèle" at St. Louis en route for New Orleans. "Story" there is practically none. The book is a potpourri of satirical commentary initiated when a deaf-mute comes on board the steamer. He carries a slate on which, in the presence of the people, he writes: "Charity thinketh no evil . . . suffereth long and is kind . . . endureth all things . . . believeth all things . . . never faileth." [149] Such conduct seems clearly insane to the other passengers, who for the most part are representative of no higher breed than the worst Americans pictured in *Martin Chuzzlewit*. The dupery practiced on board the "Fidèle" is akin to that which Mark Twain was soon to describe in the picaresque episodes of *Life on the Mississippi*. Yet Melville means his characters to be generalized: they represent humanity everywhere. Each of the sordid episodes that constitute *The Confidence-Man* is an indictment of human nature. Everywhere suspicion pollutes human intercourse. "Friendship" is only a mask for self-interest. Mark Twain's pessimistic pieces, *The Mysterious Stranger* and *What Is Man?* are forecast by Melville's ruthless exposure of the selfish motives that underlie the most plausible conduct. Yet although Mark Twain more savagely arraigned the creator of what he considered a cruelly iniquitous world, Melville exceeded him in sheer misanthropy. If the deaf-mute believed that "charity never faileth," the reader is asked to believe that the twin bearings of society are suspicion and fraud. The iteration of this baleful thesis gives *The Confidence-Man* a certain unity of tone, but in structure the book is extremely loose. As a whole *The Confidence-Man* is generally reckoned a failure. Yet there are in it many passages as brilliantly written as ever came from Melville's pen, and much of its satire rings unpleasantly true. Its fatal flaw is its lack of structural proportion. How far the book's poor structure corresponded to the dislocation of Melville's own life can only be surmised.

The Confidence-Man, notwithstanding a few favorable British notices,[150] was not reprinted until Constable brought out Melville's works in 1922-24. Its failure presaged the deepening obscurity and apathy of the last thirty-five years of his life. His personal affairs became increasingly difficult. After a somewhat cheerless tramp abroad in 1856, he had returned to America to engage in public lecturing: there was still a residuum of public curiosity about the author of *Typee* and *Omoo.* But Melville the lecturer never recovered, or sought to recover, in public the careless rapture of *Typee* and *Omoo,* and lecturing brought him so little financial return that his income had to be supplemented by the kindness of his father-in-law until 1866, when he secured the Customs appointment in New York which he retained until near the end of his life. Had he offered to take part in the literary movements of New York at that time, said Arthur Stedman, he might easily have restored his name to lustre and his purse to fulness. But Melville forbore to mingle in literary activities which must have seemed Lilliputian to the author of *Moby-Dick,* and he largely retained his privacy to the end. There were to the last emanations from his pen: the *Journal Up the Straits,* a record of part of his journey to Europe and the Near East;[151] *Battle-Pieces* (1868), being poems suggested by the fall of Richmond in the Civil War; *Clarel* (published 1876), another by-product (in verse) of his last European trip; *John Marr and Other Sailors* (1888), comprising nineteen poems; and *Timoleon* (1891), a volume of forty-three poems printed in an edition of twenty-five copies!

At the time of his death there also remained in his possession the manuscript of a short novel, *Billy Budd,* which in the opinion of one of Melville's biographers is equal to *Moby-Dick* in "loftiness of imagination." [152] The events of the story occur after the great mutiny at the Nore in 1797 which "doubtless gave the first latent prompting to most important reforms in the British navy," [153] but Melville seems to have been more deeply interested in the general problem of evil as exemplified by Billy Budd's experience. The situation is extremely tragic: an innocent and ingenuous youth is so astonished by wholly unwarranted charges against him by a petty officer that his normally slight impediment of speech increases to the point of vocal paralysis, and his face is "a crucifixion to behold." Unable to express himself otherwise, he refutes the charges by striking his accuser a blow on the forehead that proves to be mortal. The homicide has taken place in the presence of the Captain who, of course, though tempted, cannot let mercy or justice interfere with ship's discipline. He exclaims to the surgeon: "Struck dead by an angel of God. Yet the angel must hang!" [154] Obviously Melville was expounding a familiar theme: the inexplicable interaction of good and evil in "a world . . . against whose subtleties simple courage lacking experience and address and without any touch of defensive ugliness, is of little avail." [155] Billy Budd was "like a young horse fresh from the pasture" until he encountered the fatal malignancy of Claggart. After he felled his accuser, he was immediately the object of recrimination; and after his hanging (in the presence of all the crew) a news account of the episode referred to Billy as a seasoned assassin who stabbed Claggart in the back! Never did Melville write a more effective plea for humanity and seldom did he tell a better story.

This story written shortly before Melville's death proves that not all the poison bred in him by an unlucky literary career had been able to kill his artistic gift. His draughtsmanship is impeccable as ever and he retains his ability to bring a moral issue powerfully but naturally into the focus of fiction. In the merging of psychology and action only Conrad is his equal among fiction writers who have used the sea as their principal mise-en-scène.[156]

MARINER. Although Melville once remarked that he dated his life from his twenty-fifth year, he was obviously referring to his creative work as a writer. His richest experience of the objective world came during the prologue to his literary career. The voyages in the *Highlander* and the *Acushnet* opened his eyes to much that was perplexing and much that was iniquitous in life, but it also enabled him to "philosophise upon realities." [157] His experience as a sailor transformed him from a colorless amateur of letters interested in "perfect taste," into a writer capable of coping with scurvy episodes in the forecastle as well as of inviting his soul in the main-top. That Melville had need of objective reality as a mate for his speculative self is clear from *Pierre*, which although bursting with power, lacks the ballast that a work of genius should have. Most of Melville's writing circles back to his experiences before he reached the age of twenty-five. His life as a mariner at once anchored him in realities and unlocked the deepest chambers of his soul. "[T]here never was a very great man yet," cries Jack Chase, "who spent all his life inland," [158] and Melville was not the man to gainsay him. If his mature life began at twenty-five, his nonage was spent in the best possible place, for "the sea is the place to cradle genius." [159] His baptism was effective throughout his life, even if he did not return to the sea whenever he felt "a damp, drizzly November" in his soul, for the salt was in his blood permanently. It may be questioned whether his sea-faring experience was on the whole productive of personal happiness, but it created the mystic and the artist.

MYSTIC. The mystic is easily evolved from the mariner if he have the elemental stuff in him.[160] Melville, like Conrad, knew that sailors are "in character a juvenile race," [161] but he also knew that the thoughtful man gains perspective at sea, for "meditation and water are wedded forever." [162] Distance is a measuring rod. Not merely his maladjusted personal life but an instinct for wisdom sent him to escape from the "dust and reek of towns." [163] The meaning of life challenged his inquiry, but it is hard to measure life when one is in the midst of it. For the interpretation of life as a whole, a lonely night vigil fingering the sands of a desert or scanning leagues of motionless sea or guessing the depth between the stars is more effectual than listening to the hum of humanity in the bazaars and offices of crowded streets. Melville sought the atypical, the remote, the ultimate. He coveted the secrets of both the microscope and the telescope.[164] Thoreau wished to drive life into a corner; Melville yearned to track it to its sources. To this end he shipped for a long cruise on a lonely whaler to a remote island in the Pacific—and there deserted the ship. This procedure favored long, long thoughts. Melville saw life through a port-hole and from the crow's nest. He opened the hatch of the dangers over which men walk and he confronted the Master Gunner (Satan). He cut his spiritual cables to see what might be learned by a soul in isolation. He tried to understand persons on the fringes of the social order: the savage, the half-wit, the monomaniac, the half-caste. He divorced himself from the civilization that he knew in order to get a new scale of values from the mixed society of the untutored Tahitian, the Ethiopian, the Cockney, the Oriental. Like the Conrad who wrote *Youth*, he was fascinated by the East, first cradle of mysticism. Some of the spell it exerted over him he tried to express in Fedallah, one of those creatures who

> now and then glide among the unchanging Asiatic communities, especially the oriental isles to the east of the continent—those insulated, immemorial, unalterable countries, which even in these modern days still preserve much of the ghostly aboriginalness of earth's primal generations, when the memory of the first man was a distinct recollection, and all men his descendants, unknowing whence he came, eyed each other as real phantoms . . .[165]

In the little black boy Pip (whom Charles Lamb would have loved!) he embodied his affection for the lowly in estate. From them, too, one could learn eternal truths. This speck of a lad (from Tolland County, Connecticut) was almost lost in the endless reaches of the Pacific:

> By the merest chance the ship itself at last rescued him; but from that hour the little negro went about the deck an idiot; such, at least, they said he was. The sea had jeeringly kept his finite body up, but drowned the infinite of his soul. Not drowned entirely, though. Rather carried down alive to wondrous depths, where strange shapes of the unwarped primal world glided to and fro before his passive eyes; and the miser-merman, Wisdom, revealed his hoarded heaps; and among the joyous, heartless, ever-juvenile eternities, Pip saw the multitudinous, God-omnipresent, coral insects, that out of the firmament of waters heaved the colossal orbs. He saw God's foot upon the treadle of the loom, and spoke it; and therefore his shipmates called him mad. So man's insanity is heaven's sense; and wandering from all mortal reason, man comes at last to that celestial thought, which, to reason, is absurd and frantic . . .[166]

Melville sought the first frontiers of experience; he wrote from the rim of the world. But he embraced the common as well as the obviously heroic and sublime. In short, he wished to "nationalise with the universe." [167] And his purpose was much the same as that ascribed to the philosopher in *Mardi*:

> I am intent upon the essence of things; the mystery that lieth beyond; the elements of the tear which much laughter provoketh; that which is beneath the seeming; the precious pearl within the shaggy oyster. I probe the circle's centre; I seek to evolve the inscrutable.[168]

THINKER. The mystery that lay in the sea yielded meaning to Melville, but not one meaning alone. The facets of his thought are as various as the aspects of the sea, which covers "two-thirds of the fair world." [169] Sometimes, especially at first, the sea was friendly. Melville derived from it a feeling akin to that of the transcendentalists:

> And it is a very fine feeling, and one that fuses us into the universe of things, and makes us a part of the All, to think that, wherever we ocean wanderers rove, we have still the same glorious old stars to keep us company . . .[170]

Yet he learned to expect treachery as well as balm from the smiling sea, and some of his most eloquent passages voice a warning against its dangers, physical and spiritual—for the sea is a symbol as much as a reality.

In *White Jacket* when he speaks darkly of the dangers of rounding the Horn, his meaning is double. Likewise in *Moby-Dick* he often chooses to emphasize the sinister character of the sea, as in this beautifully cadenced passage:

> Consider all this; and then turn to this green, gentle, and most docile earth; consider them both, the sea and the land; and do you not find a strange analogy to something in yourself? For as this appalling ocean surrounds the verdant land, so in the soul of man there lies one insular Tahiti, full of peace and joy, but encompassed by all the horrors of the half-known life. God keep thee! Push not off from that isle, thou canst never return! [171]

The sea, like the land, contained both the good and the evil principles of existence. If it "cradled genius," it also housed monsters of sinister significance for man. It reflected the smile of God but also afforded passage to the devil. In it lurked Moby-Dick. In his great story of the whale Melville seemed strong enough to confront the full force of evil, but the outcome of the battle was at best a stalemate: who seeks the destruction of evil must himself be destroyed. The battle went on in Melville's mind, and with the passing years he sank for a time to the lowest ebb of hope. He felt that "[t]hough in many of its aspects this visible world seems formed in love, the invisible spheres were formed in fright." [172] His convictions darkened with the setting of the sun of his personal career. Like Pierre, he had "ringed himself in with the grief of Eternity," [173] and to assuage his grief he sought, sometimes vainly sought, a religion.

Melville was a skeptic but not by any means an atheist. Like many who question orthodoxy, he did so in order to prepare a place in which to build a faith for himself. Ironically, he was castigated for blasphemy when he was in search of spiritual security. If in the progress of his search he tumbled a few idols of the people, he was no mere iconoclast but hoped to replace them with worthier divinities. He had in fact a deeper need of faith than many of those who perfunctorily mumbled assent to creeds that their lives failed to translate into works. Perhaps in the end he found peace, but for many years he wandered in the desert air of skepticism without being able to arrive at an oasis of faith. Hawthorne said that he could "neither believe, nor be comfortable in his unbelief." [174] Like Pierre, Melville foolishly spent his energies in "attempts at systematising eternally unsystemisable elements." [175] He was constantly torn by the difficulty of finding a faith which would enable him to accept with something like equanimity the malign aspect

of nature and the inhumanity of man to man. His hope for immortality
fluctuated. When he met Hawthorne in England in 1856 he told him
that he had " 'pretty much made up his mind to be annihilated,' " but
Hawthorne remarked that Melville did not "seem to rest in that anticipation." Nor did he believe Melville would ever give up the quest until
he got "hold of a definite belief." [176] But Melville expressed his exasperation at his failure more than he did his need of faith. He expressed
his frustration by arraigning Fate or the Creator. Calvinism was for
him an impossible system as a whole, but Melville often excused man
as being, instead of a free agent, the mere sport of Fate:

> "we are turned round and round in this world, like yonder wind-
> lass, and Fate is the handspike." [177]

For the most part Fate is inimical (fortunate eventualities are referred
to "Providence") and inscrutable:

> Strike at one end the longest conceivable row of billiard balls in
> close contact, and the furthermost ball will start forth, while all
> the rest stand still; and yet that last ball was not struck at all.[178]

This article of determinism, in conjunction with the idea of inherent
evil, bred the deepest pessimism in Melville. The evil that men do
seemed outside their own control. To be sure, such a view dictated
charity toward sinners. Even Claggart, who was responsible for Billy
Budd's death, may be exempted from fundamental blame; evil was
"born with him and innate." For Claggart's acts the Creator is responsible:

> With no power to annul the elemental evil in himself, though
> he could hide it readily enough; apprehending the good, but
> powerless to be it; what recourse is left to a nature like Claggart's,
> surcharged with energy as such natures almost invariably are, but
> to recoil upon itself, and, like the scorpion for which the Creator
> alone is responsible, act out to the end its allotted part.[179]

What is even worse, the evil that stalks in the universe is often associated so inextricably with good or seeming good that one is at a loss to
steer a true course. For Melville, as for Hawthorne, life was a colossal
ambiguity, a parcel of paradoxes. Mankind who conceives it his business to read it aright often finds himself among insuperable difficulties.
Tension too great to endure is the result:

> Ah, muskets the gods have made to carry infinite combustions, and yet made them of clay! [180]

Against these sombre speculations what can be set down as on the side of hope if not faith? Seldom did Melville allow himself a direct expression of strong faith. Yet he has moods in which he seems to approve individual effort and to expect results to bear a proportion to effort. "Ourselves are Fate," he jauntily says in *White Jacket*.[181] In *Mardi*, he leaves a blank leaf whereon to inscribe a faith when he summarizes man's life:

> Thus with life: man bounds out of night; runs and babbles in the sun; then returns to his darkness again; though, peradventure, once more to emerge.[182]

In *Redburn* he allows himself to refer to God's care in a highly conventional manner when in speaking of the plight of sailors he postulates their ultimate improvement, for "we feel and we know that God is the true Father of all, and that none of His children are without the pale of His care." [183] Indeed throughout Melville's writings one may find little springs of hope from time to time. Occasionally, too, he found relief from his own seriousness by making jocose comments on the nature of the universe. Hardy's later speculations on possible limitations of God himself are startlingly suggested by a facetious passage in one of Melville's letters to Hawthorne:

> We incline to think that God cannot explain His own secrets, and that He would like a little information upon certain points Himself. We mortals astonish Him as much as He us.[184]

Yet the tone of this remark is unusual in Melville's religious inquiries. The matter was too serious for much jesting.

From his unreconciled opinions one must not conclude that Melville was merely inconsistent, but that he was constantly thinking and that today's thoughts were bound to conflict with yesterday's. To some extent he reserves his final judgment. When the great secret is told, he thought, it may be that evil will be accounted for. It may even be that "Sin hath its sacredness, not less than holiness." [185] Melville's pessimistic utterances must not be taken at their face value; he protests too much to be regarded as a thoroughgoing unbeliever. Even his satirical thrusts at church and creed are delivered from a tiny island of faith. His nay is not everlasting. The mark of the complete pessimist is not despair

but apathy, and Melville struggled to the end. In his epilogue written
late in life he faces the difficulties introduced by new scientific findings:

> The light is greater, hence the shadow more.[186]

Yet even here he wonders whether death "may prove unreal at the
last" with the result that "stoics" may be "astounded into heaven." [187]
Such faith as he had was inarticulate, intermittent, but real. Like Cor-
delia's love, it was lodged too deeply to be fetched up for easy expression. His religious utterances are likely to seem perverse and contradictory because he felt so deeply and because he was uncompromisingly
honest with himself. He had a certain admiration for Emerson, but he
could not adopt Emerson's metaphysics: "Nay, I do not oscillate in
Emerson's rainbow, but prefer rather to hang myself in mine own halter
than swing in any other man's swing." [188] Yet there was hope in Melville's very negation:

> For . . . all men who say *no*,—why, they are in the happy con-
> dition of judicious, unincumbered travellers in Europe; they cross
> the frontiers into Eternity with nothing but a carpet-bag,—that is
> to say, the Ego.[189]

Melville did not wish to acquire a religion by mere assent but rather
through brave encounter with such truth as he could discover. There
is reason to believe that, despite the bitterness of his later years, he
partly won the battle. Perhaps through his endless quest he (like Ahab
witnessing the death of the whale) acquired at last "a prouder, if a
darker faith." [190] And if he partially failed, he must at least have attained to a measure of tranquillity. For like the poet in *Mardi*, Melville
knew that there is no real victory without suffering, no defeat without
gain:

> "Our calms must come by storms. Like helmless vessels, tempest-
> tossed, our only anchorage is when we founder." [191]

Of storms there had been enough in Melville's life. To some critics,
these seem to be tempests in a teapot, mere emotional outbursts of
an overwrought, idealistic adolescent. "The modern reader is not
shocked," writes one critic, "by Melville's showing that society is not
governed by the Golden Rule." [192] No, indeed, for the fact of disillusionment is as old as the first man. But where would such an argument
lead if applied to artistic production in general? One is not shocked by

Shakespeare's showing that there is such a thing as filial ingratitude, but one reads with ceaseless wonder the poet's revelation of how that age-old fact came home to Lear. One knows that Hamlet was merely a super-sensitive and impractical dreamer, but one is forever moved by the drama woven round him. It is not newness of fact that counts but newness of perception and richness of report. The artist is a teller of old tales. The great artist is he who enriches an old truth. Melville was one of these.

CRITIC. The best of Melville's art came directly from the deeps of his imaginative life, his private self. Yet he devoted considerable attention to the criticism of society as he saw it. In general, man-made institutions seemed to him to exhibit grave defects. Melville's quarrel with his generation, like Thoreau's, was not that it had the wrong faith but that it failed to live up to its avowed principles. His most formidable attacks on missionaries in *Typee* and *Omoo*, the attack on the church in *Pierre*, and the satire of religion in *The Confidence-Man* are to be set down as evidences of Melville's resentment against those who for gain of some sort profess a religion that they do not practice. Frequently he was lacking in urbanity in his attacks, so that whereas he harbored few thoughts more radical than Hawthorne entertained, he brought down more wrath upon his head, for he was more contentious than Hawthorne and less given to euphemistic parleyings with the spectre of doubt. Even when he did not overtly dispense subversive doctrine, he had a profane air, and, as the *London Saturday Review* complained, his "occasional irreverent use of Scripture phrases . . . gives a disagreeable impression" to more staid and conservative readers. But Melville was no mere scoffer. Perhaps his most eloquent comment on the deficiencies of orthodox religion in practice may found in a passage in *Mardi*, in which a pagan describes a way of life and a humility and a tolerance that Melville felt were wanting in Christian lands. The passage is devastating in its implications, but it is free from the bantering tone which had irked some readers. It has beauty of language and thought:

> "Do ye then claim to live what your master hath spoken? Are your precepts practices?"
> "Nothing do we claim: we but earnestly endeavour."
> "Tell me not of your endeavours, but of your life. What hope for the fatherless among ye?"
> "Adopted as a son."
> "Of one poor, and naked?"
> "Clothed, and he wants for naught."

"If ungrateful, he smite you?"

"Still we feed and clothe him."

"If yet an ingrate?"

"Long, he cannot be; for love is a fervent fire."

"But what, if widely he dissent from your belief in Alma;—then, surely, ye must cast him forth?"

"No, no; we will remember, that if he dissent from us, we then equally dissent from him; and men's faculties are Oro-given. Nor will we say that he is wrong, and we are right; for this we know not, absolutely. But we care not for men's words; we look for creeds in actions; which are the truthful symbols of the things within. He who hourly prays to Alma, but lives not up to world-wide love and charity—that man is more an unbeliever than he who verbally rejects the Master, but does his bidding. Our lives are our Amens." [193]

In short Melville's scorn was reserved for those who had no active faith. The institution of the church, he felt, failed in one of its main objectives:

But Truth is the silliest thing under the sun. Try to get a living by Truth—and go to the Soup Societies. Heavens! Let any clergyman try to preach the Truth from its very stronghold, the pulpit, and they would ride him out of his church on his own pulpit bannister.[194]

Melville coveted for the church a higher standard of religious life than he was able to observe in it.

If insincerity was the vice of the church, bungling inefficiency seemed to characterize affairs of the state. With active politics Melville had little direct contact; he was not a man able to mix in affairs. A certain isolation was necessary for his best creative work. He was a Unionist during the War, as his *Battle-Pieces* shows, but he deplored post-war animosity toward the South.[195] Slavery he regarded as a "curse," but the Southerners were only the "fated inheritors" of the system.[196] Indeed no specific reform interested him so much as the gradual amelioration of man's state through the cultivation of finer instincts. Perhaps his relatively sequestered life failed to call forth sympathies that were strong if once appealed to. The naval abuses he attacked had come under his personal observation.[197] He was no zealous proponent of popular government. Although he said in *Redburn* that "to be a born American citizen seems a guarantee against pauperism; and this, perhaps, springs from the virtue of a vote," [198] it is doubtful if he approved of entrusting things of importance to the masses (whom he individually loved). In *Moby-Dick* he praised Andrew Jackson as an example of the Almighty's habit of selecting "champions from the kingly commons." [199] But his democracy had limits. He believed that "freedom is more social than political," [200] and no more than Lincoln did he look for complete equality among men.[201] It is doubtful if he even approved of the jury system, whereby justice is sought from the "uproar of twelve puzzled brains" and unanimity of judgment may be found in "twelve hungry stomachs." [202] Nor did he have much respect for "freedom of the press," which, he has one character say, is "on a par with *freedom of Colt's revolver*." [203] And yet, with all its imperfections, America was his country, and he would defend her against attacks by foreign writers. He was American enough to resent the superciliousness of British commentators who insinuated that Americans were a "rootless and upstart people." [204] If he was not the man to fraternize with his fellow-citizens or to follow the covered wagon, Melville at least felt that America was a land of great possibilities—especially if she cut the cable which bound her to Britain. He traveled little in his own land; yet he affirmed that "America begins with the Alleghanies."

The danger that chiefly threatened American literature was the provincialism of Americans who were unwilling to place their hopes on native productions. He of course could not approve the floods of sentimental or boudoir fiction, written by Americans, that appeared in the 1850's; and he had especial scorn for "the trash nowadays passed off for dramas." [205] What bothered him most of all was the lack of true initiative in our literary life. Publishers wished to be safe: "good" books were conventional books. Great works were not wanted, of that he was sure: "Though I wrote the Gospels in this century, I should die in the gutter." [206] Yet he felt that ultimately American literature must be independent, and he thought it a mark of provinciality to believe that when a great writer appeared amongst us, "he will come in the costume of Queen Elizabeth's day." [207] Melville came nearest to Whitman when he expressed the conviction that America was a land of unfulfilled promise deserving the confidence of the people: "Believe me, my friends, that men not very much inferior to Shakespeare are this day being born on the banks of the Ohio. And the day will come when you shall say, Who reads a book by an Englishman that is a modern?" [208] Yet this mood, which was habitual with Whitman, was only intermittent with Melville. At bottom, he was not a reformer, or a patriot, or a nationalist, but an artist who knew that his art was not beholden to his township or his era.

ARTIST. Cooper's facile production of books Melville could never have emulated. Melville's aim was to soar higher than Cooper ever contemplated—and his preparation and labor were correspondingly greater. His reading was vast and his concentration was intense. He took his books where he found them: at first, no doubt, in his home and in such second-hand shops as he could patronize; later in ships' libraries;[209] still later (at New York) in the 17,000-volume library of Evert Duyckinck.[210] His reading was catholic, including the literature of knowledge as well as the literature of power. He had a passion for documentation which fed on obscure pamphlets and archives; he used their prosaic contents to build the bony structure of stories to which he later gave imaginative form.[211] He liked plain adventure yarns. The relatively unembellished stories of Smollett he found to be absorbing.[212] Dana's *Two Years Before the Mast* he referred to as "unmatchable." [213] Despite his limitations Cooper produced "a vivid and awakening power" upon Melville's mind during boyhood.[214] The sombre technique of Hawthorne seems to have influenced "Benito Cereno" and *Pierre*. Bunyan's straightforward prose pleased him greatly. He also read books of sententious wisdom: Solomon, Plutarch, the prose of Goethe. Yet with his appreciation of sober, lucid prose and quiet tonal effects went a passion for certain writers who stimulated his imagination by their indulgence in tumultuous orgies of words: Rabelais, Shakespeare, Sir Thomas Browne, Carlyle. Though of a "meditative humour," [215] Melville at times seems intoxicated by sheer linguistic excesses. Cool, measured periods of prose give way to the most unrestrained exercise of fantasy and caprice. The literary company he kept was doubtless in part responsible. Yet when he did not drink too deeply, Melville seems to have found stimulation in these writers for some of his finest work. Browne he often seems to imitate not only in soaring passages but also in charming little disquisitions of a pseudo-scientific sort—as in the speculation as to whether amber consists of the brains of gold-fish.[216] Sometimes he piles up words, playfully or grimly, in a fashion that recalls Rabelais.[217] One never reads far in Melville without encountering the influence of Shakespeare. In *Moby-Dick* he even adopts an Elizabethan mode of introducing characters.[218] Melville had an Elizabethan wit and he had a taste for Elizabethan spaciousness in language, with an abundance of imagery and allusion. His philosophy perhaps sent him to the pages of *Timon* for company, but his favorite among Shakespearean plays was apparently *Hamlet:* he could understand times that were out of joint and the characterization of an introspective idealist unable to make adjustment to his environment. His turnkeys in *Pierre* are obviously descendants of the grave-diggers of *Hamlet. King Lear* was also much in his mind. Nor did Melville value Shakespeare only for the great tragic elements in his plays; he also produced antic trifles and gossamer fancies that distinctly recall passages in Shakespeare.[219] Other writers there were who gave him frequent inspiration—Dante, for his soundings of the after-world; Spenser for his opulence and his dreamy allegory; Sterne, for his conscienceless whims, jests, and digressions, Shelley for his Promethean treatment of the problem of evil—but most of all he seems to have delighted in the company of seventeenth-century English writers, who were kindred to him by reason of their untrammeled speculation and billowing periods of rich imaginative prose.

Melville wrote and he read and he meditated, but he theorized little. He mined the critical vein only when the creative was exhausted. It is perhaps significant that *The Confidence-Man*, the least rewarding of his long stories, contains more consecutive critical commentary than any other book he wrote. He knew, of course, the slow agony involved in the creation of an enduring work of art—whether in the shape of books or temples. "The parts of the great *Iliad*," he said, were not "put together in haste." [220] Yet he knew of no rules which would enable a writer to deliver his essential self in the medium of words. *Moby-Dick*, as has often been pointed out, contains most of the elements of a classical tragedy. Yet (for better or worse) how much more it contains! Melville's literary method was not described fully in Aristotle's *Poetics* or Longinus' *On the Sublime*. To him the process of creation was extremely complex; the demands of art seemed contradictory, paradoxical:

ART

In placid hours well pleased we dream
Of many a brave unbodied scheme.
But form to lend, pulsed life create,
What unlike things must meet and mate:
A flame to melt—a wind to freeze;
Sad patience—joyous energies;
Humility—yet pride and scorn;
Instinct and study; love and hate;
Audacity—reverence. These must mate
And fuse with Jacob's mystic heart.
To wrestle with the angel—Art.[221]

This is not to say that Melville completely ignored all ordinary rhetorical precepts. *Moby-Dick* is a gigantic unity. *Pierre*, in spite of its er-

ratic progress, moves toward a climax which brings the melodramatic
action to a definite conclusion. Most of the other books have that semblance of structural unity which is provided by the limits of the
loosely knit adventures which they recount. Yet in general Melville
seems to have paid comparatively little attention to those principles of
unity, order, and emphasis which are relied on to accommodate average
readers. His unity is not so much a unity of structure as of texture: it
may be felt but is hard to demonstrate. His thought sequences are not
controlled by logic but pour prodigally from his subconscious mind. In
a sense their source guarantees their homogeneity, but such unity as
results cannot be shown by a diagram. He valued precision less than
he valued naturalness. He wished to attain the relative roundness of
the earth rather than the perfect sphere of the demonstration laboratory. So, too, with the principles of order and emphasis. Much given
to improvising, Melville naturally had difficulty with order. His creation is often as bare of outward plan as the generation of flowers or
the journeys of the bee. He did not consistently maintain a point of
view. In its discussion of *Moby-Dick*, the London *Spectator* chided
him for "beginning in the autobiographical form and changing *ad libi-
tum* into the narrative." [222] He was a little casual, too, with respect to
emphasis. He used iteration and reduplication freely, but the essence of
what he sought to convey could not always be stated in those clear and
emphatic terms which most readers look for. The chapter on the
whiteness of the whale consists largely of illustration and analogy, but
the *thought* it conveys must be grasped imaginatively rather than rationally. Emily Dickinson's text, "The soul selects its own society,"
would have served for Melville as well. Doubtless he hoped to reach
great numbers of readers, but he could not, or would not, employ the
conventional means to that end. To a large extent Pierre was speaking
for Melville when he said: "I write precisely as I please." [223]

Naturally Melville did not undertake elaborate, formal justification
of his individual practices as a writer. Yet he filed an occasional de-
murrer against the finalities of conventional criticism. Thus he felt that
order and symmetry are the harder to attain in proportion to the scope
of a writer's intention:

> The symmetry of form attainable in pure fiction cannot so readily
> be achieved in a narration essentially having less to do with fable
> than with fact. Truth uncompromisingly told will always have its
> ragged edges; hence the conclusion of such a narration is apt to be
> less finished than an architectural finial.[224]

Similarly he believed that consistency in the abstract could be wrongly valued:

> True, it may be urged that there is nothing a writer of fiction should more carefully see to, as there is nothing a sensible reader will more carefully look for, than that, in the depiction of any character, its consistency should be preserved. But this, though at first blush seeming reasonable enough, may, upon a closer view, prove not so much so. For how does it couple with another requirement—equally insisted upon, perhaps—that, while to all fiction is allowed some play of invention, yet, fiction based on fact should never be contradictory to it; and is it not a fact, that, in real life, a consistent character is a *rara avis?* . . . That fiction, where every character can, by reason of its consistency, be comprehended at a glance, either exhibits but sections of character, making them appear for wholes, or else is very untrue to reality; while, on the other hand, that author who draws a character, even though to common view incongruous in its parts, as the flying-squirrel, and, at different periods, as much at variance with itself as the butterfly is with the caterpillar into which it changes, may yet, in so doing, be not false but faithful to facts.[225]

"Realism" was a bugaboo he had to face. He knew some readers regarded his characters as "unreal." Yet he looked for approbation to another class of readers—readers who

> look that fancy shall evoke scenes different from those of the same old crowd round the custom-house counter, and same old dishes on the boarding-house table, with characters unlike those of the same old acquaintances they meet in the same old way every day in the same old street. And as, in real life, the proprieties will not allow people to act out themselves with that unreserve permitted to the stage; so, in books of fiction, they look not only for more entertainment, but, at bottom, even for more reality, than real life itself can show. Thus, though they want novelty, they want nature, too; but nature unfettered, exhilarated, in effect transformed. In this way of thinking, the people in a fiction, like the people in a play, must dress as nobody exactly dresses, talk as nobody exactly talks, act as nobody exactly acts. It is with fiction as with religion: it should present another world, and yet one to which we feel the tie.[226]

This higher realism was Melville's quarry. He could not tell exactly how to track it down. He knew that "To produce a mighty book, you must choose a mighty theme." [227] And somehow, he felt, the writer's experience must be brought to bear on his art, for "the visible world of experience [is] that procreative thing which impregnates the muses." [228] But the process of conception and gestation he did not trust himself to dogmatize upon. Scores of passages in his books show that he brooded much and long over the development of his own art, but he hatched no manual for writers. Unremitting labor and bold intuitions served him better than any "system" of writing. He followed no formulas and he made none. He was a writer without portfolio, an artist at large. He must be judged by his achievements, not by his method.

Melville's achievement, if viewed impartially, must be accounted enormous. Even now there are those who regard him as an over-praised second-rate writer. On the other hand, there may be as many readers who share Viola Meynell's feeling (expressed in 1920) that "no greatness that has ever been surpasses his greatness." [229] Precisely where between these extremes the true estimate of Melville lies no one can say. But it is sure that after the last critic has barked and the last devotee has lit his candle, Melville's greatness as a writer will endure solidly in the candid record of time. He was a writer rare in gifts and unpredictable in performance. Even his most fervid admirers would not call him "the faultless artist." He could be discursive, quixotic, bombastic, even incoherent. Proportion he seldom achieved fully except in *Moby-Dick*. And yet (as Bacon said) "There is no excellent beauty that hath not some strangeness in the proportion." And although it is unlikely that Bacon would have approved of Melville's roving intuitions, the dictum holds good for Melville as for Da Vinci and many another artist. And Melville realized his fallibility. He may have been conscious of his great powers, but he did not look for perfection. He took himself as he was ("It is too late to make any improvements now," says Ishmael) and tried to give true expression to his inmost self. On the whole he succeeded in his aim: as much as any writer, perhaps, he wrote the books he wanted to write. The various phases of his temperament and experience found expression in his books. He would not seek a popular leverage and sustain it for profit against the instincts of his nature. No, he would write as the "fit" dictated. He would write cleanly in the narrative tradition of Defoe. He would dive recklessly into pools of fantasy which charmed some readers and frightened others. He would hurl his misanthropy fiercely into print—for this too expressed a dark corner of his nature. He would show all his holdings, the knots in the lumber as well as the even grain. No one—not even the Duyckinck brothers—should make him into a mere cabinet-maker.

He had in mind a work of greater dimensions. And there was a time when he gathered up all the diverse elements of Herman Melville and housed them permanently—in *Moby-Dick*. Here, for once at least, was harmony of all the parts. Here all Melville's styles—the playful, the ironical, the saturnine, the forthright, the tragic, the Promethean—were fused together and worked with each other to support the colossal epic of Melville's imagining. The unity of *Moby-Dick* is readily perceptible to one who reads it entire, and yet the book has been widely used in detached quotation. Preceded by a collection of passages on whaling, *Moby-Dick* has itself become an anthology of great prose. Removed from its context each passage loses a little of beauty and power, but each contains enough of the essence of Melville to suggest the great whole of which it is a part. So with the valedictory to the dying whale:

> It was far down the afternoon; and when all the spearings of the crimson fight were done: and floating in the lovely sunset sea and sky, sun and whale both stilly died together; then, such a sweetness and such plaintiveness, such inwreathing orisons curled up in that rosy air, that it almost seemed as if far over from the deep green convent valleys of the Manilla isles, the Spanish land-breeze, wantonly turned sailor, had gone to sea, freighted with these vesper hymns.
>
> Soothed again, but only soothed to deeper gloom, Ahab, who had sterned off from the whale, sat intently watching his final wanings from the now tranquil boat. For that strange spectacle observable in all sperm whales dying—the turning sunward of the head, and so expiring—that strange spectacle, beheld of such a placid evening, somehow to Ahab conveyed a wondrousness unknown before.
>
> "He turns and turns him to it,—how slowly, but how steadfastly, his homage-rendering and invoking brow, with his last dying motions. He too worships fire; most faithful, broad, baronial vassal of the sun!—Oh that these too-favouring eyes should see these too-favouring sights. Look! here, far water-locked; beyond all hum of human weal or woe; in these most candid and impartial seas; where to traditions no rocks furnish tablets; where for long Chinese ages the billows have still rolled on speechless and unspoken to, as stars that shine upon the Niger's unknown source; here, too, life dies sunward full of faith . . ."[230]

This is, perhaps, great writing, but what makes it so is scarcely capable of analysis. Certainly Melville would not be the man to explain. His instincts were against textual criticism or commentary. Great texts were to be reverenced and used, not analyzed. He hoped for no additions to the text of Shakespeare, he once exclaimed, "lest the commentators arise, and settling upon his sacred text, like unto locusts, devour it clean up, leaving never a dot over an I." [231] As for his own text, it invites analysis for biographical and historical purposes, but the real secret of its power and magic must remain, like the sea, forever inscrutable.

The Domestic Sentimentalists and Other Popular Writers (1850-1870)

In 1842 William Gilmore Simms referred to Cooper's *Precaution* as "a very feeble work, . . . a second or third rate imitation of a very inferior school of writings, known as the social life novel."[1] By the "social life novel," Simms meant a story in which the bulk of detail was made up of "the ordinary events of the household, or of the snug family circle." The action of such a story might reach its climax at a ball or a dinner party. To a man accustomed, as Simms was, to handling issues that determined the fate of states or nations, this sort of thing seemed paltry stuff, for it gave almost no play to the "imagination" or the "creative faculty." No wonder Cooper failed in *Precaution* and Scott in *St. Ronan's Well*. If such novels have to be written, let them be written by women.

Well, a few years after Simms wrote these words, women did bend themselves to producing the social or domestic novel with such zeal that they put a severe crimp in the sales of other varieties of fiction, including Simms's specialty, the historical romance. Indeed they all but pre-empted the field of fiction. The 50's and 60's saw the publication of scores of domestic novels by a variety of authors. Their sales were tremendous. Maria Cummins' *The Lamplighter* sold 40,000 copies within eight weeks. Two of Susan Warner's books, *The Wide, Wide World* and *Queechy*, sold an aggregate of 104,000 copies in three years. Mrs. Hentz's sales totalled 93,000 in three years. Mrs. Holmes's books reached a total of 2,000,000 sold copies. The demand for the books of Augusta Jane Evans Wilson may be partly judged by a notice printed in one edition of *St. Elmo:* "Special edition limited to 100,000 copies." Other writers of the school made almost comparable successes. The vogue of the form was perhaps greatest in the 50's and 60's; yet as late as 1872 the Boston Public Library "confessed . . . that the most popular authors of the day were Mary J. Holmes, Caroline Lee Hentz, and Mrs. Southworth." [2] It is no accident that Joyce's *Ulysses*, set in 1904, reports Gerty MacDowell as having read *The Lamplighter*. Nor are people lacking in the present generation even among the intelligentsia who, if pressed, will blushingly admit that they have read and enjoyed *St. Elmo*.

The productions of this prolific race of novelists have generally been dismissed briefly by historians of literature as being sub-literary, and therefore unworthy of critical attention. Granted that sales are no criterion of literary values, yet the vast popularity of these writers so affected the market for fiction and the standards of public taste that more serious artists were alarmed. In 1855 Hawthorne referred in exasperation to the authors as a "d—d mob of scribbling women." Howells later had much ado to correct false artistic standards of taste they created. Some knowledge of the origin, aims, and vogue of such an influential school is essential to an understanding of the temper of the period and of the evolution of the novel.

The domestic novel had reciprocal relationships with various other forms of fiction. A precise definition is therefore difficult, but for the moment the domestic novel may be roughly defined, in its first phase at least, as an extended prose tale composed chiefly of commonplace household incidents and episodes casually worked into a trite plot involving the fortunes of characters who exist less as individuals than as carriers of moral or religious sentiment. The thesis of such a book is that true happiness comes from submission to suffering. In its purest strain the domestic novel relied far more on religious sentiment than on romantic love, but as time went on the latter greatly increased its ratio and even an erotic element (for which the author acknowledged no responsibility) became dimly apparent between the lines. Other variations occur from author to author, but enough homogeneity obtains in the genre to give some validity to the following receipt to make a domestic novel.

First, take a young and not-too-pretty child about ten years old. Boys are possible, but girls are to be preferred, for the author and the increasing majority of women readers will be more at home in the detail. Make sure that the child is, or shortly will be, an orphan. If the mother is still living, put her to death very gradually in a scene of much sorrow and little physical suffering, uttering pious hopes and admonitions to the last. The father presumably died years ago under circumstances not well known. Now put the child under the care of a shrewish aunt, who resents being obliged to take care of her dead brother's brat. If it has been impossible to remove the father as suggested above, a reasonably good compromise will be to have him make a second marriage with a frivolous, heartless society woman. In an emergency a cruel housekeeper will do. The child is now unhappy, undernourished, and underprivileged. She is exposed to the taunts of snobbish little rich girls. It is essential that she accidentally overhear unkind comments on her awkward clothes, rustic manners, bad behavior, or even her family honor. Slander may be used freely for spicing the plot. The child's behavior may in fact be actually bad in the beginning. She may "sass" her aunt. She may even shy a stone through a window. But her worst sin is her "pride." Now introduce a young woman living not far away, who embodies all Christian virtues, especially humility. Let this lady kiss, pray over, and cry with the heroine at intervals of from three to four pages. The lady may or may not be blind; at any rate she has had her sorrows and she is destined to die about two-thirds of the way through the book of badly diagnosed tuberculosis. She will die at sunset—without a struggle. She is going home. Tears which have been flowing freely now practically inundate the book. The girl's only remaining friends are an eccentric (Barkis-like) teamster, and a wealthy (Cheeryble-like) merchant who now and then gives her a lollipop. In the meantime she has learned to subdue her pride and to submit graciously to the suffering which is the lot of all mortals in this shabby world. You may end your story here if you will, with the child on the verge of adolescence; but it is preferable to carry on a few years in order that the heroine may be menaced by a proud, handsome, moody, Rochester-like man aged about thirty who has traveled and sinned (very vaguely) in the Orient. He at first scarcely notices the meek little girl, but her bright spirit and vaguely referred to physical charms finally force him to admit to himself that he must have her. If it weren't for Queen Victoria, he would try to seduce her, but as it is he is reduced to proposing marriage. To his astonishment she refuses. This sends him darkly off on more travels. The girl meanwhile has learned to support herself by teaching, acting as governess, or writing, and she talks rather briskly about independence for women. Let her endure many trials and perform many pious acts. Monotony may be broken by a trip to Saratoga or by the introduction of some physical peril such as a carriage accident, an attack by a mad dog, or a fire. One day the moody man comes back, and finds her sitting in a cemetery. He proposes again and is accepted. Don't be alarmed at this: his pride has been humbled, too, and he is now reformed. He may even become a minister—but he has plenty of money. For her part, the heroine now drops all fantastic notions of female independence, for she realizes that a woman's greatest glory is wifely submission. The acid aunt either dies or experiences a change of heart toward the heroine. In the latter case she may be married off to the neighboring teamster (blacksmith will do). The wealthy merchant turns out to be the heroine's father: he wasn't really lost at sea! Everybody is now happy in a subdued, Christian sort of way.

This composite story is intended to give some idea of the domestic novel as it was practiced by Susan Warner, Maria Cummins, Augusta Jane Evans Wilson, E. D. E. N. Southworth, Ann Sophia Stephens, Caroline Lee Hentz, Mrs. H. B. Goodwin, Marion Harland, E. P. Roe, and others from 1850 to 1875. Its descent in the family of fiction is complicated. It is obviously related to the novel of sensibility and as such it goes back to *Pamela*. Miss Edgeworth was also an acknowledged ancestor of the type. But there are more obvious relationships with four later British writers—Bulwer, Dickens, Charlotte Brontë, and Mrs. Gaskell—whose first published novels appeared respectively in 1829, 1837, 1847, and 1848. Bulwer provided a model for drawing-room scenes and fascinating, wicked, fashionable young men; Dickens, for pathetic little girls and eccentric characters; Brontë, for the persecuted governess; and Mrs. Gaskell, for idyllic village life. From American novelists there was less that could be borrowed handily. The sensitive swooning heroine lately released from the defunct Gothic romance and the moribund historical romance could be drafted into the service of the domestic novel, given a course of intensive religious training, taught maneuvers of the heart by Jane Eyre, and assigned to heavy emotional duty on the domestic front. The kitchen realism which Miss Sedgwick employed for the benefit of readers beginning to tire of the details of military campaign and Indian adventure could be easily imitated. Yet models and inspirations outside the novel were perhaps quite as important: Mrs. Sigourney's tremendous success in poems of religious sentiment, Fanny Fern's domestic essays, Ik Marvel's dozing reveries, and the variety of sentimental pieces, whether essay, tale, or poem, which filled the literary annuals and gift-books. It is a fair guess that the domestic novel gradually took over much of the public created by the gift-book vogue, which beginning in 1825 and carrying on to the 60's, showed a marked decline shortly after 1850.[3] And when in 1852 Mrs. Stowe contributed Little Eva to the gallery of sentimental heroines, there was no stopping the lady novelists. The library of fiction which they gradually accumulated is enormous, but the basic tendencies of the genre may be judged from the production of representative authors.

SUSAN WARNER ("ELIZABETH WETHERELL") (1819-1885)

Susan Warner was born in New York City of a not-very-prosperous family whose earliest American representatives were both "Puritans" and Pilgrims.[4] Her first novel, *The Wide, Wide World*, which became possibly the second most popular novel of the century (*Uncle Tom's Cabin* being first), was rejected by several publishers before Putnam's rather casually brought it out at the end of 1850.[5] Miss Warner was herself of a sensitive temperament, and she was like the typical heroine of the domestic novel in being given to melancholy moods in which she shed tears copiously.

The Wide, Wide World made use of many of the devices that were to be standard equipment in the domestic novel for some years to come. Ellen Montgomery is not an orphan, but she is going to be soon. In the meantime the illness of her mother and the business affairs of her father make it necessary to entrust Ellen to the keeping of Aunt Fortune Emerson in a small community in New England. Since Mr. Montgomery has been slow to pay on a loan Aunt Fortune made him, she is none too gracious toward his snip of a daughter. Ellen responds to her aunt's curt treatment by being saucy and rebellious. Yet Ellen is generally sorry at her outbursts of temper, and she keeps resolving to conquer her pride. In this endeavor she is assisted by the saintly young woman Alice Humphreys. In the meantime there are endless illustrations of the day's work—washing dishes, running errands, mending clothes, cooking meals, etc.,[6] as well as incidental object lessons (recalling *Sandford and Merton*) in which Ellen learns why sheep need salt or how a horse can be made to leap a barrier. There are also interminable discussions of how to live the good life, especially by returning good for evil. There is hardly any "plot," but there are many crises. The deaths of mother and father Montgomery are reported. More directly affecting to the reader is the death of Alice Humphreys, who one day calmly announces her own imminent demise:

> "What is the matter, dear Alice? what are you thinking about?"
> "I am thinking, Ellie, how I shall tell you something that will give you pain."
> "Pain! you needn't be afraid of giving me pain," said Ellen fondly, throwing her arms around her;—"tell me, dear Alice; is it something I have done that is wrong? what is it?"
>
> .   .   .   .
>
> "Suppose Ellie," she said at length,—"that you and I were taking a journey together—a troublesome dangerous journey—and

that I had a way of getting at once safe to the end of it;—would you be willing to let me go, and you do without me for the rest of the way?"

"I would rather you should take me with you," said Ellen, in a kind of maze of wonder and fear;—"why where are you going, Alice?"

"I think I am going home, Ellie,—before you."

"Home?" said Ellen.

"Yes,—home I feel it to be; it is not a strange land; I thank God it is my *home* I am going to." [7]

With these news, Ellen

could hardly get home. Her blinded eyes could not see where she was stepping; and again and again her fulness of heart got the better of every thing else, and unmindful of the growing twilight she sat down on a stone by the wayside or flung herself on the ground to let sorrows have full sway.[8]

But when Alice dies in the arms of her brother, the spectacle is wholly edifying, and

the departing spirit had left a ray of brightness on its earthly house; there was a half smile on the sweet face, of most entire peace and satisfaction.[9]

Shortly after this Aunt Fortune decides to cast in her lot with a droll rustic and join her farm with his. It is then up to Ellen to take the advice sent her some time since by her father, to go abroad (which she does in two sentences) to search out her relatives in Edinburgh. The remainder of the book is devoted to Ellen's becoming adjusted (pleasantly, on the whole) with her Scotch relatives. It is understood, however, that after a few years she will return to the country she loves best and to Mr. Humphreys, her adopted "brother."

This story is atypical in that Ellen who is only eight or ten at the beginning of the story is spared all adult emotions of love, for the book ends with her early adolescence. *The Wide, Wide World* is a juvenile. Yet in several respects it helped to establish norms for the whole genre, especially in its casual narrative construction and its enormous content of sentimentality. Weeping and kissing are used to the point of the morbid and the unhygienic. When for example Ellen is leaving Alice Humphreys for a short time the "parting was hard. They held each other fast a good while, and kissed each other many times without speaking." [10] Ellen is also the victim of the osculatory attentions of almost all the other characters of the book. With all this kissing, which a modern psychologist might find objectionable in ways that would have surprised Miss Warner, one might assume that Ellen is a sweet girl. And so she was finally intended by her author to be. Actually she is an impossible prissy. She is even at the beginning, as the rustic Van Brunt says, about as good as anyone can safely be in this world, but Miss Warner hounds her with admonitions to subdue her pride and cultivate true humility. In short Miss Warner rants about religion. She is trying to sanctify a saint. The heroine of her story for modern readers would be Nancy Vawse, the "bad girl" who is used as a foil for Ellen. The recent exploitation of "bad" little girls (in books like Victoria Lincoln's *February Hill*, for example) is partly explicable, no doubt, as a reaction against the saccharine heroines of the domestic sentimentalists. Little Eva has suffered a similar fate: we now prefer Topsy. Each generation selects its own heroines. But certain it is that Ellen Montgomery fitted her own times and that the public found deep satisfaction in the tears and sentiment of *The Wide, Wide World*, for allusions to it occur throughout literature since 1850. The work is even cited as read by characters in other domestic novels.[11]

EMMA DOROTHY ELIZA NEVILLE SOUTHWORTH (1819-1899)

The daughter of a Virginia merchant, E. D. E. N. Southworth was born in Washington, D. C. Much of her early life was spent in Saint Mary County, Maryland, which supplied background for several of her almost innumerable novels. Her marriage to Frederick H. Southworth took her as far west as Wisconsin, where she later taught school before returning to Washington. Her literary career was stabilized in 1847 when the *National Era* published her first novel, *Retribution*. She was encouraged at the time by John G. Whittier (to whom she later gave the idea for "Barbara Frietchie"), but no person who could write such popular stories as Mrs. Southworth presently contributed (serially) to the *New York Ledger* needed encouragement very long. Her greatest success came in 1859 with *The Hidden Hand*, which was subsequently dramatized and performed by John Wilkes Booth in England. By 1877 she had written forty-two novels that seemed worth bringing out in a uniform edition (in Philadelphia) and her total output was more than sixty published novels.[12]

It is usual to include Mrs. Southworth among the group of domestic sentimentalists, but she differs from them in her emphasis on "romantic" elements. In *The Curse of Clifton* (1852), one of her best-known stories, the devious strands of action defy all attempts to see unity in them, but the principal love interest is centered on Archer Clifton, a handsome army officer of high degree, returning to marry his equally patrician cousin, Carolyn. Of course he falls in love with the beautiful daughter of a humble retainer. Of course his admiration of Kate is fiercely resented by the beautiful seventeen-year-old step-mother of Carolyn. The action later becomes more original; Clifton actually marries Carolyn, but she subsequently dies; and in the end a marriage is arranged between the scion of an aristocratic family and the daughter of a simple shepherd. Thus is the drab life of American democracy gilded with romance.

Mrs. Southworth is clearly obsessed with the affairs of characters descended from "a proud and ancient line." Not content with importing noblemen to be used in stories laid in America, she also used foreign settings (another particular in which she is different from most of her colleagues) where baronets and old castles were easy of access and France (for finishing schools) was not far away. She gave wide currency to heroines of the type of Estelle Morelle (the very names of her characters are glamorous), who is introduced as "a peerless beauty, the only child and heiress of the oldest, wealthiest and haughtiest baronet in the West of England." [13] For the period she is relatively bold in her treatment of "passion." She capitalizes directly that wicked fashionable life which most of the domestic novelists viewed with alarm. To be sure there is a republican check on all this: Mrs. Southworth does not completely forget that she is an American and a Virginian by birth. Yet many of her tales are distinctly of the type which, it is confidently believed, was read with bated breath by every chambermaid who cherished secret hopes of some day meeting, nay, even marrying, a lord. On the whole pretty cheap writing, Mrs. Southworth's, as she was not unaware. She is said to have believed that if she had been free from financial need she would have written more definitely in the interest of art and not so much to please the taste of the readers of the *New York Ledger*. Well, possibly. Yet she seems so much at home in her tawdry world of glitter and glamor that one wonders.

MARIA CUMMINS (1827-1866)

Not so prolific or indeed so long-lived as many of her kind, Maria Susanna Cummins wrote one novel, *The Lamplighter*, which with *The Wide, Wide World* and *St. Elmo*, probably represents the chief elements of the domestic novel in its most comprehensive and popular form. Miss Cummins was born at Salem, Massachusetts, and attended Mrs. Charles Sedgwick's fashionable school at Lenox. She was only twenty when she began to write stories for *The Atlantic Monthly* and only twenty-seven when she astonished and delighted an enormous public with *The Lamplighter* (1854).[14] The book was published by John P. Jewett and Company, a house that was responsible for many pious publications in the mid-nineteenth century. It sold 40,000 copies in a few weeks, and it became so well known that literary references were subsequently made to the characters of True and Gertrude without citation of the title of the book.

The little girl in this story is Gertrude, and the ogre-aunt is Nan Grant. Gertrude is rescued from a painfully sordid life on the Boston waterfront by Trueman Flint, the lamplighter, who takes her in and, though an elderly bachelor, nurses her through a three-weeks' illness brought on by exposure. Yet Trueman realizes his unfitness for bringing up a little girl properly and is delighted when Miss Emily Graham, a beautiful blind lady, takes a friendly interest in the waif. By degrees Gertrude is purged of her bad passions, such as revenge, and taught to accept suffering meekly as part of the divine plan. But other trials await her. After Trueman's orthodox sentimental death Gertrude is transferred to the bosom of Emily's family, where she receives good physical care but where she is exposed to female snobbery, the unpleasant attentions of an unworthy lover, the malicious wiles of a cruel and jealous housekeeper, and the gibes of Emily's father—who cannot understand why the independent little minx should reject a trip south in favor of staying home to nurse sick friends. The sick friends die and so does Nan Grant. Besides performing sundry holy duties, Gertrude has learned to support herself by teaching. She has also learned to love William Sullivan, an attractive young businessman whose duties have called him away for a long sojourn in the Orient. Matters of plot move toward a climax when Gertrude takes the usual trip to Saratoga.[15] Here she stumbles on a man who turns out to be her father. Before the relationship is established, however, Gertrude receives another cruel blow of fate when William Sullivan, returned after five years, not only fails to recognize Gertrude (now no child but a woman) but has the effrontery to appear to be intimate with one of the most notorious flirts who ever set foot on Saratoga soil. All is finally worked out satisfactorily, but only after the self-sacrificing Gertrude has risked her life in making sure that the flirt should be rescued from a burning ship. The dénouement demonstrates that Gertrude's father was once the suitor of Emily Graham, and the epilogue unites him in middle-aged bliss to the angelic Emily. Willie assures Gertrude that he had no idea of marrying the fashion-spoiled flirt (he was merely urging her to take care of her sick mother), and the young folks look forward to a life of sober joy. It is apparent that in their wedded life they will be above want, for Willie has made good in business, and Gertrude's father has made a fortune abroad.

The Lamplighter contains a considerable amount of petty realism, but its "morality" seems a little forced. Scenes intended to be deeply touching have a manufactured air—as in the following colloquy concerning a statue of the Infant Samuel in prayer:

> "What do you s'pose he's sittin' on his knee for?"
> Willie laughed. "Why, don't you know?" said he.
> "No," said Gerty; "what is he?"
> "He's praying," said Willie.
> "Is that what he's got his eyes turned up for, too?"
> "Yes, of course; he looks up to heaven when he prays."
> "Up to where?"
> "To heaven."
> Gerty looked up at the ceiling in the direction in which the eyes were turned, then at the figure. She seemed very much dissatisfied and puzzled.
> "Why, Gerty," said Willie, "I shouldn't think you knew what praying was."
> "I don't," said Gerty; "tell me."
> "Don't you ever pray,—pray to God?"
> "No, *I* don't.—Who is God? Where is God?"
> Willie looked inexpressibly shocked at Gerty's ignorance, and answered, reverently, "God is in heaven, Gerty."
> "I don't know where that is," said Gerty. "I believe I don't know nothin' about it."
> "I shouldn't think you did," said Willie. "I *believe* heaven is up in the sky; but my Sunday-school teacher says, 'heaven is anywhere goodness is,' or some such thing," he said.
> "Are the stars in heaven?" said Gerty.
> "They look so, don't they?" said Willie. "They're in the sky, where I always used to think heaven was."
> "I should like to go to heaven," said Gerty.[16]

The fundamental lesson of the book is to teach humble submission to suffering. The author has ransacked the poetry of sentiment to find suitable mottoes for her chapter headings, of which the following (by Mrs. Hemans) will serve as an example not only for *The Lamplighter* but in general for the whole genre:

Yet 'tis a weary task to school the heart,
Ere years of griefs have tamed its fiery spirit
Into that still and passive fortitude
Which is but learned from suffering.[17]

It seems profane to find anything false amid so much patient suffering and high testimony; yet the critical reader will be disturbed to find that a tale of moral regeneration is finally turned into a success story. Repeatedly the characters are urged to resign themselves to suffering in the confidence that only so can the soul be purified. Material goods and fashionable life are repeatedly referred to in terms of scorn. Yet here, as in most of the domestic novels, the author contrives that the hero and heroine shall have not only the satisfaction of having fought the good fight but a substantial monetary reward as well. Evidently the public approved, for *The Lamplighter* became a best seller.

CAROLINE LEE WHITING HENTZ (1800-1856)

Caroline Lee Hentz was born in Massachusetts of a family descended on her father's side from a Samuel Whiting who settled in Massachusetts in 1636. Her father fought in the Revolutionary War. Her husband, Nicholas Marcellus Hentz, was the author of an historical novel, *Tadeuskund, the Last King of the Lenape* (1825). She herself became a fairly prolific novelist. Although a Northerner by birth, Mrs. Hentz lived many years in the South, and it was an incidental purpose of some of her stories (for example, *Linda*), to lessen Northern prejudice against the South by depicting the pleasanter side of slave life on the plantation. Perhaps her best novel, however, is *Ernest Linwood* (1856).

In *Ernest Linwood* the formula for domestic romance is altered to give more prominence to story and less to religion. Sentiment, however, remains a constant, and in fact *Ernest Linwood* is possibly the most lachrymose story in the entire library of sentimental novels, there being approximately eighty references to tears in a single volume. Mrs. Hentz pretty well lives up to her promise that the story will be "full of the wildest romance" and will depict "life's deepest passions." [18] When Gabriella's mother dies, Gabriella is adopted by Mrs. Linwood, the wealthy mistress of Grandison Place. Although morbidly sensitive —a mixture of "pride and diffidence"—Gabriella is fairly well contented in her luxurious adopted home until Mrs. Linwood's son comes home. Ernest is a fascinating but jealous young man against whom Gabriella is warned—but warned in vain, for she is soon married to him.

The young couple live in New York in a sort of Asiatic palace (a familiar motif in the novel of the period) where, alienated from her friends and victimized by her sullen, suspicious husband, Gabriella is a very unhappy bride. Nor is Ernest's temper improved when they encounter the notoriety attendant on the conviction as a forger of a man who has claimed to be Gabriella's (long-lost) father. The climax is reached shortly after Richard, a young man once rejected by Gabriella, tells her that he is her half-brother and is thereupon embraced by Gabriella. Linwood, who has seen the embrace, shoots Richard almost fatally and flees. Other surprises occur—including the reappearance of Gabriella's real father (a twin brother of the forger!) and the intelligence that Richard and Gabriella are only cousins—before the story is concluded. Ernest, now thoroughly penitent and much improved in temperament, is re-united to Gabriella. Despite the sensational nature of its plot, *Ernest Linwood* is not only extremely readable but in many respects well worked out. The characterization is unusually good for the domestic novel, many of the scenes are well developed (instead of being dealt with scrappily as often in novels of the time), and the author's frequently figurative language is considerably more finished than that of the average popular writers of her day. Rather skilful imitation of other writers is obvious. Richardson is recalled by the use of the names Harlowe and Grandison, but he is less conspicuous as a model than Charlotte Brontë, who is recalled by the analogy between Jane Eyre and Gabriella as well as by Rochester-like traits in the hero. If Mrs. Hentz had not been so imbued with the idea that it is "a glorious thing . . . to touch the electric wire of sentiment, and know that thousands [will] thrill at the shock," [19] she might have made *Ernest Linwood* more than a popular book.

MARION HARLAND (MRS. MARY V. H. TERHUNE) (1830-1922)

Marion Harland was one of the most prolific as well as long-lived of all the domestic sentimentalists. She was a native of Virginia, and many of her stories, like those of Augusta Jane Evans Wilson, were laid in the South. Beginning her career as a novelist in 1854, she produced in all twenty-five or more novels, the last, *The Carringtons of High Hill*, appearing in 1919. In 1856 she married Edward Payson Terhune, the well-known minister. Finding all available household manuals utterly inadequate, she wrote one herself, *Common Sense in the Household* (1871), which not only went through several editions but deflected her for a time from fiction to home economics.[20] To meet popular demand she wrote scores of articles. She was also an indefatigable traveler and lecturer. In time she collaborated on books with her children, one of whom was Albert Payson Terhune. Her autobiography, *Marion Harland's Autobiography*, appeared in 1910.[21]

Alone (1854), Miss Harland's first book, has been called her best.[22] The heroine, Ida Ross, is no different from many sister heroines of the period in being a lonely but proud and somewhat embittered orphan girl living with a disagreeable guardian and his daughter. That she lives at Richmond, Virginia, gives her more distinction than all these traits. She presently falls in love with a young man who appears to love her equally until through the machinations of a jealous girl he is informed that Ida is engaged to another man. He therefore becomes engaged to a worthless coquette. This is the moment when the domestic novelist "regenerates" her heroine: the stricken Ida suffers fearfully for a time, but out of her suffering (and the concurrent homilies of a kindly Negro) is born a new Ida. She becomes a professing Christian and settles down on the old plantation determined to devote her life to doing good. But here again the author steps in, with a very tangible reward: the young man's fickle fiancée has jilted him and he is now free to marry Ida. And just to make the moral unmistakable, the jealous Josephine becomes a cranky old maid. True to type, also, is Ida's renunciation after her marriage of all claims to feminine independence, for she has learned that "Submission is a pleasure, not a cross." [23] The story as a whole is needlessly long and badly proportioned. The character of Miss Harland's frequently overwrought style may be judged from an observation made by Ida when she was first introduced to her adopted family: "her heart told her that the bruised tendrils which had been torn from their original support could never learn to twine around these gelid statues." [24] The Southern setting is warmly eulogized [25] if not very fully described, and Miss Harland puts into the mouth of one of her characters comments that are favorable to slavery:

> "The slave lies down at night, every want supplied, his family as well cared for as himself; not a thought of tomorrow! he is secure of a house and maintenance, without disturbing himself as to the manner in which it is to be obtained. Can the same be said of the menial classes in any other country under the sun?" [26]

But this speech is only part of a discussion in which slavery is also deplored. A little malice toward the Yankee may lurk in a quiet remark in her second novel, *The Hidden Path* (1854): "The Virginia boy is an indifferent trader—the Virginia man, seldom a sharper," [27] but Miss

Harland generally forbore to tilt openly against political convictions or social conventions. There is, as usual in the domestic novel, much discussion of feminine independence; yet Miss Harland makes it clear in the dedication to *The Hidden Path* that if she "assail[s] rooted prejudices, it is in no 'strong-minded' spirit of Reform, but through love for the truly Good and Noble." The Good and the Noble, indeed, plus a few hackneyed plot devices and the patient enumeration of detail used to illustrate the "rough discipline of Life" [28] constituted Miss Harland's stock in trade as a novelist.

ANN SOPHIA STEPHENS (1813-1886)

Ann Stephens relied on many of the same materials as the rest of the domestic sisterhood, but she added a few new touches. Her career as a periodical writer began in Portland (Maine), but she soon moved to New York, where she was named associate editor of the *Ladies' Companion*, a magazine whose circulation she greatly increased by her historical tales. In the 40's she was "one of the best known of the New York literati," [29] and she "had the first *salon* in New York." [30] She was so prolific that "between 1854 and 1880 she published more than twenty-five books in addition to the serials, poems, and articles constantly appearing in periodicals." In 1860 she published the first dime novel, *Malaeska*, which was in reality not typical of the dime novel as it later developed, for it is a story of Indian life. The most popular of her novels were *Fashion and Famine* (1854) and *The Old Homestead* (1855). *Fashion and Famine* is compounded of sterner stuff than most domestic novels. Its plot, which is too involved for a brief précis, turns on the familiar hinges of the misidentification of characters. In this case a young woman who has years before abandoned her (legitimate) infant daughter, succeeds in discovering the child, but in the process of trying to regain possession of her is involved in violent complications which cause the child's grandfather to be convicted of a murder of which he is innocent. The story owes much to Dickens. Ada Leicester (the very names are borrowed) has much in common with Lady Dedlock in *Bleak House* and there are prison scenes which recall *Little Dorrit*. The prison scenes, though courageously conceived for the time, are too much sprinkled with sentiment and melodrama to be wholly convincing. It is when Mrs. Stephens inveighs against the injustices of legal procedure that she exhibits her greatest originality and force. She was particularly incensed at a law which in effect imprisoned an innocent person for months merely because he was a witness:

It is strange—nay, it is horrible—that so much of barbarism still lingers in the laws and customs of a free land . . . In New York, the poor witness—a man who has the misfortune to know anything of a crime before the courts, is himself exactly in the place of a criminal. Like the malefactor, he must give bonds for his prompt appearance on the day of trial, or lacking the influence to obtain these, must himself share the prison of the very felon his evidence will condemn. Strangers thus—sea-faring men, and persons destitute of friends—are often imprisoned for months among the very dregs of humanity; innocent, and yet suffering the severest penalties of guilt.

This injustice, so glaring that a savage would blush to acknowledge it, exists almost unnoticed in a city overrun with benevolent societies, crowded with churches, and inundated with sympathies for the wronged of every nation or city on earth. If ostentatious charity would for a time, give way to simple justice, New York like all the American cities we know of, would obtain for itself more respect abroad and more real prosperity at home.[31]

In such diatribes as this (given as her own opinion) Mrs. Stephens is largely original. Her descriptive talent, however, is seen to the best advantage outside prison walls. The first chapter of *Fashion and Famine* contains a description of New York at dawn which, allowing for natural differences in language and data, is not far different from many modern realistic treatments of the same subject. She is also particularly skilled in the description of food. Washington Irving himself seldom provided a better stimulus to the salivary glands than Mrs. Stephens does in her account of preparations for a Thanksgiving dinner:

Mrs. Gray had done wonders that morning. The dinner was in a most hopeful state of preparation. The great red crested, imperious looking turkey, that had strutted away his brief life in the barn-yard, was now snugly bestowed in the oven—Mrs. Gray had not yet degenerated down to a cooking-stove . . . There he sat, the poor denuded monarch—turned up in a dripping-pan, simmering himself brown in the kitchen oven. Never, in all his pomp, had that bosom been so warmed and distended—yet the huge turkey had been a sad gourmand in his time. A rich thymy odor broke through every pore of his body; drops of lucious [*sic*] gravy dripped down his sides, filling the oven with an unctuous stream that penetrated a crevice in the door, and made the poor Irish girl cross herself devoutly. She felt her spirit so yearning after the good things of earth, and never having seen Thanksgiving set down in the calendar, was shy of surrendering her heart to a holiday that had no saint to patronize it.[32]

In short Mrs. Stephens had two real gifts—for trenchant criticism and for concrete descriptive detail. It is when she enters the domain of the emotions that she begins to generate that morbid psychological atmosphere which vitiates the work of so many writers of her period. As for her dime novel, *Malaeska*, posterity has long since shelved it with others of its kind, for the "power" they depended on to thrill contemporary readers seems now to have been merely rant.[33]

FANNY FERN (MRS. SARA PAYSON WILLIS PARTON) (1811-1872)

Fanny Fern was born in Portland (Maine), lived as a child in Boston, attended Catharine Beecher's school in Hartford, was first married and served her literary apprenticeship in Boston, and finally moved (in the mid-1850's) to New York, where she lived a somewhat checkered literary life until her death in 1872. Her book of collected essays, *Fern Leaves* (1853), sold 80,000 copies, a fact which seems to have encouraged many other ladies to essay an author's career. In New York she contributed copiously to the *Home Journal* and the *New York Ledger*. She was a "domestic" writer in that she celebrated the joys of home life, gardening, and country avocations; but she also wrote of the annoyances of tending home and babies, and she possessed a flair for pungent satire which found its target in cant and hypocrisy wherever she experienced them, especially among the idle wealthy and among the literary set. Another of her targets was her brother N. P. Willis, the poet, who received such ungracious treatment in *Ruth Hall* (1855), her first novel, that the author was roundly condemned.

In *Ruth Hall* Fanny Fern uses a domestic framework for her story, but she brushes in so much satire that the final result is far different from the conventional daubs of her sister novelists. The plot, largely devoid of "startling developments" and "hairbreadth escapes," is nevertheless made up mostly of stock materials. After her marriage to Harry Hall, the heroine is subjected to the pain of living with his disagreeable, gossiping, prying, and malicious parents. When her husband's death leaves her a penniless widow with two children, her brother refuses to aid her and she is forced to accept the grudgingly-given assistance of the Hall family. Her wealthy cousins allow her to use their basement to do her washing providing she brings her own soap! The only way out of such humiliating conditions is through self-support, but sewing yields too little and a teaching position is denied her. Lastly Ruth turns to journalism. She is snubbed by a number of editors, including her brother (who controls a popular magazine), but succeeds finally in marketing a few articles which are the cornerstone of a real literary success. Her brother, who had refused to permit her name to be mentioned in his columns, now tries unsuccessfully to get credit for and capitalize her success. Ruth is reunited with her kiddies in a happy ending. Maybe, too, she will marry Walters, an editor who has befriended her in darker days.

The structure of *Ruth Hall* is original only in that the inevitable unhappy childhood is not directly presented but is recapitulated after the heroine has become engaged to be married. The episodes are brief as is almost universally the case in popular feminine fiction, and the book lacks balance. The influence of Dickens is distinctly felt in several scenes, and especially in a description of a counting-house.[34] Dialogue, plentifully used throughout, is unusual in the briskness and brevity of the speeches. As for the didactic burden of the book, Fanny Fern avows that she has written the story to "fan into a flame, in some tried heart, the fading embers of hope, well-nigh extinguished by wintry fortune and summer friends," [35] but it is clear that her interest lay less in pious platitude and tender ministering to the "tried heart" of the unknown reader than in discharging her rancor against the cruel authors of her own misfortunes. Hyacinth (who stands for N. P. Willis) is represented as "a conceited jackanapes, who divides his time between writing rhymes and inventing new ties for his cravat" and (later) as "a mincing, conceited, tip-toeing, be-curled, be-perfumed popinjay." [36] He is referred to as a person without depth or integrity who writes one article a week and employs a poorly paid ghost-writer to produce the rest of his output.[37] Throughout the latter half of the book there is much discussion of the commercial aspects of contemporary literary life—the difficulty of getting the editor's ear especially if one is unknown and a woman, the poor pay accorded novices for hack-work, the tendency of reviewers either to deal in atrociously unfair abuse of a book they haven't bothered to read or to puff the productions of a writer regarded as influential. The style of the book is remarkably free from that faded-violet quality which enveloped so many books of the period. Sometimes indeed the author pursues colloquial idiom almost to the point of wilful eccentricity:

> In person Mrs. Waters was barber-pole-ish and ramrod-y, and her taste in dress running mostly to stringy fabrics, assisted the bolster-y impression she created; her hands and wrists bore a strong resemblance to the yellow claws of defunct chickens, which children play "scare" with about Thanksgiving time; her feet were of turtle flatness, and her eyes—if you ever provoked

a cat up to the bristling and scratching point, you may possibly form an idea of them.[38]

One suspects that critics were irritated by the racy, slangy, flippant manner which Miss Fern adopted in place of the decorous, flowing periods deemed appropriate to her sex. But most of all they were scandalized by her incredibly vindictive characterization not only of her brother but of her parents as well.[39] One critic asserted that "art would never admit such stony-hearted monsters in a story of real life"; another invoked the names of Goneril and Regan as the only fit analogues for Ruth's unnatural hatred.[40] Hawthorne, however, enjoyed the book "a good deal" precisely because the author wrote "as if the Devil was in her." [41] *Ruth Hall* proved Fanny Fern to be an able and provocative writer if not a good novelist. It also proved that if women were to be accepted popularly in the 1850's their best cue was to eschew satire. The common opinion of the function of women as writers had been expressed only three years before by a critic who was reviewing J. S. Hart's *Female Prose Writers of America:* "Woman," said the critic, "is eminently the author for piety and faith." [42]

MARY JANE HAWES HOLMES (1825-1907)

The muse of female inspiration behaved more normally in Mary Jane Holmes's *Tempest and Sunshine,* also published in the banner year 1854. Its author was born in Brookfield, Massachusetts. Destined to be a long-lived and prolific writer, she was also precocious, for she began writing at fifteen. *Tempest and Sunshine* was followed by a long series of stories—about forty—published between 1854 and 1905. Many of the stories were studies of small town life, and all were packed with affecting incident and wholesome ideals set forth in relatively simple language: Mrs. Holmes was no bluestocking. Perhaps the best-known among them is that "lachrymal classic," [43] *Lena Rivers* (1856).

Lena Rivers is a slightly more substantial story than is suggested by the term "lachrymal classic." It has tears, to be sure, and its plot is a pretty antiquated vehicle whose motive power is coincidence; but it also has a degree of local color, considerable realistic incident, and genuine humor (not whimsy). When Lena (Helena) Rivers, a fatherless waif whose family escutcheon is somewhat smudged, exchanges her lowly rural home in Massachusetts for the luxurious ménage of her aristocratic uncle in Lexington, Kentucky, it is obvious that she will be the victim of the snobbery and slander of her aunts and cousins (female). It is also predictable that Cinderella will grow in accomplish-

ments and beauty so that when an eligible young man comes along, she
is preferred to her haughty cousin Carrie. The persons in the story will
be surprised when Lena's father turns up, but the reader will not, for
Lena Rivers is a true romance. It is hardly necessary to add that father
not only is guiltless of the crime charged against him in earlier days but
also is pleasantly rich.

It is to be feared that our grandmothers read *Lena Rivers* for the
sake of the ingredients listed above, but they may have read it also for
its good sense of place (Mrs. Holmes had herself lived in Kentucky for
a time) and its amusing delineation of Negro life and character especially as revealed in the salty discourse of Aunt Milly, the head cook.
For whatever reason, read her they did, for the sales of her books
totaled over 2,000,000 copies, and she was next to E. P. Roe "probably
the most popular of American novelists during the period following the
Civil War." [44]

AUGUSTA JANE EVANS WILSON (1835-1909)

Of all the domestic writers whose first books appeared in the 50's,
perhaps the most talented and certainly one of the most popular was
Mrs. Wilson, author of the most celebrated book in the whole genre of
the domestic novel, *St. Elmo* (1866). Mrs. Wilson was a native of Columbus, Georgia, but moved to Texas as a girl and later lived for many
years in Alabama. She began writing at the tender age of fifteen, but
her books are not many, for like so many characters in her own and
other domestic novels, she was handicapped as an author both by delicate health and by a husband who did not approve of literary careers
for women. Her eight novels were published at fairly wide intervals
between 1858 and 1902. They show more range of interest than Mrs.
Wilson is generally credited with, but their chief popular ingredient
was sentiment.

Inez: a Tale of the Alamo (1855), Mrs. Wilson's first published novel,
did not display her most vendible qualities. It is a crudely assembled
story with little characterization, no humor, and inferior stylistic quality. Sentiment it contains, but much of the author's energy is drawn
off into an account of the siege of the Alamo and tirades against Catholicism. The historical novel was obviously not Mrs. Wilson's forte,
and to attack Catholicism was a poor way to sell novels even in the
South. But there was hope for a writer able to draw characters who
could say (as did drooping Mary when she felt a premonition of death):

. . . I know full well that my life is gradually wasting away, slowly, gently, and almost without pain. I am sinking to an early tomb. Yet I would not have it otherwise if I could. Death has long lost all terrors for me; I have no fear—all is peace and quiet.[45]

A writer capable of such effects as this should not waste her substance in historical writing. Mrs. Wilson saw the error of her ways and in *Beulah* (1859) she placed before the public one of the heaviest brews of sentiment ever offered a thirsty generation. It has most of the ingredients tried and tested by earlier sentimentalists as well as some others which were the special patent of Mrs. Wilson. The heroine is Beulah Benton, an ugly duckling, who is not only an orphan but an orphan in an asylum. With her at first are a little sister, Lilly, and a dear friend Claudia, but these companions in misery are adopted by a snobbish wealthy woman who refuses to let Beulah see them any more— even when Lilly is fatally ill of scarlet fever. Beulah herself is later sent out as nursemaid to another snobbish woman, who overworks her until she is rescued by Dr. Hartwell, a thirty-year-old handsome, moody, mysterious gentleman freely translated from Brontë's Rochester. In Hartwell's home Beulah enjoys some happiness (despite persecution by Hartwell's sister, who fears he will leave his money to Beulah) and a bond of affection is established that is obviously not merely one between guardian and ward. But friction soon arises between Beulah and her benefactor on account of the congenital flaw in a domestic heroine's character, namely, pride. An estrangement occurs when Beulah insists on teaching in a public school. Later Hartwell makes a sudden proposal of marriage, but is refused. He goes on a five-year tramp abroad (in the Orient, of course), while Beulah, more and more alone, busies herself with reading and writing. Her writing brings her money and a measure of fame, but her reading in books against which Hartwell had warned her, plunges her into atheism—Emerson being one of the contributing causes! Ultimately Hartwell's pride is relaxed and he comes back to effect a reconciliation with Beulah, whose pride is now so reduced through suffering that she meekly assents to stipulations of Hartwell that make her marriage almost tantamount to an abdication of independence. She has salvaged what she could from her wrecked faith, and one of her first tasks in wedlock will be to help restore Hartwell to orthodoxy. In the meantime the story has been filled with various strands of action not referred to in this summary, but the same overcharged emotional atmosphere envelops everything. The total effect is of course unrealistic, but the book exerts a morbid fascination which can be felt even today.

Despite her lack of success in *Inez* (which had dealt with the Mexican War), Mrs. Wilson returned to "historical" subject-matter in *Macaria: or, Altars of Sacrifice* (1864), a narrative dealing with the first phases of the Civil War. The book is in effect a Confederate document: it appeared in fact with a Confederate copyright. Its heroine passionately avows that she is willing to give up her "all on earth," praying that God will "accept the sacrifice, and crown the South a sovereign, independent nation." Mrs. Wilson reveals herself as a fierce Southern partisan, full of hatred for the "canting, puritanical hypocrisy" of the North and convinced that the War was to be explained as "the first fruits of the bigotry and fanatical hate of New England, aided by the unprincipled demagogism of the West." [46] *Macaria* was sharply criticized in the North, which could "accept her emotionalism but not her sectionalism." [47] In her next book Mrs. Wilson offered almost undiluted "emotionalism."

One year after the end of the War, Mrs. Wilson brought out her chef d'oeuvre, *St. Elmo* (1866). It is a synthesis of all the sure-fire tricks of the lady novelists except the discovery of the long-lost relative—a good riddance. There is the orphan heroine, Edna Earl, more beautiful than the formula calls for, to be sure, but soon made destitute of kindred and friends. There is the wealthy woman, Mrs. Murray, who decides to keep and train the derelict thrown accidentally on her doorstep. There is the dissolute and disillusioned but glamorous son of Mrs. Murray, St. Elmo, returned from foreign travels. There are the rude approaches of this American replica of Byron to Edna, who spurns him. There is his sullen reaction and precipitate departure for Oriental scenes, Edna meanwhile plying her books and writing articles. There is his melodramatic re-entrance—Edna being alone at the time in a Gothic chamber—and his subsequent recital of the lurid events of his past life, particularly of his having killed his rival in love and having determined to revenge himself on his faithless fiancée by making love to women chiefly for the satisfaction of breaking their hearts. From this fascinating monster of iniquity, Edna naturally flees to New York, there to act as governess (again in a wealthy home) and to minister to Felix, a little crippled boy (crippled boys being stage property in many of these dramas of the heart). She overworks, becomes famous as a "female" writer serving much the same function as present-day Dorothy Dix, and refuses various offers of marriage; but she will not see St. Elmo again—until she learns that, thoroughly reformed, he has entered the ministry! This intelligence breaks down Edna's moral scruples: she consents at last to marry him and renounce her literary career. The union of a pure if priggish girl to an overspent roué is a thought to be regarded only with loathing by the modern reader, but evidently it was romance to the fevered readers of the 1860's. Other inevitable elements in the story include a blind girl, a deaf-mute, a railway wreck, Edna's delirious fever, her almost "habitual" pallor, St. Elmo's three-weeks coma, several deaths, endless discussions of women's independence, and the trip to Saratoga. *St. Elmo* was the crowning unit in the whole structure of domestic sentimentality.

After *St. Elmo*, Mrs. Wilson's remaining books appeared at infrequent intervals. *Vashti* (1869), like its predecessors, quivers with emotion, but it deals more extensively with the subject of careers for women. The principals in *Infelice* (1875) could be interchanged with those in *Beulah* or *St. Elmo* without much alteration of character, and the story exhibits no new feature of importance unless it be the use of an incipient mother-complex in Regina. *At the Mercy of Tiberius* (1887) has Mrs. Wilson's usual sickly atmosphere, but new elements appear, including a murder charge (with trial) against the heroine, occasional flashes of humor (mostly of Negro origin), sociological comment on the state of the South during Reconstruction, and slightly freer discussions of the moral code for women.

In 1902 Mrs. Wilson's last novel, *The Speckled Bird,* was presented to a generation far different from the credulous, sentiment-sucking public that first read *Beulah:* emancipated, tight-skirted women were abroad in the land competing with men industrially and "claiming equal rights in sin." Mrs. Wilson tries in this novel to keep up with the times by varying the characters and employing topical material (strikes, socialism, political chicanery), but it is clear that despite her energetic style and often amusing comments, she is out of her element. She has survived herself.

What the public had valued in her was her analysis of the emotions. The twin bases of her vast appeal were undoubtedly religion and sex. Her "religious cast of mind" [48] made it easy for her to reach that part of the public which would touch no novel unless it were morally spotless. Excluding her Southern bias (which was not reflected strongly except in one or two of her novels) she uttered no convictions that might breed social unrest: she was against female innovators of all sorts and she denounced woman's suffrage. Likewise her code of sexual morality was rigid enough to satisfy the most conservative readers. Yet there can be no question that between the lines of her decorous discourse lay an area rich in suggestion for the minds of readers intent on the thrills of love-making. Victorian ethics forbade the seduction of the heroine and frowned upon all but the most oblique references to the mating instinct. Yet here (in *St. Elmo*, for instance) was a handsome Byronic rake palpably interested in a desirable young woman, and if the author could not say much, readers could make the most of such carefully muffled suggestions as were offered. Occasionally Mrs. Wilson does call attention to an amorous look and she allows Dr. Hartwell (in *Beulah*) to kiss the heroine "passionately," but for the most part she contents herself with setting up an atmosphere in which the reader's speculation may thrive without acknowledged help by the author. No transaction in writing remained to indict her. It may be that the excessive amount of kissing between women in the books of Mrs. Wilson and other purveyors of sentiment was a vicarious type of erotic thrill, but it was not recognized as such, and no contemporary moralist could hang anything on the author. Yet her books are more unwholesome than those of many an author who dealt more explicitly with the sexual instinct.

It is easy to sneer at Mrs. Wilson's writing as mere maudlin analyses of morbid states of mind. Yet she was in some ways a very able writer —ingenious in the invention and treatment of incident, remarkably skilled in sustaining a mood, and possessed of an easy, flexible prose style. She studded her pages with excessive allusions, for she was possessed of remarkable erudition,[49] but the enthralled reader can easily skip these in order to pick up the current of emotion. In her command of the resources of the domestic novel Mrs. Wilson was without a peer in her time. She was a first-rate writer of a second-rate type of fiction.

The fifties were the heyday of the domestic novel as far as the appearance of new authors was concerned, but the vogue of the genre continued for a number of years despite two discouragements to literary endeavor, the panic of 1857 and the Civil War. The effects of financial depression on literature are hard to trace, but apparently there was some retardation in the publishing industry, and at least one writer complained in 1857 that "literature and lecturing were both at a standstill."[50] Established writers like Longfellow and Holmes of course retained their following, but it was harder for new writers to gain a foothold. As for the domestic novelists, those who had already "arrived" continued to pile up editions, and some new ones appeared. From England, incidentally, came in 1861 one of the prime favorites of the whole school of the domestic romance, Mrs. Wood's *East Lynne*. In America, as has been seen, Mrs. Wilson made her greatest success in the 60's. Among other writers who appeared first after 1860 were Mrs. H. B. Goodwin, T. S. Arthur, J. G. Holland, and E. P. Roe.

MRS. H. B. GOODWIN (1827-1893)

Mrs. Goodwin, author of *Sherbrooke* (1866), *Dr. Howell's Family* (1868), and other stories, is of some special interest because although she dealt much in familiar plot devices and spiritual nostrums, she managed to make some of her characters a little more real and her village settings a shade less stereotyped. In these respects *Sherbrooke* is superior to *Dr. Howell's Family*.[51] It is also more interesting for another reason, namely, that its wealth of comment on books and authors provides an excellent insight into popular literary tastes and standards of its day. Tribute is paid to Longfellow, Bryant ("more thoroughly American than any other poet of ours" [52]), Richter, Mrs. Browning, Tennyson, Ik Marvel, Bayard Taylor, Mrs. Stowe, and others.[53] Of particular interest are the comments on the domestic novel. Ellen at ten years (an appropriate age) asks Hope to read Miss Warner's *Wide, Wide World* to her. Hope herself (the heroine) likes Miss Warner's *Queechy* "more than any story I have ever read," and later expresses her literary ambitions thus:

> "I even dared hope that I might leave 'foot-prints in the sands of time,' might make a name worthy of being written on the same page with Mrs. Stowe's, Miss Warner's, and Miss Cummins's." [54]

A few streaks of a dawning critical attitude toward the domestic novel are discernible in the remarks of Mr. Chapman, who thinks that religious sentiment has reached the saturation point. He is discussing Miss Warner's *Queechy* with Hope:

> Mr. Chapman: "There are some very good descriptions of every-day life in it, but many more distorted, unnatural scenes; for instance, Mrs. Evelyn's persistent annoyance of her guest, and Mr. Thorn's persecution of the lady whom he wishes to win. Then Fleda was too pretty and pious, too astonishingly capable for an ordinary mortal—"
> Hope: "Not too pious, Mr. Chapman?"
> Mr. Chapman: "Well, I didn't mean to speak lightly of genuine piety, or to affirm that a person could have too much of it; but it seems to me there is such a thing as making too great a parade of it."
>
> .   .   .   .   .   .
>
> Hope: "But you like Miss Warner's style?"
> Mr. Chapman: "It has some excellences; it is simple, unpretending,

and not too ornate, but it wants strength and vigor. The long conversations dilute and weaken it; she would have made a much
more readable book by compressing it nearly one-half." [55]

Yet the key to the popularity of these books lies more nearly in the
attitude of the frivolous, worldly girls, Virginia and Belinda, one of
whom avers that "too much critical ability spoils one's pleasure." The
other finds even Dickens dull: "he writes about such common characters—old fishermen, and paupers, and prisoners." [56] For her part, she
wants "descriptions of the best society," and she therefore "dotes" so
on Mrs. Southworth and Marion Harland that she sits up until midnight
to read them.[57] Further discussions centre in the truth of Mrs. Stowe's
depiction of slavery and the question of whether Mrs. Gaskell in her
life of Charlotte Brontë (the latter one of the models for Mrs. Goodwin's own work) did or did not "violate the sanctities of private life"
by discussing the violence of Brontë's father and the dissipation of
Branwell. If not a first-rate novel, then, *Sherbrooke* is a very interesting indication of popular trends in literature of the 1860's.

TIMOTHY SHAY ARTHUR (1809-1885)

The manifold achievement of T. S. Arthur is almost wholly without
recognition now except by a few persons who recall with a tolerant
smile his gallant effort to emphasize the importance of temperance reform in *Ten Nights in a Bar-Room* (1854). Actually he experimented
in a variety of literary forms so successfully that he had the ear of a
large public for two decades more or less. Born in New York, he lived
later in Baltimore and, after 1841, in Philadelphia. He was largely self-
educated. His business experience included watchmaking, acting as a
clerk, traveling in the West as an agent for a banking house, and editing
a newspaper. From the last vocation he moved naturally into authorship, in which he was so active that by 1875 his production had reached
the number of about seventy titles.[58] These included juvenile books,
manuals of advice to young people, hints to married folk, and miscellaneous volumes of instruction accompanied by entertaining sketches
and stories that were not intended to conceal the author's didactic purpose. In the domestic novel he was somewhat unusual in using the
theme of marital maladjustment. Sometimes as in *The Two Wives*
(1851) the marriage is blasted by the husband's weakness for liquor and
cards. But in two novels which he wrote in the 60's the basis of the
marital difficulty was extreme incompatibility in temperament. The
first of these, *The Withered Heart* (1860), tells the story of a young

wife, Jane Enfield Hardy, who has been brought up by indulgent parents. She was not grossly spoiled but accustomed to having her own way. When she marries, she encounters the cold, calculating, cruel temperament of a husband (Hardy) who insists on having *his* own way. They clash over issues that are found in much more modern novels: shall they live in a house of their own or live with Jane's parents? Shall the children be sent away to school or not? In these and other such crises, Jane pleads with her husband but Hardy is adamant. That she is brought to tears and nervous exhaustion means nothing to him: he responds harshly and stamps out of the house, embittered because his home has in it no sunshine and happiness. A few kind words from him, it is intimated, might bring them to an emotional rapport, but these are not forthcoming from Hardy, who does not understand the nervous organization of women. Jane is finally committed to an asylum, but with more realism than many of his contemporaries would have exhibited, the author brings about her virtual recovery, and, later on, after Jane makes an unexpected overture toward a reconciliation, the marriage is much improved. Both parties to the marriage are brought to the realization of the need for forbearance and sympathy. The author's own sympathies are apparently more on the side of Jane than of her husband, but it is also made clear that, partly as a result of her indulgent upbringing, she has failed as a wife. Moreover, Arthur seems to share the husband's belief that "there cannot be two heads in any government—national, municipal, or domestic." [59] This story as a whole is by no means free from defect, but it is told with much more attention to unity than most domestic novels, and despite its didactic tenor it is more realistic. Arthur was seeking to instruct rather than to thrill his readers.

Out in the World (1864) is also a story of marital maladjustment. In this case the wife, partly as the result of her association with a somewhat radical friend, insists on her rights so rigidly that there is constant friction. An estrangement occurs, after which the wife leaves home and tries to support herself. After a number of years, her husband divorces her for desertion and marries another woman, a vulgar shrew who makes life miserable for him. Madeline meantime has had a rough experience of the world. In the end a reconciliation is effected, but it comes too late. The two principals die peacefully in the knowledge that each has forgiven the other. The difficulty described in this story comes about from the mating of people of opposing temperaments. In the quarrel that ensues, the husband is partly at fault, for "when a husband puts on the tyrant, love vanishes," [60] but Arthur makes it perfectly clear that though a woman has her rights, she does not have equal rights, and she must never abandon her home and try to carry on alone. The story is ineffective artistically because of Arthur's poor command of dialogue and because of his air of reciting a case-history. Yet it is of compelling interest in its analysis of real problems of the day. Arthur is significant, too, as the first American novelist (after Imlay) to treat of divorce.[61]

JOSIAH GILBERT HOLLAND (1819-1881)

J. G. Holland's first profession was medicine, but he soon abandoned it as unsuited to him. After a period of school-teaching in Virginia and Mississippi, he returned to his native state, Massachusetts, and became an associate of Samuel Bowles, editor of the *Springfield Republican*—Bowles to handle public affairs and Holland "human interest." Holland interested his public so keenly in a number of sketches and stories, especially a series of sketches entitled *Titcomb's Letters to Young People, Single and Married* (1858), that he later largely gave up routine editorial duties in favor of creative writing. He was much in demand as a lyceum lecturer. Yet he managed to produce a great many books in prose and verse, almost all of which have such a moral and religious bias that Holland has frequently been referred to as a minister. He also wrote biographies, including a very moral life of Abraham Lincoln (1866). Although half a million copies of his books were sold, Holland's stories were "unsensational," for whatever may have been his artistic tastes, his literary aims were strictly honorable: he aimed to minister to the spiritual and moral needs of his generation.[62] Probably his best and best-known novel is *Arthur Bonnicastle* (1873). Although sub-titled "An American Novel," this story is a patent imitation of Dickens's *Great Expectations*. The narrative carries the hero from the age of ten to his marriage. Arthur is brought up with the expectation of inheriting his "aunt's" estate. The sinister effects of such expectations are shown in his conduct at school (in New Hampshire) and at college. He learns to be proud, extravagant, indolent, and ashamed of his own father. Although he has begun college with some ambition to succeed, he wastes many opportunities, and on one occasion he becomes disgracefully drunk. In all this the author has contrasted Arthur's unfortunate behavior with the exemplary conduct of one of his friends, Henry Hulm, a lad of no expectations. The inevitable reversal occurs when it is learned (partly through the inevitable family portrait) that the real heir is not Arthur but Henry. Instead of collapsing completely at this discovery, Arthur proves that he can respond to a crisis. He teaches school by day and studies law by night, and in the end he marries an ideal girl and becomes a successful lawyer. Henry remains his devoted friend. The parallel to Dickens's *Great Expectations* is obvious at a number of points (Mrs. Sanderson, Arthur's "aunt," for example, is very closely related to Miss Havisham), but the author drew on his experience in his full account of schoolboy life at the "Bird's Nest." There is a wealth of interesting detail relating to social life, religious revivals (here as elsewhere in the domestic novel condemned because of their "unwise and unworthy" methods), and life in a fashionable clique in New York City. The novel is different from many popular novels of the period in being a boy's story, in being somewhat freer from tearful sentiment, and in being an illustration not so much of a "moral" as of a theory of life and education. If its characters had been endowed with more weight, the book might have achieved permanent distinction.

EDWARD PAYSON ROE (1838-1888)

If anything were needed to give the final sanction to novel reading, it was provided when novel-writing was actually adopted as a profession by a clergyman in good standing—Edward Payson Roe. Roe was born in New York state, the son of a New York merchant. He attended Williams College for two years, but poor health prompted him to move to Auburn Theological Seminary. Ordained in 1862, he served as chaplain during part of the Civil War. In 1871 a visit to Chicago just after the great fire had begun to subside gave him the idea for his first novel, *Barriers Burned Away*, which was first serialized and then printed in book form (1872). It was received so well that he promptly wrote another novel, *Opening a Chestnut Burr* (1874), "to determine whether the amazing success of the first was an accident or the product of a dependable formula." [63] Persuaded that the latter hypothesis was correct, he resigned his ministerial duties and settled at Cornwall on the Hudson to commence work on a series of stories that reached the number of seventeen, all apparently best-sellers.

The formula of Roe has been described as follows:

> first, some topical material, historical event, or current issue; second, characters and incidents selected directly from his personal observation or from newspapers; third, an abundance of nature descriptions with much praise of the rural virtues; and fourth, plots concerned almost invariably, and never too deviously, with the simultaneous pursuit of wives, fortunes, and salvation.[64]

In *Barriers Burned Away* the first and fourth of these elements are most conspicuous; the setting in Chicago precluded much "nature" description. The fire itself is reserved for the position of climax in the last quarter of the book. In the meantime the reader has been made acquainted with a naive but determined-to-make-good rural lad trying to find a job in the vast and frequently heartless city of Chicago. He experiences the alternating rebuffs and successes that have been made familiar in scores of imitators of Roe. Suffice it to recall that although on the brink of starvation, he nobly refuses a job in a saloon. But he *will* shovel snow, and so commences his upward climb.[65] By the time he is moderately established as a young businessman, Dennis Fleet (for that, as the formula goes, is the hero's name) has painfully to learn that barriers are not only economic but social. The young lady he loves is a frivolous denizen of a social world into which he cannot penetrate—at first. But incidental business relationships and later their common interest in art bring boy and girl together. She humiliates him repeatedly, and she finally perpetrates the cruel trick of letting him make love to her so that she may paint him in the attitude of wooing. This device recoils upon its originator, for she falls in love with him in the process. But he casts her off, and it is not until the great fire breaks out that they are brought together again. But barriers are religious also; and even in the act of saving her, Dennis suffers for Christine's unregenerate state: she is an infidel. Fortunately the emergency of the fire and his admonitions during the rather long-drawn-out rescue bring Christine to a realization of the importance of true faith: consequently when he finally understands that her emotion toward him is deeper than gratitude, he is only too glad to claim her purified hand. So ends a book of absorbing interest to the public aimed at by Roe, "the young" and "the common people." [66] It is easy to see upon retrospect that its appeal, like the appeal of so many "moral" books then and now, was fundamentally grounded in a happy tie-up of religious faith and "success." Much is made of the state of Dennis's finance and one of the minor climaxes is his winning a $2,000 prize for a picture. Yet there is no hint here of the mere worship of Mammon, for Roe endows his hero with the highest motives. Dennis examines his own soul in these terms:

> "Neither do I want position and money for low, selfish purposes. My ends are the best and purest, for I am seeking my own honest living and the support of my mother and sisters . . . Take heart, Dennis Fleet: God is on your side in the struggle for an honest success in this life as truly as in your fight against sin and the devil." [67]

It does not follow that Roe was guilty of commercializing religious principles, for he seems to have been a thoroughly sincere man. In any case most ministers were ready with texts proving that there was an agreeable relationship between solvency in this world and salvation in the next. Such a conception was after all only the converse of the familiar text that the wages of sin is death. The latter text was also directly exemplified by minor episodes in the domestic novel, but the school as a whole preferred the more optimistic positive affirmation. For the rest, Roe told a good story clearly and cogently but with little imagination. The fire, which offered endless possibilities for graphic description, is treated at length but with surprisingly little success from the point of view of imagery. His principal characters tend to fade into abstractions of moral qualities, but there is undeniable life in some of the minor ones, particularly Bill Bronk, the "Good Samaritan," whose equine terminology is frequently amusing, as in his reference to a lady crying to be saved from the fire as "that young filly whinnying up there." [68] No number of such good speeches, however, can wholly redeem a book in which the heroine can say to the hero at one of the most critical moments in the fire: "You are a true knight, Mr. Fleet . . . and the need or danger of every defenceless woman is alike a sacred claim upon you." [69] Roe once said, very wisely, that "the day of prolix, fine, flowery writing" was giving way and that the new demand was for "simplicity, lucidity, strength." [70] Obviously his own dialogue did not exhibit simple strength, but his narrative was freer from embroidery than that of most of the domestic novelists. Other reforms in fiction remained for other pens. [71]

Obviously the domestic novel was not only a literary phenomenon but a social one as well. Telescoped into a few generalizations, the opinions it reflected and promoted can be seen to have been of a distinctly conservative nature. In effect the domestic novel functioned as a sort of benign moral police, whose regulations were principally comprised under the heads of religion and morality. The religion inculcated was not heavily freighted with theological doctrines; it was rather, as Gerty says in *The Lamplighter*, a "religion of the heart" and as such was available to anyone ready to listen to the voice of God. [72] Its chiefest enemies among modern writers were Goethe, Carlyle, Emerson, and various other vendors of "transcendental sophistries" devised originally in Germany. It is through Emerson that Beulah temporarily loses her faith. To be sure, Beulah is permitted to argue for his philosophy with some discernment, but she is bound to admit that "Emerson's works, collectively and individually, are aimed at the doctrines of Christianity." [73] The particular Emersonian doctrine that seemed to menace the simple structure of orthodox faith was that of compensation. To admit with Emerson that "justice is not postponed" and that "a perfect equity adjusts its balance in all parts of life" was to surrender the very citadel of the domestic novelist's belief, namely, that it is the purpose of the *next* world to redress the balance by punishing the wicked and rewarding the good. It has already been shown[74] that the good and the meek inherited considerable portions of this earth, but it was the premise of the novelist that an even more favorable adjustment was to be made hereafter. Hence a general fear of "German mysticism" [75] and cognate heresies. Yet the domestic novelists were not very prone to controversy, and they spent less time attacking "liberal" thought than in affirming their own relatively simple Christian faith. If the German vice was unorthodoxy, the threat of the French was immorality. Not that the French had not given the world their share of "infidels" in the past (especially Voltaire), but that of late they had been plying the American market with dubious novels. There was no surer way of damning a character than by showing him in the act of reading a French novel, particularly one by Eugène Sue, whose *Mysteries of Paris* and *The Wandering Jew* were promptly translated and published in this country in the middle forties.[76] Yet generally American moralists refrained from specifying the names of the obnoxious French books, and contented themselves with blanket references to the "taint of . . . loose morals or vicious philosophy which has rendered the modern literature of France the shame of genius." [77]

As for formal education there is relatively little comment on institutions of learning, for the heroine is generally shown less in her capacity as learner than, later on, as teacher or governess. The general tendency of the novelist is to endorse a simple type of curriculum in the local elementary schools. Boarding-schools are looked upon askance as places where children are underfed and poorly instructed under the orders of a tyrannical greedy headmaster.[78] Colleges are tested for their religious tone: Yale, for example, is preferred to Harvard and Columbia as the place where a lad can get "a granite foundation for . . . religion—everything solid and sound there." [79] It is conceded by another novelist, however, that a Harvard commencement is an "intellectual banquet." [80] Yet college education is in several ways suspect, and in general young girls are warned that "College boys are wild fellows." [81] Women's rights are smartly debated in practically every domestic novel. Keen feminist arguments are met by the stock replies that women have intuition but not reason,[82] that they may lose feminine graces in the pursuit of rights, and that men will deteriorate too if the need for chivalry is removed. Such sex-warfare generally ends in an ignoble truce whereby the woman barters all her advantages for a scrap of paper—a marriage certificate. As for the heroine who takes to writing as a career, she renounces that at the altar: a bluestocking she must not be.[83] Least of all should she be a reformer. The lady novelists showed their conservatism in nothing so much as their universal detestation of reform movements. Charitable Christian deeds performed by individuals and miscellaneous "errands of mercy" were acceptable, but reform movements were "radical." This attitude extended even to the subject of slavery, which forms a staple of conversation in many novels. It is argued, of course, that to hold a human being in the condition of a chattel is wrong, but nowhere is there much said for the militant abolitionist. Moreover, the Southern cause is well represented (especially since two of the principal domestic novelists, Marion Harland and Jane Wilson, were Southerners) and it is often argued that the position of a (contented) slave is considerably better than that of "the miserable, half-starved seamstresses of Boston and New York, who toil from dawn till dark, with aching head and throbbing heart." [84] In this debate, however, the novelist generally remains neutral. Other political and economic problems are but lightly touched. There are vague allusions to the beneficence of "Republican institutions" and the dignity of labor, but there is no systematic arraignment of the socio-economic order even for those evils which closely impinged upon domestic life—child labor, defective factory conditions, and miscellaneous exploitation of the poor classes—much less the growing political corruption that was to flower rankly in the Gilded Age.[85] The domestic novelists handled no inflammable social doctrine, for it was no part of their purpose to create industrial unrest or to foment class hatred.

In most respects, then, the domestic novelists were conservative socially. The pioneer spirit was not in them, and they were not concerned with "progress." Enough to be safe in the moment. Yet in one respect they exhibited, perhaps unconsciously, a tendency which has been ratified by later thinkers. This was shown in their fundamental conception of the regeneration of a person given to evil courses. Instead of trying to stamp out evil violently as a sign of innate depravity lodged in man ever since old Adam's first slip, they sought to lead the child to grace by kindly encouragement. The motive power was more often love or hope than fear. Satan's agency in sin was left out of consideration, and causes were sought for nearer at hand, specifically in heredity and environment. Vicious surroundings accounted for undesirable traits which could be removed, but only gradually, by transplantation to a more favorable environment:

> The plant that for years has been growing distorted, and dwelling in a barren spot, deprived of light and nourishment, withered in its leaves and blighted in its fruit, cannot at once recover from so cruel a blast. Transplanted to another soil, it must be directed in the right course, nourished with care and warmed with Heaven's light, ere it can recover from the shock occasioned by its early neglect, and find strength to expand its flowers and ripen its fruit.[86]

In general the novels of this school show a tendency to rely on admonition rather than punishment as a means of discipline. There is less talk of the devil and more of angels, less forcing and more leading. To be sure such positive, optimistic doctrine was not wholly new in the 1850's, but it was of some significance in a social order only recently emerged from the depressing atmosphere of Calvinistic thought.

There can be no question of the tremendous vogue of the domestic sentimentalists or of their acceptable moral teaching. What can be said of the intrinsic merit of the books themselves? Very little. Obviously they are in no cases the products of first-rate writers. Yet some abilities must be looked for in novelists who were able to command the attention not only of the average intelligent reader but of the critics as well. If they had addressed themselves only to a semi-illiterate public, their sales would not have disturbed Hawthorne by the thought of potential readers lost; if their books had been totally devoid of literary merit, Howells would not have bothered to attack them. Evidently they were read by persons who were unaware of stooping to an unworthy variety of entertainment. Why? The simplest answer (beyond the religious content of the books) is that most of the domestic novelists exhibited a fairly good prose style: their books *looked* like literature. It was perhaps as easy for the untutored reader to confuse their work with genuine literature as to mistake the popular illustrations of Currier and Ives for great art. Almost every writer in the group wrote with great facility—perhaps a fatal facility—and some of them, notably Mrs. Wilson, had a gift for phrasing that would have done credit to more important books. If an odious comparison may be admitted, it is likely that in sheer literary gifts, Mrs. Wilson excelled her present-day successors, Faith Baldwin and Kathleen Norris.

For the rest, the plot is based on a framework of trite devices, such as mistaken identity or the long-lost relative, and set into motion by coincidence. The fuel is sentiment or emotion, which is used in such a rich mixture that overheating results. No great speed is attained, but there are many melodramatic crises. The characters are generally lacking in individuality except for an occasional minor person. There is much whimsy but little humor. The description of natural scenery is slight in amount, and the sense of place is almost negligible: in this respect the domestic novelists displayed little advance over the novelists of fifty years before. The principal structural defect is the almost universal practice of chopping the action up into short scenes of approximately equal length—a method which, though perhaps dictated in part by the exigencies of serial publication, is generally fatal to proportion. The story sprawls through several years—perhaps an average of six or seven. A chronological order is observed throughout to a point about two-thirds or four-fifths of the way through the book, when the author finally vouchsafes the explanation of whatever mysteries in the plot have been arbitrarily withheld. This explanation, which generally consists of the life story of one of the characters, is so long as to throw the whole book still more askew structurally. How much better results might be obtained by the condensation or complete omission of certain scenes and the selection of others for expansion, together with the judicious use of flash-backs, remained for Howells and James to demonstrate.

The domestic novel was a popular commodity in which originality was no great virtue. Even in its period it seemed somewhat old-fashioned. As time went on, the effects of excessive inbreeding finally foreshadowed its temporary extinction. Yet the species was amazingly tenacious, and its life span extended through the 70's and even beyond. Meantime there had appeared in the late 1860's the first publications of three men—Mark Twain, Howells, and James—destined in different ways to give American fiction more vitality and greater merit. Yet none of these men immediately pre-empted the field, and one of them, James, can scarcely be said to have had a popular vogue at all. Their immediate influence, like that of Whitman, was not widespread. The gravest threats to the domestic novel in the 70's and 80's were local-color fiction (often taking the form of the short story), and the "international" or cosmopolitan novel (especially, in the popular field, the work of Francis Marion Crawford), and the historical romance, which was revived in the 1880's and 1890's. The development of the railroad contributed to the physical expansion of the country which brought the local-colorists into prominence; and the great increase in European travel in part prepared for the rise of "international" fiction. When "swaggering Americans were thronging Europe in great crowds," [87] the novelist whose characters were followed to no point more remote than Saratoga or Newport began to seem a little provincial. As for the historical romance, its occasional recurrence is inevitable. At all events new costumes, gorgeous settings, and more "personalized" characters gave the historical romance a new vogue in the 80's. A little later, the panic of 1893 doubtless made romance even more welcome as a resource against incessant discussion of wages, strikes, monopolies, and economic depression. At all events, the nineteenth-century domestic novel was by that time pretty well choked out by heavy competition except for the sporadic reappearances already noted.

Experiment and Tradition

HARRIET BEECHER STOWE (1811-1896)

Harriet Beecher Stowe, the most widely-known woman novelist of nineteenth-century America, was born in Connecticut of a gifted family. Her father, Lyman Beecher, was an able preacher who waged unceasing warfare against the encroachments of Unitarianism upon the old New England orthodoxy. Her brother Henry Ward Beecher in due time threw the weight of his powerful oratory into the Union cause. Nor was her sister Catharine without a measure of fame, for her school at Hartford (where Harriet studied and occasionally assisted) had more than a local reputation. Harriet spent most of her pre-author years at Cincinnati, where although she lost none of her loyalty to New England ("the land often spoken against yet always respected"),[1] her horizon brought Southern problems more clearly into focus: Kentucky slavery was not far off, and Ohio was a common refuge for fugitive slaves, one of whom was put into service in the Beecher household—one of the many actual episodes that were later to lend authenticity to *Uncle Tom's Cabin*. Her literary interests were nurtured by a local club whose roll included Mrs. Caroline Hentz, not yet known to fame. By 1834 she had begun publishing fiction in James Hall's *Western Monthly Magazine*. Her marriage (in 1836) to Professor Calvin E. Stowe, a scholarly widower whom she seems to have accepted partly out of zeal for Christian service, proved to be at first a stumbling block to the muse. To be sure Professor Stowe early recognized her literary flair:

> My dear [he wrote in 1842], you must be a literary woman. It is so written in the book of fate. Make all your calculations accordingly. Get a good stock of health and brush up your mind. Drop the *E* out of your name. It only encumbers it and interferes with the flow of euphony. Write yourself fully and always Harriet Beecher Stowe, which is a name euphonious, flowing, and full of meaning. Then, my word for it, your husband will lift up his

447

head in the gate, and your children will rise up and call you blessed.[2]

It was easy to drop the *E* but not so easy to "get a good stock of health," and before Mrs. Stowe's children could rise up to call her blessed, they had to be *brought* up, a procedure that she found incompatible with much writing in the by-no-means affluent establishment which the amiable professor was able to afford. Household cares in pioneer Ohio conditions oppressed the daughter of a tidy New England home:

> I am sick of the smell of sour milk, and sour meat, and sour everything, and then the clothes *will* not dry, and no wet thing does, and everything smells mouldy; and altogether I feel as if I never wanted to eat again.[3]

Illness added its burden to tedium and poverty, and she was reduced to such despair that her belief in marriage was severely tested and she felt that she was "not probably destined for long life."[4] The only thing that sustained her was an unshakable belief in the ultimate benevolence of God.

Finally her earthly troubles were mostly removed: her marriage, though temperate in its joys, proved to be a satisfactory one; good health took hold so securely that she lived to be eighty-five; poverty never really menaced her again. Even the household cares which had irked her so, later provided literary copy that appealed widely to feminine readers. Most of all, perhaps, her sufferings and her fervid religious experiences developed in her that intense emotional quality which was to lend power to her writing as soon as time and tide provided the opportunity. Religion, however, though often a theme in her novels, was not the first awakener of her crusader's instinct, for many champions of a more merciful religion had already reduced the sharpest edge of Calvinism. But slavery was a current and increasing problem, and it was this, especially after the compromise of 1850, which finally unlocked the door to her share of the powerful emotional nature that lay in the Beecher family. She had already seen much of the institution and its effects. She had heard of, read about, or actually seen slaves flogged to death, abolitionists tortured and hanged, fugitive slaves cruelly punished. She had witnessed the pathetic gratitude of Negroes rescued from unspeakable sufferings. She had regretted the fact that the Church had done comparatively little to oppose slavery—though it continued its harangues against dancing and card-playing. She had personally known some of the people who were later to figure as characters in *Uncle Tom's Cabin*. She had published her first reflections on slavery in 1836 during the Birney riots in Cincinnati. But she did not become an acknowledged abolitionist until 1850.[5] In that year she published in the *National Era* a parable, "The Freedman's Dream," a compelling statement concluding with a stern reference to those persons "who seem to think that there is no standard of right and wrong higher than an act of Congress, or an interpretation of the United States Constitution."[6] She was moving toward her supreme effort in behalf of enslaved humanity. How deeply she was affected by the crisis is clear from her statement (in March, 1851) that until then she had "dreaded to expose even [her] own mind to the full force of its exciting power."[7] But now the time had come, and she girded herself for the task of doing her part for humanity. She could not know that she was on the verge of writing what became quite possibly the "fourth in point of circulation among all the books of the world."[8]

In 1851, back in New England (for Professor Stowe had been called to Bowdoin), she first fully experienced in writing the possibilities of expressing sympathy for the victims of slavery. She at first intended that her story should run to only three or four periodical installments, but her emotional momentum carried her far beyond such limits. *Uncle Tom's Cabin* was published serially in the *National Era* between June 5, 1851, and April 1, 1852. Mrs. Stowe began to write more in love than in hatred: she meant to touch the heart of the public by presenting "pictures" of slavery—for, she said, "There is no arguing with *pictures*, and everybody is impressed . . ."[9] Her children's tears as they heard their mother read the installments must have seemed better testimony to her of the story's worth than the $300 she later received from the *National Era*. When the story appeared in book form immediately upon the conclusion of its moderately successful serial run, it leaped at once into a popularity difficult to realize fully. Cold figures tell that 300,000 copies were sold in the first year, but no figures can express the extent of its influence on the popular mind. Mrs. Stowe articulated what was already felt by millions, but she added new data so that vicariously her readers enormously extended the range of their experience. She could write with the authority and inspiration of a prophet, but she could also express herself on such a plane that her book could be "read equally in the parlour and the kitchen and the nursery of every house."[10] Like Dickens she realized how slight a partition separates the fields of humor and pathos, and she moved freely in either area. If modern readers are inclined to feel that the deaths of Eva and Tom are touched with bathos, contemporary readers saw only tragedy in them.

And even now, such was the flame of Mrs. Stowe's vehement ardor, the book is capable of enkindling the mind with strong feeling over issues that have long since become cold matter in most of the anti-slavery literature of the era, including much of Whittier's fierce invective. Imitations of Mrs. Stowe's work sprang up everywhere, but out of the immense body of "Uncle Tom literature" almost nothing has become permanent.[11] Although structurally simple, Mrs. Stowe's book was essentially inimitable.

It was not, however, immune from ferocious attack. The accuracy of its picture of slavery was first assailed in the North, and Northern feeling ran high against Mrs. Stowe in many quarters, for "There was plenty of Northern money invested in the cotton business." [12] In the South it simply wasn't safe to own *Uncle Tom's Cabin* or to display it for sale. A vast "Anti-Tom" literature quickly developed to counteract Mrs. Stowe's "poison." [13] And yet this book which made so much bad blood was not intended so to do. Its tone was very different from that of Hildreth's savagely satiric *Archy Moore*. In writing it, Mrs. Stowe had shown herself capable of deep indignation, but in general her attitude had not been belligerent; rather, the book gave expression to her great compassion. One friend, indeed, wrote naively to Mrs. Stowe that the book would be "the great pacificator" and would "unite both North and South." [14] Nor were such ideas utterly alien to the author herself, for in a four-fold statement of her purpose in writing the book she indicated that her first aim was to "soften and moderate the bitterness of feeling in *extreme abolitionists*" and her second to "convert to abolitionist views many whom this same bitterness had repelled." [15] Illogically enough, she more and more insisted, as time went on, that she was "but an instrument" in the production of the book: "The Lord Himself wrote it." [16] Whoever was responsible for *Uncle Tom's Cabin*, however great the good which it ultimately achieved, the publication of the book was an immediate cause of momentous discords and ultimately of heavy bloodshed: "From that moment the Civil War became inevitable." [17]

The virtues of *Uncle Tom's Cabin* as a novel arise from Mrs. Stowe's humanity, her ardent imagination, and her ability to finger detail sensitively; its faults are mainly attributable to the author's unwillingness to let the objective facts speak for themselves and to her always inadequate control of structure.[18] The changing locale of the action made breaks in the narrative which Mrs. Stowe spliced with so little skill that the whole structure seems to sprawl. This, however, was common enough in American fiction before the time of Howells and James. More serious is the violence done to the story by Mrs. Stowe's doc-

trinaire method. Time and again she interrupts the narrative to press
home a moral which the action itself has spelled in large enough letters.
Her apostrophes to the reader, though precedented in Dickens's similar
exhortations, do not strengthen the novel. Most serious of all is her
tendency to sacrifice character to moral crusade. A few of the minor
characters, Sam, for example, seem almost wholly real. Most of the
others have a basic strength which is impaired in varying degree as they
become the pawns of propaganda. Uncle Tom's simple affectionate
nature, his manifold troubles, and even his zeal for salvation make for
reality, but he is occasionally drafted crudely into the service of Mrs.
Stowe's Christian war. The question of whether a poorly educated
Negro who was living more comfortably under a benevolent master
than he could possibly live (at the time) as a freeman would prefer to
remain in bondage or be emancipated is difficult to answer; but it is
certain that Uncle Tom's abstract academic remarks to St. Clare on this
subject[19] have the air of a set speech prompted by the author. They
seem far less real than Hector's response to Craven in a similar situation
in Simms's *The Yemassee.* Tom's forgiveness of his enemies, though
factually credible, is too facile. So with the other characters: they suffer loss of realism when touched by the saintliness of Eva and Tom or
when used as a vehicle for polemic. Topsy's diablerie is described with
a good deal of vraisemblance, but her reform, though slow, seems a mechanical dispensation. The amiable but vacillating St. Clare is at first
a splendidly drawn character, but Mrs. Stowe, who has foreordained
his conversion, finally makes him utter religious sentiments that ring as
hollowly as his earlier opinions on slavery (pro and con)[20] had sounded
genuine. The worst of all the characters is the hypocritical Mrs. St.
Clare, who is merely a vessel into which Mrs. Stowe pours her contempt for the selfish and unthinking proponents of slavery. Even Legree, chief of the sinners in the hands of an angry Mrs. Stowe, is more
real than Mrs. St. Clare. Yet though a number of real elements went
into Legree's characterization (including his Vermont background),
the whole synthesis seems spurious. He is as wicked as Uncle Tom is
saintly.

As for sentimentalism, it was a demand of the times. There is in
Uncle Tom more sighing, sobbing, weeping, and "earnest" exhortation,
more talk of angels and glory, than goes down with readers accustomed
to the emotional understatement of many twentieth-century writers.
Exclusively solemn references to heaven are likely to seem unnatural to
a generation initiated into the quaint mixture of reverence and familiarity with which Negroes regard celestial affairs in *The Green Pastures.*
Eva is now as much an object of ridicule as Little Nell. Yet the fifties

were a decade of sentimentality in life as in literature, and what now seems mawkish (in Dickens as well as Mrs. Stowe) was then regarded as real pathos. Moreover, Mrs. Stowe's tears were no mere substitute for real emotion, for she had what few contemporary purveyors of sobs had, namely, a tremendous intensity of purpose and an unquestioned sincerity. For this reason *Uncle Tom's Cabin* has lived on as a serious, though artistically defective, book while T. S. Arthur's *Ten Nights in a Bar-Room* has been laughed into the museum. Structural faults attributable to serial publication bothered the generality not at all, nor did the average reader probably complain that two coincidences were largely responsible for Tom's tragedy. Mrs. Stowe's warm humanity so well covered the technical defects of the book that the response to it was almost wholly emotional. Seldom has a novel subsisted so largely on sheer sincerity and integrity. Its reception on the whole was dazzlingly favorable, but there were enough dissenters to evoke Mrs. Stowe's *A Key to Uncle Tom's Cabin* (1853), which gave chapter and verse for those episodes and arguments (and they were many) which could be substantiated by documents and personal observation. In her *Key* Mrs. Stowe reveals her enormous industry; yet though critics subjected it to close scrutiny, the public was less interested in sources than in results and it continued to prove its devotion to *Uncle Tom's Cabin* as an irresistible story on a great theme. Many people felt the truth of what George Sand expressed:

> I can not say she [Mrs. Stowe] has talent as one understands it in the world of letters, but she has genius, as humanity feels the need of genius,—the genius of goodness, not that of the man of letters, but of the saint. Yes—a saint! [21]

Great as was the emotional response to *Uncle Tom's Cabin*, the problem it dealt with was not to be solved soon. It was but natural, then, that Mrs. Stowe should respond to the demand for another story, especially since gathering material for the *Key* suggested many new possibilities for stories involving the slave states. She felt that there was "no ground, ancient or modern, whose vivid lights, gloomy shadows, and grotesque groupings, afford[ed] to the novelist so wide a scope for the exercise of his powers." [22] In *Dred* (1856) Mrs. Stowe looked more carefully to her art as a novelist; and she was more concerned with the white personnel of her story. Whereas in *Uncle Tom's Cabin* she had focussed her attention pretty narrowly on slavery as such, in *Dred* she tried to show the malign influence of slavery on the whole social order in the South. The story grew out of the insurrection led by Nat Turner in eastern Virginia in 1831. One of the actors in that rebellion was named Dred. In Mrs. Stowe's story he is represented as a fine type of Negro who lives in a hideout in the Dismal Swamp, brooding over the wrongs of the black race, providing sanctuary for escaped or hunted Negroes, and looking forward to the day of release, which he pictures in language perhaps too closely modeled on that of the Hebrew prophets to seem wholly natural even in a well-read Negro. On a plantation not far away lives Nina Gordon, a charming, heedless flirt. The love of Edward Clayton, however, and her gradual enlightenment with respect to slavery change her into a thoughtful character with a talent for ministering both to poor whites and to slaves whose sufferings can hope for no redress from law. There is the slave Milly, whose brutal treatment by Tom Gordon is finally sustained by the court. There are Harry and Lisette, whose marriage Tom threatens to ruin by buying Lisette. Finally there are the victims (white and black) of the cholera. These trials bring out Nina's character, but her good works avail little against the germs of cholera or the moral disease of slavery. Tom Gordon's cruelty finally drives Harry and Lisette to seek refuge in the swamp. In the slave hunt which follows, Dred is fatally wounded, but Harry escapes. Tom now foments anger against the Claytons because of their alleged abolitionist feelings, and in order to escape lynching they are forced to leave the state. In Canada, Harry Gordon ultimately manages a farm for the Claytons. But in the state of North Carolina slavery still flourishes with the support of the law and the connivance of the ministry. Nor could help be hoped for so long as the "mouth of the North [was] stuffed with cotton." [23]

Dred is structurally ineffective in that Dred's story is not successfully united with Nina's.[24] Yet there is no character in *Uncle Tom's Cabin* at once so appealing and so real as Nina Gordon, and her death, briefly described, is more tragic to modern readers than Eva's carefully ordered demise. Old Tiff is just as lovable as Uncle Tom, and he is not laid under such fearfully holy requirements. The story as a whole is not so intense as *Uncle Tom's Cabin*, but it is more comprehensive and it is well grounded. Its more objective treatment was approved by Harriet Martineau, who believed that *Dred* would do endless good "by suddenly splitting open Southern life, for everybody to look into." [25] Indeed Miss Martineau thought *Dred* "far superior" to *Uncle Tom's Cabin*, for it seemed to her "richer and more substantial." [26] Other critics of course attacked this second book mercilessly, but when Mrs. Stowe found that it had sold 100,000 copies in four weeks and promised to sell a quarter as many more, she sighed contentedly: "The fact that so many good judges like it better than 'Uncle Tom' is success enough." [27]

For a variety of reasons—including a protracted visit to Europe, domestic cares, and the death of a son—Mrs. Stowe wrote little until in 1858 she began to publish (in *The Atlantic Monthly*) her first full-length New England story, *The Minister's Wooing*.[28] In a sense this mellow book expressed Mrs. Stowe more fully than anything she had yet written, for although it is set in Newport in the latter part of the eighteenth century it reported a New England life not very different from that which she knew as a girl. In it she is less the prophet or protagonist than the chronicler. Here if ever she should prove how far she was an artist. The action is a simple one involving the hand of a girl unconsciously in love with a young man of uncertain spiritual state and at the same time governed by an admiration for a minister to such an extent that under the influence of her ambitious mother she is persuaded to plight her hand (thinking that the heart would follow) in accordance with the whisper of "duty." Intimations that the report of the young man's death by drowning may have been exaggerated are anxiously weighed in the reader's mind against the fearful blow the minister would suffer if he lost his betrothed. Ultimately, without very great sacrifice of plausibility, Mrs. Stowe manages to evolve that happy ending which was the tacit demand of so many novel readers of the period. For this story Mrs. Stowe did not have to "get up" very much of her materials. The greatest emotional episode of the book, the news of Marvin's drowning, she had twice had similar experiences of. She knew the sights and sounds of the New England sea-coast village, the well-ordered household kept tidy by the mistress's own hands, the domestic ritual of tea-drinking, the occasional quilting-party, the sobriety of the daily life of people who regarded everything "in reference to eternity," [29] the constant discussion of religion in a region "where devotion is doctrinal, not ritual," [30] and the respect accorded the minister so long as he made no attempt to show a connection between a man's soul and his business practices. Samuel Hopkins, whose "only mistake . . . was that of supposing that the elaboration of theology was preaching the gospel" [31] was real; and so was the religious conflict between love and law that was finally to relegate the austerities of Calvinism more and more to the shelves of the minister's study. The Negro cook, Candace, was out of Mrs. Stowe's own kitchen; and the superb study of Miss Prissy, the seamstress, is so full of delicate line and shading that one cannot doubt the existence of its prototype among the author's acquaintances. The glamorous, unscrupulous Aaron Burr is fully introduced, but he seems not so real as the characters of whom there is less historical record. Mrs. Stowe was always more revolted by evil-doing than adept at describing the technique of wickedness. Her urge to do good is expressed in her sympathetic treatment of Dr. Hopkins' plight after he has openly condemned the slave traffic of some of his wealthy Newport parishioners and in her evangelical concern for the state of Marvin's soul. For modern readers the book doubtless contains too much parleying on theology and a too obvious championship of right living. Indeed even Lowell, under whose benign editorial eye the story appeared serially in the *Atlantic*, felt constrained to admonish Mrs. Stowe on this score:

> As for "theology," . . . let it crop out when it naturally comes to the surface, only don't dig down to it. A moral aim is a fine thing, but in making a story an artist is a traitor who does not sacrifice everything to art . . . Let your moral take care of itself, and remember that an author's writing-desk is something infinitely higher than a pulpit.[32]

As it proved, *The Minister's Wooing* had enough charm and sincerity to compensate contemporary readers for an excess of piety, and excepting *Uncle Tom's Cabin* it is now the best-known of Mrs. Stowe's works.

A public as large as Mrs. Stowe had built up could not be denied further stories, and indeed she invested her tremendous royalties so badly that she was never wholly above financial cares. She continued to write prolifically until the last few years of her long life. Never again did she produce a novel that matched her early successes, nor did she ever improve greatly in the art of writing. Yet a warm heart, an observant eye, and a mind richly stored with the lore of New England were sufficient literary capital to warrant her continued activity.

The Pearl of Orr's Island (1862) is a mixture of idyll and tragedy experienced by the families of sea-captains and fishing folk on the coast of Maine. It was originally designed to be a sketch of the childhood of the chief characters, but Mrs. Stowe later decided to extend it to a full-length story. She did not succeed in welding together its two parts, but she did succeed in investing the book with genuine New England data. The early part is a mélange of simple characterization and homely (occasionally tragic) incident set against a background of honest Maine scenery. After an interval of ten years the same characters are seen in a situation familiar enough in the domestic novel: the love of an orphaned girl of strongly religious cast for a handsome youth of mysterious birth is marred by his occasional wildness, his religious skepticism, and his temporary attachment to a hoydenish girl, their common friend. The hoydenish girl withdraws, but the skepticism remains to cloud the heroine's happiness. She goes into a genteel decline and dies in an exemplary manner. Called by Whittier "the most charming New England idyll ever written," *The Pearl of Orr's Island* is now unduly neglected.

Begun in Florence during the winter of 1859-60, *Agnes of Sorrento* (published 1863) is one of the few stories in which Mrs. Stowe wholly forsook New England scenery and characters. The story is more continuously "romantic" than was usual with Mrs. Stowe. The beautiful heroine, Agnes, little recks that she is the daughter of a Prince who repudiated his marriage to her mother, for her grandmother is determined to bring her up in seclusion from the world of fashion which killed the girl's mother. When despite her precautions Agnes' beauty is observed by a handsome cavalier, the grandmother tries to secure her against this putative wretch by marrying her to a blacksmith. But Agnes is determined either to marry her cavalier (if he proves to be truly religious) or to enter a convent. The latter course is warmly recommended by her spiritual advisor, Father Francesco, who is worldly enough to be himself pinched by a passion for Agnes and who cannot bear the thought of her being married except to the church. Before the problem is solved, Agnes is twice kidnapped (first by the cavalier and later by one of the Pope's "nephews"), but everything comes out all right for everyone (except the blacksmith) when Agnes is married to her cavalier, whose religion, she finds, is really on a sound basis. The action is further varied by a pilgrimage to Rome to see the Pope and by considerable attention to the incarceration and martyrdom of Savonarola. In tone *Agnes of Sorrento* has much in common with the sentimental romance, and Agnes is a character not unlike some of Mrs. Wilson's patient heroines. Coincidence and melodrama are freely drawn upon to whip up a plot far more exciting superficially than those of most of Mrs. Stowe's other stories. The religious ferment of the times (which Mrs. Stowe compares with a Wesleyan revival) gives body to the book. The Italy of Savonarola's time, however, is not nearly so well called up as in George Eliot's *Romola*, nor can Mrs. Stowe's book compare with Eliot's in emotional power or depth of characterization.

A book much more natural for Mrs. Stowe to write was *Oldtown Folks* (1869), a series of sketches scarcely comprising a novel but rich in that atmosphere of a passing New England which was her best base of literary material after the Civil War. Mrs. Stowe could not forego a bit of romanticizing in her plot (the orphans turn out to belong to a wealthy English family!), but she knew every nook and cranny of the New England life to which the book was mainly devoted. She knew the history of the New England church from the days when ministers were "more statesmen than theologians" to her own more democratic era. She knew the hard-headed individualistic characters which were emerging from decades of the peculiar discipline of New England existence. She put the visionary Calvin Stowe (born in Natick, Massachusetts) into her book, and she created the shiftless Sam Lawson, a piquant character who would be a household name in New England for years to come. All these things (and others) helped to make *Oldtown Folks* a commercial success and (in the opinion of many) her best book after *Uncle Tom's Cabin*. Other personal reminiscences appeared later in *Poganuc People* (1878). In these two books Mrs. Stowe failed to prove herself a first-rate novelist, but she left a record of a way of life of the first importance to the social historian.[33]

While *The Minister's Wooing* was being serialized, Lowell remarked (anent the difficulty of handling Col. Burr in a story of village life) that "we do not want a novel of society from Mrs. Stowe . . ."[34] Yet Mrs. Stowe was finally unable to resist the temptation to do a few studies of contemporary manners. The first of these was *Pink and White Tyranny* (1871). The hero of the story is a young man who idealizes all women to such an extent that he is blind to the shallowness of the beautiful creature he chooses for his wife. Presently disagreeable discoveries begin to come home to him, among them the fact that whereas Lillie gave her age as twenty at the time she was married, actually she was then a "veteran belle" of twenty-seven whose object in marrying him was merely to insure a financial background for further selfish indulgences. Having been bred amid the luxury of New York and Newport, given to flirtation and much reading of French novels, Lillie is poorly qualified to adapt herself to the quiet pleasures of her husband's ancestral New England home—for this is a New England book in its celebration of the substantial virtues clustered in the old Seymour family and in its occasional implication that New York is more iniquitous than Boston. For a long time John allows the pink and white creature to tyrannize over him, but finally her folly and coincidental business troubles bring him tragically to the realization of facts which had long since been obvious to his friends and to his sister Gracie, the antithesis in character of the worthless Lillie. It is Mrs. Stowe's thesis in this book that in conflict between a good husband and a worthless wife the woman generally gets her way. Nevertheless she does not favor "easy dissolution of the marriage contract" for uncongenial spouses. At this time divorce was often urged by "advanced" women as a means of relief for persecuted wives; yet it is clear, says Mrs. Stowe, that if women can use it, so can men and thus women in general may be the losers. Therefore Gracie adjures John, by the portrait of his dear sainted mother, to carry on as best he can: after all he married Lillie of his own free choice and it may be necessary for individual men to endure uncongenial marriages "for the public good." The story as a whole, which Mrs. Stowe called a "parable" rather than a novel, is so foreshortened that the leading characters are little more than names representing points of view. The analysis of Lillie is too clinical to have much artistic value, but it results in clinical truth. The story is often sprightly, even humorous, in tone, and though far from great it is in fact a shrewd and readable book whether it is defined as novel, parable, or handbook for husbands.

Pink and White Tyranny notwithstanding its compression exhibits more attention to plot than do two other extended studies of social conditions, *My Wife and I* (1872) and its sequel, *We and Our Neighbors* (1875). In these books Mrs. Stowe's purpose is frankly critical rather than narrative, but since the world was at the time "running mad for Stories," [35] she must needs devise a narrative framework for her ideas. In *My Wife and I* the framework is of the flimsiest sort, being merely the progress of Harry Henderson through his childhood, his college life, his newspaper career, and his courtship of Eva Van Arsdel, a frivolous but essentially sensible "society girl" with whom he settles down in an ideal marriage after her father has lost his fortune. Since Mrs. Stowe is not interested in the story but in "the things it gives the author a chance to say," [36] the book is packed with discussion of a variety of topics: mother-love, college education, training husbands, marrying for money, Christian ideals, doubts about the Bible, Darwinism, Quakers, modern fiction, literary criticism, the corruption of newspapers, the curse of drink, the freedom of American girls in public, women in business and politics, the social emancipation of women, the advantages of simple life over fashionable life, and New England virtues. In general Mrs. Stowe appears to favor a sanely progressive attitude toward social change. She disparages Audacia Dangereyes, the bold emancipated woman, but she apparently endorses the views of Ida, who believes that only by "gradual evolution" [37] can women safely acquire those rights, social and political, that have been so long denied them. In *We and Our Neighbors* the married life of Henderson and Eva (with emphasis on the latter) is reported in a series of incidents which provoke discussion of miscellaneous problems similar to those handled in *My Wife and I*. Eva's heedless flippancy is now replaced by a serious attitude toward doing good: helping men to stabilize their religious faith, reforming a drunkard, and redeeming a fallen girl. In the latter case the girl is the daughter of Eva's servant, for Mrs. Stowe was

Victorian enough as a novelist to keep her "genteel" characters out of sordid sexual complications. The story breathes a wholesome atmosphere comparable to that of the well-bred books of Louisa Alcott and William Dean Howells. Mrs. Stowe knew little at first hand of the seamy side of human character,[38] and she didn't approve of novels of intrigue anyway, for in her opinion they could only do harm.

Besides fiction Mrs. Stowe tried her pen at a variety of things ranging from a manual of housekeeping[39] to a monograph entitled *Lady Byron Vindicated* (1870), which even her friends agreed was an unfortunate expression of her instinct for espousing the cause of the oppressed and injured. None of her other works, however, marked her as a person with literary ability much above that of scores of minor writers now almost wholly forgotten.

Seen in toto Mrs. Stowe's works reveal much of significance in the social and literary history of her time. In the twilight of Calvinism she was able to call up and report its meridian glare with rare fidelity and to prophesy a gentler tomorrow. Her innate conservatism prevented her from trafficking a great deal with transcendentalism, and the New England of *The Minister's Wooing* is a quite different one from that of Sylvester Judd's *Margaret*. She preferred to reshape the old rather than to replace it. Her earliest creed contained many of the harsher dogmas of the old theology, but long before she died she had dropped many of its dialectic bogeys. As early as 1858 she admitted that the "rigid theological discipline of New England is fitted to produce rather strength and purity than enjoyment," [40] and she speculated hopefully on the possibility that "the number of the redeemed may . . . be infinitely greater than the world's history leads us to suppose." [41] In the preface to *Oldtown Folks* she showed a tolerant view of various sects, and a gradual emancipation from strict articles of theology:

> Though Calvinist, Arminian, High-Church Episcopalian, skeptic, and simple believer all speak in their turn, I merely listen, and endeavor to understand and faithfully represent the inner life of each. I myself am but the observer and reporter, seeing much, doubting much, questioning much, and believing with all my heart in only a very few things.[42]

Yet "strength and purity" were much in her eyes, and she profoundly admired the breed of men whose road to salvation was as rocky as the soil they tilled. She looked back with an indulgent eye even upon minute inquiries into "celestial jurisprudence" [43] which so gravely con-

cerned her elders, and she liked to think of the virtues which flowered
in a simple New England meeting-house:

> Everything in their worship [writes Virginie in a letter attempt-
> ing to characterize New England ways for her French friends]
> is plain and austere; their churches are perfectly desolate; they
> have no chants, no pictures, no carvings, only a most disconsolate,
> bare-looking building, where they meet together, and sing one or
> two hymns, and the minister makes one or two prayers, all out of
> his own thoughts . . .[44]

How much better this simple sort of life than the complicated life of
cities, especially New York, where luxury and vanity led to spiritual
sloth. Mrs. Stowe was willing to relinquish the husks of the old theology, but not the fine flower of character they had borne. Its essence appeared in all her best writing. Even her anti-slavery writing was but
a transformation of the energy generated by New England spirituality.

Beyond an ability to release honest feeling Mrs. Stowe had very few
of the attributes of a first-rate writer. Doing good seemed more important to her than learning the craft of writing. Moreover there wasn't
much time to read Horace or Aristotle between the numbers of a serial
magazine. She was often repetitious and literal. Her defective knowledge of sentence-structure and syntax occasionally brought her to such
an impasse that "it sometimes needed the combined skill of all the proof-
readers and the assistant editor to extricate her." [45] She never mastered
Negro dialect or at least never learned to transcribe it accurately and
consistently. To recall Joel Chandler Harris is to realize at once Mrs.
Stowe's limitations in the treatment of Negro speech and character. Indeed she was at home only in New England. Without apparent effort
she could set down descriptions of New England scenes that wear the
face of reality, as in this charming study of changing seasons:

> Apple blossoms died quietly in the deep orchard grass, and tiny
> apples waxed and rounded and ripened and gained stripes of gold
> and carmine; and the blue eggs broke into young robins, that grew
> from gaping, yellow-mouthed youth to fledged and outflying ma-
> turity. Came autumn, with its long Indian summer, and winter,
> with its flinty, sparkling snows, under which all Nature lay a sealed
> and beautiful corpse.[46]

Yet except for those scenes which had sunk into her mind through "unconscious observation" [47] she was not skilful at conveying a feeling of
locale. With good right it was complained that *Dred* did not reveal a

thorough acquaintance with North Carolina. She never gave a comprehensive picture of actual working conditions on a plantation in the far South, nor will her New Orleans settings compare in richness with those of Cable or Tourgée or even De Forest. She was fond of dramatic crises in action; but coldly examined, most of them, including the famous ice-cake episode of Eliza, seem amateurish in technique; only the author's contagious excitement carried them off. In short Mrs. Stowe had very little to go on except a store of honest experience as an enlightened daughter of Puritanism and a simple eloquence in expressing her love of humanity.

After black humanity had been legally freed, Mrs. Stowe had to look about for new literary capital.[48] She was now in much the same position as many another novelist of the sixties and seventies, and her true stature as an artist was revealed. More often now she gave expression to her literary and social theories. In general they were conservative. Like most of the Beechers she had been a great reader. Her cultural roots lay deep—as deep as the English Bible and John Bunyan. She was an indefatigable reader of fiction. *Sir Charles Grandison* was apparently a favorite book. *The Mysteries of Udolpho,* condemned by many conservative readers of an earlier period, was acceptable entertainment to her. Miss Edgeworth she admired and imitated, and Scott she admired. Among her actual contemporaries, she naturally loved Dickens for his humanitarian sympathies, his itemized sentiment, and his low-born humorous characters. She was fond of "Washy" Irving, whose ability in describing food appealed to her feminine interest.[49] And in general she was at home in the gentle tradition of Longfellow and Whittier. Mrs. Stowe's materials were often new, but she had no new method, nor did she found a school. Indeed she was out of sympathy with much current production in the American novel. Novels for mere amusement seemed likely to run in dangerous channels. She had no objection to sentiment, but she thought true romance came from giving rein to our best impulses. She believed in the romance of the commonplace; nothing was more truly romantic than a marriage for love even if it meant living in a "little mean house on no-matter-what street . . ." In many minds, unfortunately, romance was associated with "French laces, opera boxes, and . . . Madame Roget's best gowns." [50] It was fiction dealing with such things that made Aunt Nesbit (in *Dred*) disapprove of novel-reading: "It gives false views of life, and disgusts young people with their duties." [51] Mrs. Stowe knew that there was plenty of evil in the world besides human slavery, but whereas she carried the battle against slavery right into its own territory, in the war with other types of evil she was inclined to rely on discretion rather than valor. She was not precisely prudish, but she saw no good in rehearsing evil-doing glamorously, even if punishment were to be provided at the end. Her diatribes prove that there was a great deal more reading of lurid fiction by genteel people than has generally been believed. In *My Wife and I* she has one of her characters warn a young writer against writing "the sensational novel, the blood and murder and adultery story, of which modern literature is full . . ." [52] In the same book she appears to be delivering strictures at the domestic novels represented by Mrs. Wilson etc. when Henderson condemns a novel of "the modern, hot, sensuous school, in which glowing coloring and a sort of religious sentimentalism were thrown around actions and principles which tended directly to the dissolution of society." [53] Fiction, he finds, is written for idle fashionable women, who are willing to pay for it. Hence the serial story blight:

> What [asks Ida in *My Wife and I*] are all these girls and women looking for? Amusement, excitement. What do they dread more than anything? Effort, industry, self-denial. Not one of them can read a serious book through—not because they are not able, but because it takes an effort. They read nothing but serial stories . . . [54]

The readers of serial stories, says another character in the same book, "are generally girls from twelve to twenty, and they read them with their back hair down, lounging on the bed, just before a nap after dinner, and there must be enough blood and thunder, and murder and adultery and mystery in them to keep the dear creatures reading at least half an hour." [55] The worst of it is that although here and there an editor of a popular magazine might wish to provide a more wholesome literary diet, the owners insist that the magazine "be run in the approved popular grooves that the dear thoughtless ten million prefer." [56] Nor can there be much help from professional criticism of the novel which might be "a real guide to buyers and readers, and a real instruction to writers," for as one editor explains:

> While books are a matter of commerce and trade; while magazines which criticise books are the property of booksellers, and newspapers depend on them for advertising patronage, it is too much to expect of human nature that we should always get wholly honest, unbiased opinions. [57]

In this whirl of cheap literature Mrs. Stowe naturally could not make a profitable venture of her sober stories of reality. They were not spicy enough to sell widely, and they were not brilliantly enough written to receive impartial praise. Even if they had been first-rate works of art, it is by no means sure that they would have been widely read by a generation that allowed Melville to languish in the obscurity of a New York Custom House. Her protests, however, provide a useful commentary on a deleterious trend in the evolution of the novel. They also explain why when Howells began to publish stories that combined decency with greater skill in writing there was no dearth of readers for him.

Mrs. Stowe's literary career was, then, a curious one. If she had stopped writing in 1859 (after *The Minister's Wooing*) she would have left undone no book which is valued today by any but special devotees. The first of her two themes, slavery, was removed by history; the second, the New England heritage, was discounted as time went on. She continued to mint genuine coin but the collectors gradually lost interest: they cared only for the early issues. Perhaps Mrs. Stowe was prone to insist upon too large a proportion of the gold of truth; she never learned the formulas of those alloys which have the greatest currency and are able to withstand the attrition of years. Her honest, naive studies of contemporary social life could not match those of Mary J. Holmes and Augusta Jane Evans Wilson and a number of other artful practitioners of the novel of manners who had learned how dearly the public loves the truth if it is so bundled up in sentiment as to be unrecognizable. Her reputation, therefore, rests mainly upon one book, *Uncle Tom's Cabin*, which even today glows with much of that emotional fire which at first concealed the blurred lines of Mrs. Stowe's imperfect art.

JOHN ESTEN COOKE (1830-1886)

The field of the historical romance never wholly loses its fertility, and the market it aims to supply, though it may fluctuate, will always "come back." The historical romance is a staple. There are, of course, periods of such active production that the market becomes glutted and public interest veers in other directions—as both Cooper and Simms ultimately discovered. This situation may be met in various ways—by allowing the land to lie fallow, by continuing production for a dull market, or by rotation of crops. Cooper in such an emergency tried rotation: he sowed political wild oats for a time before returning to his immensely profitable Leather-Stocking series. Simms ploughed laboriously on with meagre returns. By about 1850 the market for historical romance seemed to have reached the saturation point. Yet the public can always be beguiled by novelties, and in the very depth of the depression (1854) a partially new variety appeared which had an astonishingly large sale. The variety was a Virginia novel, and the producer was John Esten Cooke.

Virginia, preëminently the land of romantic reminiscence, had thus far been comparatively little celebrated in fiction. Cooper's Captain Lawton (in *The Spy*) had afforded a hint of the romantic possibilities of Virginian history, but no Northern writer could do full justice to the state. *The Valley of Shenandoah* (1824) by George Tucker dealt creditably with rural life. J. P. Kennedy, a Southerner by birth and a Virginian by residence, had written a distinguished work between fiction and essay, *Swallow Barn* (1832), which depicted Virginian life of the early nineteenth century. Caruthers' *The Cavaliers of Virginia* (1835), which fictionalized Bacon's Rebellion, was more "romantic" but it did not retain its hold. No one had yet fully realized the rich possibilities of a graceful romantic story set in the picturesque days immediately before the Revolution. Cooke's *The Virginia Comedians*, therefore, was in a sense first in its field. As such it was warmly welcomed on all sides. Many other stories were forthcoming from Cooke's pen, particularly a series relating to the Civil War, but after the War he was unable to compete very successfully with other new types, chiefly realistic, which were then appearing. What the public valued in Cooke above all was his charming evocation of the epoch of powdered wigs, brocaded gowns, embroidered waist-coats, Louis Quatorze chairs, the luxury and glamor surrounding aristocratic manor-house folk. *The Virginia Comedians* (1854) has been called the "best novel written in the Southern States before the civil war." [58] Such an encomium it can scarcely lay claim to in the face of the brilliant and substantial productions of Kennedy and Simms, but it contained enough of the elements of good story-writing to become the prototype of many later Virginian novels that, however inaccurate in their report of actual conditions, have satisfied an enormous public appetite for light romantic tales of the Old Dominion.

Cooke's first profession was law, which he liked so little that he eagerly interpreted a few successful magazine ventures as good enough omens for a literary career. As a lad he also wrote two romances, *The Knight of Espalion* and *Evan of Foix*, but these were never published in book form.[59] His first "serious" novel *Leatherstocking and Silk* (1854), a study of the Virginia Valley at the beginning of the nineteenth century, written when he was twenty-two, brought him no great acclaim, but *The Virginia Comedians* published in the same year struck it rich.

Though Cooke's imitation of Cooper is obvious even in the titles of his books and in the names of his characters, he utilized one avenue to popularity which for Cooper always remained secondary, namely, the love story. *The Virginia Comedians* is first of all a story of the love fortunes of Champ Effingham, the heir of Effingham Hall near Williamsburg. After Oxford and the Grand Tour, Champ has settled down to an aimless sort of manor-house existence that threatens to bore him to death despite the availability of cousin Clare Lee, a girl as fresh and unsophisticated as Champ has been dissipated. Presently Champ conceives an infatuation for a traveling Shakespearean actress, Beatrice Hallam, a young woman of fine character, who to his utter amazement rejects him (a gentleman!) because of her greater interest in a swain, Charles Waters, who has chanced to save her life. Ultimately in his desperation Champ abducts Beatrice, and in the encounter which ensues when the rescuers arrive he stabs Charles Waters through the breast. The blow having been presumably fatal, Champ now takes hasty leave of the country and has an unhappy wanderjahr in Europe and the Near East. Charles, however, recovers and is united to Beatrice, who turns out, by a formula that is an open secret among practitioners of romance, to be his cousin! In the second half of the story Charles and Beatrice, being married, possess only a reduced romantic value. Therefore the author chooses to find Beatrice's "slight cough" serious enough to warrant sending her up to the mountains for a cure. In the meantime there are hearts to mend: that of Clare Lee, wounded sorely by Champ's defection, and that of Champ himself, who is now a world-weary cynic. But he is also remorseful, and it is partly the business of the second part of the tale to transform him from the dreadful cad and worn-out roué he essentially is into a husband for the lovely if somewhat negative Clare —a proceeding which, revolting as it is to the modern reader, seems not to have shocked contemporary readers. There are other errands of Cupid, of which the most interesting is to achieve the marriage of Captain Ralph Waters (a bluff campaigner characterized chiefly by his mustache-twirling and his intermittent ejaculation of "morbleu" and "parbleu") to Henrietta Lee, a type of amiable shrew.[60] At the end there are no less than four weddings in sight. A bit of pathos tempers the shameless orgy of bliss when Beatrice, instead of recovering, goes into a fatal decline and dies an extremely elegant death offstage. The novel is one of incident and "drama," for as the author avowed, he was not equal to giving it that "nice finish which is the cameo-work of literature."[61] Accordingly characters are little more than types and their actions are reported in well-worn expressions that were clichés even in Cooke's time. Over and over again contempt is expressed by the "curling lip," mental agony by the "writhing lip," and honest love by a "chaste salute" on the mistress' brow. These are harmless iterations, but there is less excuse for the ranting melodrama in which Champ is constantly involved. His actions are incredible even in romance. Twice he actually tears at his breast until his fingers are "stained with blood." His persecution of Beatrice exceeds not only the bounds of realism but even the looser bounds of romantic plausibility. He is wholly unconvincing, and in fact he has much in common with those insolent, blasé scions of wealth in the domestic novel of that day who conduct themselves in the most incredibly malicious, dissipated, and even criminal fashion, only at the end to be united to sweet, trusting girls.

The Virginia Comedians is then a pretty flimsy story that captivated readers in its day by its clever arrangement of picturesque properties in a traditionally romantic area. Its historical aspect gave it badly needed ballast, but, one must believe, did not greatly add to its vogue. The unrest of a period when there was growing resentment against British oppression is used as a theme in the somewhat tedious conversations between Charles Waters and the "man in the red cloak," who is supposed to figure Patrick Henry. At the end of the book an exciting scene reveals Colonial hostility to the Stamp Act. Notwithstanding these, however, and frequent allusions to the *Virginia Gazette*, the Old Theatre of Williamsburg, and the Raleigh Tavern, as well as a number of incidents intended to illustrate manners, the historical background is a trifle thin. Cooke aimed to be picturesque rather than thorough. Naturally he made no such rounded study of eighteenth-century Virginia as Kennedy did of a later period; nor does his command of language in any way invite comparison with Kennedy's. Cooke did not even have the knack of giving his speech that archaic quality which so adds to the charm of Churchill's *Richard Carvel*, and the characters speak in an idiom not far different from the conventional idiom of Cooke's own day. Nor did he attempt to do much with Negro dialect; indeed his portrayal of the bottom of the social register was clearly inferior to his treatment of the aristocracy.[62] Yet his gifts, such as they were, were well enough fused to make *The Virginia Comedians* almost a household title in the period just before the Civil War.[63] It is still good reading, but it has been somewhat overrated while other Southern novels have had to struggle for their due.

The Virginia Comedians and *Henry St. John* (1859), a sequel utilizing many of the same characters but with a new hero and heroine, gave Cooke a "nation-wide" recognition.[64] He never achieved so great a success again, but his other books were well enough received to encourage him in his profession as writer. Many volumes of novels, short stories, biography, essays, and poetry appeared from his pen, and he was active until the year of his death (1886). Cooke was in fact one of the most rapid writers in American literary history. Repeatedly he wrote four or five hundred pages in a month, and he sometimes wrote a hundred pages in a day.[65] The quality of his writing never fluctuated markedly: he wrote no great books and no books without at least a modicum of merit. On the whole those novels which he wrote before the Civil War are of greater value than his later productions.

Before the War he wrote altogether eight novels. In addition to the books already mentioned, he wrote *Ellie* (1855), a not very significant domestic story set in the nineteenth century. This was followed in 1855 by *The Last of the Foresters: or, Humors on the Border,* a story of eighteenth-century Virginia intended to provide "innocent entertainment" by a study of "traits of life and manners" in a "picturesque land." [66] More than most of Cooke's books, this one seems to have suffered from rapidity of composition. A more substantial book was *Fairfax: or, The Master of Greenway Court,* not published in book form until 1868, but begun before *The Virginia Comedians* and published serially in 1859 (under the title *Greenway Court; or, The Bloody Ground*) in the *Southern Literary Messenger.* It tells the story of the sixth Lord Fairfax, then exiled in Virginia. Action is provided by Indian uprisings; mystery, by problems of character-identification. Love affairs—turbulent, comic, tragic—occupy much of the rest of the book. The Indians are finally defeated in a Cooper-like climax. Lord Fairfax learns that one Falconbridge is really his son (in the fiction, at least— in life he had none), and the reader learns that young Mr. George, who has been under the care of Fairfax, is actually George Washington. Other characters include the robust Indian-fighter, Captain Wagner; Lightfoot, the noble Indian, who gives his life for the white woman he loves hopelessly; Cannie Powell, object of Lightfoot's affection, who proves to be Fairfax's niece. There are many deaths, including those of Falconbridge and Cannie. The action occurs mainly about 1748, but in an epilogue set in 1781 Fairfax, then eighty, learns that Cornwallis has surrendered at Yorktown. A month later George Washington visits the Fairfax grave-plot and in a very moving scene mourns his lost youth and—Cannie Powell. Despite its use of old conventions, *Fairfax* is a very readable story—probably second only to *The Virginia Comedians* among Cooke's novels.

By the time of the Civil War, Cooke was well established as a novelist of old Virginia. He loved the state and was partial to it. One can fancy his agreement with one of his own characters, who thought the Shenandoah a "more noble [river] than even the Mississippi." [67] He loved, too, the olden days, and the folk of a bygone era. Indeed he became so rhapsodical as a *laudator temporis acti* that he was smartly attacked by one critic:

> Mr. Cooke's eyes are not only in the back of his head, but they are also afflicted with a pair of rose-colored goggles of enormous magnifying powers . . . And I marvel much that such a set of homely, selfish, money-loving cheats and rascals as we are, should have descended from such remarkably fine parents. No doubt it is very good noveling, but I swear it is wretched physiology.[68]

In a more reasoned comment, William Gilmore Simms called attention to Cooke's apt use of the Old Dominion, but added that "his sinews must be a little more seasoned by the proper exercise . . ." [69]

After the Civil War (throughout which he served), Cooke resumed writing as abundantly as before. He capitalized the War directly in biographies of Stonewall Jackson (1869) and Robert E. Lee (1871) as well as in a number of essays, some of which were collected in *Wearing of the Gray* (1867) and *Hammer and Rapier* (1871). Among his several novels dealing with the War, the best-known are *Surry of Eagle's-Nest* (1866) and *Mohun* (1869). Novel, biography, and essay tended to reinforce each other. Thus *Surry of Eagle's-Nest* is a "close parallel" of the life of Jackson and *Mohun* parallels Lee's life.[70] In one way or another, therefore, the Civil War occupied Cooke's pen for about five years.

The first and best of the War novels was *Surry of Eagle's-Nest*. The central character (Surry) is a staff officer whose experiences in this book duplicate in part Cooke's own experiences in the War. The action begins at Richmond in 1861 and carries on to the battle of Chancellorsville in '63. Military matters are merged with romance, however, and Surry is at last provided with the usual colorless heroine employed by Cooke. The novel made money for the author, but artistically Cooke failed to fuse "a wildly improbable Gothic tale and a record of a career in the Civil War." [71] Between *Surry of Eagle's-Nest* and its sequel (*Mohun*) appeared an undistinguished war novel, *Hilt to Hilt* (1869). Rebuked by a Boston critic for rhetorical extravagances, Cooke resolved in *Hilt to Hilt* never to "be florid or exaggerated any more," but stylistically he failed to evince any real reform. The scene of this story is the Shenandoah Valley; the action involves no great names or major military movements; the love affairs are largely routine. *Mohun; or The Last Days of Lee and His Paladins* (1869) reanimates some of the central characters of *Surry of Eagle's-Nest*. Its action has a stereotyped quality in most of its phases, but it is effective "in its depiction of the dogged determination of the lessening band of 'Lee's Miserables' as they faced defeat, and in the admirable representation of the civilian classes in Richmond." [72] All these stories had a certain topical value, and all displayed flashes of a talent that (one believes) might have shown to better advantage had the author been willing to spend more than a month or two on a novel. Even so, Cooke was not quite at his best in handling materials so close to his own experience as those of the Civil War. No one of these stories compares favorably as an account of military maneuvers with, for example, Hervey Allen's *Action at Aquila* (1937). Crane's brilliantly written *The Red Badge of Courage* was, of course, a type of novel quite beyond the range of Cooke's powers. Nor can any one of his war novels be said to equal *Miss Ravenel's Conversion* by De Forest, a contemporary of Cooke.

It was clear now that Cooke's forte lay in powdered romance of an older era. Yet *The Heir of Gaymount* (1870), his first book after *Mohun,* attempted to fictionalize the author's own experiences after the War. Problems of finance and agriculture come up for consideration, but *The Heir of Gaymount* did not turn out to be an important "Reconstruction" novel. For the rest, Cooke provided the usual love matter, and he added the (for him) new motif of buried treasure. Several other novels followed, but they revealed Cooke's inability to establish himself in an important new category or to reopen a profitable old one.[73]

Cooke hoped to do for Virginia something like what Simms had done for South Carolina. This, he thought, could not help being useful for "to know the meaning of the Republic we must go back to the States." [74] He was like Simms both a novelist and an historian. In 1856 he prophetically remarked: "It seems to me however that the time will come, when everything connected with the history and family romance (that is *truth*) of Virginia will be listened to with . . . ardor." [75] He was an ardent Secessionist, but not such a bitter partisan as Simms. He was inclined to see slavery as a benign institution, and one may believe that his views were not far different from those expressed in a colloquy between the Earl and Falconbridge in *Fairfax:*

> "Virginia, Mr. Falconbridge," [the Earl] said, "is England simply under a different form. It is true that our white retainers, essentially parts of the soil, are replaced by negroes who are legally serfs for life; but I question which is the happier of these classes."
> "I know our servants are happy," replied Falconbridge, "and we love them as they love us . . ." [76]

He resembled Simms in his theory of the historical romance. He too realized that after the historian has raked the past for factual data regarding wars and dynasties, many apparently unimportant materials could be gleaned with which the novelists might recreate the form and color of history:

> "Alas for the historians! They tell us many things, but so little! They relate with much dignity, how the battle was fought and the treaty made—they tell us the number of the combatants, and spread every protocol upon the page. But the student of the past asks for more. Of the historian we ask a picture of the elder day—portraits of the Virginian and his household. We would know the peculiarities of character and manners which marked a great race—the Worthies of Virginia. We would live again, for a time, beneath those fair or storm-convulsed skies of 'Old Virginia'; we would take the hand of the honest old planter; we would go into his library, and look over his shoulder as he reads the new Act in the 'Virginia Gazette,' and would not distain [sic] to scan critically the powdered curls and looped-back gowns, the flounces, and furbelows, and fancies of the dames." [77]

In this aim Cooke succeeded admirably when he treated old Virginia in his earliest stories. More than Simms he stressed color and atmosphere. He also took more liberties with historical fact than Simms—probably to his own disadvantage. But, as far as his Confederate stories are concerned, the Civil War was too close to him to respond to the same treatment that had succeeded in *The Virginia Comedians* and *Fairfax*. And when later he returned to olden times, he had somehow lost the formula which would enable him to recreate the old atmosphere. Moreover literary movements in the 1870's and 1880's called for new abilities to which he could not adapt himself. Yet he did not rebel at his fate:

> I still write stories for such periodicals as are inclined to accept romance [he wrote late in life], but whether any more of my work . . . will appear in book-form is uncertain. Mr. Howells and the other realists have crowded me out of popular regard as a novelist, and have brought the kind of fiction I write into general disfavor. I do not complain of that, for they are right. They see, as I do, that fiction should faithfully reflect life, and they obey the law, while I cannot. I was born too soon, and am now too old to learn my trade anew. [78]

The same detachment which permitted him to recognize his own limitations is shown in his ready vein of humor both in his novels and in

articles. He was adept at parody and raillery.[79] He was not entirely satisfied with the type of literary criticism most common in his day; and
he speculated on the immense value that would attach to causeries
modeled on those of Sainte-Beuve, which might impart tone to our
critical journals. He himself was prone to make curious literary judgments, and he once referred to *The Wide, Wide World* as "one of the
most delightful of books." Yet his taste was not generally for inferior
writers, and he emulated Simms in doing honor to Shakespeare both in
his fiction and periodical writing.[80]

Cooke's preferences among American writers were mostly of a high
order:

> My aim [he once wrote] has been to paint the Virginia phase of
> American society, to do for the Old Dominion what Cooper has
> done for the Indians, Simms for the Revolutionary drama in South
> Carolina, Irving for the Dutch Knickerbockers, and Hawthorne
> for the weird Puritan life of New England.[81]

The aim was obviously too ambitious, and it only partially suggests
Cooke's qualities. His "ultimate literary ancestor" was Scott, but neither
Scott nor Cooke's nearest relative among Virginians, Caruthers, was
apparently a close model for him.[82] Cooper, however, was an early
ideal, and he was never completely out of Cooke's mind. Yet Cooke
lacked Cooper's robustness, and he showed more interest in the amenities of life than did Cooper. Simms, whom Cooke resembled in his
voluminous and speedy production, was a writer of much more original
force. With gentle and picturesque Irving, Cooke was a trifle more in
line, but he was prone to sustained melodrama of a type that Irving
would soon have escaped from with a jest. Cooke drew from all these
writers. He also had a weather eye open for the sentimental novels of
the 1850's—those of Mary Jane Holmes, Elizabeth Wetherell, and Mrs.
Southworth—whose code of propriety he strictly observed, and whose
reeking sentiment he occasionally equalled. Along with his graceful-
ness went a certain almost feminine softness which manifested itself in
a love of small domestic detail. He also, it is very likely, learned part
of his craft from the example of Thackeray, whose *Esmond* had appeared in 1852.[83] The historical romance of Thackeray at its poorest
has an infusion of tea-partyish sentiment that appears also in Cooke's
writing. And it was probably this same softness, this delicacy, which,
when crossed with a slightly forced gusto and robustness, gave the
guise of novelty to his chef-d'oeuvre, *The Virginia Comedians*.[84]

The novelty of Cooke brought him many readers, and it inaugurated a new tradition of Virginia novels grounded in picturesqueness and sentiment: Thomas Nelson Page and Mary Johnston are approximately in the same line as Cooke. Now, when the novels of Miss Glasgow and others have revealed Virginia in more realistic outline, Cooke's type of romance seems artificial as well as outmoded. He was a facile writer of no great force or originality who reached quick success by stumbling upon a rich vein. But when that was exhausted he had neither the capacity for discipline nor the imagination to operate successfully elsewhere. At the end of his life he took more and more to writing "for checks." To compare him with Scott or Cooper or Simms is to draw attention to his essentially light gift. It is better to say that he was a writer of moderate talents who fed a harmless appetite for gingerbread romance without a grievous sacrifice of the ideals of good writing.

GEORGE WILLIAM CURTIS (1824-1892)

Popular fiction in the 1850's and 1860's was dominated by the sentimental novelists, a race of writers whose area of observation was pretty much indoors and domestic. Business and politics were little touched upon. Indeed the political novel has always been a *rara avis* in American fiction. It is the more surprising, therefore, to find that in George William Curtis's *Trumps* (1861) politics becomes a major element of interest. Curtis was not of course primarily a novelist. He is known to history for his advocacy of Civil Service reform and for his extraordinary oratorical gifts. As a literary man, he is known, even now, chiefly for his essays, especially *Potiphar Papers* (1853). *Prue and I* (1857), which has been called "the decade's finest purely sentimental masterpiece," [85] has only a gossamer thread of story, but *Trumps* is a full-bodied novel of New York (and, to a less extent, Washington) life.

The originality of *Trumps* shows but little in its plot. The central character, Abel Newt, is a scion of a family that has been "universally respectable but honest." His father is a successful New York merchant and a "Tammany Sachem." His mother belonged to stock that "came to this country at the earliest possible period." Young Newt shows undesirable traits at school (in Massachusetts), but it is confidently expected that he will make good "in the world" (in New York City). Yet through egotism and profligacy he loses not only the heiress he planned to marry but also a Southern belle whom he regarded as a tolerable compromise. Now sentimentally bankrupt, he is still a potential political asset in the eyes of certain unscrupulous men, who arrange his election to Congress on the basis of his promise to support a bill in which they are interested. He disturbs his confrères by being too drunk to respond publicly to news of his election: "if a man expects to succeed in political life he must understand when not to be drunk." [86] Later he is regarded as a successful Senator, but his own ambitions turn toward acquiring more money than he sees the hope of acquiring in politics. Finally he takes up with a lewd woman, forges his uncle's name, and plans to leave for Europe with $25,000, but on his last night before sailing he gets killed in a drunken brawl. The story contains other structural material even less original than this, but the identification theme involved in it is mercifully relegated to the secondary plot. Curtis is somewhat more independent in permitting Hope, the lovely heiress, to go husbandless to the end. For this fiction-writer's heresy he makes no apology:

> How could we help it? How could a faithful chronicler but tell his story as it is? It is not at his will that heroes marry, and heroines are given in marriage. He merely watches events and records results.[87]

Even more unusual in popular fiction was Curtis's frankly cynical representation of business methods. Abel's father, who is to be taken as something like the average merchant, gives Abel sage advice upon the latter's entrance into the business world:

> "As a rule, Abel, men are rascals; that is to say, they pursue their own interests . . . Oh! men are scamps—with some exceptions; but you must go by the rule . . . If this were the Millennium, every thing would doubtless be agreeable to every body. But it is not . . . It's a great game, business is, and the smartest chap wins. Every body knows we are going to get the largest price we can . . . I was saying that a lie well stuck to is better than the truth wavering . . . Don't misunderstand me, my son; I do not say that you must always tell stories. Heaven forbid! But a man is not bound always to tell the whole truth." [88]

Similarly Lawrence Newt, merchant brother of Boniface, remarks in a speech that "commercial honesty is not impossible, but it is rare," and adds that it is "hard for a merchant to be honest in New York." [89] Perhaps too cynical, these remarks, but a salutary note of candor amid the blind moral optimism of most of Curtis's contemporaries in the domestic novel.

The same candor marks Curtis's treatment of politics. All the evidence goes to show that the will of the people is subservient to the self-interest of party leaders. Says one of the bosses:

Speculative persons and dreamers talk about independent political action. But politics always beget parties. Governments are always managed by parties, and parties are always managed by—[90]

When the boss hesitates at this point, Abel finishes his sentence for him: "—by the managers." Abel is initiated into sound political thought in a scene which illustrates both Curtis's skeptical attitude and his delightful humor:

> "Still there are one or two points to which I would call your attention. One is, that you can not be too careful of what you say, in regard to its bearing upon the party; and the other is, a general rule that the Public is an ass, but you must never let it know you think so. If there is one thing which the party has practically proved, it is that the people have no will of their own, but are sheep in the hands of the shepherd."
> The General took snuff again.
> "The Public, then, is an ass and a sheep?" inquired Abel.
> "Yes," said the General, "an ass in capacity, and in preference of a thistle diet; a sheep in gregarious and stupid following. You say 'Ca, ca, ca,' when you want a cow to follow you; and you say 'Glorious old party,' and 'Intelligence of the people,' and 'Preference of truth to victory,' and so forth, when you want the people to follow you."
> "An ass, a sheep, and a cow," said Abel. "To what other departments of natural history do the people belong, General?"
> "Adders," returned Belch, sententiously.
> "How so?" asked Abel, amused.
> "Because they are so cold and ungrateful," said the General.[91]

And why should a great republic suffer from bad government? Curtis's answer (in a speech put into the mouth of Abel Newt) is not far different from the answer Brackenridge had made years before:

> "[N]o gentleman knows any thing of politics. Gentlemen are the natural governors of a country; and where they are not erected into a hereditary governing class, self-respect forbids them to mix with inferior men—so they keep aloof from public affairs. Good Heavens! what gentleman would be guilty of being an alderman in this town! Why, as you know, my dear Belch, nothing but my reduced circumstances induces me to go to Congress." [92]

This was a natural remark for a member of a patrician Massachusetts family to make. Curtis knew the patrician class far better than the lady novelists who so persistently denounced fashion and money. He knew their virtues as well as their vices. On the satirical side, he drew portraits of the aristocracy of wealth and rank that adumbrate Back Bay studies in Santayana's *The Last Puritan* (1936) and Marquand's *The Late George Apley* (1937).[93] The Honorable Budlong Dinks, who "untied his cravat as if he had been undoing the parchment of a great treaty," [94] is one of a group of social parasites whose trivial fashionable affairs are reported with an authenticity seldom found in the domestic novel.[95] Curtis was a master of persiflage and witty but realistic dialogue which marked him as one of the few American novelists before Howells and James to succeed in maintaining a scene on the level of high comedy. He was also one of the few nineteenth-century novelists (excepting De Forest and Henry Adams) to essay a novel in which there is considerable use of politics as seen by a trained observer.

BAYARD TAYLOR (1825-1878)

When in the 1860's Bayard Taylor reached the zenith of his career, the westering sun had already begun to warn New England that even a Golden Day must eventually give way to twilight. Emerson's prophetic utterances regarding the growth of a trans-Allegheny literature were later to prove their validity by the appearance of a host of Western writers led by Mark Twain. Yet Western writers would have to reckon with Eastern critics. New England, drained of part of its creative energy, was still asserting its patriarchal right as arbiter of the nation's literature and culture. What more natural than that Bayard Taylor, son of the middle state of Pennsylvania, should lay his hopes of recognition at the feet of the literary fathers of our country? A Western career was out of the question for one who had " 'a constitutional horror of dirty hands.' " [96] No rugged individuality could be expected of a writer whose literary appetite seems in the beginning to have been amply satisfied by such conventional caterers as Mrs. Sigourney, Mrs. Hale, Mrs. Hemans and N. P. Willis. Later his admiration for Tennyson showed Taylor's improving taste, but it also marked him more definitely as a man of essentially conservative nature. From time to time he courageously gave utterance to slightly shocking economic and social views, but on the whole Taylor conformed to the spirit of the age. The event proved that from a practical point of view at least, he was wise to aim at winning the approval of New England and New York, for he became one of the most popular writers of the century. Poet, essayist, short-story writer, novelist, traveler, lecturer, he had many avenues to publicity. His name became known wherever English was spoken; and among the literati, not to know Bayard Taylor was to argue oneself unknown. With the passage of time it has appeared that he was not only an ornament but also a victim of his age. Time has so tarnished the fame of "the laureate of the Gilded Age" that its lustre can never be restored. Viewed by posterity his actual artistic achievement seems to have warranted not one-half the acclaim it once won. Yet to neglect Taylor and his work is to remain ignorant of much of the literary history and ideals of the interim between 1850 and 1870. His four novels, not intrinsically very valuable, are useful links in any study of the evolution of fiction before the dawn of Howellsian realism.

Taylor was born in 1825 near Philadelphia in a Quaker community, Kennett Square. He inherited South German blood on both sides of his family, and Pennsylvania Dutch was spoken in his childhood home. Family finances did not permit of his going to college, but there was no need for a young man of literary ambition to despair of making a career. A literary career was no longer a fantistic notion to be sternly quashed in favor of reading law or following the plow. What with the vast growth of periodical literature in the 1830's and 1840's, there was need of young men to fill journalistic posts. If the young man could manage a trip to Europe, so much the better. Had not Irving, Longfellow, and Willis capitalized European journeys? Were not newspaper editors eager for "letters from abroad"? Let the ambitious young man first sell or give a few poems to a local newspaper. If possible let him publish a harmless book of verse. Then let him get an editor to show interest in travel letters. Taylor went abroad in 1844 with some encouragement from Horace Greeley and with the warning to send back "no descriptive nonsense. Of that I am damned sick." [97] His letters were accepted for publication—some of them in the *Tribune*—and they were later collected into a book, *Views Afoot* (1846), which subsequently had twenty editions in ten years. In spite of Greeley's warning Taylor had filled his letters with "descriptive nonsense" of a very conventional order. Time was not yet ripe when Americans, only lately the nurslings of Europe, could with impunity assert their independence by offering cool appraisals of European institutions. Cooper had proved that much. One looks in vain in *Views Afoot* for signs of the sort of irreverence that was later to enliven Mark Twain's letters to the *Tribune*. No, Taylor duly stared with awe at the cathedrals and paintings wherever he went, and he turned pretty sentences about them to the delight of conservative readers at home.

Shortly after his return to America Taylor became assistant to Horace Greeley (then editor of the *Tribune*), and for the rest of his life he was with brief interruptions constantly active in the arena of journalism. His popular style made him such a valuable asset to the

Tribune that he was repeatedly assigned long trips for the sake of the "descriptive nonsense" they would yield. To California, Egypt and the Orient, Iceland—Taylor got more "views" than he cared for, but he was anxious to make his way professionally, and he had several shares of stock in the *Tribune*. He discovered in himself also a nice talent for lecturing, and for many years he forced himself (for he finally came to regard lecturing as a bore) to endure poor accommodations and stupid audiences, on tours that carried him the length and breadth of this country. Mounting personal expenses forced him to seize every opportunity. He even undertook the hackwork of compiling a *Cyclopaedia of Modern Travel* (1860). He also received substantial sums from his various books of verse, especially *Poems of the Orient* (1854), which contained the "Bedouin (Love) Song," and *Poems of Home and Travel* (1855), as well as from innumerable articles. By 1863 (when he published his first novel), Taylor had written "six volumes of verse, nine books of travel, some five hundred newspaper and magazine articles, and more personal letters than anybody could very well count." [98] He was probably as prominent as any man of letters in America except Longfellow. Yet he was still concerned not only for the state of his finances but for his reputation in critical quarters, especially in New England.

Taylor had long contemplated putting some of his impressions of American life into the form of a novel.[99] Now in the early 1860's, when he was anxious to cut down on both traveling and lecturing, he began to carry out his plan. Doubtless he hoped for more profits than prestige from the novel, which was certainly the younger sister, if not the ugly duckling, of American literature at the time. His reputation in any case would stand (or fall) by his poetry.[100] *Hannah Thurston*, his first novel, was begun in 1861 and not published until 1863. Its actual composition, however, was carried on at a "tearing speed." [101] Two more novels, *John Godfrey's Fortunes* and *The Story of Kennett* appeared in the next two years, and a forth, *Joseph and His Friends*, was published in 1870.

Hannah Thurston was avowedly a story with a "slender plot"; in it Taylor hoped to capitalize "peculiarities of development in American life which have escaped the notice of novelists," especially "certain types of character and phases of society." [102] This kind of claim for a book was common enough by 1863, but it was as appropriate to *Hannah Thurston* as to most novels, perhaps more so. Such plot as there is, then, revolves around the central figure of Hannah Thurston, a twenty-nine-year-old spinster absorbed in women's rights, and Maxwell Woodbury, a handsome bachelor of thirty-six liberally interested in certain social questions but inclined to be a bit intolerant where women's rights are concerned. At first his admiration for Hannah as a woman is held in check by his abhorrence of her principles. Yet propinquity reduces his antagonism and qualifies her sternness, so that,. stimulated by the example of other couples and encouraged by friends, they capitulate to Cupid. Once married, they vie with one another in magnanimity, Woodbury urging "independence" on her and Hannah insisting that she no longer covets equality with him—especially when their union is blessed with a child. In order to keep this couple—who "stand up as good as married in the first chapter" [103]—apart through a long book, Bayard Taylor has not built up an elaborate plot structure but has merely filled up his text with conversation and petty episodes bearing loosely on the situation: the real obstacle to their union is the author's habit of digression. Although Taylor disclaimed opinions uttered by the characters, the work as a whole is plainly a satire on reforms and reformers observed by Taylor in Kennett Square (disguised as Ptolemy, New York, in the novel). Hunkers, abolitionists, Grahamites, spiritualists, Cimmerians, prohibitionists, and advocates of independence for women—these and other fanatics and reformers incur the author's ridicule or reproach. They are not condemned without a hearing: Seth Wattles, for example, who has a plan for the reorganization of society by means of the proper division of labor and intelligent application of machinery, is given plenty of space in which to elaborate his views before he is deflated by the caustic comments of farmer Merryfield.[104] Even Mr. Dyce is allowed to make a fairly cogent statement of certain fundamental misconceptions of society:

> "The doctrine of original sin is the basis of all the wrongs of society. It is false. Human nature is pure in all its instincts, and we distort it by our selfish laws. Our life is artificial and unnatural. If we had no rights of property we should have no theft: if we had no law of marriage we should have no licentiousness: if we had no Governments, we should have no war." [105]

So with the principal theme of discord between Hannah and Woodbury, women's rights: Hannah freely develops her arguments without being forced very often into that burlesque utterance by means of which many satirists achieve their ends. Indeed her principal speech on behalf of women's rights is almost a model of clear, reasonable argument. She does not advocate immediate extension of suffrage to women, but she believes that women should claim "an equal right to education, to employment, and reward . . . Even admitting that our sphere is limited—that there are only a few things which we may properly do—is it generous, is it even just, that man, who has the whole range of life to choose from, should crowd us out from these few chances of earning our bread? Or to force us to perform the same labor for a smaller remuneration, because we are women? Could we not measure a yard of calico as rapidly, or choose a shade of zephyr as correctly as the elegant young men who stand behind the counter?" [106]

She believes that women should be allowed to study medicine.[107] But in the course of the book she is beaten down by Woodbury (backed by the author), who more often begs the question than refutes her arguments. In his eyes "Aunt Dennison . . . was more queenly . . . than Mary Wollstonecraft or Madame de Staël." [108] He makes sneering references to a hypothetical female physician "standing at a dissecting-table, with a scalpel in her hand, and a quarter of a subject before her." [109] The solution of the problem for him is that men should adopt a chivalrous attitude toward women:

> To him . . . the relation of protector was indispensable; the rudest blows of life must first fall upon his shield. The idea of an independent strength, existing side by side with his, yet without requiring its support, was unnatural and repulsive.[110]

Other stock arguments (and fallacies) are used: Mrs. Blake, for example, is sure that if Hannah fell in love "it [would] make short work of her theories of women's rights. Our instincts are stronger than our ideas, and the brains of some of us run wild only because our hearts are unsatisfied." [111] This in fact is what happens in the story: Hannah falls in love, and in marriage she finds such completion of her life that her arguments fall away from her like faded petals and her deepest wish is to rely upon the love and the judgment of her husband—forgetting the "cold spectre of justice" and praying never again to wander from the "true path" of wifely submission.

Hannah Thurston, despite the Victorian consummation of its plot, was received rather rudely by the *Atlantic Monthly*, which found the story a "conglomeration, and partially a caricature, of the various *isms* which have disturbed the strata of our social life." [112] Yet other conservative critics—Hawthorne, Whittier, Lowell, Bryant—praised the book, and, what was perhaps quite as important in the mind of the debt-ridden author, the work sold well both in America and in England.

Hannah Thurston was even translated into German and Russian. Jubilant over the success of his first novel, Taylor proceeded with the composition of *John Godfrey's Fortunes* (1864).[113]

John Godfrey's Fortunes, as Bayard Taylor wrote to James T. Fields, hasn't "a single 'reformer' in it," [114] but it has considerable satire bearing on other matters. The story relates to John Godfrey, a delicate, studious lad whose widowed mother insists on his leaving the farm (near Philadelphia) in order to study at a boarding school. Here he meets his cousin, Alexander Penrose, a character who inevitably recalls Steerforth in *David Copperfield*. Forced by the death of his mother to give up formal education, John tries his hand as clerk in a grocery store and as school teacher. Small local successes as a poet encourage him to go to New York with the idea of making a career in literature, but experience among professional writers is of the most disillusioning sort: journalists everywhere are given to back-biting and sycophancy, and their only aim is to make a commercial success by pandering to public taste. Love ends in disillusionment, too, for the village girl of his choice marries another. He subsequently falls in love with Isabel Haworth, who suddenly terminates their acquaintance when she hears that he has formed an illicit attachment with a girl of the streets. In point of fact Godfrey has befriended a poor erring girl, Jane Berry, and tried to reclaim her from the sordid life into which she had been betrayed. Now at the lowest ebb of his idealism, Godfrey not only takes to drink but tells Jane that since the world has put the worst construction on their relationship they might as well be what they have been assumed to be. Jane refuses on the grounds that she knows he does not love her. Things are at a bad pass, but Taylor soon thereafter slams the door on realism and proceeds to devise a happy ending: Jane "explains all" to Isabel, who can now consent to marry John. Nor will the young couple have to live on love alone, for Isabel has $80,000 of her own and John comes into some of his uncle's money. The author even digs up an old sweetheart of Jane's who will marry her "as is."

The routine romantic conclusion of *John Godfrey's Fortunes* could not conceal the fact that much of the stuff of the novel was taken directly from life. Taylor, it is true, replied sharply to critics who had identified the author with Maxwell Woodbury (in *Hannah Thurston*). Critics of this ilk, he said in the preface to his second novel, would "not fail to recognize him in John Godfrey, although there is no resemblance between the two characters." [115] No student of Taylor will believe, however, that the author did not get into his own way as he was sketching John Godfrey—or that R. H. Stoddard did not sit for the portrait of the composer Swansford. "The Cave" is easily recognized as Pfaff's Beer Cellar.[116] Indeed Taylor defends himself in the same preface against "those sensitive readers who protest against any representation of 'American Life,' which is not an unmitigated glorification of the same . . ." [117] In sum *John Godfrey's Fortunes* is a combination (hardly a blend) of realism and romanticism. Taylor could command either element reasonably well, but he lacked the power to fuse the two into a convincing unit of the sort that Howells was shortly to produce.

The Story of Kennett (1866) is by common consent Taylor's best novel. It is not the most original, but it has more mellowness and depth. It grew less out of observation than out of feeling. The plot, though based in large part upon reality, follows a pretty trite pattern. Gilbert Potter, a handsome, reliable, and sturdy young man, has often besought his mother to disclose the secret of his parentage, but Mary Potter has steadily refused to do more than assure him of his legitimacy. Despite the cloud that hangs over him because of his ambiguous status in the eyes of the village, Gilbert manages to win the love of the adorable Martha Deane. Two principal obstacles confront the hero, combatting parental displeasure and paying off the mortgage on the small farm which he and his mother work. Martha's father opposes the match not only because of Potter's alleged "shameful birth," but also because of his hope that by arranging a match between Martha and her neighbor, Squire Alfred Barton, two good properties may be brought together. Gilbert finally accumulates enough money, however, to pay off the mortgage. The death of Alfred Barton's father (an octogenarian) solves the mystery of the hero's birth: Gilbert is the lawful son of Alfred Barton. On the occasion of her marriage to Barton, Mary Potter had sworn to keep the marriage secret until the momentarily expected death of the elder Barton—so that Alfred could be sure of his inheritance from a father who would not have approved his marriage with a humble girl like Mary Potter. Well, old Barton took an unconscionable time a-dying—a matter of some twenty-six years. In the meantime, Alfred had allowed his wife to live in need and opprobrium throughout all these years. In a very moving scene Mary Potter takes her rightful place at the side of her husband at the funeral of the elder Barton, but she has not forgiven his atrocious cruelty. Again Bayard Taylor is unable to resist lining the nest of his love-birds with gold as well as affection: the elder Barton had been in love with Mary also and it is to her (and therefore to the blessed couple) that the fortune of the old miser will go. Even this rather flashy fictional device, however, does not seriously detract from the solid merit that the book shows in other respects, particularly in the setting. Taylor knew and loved every inch of his mise-en-scène, for it was the environment he lived in as a boy: "The lovely pastoral landscapes which I know by heart," he wrote, "have been copied, field for field and tree for tree . . ." [118] Although the story is set in the year 1796, many of the characters were based partly upon persons he had known as a boy—some of them members of his own family. The story of Gilbert and the exploits of the bandit Sandy Flash were based upon realities that may be at least roughly checked.[119] Whether the proportion of actual fact used in the story justifies calling *The Story of Kennett* an "historical novel" [120] is extremely doubtful, but at least it makes for authenticity in atmosphere and episode. There are many homely illustrations of the quiet (Quaker) life of Kennett Square—social, religious, industrial—that ring true and that seem to be integral parts of the story instead of (as is the case in many of the conversations in *Hannah Thurston*) interpolations.[121] The book is not one of great sustained power—such power Bayard Taylor could not attain to—but it is a very readable tale delineating credible people in plausible situations. *The Atlantic Monthly* gratefully noted that the book was not burdened with "hopelessly unpicturesque" elements like "modern reformerism" or "the scarcely more attractive details of literary adventure." [122]

In his last novel, *Joseph and His Friend* (1870), Taylor did less credit to himself. Although in *The Story of Kennett* he had spoken satirically of contemporary writers who preferred to "deal with abnormal characters and psychological problems more or less exceptional or morbid," [123] in *Joseph and His Friend* he not only joined the ranks of this class of writers but also proved that his product was little if at all superior to theirs. The story is that of a young man who is inveigled into marriage with a frivolous woman much his senior. She runs him into debt, encourages him to invest in unsound stocks (promoted by her father), and in general so embitters his life that he comes to hate her. Finally, having overheard him express to another girl his feelings toward his wife, she takes arsenic and dies. Their domestic discord having been generally known, Joseph is tried for murder, but evidence is finally introduced to prove that the wife had purchased arsenic herself—which for some time she had been using as a cosmetic. Joseph is acquitted and, one may guess, is soon to be provided with another wife. His financial affairs are also restored to satisfactory condition, so that the hero, though sobered by his experiences, can look forward to an indeterminate period of domestic happiness. All this experience has been shared by a "friend," Philip Held, who is understood to have achieved a place in the hero's affections of which not even the latter's marriage can deprive him. The story is of course in effect an argument for the cultivation of those quiet virtues which lead to happiness, but in the course of the illustrations the novel traverses some rather muddy ground. The intense court-room scene is little better than melodrama. There are, in the early part of the story, a number of scenes descriptive of rural life which Taylor handles well, but these hardly serve to redeem the story as a whole. Taylor did not excel in the treatment of sophisticated characters.

Joseph and His Friend was the last of Taylor's novels. The principal literary accomplishment of his remaining years (he died in 1878) was his translation of *Faust*. Beyond that, he had projected a life of Goethe, which was never written. Clearly novel-writing had been only one phase of an exceedingly crowded literary life. A prolific man of letters, an inveterate traveler, and a popular lecturer, Bayard Taylor was not essentially a man of ideas. His incessant traveling afforded ample opportunity to observe the social order, but although he was quick to discern the picturesque wherever he was, his critical judgments were neither very acute nor very original. He was essentially a reporter. Such opinions as he held, moreover, were often in conflict with one another. In general he may fairly be labeled a middle-of-the-roader. Ever obedient to the "practical gods" who might bring about his material success, he was prone, especially in his youth, to abide by well-worn precedent. As an ambitious littérateur he felt no urge to blaze new trails: his California trip opened up new regions which a more adventurous spirit might have capitalized, but Taylor scurried back as soon as his assignment was completed and tethered himself to an office stool in Horace Greeley's *Tribune*. After New York, then Boston. It was Taylor's greatest ambition to link himself to the apostolic succession in New England. In 1851 Ticknor and Fields brought out his *Book of Romances, Lyrics and Songs,* but New England scarcely had need of a poet vending verses of the general variety that Longfellow produced and, what is more, produced without streaking them with that pagan voluptuousness which Taylor sometimes indulged in.[124] On the whole Taylor was not enthusiastically received in New England. He constantly courted the attention of the New England poets: "I am working to become one with Bryant and Longfellow, with Lowell and Whittier." And when most of the gentlemen mentioned by Taylor responded politely to one of his poems (*The Picture of St. John,* 1866), he felt himself admitted to "that small company of American poets who have some chance of life." Yet Taylor was later much grieved by the *North American Review's* treatment of his translation of *Faust*, and he came to believe that he was treated unfairly by an "exclusive Boston circle." [125]

Although temperamentally conservative, Taylor occasionally delivered vigorous strictures on the social and political order. Politically he was not tested often. In the Civil War he was a strong champion of the North, and he courageously expressed from the platform (in Philadelphia) abolitionist views so likely to anger his audience that it was necessary to provide a guard of police in order for him to proceed. He was hostile, even prejudiced, toward the South in general; and when secession was in the air, his protest was delivered in tones of angry conviction that he seldom used: "The idea of loyalty to a state is so childish that a man of ordinary intelligence should be ashamed to entertain it." [126] Centralization he deemed necessary for the successful functioning of government. Yet he deplored government "protection" of business and he made many enemies by his attacks on the corporations of the Gilded Age:

> "Our corporations are more despotic, dishonest, and irresponsible than in any other country of the civilized world. Our politicians, of whatever party, repeat the old phrases indicative of mistrust of corporations: yet we find the latter controlling entire states, electing their own legislatures and members of congress, demoralizing voters, and exercising other dangerous privileges, in utter defiance of the public interest." [127]

In making criticisms of this sort, however, Taylor was as fitful as he was in the pursuit of the art of writing. He lacked concentration and constructive ability. Similarly when he appraised the literary world in which he moved, his opinions reflected personal experience rather than critical principles. Yet he shrewdly put his finger on certain real abuses. In *John Godfrey's Fortunes* he expresses indirectly some of his contempt for the world of the literati among whom he found himself when he first moved to New York. Editors, he discovers, are wary of doing business with any but "standard" authors. Consequently the thing to do is to make a reputation by whatever vulgar means: "Write a sonnet on a railroad accident, or something else that everybody will read." Better still, discard poetry in favor of "short, sentimental stories . . . something light and airy . . . such as women like to read,—with a good deal of Millinery in them." Well, John writes a story all compact of "millinery" but finds that the ending must be changed to make it agreeable to the trade. Chiefly one must be certain that the story contains "nothing which could plant an unconventional or rebellious thought in the breast of infancy." Stories must be given "a moral turn." Articles are also in demand but honors (and emoluments) go to "weak concoctions of flashy, superficial philosophy, generally starting from the text of some trivial incident, and made piquant with a delicate flavor of slang." Articles, too, should have a moral tendency, not for the sake of virtue but for the sake of escaping censure. So long as the letter of decency is observed the spirit may go hang, the editor implies: "If you can make 'em a little racy,—you understand,—but not so that it can be taken hold of, they'll go all the better." As for book reviews, they are beneath contempt, Godfrey finds. When he publishes a volume of poems, he looks vainly among the reviews for "a single line which showed the discrimination of an enlightened critic." Indeed in Godfrey's opinion "we had no criticism, worthy of the name, at that time." [128] Under conditions such as these the new writer soon learned that he must compromise with his ideals, for although a literary reputation was worth something as a means of bringing bread and butter, fame was to be regarded as "a great humbug." [129]

Taylor soon rose somewhat above the low journalistic level on which he found himself in New York, but he never succeeded in becoming a thoroughly independent craftsman and artist responsible only to the dictates of his own artistic conscience. Financial stringency forced him to peddle gaudy wares to the distracted readers of the Gilded Age. His own restlessness and his relatively shallow mind prevented him from making a break with the petty literary world he affected to despise. Nor was he indifferent to the manifold honors and remunerations awarded him for his willingness to entertain the general with witty trifles and *morceaux de salon*. It was his fate to appear in an era of American literary history when nature did not breed many artists of heroic proportions, and it was comparatively easy for him to excel in a field of such restricted competition. Toward the end of his life he complained of the common fallacy "that a man has only to do good literary work in order to be appreciated—and rewarded." "Nothing," he added, "could be more untrue in this country at this time. The public supposes that the mere knowledge of a man's name is the token of his success. If notoriety were success this would be true; but it is sometimes the reverse." [130] Notoriety, yes, that was what Taylor achieved. Nor should he have complained. He made his choice, and he had his reward: he became an enormously popular writer. It would not have availed him to withdraw from the welter of life and consecrate himself to the highest art. In all probability he would have achieved even less than he did. No burning devotion to great art dominated his mind. He was not formed to dwell in the outermost reaches of the imagination. Whatever the form of literature he adopted, his observations remained essentially "views afoot"; for the flight to Parnassus he had no wings. This was a truth that, once at least, he himself frankly recognized:

> I have touched neither the deeps nor the heights: I have only looked down into the one and up towards the other, in lesser vibrations on either side of that noteless middle line which most men travel from birth to death.[131]

As for the novel, which in America long suffered an inferiority complex on account of the dazzling brilliance of Dickens and Thackeray and Bulwer, Taylor paid very little attention to it until he had tried his hand at many other things. His ideals of fiction were simple but mainly sound. He admired and to some extent imitated Jane Austen.[132] He was perhaps naive in failing to perceive that French novelists were interested in technical problems as well as in the analysis of emotions, but his substitute choices are good: "Give me [he says] the fresh, hearty, warm-blooded creations of Fielding and Smollett, with all their coarseness, rather than the refined and insidious immorality of modern French novelists." [133] He believed that there was an intimate connection between the tone of a book and its author's physical condition: "Byron, with all the shifting play of his wit, pathos, and passion, cannot wholly purify the pages of *Don Juan* from the smell of gin; and Mrs. Radcliffe, in the nightmare horrors of her *Mysteries of Udolpho*, betrays the suppers of raw beef in which she indulged." [134] On the whole, despite romantic caches in his stories already referred to, he was on the side of realism in fiction: "Not what ought to be, or might be, is the proper province of fiction, but what is." [135] As for writers of his own era, Taylor finds them no better than the public makes them: "The characteristic of those books which now [in 1855] best suit the popular taste in this country is morbid emotion." [136] Taylor's own novels, excepting possibly *Joseph and His Friend*, at any rate do not violate the principles here referred to. The satire in *Hannah Thurston* was at least a good tonic—if distasteful to many of the author's patients. *John Godfrey's Fortunes* was an honest attempt to tell a realistic story of adventure in a world unexploited by earlier novelists. *The Story of Kennett*, set far enough away in time to disarm Taylor the satirist, was close enough to the centre of his deepest personal reminiscences to evoke his best abilities in characterization and atmosphere. None of these books is notable for great originality or for advances in technique. Taylor anticipates Howells in protesting against the morbid tone of many novels of the 1850's and 1860's, but it remained for Howells to inaugurate a new regime in novel-writing.

THEODORE WINTHROP (1828-1861)

When at the age of thirty-three Theodore Winthrop died on the battlefield of Great Bethel in 1861, he was mourned as a brave chivalric spirit worthy to be compared with Sir Philip Sidney, but little enough was said about his literary production. Most of his work, which included three novels and two books of travel, remained in manuscript, for publishers had veered away from the risk of backing a young man whose stories, though somewhat sensational in substance, were set forth in language whose finesse seemed likely to be caviar to the general. Yet when his novels were published posthumously in 1862 they became popular so rapidly that by 1868 they had aggregated forty-four editions.[137] Nor was the popularity of Winthrop short-lived, for during the next twenty-five years the sale of his works was "positively stupendous." [138] With the opening of the twentieth century Winthrop gradually began to slip from public attention, and he is now little known. Yet from the point of view of sheer ability in language he was one of the ablest of the minor writers of American fiction. His works are more worthy of being exhumed than those of many writers who had an even greater sale in his day.[139]

His brief life was not of the happiest. Born of parents whose ancestors included the first Governor Winthrop (of whom he was a direct descendant) and Jonathan Edwards, he was possessed of a serious temperament that expressed itself in frequent "self-examination and self-accusation." [140] Enough Puritan blood still ran in his veins to create in the boy "doubts about free will." [141] He enjoyed, however, the advantages of a cultured home adjacent to the wharves and woods of New Haven. He was graduated from Yale College in 1848. Despite moments of rebelliousness, he was a prevailingly gentle youth, and he loved particularly his Greek studies, which gave him "new ideas of the exact use of words." [142] He early thought of a literary career, but delicate health, inability to focus his energies, and the need of making a living interfered with literary composition. A trip to Europe for his health's sake failed to cure his body but it satisfied many nostalgic yearnings, for he loved England almost as much as his native land. Upon his return he embarked on a commercial career, which crowded the next few years with traveling that took him as far afield as Panama, New Mexico, and California. His personal life was largely solitary, and it was at one time rendered tragic by his unfortunate engagement with a young woman who proved to be unworthy of his love—a fact which undoubtedly colored his subsequent treatment of two of his principal fictional characters.[143] Writing was a frequent but discouraging avocation during these years; except for a poem or two published in magazines (including the *Atlantic Monthly*) he elicited little hope from editors. Nor were most of his poems worthy of much more attention than they received. Finally he found a publisher for his novel, *John Brent*, but when he discovered that the publication was contingent upon the excision of an incident involving the rescue of a fugitive slave, Winthrop refused to mutilate his story.[144] When he died he left the manuscripts of three novels, none of which had the benefit of his final revision for the press.

The three novels which appeared shortly after his death have a technical homogeneity, but they represent different tendencies in fiction, and it was doubtless not so much Winthrop's verbal dexterity and charm of manner as his interesting plots which sent his books through so many editions. The first of his novels to be published (though the last to be written) was *Cecil Dreeme*. It may be roughly classified as a blending of attenuated Gothic romance with Hawthornesque fancy. The hero, a cultivated young man recently returned from Europe, takes up his residence in the apartment of an absent friend who has contrived to introduce so much exotic atmosphere and furniture into his apartment that it resembles an Italian palazzo. Romantic adventure immediately besets him in a manner that the author himself describes as "Otrantoish." With the aid of the janitor he rescues from starving a mysterious lodger on the floor above. He enters into a friendship with the lodger, Cecil Dreeme, who is a painter of real ability. At the same time he forms an acquaintance with another resident of the apartment building, a man so obviously of sinister character that Cecil Dreeme's warnings are needed by nobody but the idealistic hero. Presently Byng (the hero) finds himself involved in a complicated situation that reaches its dénouement only after the author has employed a considerable amount of stock characterization and rusty plot material: the guilty father forced by financial crimes to offer his daughter in marriage to a sleek villain; the supposed death (by drowning) of the heroine; the assumption of male clothing by the heroine; the romantic properties, such as a picture symbolizing the unhappy experience of the heroine, and the mysterious dark room kept locked; the abduction of the heroine and her imprisonment in an asylum; the violent end of the villain— done to death by an antique dagger. The elements are grim, but their treatment is quiet, and they recall not so much the power of Charles Brockden Brown as the subtle macabre effects of Hawthorne in *The Marble Faun*. But Winthrop comes nearest to Hawthorne in his philosophic treatment of the subjection of a good person to the malign influence of a fair-seeming villain. Like Hawthorne he uses symbolism to suggest sinister relationships, as in this bit of action showing how near Byng came to falling under the sway of the villain, Densdeth:

> There stood Densdeth's wine, attracting me like some magic philter. It became magnetic with Densdeth's magnetism . . .
>
> The vulgar scenery of the long dining-room faded away from my eyes . . . I was conscious of nothing but the wine—the philter—and him who had poured it out . . .
>
> I sat staring at the silly glass of wine, and began to make an unwholesome test of my self-control. I recalled the typical legend of Eve and the apple, and exaggerated the moral importance of my own incident after the same fashion.
>
> "If I resist this symbolic cup," thought I, "I am my own man; if I yield, I am Densdeth's."
>
> When a man is weak enough to put slavery and freedom thus in the balance, it is plain that he will presently be a slave.
>
> "Bah!" I thought. "What harm, after all, can this terrible person do me? Why shouldn't I accept his alliance? Why shouldn't I study him, and learn the secret of his power."
>
> My slight resistance was about to yield to the spiritual enticement of the wine, when suddenly an outer force broke the spell.[145]

Winthrop, like Hawthorne, was fascinated by the theme of moral ambiguity, but he probed his problems less deeply and sustained his enchantment less successfully. Illusion is broken by Winthrop's energetic style and by his use of local allusion. It is likely, in fact, that the popularity of *Cecil Dreeme* was due in considerable part to its vignettes of contemporary New York. For New Yorkers, although often celebrated or scourged in verse and essay, had up to this time received relatively little attention at the hands of novelists.

If Winthrop had lived to observe the immediate popularity of *Cecil Dreeme*, he might well have tried to protract his prosperity by mining further in the same vein. Yet *John Brent*, the second of his posthumous novels, brought distinction to his name in a wholly new genre. The book is full of autobiography loosely attached to a love story.[146] It opens up the romantic West. Winthrop was among the first American writers to celebrate romantic adventure set against a brilliant background of trans-Mississippi scenery. Whereas Irving had timorously and dutifully done mileage in the West and handled records of the westward course of American occupation, Winthrop was at home in the West as much as anywhere—as much and no more so, for he was a volatile and restless spirit, and his story has scarcely become thoroughly implanted in California before it begins to sweep back across the entire continent to New York and, ultimately, to London, where it ends. The action, however, is motivated by the love of John Brent for Ellen Clitheroe. John Brent, physically a splendid specimen of manhood, is a simple, noble soul who has never known love until he sees it in the kindred soul of Ellen Clitheroe, a cultivated girl of Lancashire incongruously transplanted to the deserts of Utah by the fanatical whim of her father, who thought to compensate for his financial ruin in Lancashire by a life of spiritual perfection among the Mormons. To secure Ellen against the obscene embraces of a powerful Mormon leader and rescue her from some worthless Pikes who have abducted her, involves thrilling adventures over escarpment and desert until a bloody reckoning with the kidnappers restores Ellen to the Christian personnel of the story. But John Brent is now near death from a wound. As for Ellen, her place is near her father, who is now as anxious to escape Mormon contagion as he once was to enjoy its blessings. When Brent recovers, he commences a pursuit of Ellen that ends in bliss only after Winthrop has stretched probability to extremely dangerous limits in the interests of romance. Other main characters include Richard Wade, the "first-person" of the story, who is also in love with Ellen. His nobility in this volume lies in silent renunciation: his consolation, in his ownership of Don Fulano, one of the most beautiful horses of all California.[147] There is also the rough-spoken Armstrong, whose outdoor craft seems as definitely derived from Cooper's Natty as his lust for revenge seems a literary inheritance from Bird's Nathan Slaughter.[148]

Friends of Winthrop who were disturbed by his inability to concentrate his powers[149] might well have pointed to *John Brent* as proof of the author's discursiveness. Even more than *Cecil Dreeme*, *John Brent* is a thing of brilliant shreds and patches. It is, in part at least, a story of the West told more romantically than any of Clemens' stories and less sentimentally than Bret Harte's. It has many of the markings of the historical romance, but it eludes this classification by being more concerned with psychology than most historical romances, and it finds its conclusion in a London setting which is so elaborately (and lovingly) described that the West is almost forgotten. Despite Winthrop's obvious animus against slave-owners, Pikes, and Mormons, the book is not a doctrinaire novel. Perhaps it is most of all a love story. Whatever the classification to which it belongs, the public apparently liked *John Brent*.

Edwin Brothertoft, published also in 1862,[150] is made up of almost equal proportions of the psychological and the historical and the melodramatic. Its action revolves about the fifth generation of a fine old Lincolnshire family, transplanted to a manor on the Hudson. The hero, as idealistic a young man as all of Winthrop's heroes, drifts into an "indicated" marriage with the beautiful young woman who presently proves her essential baseness by conduct so scandalous that Winthrop's pages will "not tolerate the details." [151] Unable to endure a home so degraded and unable to take comfort in a young daughter turned against him by the influence of her dissolute mother, Brothertoft enters the service of his country during the Revolution. Two years later, however, when his wife is about to marry Lucy to a worthless British officer, Brothertoft returns to thwart the plan. More or less by accident Mrs. Brothertoft gratifies a more or less subconscious desire to kill her husband by shooting him—seriously but not fatally. Lucy is carried off safely, and her mother is left bound in the house, which is subsequently set on fire by accident. Seeing the flames, Edwin rushes back to rescue his wife at the risk of his own life. She recovers but soon dies, repentant, while he lives on—"to share a little longer in the dreamy work of life." [152]

The psychological analysis of Edwin Brothertoft's character and of his ill-starred marriage is done seriously enough to create the basis for a domestic novel of more than passing interest. Brothertoft shares the family tendency toward impractical idealism:

> The Brothertoft fortunes did not wax on the new continent. Each gentle Edwin transmitted to his heir the Manor docked of a few more square miles, the mansion a little more dilapidated, the furniture more worn and broken, the name a little less significant in the pushing world of the Province . . .
> They never held their own in the world, much less took what was another's. Each was conscious of a certain latent force, and left it latent. They lived weakly, and died young, like fair exotics. They were a mild, inefficient, ineffectual, lovely, decaying race, strong in all the charming qualities, feeble in all the robust ones.[153]

Though Winthrop is seldom openly autobiographical, it is clear that much of this characterization fits his own case. His life was a tragedy of waning fortunes—material and spiritual. By an irony that is made as real as it is painful, his hero in *Edwin Brothertoft*, a chivalrous and tender spirit, is united with a coarse creature whose outward beauty temporarily blinds him to her gross selfishness. The result is a tragedy of broken ideals in domestic life. But the book is also an historical study.

Few writers of the historical romance have had more imaginative insight into the past than Theodore Winthrop. The England of Cromwell and the Great Rebellion and old Colonel Brothertoft's part in the history of the times are set forth with fine economy and poetry. With very few words Winthrop is able to evoke the scene in which men from Lincolnshire arrive in New York Harbor:

> Bluff is the bow and round as pumpkin is the stern of the Dutch brig, swinging to its anchor in the bay of New York. It is the new arrival from England, this sweet autumn day of 1665 . . .
>
> And now disembark a great company of Lincolnshire men, old tenants or old soldiers of the Colonel's. Their names are thorough Lincolnshire. Here come Wrangles, Swinesheads, Timberlands, Mumbys, Bilsbys, Hogsthorpes, Swillingores, and Galsworthys, old and young, men and women.
>
> These land, and stare about forlornly, after the manner of emigrants. They sit on their boxes, and wish they were well back in the old country. They see the town gallows, an eminent object on the beach, and are taught that where man goes, crime goes also. A frowzy Indian paddles ashore with clams to sell; at this vision, their dismayed scalps tremble on their sinciputs. A sly Dutchman, the fatter prototype of to-day's emigrant runner, stands before them and says, seductively, "Bier, Schnapps!" They shake their heads firmly . . .[154]

The Revolutionary episodes, always kept subordinate to the story of Brothertoft, are done with deftness and, although sometime humorous and even flippant in tone, without that air of factitiousness which mars many research-born romances. The plot as such, however, is poorly managed, for as in *John Brent*, Winthrop dodges the detail of many crises. He is likely at any moment to telescope important action in a word or two in order to descant on American educational opportunity compared with English, fashionable and literary life in England during the age of Johnson, or the culinary colloquies of Voltaire, Sappho, and Plato—who are in this story not historical characters but Negro aides. Before he is through he somehow fulfills the obligations of his rather melodramatic plot, and he caps the action by a full description of one of the ghastliest scenes in American fiction, namely, the scene in which Mrs. Brothertoft bound in a chair realizes that the house is afire.[155] Yet the book as a whole fails in the sense that the three elements, the psychological, the historical, and the melodramatic, are not perfectly fused. The element that finally forbids their union is the author himself: Winthrop could never submerge his own individuality. He appears every few pages as the whimsical, philosophical, or wistful commentator. He has an almost Sterne-like air of irresponsibility toward the literal progress of his story, an Oliver Alden-like impracticality.

Winthrop's interpolations spoil his stories, but they measure his strictly literary ability. Whether because of his Greek and Latin studies or not, he possessed a rare instinct for the right word. His love of language for its own sake was both his strength and his weakness. Not only Edwin Brothertoft but almost every literate character in Winthrop's books "talks powerful dictionary." [156] His excessive use of literary allusion—especially to *Hamlet,* which he sadly overworked—stamps him as somewhat juvenile, but his epigrammatic sallies betoken mastery of language. Some of his quips are gratuitous, but many of them are genuinely humorous. Some of these are isolated epigrams, such as: "No hag is a houri to her *fille de chambre.*" [157] Many of his mots are extravagantly whimsical conceits such as a more timid writer —or one destined to see his final proofs—might delete upon revision. But with a jaunty insouciance occasionally reminiscent of Sterne, Winthrop confides them all to the reader in much the same spirit as Byng speaks to Cecil Dreeme:

> "A third party would spoil the whole! What would become of our confidence, our intimate exchange of thought on every possible subject, if there were another fellow by, who might be a vulgarian or a muff? What could we do with a chap to whom we should have to explain our metaphysics, give page and line for our quotations, interpret our puns, translate our allusions, analyze our intuitions, define our God? Such a companion would take the sparkle and the flash of this rapid and unerring sympathy out of our lives." [158]

Elsewhere Winthrop's ample wit feeds on more "important" themes. George Washington, for example, who is treated with breathless adoration by most earlier writers of romance, and was still subject to panegyric that made a "stilted prig" of him, is only a fallible human being to Winthrop: "Our strapping young friend from Virginia, Master George Washington, has caracoled off, with a tear in his eye and a flea in his ear." [159] Benjamin Franklin is described, with no real disrespect, as "Ben Franklin, a shrewd old Boston-boy." [160] General Humphreys is referred to as "ridiculous, with his grand airs and his prosy poetasms." [161] Nor is this gentle de-emphasizer averse to satirizing more modern phenomena. Though himself a sinner in employing Negro dialect to excess, he inveighs with kindly humor against "Black babble" which "has become rather a bore in literature. Voltaire, therefore, will try not to talk Tombigbee." [162] He refers to the Christy minstrel Jim Crow as an "impossible buffoon" and to the Uncle Tom of "La Beecher

Stowe" as "an exceptional saint." [163] Most of this satire is more in fun than in malice, but it does not mix readily with the strictly narrative portions of Winthrop's writings.

A defective craftsman judged by the stricter canons of his profession, Theodore Winthrop was one of the most attractive of the minor novelists of the nineteenth century. His life was a series of maladjustments: he mastered neither the practical arts of living nor the rules of successful writing. He saw the imperfections of the world, but he was no whimpering fool of fortune: he took his losses with a fine pagan stoicism and he wrote them off in humor. In writing he possessed that charm which is the younger brother of great creative originality. But it was hard to sell charm to hard-headed publishers. Manfully Winthrop strove to conform to accepted narrative patterns: the historical romance, the domestic novel, the Gothic romance. The commercial success which resulted showed that he had accurately gauged the public demand. Yet in retrospect these books do not stand out as superlatively good examples in their genres. It now appears that he would have done better to relinquish his incongruous mixture of dilute Hawthornesque fantasy with mid-century Gothic and his competent but somewhat strained pseudo-historical romance in favor of the novel of manners. His gift was for finish rather than power. He had a singularly fine command of phrase, and his style is full of overtones that were partly wasted on popular stories of action. Yet his idiom seldom seemed bookish: "I wish," he said, "to form a truly American style, good and original, not imitated." [164] His descriptions of contemporary metropolitan life are brilliantly delivered in a tone of easy banter. A finely poetic note sometimes steals into his moods of reverie. Most of all he is now interesting for glints of his own sensitive, stoical, wistful, but potentially joyous individuality. In the personal essay he might have found the best synthesis of his somewhat disparate gifts.[165]

OLIVER WENDELL HOLMES (1809-1894)

Oliver Wendell Holmes's late adoption of the novel as a popular medium is a reminder not only of the slow development of the genre (except as pertains to the historical romance) but also of his limited impulse as a writer of narrative. Indeed he gave very little sign of attempting any sort of popular writing until long after he had made a career in medicine. Born in 1809, graduated from Harvard in 1829, he pursued advanced studies in medicine which ultimately brought him a Harvard M.D. but attracted few patients. He therefore presently turned his medical knowledge to the uses of writing and teaching. His monograph on puerperal fever was only one of a number of technical studies that gave him a solid reputation, and his professional work was so successful that he was advanced finally to the Deanship of the Harvard Medical School. These activities largely filled the years from 1829 to 1857.

When in the year 1857, at Lowell's request, Holmes took to the field of popular literature, he began to exercise publicly artistic gifts of which many of his friends and a small public had long been aware. As early as 1831-32 he had published in the short-lived *New England Magazine* two numbers of a projected series of essays which he entitled *The Autocrat of the Breakfast-Table*. For some reason, however, he determined to suppress these early examples of his table talk, and for the next thirty years his belles lettres efforts were confined largely to occasional verse. Finally resumed, the *Autocrat* (1857-58) was such a brilliant success that Holmes never again lost contact with a fairly large public. His first novel, *Elsie Venner* (1861), by no means proved him a master of the art of narrative, but like his two succeeding novels, *The Guardian Angel* and *A Mortal Antipathy*, it proved that the novel was a reasonably favorable medium for exploiting not only his talent for sententious commentary but even for physiological and psychological theories evolved in the course of his long experience as a professor of medicine. The rich flavor of his discourses on society and the keen edge of his sociological message compensated for his imperfect command of narrative and his shameless resort to trite fictional devices. And the fine finish of his prose, at once classically poised and charmingly intimate, lent to his novels a distinction seldom attained by more "professional" story-tellers.

When Holmes published *Elsie Venner* in 1861,[166] the vogue of the historical romance and the Gothic tale was largely over or in abeyance, and the novel of domestic life was in the ascendancy. Although, as will be seen, *Elsie Venner* possessed a vein of originality, it had much in common with the type of novel then popular. The action was in most respects conventional enough. A young woman (Elsie Venner) falls in love with a handsome young medical student (Bernard Langdon) who is temporarily teaching school. He does not return her love; but a reprobate cousin of Elsie, fearing her possible control over Bernard, decides to murder his potential rival in order to marry Elsie himself—for her financial prospects. The plot is foiled by Abel, the hired man; but, the police and the constabulary being as ineffective as in most early American fiction, the would-be murderer is ludicrously allowed to run off to South America. It remains for Elsie to make a final avowal of her love, vainly, before going into a decline accompanied by fever which ends only with her life. Most of this was not new in the novel. Nor was there novelty in the fact that Holmes often left his story idling while he stopped to study the daily life of the village folk in Pigwacket Centre and Rockland, or to elaborate certain scenes such as the parties at Colonel Sprowle's and the Widow Rowens's, or to digress on innumerable themes. What was relatively new was the character and personality of Elsie: she exhibits unmistakable ophidian characteristics. She dresses so as to suggest the appearance of a snake; walks with an undulating motion; is cold to the touch; is livelier in the summer than in the winter; and fascinates by the eye. To be sure, ophidian symbolism was familiar to readers of Hawthorne's tales, but nowhere in American fiction had the snake motif been used so vividly throughout a long story.

Holmes uses his fantastic elements in *Elsie Venner* much in the manner of Hawthorne. Thus Elsie constantly wears around her neck a chain which may or may not cover the mark of a snake bite or an ophidian feature, but when after her death the chain is removed, the sign (if any) has disappeared.[167] Again, just as in Hawthorne's "Rappaccini's Daughter," the antidote proves fatal to Beatrice, so in *Elsie Venner*, when the victim's system has been finally purged of poison, life has fled. Holmes's use of symbolism and allegory is probably less artful than Hawthorne's, but his probing of the relationship between the moral and the physical in man's nature is marked by more decisiveness. For in *Elsie Venner* the ophidian symbolism is of course used merely as a concrete way of stating an hypothesis: the fact that Elsie's mother had once been bitten by a snake is offered as a possible explanation of the girl's atrophied moral nature and her anti-social acts. Perhaps the physical details were distasteful to squeamish readers,[168] but the theory they symbolized was even more shocking to those readers who were steeped in Puritan doctrine regarding the origin of sin. Dr. Holmes's long study of the cause of physical disease had provided him with an analogy for the causes of moral obliquity. He believed that individuals are often condemned for "sinful" acts which should in all fairness be laid to their inheritance or their environment. In the preface to *Elsie Venner* he remarks that he does not wish to insist dogmatically on his thesis but rather to use it as "a convenient medium of truth rather than as an accepted scientific conclusion," [169] but it is clear from the colloquies between Dr. Kittredge and the Reverend Doctor Honeywood that his convictions concerning human responsibility were deeply rooted.[170] Thus the minister seems to be getting the worse of the argument when the doctor questions the rightness of laying human depravity to old Adam's sin or to weakness of the will:

"Ministers talk about the human will as if it stood on a high look-out, with plenty of light, and elbow-room reaching to the horizon. Doctors are constantly noticing how it is tied up and darkened by inferior organization, by disease, and all sorts of crowding inter-ferences, until they get to look upon Hottentots and Indians—and a good many of their own race—as a kind of self-conscious blood-clocks with very limited power of self-determination. That's the *tendency*, I say, of a doctor's experience. But the peo-ple to whom they address their statements of the results of their observation belong to the thinking class of the highest races, and *they* are conscious of a great deal of liberty of will. So in the face of the fact that civilization with all it offers has proved a dead failure with the aboriginal races of this country,—on the whole, I say, a dead failure,—they talk as if they knew from their own will all about that of a Digger Indian! We are more apt to go by ob-servation of the facts in the case. We are constantly seeing weak-ness where you see depravity. I don't say we're *right;* I only tell what you must often find to be the fact, right or wrong, in talking with doctors. You see, too, our notions of bodily and moral dis-ease, or sin, are apt to go together. We used to be as hard on sick-ness as you were on sin. We know better now." [171]

For Holmes to submit medical evidence as a reason for re-opening questions settled long since by synod or church council was un-doubtedly disconcerting to many conservative readers.[172] Fortunately Elsie's moral delinquency did not take forms that would shock Vic-torian readers unduly: perhaps her worst offence was biting Richard Venner's wrist. Yet the grafting of a medical and moral thesis to the novel proved almost fatal: the whole tale lacks coördination. Moreover although some of the minor characters are well drawn, notably the nurse Sophia ("Only three generations removed from cannibalism"), the major characters are pretty pallid creatures, the victims of experi-mentation, the playthings of the writer. Indeed the only individual who is alive throughout the whole book is the author himself, who bobs up aphoristically and humorously with scant regard for the welfare of his narrative. A fondness for phrase that recalls Lamb, and indulgent humor comparable to Thackeray's, an occasional passage of Dickensian satire—these literary bonnes bouches plus Holmes's native sparkling wit make for good reading even when the narrative threatens, as it often does, to break down utterly. If Holmes mixed the ingredients of a novel with an inexpert hand, he was a master of the art of seasoning and of garnishing the result.

The Guardian Angel (1867), less well known now than *Elsie Venner*, was so widely read in its time that by 1887 it had reached its twenty-third edition. It is similar to the earlier novel in stemming from a biological hypothesis. It illustrates the author's theory that "It is by no means certain that our individual personality is the single inhabitant of these our corporeal frames." Rather it seems likely that *"This body in which we journey across the isthmus between the two oceans is not a private carriage, but an omnibus."* [173] Among the ancestral passengers in this carry-all in the case of Myrtle Hazard (the heroine) are four women who may be presumed to have a great deal of influence on her life: a martyr, an alleged witch, a great beauty, and a woman said to have Indian blood in her veins. These and other strains are so mixed in Myrtle that she is the register of a variety of "inherited impulses . . . some of them dangerous. The World, the Flesh, and the Devil held mortgages on her life before its deed was put in her hands." [174] To be sure, there are also good impulses, but Myrtle goes through some pretty harassing episodes before anything like an "equilibrium" is reached in her nature. In the end it appears that beauty (in benevolent guise) is her dominant legacy—for, unlike *Elsie Venner*, this book has a happy ending.

In the beginning, not only her ancestral liabilities but her unhappy circumstances complicate Myrtle's life. Upon the death of her parents she becomes the none-too-welcome ward of her Uncle Malachi and her Aunt Silence Withers. And when Malachi hangs himself, she is the unprotected prey of Silence, a neurotic spinster, and Cynthia Badlam, a scheming shrew. Bad traits in Myrtle are explained by Cynthia as the result of her taint of Indian blood and society's failure to "break her will." As for Silence, she operates on the Puritan premise that children are fundamentally wicked and that their instincts should be "eradicated, not educated." Is it any wonder that Myrtle's soul was "chilled" and that she confided in a friend: "Aunt Silence cares for nothing but her own soul, and the other woman [*i.e.,* Cynthia] hates me, I always thought." Myrtle determines to escape her prison by disguising herself as a boy and going by small boat to Boston. Encountering a rapids, she almost loses her life, to be saved only by the prompt action of Clement Lindsay. She is presently restored to her own village through the discreet intercession of one Byles Gridley. Myrtle being an 1867 heroine, brain fever naturally ensues (Dr. Holmes is not original at all points) before Myrtle is restored to health. When she recovers, she is the cynosure of many masculine eyes. The local minister who wishes to be more than a spiritual guide to her (despite the fact that he is married and has children) Myrtle firmly rejects, once she understands his obscene attentions. Another sinister suitor is Murray Bradshaw, a young lawyer, whose perception of Myrtle's beauty is greatly sharpened by his private knowledge that she will in all probability inherit a large fortune. More and more it appears, however, that Myrtle is attracted to Clement Lindsay, her rescuer. In time all complications (and they are many) are disposed of so that the lovers may plight their troth. Murray Bradshaw achieves full-blown villainy when he tosses into the fire what he believes to be the original will providing for Myrtle's inheritance, but good old Byles Gridley, an amateur detective and Myrtle's "guardian angel," has arranged that the burnt will should be merely a copy. The Civil War now rears its ugly head over the happiness of the lovers, but Clement is finally returned to his fiancée with a few honorable wounds and a major's leaf. In the meantime the War has provided a decent death for villain Bradshaw, who expends his last breath in exhorting Myrtle, now an angel of mercy in the camps, to forgive him. There follows a shameless recital of the final fate of various characters—death, accident, marriage, repentance, reform—showing that Holmes was not above using the sort of trite narrative devices that so pained Henry James when he looked back upon the history of the novel before his time.

The measure of Holmes's inadequacy as a student of the technique of the novel is suggested by the awkward splicing of his biological theory to the objective action of the story. Myrtle's inherited traits are never wholly forgotten, but after the middle of the book they are less conspicuous and the story rambles on in familiar channels to a conventional close. The doctrine of "limited responsibility," however, was sufficiently obvious and sufficiently offensive to readers of the *Atlantic* to cause many to cancel their subscriptions.[175] In a preface to the story in book form Holmes takes pains to point out that his doctrine did not deny the existence of all "self-determining power" in individuals but merely doubts its supremacy. Yet it was unquestionably the scientific bearing of the book which was largely responsible both for repelling and attracting readers. For the rest, the story is related with an abundance of wit, wisdom, and raillery which overstep proportion but which, now that the doctrinaire content of the book has become familiar matter,[176] constitute a large part of the modern reader's interest. Like *Elsie Venner*, this book catches up many local idiosyncrasies of character and speech: to some degree Holmes was "a pathfinder for regionalists and local colorists."[177] His range of observation was not great—he was, he said, "a fowl that keeps his roost"—but his eye was sharp for people and incident within a decent radius of Boston. He has a delightful chapter on the village poet who descends patronizingly on a Boston publisher.[178] Epigrams dipped in satire are proffered from time to time. Thus:

[L]awyers half learn a thing quicker than the members of any other profession.

[Mr. Stoker] knew how to weaken his divinity, on occasion, as well as an old housewife to weaken her tea, lest it should keep people awake.

Easy-crying widows take new husbands soonest; there is nothing like wet weather for transplanting, as Master Gridley used to say.[179]

Nor did Holmes's humor consist of mere jests inserted ruthlessly: they arise out of the story. And much may be forgiven in any New England novelist of his time capable of filling in the interstices of his structure with humor rather than theology or bathos or "reform."

A Mortal Antipathy (1885) is so amorphous that it seems the *reductio ad absurdum* of Holmes's method of stretching a narrative over a framework of theory. The result in this case is that the narrative is wholly inadequate to conceal the scaffolding of the story. The fundamental idea is that a malign incident in childhood may account for an antipathy that persists for many years. In this instance a child who has been allowed to fall out of his beautiful cousin's arms and sustain an injury to his head develops such an antipathy for all beautiful young women that upon coming into their presence he suffers seizures resembling the symptoms of angina pectoris. The natural complement of such a situation is an incident in which the subject experiences a rescue at the hands of a lovely woman. This duly occurs (the hero being conveniently ill of typhoid fever in a burning house) and the antipathy is removed. The hero can now marry his rescuer, and he can also meet his cousin without so much as blanching. The objection to the story is not that it is even more furnished with clinical detail than Holmes's earlier novels but that the evolution of the narrative is needlessly neglected. Realizing its character as a miscellany Holmes calls the book a "portfolio." If it be regarded as such instead of a story it may yield much poorly related material touching on spiritualism, the evil eye, yellow fever, gynophobia, and sundry aspects of abnormal psychology. Modern notes are often struck in the psychological discussion, and the use of the rights of women as a secondary theme for the novel shows that even in his old age Holmes's mind was open to new ideas. Segregated, these materials would be interesting and useful; in *A Mortal Antipathy* they are buried in a novel to which they proved fatal.

Holmes's last novel was the worst of the three he wrote, but it differed more in degree than in kind from his others. Holmes lacked the power to enter into the minds of his characters and the will to hew to his story. He never mastered the art of illusion.[180] He was the servant of his ideas whether isolated or in the connected form of a quasi-scientific theory serving as the thesis for a novel.

As a thinker Holmes was more clear-headed than profound—an adjuster rather than a generator of thought.[181] Nevertheless he served an important function in New England during that lack-lustre period (after the Civil War) when transcendentalism had passed its zenith, by keeping speculation alive, at least in certain categories. Compared with Howells, his younger contemporary, he seems lacking in social and political vision, but he had more moral range than Howells. To his own generation he was a (sometimes embarrassing) moral question-box. Given his Calvinistic background in home and academy he naturally reacted against the religion of his father. In the 1870's he wrote to Mrs. Stowe: "I do not believe you or I can ever get the iron of Calvinism out of our souls." [182] Yet the process of purification went further in Holmes than in Mrs. Stowe.[183] To be sure the battle against Calvinistic dogma had been in full sway long before Holmes took the field; indeed he was the historian of its doctrinal decline in "The Deacon's Masterpiece" and in "Jonathan Edwards." Yet if the military front of Calvinistic doctrine had been broken before Holmes's time, the foe lingered here and there in changed uniforms, ethical and educational. It was easier to surrender the doctrine of original sin than to banish the feeling of human depravity it had engendered. Hence many ethical standards and educational procedures were still based on the premise that the human heart was naturally corrupt. Against this enfeebling conception Holmes battled with all the resources of his wit and science. This was perhaps his chief contribution to American thought. In his novels he showed that it is just as logical to correlate sin with inheritance and environment as it is to probe the causes of physical disorders. What is easily accepted by twentieth-century psychologists went down hard with many of Holmes's contemporaries, for it seemed to threaten their principal base of moral reference. Yet it was the more effective as coming from a man who was in most respects conservative and who did not allow his rationalistic thought to debouch upon atheism.

It is a commonplace to refer to Holmes as an inheritor of eighteenth-century liberalism. The reason for this is that he applied rational tests to so many things and that although he came to maturity during the very flowering of New England transcendentalism he did not avail himself of its copious lessons of mysticism. His biographical study of Emerson showed only a fractional understanding of Emerson's weltanschauung. He was perhaps most akin to the transcendentalists in his ready acceptance of changing attitudes toward the physical universe. The disclosures of science which made many Victorian writers look back wistfully to a time

> Ere microscopes had made us heirs
> To large estates of doubts and snares[184]

Holmes, himself trained in scientific method, was glad to incorporate into his belief. In him rationalism did not lead into a paralyzing skepticism such as Henry Adams suffered from. He always retained a faith. If his novels set forth the doctrine of limited responsibility, such a doctrine was not incompatible with a reliance on a beneficent creator:

> My creed . . . is to be found in the first two words of the Pater Noster . . . I see no corner of the Universe which the Father has wholly deserted. The forces of Nature bruise and wound our bodies, but an artery no sooner bleeds than the Divine hand is placed upon it to stay the flow . . . We cannot conceive of a Father's allowing so limited a being as his human child to utterly ruin himself.[185]

The centre of faith in Holmes was comforting to those readers who were occasionally rendered uneasy by the sorry exhibits resulting from his dissecting habit. A further solace was that socially, politically, and economically, he was conservative. If the theological air of Cambridge was stuffy, Holmes at least found his social milieu congenial. A Victorian decorum in the personal conduct of life was no more irksome to him than good taste in the novel. Sometimes a bit roguish on the subject of love, he could be relied upon never to treat sex objectionably.[186] If Justice Oliver Wendell Holmes inherited his father's command of phrase, his social vision must have been an acquired endowment. Politically Holmes was nearly a cipher; vaguely he believed in equality. He was "a republican, but not a democrat." [187] The leveling principle of Jacksonian democracy touched no sympathetic chord in him. The Civil War (during which his son was three times severely wounded) did not long turn his attention to national affairs. Importuned by Lowell to join the antislavery movement, he did not respond. He disapproved of slavery but believed in supporting the Fugitive Slave Law. International affairs interested him very little. In his long life he went abroad only twice, and he seldom traveled far from Boston. A broad humanity he did not possess; rather he cultivated himself in a severely limited environment. Despite his modern view of "crime," practical sociological problems seldom enlisted his attention. The dismal science of economics attracted him not at all. He seems scarcely to have been aware of the existence of a submerged tenth or even to have observed very narrowly the middle class. He was quite unable to "envisage industrial slavery or the politics of the Gilded Age." [188] Nothing he ever said or wrote was designed to create social unrest. In most respects he was a typical "Brahmin." He was, in a good sense, insular. He did not approve of a mere "millionocracy," nor did he regard it as a great menace: fortunes have a way of disintegrating. Furthermore, as a physician he recognized that an unbroken aristocratic succession is likely to wane in strength and effective intelligence, making opportunities for the less polished classes:

> A series of felicitous crosses develops an improved strain of blood, and reaches its maximum perfection at last in the large uncombed youth who goes to college and startles the hereditary class-leaders by striding past them all. That is Nature's republicanism . . . The scholar who comes by Nature's special grace from an unworn stock of broad-chested sires and deep-bosomed mothers must always overmatch an equal intelligence with a compromised and lowered vitality.[189]

But Holmes did not choose "uncombed" people for his associates. He frankly preferred the society of the rich ("rich people are apt to be so much more agreeable than others"),[190] and he felt that culture had important alliances with wealth. These beliefs together with his social urbanity, his ready store of anecdotes, his whimsical "linguacity," [191] his reliability as an after-dinner poet, even his inveterate punning, made him in almost all essentials a representation of the Brahmin aristocracy at its best.

Holmes was an aristocrat even to the extent of having a slight repugnance to people who smelled too much of mere literary pursuits. He himself was an amateur of letters (for all his activity) and like Emerson (though for different reasons) found the society of the literati apt to be a bit stupid.[192] Though associated with many writers in Cambridge and Boston, he bears less the marks of a school than of a period. Studies in the theory of technique of the novel seem to have interested him very little. In *A Mortal Antipathy* he discusses some of the problems which confront a novelist in providing a setting that will be distinct from the reader's preconceived notions, in avoiding the creation of characters who will elicit protest from people in real life, and in keeping the reader entertained when the narrative is slow.[193] It was particularly his concern to keep his reader diverted, and in *A Mortal Antipathy* he frankly comments on a device for this end:

> The holder of the Portfolio [*i.e.*, the author] would never have
> ventured to come before the public if he had not counted among
> his resources certain papers belonging to the records of the Panso-
> phian Society, which he can make free use of, either for the illus-
> tration of the narrative, or for a diversion during those intervals in
> which the flow of events is languid, or even ceases for the time to
> manifest any progress.[194]

This genial confession is a reminder of Holmes's old-fashioned, even
naive, methods as a novelist. While James and, to a lesser extent, Howells were studying point of view, mass, and proportion, Holmes was
contented with narrative devices that do not distinguish his technique
sharply from that of the domestic sentimentalists. Only his physiological theories were new in the novel and only his perfection of language was permanently valuable. His causeries (whether from the pen
of the "Autocrat" or the novelist) plus a few poems remain his most
valuable contribution to American letters.

Holmes's last novel was written in 1885. Two years later Bellamy's
Looking Backward opened the door of those economic questions from
which Holmes averted his eyes. Almost at the same time William Dean
Howells was fulminating against the execution of Chicago anarchists
and he was soon to introduce into his fiction a full reflection of the
economic unrest that preceded the panic of 1893. Such comparisons
make Holmes, with his easy acceptance of the economic status quo,
seem even more old-fashioned as a novelist. To be sure he was dimly
aware of industrial unrest. In the preface to his last novel he wrote
apropos of the imminent revolt against capitalism:

> The clouds of discontent are threatening, but if the gold-pointed
> lightning-rods are rightly distributed the destructive element may
> be drawn off silently and harmlessly.[195]

The "gold-pointed lightning-rods" did not prove to be wholly efficient to cope with the problems ahead—problems which were to be
a part of the stuff of new novelists. Holmes died in 1894. His contact
with his immediate successors in fiction was slight. In his psychological
studies he very vaguely foreshadowed the novel of the 1920's, but his
main function, so far as he was militant at all, had been to disperse the
last Calvinists.

Civil War and Reconstruction

J. W. DE FOREST (1826-1906)

Though strongly rooted in Connecticut, where he was born in 1826, John W. De Forest traveled extensively enough to acquire a cosmopolitan outlook which distinguishes him from many of his contemporaries among American novelists. Prevented by ill health from attending Yale College, he set out in 1846 for Beirut, Syria, where he visited his brother, a medical missionary. Then followed two years of traveling in the Near East before his return to Connecticut. His first book, a *History of the Indians of Connecticut From the Earliest Known Period to 1850* was so thorough-going a piece of research work that it was published (in 1851) "with the sanction" of the Connecticut Historical Society. By the time it actually appeared, however, De Forest had resumed his travels abroad—four years (1850-1855) in England and on the continent. He made it his business to steep himself in the language and culture of each country he visited. At Florence he tested the quality of his Italian by translating *The House of the Seven Gables*. In Paris he developed an interest in French authors who were later to influence the quality of his own novels—Stendhal, George Sand, and Balzac. In 1856 he returned to New Haven, Connecticut, married Harriet Shepard of that city, and commenced a literary career in earnest. Some of his time was spent in Charleston, South Carolina, where his father-in-law, a college professor (presumably drawn upon for some details in the portrait of Dr. Ravenel in *Miss Ravenel's Conversion*), spent a part of each year. Upon the outbreak of the Civil War, he left Charleston just before the firing on Fort Sumter began. His experiences during the War are partly reported in *Miss Ravenel's Conversion:* he raised a company in New Haven, fought for three years, and (like Colburne) discovered how largely military promotion depended on petty politics. After the War he continued in Federal employ at Greenville, South Carolina, where he directed the Freedmen's Bureau. He was mustered out in 1868. Thereafter his life was less colorful and his writing more prolific. He died in 1906 at New Haven.[1]

De Forest's first ventures into belles lettres ante-date the War by several years. *Oriental Acquaintance* (1856) and *European Acquaintance* (1858) are at once autobiographical and journalistic—the literary dividends of several years spent in foreign travel. *Witching Times*, De Forest's first elaborate fiction, is an historical novel laid in Salem at the time of the witchcraft trials.[2] The main narrative follows the experience of Henry More, who loses out in his battle against superstition: he is condemned and executed for witchcraft. The author notes various reactions, some of them political, to the situation created by the "discovery" of witchcraft in Salem. Cotton Mather, not entirely sure of his convictions regarding witchcraft, uses the occasion to tighten the bonds of ministerial sovereignty in Massachusetts. Judge Hathorne (called Hawthorne by De Forest), however, exhibits a "calmer and more liberal attitude." Thus the vivid representation of exciting and morbid scenes, such as the death of Giles Corey, is balanced by interpretative commentary. Nor does the story live wholly of and for itself: De Forest's keen sense of injustice and intolerance leads him to draw a not-very-successful analogy between oppression in old Salem days and in the period just before the Civil War. The novel as a whole drags a little, for despite his antiquarian interest (previously shown in *The Indians of Connecticut*) De Forest did not possess a strong sense of the historical.[3] He was more at home, therefore, in his next novel, *Seacliff; or, The Mystery of the Westervelts* (1859), a study, tragic in its outcome, of domestic complications set in contemporary southwestern Connecticut on Long Island Sound. Somewhat trite in its action devices (including a plot to change a will), resourceful in its descriptions of daily life and in its portraiture of women, *Seacliff* carries a suggestion, verified by later novels, that De Forest was less imaginative than reportorial in his gifts. His principal assets in narrative were an observant eye, a shrewd judgment, and fluency of phrase. These were qualifications that bore fruit in the novel for which he is now best remembered, *Miss Ravenel's Conversion from Secession to Loyalty* (1867).

In this book De Forest's full powers were first called into play. His intimate knowledge of New England people and places, his first-hand observation of college society at New Haven, his Southern residence, his war experiences, his wide reading, and his strictly linguistic studies all were capitalized in this, the most comprehensive literary project he ever undertook. He had already written briefly about actual warfare,[4] but to write a novel which should give adequate expression to both Southern and Northern points of view, characterize broadly both civilian and military life during the great crisis, describe the creation and maintenance of military units, trace the connection between military and political branches of Federal service, report in detail the experience of soldiers in actual battle, and at the same time to sustain a love story of uncommon interest—this was a literary enterprise which, even granting De Forest's opportunities for observation, was taxing in the extreme.

The major conflict in the story, as far as individuals are concerned, is over the hand of Lillie Ravenel, a charming, spirited, somewhat wilful girl, seventeen years old when the War breaks out. Her suitors are chiefly two, Edward Colburne, an idealistic but basically level-headed young man of conventional New England heritage; and Lieutenant-Colonel Carter, a bluff, handsome, worldly soldier-adventurer of Virginia family but Northern allegiance. Carter possesses much of the glamorousness and unscrupulousness with which Margaret Mitchell later endowed Rhett Butler in *Gone With the Wind*. The setting for the first part of the action is Connecticut (thinly disguised under the name "Barataria"), but the sentiments of the characters are mixed from the very beginning. Dr. Ravenel, father of the heroine, born in South Carolina, was for many years a professor in New Orleans, where Lillie was brought up. Unable to approve of slavery and unwilling to commit himself to "rebellion," he has been virtually forced to exile himself in New England. He settles at "New Boston" in "Barataria" as a free-lance mineralogist. Lillie, however, has brought her Louisiana loyalty and her secessionist convictions with her to the North. Colburne disapproves of her frankly Southern opinions, but falls deeply in love with her. The cool, calculating Carter is attracted by her beauty and her esprit, but he is not seriously interested in her as a prospective bride so long as her father's finances remain uncertain. In any case the War soon takes precedence over affairs of the heart. Carter's regiment is called away, but not before he has helped Colburne raise a company of volunteers, which likewise sees service promptly. Exigencies of the story require that the young people be brought together in the South, and accordingly De Forest sends the Ravenels from New England, where Lillie is persona non grata, to New Orleans, where her father is rudely treated.[5] And not only her father, for Southerners now regard Lillie also as having been contaminated by the Northern climate of opinion. It is at this time that her "conversion" commences. At first she is "unionized, but not in the least abolitionized"; later she goes over wholly to the Northern cause. At New Orleans Col. Carter helps Dr. Ravenel secure a Federal post rehabilitating Negroes. Carter's interest in Lillie increases to the point of complete infatuation, and he finally secures Dr. Ravenel's reluctant consent to an engagement. The marriage occurs suddenly, soon after Carter has been made military governor of Louisiana. Colburne, who has suffered intensely at the thought of Lillie's being married to the dissolute Carter, is let in for further anguish when he is sent to recuperate on the plantation where Lillie, now pregnant, is living under her father's care. Carter proves to be as bad a husband as Colburne has feared, for he feebly falls victim to the wiles of the siren, Mrs. Larue, and he speculates criminally with Federal funds. A good officer, however, he is finally made a Brigadier-General. When his conjugal infidelity is made clear to Lillie, she breaks with him and sets out for the North—just before Carter is fatally wounded in action. The faithful Colburne marries Lillie, who settles down with him at New Boston, now thoroughly content to be a Northerner.

The story of *Miss Ravenel's Conversion* is unfolded in a leisurely, almost negligent, fashion by De Forest, but the commentary it contains is always pointed and fresh. For the first time in the history of the American novel, war is treated with steady realism and quiet honesty. Nor does De Forest merely report the ghastly details of battle. He deals with the motives that influence men who enlist and men who direct the formation of military detachments; the internal organization of the army; the part played by official red tape and political venality; the attitudes of non-combatants on both sides; the problems of the commissary as well as of units actually engaged in battle. Not all of this was new in American fiction. Henry Morford, for example, had written three Civil War novels in which the political and industrial corruption incidental to the War were exposed to view: *Shoulder Straps* (1863), *The Coward* (1863), and *The Days of Shoddy* (1864). Sidney Lanier's *Tiger Lilies*, published in 1867, showed the condition of the Confederacy before and during the "sharp spasm of civil war." [6] Comparable problems received incidental attention in the novels of J. E. Cooke. [7] Yet no writer of De Forest's time had had the advantage of so much personal experience together with such a distinguished literary talent and such realistic fervor. To a considerable extent De Forest belied Whitman's prediction (in *Specimen Days*) that "the real war will never get in the books."

In the realistic descriptions of actual battle scenes De Forest excelled all nineteenth-century American novelists except Stephen Crane, author of *The Red Badge of Courage* (1895). The engagement at Port Hudson in *Miss Ravenel's Conversion* is reported from beginning to end with equal attention to trivia and to heart-rending suffering. The author snaps a view of Colburne in an idle moment before his company begins to move up:

Colburne has eaten his dinner of fried pork and hardtack, has washed off the grime of a three days' march, has finished his pipe, and is now dropping gently into a soldier's child-like yet light slumber. He does not mind the babble of voices about him, but if you should say "Fall in!" he would be on his feet in an instant.[8]

When his men receive their orders to "fall in" they present a picture far different from that of soldiers in the earlier historical romance:

> It was a long row of stern faces, bronzed with sunburn, sallow in many cases with malaria, grave with the serious emotions of the hour, but hardened by the habit of danger, and set as firm as flints toward the enemy. The old innocence of the peaceable New England farmer and mechanic had disappeared from these war-seared visages, and had been succeeded by an expression of hard-ened combativeness, not a little brutal, much like the look of a lazy bull-dog. Colburne smiled with pleasure and pride as he glanced along the line of his company, and noted this change in its physiognomy.[9]

The author notes, what the soldiers noted grimly as they advanced, that trees blasted by enemy batteries "seemed to give up their life with a roar of inanimate anguish." He pictures a soldier escaping to the rear, his "chin shaking," so terrified that even being struck by the angry Colburne makes no impression on him. When a man is wounded by a shot through the body, the author notes that Colburne refuses to send him back at once to the field hospital—in accordance with Army Regu-lations (which De Forest quotes) requiring that assistance to the wounded must be deferred until "after the action is decided," for the "most pressing duty is to win the victory, by which only can a proper care of the wounded be ensured." [10] A far cry, this, from the routine romantic episode in which one buddy drops everything to carry a wounded comrade to the rear lines. Nor does De Forest hesitate to describe the most extreme instances of painful wounds. At the same time, he observes that the reaction to shell wounds and painful injury ranges from the most frightful cursing and groaning to "the simple ex-clamation 'Oh!' [uttered] in a tone of dolorous surprise." Sooner or later most of the men injured "settled into the calm, sublime patience of the wounded of the battle-field." [11] Colburne, who receives a nasty arm-wound, has experience of three types of hospital, all of which are described fully. At the field hospital men in need of surgical aid are so numerous and so badly injured that, outdoors though the scene was, the "smell of blood drenched the stifling air, overpowering even the pungent odor of chloroform." [12] Grisly circumstances add to the gen-eral horror. When a patient died, "before night he was black with putrefaction, so rapid was that shocking change under the heat of a Louisiana May." [13] Alcohol, as freely given as chloroform, adds its grotesque effects when one Van Zandt drinks himself into a state of intoxication and wanders about crazily among his fellow patients. When the ambulatory patients march to a general hospital at Port Hudson, they are greeted by Confederate women—"female hyenas" De Forest cannot forbear calling them—who jeer derisively that they hope to see all the soldiers dead in order that they may dance on their graves and make rings of their bones. But De Forest the realist adds, with that instinct for proportion which always keeps him this side of melodrama, that no reprisal was offered the women: "No harm was done to them, nor any stress of silence laid upon them." [14]

In almost every aspect of his story De Forest seeks out the actual, as opposed to the traditional, state of affairs. He recognizes how much self-interest determines the "convictions" of both sides in the irrepressible conflict. He hazards the conjecture that many Northerners would not have been abolitionists had they ever owned slaves—"for what Yankee . . . was ever known to remain an abolitionist after having once tasted the pleasure of living by the labor of others?" [15] He seems to take a wry pleasure in observing how enlistments fall off after the first reports of battle conditions come in:

> Past was that springtide of popular enthusiasm when companies were raised in a day, when undersized heroes wept at being rejected by the mustering officer, when well-to-do youths paid a hundred dollars to buy out a chance to be shot at. Bull Run had disenchanted some romantic natures concerning the pleasures of war . . .[16]

His pictures of Negro life are graphic but not heightened by sentiment; he seeks merely the truth, whether it be dismal or elevating. He is capable of fine strokes of pathos when they seem called for, but balks at sentimentality. When Dr. Ravenel works among the destitute Negroes, he finds that there are "some rotten specks in the social fruit" which he is trying to raise from a "barbarous stock." In the colored Major Scott he finds a man who was in many respects "a counterpart of Mrs. Stowe's immortal idealism": yet the Major's moral strength is not proof against all temptations. Nor is his backsliding a cause of surprise to Dr. Ravenel, though it is to a visiting chaplain:

> "My dear sir," said the Doctor warmly, "renewing a man's heart is only a partial reformation, unless you illuminate his mind. He wants to do right, but how is he to know what is right? Sup-

pose he can't read. Suppose half of the Bible is not told him. Suppose he is misled by half the teaching, and all the example of those whom he looks up to as in every respect his superiors. I am disposed to regard Scott as a very fair attempt at a Christian, considering his chances . . . Uncle Tom is a pure fiction. There never was such a slave, and there never will be. A man educated under the degrading influences of bondage must always have some taint of grossness and lowness." [17]

Sooner or later, then, the social, military, political, ethical, and religious elements of *Miss Ravenel's Conversion* are at least mildly suffused with the author's satire.

All this, one must believe, was honest reporting on the part of De Forest. It constituted, as Howells noted later, one of the reasons why the book did not become popular among novel readers, now an increasingly feminine group. Another reason why De Forest failed to reach the best-seller stage is that he sprayed satire on hallowed institutions and principles. It was one thing to demonstrate plainly the horror of war, unpleasant though such a demonstration might be; it was another to pass cynical comments on New Englanders, Americans in general, and women in particular. Superficially at least, he often gives the impression of having but a poor opinion of human nature; such is the natural inference from his persistent and relentless revelations of the selfish and petty motives of most of his characters excepting Colburne. Moreover, De Forest frequently resorted to the device of irony, a device little practiced by his generation of novel-writers. When on one occasion Carter was speaking to Mrs. Larue in French—a natural procedure between them, particularly in New Orleans—he suddenly apologizes, saying that he didn't realize Colburne's lack of familiarity with the language. Then the author adds, gratuitously:

> No; Colburne did not speak French, nor any other modern language; he did not draw, nor sing, nor play, and was in short as destitute of accomplishments as are most Americans.[18]

A fine way to treat one's hero—showing him at a real disadvantage while the villain prospers. And a fine thing to say of the American people, who were struggling so seriously to acquire culture!

But New Englanders as a class come off even worse, for De Forest iterates his disdain of their cramped mode of living, their paralyzing devotion to ethics, their general lack of *savoir vivre*. The town of New Boston (New Haven) receives no very flattering characterization:

New Boston is not a lively nor a sociable place. The principal reason for this is that it is inhabited chiefly by New Englanders. Puritanism, the prevailing faith of that land and race, is not only not favorable but is absolutely noxious to social gayeties, amenities and graces. I say this in sorrow and not in anger, for New England is the land of my birth and Puritanism is the creed of my progenitors. And I add as a mere mater of justice, that, deficient as the New Bostonians are in timely smiles and appropriate compliments, bare as they are of jollities and angular in manners and opinions, they have strong sympathies for what is clearly right, and can become enthusiastic in a matter of conscience and benevolence. If they have not learned how to love the beautiful, they know how to love the good and true.[19]

Nor does the last sentence, more flattering than the rest, carry an impression which is corroborated elsewhere, for De Forest really believed that New Englanders, in their pursuit of the "good," became disagreeably zealous. More typical of his attitude throughout the book are his remarks on how "moral" people differ from corrupt people, who, says De Forest (after Balzac), are generally agreeable:

The strict moralist and pietist, on the other hand, is as hard and unyielding as a boot just from the hands of the maker; you must conform to his model, or he will conscientiously pinch your moral corns in a most grievous manner; he cannot grant you a hair's-breadth without bursting his uppers and endangering his sole.[20]

The ruinous effects of the New England climate and social regimen upon an unnamed lady are set down in terms to make one of her kind shudder:

Thin-lipped, hollow-cheeked, narrow-chested, with only one lung and an intermittent digestion, without a single rounded outline or graceful movement, she was a sad example of what the New England east winds can do in enfeebling and distorting the human form divine. Such are too many of the New Boston women when they reach that middle age which should be physically an era of adipose, and morally of charity. Even her smile was a woful phenomenon; it seemed to be rather a symptom of pain than an expression of pleasure; it was a kind of griping smile, like that of an infant with the colic.[21]

But De Forest is perfectly free from narrow sectionalism—as one might infer from his satire of his native New England. He also exposes the weaknesses of Carter, a Virginian, and of Lillie—a Louisianan, a heroine, and a woman. Lillie is a delightful creature, and as such De Forest meant, part of the time, to paint her. But she is also a real person. She has her weaknesses—arrogance, ingratitude, credulousness, selfishness—and De Forest does not propose to minimize them. The reader feels that the novelist is occasionally poking fun at her, a process fatal to the average Victorian conception of a heroine. She naively capitulates to the blandishments of a man whom she should have perceived at once to be a bounder. She rejects Colburne because he is not "magnetic." Yet she has in effect to eat her words in the end. She is often, in short, a pretty silly and vapid creature as De Forest represents her.[22] She has blundered into a graceless marriage: she is no credit to "the sex." And for De Forest to take the bloom off Lillie, his heroine, by marrying her to a cad before assigning her to her predestined Colburne was an affront to decent people. Heroines are supposed to be menaced by bad men but never to capitulate even under the auspices of the church. Or, at the very worst, if they marry them, they must reform them, as did Edna Earl in *St. Elmo*, published at the same time as *Miss Ravenel's Conversion*.[23] Lillie was sullied in the eyes of the typical Victorian reader. She was a dubious heroine, for she was real.

In all this, one may be sure, De Forest took satisfaction. For like Howells, though to a greater degree, he delighted in being openly anti-romantic. He mocked at the public's naive tendency to magnify the glamor and importance of specific military engagements in the War—to make an Austerlitz or a Waterloo of every minor episode.[24] In full view of what is probably the "greatest bombardment known in marine . . . warfare" Colburne is made to complain of a "wearisome *ennui*." [25] So with the personal relationships of the dramatis personae: the author deflates incipient romance. Folk who believe in the inevitability of true love must have been shocked at the scene in which Colburne almost proposes to the irresolute Lillie: "Ten seconds more of silence might have resulted in an engagement ring." [26] When Colburne meets Lillie in New Orleans after a long absence, there were no notable speeches or gestures:

> With the exception of Miss Ravenel's inveterate blush and of a slightly unnatural rapidity of utterance in Captain Colburne, they met in a merely friendly, commonplace manner. This is not the way that heroes and heroines meet on the boards or in some romances; but in actual human society they frequently balk our expectations in just this manner. Melo-dramatically considered real life is frequently a failure.[27]

Thus with what Howells later referred to as "scornful bluntness" and "inexorable veracity," [27a] De Forest must have alienated the affections of readers accustomed to novels in which flawless heroes and heroines steadily advance through mechanized difficulties toward a guaranteed destination—the altar—as pure and as artificial as they were at the outset. Yet *Miss Ravenel's Conversion* was to find more open-minded and more robust readers as time went on, and it has finally come into its own as a substantial social document and as a literary production of far more than average merit in its period.

The sixties and seventies were De Forest's most fertile years. During the sixties, short stories from his pen appeared frequently in *Harper's*, *The Galaxy*, and *The Atlantic Monthly*. From August, 1870, to July, 1871, *The Galaxy* ran his next novel, *Overland*, an exciting tale of adventure and mystery involving hostile Indians and Spanish plotters who menace the hero on his trek westward from Santa Fe to California—a region never traversed by the author.[28] In the following year *Kate Beaumont* appeared.

For the setting of *Kate Beaumont* (1872) De Forest had merely to recall and touch up the memories of his own residence in South Carolina. Howells called the book De Forest's "shapeliest" novel. It is certainly less intricate in pattern than *Miss Ravenel's Conversion*, for it is focussed on the obstacles confronting two lovers whose families are engaged in a feud. When Frank McAlister, a handsome and personable young man returning from study in Europe, falls in love with Kate Beaumont, also returning from abroad, his first assignment is the conventional one of rescuing her from a sinking ship. Arrived in Charleston, however, he finds that the violent Beaumont-McAlister feud is an almost insurmountable bar to his marriage with Kate. Colonel Kershaw, Kate's grandfather, who attempts to heal the rupture, is killed for his pains. Frank is shot at, challenged to a duel, and insulted on every hand. The chief ally of the lovers in their effort to reconcile the families is Nelly Armitage, Kate's half-sister, and wife of the besotted and cruel Randolph Armitage. Finally the feud is ended and the lovers are married.

Kate Beaumont is notable for its fine characterization of Southern types, both men and women, from the highest to the lowest class. Nellie Armitage suffers so terribly in her hopeless marriage to a brute that she is desperate: "Is there no such thing as separation?" [29] To a woman of her high principles, of course, no formal separation is possible (though she later leaves him), and she carries on courageously, devoting herself to the problem of making possible the union of Kate and Frank. Howells seems to have regarded her as one of the best-drawn heroines in American fiction.[30] Low life is brought into view frequently, and there is an intimate description of a "cracker ball"—a sordid kind of jollification for which the essentials were a one-room log-cabin, a pound of tallow candles, three gallons of raw whiskey, and a local fiddler. With eight couples dancing hilariously in such a small area, the effect was "nauseously . . . interesting," for even the open doors and windows "could not carry off all the mephitic steam generated by this mob of unclean people." [31] Politics are also glanced at with De Forest's customary cynicism. The backwardness of the Southern folk is shocking to Frank, who, having studied metallurgy and chemistry, wishes to test local mines and phosphate beds. But the people are indifferent to their "underground wealth," for their "eyes are bandaged with cotton." [32] The novel gives a fairly comprehensive though perhaps unnecessarily gloomy view of Carolina life in general. Yet *Kate Beaumont* is chiefly a story of a pair of star-crossed lovers (De Forest invites attention to the parallel with *Romeo and Juliet*) who work out their destiny in a region which had seldom been employed for purposes of fiction since the days when W. G. Simms had peopled it with characters, real and imagined, out of Revolutionary days.[33]

Honest John Vane (1875), De Forest's next novel of importance, is a political satire, one of the few substantial American novels of this genre to appear in the period.[34] The theme of political chicanery was not a new one to De Forest, for the crass conduct of one Gazeaway, a veteran politician, had been completely exposed in *Miss Ravenel's Conversion*. *Honest John Vane* obviously grew out of De Forest's strong convictions regarding the gross lack of intelligence and probity among the nation's law-makers. The tone of the book is cynical, but the author's earnestness is felt beneath his acid comments and his fairly engaging story. Here, as usual, De Forest is a somewhat selfconscious realist. His "hero," John Vane, is so unromantic as to be a widower encumbered with two children. His very occupation is prosaic: he is "a mere manufacturer of refrigerators, whose business was by no means colossal." [35] No wonder Olympia Smiles (the almost incredible name of the heroine) doubts his eligibility as a suitor despite his two hundred pounds of handsome masculinity. Nevertheless when John discovers a talent for politics and is pushed into candidacy for Congress (on account of his only competitor's having been *caught* in grafting operations), she makes it her business to regain his interest, for she envisages a brilliant career as a Washington hostess. But in Washington, John Vane is insignificant and his wife is unknown until he (after due pressure) finally lets it be known that he is "approachable" and his wife exerts her charms on the nation's law-givers. "Honest John" becomes an ironical sobriquet when its possessor engages in a routine peculation, changing his condition, as a result, from one of "respectable indigence into degradingly thrifty circumstances." [36] He is found out, but he bamboozles his electorate by a show of sincerity and he is again returned to a post for which he was never really fitted.

Honest John Vane clearly does not live for the originality of its plot complication. What distinguishes it is the vehemence with which De Forest denounces inefficiency and corruption in national politics, of which the career of John Vane is intended in many ways to be typical. Vane is an amiable and well-meaning person, and at first he is honest: he has never been really tested in the political fire. But he is wholly unfitted for what should be a high trust:

> He was too ignorant to be a professor in the State university, or even a teacher in one of the city schools; but it was presumed that he would answer well enough as a law-giver for a complicated Republic containing forty millions of people.[37]

Yet he is easily elevated to a position of responsibility because of the low intelligence of the electorate:

> The great majority of his constituents did not suppose that their representative needed any more intelligence or moral stamina than would just enable him to find out what were the "party measures," and faithfully to vote for them. The few who believed that he ought to be acquainted either with finance, or political economy, or constitutional limitations, or international law, and that furthermore he should be a person of tried character and honor,—these few eccentrics had no political influence.[38]

Obviously De Forest is fingering the same materials of satire that had interested Brackenridge many years before.[39] The difference between the two men in this respect is that whereas Brackenridge delivered his observations in a medium of farce, De Forest attempts to give a realistic impression of politics as he observed them in "Slowburgh" (presumably New Haven, Connecticut). He is patently disgusted at routine political maneuvers, naive in character but sinister in their effects on the body politic. Yet he does not merely sermonize on abuses, but delivers his thrusts with a phrasal ability that makes his story entertaining to read. After Vane's nomination, only he could have been surprised at the behavior of his fellow party-men:

> [L]eaders . . . hurrahed until their hard foreheads dripped with patriotic perspiration, every drop of which they meant should be paid for in municipal or State or Federal dollars.

> Many elders of the people escorted Vane home that evening, and sat up with him with a devotion which deserved no end of postmasterships.[40]

Moreover much of the cynical commentary does not emanate directly from the author but is uttered naturally enough by the crusty veteran of many campaigns, one Dorman, who keeps reminding Honest John that in due time he will see the light—*i.e.*, decide to fall in line with the gentle grafters. Dorman it is who advises John as Congressman-elect not to go in for "war memories and the nigger worshiping"—for "all those sentimental dodges are played out"—but for "questions of finance."[41] The moral fibre of typical party-men is suggested by the amusing comment one of them makes on George Washington: "A man, by George, that would cut the cherry-tree, and then tell of it, wasn't fit to guide the destinies of his country."[42] In such a murky moral climate John Vane slips, more through weakness than through viciousness, into lax practices that are finally held up as typical. For although the plot materials of the story simply crumble away at the end, the author does not relax his indignation at Congressmen who (like Vane) spend a great deal of time "enacting the national revenue into the safes of huge corporations and into the hats of individual mendicants, for the sake of a small percentage thereof . . ."[43]

Such commentary as this, though far from common in the American novel, was not wholly original in nature. More interesting to students of history is De Forest's revelation of the gradual growth of a strictly democratic tendency to return "common men" to office in place of those men of patrician lineage and (presumably) of fairly good education who, in New England at least, had held many important political offices. How gravely De Forest regarded such a movement or indeed how widespread he believed it had become is not apparent, but he reports the shift in telling terms—through the speech of one of the "common people":

> "Saltonstall is altogether too much of a gentleman to get the nomination. He's as calm and cold and dead as his buried ancestors, the old governors. You can't get the people to hurrah for a gravestone, even if it has a fine name on it. In fact, the fine name is a disadvantage; American freemen hate an aristocrat. It's really curious to see how Saltonstall's followers are killing him off. They are saying that, because he is the son of an honorable, he ought to be an honorable himself, and that he will do the right thing for the sake of his forefathers. Our voters don't see it in that light. They want plain people to become honorables."[44]

Not a cheery document, this story of "Honest John Vane." It is perhaps the more effective as representing the point of view of an enlightened citizen rather than of a profound student of political science or a politician in daily contact with the vicious conditions it depicts. The evils that it reports were symptomatic of serious disorders that menaced the nation as a whole in the Gilded Age. Other writers were treating similar abuses in various fashions—Mark Twain in the crude humor and vigorous satire of *The Gilded Age* (1873), Henry Adams in the polite revelations of *Democracy* (1881), and Edward Bellamy in the Utopian glimpses of *Looking Backward* (1888). But most of the books which treated comparable materials were to be written after 1890. In *Honest John Vane* De Forest was distinctly a pioneer in this field—the novel of political satire—as he had already been in the realistic treatment of warfare. Compared with *Miss Ravenel's Conversion,* this later book of De Forest is simpler in outline, less florid in phrase, better focussed in its satire, less youthful in its cynicism, but even deeper in its uncomfortable probing into the motives that govern men and women.[45] Yet it lacks the breadth and weight of *Miss Ravenel's Conversion,* and is on the whole the less valuable book. It can hardly be called a propaganda novel, for the author has the air of supporting a lost cause—the view of a disappointed idealist, almost of a martyr. Evidently he regarded himself as one of the "eccentric" few who realized the need of high intelligence in high office, but evidently he also shared Barnum's view of the average intelligence of the common man.[46]

A capable and in some ways a distinguished novelist, De Forest failed to win either an extremely broad popularity or the highest acclaim of critics. No record of the actual sales of his books is available, but it seems clear that they were by no means as much in demand as those of several of the "lady novelists," clearly inferior to him, who wrote so prolifically in the sixties and seventies.[47] On the other hand, though addressing himself to art rather than to commercial writing, De Forest produced no book which was an indubitable masterpiece.

De Forest was not a strongly original writer. To judge from the literary allusions in his books, he had read widely and well. Several novelists—among them Sterne, Dickens, Balzac—are referred to in terms that suggest De Forest's admiration of their work. Howells thought that he detected signs of Charles Reade's influence on De Forest, particularly in the latter's portraits of women.[48] There are traces of all these in De Forest's novels, particularly of Dickens's whimsically elaborate descriptions of persons. Yet the writer with whom he seems to have had most in common (whether there was an "influence" or not) was Thackeray. Like the Thackeray of *Vanity Fair*, he was witty, cynical, and "talky." Instead of merely presenting characters in a "dramatic" fashion through their actions, he chats with the reader about them. Frequently his little causeries consist in disclosures of the weaknesses of his characters, from the peccadillos of lovable characters like Dr. Ravenel to the major vices of Col. Carter. A certain disenchantment with human character and life in general is felt in most of his books. Romantic love often receives a mildly cynical treatment that recalls Thackeray's good-natured but penetrating satire.[49] Character-parallels there are, too; the patient Colburne, for example, often resembles the patient Dobbin. Like Thackeray, too, De Forest was restrained by the publishing mores of his era from descending as low in the scale of realism as would have been natural in a writer of his experience and convictions. Thackeray's rather sharp satire of the prurient but squeamish Victorian public which tacitly forbade him to report Becky Sharp's disreputable decline in more than the most muffled euphemisms, finds its counterpart in De Forest's complaint that he must omit not only detailed reference to the amorous technique of Mrs. Larue[50] but even such comparatively innocent items as the profane expressions of his soldiers. Both writers had to sterilize their books for a generation abnormally fearful of moral infection and none too sure, apparently, of its powers of resistance. The chief differences between De Forest and Thackeray are two. First, along with Thackeray's penetration of the vanity and selfishness of most of his characters went a certain indulgence toward erring humanity; Thackeray did not expect too much of mortal man. De Forest had far less tolerance; he could not satirize his characters without ceasing to love them. On this account, in the light of Meredith's well-known definition at least, De Forest must be regarded as a satirist rather than a comic writer.[51] Thackeray's indulgent sentimentality he could not match. Nor could he write off his discontent in merely good-humored banter, as Thackeray so often did. De Forest's humor tends to sour into cynicism.[52] Something of the Puritan censoriousness which he condemned in his characters, seems to have entered his own nature. He had a sort of youthful intolerance of error and weakness. In the second place, De Forest was more energetic in his scenes of action than Thackeray. Whereas Thackeray often prepares his stage for a "big scene" and then at the last moment evades his responsibilities by resorting to a talky interpretation or spoils the effect of the scene by artificiality,[53] De Forest compensates for his occasional garrulousness by presenting scenes of considerable dramatic energy. If Thackeray side-stepped the dramatic possibilities of Waterloo, De Forest made the most of his military maneuvers in *Miss Rav-*

enel's Conversion. His distinction in this respect entitles him to be compared favorably with Stephen Crane, whose *Red Badge of Courage* is generally regarded as containing the best realistic treatment of war scenes in the nineteenth-century novel. In psychological insight into character, however, De Forest is inferior to Crane, for like most satirists, he was more successful in the analysis of motive than in the revelation of character in its totality.

The novels of De Forest as a whole suggest that what he lacked most was a steady and all-absorbing aim. His energies were dispersed, his production miscellaneous. He experimented competently in several genres: the historical romance (*Witching Times*), the novel of contemporary social conflict (*Seacliff*), the novel of Western adventures (*Overland*), the semi-sociological novel (*Kate Beaumont*), the murder-mystery novel (*The Wetherel Affair*), political satire (*Honest John Vane* and *Playing the Mischief*), and the realistic novel of war and personal relationships (*Miss Ravenel's Conversion*). In most of these fields he worked well, in none supremely well. Possessed of a keen sense for realistic detail, a good knowledge of human character, and a distinguished prose style, he chiefly lacked a high imagination and a deeply rooted originality. His best work, however, entitles him to more consideration than he has thus far received at the hands of the historians of literature. Unable to find a completely satisfactory outlet for his roving abilities, he actually possessed powers which in the aggregate were not much less than those of his most generous critic, Howells. His temperament, too, militated against full recognition in his own time. Howells was easily able to adjust himself to the harness and check rein demanded by readers in Victorian America, but De Forest, a more mettlesome writer, was slightly irked by what he regarded as a hampering convention. It is unlikely that he wanted to delve deeply into scandalous or revolting human data, but he wished to be free to describe man in truer colors than, apparently, the public wished to pay for. America was not yet ready to view at close range the sterner manifestations of the realistic muse. In England many years were to pass before the reticence of Thackeray would be replaced by greater frankness —before a Becky Sharp could be given her full portrait. And even Hardy, who undertook to deal with morality on a realistic basis, was condemned for his pains. In America, Stephen Crane was to butt his art against a wall of convention when he produced *Maggie* in 1893. Dreiser was to recount the story of Sister Carrie to an unwilling generation in 1901. If De Forest wished to be a full-blown realist, he should have been born much earlier or much later. The sixties were dedicated to sentiment and propriety.

ALBION W. TOURGEE (1838-1905)

The problems that remained to be dealt with after the War were less spectacular than the single issue of emancipation, but they were deep-seated. The basic difficulty was that of assimilating the freed slaves into a nation which had guaranteed the Negro rights before it knew how to invest him with those rights safely and wisely. Among the novelists who employed the period of Reconstruction as a theme, few were so well equipped to treat the problem understandingly as Albion W. Tour-gée, a native of Ohio, a Northern fighter in the War, a Southern judge after the War. To a full understanding of the issues Tourgée added an extremely warm sympathy with sufferers from whatever cause. In a strictly literary sense he was also well endowed, for his pen had learned point and precision from his thorough reading, and his active life had stored his sensitive mind with memorable image and incident. In sheer command of the art of writing, in style per se, he was unquestionably superior to Mrs. Stowe. Apt expression was natural to him. Yet, like Mrs. Stowe, he gave himself first to his matter. He was only sec-ondarily interested in the novel as a type; consequently he took struc-tural liberties with the form at a time when more serious novelists were attempting to devise some sort of technical standards. The general pub-lic, however, was not finical about technique so long as a good tale was somehow told, and Tourgée's *A Fool's Errand* and *Bricks Without Straw* were compelling narratives which ranked as among the very best sellers in the early 1880's. That these and other novels of Tourgée are now seldom read argues that he was more concerned to serve his gen-eration than to perpetuate his name as an artist. He gave many years to an intensive study of the tangled pattern of life in the South after the War. What he saw he did not always report dispassionately, but he wrote with such flaming conviction that he inevitably divided his read-ers into fierce enemies and enthusiastic supporters. Indifference toward Tourgée was impossible. Yet excepting a few obviously partisan episodes in his life, he was not essentially a self-seeking or even partisan person. In his discussion of national issues he followed high ideals, and his real constituency was humanity.

Few novelists of his period led lives of such vicissitudes as Tourgée. Born in Ohio, he spent most of his boyhood in his native state; but he also lived two years in Lee, Massachusetts, studied at Rochester, New York, and taught school at Wilson, New York. He was given his A.B. degree by the University of Rochester in 1862; but he did not earn the degree in residence, for upon the outbreak of the War he had enlisted in a New York regiment. His war experiences were varied and painful. He was twice injured, the first time so seriously that his health was permanently impaired. He was a prisoner in four different Confederate prisons—"hotels" he facetiously dubbed them. Twice he was subjected to military arrest for insubordination. The occasion of his first disciplining well illustrates Tourgée's independence of character and his real sympathy with the Negro: he was arrested "for refusing to surrender a colored man who had saved [his] company." [54] He later planned to organize and lead a company of Negroes. He twice resigned from the army, believing that he had been subjected to excessive insolence by his superiors. It is not clear whether his resignation was finally accepted, but in any case he withdrew from the army in 1864—a move which should have been dictated by his physical condition if by nothing else. In the meantime he had been married (1863). A few months after leaving the army he was admitted to the Ohio bar. In 1865 he moved to Greensboro, North Carolina, where during the next fourteen years he lived an extremely active life as businessman, judge, editor, lecturer, pension agent, and author. Most of this period of life is covered in his fiction, especially in *A Fool's Errand* and *Bricks Without Straw*. His independence and his brashness frequently drew down the wrath of Southerners, but he was absolutely fearless and he continued to utter unwelcome opinions even when his life was in actual danger. In 1881, he settled down on a farm at Mayville, New York, where he lived until (in 1897) McKinley rewarded his Republican zeal (wavering though it had sometimes been) by making him Consul at Bordeaux. Tourgée never returned to America but retained his consular position until his death in 1905.

Despite his exceedingly active personal career as a politician and publicist, Tourgée was a prolific writer. At no time was he without some literary or journalistic project. Most of his political writing has slipped into limbo because of its contemporaneity and its partisanship. The same fate has overtaken much of his fiction and would doubtless have wholly swallowed him as a writer except for one fact: the burning intensity of all that he wrote touching on the problems of Reconstruction. His greatest success, *A Fool's Errand*, is often referred to as the novel which did for Reconstruction what *Uncle Tom's Cabin* did for Abolition. It was only one, however, of several novels bearing on the same problem.

Between 1874 and 1896 Tourgée wrote ten stories which may at least roughly be classified as novels. Six of these may be grouped in a loose unity.[55] They were not written in the time order of their actions, however, and the student of Tourgée would do well to consider his stories in the order in which they were written, with emphasis upon those books which exhibit best his art and influence.

His first novel, *Toinette*, written in 1868-69 and published in 1874, exhibited some of the author's typical attitudes but did not fully define them. Nor did it reach a large public. *Toinette* has been called "the first piece of fiction dealing directly with the problem of Reconstruction." [56] Its theme is the relationship between a Southern "gentleman" and a slave girl of great charm and only a trace of Negro blood. By her he has a child. But when, after the War, the girl, now free, refuses to resume their former relationship without the preliminary of marriage, the gentleman is revolted by the idea of any such bond with a "chattel." [57] When she discovers that the "royal gentleman" has in effect abdicated (left his throne of honor "vacant") she leaves him permanently —though she is without a definite place to go.[58] By his own unworthiness her "royal gentleman" was "discrowned." It was not that she demanded marriage—for she did not—but that she "insisted on the love which sanctifies that relation." That had been the kind of love which had first won her to him, a love which was so sincere on both their parts that it had made them for the time true equals—"peers and partners in heart"—for then his soul was free of the "cob-web fictions" of the Southern caste system.[59] Notwithstanding the obvious implications of the story—the folly of Southern pride etc.—Tourgée insisted that the book was "in 'advocacy' of nothing whatever; *it is a picture of facts.*" [60]

Figs and Thistles (1879) also fell short of revealing the author's forte. As he acknowledged in a Prologue, it yielded far more thistles than figs. Laid chiefly in the Western Reserve, it is autobiographical in reporting the author's Ohio boyhood. Likewise the experiences of Markham Churr, the hero, were evidently modeled partly on Tourgée's but are crowned with a higher recognition (a brigadier-generalship) than Tourgée ever achieved. Similarly the hero's post-war career carried him to a pinnacle that was an unrealized ambition of Tourgée, namely, election to Congress. The plot of the story is exceedingly casual, and the action is cluttered with legal and financial episodes of scant interest to the layman. Nor could the similarity between the hero's career and that of James Garfield—apparently an accidental parallel—give great interest to the book. It is not surprising that this dull hodge-podge made comparatively little stir—particularly since it was published only a month and a half before Tourgée's great popular success—indeed one of the most conspicuous books of its generation—*A Fool's Errand* (1879).

The conclusion reached in *A Fool's Errand* is that, after twelve years, Reconstruction has failed. The "fool's errand" referred to in the title is the attempt to harmonize two disparate civilizations by trying to "build up communities [in the South] which should be identical in thought, sentiment, growth, and development, with those of the North." [61] The fourteen years which Tourgée spent in the South qualified him to speak as a disillusioned observer of the "errand," but his book is far more than a mere portion of autobiography. All his abilities united to make this book a memorable and comprehensive study of a vast problem. He had observed conditions; he had learned to report action with a journalistic vividness; and he had studied in fullest detail the legal and economic issues involved in the problem. He knew both sections of the country, and he understood the mental and emotional attitudes of both sides. Moreover he regarded the South as a largely un-exploited region of rich possibilities for fiction. It was a natural field for writers, he was to say later, for "the downfall of empire is always the epoch of romance." [62] Moreover he believed that "the life of the Negro . . . offers undoubtedly the richest mine of romantic material" for fiction since Scott used themes from the lives of the lower classes in Scotland.[63] But most of all he was tremendously interested in the search for an equitable solution which should safeguard justice and promote happiness for the greatest number of the people in the post-war crises. Though a Northerner by birth, he held no brief for his own section.[64] His heart was stirred by the plight of the South and the Negro; and if his heart was touched, his pen was stirred also, for "Pathos lies at the bottom of all enduring fiction." [65]

The story of *A Fool's Errand* as such is by no means a good one from the point of view of novel-building. Though based on fact and re-search, it grossly neglects good narrative technique. The narrator often is replaced by the expositor. The characters are placed in real situations but are not developed beyond types. Even Comfort Servosse, the hero, who is patently Tourgée himself, is not a rounded character but is flat-tened out under a label, "The Fool," which tends to give the narrative an allegorical tone. For though strictly speaking not partisan, *A Fool's Errand* is frankly a doctrinaire work.

The story begins in the North but the author quickly telescopes the events leading to Servosse's settlement in the South for the sake of his lungs. Servosse naively believes that the immigration of Northerners into the South will assist in that general adjustment which is so needful after the War. He buys a badly run-down plantation from a shrewd Southerner, who cheats him on the transaction. He discovers that a Northern family celebrating Thanksgiving, that "relic of New-England Puritanical hypocrisy," [66] is not going to be popular with Southern neighbors—especially when its guests are six Northern young women come South to assist in reducing Southern illiteracy. He finds that he will not make himself popular by selling portions of his land to worthy Negroes. A speech in which he urges the right of the Negroes to testify in court only incenses his hearers so much that they plan to slug him to his senses—or the reverse. Threats of bodily harm by the Regulators force him to convert his home into a garrison. Yet he continues his hazardous conduct, even attending meetings of the Union League. In time he learns of the Southern point of view through discussion with an enlightened Southerner. He begins to understand the *raison d'être* of the Ku Klux Klan—and to fear the lawless brutality with which it attempts to curb "radicals" and Negroes. Two cold-blooded murders lead Servosse to write in protest to Washington—only to be reminded that the South will have to work out this problem itself. Subsequently the Klan is disbanded and its members are pardoned by Congress. Although Servosse is to some extent protected by the Southern fear of harming an influential Northerner, he is frequently in danger, and on one occasion is saved from probable injury only by the thrilling nocturnal horse-back ride of Lily, his daughter, who warns him in the nick of time. Lily is herself the centre of the "romantic" side of the story, for she is wooed by a gallant Southerner under the wrathful eye of his aristocratic father—who relents only in the last chapter. But the emphasis of the book is on the "Fool," who in twelve years has achieved nothing except to learn a little tolerance and to win a modicum of sympathy from a few Southerners. Eventually he is stricken with yellow fever, and he dies amid the sorrowing of kindly neighbors. But Reconstruction has failed—and the black belly of the South still rumbles ominously.

The story, exciting as it is often made by Tourgée's command of episode, is less important than the exposition of an attitude toward Reconstruction. Tourgée was convinced that the North had made a clumsy error in trying to bridge the enormous gulf by means of a Reconstruction Act. Servosse himself had been naive in not realizing that "the social conditions of three hundred years are not to be overthrown in a moment, and that differences which have outlasted generations, and finally ripened into war, are never healed by simple victory." [67] Now in 1867 the Republican North was preparing to solve all these intricate problems by a Reconstruction Act based largely upon "the establishment and administration of a rigorous and comprehensive military government throughout the ten states not yet restored to the Union." [68] In the next year (1868) Tourgée framed his own agenda of steps necessary to a national adjustment,[69] but in *A Fool's Errand* he emphasized chiefly the last of these, namely, efficient public education:

"The Nation [Servosse is speaking] nourished and protected slavery. The fruitage of slavery has been the ignorant freedman, the ignorant poor-white man, and the arrogant master. The impotence of the freedman, the ignorance of the poor-white, the arrogance of the late master, are all the result of national power exercised in restraint of free thought, free labor, and free speech. Now, let the Nation undo the evil it has permitted and encouraged. Let it educate those whom it made ignorant, and protect those whom it made weak. It is not a matter of favor to the black, but of safety to the Nation. Make the spelling-book the scepter of national power. Let the Nation educate the colored man and the poor-white man *because* the Nation held them in bondage, and is responsible for their education; educate the voter *because* the Nation can not afford that he should be ignorant." [70]

It should be obvious from Servosse's speech that Tourgée was not a foe of the South. He laid blame, so far as it was necessary to lay blame, on North and South alike. Elsewhere he speaks (through Servosse) of the Northern Republicans as "a party the most cowardly, vacillating, and inconsistent in its management of these questions, that has ever been known in any government." [71] He realizes the plight in which the South found herself after the War. At a number of points his description of post-war conditions parallels that of Margaret Mitchell in *Gone With the Wind*, but Tourgée did not need to rely on research: he had observed conditions:

At the South it was far different. Sadness and gloom covered the face of the land. The returning braves brought no joy to the loving hearts who had sent them forth. Nay, their very presence kept alive the chagrin of defeat. Instead of banners and music and gay greeting, silence and tears were their welcome home. Not only for the dead were these lamentations, but also for the living . . . The planter's slaves had become freedmen while he was growing into a hero, and no longer owed fealty or service to him or his family. The home where he had lived in luxury was almost barren of necessities: even the ordinary comforts of life were wanting at his fireside. A piece of cornbread, with a glass of milk, and bit of bacon, was, perhaps, the richest welcome-feast that wifely love could devise for the returning hero. Time and the scath of war had wrought ruin in his home. The hedgerows were upgrown, and the ditches stopped. Those whom he had been wont to see in delicate array were clad in homespun. His loved ones who had been reared in luxury were living in poverty. While he had fought, interest had run. War had not extinguished debt. What was a mere bagatelle when slaves and stocks were at their highest was a terrible *incubus* when slaves were no more, and banks were broken. The army of creditors was even more terrible than the army with banners, to whom he had surrendered . . . Shame and defeat were behind, gloom and apprehension before.[72]

No, although he favored abolition, Tourgée was not essentially partisan in his treatment: he was concerned for the welfare of the Nation. He was often charged with partisanship and cynicism, but actually such bitterness as the book exhibits is the result of disappointed idealism: he had hoped too much of humanity. But his aims had been high; otherwise he would not have written, "The life of the Fool proper is full of the poetry of faith." [73]

A Fool's Errand immediately became a household name throughout the country. So great was the demand for it that the publishers made duplicate plates in order that it might be printed in New York and Boston at the same time. It received the highest praise throughout the North. The author (though still anonymous) was dubbed the "Victor Hugo of America," and he was referred to as the long awaited "great American novelist." [74] Sales in the South went more slowly—by subscription. Fears were entertained for its possibly bad effect, and the *Raleigh Observer* avowed that the story was "a powerfully written work, and destined, we fear, to do as much harm in the world as 'Uncle Tom's Cabin,' to which it is, indeed, a companion piece."

Like Mrs. Stowe's *Uncle Tom's Cabin*, Tourgée's work also seemed to require a documented book as a follow-up to satisfy critics who challenged the veracity or information of the author. Tourgée's answer, no longer anonymous, to his challengers, was *The Invisible Empire*, a work approximately one-third as long as the novel which gave rise to it.[75] In it he considered some of the actual material of his invented story, but chiefly he discussed in rational though stern terms the origin and activities of the Ku Klux Klan as well as its relationship to the institutions of slavery and the statutes governing slavery. In tone it is more philosophic than *A Key to Uncle Tom's Cabin*, and in detail just as specific.

Tourgée would seem to have had his say about Reconstruction in *A Fool's Errand* and its appendix. And so he apparently believed, for he at first resisted his publishers' importunities that he write a sequel; but in the end he gave in and produced another story on the same theme—though furnished with new variations suggested by the slightly later date (1880) at which the action is set. The new work was *Bricks Without Straw*. Several elements already used by Tourgée reappear, but in this story, as if to make perfectly clear his friendliness toward the South, he made his hero a Southern gentleman, Hesden Le Moyne. His vis-à-vis is Mollie Ainslee, a Northern lady who has come South for personal reasons but has remained to act as a teacher in a small community of freed Negroes. Le Moyne's aristocratic background naturally makes him hate and fear the freed slaves; but gradually through Mollie he becomes enlightened, and he even co-operates with her by taking care of some of the Negroes after their little village has been raided by the Ku Klux Klan. When he actually arranges to send one of the Negroes North for a college education, his conversion to the cause of humanity is seen to be complete. In the interest of readers who must have a mystery, Tourgée manages to let it be discovered that Mollie is the owner of Le Moyne's estate, but the marriage of the pair soon renders the discovery unimportant.

Despite the happy solution of the problems of some of the individuals of this story, the book as a whole paints a by no means cheerful picture of Reconstruction. As the title indicates, Tourgée was impressed by the futility of expecting quick results merely upon official orders. It had been "demonstrated that in the years of Grace of the nineteenth century liberty could not be maintained nor prosperity achieved by ignorance and poverty, any more than in the days of Moses adobe bricks could be made without straw." [76] Few writers have described the plight of the manumitted slave so eloquently as Tourgée—or so often, for the author does repeat himself in however well-phrased language. The problem was a gigantic one:

> The first step in the progress from the prison-house of bondage to the citadel of liberty was a strange one. The war was over. The struggle for autonomy and the inviolability of slavery, on the part of the South, was ended, and fate had decided against them. With this arbitrament of war fell also the institution which had been its cause. Slavery was abolished—by proclamation, by national enactment, by constitutional amendment—ay, by the sterner logic which forbade a nation to place shackles again upon hands which had been raised in her defence, which had fought for her life and at her request. So the slave was a slave no more. No other man could claim his service or restrain his volition. He might go or come, work or play, so far as his late master was concerned.
>
> But that was all. He could not contract, testify, marry or give in marriage. He had neither property, knowledge, right, or power. The whole four millions did not possess that number of dollars or of dollars' worth. Whatever they had acquired in slavery was the master's, unless he had expressly made himself a trustee for their benefit. Regarded from the legal standpoint it was, indeed, a strange position in which they were. A race despised, de-

graded, penniless, ignorant, houseless, homeless, fatherless, childless, nameless. Husband or wife there was not one in four millions. Not a child might call upon a father for aid, and no man of them all might lift his hand in a daughter's defence. Uncle and aunt and cousin, home, family—none of these words had any place in the freedman's vocabulary. Right he had, in the abstract; in the concrete, none. Justice would not hear his voice. The law was still color-blinded by the past.

The fruit of slavery—its first ripe harvest, gathered with swords and bloody bayonets, was before the nation which looked ignorantly on the fruits of the deliverance it had wrought. The North did not comprehend its work; the South could not comprehend its fate. The unbound slave looked to the future in dull, wondering hope.[77]

Moreover if the national government had made the slave free in a bodily sense, the people of the South were ready with measures which would keep the slave in an inferior position for years to come:

They denied him his oath, fastened him to the land, compelled him to hire by the year, required the respectfulness of the old slave "Mahs'r" and "Missus," made his employer liable for his taxes, and allowed recoupment therefor; limited his avocations and restricted his opportunities. These would substitute serfdom for chattelism.[78]

As usual, Tourgée is ready in this novel to ply the reader with detailed exposition, but he also makes the problem concrete in the memorable portrait of the Negro Nimbus, whose life history he recounts in the introduction and whose tragic attempts to find himself in the new freedom form part of the problem of Mollie and Le Moyne. Nimbus is a real Negro—"as far from that volatile type which, through the mimicry of burnt-cork minstrels and the exaggerations of caricaturists, as well as the works of less disinterested portrayers of the race, have come to represent the negro to the unfamiliar mind, as the typical Englishman is from the Punch-and-Judy figures which amuse him." [79] His conversation with the county clerk to whom he applies for marriage registration is at once a little masterpiece of portraiture and perfect embodiment of one of the real problems of Reconstruction.[80] Ultimately Nimbus suffers severe distress because of white jealousy of his little success in establishing a tobacco plantation, for he talks too independently. This is brought out with telling irony in a colloquy between an official chairman and a sheriff:

"Well, he has as much right to talk independently as a white man. He is just as free," said the chairman sharply.

"Yes; but he ain't white," said the sheriff doggedly, "and our people won't stand a nigger's puttin' on such airs. Why, Captain," he continued in a tone which showed that he felt that the fact he was about to announce must carry conviction even to the incredulous heart of the Yankee officer. "You just ought to see his place down at Red Wing. Damned if he ain't better fixed up than lots of white men in the county. He's got a good house, and a terbacker-barn, and a church, and a nigger school-house, and stock, and one of the finest crops of terbacker in the county. Oh, I tell you, he's cutting a wide swath, he is." [81]

Thus Nimbus is marked for trouble. Yet he values his liberty, dearly bought as it is, and when a crippled Negro "pal" tries to persuade him that he was better off as a slave than he (the cripple) is under Emancipation, Nimbus replies: "I'd ruther be a hundred times wuss off ner you, an' free, than ez strong as I am an' a slave." [82] A far cry, this, from William G. Simms' sectional treatment of the manumitted slave in *The Yemassee*[83]—a far cry, and a more realistic one. Tourgée sees both sides of a question, and above it as well. The difficulties are immense, but through Mollie he voices a faith that ultimately the problems will be solved. In this book, as in *A Fool's Errand*, he looks to education as the principal instrument of reform. In *Bricks Without Straw*, however, he specifically recommends that the Federal government take the problem into its own hands by dispensing national funds to the several states in proportion to their illiteracy.[84] Only so will the bricks be made with which a permanent union may be built.[85]

Two other works of fiction Tourgée devoted chiefly to the general subject of the relationship between the South and the North. The first of these, *John Eax* (1882), a novelette, is a distinctly lesser work, much of the substance of which is clearly autobiographical. The story, a very brief one, begins before the War and carries its hero to the twin successes of a generalship in the army and marriage with a lady possessed of an ample fortune.[86] The other Reconstruction novel, the last of the group to be written, was *Hot Plowshares*, published in book form in 1883. In order of time this story belongs first in the series, for its action reaches an end at the outbreak of the War. The longest novel Tourgée wrote, it tells of the fortunes of an attractive girl who suffers under the imputation of having Negro blood in her veins but who is finally exonerated of the crime and betrothed to a strapping hero. The novel is furnished forth with much material from Tourgée's life as lawyer and businessman with a number of routine narrative devices—

the runaway horse, the fire, the abduction—thrown in for their popular effect.[87]

Having completed *Hot Plowshares*, Tourgée availed himself of hindsight to observe that he had written a group of six narratives on the "divergences" between the North and the South—those "two families under one roof," he called them in *John Eax*. In order that they might be viewed as a more or less coherent unit he arranged the books in the order of the time sequences of their actions: *Hot Plowshares, Figs and Thistles, A Royal Gentleman, A Fool's Errand, Bricks Without Straw, John Eax*. Taken together, these novels cover the period from about 1835 to 1877.[88] They do not constitute a well-integrated unit; they have no common hero (except, intermittently, Tourgée himself) and the action of one does not lead into that of another. They do not form anything closely resembling the modern "family" trilogies such as that of T. S. Stribling. Nor were they really "historical" novels, for what their author said of the last one, is equally true of the others: he was not interested in giving the history of a movement but "only a truthful picture of the life upon which it acted." [89] The whole series, he believed, would give to the public that full comprehension of the nature of two "distinct and contrasted civilizations" which he deemed an essential preliminary step to their final amalgamation. His hope—a hope often badly jarred—was that the two parts of the nation could finally be unified. In this he became definitely doctrinaire. But there can be no understanding of Tourgée without the realization that *doctrinaire* does not mean *partisan*. Tourgée insisted on viewing the evils on both sides of the Mason and Dixon line, for he found that the "*conscious* evils" of slavery were exaggerated by the North and that the "*unconscious* evils of the system—those which warped the brain and heart of the master as well as dwarfed the soul of the slave—had been allowed to drop out of sight in the heat of partisan advocacy." [90]

Probably Tourgée's fame would have been brighter today if he had written less fiction and organized his work more carefully. Yet his deracinated existence did not afford the leisure and stability which favor perfection in the arts. He wrote rapidly, from ever new inspirations. Much of his work after 1883 took the form of articles and essays published serially—sometimes in his own ill-fated periodicals.[91] A number of short stories appeared from his pen, among the most effective of which were a series of realistic episodes (frequently of a "detective" nature) from legal life, strung loosely together about the career of a single character and entitled *With Gauge & Swallow, Attorneys* (1889). The stories in this volume are perhaps too "technical" to be popular, but they contain some of his most delightful writing. Inevitably these stories constitute modified experience of their author. The same is true of the thin but amorphous *Black Ice* (1887), which begins as a quiet study of a New York farmhouse (Tourgée's own home after his return from the South) but is transformed into a mixture of melodrama and talk-fest. A more straightforward story, and an almost equally undistinguished one, was *Button's Inn* (1887), a tale set realistically enough on the Great Lakes, but drenched with a stale wash of melodramatic incident involving the missing jewels, the ghost, the mistaken identity, the desperate fight on a cliff, and the inevitable mortgaged property. Better by far than this is the long-drawn-out but thoroughly-thought-through *Murvale Eastman, Christian Socialist* (1889). If further proof of Tourgée's sincerity were needed, it could be found in this novel.

Murvale Eastman is an earnest exposition of the defects in an ailing socio-economic system, together with an eager statement of how present ills might be banished by the application of true Christian principles. The book was printed shortly after Howells' *The Minister's Charge* and Bellamy's *Looking Backward*, but it appears to have owed less to them in spirit than to the teachings of Kingsley and Ruskin.[92] Yet its message was for the times in which the book appeared. The premise of the author is that individual opportunity has been virtually stamped out in a capitalistic commonwealth in which half the wealth of the nation is controlled by a few persons and "Probably less than a score of men actually control the transportation of the United States . . ."[93] A "new feudalism" has developed in which "barons of wealth" are far more powerful than were the old feudal lords. The church, which presumably should stand in opposition to such a tendency, has accomplished little. Indeed the church itself, according to the protagonist of the story, is an egregious example of money-worship. To bring home these and related truths, Tourgée tells the story of Eastman, a minister who wishes to test the principle of whether the church can and will really aid the needy. To this end he works incognito as an employee of a street railway company. During a strike he rescues the president of the company, but he also lends his voice to workmen who wish to express their grievances. He exemplifies muscular Christianity by acting as a substitute for a tubercular worker injured in the strike. He further invites criticism from conservative and wealthy parishioners by taking the invalid into his own home. In the meantime he has established a "League of Christian Socialists." Can such a league as this function within the church?—that is the question. To this doctrinaire action Tourgée somewhat clumsily adds a fabricated "plot." Eastman is engaged to marry Lilian Kishu, daughter of one of his wealthiest parishioners; but she breaks the engagement partly because his devotion to the cause makes him seem cold and too "perfect" and partly because she is scandalized by his befriending a widow of dubious social status. In the end the widow's name is shown to be pure white—and Eastman in fact will take her as his wife. Likewise the tubercular Underwood proves to be not only the heir to a large fortune but also the father of the widow— to such lengths will Tourgée go to reach a popular audience. Not only that, but Kishu the "baron" is finally brought round, after being almost wiped out financially, to a complete faith in Christian Socialism. Thus Tourgée tacked a happy ending onto his book and sent it out into a world still suffering from those economic ills on which Eastman had sermonized so vociferously and so repetitiously. A poor novel, *Murvale Eastman* is nevertheless an interesting one and its thought is as "advanced" as its romantic plot is threadbare. The final impression it makes on the reader is that its author was in deadly earnest in his attempt to find solutions to the problems of wages and hours, bargaining with capital, the relationship between poverty and crime, the efficacy of the "dole," and the like. Tourgée leans far to the left in his general theorizing, pointing out for example that the early Christians had communism,[94] but in detail he makes practical suggestions bearing on the need of education for the poor, the establishment of the day nursery and common rooms, the promotion of profit-sharing plans, etc. Society at large is invited to view all these economic problems in the light of a truly Christian spirit, and the first article in the declaration of the League states that "the true function of Christian civilization is to equalize conditions and promote the general welfare of mankind." [95] Lacking the urbanity of Howells and the narrative gift of Bellamy, the author of *Murvale Eastman* did not succeed popularly in his economic novel. His day as a popular novelist was over. Yet the book shows the same eager desire to serve humanity that animated Tourgée's Reconstruction stories.

All Tourgée's novels were doctrinaire novels. He believed fiction should always have a moral end. It was in fact his opinion that a "novel without a purpose is the counterpart of a man without a purpose." [96] From the slashing satire in many of his books one might hastily assume that a novelist's purpose should be to destroy the enemy. Tourgée's destructive criticism has in fact been overemphasized by unfriendly critics, a classification which includes most academic critics, particularly in the South. Actually his basic aim was never to make his enemies smart, but to arouse humanity to the exertion of its finest impulses, to work toward a day when justice and peace should really reign on earth.

His diatribes against evil were always grounded in faith—faith in man's final ability to emerge from evil. He deplored determinism and pessimism, for

> that pessimistic philosophy which calls itself "realism" in art and literature, always is, and always will be, at fault when it tries to solve the riddle of humanity. It says human nature, human character, is a result of the operation of natural laws. So it is; but those laws are not all physical, nor purely mental. The soul must be taken into account if one would comprehend humanity or truly portray character. Impulse, affections, sentiments, convictions, emotions—these are more potent than all other forces in shaping the man and, if general in their application, the multitude. Every man's knowledge, almost every man's experience, is full of transformation scenes. It is a literal fact that "love works miracles;" so do hate and fear and the continuing power of cumulative ill. There is in truth no miracle about it. It is in these soul-forces, even more than in physical laws and conditions, that the secret of progress and the highest truth of human life lie hid. In a man or a people, the crises of sentiment or conviction are more important than physical conditions in determining character or prescribing the lines of truthful delineation in literature or art.[97]

Tourgée's scorn for writers who wallowed in scientific pessimism of the age of Darwin was definitely linked with his theory of "realism." Despite his own crude use of melodramatic sentiment and of the "happy ending," Tourgée thought of himself as a writer basically realistic: his books issued from a mind warm with conviction but well furnished with facts. Yet there was a kind of realism, French in origin, which he regarded as low and futile. It was a realism resting on the postulate that man is an irresponsible animal moving blindly in a shabby world. Excessive iteration of disagreeable physical facts irritated Tourgée. He deplored the apparently unanimous agreement of realistic novelists that country workmen must be dirty in their persons.[98] He complains that in novels "the 'realist' is always ready to believe anything mean . . ."[99] The realists "profess to be truth-tellers, but are in fact the worst of falsifiers."[100] Hence he had the deepest aversion to many English and continental writers—Zola, Hardy, Turgenev, Tolstoi. The last-named was anathema to Tourgée particularly because of his theories regarding love.[101] At times Tourgée seems prudish in his inability to enjoy good literature written by persons—he specifies Byron, Keats, Shelley, Coleridge, De Quincey—whose private lives he regarded as depraved.[102] At all events he was convinced that "the healthy mind . . . does . . . the best work." [103] Nor did he regard any mind as healthy which was not in harmony with the spirit. Howells and James, though free from vulgarity, were defective in that they treated people but not "souls." [104] It is clear, then, that Tourgée was a special kind of "realist"—a man with no great tolerance for practices that varied from what he conceived to be best. In fact he was a realist only in so far as he capitalized the fruit of his own observations whether on the Southern plantation, in the court-room, or on a New York homestead.[105] He believed, however, that fiction must go beyond realistic detail. It even "outranks history as a truth-teller, and teaches lessons of wisdom which philosophy strives in vain without its aid to impress upon the human mind." [106]

Critics still disagree about Tourgée's literary merits. Among his many complaints against the subject of his biography, R. F. Dibble asserts that Tourgée's novels "lack stylistic distinction." [107] This judgment can only be taken as a sign of the writer's hostility toward Tourgée or his inability to recognize distinction in style. All the charges brought against Tourgée's narrative organization and proclivity toward indoctrination can be more or less substantiated. Yet his prose style was an exceedingly good one—among the best, certainly, in his period. Even the poorest of his stories is likely to betray the author's nice discrimination of phrase, his easy cadences, his distinguished talent for epigrammatic expression. From the law Tourgée had learned precision and accuracy; the Bible had taught him dignity of accent and concreteness of expression. His emotions, not his pen, lacked poise. A firmer control of his extremely strong feelings and a more careful integration of the larger units in his stories would have placed him higher among the lists of American novelists. As it is, he will be remembered (when partisanship finally dies away) as a distinguished man of letters who not only wrote one of the most powerful novels of the nineteenth century but by his example helped to prove what a rich literary legacy belonged to the South after the painful era of Emancipation and Reconstruction had passed away.

Local-Color, Frontier, and Regional Fiction

The period of the local-color writers was roughly from the seventies through the nineties. Among the earliest were Aldrich, Woolson, and Bret Harte. The genre was also practiced with more or less conscious purpose by Cable, Eggleston, Charles Egbert Craddock, Mary Wilkins Freeman, Alice Brown, Thomas Nelson Page, Sarah Orne Jewett, Margaret Deland, Kate Chopin, and many others. Often the short story was preferred to the novel as a medium, but many of the same characteristics appear in both forms.

The colors in a local-color story are likely to be sombre. Bright interludes occur, but they serve to emphasize the seriousness more characteristic of the form. Decline and decay are often a central theme: a generation is passing away. The setting is an isolated one: a pocket in the hills, a village remote from railroad or main highway, a seaport town beyond its prime, a river hamlet, a Great Lakes outpost, a settlement begun in hope but finally bypassed by "progress." The community may have had an illustrious past, but it appears to have no future. Its inhabitants have the air of survivors. Insulated from large population centres, they live in an intellectual backwater. New currents of religious thought have only partially broken the ice of Calvinistic dogma. Economic enterprise is slack: people do the old things in the old ways. Opportunity for individual improvement is scant; escape from personal problems, difficult. Lovers are kept apart for years by a situation which a romance-writer would have solved handily in a chapter or two. Crushing burdens are patiently borne for years. A few youngsters slip out to establish themselves in an ampler area of activity, but the spirit of the community subtly discourages initiative, and in the typical local-color story the inhabitants are mostly old settlers. For them the clock is always slow. Wintry thoughts occupy their minds, and the hues of life are prevailingly sober.

Yet the author, who has probably lived in just such a milieu, has a special affection for it. A note of nostalgia crops out in his delineation of the scene and personnel of his story. The scene is often beautiful, and the characters, though outwardly "unsuccessful," are, as groups at least, strongly individualized. Living close to God and nature (including undisciplined nature) they exhibit a quiet stoicism, and they hold high the simple virtues of loyalty and response to duty. They have a strong sense of personal integrity, and a story may hinge on a point of honor. Unmodified by contact with the outer world, they develop personal traits to the point of eccentricity. But these folks are honestly derived, and their crotchety ways are as authentic as the soil that supports them. They do little that is dynamic; action in the story is precipitated by "strangers." For the writers of these stories do not excel in dramatic presentation; in scenes of violence they are likely to seem theatrical rather than dramatic. They are better in motivation than in episode. They make much of origins and aftermaths, and they excel in "atmosphere." Some of them overload their stories with description of the physical setting, but many achieve a finely poetic quality in their descriptions. Hardly less significant is the emphasis laid upon speech peculiarities. For the sense of locality may be revealed by the shape of vowels quite as definitely as by the contour of mountain, valley, or cove. Much of the folklore and superstition that characterize the local-color story is delivered orally in the special idiom of the region. All these things are noted lovingly by the author as, with a sort of pleasurable sadness, he records the passing of a generation.

The local-color story tends to be retrospective, but it need not be so. There may be local color also in stories of the frontier, of a region settled lately by people imbued with a buoyant pioneer spirit. But until "civilization" catches up with them, they will exhibit a proud sense of localism comparable to that discernible in more staid regions. Eggleston, for example, is rich in local color, but his stories are not set in a region from which the glory is departing. His people are on the upbeat; they are developing a region. They are inspired by the sense of leadership in a land whose future glows with promise and whose present is filled with vital constructive activity. Hamlin Garland's stories evoke a strong sense of place, but his people are often on the move—generally for economic reasons. They begin to study the socio-economic system for signs of injustice. Much movement and radical thought are of course inimical to the local-color story as such, and even newness is a handicap. The form developed most favorably in a sequestered region amid people bound together by tradition and generally acquiescent toward the social order in which they find themselves.

One other variety of the local-color story (for the form is a protean one) is that dealing with slightly larger population groups. H. B. Fuller has been called "the novelist of Midwest localism" partly on account of his sharply delineated study of Chicago (in *The Cliff-Dwellers*, 1893) at a time when Chicago was rather a "big town" than a city. Yet Fuller was not only a local-color writer but also a critic and a "realist"—with some pretty stern things to say about Chicago. G. W. Cable's portrayal of New Orleans in *The Grandissimes* more nearly conforms to the type of local-color story. The New Orleans he evoked was not the shiny new quasi-metropolitan centre of his own day; rather, he dipped into the past in an attempt to recover the old city just when it was awakening out of a blissful lethargy. It was a city rubbing its eyes at signs of "progress" setting in after Louisiana had been officially geared into the national life. It was a city prepared to resist innovations (including Yankees), for despite the presence of a number of nasty internal problems, it had a pride in its own past. It was a tradition-locked city, where customs and houses and people lingered on far beyond the period of their usefulness—and suffered no reproach for so lingering; where fading colors took on a romantic glow much more greatly to be prized than the glare of efficiency. In such a place an artist could settle down gratefully. In such a place "local-color" stories could be written.

EDWARD EGGLESTON (1837-1902)

"Gradually, but pretty surely, the whole varied field of American life is coming into view in American fiction; not the life of this moment, but that of half a score of years ago . . ." [1] When Howells made this observation in 1872, frontier and regional fiction had already made a good start, but the next two decades were to yield an even greater wealth of trans-Appalachian fiction. Among those writers destined to be remembered as one of the hardiest pioneers of the new school was Edward Eggleston, whose first novel had appeared in 1871. Indiana, the principal base of his regional studies, has since his time received full attention at the hands of two extremely popular American writers, namely, James Whitcomb Riley and Booth Tarkington. But Eggleston was the first writer to make his native state nationally prominent, and it is doubtful if any single book is even now so firmly associated with Indiana in the popular mind as *The Hoosier Schoolmaster*, which is still widely read as a minor American classic.

Between 1871 and 1894 Eggleston produced some eight or nine novels which brought him tremendous popularity. They were not great novels. Eggleston added virtually nothing to the technique of narrative; he was the creator of no memorable individual characters; he never quite perfected his naturally easy and effective style. His particular contribution to fiction was his vivid and realistic portrayal of the lives of frontier folk in environments which he knew well. A somewhat versatile writer, he was nevertheless influenced in practically everything he wrote by a desire to study society in relationship to an environment. That he should have devoted himself to such a theme was due partly to his having been impressed by Taine's sociological theories in *Art in the Netherlands*[2] and partly to his own experience of many classes of people in several sections of the expanding Middle West, particularly in Indiana, where he was born in the town of Vevay on December 10, 1837.[2a]

Often joshed as a Hoosier, Eggleston was proud of his native Indiana. Indeed he was once irritated by a New England reviewer who assumed that such a birthplace was a disadvantage: "Certainly I retain enough of local prejudice to feel that I should have lost more than I could have gained, had I been born near Plymouth Rock or on Beacon Hill." [3] He was educated at home and in elementary schools, but did not attend college.[4] His lack of advanced formal education he did not regard as a disadvantage, for, like Franklin, he believed that "Schools and colleges —I do not say universities—are primarily for those that cannot or will not study without them." [5] Nor, considering his home environment, could he accept the commonly applied designation of "self-made man." His father, a successful lawyer and legislator, had graduated from William and Mary College with the highest honor ever given by that institution.[6] How carefully he considered young Eggleston's intellectual progress may be judged from a provision of his will whereby at his death (which occurred when Eggleston was nine) all his law books were to be exchanged for reading matter more suitable for his son. The boy's mother was equally concerned for the development of the lad, and there can be no question of the accuracy of Eggleston's statement, that he was "born into an intellectual atmosphere." [7] Moreover Eggleston was himself an ambitious student not only of literature but of mathematics, foreign languages, geology, and theology. Born a frontiersman, he enjoyed an intellectual heritage not far different from that of cultivated men on the eastern side of the Alleghenies. Yet the religious climate in which he lived as a boy and a youth marked him in a special manner that was to have important effects upon his career. He was at first extremely, almost fanatically, devoted to religion—its special form in his home was Methodism—but in early manhood he gradually withdrew from the narrower implications of creed and theology. Yet he did not consider his submission to religious bigotry as ultimately a handicap. The "rebound" from such bondage, he believed, often "carries [the mind] for a time to a higher level than it might otherwise have attained." [8] Moreover, his knowledge of the aims and practice of Methodism was one of the chief centres of his literary material.

Born in Indiana, Eggleston became master of several milieus for fiction. For varying periods of his boyhood he lived at Albany, New York, in Wisconsin, and in Virginia. Upon his return to Indiana, he became a Bible agent. In 1856, smitten with tuberculosis, he went to Minnesota to restore his health. Later he acted as Methodist circuit-rider in Ohio and Indiana on a four-week circuit with ten "preaching places." [9] Most of his work up to 1866 was in the service of religion, and most of it was outdoor work. Yet circuit-riding in backwoods and swamp-land was as strenuous as it was poorly paid, and in 1866 Eggleston soon gave up the ministry, temporarily at least, for journalism, a move dictated by his physical condition more than by his slowly waning belief in the stricter tenets of his sect. [10] After holding one or two minor positions on educational magazines, he finally formed a connection with *Hearth and Home*, which published his first novel, *The Hoosier Schoolmaster*, in 1871. [11]

The Hoosier Schoolmaster has become an American classic. Sixteen years after its first publication, Eggleston complained: "the exasperating public still buys thousands of copies of it annually, preferring it to the most careful work I can do." [12] Undoubtedly the explanation lies in the nature of the fundamental situation. Give a spirited but none-too-muscular young man the post of schoolmaster in a hostile rural community where he is menaced first by a ferocious dog, then by a local hind of brutal instinct, and finally by the mother of a charmless slattern whom she wishes him to marry—and the framework has been provided for an exciting story. The hero may at first succeed by his friendliness and sincerity, but sooner or later he must either outwit or overpower one or more of the brutish gentry. He must also prove his intellectual calibre; and if, as in this case, there is the detailed account of a spelling bee, the interest of the general public is completely won, for a story with a spelling bee in it, like a story involving Abe Lincoln, can never be a total failure. [13] Ralph Hartsook handles his difficult situation quite capably by his wit and courage, but mostly by "sheer force of will," [14] and he even wins the respect of some of the original skeptics— though Pete Jones keeps on insisting that Ralph " 'don't lick enough. Not nigh . . . No lickin' no larnin', says I.' " Ralph's fatal error, however, lay in not loving the unlovely Mirandy Means. The girl's disgruntled mother concocts a slanderous attack which implicates the innocent young man in a robbery. A trial scene forms the climax of the story. Of course the hero is acquitted (an eye witness to the robbery gets religion and confesses), and a marriage is arranged with a bewitching little bond servant whom he has dared to prefer to Mirandy Means. The hero is given a cheer by all the citizenry except Mrs. Means. Thus Ralph Hartsook has proved himself a hero in a fashion dear to the hearts of all simple readers. In every way the ending is happy: even the chief villain, who got as near to lynching as feeling a rope around his neck, is rescued at the last moment. Bud Means, first heckler of the new schoolmaster, goes religious and accepts a post in charge of the poor-house. He is finally to become a sheriff! The inevitable little boy (after Dickens) who has been brutally mistreated in the middle of the book finds a good home at the end. Eggleston does not apologize for the Santa-Claus-like ending; he justifies it:

> We are all children in reading stories. We want more than all else to know how it all came out at the end, and, if our taste is not perverted, we like it to come out well.[15]

Eggleston knew by instinct the formula for a successful popular story. But *The Hoosier Schoolmaster* is something more than a popular story. True, its characters are but types, and the whole populace of Flat Creek has little more reality than puppets: when Eggleston chooses to pull the string, they swing completely to the hero's side. The robbery theme is carried out with no more originality or reality than similar themes in scores of novels and dime-novels.[16] It is in creating the sense of locality that Eggleston succeeds. The local customs of the uncouth folk of Flat Creek he knew by first-hand observation, and he used them plentifully—though always with a certain selectivity: he never allowed himself to descend to the "boisterousness" of the Southwest humorists.[17] But most important of all, he reported their racy idiom with faithful accuracy. His interest in speech variations had ante-dated *The Hoosier Schoolmaster*, and it was one of his articles on the subject of American dialect which had drawn the praise of James Russell Lowell—an encomium which Eggleston valued particularly as coming from "the only one of our most eminent scholars who has given careful attention to American dialects."[18] Most of Eggleston's later books evince the same interest in matters of orthography and pronunciation as *The Hoosier Schoolmaster*, and it is this aspect of his work, quite as much as his citation of native flora and fauna, which gives authenticity to the story. The book is accurately if not modestly described in Eggleston's own phrase as "the file-leader of the procession of American dialect novels."[19]

The End of the World (1872),[20] Eggleston's second novel, is a story of "religious fanaticism and racial prejudice," [21] involving the Millerites, a sect whose operations he had observed as a lad in Indiana. The theme of religion was a typical one for Eggleston, but he was to make better use of it in later stories. His third novel, however, showed Eggleston marching on to new scenes and new interests: *The Mystery of Metropolisville* was a by-product of his trip to Minnesota in search of health.

Compared with Indiana, which had entered the Union in 1816, Minnesota was an upstart territory when Eggleston first went there in 1856: two years later it was to achieve statehood. *The Mystery of Metropolisville* was a story as inchoate in structure as the Minnesota territory it described, and it employed events so loosely federated that the book seems to need nothing so much as a strong central government. The action is laid in the small boom town of Red Owl in a period "when money was worth five and six per cent a month on bond and mortgage, when corner lots doubled in value over night, when everybody was frantically trying to swindle everybody else." [22] Into this community comes Albert Charlton, an idealistic young man vehement in his vague humanitarianism but possessed of a vein of skepticism that is brought out in juvenile animadversions on the dishonesty and incompetence of lawyers, ministers, doctors, and businessmen. He has theoretical solutions for all the woes of society, but his experience in this book is discouraging enough in a turbulent commercial section of the country where "Idees is in the way—don't pay no interest." [23] He gets an inside view of ruthless methods of hardshell frontier businessmen in the person and smooth but often illegal operations of his step-father, Mr. Plausaby, a real-estate man. He finds also in his own family an example of how personal honor may be contaminated by the rude approaches of unscrupulous men, for his own sister is pursued by such an oily villain that when death by accidental drowning overtakes her, the author cannot help rejoicing at her escape. The "mystery" promised in the title receives belated and none-too-prominent treatment. When the young idealist is accused of stealing an important paper and actually goes to prison before the real culprit confesses (on her death-bed, of course), Eggleston is only retracing a familiar melodramatic pattern which he managed, with slight variations, to introduce into several of his stories. The book is realistic in its vivid description of the surface life of a small town in adolescent Minnesota. Notwithstanding his caustic exposure of duplicity in love and business, Eggleston does not convert his fiction into propaganda. He sees the good and the interesting things in frontier life as well as the sordid. In short this cluttered-up unproportioned narrative above everything testifies to the author's interest in all things human—love, commerce, religion, education. The endless conversations which mar the proportion of the story seldom reach the stage of profundity, but they report well the average opinions of pioneers in a new territory. *The Mystery of Metropolisville* is, in his own words "a contribution to the history of civilization in America." [24] As in most of his books, he contrives to give a vivid impression of people en masse without being able to create individually rounded persons. The portraiture of minor figures shows the apparent influence of Dickens, especially in the matter of speech: Smith Westcott's spasmodic utterances, for example, distinctly recall Alfred Jingle, Esq. Oral idiom and dialectical peculiarities continue to fascinate Eggleston, and it is these as much as anything which carry the ring of truth to a story whose plot has not one shred of originality. The public had enough confidence in Eggleston to order 11,000 copies of *The Mystery of Metropolisville* before publication,[25] but the confidence must have seemed misplaced.

Religion is a theme of greater or less importance in all Eggleston's novels. In *The Circuit Rider* (1874) it becomes dominant. Partly auto-biographical in its inception, the book broadens into a fairly comprehensive study of Methodism, which "was to the West all that Puritanism was to New England." [26] Yet the narrative elements are not submerged by Eggleston's social interests. Indeed Methodism does not become prominent as a factor in the plot until a very pretty complication has been set up for several young lovers. Morton Goodwin's suit for the hand of Patty Lumsden, attractive daughter of a Southern Ohio "squire," is jeopardized by his nobly opposing the squire in a shady business transaction of which the victim was Morton's friend. Discouraged by his lack of progress, Morton gets to looking "powerful dauncy," and he takes more and more to evil courses such as gambling, swearing, drinking, and baiting Methodist preachers—one of whom digresses from his sermon to assure Morton that he is "hair-hung and breeze-shaken over that pit that has no bottom." [27] Morton finally takes to the road (partly to escape Methodism, which in spite of himself he begins to be drawn toward), and experiences various picaresque adventures which culminate in his falling in with a band of robbers. He is almost hanged for a horse thief (despite his innocence in this respect) and he comes home in disgrace with fortune and men's eyes. In Patty's eyes, however, the only thing that disgraces him is his having caught the infection of Methodism shortly after his return from his ignoble Odyssey. His other sins, the routine sins of spirited young men of the region, she could forgive, but not his lapse into a dingy religion like Methodism. But Morton can't give up God even for Patty, and he sadly accepts his dismissal into an exile that will last two years. He becomes a circuit-rider and learns all the sweetness and adversity which pertain to that arduous way of life. He learns the perils not only of the fever-laden swamp-land but of even innocent friendliness with female colleagues, one of whom almost traps him into marriage. But he is saved ——frontiersman Eggleston reverts shamelessly to hereditary fictional devices for his solution—by a politician who turns out to be his long-lost brother! Patty of course is brought to her senses by this hair-breadth escape.

This is the main strand of action in a story crossed by several looser threads, chief of which is the tenuous life line of Kike, the victim of old Lumsden's shady coup. Kike, a frail lad, finally forswears his original idea of fierce revenge, turns Methodist preacher, carries on valiantly though wasted by hardship and disease, loves hopelessly a pallid saint of a girl who is formally united to him just as he is about to die beautifully in a pathetic scene while a white dove flies in at the window. For the rest, there is a diversity of minor incident and characterization which compensates for the lack of originality in the major turning points of the story. Most amusing of the minor characters is Mr. Brady, the loquacious Irish schoolmaster, who is a mine of wit, wisdom, and good will. The brief introduction of a Connecticut peddler serves to reveal the Westerner's reaction to a "pestilent peripatetic" fellow who "would work an hour to cheat you out of a 'fipenny bit.'" [28] Eggleston clearly has a measure of local pride as he paints in full detail the various activities—domestic, religious, political, commercial—which went to make up pioneer life on the Ohio border. A corn shucking or an election of very slight importance to the plot receives the minutest attention—the attention of a social historian as well as of a novelist. But in this book the most prominent theme is Methodism.

Eggleston's treatment of Methodism is full, frank, and impartial. The subject is brought into focus by the impact of Methodism on the "Old-side" believers, who had clung to Calvinistic theology and resented the "mushroom religion" which threatened the stability of the community. Even elections were rendered more violent, for a Methodist vote counted as much as any other. Captain Lumsden, who prided himself on a Virginian ancestry, naturally hated the barbarity of the new faith and all the "wrastlin' and strugglin'" that accompanied conversion. Patty, too, before her change of heart, scorned its vulgarity:

Her mother had come of an "old family"—in truth, of two or three old families. All of them had considered that attachment to the Established Church was part and parcel of their gentility, and most of them had been staunch Tories in the Revolution. Patty

had inherited from her mother refinement, pride, and a certain
lofty inflexibility of disposition. In this congenial soil Mrs. Lumsden had planted traditional prejudices. Patty read her Prayer-
book, and wished that she might once attend the stately Episcopal
service; she disliked the *lowness* of all the sects: the sing-song of
the Baptist preacher and the rant of the Methodist itinerant were
equally distasteful. She had never seen a clergyman in robes, but
she tried, from her mother's descriptions, to form a mental picture of the long-drawn dignity of the service in an Old Virginia
country church . . .

For the Methodists she entertained a peculiar aversion. Methodism was new, and, like everything new, lacked traditions, picturesqueness, mustiness, and all the other essentials of gentility in religious matters. The converts were rude, vulgar, and poor; the
preachers were illiterate, and often rough in voice and speech;
they made war on dancing and jewelry, and dancing and jewelry
appertained to good-breeding. Ever since her father had been
taken with that strange disorder called "the jerks," she had hated
the Methodists worse than ever.[29]

When Eggleston speaks *in propria persona*, however, the reader is
shown both sides of the question: early Methodism was crude but it
served an important function in its day. Eggleston clearly deprecates
religious fanaticism, but he delivers his opinions in the most diplomatic
fashion:

Now, lest some refined Methodist of the present day should be
a little too severe on our good friend Mr. Donaldson, I must express my sympathy for the worthy old gentleman as he goes riding along toward the scene of conflict. Dear, genteel, and cultivated Methodist reader, you who rejoice in the patristic glory of
Methodism, though you have so far departed from the standard
of the fathers as to wear gold and costly apparel and sing songs
and read some novels, be not too hard upon our good friend Donaldson. Had you, fastidious Methodist friend, who listen to organs
and choirs and refined preachers, as you sit in your cushioned pew
—had you lived in Ohio sixty years ago, would you have belonged
to the Methodists, think you? Not at all! your nerves would have
been racked by their shouting, your musical and poetical taste outraged by their ditties, your grammatical knowledge shocked beyond recovery by their English; you could never have worshiped
in an excitement that prostrated people in religious catalepsy, and
threw weak saints and obstinate sinners alike into the contortions
of the jerks . . . Permit me, Methodist brother, to believe that had
you lived in the days of Parson Donaldson, you would have
condemned these rude Tishbites as sharply as he did. But you

would have been wrong, as he was. For without them there must have been barbarism, worse than that of Arkansas and Texas. Methodism was to the West all that Puritanism was to New England.[30]

In *Roxy* (1878)[31] Eggleston displayed a slightly deeper interest in the psychology of individual character than any of his earlier novels had shown. Mark Bonamy, the hero, is a character neither wholly good nor wholly bad. Success comes to him quickly on account of his personal attractiveness and his versatile abilities. He wins a wife, and he attains a seat in the legislature. Yet a combination of circumstances and his weak will finally brings him to ruin. The process of his degeneration is gradual, for "No man falls like Lucifer from heaven—the progress of evil is slow and not easily perceived."[32] The embodiment of evil for Mark Bonamy is Nancy Kirtle, a poor-white woman who is physically attractive but culturally and morally deficient. When Mark drifts into a liaison with her, his only hope of regeneration lies with his wife, Roxy, a woman of natural refinement and altruistic spirit. Roxy's pride does not prevent her from offering to care for the child that Nancy bears to Mark or from receiving Mark again when after long wandering he returns to her, a prodigal husband. Victory has been won at the cost of heavy suffering; and that missionary ardor which Roxy planned to devote to unenlightened folk in Texas she has had to expend in repairing the rift in her own domestic life. Eggleston hews to his theme in *Roxy* with more than customary steadiness, but he does not fail to exhibit his remarkable gift for sketching in the daily life of the great variety of character types—of mixed racial heritage—which were to be found in southern Indiana about 1840, when Whigs, Democrats, and Loco-focos fought for political control of an exceedingly active constituency that was at the moment greatly exercised over the issues of a national bank and internal improvements. Eggleston is equally at home expounding politics in a county seat, and in describing local customs from barbecues and hoedowns to methods of "evening" shoes in order to secure greater wear. His skill in reporting native speech is at a premium in a region where pronunciation and syntax must respond to the diverse practice of gentlefolk, poor-white, Negro, French trader, and New Orleans businessmen. Few writers of the period equaled Eggleston in prodigality of realistic detail. Nature here is given more attention than in his earlier novels. Birds and flowers receive affectionate citation as adjuncts of a charmingly indolent setting in southern Indiana, where Eggleston's deepest roots lay. Strong regional love and not a little artistic skill unite to produce his description of *dolce far niente* amid the gentle valleys where he grew up:

One can never have done admiring the beauties of a late after-noon on the Ohio. In a village like Luzerne, where every house was bowered in apple-trees, and rose-bushes, and grape-vines, and honeysuckles, it was always a delight . . . At some seasons of the year, when onion buying and hay shipping were active, the town had some appearance of life; but it was never so peaceful and sleepy-looking as about the first of August. In mid-afternoon, the clerks in the stores sprinkled the floors to keep them cool, and then sat themselves down on shoe-boxes or counters to loaf away the hot and idle time, rising with reluctance to sell a half pound of eightpenny nails to some unlucky villager, into whose garden an industrious hog has forced his way, and who was obliged to exert himself enough to nail on a few palings. The roses have long ceased bloming. The red seed-vessels look bright among the green leaves of the rose-trees . . . The grapes are hardly reddening yet, but you can hear at this season the thud of the ripe summer apples, as they fall from time to time upon the ground. Nobody does anything. The boys find it too warm to play. They are up in the apple-trees, filling their hats and shirt-bosoms with the too-abun-dant fruit, or they are prowling about some garden-patch, waiting their opportunity to "hook" a great ripe water-melon. They know a good place in some retired orchard, or under a drift-pile of the river-side, where they can carry their booty, and find out how sweet are stolen melons . . .

It is a beautiful climate on this beautiful river, where the winters are never stern, and where, in the hot summer, one is absolved from responsibility and care. Nowhere is the "sweet doing noth-ing" sweeter than here. Lie down under a cherry-tree and sleep, stretch yourself near an open doorway and read, with the sound of cow-bells, and the far away cawing of crows, and the cackling of hens, and the scarcely heard and lazy hammering of the village smith floating to you out of an air full of stillness and peace. Put away your book at last. The world is too comfortable for exertion. . . . It is happiness enough to be.

It does not matter that you come of an energetic race cradled in the rocky hill-sides of New England . . . Sit down, sad soul, or lie down and slumber.[33]

The Graysons (1887) added little to Eggleston's reputation. Eggles-ton was at home in the agricultural background of Illinois where he laid his story, and as the son of a lawyer he came honestly by a knowl-edge of Tom Grayson's profession. The presence of Abe Lincoln at the climax was perhaps a deliberate play for popularity, but it is question-able whether Eggleston capitalized the situation successfully, for he used one of the hoariest pieces of Lincolniana, namely, the trial in which at a critical point Lincoln proves that there was no moonlight.

A far better story was Eggleston's last novel *The Faith Doctor* (1891). This story, set in New York, proves well enough that only part of Eggleston's success depended upon his exploitation of settings which he was among the first to describe. After his final move to the East in 1870 he had lived in Brooklyn for nine years. From 1881 on he lived at Lake George in the summer and in New York during the winter. *The Faith Doctor* is fairly rich in local color of an era in which fashionable life, having lately abandoned lower Second Avenue, was likely to centre in Washington Square. Yet the sense of place is not as strong in this novel as in the earlier novels, and it is rather Eggleston's abiding interest in religious problems which provides the solid basis of this extremely interesting story. By the time he came to the writing of *The Faith Doctor* Eggleston had broken completely away from orthodox Methodism as well as from all rigid systems of theology; and although he of course remained a sober and respectable member of society, he had come to believe that fanatical absorption in the "practical" applications of faith might be productive of much unnecessary suffering, as well as of opportunities for dangerous commercialism. In *The Faith Doctor* Phillida Callender, a charming daughter of decayed gentility, lives obscurely with her mother and sister until she is "discovered" by Charlie Millard, a cultivated and altogether attractive scion of wealth. Up to this time Phillida has been a social worker, satisfied to alleviate the miseries of the poor in various errands of mercy. But "below the philanthropic Phillida lay the devout Phillida," and when the opportunity arises to unite her religious and charitable impulses, she eagerly accepts it. In due time and under duly decorous conditions Millard and Phillida become engaged to be married. But under the malign influence of Mrs. Frankland, a fluent lecturer on religious topics of interest to the "weary rich," Phillida discovers, or thinks she discovers, that she can perform cures by faith. Thus a Hawthornesque situation is created, for out of apparent good will arise the evil which is the inevitable result of fanaticism. Once Phillida is convinced of her miraculous powers, her engagement to Millard becomes a matter of secondary importance, and he is sadly dismissed in order that she may devote herself to her sacred work. But when she learns that her faculty is powerless if germs, instead of nerves, are the cause of a disorder, she sees the error of her conduct, and she comes to understand that Mrs. Frankland's motives are not purely religious. A harrowing case in which the life of a boy is almost lost while a professional faith-healer resists the "intrusion" of a medical attendant persuades Phillida to call upon Millard to evict the woman. After the boy's life is saved, it is only a matter of time until the lovers are brought together again through the subtle and heroic stratagem of one of Phillida's unsuccessful suitors.

In *The Faith Doctor* Eggleston again revealed his weakness in story structure: most of the expository matter touching Millard's professional career at his bank is wholly out of scale though somewhat redeemed by the author's increasingly witty and epigrammatic style.[34] Once the heart of the action is reached, however, the story attains greater and more prolonged intensity than any other novel of Eggleston. The loss of the freshness and vitality characteristic of *The Hoosier Schoolmaster* is pretty well balanced by a gain in reflectiveness and weight. In his preface Eggleston declared that his "primary purpose" was "artistic, not polemical." Judged on this ground, the novel can be accorded moderate praise. Compared with the best of James's novels, *The Faith Doctor* seems a poor technical performance, but measured against the average output of the domestic sentimentalists who had recently dominated fiction it assumes a respectable stature. From the point of view of popular interest, this, the last of Eggleston's novels, was a great success, and it was noted by one contemporary critic as "quite distinctly the novel of the season when published." [35]

"If I were a dispassionate critic, and were set to judge my own novels as the writings of another, I should have to say that what distinguishes them from other works of fiction is the prominence which they give to social conditions; that the individual characters are here treated to a greater degree than elsewhere as parts of a study of a society—as in some sense the logical results of the environment . . . I am mainly interested in the evolution of society." [36] The truth of Eggleston's self-appraisal is evident to anyone who has read his novels. He has the historian's interest in environment and the sociologist's interest in group behavior. The environments he wrote about were comparatively new in American fiction: hence his fame as a pioneer local-colorist. In some measure he was animated by a competitive spirit, and in writing *The Hoosier Schoolmaster* he realized that he might help to dispel that jealousy with which Hoosier folk saw every item of New England celebrated in rhyme and tale while their own life, "not less interesting, not less romantic, and certainly not less filled with humorous and grotesque material, had no place in literature." [37] Indiana, Illinois, and southern Ohio constituted a homogeneous group of people speaking a common idiom[38] and observing the common customs. Their speech and behavior were not of course completely divorced from those of other regions, for after all the settlers of Indiana were transplanted from more eastern localities, particularly Pennsylvania.[39] Yet a certain provincialism set in which was fostered in the early part of the nineteenth century by the comparative isolation of people dependent on pre-railroad transportation. The relative simplicity of the inhabitants in this region made them easy copy for as facile a writer as Eggleston. For the most part he treated of people who corresponded to what is now known as the middle class. It was hard to set up for an aristocrat in Hoosier-land, though there were a few "professional men and people of more or less culture, chiefly from eastern Virginia and Maryland."[40] The poor-whites who thronged up to Indiana from the South in the period treated in *The Hoosier Schoolmaster* were essentially nomadic people. As early as 1845 they began drifting westward to Missouri, where, in Pike County, they acquired the name under which they were known when they appeared, during the succeeding generation, in the California stories of Bret Harte.[41] The people who remained to become more or less permanent settlers form the personnel of most of Eggleston's stories. He knew their faults: their intolerance, their commercial spirit, their uncouth manner, their narrow religious views. Had he chosen, Eggleston could have found the data for as bleak a picture of life in a small mid-West town as E. W. Howe presented in *The Story of a Country Town* (1883). But optimism ran in his blood. He had faith in the fundamental humanity of his boyhood neighbors, and he watched hopefully while education gradually obliterated the cruder features of frontier life. The virulence of the many later attacks on small-town life in the Middle West led by Sinclair Lewis in *Main Street* (1920) suggests that Eggleston's studies were in too happy a vein. The same sort of charge has often been made against James Whitcomb Riley, the Hoosier poet. Yet if examined fully, Eggleston's novels will be seen to report (in decorous terms, to be sure) most of the sordid elements of his milieu. It was his privilege not to view them hopelessly.

One of the things which gave Eggleston faith in the mid-West was its fundamental democracy. Here was no hierarchy based upon ancestry and wealth such as characterized New England and Virginia. True, he shows the narrow, sour-grapes attitude of those Westerners who belittle the things they don't possess—like Whisky Jim, the comic coach driver (from Vermont) who satirizes the useless "idees" of Boston people.[42] Yet he was skeptical of class distinction. On this point Eggleston was somewhat inconsistent. He had respect for true culture and gentility—considering his own parentage, how could he fail to?—but he enjoyed puncturing spurious claims. Thus old Lumsden in *The Circuit Rider* takes advantage of local ignorance:

When we speak of Captain Lumsden as an old Virginia gentleman, we speak from his own standpoint. In his native state his hereditary rank was low—his father was an "upstart," who, besides lacking any claims to "good blood," had made money by doubtful means. But such is the advantage of emigration that among outside barbarians the fact of having been born in "Ole Virginny" was credential enough. Was not the Old Dominion the mother of presidents, and of gentlemen? And so Captain Lumsden was accustomed to tap his pantaloons with his raw-hide riding-whip, while he alluded to his relationships to "the old families," the Carys, the Archers, the Lees, the Peytons, and the far-famed William and Evelyn Bird; and he was especially fond of mentioning his relationship to that family whose aristocratic surname is spelled "Enroughty," while it is mysteriously and inexplicably pronounced "Darby," and to the "Tolivars," whose name is spelled "Taliaferro." Nothing smacks more of hereditary nobility than a divorce betwixt spelling and pronouncing.[43]

In *The Faith Doctor* also Eggleston inveighs against pride of family. By 1891 he had seen too much of the polite world to be guilty of any low-bred slurs against people of wealth, but on the other hand he had by now crystallized his convictions on the matter, and in the following forceful passage he delivers himself of a (for him) rare passage of straight satire:

Of course there is a small set who affect not to mingle freely with newly prosperous people like the Hilbroughs. These are they in whose estimation wealth and distinction only gain their proper flavor—their bouquet, so to speak—by resting stagnant for three generations, for gentility, like game, acquires an admirable highness by the lapse of time. Descendants of the Lord knows whom, with fortunes made the devil knows how, fondly imagine that a village storekeeper who has risen to affluence is somehow inferior to the grandson of a Dutch sailor who amassed a fortune by illicit trade with the Madagascar pirates, or a worse trade in rum and blackamoors on the Guinea coast, and that a quondam bookkeeper who has fairly won position and money by his own shrewdness is lower down than the lineal descendant of an Indian trader who waxed great by first treating and then cheating shivering Mohawks. Which only shows that we are prone to plant ourselves on the sound traditions of ancestors; for where is the aristocracy which does not regard wealth won by ancient thievery as better than money modernly earned in a commonplace way? But among a gentry so numerous and so democratic, in spite of itself, as that of our American Babel, exclusiveness works discomfort mainly to the exclusive.[44]

There is no doubt that Eggleston had faith in the rank and file of humanity. He admonished them for their faults and encouraged them in their progress toward a life of simple piety and good common-sense. The bearing of his ideas throughout his fiction is of a wholesome sort.[45] He was a thoughtful person but not a profound thinker. Nor was he a radical opponent of those Eastern businessmen who gradually assumed financial control of much of the agricultural and industrial West. Treating of a slightly earlier period than Hamlin Garland, he witnessed some of the same abuses, but he did not become a spokesman against capitalism.[46] Captain Lumsden's taking advantage of Kike's mother by ordering a sale of her property might have yielded a situation comparable to the threatened dispossession of Haskins in Garland's "Under the Lion's Paw"; but whereas Garland works from the individual case of oppression to an indictment of the system which makes it possible, Eggleston shows pity for the case without showing anger toward the system. He was less the reformer than the evangelist. Economic ideologies did not interest him greatly. He merely described conditions in simple terms. None of his books would tax the intellect of the wide public at which he aimed. He loved the people, and he spoke their language.

Critics have generally agreed in their estimates of Eggleston. The commonest tag applied to him is that he was a "frontier realist." Obviously the term fits him well in most respects. He was frequently at pains to point out that his main object in telling stories was to reveal truth:

> A NOVEL should be the truest of books. It partakes in a certain sense of the nature of both history and art. It needs to be true to human nature in its permanent and essential qualities, and it should truthfully represent some specific and temporary manifestation of human nature: that is, some form of society. It has been objected that I have copied life too closely, but it seems to me that the work to be done just now, is to represent the forms and spirit of our own life, and thus free ourselves from habitual imitation of that which is foreign. I have wished to make my stories of value as a contribution to the history of civilization in America. If it be urged that this is not the highest function, I reply that it is just now the most necessary function of this kind of literature. Of the value of these stories as works of art, others must judge; but I shall have the satisfaction of knowing that I have at least rendered one

substantial though humble service to our literature, if I have portrayed correctly certain forms of American life and manners.[47]

In *The Circuit Rider* also he reminds his readers of "the solemn obligations of a novelist to tell the truth," for "no man is worthy to be called a novelist who does not endeavor with his whole soul to produce the higher form of history, by writing truly of men as they are . . ."[48] Yet this kind of avowal is *vieux jeu* in prefatory material in American fiction, and it is a poor novelist who cannot run up some such banner with a degree of plausibility. If the question be whether the novelist tells the *whole* truth and nothing but the truth, the answer may not be perfectly clear. In Eggleston's case there is certainly no perjury: he does not consciously falsify experience. Nor was he (probably) conscious of being frustrated by those public taboos or conventions which in general prevented American novelists from exploiting sex and sordidness. Eggleston was no thwarted naturalist. He was *content* with a moderate realism. To be sure he frequently goes out of his way to show how uncongenial the extremes of melodrama and romance are to him. In *The Circuit Rider*—despite its subtitle, "A Tale of the Heroic Age" —Morton Goodwin is explicitly described as "not an epic hero, for epic heroes act straightforwardly, they either know by intuition just what is right, or they are like Milton's Satan, unencumbered with a sense of duty. But Morton was neither infallible nor a devil."[49] In *The Hoosier Schoolmaster* the author pauses to admonish a hypothetical reader of melodramas:

> And you, friend Callow, who have blunted your palate by swallowing the Cayenne pepper of the penny-dreadfuls, you wish me to make this night exciting by a hand-to-hand contest between Ralph and a robber. You would like it better if there were a trapdoor. There's nothing so convenient as a trap-door, unless it be a subterranean passage. And you'd like something of that sort just here. It's so pleasant to have one's hair stand on end, you know, when one is safe from danger to one's self. But if you want each individual hair to bristle with such a "Struggle in the Dark," you can buy trap-doors and subterranean passages dirt cheap at the next news-stand.[50]

Yet, like Charles Brockden Brown, Eggleston utilized many of the very materials he affected to disparage; in *The Hoosier Schoolmaster* itself the robbery motif is carried out with a reliance upon sensation that comports rather badly with the simple entertainment values of the rest of the story. And there are lurid scenes in most of the other novels as well which show that Eggleston did not quite keep his fingers out of the pepper box. He couldn't quite resist a bit of the Gothic. Similarly he coyly affects to deflate romance:

> You expect me to describe that walk. You have had enough of the Jack Meanses and the Squire Hawkinses, and the Pete Joneses, and the rest. You wish me to tell you now of this true-hearted girl and her lover; of how the silvery moonbeams came down in a shower—to use Whittier's favorite metaphor—through the maple boughs, flecking the frozen ground with light and shadow. You would have me tell of the evening star, not yet gone down, which shed its benediction on them. But I shall do no such thing. For the moon was not shining, neither did the stars give their light. The tall, black trunks of the maples swayed and shook in the wind, which moaned through their leafless boughs. Novelists always make lovers walk in the moonlight. But if love is not, as the cynics believe, all moonshine, it can at least make its own light. Moonlight is never so little needed or heeded, never so much of an impertinence, as in a love-scene. It was at the bottom of the first hollow beyond the school-house that Ralph overtook the timid girl walking swiftly through the dark. . . .
>
> You, Miss Amelia, wish me to repeat all their love-talk. I am afraid you'd find it dull. . . .[51]

Of course Eggleston is here using the ancient trick of dodging responsibility by pretending not to do a thing he has already resolved he *will* do. The move is symptomatic of an underlying sentimentality which flows gently through most of Eggleston's books. His preference for a happy ending is also suggestive not only of Eggleston's cheerful outlook on life but of his somewhat old-fashioned story-telling technique. Most of his stories are, on one plane, simple love stories. When in *The Circuit Rider* he explains why this should be so, he reveals the light sentimental tone which was undoubtedly one of the main-springs of his popularity:

> Doubtless I shall hopelessly damage myself with some good people by confessing in the start that, from the first chapter to the last, this is a love-story. But it is not my fault. It is God who made love so universal that no picture of human life can be complete where love is left out.[52]

Eggleston was not a great novelist. Great novelists are men of deeper purpose, greater consecration to art, and fuller command of their medium. His greatest ability in sheer narrative technique was his fertile invention and vivid use of episode. He had little conception of how to build a novel. Perhaps one trouble was that he read comparatively few novels in the strict home of his boyhood. Another possible explanation is that the serial form in which his early novels appeared was no challenge to careful over-all planning: enough if each issue of the magazine carried color and action set forth in an animated style with occasional dashes of Dickensian and Hoosier humor. Serial publication may explain too his conscienceless use of a multitude of small scenes where one well-planned major scene could have done the work better. At all events Eggleston made little contribution to the sheer technique of novel-building, and in fact he seems in this respect a little old-fashioned even for his time. What he did provide that was new resulted from his exploration of new regions and new population groups. These he handled with honest attention to detail, including speech detail. He did not try to catch all the moods of the Middle West. One must look to other writers for expression of the poetry of prairie and plain on a grand scale. Eggleston was interested in "folks," and he naturally drifted to the settlements, especially medium-sized settlements such as a county-seat. Here he could find a living cross section of social organization and yet could be close to the rural scene. Under these conditions he wrote with ever-fresh inspiration and with a clear eye for the color and movement of life.

In 1879 Eggleston decided to give up novel-writing—though he did not act on the decision for several years to come. Toward littérateurs in general he had a somewhat scornful attitude,[53] and he began to feel, as the years went by, that his true métier was history. As an historian he produced several creditable works, and he was engaged on an ambitious history of the United States when death overtook him. Yet his change from novelist to historian did not at bottom imply a complete break with his habits as a writer. The distinguishing mark of his historical writing, as of most of his fiction, was its emphasis upon "the life of the people," not upon "a record of events." [54] Social history—it was what Eggleston began with and ended with. To the advantage of the American novel he used it to vivify a series of stories that form a chapter in the development of American regionalism. But he did not have the fatuously partisan spirit of that type of regionalist or local-colorist whose final aim is to celebrate a specific milieu merely because it is *his*. Eggleston, with a larger view, looked upon himself as only one of a number of regional writers who should some day complete the Americanization of the novel:

> The taking up of life in this regional way has made our literature really national by the only process possible. The Federal nation has at length manifested a consciousness of the continental diver-

sity of its forms of life. The "great American novel," for which prophetic citizens yearned so fondly twenty years ago, is appearing in sections.[55]

GEORGE WASHINGTON CABLE (1844-1925)

George Washington Cable was born of Virginian and New England parentage (on his father's and mother's side, respectively) and spent his formative years in Louisiana. In later years he lived at Northampton, Massachusetts, but even the books which he wrote in the North proved that the only region which nurtured his art was the South, and especially the exotic, magical city of New Orleans. Whatever else he produced, Cable's importance as a writer is grounded there.

His personal life was not superficially exciting. He received only informal education, and he learned early the labor and satisfaction of earning a living both for himself and for the family, his father having died in 1859. He turned his hand to various work including that time-honored occupation of American authors—the Customs. During the War he fought on the Confederate side, but the issues involved in the conflict were never simple to him. The disparity between the actual conditions of the Negro and the ideal conditions postulated for all Americans when the entire nation assented to the Constitution, troubled him. Yet at the time of the War he " 'saw no unrighteousness in fighting for slavery,' " [56] and it was considerably later that he arrived at those convictions regarding the iniquity of slavery which were to anger the South.[57] At no time, however, did he become a crusader or propagandist in his fiction, and though he was of a reflective nature his deepest instinct was the artistic. In addition he had strong antiquarian interests which enabled him to turn up data of local history that gave body to his stories of Louisiana. For Cable was no mere facile painter of surfaces but a patient craftsman who turned back fold after fold of fact in order to reach the essence that lay within.

Cable first reached a moderately large public in *Scribner's Monthly*, which printed his " 'Sieur George" in October, 1873. The time then being ripe for regional stories of all sorts, he was importuned to continue his work, but it was not until in 1879, when he collected seven stories in a volume entitled *Old Creole Days* that he was nationally acclaimed as a writer of the first order in his genre. It is obvious that his production in the seventies was not rapid. Indeed it was his creed that a writer should seek to market only his best productions:

"To use a homely parallel, the milkman who sells only cream makes as much money as the one who sells all his milk; the one lets the milk stand till the cream rises and sells the smaller quantity and better quality for the same money. So with literary work: produce the cream and sell that, instead of giving your entire life and strength to larger production and mediocre quality." [58]

The futility of applying critical tags to literary productions is well illustrated by *The Grandissimes* (1880). Denominated at different times as a romance and as a work of realism, the novel is actually such a mélange that it defies classification. A "realistic" basis it undoubtedly had, for at the time of its serial appearance the author was engaged in a statistical survey of social conditions in New Orleans for the Federal government: that he was the man best qualified to make such a study had been clear from his *Old Creole Days*. Cable had a strong historical sense. Yet fact seen from a distance may become "romantic," especially if a mellow atmosphere lies between. Atmosphere—that is what finally characterizes *The Grandissimes*. No clear-eyed journalist, however ingenious, could have written the book. No one seeking a merely exciting story can enjoy it: the book requires to be savored, like the bouquet of a rare vintage.

Certainly the story pattern never came clear. It has its prologue in very old days when "the pilgrim fathers of the Mississippi Delta" [59] were establishing their lands and their families. During an exploring expedition a feud arose, for two men of the party loved the same woman, an Indian queen. A throw of the dice determined who should win her. And the De Grapion who lost conceived a vast hatred for the ancestor of the Grandissimes, who won. A hundred years later (just after Napoleon had sold Louisiana to America) the feud still exists, to be resolved (partly by love) only after many complex involutions. Interracial marriage and extra-legal unions have by now created the tremendously intricate, almost chaotic, pattern of New Orleans society. The De Grapions are now represented by a Creole, Aurore Nancanou, a graceful creature of such natural delicacy and dignity, combined with such an endearing strain of shy playfulness, that she is one of the most charming heroines in any nineteenth-century novel. She is living, with her daughter Clotilde, in genteel poverty in a house owned by one Honoré Grandissime, a freeman of color. Only her pride has brought her so low, for the house originally belonged to her husband. Years before, he had been killed in a duel by Agricola Fusilier (uncle of Honoré Grandissime, her landlord) because having staked all his property on a game of cards and lost, he had called Agricola a cheat. Even so, Aurore could have retained her home if she had been willing to concede that Agricola had won the property fairly. But she refused. And now, eighteen years after, she is still a widow and becoming (she thinks) very, very old—why, she is thirty-five and she has a daughter of eighteen! But somehow she is so lovely and so youthful that people can't always tell which is mother and which is daughter. When her fortunes are at their worst, the Grandissimes restore the property to her, saying that it is rightly hers; and a little later Honoré's white half-brother (also called Honoré!) finally persuades her to marry him.

The feud has been resolved according to an ancient formula but amid scenes that were wholly new. The main story, indeed, is frequently submerged by a wealth of description and episode which is germane to, but poorly connected with, the main action. There is the motif of Bras-Coupé, the Ethiopian King, who for his refusal to submit to slavery had been cruelly tortured and finally killed through the instrumentality of Agricola. His widow Palmyre Philosophe, a quadroon of tiger-like power and grace—"a creature that one would want to find chained"—remains to cherish a hatred against Agricola. She is a dealer in "voudou" charms, and it is to her that Aurore goes to further her success in love. Her agent is a Negress, Clemence, who carries out errands of a grim and harrowing sort until she is caught one night skulking, knife in hand, around Agricola's home. She is cruelly shot. But Agricola himself, choleric aristocrat, goes a step too far one day when he insults Honoré Grandissime, freeman of color. Stabbed in the back, he dies praising the old days in Louisiana and cursing American efforts to establish a new régime. Through him Cable has voiced the most uncompromising arguments of the aristocratic classes in Louisiana. To Agricola, as to many patricians, the caste system was the only possible system to use among the mixture of races and part-breeds that populated Louisiana. He scoffed at the doctrine of equality as a "bottomless iniquity" and regarded efforts to educate the masses as plain "insanity." To him the Americans who endorse and disseminate such doctrine are anathema. He regards the "Yankee government" as a "drivelling failure." But on the other side Cable shows (seldom arguing on either side) the impossibility of harmonizing a social order which imposes so many hardships and disabilities on people who have merited no suffering. Even for a freeman of color like Honoré Grandissime life presents insurmountable obstacles; he later leaves the country and finally drowns himself. Slavery itself receives little direct presentation,[60] but it cannot be ignored. It may be regarded as inevitable by Agricola and as a pleasant institution by Dr. Keene—who repeats the ancient myth that slaves are "the happiest people under the sun"—but to Dr. Frowenfeld, the young German-American apothecary who finally wins Clotilde, the whole caste system is as unwise as it is iniquitous. To Clemence, the

Negress, the institution of slavery is one of complete injustice and manifold cruelty. She grants that some white folks believe with Dr. Keene, for "dey 'bleeged to b'lieb it—fo' dey own cyumfut," but she is an implacable foe of the society of which she finally becomes the victim. Indeed the whole book is full of ominous intimations of the barbaric impulses, only lightly refined, which still live in the breasts of these dealers in voudou warnings and death charms, these African exiles who rend the placid New Orleans night with savage sounds of chant and ritual dance. The resentment and the open reprisal of the Negroes have often been treated in fiction, but few novelists have capitalized so well as Cable the menace of living in permanent discord with a conquered race which might at any time rise again to take vengeance on its oppressors. As for Cable's own opinions, one can see his horror of oppression, but as novelist he refuses to lease his story for purposes of propaganda, and it is significant that (the white) Honoré Grandissime is presented as a person who is able to weigh dispassionately all the issues that are intensified by the purchase of Louisiana.[61]

But finally Cable was interested less in the problem than in place and period. New Orleans was a place which had acquired special and unique characteristics. It was composed of peoples that were desperately irreconcilable and yet inextricably commingled. Dozing in the languorous sunshine of the South, it yet was as uncertain of continued peaceful existence as a city built on a volcanic mountain. It was remote in space, and even more so in culture, from the America which had recently acquired jurisdiction over it. Unable to solve its own internal problems, it was suddenly called upon to make an adjustment with a government whose basic principles threatened to intensify local problems. It was this Louisiana, designed by nature to be a paradise but destined by fate to be the focus of governmental maneuvers, which Cable sought to record. He saw its extremes from the opulence and hauteur of the founding families to the animal menace of the conquered black—with the smouldering ambiguity of the part-breeds in between. He knew the miseries of the "black peasantry" and the shifts of decayed patricians, who must needs sell their jewels and pistols and objets d'art in order "to keep up the bravery of good clothes and pomade that hid slow starvation." [62] But he also saw the charm of the city; its physical blandishments fascinated him; the gay insouciance of its people delighted his eye and warmed his more Northern blood. Skilled as he is in reporting the piercing horror of such episodes as the shooting of Clemence, he is equally at home, and more at peace, when he lets his pen capture the subtle spell of a late afternoon:

The sun is once more setting upon the Place d'Armes. Once more the shadows of cathedral and town-hall lie athwart the pleasant grounds where again the city's fashion and beauty sit about in the sedate Spanish way, or stand or slowly move in and out among the old willows and along the white walks. Children are again playing on the sward; some, you may observe, are in black, for Agricola. You see, too, a more peaceful river, a nearer-seeming and greener opposite shore, and many other evidences of the drowsy summer's unwillingness to leave the embrace of this seductive land; the dreamy quietude of birds; the spreading, folding, re-expanding and slow pulsating of the all-prevailing fan (how like the unfolding of an angel's wing is oft-times the broadening of that little instrument!); the oft-drawn handkerchief; the pale, cool colors of summer costume; the swallow, circling and twittering overhead or darting across the sight; the languid movement of foot and hand; the reeking flanks and foaming bits of horses; the ear-piercing note of the cicada; the dancing butterfly; the dog, dropping upon the grass and looking up to his master with roping jaw and lolling tongue; the air sweetened with the merchandise of the flower *marchandes*.[63]

He could forget social and political friction while he described the old houses and noted the delicious idiom which had been evolved from its mixture of languages. For Cable is particularly happy in the description of houses. Eschewing the use of excessive formal architectural detail, he succeeds in endowing a building with a distinct individuality as well as authenticity.[64] This had been clear from his earliest stories (a good example occurs in the opening paragraphs of " 'Sieur George") and it is emphasized in *The Grandissimes*. The shop of the Apothecary Joseph Frowenfeld becomes a locus of interest (and action) not incomparable in function to the barber shop in George Eliot's *Romola:* each is fully rendered and completely individual. Cable does not aim at brilliance but at intimacy—as in his description of the house where Aurore and Clotilde are living in quiet seclusion:

It is nearly noon of a balmy morning late in February. Aurore Nancanou and her daughter have only this moment ceased sewing, in the small front room of No. 19 rue Bienville. Number 19 is the right-hand half of a single-story, low-roofed tenement, washed with yellow ochre, which it shares generously with whoever leans against it. It sits as fast on the ground as a toad. There is a kitchen belonging to it somewhere among the weeds in the back yard, and besides this room, where the ladies are, there is directly behind it, a sleeping apartment. Somewhere back of this there is a little nook where in pleasant weather they eat. Their cook and housemaid is the plain person who attends them on the street. Her bed-chamber is the kitchen and her bed the floor. The house's only other protector is a hound, the aim of whose life is to get thrust out of the ladies' apartments every fifteen minutes.

Yet if you hastily picture to yourself a forlorn-looking establishment, you will be moving straight away from the fact. Neatness, order, excellence, are prevalent qualities in all the details of the main house's inward garniture. The furniture is old-fashioned, rich, French, imported. The carpets, if not new, are not cheap, either. Bits of crystal and silver, visible here and there, are as bright as they are antiquated; and one or two portraits, and the picture of Our Lady of Many Sorrows, are passably good productions.[65]

As for the language it is of necessity a curious and colorful mixture. Probably no earlier American novel treats of such a "mingling of races: French and Spanish and German and Yankee, Creole and quadroon, Indian aborigines, and Negro slaves who speak a strange jargon of French and English . . ." [66] Aurore Nancanou speaks both French and English, but it is the latter tongue, in which she is a charming novice, that she resorts to when Honoré Grandissime makes his last attempt to win her consent. Though in love with him, she fences artfully, playfully—tremulously. She cannot marry, she says, because she thinks she is going to die: "I 'ave so mudge troub' wit dad hawt." Isn't M. Grandissime offering to marry out of a sense of duty, his uncle having wanted the marriage to take place? Has M. Grandissime said anything about love?

"An' w'en someboddie git'n ti'ed livin' wid 'imsev an' big'n' to fill ole, an' wan' someboddie to teg de care of 'im an' wan' me to gid marri'd wid 'im—I thing 'e's in love to me." Her fingers kept up a little shuffling with the fan. "I thing I'm crezzy. I thing I muz be go'n' to die torecklie." She looked up to the ceiling with large eyes, and then again at the fan in her lap, which continued its spreading and shutting. "An' daz de riz'n, 'Sieur Grandissime." She waited until it was certain he was about to answer, and then interrupted him nervously: "You know 'Sieur Grandissime, id woon be righd! Id woon be de juztiz to *you!* An' you de bez man I evva know in my life, 'Sieur Grandissime!" Her hands shook. "A man w'at nevva wan' to gid marri'd wid noboddie in 'is life, and now trine to gid marri'd juz only to rip-ose de soul of 'is oncl'—"

M. Grandissime uttered an exclamation of protest, and she ceased.

"I asked you," continued he, with low-toned emphasis, "for the single and only reason that I want you for my wife."

"Yez," she quickly replied; "daz all. Daz wad I thing. An' I thing daz de rad weh to say, 'Sieur Grandissime. Bick-ause, you know, you an' me is too hole to talg aboud dad *lovin'*, you know. An' you godd dad grade *rizpeg* fo' me, an' me I godd dad 'ighez rispeg fo' you; bud—" she clutched the fan and her face sank lower still—"bud—" she swallowed—shook her head—"bud—" She bit her lip; she could not go on . . .[67]

When M. Grandissime, realizing his "one mizteg," tells her he loves her, she demands, '*Mais,* fo' w'y you di'n' wan' to sesso?" Even then Aurore makes him wait while she recites her last doubt ("*Mais,* I was thing all dad time id was Clotilde . . .") before she finally capitulates and says "No" (meaning "Yes") as she "burst into tears, laughed through them, and let him clasp her to his bosom." Barrie himself, who greatly admired Cable's art,[68] has seldom drawn a finer illustration of the delicate coquetry of true love.

The Grandissimes is an epitome of Cable's abilities and defects: his clumsy management of plot, his superb restitution in episode and description, the extraordinarily fine word-sense which enabled him to penetrate to the smallest crevices and interstices of his subject, and the sheer charm of his literary manner. It is his best book.[69] He wrote many more novels, however, for his success in fiction, supplemented by his profitable experience as a reader (frequently on the same platform with Mark Twain) persuaded him that he could make his living permanently by literature. By the middle of the 1880's he was a made man in American letters. In England he made his way more slowly, but by 1898 (doubtless partly on account of the interest of Barrie, at whose home Cable gave readings at the time), there was a "regular Cable boom" particularly for *The Grandissimes* and *Dr. Sevier.*[70]

Dr. Sevier (1884) was the second of ten novels which proceeded from Cable's pen between 1880 and 1918. The series as a whole exhibits something like a diminuendo in Cable's art. He never wholly lost his charm of manner but his grip on the larger units of structure, never very firm, became fatally insecure in some of the stories. Leisure in the conduct of his narrative was exchanged for indolence, with resulting tedium to the reader.

Yet from this general indictment, *Dr. Sevier* must be largely excepted. It is probably Cable's best novel after *The Grandissimes.*[71] Plot it hardly has at all, but merely situation. Dr. Sevier, a middle-aged man of very definite views on philanthropy, becomes interested in the plight of a young married couple, John and Mary Richling, who are destitute a large part of the time because the husband cannot find and keep suitable employment. Believing that the hardship she is enduring is too much for Mary (now about to bear a child) Dr. Sevier sends her to Milwaukee, her original home, while John remains and is for a time indifferently successful in business. John is finally stricken with tuberculosis and Mary has much ado to get through the lines (the War having begun) to see him before he dies. At the end it is clear that Dr. Sevier loves Mary (who at first attracted him because of her resemblance to his dead wife), and that Mary has come to love him. They do not marry, but Mary remains in New Orleans to assist Dr. Sevier in his humanitarian work.

Dr. Sevier has no appreciable plot, but it has a definite theme, namely, the folly of "poverty-pride." On his death-bed Richling disclosed to Dr. Sevier (what was obvious to the reader long before) that his name was not Richling and that he was the disinherited son of "one of the proudest, most distinguished families in [Kentucky] or in all the land." [72] His family had been angered by his presuming to marry a Northern girl. Thus thrown upon the world without training, John exhibited what Dr. Sevier called a "criminal helplessness," [73] for he was unable to meet people on their own terms. He was too proud and too independent; even Mary was wise enough to tell him that "if you don't take any part or interest in the outside world it'll take none in you." [74] It is not that he is merely lazy—indeed Dr. Sevier is shocked when John demeans himself by working as a laborer—but that he is blocked by his heritage and temperament. Yet basically the fault could not be imputed to John: "There had been a crime committed somewhere in his bringing up, and as a result he stood in the thick of life's battle, weaponless," and John himself comes to realize that he is "the typical American gentleman,—completely unfitted for prosperity and totally unequipped for adversity." [75] Finally arrested for vagrancy and assaulting an officer, he is thrown into prison. Dr. Sevier, who had never been able to understand fully John's psychological blockage, realizes full well the horrors of a prison. Cable's own participation in prison reform in New Orleans is obviously responsible for the (somewhat Dickensian) prison scenes which are described and for the denunciation of the prison as "this resting and refreshing place for vice, this caucus for the projection of future crime, this ghastly burlesque of justice and the protection of society." [76] As for philanthropy in general, Dr. Sevier takes the sane view that charity should not confine itself to patching up trouble but should seek out the causes behind disaster. He recommends sensible remedies: "Do as a good doctor would. Help nature." [77]

The novel as a whole is untidy, but it contains vast stores of social commentary—on life and letters, politics, and commerce—which, were it not for its very excess, would make the book interesting. Cable had a mature and subtle mind, and even this defective book is far superior to the run-of-the-mill novels of the eighties. The characters, too, are sympathetically drawn. The relationship between the devoted, helpless young couple and Dr. Sevier is, in the beginning at least, very much like that which Barrie later established in *The Little White Bird*. Cable is more prone to let the winds of realism blow through his idyllic passages, but he has a fineness and a tenderness that easily account for Barrie's admiration of his work. His sentimentality, like Barrie's, is rescued just in time by humorous interpolation. Humor indeed is an easily available commodity in this book, what with the quaint garrulousness and eccentric conduct of Dr. Sevier's assistant, Narcisse, whose shrewd antics place him, as to literary derivation, somewhere between Sam Weller and Autolycus.[78]

In *Bonaventure, A Prose Pastoral of Acadian Louisiana* (1887), Cable puts together three stories that may be loosely described as a novel. Their hero, Bonaventure, is a teacher who dedicates his life to service among the Acadians settled in Louisiana. Lovers' misunderstandings are the main pivots of the action, but before he is through Cable has managed to touch upon many aspects of provincial life. The book is as authentic in local color as it is casual in its plot. Violence sometimes appears—including the melodramatic death of a minor character—but for the most part the book is presented in a simple fashion that tends to conceal the skill inherent in it. A Daudet-like charm and sensitivity pervade Cable's writing in *Bonaventure*.

John March, Southerner (1894) is a story of intrigue—political, personal, and financial—in a war-torn Southern town during the era of Reconstruction. More originality may be seen, if one is patient, in *The Cavalier* (1901). Cable, like Miss Murfree, tried to profit by the swing of public interest toward historical romance in the late nineties. He succeeded only moderately well from the point of view of public and critical approval, but he brought to his task far greater qualifications than Miss Murfree. Critics who had doubted Cable's Southern loyalties must have been reassured by this story, for it is distinctly pro-Southern in sympathy. At the same time Cable makes his principal Yankee character a true gentleman, and he achieves a very moving scene when on his deathbed Captain Jewett requests the heroine (a Southerner) to sing the Star Spangled Banner—a request which, with some reluctance, she grants. A love story runs through the book of course—in this case a love story complicated by the fact that the woman is a spy and is a married woman—but the book as a whole is a maze of incident, intrigue, horror, and sentiment that resists easy assimilation. Yet the War is suggested in a comprehensive, if not always comprehensible, fashion—

> those whole years of disaster and chaos; the daily shock of their news, crashing in upon the brain like a shell into a roof; wail and huzza, camp-fire, litter and grave; battlefield stench; fiddle and flame; and ever in the midst these impromptu merrymakings to keep us from going stark mad, one and all,—as so many literally did.[79]

What makes the book difficult is not only its excess of episode and lack of order, but its impressionistic method of presentation, its faithful transcription of fragmentary dialogue (and dialect), and the blurring of external action by the author's almost Jamesian proclivity for ellipsis and intimation, his expectation that the reader's inference will supply the fact he neglects to state. Its highly sophisticated literary manner and solid materials mark it as the work of a writer considerably above the average in an era when jerry-built romances sprang up by the score; and its story content could easily have pleased the populace had the author been able to order his materials in such a fashion as to put less of a strain on the reader seeking continuity. A second historical romance undertaken by Cable, *Kincaid's Battery* (1908), is less successful in every respect but is complementary to *The Cavalier* in treating of naval operations, which include Farragut's attack on the rebel fort in Mobile Bay.

Bylow Hill (1902) was the sole novel of Cable laid in New England. It differs from his other stories, too, in possessing a neatly formed and thoroughly stabilized structure. Its theme of jealousy is worked out in a series of episodes involving violence and tragedy in a small circle of characters of whom the central actor is a minister. In its materials it recalls Hawthorne, and in its bare recital of stark tragedy it looks forward to *Ethan Frome*. Unusually compact and clear for Cable, the story also posesses a certain weight, having been based on a parallel case which actually occurred and which was passed on to Cable as story material by Dr. S. Weir Mitchell. Yet, perhaps because its inspiration came from without rather than within, it lacks the overtones that characterize Cable's most effective work.

Three more novels—*Gideon's Band* (1914), *The Flower of the Chapdelaines* (1918), and *Lovers of Louisiana* (1918)—completed Cable's work as a novelist. By 1918 he had long since ceased to grow as a writer. A partial explanation of his failure to maintain or add to his stature as a writer of fiction may be the increasing attention he gave to social reform. Though not a farseeing student of the socio-economic system as a whole, Cable had a strong sense of social responsibility and he labored to support and even to initiate such movements as promised improvement in education, the status of the Negro, prison conditions, and allied subjects.[80] In later years he devoted much time and not a little publication to his deep-loved hobby of gardening. He also directed a good deal of energy into such community enterprises as "home-culture" clubs and Bible-reading classes. The devout religious spirit which had been developed in him during his early days remained to the end. He took an active part in the affairs of various churches. He was almost fanatically concerned to observe the Sabbath properly, and it was not until 1901 (when his own *Cavalier* was dramatized) that he set foot inside a theatre. Yet he was not one to examine morbidly the grounds of his religious beliefs, and he lived comfortably within the arms of Presbyterian and Congregational churches even when in his own mind he had shuffled off the stricter tenets of their theology. Finally he believed that "the effort of the wise teacher . . . will be ever toward the completer simplification of God's truth." [81] On the whole he tried to maintain an optimistic attitude toward life, and he more than once iterated his belief "in beauty and in joy." The effort to persist in such an attitude constituted the religious quest, but he knew that it was difficult, and he realized that "life is a constant beginning over again." He saw the sombreness of life and he knew the shadows that confused the direction of human effort: only faith can lead us as "We stumble upstairs." [82]

Little enough of Cable's moral earnestness receives overt expression in his fiction. He was too much the artist to relinquish story for sermon. Yet he believed that literature should have an ethical bearing:

> "The wise story-teller, though not bound to *tell* the whole truth and nothing but the truth, is bound to reverence it above all things; substituting in place of the actual the harmoniously supposable; yet only in so far as the actual is less effective for his ends— the ministry of right emotions . . . It makes nigh all the difference between life and death whether we have or have not the power and sanity of imagination daily to turn the dull intervals and ugly and commonplace things of life end on to the heart's vision and take broadside those that are strong for discipline or fine for delight." [83]

The connection between right living and good literature was observed easily and naturally by Cable; the reader never feels that the artist in him is inhibited by conscience. Perhaps Cable was diverted from art to some extent by his social interests, but for the falling off which his writing exhibits the final explanation must lie in the nature of his endowment as a writer. In one word he suffered from the fatal flaw of incoherence. From the time when he published his first story, " 'Sieur George," to the futile efforts of his old age, he constantly proved himself incapable of holding his grip on a long narrative. It may be that he would have done better to have emulated Irving and confined his efforts to the shorter tale. Certainly his *Old Creole Days* is his most nearly perfect volume. Yet the gifts which are concentrated in that volume are scattered so richly through *The Grandissimes* and through even some of his less successful novels that he takes rank as one of the best fiction writers of his day. He had the supreme gift of being able to penetrate a subject—not merely expound it or analyze it or make a report on it. He did not attempt to recreate old New Orleans by forcing facts upon the reader; rather he attempted to liberate the atmosphere which should gradually reveal an earlier civilization. He prevailed by wooing his subject instead of belaboring it. He developed a prose style which was masterful in phrase and cadence but soft in its impact. Its secret was not energy but suasion. The mark of his mastery is his effortlessness. He does not seek to grip the reader by intensity but to win him by a species of venial guile. His gentleness occasionally develops into something very like sentimentality but it is presently turned off into quiet jest or whimsicality. His humor, too, is of the sort which lives in harmony with the narrative it is intended to support instead of insisting on a separate maintenance. In short, Cable was a mature and mellowed artist in a day when the youthfulness of our nation was expressed most frequently with far greater show of vitality. The pattern of his art did not always please the popular fancy. The tendril-like spread of his imagination confused readers who were accustomed to stories more obviously derived from a single stalk of action. Yet for readers less insistent upon rigid organization there is a permanent charm in observing the sensitive processes and natural luxuriance which characterized Cable's writing. Ordinarily grouped with the local color novelists by reason of his priority in treating fully the face and fashion of old New Orleans—from levee to mansion, from quadroon to magistrate—Cable excelled most of his colleagues in the genre. By subtle mixture of his materials he achieved a range of hue and a variation of tone quite beyond the powers of most of his confrères, who in many cases were content with the quick application of primary colors.

CONSTANCE FENIMORE WOOLSON (1840-1894)

An author able to elicit the high praise of so austere a critic as Henry James may be assumed to have mastered important elements in the technique of writing.[84] Praise from such a quarter would indeed for some people be presumptive evidence that the writer was more skilled than readable. Yet Constance Fenimore Woolson was not only an able craftsman but also in the 1880's and 1890's a popular writer, especially with that relatively superior audience comprised in part of readers of magazines such as *Harper's,* in which many of her stories first appeared. Her popularity of course has long since waned, and she is now in the familiar category of the superior minor writer who is periodically "rediscovered" by a sensitive critic or a zealous historian. No number of such discoveries, of course, can make her over into a major novelist. At best her art was extremely sensitive and delicate. True, she undoubtedly won many readers by the sensational, even melodramatic, materials which she sometimes ineptly introduced into her work. Yet vigorous action was not her forte: it is vain to look in her work for any suggestion of the broad powers of her illustrious kinsman (her mother was a niece of James Fenimore Cooper). The structure of a long narrative she never mastered. It is her distinction, rather, that she skilfully employed some aspects of that type of impressionistic technique which was one of the principal interests of the more serious post-Victorian novelists. She also added to the domain of the local-color writers who were prominent in the seventies and eighties.

Miss Woolson was born in New Hampshire, educated in Ohio, "finished" at a school in New York City, lived for several years in the South (Florida and the Carolinas), and traveled extensively in Europe.[85] She practiced writing at an early age, producing rapidly a considerable number of tales and sketches, the more successful of which are set in the Great Lakes country, where she spent her childhood. Her first volume of short stories, *Castle Nowhere; Lake Country Sketches* (1875), reprinted a number of pieces that had won favorable comment upon their first appearance in *Harper's, Lippincott's, The Galaxy,* and elsewhere. Her first novel, *Anne,* was published in 1882, and her last, *Horace Chase,* in 1894, the year of her death.

Anne is a long book, presumably autobiographical in the first part and certainly set in a region which the author well knew. Its action, surprisingly enough, is often sentimental, morbid, and melodramatic. The heroine is Anne Douglas, at sixteen a very large girl regarded as a conscientious but somewhat colorless person. Unlike her immediate predecessors in popular fiction, she is not superficially alluring: "This unwritten face, with its direct gaze, so far neutralized the effect of the Diana-like form that the girl missed beauty on both sides." [86] The devoted daughter of a cultivated and amiable but eccentric old gentleman no longer gainfully employed, she does her best to stabilize his shaky personality and to bring up the four somewhat difficult children of his second marriage. Comforts are few and life is slow for Anne Douglas on the remote island (Mackinac) which is her home. Romance crosses her path in the person of a village lad named Rast, who asks her hand in marriage. But Rast must go off to college and, her father dying suddenly, Anne feels that she must accept the offer of a relative in New York who wishes to give her a year of tony schooling to the end that she may later become a teacher. New York itself proves to be a school of experience of more consequence to the story than the fussy little establishment of Mme Moreau, and Anne is involved with two men, one of them a millionaire who wishes to marry her. The other (Heathcote), to whom Anne is more drawn, is prevented from offering marriage by reason of a commitment to one of Anne's friends, Helen Lorrington. Anne, like a good domestic heroine, runs away. But Heathcote later comes back into her life: he has married Helen but loves Anne! Though now freed from her somewhat tepid engagement to Rast—whose heart has been successfully stormed by one of Anne's step-sisters, the bewitching, ruthless little quarter-breed Tita—Anne resists the entreaties of Heathcote. Ultimately the story broadens into melodrama: Helen is found murdered and it devolves upon Anne to do enough amateur detective work to prove that Heathcote did not perpetrate the deed: the real murderer was left-handed! And Anne gets Heathcote—or vice versa. The story is much too diffuse. It is best in the first part—in the charming description of Anne's circumscribed life on the island. Her queer old father is a more satisfactory character than Heathcote. The portrait of the housekeeper, Lois Hinsdale, is fine: a New England spinster whose severity in the kitchen is balanced by her High Church religious preference. Unconsciously in love with Douglas, she has bitterly resented his (second) marriage to a giddy female of French and Indian blood and of Catholic faith; but she does not weary of caring for his children, and she helps to bind together a story that often threatens to break completely into fragments.

Yet some of the fragments are precious. The opening of the story provides an excellent illustration of Miss Woolson's meticulous impressionistic method. Eschewing the traditional (Victorian) type of beginning—in which the author plainly states what he regards as essential facts for the reader: where the scene is, what sorts of persons are in it, what the time is, what the activity of the moment is, etc.—Miss Woolson, like James, begins at once to communicate an experience *in the present*. She does not wish to tell or relate an action but to present it; not to "introduce" a story but to begin it. Necessary facts will be found as experience is unfolded. Characters are not summarized but will grow out of detailed impressions.[87] The quality of the whole book will be felt from the very beginning: indeed Miss Woolson at her best concretely illustrates James's opinion that

> A novel is a living thing, all one and continuous, like any other organism, and in proportion as it lives will it be found, I think, that in each of the parts there is something of each of the other parts.[88]

Thus Miss Woolson does not begin with a statement of the "inorganic" facts (1) that it was Christmas Eve on Mackinac Island; (2) that a father was conversing affectionately with his daughter while she was decorating a provincial church; (3) that they have different opinions about a valued housekeeper named Lois, etc. etc. Instead, she opens a dialogue which begins to reveal the characters not only of the speakers but of the third person as well. It will be seen that the quality of these paragraphs is precisely that of all other valid parts of the book:

> "Does it look well, father?"
> "What, child?"
> "Does this look well?"
> William Douglas stopped playing for a moment, and turned his head toward the speaker, who, standing on a ladder, bent herself to one side, in order that he might see the wreath of evergreen, studded with cones, which she had hung on the wall over one of the small arched windows.
> "It is too compact, Anne, too heavy. There should be sprays falling from it here and there, like a real vine. The greenery, dear, should be either growing naturally upward or twining; large branches standing in the corners like trees, or climbing vines. Stars, stiff circles, and set shapes should be avoided. That wreath looks as though it had been planed by a carpenter."
> "Miss Lois made it."
> "Ah," said William Douglas, something which made you think of a smile, although no smile was there, passing over his face, "it looks like her work; it will last a long time. And there will be no need to remove it for Ash-Wednesday, Anne; there is nothing joyous about it."
> "I did not notice that it was ugly," said the girl, trying in her bent posture to look at the wreath, and bringing one eye and a portion of anxious forehead to bear upon it.

"That is because Miss Lois made it," replied William Douglas, returning to his music.[89]

It would be hard to find in fiction of the time an example of more skilful indirect characterization than is here presented. True, the reader must wait for the gradual absorption of these details into the whole body of the work to understand their full relationship to structure. True, also, Miss Woolson falls away, as *Anne* proceeds, from the high technical standard here exemplified, but the same method reappears, more evenly sustained, in her next long narrative, *For the Major* (1883).

For the Major (called by the author a "novelette") is more successful as a whole than *Anne* perhaps because its action is simpler and, except for a few exciting episodes, more suited to her special talent for finely discriminating effects. The situation fundamentally involves two venial deceptions that undoubtedly appealed to Henry James. The first is revealed shortly after Sara Carroll returns from Connecticut to Far Edgerley, a small secluded community presumably set in the mountains of North Carolina. She at first feels queerly frustrated in her attempt to resume the filial relationship with her father which had always been such a joy to her. Jealously she blames Madam Carroll, Major Carroll's second wife. When, however, the latter finally explains that the Major's mind is beginning to fail, Sara promptly co-operates with her in devising every protection for him. This involves coping with an unforeseen crisis that calls for a second deception. The appearance in Far Edgerley of a poverty-stricken, impudently vagabondish musician called Louis Dupont arouses the resentment of Far Edgerley, but Sara's step-mother astonishingly takes him up. Even more incredible to Mr. Owen, the Episcopal clergyman in love with Sara, is the fact that Sara has several clandestine meetings with the gay but sinister Bohemian. As if to end all gossip, Sara stuns the community by announcing her engagement to Dupont. Actually she has no intention of marrying him: he is the son of her step-mother! She has been conspiring with her step-mother to take care of him without revealing to the Major (or to the gossipy village) the true facts concerning Madam Carroll's first marriage. Her husband had been a rotter who had finally killed a man in a duel and fled from the law, taking their boy with him. Both were reported drowned. Left with a ten-year-old girl to support, the mother passed herself off as twenty-three (though she was thirty-five) when the Major courted her, her excuse being that she couldn't bear to destroy the pleasure the Major took in her "youth" and that she needed protection for her daughter who, however, soon died. The stratagem thus begun has to be carried out through the ensuing years by means of dye, rouge, and kindred arts. When the son turned up, the critical condition of the Major forbade an explanation. The son presently dies, but on his deathbed reports that the father had also escaped death by drowning, and was living at the time of his mother's marriage to the Major. This intelligence necessitates a formal marriage with the Major. But the Major happily wakes up one morning with his mind almost completely gone, and it is easy to arrange a ceremony in which he takes part pleasantly with no knowledge of what it signifies. Madam Carroll has had to take Mr. Owen the clergyman into her confidence, of course, but that is now an easy matter, for he will soon himself belong to the family—as the husband of Sara.

Obviously *For the Major* contains plot material which would forbid the author's throwing stones at the artificial structures of the domestic novelists. Yet in this book as in others, it is not finally the exciting plot materials that the author is concerned with, but the motives of the characters.[90] The difference between Miss Woolson and the domestic sisterhood lies in her comparatively condensed treatment of crude plot material and her artful elaboration of ethical problems created in the minds first of Madam Carroll and then of Sara. The impressionistic characterizations of the step-mother pleased Henry James:

> The conception of Madam Carroll is highly ingenious and original, and the small stippled portrait has a real fascination . . . Miss Woolson has done nothing of a neater execution than this fanciful figure of the little ringleted, white-frocked, falsely juvenile lady, who has the toilet-table of an actress and the conscience of a Puritan.[91]

Sara Carroll is almost equally well characterized, though allowed less space. Despite temperamental differences between her and the Major's wife, she willingly shares in the bizarre fiction on which the Major's tenuous happiness rests. Even when her rôle calls for action that seriously damages her in the eyes of her lover, she does not flinch. The key to her character as to that of so many characters in the novels of Henry James is high-minded renunciation.

But quite as fascinating to watch as the raveling of the fantastic fabrication of Madam Carroll is the revelation of the nature of the community in which the story takes place. Far Edgerley, as James has implied, may be a bit too steeped in Anglicanism and provided with more suggested past than a town in the New World can actually be possessed of:

. . . Miss Woolson likes little country churches that are dedicated to saints not vulgarised by too much notoriety, that are dressed with greenery (and would be with holly if there were any), at Christmas and Easter; that have "rectors," well connected, who are properly garmented, and organists, slightly deformed if possible, and addicted to playing Gregorian chants in the twilight, who are adequately artistic; likes also generations that have a pleasant consciousness of a few warm generations behind them, screening them in from too bleak a past, from vulgar draughts in the rear.[92]

Far Edgerley is brought to life perfectly with brush-strokes that are as faultless as they are gentle. Cranford is not more authentic. Much can be done by patience in a quiet community where the church is the centre of social life and where manners are so conservative that "There were persons in the congregation who considered whist-playing a test of the best churchmanship." [93] Genteel though these mountain folk be, they are so avid of personalia that the rector's every move coins local comment. Without effort Miss Woolson adjusts her tempo to miniature incident which, as in the following example, she often reports with genuine humor:

Far Edgerley was deprived of its rector. Mr. Owen had gone to the coast to attend the Diocesan Convention. But as he had started more than a week before the time of its opening, and had remained a week after its sessions were ended, Mrs. General Hibbard was of the opinion that he was attending to other things as well. She had, indeed, heard a rumor before he came that there was *some one* (some one in whom he felt an interest) elsewhere. Now it is well known that there is nothing more depressing for a parish than a rector with an interest, large or small, "elsewhere." St. John in the Wilderness was therefore much relieved when its rector returned, with no signs of having left any portion of himself or his interest behind him. And Mrs. General Hibbard lost ground.[94]

The subsequent novels of Miss Woolson do not vary greatly in quality from her first two. Her principal theme continued to be magnanimity expressed in one form or another. In *East Angels* (1886) the main character is a dauntless, an almost incredible, illustration of self-sacrifice. Margaret, the wife of Lansing Harold, has every reason in the conduct of her husband to break with him and marry the affluent and cultivated Evert Winthrop. Instead she willingly shoulders the blame for her unharmonious marriage, resists the agreeable approaches of Winthrop, and when her husband finally returns as an invalid, devotes herself to nursing him. Isabel Archer in James's *The Portrait of a Lady* (1881) is not more heroic, though she is perhaps more real. But the unhappy marriage of the Harolds is only part of the excellent social study of St. Augustine which comprises *East Angels*. The novel also reports the affairs of a giddy group of pleasure-seekers of whom the most conspicuous, Garda Thorne, is a vivacious beauty who manages to get married twice. Her wanton conduct and obvious glamour make her a foil for the resolute Margaret. The book is comprehensive in its dramatis personae, being provided also with (principal) characters from the North, as well as full-blooded Spaniards, and the quarter-Spanish Garda. The characters, though individually well done, have a certain detached or "shipwrecked air" [95] but the Floridan mise-en-scène is firmly established in all its opulence and fascination. Yet by a very fine contrast which is perhaps referable to Miss Woolson's own origin in New England, the author draws one of her most successful characters in the exiled New Englander, Mrs. Thorne, who wholeheartedly hates the entire (Florida) section. Before her death she pours out all her long repressed love of her native region in a finely conceived speech which serves to emphasize the disparities that existed in "American" character in the 1870's. Mrs. Thorne, said James, is the "tragic form of the type of which Mrs. Stowe's Miss Ophelia was the comic." [95a] Against these and other characters Margaret Harold is seen, the utmost symbol of renunciation in personal relationships. *East Angels* is perhaps the fullest, the roundest, the most significant of Miss Woolson's novels.

With what fine integrity Miss Woolson observed her own principles as a writer was amusingly illustrated in a letter written in response to one from a young person who, like a majority of popular readers, would have preferred a happy ending in *East Angels*—a consummation that could easily have been arranged if the author had been willing to decree the death of Lansing Harold. Miss Woolson replies:

> My dear Miss Ethel.
> Your letter made me laugh,—it was so frank! It would indeed have been more agreeable for everyone, if Lansing Harold could have been (as you express it) "taken." But, in real life, such fortunate takings-off seldom occur, & it is real life I was endeavoring to picture. It is seldom indeed that I ask anyone to write to me, as I find it almost impossible to answer the letters I receive. But you are so honest that I propose that, after my next novel, you send a few lines more; what do you say? About "the happy ending" you ask for, we will see! [96]

As it happens Miss Woolson's next novel, *Jupiter Lights* (1889), is equipped with a "happy ending" but only after a great quantity of trouble has been seen. The novel is interesting as a local color story "with scenes from each of the three regions with which Miss Woolson is associated: the South, the lake country, and Italy." Miss Woolson is particularly successful in her delineation of the South during Reconstruction.[97] Yet the chief power of *Jupiter Lights* derives from the concentrated study of troubled personal relations, being in this case a study of a woman who interfered disastrously in the affairs of another. A whole train of difficulty is set in motion when Eve Bruce undertakes to meddle in the affairs of Cicely Morrison, formerly the widow of Eve's dead brother, now the wife of a dipsomaniac in a small rundown town on an island off the coast of Georgia during the period of Reconstruction. Results include a shooting, a flight to the Lake Superior region, the death of the degraded husband, a love affair for Eve, her retirement to a convent in Italy, and—the happy ending—her lover's arrival at the convent, where he "batters his way to her and takes her in his arms."[98] Hemingway could have handled this strong plot in its externals much more plausibly than Miss Woolson: he might even have strengthened it by tossing in a few more shootings, stronger drinks, and more general violence. But he would have been puzzled by the ethical problems of Eve who is so troubled about a point of honor (her part in the episode that resulted in Morrison's death) that, like James's high-minded Strether, she wants to have gained nothing for herself "out of the whole affair."[99] "Can have and will not"—that would be Hemingwayese for the attitude of many of the characters in Woolson. And it is precisely in the mental struggles of persons involved in such cases of casuistry that Miss Woolson, like James, succeeds most notably. In *Jupiter Lights*, however, the problem is largely lost in the frequently improbable action, and the book remains her least valuable novel. Miss Woolson can render setting and she can characterize quiet, well-bred people, but high tensions are likely to induce erratic fluctuations in the delicate instruments of her art.

Horace Chase (1894) marks a return to the narrower scope of action in which Miss Woolson moved with greatest freedom and sureness. Fundamentally it suffers from being too studied, too conscientious. It is unique among her novels in having for its centre of interest a man instead of a woman—in this case a successful businessman of considerable intelligence but of no great refinement. In type he is not far removed from James's Christopher Newman. His language is robust and colloquial. He is frankly interested in making money for the satisfaction of his ego: "For a big pile is something more than a pile; it's a proof that a man's got brains." [100] The time comes when he must prove whether he has fineness of character as well as practical intelligence. His wife becomes infatuated with another man to the point of following him to the house of a friend—only to learn (what except for her blindness she should have known before) that he is interested not in her but in another girl, whom he is about to marry. No simple return to her own hearth is possible, for her husband untimely arrives at the house. A way out of making the embarrassing disclosure of her folly is devised by her sister, but doggedly the wife prefers to face the music, expecting to be sent away by an outraged husband. Instead, Horace Chase magnanimously but quietly indicates that he wishes her to stay: "Have I been so faultless myself that I have any right to judge *you?*" [101] This is a typical situation with Woolson: a character proves his fineness by making a difficult decision when, so far as external pressure is concerned, he is a perfectly free agent. In this case the gesture is one of forbearance rather than of renunciation. To make the scene a mess of sentimentality based upon incredible self-sacrifice would have been easy, but the author prefers to handle the situations with the quiet restraint befitting a realist. The story, she revealed in a letter to the publishers, was based on an instance "from actual life." [102] Her aim in the settings (Asheville, North Carolina, and St. Augustine) is to be utterly faithful to fact. The whole is a good miniature, possessed of much, perhaps too much, well-wrought detail. Yet that subtle process of artistic enlargement by which a work passes out of the specific into the universal is lacking in this book, as well as in most of Miss Woolson's work.

In Miss Woolson's novels the narrative situation is the thing. She carried no banners, religious, political, or sociological. Digressions seldom occur and such social criticism as she indulges in takes a subordinate place on her page. Yet her writing is informed with a realistic spirit that is gradually felt to be characteristic of her nature. Her childhood nickname "And why?" suggests in exaggerated form her critical proclivities. Thus she sees the beauty of the country but she realizes how a rural life limits the opportunities of the individual and intensifies the provincialism of the group, especially on the frontier. When in a minor matter Mlle Pitre fails to conform to village expectations, there is doubt about her integrity:

> Simple comment swelled into suspicion; the penny-saving old maid was now considered a dark and mysterious person at Lancaster. Opinions varied as to whether she had committed a crime

in her youth, or intended to commit one in her age. At any rate, she was not like other people—in the country a heinous crime.[103]

The border Indians of the Great Lakes region were not only part of her story in *Anne* but also a sociological problem. Without sentiment or romance Miss Woolson candidly reports the difficulty experienced by white folk who attempted to civilize them:

> Years before, missionaries had been sent from New England to work among the Indians of this neighborhood, who had obtained their ideas of Christianity, up to that time, solely from the Roman Catholic priests, who had succeeded each other in an unbroken line from that adventurous Jesuit, the first explorer of these in-land seas, Father Marquette. The Presbyterians came, established their mission, built a meeting-house, a school-house, and a house for their pastor, the buildings being as solid as their belief. Money was collected for this enterprise from all over New England, that old-time, devout, self-sacrificing community whose sternness and faith were equal; tall spare men came westward to teach the Indians, earnest women with bright steadfast eyes and lath-like forms were their aiders, wives, and companions . . . The missionaries worked faithfully; but, as the Indians soon moved further westward, the results of their efforts can not be statistically estimated now, or the accounts balanced.
>
> "The only good Indian is a dead Indian," is a remark that crystallizes the floating opinion of the border. But a border population has not a missionary spirit. New England, having long ago chased out, shot down, and exterminated all her own Indians, had become peaceful and pious, and did not agree with these Western carriers of shot-guns. Still, when there were no more Indians to come to this island school, it was of necessity closed, no matter which side was right.[104]

Occasionally she pauses to correct false notions implanted in the popular mind by more sensational writers. When, for example, Anne takes her place in a fashionable school in New York, her fine character does not make her either hated or sanctified. An intermediate reaction on the part of Anne's mates seems more natural to Miss Woolson:

> It was soon understood that "the islander" could sing as well as study. Tolerance was therefore accorded to her. But not much more. It is only in "books for the young" that poorly clad girls are found leading whole schools by the mere power of intellectual or moral supremacy. The emotional type of boarding-school, also,

is seldom seen in cities; its home is amid the dead lethargy of a winter-bound country village.[105]

Similarly, the common conception of a nurse's romantic rôle during the Civil War is revised when a novice reaches the front:

> But during that day, not only did the promised nurse from the Rivertown Aid Society arrive, but with her a volunteer assistant, a young girl, her face flushed with exaltation and excitement over the opportunity afforded her to help and comfort "our poor dear wounded heroes." The wounded heroes were not poetical in appearance; they were simply a row of ordinary sick men, bandaged in various ways, often irritable, sometimes profane; their grammar was defective, and they cared more for tobacco than for texts, or even poetical quotations.[106]

A fine restraint, then, distinguishes the realistic Miss Woolson from those scores of novelists who have erred on the opposite side of prolonged naturalistic descriptions of the horrors of war. Yet she does not lean over backward in this respect; and her sense of balance is shown by the fact that the same novice who found "her romance rudely dispelled" rose adequately to her situation; and since "there was good stuff in her, she would do useful work yet, although shorn of many illusions." [107] This is typical of the author in her better works: she prefers decent proportion to cheap intensity.

On the positive side (for Miss Woolson was not one to spend much time or effort upon correcting others) there was her original and vivid treatment of comparatively new regions; her pioneer studies of the difference between "the Anglo-Saxon and the Latin temperaments" in the South;[108] her faithful recording of Negro speech,[109] and her use of natural if unusually sensitive girls as heroines in place of the pasteboard saints of the popular novelists.[110] It was finally these heroines who inspired most of what was distinguished in the work of Constance Fenimore Woolson. She described their persons with a critical eye, understood the crises of their "private relations" with fine intuition, recorded their self-immolations with a quiet intensity that often lends exaltation to her page. Dynamic action jeopardized her art; larger structural units never quite found their equilibrium. But in the nooks and recesses of human experience she was wholly masterful. In *Anne* there is a church "whose steeple threw a slow-moving shadow across its garden, like a great sundial, all day." In some such sequestered place, where action is natural but unhurried, where light and shadow fulfill each other, belongs the special art of Miss Woolson.

THOMAS BAILEY ALDRICH (1836-1907)

Aldrich is the type of Indian Summer writer—warm, mellow, cherishing his security amid scenes of quiet festivity. In him sentiment and wit bring each other to a happy equilibrium. His is in part a secondary harvest of fruit from trees planted by other hands—especially Longfellow, Holmes, and Hawthorne. You are not confident that he has enough to tide you over a heavy winter, but you are content, for a time, to bask in the gentle warmth of his autumnal glow. His easy, afternoon inspiration is the trait of a writer more naturally given to summary and appraisal than to tasks calling for productive energy. Occasional verse and the personal essay were perhaps the ideal outlets for a writer of his temperament, but fictional forms (not too sternly defined) also attracted him. The novels he wrote exhibit structural flaws, but the seasoned timber that went into their making is still a delight to fanciers of New England life and letters. The interlude in American art which he represents was an interesting one, and Aldrich was articulate enough to express it in the amiable intimate terms of one who fully "belonged." He also gave voice to a few new ideas that more robust writers would soon utter with greater freedom and emphasis. But chiefly he was a charming chronicler of a season which, however brief and however unproductive, has as much right to be celebrated as any other time of the year—Indian Summer.

Aldrich the man exists in the popular mind (if at all) as a Boston Brahmin. This is pretty much as it should be, for he gave forth the special lustre that is associated with that place and type. Yet, as he himself pointed out, he was not "genuine Boston" but "Boston-plated." [111] He was born at Portsmouth, New Hampshire, and he lived there, first and last, for a good many years. When he was five, the family moved to New York, where they stayed for five years before the father's business took him to New Orleans. The three years at New Orleans (1846-1849) came perhaps a little too early in Aldrich's life (he was ten in 1846) to create strong and permanent impressions on the boy, but they did occasionally provide him with "copy" in years to come. Returned to New England, Aldrich was marked for Harvard College, but upon the death of his father he entered business instead. He also entered literature—as poet and journalist. His first book of poems appeared in 1855, and during the next twenty years or so he held a great variety of journalistic posts, including that of reporter for the New York *Tribune* during the Civil War. He became a regular resident of Boston in 1865. When Howells gave up the editorship of *The Atlantic Monthly* in 1881, the position was passed to Aldrich, who kept it until 1891. He wrote prolifically until his death in 1907. Once well started, he had been prevailingly "successful" as a writer, and he was widely honored in his later years.

Aldrich's novels may not be technically good novels, but they are good books. The reason for this is that he did not allow the laws of fiction to hamper him: he just wrote as he pleased. At least he was natural. His first long narrative, *The Story of a Bad Boy* (1872), is a bad novel if one insists on a well-regulated plot as an essential of the genre. But it is a pretty good novel if one thinks of a novel as a vivid narrative of credible people in an authentic setting. It is even an important novel if one attaches importance to a story which was among the first to carry a realistic treatment of an American boy. Such conventional plot material as the book possesses centres in the fact that Sailor Ben Watson finally turns out to be the long-lost husband of Kitty Collins, a domestic in Grandfather Nutter's household. Clearly Aldrich was not original at all points. But the Rivermouth setting is real (it is Portsmouth, New Hampshire, hardly touched by invention), and many of the characters are as real as their prototypes among Aldrich's own acquaintance. Chief among these is Grandfather Nutter, one of the earlier of our "last Puritans." The boys and girls have a slightly made-up quality about them, but their derivation is honest: they are Portsmouth people. The "shaggy yellow dog, who looked as if he had begun to unravel" also sounds real. Some of the episodes which serve in lieu of a developed plot are likewise taken out of Aldrich's own experience: the snow-fight, the amateur dramatics, the calf-love-affair, the death of Binney Wallace, the Fourth of July maneuvers. Compared to the carryings-on of some of the derelict boys washed up by recent waves of realism in American fiction, Aldrich's Tom Bailey seems a little pale to operate under such a lurid sobriquet as "bad boy." Actually, Aldrich hastens on the first page to assure the reader that Tom was "not such a very bad, but a pretty bad boy." The point is that he *was* bad compared with the sanctimonious young moral robots who had passed for boys in most earlier American fiction. For what may seem like tameness to a generation familiar with the conduct of Dead End Kids was probably a reality in Tom Bailey—for Aldrich himself was brought up under benevolent and conservative auspices in a fairly sheltered environment.

The Story of a Bad Boy is full of bright description and amusing episode, and it is mainly a boy's book excepting for its collateral comment on the sober New England life of the 1850's. It is especially good in its delineation of a characteristic Sunday in a well-conducted New England home of the period. Few writers have succeeded so well in describing the afterglow that persisted in New England long after the fiercest flames of Calvinism had died down:

At seven o'clock my grandfather comes smilelessly down-stairs. He is dressed in black, and looks as if he had lost all his friends during the night. Miss Abigail, also in black, looks as if she were prepared to bury them, and not indisposed to enjoy the ceremony. Even Kitty Collins has caught the contagious gloom, as I perceive when she brings in the coffee-urn—a solemn and sculpturesque urn at any time, but monumental now—and sets it down in front of Miss Abigail. Miss Abigail gazes at the urn as if it held the ashes of her ancestors, instead of a generous quantity of fine old Java coffee. The meal progresses in silence.

Our parlor is by no means thrown open every day. It is open this June morning, and is pervaded by a strong smell of centre-table . . . My grandfather sits in a mahogany chair, reading a large Bible covered with green baize. Miss Abigail occupies one end of the sofa and has her hands crossed stiffly in her lap. I sit in the corner, crushed. . . . If I want to read anything, I can read Baxter's Saint's Rest. I would die first. So I sit there kicking my heels, thinking about New Orleans, and watching a morbid blue-bottle fly that attempts to commit suicide by butting his head against the window-pane . . .

My grandfather looks up, and inquires in a sepulchral voice if I am ready for Sabbath-school. It is time to go. I like the Sabbath-school; there are bright young faces *there*, at all events . . .

Sabbath-school over, I go to meeting, joining my grandfather, who does not appear to be any relation to me this day, and Miss Abigail, in the porch. Our minister holds out very little hope to any of us of being saved. Convinced that I am a lost creature, in common with the human family, I return home behind my guardians at a snail's pace. We have a dead-cold dinner. I saw it laid out yesterday.

There is a long interval between this repast and the second service, and a still longer interval between the beginning and the end of that service . . .

After meeting, my grandfather and I take a walk. We visit, appropriately enough, a neighboring graveyard. I am by this time in a condition of mind to become a willing inmate of the place. The usual evening prayer-meeting is postponed for some reason. At half past eight I go to bed.

This is the way Sunday was observed in the Nutter House, and pretty generally throughout the town, twenty years ago. Persons who were prosperous and natural and happy on Saturday became the most rueful of human beings in the brief space of twelve hours.

I do not think there was any hypocrisy in this. It was merely the old Puritan austerity cropping out once a week. Many of these persons were pure Christians every day in the seven—excepting the seventh. Then they were decorous and solemn to the verge of moroseness.[112]

This is brilliant writing. What is more, it is true writing. Most of the latterday comments on Puritanism are either stodgily historical or absurdly flippant. Aldrich, who lived in the twilight of Puritanism, was able to do justice to the truth, for although he resisted what was evil in the heritage of Puritanism, he also loved the milieu of which it was a component part. The best satire generally issues from a writer who mainly cherishes the environment which in part he satirizes. Sinclair Lewis, for example, is a bitterly successful satirist of a materialistic environment which in most ways is congenial to him. Aldrich mainly loved his boyhood environment, and that fact qualified him to be its critic.

Prudence Palfrey, serialized in *The Atlantic Monthly* in 1874, was designed by Aldrich to be "a light, pleasant story for old folks, as 'The Bad Boy' was for young people." [113] During its composition the author referred to it playfully in a letter to Lowell as "The Great American Novel." [114] Of course *Prudence Palfrey* didn't become any such thing, but it did become a very readable regional story. It is as mellow and wholesome and as full of flavor as good New England cider; and if it is not a very sustaining thing, at least it has a good "bite." To make it a novel Aldrich had to have a plot, but a plot was one thing that Aldrich couldn't master. In *Prudence Palfrey* he made one of his most absurd concoctions. In its simplest terms the action is all right—even hallowed by precedent. A young man is separated from the girl he loves by a hostile uncle—made hostile by the lad's lack of economic prospects. The young man, John Dent by name, of course goes away to line his pockets. While he is away another young man of ample means pays court to the girl. Young man no. 1 returns just in time to avert a miscarriage of romance, unmask the villain, inherit some money, and marry the heroine. The blue print is all right, but Aldrich botched the building. Proportions went awry. Old Parson Wibird Hawkins, for example, isn't really important in the structure—hardly more than a gable or an alcove—but he becomes far too prominent and occupies far too much space. All he has to do, really, is to leave some money to John Dent. The villain, called James Dillingham, is just plain spurious. He is the new minister of Rivermouth, and a very good minister is he— Aldrich says so. But he is also a villain, bent upon marrying Prudence for her money—Aldrich says so. He just can't be both things at once—any more than one room can be both kitchen and parlor. Of course Aldrich makes an effort to show that such a mixture is possible, but his explanations are feeble in the extreme. For the rest, the action is advanced (when Aldrich remembers to advance it at all) by the most bare-faced coincidences, whether malign or beneficent. And the laborious stratagem which finally catches the villain's accomplice would seem amateurish to a movie-goer ten years of age.

With such a plot as this—bulging when it shouldn't and skimpy where it ought to be filled out—the reader has to fall back on the furnishings of the story for satisfaction. These are delightful. Parson Wibird Hawkins is bogus as a piece of plot but charmingly real and touching as a piece of New England of the 1850's. John Dent is for the most part only an agreeably shaped piece of protoplasm, and his adventures in Montana in quest of gold and silver have hardly any blood relationship to the rest of the story. Aldrich had to "read up" on that part of the action. Yet the author manages to make Dent's western hegira interesting by means of his witty and lightly satiric commentary on John Dent's *type* of quest:

> It was a mad idea, and John Dent's own. The day had long gone by when great nuggets were unearthed by private enterprise in California; but he had drawn the notion into his brain that his fortune was to be made at the mines. How or when the fancy first took possession of him I cannot say. Perhaps the accounts of the Australian gold-fields, then a comparatively recent discovery, had something to do with it; perhaps it was born solely of his necessity. He wanted money, he wanted a large quantity, and he wanted it immediately. A gold-mine seemed to simplify the matter. To bring it down to a fine point, it was a gold-mine he wanted. He brooded over the subject until it became a fixed fact in his mind that there was a huge yellow nugget waiting for him somewhere, hidden in the emerald side of a mountain or lying in the bed of some pebbly stream among the gulches. Æons and æons ago Nature had secreted it in her bounteous bosom to lavish it lovingly on some man adventurous and faithful above the rest. The Golden Fleece at Colchis was not more real to Jason and his crew than this nugget finally became to John Dent. He was a poet in those days. Every man is a poet at some period of his life, if only for half an hour.[115]

But Aldrich is better when he is close to home, when he is effortlessly describing a way of life in a small New England town (Portsmouth). He didn't have to get up the local color of New England. It appears as

naturally in his book as pigment in the autumn leaves of a tree. Prudence herself may be only another replica of the pretty and wholesome
girl long utilized as the heroine of New England fiction, but the house
she manages, the flowers she tends, the hours she spends on the bench
under the vines talking to Parson Hawkins or playing chess with her
uncle—these are indubitably real. So is the sound of church bells on
Sunday morning. So is the slow pulse-beat of the whole town of Rivermouth. People have the air of being quietly, dutifully busy, and yet
Rivermouth is "a town where almost literally nothing happens." Here
surely is the place not for the novelist but for the essayist. And Aldrich
fills this natural niche:

> Sometimes [in Rivermouth] somebody is married, and sometimes
> somebody dies—with surprising abruptness, as the old parson did,
> for example—and sometimes a vessel is blown on the rocks at the
> mouth of the harbor. But of those salient tragedies and comedies
> which make up the sum of life in cities, Rivermouth knows next to
> nothing. Since the hanging of a witch or two in the pre-Revolu-
> tionary days, the office of sheriff there has been virtually a sine-
> cure. The police-court—where now and then a thoughtless, light-
> fingered person is admonished of the error of his ways, and the
> one habitual drunkard is periodically despatched to the Town-
> Farm—seems almost like a branch of the Sunday-school. The com-
> munity may be said to have lived for thirty years on a single
> divorce case, growing out of the elopement of Major Tom Deer-
> ing with Mrs. Honoria Maddox . . .[116]

In such a town the arrival of a new minister (even if he weren't destined to be a villain) must be an event of enormous proportions.
Shamelessly Aldrich stops his story to descant on New England ministers and on James Dillingham in particular. By no means a rebel against
orthodoxy, Aldrich is yet too much of a shrewd Yankee not to look
clearly into the premises of some of the syllogisms by which the church
prospers. For example, what is the ratio of ability to prestige in a
young clergyman?

> The young man who, putting behind him the less spiritual re-
> wards of other professions, selects the ministry as the field of his
> labors—drawn to his work by the consciousness that it is there his
> duty points—is certain to impress us with the purity of his pur-
> pose. That he should exert a stronger influence over our minds
> than a young lawyer does, or a young merchant, or a young man
> in any respectable walk of life, is easily understood. But a young
> man, because he buttons the top button of his coat and wears a

white necktie, is not necessarily a person of exalted purpose or shining ability. Yet he is apt, without any very searching examination, to be so regarded in some of our provincial towns. I think the straight-cut black coat must possess a subtle magnetism in itself, something analogous to the glamour there is in the uniform of a young naval or army officer. How else shall we explain the admiration which we have many a time seen lavished on very inferior young men? [117]

Nor was Aldrich above referring satirically to the high moral platform from which many pious people perform petty charities. It was one of the virtues of James Dillingham (*qua* minister) that the town drunkard "was not afraid to apply to the parson for a dollar, having discovered that the coin would not be dropped upon him from such a moral height as to knock the breath out of his body and wound all his finer feelings." [118] As for the grimmer vestiges of the old Puritanism, Aldrich is aware that they linger in Rivermouth. He is too clearsighted not to observe that "To look on the darkest side of a picture is in strict keeping with the local spirit; for Rivermouth, in its shortcomings and in its uncompromising virtues, is nothing if not Puritan." [119] And yet somehow Aldrich gives the impression that he loves the town and what it symbolizes. He is inured to its sombreness, and he loves its comfort and charm. Its slow pace fascinates him. True, its people could never attain to that *dolce far niente* characteristic of more southern races, but they can cherish certain quiet satisfactions that almost amount to happiness. No New Englander of his generation, or earlier, would dare to dally with the idea of total happiness. Fractional bliss was all the Lord intended. There was a suggestion of *memento mori* in the happiest scenes. Tranquility was as much as one could safely hope for. So, at least, believes the sober young heroine:

> This tranquil picture—with that vague background of cemetery which *will* come into pictures of the future—had not been without its charm for Prudence. To grow old leisurely in that pleasant old mansion among the willows, and to fall asleep in the summer or winter twilight after an untroubled, secluded-violet sort of life, had not appeared so hard a fate to her.[120]

All these elements of New England manners and people flood those parts of *Prudence Palfrey* which are not occupied with action. And theirs is the richer content of the book. Uncle-crossed lovers and dauntless young men and nick-of-time arrivals are a dime a dozen, but the accent of life, the murmur of history in the making, the gradual incorporation of life into philosophy, the formation of regional character—these and other elements are rarer by far. It is in proportion to his success in these that Aldrich rescues *Prudence Palfrey* from being a hopelessly bad "novel."

The Stillwater Tragedy, which was serialized in *The Atlantic Monthly*, appeared in book form in 1880.[121] Written while Aldrich was at the peak of his literary career, *The Stillwater Tragedy* disclosed no new and original gifts in its author. Its structure is managed a trifle better than that of *Prudence Palfrey*, but its real values are again incidental. Its title is a misnomer, for the story is a tragedy only in the sense that the action begins with the murder of an old curmudgeon over whom no one wastes sympathy. A better title would have been "The Stillwater Murder"—doubtless too lurid a caption to be used in *The Atlantic Monthly*. And a suitable sub-title would have been "Or the Romance of Richard Shackford."

As a murder story *The Stillwater Tragedy* now seems as naive and conventional as most present-day murder stories will seem fifty years hence. When old Lemuel Shackford is found dead one morning, there are hardly any reputable clues at hand. But a professional detective who is imported to handle the case gradually assembles sufficient circumstantial evidence (as he thinks) to warrant laying the crime at the door of the deceased's young cousin, Richard Shackford, a penniless lad recently returned from a profitless four-year Odyssey at sea. Much of this evidence is "literary," but taken together it seems to show that the state has a good case: Richard had a motive and an opportunity to commit the crime, and he had no iron-clad alibi. All this is pretty shocking, for Richard is a handsome, able, and upright lad—the sort of lad that novelists like Aldrich generally use for heroes. If Richard is found to be a murderer, what will become of Margaret Slocum, obviously cast by Aldrich as a heroine? Of course this impasse has to be removed—by means as artificial as those that created it—and the young lovers must be united in connubial bliss and financial security.[122]

The detective aspect of *The Stillwater Tragedy*, though rather musty, makes fairly enjoyable reading. A more original element in the book is the economic motif, which is merged with the murder motif but which is interesting in itself. Stillwater is an unattractive "labor" town of recent growth. That Aldrich thought of himself as somewhat original in using such a milieu is clear from his comments:

> The humblest painter of real life, if he could have his desire, would select a picturesque background for his figures; but events have an inexorable fashion of choosing their own landscape. In

the present instance it is reluctantly conceded that there are few uglier or more commonplace towns in New England than Still-water—a straggling, overgrown village, with whose rural aspects are curiously blended something of the grimness and squalor of certain shabby city neighborhoods. Being of comparatively re-cent date, the place has none of those colonial associations which, like sprigs of lavender in an old chest of drawers, are a saving grace to other quite as dreary nooks and corners . . . Stillwater, viewed from a certain point, was a sort of microcosm, a little inter-national rag-fair to which nearly every country on earth had con-tributed one of its shabby human products.[123]

And Stillwater has its labor troubles. These arise out of a conflict be-tween Rowland Slocum, owner of the "Marble Works," and the union-ized organization called the Marble Workers' Association. The specific issue over which employer and employees differ is a matter of hours and wages. When the workers are told that they may have shorter hours but no wage increase, they strike. But the larger issue is that of con-trol of industry. Aldrich is reasonably objective in his treatment of the problem, but it is clear that he feels very keenly the position of Pro-prietor Slocum, who is obliged to refuse contracts for work because the union will not allow him to employ more than a stated number of apprentices each year:

The system of this branch of the trades-union kept trained work-men comparatively scarce, and enabled them to command regular and even advanced prices at periods when other trades were de-pressed. The older hands looked upon a fresh apprentice in the yard with much the same favor as workingmen of the era of Jac-quard looked upon the introduction of a new piece of machinery. Unless the apprentice had exceptional tact, he underwent a rough novitiate. In any case, he served a term of social ostracism before he was admitted to full comradeship. Mr. Slocum could easily have found openings each year for a dozen learners, had the mat-ter been under his control; but it was not. "I am the master of each man individually," he declared, "but collectively they are my master." So his business, instead of naturally spreading and becom-ing a benefit to the many, was kept carefully pruned down for the benefit of the few. He was often forced to decline important contracts, the filling of which would have resulted to the ad-vantage of every person in the village.[124]

What makes matters worse is that the strike, when it comes, is pre-cipitated not by the workmen themselves but by a man from "the great

city," a "glib person disguised as The Workingman's Friend—no workingman himself, mind you, but a ghoul that lives upon subscriptions and
sucks the senses out of innocent human beings . . ." [125] These are
strong words—stronger than Howells was to use in his labor novels
during the next decade—and they are not put into the mouth of one
of the characters. They do not of course necessarily indicate Aldrich's
state of mind regarding the underlying reasons for conflict between
labor and capital. The *ideal* relationship between labor and capital is
perhaps suggested by a speech assigned to one of the minor characters:

> "William," said Stevens meditatively, "do you know about the
> Siamese twins?"
> "What about 'em—they're dead, ain't they?" replied Durgin,
> with surprise.
> "I believe so; but when they was alive, if you was to pinch one
> of those fellows, the other fellow would sing out. If you was to
> black the eye of the left-hand chap, the right-hand chap would n't
> have been able to see for a week. When either of 'em fetched the
> other a clip, he knocked himself down. Labor and capital is jined
> just as those two was." [126]

Nevertheless Aldrich was temperamentally and environmentally unqualified to look with tolerant eyes on moves that savored of the radical. Consequently, although *The Stillwater Tragedy* is in its materials
a surprising adumbration of the labor novels of the 1920's and 1930's, its
"slant" is very different.

Aldrich's attitude toward militant labor in *The Stillwater Tragedy*
would have been dictated, if by nothing else, by the romantic needs
of his story. Slocum's Yard is owned and operated by the father of
Margaret, the not very beautiful but wholly lovely heroine of the book.
It is in this business that Richard works himself up from apprentice to
a position something like that of manager. Here he meets Margaret and
falls in love—a charming industrial idyll. It is natural that Mr. Slocum
should plan to allow Richard a share in the business. He "had not
dreamed of throwing in Margaret also," but when he gets over being
surprised at what was inevitable, he gives in gracefully. A conventional
epilogue looks forward to a time when the sign on the Yard will be
"Slocum, Shackford & Son."

Such an epilogue, however trite it now seems, must be accepted as
natural in the period. So with other now curious and quaint and out-
of-fashion things: the elementary murder, the guileless love affair. The
question remains: how well does the author handle his materials? The
answer can only be that, as usual, Aldrich has insufficient original

power to make his book seem "important" but possesses in abundance the traits of a fine craftsman. No architect, but a superior cabinet-maker—perhaps that is Aldrich. His lack of a sense of large planning is apparent in the excessively long inset narrative that follows the discovery of Lemuel Shackford's dead body. This wing of the story is essential—telling, among other things, of Richard's running away to sea under the influence of that "lying romance," *Robinson Crusoe*[127]—but a wing it should remain instead of looming almost as large as the main structure. On the other hand, once the rough work is finished, Aldrich is adept in handling those details which make a story "livable." Much of the detail is picturesque, some humorous or witty, and its effectiveness is enhanced by Aldrich's skill in phrasing. The macabre atmosphere of the house in which Shackford was found dead, for example, is created in part by a reference to one Lydia Sloper, who had also died there mysteriously:

> The coincidence struck deeply into the imaginative portion of Stillwater. "The widow Sloper and old Shackford have made a match of it," remarked a local humorist, in a grimmer vein than customary. Two ghosts had now set up housekeeping, as it were, in the stricken mansion, and what might not be looked for in the way of spectral progeny.[128]

The somewhat unaggressive Rowland Slocum is well-characterized by Richard when he says to Margaret: "If I could only have a good set of Waltham works put into your father, . . . he would go better." [129] Yet although Aldrich excels in details, his details are interdependent. They are cumulatively impressive. In *The Stillwater Tragedy* they help to support a story that falls short of great distinction but remains surprisingly readable.

Aldrich the novelist has become a part of American literary history. *The Story of a Bad Boy* lives on separately as a piece of Americana. The rest of his stories have been put away into a trunk, to be rehandled only occasionally by the connoisseur of New England antiquities—sad fate for an author so recently dead. Yet each generation must write its own books, and it is the exceptional author who can talk beyond the grave. As far as the novel per se is concerned, Aldrich left an unimportant legacy. Howells, his near-contemporary, shared many of Aldrich's predilections and skills, but Howells had more energy and achieved more momentum. In a sense Aldrich, like Holmes, was out of his métier as a novelist. A strong creative impulse of some sort the novelist must have. Aldrich was the harvester rather than the sower. He gathered up and treasured old elements of the New England heritage. Such new modes and materials as he adopted—the labor troubles in *The Stillwater Tragedy*, for example—seem finally less a part of the inner Aldrich than the shimmering recollections of Portsmouth in the 1850's. His description of the home of the labor leader Torrini, though competent in detail, is tonally as unrealistic as a Currier and Ives lithograph.[130] The industrially and socially altered New England that was emerging even in his later years, he probably understood very slightly, if at all. Fate had engineered an elegant agenda for his personal life. One sees Aldrich always in faultless attire—with a fresh buttonhole each day. One doubts if he ever spoke three words to a person observably in need of a bath. To some extent this limited, retrospective, decorous way of life is exemplified in his writing. As a writer Aldrich lived by old axioms: be clear, be controlled, be edifying. Aldrich acts as the friendly custodian of the reader's interest, chaperoning him through the book, telling him what to see and what to ignore. He does not want the reader to make discoveries for himself: the editor will sift life for the reader. Since Aldrich's time, of course, the narrative writer, in many instances, has changed from editor to reporter. The new writer (Steinbeck, for example) says in effect: here are the facts; here is the whole story; I don't presume to say what it means. Modern fiction has moved toward the front page. Aldrich stays ensconced in an amiable editorial column whence he can see life, selectively, in a mirror. He doesn't want front-page stuff. Despite the murder motif in *The Stillwater Tragedy* and the unconsummated villainy in *Prudence Palfrey*, Aldrich didn't like to handle human affairs when they took a messy turn. His characters may be warm-hearted but there is no fever in their blood. Passion is held at arm's length. The nature of ultimate evil in the world is no part of Aldrich's self-assignment. He was not troubled by the black night in which Hawthorne's lonely spirit so often brooded.[131] Aldrich's work was always done before curfew. His language is so clean, so free from vulgar suggestion, that one almost sees the author wearing gloves as he writes. Aldrich was in a sense too "nice." For him even more than for Emerson (who made the phrase for his own guidance) "a course of mobs" would have been useful. His excessively literary habit he was aware of, and he must have cried touché when Holmes gently pricked him with the criticism that he was too fond of "vanilla-flavored adjectives." [132]

Yet these faults—if they are faults—are so closely associated with definite virtues that one is at least sure of the integrity of the writer.

Aldrich may have been "just too sweet," but he was not affected or artificial. A person born and brought up in an atmosphere of old lavender, tea-roses, and pennyroyal should not be expected to excel in describing the reek of an underfed laborer's shack. Aldrich was true to his breed—and it was a patrician breed. Within his field he was masterful. He was genteel and old-fashioned but not stodgy. Clad in the garments of an older era, he could be dapper in his mien: Aldrich is not dull or slow to read. His emotions were recollected in tranquility—but not in torpor. Indeed one of his salient characteristics as a writer is his brisk pace. His phrases are nimble and his manner is often sparkling. His sentimental or nostalgic moods are as evanescent as everything else in his writings: they change as quickly as clouds reflected on the surface of a stream. His wit and his sentiment interact upon each other. In short, if Aldrich is not a rugged writer, he is at least a vital one—incapable of heavy drayage but a good carriage horse. His craftsmanship never lapsed from the high ideals he set for himself. Indeed here is perhaps the explanation of why he was not a great writer. Great writers are constantly endeavoring to write better than they have ever written before—perhaps better than they can—but Aldrich has the air of trying never to fall below a set standard of excellence. Here too he was natural. Like most New England writers up to his time, Aldrich had editorial blood in his veins: he edited as fast as he created. A descendant of the old Puritans could hardly do otherwise.

What Aldrich gave to American literature is to be measured in terms not of magnitude but of authenticity. It can be cherished and preserved for what it is—as the china ware or candle-snuffers of an earlier generation become legitimate objects of a collector's attention. Aldrich is part of a real past. He loved that past. He even wished he could have been born a little earlier—before the railroad had deprived regions of "local character." For—the secret is out—Aldrich was against progress! He congratulates himself on the fact that he can still remember the last of the town-criers. And he is a little saddened by the thought that he just missed the last of the cockades. Perhaps the best "piece" Aldrich ever wrote was not a novel at all but an essay in which he confesses these things. It is an essay on Portsmouth and it is called, in phrasing reminiscent of Longfellow, "An Old Town by the Sea." Here his writing is at its finest—clear and crisp in phrase, humorous and autumnal in tone—and here his feelings are most deeply intertwined with his language. From wharf to Governor's mansion, from Strawberry Bank to the old burying-ground, Point of Graves—he loved it every inch. He loved the golden haze of history that had settled on the town. Indian Summer was at its best in Portsmouth.

CHARLES EGBERT CRADDOCK (1850-1922)

(*Mary Noailles Murfree*)

If they formed a school, the local color writers resisted regimentation better than the individuals of most other schools—including the historical romance writers and the domestic novelists. Each member of the school has his special quality. Writing at about the same time as Eggleston, Miss Murfree is as different from Eggleston in her technique as she is in her settings. He was much at home in a bustling town or county-seat where rapid movement and crowding incident provided him with the materials for fast-revolving plots. She preferred a remote, even isolated, region where simpler action could be delineated at leisure and lonely folk could receive fuller attention. He had pace; she had penetration. His temperament was that of a gifted reporter, an inspector—almost at times an assessor—of the affairs of men; her temperament was that of a poet, seeking to record the environment she knew and to realize its meaning. She was not interested in "the evolution of society," [133] but, finally at least, in the welfare of the individual spirit.

Miss Murfree was not a native of the mountain regions she celebrated in her fiction. She was born in Murfreesboro (Tennessee). When she was six, the family moved to Nashville. Part of her education she received at Philadelphia. For about seven years she lived at St. Louis, returning to Tennessee in 1889. Consequently she had a more metropolitan background than many of the writers who wrote of the Southern "characters." Yet her acquaintance with mountain places and people began early, for as a girl she spent "fifteen pleasant summers" at Beersheba Springs in the Cumberland Mountains, which are described in her first stories.[134] She also became a visitor in the Great Smoky Mountains, the setting now more commonly associated with Miss Murfree's fiction.

Miss Murfree achieved fame at the time of a renaissance of Southern literature, particularly of the sort which emphasizes race, dialect, and economic status. The long line of local writers stemming from Longstreet, whose *Georgia Scenes* had appeared in 1835, was flowering profusely in the eighties and was winning for the South that national recognition whose lack had so long been the cause of bitterness. Tourgée, Joel Chandler Harris, Richard Malcolm Johnston, Thomas Nelson Page, and other writers were pouring forth tales, sketches, and novels with such freshness and abundance that Northern publishers and editors were fain to turn them to profit. *The Atlantic Monthly*, *The Century*, and *Harper's* no longer felt that it was an exception to give space to writers below the Mason and Dixon line. Miss Murfree first attained success by sketches and tales (collected in *In the Tennessee Mountains*) which had appeared in the *Atlantic*. Thomas Bailey Aldrich, then the editor of the *Atlantic*, was astonished one day to discover that this new find, "Charles Egbert Craddock," was a woman, but neither that fact nor the fact that she was a Southerner prevented him from serializing six of her novels.

Most of Miss Murfree's novels are now nearly forgotten: she never quite developed major powers and her undeniably excellent local color and her fine discernment of psychological detail could not sustain her. She lacked the breadth and weight to carry her down the years. Once a pupil of Bret Harte, she has lost ground equally with him; with George Eliot, who seems to have been her other earliest model she cannot well bear comparison.

Miss Murfree's best novel, probably, is *The Prophet of the Great Smoky Mountains* (1885). Its setting is vividly described; its heroine, Dorinda Cayce, is one of the best examples of Miss Murfree's not exceptionally strong characterization; and its action is exciting but plausible. Underneath the "bald" of Big Smoky Mountain, the log cabin of the Cayce family is set on a slope "sheltered by a beetling crag and shadowed by the pines." Here the rather numerous family ekes out a simple existence from agriculture supplemented by the profits from moonshine whiskey. The daughter, Dorinda, uses the same uncouth language as her kin, but she has a rare and delicate spirit. She is sought in marriage by Rick Tyler, and she is attracted by him; but affairs of the heart must wait upon the law—and Rick is at the moment a fugitive: he was known to have been in the company of a man who committed a murder. Preferring present freedom to the uncertainty of mountain justice, he eludes the sheriff's posse, but he is later captured by an acquaintance who hankered for the two hundred dollars "blood money" placed on Rick's head. He later escapes—while an extremely brutal sport called gander-pulling is going forward—and it is believed that he has been freed by Parson Hiram Kelsey, the Prophet of Smoky Mountains, who is jailed on the charge. Rick returns to claim Dorinda, who happily rejoices in her hero. But when she learns that out of jealousy of the Prophet, Rick refuses to secure the parson's release by admitting that he escaped through his own effort, she repudiates the engagement she has just made: he has fallen below her estimate of him. The Prophet is freed for lack of evidence, but when a little later the Cayce family is about to murder the man who raided and ruined their still, the parson manages to substitute himself for the intended victim and dies a Christian martyr.

The plot, though exciting enough, is hardly the best handled element in the story: interest tends to be divided between Dorinda's affairs and the Prophet's. The Prophet is a quaint and curious person in a quaint and curious community. He is credited with special powers of foresight and he acknowledges that he possesses them. In a region as religion-conscious as this of the Big Smoky he is a valued representative of the Lord. There is plenty of work for a man of God in a section where, as the storekeeper continually chants, "Satan's a-stirrin'." [135] Yet the Prophet is gnawed by doubts regarding the state of his own faith, and he frequently goes up on the "mounting" to pray. Even there he is not at rest, for "Satan hunted him like a partridge on the mountains." [136] Fanaticism and godliness mingle in him. He hates cruelty and injustice, but so loves peace that when struck by a ruffian he literally turns the other cheek. A rigid honesty compels him to announce publicly the final loss of his faith, and it is this avowal, coming at the very time when the law is about to take him up as the illegal rescuer of Rick, which causes the people to believe him guilty. His martyrdom at the end does not seem an inevitable conclusion to the story, but it seems true enough to the character of this troubled, wandering man of God. Dorinda admires him for his gifts and she is the counterpart of his finer side. It was because Rick shattered her ideal of true manhood and courage that she finally rejected him: " 'No,' she said drearily. 'I never loved ye. I loved what I thunk ye war. But ye war n't that—nuthin' like it! Ye war suthin' else. I war jes' in love with my own foolishness.' " [137] Sadly, but without complaint, she sees her dream die —for Miss Murfree (with greater firmness of purpose than Eggleston) does not manufacture a happy ending, or even such a compromise as Dorinda could have made by returning to a lad she had once refused for the sake of Rick.[138] No, Dorinda shows the same tenacity in her idealism which the rest of the Cayces showed in different ways. They are a folk long established in the region—and proud of their long tenancy. They have a strong sense of justice (not to be confused with law), but they are handy with "shootin'-irons," and they exhibit an ineradicable desire to punish any violator of their rights. When John Cayce learns that the sheriff has been needlessly cruel to Dorinda, he flares out:

> "He shell rue it!" he cried,—"he shell rue it! Me an' mine take no word off'n nobody. My gran'dad an' his three brothers, one hunderd an' fourteen year ago, kem hyar from the old North State an' settled in the Big Smoky. They an' thar sons rooted up the wilderness. They crapped. They fit the beastis; they fit the Injun; they fit the British; an' this last little war o' ourn they fit each

other. Thar hev never been a coward 'mongst 'em. Thar hev never been a key turned on one of 'em, or a door shet. They hev respected the law fur what it war wuth, an' they hev stood up fur thar rights agin it. They answer fur thar word, an' others hev ter answer." [139]

The Cayces are a homogeneous group, but each has his own pinch of individuality. The grandfather of the Prophet is a tender-hearted but rude-tongued survivor of the days when "Henry Clay shook all the life out'n" Andrew Jackson. He has a profound contempt for modern notions in general. To him the Prophet seems a little man: in the days of real men no young fellow of thirty would spend his time "idlin', an' preachin', an' convictin' his elders o' sin." When the Prophet goes out to shoot a bit of game and comes back empty-handed, the old man ridicules him in trenchant phrase: "Whenst I war young, folks ez ker-ried rifles ter git suthin' fur supper never kem home a-suckin' the bar'l." [140]

The language of the region carried a sharp edge which contact with the meagre settlements could not dull. To all intents and purposes it was as permanent as the spurs and coves of Smoky. The speech of the folk was as natural as the idiom of the mountain. Miss Murfree catches both with skill and accuracy. A score of times she pauses to describe the phases of the ever-varied mountain as it appears from hour to hour, from day to day, from season to season, in mist or in golden sunshine. A June day has its characteristic phases:

> The summer days climbed slowly over the Great Smoky Moun-tains. Long the morning lingered among the crags, and chasms, and the dwindling shadows. The vertical noontide poised motion-less on the great balds. The evening dawdled along the sunset slopes, and the waning crimson waited in the dusk for the golden moonrise.[141]

She loves the mountains in whatever mood, but most often she returns to the "illusory mists" which play about the peaks and the "elastic dis-tances" that stretch between. To her they are austere but somehow comforting: they betoken the permanence of nature (and perhaps of God) and the transience of man as he burrows in their slopes and scales their crags. She describes them with a tremulous eagerness—as if she were for the first time experiencing the beauty and wonder of earthly things. But a note of sadness creeps into her variations on this theme, and at the very top of Smoky there is a bleakness which is no more real than the sober reflections of the author:

Always enwrapped in the illusory mists, always touching the evasive clouds, the peaks of the Great Smoky Mountains are like some barren ideal, that has bartered for the vague isolations of a higher atmosphere the material values of the warm world below. Upon those mighty and majestic domes no tree strikes root, no hearth is alight; humanity is an alien thing, and utility set at naught.[142]

Not all this local description is equally well wrought. Miss Murfree writes well; and she has an eye for images. Yet perhaps by excess of zeal, she sometimes spoils her effects, and she writes with obvious effort that is revealed in an occasional angularity of phrase. She will dally with a comparison so long that its original charm is lost.[143] Yet she is always a poet at heart, and she is the tender warden of a region she loved through close intimacy. Her work has the validity that comes from fresh experience. The scenes she describes, like the customs and traditions she reports, are taken from the life and not (as too often in latter-day regional writing) dug out of "sources" in a library.

Between 1884 and 1914 Miss Murfree published some fifteen novels as well as a considerable number of short stories and sketches. Yet her work did not increase in power and significance. Indeed it is the opinion of her biographer that "if Mary Noailles Murfree had died [in 1885], or had never written another line, her reputation as a novelist would be far higher than it is today." [144] By that time she had produced four books: *In the Tennessee Mountains*, a book of short tales and sketches; *Where the Battle Was Fought*, a novel; *Down the Ravine*, a juvenile; and *The Prophet of the Great Smoky Mountains*. And of these, the more important for her present reputation are the first and the fourth. *Where the Battle Was Fought* (1884) was her first novel, having appeared one year before *The Prophet*. It is on the whole an inferior work, crowded with unproportioned incident and peopled by characters who never come quite into focus as individuals. Its best quality is a certain eeriness which is developed over the scene of Fort Despair (near Murfreesboro, the place of the author's birth), where several years after the Civil War the affairs of living men (chiefly struggles over love and property) are carried on in a desolate and stricken region. The battlefield is a maze of crabgrass and thicket that encircles yawning graves. It is a region where "spirits walk, and no hire can induce the hardiest ploughman to break the ground." [145]

Miss Murfree's later novels are, despite occasional experimentation, a fairly homogeneous group. Apparently inspired by Thomas Hardy's use of setting as a dominating force in fiction,[146] Miss Murfree frequently emphasizes background to the point of neglecting human affairs. In *In the Clouds* (1886) a peak in Great Smoky dominates the story, and in *The Mystery of Witch-Face Mountain* (1895), much is made (in a manner that recalls Hawthorne) of a Cumberland mountain that resembles a witch-face. Three later books, *The Story of Old Fort Loudon* (1899), *A Spectre of Power* (1903), and *The Amulet* (1906), were only partially successful efforts to capitalize the resurgence of the historical romance at the turn of the century. In *The Windfall* (1907), a story dealing with a street fair in a resort hotel, setting is "incidental." [147] *The Juggler* (1897) is a grim narrative of the effects of superstition. In *The Fair Mississippian* (1908) Miss Murfree based her story in part on childhood memories of planters' lives in a neighboring state. The story is very readable, but the recollections are a trifle "thin." [148]

Finally Miss Murfree excelled only in a limited milieu and with a comparatively simple plot. Excepting *The Prophet* her best novels are probably *The Despot of Broomsedge Cove* (1888) and *In the "Stranger People's" Country* (1891). In the latter the ways of mountain folk are brought into relief when an archaeologist comes to explore the graves of an extinct race of pygmies (or possibly Aztec or Indian children) called by the natives the "Leetle People." So much local superstition has grown up around the graves that the archaeologist is threatened with death if he violates them. Subsequently he digs anyway and is shot at, but shot at by robbers who have used the graves as a storehouse for booty. Politics and love also complicate existence for the archaeologist, who finally leaves the region to avoid being lynched. He promises to return, but he never does; and the uneducated girl who loved him waits vainly through the years for this stranger who so often offended her kinsmen because he misunderstood them. In this book a supernatural air hovers over all the action and seems to dominate it, but it is an atmosphere which belongs to the region. *In the "Stranger People's" Country* is no literary exercise but a true transcript of a sequestered people, their odd ways of life and their deep-rooted superstitions, their mountain-born mysticism.

For Miss Murfree could not escape her métier. Whatever she undertook as experiment or as professional makeshift failed to prosper. When she recorded the habitat, the speech, the legends, and the group conduct of primitive, isolated folk on a spur of Smoky, she was revealing her full endowment as a writer. She was weaving into the expanding web of the American novel one more strand of local color. It was of reasonably stout quality and authentic dye. But the color without the artist is bare, and in her best work Miss Murfree became a part of all she met. When she told the sombre story of a shy and uneducated but eager slip of a mountain girl destined to find final disillusionment, she was giving to a character in fiction some of the same sadness with which she herself beheld the flickering life of man. In the life of the spirit there were desolating moments which blotted out hope just as, often enough, the "dark, mysterious, heavily-wooded Cumberland spurs cancelled the rest of the universe." [149] Yellow sunshine and pockets of shadow, heartbreak and hope—Miss Murfree knew the elements of life; but it was not for her to determine their ratio. Enough if her page reflected fragments of the truth.

— XIV —

Mark Twain (1835-1910)

Compared with most of his contemporaries in the field, Mark Twain was very little conscious of his part in the evolution of the American novel. He wrote few books that could come even loosely under any classification of the novel, and those few belonged to a looser category of the novel, namely, the picaresque. He loathed reading romances, especially those of Scott and Cooper, and he read few novels of any sort —even those of Howells, his friend, whose books surely merited such a reciprocal courtesy. In general he was too explosive, too original, too impatient of restraint to submit to any rules of writing not drawn up by himself. He founded no school of fiction. He was comparatively weak in the use of traditional elements of the novel—characterization and plot. His greatest asset, his humor, was essentially inimitable even to those who had mastered the time-worn channels through which he occasionally discharged it. It was an emanation from his dynamic personality and as such it was *sui generis*. Like O. Henry's, his art seemed simpler than it was. In some ways it *was* simple and elemental—like a freshening wind—but it was for that very reason hard to imitate. Yet Mark Twain was undoubtedly one of the greatest forces in American fiction in the last quarter of the nineteenth century and after. On the whole such "technique" as he had was more distinctive in the short story or sketch than in extended fiction, but short-story writers and novelists alike were his general beneficiaries. If his specific qualities could not be duplicated, his abounding vitality and natural freedom heartened scores of later writers, and his basic reliance on colloquial idiom acted as a proclamation of emancipation to countless slavish writers who without his warrant would not have dared to depart from the "literary" language of most of his contemporaries. If Mark Twain did not "advance" the novel, he greatly strengthened it.

Mark Twain's life was in some ways the complement of that of Howells, who was two years younger. Both were born in comparatively frontier-like regions, but whereas Howells' inclination toward ordered

domesticity soon fixed him in Boston, Mark Twain moved westward
as an adventurer, and although he ended by living in the East he had
in the meantime pretty well tramped over this country and considerable
portions of the outer world. Yet Missouri, where he was born on November 30, 1835, was the most important stop he ever made. In the
absence of reliable data on his earliest years, we must pick up Mark
Twain at the age of twelve,[1] but the environment of his boyhood is
available to anyone who cares to turn back the record. Born in Florida,
Missouri, he was removed to Hannibal in early infancy, and it is in that
border village[2] that one may see retrospectively the sort of life which
Mark Twain probably led and which, freely translated by Mark Twain,
served as the literary base of most of his books.[3] Hannibal was a remote river town of a hundred inhabitants. Its boundaries were countryside, prairie, forest, and—the river.[4] The Mississippi carried practically
its only commerce, cultural as well as mercantile, with the outside
world. The region was one calculated to induce in its residents a
mixture of hope and horror. It had been only recently that the most
glamorous symbol of border lawlessness and terrorism, John A. Murrell,
was captured. Here men reached for pistols in the early stages of a dispute and Mark Twain actually witnessed brutal killings on more than
one occasion. Lynching and torture of Negroes was infrequent but
taken for granted. Abolitionists were in danger of similar violence.
Medical lore was futile against malarial fever, the scourge of many settled citizens and of almost all squatters in the picturesque but rank
bayou land of the river valley. Cultural influences made slow headway
in a region where the intelligence level was such that superstition ran
riot through all minds. Belief in witchcraft terrified young and old,
and impaired justice. Boys who were lethargic in the pursuit of the
three R's had heads crammed full of the detail of hideous spells, en-
chantments, and the grisly means one might adopt to counteract them.
Many of the "Gothic" elements in Mark Twain's stories about boyhood
were not derived from books but were transferred from the tongues of
real boys of Hannibal—of whom Sam Clemens was one. Nor did the
violence and superstition fail to leave their effect upon the nerves of the
writer Mark Twain.[5]

Yet the Mississippi region did not wholly deserve the literary black
eye administered to it by transient English observers such as Mrs.
Trollope[6] and Charles Dickens.[7] Horror was intermittent (and mostly
nocturnal) and all the disabilities of border life were compensated for
by the many opportunities for happy living in "idyllic" St. Petersburg
(Hannibal). Hannibal was a town more southern than western geo-
graphically, and its character was largely Southern.[8] "Drowsy sunlight"

favored an agreeable contemplativeness, for "life was without pressure" in this simple society which knew neither wealth nor much extreme poverty.[9] Though traditionally regarded as without a spirit of fun, these pioneer settlers had many active and some respectable amusements: theatrical performances by strolling players and minstrels, show-boats, cock-fighting, horse-racing, shooting matches, corn-shucking and roof-raising festivities, dancing—jigs, reels, and the spurious cake-walk—and singing Negro spirituals, hearing folk-tales, attending camp-meeting (which was partly, like Burns's "Holy Fair," "a social diversion, a commercial bazaar, and a focus of dynamic joy").[10] In short all the inevitable grimness of the experiences of trail-breakers must not be read into the lives of these permanent settlers. Crudity, violence, superstitions were there, but they had their tolerable counterpart in amusement and livableness. In both aspects the Negro was important. He sang the songs, recounted the charms, transmitted the superstitions, committed the occasional crime, suffered the lynching, danced the reel, provided the art, enjoyed the sunlight, and—relaxed with the boys. He was a slave, yes, but in Hannibal slavery existed "in its least repellent form," and the "slaves were . . . the happiest folk in that contented countryside. Laughter was constant among them, and singing, and horseplay. They were the nearest associates of boys." [11] From them Samuel Clemens learned much. But the best evidence that the boyhood environment was not entirely the dire and drab thing assumed by Mr. Brooks is in the words of Mark Twain himself. Even allowing for the tendency of old age to filter out the bitterness of early recollections, it is clear from a passage in his *Autobiography* that nature had many blessings to distribute to the lads of Hannibal. The ring of truth is behind these shimmering recollections:

As I have said, I spent some part of every year at the farm until I was twelve or thirteen years old. The life which I led there with my cousins was full of charm, and so is the memory of it yet. I can call back the solemn twilight and mystery of the deep woods, the earthy smells, the faint odors of the wild flowers, the sheen of rain-washed foliage, the rattling clatter of drops when the wind shook the trees, the far-off hammering of woodpeckers and the muffled drumming of wood pheasants in the remoteness of the forest, the snapshot glimpses of disturbed wild creatures scurrying through the grass—I can call it all back and make it as real as it ever was, and as blessed. I can call back the prairie, and its loneliness and peace, and a vast hawk hanging motionless in the sky, with his wings spread wide and the blue of the vault showing through the fringe of their end feathers. I can see the woods in

their autumn dress, the oaks purple, the hickories washed with
gold, the maples and the sumachs luminous with crimson fires, and
I can hear the rustle made by the fallen leaves as we plowed
through them. I can see the blue clusters of wild grapes hanging
among the foliage of the saplings, and I remember the taste of
them and the smell. I know how the wild blackberries looked, and
how they tasted, and the same with the pawpaws, the hazelnuts,
and the persimmons; and I can feel the thumping rain, upon my
head, of hickory nuts and walnuts when we were out in the frosty
dawn to scramble for them with the pigs, and the gusts of wind
loosed them and sent them down. I know the stain of blackberries,
and how pretty it is, and I know the stain of walnut hulls, and how
little it minds soap and water, also what grudged experience it had
of either of them. I know the taste of maple sap, and when to
gather it, and how to arrange the troughs and the delivery tubes,
and how to boil down the juice, and how to hook the sugar after
it is made, also how much better hooked sugar tastes than any that
is honestly come by, let bigots say what they will. I know how a
prize watermelon looks when it is sunning its fat rotundity among
pumpkin vines and "simblins"; . . . I know the taste of the water-
melon which has been honestly come by, and I know the taste of
the watermelon which has been acquired by art. Both taste good,
but the experienced know which tastes best. I know the look of
green apples and peaches and pears on the trees, and I know how
entertaining they are when they are inside of a person. I know
how ripe ones look when they are piled in pyramids under the
trees, and how pretty they are and how vivid their colors. I know
how a frozen apple looks, in a barrel down cellar in the winter-
time, and how hard it is to bite, and how the frost makes the teeth
ache, and yet how good it is, notwithstanding. I know the disposition of elderly people to select the specked apples for the
children, and I once knew ways to beat the game. I know the look
of an apple that is roasting and sizzling on a hearth on a winter's
evening, and I know the comfort that comes of eating it hot, along
with some sugar and a drench of cream. I know the delicate art
and mystery of so cracking hickory nuts and walnuts on a flatiron
with a hammer that the kernels will be delivered whole, and I
know how the nuts, taken in conjunction with winter apples,
cider, and doughnuts, make old people's old tales and old jokes
sound fresh and crisp and enchanting, and juggle an evening away
before you know what went with the time. I know the look of
Uncle Dan'l's kitchen as it was on the privileged nights, when I
was a child, and I can see the white and black children grouped on
the hearth, with the firelight playing on their faces and the shadows flickering upon the walls, clear back toward the cavernous
gloom of the rear, and I can hear Uncle Dan'l telling the immortal

tales which Uncle Remus Harris was to gather into his book and charm the world with, by and by; and I can feel again the creepy joy which quivered through me when the time for the ghost story was reached—and the sense of regret, too, which came over me, for it was always the last story of the evening and there was nothing between it and the unwelcome bed . . .

I can remember the howling of the wind and the quaking of the house on stormy nights, and how snug and cozy one felt, under the blankets, listening; and how the powdery snow used to sift in, around the sashes, and lie in little ridges on the floor and make the place look chilly in the morning and curb the wild desire to get up—in case there was any. I can remember how very dark that room was, in the dark of the moon, and how packed it was with ghostly stillness when one woke up by accident away in the night, and forgotten sins came flocking out of the secret chambers of the memory and wanted a hearing; and how ill chosen the time seemed for this kind of business; and how dismal was the hoohooing of the owl and the wailing of the wolf, sent mourning by on the night wind . . .

I remember the 'coon and 'possum hunts, nights, with the negroes, and the long marches through the black gloom of the woods . . .

I remember the pigeon seasons, when the birds would come in millions and cover the trees and by their weight break down the branches. They were clubbed to death with sticks; guns were not necessary and were not used. I remember the squirrel hunts, and prairie-chicken hunts, and wild-turkey hunts, and all that; and how we turned out, mornings, while it was still dark, to go on these expeditions, and how chilly and dismal it was, and how often I regretted that I was well enough to go. A toot on a tin horn brought twice as many dogs as were needed, and in their happiness they raced and scampered about, and knocked small people down, and made no end of unnecessary noise. At the word, they vanished away toward the woods, and we drifted silently after them in the melancholy gloom. But presently the gray dawn stole over the world, the birds piped up, then the sun rose and poured light and comfort all around, everything was fresh and dewy and fragrant, and life was a boon again . . .[12]

Here in this brief retrospect, only slightly tinted by time, is almost all that one needs to know of the nature of Mark Twain's boyhood. The known facts of his adolescence and maturity tell what happened to his body in years after he left Hannibal, but the mold of his mind and the texture of his emotional life were already set. They determined how he would react to later experience. His later life—too full in concrete data to be recorded here—was varied and brilliant. From 1853 to 1857 he shuttled from city to city—St. Louis, New York, Philadelphia, Keokuk, Cincinnati—as itinerant printer and commencing journalist. Then followed four years on the Mississippi as pilot. In 1861 began a trip westward that was protracted from its intended span of three months to a period of seven years—years during which he silvermined in Nevada (the "silver and sagebrush state"), journalized in Nevada and California, and had sundry other experiences related with considerable contempt for factual accuracy but with basic truth in his autobiographical *Roughing It* (1872). Miscellaneous but not wholly ambiguous years, these from 1853 to 1857. If he had garnered little silver either from the mines of Nevada or from the pay-envelopes of western newspapers, Clemens had learned to mine his native humor and to coin personal adventure into popular literature. His first book appeared in 1867, *The Celebrated Jumping Frog of Calaveras County*. Then came the culmination of his Wanderjahre—his trip to the Holy Land. Its religious significance for Mark Twain was nil, but his contract to describe the detail of the pilgrimage in letters for the *Alta California* proved to be an important document in his literary career. A book resulted, *The Innocents Abroad* (1869), which brought him to a peak of popularity (if not complete critical approval) from which he never thereafter descended appreciably. Following his marriage to Olivia Langdon of Elmira, New York, Mark Twain settled down to a less vagabond life. He became an Easterner—with somewhat imperfect success, for his many years in captivity under the gentle lash of Olivia never completely tamed him. A residence of twenty years in Hartford (1871 to 1891) deepened his affection for New England but did not prevent his memory from roving back to those Missouri scenes which were the foundation of some of his best books, including *Tom Sawyer* (1876), *Huckleberry Finn* (1884), and *Life on the Mississippi* (1883). Not that he was permitted to remain quietly in Hartford during these years: a great many things took him from home. Lecture tours took him the length and breadth of the land. There was Europe to visit and, after his bankruptcy in 1893, there were debts of honor (if not at law) to be paid out of royalties from a book (*Following the Equator*, 1897) based on a trip around the world. So by various stages to New York, where he settled in 1904. Living on lower Fifth Avenue, he spent most of his later years in material comfort and in the glare of considerable publicity. No abdication of his earlier modes of thought was implied by his move to New York: he did not become a "New Yorker," for, as always, he had brought his own weight and atmosphere with him. The metropolitan life held attractions for his child-like delight in mechanical novelties and gratifications to his scarcely concealed vanity. Yet countless honors and unending recognition amid metropolitan diversions could not alter the deepest interests and working habits of his eager mind. His *Autobiography*, dictated in his later years to the man (Albert Bigelow Paine) who was designated as his literary executor, is rich in the lore of his earlier days and betrays as little concern for aesthetic nicety as if he had never been lionized by the unco literary and had never received an Oxford degree. His outward life had been reasonably happy despite several encounters with adverse fate. The death of two daughters and of his wife brought on deep loneliness but did not change him basically: the rebellious tone of his expressions of grief at their loss was only a more intimate phase of a pessimistic attitude toward the meaning of life and the control of the universe which he had often revealed before. *The Mysterious Stranger* and *What Is Man?*, written late in life, are part and parcel of the man who years before had been perplexed by squalor and injustice and senseless waste at Dawson's Landing. On Fifth Avenue, too, Mark Twain recalled those happier portions of his boyhood in one of his most memorable passages.[13] It is true, as Mr. Brooks has pointed out (though not to the extent which he implies) that Mark Twain had compromised with his conscience on occasion by suppressing views that might have had an unhealthful effect on the sales of his books. But he was probably no more hypocritical than the average man, and his perturbation at his own defections was the sign of an essentially honorable man who at least retained ideals. Moreover he never lost his human sympathies, and it is clear that no matter how much he fretted and grumbled, he really loved the damned human race. He loved, too, the life which he so bitterly denounced as useless. In 1908 he moved to "Stormfield" at Redding, Connecticut: here he would have the modified solitude which became essential during his old age. He traveled, however, until the end. A year before his death he spent several months in Bermuda, returning to Redding only a week before his death. He died April 21, 1910.

The volumes that he left behind have experienced the inevitably severe re-appraisal that follows upon the death of an author. Divorced from the radiant vitality of Mark Twain in the flesh, some of his books have seriously lost prestige.[14] The greatest losses have been suffered by many hastily-written sketches, the industriously compiled *Joan of Arc*, his experiments in play-writing, the pot-boiling *Following the Equator*, the perfunctory *A Tramp Abroad*, and the later chapters of *Life on the Mississippi*. A few of the books have fluctuated—*The American Claimant* and *Pudd'nhead Wilson*—and a higher valuation has been put upon the posthumous *The Mysterious Stranger*. *The Innocents Abroad,* an uneven work, is valued as containing some of his best passages of humor. The books which approximate the novel form have been steadier than most of the others with the exception of the first extended piece of fiction, *The Gilded Age* (1873), which, though valued clinically by doctors of criticism, is now granted no great merit per se.

The Gilded Age was a neighborhood job, and such blame as it has incurred must be referred partly to Charles Dudley Warner, who lived around the corner from Mark Twain in Hartford. The novel owed its origin partly to a dinner table challenge at Mark Twain's house: wives whose literary tastes were being arraigned flared back with the rebuttal that such good judges—Mark Twain and Warner, especially—should *write* the kind of fiction they approved of. The glove was picked up by the men. Accepting the challenge was the easier for Mark Twain because he had been simmering a story in his mind for some time—a story that should centre about his mother's cousin, James Lampton, and the fate of certain unlucky Tennessee lands long in the possession of the Clemens family. Mark Twain wrote off the first eleven chapters in quick exuberance, and Warner picked up the thread where Mark Twain left it, carrying the narrative forward for twelve more. Thereafter the collaborators wrote alternate chapters in miscellaneous order until the work, about equally distributed between them, was completed. Having Warner as a collaborator had been in one sense a boon to Mark Twain, who up to this time, perhaps with an instinctive realization of his limitations, "had been unwilling to undertake an extended work of fiction alone." [15] The whole book was completed between February and April, and when the authors looked upon it, it was good in their eyes. The public also liked it, scarcely noticing the murmurs of critics, who said the book never jelled structurally.

What made it good reading was the wealth of variety—romance from Warner and satire holding both its sides from Mark Twain—that flowed into the generous lap of the plot. The nucleus of the action is a vast tract of Tennessee land which Squire Hawkins had not been wise enough to sell when a reasonable offer was made. After an attempt to develop a flourishing town had failed even with the irrepressible Col. Beriah Sellers[16] promoting it, the family hope is renewed when Laura Hawkins, adopted daughter of the Squire, reports that the government is going to buy the land through the influence of Senator Dilworthy. But the "university bill" to effect the sale is lost partly because Senator Dilworthy has been charged with vote-buying. As in many of Mark Twain's stories the outcome here is a financial fiasco: the land goes by failure to pay taxes. In the meantime Laura's personal affairs have assumed a tragic turn. In the midst of her very able political maneuvering in Washington, she is confronted by Col. Selby, a man who had years before pretended to marry her while he was already a husband. Her knowledge of his depravity cannot prevail over her love even now, but her decision to kill him prevails over both. Her trial for murder occurs at the time when the "university bill" is hanging by a thread. Major disasters in the book are balanced by the successful issue of a couple of love affairs whose complete omission, as well as that of the mystery of Laura's parentage, would have done no harm to the book. Interstices in the basic action are filled with anecdote, humorous dialogue, and rough and ready description. Relying, as often, on the popular interest in fires, Mark Twain provides two in this book, one of them involving the spectacular destruction of a steamboat. Yet he is less happy in scenes of sheer power than in humorously satirical interludes.

The Gilded Age earns its vivid title by reason of its satire, alternately jocose and caustic, of political corruption and of the sordid grab for gold when the get-rich-quick fever was epidemic in America. The subject of Congressional blunders and venality was fresh in Mark Twain's mind on account of his visit the preceding winter to Washington[17] and the notorious vote-buying tactics of Senator Pomeroy of Kansas. Mark Twain's interest in politics at this time was not that of a theorist but of a reporter with his eye cocked for specific abuses which could be ridiculed. He is never more interested in reform than he is in the humorous exposure of duplicity—a fact which sets him off from Bellamy and Henry George. Even minor matters serve a humorous purpose. When Laura tells Senator Dilworthy that she supposes that the luggage of a retiring house-member will be franked home as "public documents," the Senator replies:

> "Yes, yes, but, child, all Congressmen do that. It may not be strictly honest, indeed, it is not unless he had some public documents mixed in with the clothes." [18]

But Laura knows her Senator Dilworthy also from a remark of another lawmaker who, when asked if he would support the "university bill," replied that he " 'had no doubt it was a good thing; if Senator Dilworthy was in it, it would pay to look into it.' " [19] Mark Twain's indignation, though real, was always less in evidence than his love of fun. He is interested here not so much in the nation's loss through corruption as in the fun of deflating the guilty one—the sign of which is his habit of delivering his thrusts under a garment of pretended naiveté. This is the case when he wishes to make the point that Congressmen are as stupid as they are venal:

"That is true, Colonel [says one Hicks to Colonel Sellers]. To be sure you can buy now and then a Senator or a Representative; but they do not know it is wrong, and so they are not ashamed of it. They are gentle, and confiding and childlike, and, in my opinion, these are qualities that ennoble them far more than any amount of sinful sagacity could. I quite agree with you, Colonel Sellers." [20]

Yet the corruption of public servants and the sins of big business[21] are only part of the game of Mark Twain. After all there was no great honor attached to the effort of the Hawkins family to unload their undesirable land on the government as a site for a university. The family is here exhibiting a Midas complex which Mark Twain mercilessly satirized elsewhere, notably in *The Man Who Corrupted Hadleyburg* and *The $30,000 Bequest.* Laura Hawkins is in some ways a victim of circumstance, but she uses her wit and her beauty in an affair which reflects no great credit on her or her coadjutors. It is for this reason that she has been called "a sort of American Becky Sharp." [22] And if there is any moral in the story per se it is made specific by the final determination of Washington Hawkins and Col. Sellers to forswear all speculation (quite as characteristic of the "Gilded Age" as official corruption) and earn their livings by solid work. But even these characters are more serviceable as vehicles of humor than as moral pegs. Washington Hawkins is shown in a typical Clemensian attitude when he imagines himself as wealthy:

He got up and walked the floor feverishly during two hours; and when he sat down he had married Louise, built a house, reared a family, married them off, spent upwards of eight hundred thousand dollars on mere luxuries, and died worth twelve millions.[23]

As for Col. Sellers, he is less a piece of moral machinery than an expert in turnips (a vegetable that for some reason Mark Twain always found humorous) [24] and an apostle of optimism. It is of course this latter characteristic which has earned him the sobriquet of the American Micawber and has made him one of the few important character studies by Mark Twain. Sellers, like the Tennessee land, was out of life, and indeed the best part of *The Gilded Age* come less from Mark Twain's shrewd reporting or Warner's tender sentimentalizing than from that family history which is the substratum discoverable beneath the surface entertainment in many of Mark Twain's best books. Personal and family recollections also formed a solid basis for *Tom Sawyer.*

The Adventures of Tom Sawyer was published in London about six

months before the Hartford edition appeared.[25] The reason for delay-
ing the American edition was that Mark Twain was anxious to forestall
Canadian publishers who had already pirated almost everything he
wrote after his first success.[26] The International Copyright Law was
still fourteen years off, and Mark Twain lent his vigorous voice to the
chorus of protesters against the abuses it was aimed to regulate.[27] When
Tom Sawyer finally appeared it became despite some adverse criticism,[28] the great popular success which it has steadily remained.

For a writer like Mark Twain whose "invention was not always a
reliable quantity," [29] the best aids to composition were travel and autobiographical materials. *Tom Sawyer*, like most of Mark Twain's books
before *The Prince and the Pauper* (1881) was easily dredged up out of
the memories of boyhood in Hannibal. It was not conceived as a novel,
for Mark Twain was convinced that "it would be fatal to do it in any
shape but autobiographically . . ." He even thought that he had possibly "made a mistake in not writing it in the first person." [30] It has in
perfection the only major element of the novel which Mark Twain ever
mastered—a strongly felt and completely articulated milieu. Caricature
sometimes splashes the characters, and excessive zeal for "effect" vitiates
the action but the "community is true." [31] Its abundance of inimitably
fine episode never takes the form of a fused and proportioned action.[32]
The murder motif consumes enough space to become, what it actually
is not, the dominating factor of the book. Certainly many of the best
episodes in the book—the white-washing, the beetle at church, the conquest of Becky—would have suffered by being reduced to their proper
ranks as minor particles in a "murder story." The discipline which
might have organized the mob of Mark Twain's inspirations would have
been fatal to life not only in *Tom Sawyer* but in most of his other books
as well. Even character-development is not a principal interest in *Tom
Sawyer*. Despite use of real people as models for several of the portraits, the full panel of characterization is never achieved—or sought.
The book lives in small units, which when added up (not arranged)
equal the sum of boyhood experience. Whose boyhood? Largely
Mark Twain's, without a doubt. Yet Mark Twain was a mature man
when he wrote *Tom Sawyer*. He was also by his own testimony a
magnificent liar. His sieve-like memory was a ready accomplice of his
deliberate fabrications. If he didn't invent, he certainly embroidered.
Research into the correspondence between truth and poetry in his writings and in his life has shown the futility of accepting as gospel any
specific part of his fiction.[33] Actual events probably at first bore the
imprint of Mark Twain's own hand as he gathered up the snows of
yesterday, but in the process of rolling down hill, this small ball of fact

accumulated the weight and momentum of generalized boyhood experience. Ruses to escape school, illegal swimming, burgeoning love at ten years, campaigns against the sissy and all "snobs" who carry pocket-handkerchiefs, the fight with the new boy, the blundering discovery of a ghastly secret—if Mark Twain had kept all these items strictly intra-Hannibal, he would not have touched the main spring of memory for so many hundreds of thousands of readers young and old the world over. For to the general reader this autobiographical book has become a romantic book—an escape from the pangs of adulthood. Accuracy is not the point. What a man likes about *Tom Sawyer*[34] is its full embodiment of experience which he himself has had more or less fragmentarily—or wishes he had. Men who have seldom drawn a breath outside of the stagnant air of city apartment or downtown office read the book with the same complete abandonment to nostalgic longing as those who have actually gone cruising barefoot in a watermelon patch on an ambiguous errand. Men who as lads have lived the existence of Little Lord Fauntleroy have grinned in low appreciation of the exploits of Tom and shared his envy of the "gaudy outcast condition" of that immortal forbidden companion, Huckleberry Finn. Readers of *Paradise Lost* have no more perversely been drawn to the rebel Satan as hero than good children have regulated their adventurous ambitions by reference to those exploits of Tom and Huck which smack least of rectitude.

Tom Sawyer is an idyll, a romance. Yet some door of realism there must be which admits readers to its precincts. Mainly Mark Twain led the reader on by virtue of two things: first, the episodes, though embellished, turn on the hard hinges of true boy-psychology (not psychoanalysis). Second his endless capacity for detail, which sometimes betrayed him into tediousness, was prevailingly his friend in that it gave his episodes a Defoe-like realism. Only experience and patience, as well as utter confidence in the value of his material, could lead a writer to itemize the profits of a young white-washing "contractor":

> He [Tom] had . . . twelve marbles, part of a jews-harp, a piece of blue bottle-glass to look through, a spool cannon, a key that wouldn't unlock anything, a fragment of chalk, a glass stopper of a decanter, a tin soldier, a couple of tadpoles, six fire-crackers, a kitten with only one eye, a brass door-knob, a dog-collar—but no dog—the handle of a knife, four pieces of orange-peel, and a dilapidated old window-sash.[35]

With the same patience he observed and recorded the actual speech of boys, a form of writing which considering their authors' opportunities for practice and observation, earlier books had bungled badly. Mark Twain had never been a great reader of classic books—he had always preferred talking to reading anyway—and he was under no temptation to make children talk like a combination of the copy book and Caesar's *Gallic Wars*. He followed the colloquial idiom and colloquial syntax. Here are two real boys talking:

". . . Say—what's that?"

"Nothing but a tick."

"Where'd you get him?"

"Out in the woods."

"What'll you take for him?"

"I don't know. I don't want to sell him."

"All right. It's a mighty small tick, anyway."

"Oh, anybody can run a tick down that don't belong to them. I'm satisfied with it. It's a good enough tick for me."

"Sho, there's ticks a plenty. I could have a thousand of 'em if I wanted to."

"Well, why don't you? Becuz you know mighty well you can't. This is a pretty early tick, I reckon. It's the first one I've seen this year."

"Say, Huck—I'll give you my tooth for him."

"Less see it."

Tom got out a bit of paper and carefully unrolled it. Huckleberry viewed it wistfully. The temptation was very strong. At last he said:

"Is it genuwyne?"

Tom lifted his lip and showed the vacancy.

"Well, all right," said Huckleberry, "it's a trade." [36]

Nor did his realistic insight lapse in the more exciting moments of the Injun Joe story. No writer has equaled Mark Twain in recording the snake-like fascination that horror and cruelty have for a boy. Unwilling, frightened though he be, the boy is impelled by his nature deeper and ever deeper into horrors which will turn his young skin into goose-flesh and freeze his blood. The scene in which Tom and Becky perceive the hand bearing the moving light in the cave and realize that it is the hand of Injun Joe is, as Brander Matthews has said, "one of the very finest things in the literature of adventure since Robinson Crusoe first saw a single footprint in the sand of the sea-shore." [37]

By common consent *Tom Sawyer*, excellent as it is, must be reckoned inferior to *Huckleberry Finn*. To try to explain why this is so is merely to restate the assertion in another form: Huck is a more interesting boy than Tom. Perhaps, too, Mark Twain was on his "good behavior" more definitely in *Tom Sawyer* than in *Huckleberry Finn*. He was anxious to please the large constituency of readers represented by Howells, editor of the *Atlantic*. Tom's pious remarks to Huck in the last chapter suggest as much. It is true that on the whole the friendship with Howells was beneficial to Mark Twain. Howells was one of his best critics. It is true also that Howells valued the high spirits and mettlesomeness of Mark Twain, but there is no use in denying that he was in the beginning at least, something of a check-rein on Mark Twain. He liked Mark Twain to feel natural; he even ordered Scotch-and-soda to make him feel natural when he visited Howells. He urged Mark Twain when writing for *The Atlantic Monthly* not to "write *at* any supposed *Atlantic* audience, but yarn it off as if into [Howells'] sympathetic ear." [38] Yet general advice was one thing and editorial alertness was another. When he read the manuscript of *Tom Sawyer*, Howells wrote that it was the "best boy story" he ever read.[39] Yet when he realized that he had failed to see the word *hell* (in Huck's remark "They comb me all to hell"), he hastened to say he would "have that swearing out in an instant . . . it won't do for children." [40] A minor point this—to use or not to use "hell"—but the incident serves to illustrate a checking influence which, as Paine's biography shows, Mark Twain wrote under for some time to come. He welcomed Howells' aid,[41] but it is likely that his art suffered a little. Certainly *Tom Sawyer* is more of a "goody-goody" book than *Huckleberry Finn*.[42]

Tom Sawyer's complement, and greater part, *The Adventures of Huckleberry Finn*, appeared eight years later. In the meantime Mark Twain had published many sketches and tales as well as the reportorial *A Tramp Abroad* (1880) and *The Prince and the Pauper* (1881)[43] and *Life on the Mississippi* (1883). The last of these, the fullest expression of Mark Twain's experience of four years as a pilot, was an amplification of a series of sketches published in *The Atlantic Monthly* (January to June, 1875) as "Old Times on the Mississippi." [44] It contains a reference to Huck Finn and an adventure of that rogue (subsequently omitted from *Huckleberry Finn*) together with the comment that the adventure is "from a book which I have been working at, by fits and starts, during the past five or six years." [45] As a matter of fact he had begun to work on *Huck Finn* as early as 1876. In its original phases, however, he liked it "only tolerably well" and considered that he might "possibly pigeonhole or burn the MS when it is done." [46] These callous remarks concerning what was to be (after much revision) his chief claim to immortality!

Huckleberry Finn is of sterner stuff than *Tom Sawyer*, possibly because Huck himself was based largely on an actual boy, Tom Blankenship, who was several degrees more shady in background and more rugged in character than the Samuel Clemens who had drawn on himself so largely for Tom Sawyer's portrait. The boys' club atmosphere which hovers occasionally over *Tom Sawyer* is largely banished in *Huckleberry Finn* and is indeed most noticeable in Tom's insistence on "regularly" freeing Jim after he is already legally freed. The river flows deeper through *Huckleberry Finn*, too. If, as has been suggested, critics have exaggerated the extent of the river's influence in Mark Twain,[47] this book is a poor place to hatch a rebuttal to their argument. The river evokes the deepest romance and the most eerie moments in the book besides affording much-needed mooring for the somewhat scattered episodes of the story. The raft on the river is one of the most important pieces of machinery in American fiction and its freight, part black and part white, one of the most cherished loadings. The river, too, is the best place to look at the stars from:

> It's lovely to live on a raft. We had the sky up there, all speckled with stars, and we used to lay on our backs and look up at them, and discuss about whether they was made or only just happened. Jim he allowed they was made, but I allowed they happened; I judged it would have took too long to *make* so many. Jim said the moon could a *laid* them; well, that looked kind of reasonable, so I didn't say nothing against it, because I've seen a frog lay most as many, so of course it could be done. We used to watch the stars that fell, too, and see them streak down. Jim allowed they'd got spoiled and was hove out of the nest.[48]

Here we are not far from the centre of the epic quality of *Huckleberry Finn*—a derelict boy and a runaway slave on a makeshift raft floating perilously down the centre of the continent with the passengers giving voice to crude symbolism to express their feeling about the birth of the infinite heavens.

This tone, which is shattered elsewhere in the book, gives *Huckleberry Finn* permanent value as art, but could not make it a popular classic. There must be exciting, original narrative. The action here is perhaps better unified than in *Tom Sawyer*, but the most that can be said is that its parts are basted together. The reader is warned against looking for a plot on pain of death administered by the author.[49] The fortunes of Huck and of Jim do run through the book and the fate of Jim does provide a focal problem. But focus is lost when the reader's interest is switched to prolonged episodic treatment of the Grangerford-Shepherdson feud and (despite Jim's frequent reappearance) the picaresque plundering engaged in by "the Duke of Bridgewater" and "the late Dauphin." Jim is dumped out of the story when it is convenient to talk of other matters, that is all. Yet he is a character drawn (albeit in simple strokes) with great sympathy and understanding: he is a reminder of the fact, often lost sight of, that Mark Twain was first of all a Southerner.[50] The rogues who steal the show for so long—the Duke and the Dauphin—represent types of sharpers and fakers who actually operated up and down the Mississippi in Mark Twain's youth. Mark Twain undoubtedly had some first-hand acquaintance with their kind in his piloting days, but there is discernible in *Huckleberry Finn* also a literary strain derived from one of the few kinds of narrative Mark Twain enjoyed reading, the picaresque.[51] The cony-catching tricks and dodges employed by Mark Twain's bogus gentry are far older than the towns of Hannibal or Cairo. Even Huck exhibits a dexterity that at times casts a literary suspicion upon him—as for example when he is discovered for a boy when he closes his legs to catch the knife instead of letting the apron catch it. Yet Huck's character is not seriously flawed by literary inheritance, and his mischiefmaking like that of Tom's is comparatively mild:

> Huck . . . is a rogue with limitations. Although ready in lies, deceits, and disguises, and a petty thief, he is sound at heart. He scruples at helping to steal a "nigger;" [*sic*] he cannot bring himself to join with professional rogues in a swindle of moment; he protects the weak, and is loyal to his friends. To the Don Quixote of the imaginative Tom Sawyer he plays a delightful Sancho.[52]

But Huck is essentially an American boy, atypical perhaps in his scabrous background but fully representative of his general species in his interest in dead cats, indigenous superstitions, raft-life, petty pilfering, playing pirate, and various oddments growing out of juvenile conception of the life of chivalry and adventure. He is native too in his contempt for the alleged advantages of clean clothes and domestic security. He speaks an uncouth but serviceable vernacular. He has a wholesome resistance to surface polish and the softening effects of culture and intramural religion. He is more real in this respect than his father. For when the father discovers Huck's temporary "improvement" under the hand of Miss Watson, his remarks are carried beyond the point of such a father's natural protest. Here, as often, Mark Twain allows himself to push his fun-making beyond realistic limits:

> "Don't you give me none o' your lip," says he. "You've put on considerable many frills since I been away. I'll take you down a peg before I get done with you. You're educated, too, they say

—can read and write. You think you're better'n your father, now, don't you, because he can't? *I'll* take it out of you. Who told you you might meddle with such hifalut'n foolishness, hey?—who told you you could?"

"The widow. She told me."

"The widow, hey?—and who told the widow she could put in her shovel about a thing that ain't none of her business?"

"Nobody never told her."

"Well, I'll learn her how to meddle. And looky here—you drop that school, you hear? I'll learn people to bring up a boy to put on airs over his own father and let on to be better'n what *he* is. You lemme catch you fooling around that school again, you hear? Your mother couldn't read, and she couldn't write, nuther, before she died. None of the family couldn't before *they* died. *I* can't; and here you're a-swelling yourself up like this. I ain't the man to stand it—you hear? Say, lemme hear you read."

I took up a book and begun something about General Washington and the wars. When I'd read about a half a minute, he fetched the book a whack with his hand and knocked it across the house. He says:

"It's so. You can do it. I had my doubts when you told me. Now looky here; you stop that putting on frills. I won't have it. I'll lay for you, my smarty; and if I catch you about that school I'll tan you good. First you know you'll get religion, too. I never see such a son." [53]

The character of Huck, like that of most of Mark Twain's people, is of course finally revealed in action not in "analysis." Besides those traits already mentioned Huck displayed a superb resourcefulness in the face of difficulty, and it is this as much as anything else which makes him a hero. Mark Twain showed it in various episodes, of which the near-capture of Nigger Jim may serve as an example not only of Huck's skill in meeting an emergency but also of Mark Twain's incomparable skill in investing exciting incident with a maximum of suspense. If he was unequal to sustaining a plot, Mark Twain had few equals in the management of incident. In this case, as often, he brings his hero to within an ace of defeat only to let him recover. The process is then repeated, the tension constantly increasing, a second and sometimes a third time. Finally the reader sees no possible means of escape, but by an ingenious reversal Mark Twain saves the situation through stratagem. The situation in point is created when two men, hunting runaway Negroes, suspect that Huck (at the moment in a canoe) is harboring one on the raft. He admits that there is a man on board the raft but when asked if the man is black or white he is so clumsy and hesitating with

his lie (saying the occupant of the raft is white) that the men decide
they will go and see for themselves. This move Huck tries cannily to
forestall by telling them that the man is his "pap" and that he is sick.
But the men, though tempted not to waste the time, reckon they'll have
to go help Huck tow the raft ashore. From such dangerous co-operation Huck must now rescue the situation by devising a new stratagem.
The men have actually rowed a stroke or two toward the raft when
Huck attempts to dissuade them:

> "Pap'll be mighty much obleeged to you, I can tell you. Every-
> body goes away when I want them to help me tow the raft ashore,
> and I can't do it by myself."
> "Well, that's infernal mean. Odd, too. Say, boy, what's the
> matter with your father?"
> "It's the—a—the—well, it ain't anything much."
> They stopped pulling. It warn't but a mighty little ways to the
> raft now. One says:
> "Boy, that's a lie. What *is* the matter with your pap? Answer
> up square now, and it'll be the better for you."
> "I will, sir, I will, honest—but don't leave us, please. It's the—
> the—Gentlemen, if you'll only pull ahead, and let me heave you
> the headline, you won't have to come a-near the raft—please do."
> "Set her back, John, set her back!" says one. They backed
> water. "Keep away, boy—keep to looard. Confound it, I just ex-
> pect the wind has blowed it to us. Your pap's got the small-pox,
> and you know it precious well. Why didn't you come out and
> say so? Do you want to spread it all over?"
> "Well," says I, a-blubbering, "I've told everybody before, and
> they just went away and left us." [54]

The fear of smallpox effectually stops the slave-hunters, who now
prepare to compromise with their consciences by giving Huck elaborate
directions for a rescue at a point considerably lower on the river, ad-
vising him not to "let on" again about the smallpox. The episode is now
virtually ended, a perfect example of the creation and maintenance of
suspense. But Mark Twain cannot resist the temptation to gild the
story by having the men feel so sorry for Huck and his poor father that
each of them puts a twenty-dollar gold piece on a board for Huck to
pick up when it floats to him. Here in one incident is the method of
Mark Twain at its best—followed by a tail-piece which almost ruins the
effect by a touch of farce. Of many similar units the narratives of Mark
Twain are composed. They refuse to coalesce into one whole, but each
is in its way superb. Their effectiveness like that of the whole book
comes from the skilful ratio Mark Twain maintains between realism and

romance. His faithful attention to certain minutiae forces the reader to endorse Mark Twain as a realist, but at the same time the book is stepped up imaginatively by a subtle process which divests it of that bleak prosaicness which is just as true a part of childhood as romantic zest. In the last analysis the realism is predominant, and this is only natural, for the whole story is conveyed to the reader in that virile, colloquial idiom, frequently taking the form of authentic dialect,[55] which was one of Mark Twain's chief contributions to the novel.

The derivatives of Mark Twain's interest in "Tom Sawyer" as a fictional agent, *Tom Sawyer Abroad* (1894) and *Tom Sawyer, Detective* (1896) consist of comparatively thin humor and frothy episode which did not go down well with the public.[56] In the former Tom and Huck and Nigger Jim are more or less accidentally carried up in a balloon with a fanatical professor. The man of science attempts to murder the lads but is himself tumbled out of the basket, and the younger generation carries on alone until the balloon reaches the Sahara Desert. The story from here foregoes roguery in favor of extravaganza centred around various points of interest including the Pyramids and Mt. Sinai. The second, *Tom Sawyer, Detective*, shows Tom and Huck engaged in sleuthing a case of jewel-robbery followed by a murder trial. The action is drawn from an "old-time Swedish criminal trial" [57] modified in detail and transferred to an American setting (Arkansas). Neither book is wholly successful. Tom and Huck could be transported abroad but not transplanted there—even in a region which their globe-trotting progenitor had observed at first hand. The familiar setting of the second book is not strongly felt, and, though Tom Sawyer discourses readily on a score of topics, he seems mainly a deputy of the ever-curious and ingenious Mark Twain. Huck, whose laissez-faire grammar and syntax form the stylistic medium for both books, is somewhat better. Yet both books are "green." In order for material to be good for Mark Twain, it had to "set" a good while, and his reportorial gifts were permanently useful only when they made an alliance with his department of reminiscence.

All these books about Tom and Huck did not, of course, proceed from Mark Twain's pen in succession. After *Tom Sawyer*, his first long narrative was *The Prince and the Pauper*, conceived as a play but finally published as a story in 1881. Its foreign setting in an olden period necessitated considerable research on Mark Twain's part. He seems to have got the central idea from Charlotte M. Yonge's *The Prince and the Page*, but characteristically planned to multiply his opportunities for "situation" by having not only a prince as a beggar but also a beggar as a prince.[58] The general historical background he altered from Hume's *History of England* and the more intimate details of lowlife from Timbs' *Curiosities of London* and Richard Head's *The English Rogue*. Many of the frightful punishments described were based on comparable materials in James Hammond Trumbull's *The Blue Laws of Connecticut*, a work which, by comparing them with American laws, showed the greater cruelty of English laws.

With all these sources, however, Mark Twain did not wholly depart from the type of narrative in which he had already excelled: for *The Prince and the Pauper* is again a study of boyhood adventure. In this case the adventure is manipulated into as respectable a plot as one could wish—certainly the best plot Mark Twain ever devised. Filled with romantic tales told by Father Andrew, Tom Canty, ragamuffin of Offal Court, dreams of being King. One day he manages to get the attention of the Prince of Wales, who is inspired by Tom's eloquence (not far different from Tom Sawyer's eloquence when he wished to escape white-washing the fence) with a desire to try out the lowly life and "revel in the mud." The lads change clothes. The Prince's troubles begin at once, and he presently vows vengeance upon Tom Canty, who is now being groomed for the Kingship amid many comic scenes. The Prince, vainly asserting his true position, suffers badly at the hands of a mob until he is rescued by Miles Hendon, also fallen upon evil days through the machinations of a wicked brother. Many adventures are in store for the scion of royalty. He is impressed into picaresque service. He falls in with a crazy hermit, who prepares to carve him with an enormous knife—a Gothic scene as blood-curdling as any in Mark Twain. He endures prison life. Upon his final release he arrives at London, with Miles Hendon, just as Tom Canty is preparing to assume the Kingship. Tom's conscience has bothered him surprisingly little, but when the Prince manages to get in and assert his birth, Tom corroborates him—though general doubt remains until the Prince tells where the Great Seal is hidden. The true Prince makes Tom his ward and Miles Hendon an earl. The suspense is maintained by means of coincidence and partly by the author's arbitrary decision not to allow either lad to make a convincing statement of the true state of affairs. The Prince's conduct is managed with more verisimilitude than the pauper's. For Tom, an astute boy to begin with, has to act like a very stupid one for the sake of comic effects in his new rôle: a boy who had heard and dreamed as much of royalty should have made a quicker adaptation. Yet on the whole the action is managed more coherently than in any of Mark Twain's other long fictions. The picaresque episodes do not run away with the story; rather, they serve to characterize the Prince and to foreshadow the nature of his conduct when he shall have resumed his position. For Mark Twain's social purpose is given sharp emphasis at many points: he wishes to bludgeon mercilessly the older ideas of monarchial, aristocratic, and ecclesiastical prerogative. The reader's sensibilities are not spared in the slightest in the scene in which the Prince sees two Baptist women burned to death. The Prince is "furious" at this and other "inhumanities." Upon later assuming his Kingship he is loath, after such experiences as he has had, to inflict penalties urged upon him by "some gilded vassal of the crown":

> "What dost *thou* know of suffering and oppression? I and my people know, but not thou." [59]

Like *Tom Sawyer* and *Gulliver's Travels*, *The Prince and the Pauper* is both a boy's book and a book for adults. To some extent the same observation applies to *The Connecticut Yankee*, one of Mark Twain's funniest and saddest books.

Excepting his *Personal Recollections of Joan of Arc* no book of Mark Twain's has so divided critical opinion as *A Connecticut Yankee in King Arthur's Court* (1889). Andrew Lang could not even read a book burlesquing, albeit incidentally, such a cherished legend as Malory's *Morte d'Arthur*.[60] The book was slow to gain appreciation of the English in general, who apparently didn't want to be "pried up to a higher level of manhood." [61] DeVoto believes that "the book is chaos." [62] On the other hand William Dean Howells believed it would be "ranged . . . as a masterpiece of humor beside the great work of Cervantes." [63] Mark Twain also to his own surprise was "prodigiously pleased" with it thirty years later.[64] It was Stuart Sherman's opinion that "it represents Mark Twain more completely than any other single book on his list, and so may serve as a touchstone to distinguish those who care for the man from those who only care for some of his stories." [65] Certainly in *The Connecticut Yankee* Mark Twain expressed himself without let or hindrance.

Hank Morgan of East Hartford is admitted to the realm of King Arthur by the crude and familiar device of a blow on the head which sends him spinning backward in time thirteen hundred years. Morgan soon proves himself a greater magician than Merlin by predicting an eclipse. Then follow his various moves to improve primitive and iniquitous conditions. King Arthur is impressed by Morgan's shocking revelations and proposed reforms, but there are plenty of enemies. Sir Sagramor, returned from several years of "grailing," challenges him to a duel but is subdued, unchivalrously enough, by lariat and pistol. But the main foe of the new civilization created by Morgan is the Established Church, whose interdict finally circumvents him. A knight stabs Morgan, and Merlin casts a spell by which he will not awake for thirteen hundred years. Within this simple framework Mark Twain finds the opportunity of exercising almost all his literary talents. The book bounds recklessly from one extreme to another:

> It displays [said Stuart Sherman] every variety of his style from the mock-heroic and shirt-sleeve journalese of the Yankee's familiar vein to the careful euphonies of his descriptions of English landscape and the Dantean mordancy of the chapter "In the Queen's Dungeons." It exhibits his humour in moods from the grimmest to the gayest, mingling scenes of pathos, terror, and excruciating cruelty with hilarious comic inventions and adventures, which prove their validity for the imagination by abiding in the memory: the sewing-machine worked by the bowing hermit, the mules blushing at the jokes of the pilgrims, the expedition with Alisande, the contests with Merlin, the expedition with King Arthur, Launcelot and the bicycle squad, and the annihilation of the chivalry of England.[66]

In this book the reader gets no rest from the twin batteries of Mark Twain's humor and indignation. Refined readers are revolted by the coarse content of many of the jokes, and it must be admitted that Mark Twain often failed, here as elsewhere, to distinguish between better and worse comedy. *A Connecticut Yankee* is certainly inferior to *The Prince and the Pauper* in this respect. On the whole the social criticism interwoven with the humor has worn better than the humor. The distinguishing feature of the social diatribe is not its originality[67] but the sustained sincerity of his savage onslaught. Attacks upon monarchy had been familiar reading in America since the time of Paine and Franklin, but no one could hate special privilege more wholeheartedly than the man who wrote in deepest pity of humble folk obliged to render homage

> as if they had any more occasion to love and honor king and Church and noble than a slave has to love and honor the lash, or a dog has to love and honor the stranger that kicks him! Why, dear me, *any* kind of royalty, howsoever modified, *any* kind of aristocracy, howsoever pruned, is rightly an insult . . .[68]

To him the "aristocracy" is "but a band of slaveholders under another name." [69] Nor are the allusions to Southern slavery in his own time tempered by Clemens's own memories of reasonably contented slaves

at Hannibal, for the legal framework upholding the institution he heartily condemned and slave auctions he regarded as "hellish." [70] An elaborate, if somewhat tediously naive, discussion argues against oppression
of the wage-earning class.[71] But Mark Twain's most unrestrained satire
was directed at the Church, which, he was persuaded, was the main
cause of much injustice in the first few centuries A.D.:

> In two or three little centuries it had converted a nation of men
> to a nation of worms. Before the day of the Church's supremacy
> in the world, men were men, and held their heads up, and had a
> man's pride and spirit and independence; and what of greatness
> and position a person got, he got mainly by achievement, not by
> birth. But then the Church came to the front, with an axe to
> grind; and she was wise, subtle, and knew more than one way to
> skin a cat—or a nation; she invented "divine right of kings," and
> propped it all around, brick by brick, with the Beatitudes—
> wrenching them from their good purpose to make them fortify an
> evil one; she preached (to the commoner) humility, obedience to
> superiors, the beauty of self-sacrifice; she preached (to the com-
> moner) meekness under insult; preached (still to the commoner,
> always to the commoner) patience, meanness of spirit, non-re-
> sistance under oppression; and she introduced heritable ranks and
> aristocracies, and taught all the Christian populations of the earth
> to bow down to them and worship them.[72]

To Mark Twain the difficulty was that the Church was a "united"
Church:

> it makes a mighty power, the mightiest conceivable, and then
> when it by and by gets into selfish hands, as it is always bound to
> do, it means death to human liberty and paralysis to human
> thought.[73]

He argued in more general terms that "any Established Church is an
established crime, an established slave-pen," [74] and he believed that since
"concentration of power in a political machine is bad" and since "an
Established Church is only a political machine," the natural reform indicated was to do what had been done in modern times in America,
namely, to "have it cut up into forty free sects." [75]

Such criticism as this, tempered though it was in part by generalization, could not fail to create a formidable body of foes for Mark
Twain.[76] Moreover it is clear that his criticism of the early Church,
though in part justified by historical fact admitted by the clergy itself,
did not do justice to the good works that also distinguished the early

era of the Church. His hostility toward religious organization was only one sign of an increasing philosophical pessimism that was to find its most concentrated fictional expression in *The Mysterious Stranger*, a book which is here definitely foreshadowed by the episode in which the wife in the smallpox hut congratulates herself that husband and daughters are dead and therefore beyond the reach of inevitable unhappiness in England.[77] To him a universe is well-nigh futile in which man's intelligence is shackled by superstition and his humane impulses are trampled on in the mad pursuit of prosperity. All this, and more, provides the basis of a heavy indictment of "civilization." But critics err who find in the book, with its tags and ideas from Locke and Lecky, any original or carefully articulated criticism.[78] For finally it must be seen that in its warp and woof *A Connecticut Yankee* is emotional, not critical. Next to humor, his sensitiveness to human suffering (revealed in his rage at oppression) was Mark Twain's most distinguishing trait. And here, in this strange medley of humor and rancor, lies its most energetic expression. Its course is erratic, but its momentum is terrific, and at its centre is the boiling indignation of Samuel Clemens, son of an equalitarian frontier democracy.

Given a republican country settled by people only lately come from a nation where a titled aristocracy still obtains, it is inevitable that there will be hordes of novels whose plots hinge on the more or less hypothetical claim of American "heirs" to landed estates abroad. Most of the American novels thus conceived were developed along conventional lines with free use of not entirely accurate description of luxurious life of English gentry. Even Hawthorne used the basic theme,[79] though he gave it philosophical weight. Mark Twain, who was never very good at inventing brand new plots, was fain to use such a framework, with new effects, in *The American Claimant* (1892). Instead of capitalizing the snob-value of his theme, he sprayed the book with farce from beginning to end. When the preceding American claimant, Simon Lathers, dies, the new American claimant, Mulberry Sellers, sets about making good his alleged inheritance. In this effort he is unexpectedly aided by the Viscount Berkeley, son of the earl, for with his curious passion for plots involving duplication, Mark Twain has arranged that the young Viscount, smitten by conscience, should decide to relinquish the estate honorably and go to America at the same time that the new claimant gets ready to press his demands.[80] The enumeration of the details of this trans-Atlantic adjustment constitutes the plot of *The American Claimant*. The story takes place chiefly at "Rossmore Towers," the new name for Sellers' "rickety" frame house on "the ragged edge of Washington." [81] In the end the

Viscount, who has been disguised as the homespun "Mr. Tracy," wins the hand of "Gwendolen"—the name with which Sally Sellers had been dubbed by her optimistic father as soon as he heard of the death of the former claimant. This book, which critics have for the most part ignored in discussion beyond referring to Sellers as "an American Micawber," deserves no great praise in its entirety.[82] The horse-play of Mark Twain wears out its fun after a hundred pages. The character of Sellers also wears out and is replaced by a dummy of the same name— a very amusing dummy once it is accepted as such. In this capacity Sellers is guilty of such enormities as offering to buy Siberia and "reorganizing the climates of the earth" with a plan whereby he will "furnish climates to order, for cash or negotiable paper, taking the old climates in part payment." [83] Sellers is an irresistible clown. Yet he is honestly derived from an actual person, James Lampton, who was the "favorite cousin" of Clemens' mother. The core of his character is well enough suggested by "Lady Rossmore's" remark that "it's a blessed thing to have an imagination that can always make you satisfied, no matter how you are fixed." [84] This "real" person appears indirectly in a conversation between Mrs. Sellers and Washington Hawkins (also late of *The Gilded Age*) in the third chapter of the book, but presently is swept out of real existence by farce. If Mark Twain had wanted to do a memorable realistic portrait of an adult character out of his family materials, Sellers would have been his man. But serious portraiture he had little patience with. Pudd'nhead Wilson, the title character of his next novel, is not drawn with perfect success. Yet he was the carrier and focus of enough authentic early recollections to invest *Pudd'nhead Wilson* with a special charm that is not wholly dissipated by its ludicrous plot and the incredible Italian twins.

If Clemens hadn't been a writer, he should have been a lawyer. In that capacity he would have been able to capitalize many of his most abiding interests—money and banking, property, equity, evidence, court procedure, claims, statistics, chronology, and in general the *solution* of problems—as well as his "Indian-like . . . faculty of observing innumerable little things . . ." [85] and his aptitude for precision in the handling of minute details. His very vocabulary is unusually full of legal terms and phraseology. *Pudd'nhead Wilson* (1894) was therefore a natural book for him to have written; for it is largely centred about a lawyer, and the climax of the plot involves the legal procedure (carefully submitted by the novelist to an attorney for checking) of a murder trial [86] whose issue was determined by the (then) comparatively new device of finger-printing.[87]

The major part of *Pudd'nhead Wilson* was apparently written in haste, and its reduplicating plot—involving mixed babies and mixed twins as well—bears little of the verisimilitude which is manifested in those parts of the narrative which have to do directly with Wilson.[88] A special interest attaches to Wilson himself during his progress from Pudd'nhead to Mayor and respected lawyer. Mark Twain's sympathy evidently went out to a man who unjustly suffered considerable damage to his reputation over a period of years by reason of one spontaneous but ill-advised remark that he made upon his arrival in a provincial town.

A second major interest in *Pudd'nhead Wilson* is the character and fate of Roxana, one of Mark Twain's most real and attractive characters. The famous scene in which she is sold down the river derives from the very roots of Mark Twain's fibre.[89] Equally fine, however, is the characterization of Roxana in the earlier parts of the book. Here the author merges his humor with other elements—instead of, as often, merely pinning it to his text—and the result is the creation of a true character in a real environment. Roxana's reaction to the news that Percy Driscoll has been robbed illustrates this better method. She had not taken the money: that she knew, for she

> had been saved in the nick of time by a revival in the colored Methodist church, a fortnight before, at which time and place she "got religion." The very next day after that gracious experience, while her change of style was fresh upon her and she was vain of her purified condition, her master left a couple of dollars lying unprotected on his desk, and she happened upon that temptation when she was polishing around with a dust-rag. She looked at the money awhile with a steadily rising resentment, then she burst out with:
> "Dad blame dat revival, I wisht it had 'a' be'n put off till to-morrow!"
> Then she covered the tempter with a book, and another member of the kitchen cabinet got it. She made this sacrifice as a matter of religious etiquette; as a thing necessary just now, but by no means to be wrested into a precedent; no, a week or two would limber up her piety, then she would be rational again, and the next two dollars that got left out in the cold would find a comforter—and she could name the comforter.[90]

Nor is this a mere matter of comedy to Mark Twain. The incident leads him into a general consideration of the state of a Negro's conscience with respect to minor thefts. Here Mark Twain is his best self —humorous in his treatment, sympathetic in his attitude, and at the same time careful to make his point clear regarding the relative culpability of master and man. It is clear that he loves Roxana, that he understands Negro temperament, and that he is no fanatic in his attitude toward the ethical problems involved in slavery:

> Was she bad? Was she worse than the general run of her race? No. They had an unfair show in the battle of life, and they held it no sin to take military advantage of the enemy—in a small way; in a small way, but not in a large one. They would smouch provisions from the pantry whenever they got a chance; or a brass thimble, or a cake of wax, or an emery-bag, or a paper of needles, or a silver spoon, or a dollar bill, or small articles of clothing, or any other property of light value; and so far were they from considering such reprisals sinful, that they would go to church and shout and pray the loudest and sincerest with their plunder in their pockets. A farm smoke-house had to be kept heavily padlocked, for even the colored deacon himself could not resist a ham when Providence showed him in a dream, or otherwise, where such a thing hung lonesome and longed for some one to love. But with a hundred hanging before him the deacon would not take two—that is, on the same night. On frosty nights the humane negro prowler would warm the end of a plank and put it up under the cold claws of chickens roosting in a tree; a drowsy hen would step on to the comfortable board, softly clucking her gratitude, and the prowler would dump her into his bag, and later into his stomach, perfectly sure that in taking this trifle from the man who daily robbed him of an inestimable treasure—his liberty—he was not committing any sin that God would remember against him in the Last Great Day.[91]

In a third way *Pudd'nhead Wilson* provides critical challenge. How good was Mark Twain without his humor? Could he write straightaway description? The answer is partly here—in the first half-dozen paragraphs of the book. They illustrate what G. K. Chesterton thought one of the main virtues of the book, namely, its "true touch of the life of the Old South." [92] The description of Dawson's Landing is a page out of experience almost untouched by humor, unspoiled by the clichés which too often mar his serious descriptions. It is an illustration of the dictum of Swift—that good style is simply the right words in the right places:

> The scene of this chronicle is the town of Dawson's Landing, on the Missouri side of the Mississippi, half a day's journey, per steamboat, below St. Louis.
> In 1830 it was a snug little collection of modest one and two-

story frame dwellings whose white-washed exteriors were almost concealed from sight by climbing tangles of rose-vines, honey-suckles, and morning-glories. Each of these pretty homes had a garden in front, fenced with white palings and opulently stocked with hollyhocks, marigolds, touch-me-nots, prince's-feathers, and other old-fashioned flowers; while on the window-sills of the houses stood wooden boxes containing moss-rose plants and terra-cotta pots in which grew a breed of geranium whose spread of in-tensely red blossoms accented the prevailing pink tint of the rose-clad house-front like an explosion of flame. When there was room on the ledge outside of the pots and boxes for a cat, the cat was there—in sunny weather—stretched at full length, asleep and bliss-ful, with her furry belly to the sun and a paw curved over her nose. Then that house was complete, and its contentment and peace were made manifest to the world by this symbol, whose testimony is infallible. A home without a cat—and a well-fed, well-petted and properly revered cat—may be a perfect home, perhaps, but how can it prove title? [93]

If necessary, Mark Twain can use a metaphor—though he commonly eschewed figurative language as suspiciously "literary"—but when he does he handles it briskly:

The hamlet's front was washed by the clear waters of the great river; its body stretched itself rearward up a gentle incline; its most rearward border fringed itself out and scattered its houses about the base-line of the hills; the hills rose high, inclosing the town in a half-moon curve, clothed with forests from foot to sum-mit.[94]

Mark Twain *could* write good serious prose, as these passages prove, and if he did not do so more often[95] the explanation lies partly in the fact that although he often worked hard at his books, he generally worked sporadically. If he had been willing (and able) to sustain the mellow tone of the opening and a few other parts of the book, *Pudd'nhead Wilson*, brimful of humor as it is, could have been his best serious novel.

There were two outlets for Mark Twain's serious nature, the vitriolic and the elegaic or reverential or romantic. Doubtless it was the latter which kept him sane in a crazy world, but without question the former was, as *The Connecticut Yankee* proved, the more valuable to his art. In *Joan of Arc* (1896) he used both outlets, but the second was so much the more conspicuous that the whole book must be set down, in spite of his own opinion[96] and the pious plaudits of those who were glad to see

that the hardened humorist had a reverent side, as comparatively ineffective except as a monument to that chivalry which, in books as in
life, characterized Mark Twain's attitude toward good women.[97] As
history *Joan* is not important, for it displays the results of no more than
"sufficient" scholarship.[98] True, as an indictment of the ineffable corruption and cruelty, whether in church, state, or army, which brought
Joan low at last, it is thoroughly grounded not only in deep indignation
but also in documentary evidence. Yet the tone of the book is impaired
by that heavy-handed exaggeration which, however legitimate as an
asset of the humorous writer, may become a liability in the hands of
a serious writer engaged in a transaction largely historical. The book
opens with a blaze of overstatement which is no fit background for the
creation of a character whom, it has been a cliché to say, Mark Twain
has succeeded in making "human" for the first time. Of what use to
damn a whole century (and the people in it) by saying arbitrarily that
it was "the brutalest, the wickedest, the rottenest in history since the
darkest ages"? [99] How does it really serve Joan to pile up remorselessly
the crude contrasts that form the substance of the rest of the same paragraph? How does it make Joan "human" to set her against an unbeliev-
able background?—

> She was truthful when lying was the common speech of men; she
> was honest when honesty was become a lost virtue; she was a
> keeper of promises when the keeping of a promise was expected
> of no one; she gave her great mind to great thoughts and great
> purposes when other great minds wasted themselves upon pretty
> fancies or upon poor ambitions; she was modest, and fine, and
> delicate when to be loud and coarse might be said to be universal;
> she was full of pity when a merciless cruelty was the rule; she was
> steadfast when stability was unknown, and honorable in an age
> which had forgotten what honor was; she was a rock of convic-
> tions in a time when men believed in nothing and scoffed at all
> things; she was unfailingly true in an age that was false to the core;
> she maintained her personal dignity unimpaired in an age of fawn-
> ings and servilities; she was of a dauntless courage when hope and
> courage had perished in the hearts of her nation; she was spotlessly
> pure in mind and body when society in the highest places was foul
> in both—she was all these things in an age when crime was the com-
> mon business of lords and princes, and when the highest person-
> ages in Christendom were able to astonish even that infamous era
> and make it stand aghast at the spectacle of their atrocious lives
> black with unimaginable treacheries, butcheries, and beastialities
> [*sic*].[100]

This is rhetoric and rant—as Mark Twain would have been the first to recognize if it had been written by someone else, say Scott or Cooper. It is very carefully articulated rant, however, and this is perhaps the main point: *Joan of Arc* has been a popular book among readers who like a showy style. It was also one of the countless romances of the 1890's which were eagerly read as antidote to unpleasant economic pills that had to be swallowed in a period of depression. As for the author's own high opinion of it, that may be explained if his real love of the subject be excepted, largely by the hard work he expended not only in the research but also in rhetorical polishing. Not that the book is a complete failure. Much vigor was needed to describe the military operations, the colorful pageantry, and the painful episodes of the "history." Mark Twain was quite equal to carrying out the detail of a narrative whose framework did not have to be invented. The practice he had had in describing cruelty and oppression at Arthur's Court and in the underworld of London was serviceable when it came to reciting the even more diabolical cruelty of English soldiery and oligarchy on foreign soil. Trenchant phrase and even intermittent humor soon naturally revealed Mark Twain as the author of the book, which was first presented to the public anonymously. And yet Mark Twain's art was not sufficient to get the reader back into the fourteenth century and keep him there. He could fabricate picturesqueness but he could not sustain illusion. Surprisingly enough it was not modern ideas or American humor that exerted a baneful effect but a kind of trumped-up romanticism. W. D. Howells, kindly disposed as he was toward all of Mark Twain's books, cried "enough" at certain aspects of *Joan:*

> I am not at all troubled when he comes out with a bit of good, strong, downright modern American feeling; my suffering begins when he does the supposed mediæval things. Then I suspect that his armor is of tin, that the castles and rocks are pasteboard, that the mob of citizens and soldiers who fill the air with the clash of their two-up-and-two-down combats, and the well-known muffled roar of their voices have been hired in at so much a night, and that Joan is sometimes in an awful temper behind the scenes; and I am thankful when the brave Sieur Louis forgets himself again.[101]

What held up better than Mark Twain's romantic hocus-pocus in *Joan of Arc* was the power of his invective, his hatred of injustice. And it is finally the strength not the tenderness which accounts for the best writing in the book. As for the "radiant" Joan herself, her portrait testifies to Mark Twain's genuine feeling of reverence for an ideal. Taken together with his pessimism, to be discussed later, it perhaps shows that Mark Twain was a frustrated idealist. But he expressed his ideal best by indirection and his open adoration of Joan's sainthood seems—though the question is doubtless one of taste—fumblingly overstated and inept.[102] There are some things better left unsaid by every writer. If, as Paine said, *Joan of Arc* is a "beautiful shrine," the suspicion remains that building shrines was not Mark Twain's "gift." He was handier as an iconoclast.

After writing *Joan of Arc* (and *Tom Sawyer Abroad*) Mark Twain did not abruptly give up writing extended works, but no single long work appeared whose essential character was that of fiction. The longest, *Following the Equator* (1897), belonged in the company of *A Tramp Abroad* and *The Innocents Abroad*. The *Autobiography* he dictated during 1906-08, to be published after his death. Many short pieces continued to appear (or were written, to be published posthumously) up to the time of his death. Most famous of the short pieces definitely fictional in character were *The Man Who Corrupted Hadleyburg* (1899) and *The $30,000 Bequest* (1904). There were others that employed an interesting narrative or dialogue framework for the display of quasi-scientific or philosophical ideas: of these the most important were *The Mysterious Stranger* (written 1898) and *What Is Man?* (privately printed in 1906). In addition he wrote innumerable sketches and articles, the profits from which were essential to meet the heavy living expenses of his later years. Most of these took a humorous turn but a fair share of them give temperate expression to his somewhat unorthodox views on serious topics. All his life Mark Twain had been an interested student of man's place in a mysterious universe and man's reaction to the social framework in which he lives with his fellows. Gradually too he developed general ideas on the function and training of literary men. He was not only a humorist but also a thinker of sorts. Consequently he is not to be understood fully without some consideration of his opinions on politics, religion, and literary tradition.

Mark Twain's mind was much "on the go," but it is difficult to conceive of his mental processes apart from his dynamic personality, his magnetic temperament, and his hair-spring emotions, including humor. If, however, one tries to distinguish between his mental processes and his feelings, it becomes apparent that the prime characteristic of his mind was a comparative simplicity. He was morbidly interested in dreams and he was superstitious.[103] Mental telepathy was one of the "rages" that occupied him for a time.[104] Yet he had practically nothing of the real mystic in him—so little that his sympathetic treatment of

Joan of Arc's visions seems somewhat anomalous. Much as he was interested in the first cause of the universe, he never showed great imagination in his quest of it but kept his feet solidly on the earth and submitted cosmic problems to rudimentary rational tests. He burlesqued Melville.[105] He ridiculed Christian Science from a purely literal platform. In his literary criticism he was often shrewd but never profound. Indeed he was seldom interested for long in anything which he could not verify by fact or assess the value of by simple reasoning processes.

Within his limited range Mark Twain showed a keen active mind. In small matters he was likely to be meticulously accurate and exact; in many respects he hated slovenliness. When not disposed to be humorous he was careful of statistics and measurements—careful as a river pilot had to be. He took pride in the workings of his own mind and sometimes he tells us with naive satisfaction exactly how he arrived at a simple inference. In *Pudd'nhead Wilson* he is not trying to be humorous when he explains why a conversation outside Wilson's office disturbed him: "It was carried on in yells, which showed that the people engaged in it were not close together." [106] He took a similar (inoffensive) pleasure in detective procedure, a conspicuous feature in several of his books. He had a passion for documentation that sometimes[107] placed a tedious burden on his humorous progress. He had a peculiar interest in grammar and syntax and was even fussy about exactness in this respect. The laborious story of the translations of *The Jumping Frog* is a good instance of his capacity to be infinitely patient in small matters. He evidently enjoyed the minutiae of problems calling for ingenuity in their solution; observe the Gulliver-like care with which he worked out the literal experiences of Tom Canty and the Prince; Tom Driscoll and Roxana's child. Yet he had no stomach for protracted labors of the mind or a project of real magnitude: even for *Joan of Arc*, the principal exception to this statement, he did not study his sources with as complete thoroughness as Anatole France or Andrew Lang. There was in Mark Twain a certain juvenile quality which caused him to take pleasure in piecing things together, making them fit part for part. He was inventive in small ways. This trait, which was useful more often than not in his stories, was a mark of the literal mind of Mark Twain which operated when his humor was for the time switched off.

His opinions too were relatively simply formed. "[E]vidence," he once said, "is the bones of an opinion," [108] but he seldom used his evidence judicially: he got too excited. His general judgment of people was often good, but he was inclined to see only the larger "bones" of their structure. None of his books treats adequately a really complex character. He saw black and white—and red. Shading was foreign to his nature. The result is that he made many errors of judgment. Very much interested as he was in the copyright law reform, for example, he eagerly took part in working out a proposed revision; but he finally made a most "impracticable" suggestion.[109] According to Howells, he was "the readiest of men to allow an error if he were found in it," [110] but he gave the impression of being dogmatic by reason of his vigorous reiteration of such judgments. He practiced pretty generally the special advice he once gave his daughter Clara with respect to making speeches: "Whatever you say, say it with conviction." [111] Thoughtful deliberation was foreign to his nature. He found it an "unspeakable hardship to write editorials." [112] His thinking was fitful and fragmentary. His was "not a keen or a discriminating or even a high-grade intelligence." [113] He himself said that "life does not consist mainly—or even largely—of facts and happenings" but "of the storm of thoughts that is forever blowing through one's head." [114] The figure is a good one: Mark Twain's thinking suggests the tumult and violence and impermanence of a storm.

Notwithstanding the hurly-burly of Mark Twain's mind, however, there were two types of "storm" that he was visited with so frequently that they constituted a feature of his intellectual climate: his savage onslaughts on political injustice and his uncontrolled attacks on the hypocrisy of organized religion. Doubtless these storms were emotionally induced, but there are discernible in them certain prevailing currents of thought.

There has been difference of opinion regarding Mark Twain as a social critic. G. B. Shaw, who "regarded Clemens as a sociologist before all else," once wrote to Mark Twain: "I am persuaded that the future historian of America will find your works as indispensable to him as a French historian finds the political tracts of Voltaire." [115] Other writers, Van Wyck Brooks among them, believe that Mark Twain suppressed much of his real opinion. Both Shaw and Brooks are right: Mark Twain was enormously significant in spite of (and partly on account of) what he suppressed. In approaching the problem of suppression, one must bear in mind Mark Twain's rather delicate position. It is comparatively easy for a social outcast or an economic derelict to attack the system he thinks responsible for his failure. But Clemens was a successful writer almost from the first. As a successful author he was caught up in and to some extent dependent on the web of the very system which he castigated as so iniquitous. He was living among the pillars of the very structure he sometimes wished to demolish—an irresolute Samson. How could the man who invested in the market on tips from Henry Rogers arraign the capitalistic régime? Was it graceful in the bosom friend of Joseph Twichell, a Hartford minister, to say in print that the latter's profession was a hollow mockery? Moreover it was hard for Clemens to go counter to the wishes of one he revered so much as he did his wife, and there is no doubt that on scores of occasions Mrs. Clemens either persuaded Clemens not to publish an item which she regarded as potentially harmful to his reputation or forced him to drain off its bitterness before he gave it to his public.[116] Then there was Howells, dear Howells. Storms never came up in Howells' mind—only steady temperate breezes—and his mild editorial influence more than once helped to calm Mark Twain—especially when the latter was raging against the Almighty.[117]

All these were real restraining influences and there is no doubt that Mark Twain the writer was modified by them. It is likely too that in doing so he created in himself a state of exasperation that was only partially relieved by private expression, often extremely profane, in conversation and letters. The outlines of his political thought were simple. He believed in a democracy in which men should enjoy equal opportunities. Theoretically, at least, races were not to be discriminated against. The greatest good was liberty and the greatest evil was "slavery"—whether the slavery of Negroes in the South, or the slavery of the minions of a monarch or the spiritual slavery of church-goers, or the slavery of a corrupt nation in the Gilded Age. All types of bondage he assailed (indirectly) in his fiction. He did not advocate the overthrow of the capitalistic system but its control. Nor did he completely disapprove of the "machine age"; indeed he was with many conservative contemporaries in hoping great things from the beneficial direction of mechanical ingenuity.[118] But the accrued benefits seemed few, and Mark Twain chafed at the abuses. What, then, were the radical thoughts of Mark Twain and to what extent did he express them publicly? Mr. Van Wyck Brooks has attempted to sum up the matter:

> Turn to his letters and see what he says in the privacy of his correspondence and memoranda. He is strongly against the tariff; he vehemently defends the principle of the strike and woman suffrage; he is consistently for the union of labour as against the union of capital; he bitterly regrets the formation of the Trusts; "a ruling public and political aristocracy which could create a presidential succession" is, he says, neither more nor less than monarchism. He deals one blow after another against the tendencies of American imperialism, against the Balance of Power, against the Great Power system . . . All this in the privacy of his correspondence! In public, he could not question, he did not

wish to question, the popular drift of his age, the popular cry of his age, "Nothing succeeds like success"! [119]

This is a grim attack, but it is only a small part of a book devoted to the proposition that Mark Twain sold his birthright of love of freedom for a mess of material comfort. On the other hand V. F. Calverton asserts that "at no time did [Mark Twain] 'sell out' his philosophy to the upper bourgeoisie of the East." [120] Is Mr. Brooks too harsh? Is Mr. Calverton indulging in a little wishful thinking? The answer lies, I think, largely in chronology. Mark Twain always harbored radical ideas. In his mind he never "sold out" to special interest. In fact comparatively early in his career he looked forward to the time when he could "stop writing for print." This he planned to do "as soon as [he] could afford" it.[121] Yet, partly for reasons given above, he deferred this expensive pleasure of saying plainly what he thought. Most of his early books reflected his radical views chiefly in the mirror of history, often rather remote history. The fact is that most of his radical publications appeared within the last ten or twelve years of his life and some of the most cogent things appeared posthumously.

In his earlier attacks upon political chicanery and inefficiency he was likely to be so general that he could give offense to no particular constituency. There were slurring references to Congressmen in *Roughing It*[122] and *The Gilded Age*. He had a low opinion of politicians in general, whom he once classed with policemen as "the dust-licking pimps and slaves of the scum." [123] But this could hurt no one: it was so general. The abuses he railed at would be denounced by most progressive people. Such was the case in his ironical argument for the United States' annexation of the Sandwich Islands; we could give them three possible benefits: "leather-headed juries, the insanity law, and the Tweed Ring." [124] Many other passages in his books show his awareness of gross defects in human nature and human institutions. Yet such satire as is implicit in them is generally redeemed in one of three ways: (1) it becomes blunted by its broad application; (2) it operates in a remote arena; or (3) it is delivered from a platform of humor. All things considered the conclusion is inescapable that Mark Twain did often find it expedient to temper his radical opinions before they were given to the public. As time went on, he became more outspoken in print. Reputation had been made; financial security had finally been established. He was more independent—but no more convinced of the benevolence of man or God. As he approached the end of his life, he indulged more and more in the luxury of candor. No more would he and Howells have to "sneak off behind the barn . . . to smoke the . . .

pipe of truth." [125] Instead he exploded his opinions recklessly even in such conservative journals as the *North American Review*. There, in 1901, he published one of the most bitterly ironic pieces ever to issue from his pen, "To the Person Sitting in Darkness."

In "To the Person Sitting in Darkness" he denounces various iniquitous things: Germany's barbarous conduct in China at the time of the Boxer Rebellion, England's brutality and cupidity in the Boer War, Russia's unwarranted seizure of Port Arthur, America's bloody hand in the affairs of the Philippines and Cuba, and other activities carried on under the "Blessings-of-Civilization" banner. It amounts to a good "trade," this traffic in civilization, says Mark Twain, but it is time we called things by their true names when a nation goes on a civilizing quest "with its banner of the Prince of Peace in one hand and its loot-basket and its butcher-knife in the other." [126] He concludes by suggesting that there should be a new American flag—with a skull and crossbones on it. In this exceedingly bitter statement—sometimes Swiftian in its savage utterance and sometimes sophomorically exaggerated—Mark Twain is releasing the same sort of opinion, the same hatred of injustice which had characterized his earlier treatment of similar themes in *A Connecticut Yankee* and other books. That he waited so long to make a public statement on current subjects perhaps made him all the more vicious in statement. At all events these philippics remind the reader of Mark Twain's humorous books that his "fun" had a "bottom of fury." [127]

Much of Mark Twain's invective of men and parties is cast into language so extreme as to create the impression of rant. And yet he was basically sincere in all his tirades. He aimed at a higher standard of personal integrity than most men could achieve. This is clear from a letter he wrote Howells in 1884 urging him not to vote for Blaine:

> Somehow I can't seem to rest quiet under the idea of your voting for Blaine. I believe you said something about the country and the party. Certainly allegiance to these is well; but as certainly a man's *first* duty is to his own conscience and honor—the party of [*sic*] the country come second to that, and never first . . . It is not *parties* that make or save countries or that build them to greatness—it is clean men, clean ordinary citizens, rank and file, the masses. Clean masses are not made by individuals standing back till the rest become clean.[128]

In this letter one may perhaps see the real explanation for Mark Twain's wholesale cynicism about politics: he expected too much of mortal men—including himself. He was almost fantastically idealistic in expecting men and nations to exhibit the noble attitude he recommends to Howells' attention. "A man's first duty is to his own honor" is a reasonable statement, but to be surprised that men so often fail to live up to it is to betray a juvenile trait. Mark Twain was youthfully, almost romantically, impressed by the anomaly that "Man was born free: everywhere we see him in chains." He believed in an intelligent democracy,[129] and he was aggrieved to discover that men are not always altruistic, that governments engage in sordid dealings. He seemed perpetually surprised that God did not stamp out evil. No wonder he burlesqued Melville: he had little conception of the problems Melville treated. Compared with Henry Adams, his contemporary in disillusionment, Mark Twain seems an adolescent in the throes of his despair at discovering that the world is imperfect. That his rages do not seem childish in print more often than they do is to be explained by his emotional drive and his trenchant phrasing. If he was not a profound thinker, he was a skilled writer.

If organization of the state lent itself to abuses, there were dangers too, in religious organization. Preachers were not free even to express their honest convictions by ballot: they must "vote the ticket of their congregations."[130] He had a low opinion of the value of missionary work.[131] Nor could he accept the theology offered by the church. Mark Twain was, in his cooler moments at least, an agnostic. In his youth he had been an admirer of Robert Ingersoll, the celebrated "atheist," and he agreed with some of Ingersoll's conclusions. He did not believe in special revelation, divine "providence," or hell. Though willing to recognize the existence of a just and merciful God, he did not believe in the divinity of Christ.[132] Systems of morality he regarded as entirely the invention of man, and though he lived to the best of his ability in accordance with enlightened man-made ethics, he believed that his conduct here had no bearing upon possible future life. Whether or not there was a future life he was uncertain about in his own mind, and at one time he professed to be "wholly indifferent about it."[133] These are not the opinions of an atheist but rather of a deist and they do not differ radically from the opinions finally held by Franklin and Tom Paine. They probably represent what Mark Twain believed when not under the stress of emotion. They are typical of his rational way of approaching problems.

But these reasoned conclusions quickly melted away under emotional pressure. They could not sustain him in times of suffering or bereavement. At such times he angrily struck out in hatred of a God who could cause such needless suffering.[134] But even more conspicuous than his rebellion against the God who allowed unmerited suffering to exist was his merciless attitude toward Christianity, which he denounced as "a shell, a sham, a hypocrisy." [135] What hope could there be for frail mankind in a world operated by a merciless God whose avowed representatives on earth were themselves committed to a useless and hypocritical program? There seemed to be none, and Mark Twain at times descended into a valley of pessimism whence he thundered forth blasphemous tirades against the whole plan of the universe and the essential incorrigibility of man.

What was the basis of Mark Twain's pessimism? How deeply lodged in his nature? Mark Twain himself answered these questions in part: he believed that increasing knowledge and experience favor the growth of pessimism: "The man who is a pessimist before 48 knows too much; if he is an optimist after it, he knows too little." [136] He also recognized that a completely-absorbing pessimism is rare:

> Pessimists are born not made; optimists are born not made; but no man is born either pessimist wholly or optimist wholly, perhaps; he is pessimistic along certain lines and optimistic along certain others.[137]

In other words, Mark Twain's pessimism was largely temperamental; it could be induced by emotional states. The two things which bred the deepest pessimism in him, politics and religion, were, by his own admission, "the two things which are the peculiar domain of the heart, not the mind." [138] Yet he did not confine his expressions of pessimism to emotional outbursts but articulated them also in argumentative terms. His most formal statement on the subject may be found in the essay entitled *What Is Man?*, which is in effect a pre-Watsonian exposition of aspects of behaviorism. Unduly maligned by critics, it is at least a respectable statement, for the times, of a belief that man is essentially the toy of his environment. Man, he says, is a "machine" or an "engine":

> Whatsoever a man is, is due to his *make*, and to the *influences* brought to bear upon it by his heredities, his habitat, his associations. He is moved, directed, COMMANDED, by *exterior* influences —*solely*. He *originates* nothing, not even a thought.[139]

An obvious corollary of this proposition is that for any "worthy" deeds done by a man he himself deserves no credit. Moreover, he continues, in a proposition which is perhaps inconsistent with his fundamental belief (namely, that man is a machine), man is entirely self-seeking in his behavior:

From his cradle to his grave a man never does a single thing which has any FIRST AND FOREMOST *object but one—to secure peace of mind, spiritual comfort, for* HIMSELF.[140]

That this bleak philosophy did not at all times dominate the man who could write as rhapsodically about heroic achievement as Mark Twain did in *Joan of Arc* is obvious. All that can be said is that in his darker moments Mark Twain justified his mood by reference to such "sensational" philosophy as this.[141]

In one of his darker phases he wrote *The Mysterious Stranger* (written 1898; published 1916), a story so relentlessly sardonic that it was not published at all in Mark Twain's lifetime and is even now handled very gingerly by writers who like to regard all national heroes as "wholesome." In *The Mysterious Stranger* Mark Twain arraigns God in one of the most relentless and blasphemous pieces of writing ever produced by a major American author. The charges are preferred in the form of a narrative which though comparatively long, 140 pages, is little else than concentrated pessimism dispensed in the form of dialogue, parable, and a rather loosely contrived main plot. The scene is in Austria—a village called Eseldorf. Here Satan, a nephew of the great Satan,[142] comes to earth for a time and makes himself known to boys of the village. He cynically criticizes human beings as a worthless lot to be distinguished from animals chiefly by possessing a moral sense, which leads them generally to prefer the wrong things. They are guilty of extreme cruelty, but their cruelty, unlike that of animals, is practiced deliberately for pleasure. On one occasion he refuses to allow a wanton human act to be designated as "brutal": it would be, he says, an insult to the brutes. Man has no intellect, he says, but is merely a machine—or rather "a suffering-machine and a happiness-machine combined"—a combination which at best promises one unit of evil for every one of happiness and generally a far less favorable ratio. The consequence is that life is worth little or nothing to most people. Torture, disease, starvation, economic oppression, combine to make existence so baneful that death seems a release.[143] Such views as these make Satan's actions understandable. For example, he undertakes to "improve" the life sequence of Lisa and Nikolaus. When he tells the boys that this means taking the lives of these two, they are horrified—until they learn from him that if she had lived Lisa would have suffered thirty-six years of pain and shame and that Nikolaus' regular life would have called for him to live as a "paralytic log" (a by-product of scarlet fever) until he was sixty-two. Then they are satisfied that death is better. Yet Mark Twain takes evident savage delight in showing how this knowledge makes a hell out of the next twelve days, until, so it is appointed, Nikolaus shall die in attempting to save Lisa. The episode is made the more unbearable by a last suspense, for on the day designated Nikolaus is ordered by his father to stay at home. But the sport cannot be spoiled: the lad's mother sends him out to find Lisa—and the "mercy" is achieved. The mother giving vent to her grief, says she will never pray again—and is stoned for a heretic. What is perhaps the principal action concerns the trial of Father Peter for a theft which he did not commit. Mark Twain conducts the trial with his customary interest in matters of evidence, and proves Peter's innocence by a neat bit of detective work. But Satan, who knows the verdict of acquittal, informs the over-wrought Peter that he has lost the case. Peter goes mad in a moment. Satan's little pupils are horrified at this irony until their monitor again points the moral: only an insane man can be happy in this life. Finally the boys get the point and on one occasion they complain that Satan did not "save" a man by killing him or making him a lunatic!

Nor can the reader take any comfort in the possibility that such cruel episodes are exceptions in a world gradually improving, for "progress" as Satan shows, is a ghastly farce. Even Christianity has brought about an intensification of woe:

> "You perceive," he said, "that you have made continual progress. Cain did his murder with a club; the Hebrews did their murders with javelins and swords; the Greeks and Romans added protective armor and the fine arts of military organization and generalship; the Christian has added guns and gunpowder; a few centuries from now he will have so greatly improved the deadly effectiveness of his weapons of slaughter that all men will confess that without Christian civilization war must have remained a poor and trifling thing to the end of time.[144]

And the end of all for man is—annihilation. There is no after life. Indeed man's present life is only a "grotesque and foolish dream." But the God who dominates the dream is finally assailed in a series of propositions whose essential triteness is obscured by the audacity of the author's terms:

> . . . a God who could make good children as easily as bad, yet preferred to make bad ones; who could have made every one of them happy, yet never made a single happy one; who made them prize their bitter life, yet stingily cut it short; who gave his angels eternal happiness unearned, yet required his other children to earn it; who gave his angels painless lives, yet cursed his other children

with biting miseries and maladies of mind and body; who mouths justice and invented hell—mouths mercy and invented hell— mouths Golden Rules, and forgiveness multiplied by seventy times seven, and invented hell; who mouths morals to other people and has none himself; who frowns upon crimes, yet commits them all; who created man without invitation, then tries to shuffle the responsibility for man's acts upon man, instead of honorably placing it where it belongs, upon himself; and finally, with altogether divine obtuseness, invites this poor, abused slave to worship him! . . .[145]

Thus Mark Twain in *The Mysterious Stranger*. It is a story cumbersomely told as a whole but painfully effective in its smaller units. Fallacies fly about in his thought largely unchallenged by the reader because of the force and fervor of the author's language: no errors in logic, no juvenile exaggeration, can prevent *The Mysterious Stranger* from being a powerful expression of Mark Twain's pessimism at its depth.

Did he, Mark Twain, believe his own charges? Yes—at times. Was he really a pessimist? Yes—during the intervals of his optimism. It is probable that he overstates his actual convictions: in *The Mysterious Stranger* he writes defiantly—as if hoping that someone will contradict him. Moreover complete pessimists are seldom heard from so vigorously: their characteristic trait is a complete apathy. Nor can they joke successfully about their unbelief—as Mark Twain did when he commented on a lady's gushing apostrophe "How God must love you!" by remarking "I guess she hasn't heard of our strained relations." [146] Indeed Mark Twain conceived it as one of the functions of humor to clear the air of black thoughts. What he said of acrimonious literary disputes was just as true of weightier matters:

> Well, humor is the great thing, the saving thing, after all. The minute it crops up, all our hardnesses yield, all our irritations and resentments flit away, and a sunny spirit takes their place.[147]

There is some truth behind the remark of the lady who boldly told him: "Mr. Clemens, you are not a pessimist, you only think you are." [148] She might better have said he was a pessimist only part of the time. There are reasons why such a view must finally be taken. Even his doubt about immortality was not unshakable, and in his last moments, if family testimony may be allowed, he hung some hope on an "if." [149] Nevertheless though perhaps overstated and certainly intermittent, Mark Twain's pessimism was a formidable thing. It must be faced by anyone who wishes to understand the whole man. Traces of it appear in many of his stories, but they are generally absorbed and transformed by that buoyancy which was Mark Twain's dominating trait.

The political and philosophical conclusions arrived at by Mark Twain so warred with one another and with his business sense that his mind remained for many years divided against itself. He never achieved in his thought the harmony of an Emerson or a Whitman. His mind worked fitfully in fractions for which he could never find a common denominator. Hence he lived his intellectual life in a state of chronic exasperation. But his literary life was different. In his earliest days as a writer he knew what he wanted. He took to a congenial style as a duck to water. Not that he didn't have varied receptions at the hands of critics, but his literary manner was never frustrated by them. As a writer he wrote with that confident zest—even when he was least successful—which comes from a sense of perfect integration. From beginning to end his career as a writer was determined by a few principal impulses. These may be seen in his choice of reading, his attitude toward other writers, his impact upon New England, his humor, his style, and the evolution of his fame.

Mark Twain once said of himself that he lived constantly in a state of "excited ignorance." His customary exaggeration marks the phrase, but it is accurate in its suggestion of how little, comparatively, he learned from orthodox books. Schooling was a minor element of his boyhood, and college he knew chiefly as the recipient of a number of honorary degrees. Latin and Greek writers were unthought of. French was a difficult language with which he wrestled manfully during the composition of *Joan of Arc*.[150] Italian was a vehicle for ordering food and arguing with hotel-keepers and cabmen. German (which Mark Twain knew best of the foreign languages) was a ridiculously involved jargon whose quaint syntax obsessed him; it was not the door to the works of Goethe and Schiller. Book-learning was not his passion. To Mark Twain, the itinerant printer, the miner, the pilot, and the lecturer, books were for spare time, and even as such they came second to story-telling for real diversion. To Mark Twain, the successful author, they were unnecessary. To Mark Twain, the inveterate billiard-player, they were a comparatively dull substitute for real fun. In any case a man so restless physically that he could scarcely sit through a meal without jumping up at least once to pace the floor in eager recitation or argument was not likely to be contented for very long with a book. Outside of working hours Mark Twain was "on the go." In his study he was writing. There was evidently much truth in Howells' observation that of all the writers he had known Mark Twain was "the most un-literary in his make and manner." [151]

More important than the amount of reading Mark Twain did was the character of it. It was Howells who noted that when Mark Twain read a book, it was always a "vital book," a book which "had the root of the human matter in it." [152] This statement at least may be accepted as true. Such books as Clemens did enjoy were described generally in his famous comment:

> "I like history, biography, travels, curious facts and strange hap-penings, and science. And I detest novels, poetry, and theol-ogy." [153]

More specifically one learns that he was especially fond of Shakespeare, the Bible, *Don Quixote*, Suetonius's *Lives of the Caesars, Gil Blas*, Cellini, Casanova, Pepys, Lecky, and Carlyle (*The French Revolution*).[154] It is noteworthy that most of these favorite writers were "masculine," few were moderns, and none was American. Of the poets (excluding Shakespeare and Milton) he seems to have been passionately devoted to none but Browning, whom he was fond of reciting. Allusions to the English romantic poets occur so rarely in his writing that it gives one a start to find him on one occasion quoting Wordsworth.[155] He did not apparently read much drama, though there is one early citation of Ben Jonson.[156] As for novels, he read a few which he did not "detest." Dickens he evidently read with enjoyment.[157] And the works of Howells—there was no escaping *them*. He wrote Howells enthusiastically about *A Foregone Conclusion* as a book containing "the daintiest, truest, most admirable workmanship that was ever put on a story," [158] and he so genuinely enjoyed *The Rise of Silas Lapham* that he burst into superlative terms: "It's perfectly dazzling . . . masterly . . . incomparable." [159] Yet one cannot believe that friendship forced him to read each of Howells' books as they came out.[160] Certainly the tranquil quality of many of Howells' stories was far different from the color and vigor of the books he was able to enjoy on neutral territory. One feels sure that Howells' delicate art would leave Mark Twain with much the same opinion that Tom Canty had of the rose-scented finger-bowl out of which he essayed to drink: "it hath a pleasant flavor, but it wanteth strength." Such an inference is at least natural in view of his violent antipathy toward Jane Austen, whose charm Howells never ceased to praise and whose quiet comedy is perhaps the nearest analogy to Howells' own. Nor did Mark Twain forbear twitting Howells about his idol. When he wrote complimenting Howells on his criticism of Poe, he said:

> To me [Poe's] prose is unreadable—like Jane Austin's [*sic*]. No, there is a difference. I could read his prose on salary, but not Jane's. Jane is entirely impossible. It seems a great pity that they allowed her to die a natural death.[161]

This, clearly, is not criticism but fun-poking; yet it represents Mark Twain in that it shows his impatience with writing that lacks superficial vitality. For a similar reason he disliked George Eliot.

Mark Twain insisted on vitality, but he equally revolted against the false show of vitality. Hence his hatred of what he regarded as the spurious chivalry of Scott. He began shying rocks at the author of *Waverley* as early as 1883, when he devoted several vicious pages to him in *Life on the Mississippi*.[162] Not only did his critical sense rebel against Scott's romances,[163] but as a Southerner he held Scott responsible for the slow progress made in the South, for Scott

> by his single might checks this wave of progress, and even turns it back; sets the world in love with dreams and phantoms; with decayed and swinish forms of religion; with decayed and degraded systems of government; with the sillinesses and emptinesses, sham grandeurs, sham gauds, and sham chivalries of a brainless and worthless long-vanished society. He did measureless harm; more real and lasting harm, perhaps, than any other individual that ever wrote. Most of the world has now outlived good part of these harms, though by no means all of them; but in our South they flourish pretty forcefully still. Not so forcefully as half a generation ago, perhaps, but still forcefully. There, the genuine and wholesome civilization of the nineteenth century is curiously confused and commingled with the Walter Scott Middle-Age sham civilization, and so you have practical common-sense, progressive ideas, and progressive works, mixed up with the duel, the inflated speech, and the jejune romanticism of an absurd past that is dead, and out of charity ought to be buried.[164]

Obviously here is the (future) author of *A Connecticut Yankee* speaking.[165] To him the age of chivalry was not only a ludicrous period but a period terribly destructive to good ideals. It is for this reason that Mark Twain contrasts Scott with Cervantes:

> A curious exemplification of the power of a single book for good or harm is shown in the effects wrought by *Don Quixote* and those wrought by *Ivanhoe*. The first swept the world's admiration for the mediæval chivalry-silliness out of existence; and the other restored it. As far as our South is concerned, the good

work done by Cervantes is pretty nearly a dead letter, so effectually has Scott's pernicious work undermined it.[166]

If Mark Twain hated Scott, it was only a corollary that he should
hate Cooper, who was in some ways the standard-bearer of Scott in
America. To Mark Twain, Cooper's stories in the "Broken Twig
Series" possessed many of the same traits as Scott's: artificial plots,
impossible characters, poor mechanics, and extremely slovenly language.[167] In addition Cooper had the disadvantage of having written
about Indians who couldn't stand up under analysis engaged in activities
which could be proved impossible by actual measurements. To Mark
Twain, who had seen latter-day Indians in the sage-brush country, it
was difficult to accept Cooper's library-born red men. Moreover he
did not relish what he regarded as the sheer cant and prudery of Natty
Bumppo. But chiefly he hated Cooper (with Scott) as a clumsy con-
triver of puerile illusions that helped defeat the ends of progress. The
iconoclast could not lie down with the romanticist.

Cooper was not the only American writer whom Mark Twain treated
without respect. He was a powerfully unreverent person. Hawthorne
he passed by without enthusiasm. Melville he burlesqued. As for the
established New England writers of Concord and Cambridge, he had
little use for their wares but he could not avoid glancing at them. His
position was anomalous. When in 1871 he moved to Hartford he placed
himself at the very threshold of New England respectability. His association with Howells gave him a friend at one of the very highest
courts of opinion, *The Atlantic Monthly*. If he didn't change his formula he at least diluted his writing to make it agreeable to the tepid
tastes of the *Atlantic* subscribers. For, by a paradox, he scouted the
traditions of New England but craved her blessing. Yet he could not
force himself to read the multifarious productions of writers largely
alien to his own tastes—Longfellow, Whittier, Lowell, Emerson,[168] and
the ex-New Englander Bryant. He even burlesqued three of them in a
humorous speech which was delivered amid ghastly silence to a distinguished assemblage of literati at the Whittier birthday dinner on
December 17, 1877.[169] The reception of this speech was the measure
of New England's initial coolness toward Western brashness.[170] Not
even Whitman could have been more sternly cast upon the rock-bound
coast of New England orthodoxy. In general Mark Twain was persona
non grata in New England long after America as a whole, as well as
England, had welcomed him as a first-rate writer.[171] New England
writers had little to give Mark Twain and they found little in him.
They didn't think he was literary enough.

Another thing about Mark Twain that bothered New England considerably was his distressing humor. It was based on vulgarity or cruelty and its tone was low. It was crudely exaggerated. These things were of course true—though they do not fully cover the subject of Mark Twain's humor.

The flow of Mark Twain's humor (like that of Shakespeare) was often crude. It could hardly be otherwise, considering its source, watershed, and tributaries. Not all his humorous models were great books. The newspaper and almanac humor which started him was often clever but seldom refined. The writings of the Southwest group— J. M. Field, W. T. Thompson, G. W. Harris, Richard Malcolm Johnston, T. B. Thorpe, J. J. Hooper, Sol Smith, Davy Crockett, and A. B. Longstreet—were hardly the best training for a humorist who hoped to be read in Back Bay. They dealt in practical jokes, bodily ailments, shooting, fighting, fires, and animal adventures. Their morality was not really vicious, and there was comparatively little "sex" in them, but their spelling was poor and their cultural tone was low. Yet these were among the earliest and most important native influences on Mark Twain.[172] From these writers he presumably learned his typically American way of telling a yarn.[173] Mark Twain also knew a good deal about Down-East humor of the popular sort, particularly Haliburton's *Sam Slick*. He also knew Lowell's *Biglow Papers* and valued their rustic wit drawn, as it apparently was, partly from the same well of popular literature that Mark Twain refreshed himself at.[174] Once on a desert island (one of the Sandwich Islands, a desert as far as books were concerned) he read and almost memorized a volume of poems by Oliver Wendell Holmes.[175] Yet his roots were first nourished by the bountiful flow of Southwest humor, and the thin trickle of New England humor could do little for him. When it came to reading non-American humorists he naturally searched out those writers—Le Sage, Cervantes, Smollett, Fielding—who were capable of supplying him with the copious draughts which his nature demanded and rendered back.

No analysis of Mark Twain's humor can disclose the secret of his power. Even Howells who was constantly being inoculated with it forbore to explain the formula. All that can be said is that at its worst it was elementary, even childish, and unutterably boring, and that at its best it was capable of reaching all readers from the lowest to the highest in the scale of culture. It is easy to segregate the shoddy. The eternal boy in Mark Twain was responsible for his protracted indulgence in low forms of joking. Boys can be amused by his frequent and crude exploitation of itching, spitting, belching, vomiting, blowing one's nose, shaving, smoking, overeating and overdrinking, falling off chairs, and

similar themes involving the simpler reflexes and functions and bodily
accidents. No wonder Louisa Alcott warned readers against him. His
constant references to profanity too seem simply juvenile intrusions
in his stories. Even when he wasn't "vulgar," Mark Twain showed a
preference for humor that had a sturdy physical basis. Dozens of his
jests turn on such things as fire-arms, explosions, overturned boats, accidents to vehicles, etc. An amazing number of his stories make conspicuous use of the theme of money. Nothing apparently was funnier
to him than a man indulging in dreams of fabulous wealth which he expects to realize—only to have his hopes cruelly dashed at the last moment. Almost as numerous are his comic episodes involving dupery or
swindling—as often as not involving innocent victims whose discom-
fiture is scarcely funny. What is more, he made comic use of materials
ordinarily associated with grief or horror—insanity, murder, inhumation. He was calloused, even cruel, in his humorous exploitation of
situations implicitly tragic. Sensitive readers cannot bear to read the
cruel episode in which Tom Sawyer allows his family to believe him
drowned. Mark Twain thought it was funny. Sympathetic though he
was with actual sufferers (except readers), he could never see the line
between the comic and the grim.

His methods too are elementary. Though his gift was for episode or
incident rather than full story, he never stinted himself in the treatment
of trifling incidents. He could find eight pages of "humor" in an interview with a man who wanted to put too many lightning-rods on his
house.[176] If some of the "boners" made by school children are funny,
Mark Twain must quote not only these but a hundred more that are not
funny at all.[177] Even "The Jumping Frog" drags interminably. His
audacity was limitless. No risk of failure checked his exuberance. In
Roughing It he actually reproduced four times in five pages an inconsequential but fairly long anecdote about Horace Greeley (whom for
some reason Mark Twain always seemed to regard as funny) on the
flimsy pretext that he was showing how tedious the story could be.[178]
This sublime confidence in his capacity to inflate small matters to large
proportions was part of his heritage from the tall story-writers of the
Southwest—where the squatter sat on his haunches patiently through
no-matter-how-long stories. By their standard he succeeded: they liked
to watch the process. But the modern reader is yawning long before
Mark Twain chooses to prick the balloon.

· But Mark Twain did more than "make the unskilful laugh." Respectability drops its defenses against the irresistible quality of his humor at
its best. Nor is his best humor totally different in type from the commercial truck of his apprentice days. It stems from the twin roots of

exaggeration and understatement. Its guise is an assumed innocence or naiveté. Given as he was to the literal, the exact, even the fussily exact, in his non-humorous writing, he could never keep his humor at par with reality. He must duck under the truth or soar ludicrously above it. If a hanging is funny it is so because Mark Twain reports that the victim "received painful injuries which terminated in his death." If the catholic appetite of a jackass or a camel is funny it is because Mark Twain gives full rein to his subject:

> Sage-brush is very fair fuel, but as a vegetable it is a distinguished failure. Nothing can abide the taste of it but the jackass and his illegitimate child, the mule. But their testimony to its nutritiousness is worth nothing, for they will eat pine knots, or anthracite coal, or brass filings, or lead pipe, or old bottles, or anything else that comes handy, and then go off looking as grateful as if they had had oysters for dinner. Mules and donkeys and camels have appetites that anything will relieve temporarily, but nothing satisfy. In Syria, once, at the head-waters of the Jordan, a camel took charge of my overcoat while the tents were being pitched, and examined it with a critical eye, all over, with as much interest as if he had an idea of getting one made like it; and then, after he was done figuring on it as an article of apparel, he began to contemplate it as an article of diet. He put his foot on it, and lifted one of the sleeves out with his teeth, and chewed and chewed at it, gradually taking it in, and all the while opening and closing his eyes in a kind of religious ecstasy, as if he had never tasted anything as good as an overcoat before in his life. Then he smacked his lips once or twice, and reached after the other sleeve. Next he tried the velvet collar, and smiled a smile of such contentment that it was plain to see that he regarded that as the daintiest thing about an overcoat. The tails went next, along with some percussion caps and cough candy, and some fig-paste from Constantinople. And then my newspaper correspondence dropped out, and he took a chance in that—manuscript letters written for the home papers. But he was treading on dangerous ground, now . . .[179]

To some readers this is deplorable. Women generally, and a few men, are embarrassed by such irresponsible clowning. Some of them would laugh at comparable exaggerations in the speeches of Falstaff [180] but they cannot accept rollicking overstatement in Mark Twain. There is a curious prejudice against exaggeration in Mark Twain's humor. Granted that it is at times carried to extreme lengths in dull passages, it is no more to be condemned as a type than hyperbole in a phrase or any other literary convention—such as conventional pastoral machinery in a poem—which involves deliberate distortion of fact for the sake of vividness. The test is whether the humorous exaggeration is an extension of a true element of narrative or is a mere interpolation. In *Roughing It* Mark Twain frequently exaggerates materials that nevertheless go to make up a basically true account of real adventure. Interpolated materials partly spoil it—as they do the latter parts of *Life on the Mississippi*. Humorous exaggeration that is organically part of a story never did any harm. That is one reason why *Huckleberry Finn*, though blemished in a few spots, remains one of the great examples of humorous narrative.

Mark Twain's style varied in accordance with his purpose. His lavish reduplication and amplification of humorous materials was no more characteristic of him than his exercise of strict Franklin-like economy in the use of words when his object was merely expository. He restates thoughts for emphasis or humor, but within the sentence he is prevailingly direct and concise. His syntax is more nearly colloquial than that of most writers of his time, his rhetorical method more nearly oral. He disliked merely literary nuances. His preference for clean-cut expression caused him to "[d]amn the subjunctive. It brings all our writers to shame." [181] He rigidly excluded relative pronouns wherever possible and he aimed at that "simple and straightforward style" which he believed Cooper and Scott never could write.[182] He also aimed to use "the right word, not its second cousin." [183] Absolute clarity he regarded as essential—no matter how extravagant the tale in hand. These two qualities—mechanical precision and informality of manner—account for the vivid effects he often achieved. Consider this description of the earth from the point of view of the balloon in which Tom Sawyer and Huck Finn were ascending:

> The city went on dropping down, and down, and down; but we didn't seem to be doing nothing but just hang in the air and stand still. The houses got smaller and smaller, and the city pulled itself together, closer and closer, and the men and wagons got to looking like ants and bugs crawling around, and the streets like threads and cracks; and then it all kind of melted together, and there wasn't any city any more: it was only a big scar on the earth, and it seemed to me a body could see up the river and down the river about a thousand miles, though of course it wasn't so much. By and by the earth was a ball—just a round ball, of a dull color, with shiny stripes wriggling and winding around over it, which was rivers . . .[184]

This is close to perfection in its kind. With some right Mark Twain prided himself on the true distinction of his prose at its best.[185]

Narrative method, however, was a thing separate from precision and purity of diction. Except within a short scene or anecdote, he knew no laws of narrative writing that he thought worth repeating. This is obvious from the haphazard sequences and reckless disproportion of most of his novels. He believed that the writer who was untrammelled by rule or precedent was likely to excel in spontaneity and naturalness: in his books, as in his life, he enjoyed "roughing it." He had as little faith as skill in invention. It is better to borrow from life, for

> a fictionist *can't* invent a situation (of a *possible* sort) & get in ahead of history with it. Actual history has always arrived with it by a previous train.[186]

Despite the meticulous care he devoted to detail, therefore, Mark Twain seldom built a plot carefully before he commenced to write. It wasn't natural to do so—as he tells us in the introduction to *Those Extraordinary Twins:*

> A man who is not born with the novel-writing gift has a troublesome time of it when he tries to build a novel. I know this from experience. He has no clear idea of his story; in fact he has no story. He merely has some people in his mind, and an incident or two, also a locality. He knows these people, he knows the selected locality, and he trusts that he can plunge those people into those incidents with interesting results. So he goes to work. To write a novel? No—that is a thought which comes later; in the beginning he is only proposing to tell a little tale; a very little tale; a six-page tale. But as it is a tale which he is not acquainted with, and can only find out what it is by listening as it goes along telling itself, it is more than apt to go on and on and on till it spreads itself into a book. I know about this, because it has happened to me so many times.[187]

Here perhaps is an explanation of why in later years he came to regard dictation as a far better medium than the pen. It favored freedom that he regarded as essential:

> With the pen in one's hand, narrative is a difficult art; narrative should flow as flows the brook down through the hills and the leafy woodlands, its course changed by every bowlder it comes across and by every grass-clad gravelly spur that projects into its path; its surface broken, but its course not stayed by rocks and

gravel on the bottom in the shoal places; a brook that never goes straight for a minute, but *goes*, and goes briskly, sometimes ungrammatically, and sometimes fetching a horsehoe three-quarters of a mile around, and at the end of the circuit flowing within a yard of the path it traversed an hour before; but always *going*, and always following at least one law, always loyal to that law, the law of *narrative*, which *has no law*.[188]

Natural expression—yes, that was finally what Mark Twain held most important. The few comments he made on the technique of the novel insist on natural expression. Before he ever wrote a novel, he was burlesquing the artificiality of fictional types—the domestic, the romantic, and the Gothic—which were America's poor offerings in the fifties and sixties.[189] The nucleus of his satiric attacks on Paul Bourget was an insistence that a nation can be truly reported only by one who has learned to know not by *observation* but by *absorption* over a period of years:

> A foreigner can photograph the exteriors of a nation, but I think that that is as far as he can get. I think that no foreigner can report its interior—its soul, its life, its speech, its thought. I think that a knowledge of these things is acquirable in only one way; not two or four or six—*absorption;* years and years of unconscious absorption; years and years of intercourse with the life concerned; of living it, indeed; sharing personally in its shames and prides, its joys and griefs, its loves and hates, its prosperities and reverses, its shows and shabbinesses, its deep patriotisms, its whirlwinds of political passion, its adorations—of flag, and heroic dead, and the glory of the national name. Observation? Of what real value is it? One learns peoples through the heart, not the eyes or the intellect.
>
> There is only one expert who is qualified to examine the souls and the life of a people and make a valuable report—the native novelist.[190]

The basic truth of these remarks was illustrated by Mark Twain himself, who in Chesterton's opinion was "only a tourist in foreign countries . . . but . . . an adventurer in his own." [191] But it is not enough for the novelist to be autochthonous; he must be local as well:

> Even the native novelist becomes a foreigner, with a foreigner's limitations, when he steps from the State whose life is familiar to him into a State whose life he has not lived. Bret Harte got his California and his Californians by unconscious absorption, and put both of them into his tales alive. But when he came from the

Pacific to the Atlantic and tried to do Newport life from study—conscious observation—his failure was absolutely monumental . . .

To return to novel-building. Does the native novelist try to generalize the nation? No, he lays plainly before you the ways and speech and life of a few people grouped in a certain place—his own place—and that is one book. In time he and his brethren will report to you the life and the people of the whole nation . . . And when a thousand able novels have been written, *there* you have the soul of the people, the life of the people, the speech of the people; and not anywhere else can these be had.[192]

Here, somewhat embellished in deference to the argumentative occasion, is Mark Twain's American testament of critical principles. Their essential wisdom may be judged from the results of his wavering adherence to them. His greater work came from digested experience; his lesser, from "observation." He was a humorist, but "more richly than any earlier humorist, he revealed background." [193] He was no "psychologist" but he understood a few American boys and their adult enemies. A world-traveler, he could generalize brilliantly about the depravity and incorrigibility of human beings everywhere. Yet the Seven Seas yielded no information or wisdom half so valuable to him as the experience he "absorbed" in a tiny village on the lazy shores of the Mississippi. There he found "the whole world on a raft." There he learned to know all men, for "This Huckleberry Finn is but the race." There he became the "genius of the stream." [194]

Despite his solid pride in work well done, Mark Twain was sometimes careless of his "reputation" as a writer. Unlike Bret Harte, who deprecated the popularity of his nationally famous "Heathen Chinee" on the grounds that it wasn't his best work, Mark Twain seemed to gauge the value of most of his works by their power to please the public and bring financial returns. He seemed interested not in "the opera but the hurdy-gurdy." Generally he was satisfied to please "the masses":

My books are water; those of the great geniuses are wine. Everybody drinks water.[195]

As for critics, theirs was "the most degraded of all trades." [196] Yet there was another side (there always is in Mark Twain) to this attitude. In 1900 when he was asked to give permission for a dramatization of *Tom Sawyer*, he replied with humor and bitterness combined:

> I should like to see Tom Sawyer staged . . . You need not sub-
> mit the play to my approval . . . Turn the book upside down
> and inside out if you want to. If you wish to add people, incidents,
> morals, immorals, or anything else, do so with a free hand. My
> literary vanities are dead and nothing I have written is sacred to
> me.[197]

When did his vanities die? What or who killed them? Certainly the
critics he affected to despise had a hand in the process. Pages could be
filled with the vituperations of outraged critics who greeted almost
every book of Mark Twain with extreme denunciation of his buffoonery, vulgarity, sadism, neglect of tradition, and haphazard style. The
humorist, moreover, was seldom taken seriously—a fact bound to stick
in the craw of every "entertainer." Mark Twain's failure to carry New
England with his Western vitality was doubtless depressing even to a
man whose public embraced the world. And there is no question that
Mark Twain did care for his reputation. He occasionally struck back
savagely or humorously at some caterpillar critic, but from the time
when Anson Burlingame urged him to "refine" himself [198] and Bret
Harte "trimmed and trained and schooled" him in the technique of the
paragraph and the chapter,[199] he was always responsive to intelligent
criticism. From Howells he accepted corrections that would have irked
him in a less sympathetic editor. He worked hard to be a credit to himself, and he was sensitive to small points of criticism. His vanities did
not really die but suffered some nasty bruises. Privately he never ceased
to be proud of certain achievements. If he erred in placing *Joan of Arc*
too high, he was no more than just in looking with satisfaction upon
other productions—*Tom Sawyer, Huckleberry Finn,* and *The Prince
and the Pauper*.

Criticism of Mark Twain has been almost as erratic as he was himself.
His true significance was at first missed by many intelligent writers.
Even after the appearance of *The Innocents Abroad, Roughing It,* and
Old Times on the Mississippi, Walt Whitman, lying in the very basin of
the Mississippi, could continue to chant his routine plea for a Western
literature:

> Will the day ever come—no matter how long deferr'd—when
> those models and lay-figures from the British islands—and even
> the precious traditions of the classics—will be reminiscences,
> studies only? The pure breath, primitiveness, boundless prodigal-
> ity and amplitude, strange mixture of delicacy and power, of
> continence, of real and ideal, and of all original and first-class ele-
> ments, of these prairies, the Rocky Mountains, and of the Missis-

sippi and Missouri rivers—will they ever appear in, and in some sort form a standard for our poetry and art? [200]

In 1891 when the clamor for the great American novel was at its loudest, Andrew Lang, a great admirer of *Huckleberry Finn,* sagely queried whether the "great American novel has escaped the eyes of those who watch to see this new planet swim into their ken." [201] As late as 1911 Archibald Henderson was equally skeptical of our ability to place Mark Twain adequately:

> there is room for grave doubt whether a realization of the unique and incomparable position of Mark Twain in the republic of letters has fully dawned upon the American consciousness. [202]

Gamaliel Bradford carried the burden of conservative New England disapproval down to the year 1922, when he discharged it in heavy tones which comparatively few latter-day critics would be willing to echo in full:

> So my final, total impression of Mark is desolating . . . I cannot escape the image of a person groping in the dark, with his hands blindly stretched before him, ignorant of whence he comes and whither he is going, yet with it all suddenly bursting out into peals of laughter, which, in such a situation, have the oddest and most painful effect. [203]

Bradford's gloomy view of the great humorist seems to have been arrived at by too close a study of Mark Twain's pessimism. It is hardly the approach of a critic who wishes to evaluate Mark Twain. Nor is the critic a whit wiser who points maliciously to the many examples of juvenile humor which may be found even among the volumes of Mark Twain's "authorized edition." One does not judge Wordsworth by "Peter Bell." Mark Twain, who supplied American fiction with new energy, new horizons, and permanent inspiration, is entitled to a more fair-minded judgment. The praises which he has received for his great books no single volume could recite in full. For the quality of that work one may well go back to the testimony of an impartial friend of his (that is, an editor), William Dean Howells, who believed that this Mark Twain was a "self-lawed genius . . . who will be remembered with the great humorists of all time, with Cervantes, with Swift . . ." [204] Could he have read those words, Mark Twain might have growled, but he would have been content.

William Dean Howells
(1837-1920)

Although born in Ohio, then (in 1837) a very Western state, Howells' long life was not far different in general facts from that of many an Eastern writer except for the years of his youth. Once established as a writer in Boston, he poured forth books and articles at a rapid rate, moved from one literary "connection" to another, lived quietly in comfortable circumstances, and created a bright fame that suffered few eclipses, only gradually decreasing in brilliance until his death in 1920.

From the nature of his environment during boyhood and youth one might have expected a different sort of Howells. He was born at Martin's Ferry, but his family moved three years later to Hamilton, Ohio, described by Howells in *A Boy's Town* (1890), where his father had charge of the *Intelligencer*, a Whig newspaper. His father, Welsh by descent, was of "the philosophic rather than the imaginative temperament." [1] He embraced, and inculcated in Howells, the Swedenborgian faith. He had withal a quiet humor and an unusually wide sympathy with men, traits in which the younger Howells shared. They became good companions. Howells' mother, apparently a less dominant influence, possessed the "art of making each child feel itself the most important,"—no slight accomplishment inasmuch as there were in all eight young Howellses. The family life was, however, more agreeable than prosperous.

Like young Clemens, Howells was brought up partly in a printing office, where he began to work at the age of ten. When he was twelve, his father moved to Dayton and bought the local *Transcript*, which presently failed. Now commenced a more rugged life in a cabin on the Little Miami River, where the elder Howells unprofitably attempted to convert a sawmill and a grist-mill into paper-mills. Meantime the boys were occupied in clearing the woods, planting corn and sweet potatoes, and pursuing romantic adventures on the "Island." Here were pioneer experiences that might have turned a more adventurous lad's eyes westward. Here was literary material not far removed in type from that which Clemens capitalized in *Huckleberry Finn*. But although Howells later recounted these primitive labors and episodes in *My Year in a Log-Cabin* (1893), his inclinations were less toward forest and plain than toward the settlements. In any case the family needed his services. At fourteen he took a compositor's job on the *Ohio State Journal* in Columbus. Later moves brought him to Ashtabula (father had bought another newspaper), to Jefferson (father had moved the new sheet), and back to Columbus. At Columbus he became correspondent for a Cincinnati paper and, three years later, news editor of the *Ohio State Journal*. It was now 1859, and he was ready to try his wings as a writer.

Meantime his education had obviously been a hit-or-miss matter as far as formal schooling was concerned. He attended public schools intermittently, and at Jefferson he studied a little law. At Jefferson also he received the offer of a benevolent Scotch farmer to send him to Harvard, but he was obliged to decline the offer, for the family needed his earnings. Howells was therefore largely self-educated. The principles of self-education he learned at home, for the family was given a great deal to reading aloud. On the religious side there was the Swedenborgian *Heavenly Arcana*, which did duty in lieu of Scripture; and on the secular side there were the English poets. In addition Howells read by himself to the very limit and, even beyond, of his physical endurance. In the absence of formal education this resource became of paramount importance to the future novelist. A partial record of what he read is available in several autobiographical and critical volumes, of which the most important for the early years is *My Literary Passions* (1895).

His first love was Goldsmith, who was full of that "kindness and gentleness" which Howells thought inseparable from the "best art." [2] Cervantes' *Don Quixote* he read with rapture from the age of ten, not as "literature" but as a "forever enchanting story," long, to be sure, but cast into the form which he was later to prefer in his own writing:

> I believe that its free and simple design, where event follows event without the fettering control of intrigue, but where all grows naturally out of character and conditions, is the supreme form of fiction; and I cannot help thinking that if we ever have a great American novel it must be built upon some such large and noble lines. [3]

Then there was Irving, gentle Irving. Howells was fascinated by the *Conquest of Granada* and many of the tales, but he found the *Knicker-*

bocker History dull. Longfellow enchanted him, particularly with *The Spanish Student.* Scott was inescapable, but was read with no more than "a sobered affection." [4] The bookish Pope was more to the taste of a young man already tinkering with verse himself, and Howells remained in "long subjection" to him. *Uncle Tom's Cabin,* which he read as it came out in the *New Era,* moved him tremendously but did not for long cause him to swerve from imitating Pope's pastorals. Ossian was a good complement to Pope, for there was in his work "the light of nature." Yet tidy habits of thought and expression made him wary of a writer whose freedom verged upon a "formlessness" in which "everything spills and wastes away." [5]

Next came a sudden passion for Shakespeare. Howells later deplored the blind hero worship which apotheosized every line written by Shakespeare, but as a lad he felt that "the creation of Shakespeare was as great as the creation of a planet." What he valued most was the reality in the plays, especially the history plays containing that "gross and palpable reprobate," Falstaff—an unexpected tribute from a reader ordinarily so revolted by coarseness as Howells. He treasured Shakespeare's humor but "felt deepest those plays and passages . . . where the alliance of the tragic and the comic was closest." His devotion to Shakespeare he later proved by using Shakespeare phrases for the titles of no less than ten novels.[6]

Enthusiasms came thick and fast. He fell victim, with most of America, young and old, to Ik Marvel's sentimental reveries. Dickens, who was "more truly democratic than any American who had yet written fiction," so enthralled him that his own experiments in story imperiously took Dickensian turns of character and structure. His next prosemaster was Macaulay: stylistic graces and mannerisms learned from Goldsmith and Irving must now give way to a more energetic idiom. Thackeray Howells was devoted to, partly against his better judgment, for there was "toxic" quality in Thackeray's obvious reverence for the worldliness he affected to despise. In any case *Pendennis* was superior to *Vanity Fair,* which he thought "heavy-handed." [7] The sweet gentleness of Tennyson's lyrics and narratives inevitably became a deep solace to a young man so finely attuned as Howells. Then came a tremendous enthusiasm for Heine, who "dominated [Howells] longer than any one author." Heine was of course not acceptable to the New England literati upon whom Howells was later dependent for recognition. Yet not only was Howells captivated by Heine's wit and fancy, but he was indebted to the German poet for a liberating conception of literature that gave him the key to his own truest gifts. Before knowing Heine,

Howells had "supposed . . . that the expression of literature must be different from the expression of life." It was Heine who taught him

> that the life of literature was from the springs of the best common speech, and that the nearer it could be made to conform, in voice, look and gait, to graceful, easy, picturesque and humorous or impassioned talk, the better it was.[8]

There were other writers—De Quincey, Goethe, Bulwer, Eliot, Hawthorne, Curtis, Leigh Hunt, Hazlitt, Lamb—who so fascinated Howells that freedom from the printing office at three in the afternoon meant voluntary bondage to literature until bed-time. In odd moments he devoted himself to studies in six foreign languages. His health inevitably suffered a breakdown, but he returned to his books as soon as possible. His reading as a whole was reasonably broad in scope, but certain preferences and antipathies appear. Extremely fastidious, if not prudish, he protested against all coarseness and erotic voluptuousness; indeed he believed in expurgation of noxious passages in books for the general public. He did not relish satire, but preferred those writers who attained their moral ends by kindliness and encouragement. In matters of form, he valued "regularity, uniformity, exactness," qualities which characterized his own writing.[9] Vagueness of any sort troubled and irked him. He was not drawn to writers who indulged in "metaphysics." The broader reaches of the imagination he was not at home in; even in later years he found Dante dull. He was not strongly drawn to the classics. His reading in general was a clear indication that if he became a writer, his own work would be predominantly realistic—but not naturalistic.

Behind all his reading, in fact, there was the definite object of achieving distinction in authorship. The cultural atmosphere of Columbus was moderately stimulating, and Cincinnati, a publishing centre, was not far away; but Howells was interested in an extra-sectional reputation. The first important step, of course, was publishing a poem in the *Atlantic Monthly*. Next came a volume of poems written in collaboration with J. J. Piatt, *Poems of Two Friends* (1860). A campaign biography of Lincoln, in *Lives and Speeches of Abraham Lincoln and Hannibal Hamlin* (1860), prepared the way for political preferment in the consular service. In the meantime Howells followed his manuscripts back over the Alleghenies to meet Lowell (then editor of the *Atlantic*) and other New England worthies—Emerson, Hawthorne, Holmes, Whittier. The four years of the Civil War he spent as consul in Venice —discharging official duties, writing articles on Italian life for the *Na-*

tion, and longing for home. Upon returning, he promptly published Venetian Life (1866). This augmented his reputation, but his bread and butter depended for some years to come on journalistic posts, the first of which was given him by the *Nation* on his return to America. In 1866 he began to assist James T. Fields in editing the *Atlantic,* and in 1872 he became editor-in-chief. He was now at an important post on a main road of American letters. To follow his itinerary throughout its long extent, to note the increasing number of intersecting roads, and to summarize the results of the journey would be the work of a volume. Suffice it at the moment, to note a few principal changes of direction. In 1881 Howells resigned his editorship of the *Atlantic,* and in 1885 he moved from Boston to New York. The following year he became associated with *Harper's Magazine,* first as a contributor of fiction and then, in addition, as occupant of "The Editor's Study." An interval (in 1892) as editor of the *Cosmopolitan* preceded his re-association with the Harpers, his official publishers. In 1900 he took charge of a department called the "Easy Chair." He occupied the Chair until his death in 1920, but his arm-chair causeries and critical promulgations were only a small proportion of that prolific utterance which distinguished him from the beginning to the end of his long career.[10]

As a writer Howells matured early. He did not go through the traditional period of "youthful experimentation" in his novels. His works vary in value, to be sure, but his entire canon betrays considerable homogeneity in design and substance. The thirty-eight novels which he published between 1871 and 1920 consequently permit no easy classification according to the author's stage of development or "progress." He did not so much follow a route to a destination as function in an orbit whose beginning might have been anywhere. His first novel (if *Their Wedding Journey* is entitled to the term) revealed most of the characteristics that inhere in his later novels. A few rather shaky generalizations may be made with respect to structural outlines and subject matter. As to the structure, Howells practiced from time to time two types of development. The first, exemplified by *Their Wedding Journey,* is used in those simpler stories in which the action is "linear";[11] the second, a more complicated form, involves the use of a "double or multiple" plot.[12] This latter form was adopted in some of his most valued novels—*The Rise of Silas Lapham, A Hazard of New Fortunes* —but it is doubtful if Howells was more at home in it.[13] More often than not (especially in his earliest novels) he used a comparatively simple structure. Yet he used both types (with variations) throughout his career with no apparent adherence to a plan of self-development.

In subject-matter Howells discovered very early what was to be the most congenial to him throughout his life. From the point of view of a quick enlistment of public interest, his choice was so unexciting as to seem perverse in a day when opportunities were richly proffered by the expanding fields of fiction. The historical, the Gothic, the sentimental—these time-tested avenues to a novelist's popularity were of course unthinkable to Howells. His literary inheritance was only partly made up of fiction in any case.[14] Rather he sought his subjects in the province of "social" affairs. But even in this restricted field he imposed limitations on himself. O. W. Firkins has listed the items which for reasons of taste and expediency Howells largely excluded from his agenda:

> In these forty volumes, adultery is never pictured; seduction never; divorce once and sparingly ("A Modern Instance"); marriage discordant to the point of cleavage, only once and in the same novel with the divorce; crime only once with any fullness ("The Quality of Mercy"); politics never; religion passingly and superficially; science only in crepuscular psychology; mechanics, athletics, bodily exploits or collisions, very rarely.[15]

Thus to have stricken from his bill of fare so many tempting elements would seem to have left him little with which to cater to the popular appetite. What remained, as Firkins has shown, was perhaps more nourishing and wholesome than superficially attractive, but it afforded more variety than one might expect: love, travel, literature and art, ethics, psychology, and the "problem of self-support" together with "those inequalities of fortune which divide and disgrace our industrial civilization." [16] With these themes skilfully altered and revivified from novel to novel, Howells slowly created for himself a public which made up for its relatively slow growth by its sturdy longevity. His earliest and most pervasive theme was love—love treated tenderly, whimsically, ironically, didactically, but almost never "passionately." A certain waggish tendency to satirize the vapid sentiment of very young lovers was disconcerting to those readers able to detect its slight impact, but Howells was never the complete misogynist, and he more than balanced his occasional raillery with a fundamentally tender and respectful attitude toward "the sex." Accordingly he kept his large public of women-readers full of curiosity and he never offended them for long.

Second in importance as a theme is unquestionably the "inequalities of fortune." Himself a child of modest background translated to surroundings of comfort and even opulence, Howells made the most of his opportunities for observing economic contrasts. He never had that intimate and prolonged experience of sub-standard living conditions which forms the background of many proletarian writers, but he saw and knew enough to write with honest urgency on the side of enlightened humanitarianism. Between 1888 and 1894 he wrote five novels[17] in which economic ills form a major theme. This was the one period in his life when ideas as such seemed conspicuous in his fiction. He was not a man with a mission, not a solver of "problems." The various themes of his novels coalesce with one another in such fashion as to create an effect of homogeneity. Likewise he early attained a mastery of flexible but hard-fibred prose which, despite his very wide reading, he varied so little as time went on that it is not easy to establish the date of a volume by examining it for stylistic peculiarities. From the point of view of style, at least, even his early work seems seasoned. Popular interest has finally centred in a few books—*The Rise of Silas Lapham, A Modern Instance, A Hazard of New Fortunes*—which intrinsically are not greatly superior to others less known. In Howells a lack of one quality in a book is likely to be balanced by extra value in another category. He wrote few masterpieces and few failures. In short, his novels constitute a circular chain made of links for the most part of equal strength and lustre. Only after close scrutiny can one fix the beginning of the chain by noting a few links that are slighter (not less finished) than the others, and it is chiefly from motives of convenience that one examines first a link marked *Their Wedding Journey* (1871).

Their Wedding Journey betrays in its plot and style none of that straining after intensity or brilliance which is characteristic of the first efforts of many novelists. It merely records the impressions of Isabel and Basil March on a belated wedding journey touching, among other places, at Niagara, Montreal, and Quebec. Connected interest is maintained by the problem of keeping the nature of their expedition a secret from the other passengers. Few novelists would dare to inaugurate a career with such apparent paucity of interest-creating instruments. The principal characters are not romantic lovers but a newly married couple "no longer very young." The plot exhibits little greater originality than a railroad schedule. Not a single relative is lost at sea, and nowhere do we encounter extreme cruelty to an orphan. Incident is of such a mild order that Isabel's temporary refusal to walk back over a suspension bridge provides excitement for three pages. Nor is Howells' gift for the description of natural phenomena great enough to justify the story as a "travel" book. Yet the unhurried account of the day's events —meals, excursions, chance meetings, conversations—is invested with such quiet reality, the simple characters are revealed with such frankness and affection and penetration, that the book finally exerts a quiet fascination even over the reader who at first scoffs at its pointlessness. It is the paradox of Howells' method that by divesting himself of the habiliments of the professional entertainer and by abjuring all the tricks of his trade he holds his audience more securely bound than many a writer who resorts to the paraphernalia of "magic." He performs with a minimum of properties in a faintly colored atmosphere that the observer takes for broad daylight. He aimed to create steady attention rather than gasps of astonishment, roars of laughter, or convulsive shudders. His method was so successful in *Their Wedding Journey*[18] that Howells used it prevailingly in most of his later books. Few of his novels, however, are quite so bare of "story interest."

In *A Chance Acquaintance* (1873) the thread of action is slight, but its tiny emotional burden is so skilfully poised that a considerable suspense is created. The thread finally snaps when Kitty Ellison, a sweet girl from a small town in New York, repudiates her engagement to an essentially cold and snobbish Bostonian, whose affection for her, nurtured in isolated Quebec, quickly fades when his fashionable friends appear on the scene. Called "the American *Pride and Prejudice*," [19] this book justifies the comparison only by the material, which was drawn from Howells' own observations of a mobile American social order. As in *Their Wedding Journey*, there is no attempt here to whip up interest in the story by artificial means. Reactions are natural instead of striking. Emotional transactions take place at par value. There is much old-fashioned but apparently realistic dialogue on appropriate topics: scenery, historical backgrounds, books,[20] current events, and social customs. In many respects Howells seems to be trying to construct a story upon the lines championed by the heroine herself:

> ". . . if I were to write a story, I should want to take the slightest sort of plot, and lay the scene in the dullest kind of place, and then bring out all their possibilities. I'll tell you a book after my own heart: 'Details,'—just the history of a week in the life of some young people who happen together in an Old New England country-house; nothing extraordinary, little, every-day things told so exquisitely, and all fading naturally away without any particular result, only the full meaning of everything brought out." [21]

Such a story could have little appeal for readers accustomed to seeing passion tattered and torn to shreds in the popular domestic novel: why, there are simply no emotional crises to speak of in *A Chance Acquaintance*, and the ending is *too* disappointing! In his quiet way Howells was doing something perilously new in American fiction.

Nevertheless increasing concession to popular interest marked Howells' third novel, *A Foregone Conclusion* (1875). There is young love (instead of middle-aged affection), and not only does it prosper in the end but it is complicated by the urgent pleas of an unsuccessful suitor whose end is tragedy. No light realistic breeze here, but strong head winds. Yet Howells has the situation under control at all times and he insists, as always, that even under stress no action should overstep the modesty of nature. The story, laid in Venice, is one of several of Howells' which employ an Italian setting, but the "very Italian" Don Ippolito is Howells' only "full-length or full-dress portrait of a foreigner other than an Englishman." [22] Don Ippolito is a priest whose bonds to orthodoxy are so weak that Florida Vervain (an American girl he is tutoring) urges him to renounce his church and come to America, there to develop his inventor's genius. Misunderstandings occur which lead the priest to believe he has won her heart. But no degree of honest passion in him can change her pity into love: she finally marries the somewhat colorless American who first introduced the priest to her. The priest dies, presumably heartbroken. Howells the realist feels obliged to add that although the husband "had once imagined that the tragedy which had given him his wife would always invest her with the shadow of its sadness," their common life soon "exorcised all . . . dark associations," and Don Ippolito finally became no more than a faint, puzzling recollection. The author also feels constrained to underline the husband's discovery that even after her marriage the heroine "really had that hot temper which he had dreaded in her from the first." [23] By such uncompromising observations as this, Howells undoubtedly lost customers among the die-hard romantic readers, but he expanded his credit in critical quarters. Yet *A Foregone Conclusion* is not a novel of the first importance. Its Italian atmosphere is perhaps as authentic as that of Hawthorne's *The Marble Faun*, and its plot is managed far better. Yet the book lacks the weight and the penetration of Hawthorne's story.

Most of Howells' novels until 1882 were serialized in *The Atlantic Monthly* before being published in book form. One of them, originally called *Private Theatricals* and published serially in 1875-76, did not receive book publication until 1921, when it appeared posthumously as *Mrs. Farrell*. It is atypical also in that it contains Howells' only full-length portrait of a "bad woman." [24] Her victims are two officers of the Civil War—friends destined to be divided by her evil courses. The three principal portraits are relatively ineffective, and the story lacks the true ring of most Howellsian coin. It might be guessed that Howells forbore to republish the story because of its "unwholesome" subject matter, but actually he was threatened with legal action by persons who thought themselves the obvious models for characters in the story.[25]

The Lady of the Aroostook (1879) seems a more natural story for Howells to have written than either *A Foregone Conclusion* or *Mrs. Farrell*. Its shifting locale—from South Bradfield, Massachusetts, to Venice and back, with a California interlude—seems not at all to embarrass the author in his well-focussed study of a social situation not far removed in type from that of James's *Daisy Miller* (also published in 1879). Howells' heroine is an uncultivated back-country New England girl despatched to Venice via a freighter on which she is the only female person. Her naive unawareness of her anomalous situation makes her the subject of jesting speculation on the part of two gossipy, patrician young men. Both are attracted to the girl—much to their own surprise —but one of them, being already betrothed, beats a timely retreat, leaving Staniford to win the field after much parleying and after suitable evidence of his physical prowess: he performs a hazardous rescue of a drunken passenger fallen overboard. The Venetian entr'acte enables Howells to complete the proof of his theorem that innate fineness of character is mightier than conventional weapons. Unlike *A Chance Acquaintance*, which it closely resembles in theme, this story ends in the marriage of the socially unmated couple. The plot though smoothly handled is neither complex nor original. Creating a lovers' misunderstanding by means of a miscarried letter and confirming a hero by means of a courageous physical effort were vieux jeu even in 1879. The hoariness of the latter device is acknowledged by Howells through the remark of the hero himself: "It has been pawed over so much by the romancers that you don't feel like a hero in real life, but a hero of fiction." Yet confession is not restitution, and Howells was to recommit this type of crime many times in the future. His inventiveness is revealed rather in ways and means of keeping the story alive in those intervals between climaxes when the "romancers" in turn so often betray ineptitude. The virtue of *The Lady of the Aroostook*, called in 1898 "the most perfect story that American literature has yet produced,"[26] lies in its discerning observations on people and places in provincial communities like South Bradfield—their household detail, speech mannerisms, changing social and moral conditions ("There's a decay of the religious sentiment, and the church is no longer [in 1874] a social centre . . . Superficial humanitarianism of one kind or another has killed the good old orthodoxy"),[27] and the sturdy simplicity of rural folk. Howells not being a sea-going man, the voyage to Venice is filled with dialogue, almost none of which is nautical and almost all entertaining. Such discussions do not appear as digressions but as integral parts of the narrative. Books and writing are much discussed.[28] No American novelist has used literature as a subject of conversation so profusely or so naturally as Howells, and part of the proof of his supremacy is in *The Lady of the Aroostook*. While many novelists are concerned to show desperate people at critical moments, Howells uses the average hours of life to reveal ordinary people who are just as much alive in fair weather as foul. Storms he cannot wholly avoid but he sees his characters more clearly in a calm or amid gentle swells.

"Where Puritanism has gone out of the people in spots, there's the rankest growth of all sorts of crazy heresies, and the old scriptural nomenclature has given place to something compounded of the fancifulness of story-paper romance and the gibberish of spiritualism." This caustic generalization of Staniford in *The Lady of the Aroostook* contains the nucleus of a theme, religious variations, which informs the main body of Howells' next novel, *The Undiscovered Country* (1880). The variations involve spiritualism and Shakerism. Howells' employment of such material in fiction is not incompatible with his general attitude of indifference toward "metaphysics," for here he is interested chiefly in social behavior referable to the existence of cults; he is interested in spiritual*ists* more than in spiritual*ism*. The subject of spiritualism was not new in American fiction. Howells was evidently mindful of the precedent of Hawthorne, who is mentioned in passing in *The Undiscovered Country*, but Howells' novel is certainly inferior to *The Blithedale Romance* and probably also to James's *The Bostonians*, soon to appear (1886). The most vivid character in *The Undiscovered Country* is Dr. Boynton, an enthusiastic and sincere spiritualist, whose daughter Egeria acts as his medium. An unpleasant brush with a skeptical young journalist (Ford) visiting in Boston leads Boynton angrily to challenge Ford, whom he regards as a malign influence, to a public demonstration which shall determine whether Dr. Boynton's powers can prevail. Ford refuses—at the request of Egeria. By her act of interference Egeria virtually signs a marriage license with Ford; but the author decrees that the story must go on to a Shaker settlement, getting Dr. Boynton and his daughter there by the clumsy device of a railroading mischance and keeping them there by pleading Egeria's illness. Here Dr. Boynton arranges a séance to exhibit Egeria's powers, but, in a scene which in some ways foreshadows the climactic scene in Du Maurier's *Trilby*, Egeria for the first time fails to react properly. Of course Ford has by a Howellsian coincidence become a guest in the house, and it is presumably his presence that blasts the experiment. The overwrought Dr. Boynton is finally placated, though he dies soon thereafter. The Shakers, who are doctrinally against marriage, regard the obvious courting between Ford and Egeria as a bad example to their young folk, but after the marriage occurs, they remain friends with the young couple. Egeria and Ford engage in no more spiritualistic experiments. In the course of the latter part of the story there is considerable attention to Shakers and Shakerism, then a failing institution chiefly because, with the requirement of celibacy, it was necessary to "look for accessions from the enemy." But Shakerism is subordinated to spiritualism in the story, and over both lies the half-realistic, half-romantic love story, partly concealing the wobbly structure beneath.

Dr. Breen's Practice (1881) is better unified and more plentifully provided with good portraiture extending even to the secondary characters. A love story is again central, but its auxiliary social theme, the question of a woman's fitness to practice medicine, is harmonized with the principal motif. Dr. Grace Breen, an almost morbidly high-minded New England girl, intends to devote herself to social service by practicing medicine among needy people in a factory town. Her plans are thwarted by the arrival of her friend Louise Maynard, obviously in need of medical attention. A more immediate duty thus forces Dr. Breen to remain in her medium-fashionable summer hotel on the New England coast. Louise Maynard is not only a querulous patient but a social menace, for she is separated from her husband, whom she expects to divorce. A mildly indiscreet boating episode with Mr. Libby, a pleasant nonentity, ends disastrously when the craft overturns and Louise (later) gets pneumonia. Dissatisfied with Grace's conduct of the case, Louise demands the attentions of a male practitioner, Dr. Mulbridge, who cures her. Although he despises Grace as a colleague, Dr. Mulbridge would like her for a doctor's wife, but Grace prefers the nonentity, Libby. Louise is hustled back to her husband.

The story proves nothing, but it smells of a thesis, the exact purport of which critics cannot agree upon. If the book is aimed against women in the medical profession, it gets nowhere, for Grace's test case is a wholly unfair one;[29] if it is intended as a "satire on the medical profession in general," [30] it fails even more obviously. All that can be asserted definitely is that the women come off rather badly—not only Dr. Grace and Louise Maynard, but also Grace's nagging mother. It is not a pleasant party: what is really needed is a nerve specialist. Moreover Howells chooses to use his coast-line setting with a sombre emphasis. Amid all these causes for depression the reader is profoundly grateful for Dr. Mulbridge, who, though compared to Brontë's Rochester by one of the hotel guests, should be spared all bookish allusions, for he is one of Howells' most vital characterizations. The brief but brisk appearances of George Maynard and Barlow, the hired man, are also noted with relish. Excepting for Grace and Libby the story is rich in well-drawn characters—including the unpleasant ones. In short, though the hotel guests themselves might find *Dr. Breen's Practice* a trifle gloomy for summer reading, their "goings-on" provided Howells with the material for a substantial realistic study.

By 1882, the year in which *A Modern Instance* appeared, Howells had produced the seven novels here discussed besides a number of sketches, plays, and short stories, as well as one extended tale (whether novel or novelette), *A Fearful Responsibility*.[31] The novels are for the most part short, relatively simple stories of a "linear" type rising gradually to minor peaks of action from which, even if the remaining time is short, the author generally descends to a plane more nearly corresponding with everyday experience. The reader's pulse and respiration remain steady, for exciting episodes are few and digressions non-existent. There is an effect of moderate exhilaration, which finally wanes without leaving a sharp reaction. Love, the prevailing motif, does not often lead to unalloyed bliss or to tragedy, but what it loses in intensity it gains in reality. Its reality may be tested by the eagerness with which one tries to read results in the bland, inscrutable face of the author.

These early novels are comparatively spare in substance, but in them, as in many of Hawthorne's tales, more happens than is observed by the casual reader. They are not in most cases immature, experimental works: Howells was neither a young nor inexperienced writer when he came to the novel. His thrifty method was adopted through preference and conviction. He believed that in most big novels there is much lost energy and that with the right leverage just as much could be accomplished with far less effort. In a letter written to C. D. Warner in the midst of his first decade as a novelist he elaborated his opinion:

I still don't agree with you that a novel need be long in order to be great. I believe I grow more and more contrary-minded on this point, and it seems to me that the people of the next age will look with as much amaze upon our big novels as we do upon Richardson's. The man who has set the standard for the novel of the future is Tourguénief, whom certainly you can't blame for want of a vast outlook, or sidelight, or world. And only consider a play of Shakespeare, which is of such limitless suggestion, how short it is! No, I can't believe that I should be greater with more room . . . What one really needs is a strong *motive;* then he enlarges his territory in his reader's mind. The great art is to make your reader recur to your book with the impression that certain passages are much longer than they really are. But perhaps I'm really without desire for the sort of success you believe in for me. Very likely I don't want much world, or effect of it, in my fictions. Not that I could compel it if I did want it; but I find that on taking stock, at forty year, of my experiences, and likes and dislikes, that I don't care for society, and that I do care intensely for people. I suppose therefore my tendency would always be to get any characters away from their belongings, and let four or five people act upon each other. I hate to read stories in which I have to drop the thread of one person's fate and take up that of another; so I suppose I shall always have my people so few that their fates can be interwoven and kept constantly in common before the reader.[32]

Such a harvest of books within a decade in which he also devoted much time to the editorship of *The Atlantic Monthly* would seem to have been enough to satisfy Howells' literary conscience. Yet he gave up his editorial post in 1881 to devote himself more steadily to creative writing. Late in the same year he declined the post of literary editor of the *New York Tribune,* and in the December *Century* appeared the first installment of *A Modern Instance.*

A Modern Instance, now regarded as one of Howells' major achievements, was from a structural point of view a denial of the reasoned opinions which Howells had so lately communicated to C. D. Warner, for it is a long novel. Yet its high rank does not depend upon its relative stoutness in form, for as Firkins has pointed out,[33] the additional weight is not always well distributed. Not more weight, but greater intensity distinguishes *A Modern Instance.* Nevertheless this new intensity is not gained at the expense of naturalness: Howells is not wilfully abandoning old methods but merely applying a steadier pressure.

The problem involved in *A Modern Instance* is that of marital unhappiness leading to disastrous consequences. Howells the realist was never more courageous than in recording the gradual disintegration of the bonds that at first had held Marcia Gaylord and Bartley Hubbard in happy wedlock. Though both persons are at fault—Marcia in her jealousy and Bartley in his cruelty—neither is at the beginning endowed with more weaknesses than most persons who manage to weather the storms of matrimony. In the end Bartley is forced to bear the stigma of villainy. His downward course, which inevitably challenges comparison with that of George Eliot's "immortal Tito [Melema]"[34] is so quietly and gradually described that critics have complained of a lack of motivation.[35] His indulgence in liquor is an insufficient cause. No crushing blow of a perverse fate lays him low. There is, says Firkins, no complete "demonstration of the necessity of disaster in the marriage."[36] One must perforce lay a great deal of the trouble to inherent traits in Hubbard which needed no single event or sinister environment to make them dominant. Perhaps Squire Gaylord was right in his simple analysis when he warned Marcia against Hubbard as a "scamp" who "hasn't got the first idea of anything but selfishness." [37] Not very exciting, this, as a basis for a tragic story. So accustomed is the average reader, critic as well as layman, to expecting a heroic element in tragedy that he is inclined to feel cheated unless the victims are laid low by some ugly trick of the "President of the Immortals." There is a preference for "dramatic" situations in which gods make sport of men, using coincidence liberally. But in average life tragedy is often created by the accretion of malign particles instead of by a blow of fate; villainy is often achieved by growth. Personal behavior need not always be reckoned in terms of response to outer stimuli; it is in fact quite as often determined by inner compulsion. When, therefore, a realist like Howells has the courage to derive a true tragedy amid average circumstances without resort to spectacular episodes or egregious coincidence, it should be obvious that it is unfair to arraign him on charges of insufficient motivation. Enough that he has made the problem concrete and has presented it plausibly. There is no need to compare Bartley with the central figure in a Senecan tragedy, or to test *A Modern Instance* by the requirements of Aristotle. A more judicious comparison is to be found in *The Old Wives' Tale* of Arnold Bennett, in which the lives of Gerald and Sophia Scales are interwoven gradually with tragedy that is just as real as a catastrophe more suddenly wrought by striking and unforeseen events.

If *A Modern Instance* is imperfect structurally, the fault is not in inadequate motivation. Proportion, however, is another matter, and there is validity in the charge that the book suffers from "decentralization" largely because of the prominence of the Atherton-Halleck interest.[38] Whether the lack of a brilliant climax is a fault or a virtue is debatable. Yet no initiated reader of Howells expects the gathering of forces for a "big scene" near the end of a narrative. Howells has relatively little explosive energy, but he has an abundant vitality which is constantly at the service of the reader. At the same time he has the utmost patience, for he wishes to be convincing in little things as well as big. He never slurs details through eagerness to get ahead with the action. He does not restrict dialogue to topics bearing directly on plot. He does not confine his portraiture to a few hasty strokes. When he wishes to show that Squire Gaylord felt ill at ease in Boston, he does more than state the fact baldly:

> He [the Squire] suffered from the loss of identity which is a common affliction with country people coming to town. The

feeling that they are of no special interest to any of the thousands they meet bewilders and harasses them; after the searching neighborhood of village life, the fact that nobody would meddle in their most intimate affairs if they could, is a vague distress. The Squire not only experienced this, but, after reigning so long as the censor of morals and religion in Equity, it was a deprivation for him to pass a whole week without saying a bitter thing to any one. He was tired of the civilities that smoothed him down on every side.[39]

Of course such prolonged attention to detail is justified only in a writer whose language stands the test of a close scrutiny. In many more recent novelists, even in a writer of such power as Dreiser, atrociously inept technique makes such minuteness an impertinence; but in Howells it is a delight to observe not only the felicity of his phrasing on an average page but also passages containing those special rewards of the careful reader which Edmund Gosse described, perhaps a little too prettily, as "fairy-bells at the tips of . . . sentences, tiny wafts of perfumed wit." [40] *A Modern Instance*, though well received, was not universally applauded as an improvement over Howells' earlier stories. A typical charge was that "the author's habit of fine discrimination misled him into giving too much value in his art to the moral intention and too little to the overt act." [41] Charles F. Richardson, writing three years after its publication, felt, however, that the deepening of realism in it (which he attributed to the influence of James) was accompanied by spiritual losses:

> The men and women, boys and girls, and winter life and landscape of a typical New England village are delineated with a fidelity that would be perfect were it not that the heart and soul of New England are almost out of sight. "A Modern Instance," placed beside "The Biglow Papers," "Snow-Bound," or "The House of the Seven Gables"—all three of them minutely realistic—almost seems an artistic falsehood. Its separate elements are true, but its whole is misleading. Howells returns again and again to the porch or the heap of builders' débris, but shuts his eyes to the skyward cathedral.[42]

Criticism of emergent realism often took this direction—essentially a moral judgment rather than an aesthetic one. The moral tone of *A Modern Instance* has of course since been amply recognized. It may be admitted that Howells did not reproduce the warp and woof of New England life as understandingly as Mrs. Stowe, but in the large his fabric carries the marks of genuineness. And the superiority of his artistry is incontestable.

Between *A Modern Instance* and the at least equally memorable *The Rise of Silas Lapham* lies a largely forgotten novel, *A Woman's Reason* (1883). Its problem is to show the efforts toward self-support of a girl obviously destined to marry a handsome "Navy man." Her efforts are complicated by her appalling delicacy and her hair-trigger New England conscience. These qualities do not make her one of Howells' more attractive heroines, and the divers coincidences by means of which he pieces out his story do not add to our respect for the novelist. New scenes there are, including a coral island, but not new intrinsic values. That *A Woman's Reason* is a novel by Howells is almost a guarantee against shoddiness, but its mixture of romantic and realistic elements produced nothing of lasting value.

The Rise of Silas Lapham (1885) marked Howells' return to the same type of technique as he had used only three years before in *A Modern Instance*—a double plot and enormous amplifying detail. If not appreciably better as a novel than *A Modern Instance*, it is composed of even more popular elements and it attaches itself more firmly to certain democratic ideals. At present, a little more than fifty years after its first publication, it has every appearance of being an American classic. Its continued popularity may be accounted for partly by the fact that it is an embodiment of those elements in which Howells was most at home: comedy arising out of social incongruity, tension created by an ethical issue, anxiety over the problem of making a living, and the vagaries of young love.

Howells' own rise to social distinction was apparently an inconspicuous phenomenon attended by few embarrassing episodes. In any case the ascent was brief, for he began well above the bottom rung of the ladder and he can hardly be said ever to have reached a point of social eminence on which he could view the Lodges eye to eye. In *Silas Lapham* the rise is more disturbing. The Laphams are a family of substantial character, but in speech, manners, and general deportment they have more to learn than can be quickly acquired even after the Back Bay Coreys, first made aware of the Laphams through a business exigency, make it their pleasure to extend social invitations to them. Howells is at his best in describing, albeit at inordinate length, the painful dinner at which Lapham disgraced himself by drinking too much. Yet even at the dinner Howells typically used the minor detail rather than the crude blunder to reveal Colonel Lapham's lack of savoir faire: his "kicking out one of his legs which had gone to sleep" and his mistaking an old family portrait for a "picture" of Mr. Corey's daughter. Few story-tellers under the circumstances (certainly not Mark Twain) could have resisted exaggerating the comic to the point of the farcical, but Howells characteristically has too much regard for the reality of his characters to risk blasting their identities for the sake of a few belly laughs. Similarly Tom Corey's visits to the Laphams result in no more amusement than is consistent with character. Yet such comedy as arises from social contretemps is the more enduring because of Howells' admirable restraint.

The richness of the comic effects in *The Rise of Silas Lapham* has led to some misinterpretation of the book as a whole. It is not essentially a novel of social life, and the "rise" is not a social ascent. Howells himself felt constrained to remark, after his novel had been referred to by Francis Parkman as a study in "social recognition," that he "had supposed the rise to be a moral one." [43] Perhaps such an error as Parkman's must be laid to Howells' disproportionate attention to the Lapham's first gestures toward social prominence. Perhaps also the moral issue, which is paramount in the last part of the book, fails to receive its due because of Howells' inveterate habit of tapering off his stories instead of building them up to final climaxes. [44] Yet it should be clear that Silas Lapham's character is more important than his social rank. Although legally innocent of wrong-doing when he had forced Rogers out of the partnership, he had done a thing which (as his wife tries to make him admit) he felt to be dishonorable. It was the memory of this act which (as the minister Sewell implies) finally "strengthened" Lapham and enabled him to resist a new "emergency." The final dilemma was a cruel one: Rogers' offer to buy Lapham's mills would save the latter financially. True, Lapham suspects that Rogers will use the mills for the purposes of mulcting someone else, but of this he has no proof. On all sides he is urged to sell: "He was standing out alone for nothing, any one else would say." Yet for his high conviction he gives up all his material success and goes back to Vermont. The paint business which he described with such satisfaction to Bartley Hubbard (then a reporter) in the first chapter is gone; his house, the visible sign of his affluence, is gone; only a quiet conscience sustains him as he returns to "begin the world anew where he had first begun it, in the hills at Lapham." Not that there isn't a residue of bitterness in Lapham when he thinks of the "tens of thousands that he had gambled away in stocks, and of the commissions that the brokers had pocketed whether he won or lost," and of certain properties he held whose value was determined by the whim of a railroad. Certainly there is in his final attitude nothing superficially heroic. He seems to feel that he has been more or less mechanically impelled to act as he did: "it don't always seem as if I done it." But he sticks to his honorable compulsion to the last, resisting a final temptation to save himself by the West Virginia plan.

Even the marriage of one of his daughters to a Brahmin comes too late to be a large solace to Lapham. The whole affair had been pretty much of a fiasco anyway, what with the colossal mistake the family made in believing that Tom Corey was courting the pretty Irene instead of, as in reality, the more interesting Penelope. A certain romantic value of a Cinderella sort no doubt attaches to this misunderstanding, but it is quite likely that on the whole the "love interest" of this story, relegated to a subordinate place and tinged with satire,[45] had the effect of increasing that body of readers by whom Howells was "condemned because of his 'injustice to the finer sex.' "[46]

The Rise of Silas Lapham was anti-romantic in its revelation of a man going down to defeat in spite of his honest policy and in its almost flippant attitude toward young love. It was also criticized for its unfavorable picture of the modern industrial and financial order. Yet once these shocks were absorbed by a surprised public, it was perceived that Howells had made of Lapham a figure who might well stand as a national ideal in a democracy: a self-made man who rose to eminence but who preferred a humble competency to affluence secured at the expense of that simple code of honor which the wealthy so often subscribe to and so often, without exceeding their legal rights, violate. His cheerful resignation became a symbol: after having been a "go-getter" he became a good loser. It is perhaps for this reason that *The Rise of Silas Lapham* is held in the highest affection of all of Howells' novels.

The Rise of Silas Lapham was autobiographical to the extent that while Lapham was building a house in the novel, Howells was building one for himself on Beacon Street. His own financial security was never again seriously threatened. Soon thereafter Harper and Brothers made an apparently favorable long term contract with him.[47] His books sold widely and his critical judgments were so incisive that he was everywhere respected even by people whose respect took the outward form of opposition. When Hamlin Garland came to Boston in 1883 Howells was the reigning writer:

The most vital literary man in all America . . . was Wm. Dean Howells who was in the full tide of his powers and an issue. All through the early eighties, reading Boston was divided into two parts,—those who liked Howells and those who fought him, and the most fiercely debated question at the clubs was whether his heroines were true to life or whether they were caricatures.[48]

Both the adulation and the opposition were healthy signs, and Howells maintained his leadership in the novel for another decade more or less. His exceedingly popular *Indian Summer* appeared one year after *The Rise of Silas Lapham,* and his series of "economic" novels between 1888 and 1894 had an appeal for serious readers which could offset any disappointment felt by those ladies who, as Howells discovered to his amusement, sometimes read only the "love parts" of his books.[49]

The "love parts" of *Indian Summer* (1886) were perhaps not entirely satisfactory to the giddy adolescent reader, but the book as a whole was a boon to that adult part of the public whose taste had had comparatively little to feed upon in the sixties and seventies. *Indian Summer* is one of Howells' most mellow stories. He professed to have enjoyed its composition as much as that of any book he ever wrote, principally, doubtless, because the simple technique he adopted imposed no hardship. Moreover there was the Italian setting (Florence, this time) which evoked memories of his long residence in Italy as a young man. The characters are few, the episodes simple. Consequently most of the author's time can be devoted to pointing up, shading, and weighting those details which are finally integrated into one of the most finished chiaroscuro studies in American fiction.

The hero, Theodore Colville, is a middle-aged American with a journalistic background. He is further damaged in the eyes of the romantic reader by having been rejected as a suitor years before by a woman who regarded him as too intellectual. Mrs. Bowen, his vis-à-vis in the story, is a widow tottering on the brink of thirty-nine. It hardly seems possible that any sentimental situation involving such senile persons can be made valid for purposes of fiction, but Howells coolly sets up a very plausible triangular relationship by fixing the attractive Imogene Graham at a point equally distant from Colville and Mrs. Bowen. Colville's autumnal eye is attracted to this enchanting embodiment of eighteen springs so much that Mrs. Bowen perforce sits glooming in her corner until he should be brought to his senses. She can make no move, for although she honestly believes that a match between Imogene, her virtual ward, and Colville would be disastrous, any interference would place her in the position of seeming to be maneuvering for Colville herself. Eventually the triangle is feebly transformed into a quadrilateral through the introduction of a dim speck, Morton, between whom and Imogene a conventional line can be drawn.

The problem of course has been to make real the regard of Imogene for Colville. Sentimental readers must feel quashed when they find that the basis of her attachment was not an undying (first) love but her subconscious desire to "make up to him" for his unhappy love affair of twenty years before. Howells' finesse was never shown to better advantage than in the series of trivial accidents which serve to relax Imogene's adoration. Instead of a harsh break, there is a gradual disenchantment. Colville's clothes are not a hundred per cent contemporary; his dancing consists of walking about "as if he were a bear in a cage"; late social hours so tell on him that one day he wakes up in church thinking that the minister must have made a joke, for everyone is laughing—except Imogene. All of this implies no derogation of Imogene's charm, but it leaves her subtly deflated from a romantic point of view; and Howells is further unkind enough to show her unsuitability for Colville by an inventory of her naive intellectual equipment: for her, literary criticism consists in exclaiming that *this* author is "fascinating," and *that* author "simply weird." [50] By these and other more gentle devices Howells completes a perfect reversal which even the inevitable buggy accident does not impair: after all there *were* buggy accidents in those days. Intervals in the action are filled with the affairs of secondary characters, miniature incidents, and leisurely dialogue. Yet all of these particles range themselves flawlessly round the motivating force of the story. Whether novel or short story *Indian Summer* is close to perfection of the art of narrative. Henry James, who is referred to in terms of respect in passing,[51] could scarcely have told the story better. Certainly he would not have surpassed Howells in the naturalness of the dialogue. The following passage, though perhaps vulnerable to the charge that Howells' people are a shade *too* clever, is nevertheless superior in qualities of ease and naturalness to most dialogue in American fiction either before or after Howells:

> "I began to doubt whether Mrs. Bowen was going to bring you at all," she said frankly, with an innocent, nervous laugh, which made favour for her with Colville. "She promised it early in the evening."
>
> "She has used me much worse, Miss Graham," said Colville. "She has kept me waiting from the beginning of time. So that I have grown grey on my way up to you," he added, by an inspiration. "I was a comparatively young man when Mrs. Bowen first told me she was going to introduce me."
>
> "Oh, how *good!*" said Miss Graham joyously. And her companion, after a moment's hesitation, permitted herself a polite little titter. She had made a discovery: she had discovered that Mr. Colville was droll.
>
> "I'm very glad you like it," he said, with a gravity that did not deceive them.
>
> "Oh yes," sighed Miss Graham, with generous ardour. "Who

but an American could say just such things? There's the loveliest
old lady here in Florence, who's lived her thirty years, and she's
always going back and never getting back, and she's so homesick
she doesn't know what to do, and she always says that Americans
may not be *better* than other people, but they are *different*."

"That's very pretty. They're different in everything but thinking themselves better. Their native modesty prevents that."

"I don't exactly know what you mean," said Miss Graham, after
a little hesitation.

"Well," returned Colville, "I haven't thought it out very clearly
myself yet. I may mean that the Americans differ from other people in not thinking well of themselves, or they may differ from
them in not thinking well enough. But what I said had a very
epigrammatic sound, and I prefer not to investigate it too closely."

This made Miss Graham and Miss Effie both cry out "Oh!" in
delighted doubt of his intention. They both insensibly drifted a
little nearer to him.[52]

The Minister's Charge (1887) lacks the trim lines and good proportions of *Indian Summer*. Its surface gleams with the polish that Howells
was able to give even to his poorest structures, and many of its units are
machined with Howell's customary skill; but the assembly is imperfect.
Consequently though it is freighted with much useful reflection, its
movement is uncertain. Yet it is a better vehicle of service than of
pleasure. The story suffers from being obliged to respond to two
controls. The first is the ambition of Lemuel Barker, a raw country lad
with a faculty for writing inferior poetry. When against his better
judgment David Sewell, a Boston clergyman, praises some of Barker's
verses, the latter packs off to the city for a career in letters. Naturally
such a career is not forthcoming, and Barker is hard put to it to find a
footing in the economic anarchy into which he is plunged without
preparation or preferment—for Mr. Sewell seems a strangely impractical friend. Barker works successively at humble occupations—janitor,
elevator boy, clerk, trolley-car conductor—which give him an insight into injustice of the social order. An interval during which he
serves as a reader to Bromfield Corey (invalided out of *The Rise of Silas
Lapham*) broadens his cultural contacts and infects him with a degree of
social snobbery. The working girl for whose company he had once
been grateful no longer ranks as his social peer, and it is understood that
he rejects her, very ill though she is, for a girl (an art student) who had
formerly seemed beyond his reach. These events, with their corollaries,
would seem to have been the original basis of the novel, which was at
first entitled *The Apprenticeship of Lemuel Barker*.

The other control is the necessity of referring each of the changes in Lemuel's fortunes to the observant eye of Mr. Sewell, who having once given him false encouragement, cannot rid himself of a feeling of responsibility. Consequently each time the narrative of Lemuel gets under way, the author has to go back and pick up Mr. Sewell. Moreover Sewell is such an interesting passenger (not to mention his wife, "the custodian of their potential virtue") that he claims much of the attention which the reader uneasily thinks ought to be reserved for Lemuel. Perhaps a better manager than Howells could have devised a more efficient way of resolving these difficulties. As it is, the story shuttles back and forth so much that its absolute progress is slight.

A similar lack of co-ordination impairs the social thought of the novel. Howells refuses to be decisive even on grounds where he has genuine convictions. He wishes things to be understood or said without subscribing to them himself. The most telling criticisms of society are placed in the mouths of various characters instead of emanating from the author directly. This is of course good narrative technique—avoiding interpolations—but there is a certain amount of confusion because although the author's "proclivities are democratic . . . there is hardly a sympathetic figure in his plebs." [53] His attitude toward the working girls, Statira and Manda, is "officially lenient but instinctively severe." [54] Space is given to many views which might sit uncomfortably in the minds of aristocratic readers originally attracted to Howells by his urbanity—legal discrimination against the poor and friendless, hazardous factory conditions, long working hours for menials, social snobbery toward the servant classes, the selfish "hardness" of the rich, bribery of government officials, the buying of votes.[55] Social palliatives conceived by "official sympathy" are satirized in the person of a "benefactress" who "bestow[s] a jacqueminot rosebud on a Chinaman dying of cancer." [56] On the other hand, a whole-hearted radical would get little satisfaction from such revelations, for Howells sees the problem of social amelioration from other angles as well. The upper classes are not wholly responsible for the plight of the lower, for economic laws operate to some extent mechanically. Moreover, by one of those laws, the lower classes will eventually be the upper classes. Lemuel, says Corey, is really an "ancestor":

> "All you have to do . . . is to give him time, and he'll found a fortune and a family, and his children's children will be cutting ours in society. Half of our great people have come up in that way. Look at the Blue-book, where our nobility is enrolled; it's the apotheosis of farm-boys, mechanics, insidemen, and I don't know what!" [57]

The ultimate goal is perhaps "equality," but equality, it is implied, will never be achieved by distributing largesse to the underpaid or under-employed. A dole, Howells instructs one of his characters to believe, can only lead to "the dire life of idleness and dependence, partial or entire, which he had known so many Americans even willing to lead since the first great hard times began." [58] Howells' ideal, rather, seems to be a type of "future State, which will at once employ and support all its citizens." [59] *The Minister's Charge*, then, is no novel of purpose. It sets forth liberal views, but its liberal elements are not combined with an incendiary body of doctrine that could be of much use to a proletarian agitator. It shows Howells as an economic realist, perhaps, but certainly as no propagandist. He is by nature not a good fighter, for he "pulls his punches." He makes a better referee, for he sees both sides. *The Minister's Charge* is generally accounted one of Howells' "second-best" books, for although it has good characterization, plentiful humor, and serious thought, it is on the whole an "inartistic and confusing novel." [60] It was soon to be followed by several "economic novels" which delved even deeper into social problems. These include *Annie Kilburn* (1888), *A Hazard of New Fortunes* (1889), *The Quality of Mercy* (1892), *The World of Chance* (1893), *A Traveler from Altruria* (1894), and *Through the Eye of the Needle* (1907).[61] These novels "represent no radical break in [Howells'] development," [62] but they are sufficiently weighted with economic reflection to justify the grouping. How seriously Howells took them may be judged from his reference (in 1888) to the "miserable literary idolatries of [his] past." [63]

That Howells should have manifested so much interest in the industrial order at this time may seem somewhat surprising. He was about fifty years old—a ripe age at which to display new interests, especially in regard to the industrial order. He was comfortably off financially, and his reputation was ample. Could it be that he was beginning to weary of his rôle as purveyor of love stories for Boston matrons? Possibly this was a remote factor, but more definite influences may be cited. It was at the age of fifty that he first began to read Tolstoi, whose novels, said Howells, so profoundly affected not only his view of art but also his "ethics" that he could "never again see life in the way [he] saw it before . . ." [64] To his sister he wrote that Tolstoi's "heart-searching books" are "worth all the other novels ever written." [65] From Tolstoi he gained among other things a deepened sense of the importance of translating Christ's ethics into action, especially with respect to the laboring classes. Other European influences on Howells' social thought included theories of Ruskin and Morris. Marxian socialism also affected him indirectly. Yet the more effective influences at this period were closer to home. One of these was Henry George, author of *Progress and Poverty* (1879), a book more widely read and discussed than any work of a humanitarian character since *Uncle Tom's Cabin*. Howells could not accept wholly George's theory of the single tax, but he was in hearty agreement with George's social aims. Even more important in the chain of influence was Edward Bellamy's *Looking Backward* (1887)—"a book," said Howells, "which in the sugar-coated form of a dream has exhibited a dose of undiluted socialism." [66] Bellamy's book appeared in the midst of a period of tremendous industrial unrest arising out of the conflict between capital and labor. In the year 1886 there were more than ten thousand strikes involving mercantile and commercial enterprises.[67] In 1886, also, began a cycle of events—the Haymarket riots and their repercussions—which "dramatized for Howells the whole economic *impasse* and drove it home to his mind with the force and fervor of a religious experience." [68]

Howells was deeply moved by the fate of the "Chicago anarchists" who were condemned to die on the charge of murder as a result of their alleged participation in a bombing plot in May, 1886. He was convinced that, except for the man who had thrown the bomb, the defendants were not guilty as charged. A little slow to go into print on the matter, he at the last moment published in the *New York Tribune* a strong plea urging imprisonment instead of death for the convicted men, who in his opinion were "fairly indictable for conspiracy alone." [69] Throughout the latter part of the affair Howells repeatedly expressed himself recklessly in terms of hot indignation. Two days after the execution (Nov. 11, 1887), he wrote summarily to his father: "The historical perspective is that this free Republic has killed five men for their opinions." [70] Howells was constitutionally cautious, slow to act, but for once at least, proved himself capable of facing an angry public opinion over a case involving discrimination against white men.[71] He was now for the first time fully awakened to a realization of how important it was to understand the relationship between the "haves and the have-nots." He was ready to write his economic novels.

Annie Kilburn (1888), a story designed to "deal rather with humanity than with love," was begun at the very time of the execution of the Chicago anarchists,[72] but it does not, of course, use the event directly. It is, in fact, "the most Tolstoyan of his novels." [73] The theme of the relief of poverty is here illustrated by the efforts of Annie Kilburn, a New England girl, to use her money to the best advantage of the poor by supporting the "Social Union." But the Union is a "charity" and as such its function is comparatively disapproved by the Reverend Mr.

Peck, who believes rather in social equality, for " 'Money is a palliative, but it can't cure.' " The only real cure for social ills, he believes, is a deep-seated sympathy which " 'can spring only from like experiences, like hopes, like fears.' " [74] This view of philanthropy was not new in Howells' fiction, but it receives here an extended treatment that amounts to a debate in the form of fiction. The outcome, as often in Howells, is not a clear-cut victory for either side. The book is nevertheless most successful on the argumentative level—in its cogent (if not uncombatted) support of the thesis that "fellowship must precede service." [75] As a concrete representation it partly fails because of Howells' inability really to get himself into the minds and hearts of the poorer classes. It is even questionable whether in his persistent analysis of class distinctions Howells is not struggling with more ingrained aristocratic habits of thought than he can ever correct.[76] As story, *Annie Kilburn* is lacking in coherence, in discipline: Howells deploys his characters well in skirmishes, but he finds re-assembly difficult and an orderly march of events impossible. Yet even here he supplies one of his better characters —the pitiable, hard-drinking, sergeant-like Putney, who argues the case for the single tax.

A Hazard of New Fortunes (1889) has too much artistic merit to be concealed wholly behind the label of "economic novel." It is such a full novel—the longest Howells wrote—that the action of its "multiple" plot cannot easily be condensed. Its main lines, however, involve Basil and Isabel March, first introduced in *Their Wedding Journey* and here brought from Boston to New York, where March is finally induced to take over the editorship of a new co-operative magazine, "Every Other Week." Two principal problems arise out of the new enterprise, commercial and social. The magazine becomes rapidly profitable, but friction occurs when Lindau, a German socialist, employed as a translator, discovers that the financial backing of the magazine comes from a capitalist speculator, Dryfoos, whom Lindau despises. Rather than persecute Lindau for his opinions, March resigns. This leaves the magazine at a disadvantage until Lindau solves the problem by himself resigning. In the meantime Dryfoos's son Conrad, an "idealistic humanitarian," has become interested in labor troubles which culminate in a traction strike. In a street riot Conrad is accidentally shot and Lindau is heavily clubbed by a policeman. Both wounds prove fatal. The elder Dryfoos, though opposed to his son's socialistic views, is badly shaken by his death. He shortly sells his interest in the magazine to editor March and manager Fulkerson, who rejoice in being able to operate it independently.

The social situation is equally difficult, if not so tragic or so definitely shaped to a climax. Dryfoos and his wife are wholly untutored persons who have suddenly become affluent through the discovery of oil on Dryfoos' property in a small western town. In New York Mrs. Dryfoos generally stays upstairs to avoid social embarrassments, but when the girls go to a dance or try to steer a course in love, Howells has opportunities for a favorite exercise in pointing up social disparities, part of which are comic in their effect. The daughters do not succeed well in New York society; one of them is later married (abroad) to a European nobleman. Conrad Dryfoos instills a "society girl" with benevolent social ideals but not quite with personal love for himself. There are other persons whose affairs of the heart must be recounted with Howells' customary dispassionateness before the social entourage in which the Marches find themselves in New York is completely drawn. The tremendous bulk of the book is created not only by the bony structure of action but by the intervening tissue of discussion—much of it in the form of superb dialogue and some of it in dialect—involving domestic life chez the Marches and the Dryfooses, the mechanics of journalism, the functions of magazines, the place of art in life, the influence of New York on the literary taste of the nation, relationships of the North and the South, the true nature of democracy, and various aspects of socio-economic life, particularly the relationships between capital and labor. The discussion is leisurely, finished to the last detail. There are many observations on New York in the eighties, but Howells' descriptions *tell* more of the physical appearance of the city than they present directly to the reader's eye. Howells was not highly gifted in the art of sensory detail; and the effect of setting here as in *The Rise of Silas Lapham* is curiously forgotten as soon as the author ceases to speak of it. As usual, he is mainly interested in people and opinions. *A Hazard of New Fortunes* contains a dozen well-differentiated types among whom is the canny, plausible, humorous Fulkerson —a man as near the vulgar as Howells can go without losing verisimilitude—who must take rank as one of Howells' best portraits, and old Dryfoos, whom Lowell described as "as tragically pathetic as Père Goriot and in a more human way." [77] If this book again proves Howells' inability to subdue disparate plot materials to a common purpose, it yet shows him at the height of his power to describe real people engaged in everyday affairs no more loosely connected than average man's experience. Only churlishness could insist on a perfected "plot" amid such an abundance of life and art.

But *A Hazard of New Fortunes* is also an "economic novel." This it becomes only gradually, for at first the fortunes of the March family as they timorously abandon beatific Boston for raucous New York are of paramount significance. More general economic problems emerge from the capitalistically backed magazine. With such persons present as Lindau, who thinks American democracy a "shuffling evasion" and the United States Senate a "rich man's club," [78] and old Dryfoos, who is dead against unions, it is obvious that diversity of opinion is represented. One may take it for granted, however, that Howells' own views are substantially those of Basil March, who regards modern industrial life as a hideous struggle for existence in an "economic chance-world" for which men are somehow partly responsible and which they must seek to amend as best they can. Violence, however, is not approved, and the long account of the traction strike shows the strikers in no very pleasant light. Even his sympathy for the workers' plight cannot make Howells condone violent methods: he is "*for* the men and *against* the strike." [79] No general solution is offered by the observer Howells—is any solution possible in a "chance-world"?—but the large proportion of *A Hazard of New Fortunes* which is devoted to economic problems attests his more than passing interest.

The Quality of Mercy (1892) is more constantly focussed on a socio-economic problem. In general literary values it is not so high as *A Hazard of New Fortunes*, but it has a more coherent plot. The idea beneath the action of the book lay implicit in the remark of a trolley-car conductor in *The Minister's Charge* (1887):

> "What's the reason, if a man wants to steal, he can't steal and suffer for it himself, without throwin' the shame and the blame on a lot more people that never thought o' stealin'?" [80]

The answer, of course, is that each man is only a link in a chain of circumstances which cannot help being affected by what he does but which he cannot himself control. In *The Quality of Mercy* one Northwick absconds to Canada with a large sum of money belonging to the corporation which employed him. The story reveals the resulting embarrassment, financial and social, into which his family is thrown. It also contains much comment on the case from a variety of angles. The defalcation was not an isolated one, it is implied; and, as one of the characters says, Northwick "isn't the disease; he is merely the symptom . . ." The disease is not named, but it has invaded the whole economic structure and it is responsible for sordid eruptions on the body of business. The journalist Maxwell, who is apparently one of Howells' voices, believes society largely responsible for defaulters:

> On one hand, you had men educated to business methods which permitted this form of dishonesty and condemned that; their

moral fibre was strained, if not weakened, by the struggle for money going on all around us; on the other hand, you had opportunity, the fascination of chance, the uncertainty of punishment. The causes would continue the same . . . but it behooved society to consider how far it was itself responsible, which it might well do without ignoring the responsibility of the criminal.[81]

Even the president of the corporation refers to commerce in the large as a "repulsive" apparatus: "Some dirt seems to get on everybody's bread by the time he has earned it, or his money even when he's made it in large sums as our class do." Fixing the responsibility for economic chaos is hard. For the hard-drinking lawyer Putney "any fight against a corporation was a kind of holy war," [82] but Putney (here as in *Annie Kilburn*) often speaks without the author's blessing. As usual Howells avoids indictments except of a most general sort. His humane attitude toward the defaulter marks him with a certain courage; yet he does not really present the case for Northwick but, rather, arbitrates it. No clear-cut conclusion is reached, but at least Northwick is not hounded through the story as a vicious brute. His criminal conduct is not laid to innate depravity or original sin. In a final speech Putney very plausibly but very generally accounts for the act perpetrated by Northwick:

> "He just seems to be a kind of—incident; and a pretty common kind. He was a mere creature of circumstances—like the rest of us! His environment made him rich, and his environment made him a rogue. Sometimes I think ther*e was* nothing to Northwick, except what happened to him. He's a puzzle." [83]

Putney is inclined to refer events to the control of "Fate," but his position is challenged by an interlocutor: "Why not call it Law?" Thereupon Putney responds with a compromise solution which gives the book its title and its tone:

> "Well, I don't like to be too bold. But taking it by and large, and seeing that most things seem to turn out pretty well in the end, I'll split the difference with you and call it Mercy." [84]

Characteristically, then, the book ends on a tranquil note. The narrative has been absorbing, and feelings have not been lacerated. Howells never gave needless pain to his readers. On the positive side the story does not lack popular appeal, what with a couple of love affairs and considerable variety of scene and episode. Yet seldom did Howells adhere to his social problem so constantly and so seriously as in *The Quality of Mercy*.

In Howells' next novel, not circumstance but chance (*i.e.*, circumstance set in motion) is the controlling element. *The World of Chance* (1893) tells of the accidental rise of a young author. His novel is accepted through a chance—the publisher's sleepless night. Promotion of the book fails to give it a run, but just as the firm is on the way to bankruptcy a lucky review sends the book up to the best-selling class. In the meantime the hero (Shelley Ray) has made the acquaintance of a New York tenement family whose tragic succession of four deaths proves that chance can also be malign. Commercial life is subject to the same random fluctuation:

> "Well, it's all a game [says one of the characters], and . . . you can't bet on it with any more certainty—than you can on a trottin' match . . . I've heard about the law of demand and supply before. There's about as much of a law to it as there is to three-card monte." [85]

There is no predictable ratio between effort and success. Even "improvements" such as the invention of labor-saving machines may have dire consequences.[86] As to real improvements, one of the characters suggests (apparently with Howells' approval) the "nationalization of the telegraphs, railroads, and expresses" as the "first steps" in a gradual amelioration of the economic framework.[87] Tragic issues receive less effective treatment in this book than comic. Ansel Denton's suicide by prussic acid is perhaps "the most lurid scene in all Howells' pages";[88] but this scene is not typical, and the book as a whole possesses less philosophical weight than certain other fictional studies involving ironical chance, such as those of Hardy and Dreiser.

The crime of Northwick (in *The Quality of Mercy*) and the suicide of Denton (in *The World of Chance*) would not have occurred in "Altruria," the mythical country represented by the narrator in Howells' new economic novel, *A Traveler from Altruria* (1894). This is a kind of Utopian study in reverse: the reader does not visit the ideal commonwealth but learns about it through an Altrurian who has come to study conditions in competitive America. The setting is a summer hotel in the mountains—a favorite rendezvous for Howells' characters. The characters are not allowed to develop much beyond the types suggested by their names—Mrs. Makely, the society woman; Mr. Bullion, the banker; Mr. Twelvemough, the novelist, etc.—but they are invested with full command of Howells' harmonious and natural speech idiom. Plot is ignored, movement and incident being provided by the traveler's tour of inspection. Discussion turns on economic and sociological themes that Howells had used elsewhere: labor unions, monopolies, trusts, franchise, woman suffrage, charity, class distinctions. But in this book the abuses which arise out of the rugged individualistic American plan are seen in contrast with (reported) conditions in Altruria, where corresponding ideals exist. Altruria is a quasi-communistic state in which everyone is passing prosperous on three hours' work a day. Chance and competition are eliminated, and there is a direct ratio between effort and success. Howells is here (as elsewhere) much concerned with the doctrine of equality. The theme is basic, for, as the traveler says, " 'inequality and iniquity are the same in the last analysis.' " [89] Yet although in the Declaration of Independence we grandly affirmed equality, it was " 'rather the political than the social traditions of England that we broke with,' " [90] and our American civilization has in reality created ranks and classes of its own. The folly of class distinction is quietly brought out in dialogue between the traveler and the narrator. The narrator is of course not abjectly apologetic for our system. He thinks that America will muddle through somehow: " 'You know we are a sort of fatalists here in America. We are great believers in the doctrine that it will all come out right in the end.' " [91] Yet the result of all the parleying in this book is to show lamentable flaws in our present system. Howells does not speak bitterly of these abuses, nor does he angrily fix responsibility for their existence. He urges no immediate reforms. He looks forward to a peaceful amelioration of the state through the gradual nationalization of industry. *A Traveler from Altruria* is not a socialistic tract but a fantasy or a fable gracefully spun out of socialistic fabric. A sequel appeared in 1907, *Through the Eye of the Needle,* probably written shortly after *A Traveler from Altruria.* It is less successful for the reason that Howells undertakes in the second half of the book to show us Altruria itself. He contrives a marriage between the traveler and an American widow. The latter's letters from Altruria to Mrs. Makely disclose conditions which are ideal to the point of tedium. The author is fain to introduce incident—two American ships arrive—in order to relieve the serenity of Altruria's "ladylike" civilization. Howells' Utopian imagination is not equal to coping with that dullness which is the tax on security. The difficulty is a fundamental one, for human nature is prone to find its deepest interest in struggle. *Through the Eye of the Needle* is the least rewarding of the cycle of economic novels which it completes.

Howells was of course only an amateur "economist." There is no evidence that he ever read systematically the works of Smith, Mill, Bentham, and other political economists. Nowhere does he mention

Karl Marx, despite the prevailingly liberal tenor of his own theorizing. He does not, even in *A Traveler from Altruria*, completely outline a practical system of political economy. He seems to have had only a limited comprehension of public finance. Yet he was a keenly interested observer of the socio-economic order. He wrote pretty much from the point of view of the average man. He was himself never more than tangent to extremes of poverty and wealth. His talk was of the vast middle classes: with them any program of amelioration should start. Such a program must be an economic program, for political equality without economic equality is of negligible value. Such a program must be a comprehensive, collectivist program. It must not depend on charitable palliatives however well conceived. It must try to suppress ruthless individualism and the private control of natural monopolies. It must include provision for the solution of new problems as they arise, such as technological unemployment. Aggressive capitalism must be checked: it is as baneful to the economic order as imperialism is to the political order.[92] In short the state must be socialized. Only so will the average citizen be able to lead the measurably happy and useful life which civilization ought to afford him.

Such views as these, assembled, subscribed to, and argued for in a single document would be described as radical. Implicit in them is meat for diatribes against railroads, trusts, monopolies, and a dozen types of commercial "abominations" alleged to exploit the public. Yet Howells in retrospect appears to have had little of the radical in him, considerably less than his disciple Garland. Granville Hicks says that his "socialism was at best the vague reaction of a well-intentioned, sensitive man to the contemporary spectacle of misery and greed." [93] How can such a judgment be passed on a man armed with the incendiary doctrine summarized above? The answer is that Howells doesn't choose to fight: if he carries dynamite, he will not detonate it. It is clear from his private correspondence that he hated such enterprises as the Standard Oil Company,[94] but as a novelist he refrained from laying on hands. He did not hope to see capitalism overthrown by the confiscation of wealth or by revolution. The violence often resulting from strikes was abhorrent to him, for he believed that "every drop of blood shed for a good cause helps to make a bad cause." [95] He hoped for improvement rather by rational methods and he recommended to laborers that they "quit striking and fighting and direct their efforts toward gaining control of the government." [96] As has been shown he distributes his anti-capitalistic speeches to such a variety of characters that their author can remain in comparative anonymity. Liberal arguments are met by counter arguments almost as effective. Howells mobilizes ideas on both sides, and he does not insist on "victory": he is willing to negotiate. Nor was this merely a sign of Howells' timidity: he had shown the quality of his courage in the case of the Chicago anarchists. Rather it was his instinct as an artist not to allow ideology to destroy story. He saw the defects of our social order, and he wished to report them in general terms. It was not incumbent on him to provide remedies or even methods. It is beside the mark, therefore, to urge that "A helpful social philosophy will show not the vision of a New Jerusalem, but the steps by which it was attained." [97] Granted that the work of building the new state must some day be carried out, it is still true that the surveyor must precede the construction crew and the engineer. Nor is it more pertinent to complain that the businessman Silas Lapham should concern himself with securing social recognition at a time when "The great railroad magnates—Sage, Stanford, Huntington—robbed the government, the public, and their own stockholders." [98] Not only was it natural for Lapham to seek social success, but it was wise for Howells not to burden his text with too much allusion to robber barons. Howells, like Emerson, knew that art perishes upon too much specific analysis of contemporary issues; the proof of this lies about us now in the defunct labor novels of the 1920's. Unquestionably Howells had neither the expert knowledge nor the range of thought that could have produced important economic commentary, but time has shown that he was as much of an economist as a novelist can afford to be.

Notwithstanding his activity as a writer on socio-economic topics between 1886 and 1894 Howells had never really abandoned belles lettres. As has been shown, his so-called economic novels by no means marked a complete departure from his earlier fictional methods. Characterization, dialogue, setting—all were attended to carefully in them as in most of his stories. Moreover his pen had produced other works in the same period—travel notes, criticism, plays, short stories, and other novels. None of the other novels is now generally regarded as among his best. Yet *April Hopes* (1888) is one of Howells' most mature studies of love. He who had so often made young love the subject of easy banter, who had roguishly reveled in scenes designed to deflate the ego of an empty-headed suitor or vapid girl, who had nevertheless compromised with his conscience by repeatedly bringing about a happy ending for the sake of the "trade"—this man now resolutely faced the tragic implications of unhappy love in a story of considerable power and more than average beauty. *April Hopes* is not keyed to heroic tragedy in the grand manner, nor does it culminate in an overt tragic episode of dramatic quality. Indeed it is in many respects a "gay" book, what with its lively social intercourse between well-drawn Brahmin characters including old friends like the Coreys and the Bellinghams, as well as chit-chat among Harvard undergraduates. Moreover the "lovers" are finally married. Yet by deft psychological analysis and ingenious episode Howells has brought his readers to the realization that, as Mrs. Brinkley says, the lovers, being brought together only by passion, would be "better parted than *plighted*." The wedding can only be a prelude to marital storms.[99] Alice Pasmer, a somewhat morbid heroine possibly modeled upon Turgenev's Liza,[100] is an unusual character for Howells to have drawn, and the book as a whole carries a pinch of realism that must have been unpalatable to summer boarders who picked it up for light reading.

Three other novels appeared in this exceedingly prolific period of Howells' career. *The Shadow of a Dream* (1890), centered in a man who is the victim of an obsession that an undue affection exists between his wife and a friend, wavers somewhat unsuccessfully between romantic tragedy vaguely reminiscent of Shakespeare in tone, and psychological analysis inevitably recalling Hawthorne.[101] *An Imperative Duty* (1892) treats the theme of Negro blood in a white heroine with less strain and sensationalism than is characteristic of the genre.[102] *The Coast of Bohemia* (1893) mixes love, pride, and the artistic temperament in an amusing if not very significant story laid in and near New York City.[103]

It is convenient to use the year 1894 as a divisional line in the career of Howells. Not that he struck out into new waters; rather he tended thereafter more and more to frequent bays and inlets of a type already familiar to him. Yet if he became slightly less adventurous, he evinced little diminution of his literary powers. His personal life suffered a major change, for in this year (1894) his much-beloved father died. It was an event, said Howells, which "aged [him] as nothing else could have done." [104] It did not, however, diminish his eagerness to write.[105] His name was a shade less revered perhaps than it had been a decade earlier, and to keep his reputation alive it was necessary to continue writing, what with the great increase of young American writers in the 1890's, not to mention England's dumping on our shores a great quantity of the wares of "little British romanticists" [106] likely to seduce an uncritical public despite the wholesome counsel of his armchair critical essays collected from *Harper's* to form the volume entitled *Criticism and Fiction* (1891). Out of love and need, then, Howells continued to write novels for some twenty-five years more. Most of these later novels yield little that is wholly new to one following the evolution of Howells' art, but almost all of them reveal Howells' fine craftsman-ship, and two of them—*The Landlord at Lion's Head* and *The Son of Royal Langbrith*—come very close to his highest standards of fiction.

Of the lesser novels of the later period, one of the least is *The Day of Their Wedding* (1896). This is an airy, amorphous comedy of a pair of lovers who vainly attempt to break the (benign) fetters which bind them to Shakerism. The work is distinctly inferior to Howells' more serious treatment of Shakerism in *The Undiscovered Country*.[107] It is also inferior to his next novel, *An Open-Eyed Conspiracy* (1897). The latter is a love story set in Saratoga—a mise-en-scène by now grown pretty shabby from its constant use by nineteenth-century novelists but seen afresh in the light of Howells' unfailing vivacity. Old actors also appear—the ubiquitous Marches. In his sub-title Howells referred to the narrative as an "idyl." An idyl it may be, but not a romance, for Howells again quietly admonishes the reader not to regard the betrothed pair as destined for a happy-ever-after sort of existence. The hero is in love with the heroine's "beautiful girlhood," but "the girlhood will go . . . and the girl will remain." [108] It is in just such gentle admoni-tions that Howells not only exemplifies his critical principles as a realist but also rebuffs a large potential public among those readers who insist that the heroine must get her man and get him without any implied checks or reservations touching the promised bliss of married life. Why throw a shadow on a radiant pair of lovers? they ask in ef-fect. Howells replies (in effect) that only a shadow can prove the reality of sunlight. This is the same Howells who wrote *A Foregone Conclusion* and *April Hopes*. He avoids the blackness of pessimism but insists on the shadows of truth. Yet *An Open-Eyed Conspiracy* is a prevailingly sunny book.

For the principal actor in his next novel, *The Story of a Play* (1898), Howells re-engaged Brice Maxwell, last seen in *The Quality of Mercy*, and for his vis-à-vis, Louise (Hilary) Maxwell of the same original cast. The action (hardly a plot) is stitched together by a multitude of unimportant coincidences, but its fabric is the genuine stuff of life. Maxwell puts on a play—that is about all the action there is. Whether the production will satisfy the author—that is the main issue. Only a writer as resourceful with scant material as Howells could have straddled this issue so long without wearing out the patience of his audience. In the end the play succeeds: the novel is a comedy—and a good one.

Ragged Lady (1899) is a kind of scrap-bag—full of entertaining devices (mostly old with Howells) which resist any attempt to make of them a uniform pattern. The theme is the process of bridging class distinctions: Clementina Claxon is being "cultivated" by a wealthy couple. The theme is true love versus duty: Clementina rejects an officious young minister who criticizes her faith, and marries instead a young inventor. When the latter's death leaves her a widow, she marries the minister—but only after much discussion of the "basis" of their (re)union. The theme is one of a half dozen possibilities, for no unity is discernible in this by-no-means dull story. Never notable in his larger organization of materials, Howells made his most egregious structural failure in *Ragged Lady*.

In 1899 the Marches, Basil and Isabel, who had been allowed visiting privileges in various novels, were finally given another book of their own—or mainly their own—*Their Silver Wedding Journey*. Middle age has begun to merge into old age for this couple, who journey through Europe experiencing the pain and pleasure of recalling an earlier journey. The book achieves its very ample girth by a steady diet of anecdote, reflection, and travel minutiae, as well as by the details of a junior love affair which, though sponsored by Mrs. March, seems something of an intrusion even in this gentle pot-pourri. The lovers are united, but Howells contrives, as often, to take some of the bloom off romantic love by temporarily breaking the engagement. The Marches grow old gracefully but not without a natural broadening of Basil's mildly cynical outlook on government and politics (including Tammany Hall) and a greater awareness of the manifold approaches of death:

> He sat thinking how once the world had not seemed to have even death in it, and then how as he had grown older death had come into it more and more, and suffering was lurking everywhere, and could hardly be kept out of sight.[109]

The Kentons (1902) has been referred to as a "flawless" novel by one critic[110] and relegated by another critic to a group of novels described as being of "reduced significance." [111] Both views are tenable. The technique is flawless: Howells even conquered his old sin, poor proportion. Yet little significance attaches to the rather slight story. Ellen Kenton is sought in marriage by a somewhat plausible but insolently familiar and facetious young man of poor background (*vide* his impossible mother), from whom her frightened father finally saves her by taking her abroad. On shipboard she meets a more suitable candidate—equally flippant but basically sound—whom she eventually weds. Before she marries, Ellen insists that her parents tell her fiancé of the blot on her past, namely, the night when the former suitor had kissed her goodnight—a proceeding which had thrown the girl into hysteria, upset the whole family, and induced her brother to give the bad man a public cow-hiding. If *The Kentons* was at fault, however, it is not that its action constitutes a tempest in a Victorian teapot,[112] but that Howells somehow fails to universalize the experience: it remains a specific transaction, nothing more. It is distinctly inferior to another novel of equally light materials, *Indian Summer*. Yet it was probably "the most popular of Howells' later novels." [113]

Almost unknown but not far inferior to *The Kentons* is *Letters Home* (1903). This novel is new (for Howells) in its use of the letter form, old in raising a ruction over a comparatively trivial affair in which a young journalist worries over having caused undue flutter in the heart of a sixteen-year-old girl when his real interest lies in the more substantial daughter of a parvenu (Ralston) closely related in type to old Dryfoos of *A Hazard of New Fortunes*. *Miss Bellard's Inspiration* (1905) is an almost Quixotic narrative of a "New Woman"—a teacher who at first refuses to marry a congenial lover because she has observed what a horrible mess has resulted from the marriage of a once-devoted couple of her acquaintance. There isn't room in the world, she thinks, for two such couples. She changes her mind (can this be a "new" woman?) for a reason which forms the most absurd piece of motivation in all Howells: the other couple becomes separated. Mr. Howells' inspiration for this book was pretty feeble, but he was as successful as ever in reporting minor alterations in the social milieu, as, for example, in Mrs. Crombie's comment on whether Miss Bellard's fiancé was a religious man:

> "I suppose that once we should have considered whether he was religious or not; but the world has got to the pass where we don't consider that any more, when a man is good, and kind, and truthful, and fond of you." [114]

Through the Eye of the Needle[115] appeared in 1907, and *Fennel and Rue* in 1908. The latter tells of a girl who plays a trick on a young author[116] and gets spanked for it by Howells. The young author also rues his excessive severity toward the foolish girl. Not a pleasant book—or an important one.

Between 1908 and 1913 Howells neglected the novel in favor of travel books, verse-dialogue, and other miscellaneous items including *My Mark Twain*, published in the year of Clemens' death (1910). In 1913 he wrote *New Leaf Mills: a Chronicle*, which may be classified loosely as fiction but more fittingly as an autobiographical narrative dealing with the Ohio boyhood of Howells and the problems of the quasi-pioneer Howells family. *The Leatherwood God* (1916) also recounts early annals of Ohio, but its framework is more patently fictitious. Its centre of reference is a favorless professional evangelist (a real menace in pioneer communities of the Mid-West in the 60's and 70's), but Howells, sedulous as ever in making sure that the centre of his story does not prosper at the expense of the circumference, rounds out the community life with a wealth of authenticating detail. Both *New Leaf Mills* and *The Leatherwood God*, if not important as novels, add substantially to that literature of the middle border of which Eggleston's novels, Howe's *Story of a Country Town*, and Garland's autobiographical books are important component parts.

Two of Howells' novels were published posthumously, *Mrs. Farrell* [117] and *The Vacation of the Kelwyns* (1920). The Kelwyns take a vacation as summer boarders in a Shaker community. Here they are victimized by the Kites, who are hired (at Shaker suggestion) to cook and "do" for Professor Kelwyn's family but who prove to be hopelessly inefficient.[118] Will the Kelwyns endure such an outrage? They will—after their indignation is replaced by a measure of sympathy. An old theme is here—social responsibility for incompetents of a lower class—but it does not engross Howells to the extent of making him forget to beguile the reader with a love story and many excellent character-portraits. The portraits, indeed, were so lifelike that, again out of respect for the law[119] Howells deferred publication of the book at the instance of unwilling originals of the portraits. The book had actually been written in 1910.

The novels Howells wrote in the last twenty-five years of his life are astonishingly free from signs of a relaxed control of his art. As for deliberate pot-boilers, they were out of the question with Howells. The least of his novels reveals manifold evidence of the high powers that were his. Yet though quality is never deliberately sacrificed, some of the novels have more weight than others, and in the last period—if twenty-five years be not too many to constitute a period—Howells achieved a more comprehensive and significant synthesis of his powers in two novels, *The Landlord at Lion's Head* (1897) and *The Son of Royal Langbrith* (1904). These, together with *A Modern Instance*, *The Rise of Silas Lapham*, *A Hazard of New Fortunes*, and *Indian Summer*, are now generally considered to form the bulwark of Howells' permanent reputation.

It is typical of Howells' characterizations that he steadfastly refused to "star" one or two persons at the expense of the rest of his cast. He works more with groups (though not masses) than with individuals. His generosity toward the many is likely to obscure the fineness of his portraits separately considered. Among the few exceptions to this rule is the portrait of Jeff Durgin in *The Landlord at Lion's Head*. Indeed the book may be said to exist mainly as a character study of the hero. Other persons are well drawn, but they have few independent functions, and they are not incorporated into a plot. The book begins in a lightly described New England upland when the artist Westover settles on the Durgin farm for a week in order to paint a neighboring peak, the Lion's Head. The Durgin family and their neighbors receive leisurely introductions. Jeff appears as a thirteen-year-old boy given to teasing little girls but responsive enough to the friendly overtures of Westover. It is characteristic of Howells that in the forty-seven pages that are devoted to Westover's first visit to the Durgin farm, nothing occurs which is organically indispensable to the later action except that, more or less fortuitously, Westover has found himself in a friendly relationship (something akin to Sewell's relationship to Lemuel Barker in *The Minister's Charge*) with the Durgin family and with Jeff in particular. Five years later Westover finds the farm converted into a hotel prosperous enough to convince Mrs. Durgin that Jeff must have an education at Harvard—in law. According to the social law in and about Boston, Jeff, as a landlady's son, is a "jay." He falls in love with a "society girl," who toys with his affections before refusing his marriage proposal. He in turn trifles with the affections of another cultured flirt, finally spurning her for a plebian but charming childhood friend—who in turn finally rejects him. In the meantime the deaths of Father and Mother and Brother Durgin have made Jeff the landlord of Lion's Head. On a European trip he meets again flirt no. 1 (now the relict of a rubbishy Count) ready, when proper credentials are furnished, to marry Jeff. Jeff returns to Lion's Head, rebuilds the burnt-down hotel on modern lines, and settles down to an apparently prosperous life. His career has been steadily watched, if not materially affected, by the Coverdale-like Westover, who has his reward in a marriage with Jeff's childhood friend.

To see meaning in this succession (by no means chain) of events is difficult. The thing that really interests Howells is the character of Jeff, who is at best an honest cynic and at worst a cold, calculating individual bent on advancing his own interests in a competitive world. His conduct is not of the sort that makes a downright villain—boyish mischief, rowdyism at college, disingenuous love-making, encouraging an alcoholic Brahmin in his cups, responding to a horsewhipping at the hands of a girl's indignant brother by nearly choking the man to death. If he is a blackguard at all, he is "a blackguard in the Howells world, and this means that about half the time he is a gentleman." [120] The deeper evils he is brought to the edge of—chronic drunkenness, a sordid liaison, murder, arson—he is withdrawn from by the author. Yet he is a formidable embodiment of anti-social principles that are all the more perturbing because of his plausible manners and comparatively harmless conduct. Moreover he has an articulate philosophy which distresses that part of Westover which is in reality Howells himself:

> "You can't do a wrong thing [says Westover] and prosper on it—"
> "Oh, yes you can," Jeff interrupted with a sneering laugh. "How do you suppose all the big fortunes were made? By keeping the commandments?"
> "No. But you're an unlucky man if life hasn't taught you that you must pay in suffering of some kind, sooner or later, for every wrong thing you do—"
> "Now that's one of your old-fashioned superstitions, Mr. Westover," said Jeff, with a growing kindliness in his tone, as if the pathetic delusion of such a man really touched him. "You pay, or you don't pay, just as it happens. If you get hit soon after you've done wrong, you think it's retribution, and if it holds off till you've forgotten all about it, you think it's a strange Providence, and you puzzle over it, but you don't reform. You keep right along in the old way. Prosperity and adversity, they've got nothing to do with conduct. If you're a strong man, you get there, and if you're a weak man, all the righteousness in the universe won't help you." [121]

But Westover persists in his view of responsibility, and he asserts at the end of the story that, whether he knows it or not, Jeff will reap the evil he has sown. "The dreadful thing," adds Westover, "is that others must share in the harvest." These were problems which Howells had considered at length in some of his economic novels, in *A Modern Instance*, and in *Silas Lapham*. Here they are subordinated to the vivid presentation of a complex character. Jeff Durgin is at once a more attractive and a more disturbing "villain" than Bartley Hubbard. His full measure of reality is what chiefly makes *The Landlord at Lion's Head* "the most robust" of all Howells' novels.[122]

In *The Son of Royal Langbrith* (1904) not characterization but theme is dominant—the effect of the protracted suppression and final disclosure of the villainy perpetrated by a man long since dead. The man, Royal Langbrith, had amassed a large fortune by dishonest business practices, but his son James, kept in ignorance of seamy facts, has these many years revered the memory of his father to the point of fatuity and now wishes to bring about the erection of a public tablet in his father's honor. His move to do so brings him into opposition with

Dr. Anther, suitor to the young man's widowed mother. Dr. Anther's knowledge of the father's villainy makes him resent the proposed plan, and James Langbrith's resentment of the Doctor's coldness makes him oppose the projected marriage. At the same time James falls in love with Hope Hawberk, the daughter of Royal Langbrith's principal victim, an inventor now in an almost imbecilic state of senile decay. The evil that Royal Langbrith did, lived after him, therefore, in the memory of a number of people, but it is agreed to allow the unveiling of the tablet without apprising James of the ghastly irony it symbolizes.[123] This crisis passed, there is another threat to James's psychological security when old Hawberk, responding to improved medical treatment, recovers his wits; but Hawberk indicates that he will not bare the past, and in fact he is himself shortly merged with the past when Howells pushes him (so arbitrary is the action in effect) into a stream of ice-cold water that indirectly causes his death. The truth is finally blurted fiercely at James by his Uncle John, who under stress of a painful moment in his illness can refrain no longer. James gallantly offers to release Hope from their engagement, but she as gallantly refuses the offer.

Here was a subject worthy of Hawthorne, who is in fact mentioned in the story, or of Henry James, whose method is inevitably recalled by the opening scenes of the book. The author of *What Maisie Knew* and *The Portrait of a Lady* is brought to mind also by Howells' probing of the effect of evil upon innocent characters.[124] Strangely enough, there are dark threads in this book that recall Melville. The son's ill-founded worship of his father's memory has a certain analogy in *Pierre*, and Howells, like Melville, was troubled by the fact that an evil legacy "intertwines itself with so much of the good in the survivors that you can't strike at it without wounding the best and gentlest of them." [125] Yet the problem is ethical as well as philosophical, and (despite all possible "influences") Howells is very much himself as he struggles with its human solution. He swerves from imminent tragedy into apparent compromise. That Royal Langbrith's wicked past must be revealed to his son is a dramatic necessity (though it is brought about awkwardly), but the secret need not be spread abroad in the community. Its suppression, Howells implies, is justifiable, for evil outwardly unpunished may in effect be canceled by time:

> "How do we know [Rector Enderby asks] but that in that mystical legislation, as to whose application to our conduct we have to make our guesses and inferences, there may not be a law of limitations by which the debts overdue through time are the same as forgiven? No one was the poorer through their non-payment in

Royal Langbrith's case; in every high sort each was the richer. It may be the complicity of all mortal being is such that the pain he inflicted was endured to his behoof, and that it has helped him atone for his sins as an acceptable offering in the sort of vicarious atonement which has always been in the world." [126]

A certain charity or tolerance, it is obvious, actuates Howells in his moral decisions, chiefly, it appears, because of his theory of "complicity." [127] Yet serious as is his interest in the philosophical implications of his theme, he is chiefly concerned in *The Son of Royal Langbrith* with its concrete representation in the lives of real characters whose plight he reports with a tenderness and an understanding which he exceeded in no earlier volume. In most respects *The Son of Royal Langbrith*, written in Howells' sixty-seventh year, must be reckoned one of his best novels.

Howells wrote altogether some thirty-eight novels over a period of fifty years. They constitute a body of fiction remarkably similar in method and uniform in quality. In matters of theme, structure, characterization, setting, dialogue, diction, and tone, Howells quickly adopted practices which served him substantially from 1870 to 1920. He was not materially influenced by new "schools" of fiction. He seldom wrote experimentally or inspirationally. His methods were from the beginning adopted because of his firm convictions as to what fiction ought to be. The novelist and the critic collaborated in every story Howells wrote.[128] His principles were relatively simple at bottom, but the elaboration of them occupied a great deal of space both in his critical studies and in his novels. In a sense, therefore, his fiction may be summarized and evaluated by reference to his literary creed. For this purpose miscellaneous observations in his novels and letters are useful, in addition to more elaborate statements to be found in *Literary Friends and Acquaintance*, *Heroines of Fiction*, and *Criticism and Fiction*. The last of these, *Criticism and Fiction* (1891), is too informal, partakes too much of the nature of causeries, to be regarded as a complete system of critical thought, but it comprises most of the articles of his belief.

Central in the literary creed which Howells advocated was reverence for truth—an article of faith which was distinctly subordinate with many of the writers of domestic and historical romances before his time. In his simplest statement he denied that "literature and art are anything but the expression of life" and he refused to believe that they are "to be judged by any other test than that of their fidelity to it." An author should not, therefore, consider his work primarily in relationship to himself or to other authors but in "relation to the human nature, known to us all, which it is his privilege, his high duty, to interpret."[129] From the very beginning he was willing to act resolutely upon this principle—if need be, to the point of risking dullness. The fiction-writer, he thought, will aim to present man not only in his "heroic or occasional phases, but . . . in his habitual moods of vacancy and tiresomeness." He himself believed that men most truly reveal themselves in their "vast, natural, unaffected dullness."[130] Not only was he convinced that fiction could be made interesting on this basis (as, indeed, he proved in *Their Wedding Journey*), but he believed, with Mr. Sewell in *The Rise of Silas Lapham*, that "'The novelists might be the greatest possible help to us if they painted life as it is, and human feelings in their true proportion and relation . . .'"[131] Use—that is a thing that Howells, like Franklin, never forgot for long. He had no patience with art for art's sake, and in his opinion "the finest effect of the 'beautiful' will be ethical and not æsthetic merely."[132] Nor is there any question of the artist's being able to discern the true and the faithful for (Howells quotes Burke) "The true standard of the artist is in every man's power."[133] Often enough in the past, he admits, people have been misled by false "luminaries," but he believes that his own age is

> beginning to see and to say that no author is an authority except in those moments when he held his ear close to Nature's lips and caught her very accent.[134]

It is the obligation of every novelist to test his own work for truth, to safeguard the interest of his readers:

> The light of civilization has already broken even upon the novel, and no conscientious man can now set about painting an image of life without perpetual question of the verity of his work, and without feeling bound to distinguish so clearly that no reader of his may be misled, between what is right and what is wrong, what is noble and what is base, what is health and what is perdition, in the actions and the characters he portrays . . . I confess that I do not care to judge any work of the imagination without first of all applying this test to it. We must ask ourselves before we ask anything else, Is it true?—true to the motives, the impulses, the principles that shape the life of actual men and women?[135]

And the novelist who observes this commandment of the critic will have his reward, for "This truth . . . necessarily includes the highest morality and the highest artistry." [136] In short, Howells re-expresses an old ideal by finding an essential identity between truth, goodness, and beauty. As a critic, however, he talks most of truth. As a realist he found this imperative.

Howells has been called the father (or grandfather) of modern realism. He himself used the term "realism" freely, but he didn't profess to know exactly when the thing it stood for was originated: "no one invented realism; it came." [137] In its better phases it implied the rigorous but natural presentation of truth, in the portrayal of "men and women as they are, actuated by the motives and the passions in the measure we all know." [138] Roughly Howells used the term *realism* as opposed to *romanticism*. With romanticism he had little patience, for although it originally had the raison d'être that it was a liberating force, it "exhausted itself in this impulse," and became a convenient resort for novelists of "escape" and mere childish amusement. Consequently it devolved upon realism to "widen the bounds of sympathy, to level every barrier against æsthetic freedom, to escape from the paralysis of tradition." [139] And he is hopeful enough to assert that many good novelists have begun to show the public that the true "Romance" is in "Reality." Convinced that there need be no fear lest dull reading result from the use of "dull" subjects, he fervidly quotes Emerson's plea for the use of common material in art:

> I ask not for the great, the remote, the romantic. . . . I embrace the common; I sit at the feet of the familiar and the low. . . . Man is surprised to find that things near are not less beautiful and wondrous than things remote . . . Banks and tariffs, the newspaper and caucus, Methodism and Unitarianism, are flat and dull to dull people, but rest on the same foundations of wonder as the town of Troy and the temple of Delphos [*sic*].[140]

Nowhere did Howells so well express in his own language the meaning of Emerson's pronouncement, but it was implicit in his creed. His was a democratic creed. The artist to Howells was not a seer or a prophet but an articulator of what every man could know from his own observation and could test by his own "standard" without recourse to dialectic. Few critics were, theoretically at least, so complimentary to their public. He was also, theoretically at least, complimentary toward his fellow craftsmen when he implied that they could infallibly determine "what is right and what is wrong, what is noble and what is base, what is health and what is perdition." [141] Many American writers—Hawthorne and Melville among them—have been greatly exercised to find

out, even for themselves, "what is right and what is wrong." Howells'
theory of truth would have seemed over-simple to them.

In fact his "fidelity-to-life" theory was too broad and simple for
Howells himself, for under examination he proves to have had in mind a
selective truth. He wanted to be faithful to special facets of the truth—
as he saw them. He spoke of the malign "paralysis of tradition," but he
did not want to abolish all standards and controls. He repeatedly gave
evidence of wishing to evade the sordid and repulsive elements that
might naturally have found place in his stories. He was certain that
many nineteenth-century French "realists" had the wrong brand of
truth. There were some "motives," "impulses," and "principles" shap-
ing the lives of "actual men and women" which he did not care to
present. He was interested in "gilt-edged" ethics for most of his
heroes.[142] He even dared to lay down a statement of the sort of truth
that he thought suitable for his American colleagues in the novel:

> Our novelists, therefore, concern themselves with the more smil-
> ing aspects of life, which are the more American, and seek the
> universal in the individual rather than the social interests. It is
> worth while, even at the risk of being called commonplace, to be
> true to our well-to-do actualities; the very passions themselves
> seem to be softened and modified by conditions which formerly
> at least could not be said to wrong any one, to cramp endeavor,
> or to cross lawful desire. Sin and suffering and shame there must
> always be in the world, I suppose, but I believe that in this new
> world of ours it is still mainly from one to another one, and oftener
> still from one to one's self. We have death too in America, and a
> great deal of disagreeable and painful disease, which the multiplic-
> ity of our patent medicines does not seem to cure; but this is trag-
> edy that comes in the very nature of things, and is not peculiarly
> American, as the large, cheerful average of health and success and
> happy life is. It will not do to boast, but it is well to be true to the
> facts, and to see that, apart from these purely mortal troubles, the
> race here has enjoyed conditions in which most of the ills that
> have darkened its annals might be averted by honest work and un-
> selfish behavior.[143]

Nor did Howells really believe that truth could prevail unless adequately interpreted by the right people. He argued for objectivity in
art, and he praised Turgenev because his characters were "left to trans-
act their affair, whatever it is, with the least possible comment or explanation from the author."[144] In 1901, he observed that "[f]iction had
not yet conceived of the supreme ethics which consist in portraying
life truly and letting the lesson take care of itself."[145] Yet in his hey-

day he spoke also in another vein: he insisted on interpretation. He protested against "realism" which "heaps up facts merely, and maps life instead of picturing it." The "true realist," he said, will be "careful of every fact" and will "indicate its meaning at the risk of over-moralizing." [146] His whole critical position in fact (unlike that of James) is characterized by a schoolmasterish strain of didacticism. There is little discussion of sin in Howells' stories but much debate over ethics. He pounds no thesis, but he gently insists on interpretation. When does "interpretation" become "moralizing"? Certainly Howells' attacks on writers who in his opinion debased life do not argue his objectivity. His advocacy of expurgated editions of the classics denotes a mind toying with the idea of censorship. His preferences among novelists seem to be based upon considerations that are ethical quite as often as artistic.[147] And in his own fictional practice it is clear that the moralist is not far from the elbow of the novelist. In this respect Howells was far from as independent as James. Howells wanted the truth but not necessarily the whole truth. His critical position is not wholly invalidated by his personal squeamishness. It was salutary that Howells should have protested (in *The Rise of Silas Lapham*) against that type of untruthfulness which takes the form of sentimental mush.[148] It was salutary, too, that he should have rebuked writers bent on shocking the public by exaggerated (untruthful) scenes of violence. He was even more useful on the positive side—in holding out the promise of success to writers who should honestly exploit the "familiar" and the "commonplace." Yet a limitation surely exists in a critic unable to face "truth" in her uglier phases. Here too an Emersonian text might have helped Howells: "There is no object so foul that intense light will not make beautiful." [149]

If Howells seems a trifle tame and timid to the present generation, he was regarded as something of a literary radical in his time. His chief offense was that he sabotaged romance. He short-weighted the customers in quest of the staples of entertainment. His preference of principles to passions, his insistence on common sense, his habit of qualifying the ecstasy of his lovers, his introduction of prosy details into scenes that might otherwise be romantic, his parochial manner of pointing out moral lessons in life, his habit of subtracting a few cubits from his hero's stature and pointing out the low intelligence quotient of his heroines, his laughing at young love—all these tendencies in Howells, an acknowledged leader among novelists, aroused the wrath of readers and critics who liked stories in which wonder and beauty appeared in more traditional strains. Here was a man who deliberately clipped the wings of romance. Accordingly Howells was heartily condemned by the votaries of Stevenson, Kipling, Francis Marion Crawford, Rider Haggard, and other purveyors of marvelous adventure and sugared sentiment. The cry began as early as 1880, when *The Nation* complained of a "lack of romantic imagination" in Howells' work.[150] Toward the end of the decade, however, charges against Howells were reiterated more frequently. In 1888 he was accused of exploiting the commonplace to such an extent as to "blight germs of spirituality."[151] James Lane Allen, one of the most popular Southern romance-writers, ridiculed Howells in an article entitled "Caterpillar Critics." In 1889 a critic in *The Literary World* asserted that he read Howells "less and less with a feeling of zest, and more and more from a sense of duty."[152] This last criticism was indicative both of Howells' weakness and his strength. There were undoubtedly unexciting stretches in his novels. Yet he was not only a novelist but also a critic, able to confute his opponents in measured terms which must have impressed them almost as much as they irked his readers. For readers of the type who preferred the "realism of a very poetic sort" Howells had a reprimand that was the more effective because, as usual in his criticism of minor authors, he did not descend to personalities:

> When you have portrayed "passion" instead of feeling, and used "power" instead of common sense, and shown yourself a "genius" instead of an artist, the applause is so prompt and the glory so cheap that really anything else seems wickedly wasteful of one's time.[153]

In the long run, of course, Howells essentially won out over his adversaries. Not that protests have wholly died out: Gertrude Atherton, for example, who read Howells when his star was rising, long remembered that she "detested" him as a writer who "made all life seem commonplace."[154] Yet his unquestioned sincerity and the weight of his critical word sufficed to maintain much of his prestige during the many attacks he received in the period around 1890. Soon thereafter his position was strengthened by the creation of the international copyright law in 1891, which in effect lessened the vogue of foreign romance writers and encouraged younger American writers. Energetic followers of Howells, among them Hamlin Garland, spread and exemplified the gospel of realism. E. W. Howe, Crane, Frederic, Norris, and others added strength to the band of realists who gradually stemmed the tide of romantic fiction. To be sure, theirs was a burlier brand of "realism" than Howells'. For a time, too, Howells himself felt that his quiet voice was being drowned out by the realistic din that opened the new century. His *Kentons*, he said, was "fairly killed" by critics hostile to his theory of the "romance of the commonplace":

> I had hoped I was helping my people know themselves in the delicate beauty of their every day lives, and to find cause for pride in the loveliness of an apparently homely average, but they don't want it.[155]

Yet he had laid by enough to tide him over many rainy days of criticism and he has finally emerged with most of his reputation intact. He discouraged discipleship but he could not prevent imitation, and his immense influence on twentieth-century fiction is admitted today even by those who have little interest in his actual productions.

Finally, Howells was by all odds more important as a novelist than as a critic.[156] He announced no really important new creed of fiction or system of aesthetics, but he added richly to the domain of American fiction. Tested by whatever conventional criterion, he emerges with credit. His plots are seldom very original: he never strove to make them so.[157] They are, however, reasonably well constructed. Despite his occasional selection of unimportant scenes for expanded treatment, he definitely improved upon the practice of many predecessors and contemporaries. Lesser writers tended to employ too many "scenes" and to treat them as of equal importance—as if they were so many islands of action each of which must be touched on. Howells, on the other hand, selected for detailed examination a few larger islands, of greater elevation, whence he could view what was of importance in the lesser units. He achieves completeness without being laboriously detailed. In some ways his narrative method approaches that of the "novel démeublé" described by Willa Cather.[158]

In characterization he was even more successful. It is hard to interest the public in average well-bred citizens not bent upon adventure, throbbing with passion, or occupied in crime. Yet Howells succeeded in making normal people interesting. He drew men and women almost equally well. One of his greatest aids to characterization was his command of dialogue. Probably no American writer of the nineteenth century excelled Howells in recording the typical speech idioms of middle-class, moderately well-educated folk. With under-educated folk (not, however, the class of the very least literacy) he succeeded almost as well. Moreover he had the patience and the perceptiveness to employ dialect and broken English with ease and fidelity. In catching phonographically the colloquial idiom of a limited class of people, Mark Twain surpassed Howells, but no novelist of his time or before it surpassed him in a comprehensive command of American speech.

In his own prose style Howells was an example of quiet mastery. His lack of brilliance and obvious energy tends to obscure his great stylistic gift. Whereas many writers advertise their effort by much huffing and puffing, Howells secures his effects by nimbleness and dexterity. He prevails by craft instead of Kraft; he is the sun rather than the north wind. None of that careful inlay work which lends beauty (and sometimes virtuosity) to the style of James is apparent in Howells' prose. His prose seldom dazzles one by flaming beauty; but it sparkles and glows constantly. Almost nowhere does he lapse from his own high standards of clarity, poise, and quiet emphasis. And if he disappoints some readers by failing to rise to great heights, he is the satisfaction of others, who enjoy soaring steadily at an altitude which, though exhilarating, does not prevent the reader from keeping an eye on those mundane activities which are after all the main business of the writer *as novelist.*

Not only in style but in general effect Howells appears as an apostle of moderation. He exerts steady pressure but seeks few explosive climaxes. His action is continuous but not superficially exciting: he prefers steady progress in the foothills to a speedy ascent to great peaks of action. His usual tempo is not rapid, but he will not be hurried; and the reader who wants to go faster will lose what Howells has to offer. Like fine wines, his books require to be sipped rather than gulped; only so will they deliver up their true essence. He selects his materials with courage but not with a view to creating sensation: like Longfellow he did not test books by their "shock" value. He treats evil not in its lair but on the ambiguous line where it approaches or interlocks with good. Labor's problems he handles sympathetically, but he does not pause to hear every syllable of the strident voice of the proletariat. Although he often uses love as a major motif, his romance-nipping proclivities prevented him from descending to the mushy level of the domestic sentimentalists. He could be an advocate of right living and sound government without using the narrative structure chiefly as a pulpit or a platform. Satire he used quietly as a normal ingredient of fiction instead of as an artificial stimulant. A wide reader, he did not write bookishly but drew upon a rich deposit of experience in limited areas. He was inclined to observe more than he acted; he was an "authority" on life more than an adventurer in it. Yet he was no recluse. In all things he seems to have been held gently in check by an intuition, by an instinctive feeling that a man does his work supremely well only when he holds something in reserve.

Henry James (1843-1916)

Before the Civil War little enough attention had been paid to the novel as an art form. Novels were first of all "good stories." That meant that there must be plenty of vivid action centring around a hero and a heroine whose ultimate triumph or (more rarely) disaster was delayed a suitable length of time by certain standard devices guaranteed to generate suspense. In so far as the novel was more than this, it served often as a vehicle of morality, politics, philosophy, or propaganda. That it should ever be written in accordance with generally accepted principles of art comparable to those laid down rigidly by Poe for the short story seems not to have been seriously considered. Various writers had their little theories, but these were generally fragmentary or discursive. Nor did the varying examples of the great British novelists —Scott, Dickens, Thackeray—help to stabilize the novel as a form. There were types of fiction—the Gothic romance, the historical romance, the domestic novel—but there were few rules that pertained to the novel as a genre, and it remained by far the most flexible form of belles lettres. Probably it still is. Yet in the latter part of the nineteenth century there appeared new critical ideals intended to correct what seemed the chief defect of the novel, namely, its haphazard structure. The movement originated in France, where Flaubert and his followers experimented with a more "responsible" technique, which emphasized design more than ever before. The looseness of construction created by digression, unnecessary characters, baggy sub-plots was to be replaced by strict attention to that simplicity of design, proportion of parts, and perfection of detail of which Flaubert's *Madame Bovary* (1857) was a model. With these new ideals Henry James was in instinctive rapport. Accordingly although he could not bring himself to emulate the French realists in choice of subject-matter, he devoted himself to a type of fiction in which form should be a major desideratum. Many of the same ideals were congenial to the slightly younger Howells, who had a natural gift for design and who hated the sentimental twaddle and careless technique of earlier American novelists. Between them James and Howells carried the American novel to heights of sheer technique it had never before attained. And though they did not of course completely and permanently alter the form for all subsequent writers, their influence was largely responsible for the increased prestige of the novel as an art form toward the end of the nineteenth century. In an obvious sense James had neither forerunners nor authentic imitators: his essence was too special.[1] Yet even before James's death Howells could assert that "no American writer has been more the envy and ambition of generous youth trying for distinction as well as sincerity in their work."[2] Subsequently James has had a vast influence on the finely controlled fiction of Conrad, Mrs. Wharton, Mrs. Woolf, Elinor Wylie, Dorothy Richardson, Proust, Gide, and many other twentieth-century writers.[3] James's literary creed reduced to its simplest form was that it was wrong to regard form and substance as separate. Accordingly he brought them together and pronounced them one element, which he called art. But the marriage of form and content has been regarded askance by many readers, in whose opinion it has only led to sterility. James as the high priest presiding over this union has therefore been the object of criticism not only from the laity but also from his professional colleagues. But he has also had numberless followers who have accorded him a measure of devotion constituting little less than worship.

James is difficult to "derive" from other writers, for he was largely his own tutor. Wide reader though he was, especially in continental literature, he could be stimulated by other writers but was pupil to none. Few novelists so completely elude classification. Obviously the historical romance and the straight Gothic were alien to his interests. Nor could he approve of the tidy little domestic stories of New England life which formed one of the staples of magazine fiction.[4] There is truth in Constance Rourke's remark that James "had none of those slightly inferior forerunners in his own medium by which the great writer is often heralded. He wrote as from a fresh impulse."[5] This is to leave out of account, however, a precursor, Hawthorne, whom James never ceased to find a source of technical inspiration and even of ideas. Indeed as far as American writers were concerned, Hawthorne was the "onlie begetter" of James.[6] Even here the relationship was hardly that of master and pupil, but rather that of colleagues. Yet Hawthorne had "gone before," and the temperamental bond between the two could be attested only by James. As early as 1870 James wrote to his brother William (who had noted the resemblance between Hawthorne's style and James's) that he "mean[t] to write as good a novel one of these days (perhaps) as *The House of the Seven Gables*."[7] In 1879 he devoted a full-length study to Hawthorne, and he frequently had re-course to themes, materials, and even modes of development similar to those used by his distinguished predecessor. Both writers had the same interest in "appearances": the bare fact was less important than the gradual accumulation of impressions. At times, too, James's prolonged emphasis on one phase of an action suggests the "tableaux" of Haw-thorne. If *The Scarlet Letter* reveals more interest in the consequences of sin as such than any book of James, its perfect focus and economical use of comparatively slight substance appealed to James's sense of form, and he called it not only Hawthorne's masterpiece but "the finest piece of imaginative writing yet put forth in the country." [8] James sym-pathized with Hawthorne's complaint of the poverty of the American tradition for a fiction-writer.[9] Yet he believed that an imperfect adapta-tion to a foreign country is also baneful, and he thought that Haw-thorne "forfeited a precious advantage in ceasing to tread his native soil." [10] *The Marble Faun* he regarded as on the whole the least success-ful of Hawthorne's novels. Even so, it contained "some of the finest pages in all Hawthorne," and its use of art as a motif must have appealed to James, who occasionally worked out rather intellectualized Gothic effects in connection with portraits.[11] There is also in James a com-parable use of the spiritual domination of one character by another somewhat in the manner in which Zenobia dominates Priscilla in *The Blithedale Romance*.[12] The villains of the two writers resemble each other also—sinister men whose actions are all the more horrible for be-ing set against an evil background never fully explored.[13] Then there is the theme that obsessed Hawthorne in the latter part of his life—the recovery of an English estate by an American—which James utilized in *The Sense of the Past*. Most of all, however, Hawthorne and James were alike in their fine subordination of the merely physical fact of their stories: implications and inferences were the main thing for both men.[14] Instinctively these two great writers seem to have responded to similar ideals of art. The fact that Hawthorne wrote earlier than James makes the latter only in part his debtor.

These signs of James's kinship with Hawthorne are the more remark-able because of his almost total neglect of other American writers. In general he appears to have almost no connection with American fic-tional tradition. Obviously his bland indifference to native productions has not made for his popularity among those people whose literary in-terests are inextricably bound up with national feelings. He has had to make his way entirely on his own merits—a process attended by much debate.

Few American novelists who were not in themselves given to controversy have elicited so much sharply differing opinion as Henry James. He has been on the one hand irritably dismissed as little better than a lunatic cutting out paper dolls and submitting the results as works of art, and he has been acclaimed as "probably the most eminent man of letters America has yet to show." [15] The grounds of disapproval have often been mistaken, for his calumniators have generally been either unwilling or unable to acquaint themselves with the real quality of his art. Consequently they have most often fallen back on his lack of "action" and his preoccupation with a small corner of life. They say that his women characters are preoccupied with "doilies" and "parlor conversations" which are discussed with "precise irrelevance." [16] They also feel injured by his apparent rejection of America. The more articulate of his hostile critics say he deals with minds instead of people, points of view instead of action, building plans instead of building materials. His admirers have responded by emphasizing as virtues essentially the same things that among his detractors are regarded as defects—his preoccupation with design, his rigid economy, his sensitive fingering of detail, his deliberate but thorough interpretation of the life of Americans abroad—but they are likely in the end to confess that what most appeals to them is an indefinable essence which, once savored, demands more and more indulgence. The art of James so suffuses their being that critical judgment is finally allowed to lapse. Among his votaries James is accepted without appraisal. This of course subjects them to ridicule from the camp of the philistines, who assert that the Jamesites are sniffing a non-existent essence and are intoxicating themselves on air. Where the truth lies it is impossible to say dogmatically, but with James some thirty years in his grave and new converts appearing every year it seems idle to deny him a significant achievement in letters. When Miss Rebecca West said in 1916 that "it was given to Mr James . . . to swim longer in the sea of perfection than any other writer," [17] she expressed an opinion that has since been often echoed about the work of James. The question can no longer be, Is it art? but it may well be, Is it enjoyable art? That question each reader must settle for himself.

Besides legitimate cuts at James's professional armor there have been many foolish arguments against the man. He was, it appears, a prudish old maid capable of being shocked when Flaubert once received him at the door in his dressing-gown.[18] It also appears that he was un-American. His almost habitual rejection of the American scene as an environment suitable to artistic enterprise has rankled in many patriotic bosoms. The bourgeois mind that accepted Mark Twain's superb buffoonery as a serious measure of the value of the Old World civilization had only contempt for a man who could deliberately choose to bury himself in the musty débris of Europe when America was magnificently unrolling untold wealth and opportunity in the West. Modern critics have also assailed James on the score of his defection. His European pilgrimage, it has been implied, ended in the frustration not only of his personal happiness but also of his best artistic capabilities.[19] The point is perhaps debatable: did James's frequently deracinated personal life hamper his art? It may be granted at the outset that his quest of the most favorable milieu for his art did not bring him complete personal happiness. Socially he adapted himself with ease and suavity to most foreign environments, but he was never able to transfer his emotional and spiritual accounts wholly from one nation to another, and they remained permanently entangled. It was not possible by a mere exercise of the will to throw off one's native inheritance.[20] As late as 1900 James wrote that Howells' description of rural scenes made him "homesick for New England smells and even sounds."[21] The tower of British seclusion never quite isolated him: one window always opened on the Atlantic, over which his glance covertly strayed to the end. He ordered that after his death his ashes should be returned to America.[22] James never completely ceased being an American, and there is plenty of evidence to show that his self-imposed exile did not bring him sustained happiness. Yet life and work are in this case separate. It is significant that American characters are prominent (frequently as heroes) in most of his best novels—*The American, The Portrait of a Lady, The Wings of the Dove, The Golden Bowl, The Ambassadors.* If as his New York edition shows he more and more eschewed the American scene, he retained American characters, and his "ethics are transcendental New England."[23] Expatriate though he was, he capitalized American character in his fiction to an extent quite impossible to a foreigner. Certainly no British novelist who has assayed American character—not even Galsworthy—has done so well. And this—the interpretation of American character—was only part of an enormous artistic achievement. Let psychologists say what they will, it seems extremely doubtful that James would have accomplished more for American literature had he lived his personal life in Newport or in Zanesville, Ohio.

James spent the first twelve years of his life chiefly in New York, where he was born in 1843. From the beginning it was clear that he could not be as other American boys. Born to wealth, son of an amateur philosopher whose active Irish brain was as given to crotchets as his conscience was to the pursuit of righteousness and his pen to eloquent essays and letters,[24] brought up with brilliant but somewhat eccentric brothers and sisters in a home of piety and culture by no means typical of the throbbing commercial centre that was New York, Henry James knew an America far different from that experienced by his distinguished contemporary Howells. When he was twelve, his father's aversion to settled formal education as well as, apparently, his fear that the combination of New York and plentiful money might prove too much of a temptation for his sons as it had been for their uncles,[25] caused him to protect the boys from their tendency to "import shocking bad manners from the street" [26] by removing the entire ménage to Europe, where the family stayed three years. James made his first acquaintance with Geneva, London, and Paris. In 1858 the elder James whisked his offspring back to America, but after a year at Newport they were again in Europe. This time James submitted to courses in a rather rigorous institute at Geneva and private tutoring at Bonn. The next move was back to Newport—for four years—chiefly it appears for the sake of allowing brother William to study painting under William Hunt. Henry also dabbled in oil and pigment, but when William forswore art for science and went to Harvard, Henry also betook himself to Cambridge, where after a little profitless study of law he entered his novitiate as a literary student. The evolution of James as a writing man was slow, for although it now appears that even in 1860 his "greatest interest" was literature,[27] few people knew of his propensities or his talents until at Boston and Cambridge, stimulated by the friendship of William Dean Howells and encouraged by the success of a few magazine pieces, he finally took literary orders. The six years he spent at Cambridge (1862-1868) gave him an affection for New England which although it "never superseded . . . the native tie with New York," [28] remained fresh throughout his many years abroad. His move to Liverpool in 1868 dates his choice of writing as a vocation but it did not bring a period to his cultural Odyssey. For seven years more he fitfully shuttled back and forth between America and Europe seeking the most favorable locus for his art (which was his life). London, Paris, Rome, Florence—he tested them all and extracted from their founts what he could for his own profit.

In 1875 James had decided to adopt permanently a European residence. His first and apparently foregone choice was Paris, where he could sit at the feet of Flaubert, who taught the need of absolute objectivity, and where he could bandy critical theories with younger French novelists, followers of Balzac more than of Flaubert—Zola, Edmond de Goncourt, Daudet—all of whom, though their methods differed in various ways from James's, cherished the same hope as he did of rescuing the novel from the slough of amorphous sentimentality and clutter of specious incident into which it had slipped. Yet for all their good ideals these French masters, as well as Turgenev, were somehow circumscribed in their outlook.[29] Moreover, in Paris, as in Rome and Florence, he found difficulty in reaching intimacies with native people.[30] In short he was lonely, and in order to fill needs in his personal life he moved to England. His attitude toward his expatriation, as his letters show, was marked by inconsistency and even contradiction. He was so slow (was he too old?) to penetrate English life more than superficially that after he had been there almost a year he avowed that he had "formed no intimacies—not even any close acquaintances," and even by 1878 he was "still completely an outsider." [31] Yet he felt "more at home in London than anywhere else in the world," [32] and though he always maintained that England "never was the land of ideas," [33] it was for him pre-eminently the land for living. The English at least had been "smoothed and polished by mutual social attrition"; they had "manners and a language." [34] Manners and a language—these were after all among the essentials; and in England James settled down for the rest of his life. He never ceased to travel on the continent, of course, and he made two visits to America (in 1904-05 and 1910) but he seemed outwardly contented with the land of his deliberate adoption. Yet the extent of his divorce from America has been too much emphasized perhaps because his criticism of his native land has been too often cited. He was no fatuous Anglophile.[35] Van Wyck Brooks notes that to James "the country-house was the clew to almost everything that was distinctively British," [36] but he does not cite in this connection James's own remark that "the British country-house has at moments, for a cosmopolitanised American, an insuperable flatness." [37] As a matter of fact James felt as free to criticize England as America: he belonged to them both, loved them both, and was interested in their common welfare. Indeed he thought there was too much talk of *inter*nationalism and he looked forward to the unity of England and America:

> I can't look at the English-American world, or feel about them, any more [he wrote in 1888], save as a big Anglo-Saxon total, destined to such an amount of melting together that an insistence on their differences becomes more and more idle and pedantic . . .[38]

It was for this reason that he aspired to "write in such a way that it would be impossible to an outsider to say whether [he was] at a given moment an American writing about England or an Englishman writing about America . . ." [39] The day when the "big Anglo-Saxon total" would be reached, however, was still too distant for James ever to see it in his lifetime, and he remained to the end a man between two countries. Yet it does not follow that his art suffered correspondingly. From his splendid achievement in letters the more natural inference is that his suspension between America and England afforded the point of view that broadened his perspective and sharpened his perception of spiritual values. For, finally, who should bicker over the mortal residence of the author of such works as *The American, The Portrait of a Lady*, and *The Ambassadors?*

The canon of James's published writings is so extensive that in attempting to appraise them most critics have had recourse to considering them with respect to the various periods of his work. Nor is this a mere convenience, for few writers have so definitely altered the product of their art by careful cultivation as James. There are critics who think that the process of his artistic evolution was degenerative, and there are those who would assent to William James's jocose comment: "There *isn't* any third manner . . . Poor Harry has simply changed his stenographer, and the new one records all of his hesitancies and ellipses." [40] In any case it is obvious, as J. W. Beach has pointed out, that with respect to subject matter and content there are three rather distinct periods in James's work. In the first period (1875-1885) he used principally American characters, partly in American and partly in European settings. During the second period (1885-1901) he confined himself largely to English characters and setting. The third period (1902-1916) is characterized by a renewed preference for American characters in European (English and continental) settings.[41] Attempts to divide the novels into groups according to James's "manner" have been frequent but on the whole, unreliable. The only certain thing is that in general technique the novels exhibit a gradual evolution from a relatively "open" style of development and language in conformity at many points with the traditional English novel, toward a specialized mode of development in accordance with which almost all the common attributes of English fiction have been set aside for those subtle refinements of style, characterization, and situation that so irritate the lover of "plot stories." If there must be a dividing line between the earlier phase and the later, it may most conveniently be drawn between the publication of *The Tragic Muse* (1890) and *The Spoils of Poynton* (1897).[42] After 1897 James was beyond redemption from the point of view of the general reader; but that he regarded his own evolution as improvement is clear from the fact that in preparing the New York edition of his novels and tales (1907-1917) he not only excluded bodily a number of his earlier novels but revised others with a view to bringing them into conformity with his more mature technique. The transformation of James, however deplored by some readers and critics, was a natural organic process which he persisted in notwithstanding poor profits from the sales of his books. The New York edition, wrote James in 1915, was "practically a complete failure." [43] Nor did James's books ever make much money. His brother William frequently urged him to avoid literary manners and materials which might alienate "the great American public, to which after all you must pander for support," [44] but James went on serenely fashioning what seemed to him his true destiny.

James began his literary career writing sketches, stories, and anonymous reviews for American magazines, especially *The Atlantic Monthly* and *The Galaxy*. His first long fiction, *Watch and Ward*, a love-story published serially in *The Atlantic* in 1871, was reproduced in book form in 1878—a consummation hardly justified by its amateurish treatment of both action and dialogue. Though it carries considerable external incident, yet "the effect is of matter spread out thin, since no scene is developed according to its possibilities." [45] *Roderick Hudson* (1876), itself not one of James's best novels, seems a finished book by comparison. The latter is the story of a young sculptor whose work is so brilliant that a kindly connoisseur lifts him from his Northampton environment and sets him down in Europe, where, presumably, his genius will mature. After a brief interval of success in Europe, however, various factors operate to bring about Roderick's ultimate failure and death. Not the least of these is Christina Light, a brilliant but inconstant creature to whom Roderick plays the moth. Yet finally, if we are to believe Roderick's own suggestion, the cause of his failure was internal:

> "The whole matter of genius is a mystery. It bloweth where it listeth, and we know nothing of its mechanism. If it gets out of order we can't mend it; if it breaks down altogether we can't set it going again. We must let it choose its own pace and hold our breath lest it should lose its balance. It's dealt out in different doses, in big cups and little, and when you have consumed your portion it's as *naïf* to ask for more as it was for Oliver Twist to ask for more porridge. Lucky for you if you've got one of the big cups . . . Those of some men last for life; those of others for a couple of years . . . Nothing is more common than for an artist who has set out on his journey on a high-stepping horse to find himself all of a sudden dismounted and invited to go his way on foot . . . Who shall say that I am not one of these? Who shall assure me that my credit is for an unlimited sum? Nothing proves it, and I never claimed it . . ." [46]

In the end Roderick's vein peters out and he loses Miss Light, who gives him up when she discovers that he is "as weak as any other *petit jeune homme*." [47] In many respects this novel adumbrates the method of James's mature years. It revolves about an American who tests himself in a European mise-en-scène amid social types—artists, broken-down nobility, traveling Americans—whose counterparts often re-appear among James's dramatis personae. The narrative reaches the reader largely through the consciousness of one person, Rowland Mallet, who is himself not the chief actor. Conversation instead of incident is often the vehicle of progress. Yet there are differences also. Judging by James's later technique he was uneconomical in expending several chapters on Northampton before establishing the story in Europe. Information is frequently conveyed in blocks, which sometimes take the form of letters. The direct presentation of Roderick's death is a concession to the popular reader—a concession of the sort that James later avoided. Moreover the narrative as a whole lacks the firm focus of the best of James's books. Perhaps the problem of fusing the external and internal causes of the disintegration of Roderick's genius was too difficult. At all events *Roderick Hudson*, though not loosely assembled, is not distinguished by the unity, economy, and cohesion that marked James's major work. The author himself later referred to it as a "book of considerable good faith, but . . . of limited skill." And when he came to revise it for the New York edition in 1906 he found many parts of it "quite *vilely* written!" [48]

The American (1877) was the first novel of James's to reveal his true stature. It was widely read when it came out, and it remains one of the few books of the author which have more than a specialized public today.[49] Its popular appeal is easily understood: the attempt of Newman, a breezy, self-made Middlewestern American, to penetrate the aristocratic barriers of an ancient and vaguely sinister French family in order to carry off the beautiful "princess" Claire with the aid of the charming indolent Valentin de Bellegarde constitutes a love-story that may be enjoyed for its own sake. Of course there is a bitter draught at the end for romantic die-hards who expect a happy ending; but even after it is clear that Newman is rejected (for reasons, to be sure, that are only dimly perceived by the romantic reader), there remains the crude hope that Newman will use Mrs. Bread's dark secret to wreak a satisfactory revenge. In the meantime there has been plenty of external action described in a forthright manner instead of by indirection. There is picturesqueness and tragedy in the collateral plot involving Noémie Nioche and Valentin de Bellegarde. There are few more touching death scenes in the American novel than that of Valentin, whose life has been a tragic waste but whose finely ironic speeches betray his essentially noble character. Nor is the story without the spice of humor, for Newman's imperfect comprehension of the ways of decayed aristocracy leads to many a delightful incongruity. Newman, though as "a commercial person" he is representative of those aspects of American life which James detested, proves to be the most sympathetic hero James ever created. His fine bearing throughout the story provides early evidence of the fact that much as James prized the amenities of life, and ruthlessly as on occasion he exposed the tourist-type American, he always regarded character as finally more important than "culture." Moreover, to judge from James's stories, a delicate perception of spiritual values is more often found in somewhat ingenuous persons whose ethical sense has not been overlaid with much surface culture than in representatives of a more deeply stratified civilization. And a number of these ingenuous persons prove to be Americans. *The American,* then, is at many points akin to those later novels which he himself thought his best works of art, but even after receiving its inevitable trimming and polishing for the New York edition it retained its power to hold the attention of the general as well as the initiated reader. It probably does not represent the peak of James's art, certainly not of his most recherché manner, but it is perhaps his best-balanced novel.

It was several years before James produced a novel (*The Portrait of a Lady*, 1881) which equaled or surpassed *The American*. In the meantime he indulged his "constant impulse to try experiments of form" [50] by writing three novels, *The Europeans* (1878),[51] *Confidence* (1880), and *Washington Square* (1881), besides two volumes of criticism and a good many short stories, including the eminently readable "Daisy Miller" and "An International Episode." A fourth novel, *The Bostonians* (1886), may logically be considered in this group, for, although a more substantial work than any of the others, it shares some of their common characteristics: the use of an American setting (*Confidence* is an exception here), frequent indulgence in satire, and a certain directness of statement that is far from congenial to those initiated into James's more typical allusiveness.

The first of the novels, *Confidence*, is a story of vapory sentiment arising from lovers' misunderstanding. Though based on the theme of "love and honor," it nowhere reaches real distinction; and it is on the whole the poorest of those early novels which James later denied admission to his canon.[52] *The Europeans* is charged with airy comedy, but though the contrast between the European visitors and the Americans with whom they become entangled over love-matters provides the Baroness Münster with plenty of occasion to vent her scorn on the stunted civilization of America, the story does not rise from a medium level either in entertainment or in significance.

A better book among these experimental novels is *Washington Square*. Its setting betokens the author's affectionate remembrance of the Washington Square of his early boyhood. A somewhat bare and low-toned story, it perhaps falls into the category of those works in which James did not wish to "run the risk of wasting or gratuitously using big situations." [53] Yet its unpretentious exterior and the simple evolution of its plot cannot obscure the fact that, somehow, Catherine Sloper is molded into a very real character whose fate becomes a matter of genuine concern. And the guileless manner in which James relates the story has a charm sometimes missing from the elaborate utterance of his prime. The plot is simple: a handsome, impecunious man-about-town is determined to marry a dull-witted and superficially unattractive girl for her money, a proceeding that is favored by her match-making aunt but opposed by her father. In the end the girl loses her lover, is estranged from her father, and becomes a respectable old maid. Catherine Sloper differs from most of James's heroines in that she is not merely quiet but, in the opinion of many observers, actually "a dull, plain girl." [54] James further distinguishes her from the charming heroine of convention by the "awkward confession" that she has been "something of a glutton." Yet her lack of esprit and her proneness to overeat are not incompatible with fine qualities of character, and before the story is finished James has created a realistic heroine of quiet integrity not unlike many a girl in the early novels of Howells. Indeed *Washington Square* in its technique and in its theme of feminine independence recalls Howells' *Chance Acquaintance* (1873). Since James, who quickly felt in *Washington Square* "the want of 'paraphernalia,'" chose to ignore it when making his formal legacy to posterity, the novel may still be read in its original form, a realistic but charming period piece, appropriately illustrated in the first edition, as it happens, by the pen of Du Maurier.

In *The Bostonians* (1886), James used a theme which would have endeared the book to Hawthorne, namely, the spiritual subjection of a malleable character to the uses of a more aggressive character. Verena Tarrant is possessed of a faculty of "inspirational" speaking, but as a character she is as artless as she is charming. She is taken up by Olive Chancellor, a vigorous proponent of the emancipation of women. Despite their social disparity (Olive being of the patrician class and Verena the offspring of respectable but somewhat shabby reformers), these two girls form a spiritual union, and they plan a program based upon Verena's remarkable platform eloquence. Olive rigidly persists in her warfare on the oppressors of the sex, for she hates all men on principle. Verena, however, is a very suggestible person in more ways than one, and it finally becomes apparent that Olive will be hard put to it to maintain her ascendancy over Verena when the latter is sought in marriage by Basil Ransom, a handsome Mississippian, who openly tells Verena that he despises her program as much as he admires her. A deadly struggle for "control" of Verena ensues, which reaches its climax at the very end of the book when Verena, now fully prepared for the most important public appearances, is at the last moment prevented from addressing an enormous audience at the Music Hall in Boston—for Ransom's power over Verena has finally displaced Olive Chancellor's. James, of course, forbears to take sides openly in the controversy over women's rights, but if he is technically a neutral rather than a belligerent, he gives all aid short of war, for *The Bostonians* carries more satire than any other novel of James. Olive Chancellor is mercilessly described as a "signal old maid" who was so soured that she never laughed and who " 'would reform the solar system if she could get hold of it.' " [55] Verena's parents are palpably inferior people—and indeed her father is perfectly ready to allow Olive to "take over" Verena upon the payment of an adequate sum of money. Miss Birdseye, the aged reformer, receives mixed treatment, but it was generally believed when the book came out that in her portrait James was satirizing Elizabeth Peabody.[56] Yet most of the satire in the book, like all its other elements, is purveyed with considerable finesse. *The Bostonians* is rich in witty and epigrammatic statement, and only its extremely deliberate tempo and great length militate against its acceptance as a "good story." Those who fear James's "obscurity" will find no difficulty in this book, for the action is easy to follow. Not yet committed to consistency in his point of view, James openly dispenses facts that will aid the reader's understanding.[57]

The book as a whole has more external signs of vitality than many of his later books—more human substance and greater bulk. It is as if James here gave the reader the whole grain of life instead of submitting it first to that inexorably efficient milling process which characterized his later productions. Of course, all this is relative; and to the confirmed James-hater *The Bostonians* is just another tiny fragment of life pulverized and placed under the microscope. To contemporary readers, who encountered the story as it appeared serially in *The Century Magazine*, it was largely a failure.[58] A few critics, among them Edmund Gosse, have been generous in praise of the book, but in general it has fallen into greater obscurity than, relatively, it deserves.[59]

Coming (in 1881) in the midst of the uncertain and in some respects amateurish works just discussed, *The Portrait of a Lady* exhibited a dazzling contrast by its finish and richness and power. To many good Jamesians this book represents the height of his achievement—the first union of technical skill and emotional power. James himself thought highly of it, and although in 1898 he wrote in a moment of playful boasting "I can do better than that!" he retained his respect for it even after he had written the novels of his final period.[60] The theme was a congenial one to James—the reactions of an attractive and intelligent girl with a finely developed sense of honor to an unfortunate marriage into which she entered of her own free will. *The Portrait of a Lady* shows Isabel Archer, an American girl, coping with the cold strategy of two extremely experienced representatives of Old World culture, Gilbert Osmond and Madame Merle. The basic facts, though interesting enough, could have been reported "adequately" in a longish short story. But the gradual revelations of Isabel's plight, the steps by which she comes to realize that Osmond married her in order to provide for the illegitimate offspring of his liaison with Madame Merle, and her efforts to resolve her difficulties without sacrificing her integrity proved James's superb capability for treating situations calling for the most delicate perception of values. It is true that the story as a whole is in many respects so like a biography or "chronicle" [61] that it falls short of James's later conception of ideal technique, but it strikes a happy medium between the directness of his earliest manner and the tortuousness of his most difficult books. At all events, attention to structure did not prevent James from creating in Isabel Archer his most memorable heroine. Other heroines of James appear in situations as difficult, but to no other did James impart so much emotional warmth.[62] Seldom did he give more loving care to setting than in his treatment of the Touchett estate on the Thames or provide richer detail than in the description of Osmond's Florentine villa. In these respects *The Portrait of a Lady* is even a finer work than *The American,* and indeed it exhibits all of James's most distinguished gifts except the faultless proportion of his later masterpieces.

Between 1885 and 1901, as has been noted, James devoted himself almost entirely to portrayal of the English life with which he had by now become so thoroughly conversant. The first book in this classification, *The Princess Casamassima* (1886), stemmed from an earlier work, *Roderick Hudson,* in that the heroine of the former is that Christina Light (now the "Princess") who had proved to be such a sinister influence on the young sculptor. Nor does she prove more beneficent in her relationship with Hyacinth Robinson, the hero of the later book. Robinson, the illegitimate son of a woman serving a life-sentence for murder, is an interesting mouse-like little fellow who earns his living as a bookbinder. He becomes so involved in socialistic intrigue that he pledges himself to support a radical movement even to the extent of assassinating opposing leaders if necessary. Presently he is made the protégé of the Princess Casamassima, who finds amusement in identifying herself with the revolutionary cause. Through her, Hyacinth comes to know the delights that money can bring—art, travel, companionship of cultivated people. Likewise because of his association with her, he falls away from his middle-class friend Millicent. He finally receives the call to assassinate a certain Duke. A last visit to the Princess discloses the fact that he has been displaced in her fickle favor and that she is about to give over her socialistic experiments. In the midst of his loneliness he shoots himself, his mission unfulfilled. Despite the vague background of economic unrest the story is by no means basically a study of social or political conditions or theory.[63] Rather it is a poignant account of Hyacinth's struggle for existence as a personality. With the utmost delicacy and sympathy James follows his hero through his alliance with the radical movement, the dawn of his appreciation for the finer things of life, and the despair to which he is reduced by his dilemma. There is no wealth of dramatic action, but the people who make up Hyacinth's world are sketched in a gently humorous fashion that inevitably recalls Dickens—a writer whose technique James could not fully approve. There are few books excepting *Bleak House* which so fully render the feeling of London streets at night as *The Princess Casamassima*. In form, however, this book is a fairly definite prophecy of James's final ideals.[64]

The Tragic Muse (1890) is on the whole a less successful work despite the greater freedom James must have felt in handling familiar types—writers, artists, actors. The central idea is the conflict between the artist's and the practical view of life. The illustration is two-fold. Nick Dormer renounces a political career leading to certain distinction in favor of practicing an art (painting) for which his talents are unknown. His cousin, Peter Sherringham, a diplomat, falls in love with a distinguished actress, who refuses to give up her career for the sake of marriage. The book has a considerable interest for the large public that craves initiation into stage and studio affairs; but its reduplicating plot was hard to manage, and the first part is "too full of . . . bustle and commotion . . . to admit the kind of exposition in which James excels." [65] *The Tragic Muse* marks no essential advance in the career of James.

James's career, in fact, was frequently a cause for concern. As time went on it became more and more apparent that he could never become a "popular" novelist. Nor did he receive the critical attention he thought he deserved. His natural reaction was to "find [himself] hold-

ing the 'critical world' at large in a singular contempt." [66] He also
turned to writing short stories:

> I want to leave a multitude of pictures of my time, projecting my
> small circular frame upon as many different spots as possible and
> going in for number as well as quality, so that the number may
> constitute a total having a certain value as observation and testi-
> mony.[67]

Although the short stories of this period include the incomparably fine
"The Real Thing" (1893), he still reached a relatively small public and
he remarked acidly in 1891: "My books don't sell." [68] He also tried the
drama, a form which so exhilarated him for a time that he preferred it to
"the pale little art of fiction," [69] but after a brief flurry of popularity his
hopes of distinction in this field also were rudely quashed.[70] As far as
extended fiction was concerned James abided for a long time by his
statement (made in 1890) that *The Tragic Muse* was to be his "last
long novel." [71] Yet two pieces of fiction which he intended for short
tales outgrew the dimensions he designed for them and, more or less by
accident, established his technique in the mold which he was to prefer
for the rest of his life.

"I begin short tales as if they were to be long novels," James had once
written.[72] Some of his tales did in fact become fair-sized novels. This
was the case with three stories that were published between 1897 and
1901. The first of these, *The Spoils of Poynton* (1897), was a story
involving a girl (Fleda Vetch) whose sense of honor forbade her to
accept her lover because his faith was formally plighted elsewhere.
Begun as a tale, the story grew under James's hand until it had reached
the length at least of a short novel. The "filling" was not composed of
additional plot material but of painstaking presentation of every phase
of the entire transaction. Thus it retained a structural simplicity while
overlaid with a wealth of authenticating detail. Nor was the detail
offered point blank to the reader in blocks of information: rather it was
made available bit by bit through the reactions of the small cast of
characters participating, willingly or unwillingly, in the somewhat ignoble struggle for the furniture and art objects (the "spoils") of Poynton. The effects of the struggle on the lovers' problem are worked out
by James with a clarity of focus which he had achieved in no earlier
novel. The scene in which Fleda finally makes Owen Gereth realize
that she cannot rob Mona Brigstock of her rights is one of the most brilliant and touching in all of James. If it be complained that the strain of
concentrating on one action so long as one must in the *Spoils* is too

great for the average reader, the only reply can be that the average reader had best avoid the complex involutions of the long novels still (in spite of James's having abjured the type) to be written. *The Spoils of Poynton* therefore may be regarded as a study, a very finished study, for James's most elaborate canvases. In *What Maisie Knew* (1897) there is evidence of the author's increasing proclivity toward experiment with patterns. Here James rings the changes on a situation created when the divorced parents of a little girl use her (and sundry loose confederates drawn in from time to time) as a means of harassing each other. The relationships of the single problem shift with appalling intricacy but always with perfect definiteness—much as an expert dancer might go through many forms in a severely limited area. Yet the story proves to be more than a mere mathematical exercise on account of the tragic situation of the innocent Maisie, "a ready vessel for bitterness, a deep little porcelain cup in which biting acids could be mixed," who through the warfare of her parents has her initiation into evil. A similar but inferior work is *The Sacred Fount* (1901), which began as a short story but grew into a well-unified but somewhat taxing short novel based on the thesis that in relationships between two people, one is likely to be enriched in social and spiritual and even physical powers at the expense of the other's vitality. In this story, however, James deliberately plunges into a difficult problem by providing two more or less overlapping examples (with diverse corollaries) of the same relationship. He handles the problem with an almost scientific objectivity, and on this account the story loses in humanity as much as it gains in pattern.[73]

On account of their severely technical and occasionally experimental character, Mr. Beach plausibly regards *What Maisie Knew, The Outcry* (a much later story), and *The Sacred Fount* as "technical exercises." When, however, he includes *The Awkward Age* (1899) in the same category, there must be dissent from his opinion. Signs of professional care remain in the finished book, it is true, especially in an apparent strain to maintain a consistent objectivity. Yet within his self-imposed rules James managed to tell a story charged with strong emotion. One is first impressed by the form: the ten books each named for one of the persons brought particularly under focus at the time. The book has therefore a formidably diagrammatic appearance. In so far as it is experimental, it reveals James's attempt to graft "dramatic" technique on the novel: *The Awkward Age* contains proportionately more dialogue than any of James's novels. Moreover there is a certain monotony in the dialogue, for James has by this time almost wholly dropped the idea of differentiating his characters by tricks and mannerisms of speech: they all speak a cultivated idiom (the invention of James) marked by more elaborate sentence structure than can be regarded as realistic, but surprisingly close to an average colloquial vocabulary. Irrelevancy is rigidly excluded: no word is spoken that does not bear upon the central idea. Under these conditions James undertakes to acquaint the reader with the diverse stratagems by which Mrs. Brookenham tries to provide properly for her eighteen-year-old daughter Nanda and at the same time keep intact her own cherished social domain. It is Nanda's problem, conversely, to find her bearings in an exceedingly complex social milieu without injuring her mother. Some of Mrs. Brookenham's motives in trying to find a suitable match for Nanda are partly shared by an old friend of the family, Longdon, who has a special interest in Nanda because he was once the unsuccessful suitor of her grandmother. He wishes to rescue her from the vaguely unwholesome influence of her mother's salon. He becomes her ambassador. Nanda in turn discovers in herself a deep regard for the lonesome fifty-five-year-old gentleman who had been "no success as a young man," [74] and she resolves to "save" him. Presently Nanda, who though no beauty has great attractiveness, becomes the object of interest for various men, as well as of a deep-laid plan whereby Longdon hoped to spur the flagging interest of a suitable bachelor, Vanderbank, by settling a large sum of money on him. But Vanderbank, as part of the social circle of Nanda's mother, is unable to resist the sway of Mrs. Brookenham. Nor would Nanda have accepted him. It is a greater trial for her to see wealthy and attractive Mitchy finally awarded to the niece of a scheming Duchess, but Nanda remains loyal to her ideal of finding her place without hurting anyone else. In the end there is no one close to Nanda but Longdon, whose self-appointed guardianship has fostered in him feelings akin to those he once entertained for her grandmother Julia. Nanda "saves" him—by going away with him "never again to leave [him]—or to *be* left." A strange story and in many respects an incredible one, but, somehow, through all the complex mechanism of the narrative runs a current of feeling which transforms craftsmanship into art. Nanda Brookenham is one of James's loveliest creations and Longdon one of his dearest failures.

After completing *The Awkward Age*, which excited "little but bewilderment" and "thick-witted denunciation," [75] James, though inclined to be superior to public opinion, condescended to consider writing something that might appeal to the sluggish mind of the general reader. His best resource for this purpose was what he called the "spook" story.[76] He had already written a fairly successful "mechanical" "potboiler," "The Turn of the Screw." [77] Consequently early in 1900 he listened attentively to Howells' suggestion that he write a "terror" story that should have an international angle as well—the more so since he had by a coincidence already begun a story on that basic formula. This was *The Sense of the Past*. *The Sense of the Past* proved to require more elaborate treatment than was suitable to the serial project that Howells had in mind at the moment. On this account, as well as because of its difficulty, James set it aside, after writing a few chapters, in favor of a project more immediately congenial to him.[78] Though a "spook" story, *The Sense of the Past* has even less in common with the gooseflesh school of fiction than "The Turn of the Screw," for its philosophic implications finally crowded out the story interest. The central character, Ralph Pendrel, is a young American whose "historic passion" is so intense that Aurora Coyne, the young woman he has been wooing, believes it might stand in the way of a happy marriage. Accordingly when Ralph's inheritance of an ancestral house in London provides the opportunity, she urges him to go abroad and revel in his "sense of the past." This Ralph does to such effect that he finally succeeds in projecting himself into the early nineteenth century, and exchanging places with a young man possessed by a corresponding desire to live in the future. The trans-identification is perfect in most respects, but Ralph's intuition so far fails him as to permit his falling in love with Nan though "on the cards" he is the accepted lover of Molly. A hitch develops in the whole relationship when Ralph betrays knowledge of a vase which he could not possibly have seen. Because of his "ineffaceable margin of independence" and his "clinging taint of modernity" the orientation has been imperfect.[79] More and more he becomes suspect by the denizens of the past until finally Molly breaks the engagement. Ralph casts about for some means of extrication from a situation now hateful to him. This is to be achieved through a vaguely referred to sacrifice on the part of Nan, whom he somehow thinks of as "modern." When he is finally restored to the modern world he learns that Aurora has arrived in London and wishes to marry him. James offers no obvious interpretation of this experiment in transposed chronology. Indeed despite its invitation to philosophic speculation regarding the nature of time, there is of course no "solution." James apparently regarded the story as an innovation in its mode of achieving a "gruesome malaise." [80] Yet except in one or two scenes—notably those in which, alone in the ancestral mansion, Ralph confronts the portrait of his alter ego[81] the "spook" element is not fully developed. Certainly *The Sense of the Past* is a tale more of the arabesque than of the grotesque. Yet even pictorially it is not as rich as one is led to expect from James's remark that he wished to recapture those "little notes of truth" which can't be found in history books. There are realistic bits—indeed the Ambassador in the story is "without any effort at concealment, James's valued friend, Lowell" [82]—but the story as it was left is a little lacking in sheer entertainment values, especially comedy.[83] Consequently the reader is thrown back upon its interest as a philosophical fantasy. In this respect it possesses considerable interest, for in its use of the "continuous present" and its speculation on time values it has a partial analogy to those products of the modern school, especially the works of Proust, Stein, Mann, Dos Passos, etc., in which the "time obsession" is a central feature.[84]

"If I can't be terrible, I shall nevertheless still try to be international," wrote James to Howells (in 1900). His references were to the difficulty of completing *The Sense of the Past* or any other "international ghost" story which Howells, now "Easy Chair" editor of *Harper's Magazine*, hoped to secure from him.[85] It was by no means with a sense of complete failure that about the turn of the century, James inaugurated work on the three books, *The Wings of the Dove*, *The Ambassadors*, and *The Golden Bowl*, that displayed in their most brilliant synthesis those elements that have become known as typically Jamesian. The failure of his books to sell widely and his waning attraction for magazine readers (despite Howells' continued interest) could not shake his confidence in the essential value of the work he was doing, for even as a youthful disciple of French art he had learned, directly or indirectly, the wisdom of Flaubert's terse utterance: "il faut écrire pour soi avant tout." [86] He even found something "bracing . . . in the alpine çhill . . . shed by the cold editorial shoulder." [87] More and more the "childishness of publics" was driving him to "unfolding [his work] wholly from its own 'innards' " [88] In the long run the method he finally adopted was unquestionably wise, for these three books, together with a few earlier ones, form the foundation of his permanent reputation.

The first of the three, *The Wings of the Dove* (1902), is the poorest in construction and the most difficult to read, but many readers feel fully indemnified on account of the charm and fortitude of Milly Theale, who suffers a fate even more painful than that of the heroine of *The Portrait of a Lady*. Outline shows that the story might have been melodramatic if James had been able or willing to "let himself go." Milly is in brief the victim of a plot conceived by a somewhat heartless woman, Kate Croy, and her too pliable suitor, Merton Densher, whereby the latter shall win the affection of the dying Milly in order that Milly's millions shall later be at the disposal of Kate Croy and her suitor. The situation is the more poignant on account of Milly's desperate need of affection, her wish to "achieve, however briefly and brokenly, the sense of having lived," [89] her desire (approved by her surgeon for its possible therapeutic value) to get as much sweetness out of life as possible. In this she is thwarted by Kate Croy, who exercises over Milly a power not unlike that of Zenobia over Priscilla in *The Blithedale Romance*. The horror of the whole proceeding, however, is somewhat attentuated by James's unusually dilatory approach to the centre of his problem: the full implications·of the situation are not understood until well into the second volume. Besides having "too big a head for its body," *The Wings of the Dove* is, by James's own admission, "too inordinately drawn out, and too inordinately rubbed in." [90] Its publication elicited warm responses from many friends, including W. D. Howells, and "remarkably genial" notices from the press,[91] but its real value has finally been stabilized at a point appreciably below that of the two major novels soon to appear.[92]

The Ambassadors (1903) was begun considerably before the publication of *The Wings of the Dove*.[93] Its germ was a chance remark Howells made to a common acquaintance in Paris urging upon the young man the importance of living one's life before it is too late.[94] This simple bit of advice, which re-appears in Strether's impetuous speech to Little Bilham,[95] provided the intellectual centre around which James built up the elaborate "picture of relations" which constitutes *The Ambassadors*. Strether, a fifty-five-year-old American, a man who has not "lived," is appointed to rescue a fellow countryman, young Chad Newsome, from a presumably sordid relationship with a woman in Paris. As it happens, the "ambassador" discovers that Chad (of whom Strether is "dimly envious")[96] is in fact acting on the advice Strether later gives to Little Bilham; consequently Strether cannot bring himself to attempt to disturb a relationship which, so far from being a vulgar liaison, seems to Strether to have improved Chad: Mme de Vionnet has in fact given Chad "an immense moral lift," and has "quintupled" his value.[97] The protagonist of the story, of course, is not the rather shadowy Chad but Strether, who until now has lived an unconscious victim of the stagnated mental and spiritual atmosphere of Woollett, Massachusetts, a community where the news of Chad's attachment to Mme de Vionnet could mean only one thing. Strether's re-orientation in the ampler atmosphere of Europe, in the "civilized" life of Paris (where he discovers a man may be a "pagan" without ceasing to be a "gentleman") is a process that constitutes the essential action of the book. Everything else is subordinated to it. Mrs. Newsome, Chad's mother, doesn't even appear in the book. Strether's emancipation from the invisible fetters of Puritanism is by no means to be taken as an argument for a loose Bohemian existence among the flesh-pots of Paris: that way of life is well enough exemplified by oblique reference to the con-

duct of one Waymarsh. Chad's story is merely a concrete way of bringing into relief the transformation in Strether's intellectual and moral
outlook: he has now learned that being free is not incompatible with
being "virtuous." He now knows the value of independent judgment
and the deadening effect of the mold of tradition. Gradually Woollett
becomes a mere phantom in his mind. When Mrs. Newsome, whose
hand was to be the genteel wages of his embassy, discovers the defection
of her first ambassador, she sends reinforcements, whose assignment is
to rescue not only Chad but also Strether. The arrival in Paris of these
three raucous, inept, and hypocritical creatures completes the case
against an American way of life (not American character): it is *The
Ambassadors* as much as any book of James which (always by inference
of course) justifies his preference for Europe as a place to live.[98] *The
Ambassadors* has, then, a complete reversal in the about-face of Strether,
a reversal achieved less by violent reaction than by new light shed
on the slowly revolving sphere of Strether's life. Nor have other
matters stood still: Chad's attachment to Mme de Vionnet, however
valuable it may have been, shows signs of weakening as the story moves
toward the close,[99] and Mme de Vionnet now hopes to keep Strether in
Paris as a means of stabilizing a relationship which perhaps has already
yielded its only possible values. Strether himself has come to entertain
a high regard for Maria Gostrey, his ready confidante throughout the
period of his embassy. Yet although Miss Gostrey more than recipro-
cates his regard, Strether parries her hint that they might find happiness
together by pointing out that in order "to be right" he does not want
"out of the whole affair, to have got anything for [himself]." When
Miss Gostrey plaintively murmurs against his having to be "so dreadfully right" and against the "horrible sharp eye" which enables him
to see the right, she is bringing to the surface a quality in Strether,
his extremely delicate sense of honor, that marks his membership in the
group of the most admirable characters in James. Perhaps this is the
finer breath of Puritanism after all. Certainly it restores the self-respect
of those patriotic American readers whose sensibilities have been shocked
by the behavior of the less worthy ambassadors. The final outcome
perhaps means an "obscure victory" for Strether;[100] yet his renunciation
is actually the final proof of how much else Strether has gained from his
own embassy.

The next long novel to be produced in this astonishingly fecund
period of James's career was *The Golden Bowl* (1904). Like *The
Ambassadors* it involves an irregular sex relationship, but this time the
effect of the relationship is unequivocally malign. Of course it is no
part of James's purpose to preach "morality" any more than it was to

expound the benefits of freedom per se in *The Ambassadors*. Here his problem is to show how and why Maggie Verver's husband contracted an adulterous relationship with his wife's intimate friend and how Maggie regained him. At bottom two things seem to be major factors, Maggie's devotion to her father and her inability to perceive evil: she was "the creature in the world to whom a wrong thing could least be communicated." [101] Maggie loves and idealizes her husband, but her anxiety to compensate her father for the large void made in his life by her marriage induces her to spend more time with him than is consistent with being a good companion to her husband. Even after, largely through Maggie's insistence, her father has married Charlotte Stant, Maggie continues to be so engrossed in his welfare that it is easy for her husband and Charlotte to fill in the gaps in their leisure by resuming an illicit intimacy begun some time before. Upon discovering what has occurred, Maggie refrains from charging the lovers with their misconduct: indeed in a superbly managed scene Charlotte clearly gives Maggie to understand that bringing the matter out in the open would be an unnecessary torture to her father. Maggie, however, now as wise as she had formerly been obtuse, stoops to conquer by the stratagem of persuading her father (who probably understands her motive more clearly than she suspects) to give over his European residence and return to "American City." The situation, as usual in James, is one with special characteristics which are carefully analyzed. Charlotte is no common "home-wrecker," is not in the beginning the terrible menace she later becomes. As a single woman without money she was naturally tempted to accept the wealthy Adam Verver's proposal of marriage, but she decently tried to intimate to him that he didn't realize the implications of his step. As it proved, said Charlotte later, Mr. Verver's love for his daughter was the "greatest affection of which [he was] capable." [102] Moreover, she tried, "earnestly," to create a real partnership with him. So with Maggie: she thought "more on the whole of fathers than of husbands." [103] These conditions, plus Maggie's inveterate habit of trying to "make up" to people—first to her father, by finding him a wife and spending time with him, and then to her husband by "allowing the Prince the use, the enjoyment . . . of Charlotte to cheer his path" [104]—inevitably make for trouble. The structure of the story is well-nigh perfect. In Book First the story is told from the point of view of the amiable but flabby Prince (Maggie's husband), and in Book Second from that of the wife who must win him back. The "Golden Bowl" itself, a beautiful crystal piece whose only flaw is covered by a gold finish, is used to symbolize the whole situation somewhat in the manner in which Galsworthy later uses the "white monkey," but with far greater subtlety. The detailed development is perfect from the point of view of clarity and authenticity. Individual scenes rise to great heights; the card-room scene, for example, is in sheer technique one of the most consummate bits of artistry in the American novel. If there is any weakness in the story, it is that the emotional content, always kept at a low ratio in James, is perhaps reduced beyond the point of safety or effect.[105] That, however, is a matter of individual judgment, and true Jamesian readers have a special affection for the book.[106] James himself finally came to regard *The Ambassadors* as on the whole his best production,[107] but during the progress of *The Golden Bowl* he seemed to prefer the latter.[108] Moreover *The Golden Bowl* had the "unprecedented" distinction of reaching its fourth edition within a year[109]—a fitting climax to the period of intense activity which had resulted in the publication of three major novels in as many years. All three were marked by James's return to the theme of an earlier period, namely, the vicissitudes of an American character in the European scene, in each case, as it happens, with the finest honors "carried off" by an American. All three also represent the final synthesis of that complex literary method toward which James seems always to have been tending.

After producing his great triad of novels, James never again brought his full powers to bear on a successful long fiction. *The Outcry* (1911) is a very readable story based on a typically Jamesian theme—the debatable "right" of an owner of a rare work of art to dispose of it as he pleases, even to the extent of selling it out of the country—but though the book has a special technical interest in that it possessed many features of the dramatic form (it was first written as a play), it revealed neither novelty nor new depths. More interesting from various points of view are his two unfinished novels, *The Ivory Tower* and *The Sense of the Past*. *The Sense of the Past* is a story of an American who tries to gain his psychological equilibrium in an adventure which carries him to England and plunges him mysteriously into the past.[110] *The Ivory Tower*, its counterpart, is a study of maladjustment in the present, placed in an American setting.[111] The boldness of the latter project is a reminder of one of James's significant traits as an artist, his capacity for growth. Instead of relying upon the accumulated memories of past years, he now undertook to do a story which should take account of that newer generation in America (even to the giddy, cigarette-smoking chit of a girl) which he had taken the opportunity to observe in his visit during 1904-05.[112] Not that the modern generation, with its febrile pursuit of money and pleasure is admirable. Indeed in spite of the fact that James succeeds in imparting to the characters "the dazzling sense of their youth," [113] he is inclined to be a harsh critic of the mode of life they represent. Something of the quiet despair of Joyce's *Ulysses* is in this book.[114] The hero, Graham Fielder, finds his environment so unfavorable that he lacks the heart to carry anything through. He is a neurotic but finely sensitive youth whose inaction inevitably recalls Hamlet—a "happy Hamlet" one of his companions calls him. But he is not happy: he is too introspective. Problems which might have stimulated other heroes and heroines (Strether, Newman, Maggie Verver) only paralyze his activity and deepen his disillusionment. He is interested in his own case, but unable or unwilling to act. When he has the opportunity to expose his nefarious uncle by means of a letter, he (like Newman in *The American*) foregoes it, but he does not destroy the letter—he preserves it in his ivory tower. In short, life in the world he knows (the modern world) is so wanting in significance that he becomes inert in the midst of a corruption he can neither conquer nor condone. No wonder James was moved to relinquish such a dispiriting book as this fragment promised to be, when the outbreak of World War I called his attention to immediate horrors of even greater urgency.

For one who during most of his life lived immured in his own ivory tower, his own palace of art, James sometimes as will be seen showed a surprisingly active response to world politics and the needs of suffering humanity. When war broke out in 1914, his pen was diverted to utilitarian purposes; and the contemporary scene, not in fiction but in cold reality, became for a time his centre of interest. Yet he could not sever himself wholly from his life-work, and his life-work was nearly over. On the evening before he was stricken by his last illness, he picked up an unfinished story. The story was about a young American who was fascinated and troubled by "a sense of the past." The passionate pilgrimage had for James been accomplished long since, yes, but like Ralph Pendrel's it had never been wholly realized, never could be wholly realized—in this world. James died in 1916, his major work finished and refinished with such loving care as few authors have bestowed upon their writings. Two fragments remained, forever unfinished, forever a record of his "work in progress."

On account of the fragmentary character of his last two novels and the relatively conventional work he did in *The Outcry*, James's literary method can best be studied in the great novels he wrote at the beginning of the century and certain earlier productions. What that method was cannot be told in a few words, for James himself was voluminous in expounding his own art. Yet he more definitely knew what he wanted than almost any major American writer. His technical aims changed from time to time; but for each project they were clearly formulated in the author's mind, and the bulk if his output was governed by a few cardinal principles.[115]

The most cursory reader of James cannot but be aware of a difference between the early and later stories. The difference is not so much one of aim or of tone as of method. In a word James began by adopting the relatively direct method, open style, and flexible construction of English fiction before his time. He introduced his characters with plain itemized statements of their history, traits, opinions, and mannerisms. Action of a fairly obvious sort was set against conventional or at least fully described backgrounds. One has only to read such short stories as "The Romance of Certain Old Clothes" (1868) and "DeGrey: A Romance" (1868) to realize that young James was capable of giving his readers a round unvarnished tale—even a melodramatic tale—related for the most part in traditional fashion. To be sure even those and other early stories had a special essence which the true connoisseur can isolate and enjoy, but the characteristic flavor of James can be found abundantly only in the stories matured according to a formula which he worked out slowly over a period of years. Examples of it may best be found in the later novels.

First of all, it must be remembered that James's conception of the novelist's art was not like that of many of his predecessors. He did not wish to "copy" life in a journalistic fashion. He did not wish to point a moral or to provide a handy guide for personal conduct.[116] Nor did he think that it was the novelist's chief function to entertain by means of exciting adventures, amorous episodes, and comic interludes. Least of all did he regard the novel as a vehicle for publishing his own ideas. He utterly condemned "that accurst autobiographic form which puts a premium on the loose, the improvised, the cheap and the easy." [117] Instead of reporting life he aimed to interpret it by communicating the quality of experience. In this way, he believed, he could work for "the extension of life, which is the novel's best gift." He did not regard art as a thing separate from and feeding at the expense of life; on the contrary, he said it is "art that *makes* life, makes interest, makes importance . . . and I know of no substitute whatever for the force and beauty of its process." [118] It is the high seriousness, the almost priestly devotion, with which James spent his energies in the service of art that has won the respect even of many critics and readers to whom his literary method is anathema.

With James as with Hawthorne, a story was likely to have its inception in the chance discovery, through reading or conversation, of a provocative idea. Many of James's ideas, it may be guessed, came from notebook jottings of his observation of the social stratum in which he had his personal life.[119] Having drawn his idea from real life, James proceeded to spin from it an exceedingly elaborate web whose distinguishing feature was not superficial verisimilitude but design. The form, however, was part and parcel with the material. James's ideal in this respect may be inferred from his praise of Flaubert:

> The form is in *itself* as interesting, as active, as much of the essence of the subject as the idea, and yet so close is its fit and so inseparable its life that we catch it at no moment on any errand of its own.[120]

James is concerned, says J. W. Beach, "not with the pattern but with the texture" of life.[121] This is true in so far as it emphasizes James's love of detail, but it does not suggest his passion for order. First of all James was concerned to establish a design that has unity. For him, this implied completeness quite as much as freedom from irrelevant detail: he was not satisfied until, to use his own favorite words in this connection, a situation was fully "done" or "rendered." In *The Ambassadors,* for example, no material is admitted that does not bear definitely and *in due proportion* on Strether's curiously fated embassy; nor is James satisfied until every phase of the transaction has been "turned over." Unity of design, however, is not incompatible with division into component parts. If *The Golden Bowl* is a unified study of a broken marriage, it appears "logical" (a word often used by James in his critical self-appraisal) that the subject may be treated in two principal aspects, the conditions under which the rupture occurred and the attempt to cope with a situation thus created. Accordingly *The Golden Bowl* is divided into two parts, each complete in its way, which finally unite in perfect symmetry.[122] These in turn are subdivided into their component parts. Thus there are the various "cases" which Col. Assingham found so fatiguing to contemplate: that of Maggie and the Prince, the Prince and Charlotte, Maggie and Charlotte, Maggie and Mrs. Assingham, Charlotte and Mrs. Assingham.[123] These segments must be duly observed, measured, and evaluated before the full circle of the project is complete. The process is perhaps taxing, but it is productive of a sense of completeness and proportion that is rare in fiction.

The advantages and disadvantages of this self-imposed demand by James for unity are obvious. The rigorous attention to the specific problem does not permit of variety or even of verisimilitude: no persons in real life would ever confine themselves to the topic in hand so steadily as do the characters in James's major novels. Nor is there any relief for the reader in the rigidly focussed blocks of narrative with which in *The Golden Bowl*, for example, the sections of dialogue alternate. On the other hand the method James adopted makes for a singleness of impression and an intensity not found in many other novels of comparable length. At all events James himself was convinced that in drawing attention to the importance of design and "composition" he was doing a service to the novel, which all too often was subjected to "sentimental or conventional interference" of the sort that characterizes the works of Thackeray, Dickens, and Eliot.[124]

James achieved unity not only by eliminating much of the stock-in-trade of ordinary novelists—romantic scenery, comic relief, anecdotes and other forms of inorganic matter—but also by maintaining a consistent point of view. The average novel he believed was structurally chaotic because of careless shifts in point of view from that of the first person to the third or to the omniscient. Consequently there could not be that cohesion, that "seamless interpenetration" of parts,[125] which James deemed essential. He himself experimented with various forms. The point of view he approved least was that of the first person, for it encouraged slovenliness. To be sure, in tales such as "A Passionate Pilgrim," and "The Pension Beaurepas," he used the "I," but in these cases there is "no question of the revelation of one's own character and affairs." [126] The form he practiced least though he possibly prized it highly was that of the imagined observer, or the objective point of view, which he employed in *The Awkward Age*. In this story nothing is made available to the reader except what might have been noted by an impartial observer—a technical feat which, considering the intricacy of the plot of *The Awkward Age*,[127] must be regarded as one of the most remarkable in the Anglo-American novel. In other novels he used various methods, but generally with basic consistency. In *Roderick Hudson* the story is seen almost entirely through the consciousness of Rowland Mallet; in *The Spoils of Poynton*, of Fleda Vetch. In *The Ambassadors* the centre of consciousness, the "register of impressions," is Strether: the affairs of other characters, manifold as they are, reach the reader only in so far as they are reflected from the mind of Strether.[128] This immensely strengthens that unity of impression for which James sought, and it automatically determines a scale of values for the novel. A more difficult feat was that which James set himself in *What Maisie Knew*, in which it was his aim, at least, to bring the story to the reader through the "small expanding consciousness" of a young girl. Occasionally he used alternate points of view: in *The Golden Bowl*, for example, the husband is the roving centre of impressions in the first volume, and in the second the story is seen through the widening eyes of Maggie Verver—a procedure which accentuates the symmetry of the story without destroying its unity. In *The Tragic Muse* the rôle of "register of impressions" is allotted successively to three main characters. In *The Wings of the Dove* Milly Theale is seen "through the successive windows of [three] other people's interest in her." [129] In each of these cases (and others) James endeavors to introduce no information or other story elements except in so far as they would normally, and at the time, come within the range of the consciousness of the person selected as the point of view. It will be seen at once how this one device of a consistent point of view accounts for other characteristics of James's stories. It accounts for James's apparent niggardliness, his "doling out" information. It explains why except in the early stories setting is not provided outright by the author but is gradually built up from such glimpses of the setting as fall under the observation of the characters at specific times. It accounts for the feeling that the author is dealing with a "continuous present," and it dispenses with the need for going back to catch up dropped threads by the use of such phrases as "Now if our readers will return . . ." Suspense may be immensely, and naturally, heightened while the reader traces the consciousness of one by-no-means omniscient person. Sometimes in order to relieve the strain of maintaining consistency James creates a confidante—such as Mrs. Assingham in *The Golden Bowl*—with whom information may plausibly be exchanged for the reader's enlightenment. Sometimes the method is more or less deliberately allowed to lapse. [130] The basic reason why James favored limitation of the point of view was of course that it enabled him to achieve "that magnificent and masterly *indirectness* which means the *only* dramatic straightness and intensity." [131] He abhorred straight-away or panoramic story-telling because of its dispersion and patching; he "adore[d] a rounded objectivity . . . completely and patiently achieved." [132] Detachment and absolute objectivity—perhaps he had learned the lesson from Flaubert, who believed that the artist "doit s'arranger de façon à faire croire à la postérité qu'il n'a pas vécu." In any case no novelist in English has so resolutely devoted himself to creating a work of art that is self-sustaining or so completely effaced himself from its record. Shakespeare is not harder to find in his plays than James is in his novels. When the structure of a novel was completed no scaffolding remained to remind the reader of the builder.

James's preoccupation with unity, order, and objectivity would perhaps not have elicited so much complaint if it were not for the nature of the action he employs. His plots, it is charged, are composed of cold, juiceless elements that form a poor substitute for "real life." "Why [asks George Moore] does a woman never leave the house with her lover? Why does a man never kill a man? Why does a man never kill himself? Why is nothing ever accomplished?" [133] The answer is of course that all these tidbits *do* occur in James. The plots of James's stories, if reduced to synopses, would prove to be rich in the elements which the average reader is supposed to prefer: murder, suicide, adultery, conspiracy, fraud, revolution. How comes it, then, that the average reader finds James so difficult and lacking in action? The answer is obvious: the *presentation* of outward action seemed of secondary importance to James. Nor did he finally prize those earlier stories in which "action" was more plentiful. His evolution in this respect was similar to that of Chad Newsome's facial expression:

> He had formerly, with a great deal of action, expressed very little; and he now expressed whatever was necessary with almost none at all. [134]

In short, tangible action seemed less important to him than impressions: for "impressions *are* experience." [135] He believed it was the function of art to *represent* life not to reproduce it; consequently, like the painter in "The Real Thing," he had "an innate preference for the represented subject over the real one: [he] . . . liked things that appeared; then one was sure." [136] Therefore in his stories he eschews moments of great excitement, crises of all sorts (during which one's own perceptions are not reliable), and focusses his attention on the impressions produced by actions. He does not care for the splash of a rock thrown into a pool, but he is fascinated to watch the ripples it has created—and he throws very few stones. His stories are then "records of seeing rather than of doing." [137] The hurly-burly of life is seldom seen; the outwardly exciting grand climaxes occur off stage; and the principal actors spend their time in discourse as elaborate and poised as that of a play by Racine. No more than Hawthorne was James concerned with gratifying a popular appetite for the crude facts of experience. Thus in *What Maisie Knew* the divorce of Maisie's parents has occurred before the story opens. Chad's liaison with Mme de Vionnet, Prince Amerigo's adultery with Charlotte Stant, Milly Theale's death, these are not made the focus of big "scenes." [138] James is not interested in administering a shock but in registering the vibrations set up by a shock. His story usually commences shortly after one climax or crisis and in view of another, but his approach to the latter is exceedingly deliberate. Hence the general reader is often disgusted by James: there is not enough tangible business. The actions consist of feelings or what is worse, perceptions. Indeed James seems to have had a conception of action not far removed from that of Gabriel Nash in *The Tragic Muse:*

> "People's actions, I know, are for the most part the things they do—but mine are all the things I *don't* do. There are so many of those, so many, but they don't produce any effect. And then all the rest are shades—extremely fine shades . . . [s]hades of impression, of appreciation . . . All my behaviour consists of my feelings." [139]

There is therefore some validity in the charge that James's plots are not overtly exciting. Plot elements generally regarded as exciting are often involved but their presentation is subordinated to other purposes of the author. In the short story "Madame de Mauves," for example, a man shoots himself for the love of a woman (his wife), but his suicide as such is a comparatively unimportant incident in a story chiefly devoted to a point of honor that confronts the heroine. In short, action in James is less important than *situation.* And situation, in turn, is of paramount importance because it throws light on character.

James's characters were naturally selected from those classes of society that he knew best, and this means, in most cases, persons not immediately concerned with making their daily bread. Decayed gentlefolk there are, as well as persons who are maneuvering for property or financial security (as in *The Spoils of Poynton, The Wings of the Dove, The Portrait of a Lady,* and *The Golden Bowl*), but in no case is the real issue the disposal of property per se. Rather it is an ethical problem arising out of the material situation. More often than not—in James's best-known stories at least—the impecunious persons are European and the characters confronted by ethical problems are American. There are two large classes of American characters: those who have plenty of money but little social finesse, and those who, whatever their fiscal status, are distinguished by their finely developed ethical sense. The former (the Dodsworths of their day) are often visitors or tourists in Europe; the latter, for one reason or another, have acquired the status of more or less permanent residents in England or on the continent. James was guided by no immutable classification, however, and one of his best-loved characters, Newman in *The American,* is at once wealthy, short on social graces, and (finally) able to perceive the implications of a finely drawn problem involving a point of honor. Male and female, James created characters with about equal success. He is said to have "invented the international girl." Sometimes she is attractive (if unpolished) like Daisy Miller or, like Bessie Alden in "An International Episode," at once charming and shrewd in her ingenuous reactions to

European civilization. Sometimes she is so inept as to discredit the whole species of well-to-do young American girls, so frequently found in the eighties, spending Daddy's recently acquired wealth on a European tour. In few cases are these characters highly individualized, for James was interested, rather, in "the large, the generic, American character." [140] This is true even of the heroines of his most important novels. They are embodiments of high ideals which they exhibit not under pressure from without but from their own finely trained impulses. They act morally without being coerced or threatened or cajoled. Theological and legal implications play no part in determining their conduct. Still less could their problems be settled by the police.[141] Nor do they hope for a reward of "good conduct." There is no reward for them except in the consciousness of having acted in accordance with their best impulses. It is for this reason that Conrad called James the "historian of fine consciences." [142] Not duty but honor actuates them. Their decisions are frequently reached on the basis of sound judgment, for, asks Fanny Assingham, "what is morality but high intelligence?" [143] Yet the fine breeding and high intelligence of the characters is not incompatible with strong emotional tension, and the decision of Fleda Vetch to give up Owen Gereth, of Isabel Archer to forego the freedom she deserves, of Nanda Brookenham to resign Mitchy to Aggie—these are renunciations that cost more than the outward eye can readily observe. It goes without saying that James's portrayal of persons possessed of so much spiritual sophistication did not result in the clear-cut simplicity of characterization that readers of the American novel had been accustomed to.[144] Nor are his sinister characters splashed with obvious signs of their malignity; Charlotte Stant and Kate Croy, for example, are drawn with the same skill in chiaroscuro as the heroines. Like the persons in certain stories James once condemned, his own characters have learned to see "round several corners," [145] and the effort to follow them is often fatiguing. Not all the characters exhibit this fine spiritual poise or awareness; for James is "more forthright with his subordinate figures." [146] Obvious examples are Waymarsh (in *The Ambassadors*), Mrs. Tristram (in *The American*), and Col. Assingham (in *The Golden Bowl*). It is largely the function of these boldly drawn minor figures to serve as a foil for those more elaborate studies which distinguish James's portraiture.

But if James's themes lack interest for the casual reader and his characters lack flesh-and-blood reality, the least warranted of all criticisms is that the story stands still. James is often quiet but never languid, and he is constantly concerned with continuity and progress. The story always moves—at least in the sense that James is constantly opening up to view new areas of impressions. And, what is more, the *whole* story moves at once: there are no secondary plots requiring to be clumsily geared into the main action at stated intervals. The action moves through a series of phases. As each phase approaches its culmination, a new phase begins to be discernible. The effect is that of interlocking suspense; the execution has the effortless continuity of a violinist's "noiseless change of bow." Yet although change is constant, it must be admitted that each new phase of the action is handled with great deliberation. It is this deliberate revelation of the situation which so exasperates many readers. They feel that he is not playing the game fairly; they are spectators at a game of bridge or chess unduly protracted. Nevertheless James's method here has its own validity: the real interest in a game of bridge is not in an immediate discovery of all the cards held by each player—but in the gradual revelation of what each player holds, inferences arising from each played card, the shifting relationships created. Sooner or later of course in his "game" James must play big cards, but he does it, as it were, without adequate outward signs of emotion, and his suave discourse is always of inference instead of results. Least of all is he interested in any "money on the game": he is absorbed in the play for its own sake. And he maintains withal a mien of such gravity (such a poker face!) that he distresses those who insist that a game should be jolly and exhilarating. As he plans his finenesses, endplays, and coups, James has the impassivity of the expert—even the scientific player—and he highly disapproves of any such devices for creating excitement falsely as by the use of "deuces wild"—the deus ex machina of story. Thus the glamor of a "night at cards" is replaced by a serious session at the art (or science) of bridge. If James could be conceived of as interested in a game of baseball, he would prefer a "pitcher's battle" to a free-hitting game. His books indeed are like the technical conversation of experts *between* the innings of a game—but the average fan wants action. Conceive of James (if possible) at a prizefight. It would suffice for him to judge from the sparring, the footwork, the weight, the condition of the men, what the outcome should be, and he would leave before the end in full knowledge of the implications involved—with the excited multitude clamoring for the "kill." To James the art of the novel like that of the drama was very largely the art of preparation. Accordingly those who cannot content themselves with significant detail, find his books very short on action. To them James may be moving, but he is (like Milly Theale in *The Wings of the Dove*) "moving in a labyrinth." It is therefore the "expert" who takes most delight in James.

If obvious action is scarce in James, dialogue is plentiful. Yet it is doubtful if the general reader finds the dialogue satisfactory. Whether his characters are taking tea in the drawing room or the garden, or are talking things over in the billiard room of a country house (a very common centre for these wordy mysteries) they proceed at once to an analysis of the phase of the problem at the moment under observation. The language they speak is not realistic in the sense of reproducing actual idiom of the persons concerned. Like Santayana, with whom he had much in common, James made his characters "speak the lingo natural to [him]self." [147] Now and again a character is allowed to use a pet expression for illustration—as when Adam Verver resorts to the colloquialism "ain't" in *The Golden Bowl*, but the actors in James's stories are generally expected to adopt a special idiom of James's own invention. Contrary to common belief the vocabulary is seldom difficult to understand in itself. Monosyllables are the rule when possible, and the construction of the sentences is often colloquial.[148] On the other hand, despite colloquialism, his style is never really democratic: it gives the impression that each word has been carefully scrutinized, even fumigated, before being admitted to the text. Moreover, the vocabulary is often abstract: the business is mainly exposition. James generates power by turning over ideas, and his style is inevitably "technical" to the layman. His characters do not describe objects or narrate incidents but probe situations, and for this they sometimes use a vocabulary that is devoid of color and shape and smell to the point of desperate monotony.

The style of James has proved a terrible stumbling-block to readers. It was in no sense acquired by arbitrary adoption for the sake of eccentricity, like Carlyle's. It was organic. This much is clear from the fact that intimate personal letters betray precisely the same characteristics as those of his stories.[149] Its formality was natural—much more so than, for example, Poe's. Despite the sharp definition of his finished stories, he began a work by improvising. His habit in approaching a project was to draw up a "plan . . . as copious and developed as possible . . . in the form of an interminable garrulous letter addressed to [his] own fond fancy . . ." [150] It was his practice to *overtreat* his subject by "developments and amplifications that have, in large part, eventually to be greatly compressed." [151] In this way he achieved that saturation which gives the characteristic tone to his books. In the stage of compressing his first draft, however, it was by no means his intention to free it of all the qualifications which his extremely alert mind had originally devised. Nor did he aim to rid himself of certain mannerisms and phrases—like "lucidly concurred," "hung fire," "beautifully put it," "had a pause," "turned it over," and the like—which he found useful.

His logical habit of mind led him to place elements in exceedingly awkward combination, as in this relatively uncomplicated example: "The young man met, on it, a little, his friend's eyes." [152] At all events whether from the habit of dictating or from his innate preference for intricacy and shading, he finally attained to an involuted style which has been brilliantly described and satirized by his brother, William James:

> You know how opposed your whole "third manner" of execution is to the literary ideals which animate my crude and Orson-like breast, mine being to say a thing in one sentence as straight and explicit as it can be made, and then to drop it forever; yours being to avoid naming it straight, but by dint of breathing and sighing all round and round it, to arouse in the reader who may have had a similar perception already (Heaven help him if he hasn't!) the illusion of a solid object, made (like the "ghost" at the Polytechnic) wholly out of impalpable materials, air, and the prismatic interferences of light, ingeniously focused by mirrors upon empty space . . . But it's the rummest method for one to employ systematically as you do nowadays; and you employ it at your peril. In this crowded and hurried reading age, pages that require such close attention remain unread and neglected. You can't skip a word if you are to get the effect, and 19 out of 20 worthy readers grow intolerant. The method seems perverse: "Say it *out*, for God's sake," they cry, "and have done with it." And so I say now, give us *one* thing in your older directer manner, just to show that, in spite of your paradoxical success in this unheard-of method, you *can* still write according to accepted canons. Give us that interlude; and then continue like the "curiosity of literature" which you have become. For gleams and innuendoes and felicitous verbal insinuations you are unapproachable, but the *core* of literature is solid. Give it to us *once* again! The bare perfume of things will not support existence, and the effect of solidity you reach is but perfume and simulacrum.[153]

In its most advanced stages, its most highly finished form, James's style presents a hard slippery surface which defeats the reader's attempt to gain any traction, as in this example from *The Sense of the Past:*

> Wasn't he afterwards quite to allow to himself that he had during certain moments just then fairly invited the girl herself, so far as laughing toward her as if he desired it went, to be glad with him for his so liking what was thus promised them together, as might be—there having begun in him too, under the very sense we commemorate, who should have been able to say what instinct of the rightness of his making no sort of surrender to which he shouldn't be able to introduce her as well? [154]

Yet except in very, very few instances James is never actually lacking in clarity for the reader willing to give the text his complete attention. James bitterly complained in 1902 that the *"faculty of attention* has utterly vanished from the general anglo-saxon mind." [155] The complaint comes naturally from a novelist so dependent as James on the reader's co-operation. For the reader willing to grant such attention there are great rewards. If he was capable on rare occasions of writing in a colorless tone—the "white" tone of a singer straining at high notes —he was also capable of sustained prose which in clarity, authentic ornamentation, overtones, and cadence has seldom been equaled in English fiction. Though inclined to be sparing of imagery as such,[156] he occasionally uses appropriate figures of speech whose details enrich the text without seeming superadded. When the Duchess characterizes Mrs. Brookenham, she speaks in an idiom that is natural to her—and to James:

> As your women go she's rare. If she were French she'd be a *femme d'esprit*. She has invented a *nuance* of her own and she has done it all by herself, for Edward figures in her drawing-room only as one of those queer extinguishers of fire in the corridors of hotels. He's just a bucket on a peg. The men, the young and the clever ones, find it a house—and heaven knows they're right—with intellectual elbow-room, with freedom of talk. Most English talk is a quadrille in a sentry-box. You'll tell me we go further in Italy, and I won't deny it . . . The young men hang about Mrs. Brook, and the clever ones ply her with the uproarious appreciation that keeps her up to the mark. She's in a prodigious fix—she must sacrifice either her daughter or what she once called to me her intellectual habits.[157]

Appropriateness is indeed the key to James's style. So interdependent are the parts of his stories that excerpts seldom serve to suggest the essential quality of his writing. Nothing is inserted for the mere relief of the reader. Many of his books are fine illustrations of the comic spirit, but James almost never stooped to merely humorous interpolations. When he says of the Monarchs (in "The Real Thing") that their faces registered the "blankness, the deep intellectual repose of . . . twenty years of country-house visiting," he is not so much trying to amuse the reader as to present a picture. Similarly when he tells us that when Edward Brookenham (in *The Awkward Age*) goes out to dinner he "generally brings three pocket-handkerchiefs and six jokes," he is shrewdly touching off Mrs. Brookenham's character and situation in a few words. Most readers, however, would have been better pleased if

James had "let himself go" more often and indulged the antic mood (such as he knew it) more often. His style might have been the more readable for greater use of imagery and for more lapses from the almost pontifical solemnity of much of his utterance. It would not, however, have been more perfectly finished.

When James died, he left behind him a lasting monument to art in the form of many volumes of fiction, sketches, and critical commentary. The prefaces to his stories in the New York edition of his works are among the keenest critical documents ever written. Such was his conception of the narrative art, however, that James himself is almost never to be seen in the pages of his fiction. Of the details of his private life he left practically no immediate record in writing, except for the extremely impersonal volumes (less factual than interpretative) of autobiography, *A Small Boy and Others* (1913), *Notes of a Son and Brother* (1914), *The Middle Years* (published posthumously in 1917), and a considerable number of letters. Despite these and such hints as may be picked up from books of travel, sketches, and reviews—*English Hours* (1905), *The American Scene* (1907), *Italian Hours* (1909), *Notes and Reviews* (1921)—the man himself remains largely in shadow. He himself deliberately courted isolation, for he had a "morbid passion for personal privacy and a standing quarrel with the blundering publicities of the age." [158] Few writers have so little sought to impress their opinions on their times directly. His only voice was that of his muse.

James's observations concerning matters not germane to his art as a writer are in themselves not of great significance. He was (except in limited ways) neither a keen observer of affairs nor a learned man. He made an occasional shrewd comment on society or government, but he certainly did not show an understanding of the warp and woof of the social order as a whole. Temperamentally endowed with a strong "sense of the past," he had none of the other traits of an historian. Scientific thought seldom detained him. Of a grasp of the history of philosophy he gives no token. Even literary history was not a major interest for him. A man of great intelligence, James was "in no true sense a student save in his study of the art of fiction of his own period." [159] Intellectually he was pretty much a recluse. Such opinions as he did express, however, do not mark him as an eccentric or an ignoramus. Had he chosen to develop and express social views, he would probably have appeared as an enlightened aristocrat. Personally out of touch with "the people," he nevertheless harbored a real interest in the welfare and progress of humanity. This was to become startlingly clear in his impassioned support of the Allied cause in World War I.

In the political scene of any given moment James took little interest.

Daily politics were likely to be "awfully uninteresting" [160] or "sordid," [161] and he was glad enough to be out of the "political beargarden." [162] He had (he wrote in 1899) "no *opinions*—not even on the Dreyfus case." [163] Though he often lived at the Reform Club while he was in London, his residence there seemed singularly anomalous in view of his languid interest in practical politics. Nor did he approve of politically motivated expressions of national feeling. Blatant imperialism irritated him, and much as he admired Kipling's talent as a writer, he couldn't "swallow his loud, brazen patriotic verse." [164] Yet as James grew older he realized that he had, perhaps unconsciously, developed a deep affection for the essential values of English life and character. Throughout most of his life a spectator, he emerged from his shell of isolation during World War I. The profound concern he then felt for the state of public affairs is reflected in a number of essays written during the war and later published as a book, *Within the Rim* (1918). His Anglo-Saxon roots were deeply stirred, and he wrote, apropos of England, the "[t]he race *is* worth fighting for, immensely." [165] The cause of the Allies seemed tremendously important. When in 1915 he became a naturalized British citizen, he did so because he couldn't endure the official attitude of the United States toward the war—"sitting down in meekness and silence under the German repudiation of every engagement she solemnly took with [America]." [166]

As for James's actual political faith, he believed in democratic principles but he hoped they would be carried out by superior men. Temperamentally he was conservative, and he once referred to himself as an "old aristocrat." [167] Much of the time he was out of touch with current affairs in America, but he had his doubts about government by the people, and he once (in 1911) alluded to America as "this babyish democracy." [168] He felt that intelligence and culture must be the true governors of nations. America had a particularly difficult problem because of the untutored nature of much of the population, especially the "ragged and rudimentary" Negroes of the South. Certainly it would be a mistake, he thought, to "descend to the level of the proletariat." [169] As for England, her dangers were perhaps the snobbery and inertia of the nobility. He had lived too much among, and written too much fiction about, affluent people not to realize the connection between private wealth and cultural progress. Yet he suspected that decay was setting in among the "English upper class" and that the condition of the aristocracy was "in many ways very much the same rotten and *collapsible* one as that of the French aristocracy before the revolution . . ." [170] The ideal society, it seemed to James, was one which should be stablized by intelligence at the top and by wise guidance and control of the masses.

James's religious views were even more "private" than his political principles. One senses that he was fundamentally a religious person. Theology, however, interested him little, and those religio-philosophical questions that so absorbed Hawthorne and so tormented Melville seem not to have agitated James in the least. It was not that he failed to perceive the seriousness of life or the prevalence of evil and suffering. Indeed he once (in 1866) wrote that "the most that religion can do for any man" is to enable him to "live hopefully in the midst of a miserable world."[171] Some years later, in a letter of condolence to a friend he made an informal statement which seems to have been central in his attitude:

> I don't know *why* we live—the gift of life comes to us from I don't know what source or for what purpose; but I believe we can go on living for the reason that (always of course up to a certain point) life is the most valuable thing we know anything about, and it is therefore presumptively a great mistake to surrender it while there is any yet left in the cup. In other words consciousness is an illimitable power, and though at times it may seem to be all consciousness of misery, yet in the way it propagates itself from wave to wave, so that we never cease to feel, and though at moments we appear to, try to, pray to, there is something that holds one in one's place, makes it a standpoint in the universe which it is probably good not to forsake.[172]

This was an attitude, but not a reasoned statement of a religious faith. So with his facile "acceptance" of William James's pragmatic philosophy.[173] He could take a position on the matter, but one is sure that he devoted little time to exploring its implications. Indeed all of James's comments on the subject of philosophy, religion, government, or society in general chiefly serve to call attention to the passion with which he devoted himself to his art as a writer of fiction. To write as well as it was possible for him to write—that was little less than a religion to Henry James. This fact, which can be perceived intuitively by any reader of James, is made clear by a fragment of penciled manuscript (evidently not intended for publication) found among his papers. It is in effect addressed to himself. In it he expresses his realization of the intimate, almost sacred, relationship between him and "all the powers and forces and divinities to whom I've ever been loyal and who haven't failed me yet."[174] As he finds himself again at the threshold of a new project, he "passionately" and "tremulously" invokes the same "poor blest old Genius" which had been his guide for these many years and which, he hopes, will never let him fall below that high achievement that he always pursued with a fervid devotion. The manuscript has almost the air of a communion or a confession of faith. It expresses the inmost needs and aspirations of a man who has dedicated his life to his work.

To generalize upon and evaluate the writing of Henry James is a thankless and perhaps futile task. Those who are hostile to him can never overcome their aversion, and those who revere him need no spokesman. A case can readily be made out on either side. He is for many a purveyor of useless trifles to airy thinness beat, a writer of cryptic stories not worth the decoding. His method runs counter to natural process; he uses a pound of digestive juice for an ounce of crude material.[175] His characters are pallid parodies of reality and his actions are glacially slow. He prolongs his study of much ado about nothing until the mind revolts against another qualifying syllable. His subtlety verges upon vacuity, and he draws his wires so finely that they are almost imperceptible. To contradict all this would be as foolish as to accept it wholly. The sincerity of James as an artist will be questioned by no one, but his wisdom at all points must not be taken for granted, and his method is not above criticism. His desire to be one of those "on whom nothing is lost" perhaps betrays him into over-loading his books with the fruit of his extraordinarily acute perceptions. Though he talked of the need of selection, this principle was at war in him with an opposite principle, which was inclusiveness.[176] The penalty of thoroughness is some sacrifice of suggestion, of spontaneity. James's attention to good mechanics, to the dual process of analysis and synthesis, brought him at times perilously close to the method of the scientist. It is with an almost clinical thoroughness that he dissects the body of his story: he must finger every fibre of the organism. And if with an astonishing, an almost miraculous, skill he generally manages to restore each part to its proper place, the process has been, for many readers, a devitalizing one: the subject has become so chilled that he can never be wholly reanimated. Then, his synthesis complete, James invites us to look at the result through the microscope. Well, human tissue doesn't look like human tissue seen through the microscope. Moreover, hasn't he failed to show us the operation of the vital organs— doesn't he skip the big scenes of his stories? Thus the unsympathetic reader condemns James as a cold experimenter wholly unacquainted with the dynamic quality of life.

Yet these (debatable) faults are not wholly incompatible with corresponding or compensating gains. Granted the slight loss of energy resulting from Dr. James's analytical method, there still remains for many readers the conviction that his analysis of human life has given him an insight into the creative process such as few writers possess—an understanding of structure and of the interdependency of the marvelous mechanism of humanity that enables him to bring us into the very presence of the life process. Granted also that the subjects of his study are often special cases, rare specimens, and that he doesn't choose to study them always at the moment when their pulses are raging most violently. Yet the murmur of life is just as real as the throb, and the capillaries carry the same blood as the arteries. Who should say that Lambert Strether is not as real a figure as the most swashbuckling pirate who ever stamped his bloody way through the pages of an historical novel? As real and as finely drawn—for when James emerges from the laboratory into the studio, he proves that his understanding of human character is no greater than his instinct for order and beauty. It is finally for this reason that even those whose patience sometimes gives out revere him for his superb art. Nor do patient readers find James seriously deficient in emotion. Obvious storm and stress indeed he does not often depict, and this is a real limitation (though not defect) of James. But emotional depth is not to be judged wholly by surface agitation: choppy seas are not essential to a full tide. In many (not all) of James's stories there is a gradual rise of the tide of emotion which, though perhaps long unobserved, finally reaching its flood, and, beginning to ebb, leaves its mark of great natural forces at work. To the chance wayfarer nothing is visible except a vast calm, but to one who has learned the secret of James the margin discloses a rich record. Of late, notwithstanding a flurry of critical and publishing activity occasioned by his centennial, it has been the fashion in some circles to refer to James as an eccentric virtuoso who, thank heaven, has had his day. Yet the "day" of James bids fair to extend far into the future. For the perpetuation of a writer's fame does not depend upon his power to interest casual readers: else many a classic would have been lost to the world.

New Directions
(1890-1940)

Modern American novelists owe much to the example of Mark Twain, William Dean Howells, and Henry James. Each of these men was in fact in his own way something of an innovator. Yet even while they were in their prime—in the 80's and 90's—new forces were at work which would alter the fibre and form of the novel to a degree which they could not fully envisage. As for materials, the most fundamental change has been toward the use of economic themes. The novel has been used as a platform from which to iterate the cry for social justice. By and large the cry has been heeded; during the span of fifty years an economic revolution has occurred which has removed many of the factors that handicapped industrial workers. During the same period, however, and especially since 1920, there has been a gradual increase of pessimism in the American temper. Science, philosophy, and war have altered the faiths that men lived by. Old standards of value were cast aside, but adequate new ones have not been found—or accepted. Perhaps the curiously blended idealism of Saroyan will lead writers to happier affirmations. In the meantime the dominant note in much modern fiction has been (to use Thomas Wolfe's term) a disturbing "incertitude." Despite the attainment of certain "freedoms," there has been widespread sense of psychological insecurity and disorientation. In reflecting these revolutions in American life and thought, the novel has proved itself an extremely adaptable instrument. It has served a great variety of purposes whether as a medium of propaganda or as an art form. The past twenty years have witnessed many brilliant, and some significant, experiments in technique of the novel.

Perhaps the most striking change in the past fifty years has been the swing toward the use of socio-economic themes. The haves and have-nots have been more persistently exhibited in class relationships than ever before. The have-nots, who used to provide novelists with opportunity for interludes of pathos and picturesqueness, moved from the margins to the centre of the text. And they no longer seemed to expect to receive "handouts" from the patrician classes: they demanded their rights.

The new emphasis on labor was natural enough. There had been many economic crises during the nineteenth century which might conceivably have formed the pièce de résistance of novels. Yet the fact is that until well toward the end of the century, writers of fiction were not intimately informed on the subject of the suffering of the underprivileged. American writers in general had been of the white collar class; they knew of economic problems but their point of view was that of the salaried worker, not the wage earner. This much is clear from the treatment of labor by Howells, Aldrich, and Bellamy. But by the end of the century there were novelists who had had first-hand acquaintance with the plight of the economically oppressed. Factories were described in terms that workers could understand and corroborate. The realities of sweat and filth on farms were brought home to readers formerly accustomed to pastoral euphemisms:

> I perceived little that was poetic [wrote Hamlin Garland], little that was idyllic, and nothing that was humorous in the man who, with hands like claws, was scratching a scanty living from the soil of a rented farm, while his wife walked her ceaseless round from tub to churn and from churn to tub.[1]

The fight for economic emancipation of white workers was prosecuted with much of the same type of zeal which a few decades earlier had characterized anti-slavery writers. The cry was for tolerable working conditions and equality of economic opportunity. Writers were exhorted to abandon purely aesthetic conceptions of art. In referring to the years of his early development Hamlin Garland wrote tersely:

> Obscurely forming in my mind were two great literary concepts —that truth was a higher quality than beauty, and that to spread the reign of justice should everywhere be the design and intent of the artist.[2]

Of course it was not merely a matter of who wrote the novels. Conditions had changed. The economic phase of the novel was a reflection of a new phase in the history of the country, and indeed of the world. The complexities of modern industry and commerce had created totally new conditions: "the warrior of barbarism had given way to the priest and noble of feudalism only to yield in turn to the trader, the financier, and the industrialist." [3] In America the relatively simple economy of the early nineteenth century had been gradually replaced by an intricate but gigantic structure presenting problems for whose solution there was no precedent. Concurrently with the virtual disappearance of the frontier there had sprung up internal factors productive of angry class warfare. What at first made the worker conscious of the necessity for strife was the emergence of combinations of one sort or another:

> The 'seventies and 'eighties saw the birth of all the great monopolies—railroads, oil, steel, meat-packing, farm implements—whose growth inevitably encroached on the field of individual enterprise. The enormous flood of immigration made the pressure of population felt in the great industrial centers and tended to depress the condition of labor . . . Industrial conflict became a more prominent feature of the economic life. [4]

The elemental conflicts of pioneering days gave way to an even grimmer conflict with disquieting psychological and philosophical implications. Perhaps men were not now more conscious of the struggle for existence; but they were more keenly aware that whereas the struggle had formerly been in large part a struggle between man and nature, now it was more openly a conflict between man and man. The new conflict was a strain on the nerves as well as on muscle and bone. And psychological overtones finally crept into novels reporting the struggle. This tendency may be seen, to take an example from recent fiction, in Muley Graves (in *The Grapes of Wrath*) who is as much a psychiatric case as he is a victim of economic dispossession.

One of labor's reactions to the formation of mergers and trusts and monopolies in the post-Civil-War period of industrial expansion was to begin the formation of powerful unions. The National Labor Union, the Knights of Labor, and the American Federation of Labor appeared in 1866, 1869, and 1886 respectively. Labor also tried, ineffectively at first, to secure direct political action through the creation of parties of its own, notably the Socialist Party, which was founded in 1897. Congressional action designed to check large-scale operations detrimental to the public welfare, such as the Sherman Act, did little to improve actual conditions of the worker. Class strife continued. More and more it had become apparent that the Constitutional ideal of equality was becoming a chimera. The unequal distribution of wealth under a capitalistic system became a favorite subject of Socialistic discussion. Henry George's *Progress and Poverty* (1879) told its millions of readers that wherever "civilization" went, the rich became richer and the poor, poorer. Later on Veblen's *Theory of the Leisure Class* (1899) and Myers' *Great American Fortunes* (1901) lent data and dynamics to the crusade for "social justice." Muck-raking journalists like Lincoln Steffens and Ida Tarbell kept painful issues fresh in the public mind. Behind all these radical and reforming writers of course lay the sturdy bulk of Karl Marx's *Das Kapital* (1848), which had provided the rationale for a class war based on economic rivalry. American problems were in a sense but a counterpart of Europe's problems. Nor were European novelists lacking who had signified strong interests in problems of social reconstruction: Tolstoi, Dostoievski, Turgenev, and others.

It was inevitable that sooner or later American novelists should participate in the struggle between capital and labor. Among the earliest of the "radical" novelists were Frank Norris and Jack London. These men were not in the beginning typical Socialists. Inclined by nature to the cult of sturdy individualism and a love of primitive strength, they seem at first to have been captivated by the very concepts that threatened to submerge the working classes—especially the power ethic represented philosophically by Nietzsche. The idea of a superman was irresistibly fascinating to a certain type of unconventional thinker. Even Dreiser, who was later to evince the tenderest solicitude toward downtrodden humanity, was for a time seduced into something like admiration for glamorous big-time operators—as his Cowperwood (in *The Titan*) showed. There was certainly glamor and there was perhaps sense in the doctrine of the ethic of power. Eat or be eaten was the law of the wild; could man's law safely be much less rigorous?

Yet even while nursing adolescent admiration for the cult of primitive power, London and Norris were uneasily aware that perhaps the only effective way to combat big combinations (which were the weapon of the industrial superman) was by combinations of workers, by collective action, by Socialism. Only thus could the proletariat be saved from being crushed under the "iron heel" of business. Norris in fact served the purposes of the proletariat by revealing certain operations of big business in *The Octopus* and *The Pit*. A little later Dreiser's *Sister Carrie* showed the sad conditions under which factory girls worked and the "moral" effects of their situation. But the proletarian novel *par excellence* at the turn of the century was Upton Sinclair's *The Jungle* (1906). Equally successful in the use of the twin instruments of pity and propaganda, Sinclair described conditions in the packing industry of Chicago with such power that his book became one of the most widely read of the twentieth century. It is probable that *The Jungle* served roughly as a model for "radical" novels until the time of World War I. Even in Dos Passos' early novel, *One Man's Initiation—1917* (1920) its message was more or less standard:

> All we have now [says Dos Passos] is the same war between the classes: those that exploit and those that are exploited . . . We are too like sheep; we must go in flocks, and a flock to live must organise. There is plenty for everyone, even with the huge growth in population all over the world. What we want is organisation from the bottom . . . not socialism from the top to the ends of the governors, that they may clamp us tighter in their fetters. We must stop the economic war, the war for existence of man against man.[5]

In the early twenties, what with post-war prosperity, labor's voice was a shade less strident. There was time then for the revolt of modern youth, reflected in Fitzgerald's *This Side of Paradise* and Percy Marks's *The Plastic Age,* and for a general tendency to question the validity of conventional standards of sexual morality. People talked much about the "right to live their own lives," and popularized Freudian theories appeared to lend them support. Concurrently there was a spate of novels (*Main Street* the most conspicuous) devoted to castigating the small town for its narrowness and low cultural ceiling. Various aspects of freedom for youth and women were favorite topics in the 1920's. But the depression of the 1930's brought economic issues to the fore again, now in new areas. *Tobacco Road* (1932) symbolized wide-spread poverty in the New South; *The Grapes of Wrath* (1939) carried the problem from the Mid-West to the Pacific Coast.

All told there were hundreds of novels (not to be discussed in this survey) which in one way or another bore the plaint of the economically distressed. Loosely they may be grouped as of two main types: the labor novel of city life exemplified by Dreiser, and the land novel or the saga of the soil represented in the work of Rölvaag, Ruth Suckow, and others. The character of labor's message to the nation changed as conditions changed, notably after the depression of the 1930's. The basic struggle over wages and hours per se gradually evolved more and more into a jurisdictional dispute. One heard less and less about the struggle between capital and labor and more about disputes between labor and management. On occasion, indeed, union has bitterly fought union. This last phase of the economic battle has not fully been reflected in fiction. A comparatively new facet of fiction dealing with labor has reflected the psychological malaise created by technological development. Assembly line jitters began to assail workers forced to contract their activities to controlling the destinies of a single type of cotter-pin or king-bolt or angle-iron. The machine could menace man as well as aid him. Nevertheless, with the passage of time, substantial improvement in hours and wages has greatly reduced the grievances of labor. How the financial and political prosperity of labor in the 1940's will find its reflection in fiction is yet to be determined. In any case the proletariat has disappeared. Novelists assisted in a battle that has been largely won.

But the economic difficulties which were mobilizing man against man were only part of the grounds for pessimism that swept the intelligentsia in the late nineteenth century. Another was the philosophy of scientific determinism. Its basis was perhaps as old as Lucretius, but its new forms were terrifying. The more or less general assumptions that "through the ages one increasing purpose runs" and that "somehow good will be the final goal of ill"—which had been so comforting to the Victorians—were now becoming obsolete for many thinkers. The very concept of progress was regarded askance. Darwinism and other scientific theories were raising awkward questions. The Giant Determinism cast heavy shadows which obscured old points of reference and paths of salvation. Heredity and environment became words to conjure with. Man seemed to many observers (including Mark Twain whose *What Is Man?* was written in 1897) to be little more than a mechanism for responding to stimuli. He was not Captain of his soul or master of his domain on earth. His "little hoard of maxims" and his codes of conduct seemed irrelevant if the only constant in the cosmos was Force. Maybe the only thing that counted was the survival of the fittest. Nature which at times aided man was at other times an inscrutable "first cause"; at best she was impartial. Moreover it was a sheer matter of chance— "crass casualty," as Thomas Hardy put it—how this Force would operate at any given moment, intersecting this or that life. These and many other baleful views began to influence American fiction in the late nineteenth century. In the novel they appeared as elements of naturalism. Despite the resistance of Howells, who shuddered at the coarse aspects of life explored by the naturalists, the theories and example of Zola began to be effective in this country. The artistic mode of naturalism was objectivity. Zola had stated one of the prime articles of a new constitution for fiction:

> My study then is simply a piece of analysis of the world as it is. I only state facts. It is to be a study of man placed in a milieu, with no sermonizing. If my novel must have a result, it will be this: to tell the human truth, to exhibit our machinery, showing the hidden springs of heredity, and the play of environment.[6]

Even writers who were temperamentally unfitted to handle the sordid data which so often emanated from Zola and his more devoted worshippers followed him in emphasizing the fact that the novelist's first obligation is to tell the truth—not to sermonize and not to upholster one's books for the benefit of soft readers. The bare truth would do.

The truth was of course different for different writers. As has been suggested, men like Garland and Sinclair aimed their attacks at human betrayers of mankind. Writers under the influence of Zola tended to omit any indictment of humanity. Scientific determinism allowed for no villain—unless it were Nature, in whose vast web all things were held. Hence there was a tendency at the end of the century for the author to abdicate his office as judge of humanity and to become instead a mere observer or recorder of the somewhat lugubrious human comedy being acted before him. The editorial arm of fiction withered away, leaving the reader to find his way amid the dispiriting data of the "front page." The effect of all these changes was to increase pessimistic thinking. For although determinism might conceivably have taken an optimistic turn, actually it underlined the blacker items of man's fate. Novelists moreover have lagged behind the advance of science, deriving gloomy inferences from outmoded (Newtonian) physics while science has gone on to an "almost *mystical*" interpretation of the universe.[7]

The literary form that went arm-in-arm with scientific determinism was naturalism. This was the first new form discernible in American fiction after 1890. Beginning perhaps with Fuller's study of Chicago business and society, *The Cliff-Dwellers* (1893), naturalism underwent various changes. Stephen Crane brilliantly united a naturalistic attitude with impressionistic technique. Norris, though often detached in his point of view, was florid, even bombastic, in his phrasing, with a weakness for the grandiose in vocabulary. With the advent of Hemingway and Dos Passos and Steinbeck, some years later, came a tendency to forswear not only benign editorializing but also all purple passages. Hemingway aimed at clipped, curt statement—even understatement—of what his reporter's eye observed. A colloquial type of syntax was his ideal and practice. He was, in fact, avowedly anti-literary:

> No matter how good a phrase or a simile [the author] may have if he puts it in where it is not absolutely necessary and irreplaceable he is spoiling his work for egotism. Prose is architecture, not interior decoration, and the Baroque is over.[8]

Perhaps Hemingway's laconic delivery seemed a necessity to him. Perhaps he felt that stylistically it comported with the undertow of pessimism observable in many of his stories as well as those of other serious writers after World War I—a pessimism suggested by the very title of one of Hemingway's lesser-known works: *Winner Take Nothing* (1933). Ideologically and stylistically the naturalists refused all compromise with convention.

The 1920's were a period of tremendous expansion and prosperity for the novel. Almost anyone, it appeared, could get a novel accepted for publication. In some coteries it constituted a mark of distinction *not* to have written a novel. Adequate generalizations about so prolific a period are almost out of the question. Yet one conclusion is inescapable: it was a period of diverse and sometimes quixotic experiment in form. From novelty-mongers to genuinely original artists there were scores of writers anxious to approach the art of fiction in new manners. Perhaps the apparent lack of any rigorous requirement encouraged the innocent and the indolent just as a decade earlier free verse had proved a specious lure to amateur poets.

Readers in the 1920's were vaguely aware that certain general patterns of the novel kept repeating themselves. There was, for example, the journalistic manner, seen in the works of Sinclair Lewis and Edna Ferber. It relied in part on vivacity of tone and on the apt use of the vernacular. Like characters in Lewis's *Cass Timberlane*, its authors were "flippant and colloquial and compelled to nervous banter." The hard-boiled manner, exemplified by James Cain, also became a recognizable type. Observable intermittently also in Dos Passos, Hemingway, and Farrell, it was perhaps a later manifestation of the same spirit that had activated the naturalists at the turn of the century. Its author in effect represented himself as inaccessible to tender emotions and allergic to "culture." Diction, syntax, and grammar employed in this type of writing often conformed to those of the rough characters comprising the dramatis personae. Ethical judgments were virtually nil. As for artistic principles, the qualities aimed at were spontaneity and naturalness: none of your Aristotle-Longinus-Horace stuff for these he-men novelists. "Write as you please" was apparently a sufficient guide. This did not imply carelessness of technique, and in fact the hard-boiled writers have made a serious contribution to modern American prose. Yet too often books in this category, as well as in the journalistic, degenerated into the amorphousness complained of by Kenneth Burke:

> Why should an author spend a year or more on a single book, and end by talking as he would talk on the spur of the moment? Or why should he feel impelled to accept as the "norm" of his elucubrations that style so admirably fitted for giving the details of a

murder swiftly over the telephone and rushing them somehow into copy in time for the next edition of the news? [9]

Another sedulously cultivated manner was the epic or saga manner employed in the novels of the land which, following Ruth Suckow's *Country People* (1922), became an extremely popular type of fiction. The saga technique called for the most austere economy of statement —as if the writer were disciplining his art as stoically as the people he describes were forced to discipline their lives in order to survive under the bleak conditions of life on a Mid-Western farm. Such ornament of style as appeared was likely to be a reflection of Biblical prose. Inasmuch as the characters were often founders of a community in a remote new region, their enterprises sometimes took on an epic quality to which the novelist's style reacted appropriately. Openly ethical comment on the author's part was generally as scarce as in the hard-boiled novel, but the warmth of the author's sympathy could be felt in the sternest Dakota winter. Other writers who became at least part-time adherents to this school of novel-writing included Willa Cather, Ellen Glasgow, and Pearl Buck. The latter's *The Good Earth* (1933), though set in China, was perhaps the most popular of all the saga stories.

The framework into which the novelist cast his fictional data was a flexible one. A novelist's manner and his handling of detail seemed to matter much more than his over-all structure. Certainly the old-fashioned plot-novel was pretty much ignored by writers conscious of their art. The Aristotelian conception of a carefully articulated action having a recognizable beginning, middle, and end was often discarded as old hat. The aim of the new writers was to establish that sense of the continuous present which T. S. Eliot conveys in "Burnt Norton":

> Time present and time past
> Are both perhaps present in time future,
> And time future contained in time past.
> If all time is eternally present
> All time is unredeemable.[10]

The aim was to get at the texture of experience, not to interpret life in its totality. Gertrude Stein, who exerted a profound influence on American novelists in the 20's and 30's, especially on Anderson, Hemingway, and Caldwell, spoke disparagingly of the older type of "plot" procedure:

> I think one naturally is impressed by anything having a beginning a middle and an ending when one . . . is emerging from adoles-

cence . . . but . . . American writing has been an escaping not an escaping but an existing without the necessary feeling of one thing succeeding another thing of anything having a beginning and a middle and an ending.[11]

Novelists were not so sure exactly what time was anyway. Scientific and philosophical speculations regarding relativity and Space-Time had created a new attitude toward the nature of an "event." No doubt most novelists did not understand precisely what the newer conceptions were, but they became convinced that the old analogy between time and a ribbon being unrolled from a spool must be abolished. Hence logical coherence in the usual sense was often set aside in favor of an attempt to suggest the fractional, unordered, and blurred psychological experience, much of it inconsequential, of the average person. In Faulkner and Anderson and Saroyan, for example, the reader is sometimes at a loss to know what category of experience he is exploring at a given moment. In one of Saroyan's stories, the first person and third person are alternately employed on the same page to render the experience of one character. The important thing was to catch an experience in the act, so to speak, to pry into the very nature of consciousness. Proust's endless analyses of his characters became an inspiration for some writers. Expressionism, with its apparently arbitrary attempt to give outward form to essentially abstract experience was another challenge to the novelty seekers. The stream of consciousness technique, so brilliantly employed in Joyce's *Ulysses*, lured many artless writers to their ruin: it is a mode fraught with extreme peril for the novice. Even Thomas Wolfe occasionally bungles his use of it in *Of Time and the River*. Yet the influence of Joyce's attempt to "dramatize consciousness" [12] has been one of the most pervasive of modern times. The novel in these new guises no longer moved on a line from one point to another. Instead it was an accretion of experiential evidence centred in an individual's consciousness. It did not reach a climax in the usual sense of the word. As Hemingway explained to the Old Lady in *Death in the Afternoon,* the new-style story did not end with a "wow" as the older type did. Its climax, if any, might lie in a perception. Henry James had in a way anticipated later novelists by emphasizing perception more than action per se, but his severely selective procedure prevented his approaching the extremes later indulged in.

The modern novel not only *was* different, but it *looked* different page by page. Many special techniques and devices for handling detail were instituted and widely imitated, among them Dos Passos' "camera eye" and "newsreel" and Caldwell's trick (perhaps learned from Gertrude Stein) of deliberately repeating certain key phrases. Orthodox rhetorical practices of an earlier era were recklessly abandoned. The incomplete sentence came into its own as an art form. The dubious grammatical idiom of one of his characters (often an uneducated character) was sometimes adopted by the author without apology or explanation as if it were his own. Punctuation was altered by the omission of commas, hyphens, quotation marks, and even (for considerable sequences) periods. The formal distinction between direct and indirect discourse was broken down. Lower-case letters often took over the function of capitals. Italics, once used mainly to intensify meaning, now notified the reader that the author was in a poetical mood or that he was diving into some character's subconscious mind. The paragraph became a unit of feeling rather than of thought; the chapter marked a phase of consciousness rather than a stage in the action. Indeed there were enough novelties and oddities of typography and format to have delighted the soul of that arch-eccentric Laurence Sterne. Many of these were trivial—being the literary reflection of a gadget-minded era —but others served to emphasize the spiritual or psychological disorientation of modern man.

Changes occurring in the American novel between 1890 and 1940 by no means affected all practitioners of the form. Many a snug bourgeois novel was produced during an era of economic unrest. Many a writer of local color stories or historical romance or social manners continued to be content with well established modes of story construction. Many a writer managed to get along without adopting a startlingly new stylistic façade. Even in the 1930's it was still likely that best-sellers would not deviate radically from familiar patterns. The light popular novel designed for the circulating-library trade was inevitably conservative in form: the mass public will not tolerate anything that taxes the understanding. Books on a somewhat higher literary level might reach the best-seller class if they escaped the extremes of literary fashion, witness the commercial success of *Anthony Adverse* (1933) and *Gone With the Wind* (1937). Kenneth Roberts' *Northwest Passage* (1937), one of the finest historical novels of the period, possessed inner power and originality; but it remained on the surface a "readable" story, complete with beginning, middle, and end—and a hero or two.

Other writers, whether popular or not, went their own way regardless of the current fashions in fiction. Edith Wharton lived through many decades of changing styles but she hewed to her own course, content with what she learned from the classics, Henry James, and other conservative sources of inspiration. James Branch Cabell, called by Parrington "one of the great masters of English prose, the supreme comic spirit thus far granted us," used a good deal of structural freedom, but what is new in his books seems to be a product of his imagination rather than a reflection of his times. Most of his books might conceivably have been written twenty years earlier or twenty years later. That Santayana's *The Last Puritan*, probably one of the great narratives of the century, was published in 1936 is a fact that has only bibliographical significance. The book is essentially timeless.

Yet some of the changes surveyed in these pages have been significant. American fiction has become a new thing. Tricks and toys of style have not made it so but, rather, organic changes occurring in writers who were honestly adapting themselves to new conditions. The voice of our prose has lowered its pitch and become more husky. The sentence is now shorter, with a lower centre of gravity. Understatement and deliberate de-emphasis have become habitual with many writers. Befrilled locutions are out; diction has gone into denim. In their thoughts, novelists have tended to shun the brighter colors in favor of a dependable gray. Characters consistently heroic or utterly vicious hardly exist in the modern novel. Actions that are really concluded are rare. Finalities of whatever sort are avoided. The modern novelist doesn't "know the answers." Like Jimmy Herf in Dos Passos' *Manhattan Transfer* he knows he is on his way, but if you ask him how far, his answer will be Jimmy's: "I dunno . . . Pretty far." Even the writers who do not conform to these general practices—and they are of course in the majority—have been directly or indirectly influenced by them. Men like Hemingway, Dos Passos, Wolfe, Saroyan, and Steinbeck have permanently changed American fiction. In Steinbeck's *The Grapes of Wrath* most of the new features that have any value find a brilliant and powerful synthesis. As it happens, Steinbeck's book possesses universality as well. Perhaps that is the final responsibility of the novelist: he must be true to his times and yet save himself for Time.

Notes
CHAPTER I

1. Julian Hawthorne, *North American Review* (August, 1884), CXXXIX, 167.
2. S. E. Morison and H. S. Commager, *The Growth of the American Republic*, New York, 1936, p. 173.
3. In New York City even as late as 1820, "nearly half the children went uneducated because their parents were too poor to pay fees, and too proud to accept charity." Morison and Commager, *op. cit.*, p. 396.
4. Nor could an American writer hope to realize anything on foreign sales, for although there was a lively interest in American books abroad, especially in geography and travel, the best books were promptly translated without profit to the author. E. L. Bradsher, *Mathew Carey: Editor, Author, and Publisher*, New York, 1929, pp. 52-53.
5. In New York the first "bookmakers" who were "distinctively publishers" were established about 1815. *Cambridge History of American Literature*, IV, 537.
6. Bliss Perry, *The American Mind*, Boston, 1912, p. 17.
7. William Cullen Bryant, "An Essay on American Poetry," *North American Review* (July, 1818), VII, 200.
8. See below, pp. 5-7.
9. Carl Van Doren, *The American Novel* (New York), 1924, p. 2.
10. Josephine Fisher (ed.), "The Journal of Esther Burr," *The New England Quarterly* (April, 1930), III, 301.
11. Van Doren is misleading when he implies (*The American Novel 1789-1939*, New York, 1940, p. 3) that a widespread acquaintance with the English eighteenth-century novelists was deferred until after the Revolution. Newspapers before the War show that novels were frequently advertised in the lists of booksellers and stationers. Records of loans by subscription libraries even before the Revolution show a lively interest in Richardson, Fielding, Sterne, Smollett, Brooke, and others. See especially Chester T. Hallenbeck (ed.), "A Colonial Reading List," *The Pennsylvania Magazine of History and Biography* (1932), LVI, 289-340.
12. In 1794, for example, when the Montpelier (Vermont) library was established, the authorities regarded it as expedient to banish the novels of both these men. E. Flitcroft, *The Novelist of Vermont, a Biographical and Critical Study of Daniel Pierce Thompson*, Cambridge, 1929, pp. 29, 40 (and note).
13. Lyle H. Wright, "A Statistical Survey of American Fiction, 1774-1850," *The Huntington Library Quarterly* (April, 1939), II, 311.
14. Milton's *Areopagitica*.
15. Cf. Lyle Wright, *loc. cit.*, p. 311.
16. Timothy Dwight, *Travels; in New-England and New-York*, New Haven, 1821, I, 518.
17. Between 1791 and 1800 there were no fewer than fifty-eight new periodical ventures. J. T. Winterich, *Early American Books and Printing*, Boston, 1935, pp. 121-22. Many of these ventures were destined to disappear so promptly that Noah Webster remarked: "The expectation of failure is connected with the very name of a Magazine." Quoted in Winterich, p. 124. According to the compilation of F. L. Mott, there were five magazines in 1794; twelve in 1800; about forty in 1810; and nearly a hundred in 1825. *A History of American Magazines 1741-1850*, New York, 1930, p. 120.

18. For a full discussion of early attacks on the novel see G. Harrison Orians, "Censure of Fiction in American Romances and Magazines, 1789-1810," *PMLA* (March, 1937), LII, 195-214. For examples of censure of the novel occurring at later dates, see H. M. Jones, *American and French Culture 1750-1848*, Chapel Hill, 1927, pp. 58-60. For, although the prejudice against the novel slackened, it did not disappear. It went westward with emigration and cropped up with surprising strength many years later. The novelist Eggleston, for example, was discouraged from reading fiction as a boy. See below, Chapter XIII, note 7.

19. *The Ladies Magazine* (1792), I, 264. Quoted in Orians, *loc. cit.*, p. 198.

20. *Philadelphia Repository and Weekly Register* (June 6, 1801), I, 238. Quoted in H. M. Jones, *op. cit.*, p. 59.

21. G. H. Orians, *loc. cit.*, p. 199.

22. America was not, of course, alone in condemning the novel, for British writers also viewed the form askance. The London *Monthly Mirror* for November, 1797, for example, printed a vigorous article on "Novel Reading a Cause of Female Depravity," which was reprinted by many American periodicals: see F. L. Mott, *op. cit.*, p. 174. For a comprehensive discussion of the subject as it concerns early British fiction, see W. F. Gallaway, Jr., "The Conservative Attitude Toward Fiction, 1770-1830," *PMLA* (Dec. 1940), LV, 1041-59.

23. Quoted in Orians, *loc. cit.*, pp. 208-09.

24. "If any lady is desirous to know how to avoid the delusive snares of man, let her attend to the story and imitate the character of Clarissa; and if any man is desirous of learning how to deceive innocence and betray unguarded female virtue, and in a word to become an incarnate devil, let him attend to the observations and imitate the character of Lovelace." *The Boston Chronicle* (January 18-22, 1770), III, 25.

25. J. T. Adams, *The Founding of New England*, Boston, 1926, p. 121.

26. Orians, *loc. cit.*, p. 209.

27. *The Diaries of Julia Cowles, a Connecticut Record, 1797-1803*, ed. by Laura H. Moseley, New Haven, 1931, p. 31.

28. *Ibid.*, pp. 39, 40.

29. Lillie Loshe, *The Early American Novel*, New York, 1930, p. 26.

30. John Davis, *Travels of Four Years and a Half in the United States* . . . London, 1803, p. 204. Quoted by Orians, *loc. cit.*, p. 213. For a detailed study of Caritat's library, see George G. Raddin, *An Early New York Library of Fiction*, New York, 1940.

31. *The Boston Weekly Magazine* (June 16, 1804), II, 136. Quoted by Orians, *loc. cit.*, p. 214, note.

32. For a discussion of *The Female Quixote*, see Miriam R. Small, *Charlotte Ramsay Lennox*, New Haven, 1935, Chapter III.

33. Patently modeled on Arbuthnot's *History of John Bull*, Hopkinson's work was probably not regarded as a novel by its author. Nor is it so designated by Hopkinson's biographer, George E. Hastings, who discusses the work in *The Life and Works of Francis Hopkinson*, Chicago, 1926, pp. 193-99.

34. The author was probably Thomas Atwood Digges. See Robert H. Elias, "The First American Novel," *American Literature* (January, 1941), XII, 419-34.

35. *Charlotte Temple* is discussed below, pp. 12-14.

36. Isaiah Thomas, who printed the book, had no hesitation in advertising it as "the first American novel." *American Literature* (January, 1938), IV, [359].

37. It is almost inconceivable that Mrs. Morton, a woman of strong pride in family, should have written a book containing, as *The Power of Sympathy* does, a scandalous story based upon a real incident involving her own relatives. Moreover there are no contemporary records suggesting that she was regarded as the author. Had she been known as the author, it is almost certain that Mrs. Sally Wood would have referred to the fact in her novel *Julia, and the Illuminated*

Baron (1800) in which Mrs. Wood represents a character as visiting Mrs. Morton and finding her established as one of "the first grade of poets." See *Julia*, p. 81. No printed reference to Mrs. Morton as the author occurred until 1878, and then on the slightest basis of conjecture. The case for Brown's authorship rests partly on the direct testimony of Brown's niece, but it has much collateral support. For a full discussion of the point, see Milton Ellis and Emily Pendleton, *Philenia, The Life and Works of Sarah Wentworth Morton 1759-1846*, Orono (Maine), 1931, and Milton Ellis, "The Author of the First American Novel," *American Literature* (January, 1933), IV, 359-68. A brief résumé of the problem (also written by Mr. Ellis) appears as a prefatory Bibliographical Note to the Facsimile Text Society reprint of *The Power of Sympathy*, New York, 1937, 2 vols.

38. The fact that William H. Brown's novel *Ira and Isabella* also impinges on the theme of incest has been advanced as collateral evidence of his authorship of *The Power of Sympathy*. The point is a poor one, however, for narrowly averted incest was one of the favorite elements in the early novel. Indeed it continued to be used as a means of creating morbid thrills until late in the nineteenth century. Denied the use of erotic detail in ordinary relationships, the authors seem to have compensated by trading on the unwholesome dilemma of a heroine who is suddenly called upon to regard as a brother the man to whom she has been bound by romantic love. See *The Power of Sympathy*, Letter L.

39. Additional food for the appetites of the curious was the inclusion of a rather long note on the unfortunate case of Elizabeth Whitman of Hartford, whose ruthless seduction was soon to provide the theme for another novel in the same tradition. See below, pp. 15-16.

40. For a discussion of the letter-form in early fiction, see H. R. Brown, *The Sentimental Novel in America 1789-1860*, Durham (North Carolina), 1940, Chapter III.

41. From the title page of *Clarissa Harlowe*.

42. See young Harrington's comment on the danger of "inequality among mankind" in Letter XVII.

43. *The Conquest of Canaan* and *The Vision of Columbus* were published in 1785 and 1787 respectively.

44. Letter XXIX.

45. *The Power of Sympathy*, New York, 1937, Bibliographical Note. Copies of the original edition are extremely rare. The work was twice reprinted (once serially) in 1894.

46. Elias Nason, *A Memoir of Mrs. Susannah Rowson*, Albany, 1870. See also *Dictionary of American Biography*, XVI, 203-04.

47. *Charlotte Temple* (New Haven, 1813), p. 81.

48. Chapter XXXIV. A tombstone in Trinity Churchyard actually bears the name of Charlotte Temple, but it probably marks the resting place of Charlotte Stanley, who experienced a fate very similar to that of the heroine of the novel. Tradition also makes Charlotte Stanley the mother of that Elizabeth Whitman of Hartford who was the subject of *The Coquette*. Montraville seems also to have been drawn from an actual person, one Col. Montrésor, a kinsman of Mrs. Rowson. For a full discussion of the relationship of the characters in the novel to real persons, see the introduction to F. W. Halsey's edition of *Charlotte* (New York, 1905).

49. Chapters XX, XXXIII.

50. *Charlotte Temple* (New Haven, 1813), p. 75.

51. Chapter XX.

52. Of these, some 158 have been located and described by R. W. G. Vail in *Susanna Haswell Rowson, The Author of Charlotte Temple: a Bibliographical Study*, Worcester, 1933, pp. 47-85.

53. *Charlotte Temple* (New York, 1905), Introduction, p. cviii. The story has

been sold at ten-cent-store counters within recent years. No such praise can be accorded to the sequel to *Charlotte*, published posthumously in 1828 as *Charlotte's Daughter, or The Three Orphans*, and subsequently under titles which vary slightly. A much more complicated and much less effective story than *Charlotte*, it tells of Lucy's blasted happiness upon her discovering from the now dying Montraville that her prospective husband is her half-brother. Finally Lucy settles down to atone for her mother's sin by leading a life of pious resignation and humanitarian effort which is not without its compensation, for "she has learned the great secret of woman's happiness, to enjoy the happiness of others." *Lucy Temple*, Philadelphia, 1874, p. 124.

54. For a detailed discussion of these, see A. H. Quinn, *American Fiction*, New York, 1936, pp. 15-19.

55. The story was published in book form in 1813. An early novel with auto-biographical elements, *Rebecca: or The Fille de Chambre* (1792?), had treated of the difficulties which she and her father experienced during the Revolution. It was written while the author was abroad.

56. Hannah Foster (1758-1840) was a cultivated woman descended from an early Massachusetts family. Besides *The Coquette* she wrote one other book, *The Boarding School* (1798), a causerie on female education; but thereafter she seems to have devoted her literary talents to newspaper articles and to helping two daughters in their novel writing. R. L. Shurter, "Mrs. Hannah Foster and the Early American Novel," *American Literature* (November, 1932), IV, 306-08.

57. The death was reported in *The Salem Mercury* for July 29, 1788.

58. For a detailed discussion of Elizabeth Whitman's life together with conjectures concerning her seducer, see C. H. Dall, *The Romance of the Association*, Cambridge, 1875, and C. K. Bolton, *The Elizabeth Whitman Mystery*, Peabody (Mass.), 1912.

59. *The Massachusetts Centinel*, Sept. 20, 1788. Quoted in H. R. Brown's Introduction to the facsimile reprint of *The Coquette*, New York, 1939, p. xii.

60. H. R. Brown, Introduction to *The Coquette*, p. xiv.

61. In 1833 there appeared an edition referred to on the title page, apparently by a misprint, as the "30th ed." In reality this was the thirteenth edition. See H. R. Brown, *loc. cit.*, p. viii. The last known edition of the novel (prior to the 1939 reprint of the original) was made in 1874.

62. Quoted by H. R. Brown, *loc. cit.*, p. viii.

63. *Memoirs of the Bloomsgrove Family*, Boston, 1790, I, 15.

64. *Ibid.*, I, 47.

65. *Ibid.*, I, 52-53.

66. *Ibid.*, I, 91.

67. *Diaries of Julia Cowles*, p. 31. Hitchcock was also the author of *The Farmer's Friend, or the History of Mr. Charles Worthy* (1793), a sort of manual on how to succeed by one's own efforts, and *The Art of Courting*, designed to show, by seven typical examples, what courtship should and should not be. See Loshe, *op. cit.*, pp. 21, 22.

68. Little is known of the author's life, but she referred to herself on the title page of her first book as "of Charlestown, South Carolina."

69. *The Gamesters*, Boston, 1805, p. 3.

70. *Ibid.*, p. 6.

71. Loshe, *op. cit.*, p. 14.

72. *The Gamesters*, pp. 159, 160.

73. *Ibid.*, pp. iv, v.

74. Quoted in Loshe, *op. cit.*, p. 18.

75. For other titles in the same genre, see Loshe, *op. cit.*, p. 17, n.

76. See above, p. 19.

77. Though Brown appeared early, discussion of his work is reserved for Chapter III, below.

78. *The Ladies Magazine* (1792), I, 296.

79. In *Arthur Mervyn*, for example, Welbeck is left in the awkward possession of certain papers which prove to be stolen Italian manuscripts. See below, p. 80.

80. G. H. Orians (*loc. cit.*, p. 202) has noted the severe strictures of American critics on such American reprints.

81. Modified Gothic elements of course were used later by various American writers, notably Poe, Hawthorne, Cooper, and Lippard. See below, *passim*.

82. *Julia* (Portsmouth, 1800), p. iii.

83. *Ibid.*, p. 47.

84. This cliché appeared in practically all American novels of the period. Mrs. Wood on one occasion alters the epithet to read "the illustrious farmer of Mount Vernon." *Julia*, p. 131.

85. *Ibid.*, p. 135.

86. The Illuminati were first heard of in the Middle Ages. They flourished in various European countries, particularly in Germany. At times their doctrines were merged with those of the Rosicrucians, and generally they conflicted with Jesuitism. Their beliefs have been much enshrouded in mystery, but basic among their objectives seems to have been the propagation of atheism. Their activities have also been associated with miscellaneous terrorism. Charles Brockden Brown also used their vague menace as a background in his Gothic tales. See below, p. 77. For a discussion of late eighteenth-century activities of the Illuminati in Europe and America, see Vernon Stauffer, *New England and the Bavarian Illuminati* (Columbia University Studies in History, Economics and Public Law, vol. LXXXII), New York, 1918, Chapters III, IV.

87. *Julia*, p. 204.

88. It was Mrs. Morton to whom, years later, *The Power of Sympathy* was ascribed. See above, p. 10.

89. "The elegance, taste, fancy and art that were here displayed; rural beauty mingled with grandeur and magnificence, elevated the mind, while they charmed the eye: every necessary and real convenience were conspicuous, and at the same time rendered so ornamental, that it was impossible for a person who has seen the world and been most acquainted with the grand, and the noble, not to admire it. The connoisseur and the critic sought in vain for faults, and vainly wished to find something to blame, that they might display their own talents: but they returned disappointed, though not chagrined, for the hospitality and benevolence of the Countess, overpaid them for being obliged to commend, when they meant to condemn." *Julia*, pp. 32-33.

90. *Ibid.*, p. 153.

91. Quinn, p. 21.

92. A Maine snow-storm receives brief (epistolary) attention in *Julia* (p. 79). But the home scene lacked glamor; and glamor, it was assumed, was what readers wanted.

93. The date of this novel is generally given as 1808, but the book first appeared at Boston in 1801.

94. *Female Quixotism* (Boston, 1841), III, 4.

95. See below, Chap. X. A secondary lesson in Mrs. Tenney's book is implied in her protest against "Jacobinism, atheism, and illuminationism." *Female Quixotism*, p. 70. Quoted in Loshe, p. 52.

96. Oscar Wegelin, *Early American Fiction 1774-1830*, New York, 1929, p. 33. See also E. A. and G. L. Duyckinck, *Cyclopaedia of American Literature*, New York, 1856, I, 504, note. Duyckinck implies that the work went through a number of editions.

97. Anna Cora Mowatt, *Autobiography of an Actress*, Boston, 1853, p. 196.

98. For a list of such novels see R. B. Heilman, *America in English Fiction 1760-1800: The Influences of the American Revolution*, Baton Rouge (Louisiana State University Studies, no. 33), 1937, Appendix C (pp. 439-42).

99. Heilman, *op. cit.*, p. 165.

100. *Ibid.*, p. 196.

100a. *The Foresters* first appeared serially in *The Columbian Magazine* in 1787. Quinn, *op. cit.*, p. 5. In its revised and enlarged edition (1796) it had considerable success. Cf. Lyle H. Wright, *American Fiction 1774-1850*, San Marino, 1939, p. 20.

101. *Amelia* was first printed in the *Columbian Magazine* for October, 1787; it was issued in book form in 1798. Quinn, p. 5.

102. See below, p. 33.

103. *Miss MacRae* is melodramatic in tone and action, but it really makes use of scenes and persons in the Revolution. The story is fully summarized in Loshe, pp. 61-64.

104. Quoted in Loshe, p. 64.

105. Percy Boynton, *Literature and American Life*, Boston, 1936, p. 195.

106. A fuller discussion of *The Female Review* may be seen in Loshe, pp. 65-66.

107. Albert Keiser, *The Indian in American Literature*, New York, 1933, p. 10.

108. For a discussion of the Indian in British fiction before 1800, see Benjamin Bissell, *The American Indian in English Literature of the Eighteenth Century*, New Haven, 1925, pp. 78-117.

109. Keiser, *op. cit.*, p. 19.

110. That she was regarded as an American is clear from a hostile review of her book in the (London) *Critical Review* of 1767. See Bissell, *op. cit.*, p. 99. Oscar Wegelin lists the work as an American production. *Early American Fiction*, p. 36. Wegelin also notes a later edition, at Vergennes, Vermont, in 1814.

111. The story is summarized in Bissell, pp. 99-103.

112. Quoted in Bissell, p. 100.

113. Mrs. Bleecker was not herself the victim of outrages paralleling those perpetrated by the Indians on Mrs. Kittle and family, but she endured a shocking and dangerous experience when she attempted to rescue her husband after he was abducted by the British marauders north of Albany in 1781. See Duyckinck, *Cyclopaedia*, I, 366.

114. Keiser, *op. cit.*, p. 33.

115. See below, p. 47.

116. See below, p. 39.

117. See below, p. 83.

118. Quoted in Quinn, p. 38.

119. Loshe, p. 74.

120. Keiser, p. 10.

121. *The First Settlers of Virginia*, New York, 1806 (second edition), p. 53.

122. *Ibid.*, pp. 54-55.

123. *Ibid.*, pp. 272-73.

124. Quoted in Loshe, p. 75.

125. *The First Settlers of Virginia*, p. [v].

CHAPTER II

1. The original printing of the book is extremely rare, not more than half a dozen copies being known. A second edition appeared at Dublin in 1794, but the work appears not to have been reprinted since. Doubt has sometimes been expressed as to whether Imlay should be regarded as an American novelist. His name is omitted from Van Doren's *American Novel* and from Lyle Wright's *American*

Fiction 1774-1850. On the other hand an attempt has been made, on poor grounds, to show that Imlay was not only an American writer but also the author of "the first American novel." See *The Atlantic Monthly* (Oct., 1929), CXLIV, 466-75. Refutation of the claim may be found in *ibid.* (Dec., 1929), p. 864. On grounds already discussed in the present work it seems only natural to regard the book as an American novel—though of course not the first.

2. There are, however, two carefully considered biographical articles: Ralph Rusk's "The Adventures of Gilbert Imlay," *Indiana University Studies* (March 1923), and Oliver Farrar Emerson's "Notes on Gilbert Imlay, Early American Writer," *PMLA* (June, 1924), XXXIX, 406-39. Both of these are indebted to J. W. Townsend's *Kentuckians in History and Literature*, New York, 1907.

3. *PMLA* (June, 1924), XXXIX, 413.

4. It is certain that a "Gilbert Imlay" died in Jersey during this year, but no conclusive evidence shows that he was the author of *The Emigrants.*

5. O. F. Emerson, *loc. cit.,* p. 425.

6. He was probably stimulated, however, by the *Letters From an American Farmer* by Crèvecoeur, whom he knew.

7. *The Emigrants* (Dublin, 1794), Preface, p. v.

8. *Ibid.,* pp. v, vi.

9. *Ibid.,* p. 18.

10. *Ibid.,* pp. 18-20.

11. *Ibid.,* pp. 133-34.

12. *Ibid.,* p. 138.

13. In some respects Imlay's views are similar to those expressed by William Godwin, whose *Political Justice* (which described marriage as a "fraud") appeared in the same year as *The Emigrants.* Charles Brockden Brown discussed comparable "advanced" views in books written a few years later. See below, pp. 77-78, 88-89, 93-94. In recent years, remarkably similar views have received fictional treatment in A. P. Herbert's *Holy Deadlock* (London, 1934).

14. *The Emigrants,* pp. 179, 180.

15. *Ibid.,* p. 291.

16. *Ibid.,* p. 283.

17. *Ibid.,* p. 259. Before he is through his travels Arl—ton has explored territory as far south as New Orleans.

18. Moore, who came to America in 1803, complained that his observation could not confirm the impression he had gained from books. He finally "ascribed the popularity of the American legend to 'such romantic works as *The American Farmer's Letters* and the account of Kentucky by Imlay,' which 'would seduce us into a belief, that innocence, peace and freedom had deserted the rest of the world for Martha's Vineyard and the banks of the Ohio.'" H. N. Fairchild, *The Noble Savage, A Study in Romantic Naturalism*, New York, 1928, pp. 268-69.

19. *The Emigrants,* pp. 24, 27, 90.

20. *Ibid.,* p. 318.

21. Of these, the best known were Basil Hall's *Travels in North America* (1829) and Mrs. Trollope's *Domestic Manners of the Americans* (1832). Dickens' somewhat discouraging *American Notes* came in 1842. For a study of early travel-writers, favorable and unfavorable to America, see Jane L. Mesick, *The English Traveller in America 1785-1835*, New York, 1922.

22. The Indians receive scant attention in *The Emigrants.* Only a brief account is given of Caroline's abduction and rescue. In general Imlay preserved the "noble savage" conception of the Indian, and he has Caroline avow (p. 258) that her captors treated her with "the most distant respect and scrupulous delicacy."

23. *The Monthly Review* (of London) for August, 1793, first called attention to the novelty of *The Emigrants:* "In a novel written by the intelligent and lively author of the topographical description of the western territory of America, the

public will look for something more than a sentimental tale; and we can assure our readers that they will find in these volumes many things which are not commonly to be perceived in writings of this class. He comprehends within the plan of his work many . . . objects . . . which will render it interesting to the philosopher as well as to the lover." Quoted by O. F. Emerson, *loc. cit.*, p. 438.

24. The periodical, *The United States Magazine*, lasted less than a year (in 1779). In it appeared eight of Freneau's earliest poems.

25. Quoted in *Modern Chivalry*, ed. by Claude M. Newlin, New York, 1937, Introduction, p. xvi. The facts of Brackenridge's life are recorded briefly in this Introduction. For a fuller treatment, see C. M. Newlin, *The Life and Writings of Hugh Henry Brackenridge*, Princeton, 1932.

26. Such was his reaction against the French Revolution that when, as it seemed to him, Pennsylvania also seemed on the verge of civil strife, he "could scarcely bear to cast [his] eye upon a paragraph of French news." *Incidents of the Insurrection in the Western Parts of Pennsylvania in the Year 1794*, Philadelphia, 1795, I, 86. Quoted in Newlin, p. 152. Brackenridge's fears were perhaps exaggerated, but they were not groundless, for democratic societies modeled upon French radical clubs were being founded in Pennsylvania, the first one being formed at Mingo Creek, near Pittsburgh, in 1794. Newlin, p. 134.

27. This volume, which came out at Pittsburgh, was "the first literary work published west of the Alleghenies." *Modern Chivalry* (New York, 1937), Introduction, p. xxiv.

28. The 1815 edition contained all the parts published up to that time together with considerable additions to and revisions of the earlier parts. The bibliography of the whole work is extremely complicated on account of the sporadic appearance of the various volumes, the frequent re-issues of older volumes, the inconsistent numbering of the volumes, and the author's constant revision of the whole. For a complete bibliography of the writings of Brackenridge, chronologically arranged, see C. M. Newlin, *The Life and Writings of Hugh Henry Brackenridge*, pp. [316]-322.

29. *Modern Chivalry*, p. 6. References are to the New York 1937 edition.

30. *Ibid.*, p. 16.

31. *Ibid.*, p. 30.

32. *Ibid.*, p. 34.

33. *Ibid.*, pp. 55-57.

34. *Ibid.*, pp. 61-62.

35. For a brief description of Brackenridge's difficult position during the affair, see C. M. Newlin, *The Life and Writings of Hugh Henry Brackenridge*, Chapter XIV. For an impartial and detailed study of the Insurrection, see Leland D. Baldwin, *Whiskey Rebels: The Story of a Frontier Uprising*, Pittsburgh, 1939.

36. *Modern Chivalry* (New York, 1937), Introduction, p. xxv.

37. *Modern Chivalry*, p. 343.

38. *Modern Chivalry* (New York, 1937), Introduction, p. xviii.

39. *Modern Chivalry*, p. 357. Cf. Newlin, p. 252. At a later point in his work, at the opening of vol. II of Part II, Brackenridge made a still more vigorous attack on the economy program of Jefferson. See *Modern Chivalry*, pp. 467-74. Brackenridge's customary insistence upon sanity and proportion is exemplified here also: "There may be *an extreme in oeconomy*, as well as in expenditure." (P. 472).

40. *Ibid.*, pp. 367-68.

41. *Ibid.*, p. 419. In his occasionally despairing attitude toward popular enlightenment Brackenridge adumbrates comparable points of view in Melville, whom he resembles also in the fullness of his writing and in his proneness to canvass antiquity to find appropriate analogies for present discourse.

42. Quoted in Parrington, *Main Currents in American Thought*, I, 353.

43. *Modern Chivalry*, pp. 372-73.

44. *Modern Chivalry* (New York, 1937), Introduction, p. xxvi.

45. *Ibid.*, pp. xxvi, xxvii.

46. *Modern Chivalry*, p. 487.

47. *Ibid.*, p. 717. A sign of the widespread failure to understand Brackenridge is C. M. Newlin's remark that this passage constitutes a surprising revelation of Brackenridge's purpose in using animals as characters. In point of fact the explanation here given has been implicit in thirty pages of the preceding text. See *The Life of Brackenridge*, p. 300.

48. *Modern Chivalry*, p. 481.

49. *Ibid.*, p. 350.

50. *Ibid.*, p. 20. Brackenridge does not of course mean a "*simple* democracy," for that is a form of government which "has never been able to exist long" (p. 507) but rather a government based upon popular representation—what would be more precisely called a "republic."

51. *Ibid.*, p. 19.

52. *Ibid.*, p. 21.

53. *Ibid.*, p. 507. Elsewhere Brackenridge observes that the demagogue in a democracy and the courtier in a monarchy are the same.

54. In an argument over Negro slavery, Captain Farrago, the mouthpiece of Brackenridge, calls attention to the essential meaninglessness of the term "the natural rights of man." He even goes so far as to assert that "a state of liberty is an unnatural state" (p. 136). An interesting analogy to this point of view was later expressed by Poe, who in "Mellonta Tauta" wrote satirically of the "queerest idea conceivable, viz.: that all men are born free and equal—this in the very teeth of the laws of *gradation* so visibly impressed upon all things both in the moral and physical universe." Brackenridge further enters upon a philosophic defense (partly ironical) of the institution of slavery. *Modern Chivalry*, pp. 134-35. One of the most humane of men, Brackenridge was not primarily a humanitarian.

55. *Modern Chivalry*, p. 740.

56. *Ibid.*, p. 297.

57. *Ibid.*, p. 806.

58. *Ibid.*, p. 507.

59. *Ibid.*, p. 497.

60. *Ibid.*, p. 611.

61. *Ibid.*, p. 803. He also inveighed (p. 448) against the long-windedness of lawyers, and he suggested (p. 807) that there be a tax on Congressional debate.

62. For elaboration of this contrast, see Tremaine McDowell, "Sensibility in the Eighteenth Century Novel," *Studies in Philology* (1927), XXIV, 383-402.

63. Indeed Brackenridge, an apostle of common sense, was deliberately anti-romantic. He disapproved of the treatment of love in most fictitious works, particularly on the grounds that parental opposition is almost always represented ludicrously. Consequently when on one occasion a young lady of good family falls in love with Teague and has to be saved from her own folly by the Captain, Brackenridge presses home the point sharply: "I have thought it worthwhile to give this hint; because the greater part of our romances and comedies in the English language are calculated to depreciate the respect which a young lady ought to have for the opinion of aged and grave persons; and to confirm her in taking the Teague O'Regan of her own choice. For all such are usually represented as old humdrum curmudgeons, or grannys, whose judgment is not worth regarding, and whose taste, in affairs of love, as in their dress, is antiquated, unfashionable, and absurd; but the adventurers, and fortune hunters, are all possessed of taste, and spirit, and gallantry, and carry off the damsel and make her happy. They stop just at the marriage, and give no view of the disgust, repentance, and unhappiness that ensues." (*Modern Chivalry*, p. 242.)

64. *Modern Chivalry*, p. 471.

65. *Ibid.,* pp. 4, 5.

66. *Law Miscellanies,* Philadelphia, 1814, pp. xii, xiii. Quoted in *Modern Chivalry* (New York, 1937), Introduction, p. xl.

67. *Modern Chivalry,* p. 161.

68. *Ibid.,* p. 163. Cf. also pp. 77, 355.

69. *Ibid.,* p. 163.

70. *Ibid.,* p. 163.

71. He often referred nostalgically to the ancient conception of democracy. After complaining on one occasion that in the backwoods one had to choose between a weaver and a whiskey distiller, and that in Philadelphia elections always went to "fat swabs, that guzzle wine and smoke segars," he added plaintively, "It was not so in Greece . . . or in Rome." (*Modern Chivalry,* p. 105). His emphasis on a system of checks and balances was inspired largely by Polybius (*ibid.,* p. 414). Horace taught him not only the ways of wit but also the importance of the golden mean. Many of his political ideas came from Plutarch's *Lives,* which he regarded so highly that he wished he could "see an edition of 10,000 volumes bought up in every state." (*Ibid.,* p. 433.) For a general encomium on classical writers, see *ibid.,* pp. 720 ff.

72. See, for example, *Modern Chivalry,* pp. 256, 389, 392, 783.

73. *Ibid.,* p. 43. Brackenridge's own experience proved the danger of possessing such "talents" as these, for when during the Whiskey Insurrection he at one time tried to use humor as a way of relaxing the tension of the crowd, he found that his innocent pleasantry (which happened to include a reference to the President) was later reported and used against him as evidence of his being a dangerous insurgent. Newlin, pp. 142 ff.

74. His persistent criticism of the Order of the Cincinnati stemmed from his conviction that such an order, being essentially an order based upon the recognition of class distinctions, could not help doing harm, for it "cut men from the common mass." *Modern Chivalry,* p. 71.

75. *Ibid.,* p. 78.

76. One of the principal exceptions is Thomas Paine, in whose radical doctrine, naturally enough, he found more to dissent from than to endorse. See *ibid.,* pp. 260, 312, 573, 786.

77. *Main Currents,* I, 391.

78. *Modern Chivalry,* p. 405.

79. *Ibid.,* p. 171.

80. *Ibid.,* p. 807.

81. *Ibid.,* p. 805.

82. *The Monthly Anthology and Boston Review* (Oct. 1808), V, 558.

83. Abigail later married a Col. Smith in London, with none too happy results; Tyler married Mary Palmer, whom he picked out for his wife when she was a babe in arms. Their marriage was a happy one, and the wife lived on until 1866. She was the author of many "recollections" which were finally published as *Grandmother Tyler's Book,* ed. by Frederick Tupper and Helen Tyler Brown, New York, 1925.

84. Quinn, *American Fiction,* pp. 12, 13.

85. In a long passage Tyler sketches Paine as a brilliant but somewhat irascible person—a "fiery Hotspur"—whose books were more shocking than his conversation. *The Algerine Captive,* Walpole (New Hampshire), I, 182.

86. Morison and Commager, *The Growth of the American Republic,* pp. 271, 272.

87. *The Algerine Captive,* II, 161.

88. *Ibid.,* I, 201.

89. *Ibid.,* II, 29.

90. *Ibid.,* II 39.

91. *Ibid.*, I, 126.

92. *Ibid.*, I, 63.

93. *Ibid.*, I, 65, 66.

94. *Ibid.*, I, 115.

95. *Ibid.*, I, 74.

96. *Ibid.*, I, 98, 99.

97. *Ibid.*, I, 107, 108.

98. *Ibid.*, I, 171-73. Tyler later made an extended analysis of English character in a volume of humorous comment, *The Yankey in London* (New York, 1809). Tyler, however, had never been in London.

99. *The Algerine Captive*, I, 183.

100. *Ibid.*, Preface, p. vii.

101. *Ibid.*, pp. ix-xi. This theme, *i.e.*, the importance of cleaving to native strength and simplicity, was not new in Tyler's writing, for his play *The Contrast* (1787) had embodied in very amusing fashion the same sort of counsel.

102. *The Algerine Captive*, Preface, p. xi.

103. *Ibid.*, p. xii.

104. At the end of *Roderick Random*, a wealthy trader turns out to be Roderick's father. In scores of eighteenth-century English novels some such conclusion as this is tacked to a loose and rambling narrative in order to carry out the pretense of fiction. Plot in the sense of single action properly motivated and proportioned so as to create interdependence of its component parts was largely unattempted until well into the nineteenth century. The early novel both in England and America appears to have had a closer relationship with the tale of travel or adventure than with its more compact cousin, the drama. Literary historians have not yet taken full cognizance of the real aims of eighteenth-century writers casually referred to as "novelists."

105. *The Algerine Captive* was well received abroad (*Grandmother Tyler's Book*, p. 258 n.), but it does not seem to have taken the American public by storm, for there is no record of its having been reprinted here until 1816. The explanation doubtless lay partly in faulty distribution and promotion of the book. Shortly after its first appearance, Joseph Dennie wrote the author from Boston: "Your novel has been examined by the few and approved. It is, however, extremely difficult for the Bostonians to supply themselves with a book that slumbers in a stall at Walpole . . . 400 miles north . . ." *The Letters of Joseph Dennie, 1768-1812*, ed. by L. G. Pedder, *University of Maine Studies* (second series), vol. XXXVIII, no. 36, p. 165. Perhaps, too, Tyler's failure to invest the tale with a "love interest" militated against its popular appeal. Perhaps the Algerine atrocities were too remote to interest the *average* American reader. Certainly Tyler did not go out of his way to catch the general public, and it is likely that his finely wrought satire was caviar to readers who grasped eagerly at the wares of facile mystery-mongers and "heart" specialists of the day.

CHAPTER III

1. *The Works of Thomas Love Peacock*, London, 1934, VIII, 78.

2. William Dunlap, *The Life of Charles Brockden Brown*, Philadelphia, 1815, 2 vols., I, 13. For a brief sketch of Brown's life, see F. L. Pattee's Introduction to *Wieland*, New York, 1926, pp. ix-xxv.

3. Dunlap, *op. cit.*, I, 17.

4. *Ibid.*

5. *Ibid.*, I, 18.

6. Godwin's philosophical temper has often been misinterpreted. He uttered a great many radical opinions, but his bark was worse than his bite. Quite as real a part of his make-up was a benevolent, almost sentimental, strain which caused him to react sympathetically to theories regarding man's innate goodness. He was finally more of a visionary than a radical. The extent of Godwin's influence on Brown has been a matter of debate. See Brown's *Ormond*, ed. by Ernest Marchand, New York, 1937, Introduction, p. xxxvii.

7. The book was probably "Carsol," a work never completed. Between 1789 and 1799 Brown produced many miscellaneous and fragmentary pieces some of which were later drawn upon for use in his novels. The episode recounted in Chapter VII of *Ormond*, for example, was "lifted bodily" from "The Man at Home." See Harry R. Warfel (ed.), *The Rhapsodist and Other Uncollected Writings by Charles Brockden Brown*, New York, 1943, Introduction, p. x.

8. Pattee, *loc. cit.*, p. xvii.

9. This book, "the first published volume of the first professional author in America," was written at least as early as the spring of 1797; and it was published in 1798, presumably in May. See *Alcuin, A Dialogue*, "A Type Facsimile Reprint of the First Edition Printed in 1798," New Haven, 1935, Introduction, p. xi.

10. Quoted in David L. Clark's Introduction to *Edgar Huntly*, New York, 1928, p. x.

11. Dunlap, II, 58.

12. Ernest Marchand, "The Literary Opinions of Charles Brockden Brown," *Studies in Philology* (October, 1934), XXXI, 554.

13. *Ibid.*, p. 553.

14. *Ibid.*, pp. 554, 556.

15. After completing *Alcuin*, Brown had begun a tale, possibly "Jessica," which he gave up in discouragement: "When I revolve the transcendent merits of Caleb Williams, my pleasure is diminished, and is preserved from a total extinction only by the reflection that this performance is the first." Quoted in Pattee, *loc. cit.*, p. xix.

16. Harry R. Warfel, "Charles Brockden Brown's German Sources," *Modern Language Quarterly* (September, 1940), I, 361.

17. Annie R. Marble, *Heralds of American Literature*, Chicago, 1907, p. 296. In his "Advertisement" to the reader, Brown himself capitalized the news by referring to "an authentic case, remarkably similar to that of Wieland." For details of the Tomhannock murder see *The Nation* (November 12, 1914), XLIX, 577. For a further note suggesting that Ann Eliza Bleecker, author of *The History of Maria Kittle*, was cognizant of the same shocking facts, see *American Literature* (November, 1936), VIII, 305-06.

18. See *Wieland* (New York, 1926), p. 52 n.

19. Cf. Pattee, *loc. cit.*, pp. xlii, xliii.

20. The narrative of Carwin grew under Brown's hand to such an extent that he temporarily set it aside and "improvised" a new ending for *Wieland*. Later he added to the Carwin narrative, which, though he never completed it, was published serially in *The Literary Magazine* from November, 1803, to May, 1804. See Pattee, *loc. cit.*, p. xliv.

21. The reader naturally agrees with Mr. Cambridge, who ascribes Wieland's behavior to a "maniacal illusion . . . indirectly but powerfully" affected by Carwin's actions. *Wieland*, pp. 267-68. The principal narrator, Clara, herself the bewildered subject of Carwin's experimentation, expresses various opinions about the causes of her brother's condition, but she finally emphasizes Carwin's responsibility. See especially *ibid.*, pp. 39-40, 211, 261.

22. *Ibid.*, pp. 193-94.

23. "Fanaticism," *The Writings of John Greenleaf Whittier*, Cambridge, 1888,

VII, 393. Whittier also adds that *Wieland* resembles *Wuthering Heights* in its "great strength and power" and that although it has "no beauty" it contains "an important and salutary moral . . . a warning to all who tamper with the mind and rashly experiment upon its religious element." *Ibid.*, p. 395. Cf. Hawthorne's similar warning, below, p. 348.

24. *Wieland*, p. 231.

25. *Ibid.*, 242. In these words, so it has been surmised, Mary Shelley found the germ of the idea which she developed in *Frankenstein. American Literature* (May, 1930), III, 172-73.

26. Brown's friend and first biographer, Dunlap, commented on Carwin as "a character approaching the sublime, from the mystery thrown around him, and yet at times inspiring sentiments of disgust, and even contempt." *Op. cit.*, II, 15.

27. Thomas Love Peacock, *Gryll Grange*, London, 1924, p. 358.

28. For general remarks on Brown's use of Gothic effects, see Oral S. Coad, "The Gothic Element in American Literature Before 1835," *JEGP* (1925), XXIV, 80-82.

29. *The Diamond Lens and Other Stories*, New York, 1932, p. 199.

30. In actual composition, the novels seem to have overlapped each other, but Marchand (*Ormond*, Introduction, p. xxix n.) offers a tentative statement of their order.

31. Dunlap, II, 13.

32. *Ormond* (ed. by Ernest Marchand), New York, 1937, p. 101.

33. Dunlap calls attention to the parallel between Ormond and Godwin's Falkland—at first attractive and then "monsters of depravity." But he finds this reconcilable with the principle that a man may act honorably as long as honor succeeds but may be pushed into brutality by circumstance, for "character takes its complexion from" events. *Op. cit.*, II, 15, 16.

34. D. L. Clark refers to him as "the prototype of Nietzsche's superman, whose actions are beyond good and evil." *Loc. cit.*, p. xvii.

35. It is Peacock's testimony that "Nothing stood so clearly before [Shelley's] thoughts as a perfect combination of the purely ideal and possibly real, as Constantia Dudley." *Works*, VIII, 79. For a detailed study of Brown's influence on Shelley, see Melvin T. Solve, "Shelley and the Novels of Brown," *The Fred Newton Scott Anniversary Papers*, Chicago, 1929.

36. *Ormond*, p. 55.

37. *Ibid.*, Introduction, p. xxxvii.

38. John T. Winterich, *Early American Books and Printing*, Boston, 1935, p. 155.

39. It was doubtless the phantasmagoric quality of the story which led Hawthorne to allot a place in his "Hall of Fantasy" to "the author of Arthur Mervyn." *Mosses from an Old Manse*, Boston, 1864, I, 201.

40. *Arthur Mervyn* (Philadelphia, 1887), I, 173-74.

41. Quinn asserts that Brown's "realistic description of the plague [was] not to be surpassed until Weir Mitchell wrote *The Red City.*" *American Fiction*, pp. 29-30.

42. *Arthur Mervyn*, I, 3.

43. *Ibid.*

44. Like *Arthur Mervyn* it had been published in part in *The Monthly Magazine and American Review*. Pattee, *loc. cit.*, p. xxii.

45. This idea had already turned up in *Wieland*, p. 201.

46. *Edgar Huntly* (New York, 1928), "To the Public," p. xxiii. Most of the American novelists who used the Gothic form laid their scenes in America, and it is probably true that "the persistence with which they followed this practice, while the great majority of [Gothic] poets and playwrights went to Europe, is owing in no small measure to Brown." Oral S. Coad, *loc. cit.*, p. 91.

47. Dunlap, II, 30.

48. *The Monthly Magazine and American Review*, 1799. Quoted in Pattee, *loc. cit.*, p. xxii.

49. For a discussion of the latter parallel, see D. L. Clark, "Sources of Poe's 'The Pit and the Pendulum,'" *Modern Language Notes* (June, 1929), XLIV, 351-56.

50. *Edgar Huntly*, p. 165.

51. In the original preface to *The Spy*. See *American Literature* (November, 1931), III, 334.

52. John Neal, *American Writers, A Series of Papers contributed to Blackwood's Magazine (1824-1825)*, ed. by F. L. Pattee, Durham (N. C.), 1937, p. 68.

53. "I find to be the writer of Wieland and Ormond is a greater recommendation than I ever imagined it would be." Letter to James Brown, February 15, 1799. Dunlap, II, 98.

54. *Ibid.*, II, 100.

55. Joseph Dennie, living in Philadelphia at the time, frequently reviled America as a place where no author could have the chance that he might have had in England. See *The Letters of Joseph Dennie 1768-1812*, ed. by L. G. Pedder, *University of Maine Studies*, second series, vol. XXXVIII, no. 36, pp. 182, 189, 190. *Edgar Huntly* was one of the few American novels praised by Dennie. See H. M. Ellis, *Joseph Dennie and his Circle, Bulletin of the University of Texas*, no. 40, July 15, 1915, p. 125.

56. Dunlap, II, 100. Extravagance and improbability apparently continue to be the grounds of disapproval of Brown during years to come. George Watterston, one of the few contemporaries of Brown who wrote in the Gothic vein, complained of Brown on this score in *Glencarn* (1810), I, 91-92. Cf. below, p. 110.

57. *Ormond*, p. 218.

58. *Clara Howard, or, The Enthusiasm of Love* (Philadelphia, 1887), pp. 407, 409.

59. *Ibid.*, p. 329.

60. See below, Chapter X.

61. *Jane Talbot* (Philadelphia, 1887), p. 97.

62. See *ibid.*, pp. 42-43.

63. See above, p. 78.

64. *Edgar Huntly* (New York, 1928), Introduction, pp. xi, xii.

65. He had never wholly relinquished periodical writing, and even in 1802 he complained of the "irksome undertaking" of reviewing personally a great many books under great pressure while the magazine was "exceedingly behind hand." *Ormond* (New York, 1937), Introduction, facsimile facing p. xl.

66. Cf. F. L. Mott (*A History of American Magazines*, New York, 1930, p. 54): "As to . . . the field of criticism, it was tilled but little, and that little by workmen from over-seas . . . [T]he art of book reviewing was, generally speaking, unpracticed in America before Charles Brockden Brown's *Monthly Magazine* of 1799."

67. Dunlap, II, 60.

68. D. L. Clark, "Brockden Brown and the Rights of Women," *University of Texas Bulletin*, no. 2212, March 22, 1922, p. 30.

69. For comments on Brown's interest in the "Illuminati," a German society which aimed at "regeneration of the world by faith, the dagger, and poison," see Loshe, p. 43. See also above, pp. 24, 77. This influence was rather an artistic than a political one, however, and the "mingling of idealism and infamy" which was characteristic of their society was peculiarly adapted to fascinate the progenitor of such high-minded, glamorous villains as Welbeck and Ormond.

70. Marchand, *loc. cit.*, p. x.

71. On this subject, see Allene Gregory, *The French Revolution and the English Novel*, New York, 1915.

72. How different Brown's somewhat idealistic conception of human nature was from a common view at the time may be inferred from a criticism passed on him by a friend of Dunlap: "Whatever of defect was discernible in existing systems, he [Brown] imputed to the wrong cause . . . and not to the depravity of our common nature, so capable of perverting the best systems to the worst purposes." To this critic Brown seemed "ardently romantic." Dunlap, I, 70.

73. Cf. his remark in "Fragments": "It is not in human nature to resist persevering benevolence." Quoted in *ibid.*, II, 149.

74. Marchand, *loc. cit.*, p. xiv.

75. See *ibid.*, pp. xiii-xv.

76. It would surely be injudicious to infer Brown's religion from the unorthodox opinions ascribed to Colden, for example. See above, p. 89.

77. Cf. Marchand, *loc. cit.*, p. xiii.

78. Godwin had said, for example, "The institution of marriage is a system of fraud, . . ." *Political Justice* (New York, 1926), II, 272.

79. Dunlap, I, 102. Dunlap published a portion of *Alcuin,* consisting of a few introductory pages from Part I and the rest from Parts III and IV.

80. In *Ormond,* Constantia expresses the opinion that "to vow an affection that was not felt and could not be compelled, and to promise obedience to one whose judgment was glaringly defective, were acts atrociously criminal." P. 69. In the passage from which this statement is taken Brown iterates many of the arguments used in *Alcuin.*

81. Dunlap, I, 101.

82. Inklings of a revised attitude toward French radicalism may be discerned even in his novels. See *Arthur Mervyn,* II, 209, and *Ormond,* pp. 170, 171. Foreign doctrine had never made him completely out of sympathy with America. Indeed in the preface to *Arthur Mervyn* he took pains to point out America's advantage in not being bound by "the artificial degrees of esteem or contempt which connect themselves with different professions and ranks" in Europe. See also above, p. 87, for Brown's "prejudice" against Europe.

83. Letter to (his father-in-law) J. B. Linn, July 4, 1804. Dunlap, II, 112. In the *Monthly Magazine* (II, 96) he announced a neutral policy, says Marchand, *loc. cit.*, xliii.

84. Quoted in Dunlap, II, 61.

85. *An Address to the People of the United States on the Cession of Louisiana* (1803), *The British Treaty of Commerce and Navigation* (1807), and *An Address to the Congress of the United States on the Utility and Justice of Restrictions Upon Foreign Commerce* (1809).

86. From *An Address to the People of the United States on the Cession of Louisiana,* quoted in Dunlap, II, 66.

87. See above, pp. 72, 90-91.

88. Cf. Marchand, "The Literary Opinions of Charles Brockden Brown," *Studies in Philology* (October, 1934), XXXI, 554-57, 565-66. See further in this article for a discussion of Brown's criticism both in periodicals and elsewhere.

89. Quoted in Pattee, Introduction to *Wieland,* p. xxvi.

90. Quoted in *ibid.*, p. xx.

91. Quoted in *ibid.*, p. xxvi.

92. *Ibid.*

93. *Ibid.*, pp. xxvii, xxviii. Cf. his statement to his brother James regarding *Arthur Mervyn:* "to excite and baffle curiosity, without shocking belief, is the end to be contemplated." Dunlap, II, 97.

94. Quoted in Dunlap, II, 329, 330.

95. *Ibid.*, II, 97.

96. Joseph Dennie, for example, writing in the (Philadelphia) *Port Folio,* vigorously condemned Gothic writers for their proneness to "go out of the walks of

nature." Quoted in Pattee, *loc. cit.*, p. xxvii. Jane Austen's *Northanger Abbey*, a burlesque, begun in 1798, was published in 1818.

97. The passage is quoted above, p. 84.

98. Such as above, pp. 85-86.

99. W. B. Cairns, *British Criticisms of American Writings 1783-1815*, p. 91. See also *Edgar Huntly* (New York, 1928), p. xxi.

100. W. B. Cairns, *op. cit.*, pp. 91, 92.

101. A. R. Marble, *Heralds of American Literature*, p. 316.

102. See *American Literature* (May, 1930), II, 172.

103. Cf. above, note 25. Her *Frankenstein* appeared in 1818.

104. Quoted in Loshe, p. 51.

105. *The Letters of John Keats* (ed. by M. B. Forman), New York, 1935, p. 390.

106. *Ibid.*

107. Cf. William B. Cairns, *British Criticisms of American Writings 1815-1833*, *University of Wisconsin Studies in Language and Literature*, no. 14, Madison, 1922, pp. 193-200.

108. *Ibid.*, p. 206.

109. S. G. Goodrich, *Recollections of a Lifetime*, New York, 1857, II, 203-04. For comments on this conversation, see *Modern Language Notes* (January, 1930), XLV, 18-20.

110. John Neal, *American Writers*, p. 61.

111. *Ibid.*, pp. 61-68.

112. *Ibid.*, p. 62.

113. Quinn, p. 732.

114. Cf. William Charvat, *The Origins of American Critical Thought, 1810-1835*, Philadelphia, 1936, p. 153.

115. By 1850 even conservative Richard Henry Dana, Senior, who was hostile to Brown's social thought, praised him highly as an imaginative writer. "The Novels of Charles Brockden Brown," *Poems and Prose Writings*, New York, 1850, II, 325-43. Dana had already (badly) imitated Brown in his *Paul Felton* (*ibid.*, I, 270-374). See *Edgar Huntly* (New York, 1928), Introduction, p. xxi.

116. Hervey Allen, *Israfel*, New York, 1926, II, 430.

117. *The Broadway Journal*, October 4, 1845. Quoted in W. P. Trent's *William Gilmore Simms*, Boston, 1892, p. 151. For other references to Brown by Poe, see *The Complete Works of Edgar Allan Poe* (New York, 1902), XI, 206; XII, 224; XVI, 41.

118. *Mosses from an Old Manse*, II, 161. Cf. Hawthorne's praise of *Arthur Mervyn*, above, note 39.

119. A proposed edition of Brown's works, however, referred to in 1846 by Hawthorne (*Mosses*, II, 161) did not materialize until 1857. It was reprinted in 1887.

120. *The Writings of . . . Whittier*, VII, 392.

121. In that year appeared Martin S. Vilas, *Charles Brockden Brown: A Study of Early American Fiction*, Burlington (Vermont), 1904.

122. Dunlap, II, 120.

123. *Ibid.*, I, 107.

124. *Arthur Mervyn*, II, 49.

125. "Memoirs of Stephen Calvert," in Dunlap, II, [274].

126. *Edgar Huntly*, p. 165.

127. *Edgar Huntly*, p. 166.

128. John Neal, *American Writers*, p. 57.

129. See *Ormond*, pp. 231, 232.

130. *Ibid.*, Introduction, pp. xl-xlii.

131. "Every publisher became eager to get large profits out of the few popular books instead of small profits from an extended general list. Byron and Scott

became the special booty fought for . . ." H. W. Boynton, *Annals of American Bookselling 1638-1850*, New York, 1932, p. 139.

132. Mott, *A History of American Magazines 1740-1850*, p. 174. Actually there were published between 1800 and 1819 some fifty-three titles of "American fiction" (Lyle Wright, *Huntington Library Quarterly*, April, 1939, p. 309), but many of these elicited scarcely a ripple of attention.

133. Jackson, who evidently plagiarized Mitchell's book, brought out his version of the story at Plattsburg (New York) in 1811 under the title *A Short Account of the Courtship of Alonzo and Melissa*. In the same year Mitchell also brought out his story in book form. A grandson of Jackson stoutly defended his forbear's claim to the original authorship, but it would seem that the claim must be dismissed in the light of one significant fact, namely, that the serial publication of the story occurred when Daniel Jackson was fourteen years old. Perhaps, however, he deserves a modicum of credit for having shortened an old romance. For the details of the controversy, see *Dictionary of American Biography*, XIII, 48-49.

134. In *Queer Books* (New York, 1928, p. 47) Edmund Pearson refers to Alonzo as "probably the first Yale man to appear in fiction." That honor, however, belongs to Mr. Boyer in Hannah Foster's *The Coquette* (see above, p. 16). One of the principal characters in Mrs. Tenney's *Female Quixotism* (cf. above, p. 27) also preceded Alonzo in this capacity.

135. *Alonzo and Melissa* (Boston, 1839), p. 103.

136. *Ibid.*, Preface.

137. *Ibid.*, pp. 13, 14.

138. Edmund Pearson, *Queer Books*, p. 55.

139. *Ibid.*, pp. 14, 15.

140. *Ibid.*, p. 206.

141. Lyle Wright, *American Fiction*, pp. 141-43.

142. *Queer Books*, p. 43.

143. Oliver Wendell Holmes notes one such instance in *Elsie Venner* (II, 83, 1865 edition), in which *Alonzo and Melissa* appears on the same shelf with Cowper's *Task*, Thomson's *Seasons*, Young's *Night Thoughts* and other standard works. The work is also cited as an example of "female" reading in Bayard Taylor's *The Story of Kennett*, New York, 1866, p. 86.

144. *Glencarn*, Alexandria, 1810, Preface, p. [3].

145. *Ibid.*, I, 22.

146. *Ibid.*, 121, 122; III, 221. Godwin's *Caleb Williams* is definitely brought to mind by Glencarn's subsequent intercourse with the robbers, whom he joins temporarily.

147. In a passage apparently intended to be humorous, there is a political argument between a Frenchman, an Irishman, a Dutchman, and a Scotchman, in which it falls to the lot of the Irishman to proclaim—in crude dialect—that "Jefferson must be our next President" for "By Jasus! if we don't have Jefferson our country's sould to the Dutch." III, 117 [*sic*—misprint for 217].

148. *Ibid.*, I, 92-93.

149. *Ibid.*, II, 207. The dearth of native production is also ascribed to a "lack of encouragement" to American writers and to the fact that American people are addicted to other "pursuits, such as politics and the acquisition of wealth." *Ibid.*, II, 189.

150. *Ibid.*, I, 30, 31.

151. *Ibid.*, I, 44-45.

152. Both of these were reprinted in 1829.

153. The most notable of these was the *New York Mirror*, founded in 1823 by Woodworth and G. P. Morris (author of the immortal sentimental lyric, "Woodman, spare that tree.")

154. Oral Coad, "The Plays of Samuel Woodworth," *The Sewanee Review* (April, 1919), XXVII, 166.

155. *The Champions of Freedom*, [1816], [n.p.], I, [iii].

156. *Ibid.*, I, v.

157. *Ibid.*

158. *Ibid.*, I, 8.

159. *Ibid.*, I, 28.

160. *Ibid.*, I, 47.

161. *Ibid.*, I, 37.

162. Cf. his remark in the Preface (p. viii): "For the biographical facts interspersed throughout the work, I most gratefully acknowledge that I am indebted to two of the first literary publications in this country—the Port Folio and the Analectic Magazine." Doubtless the need of relying on periodicals rather than on books, accounts for some of the author's troubles in constructing the novel.

CHAPTER IV

1. Stanley T. Williams, *American Literature*, Philadelphia, 1933, p. 61.

2. For a discussion of the relative importance of the various elements of the historical romance, see Paul Leicester Ford, "The Historical Romance," *The Atlantic Monthly* (December, 1897), LXXX, [721]-728. For a general discussion of the form, see also Brander Matthews, *The Historical Novel and Other Essays*, New York, 1914, pp. 3-28.

3. S. G. Goodrich, *Recollections of a Lifetime*, II, 110-11. The period referred to by Goodrich is just prior to 1820.

4. He was the author of *A Guide in the Wilderness* (Dublin, 1810), a book which recounted the history of settlements in western New York.

5. Quoted in Gregory L. Paine, Introduction to *The Deerslayer* (New York, 1927), p. x. This introduction contains a convenient sketch of Cooper's life. For a fuller account see the standard work (in the *American Men of Letters* series): Thomas Lounsbury's *James Fenimore Cooper*, Boston, 1882. There is no official biography of Cooper. Nor is Lounsbury's biography full enough or modern enough to do justice to the subject. Until a comprehensive and detailed "life" appears, the student must consult special biographical and critical studies which supplement Lounsbury. A good bibliography may be found in R. E. Spiller and J. D. Coppock (eds.), *Satanstoe* (New York, 1937), pp. xxiii-xli.

6. Tremaine McDowell (ed.), *The Spy* (New York, 1931), A Historical Introduction, p. xi.

7. Quoted by Paine, *loc. cit.*, p. xii.

8. Lounsbury, *op. cit.*, p. 9. The point is a dubious one. Interest in "form" is independent of training, as countless writers have proved, among them Irving. Nor was Yale equipped to teach literary form successfully in 1806.

9. James Fenimore Cooper (ed.), *Correspondence of James Fenimore-Cooper*, New Haven, 1922, 2 vols., I, 81. This, the only collection of Cooper's letters, is not only incomplete but bowdlerized. Among the principal groups of unpublished letters, that at Yale University is the fullest. In particular Cooper was irked because Congress failed to support naval needs financially. Paine, *loc. cit.*, p. xiii.

10. Henry W. Boynton, *James Fenimore Cooper* (New York, 1931), p. 34. Nor was he greatly concerned with the status of the common seaman. Whereas Melville brooded over flogging, Cooper was, as often, able to see the position of those

in authority. In the preface to *The Pilot*, for example, he wrote: "It is not easy to make the public comprehend all the necessities of service afloat. With several hundred rude beings confined within the narrow limits of a vessel, men of all nations and of the lowest habits, it would be to the last degree indiscreet to commence their reformation by relaxing the bonds of discipline, under the mistaken impulses of a false philanthropy. It has a lofty sound, to be sure, to talk about American citizens being too good to be brought under the lash, upon the high seas; but he must have a very mistaken notion who does not see that tens of thousands of these pretending persons on shore, even, would be greatly benefited by a little judicious flogging . . ." Preface to the 1859 edition, p. xi.

11. Boynton, *op. cit.*, p. 57.

12. The Cow-Boys were in general severely condemned, however, and after the War, Governor Clinton remarked, apropos of their leader, that "De Lancey is a very bad name." Quoted in McDowell, *loc. cit.*, p. x.

13. *Correspondence*, I, 82.

14. *Ibid.*, I, 83.

15. What book he had been reading when he decided to turn author, and of what book he produced an "elaborate imitation in plot and character" have been the subject of a number of articles, all of which are referred to in the most recent (and most conclusive) article on the subject, namely, George E. Hastings, "How Cooper Became a Novelist," *American Literature* (March, 1940), XII, [20]-51. It is Mr. Hastings' opinion that the book Cooper attempted to imitate (not necessarily the one he threw down as tripe) was Jane Austen's *Persuasion,* to which, as Mr. Hastings shows, *Precaution* bears many striking resemblances.

16. *Precaution* (New York, 1861), p. 69.

17. F. L. Pattee, "James Fenimore Cooper," *American Mercury* (March, 1925), IV, 292-93.

18. *Precaution*, p. 78.

19. As late as 1839 Cooper, perhaps out of partiality for a weaker child, insisted on the appearance of a new edition. His excuse (as he said in the Preface) was that "no novel of our times was worse printed than the first edition. . . ." He recognized also that the story *per se* contained many "inherent defects" attributable to his having been a "novice," but his corrections were chiefly confined to matters of punctuation and paragraphing. Needless to say, the new edition did not take hold; it is now generally regarded as an interesting erratum.

20. McDowell, *loc. cit.*, p. xiv.

21. Some idea of book sales and distribution in those days in New York may be gained from publisher Wiley's letter of January 7, 1822, to Cooper: " 'The Spy' has succeeded over and beyond my own expectations, and they were not easily to be exceeded. We have sold 100 to M. Carey and Lee, 100 to Lackwood, each at six months, 50 to Gilley, at three months, besides 24 copies to several others. We have also retailed a very considerable number ourselves. A number of copies have been sent on commission to the principal towns in different States. We have sold and sent off on commission about 600 copies, and think it very probable that the whole edition will be sold in three months. This, I think, is doing as well as you yourself could have expected." Boynton, *op. cit.*, p. 94.

22. Cooper wrote new prefaces for the second and third editions, but no radically revised edition appeared until the Bentley (London) edition of 1831. The first "genuine American revision" was the Putnam edition of 1849. R. E. Spiller and P. C. Blackburn, *A Descriptive Bibliography of the Writings of James Fenimore Cooper*, New York, 1934, pp. 21-22.

23. McDowell, *loc. cit.*, p. xvi.

24. Boynton, *op. cit.*, p. 95.

25. *North American Review* (July, 1822), VI (n.s.), 250-82. Charles Brockden Brown was not forgotten by the reviewer but was denied distinction as

an "American" novelist. Despite the "encouraging" nature of many of Gardiner's remarks, Cooper was not pleased by the piece as a whole: it was a "review which Cooper neither forgot nor forgave." Marcel Clavel, *Fenimore Cooper and His Critics*, Aix-en-Provence, 1938, p. 7.

26. See Cairns, *British Criticisms of American Writings 1815-1833*, pp. 114-19.

27. Quoted in McDowell, *loc. cit.*, p. xxiv.

28. Quoted in Cairns, *op. cit.*, p. 116.

29. *North American Review*, p. 259. The identity of a possible prototype of Harvey Birch has been a subject of much speculation. Was Birch the patriot spy whose story Cooper had heard personally from John Jay? Was he the Enoch Crosby described by H. L. Barnum in *The Spy Unmasked; or, Memoirs of Enoch Crosby, alias Harvey Birch* (1828)? For a thorough analysis of these and other relevant matters, see Tremaine McDowell, "The Identity of Harvey Birch," *American Literature* (May, 1930), II, 111-20. It is Professor McDowell's final opinion that Birch is "the original creation of Cooper's imagination."

30. One of the commonest misconceptions about Cooper is that he had little or no humor. Bryant, for example, said that humor "formed no considerable element in his works." *William Cullen Bryant* (ed. by Tremaine McDowell), New York, 1935, p. 283. To one who has read Cooper this judgment is palpably false. The bulk of Cooper's humorous material is more than "considerable." Its quality, of course, is another matter. What most misleads commentators is not a lack of humor in Cooper but a lack of good-natured humor.

31. Although it was probably true that "no military commander ever availed himself of *espionage* with more consummate address, or greater advantage to his cause, than General Washington," nevertheless Washington should have been used, if at all, in a capacity more appropriate to his station—"at the head of armies, or in the dignity of state." (*North American Review*, 259, 261.) To have shown him skulking awkwardly in the Wharton home was, as Cooper admitted later, "a sad, sad mistake."

32. Neal's observation in *Blackwood's* magazine in 1824 (XIV, 415), quoted in Cairns, *op. cit.*, p. 117. John Neal thought the book in most respects, however, a "capital novel."

33. Cooper's sympathetic treatment of the Loyalist Wharton family may have been in part conditioned by his association with the De Lanceys (his wife's family), but it was perfectly obvious to any student of the period (1780) how difficult was the decision whether to go Whig or Tory. As for Mr. Wharton, who had "friends in both armies," he would naturally "dread a victory of either [side] as a source of misfortune," and of course his estate was endangered by the conflict. Such frank recognition of difficult issues naturally lent interest and authenticity to *The Spy* as a fundamentally patriotic book.

34. Cooper's extensive use of Negroes throughout his novels has never received the attention it deserves. Gaines, for example, says that Cooper was "interested mildly in negro character." *The Southern Plantation*, New York, 1925, p. 21. Actually Cooper was not greatly concerned over Negro rights but was greatly interested in Negro character.

35. *North American Review*, VI, 258.

36. Quoted in Henry A. Beers, *A History of English Romanticism in the Eighteenth Century*, New York, 1916, p. 9.

37. One contemporary (possibly the poet Percival) charged Cooper with an egotism so gross that "he writes his Novels in the street, leaning against a lamppost." Boynton, p. 111.

38. For accounts of this extremely interesting club, see N. F. Adkins, "James Fenimore Cooper and the Bread and Cheese Club," *Modern Language Notes* (February, 1932), LXVII, 71-79, and A. H. Marckwardt, "The Chronology and Personnel of the Bread and Cheese Club," *American Literature* (January, 1935), VI, 389-99.

39. It should be noted that the full title at first ran: *The Pioneers; or the Sources of the Susquehanna. A Descriptive Tale.*

40. Shortly after the publication of *The Pioneers,* R. H. Dana wrote to Cooper that the mixture of traits in Natty created in the reader "a grateful and peculiar emotion made up of admiration and pity and concern." *Correspondence of Cooper,* I, 94. Later the ratio of admiration was to be stepped up.

41. Lounsbury, p. 41. In London, Murray, who had refused *The Spy,* condescended to stand behind *The Pioneers,* which was at least as well received by the British press as *The Spy.*

42. *North American Review,* VI, 276.

43. Boynton, p. 111.

44. *Koningsmarke, The Long Finne,* II, 67-71 (quoted in A. L. Herold, *James Kirk Paulding,* New York, 1926, p. 119). *Koningsmarke* was published only a few months after *The Pioneers.* Cooper's high opinion of Paulding, who was a fellow Bread and Cheese-er, is suggested by his use of a passage from the latter as a title-page motto for *The Pioneers.*

45. Nevertheless there are modern critics who have granted high praise to *The Pioneers,* among them D. H. Lawrence, whose sometimes inaccurate but finely intuitive comments on Cooper have not yet been fully appreciated in this country. Lawrence loved the descriptive parts of *The Pioneers:* "Perhaps my taste is childish, but these scenes in *Pioneers* seem to me marvellously beautiful. The raw village street, with woodfires blinking through the unglazed window-chinks, on a winter's night. The inn, with the rough woodsmen and the drunken Indian John; the church, with the snowy congregation crowding to the fire. Then the lavish abundance of Christmas cheer, and turkey-shooting in the snow. Spring coming, forests all green, maple-sugar taken from the trees: and clouds of pigeons flying from the south, myriads of pigeons, shot in heaps; and night-fishing on the teeming, virgin lake; and deer-hunting.

Pictures! Some of the loveliest, most glamorous pictures in all literature." *Studies in Classic American Literature* (New York, 1923), p. 80.

46. The title page carries the date 1823, but the book was published on January 7, 1824. Spiller and Blackburn, p. 34. At some time in 1823 Cooper also wrote (under the pseudonym of "Jane Morgan") an unimportant little volume, containing two stories, called *Tales for Fifteen,* one of a number of volumes written by friends of publisher Wiley to help him out of his financial difficulties, which culminated in bankruptcy about this time. Boynton, p. 99.

47. Ludwig Lewisohn's frequently splendid intuitions and brilliant phraseology should not be permitted to obscure his essential unfairness to many writers. To Cooper, for example, he denies "depth of characterization" (*Expression in America,* New York, 1932, pp. 55-56), forgetting that simplicity is not incompatible with depth.

48. Quoted in Boynton, p. 121. See also *ibid.,* p. 116.

49. He also used Long Tom in the first whaling scene written by a major American novelist—a fact which Melville probably did not fail to note.

50. *The Ariel* (March 6, 1830), p. 183.

51. The partial failure of *Lionel Lincoln* was largely an artistic failure. The book was for a time well received, and it "created in Boston and throughout New-England, a popularity for Mr. Cooper's works, at one period so great, as to become among novel readers, almost a mania." *The Southern Literary Messenger* (June, 1838), IV, 375, quoted in E. E. Leisy, *The American Historical Novel (on American Themes) Before 1860,* Urbana, Illinois, [1923], p. 16. A play based on the novel, *The Leagues of Boston,* seems also to have been well received. *Ibid.*

52. Two months after publication "the demand had grown large enough to call for a stereotype edition—a rare thing in those days." Boynton, p. 138.

53. *William Cullen Bryant* (ed. by Tremaine McDowell), New York, 1935, p. 283.

54. Quoted in Boynton, p. 149.

55. Boynton, p. 154.

56. Boynton, p. 159. Susan Cooper wrote that Scott reminded her of "one of our country Presbyterian Parsons." *Ibid.*

57. In years to come, Cooper, no doubt irritated at being everywhere called "the American Scott," changed his attitude toward the "Antiquary." A more important factor was his disapproval of Scott's Toryism. Cf. Dorothy Waples, *The Whig Myth of James Fenimore Cooper*, New Haven, 1938, pp. 56-57.

58. Lounsbury, p. 104.

59. *Notions of the Americans* (1838 ed.), pp. 90-110.

60. *The Philadelphia National Gazette*, February 18, 1826. Quoted in Boynton, p. 139.

61. *Ibid.*

62. D. H. Lawrence erred in saying that Cooper "saw the prairies, and camped with the Indians." *Classic American Literature*, p. 83.

63. The parallel is noted promptly: "The earth was not unlike the ocean, when its restless waters are heaving heavily, after the agitation and fury of the tempest have begun to lessen. There was the same waving and regular surface, the same absence of foreign objects, and the same boundless extent to the view. Indeed so very striking was the resemblance between the water and the land, that, however much the geologist might sneer at so simple a theory, it would have been difficult for a poet not to have felt, that the formation of the one had been produced by the subsiding dominion of the other." *The Prairie* (New York, 1859), pp. 14-15.

64. Van Doren, *The American Novel* (1940), p. 31.

65. *The Prairie*, p. 72.

66. *Ibid.*, p. 478. Thackeray, who once parodied *The Last of the Mohicans* (in a sketch called "The Stars and Stripes, by the author of the Last of the Mulligans") did Cooper the (further) honor of imitating Natty's death in his description of the last moments of Col. Newcome, who responds to an imagined roll-call with "Adsum."

67. Melville, who, though not blind to Cooper's faults, discerned in him a "pervading greatness," reviewed an edition of *The Red Rover* favorably in *The Literary World* (Boston), and he was to perform a similar service for Cooper's *The Sea Lions* (1849). *The Pilot*, also, Melville knew, for he included a passage from it in the "Extracts" on cetology which are prefaced to *Moby-Dick*. For other notes on Melville's attitude toward Cooper, see *Notes and Queries* (January, 1932), CLXII, 39.

68. Lounsbury, p. 75. R. E. Spiller has further explained (*Fenimore Cooper: Critic of his Times*, New York, 1931, p. 313) the chief reason for Cooper's inability to do justice to New England: "Toward New Englanders he had an instinctive antipathy because he realized that the middle class ideal had been brought to America by the Pilgrim and Puritan fathers; and toward the Episcopal Church he felt an irresistible attraction because it was the religion most clearly integrated with the social tradition of which he was a part and of which he preached the doctrine." For Cooper's social views, see below, pp. 155 ff.

69. For a discussion of various uses to which this theme was put see G. H. Orians, *American Literature* (November, 1932), IV, 257-69 and Frank Davidson, *American Literature* (November, 1935), VII, 330-32.

70. *North American Review*, VI, 255-57.

71. Cooper was accused of plagiarizing Miss Sedgwick's popular *Hope Leslie* (1827), doubtless because Ruth Heathcote, like Faith Leslie, is abducted by Indians and married to one of the braves. (*The Ariel* [December 26, 1829], III, 141.) The charge seems idle, for inter-racial marriage was common in early annals, and in any case why plagiarize a recent novel of wide circulation?

72. Cooper proposed to publish it at Rome, but the censor denied permission

unless Cooper should delete various passages reflecting on Rome as a city of vanished glory and present decay—"youthful" America, of course, pointing the contrast. Lounsbury, p. 123.

73. Quoted in Boynton, p. 205.

74. *Ibid.*, p. 206.

75. See above, p. 133.

76. R. E. Spiller, *Fenimore Cooper: Critic of his Times*, p. 217.

77. Boynton, p. 223. See also Spiller, *Fenimore Cooper: Critic of his Times*, pp. 174-81 for a detailed discussion of Cooper's interest in Poland, an interest which kept him for some time in close association with Lafayette.

78. R. E. Spiller goes so far as to say that *The Bravo* is "one of the best of Cooper's romances." *Ibid.*, p. 218.

79. Lounsbury, p. 109. Cooper himself conceded that *The Heidenmauer* was not so good as *The Bravo*, but he thought it "a good book and better than two thirds of Scott." *Correspondence*, I, 283.

80. For brief analyses of these stories, see Quinn, pp. 71-72; Spiller, *Fenimore Cooper*, pp. 218-22.

81. *Views and Reviews* (first series), New York, 1845, p. 224.

82. In *The Heidenmauer* he aimed "to show how differently a democrat and an aristocrat saw the same thing"—that is, the dissolution of medievalism. *Correspondence*, I, 283.

83. Quoted in Spiller, *Fenimore Cooper*, p. 220.

84. Boynton, p. 231.

85. Quoted in Spiller, *Fenimore Cooper*, p. 215.

86. He was particularly enraged by a sharp criticism of *The Bravo* published in *The New York American*, and he wrote a vitriolic reply (for *The Albany Daily Advertizer*) in which he not only excoriated the author of the article but spread his fire to cover "the venality of French and English reviews." Quoted in Spiller, *Fenimore Cooper*, pp. 224-25.

87. *Correspondence*, I, 328.

88. Parrington, *Main Currents*, II, 229.

89. *Views and Reviews* (second series), p. 229.

90. Quoted in Boynton, p. 261.

91. Spiller, *Fenimore Cooper*, p. 237.

92. *Ibid.*, p. 238. For a full discussion of *The Monikins*, see *ibid.*, pp. 237-43.

93. For bibliographical details of these publications, see Lounsbury, pp. 292-93, and Spiller and Blackburn, *op. cit.*, pp. 84-96. Even the travel books, of course, could serve in part as vehicles of political discussion. Cf. Dorothy Waples, *The Whig Myth of James Fenimore Cooper*, pp. 159 ff.

94. Lounsbury, p. 178.

95. *The American Democrat, or Hints on the Social and Civic Relations of the United States of America*, Cooperstown, 1838, p. 131. This book, which contains the core of many of Cooper's opinions, was reissued with an introduction by H. L. Mencken at New York in 1931.

96. Cooper was thus, Spiller points out (*Fenimore Cooper*, p. 259), in a sense a pioneer in the international novel of manners (although "in reverse") later to be practiced by James and Howells. The type had begun much earlier, however—in fact with *The Emigrants*.

97. *Home As Found* (New York, 1860), p. 427.

98. For a detailed documentary study of the whole matter of the controversy, see Ethel R. Outland, *The "Effingham Libels" on Cooper* (University of Wisconsin Studies in Language and Literature, no. 28), Madison, 1929.

99. Cooper had his defenders, both of his legal moves and of his novel, among them Bryant. But most of his friends must have agreed with the shrewd comments of W. G. Simms anent the social criticism of *Home As Found:* "The tone of

'Homeward Bound,' and 'Home As Found,' was bad. It expressed the language of querulousness and distaste, if not disgust. It was written less in sorrow than in anger, as if the writer took a malicious delight in singling out the sore spots, which it had been the better purpose of the patriot to hide if he could not heal. He showed himself more disposed to revenge his own hurts and injuries than to amend the faults of his countrymen. Besides, as we have already said, he was unjust because too sweeping in his condemnation. This was the consequence of writing in his anger. Passion has no powers of discrimination, and the wilful mind will exercise none. But if Mr. Cooper's censure had been just in all respects, and in its entire application, it must have failed of any good result at the time of its utterance. It was unseasonable, and therefore impolitic and unwise." *Views and Reviews*, I, 236.

100. Cooper had not forgotten his hero during the interval since the publication of *The Prairie* (1827). Natty is mentioned several times in *Home As Found*, where one of the characters is made to compare him with Washington, Jackson, Jefferson, and Napoleon Bonaparte. *Home As Found*, pp. 211-12, 215, 216.

101. *The Pathfinder* (New York, 1860), p. 503.

102. D. H. Lawrence, *op. cit.*, p. 72.

103. Balzac was quite carried away by *The Pathfinder:* "It is beautiful, it is grand. Its interest is tremendous. [Cooper] surely owed us this masterpiece after the last two or three rhapsodies he has been giving us . . . I know no one in the world, save Walter Scott, who has risen to that grandeur and serenity of colors . . . Never did the art of writing tread closer upon the art of the pencil. This is the school of study for literary landscape-painters." Quoted in Lounsbury, pp. 240-41.

104. Between the publication of *The Pathfinder* and *The Deerslayer* had appeared *Mercedes of Castile* (1840), one of Cooper's least rewarding stories—another proof that Cooper was unequal to producing a good novel based chiefly on research. An ineffective blend of epic, romance, and history, it tells (finally) the story of Columbus' first voyage to America: the introductory matter (of 230 pages) constitutes one of the bleakest deserts in Cooper. Nor does the feeble love triangle established between Mercedes, Don Luis, and Ozema take rank as an oasis. Students of early sailing ships alone can find use for this tale.

105. The reader who wishes to observe Cooper's evolution from a realistic to an idealistic attitude would do well to read the series not in their narrative order (*The Deerslayer, The Last of the Mohicans, The Pathfinder, The Pioneers,* and *The Prairie*), but in the order (used in this chapter) of their composition. Cf. Paine, *loc. cit.*, p. xxi. Then the series exhibits "a *decrescendo* of reality, and a crescendo of beauty." D. H. Lawrence, *op. cit.*, p. 72.

106. *Correspondence*, II, 449-50.

107. *The Deerslayer* (New York, 1861), Preface, p. vi.

108. In his analysis of the component parts of Natty Bumppo, G. L. Paine notes (cf. above, p. 127) that the physical "models" included Shipman (the New York hunter) and Daniel Boone. Two less specific elements are also noted by Mr. Paine. One of these is the concept of "nature's gentleman"—a youth of "unknown, humble parentage [who] has been ennobled by living in the virgin forest and by years of companionship with those true sons of nature, the Indians." He is both Christian and pantheistic, and he "scorns the wranglings of the various sects." The final element is the "idealistic spirit of American manhood" as seen particularly by friendly European observers. *The Deerslayer* (New York, 1927), Introduction, pp. xxix-xxxi.

109. *The Deerslayer* (1861 ed.), Preface, p. ix.

110. "You have the advantage over me," he once remarked to a friend, "for I never was among the Indians." J. G. Wilson, *Bryant and His Friends*, New York, 1886, p. 337.

111. Paine, *loc. cit.*, p. xxv.
112. Quoted in Gregory L. Paine, "The Indians of the Leatherstocking Tales," *Studies in Philology* (January, 1926), XXIII, 28. This article contains a full account of the whole matter.
113. Quoted in Keiser, *The Indian in American Literature*, p. 106.
114. Quoted in *ibid.*, p. 142.
115. In the original preface to *The Spy* he had said that Brown's cave scene "contain[ed] an American, a savage, a wild cat, and a tomahawk, in a conjunction that never did, nor ever will occur . . ." Quoted in *American Literature* (November, 1931), III, 334. The passage was omitted from later prefaces: doubtless Cooper perceived that some of the "conjunctions" in his own novels would not bear similar examination.
116. *The Deerslayer* (New York, 1927), Introduction, p. xxvii.
117. See below, p. 254.
118. Cf. *Studies in Philology*, XXIII, 34 ff.
119. *The Deerslayer* (New York, 1927), Introduction, p. xxvii.
120. Keiser, *op. cit.*, p. 101.
121. *The Deerslayer* (1861 ed.), Preface, p. x.
122. Cf. below, p. 412.
123. Boynton, p. 333.
124. *The Literati*, pp. 389-400.
125. It is true that the glorification of New York is not achieved without some satire at the expense of New England (now increasingly the object of Cooper's ill-humor), but the extent to which partisanship vitiates *Wyandotté* has been over-emphasized by Lounsbury (pp. 244-46).
126. *Wyandotté* (New York, 1859), pp. 9-10. There were in the novels many other disparaging comments on America. Lounsbury (pp. 164, 249, 254) notes, for example, Cooper's offensively repetitious praise of the Bay of Naples as contrasted with New York Harbor. Sometimes the attack became picayune indeed, as when in *Satanstoe* (1845) Cooper pauses in a footnote to observe that Broadway is "certainly not more than a third-class street, as streets go in the old world." *Satanstoe* (New York, 1937), p. 89.
127. *The Pathfinder* (New York, 1860), p. 3.
128. Boynton, p. 338. Royalties therefore fell off, so that even when his books were selling, Cooper received only trifling returns or none. The situation on one occasion led him to observe in a letter to his wife: "I am afraid all booksellers are rascals." *Correspondence*, II, 522.
129. Letter to J. K. Paulding, quoted in *Satanstoe* (New York, 1937), opposite p. 62.
130. Quoted in Boynton, pp. 333-34.
131. The second of the series is now most commonly designated as *Miles Wallingford* in American editions, in England as *Lucy Hardinge*. Lounsbury, p. 249.
132. Cf. Lounsbury, pp. 250-51.
133. In 1846 also appeared the two-volume *Lives of Distinguished American Naval Officers*.
134. Spiller, *Fenimore Cooper*, p. 317.
135. Parrington, *Main Currents*, II, 235.
136. *The Redskins* (New York, 1860), Preface, p. xvi.
137. *Ibid.*, p. 461. Quoted in Parrington, II, 231.
138. *The Redskins*, Preface, p. xvi. Cooper does not here use the word "patriarchal," but he is evidently swayed by Biblical authority for a patriarchal government.
139. *The Chainbearer* (New York, 1860), Preface, pp. viii-ix.
140. *Satanstoe*, Preface, p. 3.
141. On account of its emphasis upon local tradition and geography, *Satanstoe*

may well be grouped with the works of several historical novelists who in the thirties and forties began to modify the earlier "Scott-Cooper pattern" of the historical romance by giving it a greater content of regionalism. Cf. E. E. Leisy (ed.), *Horseshoe Robinson* (New York, 1937), Introduction, p. xviii. Another book in the same tradition is Paulding's *The Dutchman's Fireside*. See below, p. 191-92.

142. *Correspondence*, II, 574.

143. *Jack Tier* was first published as a serial in *Graham's Magazine* (November 1846-March 1848) under the title *The Islets of the Gulf*. Spiller and Blackburn, *op. cit.*, p. 148.

144. The religious theme of *The Sea Lions* was not perfunctorily introduced, however, for Cooper gave a good deal of thought to religion in his last days. In 1851 he became a communicant in the Episcopal Church, a move he had long contemplated. Lounsbury, p. 266.

145. Lounsbury, p. 260. There are allusions to whaling, an interesting fictional element to be used in *Moby-Dick* the next year.

146. The abuses of trial by jury were to receive attention a little later at the hands of another distinguished democrat, Herman Melville—in *Mardi*. See below p. 404.

147. Chapter XXVII.

148. Until recently, *Upside Down* has been known by title only. Part of the play has been published, however, and its general bearing as a protest against Fourierism and other newfangled ideas is discussed in John Kouwenhoven, "Cooper's 'Upside Down' Turned Up," *The Colophon*, n.s., III, 524-30.

149. In a candid but private letter to J. K. Paulding in 1846 Cooper wrote bitterly: "If I were fifteen years younger, I would certainly go abroad, and never return . . . You and I have committed the same error; have been Americans—whereas our cue was to be European, which would have given us success at home." Facsimile reproduced in *Satanstoe* (New York, 1937, opposite p. 62). Yet this remark is of the sort which obviously is an overstatement intended to elicit protest and reassurance from the person addressed.

150. *Ways of the Hour* (New York, 1861), Preface, p. vii.

151. Waples, *op. cit.*, p. 41.

152. Cf. Cooper's remark to S. M. Shaw that it "takes a first-class aristocrat to make a first-class Democrat." Quoted in Waples, p. 50.

153. Waples, p. 60.

154. *The American Democrat* (New York, 1838), p. 97. Quoted in *Satanstoe* (New York, 1937), Introduction, p. xvi. Cf. also John Effingham's remark in *Home As Found* (p. 242): "Of all tyranny, a vulgar tyranny is to me the most odious."

155. The point affords as good an example of apparent inconsistency as any in Cooper. For, ceaselessly as he castigated his fellow countrymen for their servile truckling to foreign political opinion, he also laid equal emphasis upon corruption at home. His conclusion seems to have been that domestic perils were finally the greater: "There is now no enemy to fear," he wrote in the preface to the 1849 edition of *The Spy*, "but the one that resides within."

156. Cooper was keenly aware of such a danger: "The great practical defect of institutions like ours, is the circumstance that 'what is everybody's business, is nobody's business;' a neglect that gives to the activity of the rogue a very dangerous ascendancy over the more dilatory corrections of the honest man." Preface to *Satanstoe*, p. 4.

157. Waples, p. 49.

158. *Ibid.*, p. 61. The whole question of Cooper's political allegiance is an extremely involved one, made so by conflicting assertions of Cooper, his friends, and the press. Cooper himself frequently disavowed party affiliation, referring to himself in 1834, for example, as "a man who is perfectly free from all party connec-

tions, party feelings, or party designs." Quoted in Waples, p. 148. Miss Waples' book contains the most detailed discussion of the whole matter. In her zeal Miss Waples perhaps overstates matters by insisting that Cooper was evidently "a staunchly reliable party man" (p. 5), but she well indicates why Cooper should have found so much that was attractive in Jackson. For despite the atmosphere of utter equalitarianism now associated with his name, Jackson stood for a strong central (benevolent) government, and personally he preferred, as his "Hermitage" suggests, a life not unlike that of the country gentleman so dear to Cooper's heart.

159. *Notions of the Americans*, II, 131-32.

160. Preface to *Satanstoe*, p. 3.

161. Preface to the 1823 edition of *The Pilot*, quoted in William Charvat, *The Origins of American Critical Thought*, Philadelphia, 1936, p. 144.

162. *Afloat and Ashore*, Preface, p. vi.

163. Preface, p. vii. In this preface also Cooper insisted that patriotism is ill served by any suppression of the truth: "Although the American revolution was probably as just an effort as was ever made by a people to resist the first inroads of oppression, the cause had its evil aspects, as well as all other human struggles. We have been so much accustomed to hear everything extolled, of late years, that could be dragged into the remotest connexion with that great event, and the principles which led to it, that there is danger of overlooking truth, in a pseudo-patriotism. Nothing is really patriotic, however, that is not strictly true and just; any more than it is paternal love to undermine the constitution of a child by an indiscriminate indulgence in pernicious diet. That there were demagogues in 1776, is as certain as that there are demagogues now, and will probably continue to be demagogues as long as means for misleading the common mind shall exist." *Ibid.*, pp. v, vi. Similarly in connection with the Anti-Rent series, he avowed that "true patriotism consists in laying bare every thing like public vice." *Satanstoe*, Preface, p. 4.

164. P. viii.

165. See above, p. 147.

166. "Lockhart's Life of Scott," *The Knickerbocker, or New-York Magazine* (October, 1838), XII, 364. Both these qualities he ascribed to Scott.

167. *Satanstoe*, Preface, p. 3.

168. *The Pilot*, p. 105.

169. "Home As Found. Lost Chapter," *Brother Jonathan* (January 1, 1842), I, 17.

170. *Correspondence*, II, 493.

171. Bryant aptly characterized Cooper's stories in this respect: "The progress of the plot, at first, is like that of one of his own vessels of war, slowly, heavily, and even awkwardly working out of a harbour. We are impatient and weary, but when the vessel is once in the open sea, and feels the free breath of heaven in her full sheets, our delight and admiration are all the greater at the grace, the majesty and power with which she divides and bears down the waves, and pursues her course, at will, over the great waste of waters." McDowell (ed.), *William Cullen Bryant*, p. 283.

172. Among the most skilful and entertaining parodies is Bret Harte's "Muck-a-Muck" (in *Condensed Novels*).

173. Quoted in Brownell, *American Prose Masters* (New York, 1923), p. 20.

174. Said of Scott's characters by James Hilton, *New York Times*, May 1, 1938.

175. Quoted in Brownell, *op. cit.*, p. 28.

176. Preface to 1849 edition, p. x.

177. Lawrence, *op. cit.*, p. 88.

178. Lewisohn, *op. cit.*, p. 56.

CHAPTER V

1. Neal never was sure what strain predominated, but he inclined to regard himself as Scotch.

2. "P's Correspondence," *Mosses from an Old Manse* (Boston, 1864), II, 159.

3. John Neal, *Wandering Recollections of a Somewhat Busy Life: An Autobiography*, Boston, 1869, pp. 193-95.

4. *Ibid.*, p. 221.

5. His first book of verse, *The Battle of Niagara*, appeared in 1818.

6. Neal, however, "opposed the extreme abolitionist views of William Lloyd Garrison" just as he also disapproved "the extreme prohibitionism of his distant cousin Neal Dow." Irving T. Richards, "The Life and Works of John Neal," *Summaries of Harvard Theses 1933*, Cambridge, 1934, p. 297.

7. *Logan*, Philadelphia, 1822, I, 242.

8. *Ibid.*, I, 216.

9. *Ibid.*, I, 291-94.

10. *Wandering Recollections*, p. 224.

11. "I had got charged to the muzzle with the doings of our Revolutionary fathers, while writing my portion of 'Allen's History,' and wanted only the hint, or touch, that Cooper gave in passing, to go off like a Leyden jar, and empty myself at once of all the hoarded enthusiasm I had been bottling up, for three or four years." *Wandering Recollections*, p. 224.

12. *Seventy-Six* seems to have had its extremely loyal devotees. Of one lady reader, it was said—in phrasing slightly ambiguous—that she "died with 'Seventy-Six' in her hand." *Ibid.*, p. 228.

13. *Ibid.*, p. 229.

14. *The United States Literary Gazette* (April 1, 1824) I, 6.

15. *Ibid.*

16. *Wandering Recollections*, p. 238.

17. See Cairns, *British Criticisms of American Writings 1815-1833*, pp. 208-10.

18. *Wandering Recollections*, p. 239.

19. *The New York Mirror* (September 28, 1833), XI, 101, quoted in *American Writers, A Series of Papers Contributed to Blackwood's Magazine (1824-1825) by John Neal*, ed. by F. L. Pattee, Durham (N. C.), 1937, Introduction, p. 15.

20. The articles Neal wrote for *Blackwood's* have been collected and reprinted by F. L. Pattee. See note above. Neal seems to have written for a number of other periodicals as well (see Pattee's Introduction, p. 19, n. 18), but he addressed himself chiefly to *Blackwood's* as "the cleverest, the sauciest, and the most unprincipled of all our calumniators." *Wandering Recollections*, p. 245.

21. *Wandering Recollections*, p. 246.

22. Indeed the entire subject of Neal as a New England writer still awaits detailed treatment. In his *Flowering of New England* Van Wyck Brooks refers to Neal's novels as valueless. Actually there is in them a great deal of native material which would have been germane to Mr. Brooks' study.

23. *Brother Jonathan*, Edinburgh, 1824, I, 17.

24. *Ibid.*, I, 52, 53 ff.

25. *Ibid.*, II, 166-70.

26. *British Critic* (April, 1826) II, 53, quoted in Cairns, p. 212.

27. *Ibid.*, II, 406. Quoted in Cairns, p. 213.

28. In 1829 he was accorded these plain terms of contempt: "Your ravings are the dreams of a sick monkey—and your ideas hang as awkwardly together as so many bits of old rope spliced by a land lubber. Look at your novels. Why, you can't, to save your ears, sell them for four-pence the bushel. After having been a 'poor Devil Author' so long as to be starved first out of America into G. Britain, and back again into America, it hardly looks well in you to put on airs, and swagger as is your wont. Be modest, John, be modest—you never *did* support yourself by your pen, and you never *will* . . ." Quoted in *The Ariel, A Semimonthly Literary and Miscellaneous Gazette* (July, 1829) III, 44.

29. A. H. Quinn, *Edgar Allan Poe, a Critical Biography*, New York, 1941, p. 154. The favorable notice appeared in *The Yankee* in September, 1829.

30. *Rachel Dyer: A North American Story*, Portland, 1828, Preface, p. iv.

31. *Ibid.*, p. 22.

32. Although for the most part calm in his treatment of the Massachusetts elders, Neal allows himself to draw a rather satiric portrait of Governor Phipps, who is represented as unduly covetous of power and rank. Indeed Neal enlarges his satire at one point to include all New England—a place, he says, "where birth is now, and ever will be a matter of inquiry and solicitude, of shame perhaps to the few and of pride to the few, but of inquiry with all, in spite of our ostentatious republicanism." *Rachel Dyer*, p. 45.

33. In an appendix Neal supplies certain "Historical Facts" which he used or altered for purposes of his story.

34. *Rachel Dyer*, p. 148. Rachel's lack of physical charm makes it the harder for her to secure a fair trial, for (she says) although there might be "some hope on earth for a beautiful witch . . . . with golden hair . . . . with large blue eyes . . . . and a sweet mouth," there can be no real hope for "a freckled witch . . . . with red hair and a hump on her back." *Ibid.*, p. 262.

35. Oddly enough, *Rachel Dyer* turns up in the conversation of two characters in a novel published in 1861—G. W. Curtis's *Trumps*.

36. Poe, who recognized Neal's limitations, was nevertheless "inclined to rank John Neal first, or at all events second, among our men of indisputable *genius*." *Marginalia*. As late as 1843 Poe was hoping to secure the aid of Neal for his projected *Penn Magazine*. Quinn, *Edgar Allan Poe*, p. 366.

37. For his satirical comments on New York, see *Brother Jonathan*, II, 336 ff.

38. *Rachel Dyer*, Portland, 1828, Unpublished Preface to the North-American Stories, p. xv.

39. *American Writers*, ed. by Pattee, pp. 236-37.

40. *Mosses*, II, 159.

41. See *Dictionary of American Biography*, IV, 67-69, for a sketch of her life.

42. Quoted in Keiser, *The Indian in American Literature*, pp. 43, 44.

43. These items are pointed out by Quinn, p. 155. In addition it should be noted that in "The Theologian's Tale" Longfellow avowedly used Mrs. Child's *Hobomok* as a source. In the "Interlude" which follows his tale he pays tribute to the "skilful hand" that wrote *Hobomok*. *Longfellow's Complete Poetical Works* (Cambridge ed.), p. 275.

44. See below, p. 204.

45. *Hobomok*, [Boston, 1824], p. 26.

46. *Ibid.*, p. 74.

47. *Ibid.*, 97-98. Probably it was this sort of passage which led a reviewer to give the author the gentle criticism that her style could be "improved by careful cultivation." *The United States Literary Gazette* (June, 1824), I, 71.

48. *Hobomok*, p. 23.

49. *Ibid.*, p. 6.

50. *The Rebels*, Boston, 1825, Preface, p. vi.

51. *Ibid.*, p. 22.

52. *The North American Review* (April, 1826), XXII, 401-02. Yet this high-flown rhetoric long took rank as literary art, as T. W. Higginson had reason to note. *The Rebels*, he said, "contained an imaginary sermon by Whitefield and an imaginary speech by James Otis. Both of these were soon transplanted into 'School Readers' and books of declamation, and the latter, at least, soon passed for a piece of genuine revolutionary eloquence. I remember learning it by heart . . ." *Contemporaries*, Boston, 1899, p. 115.

53. Mrs. Child had a high opinion of Miss Sedgwick, whom she referred to as "our own admirable and excellent Catherine Sedgwick" and whom she compared with Maria Edgeworth, Mary Howitt, and Fredrika Bremer, as examples of women who though "placed in the genteel ranks of society by birth" have done such useful work as writers that they "are universally regarded with increased respect." *Letters From New York* (Second Series), New York, 1845, p. 283.

54. There were two series (1843, 1845) of *Letters From New York*. Lyle Wright notes (*American Fiction*, pp. 39, 40) ten editions of the former, eleven of the latter, all before 1850.

55. The early twenties had been so unproductive that in 1825 one observer reguarded ten American novels as "a striking output for one year." Van Doren, *op. cit.*, p. 44.

56. Novels with a Greek background were extremely rare in the early and mid-nineteenth century. There was, however, something of a vogue for stories of Hebrew history, the early Christians, and the Romans. See, for example, William Ware's *Probus; or, Rome in the Third Century* (1838); Eliza Buckminster Lee's *Parthenia: or, The Last Days of Paganism* (1857); and Joseph Holt Ingraham's *The Pillar of Fire* (1859) and *The Throne of David* (1860). *Parthenia* includes scenes set in Athens.

57. Cf. Quinn, pp. 105-06.

58. *The Literati*, p. 99. See also Duyckinck, II, 388, for favorable comment.

59. T. W. Higginson, *op. cit.*, p. 137.

60. See below, p. 506.

61. *Letters From New York* (Second Series), pp. 279-80.

62. *Ibid.*, pp. 280-81.

63. *Letters From New York* (First Series), New York, 1843, pp. 193-94. Compare Cooper's similar strictures, above, pp. 141, 155-56.

64. *Ibid.*, p. 192.

65. *Ibid.*, p. 177.

66. See below, Chapter X, *passim*.

67. *A Fable For Critics*.

68. *The Literati*, p. 574.

69. Paulding is now known best for one or two novels, but he was also an indefatigable writer of short-stories, the best of which, *The Merry Tales of the Three Wise Men of Gotham* (1826) and *Tales of the Good Woman* (1829), possess a value quite independent of the fact that they were published before either Poe or Hawthorne had won distinction in the field.

70. Amos L. Herold, *James Kirke Paulding, Versatile American*, New York, 1926, p. 137.

71. *Ibid.*, p. 97.

72. See below, p. 188.

73. In *Koningsmarke*, Paulding pauses to pay his devoirs to "the popular author of the PIONEERS" but begs to be excused from the charge of imitating Cooper's description of the seasons, for "we only copy from the same original." *Koningsmarke* (New York, 1836), I, 124-25. Cooper had already complimented Paulding by using four lines from *The Backwoodsman* on the title page of *The Pioneers*.

74. See especially a passage in praise of Penn: *Koningsmarke*, II, 51, 52.

75. *Koningsmarke*, I, 119.

76. *Ibid.*, II, 135.

77. *Ibid.*, II, 107-08.

78. *Ibid.*, I, 32.

79. *Ibid.*, I, 97.

80. *Ibid.*, I, 178.

81. *Ibid.*, I, 73.

82. *Ibid.*, II, 128.

83. *The New York Mirror* reviewed the book favorably in November, 1823, as being possibly the production of another "great unknown." Quoted in Herold, p. 97.

84. *The New England Magazine* (July, 1831), I, 88.

85. Cairns, *British Criticisms of American Writings 1815-1833*, pp. 206-07.

86. *The New England Magazine* (Nov. 1832), III, 424.

87. See below, p. 258.

88. The place is probably Hadley, Massachusetts. A. L. Herold (*James Kirke Paulding*, p. 109) tentatively but erroneously refers the setting of the last part of the story to the Mississippi Valley. Cf. Frank Davidson, "Paulding's Treatment of the Angel of Hadley," *American Literature* (Nov. 1935), VII, 330-32.

89. *Koningsmarke*, II, 160.

90. *The New England Magazine* (July, 1831), I, 88.

91. For Paulding's carefully worked-out if not deeply felt arguments in partial support of slavery, see his *Slavery in the United States* (New York, 1836), a work which Mrs. Stowe found it convenient to cite in her *Key to Uncle Tom's Cabin* (Chapter III) as a sign of her open-mindedness.

92. Observing the contented air of banjo-playing Negro slaves at Richmond, Paulding was led to wonder whether as a class they suffered so much as had been asserted: "How would it mortify the pride of the white man, and humble his lordly sense of superiority, if it were indeed found, that these poor fellows were happier than those who affect to pity their miseries." *Letters from the South*, New York, 1835, I, 97. Certainly they were far better off than the dispossessed Indians. The slaves in *Koningsmarke* are represented on one occasion as gaily participating in a "Pinckster" frolic, but the Indians are always, in Christina's phrase, "the sad people." *Koningsmarke*, I, 157, 172.

93. *Letters from the South*, II, 79.

94. *Koningsmarke*, II, 75.

95. *Salmagundi*, Second Series, New York, 1835, II, 267.

96. *Ibid.*, II, 266.

97. *Letters from the South*, I, 195-96.

98. *Koningsmarke*, I, 147-48, II, 62-64.

99. *Ibid.*, I, 50.

100. Quoted in Herold, *op. cit.*, p. 111.

101. *Ibid.*, p. 143.

102. Henry Ward Beecher, *Norwood*, New York, 1868, end papers.

103. In 1832 (eight years after Miss Sedgwick's first successful novel) Mrs. Trollope wrote that the Americans "are great novel readers, but the market is chiefly furnished by England." *Domestic Manners* (New York, 1927), p. 270.

104. Poe, *The Literati*, p. 109.

105. *Life and Letters of Catharine M. Sedgwick*, ed. by Mary Dewey, New York, 1871, p. 14.

106. *Life and Letters*, p. 49.

107. *Ibid.*, p. 153.

108. *Ibid.*, p. 153.

109. "Reminiscences of Miss Sedgwick," in *Life and Letters*, p. 439.

110. *Redwood: A Tale* (New York, 1850), Preface to the First Edition, pp. [vii]-ix.

111. *Ibid.*, p. ix.

112. *Life and Letters*, p. 168.

113. *Ibid.*, pp. 169, 170.

114. This controversy moved Miss Sedgwick to the quip that she hoped Mr. Cooper's "self-complacency will not be wounded by this mortifying news." *Ibid.*, p. 172.

115. *Redwood*, New York, 1824, Preface, p. x, and I, 129.

116. After *Redwood* she wrote *The Travelers,* the first of a number of juvenile stories which won great popularity.

117. *Hope Leslie: or, Early Times in the Massachusetts* (New York, 1872), I, 80.

118. Cf. G. H. Orians, "The Cult of the Vanishing American," *Bulletin of the University of Toledo,* November, 1935, pp. 10-11.

119. *Hope Leslie,* I, 118.

119a. *Domestic Manners,* p. 147.

120. *Life and Letters,* p. 187. The author's allusion to her "oppressed state" may be a reference to the pressure her brother Robert exerted to prevent her from marrying—so that she might continue to exercise her literary talents, which, he assured her, were a "national blessing." *Ibid.*, p. 189.

121. See, for example, *Hope Leslie,* I, 105-06.

122. *Life and Letters,* pp. 192-93.

123. *The Literati,* p. 106.

124. An edition appeared as late as 1872.

125. *Hope Leslie,* I, 210. Cf. Miss Sedgwick's later tribute to Cooper's great superiority to all other novelists in handling the sea. *The Linwoods; or, "Sixty Years Since" in America* (New York, 1835), II, 248.

126. *Life and Letters,* p. 205.

127. *Clarence; or, A Tale of Our Own Times,* Philadelphia, 1830, p. 147.

128. *Clarence,* I, 51.

129. *Ibid.*, II, 155.

130. *Ibid.*, II, 147.

131. *Life and Letters,* p. 205.

132. *Ibid.*

133. Bryant, "Reminiscences," p. 443.

134. When the author does essay an account of military operations, she interlards it with plenty of personal comment. See, for example, *The Linwoods,* I, 164 ff.

135. *The Linwoods,* II, 284.

136. *Ibid.*, II, 209.

137. *Life and Letters,* pp. 30 ff.

138. *The Literati,* p. 106.

139. In this respect Miss Sedgwick was especially qualified to write with verisimilitude for she had witnessed mental breakdowns both in her mother and in one of her brothers. *Life and Letters,* pp. 28, 185.

140. Poe called attention to a fault that Miss Sedgwick shared with Cooper, namely, letting the same character speak on one occasion in the most meticulously phrased expression and on other occasions in an extremely colloquial idiom. *The Literati,* p. 107. In this respect, however, Miss Sedgwick erred less than Cooper.

141. In commenting on the early education of the Sedgwick children, she remarked that their "minds were not weakened by too much study," *Life and Letters,* p. 44.

142. *Live and Let Live,* New York, 1837, Preface, p. [v].

143. *Ibid.*

144. Cf. a similar plea for a more liberal course for women in *The Linwoods,* II, 260.

145. *Life and Letters,* p. 271.

146. See below, Chapter X, *passim*.

147. *Life and Letters*, pp. 312-22.

148. Miss Bremer appears to have regarded her chiefly as a social historian and critic in 1849 (*America in the Fifties*, New York, 1924, pp. 17-18), but she recalled the pleasure she had received from *Redwood* and *Hope Leslie*. *Ibid.*, p. 10.

149. *The Linwoods*, II, 170.

150. *Life and Letters*, pp. 249-50.

151. *Ibid.*, pp. 345, 97.

152. *Ibid.*, pp. 328-29.

153. *Ibid.*, pp. 382, 394.

154. See for example her praise of *Villette* in *Life and Letters*, p. 349.

155. *The United States Literary Gazette* (July 15, 1824), I, 101.

156. Rufus W. Griswold, *The Prose Writers of America*, Philadelphia, 1847, p. 30.

157. Griswold, *loc. cit.*

158. Daniel Drake, *Discourse on the History, Character, and Prospects of the West*, 1834, p. 55, quoted in Ralph L. Rusk, *The Literature of the Middle Western Frontier*, New York, 1925, I, 272.

159. *Ibid.*, I, 273.

160. "The few self-conscious writers of the frontier, striving ineffectively for a certain artistic achievement, had their eyes fixed on an ideal rather than a reality . . . The few who acquired a style of any charm were usually those who were . . . incapable of picturing the real West." *Ibid.*, I, 77, 78.

161. *Ibid.*, I, 282. The problem of veracity was one which would harass Western writers for a long time to come. Even Hamlin Garland's realistic studies of Middle Western farm life in *Main-Travelled Roads* (1891) drew forth the angry criticism that the author was "a bird willing to foul his own nest." *A Son of the Middle Border* (New York, 1927), p. 415.

162. Harriet Beecher Stowe, who contributed sketches to Ohio periodicals during her early residence in Cincinnati, can hardly be considered a member of the group.

163. J. E. Kirkpatrick, *Timothy Flint, Pioneer, Missionary, Author, Editor*, Cleveland, 1911, pp. 42-44. This fully documented work is the only extended biography of Flint. Autobiography is to be found in Flint's *Recollections of the Last Ten Years* and in the author's "most autobiographic" story, *George Mason*. Cf. Kirkpatrick, *op. cit.*, p. 44.

164. *Ibid.*, Chapter XIV *et passim*.

165. *Recollections of the Last Ten Years . . . in the Valley of the Mississippi*, Boston, 1826, p. 38. Since the time when Flint had first visited it (1815-16) it had about doubled its population.

166. Quoted in Kirkpatrick, pp. 186-87. The title was at first *The Western Magazine and Review*. Rusk, I, 168.

167. Kirkpatrick, p. 187.

168. Rusk, I, 170.

169. *Francis Berrian*, Boston, 1826, I, 16.

170. *Ibid.*, I, 118.

171. *Ibid.*, II, 279-80.

172. *Ibid.*, I, 68.

173. *Ibid.*, I, 104. It wasn't necessary, of course, to go so far as New Spain to hear reflections on Yankee character. Indeed Flint himself noted in his *Recollections* (p. 32) the belief of Ohioans that the Yankees were unscrupulous purveyors of "wooden nutmegs, and pit-coal indigo, and gin made by putting pinetops in the whiskey."

174. *Ibid.*, I, 88.

175. *Ibid.*, I, 131.

176. It had already been noted that Cooper's Uncas provided an "interesting" parallel to "the sentimental hero of M. Chateaubriand's Atala." Quoted in Waples, *The Whig Myth of James Fenimore Cooper*, p. 64. Yet Cooper was too dynamic to be an imitator *par excellence* of Chateaubriand.

177. *Francis Berrian*, I, 133-34.

178. *The Life and Adventures of Arthur Clenning*, New York, 1828, I, 210.

179. *Ibid.*, II, 143.

180. *Ibid.*, II, 156.

181. *Ibid.*, II, 79.

182. It seems to have made only a moderate stir upon its publication. *The New York Mirror* (vol. VI, p. 33, August 9, 1828) noted that it was "written with spirit," but made no great claims for it. James Hall, however, preferred it to *Francis Berrian*. Rusk, *op. cit.*, I, 293. More recently its "imaginative art" elicited praise from Henry A. Beers. Quoted in Kirkpatrick, *op. cit.*, p. 253.

183. Flint's biographer called *George Mason* the author's "most autobiographic" story. Kirkpatrick, p. 44.

183a. Quoted in Kirkpatrick, pp. 44-45.

184. For comment on its probable contents, see Rusk, I, 290-91. Recently the Yale University Library has found record of a copy which may be available for examination in the near future.

185. For full statistics of the morbidity of this story, see Rusk, I, 291-92.

186. *Ibid.*, I, 293.

187. See Kirkpatrick, Chap. XVI, *passim.*

188. *Ibid.*, p. 257.

189. Quoted in *ibid.*, p. 261.

190. B. M. Fullerton, *Selective Bibliography of American Literature 1775-1900*, New York, 1932, p. 103.

191. *Domestic Manners of the Americans*, New York, 1927, pp. 73-4, 147, 270.

192. Quoted in Rusk, I, 294. Oddly enough, however, Flint is accorded a very respectable notice, with several selections from his books, in Griswold's anthology, *Prose Writers of America* (1847).

193. In the advertisement to *Arthur Clenning* (p. 6), Flint testily imagines the type of comment made on his works: "He has been an exact and humble copyist of Sir Walter Scott, though he is just a thousand leagues behind him . . . He is nine hundred miles behind Mr. Cooper, dear man."

194. The comment is quoted in Kirkpatrick, p. 254.

195. *Arthur Clenning*, II, 148. Quoted in Kirkpatrick, p. 250.

196. Quoted in Rusk, I, 206.

197. Quoted in Rusk, I, 207.

198. Quoted in Kirkpatrick, p. 253.

199. Cf. above, p. 216.

200. *Dictionary of American Biography*, VIII, pp. 134-35.

201. Quoted in Rusk, I, 279. This book is the source for much of the present discussion of Hall.

202. Cf. above, p. 213.

203. Quoted in Rusk, I, 277. For a more realistic camp-meeting description written in the same period, see Mrs. Trollope's *Domestic Manners of the Americans*, pp. 138 ff.

204. Quoted in Rusk, I, 277.

205. *Ibid.*, I, 278.

206. *The Harpe's Head* (Philadelphia, 1833), pp. vii-viii, quoted in Rusk, I, 295-96.

207. *The Hesperian* (November, 1839), III, 463, quoted in Rusk, I, 282.

208. Quoted in *ibid.*, I, 282.

209. John T. Flanagan, *James Hall, Literary Pioneer of the Ohio Valley*, Minne-

apolis, 1941, p. 90. This work presents a comprehensive view of Hall as traveler, lawyer, journalist, banker, story-teller, critic, and poet. See also *America is West* (ed. by John T. Flanagan), Minneapolis, 1945, pp. 138-50.

210. The book appeared over the pseudonym "Mrs. Mary Clavers."

211. *A New Home—Who'll Follow?* (New York, 1850), p. 3.

212. The authors who were read by these settlers in farthest Michigan were by no means Western: Ainsworth, G. P. R. James, Bulwer, Cooper, Sedgwick, Willis. *A New Home*, pp. 163, 232.

213. *A New Home*, p. 11. Mrs. Kirkland here refers to Captain Basil Hall.

214. Quoted in Rusk, I, 285.

215. *A New Home*, chapter XX.

216. *Ibid.*, p. 290.

217. *Ibid.*, p. 291.

218. Rusk, II, 18.

219. *Ibid.*, I, 300. Thomas's novels are discussed by Rusk in some detail. The most popular was *Clinton Bradshaw* (1835), a novel emphasizing the adventures of a young law student in a wicked (Eastern) city. The setting of *East and West* (1836) lives up to its title, the second part ranging through Kentucky and the lower Mississippi region, and including a steamboat race on the Ohio. Thomas's *Howard Pinckney* (1840) is centred in a love affair, the setting for which is indefinite.

220. See below, pp. 422-23, for a brief discussion of Mrs. Hentz.

221. The term "West" must be broadly interpreted in this period. Mrs. Kirkland herself puts the question—"how much does that expression mean to include? I have never been able to discover its limits." *A New Home*, p. 11 (1850 ed.). At times the "West" seems to mean as little as the principal settlements in what is now Ohio, at other times everything between the Alleghenies and the Rocky Mountains. There was no settled point of view among such a mobile population as flowed over the Alleghenies before 1850.

CHAPTER VI

1. From a memorandum of Simms printed in William P. Trent, *William Gilmore Simms*, Boston, 1892, p. 5.

2. *Ibid.*, p. 73.

3. It pleased his fancy to believe that an old grave on which his father stumbled was that of De Soto. Trent, *op. cit.*, p. 15.

4. Simms wrote verse so prolifically that by 1860 he had produced eighteen volumes. Although he was but a mediocre poet, he persisted in believing that his poetry was more valuable than his prose. For a discussion of his poetry, see Edd W. Parks, *Southern Poets*, New York, 1936, pp. xci-xciii.

5. Trent, pp. 220-22.

6. During the War Simms's house was partly burned (apparently by accident) and it was later completely destroyed by an incendiary fire which entirely consumed his library of about ten thousand volumes.

7. Simms's analysis of the causes of crime in this book suggests that he was inspired partly by Godwin's *Caleb Williams*. He was also charged, unjustly, it appears, of plagiarizing a more recent book, F. M. Reynolds' *Miserrimus*. Trent, pp. 77-80.

8. *Guy Rivers: A Tale of Georgia* (New York, 1855), Dedicatory Epistle, p. 10. References to Simms's novels (unless otherwise stated) are to the most nearly complete edition of his novels, an edition consisting of twenty-two volumes published from time to time between 1853 and 1866 by J. S. Redfield and his successor W. J. Widdleton.

9. Robin Hood is in fact mentioned in the story (p. 29). It is possible that Simms had read a review of Cooper's *Red Rover* in which complaint was made of the fact that in America we had "no bands of merry archers whose very thievery is full of romantic adventure . . . no Robin Hoods . . ." See *American Literature* (January, 1932), III, 423-24. At all events, his forest outlaws in this book occasionally suggest those of Robin Hood. In *The Yemassee* also Robin Hood is at least vaguely recalled by the jolly Craven's attitude toward his forest henchmen.

10. The story was a timely one, for gold-mining had begun in Georgia in 1829.

11. Many of the elements later used in fiction dealing with the Western frontier are apparent in *Guy Rivers*. H. M. Jarrell goes so far as to say that "most of the elements of western fiction of today existed as far east as Georgia a hundred years ago." "William Gilmore Simms, Realistic Romancer" (manuscript), p. 135.

12. Its reception was exceedingly enthusiastic not only in the South but also in New York, where most of Simms's books were published, and in London, where *Guy Rivers* was printed in the next year. Trent, p. 83.

13. *Ibid.,* p. 89. Although the first edition (of 2500 copies) was twice as large as that of comparable foreign novels published in America, a second edition was called for within three weeks. On August 17 (1835) the story was dramatized at the Bowery Theatre in New York. By the end of a year the book had reached its third American edition and its first English edition. Further signs of its popularity were a second English edition in 1844 and a German translation in 1847. In 1853 Simms revised it for the Redfield edition, which, like each of its companion volumes, had two illustrations by F. O. C. Darley.

14. *The Yemassee,* ed. by Alexander Cowie (New York, 1937), p. 16.

15. *Ibid.,* p. 87.

16. Albert Keiser believes that Simms gives the "most balanced" view of the Indian in American romance. *The Indian in Literature* (New York, 1933), p. 296.

17. See *The Yemassee,* Prefatory Letter, p. 4. For a detailed commentary on Indian gifts and a sympathetic analysis of their plight, see Simms's "Literature and Art Among the Aborigines." *Views and Reviews,* New York, 1845, I, 102-17.

18. In Trent's classification of Simms's stories there are only six Revolutionary tales. He omits *The Scout* as being more akin to the border romances. (See *op. cit.,* pp. 121-22, 201.) In the advertisement to the revised edition of Simms's works, however, it is listed as the fourth of the "Revolutionary Tales." *Beauchampe* (1856 edition), end pages. See also *American Literature* (May, 1931), III, 204.

19. In those respects in which Porgy differs from his prototype he is apparently a combination of Simms in self-portrait and of Simms's ideal of a South Carolinian gentleman. See Trent, *op. cit.,* p. 109; American Literature (May, 1931), III, [204]-212.

20. As units in the Revolutionary series they belong after *Katharine Walton; Woodcraft,* which was published earlier, belongs last. H. M. Jarrell omits *Woodcraft* from the list of Revolutionary romances, but it is generally included because of its treatment of the conditions in South Carolina between the time of the close of the War and the treaty of peace.

21. In *The Partisan* (Chapter XLII), for example, he gives in detail General Gates's orders to the army at Camden. Other signs of Simms's interest in military minutiae may be seen in *The Life of Francis Marion* (New York, 1845) and *The Life of Nathanael Greene* (New York, 1849), the latter of which is so packed with technical discussion as to be all but unreadable to the layman. Simms was an able student of tactics, and at the time of the Civil War he anticipated some of the

moves made by the Confederate staff in connection with the relief of Fort Sumter. See Trent, *op. cit.*, pp. 261 n, 267.

22. *The Partisan* (1835), Preface, p. x.

23. Simms also knew personally Virgil A. Stuart, the captor of Murrell, the bandit on whom Foster was modeled. Trent, *op. cit.*, p. 116.

24. For a brief summary of the various literary forms in which this exceedingly popular story appeared see S. Foster Damon, *Thomas Holley Chivers*, New York, 1930, p. 72 n.

25. Simms retained some of the actual names, but "Margaret Cooper" was in reality Anne Cooke.

26. A difficult bibliographical problem has arisen because of the rarity of the first edition of *Beauchampe*, which included all the story outlined above. Subsequently the first part of the story was published separately (with revisions) in a volume entitled *Charlemont* (1846). The second part of the story was also published separately, as *Beauchampe*. Following Trent (pp. 210, 337) bibliographers and historians of the novel (including the present writer) have made the error of implying that the story contained in *Charlemont* was first published in 1856. A. H. Quinn gives the full facts in his *American Fiction*, p. 122 and note.

27. Cf. Quinn, *op. cit.*, p. 123.

28. Trent, pp. 118, 211; Van Doren, *The American Novel*, p. 55.

29. *Confession*, Preface, p. 9.

30. Trent, pp. 206-09.

31. See above, note 3.

32. *The Broadway Journal* (October 4, 1845), II, 190. Characteristically Poe later changed his phrasing and asserted that "Grayling" was "the best ghost-story ever written by an American." *The Literati*, p. 275. The story appeared in the second series of *The Wigwam and the Cabin* (1846). For a brief but thorough study of the canon of Simms's short stories (fifty-nine in all), see J. Allen Morris, "The Stories of William Gilmore Simms," *American Literature* (March, 1942), XIV, 20-35.

33. He deplored the fact that Cooper had "hobbies on which he rode too often." *Views and Reviews*, I, 218.

34. Some of the best of these were printed in Simms's *Views and Reviews*, and others are listed in Trent (*op. cit.*, pp. 339-40), but a complete bibliography is not available. Besides being solicited for articles, Simms wrote constantly for various organs (nine in all) of which he was editor. Some idea of how prolific he was may be gained from the fact that in 1837 he "appeared as a contributor twenty-two times in three magazines." *Ibid.*, p. 114.

35. He was once elected to the state legislature of South Carolina. *Ibid.*, pp. 62-64, 141.

36. *The Southern Quarterly Review* (July, 1850), I, new series, 320, 323.

37. *Ibid.*, p. 316.

38. *Ibid.*, p. 318.

39. In the advertisement to the revised edition of *Mellichampe*, p. 2.

40. In a review of Guizot's "Democracy in France" he referred to the "principle of states' rights" as the "grand conservative feature of the American system." *Southern Quarterly Review* (April, 1849), XXIX, 164.

41. *Views and Reviews*, I, 73, 149, 150.

42. *Guy Rivers*, Dedicatory Epistle, p. 9.

43. *Views and Reviews*, I, 2.

44. *Ibid.*, I, 5.

45. Trent, p. 180.

46. He had always favored reasonable observance of states' rights, but he was slow to endorse nullification (see *ibid.*, pp. 60-63).

47. *Southern Quarterly Review* (September, 1850), II, 199.

48. *Ibid.* (September, 1850), II, 32.
49. *Ibid.* (April, 1850), I, 197.
50. *Ibid.* (September, 1850), II, 199.
51. *Ibid.* (July, 1850), I, 392.
52. *Ibid.* (September, 1850), II, 198.
53. *The Yemassee* (New York, 1937), pp. 391-92.
54. This first appeared in the *Southern Literary Messenger* (November, 1837), III, 641-51, but it was reprinted separately with some additions as *Slavery in America* (Richmond, 1838) and as part of a symposium, *The Pro-Slavery Argument* (Charleston, 1852).
55. *Southern Quarterly Review* (September, 1850), II, 28.
56. *The Pro-Slavery Argument*, p. 217.
57. *Southern Quarterly Review* (September, 1850), II, 28-30.
58. Quoted in Trent, *op. cit.*, p. 173. For more temperate expressions of basically similar views by Southern novelists, see below, pp. 261, 276-78.
59. Trent, p. 249.
60. See, for example, the preface to *Charlemont* (1856), pp. 10-12.
61. Trent, p. 326.
62. *Views and Reviews*, II, 40, 41.
63. In one of his early papers Simms actually speculated on the possible benefits of miscegenation between the Puritans and the Indians: "Properly diluted there was no better blood than that of Cherokee and Natchez. It would have been a good infusion into the paler fountain of Quaker and Puritan . . ." *Views and Reviews*, I, 110-11.
64. *Ibid.*, II, 40.
65. Poe (the kettle) called Simms (the pot) black in his *Marginalia* in which he referred to the latter's "proneness to revolting images." (*The Literati*, p. 510).
66. See *Beauchampe*, pp. 335-37.
67. *Guy Rivers*, p. 284.
68. *Beauchampe*, pp. 342, 343.
69. *The Partisan*, Advertisement, p. xii.
70. See especially *Mellichampe* (1836), Advertisement, pp. xi, xii; *Richard Hurdis* (1888), Advertisement, p. 10.
71. *Views and Reviews*, I, 8.
72. For an exhaustive analysis of the train of evils attributable in part to the lack of an international copyright law, see Simms's vigorous series of papers in the *Southern Literary Messenger* (January-August, 1844), X, 7-17, 137-50, 340-49, 449-69. Other factors that militated against the growth of a national literature were the conquest of the Atlantic by steam navigation, which in effect made America "a suburb of London" (N. P. Willis, *Letters from Under a Bridge*, London, 1840, p. 125); and the reaction against aggressive nationalism led by Lowell and Longfellow (see Benjamin T. Spencer, "A National Literature, 1837-1855," *American Literature* (May, 1936), VIII, 147-56).
73. *The Damsel of Darien*, Preface, p. 9.
74. *Views and Reviews*, I, 227. Obviously this mode of achieving fame would fit no American author (of eminence) so well as Washington Irving. Although Trent remarks that Simms's relations to Irving were "friendly," neither Trent's life of Simms nor Stanley Williams' *Life of Washington Irving* (New York, 1935) affords any sign of intimacy between the men.
75. *Views and Reviews*, I, 36.
76. *Ibid.*, I, 27.
77. *Ibid.*, I, 25.
78. *Ibid.*, I, 42.
79. Simms wrote a considerable number of historical pieces, including an ex-

tended *History of South Carolina* (Charleston, 1840). For his other historical publications, see Trent, *op. cit.*, p. 337.

80. *Views and Reviews*, I, 42.

81. *Southern Quarterly Review* (April, 1849), XV, 52.

82. See *The Yemassee* (New York, 1937), Prefatory Letter, pp. 4, 5.

83. *Ibid.*, p. 6.

84. *Southern Quarterly Review* (April, 1849), XV, 72. His own Gothic effects, if often crude, were rationally explicable.

85. *The Yemassee*, Prefatory Letter, p. 6.

86. Cf. his reference to *Robinson Crusoe* as "that dear little book of details." *Views and Reviews*, I, 82.

87. *Aristotle's Poetics*, XXIV. In his preface to *The Yemassee*, Simms appears to have Aristotle's *Poetics* much in mind.

88. *Katharine Walton*, Preface, pp. 3-4.

89. *Southern Quarterly Review* (April, 1849), XV, 45. See also *ibid.* (April, 1845), VII, 340, 344, and *Views and Reviews*, I, 214, 218.

90. *The Partisan* (1835), Preface, p. x. In this respect also Simms seems to have been influenced in romance by Aristotle's rules for tragedy and epic. Cf. Aristotle's *Poetics*, VI: "Tragedy is essentially an imitation not of persons, but of action and life . . . all human happiness or misery takes the form of action." In his more psychological studies, however, Simms recognized the importance of characterization. In *Beauchampe* (p. 46), for example, he says: "The novel only answers half its uses when we confine it to the simple delineation of events . . ." Cf. also *Confession*, Preface, pp. 8-9.

91. *Views and Reviews*, I, 215, 216. In Simms's opinion, Cooper was often inferior in both invention and design, for he tended "to rely wholly on the spirit and success of certain scenes." *Ibid.*, p. 212. Cf. also Simms's comment on Cooper's failure when he undertook to "deal with groups" in *Lionel Lincoln. Ibid.*, p. 223.

92. *Southern Quarterly Review* (April, 1849), XV, 45.

93. *Ibid.* He himself found that it was "much easier to invent a new story than to repair the defects of an old one." *The Wigwam and the Cabin*, Preface, p. 4.

94. *Richard Hurdis*, Preface, p. 8.

95. *Views and Reviews*, I, 38.

96. *The Partisan*, p. 104.

97. For comment on Simms's skilful use of colloquial idiom, see Parrington, *Main Currents*, II, 130-31.

98. For example, he anticipated objections to the violence of *Border Beagles* by saying that "Nature has her sports, no less than Art, and it is in her extravagancies that Art must find her justification." *Border Beagles* (Chicago, 1885), Advertisement, p. 1.

99. *The Literati*, p. 273.

100. *Ladies' Vase: or Polite Manual for Young Ladies*, Lowell, 1843, p. 113. Cf. R. W. Griswold's complaint in 1847 that Simms "gives us too much of ruffianism." *Prose Writers of America*, p. 504.

101. Cf. "A Note on Simms's Novels," *American Literature* (May, 1930), II, 173-74.

102. Upon revising *Guy Rivers* for a new edition in 1855 he decided that the book suffered from "truant twigs and . . . overmassed intricacies." Dedicatory Epistle, pp. 10, 11. He also labored to improve the "stiltish style" which at first marred his tales. *Ibid.*, p. 10.

103. Clement E. Foust, *The Life and Dramatic Works of Robert Montgomery Bird*, New York, 1919, p. 7. Much of the early portion of *Robin Day* is autobiographical. *Ibid.*, p. 8 n.

104. Foust, *op. cit.*, p. 77.

106. W. H. Prescott, *History of the Conquest of Mexico*, Philadelphia, 1873, III, 134.

107. Foust, p. 90.

108. Bird was sanguine enough about *Calavar* even before it had appeared, to go abroad to arrange for an English edition, but the British superciliousness toward unknown authors and Bulwer Lytton's languid attitude toward the young American writer gave him a distaste for English literary practice that he did not soon forget. Foust, pp. 82-86. Nevertheless English editions of both *Calavar* and *The Infidel* appeared in 1835.

109. *The Conquest of Mexico*, II, 324 n.

110. Quoted in Foust, p. 89.

111. *The Literati*, p. 259.

112. Foust, p. 91.

113. Quoted in Foust, pp. 90-91.

114. *The Hawks of Hawk-Hollow*, Philadelphia, 1835, II, 191.

115. Foust, p. 93.

116. This episode may have influenced Poe's "The Gold-Bug." Cf. Killis Campbell, *The Mind of Poe*, Cambridge, 1933, p. 172, text and note 3.

117. *Sheppard Lee*, New York, 1836, I, 67.

118. Poe's "Metzengerstein," a story employing metempsychosis, antedated *Sheppard Lee* by three years.

119. *The Literati*, p. 261.

120. Crockett, the "Robin Hood of the Canebrake" (the phrase is Hamlin Garland's), died in 1836.

121. Between 1834 and 1836 sales of public lands jumped from less than $5,000,000 to $24,000,000. D. S. Muzzey, *An American History*, Boston, 1925, p. 235.

122. *Nick of the Woods* (New York, 1928), Preface, p. 8. Constance Rourke credits Bird with having "tapped a deep fund of comic talk and character." *American Humor, A Study of the National Character*, New York, 1931, p. 201.

123. Chapter XXIX.

124. Bird MSS. at the University of Pennsylvania, quoted in *Nick of the Woods* (New York, 1939), ed. by C. B. Williams, Introduction, p. xxxi. The Introduction to this edition contains an excellent study of *Nick of the Woods*.

125. *Nick of the Woods* (New York, 1928), Preface, p. 9.

126. *Ibid.*, editor's note. Bird's widow said that *Nick* sold more than 10,000 copies in Germany, but from its sale in Germany (as in England) Bird of course received "no substantial return." Foust, p. 155.

127. The experience of Nathan's family is said to have been based on a real case in Pennsylvania history. *Nick of the Woods* (New York, 1928), Preface, p. 9.

128. For a discussion of the domestic novel, see below, Chapter X.

129. Bird's severe strictures on educational methods inevitably recall Dickens' account of Dotheboys Hall in *Nicholas Nickleby* (published 1838-39). See *The Adventures of Robin Day*, Philadelphia, 1839, I, 42-92.

130. "I am entirely of too discursive and diffuse a turn . . . to shine in a nutshell." Foust, p. 112.

131. *Nick of the Woods* was re-published in 1853 by the enterprising J. S. Redfield of New York.

132. "I do verily believe that much of the evil and good of man's nature arises from causes and influences purely physical; that valour and ambition are as often caused by a bad stomach as ill-humours by bad teeth." *Sheppard Lee*, I, 181.

133. He even wrote part of a novel (to be called *The Celebrated Mrs. Munchary*) satirizing "the new woman." Foust, p. 126.

134. *The Hawks of Hawk-Hollow*, I, 35.

135. Foust, p. 127.

136. Cf. *The Adventures of Robin Day*, I, 124-27. This is of course inference: the author does not speak in his own person.

137. In *Sheppard Lee* (I, 23) he amusingly represents the Negro Jim as protesting at emancipation: Jim "burst into a passion, swore he would *not* be free, and told me flatly I was his master, and I should take care of him: and the absurd old fool ended by declaring if I made him a free man he would have the law of me . . ." Cf. a similar scene in Simms's *The Yemassee*, above, p. 239.

138. He was not surprised that his Mexican stories were not appreciated by the "Johnny Raws of the States" (quoted in Foust, p. 89), and he complained, as a dramatist, that it was degrading to "write for and be admired by the groundlings." (*Ibid.*, p. 51.)

139. "We have always held the Delaware to be the finest and noblest river in the world . . ." *The Hawks of Hawk-Hollow*, Introduction, p. iv.

140. *Ibid.*, p. v.

141. *The Hawks of Hawk-Hollow*, Introduction, pp. v-vi.

142. Cf. above, p. 247. See also Foust, pp. 73-74.

143. Quoted in Foust, pp. 74-75.

144. *The Hawks of Hawk-Hollow*, Introduction, p. iv. Reference has already been made (above, p. 251) to Bird's approval of an "avalanche" technique—a type no more favorable to good design than the "mosaic."

145. Quoted from Lounsbury by Foust, p. 84.

146. *Sheppard Lee*, I, 83. For further evidence of Bird's gift for satire, see his amusing characterization of the physician in *The Hawks of Hawk-Hollow*, I, 114 ff.

147. J. E. Uhler, "Kennedy's Novels and his Posthumous Works," *American Literature* (January, 1932), III, 472.

148. J. P. Kennedy, *Swallow Barn* (ed. by Jay B. Hubbell), New York, 1929, Introduction, p. ix.

149. *American Literature*, III, 474.

150. Kennedy also wrote a great deal of non-fictional prose, which is briefly discussed by Uhler, *loc. cit.*, and in Ernest E. Leisy's Introduction (pp. xi-xiii) to *Horse-Shoe Robinson*, New York, 1937.

151. Hubbell, *loc. cit.*, p. xi.

152. Edward M. Gwathmey, *John Pendleton Kennedy*, New York, 1931, pp. 59-61.

153. *Swallow Barn* (New York, 1929), p. 10.

154. It is listed as a "semi-historical" novel in Jonathan Nield, *A Guide to the Best Historical Novels and Tales*, London, 1904, p. 122.

155. *Swallow Barn*, pp. 378-83.

156. See below, p. 269.

157. Hubbell, *loc. cit.*, p. xxv.

158. *Ibid.*, pp. xxv, xxvii.

159. Fiction followed the migratory movement, and one of the most popular romances of the period, *Nick of the Woods*, deals with Virginian emigrants. See above, p. 253.

160. Hubbell, *loc. cit.*, xxvi, xxvii.

161. Cf. the observation of J. E. Cooke in 1883: "Swallow Barn remains the best picture of Virginia country life in literature." *Virginia: A History of the People* (Boston, 1887), p. 496.

162. *Horse-Shoe Robinson, A Tale of the Tory Ascendency*, New York, 1937, ed. by E. E. Leisy, Preface to the First Edition, p. 11. In his Preface, Kennedy notes that up to that time "only the political and documentary history of that war [had] been written."

163. Even so W. G. Simms, whose *Partisan* (1835) treated much the same ma-

terials as *Horse-Shoe Robinson*, complained in a review of a revised edition of the latter that there were a good many errors with respect to South Carolinian history. See *Southern Quarterly Review* (July, 1852), VI, n.s., 207 ff.

164. *Horse-Shoe Robinson*, p. 27.

165. *Ibid.*, Introduction, p. xx.

166. One of the conditions of the successful revival of the historical romance in the 1930's has been the creation of hero and heroine who are more than rubber-stamp patterns of assorted virtues, witness *Anthony Adverse, Northwest Passage, Paradise*, etc.

167. *Horse-Shoe Robinson*, p. 80.

168. *Ibid.*, p. 70.

169. *Ibid.*, pp. 5-10. Differences between Natty and Robinson were noted by Simms: "[Robinson] is quite as ready and practical as Cooper's Hunter, but not so poetical. Where the latter dealt in musings, the former dealt in argument. While Natty Bumppo nursed the solitude, Horse-Shoe was eminently social; and while the one inclined to melancholy, the other was the very personification of *bonhommie*." *Southern Quarterly Review*, VI, 204-05.

170. Gwathmey, p. 115.

171. *Southern Literary Messenger* (May, 1835), I, 523. This panegyric may have been based partly on gratitude. See Hervey Allen, *Israfel*, New York, 1926, I, 354, 366.

172. *Southern Literary Messenger*, I, 524.

173. It went into three editions within the first two years. In 1851 the *American Review* referred to it as equal in popularity to all but two of Cooper's novels. (Gwathmey, *op. cit.*, p. 114.) A new edition with a new introduction appeared in 1852. In 1856 the story was dramatized. Subsequent editions of the novel appeared in 1872, 1883, 1891 (in serial form), 1893, 1897 (for school use), 1906, and 1937.

174. Gwathmey, p. 125.

175. *Rob of the Bowl*, New York, n.d., pp. 74, 75.

176. *The North American Review* (April, 1833), XXXVI, 519, quoted in Gwathmey, p. 154.

177. Gwathmey, p. 58.

178. Parrington, *Main Currents*, II, 56.

179. Gwathmey, p. 150. The other four were Irving, Paulding, Cooper, and John Quincy Adams.

180. Legend once ascribed the writing of the fourth chapter of *The Virginians* to Kennedy, but the story is apparently apochryphal. Hubbell, *loc. cit.*, p. xxiv.

181. Gwathmey, p. 156.

182. *Ibid.*, pp. 158-59.

183. *Ibid.*, p. 160.

184. *Israfel*, I, 350, note.

185. Quinn, *Edgar Allan Poe*, p. 240.

186. See above, p. 264.

187. Gwathmey, p. 182.

188. *Ibid.*, pp. 49, 50.

189. *Ibid.*, p. 161.

190. Carl Van Doren, *The American Novel*, p. 48.

191. John E. Flitcroft, *The Novelist of Vermont*, Cambridge, 1929, *passim*. See also Duyckinck, *Cyclopaedia*, II, 216.

192. Flitcroft notes, *e.g.*, that although Allen once followed up a military victory by burning houses, destroying corn, and wrecking a grist-mill, Thompson generously ignored these unpleasant details. *Op. cit.*, pp. 102-03.

193. Flitcroft, *op. cit.*, p. 93.

194. *Locke Amsden* (Boston, 1850), Chapter V.

195. In this scene Saint-Pierre's *Paul and Virginia* is recalled when Locke's sweetheart almost perishes because she "ran back to add another article to her scant dress." *Locke Amsden*, p. 211.

196. *Ibid.*, pp. 5, 6.

197. See *The North American Review* for January, 1848.

198. Flitcroft, *op. cit.*, pp. 125-27. It may be added that the trials of the young schoolmaster in Holmes' *Elsie Venner* (1861) are not unlike those that befell Locke Amsden.

199. T. S. Arthur's *Ten Nights in a Bar-Room* had appeared but two years before.

200. *Gaut Gurley* (Philadelphia, 1860), p. 1.

201. At the time of his death Thompson was engaged in writing *The Honest Lawyer*, a novel of which a rather considerable fragment has been published posthumously in Flitcroft, *op. cit.*, pp. 161-299.

202. Flitcroft, *op. cit.*, pp. 91, 92.

203. *Ibid.*, p. 92.

204. Thompson used these terms in a lecture, "American Romances," first printed in Flitcroft, *op. cit.*, pp. 309-15.

205. *Ibid.*, pp. 310-12.

206. *Ibid.*, p. 314.

CHAPTER VII

1. Cf. Ellen Glasgow's comment on the South as a whole: "From the beginning of its history the South had suffered less from a scarcity of literature than from a superabundance of living. Soil, scenery, all the color and animation of the external world, tempted a convivial race to an endless festival of the seasons . . . Life, for the ruling class at least, was genial, urbane, amusing." *Harper's Monthly Magazine* (December, 1928), CLVIII, 94.

2. J. B. Hubbell (ed.), *Swallow Barn*, New York, 1929, Introduction, p. xxvi. The remark is made with special reference to the interpretation of the Virginian social order.

3. For still earlier use of a Virginian background, see above, pp. 34-36, 260, and below, p. 277.

4. The spelling *Carruthers* has been widely used, but V. L. Parrington (*Main Current*, II, 46) notes some warrant for believing that Caruthers himself used only one "r." The author's name did not appear on the title pages of his novels.

5. See *Dictionary of American Biography* for a brief biography.

6. Parrington, *op. cit.*, II, 45.

7. J. B. Hubbell, *loc. cit.*, p. xxv.

8. His *The Partisan Leader* has since been called (by another Southerner) a "textbook of rebellion in disguise." Montrose Moses, *The Literature of the South*, New York, 1910, p. 253.

9. *The Kentuckian in New York*, I, 181. Quoted in Parrington, II, 42.

10. Quoted in Parrington, II, 42-43. Other quotations in this paragraph are from the same source, pp. 42-45.

11. *The Cavaliers of Virginia*, New York, 1834, I, 12, 13.

12. *Ibid.*, II, 50, 51.

13. *Ibid.*, I, 69.

14. *Ibid.*, I, 87-88. For further comments on the Indian problems, see vol. II, pp. 73-74, 75-79, 82-84, 243.

15. *Ibid.*, I, 153.

16. *Ibid.*, I, 14, 15.

17. *Ibid.*, I, 21.

18. *The New England Magazine* (January, 1835), VIII, 324.

19. *Harper's Magazine* (December, 1928), CLVIII, [93].

20. *The Cavaliers*, I, 4.

21. Quinn, *American Fiction*, pp. 713-14.

22. Cf. Lyle Wright, "A Statistical Survey of American Fiction, 1774-1850," *Huntington Library Quarterly* (April, 1939), II, 317.

23. Perhaps the origin of Fay's interest in duelling may be referred to the fact that his father had once worked in the law office of Alexander Hamilton.

24. R. W. Griswold, *The Prose Writers of America*, Philadelphia, 1847, pp. 447-48.

25. *Norman Leslie*, New York, 1835, Preface, p. [8].

26. *Ibid.*, I, 137.

27. *Trumps* is discussed below, pp. 472-75.

28. *Norman Leslie*, I, 157.

29. *Ibid.*, I, 27. Cf. also Rosalie's interest in circulating-library books plentifully provided with titled characters. *Ibid.*, I, 52.

30. *Ibid.*, II, 34, 35, 145.

31. On the very first page, Fay, himself a world-traveler, asserts that New York city provides a scene of "splendor which when the western continent shall be better known to European tourists, will be acknowledged to lose nothing by comparison with the picturesque views of Florence and Naples." *Ibid.*, I, 9, 10. For further eulogy of the American scene, see *ibid.*, II, 34.

32. *Ibid.*, I, 8.

33. *Southern Literary Messenger* (December, 1835), II, 56.

34. Hervey Allen, *Israfel*, I, 404 ff.

35. *Norman Leslie* was reprinted within a few months of its publication. There were also editions in 1836 and 1841. R. W. Griswold, *op. cit.*, and Lyle Wright, *American Fiction*, p. 67.

36. A detailed evaluation of Ingraham's enormous output has yet to be made. See *Dictionary of American Biography* for a brief bibliographical note.

37. Lyle Saxon published an extended life, *Lafitte, The Pirate*, at New York in 1930.

38. Jackson later wrote that Lafitte was "one of his ablest men on that morning . . ." Lyle Saxon, *op. cit.*, p. 182.

39. Albert Phelps, *Louisiana*, Boston, 1905, p. 260.

40. The "best," though "far from conclusive," evidence is that Lafitte died in 1826 in Yucatan. Lyle Saxon, *op. cit.*, pp. 262-63.

41. *Ibid.*, p. 271.

42. For bibliographical details see *American Literature* (Nov., 1937), IX, 351-53.

43. Two lines from Byron's *The Corsair* formed the title page motto of *Lafitte:*
> "He left a Corsair's name to other times
> Link'd with one virtue and a thousand crimes."

44. Ingraham, who lived much of his life in the South, was born in Maine.

45. When, for example, Achille thrusts Henri away from him violently, the author writes:
> The poor boy, reeling, fell forward, striking his forehead violently against a marble pedestal upon which stood an alabaster statue of the Madonna, and the warm blood spouted from his gashed temples over the cold, white robes of the image.
>
> It was a spectacle of horror! and the guilty being gazed wildly upon his prostrate brother, and thought of Abel and his murderer—upon the red-sprinkled image, and laughed, "Ha! ha! ha!" as maniacs laugh, at the fitness

of his first offering—a mangled brother—at the shrine of the virgin mother. *Lafitte: The Pirate of the Gulf*, New York, [1853], p. 16.

46. *Southern Literary Messenger*, II, 595. Unsigned but obviously by Poe.

47. Ingraham also "changed Captain Kidd beyond recognition in a romantic novel." Lyle Saxon, *op. cit.*, p. 273. Ingraham's *Captain Kidd; or, The Wizard of the Sea* appeared in 1839. Many other stories by Ingraham dealt with pirates and freebooters. See Lyle Wright, *American Fiction*, pp. 93-103, *passim*.

48. *Lafitte*, p. 57.

49. Longfellow was impressed: "In the afternoon, Ingraham the novelist called. A young, dark man, with soft voice. He says he has written eighty novels, and of these twenty during the last year; till it has grown to be merely mechanical with him. These novels are published in the newspapers. They pay him something more than three thousand dollars a year." Journal entry for April 5, 1846. *Life of Henry Wadsworth Longfellow*, ed. by Samuel Longfellow, Boston, 1886, II, 35.

50. The title of subsequent editions varied; now the book is most commonly known as *Archy Moore*.

51. *The Slave: or Memoirs of Archy Moore* (Boston, 1840), I, 15.

52. *Ibid.*, I, 18.

53. *Ibid.*, I, 10.

54. *Ibid.*, I, 25.

55. *Ibid.*, II, 22.

56. Quinn, p. 107.

57. *The Slave*, II, 59.

58. *Ibid.*, II, 104.

59. In 1852 there appeared an edition of the story to which was added a "happy" ending: Archy comes back, finds his family, and returns to live in "free England." This new material, the "Advertisement" asserted, was "originally intended, and often called for." The 1852 edition bears the title *The White Slave; or, Memoirs of a Fugitive*.

60. *The Slave* (Boston, 1840), I, 31.

61. *Ibid.*, I, 111.

62. *Ibid.*, II, 28.

63. Apropos of gay talking during a sale of slaves Hildreth writes: "An apologist for tyranny, would no doubt, rejoice in such a spectacle, and would be emboldened to argue, that after all being sold at public auction is not so terrible a thing, as some weak people are apt to imagine . . . The truth is, that the human mind, in its eager, though too often unavailing struggle after happiness, will still make the most of its means;—and even in the valley of despair, or under the ribs of death itself, still strives to create some matter of enjoyment. Even the slave will sing at his task; he can laugh too, though he find himself sold like an ox in the market. The tyrant discovers that all his wrongs and oppressions have not been able to extinguish in the soul of his victim, the capacity of enjoyment; and he points you to these outbursts of a nature not yet totally subdued, and dares to boast of the happiness he causes!" *Ibid.*, I, 71.

64. *Ibid.*, II, 31.

65. *Ibid.*, I, 62.

66. *Ibid.*, I, 96. A few years earlier, young Ralph Waldo Emerson was observing an even more striking incongruity in St. Augustine, Florida, when a slave-auction and a meeting of the Bible Society occurred "at the same time and place, one being in the Government house, and the other in the adjoining yard." *Journals of Ralph Waldo Emerson*, Boston, 1909-14, II, 177.

67. *The Slave*, I, 25.

68. *Ibid.*, II, 114.

69. "Thank God, tyranny is not omnipotent! Though it crush its victims to the earth; and tread them into the dust; and

brutify them by every possible invention; it cannot totally extinguish the spirit of manhood within them. Here it glimmers; and there it secretly burns; sooner or later, to burst forth in a flame, that will not be quenched, and cannot be kept under!" (II, 68).

70. *Literary Friends and Acquaintance*, New York, 1900, p. 97.

71. *The Slave*, I, 68, 73, 88; II, 64, 98.

72. *Ibid.*, I, 67, 68.

73. *Ibid.*, I, 73.

74. *Ibid.*, I, 91.

75. *Ibid.*, I, 45. Nor does Hildreth fail to point the moral. When Archy later reaches Connecticut, he observes the "unusual thrift and industry of the inhabitants. When freedom nerves the arm, it is in vain that rocks and hills of granite, oppose the labors of cultivation." *Ibid.*, II, 103.

76. *Ibid.*, I, 94.

77. Thus one of Archy's masters, living west of Richmond, in "Middle Virginia," was "not a planter;—that is to say, he did not make tobacco, and he chose to call himself a farmer." *Ibid.*, I, 74.

78. *Ibid.*, I, 98. For Caruthers' somewhat similar explanation of Virginia's economic decline, see above, pp. 278-79.

79. In the writing of history, in which he was prolific, Hildreth wrote a "plain business style" which puzzled people who knew his belligerent activities in politics. Van Wyck Brooks, *The Flowering of New England*, p. 327. See also A. M. Schlesinger, Jr., "The Problem of Richard Hildreth," *The New England Quarterly* (June, 1940), XIII, 223-46.

80. In the advertisement to the second edition of *The Slave* he said that the book was written "in the midst of scenes, similar to those which it attempts to describe."

81. *American Authors 1600-1900* (ed. by Kunitz and Haycraft), New York, 1938, p. 367.

82. Advertisement to second (1840) edition.

83. *Ibid.*

84. *Huntington Library Quarterly* (April, 1939), II, 317.

85. Howells, *op. cit.*, p. 97.

86. Quinn, p. 107. F. P. Gaines refers to it (*The Southern Plantation*, p. 31) as the "most effective piece of abolition fiction of the early period."

87. *American Authors 1600-1900*, p. 367.

88. *The Slave*, I, [5].

89. Quoted in A. H. Quinn, *Edgar Allan Poe*, New York, 1941, p. 251.

90. Poe had only a limited tolerance for those "wire-drawn romances which have been so long fashionable (God only knows how or why) . . ." Written in 1841. See M. Alterton and H. Craig, *Edgar Allan Poe*, New York, 1935, p. 309.

91. *Graham's Magazine*, April, 1841, quoted in Alterton and Craig, *op. cit.*, p. 309. Cf. his later (1847) reference to the novel form as "objectionable . . . for reasons analogous to those which render length objectionable in the poem." *The Complete Works of Edgar Allan Poe* (New York, 1902), XIII, 152.

92. Cf. above, Chapter VI, note 171.

93. Review of *Barnaby Rudge*, quoted in Alterton and Craig, *op. cit.*, p. 334.

94. "The interest of plot, referring, as it does, to cultivated thought in the reader, and appealing to considerations analogous with those which are the essence of sculptural taste, is by no means a popular interest; although it has the peculiarity of being appreciated in its atoms by all, while in its totality of beauty it is comprehended but by the few. The pleasure which the many derive from it is disjointed, ineffective, and evanescent; and even in the case of the critical reader it is a pleasure which may be purchased too dearly. A good tale may be written without it. Some of the finest fictions in the world have neglected it altogether.

We see nothing of it in 'Gil Blas,' in the 'Pilgrim's Progress,' or in 'Robinson Crusoe.' Thus it is not an essential in story-telling at all; although, well managed, within proper limits, it is a thing to be desired. At best it is but a secondary and rigidly artistical merit, for which no merit of a higher class—no merit founded in nature—should be sacrificed." Review of Bulwer's *Night and Morning*, quoted in Alterton and Craig, *op. cit.*, p. 308. Cf. also *The Literati*, p. 392.

95. Cf. above, p. 149, for Poe's low opinion of the plot of *Wyandotté*.

96. Cf. his observation that in *Night and Morning* Bulwer "merely concentrated into his book all the *necessary evils* of the stage . . . The overstrained effort at perfection of plot has seduced him into absurd sacrifices of verisimilitude . . ." Quoted in Alterton and Craig, *op. cit.*, p. 310.

97. Cf. H. S. Canby: "For the visions of Poe differ from the visions of irrational dreamers because they have order." *Classic Americans*, New York, 1931, p. 302.

98. Poe uses the term "severity" in his "Poetic Principle."

99. The verisimilitude of the story, particularly touching the New Bedford part, was in fact so striking that a brother of O. W. Holmes refused to regard the book as a fabrication. See H. Allen, *Israfel*, II, 420, n. 504.

100. *Ibid.*, II, 420.

101. Aubrey Starke, "Poe's Friend Reynolds," *American Literature* (May, 1939), XI, 152.

102. *The Narrative of A. Gordon Pym*, in *Complete Works of Edgar Allan Poe*, ed. by J. A. Harrison, New York, 1902, II, 53.

103. *Israfel*, II, 420.

104. James refers to the white curtain in *The Golden Bowl*, I, 22. A journalistic allusion to the same phenomenon may be found in an account of Richard Byrd's recent flight across the South Pole. Russell Owen, who reported the flight, says that a certain screen of frost smoke rose from the water making the observer think of Poe's Pym and "the mysterious curtain through which he vanished in the south." *South of the Sun*, New York, 1934.

105. There is some resemblance too between the machinery whereby Melville introduced (the real) Tobias Greene (of *Typee*) and Poe's journalistic use of Pym as the purported hero of his adventure. A trifling similarity lies in the fact that both Poe and Melville employ the name Enderby in connection with shipping.

106. More recently, H. G. Wells has written a book, *Mr. Blettsworthy on Rampole Island*, which, coincidentally or not, employs a number of the same devices and situations as Poe's *Narrative*.

107. Poe applied this stinging comment to Bulwer Lytton. See Alterton and Craig, *op. cit.*, p. 317.

108. *Israfel*, II, 846-47.

109. "His authorized biographer, Dr. Bucke, was searching for the book for twenty years." *Franklin Evans, or the Inebriate* (New York, 1929), ed. by Emory Holloway, Editor's Introduction, p. x.

110. *Franklin Evans* (New York, 1929), Introductory, p. 5.

111. The volume was advertised to sell at 12½ cents, for it was only by keeping prices low that publishers could gain headway with American books which had to compete with pirated editions of the extremely popular books of Dickens, Bulwer, Dumas, and the Countess of Blessington. Holloway, *loc. cit.*, pp. xvii, xviii.

112. T. S. Arthur had recently published *Six Nights with the Washingtonians*, hardly a novel but certainly a success as an exploitation of the theme of temperance. No New York publisher, however, seems to have brought out a temperance story before Whitman's appeared. Holloway, *loc. cit.*, p. xx.

113. *Franklin Evans*, p. 118.

114. *Ibid.*, pp. 90-91.

115. One of these, an Indian story related in Chapter II, is a fairly successful story presaging Whitman's more elaborate experiment in the Indian tale, *The Half-Breed* (1845).

116. Chapters XVI, ff.

117. *Franklin Evans*, Editor's Introduction, p. xi.

118. The story was used in the *Eagle* under the title "Fortunes of a Country Boy."

119. He once went so far as to say that "the puritan is only another kind of toper." Quoted by Holloway, *loc. cit.*, p. ix. Finally Whitman became impatient of all reformers who with a "farthing rushlight . . . seek to illumine the illimitable caverns of the infinite." *Ibid.*, p. viii. Himself unable to probe the origins of evil, he at least realized the difficulty of the problem.

120. *Hyperion, A Romance*, in *Prose Works of Henry Wadsworth Longfellow*, Boston, 1864, II, 16.

121. *Ibid.*, p. 312.

122. *Ibid.*, p. 20.

123. *Ibid.*, p. 53.

124. *Ibid.*, pp. 27-28.

125. *Ibid.*, pp. 55-56.

126. *Ibid.*, p. 79.

127. *Ibid.*, p. 42.

128. *Ibid.*, p. 194.

129. *Kavanagh*, in *Works*, II, [325]-326.

130. *Ibid.*, p. 354.

131. *Ibid.*, p. 466.

132. *Ibid.*, p. 363.

133. *Ibid.*, p. 453.

134. Samuel Longfellow, *Life of Henry Wadsworth Longfellow*, II, 295 n.

135. *Ibid.*, p. 140.

136. *Ibid.*, p. 141.

137. *My Literary Passions*, p. 147.

138. *Kavanagh*, pp. 414-17.

139. *Ibid.*, p. 371.

140. This work has become more generally known by the title of the 1845 edition: *The Quaker City; or, The Monks of Monk-Hall, A Romance of Philadelphia Life, Mystery, and Crime.*

141. *Dictionary of American Biography*, XI, 285-86.

142. Lippard's name does not sully the pages of Barrett Wendell, C. F. Richardson, W. P. Trent, William B. Cairns, or any of a dozen other early historians and custodians of American literature who yet give space to the discussion of writers no more talented or widely read.

143. *The Quaker City*, Preface to the 27th American edition, Philadelphia, [1849], p. [2].

144. *Ibid.*, p. 447.

145. Lippard did not confine his diatribes on social corruption to the Philadelphia scene; his *Empire City* and *New York: Its Upper Ten and Lower Million* ascribed to New York a similar catalogue of abuses.

146. *The Quaker City*, p. 48.

147. *Ibid.*, p. 174. This speech contains an indirect allusion to the fact that a performance of a play based on the story of *The Quaker City* was prevented by municipal action.

148. *Ibid.*, pp. 189-90. A good deal of Lippard's animosity is directed against members of the professions. For a comprehensive illustration of this sort, though more restrained in tone, see *New York: Its Upper Ten* (Cincinnati, 1854), p. 108. In general Lippard champions the artisan class; his was distinctly a class crusade.

Thus, for example, when he refers to Byrnewood's having seduced a servant girl (whom he later protected) Lippard says: "In crushing the honor of an unprotected girl, he had only followed out the law which the Lady and Gentleman of Christian Society recognized with tacit reverence." *The Quaker City*, p. 352.

149. *New York: Its Upper Ten*, p. 206.

150. His serious conception of the vocation of authorship he expressed in *The Empire City, or New York by Night and Day* (New York, 1850), p. 202: "If there is a pursuit in this world especially set apart by God to minister to his worship—a pursuit which directly derives its authority from God—that pursuit is found in the profession of the Author."

151. *The Quaker City*, pp. 9-10.

152. Dickensian characters of the less savory sort, such as Uriah Heep and Alfred Jingle, were apparently used as models by Lippard.

153. *The Quaker City*, p. 220, author's footnote.

154. Poe was personally acquainted with Lippard, and the latter did Poe a good turn when Poe was at a very low ebb at Philadelphia in 1849. See H. Allen, *Israfel*, II, 817-18.

155. That market was apparently supplied in part also by the romances of Eugène Sue, a volume of whose novels was published in Philadelphia in 1845.

CHAPTER VIII

1. "I do abhor an Indian story." "Sketches from Memory" (1835), *Mosses From an Old Manse*, p. 483. Page references are to the standard edition of Hawthorne's works, Boston, 1883, unless otherwise noted.

2. Though he did not modify his art to please a special public, Hawthorne bitterly resented the neglect he suffered. See G. E. Woodberry, *Nathaniel Hawthorne*, Boston, 1902, pp. 158, 176-77.

3. Reading in his great models—Spenser, Milton, Bunyan—came later. For a detailed study of Hawthorne's reading, see Austin Warren, "Hawthorne's Reading," *New England Quarterly* (December, 1935), VIII, 480-97.

4. Woodberry, *op. cit.*, p. 14.

5. *Ibid.*, pp. 14-16.

6. *Ibid.*, p. 18.

7. *Ibid.*, p. 21. The amusing details of this sordid lapse may be seen in *ibid.*, pp. 18-21.

8. Lloyd Morris, *The Rebellious Puritan*, New York, 1927, p. 38.

9. Newton Arvin, *Hawthorne*, Boston, 1929, p. 44.

10. The book was printed by Marsh and Capen of Boston for $100; recently a copy of this, Hawthorne's first novel, was offered at a sale for $5000.

11. Arvin, *op. cit.*, pp. 44-45.

12. Woodberry, *op. cit.*, p. 32.

13. How Hawthorne's practice differed from Scott's may be observed in his treatment of the "Gray Champion," which he evidently modeled in part upon a similar legend in *Peveril of the Peak*. See G. H. Orians, "The Angel of Hadley in Fiction," *American Literature* (May, 1932), IV, [257]-269.

14. Though Hawthorne rescued himself soon from excessive use of Scott as a model, and he later felt that "the world . . . requires a more earnest purpose, a deeper moral, and a closer and homelier truth than he [Scott] was qualified to supply it with" (*Mosses*, p. 416), he retained his admiration for the Waverley

novels to the end of his life. Julian Hawthorne, *Nathaniel Hawthorne and His Wife*, Cambridge, 1884, II, 269.

15. *Ibid.*, I, 97. On one occasion he got as far west as Detroit.

16. Morris, *op. cit.*, p. 46.

17. "Journal of a Solitary Man," quoted in Woodberry, *op. cit.*, p. 53.

18. *The Saturday Review of Literature* (April 16, 1927), III, 727-28.

19. "The Gentle Boy," "Major Molineux," "Roger Malvin's Burial," and "The Wives of the Dead."

20. Woodberry, *op. cit.*, p. 34.

21. Benjamin referred to Hawthorne as "the most pleasing writer of fanciful prose, except Irving, in the country." Morris, *op. cit.*, p. 62.

22. *The Snow-Image and Other Twice-Told Tales*, p. 580. There is undoubtedly autobiographical fervor in this imprecation. Cf. Woodberry, *op. cit.*, p. 50.

23. S. G. Goodrich, cited in Woodberry, *op. cit.*, p. 49. It seems likely that professional discouragement rather than "some secret" postulated by Melville (cf. Julian Hawthorne, *Hawthorne and His Circle*, New York, 1903, p. 33) was the chief cause of Hawthorne's gloom. Julian Hawthorne has persistently attacked attempts to "psychoanalyze" his father. (Cf. *Saturday Review of Literature*, cited above.)

24. *The North American Review* (July, 1837), XLV, 59-73. Longfellow had now won some fame with his *Outre Mer*. Longfellow does not seem to have valued Hawthorne highly. William Dean Howells noted in later years that he "never heard him mention Hawthorne." *Literary Friends and Acquaintance*, New York, 1900, p. 200.

25. S. G. Goodrich, cited in Woodberry, *op. cit.*, p. 69.

26. The obscurity in which he had lived up to this time may be inferred from the common belief that "Nathaniel Hawthorne" was a pen-name. Randall Stewart (ed.), *The American Notebooks of Nathaniel Hawthorne*, New Haven, 1932, p. [283].

27. Woodberry, *op. cit.*, pp. 50, 55.

28. *Hawthorne and His Wife*, I, 178.

29. *Ibid.*, p. 180.

30. *Ibid.*, p. 195.

31. "Oh, labor is the curse of the world, and nobody can meddle with it without becoming proportionably brutified!" *Passages from the American Note-Books*, Boston, 1883, p. 235. Moreover, Hawthorne was not a good mixer, whatever the motive. Cf. Coverdale's remark on the likelihood that Brook Farm would not last long: "Persons of marked individuality—crooked sticks, as some of us might be called—are not exactly the easiest to bind up into a fagot." *The Blithedale Romance*, p. 390.

32. *Modern Language Notes* (May, 1932), XLVII, 314-16.

33. A bitterly satirical account of this procedure appeared later in the preface to *The Scarlet Letter*.

34. Arvin, *op. cit.*, p. 152.

35. "Hawthorne and his Mosses" in Melville's *Works* (Constable edition), XIII, 143.

36. *Twice-Told Tales*, Preface, p. 16.

37. Cf. Hawthorne's observation (in 1851) that "ever since [his] youth" he had "been addressing a very limited circle of friendly readers, without much danger of being overheard by the public at large." *The Snow-Image*, Preface, p. [385].

38. *Mosses From an Old Manse*, p. 44.

39. Dickens, for example, was surprised to find how popular circulating libraries were with working girls. *American Notes* (London, 1910), p. 79.

40. Edwin Whipple, *Lectures*, Boston, 1849, p. 81. This lecture was first delivered in 1844.

41. *The Scarlet Letter*, p. 241.

42. Cf. his reference to himself as a writer of "psychological romance." *The Snow-Image*, Preface, p. 386.

43. *Not Under Forty*, London, 1936, p. 53-54.

44. *Mosses*, p. 13.

45. *The Scarlet Letter*, p. 234. This passage has evoked a great deal of comment. In Hawthorne's day it was used as a text by persons who regarded *The Scarlet Letter* as an immoral book: Hawthorne seemed to condone free love. More disinterested scholars have also tended to stress unduly the "tolerance" of Hawthorne. The probability is that Hawthorne wrote the passage in all honesty, and that he felt the truth of the lovers' plea. But it was only a partial truth. To Hawthorne the most basic quality of human life was its ambiguity. He sympathized with Hester, but he knew that she was prone to error. Moreover she had "assumed a freedom of speculation" (*ibid.*, p. 199) which he probably thought dangerous. Cf. N. F. Doubleday, "Hawthorne's Hester and Feminism," *Publications of the Modern Language Association* (September, 1939), LIV, 825-28. As for Hester's assertion that the lovers' conduct "had a consecration of its own," the novel provides an opposite (or complementary) view in the final words of Dimmesdale, who acknowledged that the lovers had " 'violated [their] reverence each for the other's soul.' " (*The Scarlet Letter*, p. 304.) These words Hawthorne seems to have written with quite as much assent to their purport as he had earlier given to Hester's plea. Hawthorne did not solve a problem; he presented an ugly dilemma.

46. Cf. Herbert J. Muller: "Although men's notions of right and wrong are relative and mutable, a line is inevitably drawn somewhere, and he who crosses it suffers; conscience remains an inexorable fact of human nature even in this emancipated age. That the grounds and appearances of guilt have shifted does not destroy the validity of Hawthorne's demonstrations of the psychological consequences of the consciousness of guilt." "The New Psychology in Old Fiction," *Saturday Review of Literature* (August 21, 1937), XVI [3], 4.

47. *The Scarlet Letter*, p. 307.

48. Julian Hawthorne, "The Making of 'The Scarlet Letter,'" *The Bookman* (December, 1931), LXXIV, 401-11.

49. *The Scarlet Letter*, pp. 307-08.

50. "I doubt [wrote Hawthorne in 1851 in a letter probably addressed to R. W. Griswold] whether my romances would succeed in the serial mode of publication; lacking, as they certainly do, the variety of interest and character which seem to have made the success of other works, so published. The reader would inevitably be tired to death of the one prominent idea, if presented to him under different aspects for a twelve-month together. The effect of such a story, it appears [to] me, depends on its being read continuously." *Passages from the Correspondence . . . of Rufus W. Griswold*, Cambridge, 1898, p. 280.

51. *The Scarlet Letter*, p. 306.

52. A pathetic episode is that of Hawthorne's acceptance of a sum of money discreetly tendered him in 1850 in recognition of what he had "done for American literature." Woodberry, *op. cit.*, pp. 185-87. Hawthorne later returned the money.

53. Cf. F. L. Pattee, *The First Century of American Literature*, New York, 1935, p. 546.

54. Woodberry, *op. cit.*, p. 189.

55. *Hawthorne and His Wife*, II, 1.

56. Norman H. Pearson (ed.), *The Novels and Tales of Nathaniel Hawthorne*, New York, 1937, Introduction, p. xii.

57. Cf. Edward Mather, *Nathaniel Hawthorne, A Modest Man*, New York, 1940, pp. 21, 51, 114.

58. F. W. Chandler, who calls Holgrave a "colorless picaro" (*The Literature of Roguery*, London, 1907, II, 376), remarks that Hawthorne was "too much of an idealist" to develop the strain fully (*ibid.*). Indeed Hawthorne plainly says that "A romance on the plan of Gil Blas, adapted to American society and manners, would cease to be a romance." (*The House of the Seven Gables*, p. 211.)

59. *The House of the Seven Gables*, p. 59. Nevertheless some readers, among them Miss Sedgwick, complained that the book was morbid. See above, pp. 210-11.

60. "The Public . . . prefers forgery to fact," said Julian Hawthorne with some asperity in regard to the demand for the "original" of the House of the Seven Gables. See *The Bookman*, LXXIV, 401.

61. Quoted in R. M. Weaver, *Herman Melville, Mariner and Mystic*, New York, 1921, pp. 315, 317.

62. *The Blithedale Romance*, p. 434. Cf. his satire of reformers in "Earth's Holocaust." (*Mosses*, pp. 430-56).

63. Austin Warren (ed.), *Nathaniel Hawthorne*, New York, 1934, Introduction, p. xliv.

64. An unpleasant note is struck, for example, when at the grave of Zenobia, Hawthorne observes that "Nature . . . is just as well pleased, for aught we can see, with the tuft of ranker vegetation that grew out of Zenobia's heart, as with all the beauty which has bequeathed us no earthly representative except in this crop of weeds." (P. 596.) No pretty sentiment glosses the sorrow as in much popular literature of the day. Moreover Hollingsworth is seen in permanent penance at the end, recognizing himself as in effect the "murderer" of Zenobia.

65. Oscar Cargill (*Publications of the Modern Language Association* [Sept., 1937], LII, 848 ff.) presses the analogy. Austin Warren (*ibid.* [June, 1939], LIV, 615-18) wisely corrects Cargill's overemphasis. Edward Mather (*op. cit.*, pp. 210-11, 217-18) thinks Zenobia was based on Margaret Fuller and Fanny Kemble.

66. For an account, more fearful even than the fiction, of the espisode on which Zenobia's death is based, see *The American Notebooks* (ed. by R. Stewart) pp. 112-15.

67. *The Blithedale Romance* is less realistic than *Trilby*, another novel in which mesmerism is a significant motif. It is more nearly comparable in this respect to Howells' *The Undiscovered Country*.

68. Henry James, *Hawthorne*, New York, 1880, p. 128.

69. Parrington, prone to find artistic failure in works that are economically "unsound" or deficient, was disappointed at Hawthorne's failure to view the economic experience of Brook Farm more favorably; he accordingly called *The Blithedale Romance* "as thin and unreal" as any book Hawthorne wrote. *Main Currents*, II, 448. It is hardly surprising, considering the slow development of economic themes in the American novel, that Hawthorne did not make more capital of the Brook Farm experiment per se. E. O. Smith's *Bertha and Lily* (1854) glances at the subject but makes even less of it than does *The Blithedale Romance*. See Mary Alice Wyman, *Two American Pioneers*, New York, 1927, pp. 185-86. In 1927 Joseph Hergesheimer published a short story (constituting section X of *Quiet Cities*) which is set in, and makes considerable use of, Brook Farm.

70. *Hawthorne and His Wife*, II, 2.

71. Caroline Ticknor, *Hawthorne and His Publisher*, Boston, 1913, p. 229.

72. *The Marble Faun*, p. 125.

73. *The Marble Faun*, Preface, p. 15.

74. The plight of Melville's Benito Cereno is distinctly recalled by Hawthorne's comments (p. 132) on her relationship to her pursuer: "But, allowing that he had caught a true glimpse into the hidden significance of Miriam's gesture, what a terrible thralldom did it suggest! Free as she seemed to be,—beggar as he looked,—

the nameless vagrant must then be dragging the beautiful Miriam through the streets of Rome, fettered and shackled more cruelly than any captive queen of yore following in an emperor's triumph." Hawthorne was abroad when "Benito Cereno" was published in 1855. The passage also recalls, of course, the Cleopatra of Shakespeare.

75. *The Marble Faun*, p. 135.

76. Cf. Thoreau's characteristically paradoxical epigram: "We cannot well do without our sins: they are the highway of our virtue." *Heart of Thoreau's Journals*, ed. by Odell Shepard, Boston, 1927, p. 44.

77. Howells, *Literary Friends and Acquaintance*, p. 62.

78. *The Marble Faun*, p. 65.

79. *Hawthorne and His Publisher*, p. 223.

80. *Ibid.*, p. 329.

81. "Browne's Folly," in *Works*, XII, 131 (*Tales and Sketches*).

82. Letter to Ticknor quoted in *Hawthorne and His Publisher*, p. 235.

82a. *Dr. Grimshawe's Secret* (Boston, 1900), p. 152.

83. *The Dolliver Romance*, p. 42.

84. *Dr. Grimshawe's Secret*, Preface, p. viii.

85. Cf. his remark that New England was "the largest lump of earth his heart could hold." Quoted in Odell Shepard, *Connecticut Past and Present*, New York, 1939, p. 6.

86. See above, pp. 342-43.

87. Harris's bitterly ironical comment on James's remark contains some of the finest praise ever accorded Hawthorne: "Why should Americans strive to be anything else than American? Why not insist that the provinciality of American literature is the essential quality of all literature—the one quality that gives distinctiveness to literary efforts?

"It seems almost like sacrilege to hear Mr. James making excuses for Hawthorne to English readers by enumerating the surroundings that the Americans lacked. He had no sovereign, no court, no personal loyalty, no aristocracy, no church, no clergy, no diplomatic service, no palaces, no castles, no manors, no cathedrals, no abbeys, all these things and many more are catalogued by Mr. James to show the difficulties under which Hawthorne labored—this man who had before him all the ruins of human passion, and who was surrounded by the antiquity of the soul. How paltry—how shriveled and shrunken does the swallow-tailed-culture of the literary snob appear in contrast with the provinciality which invests the works of Hawthorne with the swift passion of New England summers, the wild, desolate beauty of her autumns, and the strange, penetrating gloom of her winters!" *Joel Chandler Harris, Editor and Essayist* (ed. by Julia C. Harris), Chapel Hill, 1931, pp. 189-90.

88. Lowell said it was the "most valuable contribution to New England history that has been made." *Hawthorne and His Wife*, II, 391. Such a statement, however, does not imply literal conformity to source material. It has recently been pointed out with reference to the scarlet "A," for example, that "In the entire court records of the Puritans of Massachusetts Bay Colony, of which Boston was the capital, there is not a single instance of the scarlet letter being attached." The practice referred to did occur at Plymouth Colony, but even there it was rare and the token was not "A" but "AD." Gustavus Meyers, "Hawthorne and the Myths about Puritans," *The American Spectator* (April, 1934), II, 1.

89. *The House of the Seven Gables*, Preface, p. 15. With a fine perception of Hawthorne's artistic use of Rome as a setting in *The Marble Faun*, Howells protested (through Colville in *Indian Summer*, p. 311) against a too literal study of the mise-en-scène: Colville, says Howells, "had his opinion of people who illustrated *The Marble Faun* with photographs . . ."

90. Arvin, *op. cit.*, p. 210.

91. *The Marble Faun*, p. 39.

92. *The American Notebooks* (ed. by Stewart), p. 106.

93. In order to develop the skill which enables him "to see the inmost soul," the painter has "insulated himself from the mass of mankind"—almost always a prophecy of evil in a Hawthorne tale. Indeed "The Prophetic Pictures" reveals several key elements in Hawthorne's art and heritage. It reflects the Puritan distrust of pictorial art: for "Some deemed it . . . a presumptuous mockery of the Creator, to bring into existence such lively images of his creatures." An artist's more or less necessary isolation, Hawthorne believed, is in itself unfortunate, for "It is not good for man to cherish a solitary ambition." At the end of "The Prophetic Pictures" a characteristic scene occurs in which the painter is obliged to restrain Walter from a murderous assault upon his wife. This scene, it may be added, provides the closest link between Hawthorne and Charles Brockden Brown, for when the painter cries "Hold, madman!" he inevitably recalls a comparable command by Carwin (in *Wieland*)—another character who indiscreetly cultivated a gift verging on the supernatural. For Hawthorne's favorable comment on Brown, see above, p. 101.

94. See "Dr. Heidegger's Experiment," "The Birthmark," "Rappaccini's Daughter," etc.

95. How seriously he regarded mesmerism may be judged from his solemn admonition to Sophia Peabody not to attempt to cure her headaches by mesmerism lest the "sacredness" of her individuality be "violated." Letter quoted in *The American Notebooks*, Introduction, p. lxxv.

96. See "Dr. Heidegger's Experiment," *Septimius Felton*, *Dr. Grimshawe's Secret*, *The Dolliver Romance*. Cf. also *The Scarlet Letter*, p. 147.

97. Beatrice and Giovanni, typical of Hawthorne in this respect, are presented as an "insulated pair" being experimented upon by Dr. Rappaccini in "an utter solitude." *Mosses*, p. 145. Almost the identical phrasing is used to describe the situation of Miriam and Donatello in *The Marble Faun*, p. 114.

98. For a comprehensive treatment of Hawthorne's themes, see *The American Notebooks, Introduction*, pp. [lxviii]-lxxxix.

99. *The Blithedale Romance*, pp. 391.

100. It is with a distinct sense of incongruity that one reads Miriam's full name on the doorplate of her studio: "Miriam Schaefer." *The Marble Faun*, p. 55.

101. The finding of Zenobia's body in *The Blithedale Romance* and the death scene of the Capuchin monk in *The Marble Faun* are examples. See *Hawthorne and His Publisher*, pp. 217-18.

102. *The American Notebooks*, Introduction, p. lxvii.

103. It is idle to complain, as does Granville Hicks, of the lack of superficial realism in Hawthorne's characters: "With few exceptions they never suggest a capacity to step, robust and insistent, out of their books and into our lives." *The Great Tradition*, New York, 1933, p. 6. As well to complain that the shepherds in "Lycidas" could not go readily to work on a farm. Hawthorne was not trying to copy life in this sense. For further adverse comment on Hawthorne's characterization, see Newton Arvin, *op. cit.*, p. 206. It is Mr. Arvin's contention that "[a]s a writer of fiction, Hawthorne is plainly not of the first order." *Ibid.*, pp. 206-07.

104. Graham Balfour, *The Life of Robert Louis Stevenson*, New York, 1901, II, 168-69.

105. This is obvious from Hawthorne's comments in his *Notebooks* and from his practice. Cf. Henry A. Beers, quoted in *The American Notebooks*, Introduction, p. xlii. That Hawthorne continued this practice until late in life is clear from *Septimius Felton*, which is complete in "plot" and in rationale but wanting in concrete material which Hawthorne supplied, more or less niggardly, in most of his stories.

106. "It is politic, however, to make few allusions to such a past; nor, if we would create an interest in the characters of our story, is it wise to suggest how Cicero's foot may have stepped on yonder stone, or how Horace was wont to stroll near by, making his footsteps chime with the measure of the ode that was ringing in his mind." *The Marble Faun*, p. 189.

107. Hawthorne himself realized as much, and he wrote in a moment of candor: "If I were to meet with such books as mine by another writer, I don't believe I should be able to get through them." Letter to J. T. Fields, quoted in Arvin, *op. cit.*, p. 207.

108. *Mosses From an Old Manse*, p. [347].

109. *Ibid.*, p. 359.

110. Preface to *The Blithedale Romance*, p. 322.

111. Even Hawthorne's friends commented on the slowness of his stories. Ellery Channing was quoted as having said that Hawthorne had "the undeniable test-faculty of narration, one event to every one hundred and forty pages; a cough took up ten pages, and sitting down in a chair six more." E. W. Emerson, *The Early Years of the Saturday Club*, Boston, 1918, p. 211.

112. *Works*, VII, 16.

113. Perhaps Hawthorne's early reading of Spenser and Bunyan accounts for his frequent use of allegory. For Spenser's influence, see Randall Stewart, "Hawthorne and *The Faerie Queene*," *Philological Quarterly* (April, 1933), XII, 196-206.

114. "The Prophetic Pictures," *The Marble Faun*, "Major Molineux," "Bald Eagle," "David Swan," "The Canterbury Pilgrims," etc.

115. *The Marble Faun*, p. [97].

116. *The Literati*, p. 202.

117. *The Marble Faun*, pp. 139, 145.

118. *Ibid.*, p. 57.

119. *Ibid.*

120. Cf. Lewis Mumford, *Herman Melville*, New York, 1929, p. 203.

121. A good example of this occurs when Hawthorne evades a definite statement regarding the identity of Donatello. *The Marble Faun*, p. 51.

122. *Hawthorne and His Wife*, II, 250.

123. *The Marble Faun*, p. 524.

124. *Ibid.*, p. 523.

125. "A high truth . . . is never any truer, and seldom any more evident, at the last page than at the first." *The House of the Seven Gables*, Preface, p. 15.

126. H. S. Canby, *Classic Americans*, New York, 1931, p. 227.

127. *Hawthorne and His Publisher*, p. 223.

128. *The Marble Faun*, p. 117.

129. W. D. Howells, *Heroines of Fiction*, New York, 1901, II, 174.

130. Cf. "Roger Malvin's Burial," "The Bosom Serpent," *The House of the Seven Gables, The Marble Faun*. Cf. also the contrast Dimmesdale draws between Hester, whose shame is known, and himself, whose sin has been concealed: "Happy are you, Hester, that wear the scarlet letter openly upon your bosom! Mine burns in secret!" *The Scarlet Letter*, p. 230.

131. *The Marble Faun*, p. 491. Even in the natural innocence and happiness of children Hawthorne cannot take complete satisfaction. In *The Scarlet Letter* (p. 221) he speaks significantly of the "metallic lustre" of Pearl's character and gives it a sober explanation: "She wanted—what some people want throughout life—a grief that should deeply touch her, and thus humanize and make her capable of sympathy."

132. "Hawthorne and His Mosses," Melville's *Works*, XIII, 129.

133. "Graves and Goblins," Hawthorne's *Works*, XII, 69.

134. *Mosses*, pp. 28, 29.

135. Julian Hawthorne never knew his father to go to church. *Hawthorne and His Wife*, II, 22.

136. *Ibid.*, II, 252. This theme is elaborated in *Sorrow Built a Bridge* by Katherine Burton, New York, 1937.

137. *The English Notebooks by Nathaniel Hawthorne* (ed. by Randall Stewart), New York, 1941, p. 451.

138. *Mosses*, p. 13.

139. Austin Warren, (ed.) *Nathaniel Hawthorne*, Introduction, p. xxvii. See also Melville's comment on Hawthorne's use of the idea of original sin. Melville's *Works*, XIII, 129.

140. *The Marble Faun*, p. 104. See also *ibid.*, pp. 99, 109, 111, 491, *et passim*.

141. *Ibid.*, p. 141.

142. *Passages From the American Note-Books* (Boston, 1900), p. 39.

143. "Wakefield," *Twice-Told Tales*, p. 160.

144. "He Did Not Know Me," *Winter Words*, New York, 1928, p. 71.

145. *The Marble Faun*, p. 191.

146. *Ibid.*, p. 1.

147. "John Inglefield's Thanksgiving," in *The Snow-Image*, p. 590.

148. "Earth's Holocaust," *Mosses*, p. 455.

149. "The Maypole of Merry Mount," *Twice-Told Tales*, p. 84.

150. *The Marble Faun*, p. 99.

151. *Ibid.*, p. 64.

152. *The Life of Pierce* was a Democratic document pure and simple.

153. *Sketches*, p. 319. Quoted in *The American Notebooks*, p. 291.

154. *Ibid.*

155. In "The Hall of Fantasy" he harshly satirized "the abolitionist, brandishing his one idea like an iron flail." *Mosses*, p. 205.

156. *The American Notebooks*, p. 48.

157. R. C. Beatty, *Bayard Taylor*, Norman (Oklahoma), 1936, p. 91.

158. Quoted in Warren, *loc. cit.*, p. xlix.

159. *The House of the Seven Gables*, p. 216.

160. *Love Letters of Nathaniel Hawthorne*, Chicago, 1907, I, 149, quoted in Warren, *loc. cit.*, p. xlviii.

161. Cf. above, note 45.

162. "It was a woeful thought, that a woman of Zenobia's diversified capacity should have fancied herself irretrievably defeated on the broad battle-field of life, and with no refuge, save to fall on her own sword, merely because Love had gone against her. It is nonsense, and a miserable wrong,—the result, like so many others, of masculine egotism—that the success or failure of woman's existence should be made to depend wholly on the affections, and on one species of affection, while man has such a multitude of other chances that this seems but an incident. For its own sake, if it will do no more, the world should throw open all its avenues to the passport of a woman's bleeding heart." *The Blithedale Romance*, p. 593.

163. "It is especially singular that Americans should care about perpetuating themselves [in marble busts] . . . The brief duration of our families, as a hereditary household, renders it next to a certainty that the great-grandchildren will not know their fathers' grandfather, and that half a century hence at furthest, the hammer of the auctioneer will thump its knock-down blow against his blockhead, sold at so much for the pound of stone!" *The Marble Faun*, p. 144.

164. *Our Old Home, passim*. See also *New England Quarterly* (March, 1935), VIII, 3-13.

165. See "The Haunted Quack," "Rappaccini's Daughter," *The Scarlet Letter*, etc.

166. See above, pp. 355-56.

167. *The House of the Seven Gables*, pp. 219-20.

168. *Mosses*, p. 30.

169. In the same passage Hawthorne referred to "the controversial works of Unitarian ministers" as "trash." Austin Warren, *loc. cit.*, p. xxii. In the standard edition of his works (*Mosses*, p. 29) the passage is greatly altered.

170. *Ibid.*, p. 224.

171. *Ibid.*, p. 42.

172. "Let him mend his pen, get a bottle of visible ink, come out from the Old Manse, cut Mr. Alcott, hang (if possible) the editor of 'The Dial,' and throw out of the window to the pigs all his odd numbers of 'The North American Review.'" *The Literati*, p. 202.

173. *Mosses*, pp. 80, 428, 426.

174. *Ibid.*, p. 426.

175. *Ibid.*, pp. 42, 422-23.

176. *Ibid.*, p. 427.

177. *Ibid.*, p. 260.

178. Caroline Ticknor, *Hawthorne and His Publisher*, p. 141.

179. "Nathaniel Hawthorne's reputation [wrote Emerson in 1842] as a writer is a very pleasing fact, because his writing is not good for anything, and this is a tribute to the man." *Journals of Ralph Waldo Emerson*, Boston, 1909-1914, VI, 240. When Hawthorne died Emerson was still of the opinion that he had never revealed that "purer power" which, Emerson thought, lay latent in him. *Ibid.*, p. 306.

180. "Hawthorne and His Mosses," Melville's *Works*, XIII, 78. Written in 1850.

181. ". . . He is a tale writer, rather than a novelist, and exhibits some very peculiar endowments in this character. He has a rare and delicate fancy, with an imagination capable, in particular, of that curious distribution of light and shade— 'that little glooming light, most like a shade,'—which constitutes the singular faculty of some of the most remarkable of the Italian painters. He is truthful, also, in his delineation of character, though his range is a limited one. He enters, with the art of Sterne, into the heart of his single captive, and, with exquisite adroitness, unfolds to you, and to the victim's self, the hurts of the secret nerve, its morbid condition, and how it operates upon, and affects by sympathy, the whole system. . . . As a story, the 'House of the Seven Gables' will probably prove less attractive to the general reader than the 'Scarlet Letter,' as exhibiting a less concentrative power; but it is a less truthful book, and, if less ambitious in plan and manner, is not less earnest of purpose, nor less efficient in the varieties of character." *Southern Quarterly Review* (July, 1851), IV, 7-8.

182. *Hawthorne*, London, 1879, p. 2. In such a comparison, of course, Hawthorne would have to be weighed with Whitman and Melville, not to mention three distinguished younger men on the threshold of their fame, namely, Mark Twain, Howells, and James.

183. Raymond M. Weaver, *Herman Melville, Mariner and Mystic*, p. 318. Cf. Hawthorne's own reference to his "life of much smoulder and scanty fire." *Hawthorne and His Publisher*, p. 309.

184. Cf. Holgrave's speculation that "a man's bewilderment is the measure of his wisdom." *The House of the Seven Gables*, p. 214.

CHAPTER IX

1. *Mardi*, II, 71. Unless otherwise noted, references are to the standard (Constable) edition: *The Works of Herman Melville*, 16 vols., London, 1922-24.

2. F. J. Mather had been discouraged from writing a biography of Melville in 1904 because Melville was a "hopelessly poor risk." *Saturday Review of Literature* (April 27, 1929), V, 945. For a detailed discussion of Melville's reputation before 1920, see O. W. Riegel, "The Anatomy of Melville's Fame," *American Literature* (May, 1931), III, [195]-203, and William Braswell, "A Note on 'The Anatomy of Melville's Fame,'" *ibid.* (January, 1934), V, 360-64.

3. Even so late as 1921 Carl Van Doren, who appreciated much of Melville's ability, could speak of him as one of America's "most promising and yet most disappointing figures." *The American Novel* (New York, 1924), pp. 75-76.

4. Raymond M. Weaver, *Herman Melville, Mariner and Mystic*, New York, 1921, p. 18.

5. Weaver, *op. cit.*, pp. 22, 27.

6. London *Nation*, January 22, 1921. Quoted in Weaver, *op. cit.*, p. 21.

7. John Freeman, *Herman Melville*, New York, 1926, p. 1.

8. Lewis Mumford, *Herman Melville*, New York, 1929, p. 4.

9. Freeman, *op. cit.*, pp. 1-3. It is perhaps worth observing that the original subtitle of the partly autobiographical *Redburn* (1849) referred to the book as "Reminiscences of the Son-of-a-Gentleman."

10. Weaver, *op. cit.*, p. 77.

11. Charles R. Anderson, *Melville in the South Seas*, New York, 1939, p. 12.

12. *Redburn*, p. 54. Details of Melville's trip on the *Highlander* are not known except in so far as *Redburn* may be regarded as autobiographical.

13. These are preserved in part in *Billy Budd and Other Prose Pieces*, pp. 382-99.

14. *Pierre*, p. 342. The phrase occurs in a section of *Pierre* which is apparently autobiographical.

15. *Billy Budd*, p. 388.

16. Freeman, *op. cit.*, p. 20.

17. *Moby-Dick*, I, 7.

18. *Ibid.*, I, 7.

19. Anderson, *op. cit.*, p. 12.

20. See *ibid.*, pp. 14-21.

21. Charles R. Anderson's *Melville in the South Seas* (cited above) is the definitive study of this period in Melville's life.

22. The phrase is from *Moby-Dick*, in which the *Acushnet* is called "The Pequod." In *Typee* the ship is called "The Dolly."

23. In *Typee* Melville referred to his stay as having been one of "four months," but Anderson has shown (*op. cit.*, p. 70) that the period must have been between four and eight weeks. Many comparable discrepancies occur in the stories relating to Melville's experience. Not poor memory on his part but the needs of his narrative seem to have dictated the alterations.

24. Weaver, *op. cit.*, p. 251.

25. *Typee*, p. 286.

26. *Typee*, pp. 168-69. Rousseau is mentioned in *Typee* (p. 170). On Melville's debt to Rousseau see also Anderson, *op. cit.*, pp. 178, 276.

27. *Typee*, pp. 262-68.

28. *Some Personal Letters of Herman Melville* (ed. by M. Minnegerode), New York, 1922, p. 107. See also Anderson, *op. cit.*, pp. 179-81.

29. *Omoo*, 1847, fifth edition, end pages. Some idea of the widespread attention accorded *Typee* may be gained from the excerpts from the British press here collected, including notices from *The London Times, The Shilling Magazine, Beckett's Almanac for the Month, The London Sun, The London Athenaeum, The London Examiner, The London Spectator, The London Critic, The London Eclectic Review, Tait's Edinburgh Magazine, Simmons's Colonial Magazine, The Gentleman's Magazine,* and *John Bull.*

30. *Omoo* (1847 edition), end pages, p. xxiii.

31. The English rights to the book were sold before Wiley and Putnam bought the American rights. Minnegerode, *Personal Letters*, p. 105.

32. In England these deletions were not made. *Personal Letters*, p. 109.

33. Anderson, *op. cit.*, p. 238.

34. *Herman Melville* (ed. by Willard Thorp), New York, 1938, Introduction, p. xli. See this volume (pp. cxxxiii-clxi) for a useful selected bibliography of Melville.

35. By 1849 *Typee* had sold 6392 copies in America. Weaver, *op. cit.*, p. 253.

36. *Personal Letters*, p. 130.

37. Anderson, *op. cit.*, p. 199.

38. Mumford, *op. cit.*, p. 82.

39. *Studies in Classic American Literature*, New York, 1923, p. 207.

40. *Personal Letters*, p. 132.

41. Duyckinck, *Cyclopædia of American Literature*, II, 673.

42. Freeman, *op. cit.*, p. 44.

43. *Mardi*, Preface, p. [vii].

44. *Personal Letters*, p. 40.

45. Anderson, *op. cit.*, p. 344. See especially *Mardi*, Vol. II, Chapter LIV.

46. *Mardi*, II, 380.

47. *Ibid.*, II, 376.

48. The phrase occurs in *Mardi*, II, 377.

49. *Ibid.*, I, 345.

50. *Ibid.*, I, 268-69.

51. *Personal Letters*, p. 40.

52. *Ibid.*, p. 41.

53. *Mardi* (ed. by R. M. Weaver), New York, 1925, Introduction, p. viii.

54. *Personal Letters*, p. 42.

55. *Ibid.*, p. 144.

56. *Redburn*, p. 246.

57. *Ibid.*, pp. 175 ff., 227.

58. *Ibid.*, p. 198.

59. *Personal Letters*, p. 50.

60. Although he much admired Smollett, who was relatively realistic, Melville takes occasion to refer to "the exaggerated sailors of Smollett." (*Redburn*, p. 177.) In *Omoo* (p. 347) Melville tells of the eagerness with which he read Smollett.

61. *Personal Letters*, p. 52.

62. Freeman, *op. cit.*, p. 45.

63. Weaver, *op. cit.*, p. 273.

64. *White Jacket*, p. 59.

65. This was clearly inspired by a comparable (if inferior) scene in *Roderick Random*. For the official record, see Charles R. Anderson (ed.), *Journal of a Cruise to the Pacific Ocean, 1842-1844, in the Frigate United States*, Durham, (N. C.), 1937.

66. For a detailed discussion of the proportion of fact and fiction in *White Jacket*, see C. R. Anderson, *Melville in the South Seas*, Chapters XIII-XVI.

67. *White Jacket,* Chapter LXVII.

68. This manuscript has been printed by Charles R. Anderson. See *American Literature* (May, 1935), VII, [123]-144.

69. *White Jacket,* p. 206.

70. *American Literature,* VII, [123].

71. *White Jacket,* p. 405.

72. *Ibid.,* p. 27.

73. *Ibid.,* p. 205.

74. *Ibid.,* Chapter LXIII.

75. *Ibid.,* Chapter XXXI.

76. *Billy Budd,* p. 92.

77. Thorp, *loc. cit.,* p. xxxvi.

78. Newton Arvin, *Hawthorne,* p. 169.

79. *White Jacket,* p. 356.

80. *Personal Letters,* pp. 55, 66.

81. Weaver, *op. cit.,* p. 319.

82. Randall Stewart, "Hawthorne's Contribution to *The Salem Advertiser*," *American Literature* (January, 1934), V, 328-29.

83. Quoted in *The American Notebooks* (ed. by R. Stewart), p. 307.

84. *Personal Letters,* p. 52.

85. *Ibid.,* pp. 53, 54.

86. Freeman, *op. cit.,* p. 50.

87. Chapter VII.

88. Weaver, *op. cit.,* p. 137.

89. Leon Howard, "A Predecessor of Moby-Dick," *Modern Language Notes* (May, 1934), XLIX, 310-11.

90. It was reprinted in book form by Scribner in 1932.

91. This may be the legend of the white whale to which Emerson referred in his *Journal* for February 19, 1834.

92. *The Examiner,* November 8, 1851, p. 709. Quoted in *American Literature,* III, 196.

93. The simple-minded Stubb, indeed, takes him to be the devil—with his tail tucked up and "coiled away in his pocket." He adds that Fedallah is trying to get Ahab to "swap away his silver watch, or his soul, or something of that sort, and then he'll surrender Moby-Dick." *Moby-Dick,* II, 55-56. This Faustian motif is an integral element of the book often overlooked by critics.

94. *Moby-Dick,* II, 57.

95. Weaver, *op. cit.,* p. 327.

96. *Ibid.*

97. Freeman, *op. cit.,* p. 130.

98. For the details of this incredible expurgation, see William S. Ament, "Bowdler and the Whale," *American Literature* (March, 1932), IV, 39-46.

99. Freeman, *op. cit.,* p. 130.

100. Weaver, *op. cit.,* p. 327.

101. *Moby-Dick,* I, 257.

102. Cf. his words to Mrs. Hawthorne: "I had some vague idea while writing it, that the whole book was susceptible of an allegorical construction, & also that parts of it were—but the speciality of many of the particular subordinate allegories were first revealed to me after reading Mr. Hawthorne's letter, which, without citing any particular examples, yet intimated the part-&-parcel allegoricalness of the whole." Letter to Mrs. Hawthorne, January 8, 1852. *The Saturday Review of Literature* (April 25, 1931), VII, 775.

103. Melville himself invites the interpretation when he notes that the crew (who had no "personal quarrel" with Moby-Dick) finally regarded Moby-Dick as "as much their insufferable foe as his [Ahab's]." *Moby-Dick,* I, 233.

104. H. A. Myers, "Captain Ahab's Discovery," *New England Quarterly* (March, 1942), XV, 28.

105. *Moby-Dick*, II, 366.

106. *Ibid.*

107. Myers, *loc. cit.*, p. 31.

108. *Moby-Dick*, II, 367.

109. Myers, *loc. cit.*, p. 32.

110. *Moby-Dick*, I, 253.

111. *Ibid.*, II, 352.

112. *Ibid.*, I, 270.

113. *Ibid.*, I, 233.

114. Myers, *loc. cit.*, p. 19.

115. Thorp, *loc. cit.*, p. cxxiii.

116. *William Gilmore Simms*, Boston, 1892, p. 330. It is only fair to add that Trent later revised his estimate of Melville somewhat and gave *Moby-Dick* a cool encomium as an "uneven, but on the whole genuine, work of genius." (*A History of American Literature*, New York, 1923, p. 391).

117. *A Literary History of America*, New York, 1914, p. 229.

118. *Heroines of Fiction*, New York, 1901, II, 152.

119. See O. W. Riegel, *American Literature*, III, 198. *Typee* and *Omoo* retained a fair degree of popularity, but *Moby-Dick* was slighted. Charles Anderson asserts (*Melville in the South Seas*, p. 439) that "the popularity of . . . *Moby-Dick* has been consistent all along," but he admits (on the same page) that there were no editions of it in the 1870's and 1880's. A book not re-edited for twenty-nine years (see dates in text above) can scarcely be designated as "popular."

120. Freeman, *op. cit.*, pp. 116, 131. Cf. A. Edward Newton, *This Book-Collecting Game*, Boston, 1928, p. 286.

121. *American Literature* (May, 1931), III, 203. Among the recent discussions of Melville which treat him with tolerance but without enthusiasm is that of A. H. Quinn (*American Fiction*, New York, 1936, pp. 149-58), who not only finds Melville relatively deficient in imagination but also lacking "the artistry of form which distinguished Bret Harte." Although Mr. Quinn refers to *Moby-Dick* as a work of "sustained greatness," he complains of "confused introductory chapters," "tiresome lectures on . . . whales," "lack of a sense of proportion," and of Melville's "inability to distinguish fact from fiction." (*Ibid.*, pp. 151-52.) His imperfect sympathy with *Moby-Dick* is suggested by his caption reference to Melville as a writer of "exotic romance," a phrase which fits *Typee* and *Omoo* fairly well.

122. Weaver, *op. cit.*, p. 326.

123. See Mumford, *op. cit.*, Chapter VIII, *et passim*.

124. *Personal Letters*, p. 71.

125. Weaver, *op. cit.*, p. 341.

126. Cf. *Pierre, or the Ambiguities* (ed. by Robert S. Forsythe), New York, 1930, Introduction, pp. xx, xxiii, xxv.

127. Cf. Weaver, *op. cit.*, p. 342.

128. The important point here is Melville's frankness, for it is clear that the theme of incest could be employed in fiction designed for the home reading table if the author glossed the facts. See above, p. 10 and note 38.

129. *Pierre*, p. 499.

130. *Pierre* (New York, 1929), Preface (by H. M. Tomlinson), p. xiii.

131. *Ibid.*, p. ix.

132. *Cyclopaedia*, II, 674.

133. Tomlinson, *loc. cit.*, p. xvi.

134. *Pierre*, p. 489.

135. Weaver, *op. cit.*, p. 342.

136. See his favorable preface in the Dutton (1929) edition of *Pierre*.

137. Weaver, *op. cit.*, p. 323.
138. *Ibid.*, p. 348.
139. *Personal Letters*, p. 170.
140. Weaver, *op. cit.*, p. 347.
141. Mumford, *op. cit.*, p. 241.
142. *Israel Potter*, p. 62.
143. It was first printed in *Putnam's Magazine* for October, November, and December, 1855.
144. For a discussion of Melville's use of Delano's Journal see H. H. Scudder, "Melville's *Benito Cereno* and Captain Delano's Voyages," *PMLA* (June, 1928), XLIII, 502-32.
145. *PMLA*, XLIII, 502.
146. Freeman, *op. cit.*, p. 148.
147. *Loc. cit.*, p. 529.
148. Freeman, *op. cit.*, p. 145.
149. *The Confidence-Man*, pp. 1-3.
150. *Personal Letters*, pp. 175-76.
151. This was first published in 1935 by The Colophon with an introduction by Raymond Weaver.
152. Freeman, *op. cit.*, p. 70. *Billy Budd* was published in 1927.
153. Preface, p. 4.
154. *Billy Budd*, p. 75.
155. *Ibid.*, p. 38.
156. There is an exceedingly close parallel between *Billy Budd* and Conrad's "The Secret Sharer." In the latter, however, the unintentional killer is a fugitive who, unknown to other members of the ship, seeks the Captain's aid, and is at last set free.
157. *Billy Budd*, p. 29.
158. *White Jacket*, p. 341. Cf. also *Moby-Dick* (I, 133): "But . . . in landlessness alone resides the highest truth, shoreless, indefinite as God . . ."
159. *White Jacket*, p. 341.
160. From the first, Melville's more discerning critics realized that he was no mere writer of sea-adventure stories. Cf. the comment of *The London Times* that Melville was "a very uncommon common sailor." Quoted in *Personal Letters*, p. 108.
161. *Billy Budd*, p. 59.
162. *Moby-Dick*, I, 3.
163. *White Jacket*, p. 97.
164. *Mardi*, II, 71.
165. *Moby-Dick*, I, 291-92.
166. *Ibid.*, II, 169-70.
167. *White Jacket*, p. 96.
168. *Mardi*, II, 36.
169. *Moby-Dick*, I, 348.
170. *White Jacket*, p. 96. He later remarked to Hawthorne, however, that "the *all* feeling" is only "a temporary feeling, or opinion." (Weaver, *op. cit.*, p. 324.)
171. *Moby-Dick*, I, 349.
172. *Ibid.*, I, 243.
173. *Pierre*, p. 424.
174. *The English Notebooks* (ed. by Randall Stewart), New York, 1941, p. 433.
175. *Pierre*, p. 198.
176. *The English Notebooks*, p. 432.
177. *Moby-Dick*, II, 330. Cf. also *ibid.*, I, 7; *White Jacket*, pp. 161, 502.
178. *Pierre*, p. 254.
179. *Billy Budd*, p. 49. See also *ibid.*, p. 46.

180. *Pierre*, p. 150.
181. *White Jacket*, p. 404. See also the last page of *White Jacket*.
182. *Mardi*, I, 272. See also *ibid.*, I, 344; II, 54.
183. *Redburn*, p. 179.
184. Weaver, *op. cit.*, p. 316. In his long and difficult philosophical poem *Clarel* (published 1876) Melville takes account, among other things, of the impact of science on religion. Science, however, could not alone solve Melville's problem. For a brief discussion of *Clarel*, see Thorp, *loc. cit.*, pp. lxxxviii-xcii.
185. *Pierre*, p. 248. Cf. similar views in Hawthorne and Thoreau, above, p. 344 and note 76.
186. *Clarel*, II, 297.
187. *Ibid.*, II, 298.
188. *Personal Letters*, p. 32. Moreover Melville a little resented Emerson's tacit "insinuation that had he lived in those days when the world was made, he might have offered some valuable suggestions." (*Ibid.*, pp. 33, 34.)
189. Quoted by Weaver, *op. cit.*, p. 317.
190. *Moby-Dick*, II, 270.
191. *Mardi*, II, 359.
192. *Pierre* (ed. by R. S. Forsythe), Introduction, p. xxxiv.
193. *Mardi*, II, 365.
194. Letter to Hawthorne, quoted in Weaver, *op. cit.*, pp. 320-22. Melville's remarks were not, of course, intended for publication. Oddly enough, they were almost exactly paralleled by Thoreau in *A Week on the Concord and Merrimack Rivers* (1849), in which the author, after quoting Christ's injunctions regarding the spiritual life, asserts that Christians do not dare read such injunctions aright:

Let but one of these sentences be rightly read from any pulpit in the land, and there would not be left one stone of that meeting-house upon another.

A Week on the Concord . . . (New York, 1921), p. 50.

195. *Poems*, pp. 183 ff.
196. *Ibid.*, p. 185. The remark of the herb-doctor in *The Confidence-Man* seems to carry Melville's conviction: "If by abolitionist you mean a zealot, I am none; but if you mean a man, who . . . feels for all men . . . then am I what you say." (*The Confidence-Man*, p. 149.)
197. See above, p. 379.
198. *Redburn*, p. 259. See also "Poor Man's Pudding" for modification of this view. (*Billy Budd*, pp. 201-02.)
199. *Moby-Dick*, I, 144.
200. *Mardi*, II, 244.
201. *Ibid.*, II, 367.
202. *Ibid.*, I, 215.
203. *The Confidence-Man*, p. 221.
204. Weaver, *op. cit.*, p. 48.
205. *White Jacket*, p. 208.
206. Quoted in Weaver, *op. cit.*, p. 322. Cf. Mrs. Melville's bitter supposition that "if John Milton were to offer 'Paradise Lost' to the Harpers tomorrow, it would be promptly rejected as 'unsuitable,' not to say denounced as dull." *Personal Letters*, p. 87.
207. *Billy Budd*, p. 132.
208. *Ibid.*
209. In *White Jacket* (pp. 207-09) he tells of his delight in turning over a "Man-of-War Library."
210. Thorp, *loc. cit.*, p. xxv.
211. See for example the comments on the sources of *Israel Potter* and "Benito Cereno," above, pp. 390-92.
212. Cf. *Omoo*, p. 347.

213. *White Jacket,* p. 124.

214. *Notes and Queries* (January 16, 1932), CLXII, 39.

215. *White Jacket,* p. 96.

216. *Mardi,* II, 61. See also his studies of the dragon fly's eyes and the flea's leg muscles. *Ibid.,* II, 71.

217. For a partial study of Rabelais' influence on Melville, see W. H. Wells, "*Moby Dick* and Rabelais," *Modern Language Notes* (February, 1923), XXXVIII, 123.

218. Chapters XXXVI-XL.

219. See for example the "Queen Mab" in *Moby-Dick* (Chapter XXXI) and Yoomy's delightful legend in *Mardi,* Chapter XCIII. Melville was not, however, a blind worshipper of Shakespeare. See the judicial discussion of Polonius and Autolycus in *The Confidence-Man* (Chapter XXX).

220. *Mardi,* I, 268.

221. *Poems,* p. 270.

222. Quoted by Riegel, *American Literature* (May, 1931), III, 196.

223. *Pierre,* p. 341.

224. *Billy Budd,* p. 109.

225. *The Confidence-Man,* pp. 89, 90.

226. *Ibid.,* pp. 243-44.

227. *Moby-Dick,* II, 220.

228. *Pierre,* p. 361.

229. *The Dublin Review* (January-March, 1920), CLXVI, 98. Quoted in *American Literature,* V, 363 n.

230. *Moby-Dick,* II, 269-70.

231. *White Jacket,* p. 209.

CHAPTER X

1. *Views and Reviews,* New York, 1845, I, 210.

2. *The Reinterpretation of American Literature* (ed. by N. Foerster), New York, 1928, p. 176.

3. Ralph Thompson, *American Literary Annuals & Gift Books 1825-1865,* New York, 1936, p. [167].

4. Anna B. Warner, *Susan Warner ("Elizabeth Wetherell"),* New York, 1909, p. 1. This book gives a vivid impression of more or less typical struggles of an unknown young woman to gain recognition in the mid-nineteenth century.

5. *Dictionary of American Biography,* XIX, 469. George Putnam later confessed to the "sad want of faith and good judgment" which had prevented his recognizing in the book an exceedingly good commercial risk. He also paid Miss Warner "ten thousand dollars above his contract." Warner, *op. cit.,* pp. 346, 351. Her other novels include the extremely popular *Queechy* (1852) and *Melbourne House* (1864).

6. A chapter-head motto which Miss Warner rather surprisingly chose from *The Merry Wives of Windsor* well characterizes much of the filler material not only in this but in many other domestic novels: "I keep his house, and I wash, wring, brew, bake, scour, dress meat, and make the beds, and do all myself." *The Wide, Wide World,* New York, 1852, II, 74.

7. *Ibid.,* II, 161, 162.

8. *Ibid.,* II, 165.

9. *Ibid.*, II, 179.

10. *Ibid.*, II, 74.

11. Jo March, in *Little Women*, for example, "spent the morning on the river . . . and the afternoon reading and crying over 'The Wide, Wide World,' up in the apple-tree." Louisa M. Alcott, *Little Women*, p. 124 (1907 ed.).

12. *Dictionary of American Biography*, XVII, 414-15.

13. *The Lady of the Isle: a Romance of Real Life*, Philadelphia, 1859, p. 33. The scene of the story is Devonshire.

14. *Dictionary of American Biography*, IV, 600.

15. No self-respecting domestic novel omits the trip to Saratoga. Usually the itinerary also includes visits to Niagara Falls and the White Mountains, but these are optional, whereas Saratoga is required. Sometimes a character is sent abroad by the author, but the European trip is seldom described, doubtless because the author could not command the detail. Most of the authors grew up in a time (1820-1840) when "Europe was an experience which came to few, and to them as the event of a lifetime." C. R. Fish, *The Rise of the Common Man 1830-1850*, New York, 1927, p. 19.

16. *The Lamplighter*, Boston, 1854, pp. 43-44.

17. *Ibid.*, p. [449].

18. *Ernest Linwood*, Boston, 1856, p. 48.

19. *Ibid.*, p. 69.

20. Yet this work is no mere compendium of recipes, but a lively book of table talk on a variety of topics from interior decoration to habits of speech. It is very amusingly written, and contains many literary allusions and aperçus. Many parts of the book indeed make better reading than Miss Harland's novels.

21. *Dictionary of American Biography*, XVIII, 376-77.

22. *Ibid.*

23. *Alone* (New York, 1887), p. 381.

24. *Ibid.*, p. 11.

25. See, for example, *ibid.*, pp. 116, 222.

26. *Ibid.*, p. 116.

27. *The Hidden Path* (New York, 1855), p. 21.

28. *Ibid.*, Dedication.

29. *Dictionary of American Biography*, XVII, 576.

30. Quoted in Edmund Pearson, *Dime Novels*, Boston, 1929, p. 7.

31. *Fashion and Famine*, New York, 1854, p. 282. For further examples of Mrs. Stephens' interest in the need of reform, see *The Old Homestead*, the first half of which is almost completely doctrinaire in its emphasis on the malign effect of municipal graft on the social order.

32. *Fashion and Famine*, pp. 130-31.

33. For a discussion of *Malaeska*, see Pearson, *op. cit.*, pp. 8-13.

34. *Oliver Twist* is in fact referred to by the author. *Ruth Hall: A Domestic Tale of the Present Time*, New York, 1855, p. 182.

35. *Ibid.*, Preface, p. iv.

36. *Ibid.*, pp. 26, 134.

37. *Ibid.*, pp. 302-03.

38. *Ibid.*, p. 216.

39. For a "Key" to *Ruth Hall*, see *Life and Beauties of Fanny Fern*, New York, 1855, Chap. XII. Her father, Nathaniel Willis, was the founder of the *Youth's Companion*.

40. *Ibid.*, p. 63.

41. *Hawthorne and his Publisher*, p. 142.

42. *Southern Quarterly Review* (1852), VI, 120. It was this sort of attitude toward women that angered the stormy Fanny Fern. It is not surprising that she was an admirer of Walt Whitman. The suggestion has been made that Whitman

imitated the title *Fern Leaves* in his *Leaves of Grass. New York Dissected, By Walt Whitman*, ed. by Emory Holloway and Ralph Adimari, New York, 1936, pp. 152, 162-65, 239 (note 17).

43. E. Douglas Branch, *The Sentimental Years, 1836-1860*, New York, 1934, p. 131.

44. *Dictionary of American Biography*, IX, 168.

45. *Inez*, Rahway (New Jersey), [n.d.], p. 179.

46. *Macaria* (New York), 1896, pp. 340-41.

47. Montrose Moses, *The Literature of the South*, New York, 1910, p. 335.

48. Moses, *op. cit.*, p. 333.

49. Mrs. Wilson probably exceeded all other American fiction-writers in frequency of allusion, using at times as many as fifteen allusions on one page and approximately five hundred in one book (*St. Elmo*). She drew upon philosophy, religion, mythology, music, literature, and occultism.

50. R. C. Beatty, *Bayard Taylor*, Norman (Okla.), 1936, p. 210.

51. One relatively new element later to be heavily capitalized in fiction and on the stage, is introduced into *Sherbrooke* when the railroad buys the dear old mortgaged farm.

52. *Sherbrooke*, New York, 1866, p. 253.

53. It is significant that the domestic novelists did not respond quickly to "the freshest European interpreters." Balzac, Stendhal, Flaubert, Turgenev, all of whom were available in the fifties, might just as well not have existed for them. Cf. Mary Moss, "An Impression of the Fifties," *Putnam's Monthly* (January, 1908), III, 399. Perhaps the greatest women's favorite of all, judging from the comments in popular fiction, was Tom Moore. The great names of American letters—Emerson, Thoreau, Hawthorne, Melville, Whitman—are scarcely alluded to. Even Poe's name is seldom invoked except in an occasional Gothic or macabre scene.

54. *Sherbrooke*, p. 349.

55. *Ibid.*, p. 129.

56. Dickens was nevertheless one of the mainstays of the domestic novelists. His Mr. Pickwick was inimitable, but Little Nell was not. And although little given to humor, the ladies of the novel frequently drew eccentric characters of the order of Mr. Turveydrop and Jerry Cruncher. Most of all Dickens was valued for his humanitarianism.

57. *Ibid.*, p. 340.

58. *Dictionary of American Biography*, I, 377.

59. *The Withered Heart*, Philadelphia, 1860, p. 71.

60. *Out in the World* (New York, 1865), p. 78.

61. Arthur's first divorce novel appeared in 1858: *The Hand but Not the Heart*. In general divorces are rare in the popular novel of the period. There was moreover a "lag of ten to twenty years between the general concern over divorce (1860-1875) and reflection of this in . . . divorce novels." J. H. Barnett, *Divorce and the American Divorce Novel 1858-1937*, Philadelphia, 1939, pp. 71, 139.

62. *Dictionary of American Biography*, IX, 146-48. For a full discussion see H. H. Peckham, *Josiah Gilbert Holland*, Philadelphia, 1940, Chapters V, VII.

63. *Dictionary of American Biography*, XVI, 84.

64. Van Doren, p. 113.

65. Stephen Leacock's "Hero in Homespun" (in *Nonsense Novels*) reads unmistakably like a parody of *Barriers Burned Away*, though in a letter to the present writer Mr. Leacock denied ever having read Roe's novel.

66. E. P. Roe, "A Native Author Called Roe," *Lippincott's Monthly Magazine* (October, 1888), XLII, 489.

67. *Barriers Burned Away* (New York, 1886), pp. 52, 53.

68. *Ibid.*, p. 386.

69. *Ibid.*, p. 410.

70. *Lippincott's Monthly Magazine*, XLII, 493.

71. Among the better domestic stories of the period were the juveniles of Louisa May Alcott. Not that Miss Alcott's stories were free from excessive emotional tension and even sentimental tosh. *Little Women* (1868) has the tears, the illnesses, the instructive episodes, the domestic detail, and the prevailingly moral and religious atmosphere of scores of contemporary novels. On the other hand it is blessedly free from many outworn plot devices, as well as from extremely morbid elements. Moreover it possesses genuine humor. Its characters, if not very complex, are individualized. They could not possibly be interchanged with characters in any other story—a test which few characters in domestic stories could meet successfully. In a later period, the best traits of the domestic novel were happily synthesized in Kate Douglas Wiggin's *Rebecca of Sunnybrook Farm* (1903).

72. For this reason the elaborate soul-saving machinery of evangelists was generally presented unfavorably. See, for example, the condemnation of messy emotionalism and sheer hypocrisy in Marion Harland's *Alone*, pp. 103 ff.

73. *Beulah*, New York, [n.d.], p. 237.

74. See above, pp. 218, 414-15, 421, 430.

75. Caroline Hentz, *Ernest Linwood*, p. 109. See also Mrs. Goodwin's *Dr. Howell's Family*, Boston, 1869, pp. 239-40, for criticism of a college course treating of "the miscalled liberal school of writers" who "becloud and daze their own and their readers' intellects."

76. Cf. Ann Stephens, *Fashion and Famine*, p. 293.

77. *Ibid.*, p. 148. For a study of American attitudes toward George Sand, Paul de Kock, Victor Hugo, and other French writers, see H. M. Jones, "American Comment on George Sand, 1837-1848," *American Literature* (January, 1932), III, 389-407.

78. For a typical diatribe against "the arrant, monstrous humbug of fashionable female education" see Marion Harland, *The Hidden Path*, p. 113.

79. Ann Stephens, *The Old Homestead*, p. 236.

80. Caroline Hentz, *Ernest Linwood*, p. 116.

81. *Ibid.*, p. 84.

82. Cf. a comment in Marion Harland's *Alone* (p. 222): "If there is an enjoyment, which is purely of the intellect, its usurpation is man's high prerogative; the sticklers for woman's 'equal rights' will never establish her title to it."

83. The heroine often makes a gallant effort to establish herself as a writer, and she occasionally succeeds for a time. Yet such a course brings her into sharp competition with men, and in the end she is generally defeated by the age-old argument that a woman's "gift" is affection, not intellect—a consummation that was doubtless agreeable to the vast public of female readers, few of whom could hope to be writers. In *The Hidden Path* the heroine freely admits her error: "Had you intimated that I was separating myself from the delicate and good of my sex; establishing myself without the pale of the privileges accorded as the due of their modesty and helplessness; setting myself up as a target for envy and malice and contemptuous pity—above all, excluding myself from that which you knew was as my very life—the affection of my kind—how thankfully would I have remained in the obscurity of my home!" *The Hidden Path*, p. 314.

84. A. J. E. Wilson, *Inez*, p. 35.

85. Among the "reform" novels of the period, Elizabeth Oakes Smith's *The Newsboy* (1854) was among the most popular, having had twelve editions in the first year. Mary A. Wyman, *Two American Pioneers*, New York, 1927, pp. 187-88. This book exhibits some of the traits of the domestic novel, but it is different in being more strongly sociological and in employing a boy for the central figure. The immense possibilities in stories about underprivileged, ambitious boys were soon to be realized by Horatio Alger, Jr., whose books appeared in 1867 ff.

86. *The Lamplighter*, p. 47. The point was of course not a wholly new one even in the American novel. See, for example, the allusion to society's responsibility for criminal behavior in *Guy Rivers*, above, p. 241. In the domestic novel, however, although environment may be used as an explanation of bad behavior, it cannot be used as an excuse for it. In any case the redemption of the individual interested the author more than the indictment of society. There was a perceptible swing from a theological to a scientific conception of the proper control of mental and moral states for "'There is mental as well as bodily sickness, and a true physician should minister to both.'" T. S. Arthur, *The Withered Heart*, p. 216. Cf. O. W. Holmes's elaboration of this view in *Elsie Venner*, below, p. 497.

87. A. C. Cole, *The Irrepressible Conflict 1850-1865*, New York, 1934, p. 198.

CHAPTER XI

1. Harriet Beecher Stowe, *Stories, Sketches, and Studies*, p. [1]. References are to the uniform edition of Mrs. Stowe's works published in sixteen volumes at Cambridge in 1896.

2. Forrest Wilson, *Crusader in Crinoline: The Life of Harriet Beecher Stowe*, Philadelphia, 1941, p. 213. The "E" referred to by Professor Stowe stood for her middle name, Elizabeth.

3. Charles Edward Stowe, *Life of Harriet Beecher Stowe*, Boston, 1889, p. 111.

4. *Ibid.*, p. 106.

5. Wilson, *op. cit.*, p. 190.

6. Quoted in L. D. Turner, *Anti-Slavery Sentiment in American Literature Prior to 1865*, Washington, 1929, p. 59.

7. Wilson, *op. cit.*, p. 260.

8. Kirk Munroe's statement, quoted in Wilson, *op. cit.*, p. 635.

9. Wilson, *op. cit.*, p. 260.

10. Emerson's *Journals* (November [?], 1852), VIII, 346.

11. For a brief discussion of some of the best books to come in the wake of *Uncle Tom's Cabin*, see F. P. Gaines, *The Southern Plantation: A Study in the Development and the Accuracy of a Tradition* (New York, 1925), pp. 41-49. Of course much of the influence of *Uncle Tom's Cabin* was generated by dramatic versions of the story, the first of which appeared in 1852. Mrs. Stowe gave her sanction to none of these, and she attended, so far as is known, only one performance.

12. Wilson, *op. cit.*, p. 297.

13. This literature included "at least fourteen proslavery novels." H. R. Brown, *The Sentimental Novel in America 1789-1860*, Durham (N. C.), 1940, p. 243.

14. Catherine Gilbertson, *Harriet Beecher Stowe*, New York, 1937, p. 166.

15. *Ibid.* Her own solution of the problem of freed slaves, as *Uncle Tom's Cabin* shows, involved the education of the Negroes in the United States as a preliminary step to their colonization in Liberia.

16. Wilson, *op. cit.*, p. 270.

17. *Ibid.*, p. 297.

18. Cf. Howells' comment: "*Uncle Tom's Cabin* . . . is almost the greatest work of imagination that we have produced in prose . . . I do not call it a novel, however." *Literary Friends and Acquaintance*, p. 118.

19. See Chapter XXVIII. Although other Negroes more plausibly based their request for freedom on the grounds that a benevolent master might die, Tom is

interested in "bein' a *free man*" for its own sake. Cf. Candace's quick acceptance of manumission at the hands of a good master in *The Minister's Wooing*, Chapter XI.

20. It must not be forgotten that Mrs. Stowe was wise enough (and honest enough) to depict the more attractive aspects of the master-slave relationship. There is more than a modicum of truth in J. C. Harris's comment: "The real moral that Mrs. Stowe's book teaches is that the possibilities of slavery anywhere and everywhere are shocking to the imagination, while the realities, under the best and happiest conditions, possess a romantic beauty and a tenderness all their own . . ." *Joel Chandler Harris, Editor and Essayist* (ed. by Julia Collier Harris), Chapel Hill, 1931, p. 117.

21. Quoted in Wilson, *op. cit.*, p. 329.

22. *Dred; a Tale of the Great Dismal Swamp*, I (Author's Preface), [xiii].

23. *Dred*, II, 192.

24. So obvious was the importance of Nina's story, that the novel was listed for a time as *Nina Gordon*, and it was so republished in 1866 in England.

25. *Dred* (Cambridge, 1896), I, ix.

26. *Ibid.*

27. C. E. Stowe, *op. cit.*, p. 279.

28. The story appeared in book form in 1859.

29. *The Minister's Wooing*, p. 62.

30. *Ibid.*, p. 9.

31. *Ibid.*, p. 68.

32. C. E. Stowe, *op. cit.*, pp. 333-34, 335.

33. Cf. Parrington, *Main Currents*, II, 372.

34. C. E. Stowe, *op. cit.*, p. 331.

35. *My Wife and I*, Introductory Note, p. viii.

36. *Ibid.*, p. xii.

37. *Ibid.*, p. 275.

38. In spite of formidable documentary evidence pointing toward the guilt of her brother, Henry Ward Beecher, in the Tilton scandal, Mrs. Stowe refused to believe the slightest evil of her brother, and she referred to him as a man of "almost childlike innocence." C. E. Stowe, *op. cit.*, p. 480.

39. *Principles of Domestic Science*, New York, 1870, written in collaboration with Catharine E. Beecher.

40. *The Minister's Wooing*, p. 17.

41. C. E. Stowe, *op. cit.*, p. 340. Cf. Candace's encouraging remark in *The Minister's Wooing* (written in the same year): "I'm clar dar's consid'able more o' de 'lect dan people tink." *The Minister's Wooing*, p. 254.

42. Oldtown Folks, p. xxiv.

43. *The Minister's Wooing*, p. 243.

44. *Ibid.*, p. 353.

45. Howells, *Literary Friends and Acquaintance*, p. 138.

46. *The Minister's Wooing*, p. 226.

47. Lowell's phrase quoted in C. E. Stowe, *op. cit.*, p. 329.

48. Mrs. Stowe did not cope with the problems of Reconstruction. Nor did she turn her attention to the wage-slavery of the North, which was beginning to form the subject matter of fiction. In 1871, Mrs. Elizabeth S. Phelps's *The Silent Partner* discussed capital-and-labor problems in some detail, whereas Mrs. Stowe's *Pink and White Tyranny*, published in the same year, gave only casual attention to a similar problem that was germane to her subject.

49. *The Minister's Wooing*, p. 333.

50. *Ibid.* p. 88.

51. *Dred*, I, 150. In *The Pearl of Orr's Island* (p. 309) Mrs. Stowe corroborates Aunt Nesbit and explains in detail how fiction may corrupt the life of a

young girl by giving her notions that do not comport with the seriousness of life.

52. *My Wife and I*, p. 96.
53. *Ibid.*, p. 151.
54. *Ibid.*, p. 205.
55. *Ibid.*, p. 347.
56. *Ibid.*, p. 348.
57. *Ibid.*,.p. 190.
58. C. F. Richardson, *American Literature 1607-1885*, New York, [1888], Part II, p. 401.
59. John O. Beaty, *John Esten Cooke, Virginian*, New York, 1922, pp. 24-26.
60. This match was evidently to be the climax of the second volume, for it provided a title when the two volumes were issued separately: *Captain Ralph*.
61. *The Virginia Comedians* (New York, 1883), Author's Preface, p. viii. See also *ibid.*, I, 240, for Cooke's preference for characterization by direct methods, especially through speech, rather than by character "analysis."
62. Cf. Beaty, *op. cit.*, p. 41.
63. The story was dramatized by C. W. Tayleure, and presented at Richmond, April 29, 1857, with Joseph Jefferson playing a comic part. Beaty, *op. cit.*, p. 46.
64. *Dictionary of American Biography*, IV, 385.
65. Beaty, *op. cit.*, p. 40, *et passim*.
66. *The Last of the Foresters*, New York, 1856, Preface, p. [v].
67. *Ibid.*, p. 43.
68. Quoted in Beaty, *op. cit.*, p. 70.
69. *Ibid.*, pp. 71-72.
70. *Ibid.*, p. 87.
71. *Ibid.*, pp. 94, 95.
72. *Ibid.*, p. 106.
73. These novels are discussed briefly in Beaty, *op. cit.*, pp. 128 ff.
74. *Henry St. John, Gentleman* (New York, 1860), p. vi.
75. *Southern Literary Messenger*, XXII and XXIII, 68-72 (July, 1856). Cooke's *Virginia: A History of the People* appeared in 1883.
76. *Fairfax; or The Master of Greenway Court*, New York, 1868, p. 193.
77. *Henry St. John, Gentleman*, pp. vi, vii.
78. Quoted in Beaty, *op. cit.*, p. 161.
79. See, for examples of his burlesque, *Southern Literary Messenger* (January, 1849), XV, 16-22, and *ibid.* (November, 1858), XXVII, 334-48.
80. In *The Virginia Comedians* there is considerable allusion to Shakespeare since his plays comprise the repertory of the Hallam troupe at Williamsburg. In general Cooke seems to have preferred Shakespeare's comic gift to his tragic. See for example his discussion of Jaques and Touchstone, *Appleton's Journal* (February 5, 12, 1876), XV, 175-78, 211-13. See also a charming interlude with Shakespeare at the Mermaid Tavern in *My Lady Pokahontas* (Boston, 1885), Chapter II, and an imaginary performance of *The Tempest* at the Globe Theatre (Chapter XXIV).
81. Quoted in Beaty, *op. cit.*, p. 160.
82. Cf. *ibid.*, p. 161.
83. It is perhaps not accident that Cooke used the names Beatrice and Mohun (cf. Beatrix and Mohun in *Esmond*). Cooke later met Thackeray when the latter visited America. See "An Hour with Thackeray," *Appleton's Journal* (September, 1879), XXII, 248-54.
84. The *New York Courier and Enquirer*, for example, referred to it as "a new book—new in style; new in its construction; new in character." *The Virginia Comedians*, end pages of the 1883 edition.
85. Carl Van Doren, *The American Novel* (New York, 1924), p. 117.

86. *Trumps*, New York, [1861], p. 399.

87. *Ibid.*, p. 499.

88. *Ibid.*, pp. 86, 89, 90.

89. *Ibid.*, pp. 342, 344.

90. *Ibid.*, p. 379.

91. *Ibid.*, pp. 413-14.

92. *Ibid.*, pp. 415-16.

93. After the first few chapters the scene of *Trumps* is New York City. For a comparable study of New York society at an earlier date, see Theodore Fay's *Norman Leslie* (1835).

94. *Trumps*, p. 124.

95. Some of these portraits so resembled actual persons that the *North American Review* (July, 1861, XCIII, 288) questioned their propriety, but it nevertheless called *Trumps* "among the very best of American novels."

96. Richmond Croom Beatty, *Bayard Taylor, Laureate of the Gilded Age*, Norman (Oklahoma), 1936, p. 289.

97. *Ibid.*, p. 31.

98. *Ibid.*, p. 229.

99. *Life and Letters of Bayard Taylor*, ed. by Marie Hansen-Taylor and Horace E. Scudder, Boston, 1884, I, 374.

100. Cf. A. H. Smyth, *Bayard Taylor*, Boston, 1896, p. 163.

101. *Ibid.*, p. 163.

102. *Hannah Thurston* (New York, 1864), Dedication, p. 4.

103. *The Atlantic Monthly* (January, 1864), XIII, 133.

104. *Hannah Thurston*, pp. 263 ff.

105. *Ibid.*, p. 179. The author pretty well places himself by vouchsafing that these opinions are "absurd."

106. *Ibid.*, p. 70.

107. A few years later Howells was to use this theme for his novel, *Dr. Breen's Practice*, see below, p. 664.

108. *Ibid.*, p. 62.

109. *Ibid.*, p. 63.

110. *Ibid.*, p. 62. This was a familiar attitude in the domestic novel. Cf. William Grey's protest against women who "act as extinguishers upon the feeble, flickering flame of chivalry, which modern degeneracy in manners and morals has almost smothered." Augusta Evans Wilson, *Vashti*, New York, [n.d.], p. 65.

111. *Hannah Thurston*, p. 276.

112. *The Atlantic Monthly*, XIII, 132.

113. For further examples of Taylor's (often amusing) satire of reformers in general and women's rights in particular, see his short stories, "The Experiences of the A. C." and "Mrs. Strongitharm's Report" in *Beauty and the Beast* (1872).

114. *Life and Letters*, II, 420.

115. *John Godfrey's Fortunes* (New York, 1865), Dedicatory Letter "to James Lorimer Graham, Jr., Esq.," p. [iii].

116. Beatty, *op. cit.*, p. 238.

117. Dedicatory Letter, p. [iii].

118. *The Story of Kennett*, New York, 1866, Prologue, p. [iii].

119. A. H. Smyth, *op. cit.*, pp. 167-68.

120. Beatty, *op. cit.*, p. 238.

121. Whittier went on record as approving *The Story of Kennett* "for its fidelity to Quaker character in its less amiable aspects." W. D. Howells, *Literary Friends and Acquaintance*, p. 135.

122. *The Atlantic Monthly* (June, 1866), XVII, 776.

123. *The Story of Kennett*, Prologue, pp. iv. v.

124. For the "free" tendency of his Oriental poems Taylor was on one occasion

chided by Lowell: "Beware of becoming too deeply enamored of the sensuous in poetry. It is natural that the pendulum of us Yankees should swing very far away from our Puritan and Quaker extreme—only we must remember that Bacchus was the God of severe tragedy also. What I mean is that you must not trust too far to your own purity, because few of your readers will be able to match it." Quoted in Beatty, *op. cit.,* p. 178.

125. Beatty, *op. cit.,* pp. 244, 245, 96.

126. *Ibid.,* p. 158.

127. *Ibid.,* p. 285.

128. That Taylor held a similar opinion of professional critics is apparent from his own statement that when he and his friend Stoddard discussed criticism together the "most complimentary" term they used toward the critic was "to call him a 'lousy son of a bitch!'" *Ibid.,* p. 186.

129. Quotations in this paragraph are from *John Godfrey's Fortunes,* pp. 183, 182, 199, 355, 356, 227, 267. For comparable complaints by Fanny Fern (in *Ruth Hall*), see above, pp. 427-28.

130. Beatty, *op. cit.,* pp. 327-28.

131. *John Godfrey's Fortunes,* p. 320; quoted in Beatty, *op. cit.,* p. 242. The hero is here clearly speaking for the author.

132. *Ibid.,* p. 230.

133. From a lecture of 1855, quoted in Beatty, *op. cit.,* pp. 151-52.

134. *Ibid.,* p. 151.

135. *John Godfrey's Fortunes,* Dedicatory Letter, p. iv.

136. Beatty, *op. cit.,* p. 151.

137. Elbridge Colby, *Bibliographical Notes on Theodore Winthrop,* The New York Public Library, 1917, p. 6.

138. Elbridge Colby, *The Plates of the Winthrop Books,* The New York Public Library, 1918, p. 3.

139. Cf. Mary Moss's observation: "Theodore Winthrop, underrated and forgotten, belonged in his mental processes to our world rather than his own." "An Impression of the Fifties," *Putnam's Monthly* (January, 1908), III, 400.

140. *The Life and Poems of Theodore Winthrop, Edited by his Sister,* New York, 1884, p. 20.

141. *Ibid.,* p. 19.

142. *Ibid.,* p. 21.

143. *Ibid.,* pp. 264-65, 274.

144. *Ibid.,* p. 273.

145. *Cecil Dreeme,* Boston, 1862, pp. 66-67.

146. *Life and Poems,* p. 163.

147. In a brief but merry sequel, *Love and Skates,* Richard Wade is also provided with a wife. *Love and Skates,* accepted by James Russell Lowell before Winthrop's death, appeared first in *The Atlantic Monthly* (January, February, 1862), IX, 70-85, 223-40. It was also published in Winthrop's *Life in the Open Air, and Other Papers,* Boston, 1863.

148. Winthrop indicates his awareness of the similarity of some of his material to Cooper's in an apostrophe to "Fenimore." *John Brent,* Boston, 1862, p. 38.

149. G. W. Curtis, "Biographical Sketch of the Author," *Cecil Dreeme,* p. 6.

150. With *John Brent, Edwin Brothertoft* was intended to be part of a series of tales "bound together by their connection with an old house on the Hudson." *Life and Poems,* p. 277. The third was to be *Love and Skates.* The plan was abandoned, but signs of it remain in the duplication of certain characters.

151. *Edwin Brothertoft,* Boston, 1862, p. 71.

152. *Ibid.,* p. 360.

153. *Ibid.,* pp. 16, 17.

154. *Ibid.,* pp. 13, 14.

155. *Ibid.*, Chapters XXI, XXII.
156. *Ibid.*, p. 301.
157. *Ibid.*, p. 150.
158. *Cecil Dreeme*, p. 243.
159. *Edwin Brothertoft*, pp. 26, 98.
160. *Ibid.*, p. 67.
161. *Ibid.*, pp. 240-41. See also p. 123.
162. *Ibid.*, p. 74.
163. *Ibid.*, pp. 138-39.
164. *Life and Poems*, p. 277.
165. Winthrop's *The Canoe and the Saddle* (1863), a vivid account of some of his western travels, does not exhibit his best writing. The book was, however, exceedingly popular. There is also a journal, incorporated in the 1863 edition of *The Canoe and the Saddle.*
166. The novel had first appeared serially in *The Atlantic Monthly* (1860-61) as *The Professor's Story.*
167. For signs of Hawthorne's apparent influence on Holmes, see especially *Elsie Venner: A Romance of Destiny*, Cambridge, 1891, pp. 260-62. All references are to the Riverside Edition: *The Writings of Olive Wendell Holmes*, Cambridge, 1891-92, 14 vols.
168. Complaint was made of the "cruel" conception of "an alien element introduced into the blood of a human being before that being saw the light." *The Guardian Angel*, "To My Readers," p. [vii].
169. *Elsie Venner*, Preface, p. [vii].
170. Moreover he used a comparable theme in *The Guardian Angel.* See below.
171. *Elsie Venner*, p. 323. Cf. also *ibid.*, pp. 225-28. These same ideas crop up in Holmes's other writing, especially the essays "Crime and Automatism," "Jonathan Edwards," and "Mechanism in Thought and Morals." (These essays appear in *Pages From an Old Volume of Life, Writings*, vol. VIII.) "Moral idiocy," he wrote in "Crime and Automatism," "is the greatest calamity a man can inherit, and the subjects of it deserve our deepest pity and greatest care." A "moral hospital" rather than a prison would seem to be the place for such unfortunate persons. Their actions in many cases are determined quite independently of their wills. Dr. Holmes did not utterly deny freedom of the will, but he thought it was reduced to a very low ratio. "We are getting to be predestinarians as much as Edwards or Calvin was," he wrote in the essay on Edwards, "only instead of universal corruption derived from Adam, we recognize inherited congenital tendencies." Consequently he wished to "punish" the crime rather than the criminal. Holmes discussed morality from the point of view of a scientist rather than a theologian. For an elaboration of these views, see H. H. Clark, "Dr. Holmes: A Re-Interpretation," *The New England Quarterly* (March, 1939), XII, 19-34.
172. In a latter-day New England story, *The Last Puritan*, Santayana also represents medical science as getting the better of theology on a point involving education. See *The Last Puritan*, New York, 1936, Chapter III.
173. The *Guardian Angel*, pp. 22, 23.
174. *Ibid.*, p. 27.
175. W. D. Howells, *Literary Friends and Acquaintance*, p. 153.
176. The *Nation* complained in 1867 that even then Holmes was belaboring a dead horse: "Dr. Holmes . . . goes through his story,—too often bearing on hard when only the lightest touch would have been pleasing, not to say sufferable; sternly breaking on his wheel the deadest of bugs and butterflies." Quoted in W. S. Kennedy, *Oliver Wendell Holmes*, Boston, 1883, p. 179.
177. H. H. Clark, *loc. cit.*, p. 27.
178. Chapter XVIII. It was the elaboration of this sort of light mockery which led a reviewer in the *Nation* to remark in 1867: "We speak of the author as a

satirist. That he is, mainly; he is hardly to be called a novelist." Kennedy, *op. cit.*, p. 180.

179. *The Guardian Angel*, pp. 138, 158, 230.

180. Cf. Leslie Stephen: "He [Holmes] did not get fairly absorbed in his story and feel as though he were watching, instead of contriving, the development of a situation . . . Holmes is distinctly a spectator from outside, and his attention is too easily distracted." *Studies of a Biographer*, New York, 1899, II, 175.

181. W. D. Howells remarked that Holmes "was not constructive; he was essentially observant, and in this he showed the scientific nature." *Literary Friends and Acquaintance*, p. 171.

182. J. T. Morse, Jr., *Life and Letters of Oliver Wendell Holmes*, Boston, 1896, II, 246. The letter is undated.

183. It is interesting to observe, however, that Mrs. Stowe, surrounded by ministers as she was, could be so impressed by Holmes's use of medical correctives to theology as to be able to say after reading *Elsie Venner* that a "course of medical study ought to be required of all ministers." C. E. Stowe, *op. cit.*, p. 360.

184. Lowell, "Credidimus Jovem Regnare."

185. J. T. Morse, *op. cit.*, II, 245-46.

186. Though he granted them a measure of skill, Holmes violently objected to the novels of Flaubert and Zola on account of their "realistic" exploitation of sex and of horror. *Over the Teacups*, pp. 106-07, 108-10.

187. *Oliver Wendell Holmes* (ed. by S. I. Hayakawa and Howard M. Jones), New York, 1939, Introduction, p. xvii.

188. *Ibid.*, p. xxii.

189. *Elsie Venner*, p. 5.

190. *The Professor at the Breakfast-Table*, p. 133. See also his verbal quibble: "I go politically for equality . . . and socially for *the* quality." *Ibid.*

191. Holmes's own term. Morse, *op. cit.*, I, 247.

192. See *The Professor at the Breakfast-Table*, pp. 135-36.

193. *A Mortal Antipathy*, pp. 34, 35, 106, 108 ff.

194. *Ibid.*, p. 106.

195. *Ibid.*, p. 32.

CHAPTER XII

1. J. W. De Forest, *Miss Ravenel's Conversion from Secession to Loyalty*, New York, 1939, Introduction, pp. x, xi. This novel, originally a Harper book, was reissued (with many important corrections of the text) by the same house with a brief introduction by Gordon S. Haight. For biographical facts concerning De Forest, see also *Dictionary of American Biography*. Very little has been written on De Forest, and that little not always factually consistent.

2. *Witching Times* was serialized in *Putnam's Magazine* between December, 1856, and September, 1857.

3. Cf. Quinn, *American Fiction*, pp. 166-67.

4. "The First Time Under Fire," *Harper's Magazine* (September, 1864), XXIX, 475-82.

5. A good example of De Forest's ironical style may be found in the comment of Dr. Ravenel after he has been clubbed by a ruffian. In complimenting Colburne on his manners, the Doctor observes: "He doesn't know all the pretty manners and customs of the place . . . He hasn't yet learned to knock down

elderly gentlemen because they disagree with him in politics. They are awfully behind-hand at the North, Mrs. Larue, in those social graces. The mudsill Sumner was too unpolished to think of clubbing the brains out of the gentleman Brooks. He boorishly undertook to settle a question of right and justice by argument." *Miss Ravenel's Conversion from Secession to Loyalty* (New York, 1939), p. 134.

6. Edwin Mims, *Sidney Lanier*, Boston, 1905, p. 36.

7. For Cooke's use of the Civil War as a theme, see above, pp. 468-69.

8. *Miss Ravenel's Conversion*, pp. 243-44.

9. *Ibid.*, p. 246.

10. *Ibid.*, p. 251.

11. *Ibid.*, p. 255.

12. *Ibid.*, p. 257.

13. *Ibid.*, p. 259.

14. *Ibid.*, p. 261.

15. *Ibid.*, p. 100.

16. *Ibid.*, p. 74.

17. *Ibid.*, pp. 235-37. De Forest comments intelligently upon post-war sociological problems, but he did not become absorbed in them, like Tourgée. Human nature, rather than human "problems," interested De Forest.

18. *Ibid.*, p. 156.

19. *Ibid.*, p. 14. For Mrs. Stowe's similar views, see above, pp. 459-60.

20. *Ibid.*, p. 85.

21. *Ibid.*, p. 16.

22. At the end of the story she is only twenty-three years old—a partial explanation of her limitations in the eyes of the author, for De Forest plainly states that "women are most interesting at thirty." Howells, a slightly later realist and an admirer of De Forest, held a similar view of women. See below, pp. 671, 685.

23. For the typical heroine of the period, see above, pp. 413-15.

24. *Miss Ravenel's Conversion*, pp. 72, 73.

25. *Ibid.*, p. 102.

26. *Ibid.*, p. 87.

27. *Ibid.*, pp. 128-29.

27a. *Heroines of Fiction*, II, 153, 162.

28. Quinn, p. 169.

29. *Kate Beaumont*, Boston, 1872, p. 102.

30. *Heroines of Fiction*, II, 152-63.

31. *Kate Beaumont*, p. 98.

32. *Ibid.*, p. 65.

33. De Forest wrote one other novel laid in South Carolina, *The Bloody Chasm* (1881).

34. The novel most nearly akin to it in the same period is G. W. Curtis's *Trumps* (1861), which is discussed above, pp. 472-75.

35. *Honest John Vane*, New Haven, 1875, p. 11.

36. *Ibid.*, p. 187.

37. *Ibid.*, p. 46.

38. *Ibid.*, pp. 46-47.

39. See above, pp. 43 ff.

40. *Honest John Vane*, p. 28.

41. *Ibid.*, p. 29.

42. *Ibid.*, p. 18.

43. *Ibid.*, pp. 257-58.

44. *Ibid.*, p. 22.

45. Not the least cynical aspect of the book is the revelation of Olympia Vane's character. After John goes to Washington, she becomes quickly discontented with her lot as the wife of an ordinary Congressman. Nor can she be sat-

isfied with his comparative success but longs for "her own separate empire and glory." (P. 69.) Like most of De Forest's female characters, Olympia comes off badly.

46. In another political satire, *Playing the Mischief* (1875), De Forest devotes further attention to the welter of corruption—major and minor—in Washington. Female lobbying proves to be part of the "mischief."

47. See above, Chapter X.

48. *Heroines of Fiction*, II, 157.

49. The parallel extends even to certain specific scenes. For example when Colburne is more or less fortuitously prevented from proposing to Lillie near the beginning of *Miss Ravenel's Conversion* (cf. above, p. 513), De Forest's narrative strategy distinctly recalls the scene in which the untimely entrance of George and Amelia helps to prevent Joseph Sedley from coming forth with a declaration which would have committed him to Becky's designing heart and so ended Thackeray's story before it was well begun. *Vanity Fair*, Chap. IV. Both writers were fond of suggesting that the flowering of young love is more dependent on chance and environment than on inevitable and star-constant attraction.

50. Even so, Mrs. Larue was too rich for the blood of Howells. It is amusing to note that in his reference to this woman—whom, he said, he could not think of "without shuddering"—Howells made what will now be regarded as a Freudian slip, for he even misspelled her name, writing Mrs. "Leroy" instead of Mrs. "Larue." *Heroines of Fiction*, II, 157.

51. Cf. Meredith's observation: "You may estimate your capacity for comic perception by being able to detect the ridicule of them you love without loving them less." *An Essay on Comedy and the Uses of the Comic Spirit* (New York, 1918), p. 133; see also p. 120.

52. There is validity in Howells' criticism that in De Forest's treatment of "bad" characters "the artist's contempt for their duplicity masters his sense of the goodness, the sincerity indeed, which consists with that duplicity." *Op. cit.*, p. 162. Cf. also the opinion of a reviewer (presumably Howells) of *Overland*, who complained that the unpleasant people, though well drawn, are "hardly balanced by the good people of the story." *The Atlantic Monthly* (January, 1872), XXIX, 111.

53. For a discussion of Thackeray's comparative failure in "performance," see Percy Lubbock, *The Craft of Fiction*, pp. 93 ff. Thackeray was one of those writers whose somewhat indolent narrative technique caused Henry James to feel that the form of the novel needed artistic disciplining. Cf. below, pp. 702, 729.

54. Quoted in Roy F. Dibble, *Albion W. Tourgée*, New York, 1921, p. 26. This study is the best source of external facts concerning Tourgée's life. The author's strangely hostile attitude, however, prevents his book from being a satisfactory biography.

55. See below, p. 531.

56. Dibble, *op. cit.*, p. 145.

57. *Ibid.*, p. 49. *Toinette* was reissued in 1881 as *A Royal Gentleman*.

58. *A Royal Gentleman*, New York, 1881, p. 465.

59. *Ibid.*, pp. 446-47, 463.

60. *Ibid.*, Preface, p. ix.

61. *A Fool's Errand*, New York, 1879, p. 341.

62. "The South as a Field for Fiction," *The Forum* (December, 1888), VI, 404-13.

63. *Ibid.*, p. 410. He also predicted later that the South would be "the Hesperides Gardens of American literature." *Ibid.*, p. 413.

64. Despite Tourgée's service to the state of North Carolina in codifying the state laws (Dibble, *op. cit.*, p. 40), and despite other evidences of his true interest in the South, he has seldom received fair treatment at the hands of critics. By many writers he has been regarded as little less than a carpet-bagger. His honest

motives were overlooked; enough that he called attention to the South's occasional mistreatment of the Negro and her general inability to cope with the entire problem of Reconstruction.

65. *The Forum*, VI, 411.
66. *A Fool's Errand*, p. 46.
67. *Ibid.*, p. 20.
68. Quoted in Dibble, *op. cit.*, p. 65. The fifth provision of the Act was for "general negro enfranchisement and limited rebel disfranchisement."
69. They are quoted in Dibble, p. 66.
70. *A Fool's Errand*, pp. 346-47.
71. *Ibid.*, p. 152.
72. *Ibid.*, pp. 113-14.
73. *Ibid.*, Letter to the Publishers, p. [3].
74. Dibble, p. 68.
75. *The Invisible Empire* appeared in 1880 as "Part II" of *A Fool's Errand*.
76. *Bricks Without Straw*, New York, 1880, p. 401.
77. *Ibid.*, pp. 34-35. Cf. also these moving lines from a poem by Tourgée:

> Yet up from the Southland comes a moan
> Like Yesterday's ceaseless monotone.
> Hark! 'Tis the half-freed Slave's lament. [*sic*]
> For the bliss we promised and woe we sent.

Quoted in Dibble, p. 145.
78. *Bricks Without Straw*, p. 41.
79. *Ibid.*, pp. 26-27.
80. *Ibid.*, Chap. V.
81. *Ibid.*, p. 48.
82. *Ibid.*, p. 56.
83. See above, p. 239.
84. *Ibid.*, Chap. LVII. In later years Tourgée admitted with bitter irony that education and Christianity did not seem equal to their obligations, but Mr. Dibble's comments on Tourgée's apparent renunciation of his principles are heavily prejudiced and utterly misleading. *Op. cit.*, pp. 126-27.
85. The emblem at the end of the novel is an open spelling-book reading "In Hoc Signo Vinces."
86. For an analysis of the story, see Dibble, *op. cit.*, pp. 54-55. In the same volume with *John Eax* there appeared another novelette, *Mamelon*, which with its twin story comprised (as the Preface states) two "rifts in the shadow" that overlay the South. Later in the same year a third rift was added, *Zouri's Christmas*, in a volume given the sub-title *Life Sketches*.
87. Dibble, pp. 86-87.
88. *Hot Plowshares* (New York, 1883), Preface. Tourgée implies that he had planned the series years before, but it seems likely (see Dibble, pp. 61-62) that he was indulging in a bit of hindsight. Indeed he admits as much by saying in the Preface (p. vi) to the 1881 edition of *A Royal Gentleman* that his stories were "an unpremeditated 'series.'"
89. *Hot Plowshares*, Preface.
90. *A Royal Gentleman*, Preface (to the 1881 edition), pp. iii-iv.
91. For a discussion of the most important of Tourgée's periodical ventures, *Our Continent*, see Dibble, pp. 84-91.
92. Dibble, pp. 113, 115.
93. *Murvale Eastman, Christian Socialist* (New York, 1890), Preface, pp. [i], ii.
94. *Ibid.*, pp. 454-55.
95. *Ibid.*, p. 318.

96. Quoted in Dibble, p. 135.

97. *Murvale Eastman*, pp. 113-14.

98. In *Button's Inn* Tourgée writes that a certain young man's hands "were scrupulously clean except for traces of his recent occupation [slaughtering a lamb]; for the day of the 'realistic' novel had not yet dawned, and there were yet people living even in country places who sometimes washed their hands." (P. 24.)

99. *Murvale Eastman*, p. 165.

100. "The South as a Field for Fiction," *The Forum*, VI, 411.

101. Dibble, pp. 139-40.

102. *Murvale Eastman*, p. 415.

103. *Ibid.*

104. Dibble, p. 138.

105. For further comments by Tourgée on the nature of realism, see the Preface to *With Gauge & Swallow, Attorneys*.

106. *Murvale Eastman*, p. 420. He was also a trifle skeptical of the uses of biography, for "Biography covers the whole area of History with private landmarks." *Hot Plowshares*, Preface.

107. Dibble, p. 133.

CHAPTER XIII

1. William Dean Howells, "Recent Literature," *The Atlantic Monthly* (Oct. 1872), XXX, 487.

2. "Books That Have Helped Me," *The Forum* (August, 1887), III, 584.

2a. For an extended biographical study of Eggleston, see W. P. Randel, *Edward Eggleston, Author of The Hoosier School-Master*, New York, 1946.

3. Edward Eggleston, "Formative Influences," *The Forum* (November, 1890), X, [279].

4. He once refused an offer to send him to the University of Virginia on account of his hatred of the institution of slavery, to which the state subscribed. *Dictionary of American Biography*, VI, 52. Chronic ill health also forbade a regular college course.

5. *The Forum*, X, 283. Cf. also Albert Charlton's remarks in *The Mystery of Metropolisville* (p. 41): "I learned six times as much as some of the dunderheads that got sheepskins, and the professors knew it, but they do not dare to put their seal on anybody's education unless it is mixed in exact proportions—so much Latin, so much Greek, so much mathematics. The professors don't like a man to travel any road but theirs. It is a reflection on their own education."

6. *The Forum*, X, 280.

7. *Ibid.* Fiction, however, was viewed with a hostile eye. Eggleston reported that when he was a youngster "religious prejudices made [him] shrink from novels." *Ibid.*, p. 284.

8. *Ibid.*, p. 285.

9. *Ibid.*, p. 289.

10. Later Eggleston returned to the ministry as pastor of The Church of Christian Endeavor in Brooklyn (1874-1879).

11. The story was serialized between Sept. 30 and Dec. 30, 1871. In book form it carries the imprint 1871.

12. *The Forum*, III, 584.

13. The spelling bee in *The Hoosier Schoolmaster* seems to have been in large

part the cause of an enormous revival of spelling bees throughout the country. *PMLA* (June, 1941), LVI, 506.

14. *The Hoosier School-Master*, New York, 1871, p. 184.

15. *Ibid.*, p. 224.

16. Van Doren perhaps errs in drawing a sharp line between Eggleston and the writers of penny dreadfuls. *American Novel*, p. 119. Eggleston often helped himself to stereotyped Gothic night scenes involving desperadoes.

17. *The Hoosier Schoolmaster* (Chicago, 1901), Preface, p. 8.

18. *The Hoosier School-Master*, New York, 1871, Preface, p. 6. In his (1892) preface to the "library edition" of *The Hoosier Schoolmaster*, Eggleston gave a detailed account of the genesis and development of his novel, and he added numerous comments on the special peculiarities of the frontier.

19. *The Hoosier Schoolmaster* (Chicago, 1901), Preface, p. 6. This is not to say, of course, that dialect had not been used frequently as an accessory to novels whose main bearings were quite different.

20. Like *The Hoosier Schoolmaster*, this novel was serialized in *Hearth and Home*.

21. *Dictionary of American Biography*, VI, 53

22. *The Mystery of Metropolisville* (New York, 1873), p. 13.

23. *Ibid.*, p. 21.

24. *Ibid.*, Preface, p. 7.

25. *Scribner's Monthly Magazine* (September, 1873), VI, 563.

26. *The Circuit Rider*, New York, 1874, p. 159.

27. *Ibid.*, p. 74.

28. *Ibid.*, p. 214.

29. *Ibid.*, pp. 173-74.

30. *Ibid.*, pp. 158-59.

31. That *Roxy* was serialized in *The Century* is an indication of the growth of Eggleston's reputation among more conservative critics, who had at first "affected to look on Eggleston as an undisciplined product of the Wild West." H. C. Vedder, *American Writers of Today*, New York, 1894, p. 254. In his earlier days Eggleston was inclined to wear a chip on his (Western) shoulder. See, for example, his irritable suggestion that a man "who had the unhappiness to be born in longitude west from Washington" would probably not be accepted as an author. *The Mystery of Metropolisville*, p. 125.

32. *Roxy*, New York, 1878, p. 271.

33. *Ibid.*, pp. [424]-25. Not only Eggleston's reference to the sweetness of stolen water-melon, but the whole tone and much of the detail of this passage bear a close relationship to the terms in which Mark Twain was to celebrate similar delights in similar latitudes a few hundred miles farther west. Cf. below, pp. 601-03.

34. Eggleston did not pull up all his literary stakes when he moved to New York for the setting of *The Faith Doctor*. The cracker-box philosophy and homely wisdom associated with the Hoosier state, crop out from time to time in metropolitan scenes. Thus the author notes at the very beginning that "every fairly dressed man is a dude to somebody," and he introduces one Sampson as "a quiet man with the air of one who knows it all and is rather sorry that he does." *The Faith Doctor*, New York, 1891, pp. [7], 19.

35. Vedder, *op. cit.*, p. 255.

36. *The Forum*, X, 286-87.

37. *The Hoosier School-Master*, New York, 1871, Preface, p. [5].

38. *The Hoosier Schoolmaster* (Chicago, 1901), Preface, p. 7.

39. *Ibid.*, p. 20.

40. *Ibid.*

41. *Ibid.*, pp. 20, 21.

42. *The Mystery of Metropolisville*, p. 21.

43. *The Circuit Rider*, p. 13.

44. *The Faith Doctor*, pp. 55-56.

45. Cf. his remark in the Preface to *The Circuit Rider*: "The story of any true life is wholesome."

46. Cf. V. F. Calverton, *The Liberation of American Literature*, pp. 340 ff. On several occasions, however, Garland acknowledged Eggleston's inspiration. See especially *Roadside Meetings*, pp. 94, 111, and *A Son of the Middle Border*, p. 243.

47. *The Mystery of Metropolisville*, Preface, p. 7.

48. *The Circuit Rider*, Preface, pp. vi-vii.

49. *Ibid.*, p. [243].

50. *The Hoosier Schoolmaster*, pp. 109-10. Cf. also Eggleston's protest against "such novels as 'The Pirate's Bride,' 'Claude Duval,' 'The Wild Rover of the West Indies,' and the cheap biographies of such men as Murrell." *Ibid.*, p. 255. In *The Mystery of Metropolisville* (p. 124) he satirizes the female reader of sensational literature with its "labyrinthine plots and counterplots."

51. *The Hoosier Schoolmaster*, pp. 90, 91.

52. *The Circuit Rider*, Preface, p. vii.

53. Cf. his remarks on the literary life in New York: *The Faith Doctor*, pp. 21-26.

54. H. C. Vedder, *op. cit.*, p. 260.

55. *The Hoosier Schoolmaster*, Preface to the Library Edition, pp. 6-7. On the subject of Eggleston's nationalism, see further *The Circuit Rider*, p. 55.

56. Lucy Leffingwell Cable Biklé, *George W. Cable, His Life and Letters*, New York, 1928, p. 155.

57. Feeling against Cable persisted for a long time even in literary histories written by Southerners. See for example Montrose Moses, *The Literature of the South*, pp. 434-35. Mrs. Biklé's biography amply shows that Cable did not develop an animus against the South.

58. Biklé, *op. cit.*, pp. viii, ix.

59. *The Grandissimes, A Story of Creole Life* (New York, 1884), p. 27.

60. Cf. Gaines, *The Southern Plantation* (p. 70): "The plantation as a definite locale is largely missing from the work of George W. Cable." Yet, as Gaines adds, Cable succeeded in presenting the "social manifestations" of slavery extremely well by means of his emphasis on "its caste structure and its race relations."

61. For all his discretion in this book, Cable was harshly criticized for his "unfairness" to the South. Subsequently in a number of articles (later collected into a volume, *The Silent South*) he considered some of the problems which faced the South during Reconstruction. Although during the actual composition of *The Grandissimes* he was still in the stage of "very slowly and painfully guessing out the riddle of our Southern Question (Biklé, *op. cit.*, pp. 158-59), he came to have certain very definite convictions regarding the South's obligation toward freed slaves—convictions which were probably strengthened by his residence in New England, where he observed "that kind of American civilization founded on the Village, the antipode of the Plantation." (*Ibid.*, p. 161.) In particular he was distressed by the Negroes' "unequal chances in the courts of law." (*Ibid.*, p. 160. Cf. Tourgée's similar conclusion, above, pp. 528-29.) These and other avowals (as well as his Northern residence, no doubt) brought Cable into odium with Southerners, but he insisted that his motives were purely humanitarian: he was interested not in "party exigency" but in "political ethics." (*Ibid.*, p. 164.) For an explanation of why Creoles to this day hate the very name of Cable, see E. L. Tinker, "Cable and the Creoles," *American Literature* (January, 1934), V, [313]-326. Principally they held it against him that he was the first Southerner to espouse the cause of the Negro and the quadroon in fiction. They also feared that Cable's harping on the theme of miscegenation might give "the impression that their race [*i.e.*, the Creole's] was not of unsullied descent." So high was the feeling against Cable that

printed attacks on him carried the most offensive terminology, one pamphlet-writer comparing Cable to a "buzzard" and a "jackal" and alluding to his extremely short stature by calling him a "grim-humored dwarf." *Ibid.*, pp. 319, 322-32.

62. *The Grandissimes*, p. 144.

63. *Ibid.*, p. [439].

64. It was Lafcadio Hearn who first called attention to the "strict perfection of [Cable's] Creole architecture." *The Century*, V, 40. Quoted in Pattee, *American Literature Since 1870*, p. 248.

65. *The Grandissimes*, pp. [78]-79.

66. Van Doren, p. 195.

67. *The Grandissimes*, pp. 446-47.

68. Barrie visited Cable at Northampton in 1896. See Biklé, *op. cit.*, pp. 217 ff.

69. It was enthusiastically received upon its first appearance in *Scribner's Monthly* (beginning November, 1879) and it was greeted by *Harper's* as "one of the great novels of our times." Quoted in Gaines, *The Southern Plantation*, p. 70. At almost the same time, the author of *A Fool's Errand* was being called "the great American novelist." Cf. above, p. 527. It was a period when there was a feverish search on all sides for a novel which could be accorded the superlative designation. For a discussion of the whole subject, see Herbert R. Brown, "The Great American Novel," *American Literature* (March, 1935), VII, 1-14.

70. Biklé, *op. cit.*, p. 226, note.

71. Cable's "Madame Delphine," a superbly finished novelette on the subject of miscegenation appeared in 1881. It is now generally reprinted in the volume called *Old Creole Days*.

72. *Dr. Sevier* (Boston, 1885), p. 448.

73. *Ibid.*, p. 143.

74. *Ibid.*, p. 85.

75. *Ibid.*, pp. 122, 200.

76. *Ibid.*, p. 216. For a discussion of the strong sense of community responsibility which led Cable to work for reform of prison and asylum in New Orleans, see Biklé, pp. 159-60.

77. *Dr. Sevier*, p. 290.

78. See especially Chapter XXII in which Narcisse "touches" Richling for a loan.

79. *The Cavalier*, New York, 1901, p. 213.

80. For a bibliography including most of Cable's papers on social reform, see Biklé, *op. cit.*, pp. 303-06.

81. *Ibid.*, pp. 200-01.

82. Letter to his daughter, *ibid.*, p. 174.

83. *Ibid.*, p. xiii.

84. See James's *Partial Portraits*, London, 1888, Chapter VI.

85. For a study of her life and writings see John Dwight Kern, *Constance Fenimore Woolson: Literary Pioneer*, Philadelphia, 1934. For such autobiography as is available in the abridged letters of Miss Woolson, see Clare Benedict (ed.), *Constance Fenimore Woolson*, London [1930]. This latter work is the second part of a three-volume study entitled *Five Generations* (*1785-1923*). For a brief biographical and critical study, see Lyon N. Richardson, "Constance Fenimore Woolson, 'Novelist Laureate' of America," *South Atlantic Quarterly* (January, 1940), XXXIX, 18-36.

86. *Anne, A Novel*, New York, 1882, pp. 2, 3.

87. Cf. an observation in one of her notebooks: "Character . . . should . . . grow and develop on the scene; in the book. Not to be introduced completely formed in the beginning." Clare Benedict (ed.), *Constance Fenimore Woolson*, p. 99. Few novelists of the nineteenth century (except Hawthorne and James) have

left such copious laboratory or workshop notes—comment on technique, ideas for stories, etc.—as Miss Woolson. These may be found in the work cited, pp. 95-150. At many points her notes distinctly show her kinship with Hawthorne and James. Hawthorne might have been interested by this (*ibid.*, p. 137): "To imagine in an old Italian palace or villa a bell which rang at the top of a very high ceiling, now and then. No one can find any cord or handle to it!" A turn of thought that James might have found interesting (*ibid.*, p. 138): "An American who has lived so long abroad that he is almost de-nationalized, and *conscious of it fully;* which makes him an original figure."

88. "The Art of Fiction," *Partial Portraits*, p. 392.

89. *Anne*, pp. 1, 2.

90. Cf. a comment in her notebook: "I care only for motives; why a man or woman does or has done so and so. Ditto a nation. It is the mental state—the mental problem that interests me." *Constance Fenimore Woolson*, pp. 118-19.

91. *Partial Portraits*, p. 183. As it happens, James achieves this neat antithesis at some slight expense of truth. It was the daughter who was really the Puritan, as Madam makes it clear when she says in discussing her stratagem with Sara: "Under the same circumstances you would never have done it, nor under twenty times the same circumstances. But I am not you; I am not anybody but myself. That lofty kind of vision which sees only the one path, and that the highest, is not mine; I always see . . . the cross-cuts." *For the Major*, New York, 1883, p. 160.

92. *Partial Portraits*, p. 184.

93. *For the Major*, p. 179.

94. *Ibid.*, p. 131.

95. James, *op. cit.*, p. 187.

95a. *Ibid.*, p. 191.

96. Kern, *op. cit.*, p. 88.

97. Indeed among Northern writers it was Miss Woolson who had the "surest grip upon a mood of plantation life, the bewildering numbness of that civilization after the full import of the change was realized." Gaines, *The Southern Plantation*, pp. 68-69. The poignant suffering of the South (spiritual and material) after the War is brought out in an almost perfect short story, "Old Gardiston" (published first in *Harper's Magazine* in 1876; collected in *Rodman the Keeper*, 1880).

98. Kern, *op. cit.*, p. 91.

99. Cf. below, p. 723.

100. *Horace Chase, A Novel*, New York, 1894, pp. 269-70.

101. *Ibid.*, p. 419.

102. Kern, *op. cit.*, p. 94.

103. *Anne*, pp. 185-86.

104. *Ibid.*, pp. 53-54.

105. *Ibid.*, p. 156.

106. *Ibid.*, p. 368.

107. *Ibid.*

108. Cf. Kern, *op. cit.*, p. 176.

109. In this, observed James, Miss Woolson antedated J. C. Harris. *Partial Portraits*, pp. 180-81.

110. Cf. Miss Vanhorn's comment on another character in *Anne*, a character who reminds her of the "creole" type of beauty: "It is a novelty . . . which has made its appearance lately; a reaction after the narrow-chested type which has so long in America held undisputed sway. We absolutely take a quadroon to get away from the consumptive, blue-eyed saint, of whom we are all desperately tired." *Anne*, p. 196. The Creole was at about the same time making her fascinating appearance, it may be noted, in the works of G. W. Cable. See above, pp. 557-58, 561-62.

111. Ferris Greenslet, *Thomas Bailey Aldrich*, Boston (1928) (American Men of Letters Series), p. [78]. A good brief critical biography, though it makes Aldrich out as more of a poet than he was.

112. *The Story of a Bad Boy*, pp. 67-70. References are to *The Writings of Thomas Bailey Aldrich*, Cambridge, 1897-1907, 9 vols.

113. Greenslet, *op. cit.*, p. 104.

114. *Ibid.*

115. *Prudence Palfrey*, pp. 54-55.

116. *Ibid.*, p. [141].

117. *Ibid.*, pp. 154-55.

118. *Ibid.*, pp. 162-63.

119. *Ibid.*, p. 124.

120. *Ibid.*, p. 87.

121. Between *Prudence Palfrey* and *The Stillwater Tragedy* came another long story, *The Queen of Sheba*, serialized and book-published in 1877. A story of a young man attracted by a young woman who has lost her mind, *The Queen of Sheba* contains passages of Aldrich's best writing but is not his best novel. Aldrich planned a tragic ending for the book but was persuaded by Howells and Osgood to change it.

122. In his novels Aldrich goes in shamelessly for the live-happily-ever-afterward ending, but he knew that life does not always order things so neatly and blissfully. In his short-story "A Rivermouth Romance," for example, he wrote: "Yet when the average sentimental novelist has supplied his hero and heroine with their bridal outfit and arranged that little matter of the marriage certificate, he usually turns off the gas, puts up his shutters, and saunters off with his hands in his pockets, as if the day's business were over. But we, who are honest dealers in real life and disdain to give short weight, know better. The business is by no means over; it is just begun." *Writings*, IV, 288.

123. *The Stillwater Tragedy*, pp. [38], [223].

124. *Ibid.*, pp. 63-64.

125. *Ibid.*, p. 171.

126. *Ibid.*, p. 191.

127. *Ibid.*, p. 56.

128. *Ibid.*, p. 10.

129. *Ibid.*, p. 186.

130. *Ibid.*, Chapter XXIII.

131. Ironically enough, Aldrich was strongly attracted by Hawthorne. The author of "The Birth-Mark" is called to mind by Aldrich's treatment of the casting of Margaret's hand in *The Stillwater Tragedy* (Chapter IX) and in the same novel one finds the heroine reading *The House of the Seven Gables* aloud to the hero. *The Queen of Sheba*, with its plot involving the mental aberration of the heroine, could have served Hawthorne for many a grim and mystical text, but in Aldrich's hands the story remains a cheerful fantasy. In 1897 Aldrich wrote that *The Scarlet Letter* was one of "the two chief pieces of American fiction" (Greenslet, p. 201), but whether he valued *The Scarlet Letter* for its essential content may be doubted when one reads that the other "chief piece of fiction" was Mitchell's *Hugh Wynne*! One guesses that Aldrich was charmed by the sunlight playing about the threshold of Hawthorne but that he could never penetrate to the darker chambers of Hawthorne's thought and feeling.

132. Letter to Aldrich, Greenslet, *op. cit.*, p. 65.

133. Cf. above, p. 555.

134. E. W. Parks, *Charles Egbert Craddock (Mary Noailles Murfree)*, Chapel Hill, 1941, pp. 14, 177-78, 198.

135. *The Prophet of the Great Smoky Mountains* (Boston, 1886), p. 56.

136. *Ibid.*, p. 79.

137. *Ibid.*, p. 284.

138. W. D. Howells had a phrase for Miss Murfree's heroines which applies well to Dorinda, for in the midst of a "savage rudeness" of environment she was a girl with "a sort of martyr-grace and angelic innocence that touch the heart to pity rather than passion." *Heroines of Fiction*, II, 234-35.

139. *The Prophet of the Great Smoky Mountains*, p. 33.

140. *Ibid.*, p. 85.

141. *Ibid.*, p. 35.

142. *Ibid.*, p. 1.

143. In the following passage, *e.g.*, a good image got stale:
"The moon, still in the similitude of a silver boat, swung at anchor in a deep indentation in the summit of Chilhowee that looked like some lonely pine-girt bay; what strange, mysterious fancies did it land from its cargo of sentiments and superstitions and uncanny influences!" *Ibid.*, p. 33.

144. Parks, *op. cit.*, p. 172.

145. *Where the Battle Was Fought*, Boston, 1884, p. 2.

146. Cf. Parks, *op. cit.*, p. 109 n.

147. *Ibid.*, p. 222.

148. *Ibid.*, p. 224.

149. *Where the Battle Was Fought*, p. 328.

CHAPTER XIV

1. Bernard DeVoto, *Mark Twain's America*, Chautauqua, New York, 1933, p. [78].

2. The term "frontier" is only loosely applicable to the region, for by 1835 the "line of hazard" had moved farther west. DeVoto, *op. cit.*, p. 30. See also William D. Howells, *My Mark Twain*, New York, 1910, p. 127. Hannibal was, however, marked by "a condition of simplicity, isolation, and noncompetitive society."

3. Five-sevenths of Mark Twain's books, says DeVoto (p. 30), deal with his first environment. In the early 1930's a rancorous debate was rife as to the relative wholesomeness of Mark Twain's boyhood environment. In a word, Van Wyck Brooks (see *The Ordeal of Mark Twain*, New York, 1933, p. 45) condemned it as "drab" and "tragic"; DeVoto assented in part, but asserted its comparative "joyfulness"; and Mumford showed that both men were wrong, favoring, however, Mr. Brooks. The evidence finally favors DeVoto, whose *Mark Twain's America* is indispensable to anyone who wishes to get a quick survey of the mottled scene of Mark Twain's boyhood. Van Wyck Brooks seems to be recording the revulsion he himself would feel if suddenly deprived of all the "civilization" he now enjoys, forgetting that Mark Twain as a boy *grew* into his environment.

4. DeVoto, *op. cit.*, p. 29.

5. *Ibid.*, pp. 76-77.

6. In *Domestic Manners of the Americans*, 1832.

7. In *American Notes*, 1842, and *Martin Chuzzlewit*, 1844.

8. Cf. Minnie M. Brashear: "The southern element in Mark Twain's inheritance and training, often lost sight of because of the emphasis put upon his significance as a western writer, has constantly to be stressed in any attempt to account for [Mark Twain's] temperament and personality." *Mark Twain, Son of Missouri*, Chapel Hill, 1934, p. 59. See also p. 195.

9. DeVoto, *op. cit.*, p. 46.

10. *Ibid.*, p. 43.

11. *Ibid.*, pp. 37, 65.

12. *Mark Twain's Autobiography* (ed. by A. B. Paine), New York, 1924, I, 109-115.

13. Quoted above, pp. 601-03.

14. For a somewhat severe re-valuation of Mark Twain's books eighteen years after his death, see F. L. Pattee, "On the Rating of Mark Twain," *American Mercury* (June, 1928), XIV, 183-91.

15. A. B. Paine, *Mark Twain, A Biography*, New York, 1912, I, 477. Thus far Mark Twain's only long books had been the semi-autobiographical: *The Innocents Abroad* (1869) and *Roughing It* (1872).

16. Sellers was called Eschol Sellers in the first edition of the book, but Mark Twain was induced to change his name to Beriah by a "request—backed up by threat of a libel suit" to change it so as to oblige a real person named Eschol Sellers. Subsequently the "Beriah" gave way to "Mulberry," the name used in the stage version of *The Gilded Age* and in *The American Claimant*.

17. Paine, *op. cit.*, I, 478-79.

18. *The Gilded Age*, II, 50. All references except as noted are to the "Author's National Edition" of *The Writings of Mark Twain*, New York, 1907-18, 25 vols.

19. *Ibid.*, II, 49.

20. *Ibid.*, II, 54. The tone of *The Gilded Age* is thus to be contrasted with that of De Forest's *Honest John Vane*, a thoroughly serious political satire. Cf. above, pp. 515-18.

21. V. F. Calverton regards *The Gilded Age* not only as an attack upon corruption in Mark Twain's own time but also as "the precursor of those many attacks upon the exercise of power, which were to be made by the novelists and politicians of later generations." *The Liberation of American Literature*, p. 327.

22. Paine, *op. cit.*, I, [479].

23. *The Gilded Age*, II, 45.

24. Cf. *Roughing It*, II, 266 ff. The famous turnip dinner in *The Gilded Age* occurs in Chapter XI of the first volume.

25. The London edition, an authorized edition by Chatto and Windus, appeared on June 9, 1876. I. R. Brussel, *Anglo-American First Editions* (Part Two: West to East 1786-1930), London and New York, 1936, p. 5.

26. Paine, *op. cit.*, II, 570.

27. For an example of his ironical treatment of the subject see pp. 232-33 of *Sketches New and Old*, a volume which appeared between the completion of *Tom Sawyer* and its American publication. A more substantial paper by Mark Twain on copyright appeared in *The North American Review*, January, 1905. See also Paine, *op. cit.*, I, 552-53, and *Mark Twain's Letters* (ed. by A. B. Paine), New York, 1917, I, 261-62.

28. Regarded as unwholesome, both *Tom Sawyer* and *Huckleberry Finn* were at one time removed from the Children's rooms in a branch of the Brooklyn Public Library. *Huckleberry Finn* was also "flung out" of libraries at Concord and at Denver. *Autobiography*, II, 333 ff.

29. Paine, *op. cit.*, II, 585.

30. *Ibid.*, I, 547. This was a "mistake" he remedied in *Huckleberry Finn*.

31. DeVoto, *op. cit.*, p. 307.

32. A rough unity is achieved, however, by Mark Twain's apparent purpose of writing a realistic counterpart to the moralizing juvenile stories that were popular in the sixties and seventies. See Walter Blair, "On the Structure of *Tom Sawyer*," *Modern Philology* (August, 1939), XXXVII, 75-88.

33. "But though the books of Mark Twain were conditioned by experience, guessing that any given incident in them actually happened to Samuel Clemens is a precarious business." DeVoto, *op. cit.*, p. [78].

34. Mark Twain was partly right in saying that *Tom Sawyer* is "not a boy's book at all. It will only be read by adults. It is only written for adults." Paine, *op. cit.*, I, 547, from a letter of July 5, 1875. Later Mark Twain changed his mind, apparently at Howells' suggestion, and decided to make it a boy's book (*Letters*, I, 273), but readers' experience has proved the book to be rather a boy's book for adults—with the qualification that it was made a little goody-goody for the trade. Though given to young boys as a present it is surreptitiously (re)read by daddy until the boy gets to be fifteen or sixteen (*i.e.*, adult) and can read it with full appreciation. Mark Twain might have added that it was not written for female adults: ladies almost uniformly sheer away from its unreliable jokes and cruel humor.

35. *Tom Sawyer*, pp. 32-33.

36. *Ibid.*, p. 76.

37. Quoted in Paine, *op. cit.*, II, 585.

38. Paine, *op. cit.*, I, 533.

39. *Ibid.*, I, 548.

40. *Ibid.*, I, [549].

41. In acknowledging Howells' advice on the manuscript of *Tom Sawyer*, Mark Twain wrote that "instead of *reading* the MS," he merely "hunted out" the editor's penciled suggestions and followed them. See *Letters*, I, 272.

42. The extent to which Mark Twain chafed under the need of preserving decorum has been endlessly debated. Brooks (*The Ordeal of Mark Twain*) thinks that much was unhappily suppressed in the author. DeLancey Ferguson ("Huck Finn Aborning," *The Colophon* [Spring, 1938], III, n.s., 171-80) argues that Mark Twain made most of his manuscript changes in the interest of art, not morals or taste. Alexander Cowie (*American Literature* [January, 1939], X, 488-91) believes that Mark Twain would have liked to write in a more robust vein (as in fact he did privately) but that as a practical man he easily learned to control himself. Mark Twain must certainly have known that "nowhere in America" would an editor or publisher have printed his raciest passages. DeVoto, *op. cit.*, p. 209.

43. *The Prince and the Pauper* is discussed below, pp. 617-19.

44. "Old Times" constituted Chapters IV to XV of *Life on the Mississippi*. The papers were published as a (pirated) book in Toronto in 1876.

45. *Life on the Mississippi*, p. 31.

46. Bernard DeVoto, *Mark Twain at Work*, Cambridge, 1942, p. 50.

47. By DeVoto (*Mark Twain's America*, p. 107) and Minnie Brashear, *op. cit.*, pp. 194-95. The fact that he "did not return to piloting after the war, even when he had an opportunity to do so" (Edward Wagenknecht, *Mark Twain, The Man and His Work*, New Haven, 1935, p. 11) has little to do with the imaginative results of his earlier experience with the river. Critics prone to discount the emotional importance of the piloting years have generally failed to note that five years after his release from it he wrote nostalgically to his mother: "I wish I was back there piloting up and down the river again. Verily, all is vanity and little worth —save piloting." *Letters*, I, 101.

48. *Huckleberry Finn*, p. 163.

49. "NOTICE. Persons attempting to find a motive in this narrative will be prosecuted; persons attempting to find a moral in it will be banished; persons attempting to find a plot in it will be shot. BY ORDER OF THE AUTHOR, Per G.G., Chief of Ordnance." *Huckleberry Finn*, p. iii.

50. Cf. Brashear, *op. cit.*, pp. 59, 60.

51. O. H. Moore insists that Mark Twain's European sources even for *Tom Sawyer* and *Huckleberry Finn* were far greater than has been supposed. See *PMLA* (June, 1922), XXXVII, 324-46. He cites as evidence various sources together with Mark Twain's own statement (in *Literary Essays*, p. 148): "There isn't a single human characteristic that can be safely labeled 'American.'" That

Mr. Moore has overstated a partial truth (Mark Twain's word cannot be accepted) is obvious from an examination of such books as DeVoto's *Mark Twain's America* and Walter Blair's *Native American Humor (1800-1900)*, New York, 1937. For further comments on Mark Twain's reading, see below, pp. 640-44.

52. F. W. Chandler, *The Literature of Roguery*, London, 1907, II, 488. The deeper dyes which Mark Twain used in *Huckleberry Finn* and later expunged may be only guessed at from his daughter Susan's comments on many a "delightfully terrible part" ordered cancelled by Mrs. Clemens. Paine, *op. cit.*, II, 775.

53. *Huckleberry Finn*, p. 39.

54. *Ibid.*, pp. 128-29.

55. DeVoto's *Mark Twain's America*, p. 34. See also Mark Twain's own claim to accuracy, *Huckleberry Finn*, "Explanatory" note.

56. For the facts concerning other projected narratives involving Tom and Huck, see DeVoto, *Mark Twain at Work*, pp. 48-50.

57. *Tom Sawyer, Detective*, p. 137 n.

58. Cf. his use of a similar situation in *Pudd'nhead Wilson;* see below, pp. 623-24.

59. *The Prince and the Pauper*, p. 308.

60. Mark Twain's book was written partly at the suggestion of his partner on one of his reading tours, G. W. Cable, who called Malory's tale to his attention.

61. *Letters*, II, 525.

62. *Mark Twain's America*, p. 277.

63. *My Mark Twain*, p. 151.

64. Clara Clemens, *My Father, Mark Twain*, New York, 1931, p. 289.

65. *Cambridge History of American Literature*, III, 17.

66. *Ibid.*

67. The place of *A Connecticut Yankee* in the very extended literature of Utopian and other social satire following Edward Bellamy's *Looking Backward* (1887) has been fully indicated in DeVoto, *Mark Twain's America*, pp. 272-73. Whether Mark Twain was actually influenced by *Looking Backward* is discussed by R. L. Shurter in "The Literary Work of Edward Bellamy," *American Literature* (November, 1933), V, 233 n.

68. *A Connecticut Yankee*, p. 65.

69. *Ibid.*, pp. 216-17.

70. *Ibid.*, pp. 319-20.

71. *Ibid.*, pp. 294 ff.

72. *Ibid.*, p. 67.

73. *Ibid.*, p. 78.

74. *Ibid.*, p. 124.

75. *Ibid.*, p. 142.

76. With similar recklessness he attacked the doctrine of Christian Science in a series of articles dating from 1897. His book *Christian Science* appeared in 1907. In a letter written in 1909 he made it clear that he did not scoff at all mental healing but that, characteristically enough, he objected to the organization that had grown up about its leader. *Letters*, II, 832-33.

77. *A Connecticut Yankee*, Chapter XXIX. In *The Mysterious Stranger* insanity is held up as a comparable blessing. See below, p. 638.

78. Parrington is inclined to overrate it from this point of view. See *Main Currents in American Thought*, III, 97-98.

79. See above, p. 345.

80. A comparable exchange of rôles occurs in *The Prince and the Pauper* and *Pudd'nhead Wilson*.

81. *The American Claimant*, p. 18.

82. Mark Twain himself "thought the Claimant bad" when he saw it in print. *Letters*, II, 579.

83. *The American Claimant*, p. 228.

84. *Ibid.*, p. 42.

85. Quoted in *Mark Twain's America*, p. 32. Mark Twain's interest in the law crops out frequently in other writings; and it is noteworthy that he believed the major issue in the Baconian-Shakespeare controversy (which he recapitulated in part in *Is Shakespeare Dead?*) to be the question of whether or not Shakespeare had a legal training.

86. Mark Twain's third major murder trial by this time. Others occur in *Tom Sawyer* and *The Gilded Age*.

87. Mark Twain's interest in thumb-printing dated back at least to 1883, when it appeared in an episode of *Life on the Mississippi* (Chapter XXXI).

88. Mark Twain realized, as he tells in an introduction, that the Italian twins were an added burden to the story, but he excised them too late—the story was already seriously damaged—and *Pudd'nhead Wilson* never really recovered.

89. It is noteworthy in any study of increasing realism in the American novel that Roxana's fifteen parts of white blood, which were "outvoted" by the black sixteenth, did not tempt Mark Twain to do a novel of miscegenation, a popular type of nineteenth-century fiction. Cf. Gaines, *The Southern Plantation*, pp. 221-22.

90. *Pudd'nhead Wilson*, pp. 26-27.

91. *Ibid.*, pp. 27-28. Cf. De Forest's defense of "Major" Scott in *Miss Ravenel's Conversion*. See above, pp. 510-11.

92. *Pudd'nhead Wilson* (Stormfield ed.), "An Appreciation," p. xii. The Stormfield edition of Mark Twain's writings, comprising 37 volumes, appeared in 1929.

93. *Pudd'nhead Wilson*, pp. 11-12.

94. *Ibid.*, pp. 12-13.

95. A. B. Paine is clearly beside the mark in asserting that Mark Twain was "always at his best" in the "poetic and contemplative." *Op. cit.*, I, 454.

96. "I like *Joan of Arc* best of all my books; and it *is* the best; I know it perfectly well. And besides, it furnished me seven times the pleasure afforded me by any of the others; twelve years of preparation, and two years of writing. The others needed no preparation, and got none." *Joan of Arc* (Stormfield ed.), "Introduction," p. xx.

97. Sometimes his chivalry got tangled up with his argument as in his "In Defence of Harriet Shelley," *Literary Essays*, pp. 16-77.

98. *Joan of Arc* (Stormfield edition), "An Appreciation" (by Henry van Dyke), p. xii.

99. "Translator's Preface," p. v. Twain was of course his own "translator" for he adopted in this book the somewhat trite device of passing the whole off as "personal recollections" of a contemporary who knew Joan.

100. "Translator's Preface," pp. vi-vii.

101. *My Mark Twain*, pp. 152-53.

102. When in a serious moment Mark Twain casts aside the last garment of his reticence, his display of emotion renders the reader uncomfortable, as, for example, in his remarks after the death of his daughter Jean—which are almost too painful to read.

103. Wagenknecht, *op. cit.*, pp. 196-97.

104. Paine, *op. cit.*, I, 542.

105. DeVoto, *Mark Twain's America*, p. 285 n.

106. *Pudd'nhead Wilson*, p. 21.

107. His treatment of the Mormon Bible is an example. See *Roughing It*, I, 132 ff.

108. *Joan of Arc*, I, 24.

109. Robert Underwood Johnson, *Remembered Yesterdays*, Boston, 1923, p. 320.

110. *My Mark Twain*, p. 31.

111. Clara Clemens, *op. cit.*, p. 134.

112. *Roughing It*, II, 139.

113. *New York Times*, Oct. 27, 1935, "Book Review," p. 22.

114. *Autobiography*, I, 283.

115. Quoted in Paine, *op. cit.*, III, 1398.

116. Mrs. Clemens persuaded him not to publish *What Is Man?* lest it "have a harmful influence on many people, and according to her understanding of human beings the article was not true, anyway." Clara Clemens, *op. cit.*, p. 208.

117. Howells it was who counseled against the American publication of *Captain Stormfield's Visit to Heaven* without the precaution of having it tried out in England: "[A]sk Dean Stanley to endorse it, which will draw some of the teeth of the religious press, and then reprint it in America." (*Letters*, I, 323.)

118. "As a business man, he joined his contemporaries in glorifying the machine, fascinated with the possibilities of exploiting it and of controlling nature through it. As a satirist, he joined his contemporaries in attacking, never the machine itself, but certain economic abuses . . ." Walter F. Taylor, "Mark Twain and the Machine Age," *South Atlantic Quarterly* (October, 1938), XXXVII, 396.

119. Brooks, *op. cit.*, pp. 175-76.

120. *The Liberation of American Literature*, p. 327.

121. Quoted in Brooks, *op. cit.*, p. 182. Strongly as Mark Twain felt about politics, he frankly hadn't much taste for martyrdom. This is clear from the readiness with which he absolved his friend Twichell for the latter's having voted his congregation's political ticket—after one disastrous show of independence. "His very first duty," said Mark Twain, "was to his family, not to his political conscience." *Autobiography*, II, 25.

122. I, 176.

123. *Ibid.*, II, 135.

124. Printed first in *The New York Tribune*, quoted in Paine, *op. cit.*, I, 474. In *Roughing It* (II, 74 ff.) he commented at length on the absurdity of trial by jury—that "palladium of our liberties"—and gave in some detail a (typically) extreme example of its blundering operation in Nevada. Cf. also his jibe at the corrupt jury system in his burlesque sketch, "The Judge's 'Spirited Woman,'" *Sketches New and Old*, pp. 149-51.

125. Brooks, *op. cit.*, p. 161.

126. *North American Review* (February, 1901), CLXXII, 169. In his *Autobiography*, which, though not published until after his death, was dictated in 1906-08, Mark Twain gives vent to his hatred of turn-of-the-century imperialism and political corruption in general. See especially the *Autobiography*, I, 284, 293, 345; II, 187 ff. For his devastating epitaph on King Leopold of Belgium, see Wagenknecht, *op. cit.*, p. 101.

127. The phrase is from Howells. *Letters* (of Mark Twain), I, 390.

128. *Letters*, II, 445.

129. Intelligence, he thought, was man's best weapon against corruption in the state. In his Utopian state of Gondour "ignorance and incompetence had no place" largely because of the system of suffrage, whereby every man had one vote but was entitled to additional votes in proportion to his education. "The Curious Republic of Gondour," *Atlantic Monthly* (October, 1875), XXXVI, 461-63.

130. *Autobiography*, II, 25.

131. See *Mark Twain's Notebook* (ed. by A. B. Paine), New York, 1935, p. 325, and *Roughing It*, II, 233.

132. He believed, however, that Jesus had had a profound influence on the world. *Letters*, II, 817.

133. Paine, *op. cit.*, III, 1583. This phrase is part of a religious creed drawn up by Mark Twain, probably in the early eighties, embodying "conclusions from which he did not deviate materially in after years." *Ibid.*, III, 1582 ff.

134. Clara Clemens, *op. cit.*, p. 180.

135. *Autobiography*, II, 292.

136. *Mark Twain's Notebook*, p. 380. A little later another aphorism restates the view: "There is no sadder sight than a young pessimist, except an old optimist." *Ibid.*, p. 385.

137. *Letters*, II, 785.

138. *Mark Twain's Notebook*, p. 307.

139. *What Is Man? and Other Essays* (Stormfield edition), p. 5.

140. *Ibid.*, p. 15. In less serious vein Mark Twain expressed his opinion of the self-seekers who infested his mail when he first became famous: "The symbol of the race ought to be a human being carrying an ax, for every human being has one concealed about him somewhere, and is always seeking the opportunity to grind it." Paine, *op. cit.*, II, 564.

141. "Mark Twain was no systematic student of science," but "the theories of science confirmed his pessimistic suspicions about life." H. H. Waggoner, "Science in the Thought of Mark Twain," *American Literature* (January, 1937), VIII, 369.

142. For observations regarding the fascination that Satan had for Mark Twain, see Brashear, *op. cit.*, pp. 84, 208, 214. See also *Letters*, II, 817.

143. Pessimistic utterances on the theme of the boon of death were frequent in Mark Twain's conversation and correspondence as well as implicit in fiction such as *A Connecticut Yankee*. Some of those aphorisms of Pudd'nhead Wilson which Mark Twain used as chapter heads carry a similar ring, *e.g.*: "Whoever has lived long enough to find out what life is, knows how deep a debt of gratitude we owe to Adam, the first great benefactor of our race. He brought death into the world." *Pudd'nhead Wilson*, Chapter III.

144. *The Mysterious Stranger* (Stormfield edition), p. 110.

145. *Ibid.*, p. 139.

146. Clara Clemens, *op. cit.*, p. 259.

147. *Literary Essays*, p. 163.

148. Quoted in Paine, *op. cit.*, III, 1581.

149. Clara Clemens, *op. cit.*, p. 291. See also p. 177.

150. French he must have begun early, for he amused himself by translating his *Jumping Frog of Calaveras County* (1867) into it—only to "claw" it back into English at once.

151. *My Mark Twain*, p. 17. Mark Twain probably did not have a really wide familiarity with books. Pilots on the river regarded him as a "great reader" (Paine, *op. cit.*, I, 151), but such a reputation was too easily secured to be significant. Rather impressive data on his reading have been compiled by scholars. Yet in a life-time of seventy years a man must read *something*. His biographer's testimony is that he "read not so many books . . . but read a few books often." (Quoted in Wagenknecht, *op. cit.*, p. 46).

152. *My Mark Twain*, p. 15.

153. Paine, *op. cit.*, I, [512].

154. *Cambridge History of American Literature*, III, 6. See also Paine, *op. cit.*, II, 579.

155. *Letters*, II, 808.

156. *The Gilded Age*, I, 92.

157. *Cambridge History of American Literature*, III, 6. His favorite was *A Tale of Two Cities*, which he read "'at least every two years.'" (Quoted in Brashear, *op. cit.*, p. 212 n.) He seems to have thought little, however, of *Pickwick Papers*. (*Ibid.*, p. 218.)

158. *Letters*, I, 222.

159. *Ibid.*, I, 421.

160. His "William Dean Howells" (in *What Is Man? and Other Essays*) is not a comprehensive criticism but an appreciation based on passages in a few books.

161. *Letters*, II, 830. On another occasion he remarked that one could make a fairly good library just by leaving out Jane Austen. In spite of his strictures on Poe, Mark Twain did read Poe and he was not unlike him in his interest in bizarre adventures and his fondness for ratiocination. The unwritten story about an iceberg outlined in the *Notebook* (pp. 169-70) might have been written by either man. The balloon ascent in *Tom Sawyer Abroad* also suggests Poe. For a reference to Mark Twain's burlesque of Poe, see Brashear, *op. cit.*, pp. 212-13 (note).

162. *Life on the Mississippi*, pp. 308, 342, 347 ff.

163. See *Letters*, II, 737-38, for an itemized list of charges against Scott as a novelist. Scott, had he been alive, could have picked up some of the stones cast at him and returned them at Mark Twain's *Joan of Arc*, which was at least partly a glass house.

164. *Life on the Mississippi*, p. 347. The only novel of Scott that he regarded as "living" was *Quentin Durward*. Paine, *op. cit.*, III, 1198.

165. In *A Connecticut Yankee*, however, there is only one brief fling at Scott —for his unreal language (pp. 38-39).

166. *Life on the Mississippi*, p. 349. For observations on the tremendous vogue of Scott in the South, see Grace W. Landrum, "Sir Walter Scott and His Literary Rivals in the Old South," *American Literature* (November, 1930), II, 256-76. Miss Landrum believes that "the devotion of the South to Sir Walter was for good, not for ill." See *ibid.* (March, 1931), III, 66.

167. For Mark Twain's extremely humorous treatment of "Fenimore Cooper's Literary Offences" see *Literary Essays*, pp. 78-96. Though unfair (as usual), it contains some of Mark Twain's best literary criticism.

168. Holmes and Lowell were to some extent exceptions. See below, p. 644.

169. The speech is reprinted in Paine, *op. cit.*, III, 1643-[1647].

170. There were sporadic exceptions: Lowell, for example, had publicly praised *The Celebrated Jumping Frog of Calaveras County*. DeVoto, *Mark Twain's America*, p. 188 n.

171. For observations by an eye-witness of the imperfect New Englandization of Mark Twain, see Howells, *My Mark Twain*, pp. 46-47.

172. Walter Blair, *Native American Humor*, p. 153. Chapter VII of the Introduction to this book analyzes fully Mark Twain's American sources. Cf. also DeVoto, "The Matrix of Mark Twain's Humour," *The Bookman* (October, 1931), LXXIV, 172-78. The danger of assuming that all these "native" tales and anecdotes were *originally* American is pointed out by J. De Lancey Ferguson, who supplies many British sources. See "The Roots of American Humor," *The American Scholar* (Winter, 1935), IV, 41-49.

173. The essence of that method is stated in his "How to Tell a Story," *Literary Essays*, p. 11: "To string incongruities and absurdities together in a wandering and sometimes purposeless way, and seem innocently unaware that they are absurdities, is the basis of the American art ... ."

174. DeVoto observes that Lowell "seems to have read appreciatively the popular fiction and humor of the uncouth Fifties." *Mark Twain's America*, p. 188.

175. His later unintentional plagiarism of Holmes is recounted in *Autobiography*, I, 238-42.

176. *Sketches New and Old*, pp. 16-24.

177. "English as She Is Taught," *What Is Man? and Other Essays*, pp. 240-55.

178. He had already had a "narrow escape" with the same dull story on the lecture platform. The audience pitied him for repeating such trite stuff, but with sheer audacity Mark Twain repeated it until he succeeded finally in making them laugh. Paine, *op. cit.*, I, 303.

179. *Roughing It*, I, 32-33.

180. The scene in which Mark Twain was robbed by disguised friends at midnight near Gold Hill was based on actuality, but Mark Twain could not have written it (*Roughing It*, II, 333 ff.) without recalling a more famous hold-up at Gadshill.

181. *Mark Twain's Notebook*, p. 303.

182. *Literary Essays*, p. 81.

183. *Ibid.* On the few occasions when he could take time to read the books sent to him by young novelists he was likely to dwell on the need of using the exact word. See, for example, *Letters*, II, 497-99.

184. *Tom Sawyer Abroad*, pp. 21-22.

185. Nothing flattered him more than a compliment on his style. He was boyishly pleased at a certain biographical sketch of himself: "For it contained praises of the very thing which I most loved to hear praised—*the good quality of my English;* moreover, they were uttered by four English and American literary experts of high authority." *Autobiography*, I, 175-76.

186. *Saturday Review of Literature*, May 7, 1932, p. 722. This in a letter to a critic who had questioned an improbability in "A Double-Barrelled Detective Story." Mark Twain pointed out that the "improbable" incident was the only truthful one in the story, and he concluded that "where it comes to the contriving of extravagances & apparent impossibilities Fiction is n't 'in it' with fact." *Ibid.*

187. *Pudd'nhead Wilson and Those Extraordinary Twins*, p. 229.

188. *Autobiography*, I, 237. Cf. Howells's mild understatement that Mark Twain "was not enslaved to the consecutiveness in writing which the rest of us try to keep chained to." *My Mark Twain*, p. 17.

189. See his tedious account of how the staff of the Virginia City *Weekly Occidental* planned to write a novel in collaboration. *Roughing It*, II, 96-105.

190. *Literary Essays*, pp. 145-46.

191. *Pudd'nhead Wilson* (Stormfield edition), "An Appreciation," p. x.

192. *Literary Essays*, pp. 146-47. In words omitted from the above quotation Mark Twain itemizes the things remaining to be done in American fiction—the regional, racial, religious elements still to be taken stock of.

193. Blair, *op. cit.*, p. 160.

194. The quotations are from the poems of another American vagabond who was a native of a near region, Vachel Lindsay. *Collected Poems*, New York, 1923, pp. 259, 260, 261.

195. Quoted in *The Saturday Review of Literature*, October 12, 1935, p. 4. See also *Letters*, II, 527.

196. *Autobiography*, II, 69.

197. *The New Yorker*, March 12, 1938, p. [11].

198. Paine, *op. cit.*, I, 287.

199. *Letters*, I, 182-83.

200. Walt Whitman, *Specimen Days, Democratic Vistas, and Other Prose* (ed. by Louise Pound), New York, 1935, p. 194.

201. *The Critic* (July 25, 1891), XVI, n.s., 46.

202. Archibald Henderson, *Mark Twain*, London, 1911, p. 4.

203. "Mark Twain," *American Portraits 1875-1900*, Boston, 1922, p. [28].

204. *My Mark Twain*, p. 13. Kipling, who said Mark Twain was the "biggest" American writer "by a damn sight," added that "Cervantes was a relation of his." (Mark Twain's) *Letters*, II, 747 n.

CHAPTER XV

1. Quoted in Delmar Gross Cooke, *William Dean Howells, A Critical Study*, New York, 1922, p. 11.

2. *My Literary Passions*, New York, 1895, p. 17.

3. *Ibid.*, p. 26.

4. Scott's fault was longwindedness; he would go "about half a mile to express a thought that could be uttered in ten paces across lots." *Criticism and Fiction*, New York, 1891, p. [21].

5. It was formlessness which Howells found the "fatal defect of our American Ossian, Walt Whitman, whose way is where artistic madness lies." *My Literary Passions*, p. 68.

6. See also his fantasy: *The Seen and Unseen at Stratford-on-Avon*, New York, 1914.

7. Howells also objected to Thackeray's proneness to "stand about in his scene, talking it over with his hands in his pockets, interrupting the action, and spoiling the illusion in which alone the truth of art resides." *Criticism and Fiction*, p. 76.

8. *My Literary Passions*, p. 172.

9. Cf. his admiration for Defoe's style in *Roxana*—"the best and most natural English that a book was ever written in." Letter to Mark Twain, August 9, 1885. *Life in Letters of William Dean Howells* (ed. by Mildred Howells), New York, 1928, I, 371. Cf. also his admiration for "divine" Jane Austen, whom he seems finally to have considered the greatest English novelist. *Criticism and Fiction*, pp. [73]-75. See also *My Literary Passions*, p. 247.

10. For the details of Howells' life, see Cooke, *op. cit., passim*. The latter part of his life has never received full biographical treatment.

11. O. W. Firkins, *William Dean Howells, A Study*, Cambridge, 1924, p. 75.

12. *Ibid.*, p. 69.

13. Firkins (*op. cit.*, p. 69) goes so far as to say that in "no case whatever has [Howells] been wholly fortunate in the conduct of a double or multiple plot." Howells himself expressed doubt of his "fitness for a sustained or involved narration." *Their Wedding Journey* (Boston, 1895), p. [1].

14. Note the preponderance of essayists, poets, and short story writers mentioned in the first part of *My Literary Passions*.

15. Firkins, *op. cit.*, p. 65. The number of novels (as opposed to novelettes) written by Howells is variously stated. Firkins' bibliography (*op. cit.*, pp. [339], 340) lists thirty-eight.

16. *Ibid.*, p. 66.

17. See below, pp. 676-85.

18. See *Life in Letters*, I, 163. Of course the sale was not phenomenally large, for as P. Boynton has pointed out, Howells' books generally placed him not in the best-selling class but the "best-reading" class. *Literature and American Life*, Boston, 1936, p. 748.

19. Cooke, *op. cit.*, p. 162.

20. One of Howells' earliest references to Mark Twain's writings occurs when the somewhat naive Col. Ellison refers to *The Innocents Abroad* as a "travel" book "so good . . . that he need never read anything else about the countries of which it treated." *A Chance Acquaintance*, Boston, 1873, p. 101. Howells first met Mark Twain in the following year.

21. *Ibid.*, pp. 163-64.

22. Firkins, *op. cit.*, p. 86.

23. *A Foregone Conclusion* (Boston, 1881), pp. 260-61.

24. Firkins, *op. cit.*, p. 89.

25. "Ricus" (pseud.), "A Suppressed Novel of Mr. Howells," *The Bookman* (October, 1910), XXXII, [201]-203.

26. Quoted from Harry Thurston Peck by Cooke, *op. cit.*, p. 177. Matthew Arnold also found *The Lady of the Aroostook* a "charming" story. *Discourses in America* (New York, 1924), p. 187.

27. *The Lady of the Aroostook* (Boston, 1879), pp. 70, 71.

28. See especially *ibid.*, pp. 61, 68, 91-92, [192].

29. Cf. Firkins, *op. cit.*, pp. 96, 97. The subject of women as physicians was much in the air at the time. Elizabeth S. Phelps's *Doctor Zay* was written at almost the same time and with much the same plot as *Dr. Breen's Practice*. Still another book with a similar plot was withheld from publication because Howells' story had a "first claim." See *Life in Letters*, I, 299. For an extremely conservative discussion published a few years earlier, see G. B. Woods, "Women in Medical Schools," *Essays, Sketches, and Stories*, Boston, 1873, pp. 38-40.

30. This is Cooke's view, *op. cit.*, p. 192.

31. This appeared in a volume entitled *A Fearful Responsibility, and Other Stories* (1881). The "responsibility" is an American girl who must be saved from an unsuitable match with an Austrian officer. The story is rather poorly done (Cooke, *op. cit.*, pp. 199-201), but Howells intrepidly hews to his realistic course by refusing to allow his heroine to be heartbroken over her loss.

32. *Life in Letters*, I, 232-33. The letter is dated April 1, 1877.

33. Firkins, *op. cit.*, pp. 70, 71.

34. Howells used this term in a study of Robert Herrick, *North American Review* (June, 1909), CLXXXIX, 816.

35. His "deterioration is not explained by his circumstances," for the "circumstances do not favor depravation; they favor uprightness." Firkins, *op. cit.*, p. 103.

36. *Ibid.*, p. 105.

37. *A Modern Instance*, Boston, 1882, p. 110. Cf. Cooke, *op. cit.*, p. 241.

38. Firkins, *op. cit.*, p. 101.

39. *A Modern Instance*, pp. 273-74.

40. *The Life and Letters of Sir Edmund Gosse* (ed. by Evan Charteris), New York, 1931, p. 163.

41. "Recent American Fiction," *The Atlantic Monthly* (October, 1885), LVI, 555.

42. *American Literature 1607-1885* (2 vols. in one), New York, 1888, II, 438. R. L. Stevenson, per contra, appears to have thought that Howells' vision was too much "skyward." Himself the husband of a once-divorced woman, he wrote Howells an extremely disagreeable letter concluding with the statement that he wished "to know no one who considers himself holier than my wife." (Howells') *Life in Letters*, I, 332-33.

43. *Literary Friends and Acquaintance*, New York, 1900, p. 141.

44. Firkins, *op. cit.*, p. 112.

45. Observe, for example, how Howells makes gentle fun of Irene's naive literary conversation. *The Rise of Silas Lapham*, Chapter IX. See a comparable treatment of Imogene in *Indian Summer*, below, p. 673.

46. Hamlin Garland, *A Son of the Middle Border* (New York, 1927), p. 383. Editors, too, were wary of Howells on this score. The editor of *Harper's Monthly*, for example, indicated that he would "reconsider" *The Minister's Charge* if Howells consented to making more of the hero and heroine. Howells' response to the idea was typical: "I don't believe in heroes and heroines, and willingly

avoid the heroic . . . Nothing in a story can be better than life." *Life in Letters*, I, 361. It is characteristic of Howells, too, that he presents Tom Corey not as a "fairy prince" but as "an energetic fellow . . . with the smallest amount of inspiration that can save a man from being commonplace." *The Rise of Silas Lapham*, Boston, 1885, pp. 177-78.

47. *Life in Letters*, I, 372.

48. Garland, *op. cit.*, p. 383.

49. *Life in Letters*, I, 365.

50. The book was nevertheless a favorite with women readers, one of whom wrote a letter that throws an interesting sidelight on Howells' vogue. The woman begged to be allowed to see the advance sheets (the story was being serialized) on the plea that she was dying and that the thought of dying without knowing the conclusion was "perfectly insupportable." Howells consented, but his publishers detected the hoax. *Life in Letters*, I, 374. Howells thriftily used the incident in a later story, *Fennel and Rue.*

51. *Indian Summer* (Boston, 1914), p. 243.

52. *Ibid.*, pp. 39-41.

53. Firkins, *op. cit.*, p. 121.

54. *Ibid.*, p. 122.

55. *The Minister's Charge*, Boston, 1887, pp. 61 ff., 218, 223, 275, 182, 236, 237.

56. *Ibid.*, pp. 444-45.

57. *Ibid.*, p. 368. The same idea turns up later in *A Hazard of New Fortunes* (New York, 1899), II, 37-38. Cf. also Holmes's *Elsie Venner*, above, p. 503.

58. *The Minister's Charge*, p. 130.

59. *Ibid.*, p. 241.

60. Firkins, *op. cit.*, p. 123.

61. As has been shown above, *The Minister's Charge* might almost as well be included in this group. *Annie Kilburn* was, however, "the first of the definitely economic novels." W. F. Taylor, *The Economic Novel in America*, Chapel Hill, 1942, p. 244. Taylor's book offers a full discussion of Howells' "labor" novels. For modifying views and additional material—especially touching the influence of Laurence Gronlund and Björnstjerne Björnson—see George Arms, "The Literary Background of Howells's Social Criticism," *American Literature* (November, 1942), XIV, [260]-276.

62. Taylor, *op. cit.*, p. 230.

63. *Life in Letters*, I, 408.

64. *My Literary Passions*, p. [250]. Cf. his observation in 1910 that Tolstoi's "moral influence was like a 'religious experience.'" W. L. Phelps, *Autobiography With Letters*, New York, 1939, p. 504.

65. *Life in Letters*, I, 405.

66. Quoted in Taylor, *op. cit.*, p. 240.

67. *Ibid.*, p. 237.

68. *Ibid.*, p. 241.

69. *Life in Letters*, I, 399.

70. *Ibid.*, I, 402.

71. "[S]ome of the papers abused me as heartily as if I had proclaimed myself a dynamiter." *Ibid.*, I, 413.

72. *Ibid.*, I, 405. The letter here quoted was dated November 18, 1887.

73. Taylor, *op. cit.*, p. 233.

74. *Annie Kilburn*, New York, 1888, p. 65.

75. Firkins, *op. cit.*, p. 143.

76. Cf. *ibid.* (p. 144): "I am not sure that an endless probing of differences of caste . . . is not a final subterfuge of the aristocratic impulse."

77. *New Letters of James Russell Lowell* (ed. by M. A. DeWolfe Howe), New York, 1932, p. 335. Howells' own view of *Père Goriot* was that it was "full

of a malarial restlessness, wholly alien to healthful art." *Criticism and Fiction,* p. [25].

78. *A Hazard of New Fortunes,* II, 57.

79. Firkins, *op. cit.,* p. 168.

80. *The Minister's Charge,* p. 184-85.

81. *The Quality of Mercy,* New York, 1892, p. 161.

82. *Ibid.,* p. 208.

83. *Ibid.,* p. 474.

84. *Ibid.*

85. *The World of Chance,* New York, 1893, p. 22.

86. W. F. Taylor points out that *The World of Chance* affords the first instance of technological unemployment in the American novel. "William Dean Howells and the Economic Novel," *American Literature* (May, 1932), IV, 111.

87. *The World of Chance,* p. 120.

88. Cooke, *op. cit.,* p. 232.

89. *A Traveler from Altruria,* New York, 1894, p. 12.

90. *Ibid.,* p. 13.

91. *Ibid.,* p. 15. Cf. this typical remark with the concluding comment of Putney in *The Quality of Mercy* quoted above, p. 681.

92. He was opposed to the Spanish-American War: "After war will come the piling up of big fortunes again; the craze for wealth will fill all brains, and every good cause will be set back. We shall have an era of blood-bought prosperity, and the chains of capitalism will be welded on the nation more firmly than ever." *Life in Letters,* II, 90.

93. *The Great Tradition,* New York, 1935, p. 98. Hicks' statement is in sharp contrast to the statement of W. F. Taylor (*op. cit.,* p. 260): "Howells' destructive criticism of industrialism is . . . the most thoroughgoing by far that appeared in our literature before 1900 . . ." Actually, Howells is by no means "vague," but he has too little of the dynamic to be well described as "destructive."

94. *Life in Letters,* II, 54.

95. *Ibid.,* II, 25.

96. Taylor, *op. cit.,* p. 269.

97. Cooke, *op. cit.,* p. 236. Cf. Granville Hicks' similar comment, *op. cit.,* p. 97.

98. Hicks, *op. cit.,* p. 75.

99. Cf. Howells' criticism of the "happy ending" in connection with a study of Valera's *Pepita Ximenez* in *Criticism and Fiction,* p. 85.

100. Cooke, *op. cit.,* p. 207.

101. Cf. Firkins, *op. cit.,* p. 135; Cooke, *op. cit.,* p. 158.

102. The theme of miscegenation was of course commonly related more closely to the abolition movement in other novels. Frequently, moreover, the octoroon-heroine was subjected to offensive advances from white men. Cf. Gaines, *The Southern Plantation,* pp. 221-22. Howells characteristically keeps his story chiefly within the ethical problem of the girl herself: shall she reveal to her lover the cloud on her ancestry?

103. Critics vary in their estimate of *The Coast of Bohemia.* Firkins, who is not given to superlatives, calls it a "failure" (*op. cit.,* p. 172), but Cooke refers to it as "one of the most delightful of [Howells'] lighter transcripts of manners" (*op. cit.,* p. 208). The unexciting truth is that the story is little above or below the average of Howells' novels.

104. *Life in Letters,* II, 53.

105. "For the present [he wrote to Henry James in December, 1894], I am doing short things; odds and ends of fiction; but I hope soon to get at a novel. It is strange how the love of doing it survives. Of course, there is the need, too, but the love seems as great as ever." *Ibid.,* II, 56.

106. *Ibid.*, II, 55.

107. See above, p. 663.

108. Cf. Firkins, *op. cit.*, p. 176.

109. *Their Silver Wedding Journey*, New York, 1899, I, 99-100. As for Basil's cynicism, it parallels a strain of skepticism that often appears in Howells' letters at the turn of the century. Nowhere does he show a pessimism equal to Mark Twain's at the same period, but he felt that America had "a long way to come toward civilization." *Life in Letters*, II, 147, *et passim*.

110. Carl Van Doren, *op. cit.*, p. 134.

111. Firkins, *op. cit.*, p. 195.

112. The period of the action and the quality of the Kentons are well defined when Lottie Kenton in a moment of impatience permits herself to say "pshaw" but will not go so far as "rats." *The Kentons*, New York, 1902, p. 109.

113. Cooke, *op. cit.*, p. 210.

114. *Miss Bellard's Inspiration*, New York, 1905, p. 202.

115. See above, p. 683.

116. Cf. above, note 50.

117. See above, pp. 661-62.

118. Cf. a more serious treatment of a similar situation in James's tale, "The Real Thing" (1893).

119. Cf. above, pp. 661-62.

120. Firkins, *op. cit.*, p. 183. Cf also Cooke, *op. cit.*, pp. 251-52.

121. *The Landlord at Lion's Head* (New York, 1900), pp. 345-46.

122. Firkins, *op. cit.*, p. 183.

123. Howells closely resembles Holmes when (in Chapter XIV) he brings together Dr. Anther and Judge Garley in a discourse on responsibility. Cf. above, pp. 496-97.

124. Cooke observes (*op. cit.*, p. 212) that two of Howells' comparatively late stories, *Miss Bellard's Inspiration* and *Fennel and Rue*, marked "a sort of decadence into the psychological manner"—reflecting "more of Henry James and less of Jane Austen." Yet *The Son of Royal Langbrith* is patently the closest approximation Howells ever made to James in a full-length novel. Individual scenes are frequently as finished in Howells as in James, but their relationship to the whole story is generally not so well worked out. Howells, it may be added, appeared to regard himself as pupil and James as master.

125. *The Son of Royal Langbrith*, New York, 1904, p. 112.

126. *Ibid.*, p. [369].

127. Cf. Mr. Sewell's views on the same subject (*The Minister's Charge*, pp. 457-59) and the concluding note of *The Quality of Mercy* (quoted above, p. 681).

128. Cf. Cooke, *op. cit.*, p. 43.

129. *Criticism and Fiction*, p. 8.

130. *Their Wedding Journey*, p. 106.

131. *The Rise of Silas Lapham*, Boston, 1885, p. 278.

132. *Criticism and Fiction*, p. 83.

133. *Ibid.*, p. 8.

134. *Ibid.*, p. 14.

135. *Ibid.*, pp. 98-99.

136. *Ibid.*, p. 99.

137. *Life in Letters*, I, 378. For an inquiry into the origin of the term realism as applied to modern fiction, see Edward E. Hale, "The Earlier 'Realism,'" *Union College Bulletin* (January, 1932), XXV, 5 n.

138. *Criticism and Fiction*, p. 104.

139. *Ibid.*, p. 15.

140. Quoted in *Criticism and Fiction*, p. 79.

141. Quoted above, p. 695.

142. The term was used by Edmund Gosse (*op. cit.*, p. 153), who once offered to supply Howells with some Zolaesque details for a story about Hong-Kong!

143. *Criticism and Fiction*, pp. 128-29.

144. *My Literary Passions*, p. [229].

145. *Heroines of Fiction*, New York, 1901, I, 26.

146. *Criticism and Fiction*, pp. 15, 16.

147. Cf. Alexander Harvey's (somewhat unfair) complaint that whenever Howells granted approval to a writer "he turns out to be a member of the sissy school." *William Dean Howells*, New York, 1917, p. 196.

148. When it is proposed that Penelope "give up" Tom Corey to Irene, Mr. Sewell (with Howells' apparent backing) protests against the "false ideal of self-sacrifice" that people are likely to get "from the novels that befool and debauch almost every intelligence in some degree." *The Rise of Silas Lapham*, pp. 338-39.

149. Emerson's "Nature."

150. Quoted in Herbert Edwards, "Howells and the Controversy over Realism in American Fiction," *American Literature* (November, 1931), III, [237].

151. *Ibid.*, p. 238.

152. *Ibid.*, pp. 239, 240.

153. *Ibid.*, p. 240.

154. *Adventures of a Novelist*, New York, 1932, pp. 101-02.

155. *Life in Letters*, II, 161. It is a fair guess that about the turn of the century Howells also began to lose readers to Booth Tarkington, who shared some of Howells's gifts but offered new elements as well. A little later the projected 31 or 32-volume "Library Edition" of Howells' works was abandoned after only six volumes had been issued (in July, 1911). See George Arms, "Howells's Unpublished Prefaces," *The New England Quarterly* (December, 1944), XVII, 580-91.

156. This fact was insisted on by James, who wrote in a rare moment of peevishness:

I had n't seen [Howells'] "tribute" in the September *Harper's*, but I have just looked it up. It gives me pleasure, but does n't make me cease to deplore the figure that Howells makes every month in his critical department of *Harper's*. He seems to me as little as possible of a critic and expresses himself so that I wish he would "quit," and content himself with writing the novel as he thinks it should be, and not talking about it: he does the one so much better than the other. He talks from too small a point of view, and his examples (barring the bore he makes of Tolstoi) are smaller still. There is, it seems to me, far too much talk around and about the novel in proportion to what is done. Any *genre* is good which has life. . . . *The Thought and Character of William James* (ed. by R. B. Perry), Boston, 1936, I, 399-400. From a letter to William James, October, 1887. The tone of this passage is not, of course, typical of James's comments on Howells, for whom he had much admiration. For more complimentary comments, see *The Letters of Henry James, passim.*

157. Cf. his remark in an article on James: it is "after all, what a writer has to say rather than what he has to tell that we care for nowadays. In one manner or other the stories were all told long ago; and now we want merely to know what the novelist thinks about persons and situations." "Henry James, Jr.," *Century Magazine* (November, 1882), III (new series), 29. See also the discussion of *A Chance Acquaintance*, above, p. 660.

158. Cf. Cather's *Not Under Forty*, London, 1936, pp. 47-56.

CHAPTER XVI

1. This is not to leave out of account his association with the Impressionists of the Crane-Conrad-Hueffer school that became prominent in the 1890's. For commentary on James's association (not alliance) with this group, see Ford Madox Hueffer, *Thus to Revisit*, New York, 1921, Part II, Chapter IX. See also Ford Madox Ford's *Portraits From Life*, Boston, 1937, Chapter I.

2. *Heroines of Fiction*, II, 165.

3. Cf. Gertrude Stein's remark that James was "the first person in literature to find the way to the literary methods of the twentieth century." *The Autobiography of Alice B. Toklas*, New York, 1933, p. 96. See also G. E. De Mille, *Literary Criticism in America*, New York, 1931, pp. 180-81.

4. Cf. his approving comment on one of his own characters, Mrs. Stringham— a writer who practiced "the art of showing New England without showing it wholly in the kitchen." *The Wings of the Dove*, I, 107. (References are to the New York edition (Scribner), 1907-17, except as noted.)

5. Constance Rourke, *American Humor*, New York, 1931, p. 237.

6. Later on, James was much attracted by Howells, and he wrote in 1884 that Howells was "the only English novelist" he read "except Miss Woolson." *The Letters of Henry James* (ed. by Percy Lubbock), New York, 1920, I, 105. James's admiring study of Miss Woolson appears in *Partial Portraits*. James's rather surprising reference to Poe in *The Golden Bowl* has been noted above, p. 305 and note 104.

7. R. B. Perry, *The Thought and Character of William James*, Boston, 1936, I, 316, 319.

8. *Hawthorne*, London, 1879, p. 111. It is an interesting question whether the life of little Pearl may not have been in the back of James's mind when he undertook to show the effect of evil on a little girl in *What Maisie Knew*.

9. Cf. his observation (*Hawthorne*, p. 3) "that the flower of art blooms only where the soil is deep, that it takes a great deal of history to produce a little literature, that it needs a complex social machinery to set a writer in motion."

10. *Ibid.*, p. 165.

11. See especially *The Wings of the Dove*, I, 221, II, 144; *The Tragic Muse*, II, 412, [413]; *The Sense of the Past*, pp. 86 ff. It is perhaps no accident that in *The Tragic Muse* the chief female character is not only given the name of Hawthorne's heroine in *The Marble Faun* (Miriam) but also has like Miriam a tincture of Jewish blood.

12. Cf. the relationship between Kate Croy and Milly Theale in *The Wings of the Dove* as well as Olive Chancellor's domination over Verena Tarrant in *The Bostonians*.

13. Cf. Lionel Croy (in *The Wings of the Dove*) and Hollingsworth (in *The Blithedale Romance*). Hawthorne would have been fascinated by the vague but fearful grip of evil in "The Turn of the Screw."

14. Just as readers of *The Marble Faun* clamored for a literal statement at the end of the story, so the uninitiated reader of James wishes to know exactly whether Isabel Archer will ever return to Caspar Goodwood (in *The Portrait of a Lady*) and whether Chad Newsome really will abandon Mme de Vionnet at the end of *The Ambassadors*. To the authors these material points were immaterial.

15. Ludwig Lewisohn, *Expression in America*, New York, 1932, p. 255.

16. Charles Angoff, "Three Notes on American Literature," *North American Review* (Spring, 1939), CCXLVII, 39.

17. *Henry James*, New York, 1916, pp. 89-90.

18. Van Wyck Brooks, *The Pilgrimage of Henry James*, New York, 192 p. 59.

19. In Van Wyck Brooks's *The Pilgrimage of Henry James* overt statement is avoided, but there is a critical undertone of displeasure, even irritation, at James's having bartered his American birthright for a mess of internationalism. In *New England: Indian Summer* (p. 294) Mr. Brooks incredibly asserts that "[w]hat seemed to James really important was not morals but manners."

20. Cf. Ralph Touchett's remark in *The Portrait of a Lady* (I, 125): "Ah, one does n't give up one's country any more than one gives up one's grandmother. They're both antecedent to choice—elements of one's composition that are not to be eliminated."

21. *Letters*, I, 353.

22. Van Wyck Brooks, *Opinions of Oliver Allston*, New York, 1941, p. 104.

23. Joseph W. Beach, *The Method of Henry James*, New Haven, 1918, p. 168.

24. For an admirable study of Henry James's distinguished father, see Austin Warren's *The Elder Henry James*, New York, 1934.

25. Van Wyck Brooks, *The Pilgrimage of Henry James*, pp. 15 ff.

26. Warren, *op. cit.*, p. 134.

27. *Letters*, Preface, I, 8.

28. *Ibid.*, I, 10.

29. *Letters*, I, 42. It was not, of course, the "immorality" of French novelists that held James off. Indeed he later defended Zola against attack on this ground. *Atlantic Monthly* (August, 1903), XCII, 193-210. Rather there were temperamental differences, and James finally felt that these writers were provincial.

30. From Florence he had written in 1874: "I have been nearly a year in Italy and have hardly spoken to an Italian creature save washerwomen and waiters." *Letters*, I, 36.

31. *Ibid.*, I, 55, 59.

32. *Ibid.*, I, 54.

33. *Ibid.*, II, 11.

34. *Ibid.*, I, 22.

35. It is true that late in life (1915) he referred to himself as a "poor old Anglo-maniac" (*Letters*, II, 463), but this was after America's dilatory attitude toward World War I had angered him, and it is not characteristic.

36. Brooks, *The Pilgrimage of Henry James*, p. 75.

37. *Letters*, I, 64.

38. *Ibid.*, I, 141.

39. *Ibid.*, I, 141-42.

40. Bliss Perry, *And Gladly Teach*, Boston, 1935, p. 225.

41. *Cambridge History of American Literature*, III, 98.

42. *Ibid.*, III, 103.

43. *Letters*, II, 497. So obvious was the public and even critical indifference to the edition that it was never completed as planned. *Ibid.*, 498-99.

44. R. B. Perry, *op. cit.*, I, 370, *et passim*.

45. Beach, *op. cit.*, p. 182.

46. *Roderick Hudson*, pp. 230-31.

47. *Ibid.*, p. 259.

48. *Letters*, I, 132; II, 55.

49. It was published in *The Atlantic Monthly*. Most of James's novels before 1904 were first serialized. Since most of his books sold but poorly on the whole, it may perhaps be inferred that the ready acceptance of his long fiction by editors is to be explained by the success of a few of his short stories such as "Daisy Miller" (1879) and "An International Episode" (1879) and the relative readability of a few of the novels of his early period, especially *The American* and *The Portrait of a*

Lady. As time went on, James increasingly "hated the magazine form, magazine conditions and manners, and much of the magazine company," and as his serial popularity waned, he became more and more interested in his "book-position." *Letters,* I, 231.

50. *Letters,* I, 66.

51. Unless otherwise specified the dates are those of book publication.

52. Cf. Beach, *op. cit.,* p. 223.

53. *Letters,* I, 66.

54. *Washington Square,* New York, 1881, p. 20.

55. *The Bostonians,* London and New York, 1886, pp. 17, 6.

56. Miss Birdseye receives about as severe a frontal attack as any character in James when she is described as "a confused, entangled, inconsequent, discursive old woman, whose charity began at home and ended nowhere, whose credulity kept pace with it, and who knew less about her fellow-creatures, if possible, after fifty years of humanitary zeal, than on the day she had gone into the field to testify against the iniquity of most arrangements." *Ibid.,* p. 27. Fashionable New York society comes in for its share of satire. See Chapter XXVI.

57. Many years later James spoke of *The Bostonians* as "rather a remarkable feat of objectivity" (*Letters,* II, 498), but actually he intruded upon its objectivity more than he probably remembered. For examples of such violation see *The Bostonians,* pp. 164, 176, 186, 189, 230, 247, 311, 337.

58. R. W. Gilder, editor of *The Century,* wrote to James that "they had never published anything that appeared so little to interest their readers." *Letters,* II, 498. Doubtless it was the serial experience of the book which persuaded James and the Scribners to omit it for the time being from the New York edition. James planned some day to revise the book for use in the complete edition, but the publication of the edition was never completed.

59. *Letters,* II, 498.

60. *Ibid.,* I, 132-33, 279; II, 333.

61. Beach, *op. cit.,* p. 205.

62. It is interesting to note that even Joel C. Harris, who objected to James's "snobbery" and to his difficult diction, referred to *The Portrait of a Lady* as "that fine book." Julia C. Harris, *The Life and Letters of Joel Chandler Harris,* London, 1919, p. 575. See also *Joel Chandler Harris, Editor and Essayist,* (ed. by Julia Collier Harris), Chapel Hill, 1931, pp. 185-91.

63. To present a graphic account of the economic woes of the submerged tenth in London was no part of James's purpose; consequently Pelham Edgar is beside the point in charging James with "evasion of the central issues." *Henry James: Man and Author,* Boston, 1927, p. 269.

64. Beach, *op. cit.,* p. 5. The book was somewhat harshly received by English critics. James R. Lowell, however, took issue with the critics and himself found the story "admirable." *New Letters of James Russell Lowell* (ed. by M. A. DeWolfe Howe), New York, 1932, p. 296. In Lowell's opinion James had by now "conceived more original characters and situations than all the [modern] English school put together."

65. Beach, *op. cit.,* p. 217.

66. *Letters,* I, 136.

67. *Ibid.,* I, 138.

68. *Ibid.,* I, 176.

69. *Ibid.,* I, 180.

70. For a discussion of James's ventures in the drama, see *Henry James* (ed. by Lyon N. Richardson), New York, 1941, Introduction, pp. lxii-lxviii.

71. *Letters,* I, 163.

72. *Ibid.,* I, 104.

73. *The Sacred Fount* is in fact less a novel than a demonstration (inordinately

drawn out) of James's conception of the relationship between life and the novel. For an excellent study of the story see Wilson Follett's "Henry James's Portrait of Henry James" in *The New York Times*, August 23, 1936.

74. *The Awkward Age*, p. 30. In some respects Longdon is akin to Strether in *The Ambassadors*, a character almost certainly containing a good deal of self-portraiture of James. The relationship between Nanda and Longdon distinctly recalls that of Imogene and Colville in Howells' *Indian Summer* (1888), but Howells resolved the situation differently. See above, pp. 672-73.

75. *Letters*, I, 333.

76. The historical romance which had a lively revival at the end of the nineteenth century, was of course out of the question. Cf. his bitter indictment of tawdry romance: "I do hunger and thirst, in this deluge of cheap romanticism and chromolithographic archaisms (babyish, puppyish, as evocation, all, it seems to me) for a note, a gleam of the life *we* live." Quoted by De Mille, *Literary Criticism in America*, p. 173. Stevenson, however, who was in part responsible for the revival, James admired for his good technique.

77. *Letters*, I, 300. Though called a "pot-boiler" by its author, "The Turn of the Screw" has gradually come into its own as one of the most distinguished modern short stories.

78. He resumed (but did not complete) *The Sense of the Past* in 1914. *Letters*, I, 349-60, *et passim*. The finished portion, about 30,000 words, is followed in the New York edition by James's elaborate notes for the rest.

79. *The Sense of the Past*, p. 322.

80. Edgar, *op. cit.*, p. 184.

81. *The Sense of the Past*, pp. 86 ff.

82. Edgar, *op. cit.*, p. 186.

83. The popular possibilities of the theme have since been more richly capitalized by John L. Balderston in a stage-play *Berkeley Square* (1928). The outline of the play, however, follows the story very closely excepting for the fact that Balderston pushes the time back from the early nineteenth century to the eighteenth.

84. Cf. Stephen Spender, *The Destructive Element*, Boston, 1936, p. 105. See also Wyndham Lewis, *Time and Western Man*, New York, 1928, *passim*.

85. *Letters*, I, 351, 353. James's difficulty with stories of sheer horror is further explained by the fact that he didn't "care for 'terror' . . . without 'pity.'" *Ibid.*, I, 357.

86. Abry, Audic, and Crouzet, *Histoire Illustrée de la Littérature Française*, Paris, 1918, p. 618.

87. *The Wings of the Dove*, Preface, p. xii.

88. *Letters*, I, 407-08.

89. *The Wings of the Dove*, Preface, p. v.

90. *Letters*, I, 403.

91. *Ibid.*, I, 407.

92. Cf. Beach, *op. cit.*, pp. 262-63.

93. First conceived and briefly developed in 1899, it was subsequently resumed with such enthusiasm that by August, 1900, it had become "the greatest obsession." *Letters*, I, 357, 358. Parts of it were written concurrently with *The Wings of the Dove*. It was published in *The North American Review* from January to December, 1903.

94. *Letters*, I, 376. For a full account (mostly by James) of the project of *The Ambassadors*, see *Hound & Horn* (April-May, 1934), VII, [541]-562.

95. *The Ambassadors*, I, 217-18.

96. *Letters*, II, 245.

97. *The Ambassadors*, I, 284; II, 312.

98. Cf. Beach, *op. cit.*, p. 267.

99. It is typical of James's method that the reader is never fully apprised of the ultimate fate of Chad or his mistress. Strether has been the main object, and his work is over. This concentration on Strether is one of the marks of the final phase of technique which *The Ambassadors* shares with the two other books in James's major triad. That technique is discussed below, pp. 726 ff.

100. The phrase is Glenway Wescott's: *Hound & Horn,* VII, 525.

101. *The Golden Bowl,* I, 384.

102. *Ibid.,* I, 262.

103. *Ibid.,* I, 257.

104. *Ibid.,* I, 394-95.

105. Cf. Rebecca West, *op. cit.,* pp. 110-13.

106. For detailed criticism of *The Golden Bowl* from a sympathetic point of view, see Ferner Nuhn, *The Wind Blew From the East,* New York, 1942, Chapter VI, *passim.*

107. *The Ambassadors,* Preface, p. vii.

108. *Letters,* II, 15.

109. *Ibid.,* II, 30.

110. *The Sense of the Past* is discussed above, pp. 720-21.

111. The idea for *The Ivory Tower* was in James's mind as early as 1908 (*Letters,* II, 98), but he apparently did not proceed to actual composition until 1914.

112. From this trip grew also his volume of description and interpretation, *The American Scene* (1907).

113. Spender, *op. cit.,* p. 103.

114. *Ibid.,* p. 104.

115. A great deal of his critical comment appears in the extremely elaborate prefaces to the stories in his New York edition. These have been conveniently assembled in a single volume edited with an introduction by Richard P. Blackmur: *The Art of the Novel: Critical Prefaces by Henry James,* New York, 1934. Among other works of James which reveal his critical theory are "The Art of Fiction" (in *Partial Portraits,* 1888), *French Poets and Novelists* (1878), *Notes on Novelists* (1914), *The Letters of Henry James* (ed. by Percy Lubbock), and Perry's *The Thought and Character of William James.* In addition, of course, his theory may be to some extent inferred from passages in many of his stories, especially "The Figure in the Carpet" and *The Sacred Fount.*

116. Cf. his sympathetic comments on those writers in Flaubert's circle whose conviction was that "art and morality are two perfectly different things, and that the former has no more to do with the latter than it has with astronomy or embryology . . ." *Atlantic Monthly* (January, 1884), LIII, 46, quoted in *American Literature* (May, 1932), IV, 118.

117. *Letters,* II, 181.

118. *Ibid.,* II, 490.

119. The idea for *The Ambassadors* (see above, p. 722) came from a remark of Howells; "The Turn of the Screw" had its nucleus in a story told James by the Archbishop of Canterbury (see E. F. Benson, *As We Were,* New York, 1930, pp. 278-79. Cf. New York edition, vol. XII, Preface, pp. xiv-xvi). The situation of his cousin, Minnie Temple, gave James the central idea for *The Wings of the Dove* (Edgar, *op. cit.,* p. 301).

120. *Notes on Novelists,* New York, 1914, p. 80.

121. J. W. Beach, *op. cit.,* p. 148.

122. For further comment on James's fondness for symmetrical design, see Beach, *op. cit.,* pp. 251-52, Stephen Spender, *The Destructive Element,* pp. 87-88, Wilson Follett, "Henry James's Portrait of Henry James," *The New York Times,* August 23, 1936.

123. *The Golden Bowl,* I, 75.

124. Cf. *Letters,* II, 40.

125. Lewisohn, *op. cit.*, p. 269.

126. Beach, *op. cit.*, p. 69.

127. See above, pp. 718-19.

128. James's technical problem in this book is fully analyzed in Percy Lubbock's *The Craft of Fiction*, New York, 1921, pp. 156-71. See also F. O. Matthiessen, *Henry James: The Major Phase*, New York, 1944, Chapter II.

129. Preface, p. xxii. Pelham Edgar notes (*op. cit.*, p. 308) that James's plan of excluding Milly's consciousness as a focus for the book was violated only twice throughout the entire narrative. The reason for not using Milly's point of view is, of course, that the real "subject is not in Milly herself, but in her effect upon the relation existing between Densher and Kate." Lubbock, *op. cit.*, p. 183.

130. This is especially true at the beginning of stories. In *The American* (1877) so far was James from having adopted the most exacting method in this respect that shortly after the beginning of the story four pages are devoted to an "itemized" description of the hero. The opening of *The Ambassadors* (1903) shows the method almost perfected. James supplies the characters but he does not even "introduce" them; they introduce each other. (Cf. Beach, *op. cit.*, p. 102.) Even in *The Ambassadors*, however, James has recourse to giving arbitrarily a bit of information about Strether that "had better be confessed at the outset."

131. *Letters*, I, 322. For further comment on James's indirect method, see Lubbock, *op. cit.*, pp. 147-50.

132. *Letters*, II, 334.

133. Quoted in D. G. Cooke, *William Dean Howells*, New York, 1922, pp. 97-98.

134. *The Ambassadors*, I, 152.

135. "The Art of Fiction," *Partial Portraits* (London, 1888), p. 389.

136. "The Real Thing" (New York edition, vol. XVIII), p. 317.

137. Beach, *op. cit.*, p. [56].

138. This perhaps partially explains his frequent ill-success with the serial form.

139. *The Tragic Muse*, I, 31.

140. Rourke, *op. cit.*, p. 238.

141. Cf. *The American*, p. 462.

142. Joseph Conrad, *Notes on Life and Letters*, New York, 1924, p. 17.

143. *The Golden Bowl*, I, [88].

144. Cf. Constance Rourke's observation (*op. cit.*, p. 261) that the "later novels are full of the unsaid and understated; they are full of complex moods and states of inner feeling revealed by the slightest and most ephemeral of notations."

145. *The Wings of the Dove*, I, 201.

146. Edgar, *op. cit.*, p. 223. Edgar applies this remark to *The Wings of the Dove* but it has general validity.

147. George Santayana, *The Last Puritan*, New York, 1936, p. 600.

148. The revision of *The American* shows that he often substituted an Anglo-Saxon expression for a Latin word. *Letters*, II, facsimile facing p. 70. See also L. Richardson, *loc. cit.*, p. lx n.

149. See for example an amusing letter to his nephew, on naming a baby, and a letter to Howells condoling with Mrs. Howells on the subject of dentistry. *Letters*, II, 314-15, 103.

150. *Letters*, I, 405.

151. *Ibid.*, II, 15.

152. *The Ambassadors*, I, 202.

153. *The Letters of William James* (ed. by Henry James), Boston, 1920, II, 277-78. A delicious burlesque of James's style may be found in Max Beerbohm's *A Christmas Garland*, New York, 1925, pp. 3-10. James was not convinced by William and he continued to express his contempt for the "two-and-two-make-

four system on which all the awful truck that surrounds us is produced." R. B. Perry, *op. cit.*, I, 424.

154. *The Sense of the Past*, p. 230.

155. *Letters*, I, 408.

156. As early as 1873 James noted his diminishing interest in sheer image: "The *keen* love and observation of the picturesque [he wrote to his brother William] is ebbing away from me as I grow older, and I doubt whether a year or two hence I shall have it in me to describe houses and mountains, or even cathedrals and pictures." R. B. Perry, *op. cit.*, I, 345.

157. *The Awkward Age*, p. 255.

158. *Letters*, I, 198.

159. Richardson, *loc. cit.*, p. lxxxiii.

160. *Henry James: Letters to A. C. Benson and Auguste Monod* (ed. by E. F. Benson), London, 1930, p. 47.

161. *Letters*, I, 207.

162. *Ibid.*, I, 246.

163. *Ibid.*, I, 310-11.

164. *Ibid.*, I, 341.

165. *Ibid.*, II, 443.

166. *Ibid.*, II, 449.

167. *Ibid.*, II, 186.

168. *Ibid.*

169. Richardson, *loc. cit.*, p. lxxv.

170. *Letters*, I, 124.

171. *Notes and Reviews*, Cambridge, 1921, p. 185.

172. *Letters*, I, 100-01.

173. See *ibid.*, II, 83.

174. *Letters*, Introduction, I, xx.

175. Cf. the remark of Mrs. Henry Adams: "It's not that he 'bites off more than he can chaw,' . . . but he chaws more than he bites off." *The Letters of Mrs. Henry Adams 1865-1883*, Boston, 1936, p. 306.

176. "The Art of Fiction," p. 398.

CHAPTER XVII

1. Hamlin Garland, *A Son of the Middle Border* (New York, 1927), p. 375.

2. *Ibid.*, p. 374.

3. Alfred Kazin, *On Native Grounds*, New York, 1942, p. 137.

4. Ernest Marchand, *Frank Norris: A Study*, Stanford, 1942, p. 54.

5. Quoted in Harry Hartwick, *The Foreground of American Fiction*, New York, 1934, pp. 290-91. See this book for a study of many novels dealing with the "insurgence." For a thoroughgoing survey of the economic and political novel in the latter part of the nineteenth century, see Lisle Abbott Rose, "A Bibliographical Survey of Economic and Political Writings 1865-1900," *American Literature*, XV (January, 1944), [381]-410. It is apparent from Mr. Rose's study that few literary historians have found it possible to examine more than a small proportion of the hundreds of novels dealing with economics and politics. Yet it is likely that a careful evaluation of all such novels would "not disturb the esthetic primacy of Twain, Howells, Bellamy, and Garland." *Ibid.*, p. 392.

6. Matthew Josephson, *Zola and His Time*, New York, 1928, p. 148.

7. Hartwick, *op. cit.*, p. 13.

8. Ernest Hemingway, *Death in the Afternoon*, New York, 1932, p. 191.

9. *Saturday Review of Literature*, March 19, 1932, p. 604.

10. T. S. Eliot, "Burnt Norton," *Collected Poems 1909-1935*, New York, 1936, p. 213.

11. Gertrude Stein, *Narration*, Chicago, 1935, pp. 23-25.

12. Herbert J. Muller, *Modern Fiction*, New York, 1937, p. 292.

Bibliography

The following list is confined to some of the more general books in the field of the American novel. In a few of the books English and American novels are treated together. Readers wishing to pursue the study of individual novelists are referred to the detailed documentation to be found in the Notes. Although by no means bibliographically complete, the Notes should provide a convenient starting place for further study.

Barnett, James H.: *Divorce and the American Divorce Novel 1858-1937* (Philadelphia, 1939).

Beach, Joseph Warren: *The Twentieth Century Novel: Studies in Technique* (New York, 1932).

Beach, Joseph Warren: *American Fiction 1920-1940* (New York, 1941).

Birkhead, Edith: *The Tale of Terror: A Study of the Gothic Romance* (London, 1921).

Black, Frank Gees: *The Epistolary Novel in the Late Eighteenth Century* (Eugene [Oregon], 1940).

Boynton, Percy H.: *America in Contemporary Fiction* (Chicago, 1940).

Brown, Herbert Ross: *The Sentimental Novel in America 1789-1860* (Durham [North Carolina], 1940).

Burgum, Edwin Berry: *The Novel and the World's Dilemma* (New York, 1947).

Cooper, Frederic Taber: *Some American Story Tellers* (New York, 1911).

Drew, Elizabeth A.: *The Modern Novel: Some Aspects of Contemporary Fiction* (New York, 1926).

Du Breuil, Alice J.: *The Novel of Democracy in America* (Baltimore, 1923).

Dunlap, George A.: *The City in the American Novel 1789-1900* (Philadelphia, 1934).

Edgar, Pelham: *The Art of the Novel from 1700 to the Present Time* (New York, 1933).

Erskine, John: *Leading American Novelists* (New York, 1910).

Fiske, Horace S.: *Provincial Types in American Fiction* (Chautauqua, 1903).

Geismar, Maxwell: *Writers in Crisis: The American Novel Between Two Wars* (Boston, 1942).

Hartwick, Harry: *The Foreground of American Fiction* (New York, 1934).

Hatcher, Harlan: *Creating the Modern American Novel* (New York, 1935).

Knight, Grant C.: *The Novel in English* (New York, 1931).

Loshe, Lillie Deming: *The Early American Novel* (New York, 1907).

McCole, C. John: *Lucifer at Large* (New York, 1937).

Marble, Annie Russell: *A Study of the Modern Novel, British and American, Since 1900* (New York, 1928).

Michaud, Régis: *The American Novel To-day: A Social and Psychological Study* (Boston, 1928).

Monroe, N. Elizabeth: *The Novel and Society: A Critical Study of the Modern Novel* (Chapel Hill, 1941).

Muller, Herbert J.: *Modern Fiction, A Study of Values* (New York, 1937).

Norris, Frank: *The Responsibilities of the Novelist, and Other Literary Essays* (New York, 1903).

Pearson, Edmund: *Dime Novels; or, Following an Old Trail in Popular Literature* (Boston, 1929).

Quinn, Arthur Hobson: *American Fiction: An Historical and Critical Survey* (New York, 1936).

Singer, Godfrey F.: *The Epistolary Novel: Its Origin, Development, Decline, and Residuary Influence* (Philadelphia, 1933).

Snell, George: *The Shapers of American Fiction: 1798-1947* (New York, 1947).

Speare, Morris E.: *The Political Novel: Its Development in England and in America* (New York, 1924).

Taylor, Walter Fuller: *The Economic Novel in America* (Chapel Hill, 1942).

Van Doren, Carl: *The American Novel* (New York, 1921).

Van Doren, Carl: *Contemporary American Novelists 1900-1920* (New York, 1922).

Van Doren, Carl: *The American Novel 1789-1939* (New York, 1940).

Index

Numbers in italics refer to material in the Notes

Wyandotté, 147, 148-50, 159
Wylie, Elinor, 703

Yemassee, The, 231-33, 239, 451, 530, 795
Yonge, Charlotte M., 617
Young, Edward, 771

"Young Goodman Brown," 320, 334, 347, 350, 354
Youth, 396

Zola, Émile, 534, 707, 748, 749, *828*
Zouri's Christmas, *831*
Zury, 226, 227

~~20764~~
1177